HENRY OF KIRKESTEDE,
CATALOGUS DE LIBRIS AUTENTICIS ET APOCRIFIS

CORPUS OF BRITISH MEDIEVAL LIBRARY CATALOGUES

Volumes published

1. The Friars' Libraries (1990),
   edited by K. W. Humphreys

2. *Registrum Anglie de libris doctorum et auctorum ueterum* (1991),
   edited by R. A. B. Mynors, R. H. Rouse and M. A. Rouse

3. The Libraries of the Cistercians, Gilbertines and Premonstratensians (1992),
   edited by David N. Bell

4. English Benedictine Libraries. The Shorter Catalogues (1996),
   edited by R. Sharpe, J. P. Carley, R. M. Thomson and A. G. Watson

5. Dover Priory (1999),
   edited by William P. Stoneman

6. The Libraries of the Augustinian Canons (1998),
   edited by T. Webber and A. G. Watson

7. The Libraries of King Henry VIII (2000),
   edited by James P. Carley

8. Peterborough Abbey (2001),
   edited by Karsten Friis-Jensen and James M. W. Willoughby

9. Syon Abbey (2001), *edited by* Vincent Gillespie,
   with The Libraries of the Carthusians, *edited by* A. I. Doyle

10. The University and College Libraries of Cambridge (2002),
    edited by Peter D. Clarke, *with an introduction by* Roger Lovatt

11. Henry of Kirkestede, *Catalogus de libris autenticis et apocrifis* (2004),
    edited by Richard H. Rouse and Mary A. Rouse

Volumes in preparation
Christ Church, Canterbury
St Augustine's, Canterbury
Durham Cathedral Priory
Secular Cathedrals, Colleges and Hospitals
The University of Oxford
The Libraries of Scotland
General indexes

GENERAL EDITOR   R. Sharpe   ASSISTANT EDITOR   J. M. W. Willoughby

EDITORIAL COMMITTEE

A. I. Doyle   J. Durkan   J. C. Higgitt   K. Jensen
H. M. R. E. Mayr-Harting (Chairman)   A. J. Piper   M. D. Reeve
R. H. Rouse   R. Sharpe   J. B. Trapp   A. G. Watson
M. T. J. Webber (Secretary)

CORPUS OF BRITISH
MEDIEVAL LIBRARY CATALOGUES
11

HENRY OF KIRKESTEDE,
CATALOGUS DE LIBRIS AUTENTICIS ET APOCRIFIS

Edited by
RICHARD H. ROUSE
and MARY A. ROUSE

THE BRITISH LIBRARY
in association with
THE BRITISH ACADEMY
2004

First published 2004
by The British Library
96 Euston Road
London NW1 2DB

in association with
The British Academy

© 2004 The British Library Board

British Library Cataloguing in Publication Data
is available from The British Library

ISBN 0 7123 4837 9

Designed by John Mitchell
Typeset in Baskerville MT
by Hope Services (Abingdon) Ltd
Printed in England
by St Edmundsbury Press, Bury St Edmunds

For Paul Meyvaert
and in memory of
Leonard E. Boyle OP

N   Radulphus de Diceto Decanus Ecclesiæ S. Pauli London. floruit A. Ch. 1147. et scripsit
    Librum Cronicorum qui dicitur Ymagines
    Historiarum   Cronica sunt ymagines Historiarum et finit A.Ch. 1199.

N   ..... de Fresingfeld floruit circa A. Ch.   et scripsit
    Librum metricum qui dicitur Practica
    Grammaticæ   Commoda   per sæcula cuncta
    Librum prosaicum qui vocatur Verbarius -   Cum sit necessarium per æterna sæcula.

N   Ricardus de Cyrencestria
    De officio Ecclesiastico . . . . .   lib. 7. Officium ut

    Rathamius floruit circa A. Ch.   et scripsit
    De Anima . . . .   lib. 1. Suo quantum   argutiis. 19. 63. 82.
    De eo quod Christus de Virgine natus est
    per naturalem corporis partem . . .   lib. 1. Fama est   complacuit. 19. 63. 82.

N   Ricardus de Withringsete Cancellarius Cantebriggiæ floruit   et scripsit
    De vitiis et virtutibus et de sacramentis lib.   Qui bene præsunt erit consummatus.

N   Robertus Lincoln. Episcopus qui et Grosteste dicitur floruit A. Ch. 1250. et obiit
    anno 1253. et scripsit multa. Hic fuit Doctor in Theologia in triplici lingua eruditus, Latina,
    Hebraica, et Græca. Multa de Glosis Hebræorum extraxit, de Græco multa transferri fecit,
    utpote Libros Dionysij quorum novam translationem perluculde commentavit. Item in Logica
    et Astrologia et in cunctis liberalibus Artibus excellenter erat eruditus. Ad Papam Innocentium
    misit Epistolam invectivam satis tonantem pro eo quod Ecclesias Angliæ exactionibus indebitis
    vexare videatur. Hac de causa vocatus est ad Curiam, et cum ibi molestaretur appellavit
    constanter a Curia Papæ Innocentij ad Tribunal Christi, unde contigit quod eadem Roberto
    in Anglia obeunte audita est vox in Curia Papæ Vani miser ad judicium et Papa in
    crastino invenitus est examinis, quasi cuspide baculi in latere percussus. His de causis licet
    perspicuus effulserit Robertus miracula transferri, tamen nec in Sanctorum Cathalogos poni
    non est a Curia permissus.

    Tithulus librorum   Num.   Princ. librorum   Finis libr.
    Rob. Lincoln.   Libr.   Rob. Lincoln.   Rob. Linc.

    Super Dionisium de Cœlesti et Ecclesiastica
    Gerarchia   lib. 2.
    De originali peccato . . . . . .   lib. 1. Quocirca
    Super Dionisium de Divinis nominibus
    De libero arbitrio quæstiones   lib. 1. Cum per   contrarium.
    De Spæra . . . .   lib. 1. Intentio
    De Astrolabio   lib. 1.
    De Composto   lib. 1.
    Super librum Posteriorum . . . .   Intentio   posteriorum.
    Super libros Physicorum notulas   Cum scire
    Super Dionisium de Mistica Theologia
    Super Prologum Biblice   Expos. 1. Hanc epistolam pleni sunt sensibus. 168.
    Examæron
    Super Psalterium   Beatus vir
    Super Epistolam ad Galathas   ut Apostolus   Quod doceatur
    De 10. præceptis   Sicut dicit   sex mandatis.
    De cessatione legalium   Fuerunt
    De Confessione   Tract. 1. Quum cogitabo   potentiam.
    De cura Pastorali
    De eo quod oportuit Deum fieri hominem.
                                                                  De veritate

CUL MS Add. 3470 p. 126. The Catalogus *as transcribed by Thomas Tanner.*

CONTENTS

Prefatory Note   viii
Acknowledgements   ix
Table of Authors   xi
List of Abbreviations   xix
List of Plates   xxvi

INTRODUCTION

1. Henry of Kirkestede   xxix
Appendix. Kirkestede's Hand   lxxxiii
2. Compiling the *Catalogus*   lxxxiv
3. Kirkestede and the *Speculum coenobitarum*   cxxvi
Appendix. The List of Monastic Authors in the Revised *Speculum Coenobitarum*   cxliv
4. The History of the Text of the *Catalogus*   clxxiv
5. The Edition of the *Catalogus*   ccxi

THE PLATES

CATALOGUS DE LIBRIS AUTENTICIS ET APOCRIFIS

APPENDIX   Kirkestede's Location Numbers   540

Alphabetical List of Houses   575
Alphabetical List of Authors   577
Index of Manuscripts   585
General Index   592

PREFATORY NOTE

The *Catalogus de libris autenticis et apocrifis* by Henry of Kirkestede is a text that has held a near legendary place in the imaginations of English bibliographers for more than four centuries, so it is a remarkable fact that this volume should represent its first full edition. Henry of Kirkestede's *Catalogus* occupies a slightly anomalous place in the present series, for it is more a work of bibliography than a catalogue of shelved books. But it was part of Henry's method to record the presence of certain works in the libraries of which he had personal knowledge, and the editors have been able to assess where he was reporting on actual books. Richard and Mary Rouse have laboured long to bring Henry of Kirkestede's life and work into the scholarly mainstream, and the Committee is delighted to express its gratitude to them for the triumphant conclusion to their labours. Their edition takes its place next to the *Registrum Anglie*, the Franciscan union-catalogue that was a chief source for Henry's *Catalogus*, and which was published as the second volume in the present series.

The Committee also expresses its great thanks to the General Editor of the series, Richard Sharpe, who has brought his usual learning and acumen to bear on this volume. Its publication also provides the first opportunity to express the Committee's gratitude to the Gladys Krieble Delmas Foundation of New York for its most generous grant in aid. With this grant we have been enabled to continue with our excellent Assistant Editor, James Willoughby, who has expedited work on this volume with great energy and good judgement. As always, we are greatly indebted to the encouragement of David Way.

HENRY MAYR-HARTING

ACKNOWLEDGEMENTS

This edition of the *Catalogus scriptorum ecclesiae* is the product of two widely separated campaigns of work. The first, in 1960–63, was completed as Richard Rouse's doctoral dissertation for Cornell University, and the second, leading to publication, was completed forty years later in 2003. The George Lincoln Burr Fellowship from Cornell University and a grant from the Association of College and Research Libraries enabled us to spend 1961–2 at St Antony's College, Oxford. Our debt to a large number of scholars encountered then, who generously shared with us their knowledge of medieval authors and medieval texts, was acknowledged in the 1963 dissertation. With continued gratitude we thank Giles Constable, Antonia Gransden, Susan Hall, Françoise Hudry, Malcolm Parkes, and Brian Scott. The following scholars are regrettably no longer with us: Marie-Thérèse d'Alverny, Doris Bains, Ignatius Brady OFM, Julian Brown, Ruth Dean, A. B. Emden, Margaret Gibson, Beatrice M. Hirsch-Reich, N. R. Ker, Jean Leclercq OSB, Eric G. Millar, William A. Pantin, Graham Pollard, Marjorie Reeves, and Beryl Smalley.

Our revision of the dissertation began indirectly in 1980, with our edition in the present series of the Franciscan *Registrum Anglie*, a source that was almost entirely integrated by Kirkestede into his *Catalogus*. We have benefited frequently from the other editions in this series, and from the research tools developed for it by Richard Sharpe. It is a pleasure to acknowledge the continuing support throughout our work of the Council on Research, Academic Senate, of the University of California, Los Angeles. A grant from the National Endowment for the Humanities in 1984–6 supported our research jointly on the *Catalogus* and on the *Registrum*. We thank the Master and Fellows of Pembroke College, Cambridge, for our appointments as Visiting Fellows for 2000–2001. We are indebted to Trinity College, Cambridge, for a summer grant in 2002. Numerous librarians extended us courteous assistance. We are especially grateful for the help afforded to us at Cambridge by Pamela Judd, former Assistant Librarian, Pembroke College; Jayne Ringrose, Pembroke College Archivist; Gill Cannell, Parker Sub-Librarian of Corpus Christi College; and Godfrey Waller, Superintendent of the Manuscripts Reading Room, Cambridge University Library. The present edition could not have been completed without the generous assistance over the years of the Section Latine of the Institut de recherche et d'histoire des textes, Paris, and the staff of the Young Research Library of the University of California, Los Angeles.

An edition of the *Catalogus* was proposed at the end of the nineteenth century, announced for publication in 1917, and begun afresh in the 1930s, an effort renewed in 1961 and eventually formalized in 1980 with the establishment of the British Academy Committee to edit the medieval British library catalogues. It is pleasing to remark that two members of the present committee, Ian Doyle and Andrew Watson, as well as one of the current authors, Richard Rouse, attended that first meeting of the British Academy Committee; and it is altogether fitting that the present edition should be printed in Bury St Edmunds, where the *Catalogus* was compiled more than 600 years ago. We are grateful for the erudition and encouragement of the series editor Richard Sharpe; and our debt to the detailed assistance of James Willoughby cannot be overstated. Together they have saved us from numerous errors and oversights.

For permission to reproduce photographs of documents, we are most grateful to the Bodleian Library of the University of Oxford, The British Library Board, Cambridge University Library, the Master and Fellows of Corpus Christi College, Cambridge, the Master and Fellows of Pembroke College, Cambridge, the College of Arms, and to the Wisbech and Fenland Museum. Among the scholars we have met in the course of revising an elderly dissertation for publication, we are especially indebted to the learned and considerate help of Rod Thomson and Tessa Webber. The memory of Richard Hunt and Roger Mynors figured largely in our commitment to completing this edition.

We dedicate this book to two scholars whose research we first encountered as graduate students working on the *Catalogus*, and who became and remained the dearest of friends through long years, Paul Meyvaert and the late Leonard E. Boyle OP.

TABLE OF AUTHORS

In the table below the authors included in the *Catalogus* are listed in the order and form in which they appear in the text. In many cases, the 'author' named is either a conflation or a phantom. A full alphabetical listing of identified authors is given at the back of this volume.

 1 Augustinus
 2 Ambrosius
 3 Anselmus
 4 Alexander Nequam
 5 Adelredus
 6 Athanasius
 7 Alcuinus
 8 Aldhelmus
 9 Abbo
10 Angelonius
11 Avitus
12 Antonius
13 Andreas S. Victoris canonicus
14 Amalarius
15 Alanus
16 Alanus Porrens
17 Apollinaris
18 Apringius
19 Achacius
20 Ambrosius Alexandrinus
21 Ansbertus
22 Arator
23 Apyon
24 Anatholius Alexandrinus
25 Amphilocius
26 Arnobius
27 Atticus
28 Anthiochus
29 Audentius
30 Ammonius
31 Arnulphus vel Arnaldus
32 Affricanus
33 Adamantius
34 Asclepius
35 Apollinaris
36 Apollonius

37 Ambrosius
38 Apollonius
39 Alexander Martir
40 Arabianus
41 Agrippa
42 Archelaus
43 Achillius Severus
44 Aptatus vel Optatus
45 Adrianus
46 Aristotiles
47 Apuleius
48 Agellius
49 Aristides
50 Ansegisus
51 Adelardus
52 Alexander Altisiodorensis
53 Adalbertus
54 Alexander de Hales
55 Alexander Magnus
56 Albertus Teutonicus
57 Albertus Erfordensis
58 Albertus Lumbardus
59 Arnaldus Laudiensis
60 Albrandinus Lumbardus
61 Augustinus Dacus
62 Absolon
63 Albumasar
64 Anticlaudianus
65 Aluredus Anglicus
66 Aquila Ponticus
67 Albertanus Causidicus Brixiensis
68 Avicenna
69 Algazel
70 Alkindus
71 Achardus
72 Astulphus

73 Albericus
74 Alfridus Beverlacensis
75 Alpharabius
76 Aluredus rex
77 Alvarus
78 Basilius Archiepiscopus Cappadociae
79 Basilius Anchiranus
80 Baldwinus
81 Bacharius
82 Berengarius
83 Berillus
84 Beda
85 Bernardus
86 Bernardus Cassinensis
87 Bernardus Silvestris
88 Bernardus Morlanensis
89 Bonaventura
90 Bridferthus
91 Bruno Sigiensis
92 Buconius
93 Bartholomaeus
94 Boetius
95 Bardesanes
96 Berengarius
97 Bernardus de Trilia
98 Bernardus Claremontensis Episcopus
99 Bochardus Theutonicus
100 Bartholomeus Pisanus
101 Boetius Dacus
102 Bumbalonius Bononiensis
103 Byardus
104 Bachillus
105 Bellator
106 Burcardus
107 Babio
108 Bernardus Papiensis
109 Bartholomeus Brixiensis
110 Brida
111 Cassiodorus
112 Ciprianus Afer
113 Clemens papa
114 Clemens Stromates
115 Clemens Lantoniensis
116 Columella
117 Curtius
118 Cornelius
119 Claudius
120 Claudius vel Claudianus
121 Claudianus Viennensis
122 Cato
123 Candidus
124 Constantius
125 Celius Aurelius
126 Cirillus Alexandriae Episcopus
127 Crispinus
128 Celestius
129 Comodianus
130 Cirillus Jerosolymitanus
131 Celestius papa
132 Cirus Alexandrinus
133 Caecilius
134 Cherealis
135 Cesarius Arelatensis
136 Constantinus Cassinensis
137 Censorinus
138 Columbanus
139 Dionisius Areopagita
140 Dionisius Alexandriae
141 Dionisius Monachus
142 Dionisius Corinthiorum Episcopus
143 Damasus papa
144 Didimus Alexandrinus
145 Didimus Grammaticus
146 Durandus
147 Diacontius
148 Diodorus
149 Diomedes
150 Donatus
151 Dorotheus
152 Dares Frigius
153 Dites
154 Diascorides
155 Effrem
156 Euagrius
157 Euagrius
158 Epiphanius
159 Eusebius Caesariensis
160 Eusebius presbyter
161 Eusebius
162 Eusebius Emissenus

163 Egesippus
164 Eucherius Lugdunensis
165 Eusebius Arelatensis
166 Eutropius
167 Eugipius
168 Ernaldus Bonevallensis
169 Egidius
170 Esicius
171 Edmundus Cantuariensis
172 Egidius de Listiniis
173 Egidius Aurelianus
174 Elizabeth
175 Eugenius Cartaginensis
176 Eutropius
177 Eustasius
178 Emilianus
179 Eutices
180 Excolio
181 Euclides
182 Erodotus
183 Ethicus
184 Fulgentius Ruspensis
185 Fabius Planciades Fulgentius
186 Fulbertus Carnotensis
187 Faustus
188 Faustinus
189 Firmianus
190 Fastidius
191 Fortunatus
192 Frigius Dares
193 Flavianus
194 Flaccianus
195 Florentius Wigorniensis
196 Flavius
197 Ferrandus Carthaginensis
198 Frethulfus Luxoniensis
199 Fulgerius Carnotensis
200 Facundus Ermanensis
201 Fortunatianus
202 Focas
203 Gregorius papa
204 Gregorius Nazanzenus
205 Gregorius
206 Gregorius Emisenus
207 Gregorius Boeticus

208 Gregorius de Bridelington
209 Gregorius Turonensis
210 Genadius
211 Gelasius papa
212 Gilbertus Albus
213 Gilbertus Londoninensis
214 Gilbertus Westmonasteriensis
215 Gilbertus Porree
216 Galfridus Claraevallensis
217 Gracianus
218 Galienus
219 Galfridus Monumutensis
220 Guymundus
221 Gervasius
222 Gorgias Rethor
223 Gerardus Teutonicus
224 Guydo Argominensis
225 Gregorius Viennensis
226 Godius
227 Galfridus Vinesauf
228 Gaius
229 Gildas
230 Gargilius Martialis
231 Godardus Malmesbiriae
232 Giraldus Cambrensis
233 Guido Aretinus
234 Godefridus Parisiensis
235 Gundisalvus Tholetanus
236 Guido de Columpnis
237 Guido abbas S. Dionisii
238 Gaufridus Altisiodorensis
239 Guido prior Cartusiae
240 Haimo
241 Hamonius
242 Hillarius Pictavensis
243 Hillarius Arelatensis
244 Hugo S. Victoris Canonicus
245 Hugo de Folieto
246 Hildefonsus
247 Hildebertus Cenomanensis
248 Helynandus
249 Hildegardis
250 Heliodorus
251 Heliodorus Antiochiae
252 Haly

253 Hermannus
254 Hugo Pisanus
255 Hereneus Lugdunensis
256 Heraclidis
257 Hermes
258 Hesopus
259 Hermes Trismegistus
260 Henricus Huntedoniensis
261 Humbertus
262 Hugo de Vienna
263 Hambaldus
264 Hugo
265 Herveus Brito
266 Hugo Argentinensis
267 Hispanus
268 Hermannus Teutonicus
269 Heilwicus
270 Henricus Teutonicus
271 Henricus de Costeseye
272 Helprlcus
273 Heraclitus
274 Honoratus
275 Homerus
276 Henrlcus de Gandavo
277 Holcote
278 Hesiodus
279 Hildewinus
280 Houden
281 Jeronimus
282 Johannes Crisostomus
283 Innocentius III papa
284 Ignatius
285 Johannes Cassianus
286 Johannes Damascenes
287 Johannes Scotus
288 Johannes Sarisburiensis
289 Johannes Gerundiensis
290 Johannes Beleth
291 Johannes Antiochenae
292 Jacobus Sapiens
293 Joachim
294 Johannes Jerosolymitanus
295 Johannes Constantinopolitanus
296 Josephus
297 Justinus
298 Justinianus
299 Justus
300 Justinianus
301 Julius Firmicus
302 Julius Affricanus
303 Julius Frontinus
304 Julius Celsus
305 Julius papa
306 Julianus Pomerius
307 Junilius
308 Jordanus
309 Johannes de Deo
310 Juvencus
311 Juvenalis
312 Jordanus
313 Johannes Parisiensis
314 Innocentius V papa
315 Johannes de Erdenbers
316 Johannes Faventinus
317 Johannes Pingens
318 Jacobus de Benevento
319 Jacobus de Frumanno
320 Jacobus Januensis
321 Johannes Teutonicus
322 Johannes de Fano
323 Johannes Januensis
324 Jacobus de Vitriaco
325 Johannes de Saxonia
326 Izachius
327 Judas
328 Johannes Cornubiensis
329 Jacobus de Viterbio
330 Johannes de Rupella
331 Johannes de Garlandia
332 Johannes Scolasticus
333 Johannes Manduyt
334 Johannes de Alba Villa
335 Johannes Carpinus
336 Johannes Ocreatus
337 Johannes Walensis
338 Johannes de Bromyerd
339 Johannes Peccham
340 Ignius
341 Johannes Anglicus
342 Johannes de Hovden

343 Leo papa II
344 Lanfrancus
345 Lactantius Firmianus
346 Leander
347 Lucianus
348 Lucanus
349 Ludoldus
350 Lentius
351 Lucianus
352 Lucifer Caralitanus
353 Lucius Alexandrinus
354 Leporius
355 Licinianus
356 Longus
357 Luitprandus
358 Laurentius Dunelmensis
359 Maximus Tauriensis
360 Maximus
361 Methodius
362 Macharius
363 Macharius Alexandrinus
364 Martinus Dumiensis
365 Marcus Varro
366 Marcellinus Illiricanus
367 Marianus Scotus
368 Marcion
369 Macrobius
370 Macrobius Ambrosius Theodosii
371 Mileto vel Miletus
372 Musseus Massiliensis
373 Militiades
374 Minucius Felix
375 Monagaldus
376 Martinus Polonus
377 Moneta
378 Matheus Ripensis
379 Matheus Parisiensis
380 Musanus
381 Modestus
382 Marcellus Ancheranus
383 Mothunus
384 Mennadius
385 Maximus Augustanae episcopus
386 Maximus
387 Martirius

388 Macer
389 Marcius Valerius Martialis Cocus
390 Marcianus Felix Capella
391 Marbodius
392 Marcus Paulus de Venetiis
393 Marius Salernitanus
394 Mauricius
395 Maximianus
396 Novatianus
397 Nicholaus Ambianensis
398 Nicholaus Trivet
399 Nicholaus de Gorham
400 Niceas
401 Nicetus
402 Nennius
403 Nicholaus de Lyra
404 Origines
405 Odo Cluniacensis
406 Odo de Tyrentona
407 Orosius
408 Odo Vienensis
409 Ossius Cordubensis
410 Odilo Cluniacensis
411 Oratius Flaccus Satirus
412 Ovidus Publius Naso
413 Oliverus Brito
414 Oresiesis
415 Olimpius
416 Orianus
417 Osbertus de Clara
418 Osbernus
419 Papias
420 Papias
421 Pachomius
422 Palladius
423 Palladius
424 Paulinus Nolanus
425 Paulinus
426 Paulus Cassinensis
427 Paulus
428 Petrus Edissenus
429 Possidonius
430 Pascasinus Ciciliensis
431 Pastor
432 Paulus natione Pannonius

433 Petrus Abelardi
434 Patricius archiepiscopus Hiberniae
435 Papirianus
436 Paschasius Radbertus
437 Paterius
438 Pamphllius
439 Petrus Lumbardus
440 Petrus Commestor
441 Petrus Pictavensis
442 Petrus Cantor
443 Petrus Damianus
444 Petrus Blesensis
445 Petrus Afulfi
446 Petrus de Tharenta
447 Petronius
448 Petrus Heli
449 Persius
450 Petrus abbas S. Remigii
451 Petrus Ravennatis episcopus
452 Philo Judaeus
453 Phileas
454 Philippus Cretensis
455 Pontius
456 Philippus
457 Pierius
458 Policarpus
459 Porphirius
460 Policrates
461 Porchetus
462 Plinius Secundus
463 Plutarchius
464 Plato
465 Placentinus Barre
466 Prosper natione Aquitannicus
467 Primasius
468 Promeritus
469 Prudentius
470 Priscianus
471 Prepositinus
472 Proba
473 Pebadius
474 Pacacianus
475 Pinitus Cretensis
476 Panthenus
477 Priscillianus
478 Pelagius
479 Poterius
480 Petrus abbas Tripolitanae
481 Petrus de Aureola
482 Parisiensis episcopus dictus Willelmus de Avernys
483 Petrus Carnotensis
484 Petrus de Vineis
485 Plautus
486 Proculus
487 Portumanus
488 Pomponius Porphirionis
489 Quadratus
490 Quintilianus
491 Quintus Curtius Rufus
492 Rabanus
493 Raby Moyses
494 Radulfus Flaviacensis
495 Radulphus Niger
496 Radulfus Westmonasteriensis
497 Remigius Altisiodorensis
498 Richardus de S. Victore
499 Ricardus de Media Villa
500 Radulphus de Diceto
501 [R] . . . de Frisingfeld
502 Ricardus de Cyrencestria
503 Rathamius
504 Ricardus de Withringsete
505 Robertus Grosteste
506 Robertus Molendinensis
507 Robertus Pullus
508 Rufinus
509 Raymundus
510 Robertus Kylwardeby
511 Robertus Tracensis
512 Ricardus de Capwell
513 Ricardus Fichacre
514 Robertus de Oxford
515 Robertus de Holcote
516 Robertus Curson
517 Rhodon
518 Rethicius
519 Robertus de S. Victore
520 Ridevales
521 Regio

522 Robertus abbas de Monte S. Michaelis
523 Ricardus Barre
524 Robertus rex Franciae
525 Ricardus Armachanus
526 Rlcardus Prior Eliensis
527 Ricardus de Bury
528 Rlcardus Heremita de Ampole
529 Salustius
530 Salmanus Massiliensis
531 Sedulius
532 Sabbatius
533 Severianus
534 Severus
535 Severus Sulpitius
536 Severinus episcopus
537 Sergius
538 Sextus
539 Servus Dei
540 Samuel
541 Simplicianus
542 Siricius papa
543 Seneca
544 Sidonius
545 Siagrius
546 Simachus
547 Serapion Scolasticus
548 Serapion Antiochenus
549 Socrates
550 Sibilla
551 Sofronius
552 Strabus
553 Smaragdus
554 Stephanus de Langeton
555 Stephanus Burgundus
556 Stephanus Gallicus
557 Symon de Borastona
558 Solinus Flaccus Gaius Julius
559 Servius
560 Statius
561 Secundus Philosophus
562 Serlo
563 Suetonius Gaius Tranquillus
564 Scipio
565 Sigebertus
566 Symphosius

567 Thomas de Aquino
568 Tatianus
569 Thomas Sarisberiensis
570 Thomas archiepiscopus Cantuariae
571 Theodorus Siriae
572 Theodorus Heracliae
573 Theodorus
574 Theophilus Antiochenus
575 Thimotheus
576 Theophilus Alexandrinus
577 Terentius
578 Tertullianus
579 Tholomaeus
580 Triphon
581 Triphilius
582 Tullius Marcus qui et Cithero
583 Tyconius
584 Thomas de Sutton
585 Thomas de Linduno
586 Thomas Waleys
587 Theodoricus Theutonicus
588 Trogus Pompeyus
589 Tullianus
590 Theodorus papa
591 Theodorus archiepiscopus Cantuariae
592 Tremegistus
593 Theodorus
594 Theophilus
595 Titus Bostrenus
596 Theotimus
597 Titus Livius
598 Theodorus Antiochenus
599 Theodorus Anchiranus
600 Theodorus
601 Theoctiscus
602 Theofrastus
603 Thinredus
604 Trota et Trotula
605 Turpinus
606 Valerius Maximus Gayus Valerius
     Flaccus Balbus Sennus
607 Walterus de Mauritania
608 Warnerius Westmonasteriensis
609 Varro
610 Vegetius Renatus

611 Velius
612 Victor Mauritaniae episcopus
613 Victor papa
614 Victor
615 Vincentius Lirinensis
616 Victorius Massiliensis
617 Victorius natione Aquitannicus
618 Victorius Pictavensis
619 Victorinus
620 Victorinus
621 Victruvius
622 Vigilius papa
623 Vigilius
624 Vigilius
625 Wilhelmus de Monte vel Montibus
626 Wilhelmus de Burgo
627 Wilhelmus Parvus
628 Valeranus
629 Wilhelmus de Pagula
630 Virgilius Maro
631 Vitellius
632 Wilhelmus de S. Theodorico
633 Wilhelmus Durandus
634 Ursinus
635 Vigillius
636 Vincentius Burgundus Alias Belvacensis
637 Wilhelmus de Hothun
638 Wilhelmus de Altona
639 Wilhelmus de Maunfeld
640 Wlricus
641 Wilhelmus Lumbardus
642 Wilhelmus de Paraldo
643 Wilhelmus Aurelianensis
644 Wilhelmus Gallicus
645 Wilhelmus Brixensis
646 Wilhelmus Parisiensis
647 Wilhelmus Gallicus
648 Wilhelmus de Enkourt
649 Wilhelmus de Kingesham
650 Wilhelmus Brumyard
651 Wilhelmus Brabantinus
652 Wido
653 Walterus de Bokedene
654 Wilhelmus Gemeticensis
655 Wilhelmus de Conches
656 Verecundus
657 Wilhelmus de Malmesbiria
658 Wilhelmus Neubrigensis
659 Walterus Exoniensis
660 Wilhelmus Rivallensis
661 Windichindus
662 Windocinensis
663 Usuardus
664 Xpoforus Nolhamsensis
665 Xpoforus Lumbardus
666 Ysidorus
667 Yvo Belvacensis
668 Ypolitus
669 Ysaac
670 Ysaac Antiochenus
671 Ypocras
672 Ysichius
673 Zacharias Crisopolitanus
674 Zoroastes qui et Cham

LIST OF ABBREVIATIONS

Catalogues and other lists of books published in this series are generally designated by letters and numbers:

A	Augustinian canons
B	Benedictines: shorter catalogues
BM	Dover priory
BP	Peterborough abbey
C	Carthusians
G	Gilbertines
H	Henry VIII
K	Henry of Kirkestede
P	Premonstratensians
R	*Registrum Anglie*
SS	Syon abbey
UC	Cambridge
Z	Cistercians

Abh.	Abhandlung(en)
AFP	*Archivum Franciscanum Historicum* 1– (Quaracchi 1908–)
AH	*Analecta Hymnica Medii Aevi*, ed. G. M. Dreves & others, 55 vols (Leipzig 1886–1922)
AHDLMA	*Archives d'histoire doctrinale et littéraire du moyen âge* 1– (Paris 1926–)
AL	*Aristoteles Latinus*, 31 vols (Brugge, Paris, Leiden 1961–); volumes to appear are listed in L. Minio-Paluello, *Opuscula* (Amsterdam 1972), 471–3
AL Codd.	G. Lacombe & others, *Aristoteles Latinus. Codices*, 2 vols (Rome, Cambridge 1939–55)
AL Supp.	L. Minio-Paluello, *Aristoteles Latinus. Codices, Supplementa altera* (Brugge, Paris 1961)
Arnold, *Memorials*	*Memorials of St Edmund's Abbey*, ed. T. Arnold, RS 96, 3 vols (London 1890–96)
attrib.	attributed
Bale, *Index*	J. Bale, *Index Britanniae scriptorum*, ed. R. L. Poole & M. Bateson (Oxford 1902; repr. with introduction by C. Brett & J. P. Carley, Woodbridge 1990)
Bale, *Scriptores*	J. Bale, *Scriptorum illustrium Maioris Britanniae catalogus*, 2 vols (Basel 1557–9 / repr. Farnborough 1971)
BAV	Biblioteca Apostolica Vaticana, Rome

Bell, *Cistercians*	D. N. Bell, *The Libraries of the Cistercians, Gilbertines and Premonstratensians*, Corpus of British Medieval Library Catalogues 3 (London 1992)
BHL	[A. Poncelet & others], *Bibliotheca Hagiographica Latina* (Brussels 1898–1901), with supplement (1911); further supplemented by H. Fros, *Bibliotheca Hagiographica Latina. Novum supplementum* (Brussels 1986) [cited by no.]
BL	British Library, London
Bloomfield	M. W. Bloomfield & others, *Incipits of Latin Works on the Virtues and Vices, 1100–1500 A.D.* (Cambridge, MA, 1979) [cited by no.]
BM *Cat. Royal*	G. F. Warner & J. P. Gilson, *British Museum, Catalogue of Western Manuscripts in the Old Royal and King's Collections*, 4 vols (London 1921)
BNF	Bibliothèque nationale de France, Paris
Bodl.	Bodleian Library, Oxford
Bressie, 'Textual corruption'	R. Bressie, 'Modern textual corruption in MS. Cambridge Additional 3470', *Modern Language Notes* 60 (1945) 248–54
BRUO	A. B. Emden, *A Biographical Register of the University of Oxford to A.D. 1500*, 3 vols (Oxford 1957–9)
Camd.	Camden Society, Publications 1–105, new ser. 1–62, 3rd ser. 1–94, 4th ser. 1–44, 5th ser. 1– (London 1838–)
Carmody	F. J. Carmody, *Arabic Astronomical and Astrological Sciences in Latin Translation: a critical bibliography* (Berkeley, CA, 1956) [cited by page]
Cassiodorus	*Cassiodori Senatoris Institutiones*, ed. R. A. B. Mynors, 2nd edn (Oxford 1961)
CCCM	*Corpus Christianorum, Continuatio Medievalis* 1– (Turnhout 1971–)
CCSL	*Corpus Christianorum, Series Latina* 1– (Turnhout 1954–)
CMA *Gallia*	M.-H. Jullien & F. Perelman, *Clavis scriptorum Latinorum medii aevi. Auctores Galliae 735–987*, 1– (Turnhout 1994–)
CPG	M. Geerard, *Clavis Patrum Graecorum*, 2nd edn, 5 vols (Turnhout 1974–87); *Supplementum* (Turnhout 1998)
CPL	E. Dekkers, *Clavis Patrum Latinorum*, 3rd edn (Steenbrugge 1995)
CPPM	J. Machielson, *Clavis Patristica Pseudepigraphorum Medii aevi* 1– (Turnhout 1990–) [cited by no.]
CSEL	*Corpus Scriptorum Ecclesiasticorum Latinorum* 1– (Vienna 1892–)
CUL	Cambridge University Library
Diaz	M. C. Diaz y Diaz, *Index scriptorum Latinorum medii aevi Hispanorum* (Salamanca 1958)
DS	*Dictionnaire de spiritualité*, ed. M. Villers & others, 1– (Paris 1932–)
DTC	*Dictionnaire de théologie catholique*, ed. A. Vacant & E. Mangenot, 15 vols (Paris 1899–1950); tables générales, 3 vols (Paris 1951–72)
Duchesne	*Liber pontificalis*, ed. L. Duchesne, revd. C. Vogel, 3 vols (Paris 1955–7)

Ely extracts	Extracts from a lost copy of the *Catalogus* copied into a manuscript from Ely in the mid-15th cent., Lambeth Palace Library, MS 448, fols. 118v, 119v, and 149v
Étienne de Bourbon	É. de Bourbon, *Tractatus de diuersis materiis praedicabilibus*, ed. A. Lecoy de La Marche, Société de l'histoire de France 185 (Paris 1877)
Fleming, *Prophecies*	M. H. Fleming, *The Late Medieval Pope Prophecies: The* Genus nequam *Group*, Medieval & Renaissance Texts & Studies 204 (Tempe, AZ, 1999)
Friedberg	E. Friedberg, *Corpus iuris canonici*, 2 vols (Leipzig 1879, 1881/repr. 1922–8)
Friis-Jensen & Willoughby, *Peterborough*	K. Friis-Jensen & J. M. W. Willoughby, *Peterborough Abbey*, Corpus of British Medieval Library Catalogues 8 (London 2001)
Fulgentius	Fulgentius, *Sermones antiqui*, ed. R. Helm (Leipzig 1898) [cited by page]
Gale extracts	Extracts from the lost Bale/Ussher manuscript of the *Catalogus*, recorded by Thomas Gale (d. 1702) on four unnumbered front and back flyleaves of his copy of Bale's *Scriptores*, CUL F156.a.3.1
Gennadius	Gennadius, *De uiris inlustribus*, ed. E. C. Richardson, Texte und Untersuchungen 14 (Leipzig 1896)
GL	*Grammatici Latini*, ed. H. Keil, 7 vols (Leipzig 1857–80)
GL Supp.	*Grammatici Latini: Supplement*, ed. H. Hagen (Leipzig 1870)
Glorieux, *Rép.*	P. Glorieux, *Répertoire des maîtres en théologie de Paris au XIIIe siècle*, 2 vols (Paris 1933–4)
Goff	F. R. Goff, *Incunabula in American Libraries, a third census* (New York 1964/repr. with additions, New York 1973)
Gransden, *Bury St Edmunds*	A. Gransden (ed.), *Bury St Edmunds: Medieval Art, Architecture, Archaeology, and Economy*, British Archaeological Association, Conference Transactions 1994 (1998)
Gransden, 'Some manuscripts'	A. Gransden, 'Some manuscripts in Cambridge from Bury St Edmunds abbey: exhibition catalogue', in Gransden, *Bury St Edmunds*, 228–85
GW	*Gesamtkatalog der Wiegendrucke*, 7 vols (Leipzig 1925–38); 8– (Stuttgart 1978–)
Hain	L. Hain, *Repertorium Bibliographicum*, 4 vols (1826–38/repr. Milan 1948)
Hall	A. Hall, *Nicolai Triveti Annalium continuatio, ut et Adami Murimuthensis Chronicon . . .* (Oxford 1722)
Harvey, *Living and Dying*	B. Harvey, *Living and Dying in England, 1100–1540: the Monastic Experience* (Oxford 1993)
Higden	Ranulf Higden, *Polychronicon*, ed. C. Babington & J. R. Lumby, 9 vols, RS 41 (1865–86) [cited by volume and page]
Hunt, *Teaching Latin*	A. B. Hunt, *Teaching and Learning Latin in Thirteenth-Century England*, 3 vols (Cambridge 1991)

inc.	incipit
Isidore	Isidore of Seville, *De uiris illustribus*, ed. C. C. Merino, *El 'De viris illustribus' de Isidoro de Sevilla: Estudio y edición crítica* (Salamanca 1964)
James, *Caius*	M. R. James, *A Descriptive Catalogue of the Manuscripts in the Library of Gonville and Caius College*, 2 vols (Cambridge 1907–8); Supplement (Cambridge 1914)
James, *Corpus*	M. R. James, *A Descriptive Catalogue of the Manuscripts in the Library of Corpus Christi College, Cambridge*, 2 vols (Cambridge 1912)
James extracts	Extracts from the lost Bale/Ussher manuscript of the *Catalogus*, recorded by Richard James (d. 1638) in one of his notebooks, Bodl. MS James 11, pp. 195–200 (*al.* 240–245)
James, *Lambeth*	M. R. James & C. Jenkins, *A Descriptive Catalogue of the Manuscripts in the Library of Lambeth Palace* (Cambridge 1932)
James, 'List of libraries'	M. R. James, 'The list of libraries prefixed to the *Catalogus* of John Boston and the kindred documents', *Collectanea Franciscana* 2 (1922) 37–60
James, *Pembroke*	M. R. James, *A Descriptive Catalogue of the Manuscripts in the Library of Pembroke College, Cambridge* (Cambridge 1905)
James, *St Edmund*	M. R. James, *On the abbey of S. Edmund at Bury*, Octavo publications of the Cambridge Antiquarian Society 28 (Cambridge 1895)
James, *St John's*	M. R. James, *A Descriptive Catalogue of the Manuscripts in the Library of St John's College, Cambridge* (Cambridge 1913)
Jerome	Jerome, *De uiris inlustribus*, ed. E. C. Richardson, Texte und Untersuchungen 14 (Leipzig 1896)
JTS	*Journal of Theological Studies* 1–50 (Oxford 1899–1949); new ser. 1– (Oxford 1950–)
Kaeppeli	T. Kaeppeli, *Scriptores Ordinis Praedicatorum Medii Aevi*, 4 vols (Rome 1970–93)
Ker, *MLGB*	N. R. Ker, *Medieval Libraries of Great Britain*, 2nd edn (London 1964); Supplement, ed. A. G. Watson (London 1987)
Ker, *MMBL*	N. R. Ker, *Medieval Manuscripts in British Libraries*, 4 vols (Oxford 1969–92); index (Oxford 2003)
Knowles, *Monastic Order*	D. Knowles, *The Monastic Order in England: a history of its development from the times of St. Dunstan to the Fourth Lateran council, 943–1216*, 2nd edn (Cambridge 1963)
Knowles, *Religious Orders*	D. Knowles, *The Religious Orders in England*, 3 vols (Cambridge 1948–59)
Lambert	B. Lambert, *Bibliotheca Hieronymiana Manuscripta*, Instrumenta Patristica 4, 4 vols in 5 (Steenbrugge 1969–72) [cited by no.]
Landgraf	A. M. Landgraf, *Introduction à l'histoire de la littérature théologique de la scolastique naissante*, Université de Montréal, Publications de l'Institut d'études médiévales 22 (Montréal/Paris 1973)

Lapidge/Sharpe	M. Lapidge & R. Sharpe, *A Bibliography of Celtic–Latin Literature 400–1200* (Dublin 1985)
Mariale	An unedited collection of Marian material cited here from the Bury manuscript, Cambridge, Pembroke College, MS 22
MARS	*Mediaeval and Renaissance Studies* 1–6 (London 1941–68)
Martène & Durand	E. Martène & U. Durand, *Veterum scriptorum et monumentorum . . . collectio*, 9 vols (Paris 1724–33)
Med. Stud.	*Mediaeval Studies* 1– (Toronto 1939–)
MF	Thomas of Ireland, *Manipulus florum*. Reference is to the discussion by R. H. & M. A. Rouse, *Preachers,* Florilegia, *and Sermons: Studies on the* Manipulus Florum *of Thomas of Ireland* (Toronto 1979); unless otherwise specified, reference is made to the 'List of Authors and Works' edited on pp. 251–310
MGH	Monumenta Germaniae Historica
OMT	Oxford Medieval Texts (Oxford 1967–)
PAL	C. B. Schmitt & D. Knox, *Pseudo-Aristoteles Latinus. A guide to Latin works falsely attributed to Aristotle before 1500* (London 1985)
Pantin, *Documents*	W. A. Pantin, *Documents illustrating the Activities of the General and Provincial Chapters of the English Black Monks 1215–1540*, 3 vols, Camd. 3rd ser. 45, 47 and 54 (1931–7)
Pantin, 'English treatises'	W. A. Pantin, 'Some medieval English treatises on the origins of monasticism', in *Medieval Studies Presented to Rose Graham* (Oxford 1950), 189–215
Paulus Diaconus	Paulus Diaconus, *Historia Langobardorum*, ed. G. Waitz, MGH *Scriptores rerum Germanicarum in usum scholarum editi* (1878)
Pign.	L. Pignon, *Catalogus fratrum qui claruerunt doctrina*, in G. Meersseman, *Laurentii Pignon catalogi et chronica*, Monumenta Ordinis Fratrum Praedicatorum historica 18 (Rome 1936) 21–33
Pitra, *Analecta sacra*	J.-B. Pitra, *Analecta sacra spicilegio Solesmensi parata*, 5 vols (Paris 1876–91)
PG	J.-P. Migne, *Patrologia Graeca*, 161 vols and index (Paris 1857–66)
PL	J.-P. Migne, *Patrologia Latina*, 217 vols (Paris 1844–55); Index, 4 vols (Paris 1864)
RB	*Revue Bénédictine* 1– (Maredsous 1885–)
Registrum	*Registrum Anglie*, ed. R. A. B. Mynors, R. H. & M. A. Rouse, Corpus of British Medieval Library Catalogues 2 (London 1991)
Rouse, 'Bostonus Buriensis'	R. H. Rouse, 'Bostonus Buriensis and the author of the *Catalogus scriptorum ecclesiae*', *Speculum* 41 (1966) 471–99
Rouse & Rouse, *Authentic Witnesses*	M. A. Rouse & R. H. Rouse, *Authentic Witnesses: Approaches to Medieval Texts and Manuscripts* (Notre Dame, IN, 1991)
RS	Rolls Series, 99 vols in 259 (London 1858–1911, 1964)

SAO	*Sancti Anselmi Opera*, ed. F. S. Schmitt, 6 vols (Seckau, Rome, Edinburgh 1938–61)
SBO	*Sancti Bernardi Opera*, ed. J. Leclercq & others, 8 vols (Rome 1957–77)
SBonO	*S. Bonaventurae Opera omnia*, 10 vols (Quaracchi 1882–1902)
SC	*Speculum coenobitarum*, Oxford, The Queen's College, MS 304, fols. 62r–65v; numbered references correspond to the list of monastic authors and works edited in the appendix to chapter 3 of the Introduction in the present volume
Schanz	M. von Schanz, *Geschichte der Römischen Literatur*, Handbuch der Altertumswissenschaft, 8 bd. in 4 vols (Munich 1896–1920)
Schenkl	H. Schenkl, *Bibliotheca patrum Latinorum Britannica*, 3 bde. in 10 parts (Vienna 1891–1908)
SChr	Sources chrétiennes 1– (Paris 1941–)
Schulte	J. F. von Schulte, *Die Geschichte der Quellen und Literatur des canonischen Rechts von Gratian bis auf die Gegenwart*, 3 vols (Stuttgart 1875)
Script. Ord. Praed.	The non-extant *Scriptores Ordinis Praedicatorum* compiled by the English Dominicans; see chapter 2 of the Introduction in the present volume
Speculum coenobitarum	*Speculum coenobitarum*, ed. A. Hall, *Nicolai Triveti Annalium continuatio ut et Adami Murimuthensis chronicon* (Oxford 1722) 157–92
Sharpe, *Latin Writers*	R. Sharpe, *A Handlist of the Latin Writers of Great Britain and Ireland before 1540* (Turnhout 1997)
Sharpe, 'Reconstructing the medieval library'	R. Sharpe, 'Reconstructing the medieval library of Bury St Edmunds abbey: the lost catalogue of Henry of Kirkstead', in Gransden, *Bury St Edmunds*, 204–218
Sharpe & others, *Benedictines*	R. Sharpe, J. P. Carley, R. M. Thomson & A. G. Watson, *English Benedictine Libraries: the shorter catalogues*, Corpus of British Medieval Library Catalogues 4 (London 1996)
Stams	*Catalogus Stamsensis*, in G. Meersseman, *Laurentii Pignon catalogi et chronica*, Monumenta Ordinis Fratrum Praedicatorum historica 18 (Rome 1936) 56–67
Stegmüller *Bibl.*	F. Stegmüller, *Repertorium Biblicum Medii Aevi*, 11 vols (Madrid 1940 [*recte* 1950]–80)
Stegmüller *Sent.*	F. Stegmüller, *Repertorium commentariorum in Sententias Petri Lombardi*, 2 vols (Würzburg 1947); supplement by V. Doucet (Quaracchi 1954)
Tanner, *Bibliotheca*	T. Tanner, *Bibliotheca Britannico-Hibernica, siue De scriptoribus, qui in Anglia, Scotia, et Hibernia ad saeculi XVII initium floruerunt, commentarius*, ed. D. Wilkins (London 1748)
Teubner	*Bibliotheca scriptorum Graecorum et Latinorum Teubneriana* (Leipzig, Stuttgart, 1849–)

Texts and Transmission	*Texts and Transmission: a Survey of the Latin Classics*, ed. L. D. Reynolds, revd. edn (Oxford 1986)
Thomson, *Archives*	R. M. Thomson, *The Archives of the Abbey of Bury St Edmunds* (Woodbridge 1980)
Thomson, 'Obedientiaries'	R. M. Thomson, 'Obedientiaries of St Edmund's abbey', *Proceedings of the Suffolk Institute of Archaeology and History* 35 (1982) 91–103
Thorndike/Kibre	L. Thorndike & P. Kibre, *A Catalogue of Incipits of Mediaeval Scientific Writings in Latin*, 2nd edn (London 1963)
Twyne extracts	Extracts from the lost Bale/Ussher manuscript of the *Catalogus*, recorded by Brian Twyne (d. 1664) in one of his notebooks, Bodl. MS Twyne 22, pp. 403, 406
Twysden, *Scriptores*	Roger Twysden, *Historiae Anglicanae scriptores X* (London 1652)
UL	University Library
VCH	*The Victoria History of the Counties of England* (London 1900–)
Vincent	Vincent of Beauvais, *Speculum historiale*, pr. [Strassburg]: Johann Mentelin, [1473]
Ware extracts	Extracts from the lost Bale/Ussher manuscript of the *Catalogus*, recorded by James Ware (d. 1666) in one of his notebooks, BL MS Add. 4787, fols. 132r–133v
Webber & Watson, *Augustinians*	T. Webber & A. G. Watson, *The Libraries of the Augustinian Canons*, Corpus of British Medieval Library Catalogues 6 (London 1998)

LIST OF PLATES
(between pages ccxiv–1)

Frontispiece. CUL MS Add. 3470, p. 126

1. *a.* Cambridge, Pembroke College, MS 28, fol. [69r]. (See p. xxxiii.)
   b. Bodl. MS Bodley 297, p. 345. (See p. xli.)
2. Cambridge, Pembroke College, MS 23, fol. 1r. (See p. xlv.)
3. *a.* BL MS Harley 1005, fol. 35v. (See p. xlix.)
   b. Wisbech & Fenland Museum, Town Library, MS 1, fol. i^r. (See p. xlix.)
4. *a.* Cambridge, Pembroke College, MS 25, fol. 3r. (See p. lii.)
   b. Cambridge, Pembroke College, MS 313, fol. 1r. (See p. liii.)
   c. Cambridge, Pembroke College, MS 313, fol. 8v. (See p. liii.)
5. Cambridge, Corpus Christi College, MS 404, fol. 7r. (See p. lviii.)
6. *a.* Bodl. MS Bodley 833, fol. 1r. (See p. lix.)
   b. BL MS Harley 1005, fol. 115r. (See pp. xlvii, lxxiii.)
7. Bodl. MS Lat. hist. d. 4, fol. 224r. (See p. lxvi.)
8. *a.* Cambridge, Corpus Christi College, MS 404, fol. 41r. (See p. lxxxi.)
   b. College of Arms, MS Arundel 30, fol. 8v. (See p. lxxxiii.)

INTRODUCTION

CHAPTER I

HENRY OF KIRKESTEDE

Henry of Kirkestede, compiler of the *Catalogus de libris autenticis et apocrifis*, was a Benedictine monk, and eventually the prior, of the royal abbey of St Edmund at Bury in Suffolk.[1] His life spanned some sixty-five years across the middle of the 14th cent., from around 1314 or before to 1378 or after, making him a close contemporary of Edward III's (1312–77). To us who view it in retrospect, his lifetime seems an era of chronic turmoil.

Henry of Kirkestede lived through the coup that removed Edward II from the throne in 1327. In that same year he witnessed, as an adolescent growing up on Bury land, the sack of the abbey by local rebels exploiting the absence of royal protection. He observed the opening years of the Hundred Years War, and the gradual empowerment in Parliament of those whose taxes paid for the war's expensive alliances and campaigns. He survived the devastation inflicted by the Black Death in the middle of the century and the social unrest that followed. As a Benedictine he was affected by the strains besetting organized religion: the losing struggle of the old orders with the mendicants; the constant after-effects of the relocation of the papacy in 1309 from Rome to Avignon, where it functioned under the domination of England's adversary, France; and, near the end of his days, the opening of the Great Schism in 1378. He surely heard of the teachings of John Wyclif at Oxford, and their initial condemnation by the pope (apparently at Benedictine instigation). And he may have lived to witness the Peasants' Revolt at Bury in the summer of 1381, a much more violent recurrence of the destructive Bury uprising of 1327–31 that had marked his early years. It

---

1. The *Catalogus*, previously ascribed to 'Boston of Bury', was attributed to Henry of Kirkestede by R. H. Rouse, 'Bostonus Buriensis and the author of the *Catalogus scriptorum ecclesiae*', *Speculum* 41 (1966) 471–99. John Boston, nevertheless, continues to appear in current biographical dictionaries; see T. Copsey, *Suffolk Writers from the Beginning until 1800: a Catalogue of Suffolk Authors with Some Account of their Lives and a List of their Writings* (Ipswich 2000), 66: 'Boston, John of Bury fl. 1410', where he is called 'a native of Bury St Edmunds and an Augustinian monk belonging to the Abbey at Bury'. Copsey states that much of the information for his new dictionary comes from the eighteenth-century Suffolk antiquary David E. Davy's unpublished biographical register.

is against this turbulent backdrop that we examine the career of the founder of English bibliography and librarian of Bury St Edmunds.[2]

Henry of Kirkestede's name appears in full, or close to it, in six examples written either in his own hand[3] or by contemporaries in formal circumstances.[4] At Bury, as in other monasteries, recruitment was resolutely local;[5] for example, Bury's 14th-cent. priors and sacrists were all Norfolk and Suffolk men.[6] It is not surprising in these circumstances that Kirkestede's birthplace—the source of his surname—was a Bury dependency in Norfolk, *Kirkestede* or *Kerkestede* (now Kirstead Green), which appears in the Bury archives from as early as 1095;[7] there is even another 'Henricus de Kirkestede'

---

2. For a view of the central years of the 14th cent., see W. A. Pantin, *The English Church in the Fourteenth Century* (Cambridge 1955), and S. L. Waugh, *England in the Reign of Edward III* (Cambridge 1991).
3. See Appendix to this chapter.
4. The following examples are in his hand. Cambridge, Corpus Christi College, MS 404, fol. iiiv (P. 163), 'ffrater Henricus de Kirkestede'; see Rouse, 'Bostonus Buriensis', pl. I, note printed by James, *Corpus Christi*, 2. 269. BL MS Royal 8 B. IV, fol. 72r (S. 184), 'de procuracione fratris Henrici de Kirkested'; printed in BM *Cat. Royal*, 1. 220. Cambridge, Pembroke College, MS 92, fol. iv, to his prescription, 'de procuracione fratris Henric. de Kirkestede'; printed by James, *Pembroke*, 85; Gransden, 'Some manuscripts', pl. LXXIXc. These agree with the spelling of his name in the record of his ordination, 'Henricus de Kyrkestede'; in the record of a miracle of St Edmund that he confirmed, 'fr. Henricus de Kirkestede', in Bodl. MS Bodley 240, p. 675; and as witness in the record of the settlement of the tithe of Woolpit, 'Henricus de Kirkestede'.
5. In general, 'for every house ... the vast majority of recruits came from the manors and estates owned by the monastery and (in the case of urban sites) from the town or city and its environs' (Knowles, *Religious Orders*, 2. 229). In a specific case, 'the Abbey's precinct, the town of Westminster, and the City of London' provided perhaps half the recruits at Westminster abbey, with 'its country estates' providing the other (B. Harvey, *Living and Dying in England, 1100–1540: the Monastic Experience* (Oxford 1993), 76).
6. Edmund of Brundish (Norf), Ralph of Caston (Norf), Peter of Clopton (Suff), Reginald and Richard of Denham (Suff), John of Gosford (Suff), Geoffrey of Hemblington (Norf), Robert of Icklingham (Suff), Simon of Langham (Suff), John of Lavenham (Suff), William of Rockland (Norf), Hugh of Saxham (Suff), William of Stow (Norf), and Nicholas of Wortham (Suff); the one exception, Prior John of Cambridge, came from just across the west Suffolk boundary in Cambridgeshire. This sample listing could doubtless be extended to encompass abbots and other obedientiaries among local recruits.
7. D. C. Douglas, *Feudal Documents from the Abbey of Bury St Edmunds* (London 1932), 14 and n. 22, citing a 13th-cent. transcript of the feudal book of Baldwin, abbot of Bury (1065–98), under the heading 'Hec sunt maneria que habuit sanctus Ædmundus in suo dominio et hec sunt terre suorum hominum quas ipsi etiam tenuerunt' ('Kerkestede'), and referring to the comparable passage in the 14th-cent. Pinchbeck Register ('Kirkestede'). See also the entry for Kirstead in E. Ekwall, *The Concise Oxford Dictionary of English Place-names*, 4th edn (Oxford 1960), 281.

from this dependency who witnessed a mid-13th-cent. record.[8] The identity of this village is corroborated by a 13th-cent. Bury record that calls it *Kyrksted juxta Brok* (Kirstead Green is about one mile from Brooke).[9]

The approximate date of Kirkestede's birth can be surmised from the record of his ordination to the priesthood on Saturday 19 September 1338 at Ely Cathedral.[10] Since twenty-four was the earliest canonical age for ordination, we can presume a birthdate of around 1314.[11] If he followed the normal practice, he would have become a novice sometime between the ages of seventeen and twenty-one, with ordination occurring about seven years later.[12]

Kirkestede would presumably have entered the community *c.* 1331, when the legal and financial ramifications of the town's attack on the abbey in 1327 were still being worked out by both sides. The initial violence of the Bury rioters, beginning in January 1327, saw the abbey invaded and plundered. The book-chests were smashed, the books stolen or thrown about, and many registers, charters, and muniments were destroyed. The rebels continued to control the borough and to harass the monks during the months of interregnal uncertainty while the deposed Edward II was alive but imprisoned, until the new royal government managed to impose a degree of order

8. In a charter of gift (*c.* June 1252) to the Cistercian abbey of Sibton that included property at Kirstead, one of the local witnesses is 'Henricus de Kirkestede'; P. Brown, *Sibton Abbey Cartularies and Charters*, Suffolk Charters 7–10 (Woodbridge 1985–8), 4. 44 no. 997. See also charter no. 25, *c.* 1291 (ib. 2. 24, 'Kirksted') and charter no. 29(ii), May 1323 (ib. 2. 37, 'Kirkestede').
9. Printed in W. Dugdale, *Monasticon Anglicanum*, ed. J. Caley & others (London 1817–30), 3. 161 no. XXIX, note at the end. We had previously thought Kirkestede's birthplace to be the village of Kirkstead in Lincolnshire (see, for example, Rouse, 'Bostonus Buriensis', 480, and Sharpe, *Latin Writers*, 172); at the time we were unaware of the Norfolk village.
10. His name appears in the ordination lists of Simon de Montacute, bishop of Ely (1337–45); Montacute Register, fol. 102ra. We are grateful to the late A. B. Emden for this reference. Ordination in practice marked the beginning of a monk's full membership in the community; Knowles, *Religious Orders*, 2. 233. The statutes of the general chapter in 1277 had not required monks to seek ordination (see Pantin, *Documents*, 1. 73), but sixty years later in Kirkestede's day ordination was routine.
11. See Harvey, *Living and Dying*, 118–20. Harvey cites exceptions and dispensations permitting ordination at an earlier age, but they are few in number and late in date, most of them post-dating the Black Death (see below).
12. Knowles, *Religious Orders*, 2. 232–3. The series of statutes of General Chapters printed by W. A. Pantin, *Documents illustrating the Activities of the General and Provincial Chapters of the English Black Monks 1215–1540*, 3 vols, Camd. 3rd ser. 45, 47 and 54 (1931–7), routinely repeat that no one be accepted as a monk under the age of 20, but there are exceptions that seem to have been customarily exploited (that one may be admitted on probation at 19, that no one may be professed—rather than received—before the age of 20, that exception may be made for good reason or for necessity); see, for example, Pantin, *Documents*, 1. 10, 99.

in late October (after Edward II's death in late September). Amid the trials and accusations that followed in 1328 there were renewed outbreaks of violence, and in 1329—a bizarre occurrence—the abbot of Bury was kidnapped, spirited across the Channel, and hidden away, and his release was secured only in 1330. At the time when Kirkestede entered the noviciate, perhaps in 1331, the abbey was demanding from the borough a massive fine of £140,000, which it is safe to say the town could not have paid off in a generation or more. Edward III came in person to Bury in June 1331, to impose on abbey and town a more equitable and realistic settlement that might, at last, put an end to the drama begun in 1327.[13] The abbey's recovery from the physical damage of the incursions, however, continued long after Kirkestede entered the house.

After his noviciate, Kirkestede's brothers would have considered him a junior member of the community until his ordination in 1338. By the 1330s ordination was probably an expected step for Bury monks, rather than an exception. This was necessary, not so much for serving parishes in the neighbourhood, as for celebrating at abbey altars the requisite masses for the deceased, both monks and lay patrons of the abbey. Bury is located in the diocese of Norwich, but it was no accident that Kirkestede was ordained instead by the bishop of Ely: as a royal abbey, Bury was exempt from episcopal oversight, and did not wish to afford the bishop of Norwich any encouragement to think his authority extended to Bury monks even in so routine a matter as ordination.[14]

Novice Master and Librarian 1338–61

In common with the rest of his generation Kirkestede's life was divided into two parts, with the Black Death in 1349 and the subsequent decade of recovery marking the rupture. Kirkestede lived his most productive years in the tenure of Abbot William of Bernham (1335–61), during which time he was chaplain to the abbot, novice master, and custodian of the abbey books, while the abbey itself withstood attacks from the bishop of Norwich and the devastating onset of the Black Death. The second part of Kirkestede's career

---

13. The contemporary account written from the abbey's point of view, *Depraedatio abbatie Sancti Edmundi*, is printed in *Memorials of St Edmund's Abbey*, ed. T. Arnold, RS 96, 3 vols (London 1890–96), 2. 327–54. The various contemporary reports conflict on many details. M. D. Lobel, 'A detailed account of the 1327 rising at Bury St Edmund's and the subsequent trial', *Proceedings of the Suffolk Institute of Archaeology* 21 (1933) 215–31, comes closest to making sense of them all.
14. That the diocesan has no special authority in this matter was deliberately emphasized in the ordinations of 1351; see below, p. lxiv.

filled the years from 1361 until his death after 1378, when he replaced a prior killed by another virulent outbreak of plague and helped his new abbot John Brinkley with the regeneration of the abbey.

It is possible that Kirkestede, presumably before his ordination in 1338, spent some time at university. Despite the proximity of Cambridge, student-monks from Bury were regularly sent to Gloucester College at Oxford, the Black Monks' house of study established in 1286 and jointly supported by the Benedictine abbeys of England. A Master P. from Bury was regent of Gloucester College in the second decade of the 14th cent.;[15] and Bury had an exceptional record for sending both students and financial support to the college throughout the 14th cent., following the injunction of Benedict XII (1336) that one of every twenty Benedictines be sent for a degree in either theology or canon law, and the enactment of legislation to that effect (1338) by the English general chapter.[16] No explicit statement ties Kirkestede to university training, but a stay at the school would help to explain his seeming acquaintance with the books of the Oxford Greyfriars.[17] The Bury manuscript of Peter Lombard's Sentences offers another hint.[18] Written in the 13th cent., probably on the Continent, this manuscript had already been at the university where it was heavily annotated by perhaps two student hands;[19] to these Kirkestede added annotations of his own, including a great many that add bibliographical references or clarify existing ones. For example, above an anonymous passage in the text he wrote, 'This is Hugh's *De sacramentis* Book I part 1 ch. 4';[20] and as an addition to references to 'Augustine in the book of Retractations' in the text and the marginal rubric, his annotation specifies 'book 1, chapter 12'.[21] Whether Kirkestede annotated the volume at Oxford or at Bury one cannot say; perhaps he was sent to Oxford for one year of theology, a common practice. Kirkestede's addressing the

---

15. Pantin, *Documents*, 1. 174.
16. Knowles, *Religious Orders*, 2. 15, 18–19; Pantin, *Documents*, 2. 17–18.
17. For Kirkestede and the books of Greyfriars see pp. lvii and cxiv below.
18. Cambridge, Pembroke College, MS 28 (Bury P. 64; s. xiii^{in}).
19. Gransden, 'Some manuscripts', pl. LXXIIA.
20. See plate 1a: 'Istud est Hugo De sa[cramentis] lib. i parte prima capitulo 4to'. Hugh's *De sacramentis* was a work Kirkestede knew well; extracts from it are among the works in a manuscript that Kirkestede purchased for the abbey, BL MS Royal 8 F. xiv, fol. 71r (Bury G. 15), and it is the first of Hugh's works listed in the *Catalogus*, *244.1*.
21. Pembroke College, MS 28, fol. 112v, top of col. 1: internal reference, 'videtur in li. retractationum' and rubric in the adjacent margin, 'Augustinus in li. retractationum'; Kirkestede's interlinear addition, 'li. 1 capitulo 12'. See another example on the facing fol. 113r col. 1: to a citation, 'Augustinus qui dixerat in li. lxxxiiii questionum quod . . .', Kirkestede interlines 'q. 29 capitulo 26'. Examples are plentiful.

Catalogus 'for the use and convenience of students and preachers'[22] anticipates the support expressed by the General Chapter in 1363 for those monk-students whose brief Oxford training was aimed not at a degree, but at learning to preach effectively, 'aliis rite proponere verbum Dei'.[23] All told, the evidence is general and vague, a basis for speculation and nothing more.

Following his ordination in 1338, the next fixed date in Kirkestede's life (1341) is one he recorded himself. Bodl. MS Lat. hist. d. 4 (Bury C. 59), a collection of histories including Martinus Polonus and an excerpt from William of Malmesbury's *Gesta pontificum*, concludes with the *Flores historiarum* and its continuations.[24] As a further continuation, Kirkestede marked off the blank folios at the end on which to keep annals of his own, at a rate of two years per page (foot of fol. 219r through fol. 224v). He labelled the first year 1341, and numbered in advance the rest of the blank half-pages to 1363. In practice, however, he wrote only four entries over twenty-three years: for the years 1341 (the prior of Ely died and the sacrist was chosen to replace him) and 1342 (Pope Benedict XII died), and then again for 1361 and 1362, when the theme was death and destruction at Bury itself.[25] The entries suggest that by 1341 Kirkestede was already reflecting seriously on the history of his abbey and his country.

Kirkestede first appears in a dated document from the abbey on 13 November 1346, which survives in a 15th-cent. copy. The church of Woolpit owed 20 marks per annum, in two instalments, to the Bury guest-master or hosteller; the early 15th-cent. guest-master Andrew Ashton copied into his register the abbey's charters and records concerning this revenue (1161–1402).[26] Among these is the promise of the rector John Totyngton to

---

22. 'Utilitati et expeditione studencium et predicancium', opening words of the introductory paragraph; see below p. xci.
23. Pantin, *Documents*, 2. 76. Monk-students training in this situation are enjoined to preach more frequently in Latin than in the vernacular so they can quickly hone their skills to preach to their brothers when they are called back to the monastery.
24. Bought by William of Colchester, a Bury monk: 'Liber monachorum Sancti Edmundi de empcione fratris Willelmi de Colcestrie', containing on fols. 1r–48v Martinus Polonus, *Chronicon summorum pontificum et imperatorum*, copied in Italy. The book was bound before the mid-14th cent. with these works copied in England: fol. 50r, chronicles of archbishops and bishops of England taken from William of Malmesbury's *Gesta pontificum*; fol. 59r, laws of Edward confirmed by the Conqueror; fol. 66r, descriptions and wonders of Britain, and fol. 67v, founders of English monastic houses, all taken from Ralph de Diceto; fol. 72r, prophecies; fol. 76r, *Flores historiarum* and its continuations (202v, 205v, 218r–219r); fols. 219v–224v, originally blank.
25. For the reports of plague and tempest in these later entries, see pp. lxvi and lxx below.
26. In the Register of Andrew Ashton, *c*. 1428 (BL MS Cotton Claudius A. xii, fols. 86r–99v [Bury —]); the Woolpit segment is printed by Arnold, *Memorials*, 3. 77–112. For Kirkestede's appearance see Claudius A. xii, fol. 92r (Arnold, 3. 100).

pay the set amount at the set times, an oath sworn in 1346 in the cloister at Bury in the presence of the abbey officials of Kirkestede's day: Edmund Brundish, prior, Adam of Hempnall, subprior, John of Snailwell, precentor, and John Ernstede cellarer; those who signed as witnesses were Robert Lyrlyngges and John Totyngton, clerics of the Norwich diocese, and Master William Wyvelyngham and Henry of Kirkestede of the abbey, along with the notary.

By this date, 1346, Kirkestede was an active senior member of the community, who would have been involved in the joint defence of the abbot and convent in repelling the attack on their privileges (and their income) waged tenaciously by the bishop of Norwich.[27] Perhaps it was then, or soon after, that Kirkestede became one of the abbot's chaplains; we know for certain only that he held that post sometime before 1361, in a term that overlapped with the service of John Ernstede (sometime cellarer; see above) and others in the same post.[28] The abbot's chaplains are said to have combined 'the functions of secretary and bursar to the abbot' with that of 'liaison officer between abbot and convent'.[29] If he held this position at any time in the later 1340s, Kirkestede would have experienced the bishop's tactics at close quarters.

The quarrel (1345–51) between William Bateman, bishop of Norwich, and William of Bernham, abbot of Bury, turned on the always controversial issue of monastic exemption: Bateman attempted to levy an aid from Bury, along with all the other establishments in his diocese. The abbey refused, on the grounds that it was exempt from diocesan obligations and oversight. The bishop then 'investigated' the abbey's conduct and morals, on the basis of testimony from priests in the surrounding parishes, among whom deep-seated resentment of the abbey was a way of life. The investigators reported that 'very many' (*quamplures*) Bury monks lived outside the abbey in neighbouring villages, where they were guilty of an energetic array of crimes. The accusations included adultery, fornication, incest, kidnapping,

---

27. In 1345 and earlier in 1346 the abbey had been engaged in bitter verbal and legal hostilities with the bishop of Norwich, over the perpetually vexing matter of the abbey's exemption from episcopal control and therefore from episcopal levies. See Arnold, *Memorials*, 3. x–xv for the facts (though one must discount Arnold's enthusiastic bias in favour of the secular clergy, which pits 'the brave and vigorous bishop' against William of Bernham, 'the worst [choice of abbot] that the monks ever freely made during the whole existence of the abbey'), and ibid. 56–73 for an edition of several of the pertinent documents.
28. See BL MS Harley 1005, fol. 67v, recording a visitation that occurred in the abbacy of William of Bernham (1335–61) and in the time of four named abbot's chaplains, including Kirkestede: 'Visitacio domini W. abbatis temporibus fratrum H. de Lakingham, Iohannis de Ernsted, H. de Kirk. et G. de Haliswell capellanorum'.
29. Knowles, *Religious Orders*, 1. 274.

rape, deflowering virgins, engendering bastards, carrying offensive weapons, highway robbery, being out of habit, and two perennial favourites for good measure, simony and usury. (Inevitably, some of these charges were true, just as, inevitably, most of them were not.) The bishop's commissioners therefore ordered Abbot William of Bernham (who was not subject to such an order) to come at a time and place that they specified, to justify himself and his monks. Instead, Bernham petitioned the king's justices to enjoin the bishop to cease from harassing the abbey, while the bishop for his part appealed to the pope for support. The stakes were raised when the bishop excommunicated the royal messenger bearing the injunction, and the king's men responded by confiscating the bishop's estates in four counties. The pope, frustrated by his distance from events, repeatedly ordered fact-finding reports concerning problems that had long since been superseded by other problems.[30]

We do not know how the impasse was resolved, but it must have involved a satisfactory compromise all around. Certainly Bury continued to enjoy its exempt status until the Dissolution, while Bishop William Bateman later on can be seen still, or once more, in Edward III's good graces. Although the manifestations of this quarrel seem farcical at times, the principles were serious and the protracted affair must have been expensive to both sides, involving lawyers' fees for at least six years, the searching out and recopying of documents, the sending of numerous messengers to Westminster and Avignon, and the providing of the sorts of gifts to middle- and high-level bureaucrats that assured one's suit a steady advance through the papal or royal administrative process. Ever after, the matter survived in abbey legend as one of St Edmund's miracles: when the bishop threatened the abbey's rights, one of the keepers of the shrine, William Hengham,[31] had a vision of the saint rising up from his sepulchre fully armed and drawing his sword from its sheath; and, sure enough, the bishop of Norwich died. Nine years later.[32]

---

30. Large parts of this confrontation are recorded in the obviously biased Bury Chronicle (CUL MS Add. 850, fol. 217ff.; ed. Arnold, *Memorials*, 3. 56–73), which reproduces many of the relevant documents from both sides under the heading, 'The burdensome persecution against the monastery of St Edmund by the bishop of Norwich' (*Grauis persecutio contra monasterium sancti Edmundi per episcopum Norwicensem*). For a summary of the other records, including papal commissions to various English bishops and the archbishop of Canterbury in 1349, 1350, and 1351, see *VCH Suffolk* 2 (1907) 63–4.
31. Ordained deacon 13 March 1339, priest 24 March 1340; Montacute register, fols. 103va, 107vb.
32. Bodl. MS Bodley 240, pp. 670–672, with the rubric 'The calumnies and insults inflicted on the monastery of St Edmund by Bishop William of Norwich and miraculously brought to an end by the merits of Saint Edmund' (*De calumniis et injuriis per Willelmum Norwici episcopum*

A. *Novice Master*

At some time, probably at several different times, Henry of Kirkestede served as a master of novice monks. He is nowhere given this title, but the circumstantial evidence is clear. At Bury, as at most English Benedictine houses, the novice master was not an obedientiary and the post was not a prominent one.[33] Instead, the role of novice master was a rotating duty that the senior monks shared, each novice master keeping responsibility for one 'class' of incoming novices until they had progressed to the point where they no longer needed his tutelage (often at ordination, as we have seen).[34] The English Benedictine statutes speak of novice masters in the plural, in describing their charge: 'In choir, cloister, and refectory, the masters of the novices should continually stand or sit in the midst of them, giving them attentive and discerning supervision until such time as they are fully instructed in matters pertaining to the order'.[35] The task was obviously one to Kirkestede's liking, and we suspect that he served repeatedly. He retained a keen interest in the process of 'fully instructing' new monks even when he held other posts, and he personally procured for the abbey three manuscripts specifically intended for novices.

The first of these, Cambridge, Pembroke College, MS 92 (Bury J. 35), contains Cassian's *Collationes patrum*, a work that both St Benedict and Cassiodorus had recommended for monastic instruction. On its flyleaf is Kirkestede's informal account for the making of the manuscript:

---

monasterio sancti Edmundi illatis, et per merita sancti Edmundi miraculose finitis); it is one of the many interpolated St Edmund legends, in this abbreviated Bury copy of John of Tynemouth's *Historia aurea* dating from 1377. Bateman's actions sufficed to earn him a place on the list (which is recited) of those, beginning with King Sweyn, who had defied the protection of St Edmund and paid the ultimate penalty with their lives. Ed. Arnold, *Memorials*, 3. 320–27.

33. Knowles, *Monastic Order*, 422–3 and notes; for instructing novices in batches, Harvey, *Living and Dying*, 74.
34. 'Ordination, the event which in principle marked the novice's final emergence from tutelage'; Harvey, *Living and Dying*, 118, and see 73. Although it is late in date (1492), a list of monks and their posts at St Albans exemplifies the details noted above. Two of the monks are associated with training new monks—William Andrew, novice master, and John Erly, novice instructor—each of whom was probably responsible for a different small group of novices from their entry into the abbey until they attained senior status. Moreover, at the end of the list of monks is the note, 'All these are priests' ('Omnes isti sunt sacerdotes'), followed by a further six names labelled 'Novices who are not priests' ('Nouicii non presbiteri'). See Pantin, *Documents*, 3. 232–4.
35. 'Magistri nouiciorum in choro claustro et refectorio stent vel sedeant iugiter inter eos diligentem et discretam custodiam adhibentes eisdem, donec in hiis que sunt ordinis plenius fuerint informati'; Pantin, *Documents*, 1. 73, Version B (1278).

'Memorandum: Brother H. of K. paid, for the writing and other expenses of this book, 22 s.'; and the copyist who wrote the flyleaf table of contents in red wrote an *ex dono* inscription at its head, in the same ink: 'Book of the monks of Saint Edmund, purchased by Brother Henry of Kirkestede'.[36] On the next flyleaf, recto and verso, is a defence of Cassian's orthodoxy in Kirkestede's hand, a subject on which Kirkestede was insistent. This note, partly from Vincent of Beauvais and partly from an unidentified source, reappears twice in the *Catalogus*;[37] and Kirkestede copied Vincent's vindication of Cassian a second time, on the flyleaf of a manuscript of Prosper of Aquitaine, who had attacked Cassian's orthodoxy.[38]

Another manuscript purchased by Kirkestede, BL MS Royal 8 F. xiv (Bury G. 15), is an introduction to ecclesiastical literature and the monastic ideal. The book is composed of separate booklets of the 13th and 14th cent., bound together at Kirkestede's direction, and having an *ex dono* note on the flyleaf, 'Per fratrem H. de K.'.[39] Among its contents are Gregory's *Dialogi*, Hugh of Saint-Victor's *De arca Noe, Didascalicon* and *De institutione nouiciorum*, and extracts from Hugh's *De sacramentis*, along with Bernard's *De dispensatione et praecepto*, Martin of Braga's *De formula honestae uitae*, Innocent III's *De contemptu mundi*, the *Admonitio ad filium spiritualem* falsely attributed to St Basil, and the rule of St Francis,[40] all works suited to instruction of novices. Kirkestede extensively annotated all the parts of the manuscript, supplying titles of works and incipit, explicit, and location notes, and he copied with his own hand (fols. 138r–139r) a brief tract *De septem gradibus contemplationis*.[41]

Kirkestede itemized on a back flyleaf (fol. 147v) his payment for Cambridge, St John's College, MS G. 2 (Bury H. 56): 'Brother H. of K. paid, for the writing of this book, 8 s. 6 d.; for the parchment, 2 s. 8 d.; for the binding, 8 d.; total, 11 s. 10 d.'; the *ex libris* on the front flyleaf formally records his participation, 'Book of the monks of Saint Edmund which Brother H. of K. caused to be written'.[42] This volume contains another selection of novice treatises: Hugh of Saint-Victor's *De institutione nouiciorum*, John of Wales'

---

36. Both notes are reproduced in Gransden, 'Some manuscripts', pls. LXXIXB and LXXIXC.
37. See below, pp. 17 and 313. See also Rouse, 'Bostonus Buriensis', pls. II, X–XI, and Gransden, 'Some manuscripts', pl. LXXIXD. The Cassian note is discussed below, p. lxi.
38. Wisbech, Wisbech and Fenland Museum, Town Library, MS 1, fol. ii^v; see below, p. lxiii.
39. See also Rouse, 'Bostonus Buriensis', pl. VI.
40. The manuscript now also contains the *Philobiblon* of Richard de Bury; one of the volume's separate booklets, it does not appear in the table of contents and was evidently added after Kirkestede had these works bound together. It may thus have no connexion with him.
41. Concerning the authorship of this work see S. H. Thomson, *The Writings of Robert Grosseteste* (Cambridge 1940), 250–51.
42. See also Rouse, 'Bostonus Buriensis', pls. III–IV. The notes are printed by James, *St John's*, 204–205.

Ordinarium uitae religiosae, a tract entitled *Forma uitae regularis*, and a tract attributed to David ab Augusta, *Formula nouiciorum*. Kirkestede added running headlines throughout the text, as well as some corrections and division into chapters. For the *Formula nouiciorum* he compiled a thirteen-page table of chapters, and a subject index (fols. 64r–70r), alphabetically arranged according to the first two letters of each entry. The margins of the treatise itself are filled with index notes and topic-headings in Kirkestede's hand, annotations that he made as he constructed the indexes.

Notes in other manuscripts also often pertain, directly or indirectly, to the training of novices. In BL MS Harley 1005, the *Liber albus* which is essentially an administrative handbook, Kirkestede noted at the head of a 13th-cent. custumal, 'See the important information about the entrance of novices, in a parchment quire of the lord abbot's that begins *Unumquodque scimus etc.*'—a reference presumably to the *Doctrina nouiciorum* in the abbot's custumal.[43] Another work in the *Liber albus*, the *Liber de signis monachorum*, describes the system of hand-signs that monks used during the silent period and at all other times and places where unnecessary talk was discouraged; it was one of the novice master's tasks to introduce the novices to this sign language. Two Bury versions of this widely-disseminated tract survive (including CUL MS Add. 6006). The version of the Book of Monks' Signs in the *Liber albus* (fols. 203r–210r) is copied in Kirkestede's hand, and above the title he later added reference to his personal copy, now lost: 'This tract can be found in better and fuller form in a paper copy belonging to Henry of Kirkestede'. He twice more mentions this better book, which was perhaps the copy he used for instructing novices: 'A significant passage missing here is found in the paper copy of H. of Kirkestede', and, at the end, 'See the better collection of signs in H. of Kirkestede's paper copy'.[44]

---

43. 'Vide notabilem informacionem pro ingressu nouiciorum in quodam quaterno domini abbatis in pergameno, et incipit sic: Unumquodque scimus etc.'; BL MS Harley 1005, fol. 200r. For the tract in the abbot's custumal, see BL MS Harley 3977, fol. 3r, beginning 'Unumquodque scimus'. R. M. Thomson, *The Archives of the Abbey of Bury St Edmunds* (Woodbridge 1980), 145, suggests the connexion.

44. 'Iste tractatus melius et plenius habetur in quodam papiro H. de K.' (Harley 1005, fol. 203r); 'Deficit hic notabile passus qui [est] in papiro H. Kirk.', and 'Vide signa melius collecta in papiro quodam H. de Kirk.' (fol. 207r, respectively top and bottom). The version of the *Liber de signis* in CUL MS Add. 6006, fols. i^v–xi^v and 76v–80r (Bury C. 63) has a note in Kirkestede's hand at the end of the prologue (fol. xiv) sending readers to the beginning of the tract proper on fol. 76v. The body of the tract (fols. 76v–80r only) has been edited and translated by D. Sherlock and W. Zajac, 'A fourteenth-century monastic sign list from Bury St Edmunds abbey', *Proceedings of the Suffolk Institute of Archaeology and History* 36 (1985–8) 251–73; their suggestion (ib. 252) that Kirkestede's copy be identified with the Book of Signs in CUL MS Add. 6006 ignores Kirkestede's repeated statements that his copy was on paper.

Kirkestede's conspicuous interest in the history of his abbey and of his order coincides with the statutory prescription that novices be 'fully instructed in matters pertaining to the order'.[45] The historical starting point for all monks of Bury was the legend of St Edmund, and Kirkestede's annotations are everywhere present in the surviving Bury manuscripts of their patron's life and miracles. In BL MS Cotton Tiberius B. II, fols. 2r–85r (Bury S. 155), the *Vita et miracula S. Edmundi* composed by the hagiographer Archdeacon Herman, the saint's name was painted in gold capitals on a purple ground each time it appears; towards the end, where the illuminator failed in his job, Kirkestede has added the name in his large uneven hand wherever it was lacking.[46] Another manuscript of St Edmund's life and miracles, BL MS Cotton Titus A. VIII (Bury S. 153), contains Kirkestede's glosses on Anglo-Saxon names and notes on persons connected with the history of St Edmund. Others of Kirkestede's notes pertain to the foundation and history of the abbey itself, with lists of successive abbots down to John Brinkley (1361–78).[47]

Kirkestede wrestled, over many years it seems, with a chronological discrepancy among the various accounts of the three-year temporary translation of St Edmund's body to London by the monk Ailwin for safe-keeping from seafaring raiders. The question focused on events of the first two decades of the 11th cent.—specifically, on whether the temporary removal occurred before or after Edmund's apparition miraculously killed the tyrant Sweyn and saved Bury from unlawful taxation. Some 350 years later, one sees Kirkestede defending the authority of the Bury chroniclers against an external tradition. In a marginal comment to the chronicle of 'Marianus'

---

45. See n. 35 above.
46. He also glossed the names of Anglo-Saxon monarchs, adding a long marginal gloss on King Edmund II and the donation of Aethelstan. Herman's *Life and Miracles* are printed by Arnold, *Memorials*, I. 26–92; Kirkestede's note is printed, ibid. 29. The note and charter of King Edmund II are both probably taken from the additions to the Bury manuscript of John of Worcester, Bodl. MS Bodley 297 p. 327 (Bury C. 53); see Arnold, *Memorials*, I. 340–41. Concerning Archdeacon Herman see Sharpe, *Latin Writers*, 178.
47. The chronicle of John of Everisden in London, College of Arms, MS Arundel 30 (Bury —), contains two long notes of historical interest. On fol. 131v, next to a notice of the foundation of the abbey in 1020 by Cnut, Kirkestede entered the list of abbots, connected by a tie mark with a list in a different hand that he was correcting. On fol. 132v, annals for 1037–51 which mention Stigand, Kirkestede copied a long excerpt from John of Worcester concerning the bishops of East Anglia in the time of Edward the Confessor and the episcopate of Stigand; ed. and trans. A. Gransden, *Chronica Buriensis: the Chronicle of Bury St Edmunds, 1212–1301* (London 1964). In earlier years only members were permitted to use the library of the College of Arms; we are grateful to Dr Gransden for having allowed us in that era to consult her transcripts of these notes. See also Gransden, 'The legends and traditions concerning the origins of the Abbey of Bury St Edmunds', *EHR* 100 (1985) 1–24.

(i.e. John of Worcester [Bury C. 53]), he scornfully dismissed that chronicle's sequence of events, which put the death of Sweyn (1014) after the translation to London:

> Note that the standard history and the accounts of the monk Ailwin are, without a doubt, more to be believed than these chronicles of Marianus, since this Marianus had not even been born at the time to which the miracle pertains. He was born later, in 1028. And so, being thus situated and far removed, he could not verify anything about this miracle for himself, nor could he even have heard about it—no more than could all the other chroniclers who follow his version.[48]

The 'standard history' Kirkestede had in mind was Herman's narrative (written after 1097), whose sequence of events was followed also in Abbot Samson's account of the miracles of St Edmund.[49] Although Herman and Samson likewise 'had not even been born' in 1014—they were indeed further removed chronologically than 'Marianus'—Kirkestede preferred them because they knew local lore, both oral and written. Amusingly, years later (probably after 1368) an older Kirkestede spotted an internal contradiction in Herman's narrative and acknowledged that, after all, Herman was mistaken: 'It is evident here that the translation of St Edmund from Bury to London must have preceded the death of Sweyn, even though the sequence related above indicates the contrary—because this St Alfegus, who wanted to acquire the martyr's cross when Ailwin was in London [the point in the text to which the note refers], was himself martyred nearly three years before Sweyn's death'.[50]

48. Bodl. MS Bodley 297, p. 345 (see plate 1b): 'Nota quod absque dubio plus credendum est communi historie et relacionibus Ailwini monachi quam hiis cronicis Mariani que quidem Marianus tempore quo contigit hoc miraculum nondum natus erat. Natus enim erat postea anno domini M°xxviij°. Et sic non potuit sibi tamquam stato et multum remoto constare de isto miraculo nec per auditum sicut nec aliis sequacibus omnibus cronographis'.

49. Arnold, *Memorials*, I. 32–46 (Herman) and I. 114–25 (ascribed to Samson by Arnold). See in the Bury manuscript of William of Malmesbury (BL MS Harley 447 [Bury C. 49]), in the margin beside the report of Sweyn's death, Kirkestede's note '[Sic] Marianus Scotus; sed plus credendum est Alwino quam eo (?) vel sequacibus suis'; and in the miracle collection in BL MS Cotton Titus A. VIII, fol. 89r (Bury S. 153), in the margin beside the chapter describing the translation to London, Kirkestede's note 'Ista historia post c// sit interfeccionem Suani per IIIIor annos iuxta omnia cronica'.

50. BL Cotton Tiberius B. II, fol. 45r (Bury S. 155): 'Hic patet quod translatio Sancti Edmundi de Beodricesworth ad Londinium precessit occisionem Suani, licet hic superius in processu habeatur contrarium, quia Sanctus Alfegus qui voluit crucem ab Ailwino London. comparasse, martirizatus fuit fere per tres annos ante occisionem Suani'; printed by Arnold, *Memorials*, I. 53 note *a*. This manuscript of Herman's *Miracula* belonged to the shrine-keepers (*feretrarii*)

Kirkestede's interests in the history of his order and in the training of young monks converge in the *Speculum coenobitarum*, a history of Benedictine monks, validated by Joachim of Fiore's explanation of history and of the role of monks in God's plan. The work served novices as a basic handbook of monastic history and a roll of honour of famous monks (monk-writers, monk-saints, etc.). Kirkestede was perhaps the author, but more likely the compiler of a major revision, of the *Speculum coenobitarum*, a question to which we shall devote a later chapter,[51] but we wish at least to note here the *Speculum*'s relationship to Kirkestede's role as novice master. It underscores the combination of history and instruction exemplified by his notes in manuscripts and his manuscript purchases, revealing Kirkestede as a traditionalist bent on instilling in his novices an admiration for the founders and martyrs of their house and their order, and a respect for the traditional Benedictine labours of reading and copying the scriptures and the heritage of the Christian past.

B. *Librarian*

In the first half of his career, Kirkestede's principal role at the abbey was that of librarian; with the advantage of hindsight, we should rate it as unquestionably the most important role of his life. The destructive incursion of 1327 had left Bury's books in chaos, or so the records, all admittedly partisan, reiterate. Thus, the *Depredatio abbatie Sancti Edmundi*: 'When they had entered the cloister, they smashed the boxes and the bookchests, and carried off the books and everything else found in them'.[52] The context makes it clear that 'cloister' here does not mean the monastic enclosure in a general sense but the specific place within it, the enclosed and covered passageway with central court. The *Chronica Buriensis* echoes the complaint: 'They smashed the book-cupboards and carrels and the treasures kept in

---

of St Edmund. The date of Kirkestede's note is strongly suggested, though not proved, by the fact that he has noted at the end of Herman's work (fol. 85v), 'Deficiunt hic .vi. miracula', and added, 'qui sunt in libro domini Johannis de C. prioris'. John of Cambridge was prior of Bury from the unknown date of Kirkestede's retirement as prior (after 1368) until John's own death in 1381; see below.

51. Chapter 3 below.
52. 'Deinde claustrum ingressi, cistulas, id est caroles, et armoriola (*sic*) fregerunt, et libros ac omnia in eis inuenta similiter asportauerunt'; *Depredatio Abbatie Sancti Edmundi*, BL MS Cotton Claudius A. XII, fol. 117r (Bury —), cited from Arnold, *Memorials*, 2. 330. See the references to images of bookchests in n. 75 below.

xlii

them'.⁵³ And a Bury record itemizes the articles broken, stolen, or destroyed: '20 chests, 30 strongboxes, 40 carrels . . . and gold and silver chalices, books, vestments, and ornaments of the church—namely, 3 golden chalices, 40 silver chalices, 20 missals, 24 portiforia, 12 bibles, 20 psalters, 10 diurnals, 7 sets of Decrees, 10 sets of Decretals, and many other books of various disciplines in various volumes'.⁵⁴

The after-effects of the riots on the abbey's archives were plainly noted in the prologue to the register of Walter Pinchbeck, who set out in 1333 to locate and copy the main documents defining the abbey's rights and its relations with the town 'from the creation of the world to the present', as he put it. While he never finished this large undertaking, others continued the task and the reorganization was finally completed by John Lakenheath, shortly before 1381. Lakenheath's introduction to his new register explicitly ties it to the destruction and plunder of the registers and muniments in 1327.⁵⁵

i. Classifying the books

In response to the same stimulus and presumably not long after his ordination in 1338, Kirkestede began to organize the abbey's book collection. He left no overt statement like the prologues of Pinchbeck and Lakenheath but the goal was the same, to bring order out of confusion. Despite the exaggerated reports of the riots of 1327, the great majority of the books either had not been carried off or else they were soon recuperated, although they were left in thorough disarray. Even before the uprising, however, the abbey had not catalogued its books since the late 12th cent.⁵⁶ That catalogue was added to, briefly, in the opening years of the 13th cent., and

---

53. 'Necnon armariola et karolla et thesaurum eorum fregerunt'; CUL MS Add. 850, fol. 110v (Bury —), cited from Arnold, *Memorials*, 3. 38.
54. 'xx cistas, xxx forceria, xl carulas . . . et calices aureos et argenteos, libros, vestimenta, ornamenta ecclesie, videlicet: iii calices aureos, xl calices argenteos, xx missalia, xxiv portiforia, xii bibulas, xx psalteria, x jornalia, semptem paria decretorum, x paria decretalium et alios plures libros diuersarum scientiarum et voluminum'; found in the Pinchbeck Register, CUL MS Ee. 3. 60, fol. 65r (Bury —); cited from James, *St Edmund*, 163.
55. Relevant portions of the prologues to these registers are printed and discussed by Thomson, *Archives*, 21 and 23; the registers themselves are described ibid. 123–6 and 129–30 (nos. 1280, 1283).
56. The catalogue, which survives in Cambridge, Pembroke College, MS 47, fols. 117r–119v (Bury B. 40), was first discussed and edited by James, *St Edmund*, 23–34; a corrected version was edited by Sharpe & others, *Benedictines*, B13, whose dating (pp. 46–7) we follow for the early catalogue, its addenda, and the early *ex libris* notes. Pages are reproduced ibid. pls. 3–4, and a detail in Gransden, 'Some manuscripts', pl. LXXIIIA.

around 1200 the first *ex libris* notes were inscribed, 'Liber Sancti Ædmundi regis et martyris', after which both efforts were abandoned.[57] By Kirkestede's day, the 261 codices listed in that early catalogue[58] had increased in number to something between 1,500 and 2,000 manuscripts, with no sort of structure governing their use and no inventory documenting their existence. The effects of the riots of 1327–31, therefore, provided the necessary impetus to deal with a problem that had been growing for more than a century. The librarian was never an obedientiary of the abbey; the creation of the late 12th-cent. inventory, the additions to it, the marking of the early *ex libris* notes *c.* 1200—these represented the occasional efforts of interested individuals, and Kirkestede's work as well was the response of the right man to a set of circumstances.

Kirkestede's organization of the Bury books marked a major turning-point in the abbey's book provisions, affording effective control over the collection and facilitating access to it. In each of Bury's 1,500 to 2,000 manuscripts he inscribed an *ex libris* note, he listed the contents of each, and assigned to each a class-mark. Whether he did all three tasks at once or *seriatim* is not clear—and it probably differed from one case to another—but for clarity of understanding we shall look at them individually. He began the task of adding an *ex libris* by using the formula of the early 13th cent., 'Liber Sancti Edmundi regis et martyris', or variations of it.[59] But he preferred the phrase 'Liber [*or* Quaternus] monachorum Sancti Edmundi',[60] which he entered in the majority of surviving Bury manuscripts, going so far as to update several of the older *ex libris* by inserting 'monachorum'.[61] This new emphasis on the community rather than the saint is intriguing, although its immediate import is obscure. The *ex libris* in whatever form is most apt to be found at the head of a book's opening page, above the text.

---

57. See Cambridge, Pembroke College, MSS 17, 24, 25, 26, 59 (*L. S. Æ.*), 84, 88, and Bodl. MS e Musaeo 31 (*L. S. Æ.*).

58. This number is higher than it should be, because the list of 261 codices in B13 includes a certain amount of duplication.

59. In Kirkestede's hand, *L. S. E. r. et m.*: Cambridge, Corpus Christi College, MS 135, fol. i^v (Bury A. 83), Cambridge, Pembroke College, MSS 29, fol. i^v (Bury R. 14), 47, fol. i^v pastedown (Bury B. 40), 49, fol. 1r (Bury B. 48), 84, fol. i^v (Bury B. 319); *L. S. E. r.*: Pembroke College MS 107, fol. ii^r (Bury B. 328); *L. S. E.*: Pembroke College MSS 27, fol. i^v (Bury P. 25), 42, fol. i^v pastedown (Bury A. 61), 118, fol. i^v (Bury Y. 12), Cambridge, St John's College, MS D. 19, fol. iii^r (Bury Y. 24), Lambeth Palace Library, MS 67, fol. 2r (Bury B. 318). For a reproduction see Rouse, 'Bostonus Buriensis', pl. XIII.

60. See, for example, Gransden, 'Some manuscripts', pl. LVIIIA.

61. Cambridge, Pembroke College, MSS 18, fol. i^v pastedown (Bury J. 28), 47, fol. i^v pastedown (Bury B. 40), 49, fol. i^r (Bury B. 48). Rouse, 'Bostonus Buriensis', pl. XII.

Kirkestede listed each book's contents on an opening flyleaf, seeming to prefer the verso of the flyleaf opposite the first page of the text. He nearly always incorporated a duplicate *ex libris* note into the table, 'Book [or Quire] of the monks of St Edmund, in which are contained . . .', followed by a list of the works that gives the author's name, the title, the number of homilies, sermons, or books, and occasionally the folio number on which the work begins. Whenever a list provides folio numbers, the foliation of the manuscript is often found to be in Kirkestede's hand as well. Most contents lists are thorough, though some list only the main works in the codex or omit works for no evident reason. In Bodl. MS Laud Misc. 233, fol. i^v (Bury Y. 7), Kirkestede supplied in the table the incipits of an anonymous tract and the individual sermons in two collections. His most elaborate contents lists appear on the flyleaves of a two-volume 11th-cent. collections of sermons, Cambridge, Pembroke College, MS 23, fol. i^r (Bury O. 52), *Sermones de tempore* (plate 2), and Pembroke College, MS 24, fol. i^r (Bury O. 54), *Sermones de sanctis*, brought from Saint-Denis by Abbot Baldwin. In each of these Kirkestede compiled two complementary lists of the sermons, one arranged by author and the other arranged according to the liturgical year. For example, on the flyleaf of Pembroke 23 Kirkestede grouped seventy homilies under the names of the eight authors represented in the collection; then, with the heading 'Order and position of these homilies and sermons in this volume', he listed the same sermons in the order of the liturgical year (which is the order of the manuscript).[62] The omnipresence of Kirkestede's hand in the *ex libris* notes and contents lists indicates that he accomplished these tasks virtually unaided.

In addition to these badly needed but unexceptional tasks, Kirkestede's innovation was to classify all the Bury books according to their contents. Identifying marks in manuscripts (inventory marks or press-marks) were not new, and even the combination of letters and numbers was known elsewhere. Kirkestede's, however, is the earliest known system that served jointly to identify the individual book with a unique mark and to group books by category.[63] His identifying marks, which may appropriately be called classmarks, consist of a letter that refers either to the author or the subject-matter (A for Augustine or Astronomy, B for Bede or Bible, etc.), and an arabic numeral specific to the volume itself within the class. Initially, at least, similar books within a classification were numbered in sequence. For example, glossed books of the bible bear class-marks ranging between B. 40 and B. 207, biblical commentaries between B. 220 and B. 252, and works of Bede

---

62. For other contents lists in Kirkestede's hand see Rouse, 'Bostonus Buriensis', pls. I, IV–VIII.
63. For a survey of English monastic practice see R. Sharpe, 'Accession, classification, location: shelfmarks in medieval libraries', *Scriptorium* 50 (1996) 279–87.

between B. 280 and B. 296. In some instances the higher numbers may represent the more recent acquisitions, but this is never a dependable assumption.[64] In addition to planning the system, Kirkestede entered the class-mark in almost every Bury book himself, usually placing it to the right of the *ex libris* inscription.[65]

The creation of this system of class-marks was presumably linked to the preparation of a new catalogue of the abbey's books. Although no such catalogue survives, a contemporary note in a Bury copy of John Cassian's *Collationes* (Lambeth Palace Library, MS 218 pt 2 [Bury J. 23], fol. 90v) refers by class-mark to another Cassian (J. 35 = Pembroke College, MS 92) said to appear 'in the register of books'.[66] An attempt has been made to reconstruct the lost register, as far as one can do so on the basis of surviving manuscripts and incidental mentions of class-marks,[67] and the classification system would have served to permit the taking of inventory with this new register.[68] But a second purpose, we suggest, may have been to serve as a device for locating the books, physically, in the book-cupboards.[69]

That class-marks were a finding device is suggested by analogy with the Bury archives. In the year 1379 or 1380, around the time of Kirkestede's death, a system of press-marks was assigned to the documents.[70] The classification, comprising letters and arabic numerals in imitation of the system Kirkestede had devised for the manuscripts, was probably applied to the archives by the abbey baroner, or keeper of the barony, John Lakenheath (d. 1381),[71] and the

---

64. See the instances of late manuscripts with low numbers noted in Sharpe & others, *Benedictines*, 45.
65. See examples in Rouse, 'Bostonus Buriensis', pls. I, IV–VIII, XII–XIII; Gransden, 'Some manuscripts', pls. LXIVB, LXIXB, LXXIXC; *New Palaeographical Society* 1 (1903), pl. 17 no. 8 a–c; and E. G. Millar, *The Library of A. Chester Beatty* (London 1927), pl. 73.
66. 'Vide originaliter xxiiii collaciones patrum in registro librorum in J. 35'; printed also by Sharpe & others, *Benedictines*, 44; and by James, *Lambeth*, 2. 250. Cambridge, Pembroke College, MS 92 (Bury J. 35), does indeed include the twenty-four collations.
67. R. Sharpe demonstrated the catalogue's existence and reconstructed what was recoverable: 'Reconstructing the medieval library of Bury St Edmunds abbey: the lost catalogue of Henry of Kirkstead', in Gransden, *Bury St Edmunds*, 204–218.
68. 'The primary function of library marks was to allow an individual book to be easily matched with its entry in a catalogue'; Sharpe, 'Reconstructing the medieval library', 206.
69. A simple sequence of numerals, running from 1 to 2,000 or whatever was necessary, would have sufficed for a register or catalogue, it seems to us; only an attempt to group the books physically by subject would require class-marks (i.e. press-marks that classify).
70. Thomson, *Archives*, 30.
71. 'It is hard to avoid the assumption that Lakenheath took his ideas for the cataloguing of the charters from Kirkestede's system for the library-books'; Thomson, *Archives*, 30–31. Thomson adds 'or vice versa', but he was unaware at the time that Kirkestede had died in or shortly after 1378.

items in the archives were housed in the order of their classification, in upright wooden chests (*cophina*) subdivided into smaller compartments or pigeon holes (*cista*), in the vestiary.[72] Chance remarks in the early 15th-cent. register of Abbot William Curteys (d. 1446) confirm the assumption, alluding for example to a record that was found 'in the vestiary, in box A with the number 6'[73]—and revealing unmistakably the practical meaning of the mark 'A 6' on a document.[74]

We think it plausible that Kirkestede's class-marks for the books also referred to a physical place. Kirkestede, we suggest, may have rehoused the books in the repaired or newly built *armaria*, upright wooden cupboards with doors.[75] Although one had not yet reached a time when abbeys had dedicated rooms for book storage, the place where the books were kept in the cloister at Bury was already assuming an identity as 'the library' by Kirkestede's day. In the *ex libris* that he employed, at least nine read, 'Book from the cloister bookchest of the monks of St Edmund'.[76] In one reference to a Bury book Kirkestede employed the word *librarium*, documenting the source of a passage that he had transcribed into his handbook (BL MS Harley 1005, fol. 115r; plate 6b): 'From the *Traditiones patrum* in the keeping of T. de Saxham, on parchment, marked with the letter C. 64 in the

---

72. Thomson, *Archives*, 19.
73. 'In vestiario, cophino A sub figura 6'; CUL MS Add. 4220, fol. 61r, the register of Abbot Curteys (d. 1446), printed by Thomson, *Archives*, 36. See also the similar references on fol. 61v, 'in vestiario, cophino A sub figura 24', 'in vestiario, cophino B sub figura 55', 'in vestiario, cophino C sub figuris 19 et 80', etc.
74. The marks in this system are press-marks—that is, they refer to the presses or cupboards in which documents were kept—rather than class-marks that refer to the category to which a document belongs.
75. For photographs of the 14th-cent. horizontal bookchest from Hereford cathedral see R. A. B. Mynors and R. M. Thomson, *Catalogue of the Manuscripts of Hereford Cathedral Library* (Cambridge 1993), pl. 19; W. Löschburg, *Historic Libraries of Europe* (Leipzig 1974), 51; and M. Baur-Heinhold, *Schöne alte Bibliotheken* (Munich 1972), 40 pls. 27–8. No English examples of upright or vertical medieval book-cupboards are known to survive. For two large *armaria* from Bayeux and Obazine that may have served as bookchests, see J. W. Clark, *The Care of Books*, 2nd edn (Cambridge 1902), discussed on pp. 87–8 along with a third in Paris at St-Germain-l'Auxerrois. See also E. Viollet-le-Duc, *Dictionnaire raisonné du mobilier français de l'époque carlovingienne à la Renaissance*, 6 vols (Paris 1926), 1. 3–18, s.v. 'Armoire'.
76. 'Liber de armario claustri monachorum Sancti Edmundi', or variants thereof: Cambridge, Pembroke College, MSS 16, 44 (*de armario claustri monachorum S.E.*), 72 (*de armario S. E.*; reproduced in Gransden, 'Some manuscripts', pl. LXIXB), and 105 (*de claustro S.E.*); BL MSS Egerton 3776 (*in armario nostro S.E.*) and Royal 6 C. II (*de communi armario claustri S. E. r. et m.*); Bodl. MSS Bodley 130 (*de armario monachorum S.E.*), e Musaeo 7 (*de armario claustri S. E.*), and e Musaeo 8 (*de claustro S.E.*).

librarium'[77]—meaning perhaps no more than 'in the abbey's book collection', but there does seem to be an overtone of place.[78]

The site where the Bury book cupboards were kept did not change much in the course of the 14th cent. In the description of the depredations of 1327, nearly all of the books (save liturgical) were associated with a single location, the cloister.[79] The cloister was situated on the north side of the abbey church.[80] A contemporary record describes it as '145 feet across, and 14 feet between the columns and the wall, excluding the benches'.[81] The book-

77. 'Ex traditionibus patrum in custodia T. de Saxham in pergameno cum littera C. 64 intitulatis in librario', and see also below. The passage is repeated in virtually the same words at the bottom of fol. 116r.

78. He used the same term several other times on the flyleaf of Cambridge, Pembroke College, MS 29 (Bury R. 14), where he copied from the Franciscan *Registrum Anglie* a list of the works of Ralph of Flaix. Instead of copying there the numbers that the *Registrum* used to designate locations, Kirkestede transformed them into place-names, and he located various of Ralph's works 'in the *librarium* of St Edmund', 'in the *librarium* of the Witham charterhouse', and 'in the *librarium* of the monks of Battle abbey'. These instances would seem merely to refer to the various book collections.

79. One can trace the physical path of the break-in on that first day of rioting, Wednesday 14 January 1327 (NS), in Arnold, *Memorials*, 2. 330–31. The rioters smashed in the great gate, broke into the cellar, then in sequence into the cloister, the prior's *camera*, the sacristy, and finally the offices of the chamberlain and the infirmarer and 'other offices', roughing up monks or taking them captive along the way. Smashing the cloister book-cupboards and carrying off the books may have been acts of frustration at not finding the archives and valuables they were looking for. It was the next day, Thursday, when they discovered and carried off the royal charters and papal bulls from the treasury.

80. Concerning English monastic libraries in the 14th cent., see F. Wormald, 'The monastic library', in *The English Library before 1700*, ed. F. Wormald and C. E. Wright (London 1958), 15–31; and Knowles, *Religious Orders*, 2. 331–53. G. Hills states that Bury's library was over the chapterhouse on the east side of the main cloister, but he gives no evidence for this and is probably incorrect; *Journal of the British Archaeological Association* 21 (1865), 129. James, *St Edmund*, 146, assumes that the library was in the cloister.

81. The measurement of the cloister occurs in London, College of Arms, MS Arundel 30 (Bury —), on fol. 214r, one of the final pages in a gathering of guard-leaves, amidst notes on the dimensions of other buildings (the length and width of the halls of Westminster and of York, of the hospice and the cloister at Durham, of the castle hall at Newcastle): 'latitudo claustri S. Eadmundi .vii^{xx} v. / inter columpnas et murum xiiii [pedes]', the two lines bracketed with the note 'preter bancos'. The hand, late 13th- or early 14th-cent., is not Kirkestede's. The note is printed by James, *St Edmund*, 203. Built probably under Abbot Robert (1102–1112) by his sacrist Godefridus, the cloister was rebuilt in the last decades of the 14th cent. by Prior John Gosford (1382–after 1405); James, *St Edmund*, 145–6. It probably resembled the cloister at Durham cathedral; see the contemporary description in *The Rites and Monuments of the Cathedral Church of Durham*, ed. J. Raine, Surtees Soc. 15 (1842) 70–71; and Wormald, 'The monastic library', 18, and plate III depicting the well-known carrel niches in Gloucester cathedral.

cupboards would have been on the south side of the main cloister along the church wall, with the wooden carrels, at least forty at Bury, built in the window niches of the inner wall.[82] We can see that a few books were housed, instead, in the place of their use. For example, three manuscripts bear Kirkestede's designation 'Liber de refectorio Sancti Edmundi', the texts that were kept in the refectory for reading aloud during meals.[83] One of these, Wisbech and Fenland Museum, Town Library, MS 1 (Bury P. 119), can be identified in a list in Kirkestede's hand of seventeen books to be read in the refectory for a period of three liturgical years (plate 3a),[84] and Kirkestede copied a note from the list onto the *ex libris* of Wisbech Museum 1: 'This is read at the community's collation from Easter until the Translation of St Benedict. After this comes Odo's book *De uiciis uirtutibusque anime*' (plate 3b).[85] The splendid book of Edmund-legends including the Life by Archdeacon Herman, BL MS Cotton Tiberius B. II, fols. 2r–85r (Bury S. 155), was kept by the keepers of St Edmund's shrine, according to Kirkestede's inscription, 'Liber feretrariorum sancti Edmundi'.[86] The growing problem of housing the books was somewhat mitigated as well by the fact that at any given moment a share of the abbey's total collection would have been in the hands of individual monks.[87] For the most part, however, the books remained in the cloister in Kirkestede's time.

The cloister's book-cupboards may have been marked on their exteriors with conspicuous letters of the alphabet referring to the class-marks of the books they contained. If a class were large (for example, A, perhaps exceeding 200 volumes; or B, perhaps exceeding 300), one might have had several *armaria* marked with the same letter.[88] The volumes would presumably have

---

82. See the references in n. 75 above.
83. The three surviving refectory books are Cambridge, St John's College, MS B. 13 (Gregory on Ezekiel [Bury G. 6]), BL MS Egerton 2782 (Haimo [Bury H. 1]), and Wisbech, Wisbech and Fenland Museum, Town Library, MS 1 ('Prosper', *De uita actiua et contemplatiua* [Bury P. 119]).
84. BL MS Harley 1005, fol. 35v. The list is printed by James, *St Edmund*, 111–12; and Sharpe & others, *Benedictines*, B14.
85. 'Et legitur ad collacionem conuentus a Pascha usque ad translationem sancti Benedicti; post istum ponatur liber sancti Odonis de uiciis uirtutibusque anime'; James, *St Edmund*, 71; Sharpe & others, *Benedictines*, 88.
86. The manuscript contains, fols. 2r–19v, the *Passio* written by Abbo of Fleury (*BHL* 2392) and, fols. 20r–85v, the *Miracula* written by Archdeacon Herman, now incomplete (*BHL* 2395).
87. In the 14th cent. Bury had not yet divided its books into two parts, one a circulating library and the other a library of chained books housed in a special library room. This division occurred much earlier at the schools, where one sees chained collections both at the Sorbonne in Paris and at Merton College in Oxford before the end of the 13th cent.
88. Concerning the numbers in the classes see n. 91 below.

been on their sides on the shelves of the book-cupboard rather than upright, since one could not easily maintain scores of upright volumes side by side, large, small, fat, thin, many bound in bevelled boards. Twenty-one Bury manuscripts—the majority of its pre-1400 manuscripts for which medieval bindings survive—have their class-mark and author's name written in large letters along the spine or on the cover, so that they might be identified from their outside when housed in this fashion.

There are difficulties, to be sure, with the notion that the class-marks were also press-marks. For example, we referred above to manuscripts that were kept in special locations—the Wisbech manuscript of Prosper in the refectory, rather than in a cupboard marked P, or the saint's legends in the shrine, rather than in a cupboard marked S. Moreover, we are not convinced that all the volumes were once marked on their spines. Nevertheless, if the books were principally sorted by category into cupboards marked with the corresponding letter, searching through them to find a specific volume would be a much easier task than searching the whole collection.

It is difficult to gauge with any precision the total number of books in Kirkestede's care. An attempt has been made: by adding the highest numeral that survives in each letter-class, one arrives at a total of 1,929 books. But this begs the question 'whether the numbers can be assumed to be continuous'.[89] Such an assumption is not always warranted. With surviving books of Augustine's works numbered A. 27, A. 31, and A. 52 (for example), it is safe enough to suppose that the intervening numbers were applied to now-lost books of Augustine. However, Kirkestede often gave sequential numbers within a classification to books with the same author or on the same subject, and he may well have left gaps in the numbering sequence to accommodate later additions (additions that, for the most part, his successors did not make). In most cases the gaps would be insignificant in the absolute, accounting for only two or three here and there. Some gaps look quite suspicious, however—for example, the gap in the G class which, in practice, reports only works of Gregory the Great: the latest number surviving from Kirkestede's lifetime is G. 18, with a gap of 111 numerals before a work of Gregory's added in the 15th cent., G. 129—almost surely an error by someone unfamiliar with the class-mark system.[90] No such explanation accounts for other breaks in the sequence, such as the gap of fifty-seven numerals between A. 143 ('Armachanus', i.e. Richard Fitzralph) and the last three survivors from that class (Avicenna, astronomy, and an almanach: A. 200, 222,

---

89. Sharpe, 'Reconstructing the medieval library', 216. We use Sharpe's figures below.
90. ibid.

229).⁹¹ Especially troublesome is the gap in the B classification, with nearly one hundred numbers absent between the last glossed gospel (B. 109) and the first glossed Pauline epistles (B. 205)—implying, quite improbably, the loss of ninety-five glossed books of the bible in numerical order. Tendencies toward overcounting are accompanied, but probably not counter-balanced, by under-representations among the survivors: in the G classification, as we have noted, but also in D, E, and F, while the classifications N, Q, and Z are lacking altogether. In sum, it would be imprudent to say whether the total was closer to 1,500 or to 2,000; but it is obvious that Bury's collection of books was very large relative to those of other English abbeys.

ii. Bibliographic notes

The organization and registering of the abbey's book collection was surely Kirkestede's most significant undertaking as librarian. As we have seen, he added the *ex libris* notes, class-marks and tables of contents; he purchased books for the abbey; and he copied books or parts of books in his own hand. Above and beyond these tasks, however, he worked continually to provide access to correctly described texts, by means of a myriad of other practical actions designed to straighten out problems and to offer the necessary information and guideposts to his novices and fellow monks.[92]

Kirkestede routinely noted dislocation or loss, a near-universal practice among medieval readers. Thus, for example, in a manuscript of Alexander of Hales's *Summa*, Kirkestede noted, '15 *quaestiones* are missing here. See below near the end at this sign Ø'.[93] Fifty folios farther on, he marked the place where the missing fifteen *quaestiones* have been added out of order with the note, 'This sermon ends here', and a large Ø.[94] In BL MS Royal 7 C. II, fol. 57v (Bury R. 40), the *Summa* attributed to Robert of Melun, he referred to a complete text in the Bury library: 'This *summa* lacks three parts or books

---

91. Others include class C, with only one surviving author-entry (Claudius, C. 16) before the subject classifications begin at C. 43 (chronicles and custumals); or class S, which, after the long, convincing sequence of sermons ending with S. 78, is followed by the Saints' Lives at S. 146—a near-total blank of sixty-eight numbers, interrupted only by BL MS Harley 4025 pt 1 (Bury S. 97), which Kirkestede purchased after 1360.
92. We shall simply give examples here of the various tasks Kirkestede performed in the Bury manuscripts, for the cases are too many to discuss individually.
93. 'Hic deficiunt xv. questiones. Vide infra circa finem ad tale signum Ø'; Cambridge, Pembroke College, MS 43, fol. 60r (Bury A. 114).
94. 'Explicit hic sermo ista'; ibid. fol. 110v. See the similar note in Cambridge, Pembroke College, MS 18, fol. 56v (Bury J. 28), concerning twelve missing homilies of Chrysostom on Matthew 23–25, to which he adds 'Hic deficiunt ut credo quatuor quaterni, ut patet in alio libro ad signum . . .' and draws the sign; printed by James, *Pembroke*, 16.

at the end, and eleven parts or books at the beginning. See the full and complete copy of this *summa* in the cloister book-cupboard, in two large handsome volumes'.[95] Kirkestede continued to record this sort of information late in life even after he retired as prior: thus, in BL MS Cotton Tiberius B. II, fol. 85v (Bury S. 155), another collection of St Edmund legends, he noted that the last six miracles were lacking; but he later added that he had found them in a book belonging to John of Cambridge (d. 1381), who had succeeded him as prior by 1374/5: 'qui sunt in libro domini Iohannis de C. prioris'.

A number of manuscripts were provided with marginal annotations to mark the beginning and end of each work, essential when the original rubrics are lacking or unclear. For example, each of the eleven works whose titles appear in Kirkestede's contents list in BL MS Royal 6. B x (Bury A. 88) has also been given a marginal short-title marking the place where the text begins.[96] Similar titles appear in a two-volume collection of *Sermones de tempore* and *de sanctis* mentioned above. Marginal notes like these were made as aids to compiling the table of contents, but they also served readers searching for a specific work in the codex. Each of the twenty-one miracles of St Edmund compiled by Osbert of Clare can be easily located in BL MS Cotton Titus A. VIII, fols. 65r–145v (Bury S. 153), with the aid of Kirkestede's marginal index notes.

It is apparent that Kirkestede handled every book in the library at least once, in the process of organizing the collection. But he seems in addition to have handled some of the books repeatedly, as new information came to hand. An example is Cambridge, Pembroke College, MS 25, an 11th-cent. homiliary. Bound at the end is a stray quire from an early 13th-cent. preachers' handbook, containing the final half-column from the end of Petrus Cantor's *Verbum abbreuiatum* (without an identifying colophon) followed by the beginning of Alanus Porretanus's *De arte praedicandi* (without an identifying rubric). To the early 13th-cent. *ex libris* at the top of the manuscript's opening page (fol. 3r), 'Liber sancti Edmundi regis et martyris', Kirkestede added 'in quo continentur omelie [vel sermones *added above the line*] xcv. Item tractatus Alani Porrei de arte predicandi'; and above this the class-mark, O (for *Omeliae*) 55 (plate 4a). At this time, then, he had already identified the *Ars praedicandi*, but not the other fragment. Later, however, the book passed through his hands again, and he took advantage of the space afforded by

---

95. 'Deficiunt de ista summa partes siue libri tres de fine, et xi partes siue libri de principio. Vide summam istam plenarie completam in armario claustri in duobus pulcris et magnis uoluminibus'; printed in BM *Cat. Royal*, 1. 176.
96. See folios 1r, 9r, 7r, 9v, 14v, 21v, 22v, 23r, 24r, 26v, 34r–v, 35v, 43v (for which space is left in the contents note), and 93r.

a front flyleaf (fol. 2v) to enter the 14th-cent. version of the *ex libris* and a much fuller contents list, facing the first page of text: 'Liber monachorum S. Edmundi in quo continentur Omelie uel sermones xcv ab aduentu Domini usque ad festum S. Andree, et de apostolis, martyribus, confessoribus et uirginibus, et de dedicacione ecclesie. Rabanus de officio misse et eius misterio, et [Amalarius] de significatione canonicarum horarum', adding once again the class-mark, O. 55. He did not include the extraneous quire in the contents list, however, having perhaps decided that it was irrelevant to the codex. But he had by then, or shortly thereafter, identified both of the texts; and for the sake of completeness he recorded that information in the margin on the first page of this displaced quire, opposite the junction between the first text and the second: 'Hic est finis illius notabilis summe que uocatur uerbum abbreuiatum quem quidem continent cii capitula' (plate 4b). At the end of the separated quire, where the text of Alanus's *De arte praedicandi* breaks off incomplete, he wrote, 'Nota quod deficiunt hic de isto tractatu xxxxiiii capitula' (plate 4c). Evidently Kirkestede had taken the trouble to compare the fragment with a Bury manuscript containing complete copies of the two works, BL MS Royal 7 C. xi (Bury V. 21). Not surprisingly, he recorded *De arte praedicandi* and *Verbum abbreuiatum* in the *Catalogus*.[97]

Kirkestede's efforts to identify texts at times led him into problems that simple collation with a better manuscript would not solve. One free-floating passage from Hugh of Saint-Victor gave him repeated difficulty. The scribe of BL MS Royal 8 F. xiv (Bury G. 15) wrote two brief extracts from Hugh's *De sacramentis* (fols. 70v–71v), beginning 'Postquam primus parens', continuous with the end of Hugh's *De arca Noe*, and presented as belonging to that work, concluding the whole with 'Explicit de arcis'. Kirkestede inserted a note, 'explicit .iiii[us]. liber', at the end of the *De arca Noe* proper (fol. 70v, before the 'Postquam' passage), adding in the margin that, according to some authorities, the fifth book ought to follow at this point.[98] He recognized the origin of the 'Postquam' extract, and added, 'This chapter beginning 'Postquam' appears in Book I part 8 of Hugh's *De sacramentis*'.[99] To his dismay he later located that same extract in another of Hugh's works, and added, 'But in other codices this chapter beginning 'Postquam' is chapter 1 book 4 of Hugh's *De uanitate rerum mundanarum*'.[100]

---

97. See *Catalogus 16.1* and *442.14*. Kirkestede also knew of the *Verbum abbreuiatum* through the *Registrum* and through a copy at Ramsey abbey with forty chapters (see Catalogus *442.14*).
98. 'Hic debet continuari quintus liber, secundum quosdam', i.e. *De arca Noe mystica*; PL 176. 681–704.
99. 'Istud capitulum *Postquam* scribitur in primo libro Hugonis de sacramentis parte VIIIa'.
100. 'Item in aliis codicibus istud capitulum *Postquam* est primum capitulum quarti libri Hugonis de uanitate rerum mundanarum'. The notes are printed in BM *Cat. Royal*, I. 270.

And there the problem remained, because—as often happened with the *Catalogus* as well—he had reached the limit of the resources available to him.

His marginal annotations often supply elements missing from a rubric, either the name of the author or title of the work; and they make corrections and provide additional information, bespeaking a close comparison with other copies of the same work. He added author and title to an 11th-cent. text that lacked both (Cambridge, Pembroke College, MS 41, fol. 11r), 'Encheridion Augustini'.[101] To a *De sacramentis* in verse he prefixed the explanation, 'These books are compiled from Hugh's *De sacramentis*'.[102] In a copy of Gregory's *Dialogi*, Kirkestede copied into the margins of Book II the rubrics from a manuscript of the work that was divided in a different fashion.[103] In the same manuscript he completed the text of Hugh of Saint-Victor's *De quinque septenis* by adding the last two sentences in the margin (fol. 73r) from another copy.[104] His explicits can also serve as informative colophons: for example, 'Here ends the Life and Passion of St Edmund written by the monk Abbo of Fleury at the request of King Etheldred and St Dunstan, the archbishop, about AD 985'.[105] If he could, he also noted when a work was incomplete—for example, at the end of an incomplete commentary on the book of Esther, 'Four chapters are missing here';[106] in a manuscript of Abbot Samson's Miracles of St Edmund (one of Kirkestede's principal interests as novice master), on fol. 67r he wrote, 'A great deal is missing here', and on fol. 145r, 'The total number of miracles is 37'.[107] Sometimes Kirkestede pointed out where physical portions of a manuscript were missing, with remarks such as, 'Eight short chapters are missing from

---

101. See Gransden, 'Some manuscripts', pl. LXVIIA; and James, *Pembroke*, 41.
102. 'Isti libri collecti sunt de libris Hugonis de sacramentis'; Cambridge, Gonville and Caius College, MS 145/195 fol. i^r (Bury H. 31), printed by James, *Caius*, I. 163.
103. BL MS Royal 8 F. xiv, fols. 15v–24r (Bury G. 15).
104. BL MS Royal 8 F. xiv, fol. 73r, bottom margin, 'Ecce frater peticionem tuam non qualiter debui sed qualiter interim potui adimpleui. Accipe munusculum (?) de quinque septenis quod postulasti et cum illud respexeris memento mei. Gratia dei sit tecum, Amen. *Explicit liber Hugonis de quinque septenis*'.
105. 'Explicit uita et passio sancti Edmundi scripta ab Abbone floriacensis monacho ad instanciam regis Etheldredi et sancti Dunstani archiepiscopi circa annum Christi 985'; BL MS Cotton Tiberius B. II, fol. 19v (Bury S. 155).
106. 'Hic deficiunt quatuor capitula'; Cambridge, Pembroke College, MS 63, fol. 89r (Bury B. 69). Printed by James, *Pembroke*, 56.
107. 'Deficit hic multum' and 'Summa miraculorum xxxvii'; BL MS Cotton Titus A. VIII, fols. 67r, 145r (Bury S. 153). A second note on fol. 145r is in a 14th-cent. hand, but probably not Kirkestede's: 'Hic deficit miraculum factum per sanctum Edmundum in Henricum de Exsexia sed [et alia?] innumerabilia'; printed by Arnold, *Memorials*, I. 207.

this work, that is, one and a half folios',[108] or simply, 'A quire is missing here'.[109] And occasionally he performed all these tasks together in the service of a single manuscript. Thus, for a poorly-presented text of Alan of Lille's *Theologicae regulae* Kirkestede corrected its title as listed in an earlier table of contents; he added the missing rubric at the head of the work, and then noted in the margin where the prologue ends and the text proper begins ('Hic incipit liber'); and at the end he called attention to the fact that the work is incomplete ('Finis deficit').[110]

iii. Location notes

Most intriguing are Kirkestede's notes reporting that missing portions or a complete text could be found elsewhere. In compiling the *Catalogus* he was providing his fellow monks and his novices with a list of authoritative writers and their works, described in such a way as to be identifiable and physically located. Notes in his hand mentioning physical location are, thus, very much in character, and notes revealing his knowledge of books in other abbeys are especially closely tied to his work in compiling the *Catalogus*.

Kirkestede was acquainted with the libraries of several other religious houses, especially those near Bury, and he referred explicitly to texts located there. In connexion with this it should be understood that being 'cloistered' did not imply the strict enclosure of earlier centuries. Not only were contemporary Benedictines released from enclosure to attend the university, but it had become the practice for monks to visit their families and even to take what amounted to vacations.[111] At the time when the burgesses burst into the abbey in 1327, the Bury Chronicle records that no fewer than thirty-two of the monks were 'outside of the monastery walking in various places'.[112] Under such conditions Kirkestede would have had no difficulty obtaining permission for travel. The depth and breadth of his reports from other libraries suggests that his knowledge of them was largely incidental, that is, that he took advantage of trips possibly made on abbey business to make a

---

108. 'Deficiunt viii° capitula parua de isto opusculo, uidelicet i folium et dimidium'; at the end of a copy of Petrus Alphonsus's *Disciplina clericalis*, BL MS Royal 10 B. xii, fol. 19v (Bury D —); printed in BM *Cat. Royal*, 1. 322.
109. 'Deficit hic i quaternus'; Berengaudus, *Expositio super Apocalypsin*, in Cambridge, Pembroke College, MS 85 pt 3, fol. 16v (Bury B. 340).
110. Cambridge, Pembroke College, MS 87 (Bury E. 11), fols. iv, 178r, 192v. He probably compared this text with the better copy at Babwell near Bury, upon which he based the entry for this work in the *Catalogus* (see Alanus *15.1*).
111. Knowles, *Religious Orders*, 2. 284–5.
112. 'Extra ad spatiandum per diuersa loca xxxii monachi ejusdem'; Arnold, *Memorials*, 3. 39.

note of interesting books that caught his eye. Often his knowledge of other monastic libraries was manifestly related to his gathering of information for the *Catalogus*. He knew best the books of the Franciscan house at Babwell, just outside the walls of the town of Bury, and he made casual reference to them more than once. For example, a manuscript of excerpts from Augustine's works, Cambridge, Pembroke College, MS 87 (Bury E. 11), was compared with a similar collection at Babwell, and he recorded on fol. 188r of the Bury copy, 'The Babwell book ends here' ('Hic finit liber de Babewell'). The abridgment of Richard of Saint-Victor's *Beniamin maior* in BL MS Royal 8 F. xiv, fol. 132r (Bury G. 15), likewise has Kirkestede's note, 'This book is complete and whole at Holme St Benets, and at Babwell in the codex with Maimonides';[113] Kirkestede reported the copy at St Benets (**74**) in the *Catalogus* entry for Richard of Saint-Victor (*498.3*), and he evidently used the Babwell Maimonides in the *Catalogus* as well (Raby Moyse *493.1*, without location numbers). It is ironic that Kirkestede should have enjoyed such easy familiarity with the Babwell books. A century earlier, in 1257, the Franciscans had attempted to establish a priory within the town of Bury, and the Benedictines were determined to prevent it. A dispute, bitterly fought out on the ground (more with pushes and shoves than with bloodshed) and in the courts both royal and ecclesiastical, finally resulted in a compromise in 1263 that permitted the Franciscans to establish themselves at Babwell, two or three miles outside the abbey's town.[114] And sixty years later, when the burgesses of Bury invaded the abbey in 1327, beat and imprisoned monks, and destroyed monastic documents and other possessions, the Babwell Franciscans gave overt support to the town rebels.[115] The contrasting routine cooperation implicit in Kirkestede's knowledge of the Babwell books reflects a difference between public institutional attitudes, on the one hand, and on the other the actualities of personal relations between Kirkestede and an unknown Franciscan.[116]

Kirkestede's notes mention other establishments as well. We have already seen his reference to a book at Holme St Benets (Norfolk); this was the abbey from which Bury had been founded in the 11th cent., and the two houses maintained close ties. At the end of Bury's *Epistolae Alexandri*, Kirkestede noted that 'the other epistles between Alexander and Dindimus

---

113. 'Iste liber est perfectus et integre scriptus apud Hulmum et apud Babewell cum Raby Moyse'; BL MS Royal 8 F. xiv, fol. 132r. Printed in BM *Cat. Royal*, 1. 271.
114. Arnold, *Memorials*, 2. 263–70 and 271–85.
115. Arnold, *Memorials*, 2. 336.
116. Similarly, the Franciscan surveyors for the *Registrum* clearly enjoyed free access to the Bury books; see p. lxxxv below.

are missing here. See them at Saffron Walden'.[117] Saffron Walden (Essex), along with Bury itself, is the only location cited in the *Catalogus* entry for Alexander the Great (55). A more elaborate example of this type of knowledge appears at the end of a Latin translation of the *Suidas* that Kirkestede himself had bought for the abbey, BL MS Royal 8 B. IV, fols. 72r–80r (Bury S. 184);[118] at the end Kirkestede added, 'There is no more than this at King's Lynn [Norfolk], but the rest can be found at Oxford';[119] however, Kirkestede seems to have used the Bury copy for his description of the *Suidas* in the *Catalogus* (Robertus Lincolniensis *505.37*). Besides other religious houses, Kirkestede showed his acquaintance with the books of his friends and colleagues; for example, in BL MS Royal 12 C. VI (Bury M. 83), another manuscript that he acquired for the abbey and annotated heavily, at the end of a *pseudo*-Aristotelian *Phisionomia* (fol. 49r) Kirkestede noted, 'There is something shorter and better on physiognomy in a small quire that belongs to Master John Tebaud, the rector of Elmswell [Suffolk], beginning *Matrix est embrion* and ending *expellere*'.[120]

Similar notes appear in Cambridge, Corpus Christi College, MS 404 (Bury P. 163), a collection of prophecies largely copied in Kirkestede's own hand. Following a short tract on the coming of Antichrist he notes, 'This tract is very defective. See the noteworthy tract on the Antichrist, along with

---

117. 'Deficiunt hic alie epistole inter Alexandrum et Dindimum. Vide apud Waldenum'; Cambridge, Gonville and Caius College, MS 154/204, fol. 150r (Bury P. 162); reproduced in Gransden, 'Some manuscripts', pl. LXIIA, and see James, *Caius*, I. 179. The manuscript at Walden must have resembled in part London, College of Arms, MS 1, which contains (among other items) not only the added correspondence attributed to Alexander and Dindimus but also the only three *Catalogus* entries (*Catalogus* 55.3, 55.4, and 152.1) that Kirkestede located at **68** Walden.

118. He added the opening rubric as well, 'Narracio libri de Suda quem Robertus episcopus Lincolniensis [Robert Grosseteste] de greco transtulit in latinum'; printed in BM *Cat. Royal*, I. 220.

119. 'Non plus habetur apud Lenniam, sed residuum est Oxonie'; printed in BM *Cat. Royal*, I. 220. The manuscript referred to in Oxford evidently survives in Bodl. MS Digby 11, fols. 33r–43r, which belonged to the Oxford Greyfriars and which is now itself incomplete, containing chs. 32–71 only. The Bury manuscript of the *Suidas* (BL MS Royal 8 F. XIV, fols. 73r–80r) contains only eight chapters of the work. A contemporary of Kirkestede added a separate list of seventy-one chapters, of which chs. 32–71 agree with the surviving chapters in Digby 11, suggesting that the list was copied from it. See H. H. E. Craster, 'Liber Suda,' *Bodleian Quarterly Record* 3 (1920), 51.

120. 'Vide de phisonogmia breuius et melius in quodam paruo quaterno magistri Iohannis Tebaud rectoris de Elmeswell, et incipit sic, Matrix est embrion etc., finis expellere'; printed in BM *Cat. Royal*, 2. 24. He also reported the Aristotelian tract in the *Catalogus* (*46.41*, with a location number for St Botulph's Colchester).

a bestiary in French, in a small black book belonging to H. de Brigham'.[121] At the beginning of the next work, *De duracione mundi secundum Eusebium*, he notes, 'This tract is defective, too', and at its conclusion, 'The end is missing'.[122] Once again he drew attention to a Babwell text on the appearance of the Antichrist; on a scrap of parchment inserted after fol. 6r he gave a detailed description of the book (plate 5):

> Concerning the Antichrist, see the small quire at Babwell that begins *Quem phiseus* [?] *de iusticia*, or on the third folio after the beginning, *Nichil amarius peccato* etc. At the end of the quire is a brief versified tract called *Breuis ortulus* with this rubric: *Incipit libellus qui potest dici breuis ortulus eo quod breuiter in eo tanquam in ortulo fructus dulces excerpantur*; the verse at the end of the booklet, *Non me despicias quia non sum corpore magnus ortulus iste breuis micia poma gerit*. The tract on the Antichrist begins *De antichristo scire uolentes* etc., and ends *seculum iudicabit et ita esse prefixit* and is attributed to Albinus.[123]

In his quest for material on the Antichrist, Kirkestede had also seen books at two East Anglian Cistercian abbeys (or else he had discussed the matter seriously with someone who had done so); for he noted, with respect to another brief tract on the subject, 'This is in the book of visions at Sibton [Suffolk] and at Coggeshall [Essex]'.[124] The tract in question comprised an excerpt from the *Chronicon* of Ralph, abbot of Coggeshall, relating his interview with Joachim of Fiore, so it is not surprising that it should have been found at Coggeshall.[125]

Many of the manuscript annotations we have discussed are physical manifestations of the interests that produced the *Catalogus*; and many of the same motives, same methods, and even the same words evident in Kirkestede's

---

121. 'Iste tractatus est valde defectiuus. Vide tractatum de Antichristo notabilem in paruo libro nigro cum bestiario in gallicis quondam H. de Brigham'; Cambridge, Corpus Christi College, MS 404, fol. 7r. For a discussion of MS 404 and its contents see p. lxxvii below.
122. 'Iste tractatus similiter est defectiuus' and 'Deficit finis'; ibid. fols. 7v, 8v.
123. 'Vide de Antichristo in quodam paruo quaterno apud Babewell qui sic incipit Quem phiseus [?] de iusticia, uel sic in 3° folio post principium Nichil amarius peccato etc. In fine quaterni habetur breuis tractatus metricus qui dicitur Breuis ortulus, cuius rubrica est hec: Incipit libellus qui potest dici breuis ortulus eo quod breuiter in eo tanquam in ortulo fructus dulces excerpantur. Versus in fine libelli, Non me despicias quia non sum corpore magnus ortulus iste breuis micia poma gerit. Tractatus de antichristo sic incipit, De antichristo scire uolentes etc., finis, seculum iudicabit et ita esse prefixit et attitulatur albino'. This note and others from Corpus Christi 404 are printed by James, *Corpus Christi*, 2. 270.
124. 'Hec in libro uisionum apud Sibetone et apud Coggeshale'; ibid. fol. 66v.
125. M. Reeves, *The Influence of Prophecy in the Later Middle Ages* (Oxford 1969), 94.

annotations recur in the *Catalogus*. Moreover, we note in the edition unmistakable examples in the *Catalogus* of his having seen, not just any manuscript, but one or other specific manuscript that had belonged to the house whose location he gives. The most unexpected physical evidence of Kirkestede's bibliographical travels, however, appears in a surviving book. Kirkestede reported first-hand in the *Catalogus* 125 works from the Benedictine house at Ramsey in Cambridgeshire, suggesting that he had frequently visited the abbey. Bodl. MS Bodley 833, an early 13th-cent. manuscript from Ramsey, seems to be the only surviving copy of the *Euphrastica*, a treatise explaining difficult passages in the bible, written by the Ramsey monk William of Peterborough; in the *Catalogus (626.1)*, Kirkestede recorded Ramsey (**65**) as the *Euphrastica*'s sole location. None of this is singular. The surprise appears in the Ramsey manuscript: across the top of folio 1r of Bodley 833 is an *ex libris* in Kirkestede's hand, 'Liber monasterii de Rames.' (plate 6a). Kirkestede was not, as one might suspect, simply taking it upon himself to remedy an oversight by the Ramsey librarian, for Ramsey had no tradition of recording *ex libris* notes. The common identifying feature of Ramsey books is an *ex dono* note, and indeed a typical example appears on fol. iii^r of Bodley 833, 'Eufrastica inter libros Magistri Willelmi de Burgo'.[126] A possible explanation is that Kirkestede took the book on loan from Ramsey back to Bury, to read or to have a copy made for Bury, and that he inscribed the *ex libris* to ensure that the Ramsey book would be returned to its owners. Whatever the motive for this inscription, here is one book from another abbey that Kirkestede demonstrably held in his hands.

iv. Gathering information for the Catalogus

Kirkestede's interests in classifying the abbey's books, in correcting rubrics and supplying tables of contents, in finding and comparing books in other

---

126. Concerning Ramsey's standard practice see Sharpe, *Latin Writers*, 800–801, and esp. Sharpe, *Benedictines*, 328 and 415. In Ker, *MLGB*, the surviving Ramsey manuscripts (pp. 153–4) marked with an italic *e* (meaning 'evidence from an *ex libris* inscription or note of gift') nearly all have the latter, notes of gift. Even Bodley 833 has, along with Kirkestede's *ex libris* inscription, the usual Ramsey note of gift. In something of a contradiction, Sharpe, *Benedictines*, 327, also says that 'one quarter of the [Ramsey manuscript] survivors are attributed to Ramsey on the evidence of *ex libris* inscriptions; another quarter were inscribed with the names of Ramsey monks'. This has not been our experience. Although we have not seen all surviving Ramsey books, nevertheless from those in the Bodleian Library, the British Library, and the Cambridge university and college libraries we saw only one manuscript with an *ex libris* note: BL MS Royal 3 B. xi (Ramsey s. xii/xiii), a psalter commentary attributed to Richard of Saint-Victor, in which a note formerly on a pastedown has been pasted to the top of fol. iv, with 'Liber monasterii Rameseye' written in a tiny hand, its appearance unlike the Kirkestede note in the *Euphrastica*.

libraries—all of these form a context, and a recurring pattern of behaviour, that frame his compiling of the *Catalogus*. One final group of flyleaf notes in Bury manuscripts seems to show Kirkestede in the act of collecting information for the *Catalogus*. Unlike the various notes we have already discussed, these do not pertain to the work(s) in the manuscript, but rather they are extended biographical and bibliographical notes concerned with the author, and they reappear in similar prose in the *Catalogus*. Kirkestede entered a note of this sort on the flyleaf of a manuscript containing one or more of the author's significant works. Some seven notes of this type are known, and presumably there once were others in Bury manuscripts that no longer survive.

The longest of Kirkestede's flyleaf compositions reappears in large part in the *Catalogus* entry for Bede (*84*); it deals primarily with the problem of the authorship of the collections of extracts on the Pauline epistles taken from the works of Augustine.[127] On a flyleaf (p. vii) of Bodl. MS e Musaeo 9 (Bury B. 290),[128] which he thought contained Bede's *Super epistolas Pauli ex operibus Augustini*, Kirkestede noted that Bede himself said in his *Historia ecclesiastica* (V 24) that he had written such a work.[129] However, Kirkestede added that the work is ascribed by some to Petrus Tripolitanus, as is seen in Cassiodorus (*Institutiones* I. 8. 9). This remark he crossed out, and he replaced it with the full quotation from Cassiodorus. In the Bury manuscript of Cassiodorus Kirkestede marked the passage with a running line and the words, 'Note with regard to the exposition of the Pauline epistles attributed to St Augustine, although according to all the sources Augustine commented only on Romans and Galatians'.[130] The compilation by Petrus Tripolitanus is not known, and, understandably, Kirkestede could not locate a text of it; thus, he added to the Bede flyleaf note, in bold, underlined letters, 'This book of Peter's is extremely rare'.[131] Following this discussion he copied Bede's list of his own works from *Historia ecclesiastica* V 24, introduced by an excerpt from Bede's introductory comments. Kirkestede carefully singled out from the list the *Super epistolas Pauli* with a pointing hand and the words, 'Nota pro ista expositione'. The information found on this flyleaf appears in two places in the *Catalogus*, the list of Bede's works in

---

127. Cf. *CPL* 360.
128. Reproduced in Rouse, 'Bostonus Buriensis', pl. VIII.
129. The manuscript contains the similar work by Florus of Lyon. In addition to the bibliographic discussion Kirkestede recorded the Bury *ex libris* and contents note.
130. 'Nota pro expositione super epistolas Pauli que ascribitur beato Augustino, cum tamen beatus Augustinus iuxta omnes doctores non scripserit nisi tantum super epistolam ad Romanos et ad Galathas'; Bodl. MS e Musaeo 31 (Bury A. 31), p. 94.
131. 'Iste liber Petri rarissimus est'.

the Bede entry (*84*) and the note from Cassiodorus's *Institutiones* in the entry for Petrus Tripolitanus (*480*).

A bibliographical note related to the *Catalogus* entry for Boethius (*94*) appears on fol. i^v of Lambeth Palace Library, MS 67 (Bury B. 318), which contains Boethius, *De musica* and *De arithmetica*.[132] Kirkestede copied a short biographical notice from Vincent of Beauvais' *Speculum historiale* XXII 15, and followed this with the titles that appear in the *Catalogus* as works *94.1, 2, 4, 6, 7, 9, 10, 14, 12*, and *5* in the Boethius entry, the first four in the flyleaf list being supplied with incipits and explicits. The wording there is slightly fuller than that in the *Catalogus*, and two of the incipits are longer. Interestingly, Kirkestede compiled the flyleaf note not from a single source but from a combination of the *Manipulus florum*, the *Speculum historiale*, and the *Registrum*, all major sources for the *Catalogus*.[133] When he created the Boethius entry in the *Catalogus*, he added to the list another eight works from Bury manuscripts.[134]

Cambridge, Pembroke College, MS 92 (Bury J. 35), a copy of Cassian's *Collationes patrum* that Kirkestede personally commissioned for the abbey, contains on fol. ii^r a partly biographical note that discusses Cassian's orthodoxy; it was compiled from Gennadius, *De uiris illustribus* c. 85, the *Speculum historiale* XX 14, and the Gelasian decretal *De libris recipiendis*, and written in the hand of the text scribe (no doubt at Kirkestede's direction). At the end of this note, and extending on to the verso of the folio, Kirkestede added in his own hand a paragraph taken from an unidentified source defending the orthodoxy of Cassian's *Collationes*. The final sentence of the scribal portion along with all of Kirkestede's addition appears at the end of the introduction to the *Catalogus*; and the last half of this section he employed again, in the Cassian entry (*285*).[135] It is obvious, from Kirkestede's repeated reworking of this statement and from his commissioning of a manuscript of the *Collationes*, that Cassian figured prominently in Kirkestede's pantheon of authors, as a leading exponent of the monastic life.

132. The note is separate from the *ex libris* and contents notes on fol. ii^r; printed by James, *Lambeth*, 106, and reproduced in Rouse, 'Bostonus Buriensis', pl. IX.
133. For Kirkestede's use of these works in compiling the *Catalogus* see chapter 2 below.
134. Works *94.3* and *8* from Cambridge, Pembroke College, MS 84 (Bury B. 319), and Lambeth Palace Library, MS 67 (Bury B.318); *94.11* from Vincent and another Bury manuscript; *94.13* from a manuscript; *94.15* from an unidentified source; and *94.16–18* from Pembroke 84 again.
135. Reproduced Rouse, 'Bostonus Buriensis', pls. X–XI; and Gransden, 'Some manuscripts', pl. LXXIX_B–D, with discussion pp. 264–5. The portion of the note written by the scribe of Pembroke 92 has been copied from this manuscript into Lambeth Palace Library, MS 218 pt II, fol. 90r (Bury J. 23), Cassian's *De septem collationibus patrum*, by an early 15th-cent. scribe who added 'Vide originaliter xxiiii collaciones patrum in registro librorum in J. 35'. Extracts from the note were copied from the introduction to the *Catalogus*, Add. 3470 p. 10, by a mid-15th-cent. monk of Ely, in Lambeth Palace Library, MS 448, fol. 139r (Ely Cathedral).

Kirkestede's note in the *Catalogus* that follows, and comments on, the entry for Chrysostom's *Super Mattheum opus imperfectum (282.4)* indicates that, like so many others, he had struggled with the homilies of *ps.*-Chrysostom. He had written this note in slightly fuller form on fol. i^v (the front pastedown) of Cambridge, Pembroke College, MS 18 (Bury J. 28),[136] which contains twenty-one homilies of *ps.*-Chrysostom on Matthew 19–23.[137] This, like the note concerning Bede's writings, shows both Kirkestede's awareness of a bibliographical problem and the limitations of his resources for solving it. He had before him in Pembroke 18 a text entitled 'Omelie Crisostomi super Matheum in imperfecto .xliii.' But the text was incomplete, and the further he pursued the matter the more confusing it turned out to be. Somewhat uncharacteristically, he set forth the problem in the midst of the table of contents, before listing the other works in the codex, adding to the title, in slightly reduced script,

> That is to say, from homily 23 to homily 43, according to the numbering in this codex, for different codices do not number the homilies identically; thus, one codex will count three or four homilies where another codex counts only one. And the homilies are not even arranged in the order of the text of Matthew. Thus, from the first to the eighth chapter of Matthew there are 22 homilies, which expound the text sequentially. But from that eighth chapter to the end of the work there are 61 homilies, in some codices, in which the homilies do not follow the order of the Gospel; because from the eighth chapter they go to the nineteenth and continue to the twenty-second, then return to chapter 10 continuing to the twenty-first, twenty-third, twenty-fourth and so on. Note that in this present volume 22 homilies are missing from the beginning and 18 homilies from the end.[138]

---

136. Reproduced in Rouse, 'Bostonus Buriensis', pl. XII.
137. The note is printed by James, *Pembroke*, 15–16.
138. Cambridge, Pembroke College, MS 18, pastedown: 'Videlicet ab omelia xxiii^a usque ad omeliam xliii, iuxta quotacionem istius libri. Non enim seruatur idem numerus omeliarum in diuersis libris, quia in aliquo libro quotantur tres vel iiii^{or} omelie ubi in alio libro non quotatur nisi una omelia. Nec etiam omelie ponuntur in ordine iuxta textum Mathei. A primo enim capitulo Mathei usque ad viii capitulum sunt omelie xxii et exponunt textum consequenter. Et ab illo capitulo viii^o usque in finem operis sunt omelie lxi iuxta quosdam libros in quibus omeliis non seruatur ordo textus euangelii; quia ab viii capitulo itur ad xix^m et continuatur usque ad xxii^m, deinde redit ad x capitulum continuans usque ad xxi^m, xxiii et xxiiii et sic procedit diuersimode etc. Nota quod xxii omelie de principio istius operis deficiunt in hoc volumine, et xviii omelie de fine'.

Only then did he list, in a return to the full-size script, the titles of the two other works in the codex.

Two long extracts from Vincent's *Speculum historiale* appear on fol. ii^v of Wisbech and Fenland Museum, Town Library, MS 1 (Bury P. 119),[139] which contains Prosper's *De uita contemplatiua et actiua* (i.e. Julianus Pomerius). The first, from *Speculum* XXI 58 reporting the works of Prosper of Aquitaine, forms the basis of the Prosper entry in the *Catalogus* (*466*). This passage continues with the second, an excerpt from XX 14 supporting the orthodoxy of Cassian's *Collationes patrum* which Prosper had condemned. This is the same extract from Vincent that we have seen in Kirkestede's hand on the flyleaf of Cambridge, Pembroke College, MS 92, and repeated in the *Catalogus*, both in the introduction and in the entry for Cassian (*285*).

Perhaps the most interesting of Kirkestede's pre-*Catalogus* notes appears on the flyleaf (fol. i^v) of Cambridge, Pembroke College, MS 29 (Bury R. 14),[140] which contains Ralph of Flaix *Super parabolas Salomonis*.[141] The note closely parallels the entry for Ralph of Flaix in the *Catalogus* (*494*). Following a biographical notice (the version in the *Catalogus* is briefer), Kirkestede lists in this sequence *494.1*, *sermones et epistolas ad diversos*, *494.6, 7, 4, 8, 2, 3*, *De re militari* and comment, *494.9, 10, 14, 15*, and another comment. That is, he lists eleven of the *Catalogus*'s fifteen titles. The majority of these were taken from the list in the *Registrum*, but the others come from the same unidentified source that provided titles for the *Catalogus* entry. Following several of the titles, Kirkestede has spelled out *in extenso* the names of the libraries represented by the location numbers found with this entry in the *Registrum*. After he had copied the list onto the flyleaf, Kirkestede corrected it by crossing out *De re militari* (a title from the *Registrum*'s list), commenting in the margin, 'Ralph of Flaix did not write *De re militari* but another Ralph named Niger'.[142] The flyleaf contents-note of another Bury manuscript, Pembroke College, MS 27 (Bury P. 25), has similarly been corrected from 'Radulfus de re militari' to 'Radulfus Niger de re militari', and in the *Catalogus* Kirkestede naturally omits the work from the entry for Ralph of Flaix and records it among the works of Ralph Niger (*495.5*). The title *De sanctuario* appears in the Ralph of Flaix flyleaf list in Pembroke 29, along with Kirkestede's comment that some authorities ascribe this work to Hildefonsus. Since he was

---

139. Reproduced in Rouse, 'Bostonus Buriensis', pl. XIV.
140. Reproduced in Rouse, 'Bostonus Buriensis', pl. XIII.
141. Actually the work of Radulfus Pratellensis. The note is printed by James, *Pembroke*, 32, and id. *St Edmund*, 72.
142. Cambridge, Pembroke College, MS 29, fol. i^v: 'Radulfus Flauiacensis non scripsit de re militari sed alius Radulfus cognomine Niger'. Bale (*Index*, 331) noted that Ralph Niger came from Bury, but there is no corroboration of this claim.

unable to settle the question of attribution, he entered *De sanctuario* and a longer version of the note in the *Catalogus* entries for both Flaviacensis (*494.15*) and Hildefonsus (*246.13*). Beside the mention of Radulfus's commentary on Leviticus in twenty books Kirkestede noted that this was 'in librario sancti Edmundi in .ii. pulcris et magnis uoluminibus'.[143]

Clearly these flyleaf notes were not simply excerpted from the *Catalogus*, for their lists of works are uniformly shorter. Likewise, the *Catalogus* entries are not direct copies from the manuscript flyleaves. In these notes Kirkestede treated the flyleaves as convenient places to store information concerning the authors whose works appeared in the manuscripts. Whether he wrote the notes with the *Catalogus* in mind or as draft entries is not known. What is known is that significant portions of them reappear in the *Catalogus*.

C. The Black Death at Bury St Edmunds

The outbreak of plague at mid-century marked the end of Kirkestede's young manhood. In dealing with the subject, we can only reiterate the comment of David Knowles that when the fearful severity of the scourge is borne in mind it appears strange that it has left such scanty traces in the monastic records. Kirkestede's only activity that can be securely dated to the year 1349 was totally unrelated to the plague, confirming that, yes, he did know a Bury resident who in that year claimed that he had been favoured, as a boy, by a miraculous intervention of St Edmund.[144] No plague miracles are associated with Edmund.[145] Nevertheless, the experience changed Kirkestede's abbey and ultimately changed his life.

Hard information about the severity of the Black Death at the abbey of Bury St Edmunds in 1349–50 is almost non-existent. The only precise figure specifically related to the plague consists in the fact that in January 1351 Abbot William of Bernham received papal permission to ordain as many as ten monks who had not yet reached the canonical age of 24—indeed, to reduce the age to 19 'or beyond', which is to say, even younger[146]—for the

---

143. And he noted in Bury's two-volume glossed Leviticus that 'Ralph, monk and abbot of Flaix, expounded this book'; Cambridge, Pembroke College, MSS 49, fol. 72r (Bury B. 48) and 50, fol. 54r (Bury [B. 49?]), 'Hunc librum exponit etiam Radulfus Flauiacensis monachus et abbas' ('. . . exponit plenius Radulfus abbas flauiacensis' in MS 50).

144. See below, p. cxxix.

145. With the curious exception of the plague miracles wrought at Toulouse in the 17th cent. by the fraudulent bones of Edmund there; R. Gem, 'A scientific examination of the relics of St Edmund at Arundel Castle', in Gransden, *Bury St Edmunds*, 45–56, esp. 51.

146. The figures are customarily stated as 'in the twenty-fifth year' and 'in the twentieth year' which means those who had reached their twenty-fourth and their nineteenth birthdays, respectively.

express reason that death from plague had left too few ordained monks to celebrate masses.[147] (Plague or not, the abbot secured explicit permission that the ordination could be at the hands of any bishop in good standing with the Holy See—that is to say, he confirmed that, as usual, it was not necessary to apply to his local bishop, in Bernham's case his adversary Bishop Bateman of Norwich, and he did not.) And in the event, nine Bury monks were ordained priest in 1351 by the bishop of Ely, when the previous average had been two or three annually, sometimes fewer.[148]

It happens that there are printed statements of a fifty per cent mortality rate at Bury claiming the lives of forty monks in 1349; and further assumptions have been built upon these 'facts'. These figures are mistaken, however, and there are regrettably no dependable figures about the mortality rate or about the total number of monks at Bury at mid-century.[149] The population of the borough at the time, potentially useful for comparison, is likewise unknown. The Bury chronology marked the year 1349 with the stark comment, 'In England there was enormous loss of life', and it is difficult to be more precise than that.[150] Whatever the exact dimensions of the blow to the community, one cannot doubt its severity; the abbot's ordination of teenagers speaks for itself.

The experience was one that marked Kirkestede's outlook, and before his life ended he experienced three further outbreaks of plague at Bury, a cumulation of signs that encouraged him to anticipate the Last Judgement. After the initial major outbreak at mid-century, the survivors at Bury as elsewhere picked up the pieces and attempted to return as quickly as possible to a normal life under the rule, with senior monks (now including Kirkestede) obviously having to take up more of the numerous tasks necessary to the abbey's life in order to compensate for those who had been lost. The documented lack of enough priests to say the requisite masses for the dead at Bury's altars can be taken as symptomatic of deficiencies overall. Kirkestede also seems to have persisted in his work on the *Catalogus* and on his organization of the library through the course of the 1350s. In this post-plague climate, however, one might suppose that his days of energetic innovation had ended.

147. C. Ritchie, 'The Black Death at St. Edmund's abbey', *Proceedings of the Suffolk Institute of Archaeology* 27 (1958) 47–50, at 48–50 edits and translates the papal bull. Bury was not unique in petitioning the pope on this matter, of course: see, for example, Knowles, *Religious Orders*, 2. 12.
148. See the Lisle register, fols. 97va and 98ra; and see the Montacute and Lisle registers passim.
149. R. H. and M. A. Rouse, 'Plague at the abbey of Bury St Edmunds, 1348 and 1361' (forthcoming).
150. 'In Anglia fuit maxima mortalitas hominum'; BL MS Campbell Roll XXI.1, on verso of the last membrane.

Prior of Bury, from 1361

The second part of Kirkestede's life began in earnest in 1361.[151] The abbey in that year underwent a dramatic and thorough change of its administration, which raised Henry of Kirkestede to the office of prior and his long-time friends and associates to other positions of authority. The shift in Kirkestede's own priorities was a major one.

The process began as a routine transfer of power: Abbot William of Bernham, then perhaps in his sixties,[152] died on 28 February 1361 (NS) after holding office for twenty-six years, the longest tenure of any abbot since Abbot Samson (1182–1211). Bernham's death had been anticipated, clearly, because the abbey had already sent its petition to the king and received his permission to elect a successor by 3 March. But thereafter an unexpected sequence of further deaths left the abbey reeling, as another major outbreak of plague swept across Europe, second in virulence only to that of 1349. We have mentioned previously the meagre annals, twenty-three years' worth from 1341 through 1363, that Kirkestede had marked off at the end of a Bury collection of histories (Bodl. Lat. hist. d. 4), but that he had left blank after two brief notes.[153] The events of 1361–62 stirred him to make renewed entries, not hitherto noticed by scholars, documenting in laconic prose the disasters at Bury (plate 7).

Bury's new abbot-elect Henry of Hunstanton,[154] journeying to Avignon to gain papal confirmation of his election, fell ill and died of plague on 24 July just as he reached the outskirts of the city.[155] And at Bury itself, as Kirkestede recorded in his annal for 1361, the local outbreak killed many monks and the abbey's senior dignitary, Prior Edmund Brundish: 'A general pestilence, in which the prior and 18 monks of St Edmund's died. After the death of lord Henry of Hunstanton, abbot elect, who died at

---

151. We earlier called Kirkestede a subprior; Rouse, 'Bostonus Buriensis', 481–2. The error was corrected by Thomson, 'Obedientiaries', 93.
152. Bernham was already serving as subprior when he was elected abbot in 1335.
153. See above at nn. 24–5.
154. Hunstanton must have been a Bury monk for at least three years when he was ordained priest on 17 March 1347 (NS); see the Lisle register, fol. 95vb.
155. Bury, as an 'exempt abbey', had the pope, instead of a bishop, as its direct superior. This situation entailed a trip to the papal curia by each newly-elected abbot. Concerning Hunstanton see *BRUO* 985 and *VCH Suffolk* 2 (1907), 64; and for his election and for the death dates of both abbots, see Kirkestede's annals in Bodl. MS Lat. hist. d. 4, fol. 224r, under the year 1361.

the curia, Pope Innocent VI conferred the abbacy of St Edmund's on lord John of Brinkley, monk of St Edmund's and bachelor in both laws'.[156]

In numbers, then, with the loss of eighteen monks and the prior and the abbot-elect, the abbey must have lost between a quarter and a third of its population in the plague of 1361.[157] In addition to the quantitative loss, the abbey lost its mature leadership: Abbot William of Bernham, Abbot-elect Henry of Hunstanton, Prior Edmund Brundish, and probably the sacrist Simon of Langham, although Kirkestede does not say so (his successor is mentioned before the end of 1361);[158] at Bury the sacrist ranked next after the prior in administrative importance.[159] Within six months or so, therefore, not only did the abbey lose a third of the community, but the survivors were left without abbot or prior and, probably, without sacrist as well.[160]

156. Bodl. MS Lat. hist. d. 4, fol. 224r: 'Pestilencia generalis in qua prior et XVIII monachi Sancti Edmundi obierunt. Innocencius VI papa contulit abbatiam Sancti Edmundi, post mortem domini Henrici de Hunstanton' electi et in curia defuncti, domino Johanne de Brinkele monacho Sancti Edmundi et in utroque iure baculario'; see plate 7.

157. Concerning the size of Bury's population in the 1370s see our 'Plague at the abbey' (forthcoming).

158. Simon of Langham, monk of Bury, was ordained an acolyte in 1340; see Montacute register, fol. 106vb. According to the published calendar of probate records at Bury, Langham was the abbey's sacrist from the time when the will of Richard le Palmer was proved on 13 February 1357 until the will of Gilbert le Barbour was proved on 4 July 1361 (and an undated will on the following folio); V. B. Redstone, 'Registers of testaments, wills, and probates at Bury', *Proceedings of the Suffolk Institute of Archaeology* 12 (1906), 1–3. But intruded out of sequence on folios 17 and 18, between a will dated 13 June 1361 and another dated 2 July 1361, there are three wills proved on 23 and 24 December 1361, ostensibly during Langham's tenure; this conflicts with the fact that John of Lavenham is recorded as sacrist for proving the will of Thomas of Sutton on 9 August 1361, as well as more than two dozen undated probates that may have belonged to that plague summer and autumn of 1361 (Redstone, 3–4). It is plausible that the three December probates were inscribed out of sequence, among the wills that had been proved during Simon of Langham's term of office at the beginning of the summer, and that Langham himself died of plague at Bury in July at about the same time that his abbot-elect Hunstanton died of plague in Avignon. It is possible, instead, that Simon of Langham and John of Lavenham exercised the office of sacrist jointly; see Thomson, 'Obedientiaries', 95.

159. Thomson, 'Obedientiaries', 91.

160. See the comparable effect of the 1361 plague on high civil servants in England: W. M. Ormrod, 'The politics of pestilence', in *The Black Death in England*, ed. W. M. Ormrod and P. G. Lindley (Stamford 1996), 147–81, esp. the tables on pp. 178 and 180. The size of Bury's monastic community in 1361 can only be an estimate; a figure between sixty and eighty seems a conservative estimate.

Because Henry of Hunstanton died at the curia, the pope had the right to name his successor. Innocent VI (1352–62), within eleven days of Hunstanton's death, named as abbot the Bury monk John of Brinkley (4 August 1361–31 December 1378). Brinkley had been ordained priest in 1351; although this was during the period when Bury had received dispensation to ordain ten priests below the canonical age, Brinkley was not one of these exceptions (he had been ordained subdeacon the previous year and thus was already on the rungs of the ordination ladder).[161] At the time of his provision by the pope he was just completing his university studies at Oxford, trained in both laws; elevation to the abbacy prevented him from incepting in 1361.[162] The most plausible reason for the swift choice of this promising but (so the university record suggests) young and inexperienced administrator is that Brinkley was there, on the spot, when Hunstanton fell mortally ill. Brinkley must have travelled to Avignon with Hunstanton (who also was an Oxford-trained lawyer, an inceptor in both laws), as a hand-picked member of the abbot-elect's entourage. It is conceivable that Hunstanton on his deathbed may have recommended Brinkley to the pope as a worthy replacement.

Ablest of the abbots of Kirkestede's day, Brinkley was soon chosen as one of the three presidents of the English Benedictine province and served in that capacity for ten years (from c. 1366);[163] he was heavily involved in administration in the province.[164] Brinkley left tangible evidence of an interest in the Bury library: he personally procured at least four surviving manuscripts for the abbey, and he appears in a list of benefactors as having purchased books for the abbey valued at no less than £150.[165] It is tempting to see here the influence of Kirkestede the novice master on the younger Brinkley.

---

161. See above at nn. 146–8. For other monasteries ordaining underage priests see C. Harper-Bill, 'The English church and English religion after the Black Death', in *The Black Death in England*, ed. W. M. Ormrod and P. G. Lindley (Stamford 1996), 79–123, at 97. For Brinkley as subdeacon, see the Lisle register, fol. 97ra.
162. *BRUO* 267.
163. *VCH Suffolk* 2 (1907), 64. Presidents of the English provincial chapter of the Benedictines were three in number for the whole of Kirkestede's lifetime, ostensibly two from the south and one from the north; see Knowles, *Religious Orders*, 2. 7.
164. Pantin, *Documents*, 3. 72, 76 n. 1, 77–8, 277, and cf. 260.
165. Cambridge, Pembroke College, MSS 1 (Bury A. 92) and 40 (Bury T. 47), Glasgow UL MS Hunterian 209 (Bury B. 332), and BL MS Royal 8 E. x (Bury M. 12). Probably also Ipswich Central Library, MS 4 (Bury M. xi), 'J. abbas', and perhaps Bodl. MS Bodley 216 (Bury B. 46) 'per J. abbatem'. The list of benefactors is printed from Douai BM MS 553 (Bury —) by James, *St Edmund*, 7–8.

It must have been Brinkley who proposed Henry of Kirkestede to fill the post of prior upon the death of Edmund Brundish.[166] By the late 14th cent. a Benedictine abbot did not wield absolute power in the choice of his officials but shared such decisions with the chapter. The chapter could even act alone in choosing a prior during a vacancy (as Bury's chapter was to do in 1381);[167] and at Bury it was 'the approved custom of the abbey from ancient times' that the prior install the abbot, rather than the reverse.[168] But given the decimation of the abbey's highest officers in 1361, Brinkley no doubt had unusual moral authority in imposing his choices.

The prior was the most important officer of the abbey, saving only the abbot. Like the abbot, the prior had his own establishment, which included a separate house within the abbey precinct (east of the dormitory, which was north of the church) and his own stables.[169] In a large and important abbey such as Bury, whose abbot habitually spent much of his time in London and Westminster, at parliament and in attendance on the court, and as visitor or president of the provincial chapter, the day-to-day management and governance of the abbey rested primarily in the prior's hands. The choice suggests a previous association of some sort, and it was doubtless advantageous for the new abbot to have as his second in command a reliable senior monk with intimate and long-term knowledge of the abbey's innermost workings and its personalities—the sort of direct knowledge that Brinkley himself lacked because of long absences at Oxford.

In his years as prior under Abbot Brinkley, Kirkestede's associates in administering the abbey—most of whom must also have been Brinkley's choice in late 1361—were Edmund Wirlington, infirmarer (by 1362/3); John of Snailwell, former precentor (known 1346) who became Kirkestede's subprior (by 1362/3), perhaps at Kirkestede's own suggestion; John of Lavenham,

---

166. The fact that Kirkestede immediately succeeded Brundish is implicit in a note in his hand, which dates a prior's visitation as taking place 'in the times of Edmund Brundish and Henry of Kirkestede, priors', a note presumably begun by the first before his death and completed by the second ('Visitacio prioris temporibus domini E. de B. et H. de K. priorum'; BL MS Harley 1005, fol. 67v [Bury C. 68]). The 15th-cent. cellarer's register, CUL MS Gg. 4. 4, fol. 340r (modern foliation 243r), gives incidental reference to Kirkestede as prior in 1362/3; Thomson, 'Obedientiaries', 93.

167. John Timworth was elected abbot in 1379 but not approved by the pope until 1384, and the abbey, at least officially, treated this as a vacancy. Prior John Cambridge was killed in 1381, and newly-elected Prior John Gosford thereafter managed the abbey's affairs until approval for Timworth was secured three years later. See *VCH Suffolk* 2 (1907), 64–5, and Arnold, *Memorials*, 3. 113–37.

168. 'Secundum consuetudinem monasterii antiquitus approbatam'; Arnold, *Memorials*, 3. 119.

169. A. B. Whittingham, 'Bury St Edmunds abbey: the plan, design and development of the church and monastic buildings', *The Archaeological Journal* 108 (1951) 168–87, esp. 179.

former guestmaster who was named sacrist in 1361 and retained that post until after 1383; and John of Cambridge, cellarer (by 1362/3),[170] who would become Kirkestede's immediate successor as prior.[171] Among this group, John of Lavenham and John of Cambridge in particular were powerful and trusted figures, responsible respectively for the care of the abbey's fabric and the administration of the abbey's revenues. These three, Kirkestede, Lavenham, and Cambridge, prior, sacrist, and cellarer, were the inner circle who oversaw the affairs of the house in the absence of Abbot Brinkley.

Kirkestede's term as prior was not uneventful. Following upon the change of administration, the abbey was saddled almost immediately with an unexpected financial blow in the loss of the central bell-tower of the abbey church, which toppled in a winter gale at the beginning of 1362, damaging other parts of the fabric as it fell. The destructive storm, also remarked by other observers including William Langland and Thomas Walsingham,[172] was recorded by Prior Kirkestede in his brief annals: 'On 15 January a tempestuous wind blew down the great bell-tower of St Edmund's, along with the presbytery and the Lady Chapel, and many other great bell-towers of England. It toppled many buildings and woodlands'.[173] The bell-tower's collapse in 1362, not previously mentioned in histories of the abbey, was presumably also the occasion of an undated 'miracle of St Edmund', whose

170. John of Cambridge had been a Bury monk from before 17 March 1347 (NS), when he was ordained subdeacon by Bishop Thomas Lisle of Ely; Lisle register, fol. 95ra (ordained deacon 14 June 1348, ibid. fol. 96rb).

171. In the 36th year of Edward III (i.e. 1362-3) Wirlington and Cambridge reached an amicable division of property disputed by the infirmarer's office and the cellarer's, agreed in the presence of abbot, prior and subprior (Brinkley, Kirkestede, Snailwell)—in other words, except for the sacrist (Lavenham) the abbey's entire cadre appears in this one document; CUL MS Gg. 4. 4, fol. 340r (modern foliation 243r), a 15th-cent. transcript in the cellarer's register; see Thomson, 'Obedientiaries', under the individual names.

172. See W. W. Skeat (ed.), *The Vision of William concerning Piers the Plowma.*, 10th revd. edn (Oxford 1964), 130, whose note to Passus V verse 14 ('And the southwest wynde . on saterday at euene') cites these and at least five other contemporary accounts of the tempest. A note in the calendar of a 15th-cent. Wycliffite New Testament, Bodl. MS Rawlinson C. 259, at the bottom of the January/February page, records that 'Anno domini MCCCLXI in festo sancti Mauri abbatis erat ventus validus'; this is written in a formal bookhand by the hand of the calendar, and was probably copied along with the calendar from its exemplar; see C. F. R. De Hamel, *The Book* (London 2001), 187.

173. Bodl. MS Lat. hist. d. 4, fol. 224r, under the heading '1361' (which in January became 1362): 'Eodem anno XVIII Kal. Februarii [15 January 1362, New Style] ventus tempestuosus prostrauit magnum campanile Sancti Edmundi presbiterum et capellam beate Marie et alia plura et magna campanilia Anglie. Edificia quoque et nemora plura obuertit'; see plate 7. The path of destruction suggests that the gale hit the abbey from the southwest. The spire of Norwich cathedral was toppled as well; Skeat (as n. 172).

timing has eluded students of Bury's history; like Kirkestede's account, the miracle story emphasizes the magnitude of the storm (called a *tempestas inaudita* and a *tempestas horrenda*), and mentions damage to the Lady Chapel and the presbytery; and it thanks the miraculous intervention of the saint for changing the direction of the wind so that the bell-tower's fall spared the high altar and preserved the lives of all the monks (in fact, the legend continues, there was no death nor even serious injury to any servant nor to the least of the abbey's creatures).[174] Repairs cost the abbey a large sum that Lavenham the sacrist had to scrape together: £866 13s. 4d. for the tower itself (and presumably the other structural repairs), with an additional £133 6s. 8d. for the great bell that weighed about three tons.[175] Other expenditures on the fabric during Lavenham's term as sacrist may also have been connected to the storm damage, such as providing a new screen for the Lady Chapel and repainting the ceiling of the choir.[176]

Later in Kirkestede's term of office, perhaps in the second half of 1368, a serious internal scandal occurred. In the dormitory a fight broke out involving three monks, John of Grafton, William of Blundeston, and John of Norton, at night while the others slept, and Grafton stabbed Norton to death, with Blundeston's help. Abbot Brinkley and the chapter then secretly buried the victim in the monastic cemetery, hoping (they later explained) to avoid 'scandals and damages' and 'thinking the crime could be concealed'; and with the community's assent, the abbot imprisoned Grafton and Blundeston in the abbey prison.[177] With over a hundred lay servants

---

174. 'Neque famulus aliquis vel catulus ullam sensit lesionem qua mortem vel mutilacionis discremen incurrit'; the account of the miracle appears in Bodl. MS Bodley 240, p. 677. Both James, *St Edmund*, 203, and Arnold, *Memorials*, 3. 345–6, print transcriptions; neither one could have known of Kirkestede's notes. James hazards a guess that the miracle refers to the collapse of 1210, although he notes that the mention of a storm does not fit the earlier occasion, while Arnold opts for the collapse in 1430, and on that basis proposes to move to the 15th cent. the date of Bodley 240, dated 1377.

175. Added together, these two precise-looking sums total £1000 to the penny—perhaps a bit suspicious. The sacrist John Lavenham is said to have spent twenty-six years in the rebuilding, which may mean that Kirkestede did not live to see its completion; John Leland, *Itinerary*, 4. 153–5, cited here from James, *St Edmund*, 167–8. Leland mistakenly regarded the sacrist's building efforts as a benefaction, interpreting the phrase 'Ioannes Lavenham sacrista fecit et fieri procuravit' as 'John Lavenham gave . . .'; James, 168. James supposed that Lavenham's rebuilding replaced the tower destroyed in 1210 (ib. 167); Whittingham, 'Bury', 175, accepted this suggestion without question.

176. See the documents printed or translated by James, *St Edmund*, esp. 182, and cf. 133, 143–4. Perhaps Lavenham's outlay of £100 to paint the ceiling of the nave was also necessitated by the storm's damage (ib. 130).

177. *Cal. Pat. Rolls 1367–1370*, 186.

passing in and out of the abbey gates each day, the 'secret' became public at once, and the crown's officers took a hard look. Investigating this situation must have been the motive for the undated visit (not quite a formal visitation) by Thomas de la Mare—long-serving abbot of St Albans, president of the English Benedictine province, and privy councillor—who was sent to Bury at Edward III's behest, at some date between *c.* 1366 and late 1368. De la Mare had also been sent by the king earlier in this period to the abbeys of Eynsham, Abingdon, Battle, and Reading; the Bury visit is the only one whose purpose is not stated.[178] The abbot and convent claimed they had been unaware that it was a crime not to report a homicide to the coroner; the king was content to accept this disingenuous plea from Brinkley the lawyer-abbot, and to deal with the matter quietly. Prior Kirkestede wanted to resign, however, but the visitor Abbot de la Mare persuaded him to remain in office.[179] Our knowledge of the incident, and of the abbey's rationalization of its actions, stems from a royal letter of pardon to all concerned, dated 8 January 1369.[180] One can read between the lines that the abbey made an appropriate payment for the king's forgiveness. Prior Kirkestede was fortunate that the abbot was present to shoulder responsibility for the abbey's folly; but if this was, as the timing suggests, the incident over which he sought to resign, then he obviously felt his own responsibility in the matter.

Kirkestede's routine duties as prior, in contrast to these extraordinary occurrences, are reflected in a record mentioned above called the *Liber albus*—a collection of miscellaneous 13th-, 14th-, and early 15th-cent. documents and texts concerning the history of the abbey, its customs, offices, and benefactors; the most famous of the texts is the only complete copy of Jocelin of Brakelond's Chronicle (fols. 127r–170r), to which Kirkestede has supplied

---

178. Concerning this visit, Knowles says vaguely that de la Mare at Bury 'helped to compose the differences that were distracting the abbey at the time'; Knowles, *Religious Orders*, 2. 205.
179. 'Priorem Henricum Kirkstede qui cessisse voluit ad regendum suum officium animauit'; Thomas Walsingham, *Gesta abbatum monasterii sancti Albani*, ed. H. T. Riley, RS 28/4 (1867–9), 2. 406. Walsingham specifies that although de la Mare visited, he did not make a visitation: 'inuenit omnes paratos ad se submittendum sue visitationi, non tamen visitauit'. See the brief reference to the Bury visit in Pantin, *Documents*, 2. 34 (based on Walsingham), who gives a date of *c.* 1362–6 for de la Mare's earlier visitations of Eynsham, Abingdon, and Battle. Walsingham mentions these others and says that the visit to Bury occurred 'finally' (*postremo*). For a biography of Thomas de la Mare see Knowles, *Religious Orders*, 2. 39–48. For an appreciation of Walsingham see J. G. Clark, 'Thomas Walsingham reconsidered: books and learning at late-medieval St. Albans', *Speculum* 77 (2002) 832–60.
180. The incident is not dated. The royal exoneration, summarized in the *Calendar of Patent Rolls 1367–1370*, 186, says the homicide occurred 'lately'—although the letter also says that Grafton and Blundeston have 'long' been imprisoned.

marginal headings. It has been said that by Kirkestede's day the *Liber albus* was, and may have been from its creation in the 1270s, the prior's custumal that was passed from one prior to the next.[181] The extent to which Kirkestede annotated the manuscript shows that he considered it his own working handbook, a record to revise and keep up to date, and a notebook in which to enter memorable information and to copy documents, statutes, tracts, or customs that might be of use to him as prior.

Among his notes in the *Liber albus* are a great many that reflect the everyday business of the abbey. There is nothing remarkable here, but the very banality of Kirkestede's notes and additions is the clearest indication of his immersion in the established routine of the monastery: visitation records (fol. 67v); a note concerning the removal of lepers to the hospitals of St Nicholas and St Peter (fol. 101v); numerous ordinances, both general (fol. 195v) and specific—for lighting the refectory, for distribution of money to the abbey's officers (fol. 84r), for the disposal of the goods of deceased monks (fol. 67v), for the number of candles to be provided for each altar on specified feast days (fol. 67r, copied 'from the sacrist's register, and from an old custumal of the third prior in a shabby quire'[182]). The prior's concern with guarding the abbey's rights is everywhere manifest—in his correction and updating of an early 14th-cent. list of duties and taxes owed to the monks of Bury (fols. 63r–64r), for example, or in his copying into this custumal (fols. 280v–281v) three lengthy charters of Abbots Anselm, Samson, and Hugh, fixing the rights of the burgesses of Bury.

Notes in the *Liber albus* illustrate Kirkestede's concern with administrative customs of the abbey and the duties of its various officers and servants, which were major responsibilities under the prior's charge. He added to a late 13th-cent. list of abbey officers (fol. 43r–v), and he himself copied a list of the duties of the keepers of the shrine of St Edmund (fol. 44r) and a list of the festivals on which the monks were permitted to eat twice (fol. 115r), 'copied from an old quire of customs with the shelf-mark C. 78, and from the *Traditiones patrum* in the keeping of T. de Saxham, on parchment, marked with the letter C. 64 in the library' (see plate 6b).[183] From another custumal he excerpted a further page of notes dealing with the abbey's officers

---

181. See the detailed description by Thomson, *Archives*, 142–5 no. 1293, and see Thomson's discussion of its history, ibid. 17–19.

182. 'Ex registro sacriste et ex antiquo consuetudinario tercii prioris in turpi quaterno'; James, *St Edmund*, 161.

183. 'He scripte sunt de antiquo quaterno consuetudinum cum littera C. 78. intitulato et ex traditionibus patrum in custodia T. de Saxham in pergameno cum littera C. 64. intitulatis in librario'; ibid. 55, and see above at n. 77. Concerning lost custumals of Bury see Thomson, *Archives*, 9–10.

and their duties (fol. 44v) that he continued later in the manuscript (fol. 210v), verifying that 'this has been corrected against the exemplar in a very old roll belonging to the lord abbot'.[184]

Obviously, there can be no clear boundary between Kirkestede's concern with the abbey's customs as prior and his emphasis on the abbey's history as novice master, and he can often be seen pursuing both interests jointly— or the same interest to dual purpose—in his notes in the 'prior's custumal', the *Liber albus*. Thus, Kirkestede heavily annotated an early 14th-cent. list of 11th-cent. benefactors of the abbey, supplying the dates of each and noting whether the grant was confirmed by an extant charter (fols. 81r–83r). He recorded (fol. 126v) the history of the donation of Mildenhall, the abbey's most profitable estate, and from another source he glossed a 13th-cent. text (fols. 217v–218v) concerning the dedications of altars in the chapel and the crypt of Bury. He annotated a text on the foundation of Ely and St Aetheldrytha (fol. 193r), recording that 'these chronicles are taken from an ancient text at Ely concerning the realm of the East Angles'.[185] Certain of his annotations in Harley 1005 suggest that he continued to treat it as his own even after he had been succeeded as prior. On fol. 195v, a document dated 1372 that was copied (according to its heading) from a version written in the hand of 'J. de C. prior', which is to say, John of Cambridge. The words do not say that John had become prior by 1372, but the note is written in Kirkestede's hand. And a note of accounts in his hand (fol. 84r) he dated 1375.

We do not know how long Kirkestede continued as prior. Documents settling the homicide suggest that he remained through 1369 at least, and perhaps in total as many as a dozen years or more from his appointment in 1361. By 1374/5 John of Cambridge, the former cellarer, is mentioned as prior. Kirkestede may have resigned because of age or ill health, since he apparently did not live many years thereafter. For whatever the reason, Kirkestede left the office of prior in time to escape the fate of his successor, who (in the abbot's absence) was executed, as the most visible target, by John Wrawe's army in the Peasants' Revolt of 1381.

In Old Age, the 1370s

Kirkestede seems to have worked on, or at least continued to annotate, the *Catalogus* until his death. He was perhaps relieved to relinquish the office of

---

184. 'Correcta est ista scripta per exemplar in rotulo uetustissimo domini abbatis'; BL MS Harley 1005, fol. 210v (James, *St Edmund*, 87), with corrections in Kirkestede's hand in the margins.

185. 'Ista cronica sumpta sunt de quodam textu ueteri apud Ely. De regno estanglorum.'

prior, but his annotations in Bury manuscripts indicate that he retained his interests in the abbey's books and its novices until the last years of his life.[186] At an undatable time in the 1370s his hand acquired a noticeable tremor, caused perhaps by a stroke or other illness, or simply by the weakness of old age. The tremor is quite pronounced in some manuscripts, which can be dated as the latest of his annotations.[187] He had earlier (*c*. 1368) been dissuaded from resigning the priorate, and infirmity may eventually have given him an honourable excuse for retirement (if such it was). The last datable note in his hand, a good example of the tremor, occurs in Cambridge, Corpus Christi College, MS 404 (Bury P. 163); at the bottom of fol. 94v he added the death date of Pope Gregory XI (d. March 1378), and at the top of fol. 95r he entered the name of Gregory's successor, 'Urbanus VI^{us}', as the running headline over a still-blank page.

We do not know how much longer Kirkestede lived beyond this date. It is not unlikely that he saw, a few months later, the start of the Great Schism, with the election of a French antipope at Avignon in September 1378, to parallel the papacy of Urban VI in Rome that was supported by England.[188] Perhaps he lived to see the death of Abbot Brinkley on the last day of December 1378, which initiated a lengthy and bitter dispute over Bury's abbacy. The king's officers imprisoned the pope's nominee Edmund Bromfeld under the Statute of Provisors, after Urban VI had refused to confirm the man elected by the monks (and favoured by the king), John of Timworth.[189] Bromfeld had entered the realm illegally and, knowing that he lacked support from a majority of the monks, he successfully courted the burgesses of Bury; the town's support of the interloper was added to the list of the perpetual grievances between town and monastery. Kirkestede may have lived into this period, when his abbey was officially headless for a number of years.

---

186. See, for example, his note in BL MS Cotton Tiberius B. II (n. 50 above), written after John of Cambridge had replaced him as prior.
187. CUL MS Add. 6006, fol. xviii^v (Bury C. 63), Cambridge, Corpus Christi College, MS 404, fol. iii^v (Bury P. 163), Cambridge, St John's College, MS G. 2, fols. 64r–70r (Bury H. 56), BL MS Harley 1005, fols. 9r, 80v–81v (Bury C. 68).
188. If he did live until the beginning of the Great Schism, it is unlikely that Kirkestede would have assigned undue importance to it; antipopes were not unknown (there had been an antipope earlier in Kirkestede's lifetime, in 1328–30), and he could not have imagined how remarkably long this new division was to last.
189. Bromfeld (also Bromfield, Brounfield) was a monk of Bury by 18 December 1349 or 1350, when he was ordained subdeacon; Lisle register, fol. 96v. The keeping and dating of this record was briefly thrown into disarray by the Black Death, and it is not immediately clear which of the two years is referred to.

He may well have seen the violence of 1381. It would have been a bitter symmetry had Kirkestede come full circle, to have entered the monastery *c.* 1331, when punishments for the riots of 1327–31 were still being determined and exacted, and then to have ended his days in the bloody Peasants' Revolt of 1381.[190] For a period of ten days, between 13 June 1381 with the arrival of John Wrawe's band at Bury and 23 June when the earl of Suffolk and his retainers relieved the abbey, the rebels had free reign. Since the abbacy was still vacant, in the abbot's stead they captured the prior, John of Cambridge, at Bury's estate of Mildenhall, beheading him and taking his head back to Bury where it was mounted next to the head of the abbey baroner John of Lakenheath, and that of Sir John Cavendish, Chief Justice of the King's Bench.[191] The rebels extorted from the terrified monks gold and jewelled objects; and then, prodded by Bury burgesses with the same object in mind as their fathers had had in 1327, the rebels also destroyed Bury documents and demanded a charter of liberties for the town. For good measure, they demanded that Edmund of Bromfeld (the town's favourite in the disputed election two years before) be released from imprisonment and installed as abbot so that he could seal the new charter. It did not happen. And despite blanket protestations of innocence, the burgesses' overt collaboration with the rebel army was so flagrant that Bury St Edmunds was the only town in England excluded from the eventual royal amnesty, and it spent the next five years paying the fine levied against it.

Already elderly, Kirkestede may have collapsed and died under the terror and violence of those days. Or perhaps, instead, he lived on, to see the magnificent visit to Bury of King Richard II, his new queen Anne of Bohemia, and their entourage, for a ten-day period in 1383. (Such signs of royal favour always cost the abbey dear: 800 marks, in this instance.[192]) He may even have lived until 1384, to see the matter of the disputed election finally resolved in John Timworth's favour.

Conversely, he may have experienced none of this. There is no datable evidence that Henry of Kirkestede was alive after April 1378. Within the provincial Benedictine structure that framed his life, his career was one of modest achievement, even of modest distinction. At the end of it all, he

---

190. For the events at Bury see A. Réville, *Le soulèvement des travailleurs d'Angleterre en 1381* (Paris 1898), esp. 58–77; and the briefer treatment of M. D. Lobel, *The Borough of Bury St. Edmunds* (Oxford 1935), 150–55, and R. Hilton, *Bond Men Made Free* (London 1973), esp. 140–41. R. B. Dobson translates the portion of Thomas Walsingham's history pertaining to these events: *The Peasants' Revolt of 1381*, 2nd edn (London 1983), 243–8.
191. A Bury monk named John of Lakenheath, presumably the same man, was ordained priest on 28 March 1338 (Montacute register, fol. 101ra), six months earlier than Kirkestede.
192. Arnold, *Memorials*, 3. xxvii.

must have been pleased; but of course he does not say so. He must also at the end have been worried, perhaps even fearful, as well; and this he does come very close to revealing. Kirkestede had survived a series of traumatic events in his life. The town, with unrestrained malice, inflicted great damage on his abbey in 1327–31. The plague of 1349 swept away great numbers of his brother-monks. A dozen years later, another outbreak took perhaps a third of his confreres, and that year of 1361 saw the deaths of two Bury abbots within an interval of less than five months. Any personal satisfaction Kirkestede may have felt on being named prior was quickly blunted by the inauspicious fall of the bell-tower before he had been six months in office. A monk under his charge was knifed to death by two other Bury monks, also under his charge. The plague came again in 1368–9. And in 1375 it came yet again. In 1377 Edward III, enfeebled but symbolic of a half-century's continuity in the realm and at the royal abbey, died to be replaced by a child on the throne.

These were calamitous events, both natural and man-made. But for Kirkestede and his contemporaries, they were also portents. It was commonplace among the survivors of famine, plague, and war to fear that the Day of Judgement might be near, and to question when and where the Antichrist would make his appearance and how he should be recognized. In revising the *Speculum coenobitarum*, Kirkestede earlier in his life had come into contact with the historical structures of Joachim of Fiore.[193] At the end of his life, however, he was captivated instead by *pseudo*-Joachimite prophecies of the most extravagant sort, devoted especially to considerations of the Last Days. We see this clearly in the collection of prophetic texts which Kirkestede copied himself, 'for the most part', in Cambridge, Corpus Christi College, MS 404; and in practice, this meant all save fol. 39 (a separate sheet added to the end of quire 4) and fols. 88–95 (an added quire of papal prophecies).[194] His table of contents on the front flyleaf reveals the tone of the collection:[195]

---

193. See above at p. xlii and especially p. cxxxviii below.
194. For the collation see James, *Corpus*, 2. 269; who describes the quire containing fols. 27–39 as '4¹² (+ 1)'. James sees further changes of hand in a note at the bottom of fol. 7r and the text on fols. 7v–8v, both of which we would attribute to Kirkestede. In addition, three or four short texts (the division is not clear) were later written on blank folios at the end, fols. 104–107. Concerning this manuscript see Reeves, *Influence of Prophecy*, 402–403; for a reproduction of fol. 88v with Kirkestede's rubric see Gransden, 'Some Manuscripts', pl. LXIA, and for a description of the manuscript, p. 248. For recent bibliography see M. H. Fleming, *The Late Medieval Pope Prophecies: The* Genus nequam *Group*, Medieval & Renaissance Texts & Studies 204 (Tempe, AZ, 1999), 44–51.
195. The table of contents is reproduced in Rouse, 'Bostonus Buriensis', pl. I.

Quaternus monachorum sancti Edmundi quem scripsit pro maiori parte frater Henricus de Kirkestede in quo subscripta continentur, videlicet

1, fols. 1r–3v]	Prophetia Sibille. fo. primero.
2, fols. 4r–6v]	Liber sancti Methodii martyris de principio et fine mundi. fo. 4.
3, fol. 7r]	Quibus dies iudicii manifestabitur et per quem. 7°.
4, fols. 7v–8v]	De duracione mundi secundum Eusebium. 7°.
5, fols. 9r–38v]	*Nota* [in margin]: Liber qui dicitur pentacronon siue speculum temporum futurorum de prophetiis sancte Hildegardis virginis. 9°. et 38°.
6, fol. 39r–v]	Reuelacio super statu tocius ecclesie et precipue super hiis que contingent in diebus fratrum predicatorum et minorum. 39°.
7, fols. 88r–95r]	Prophetie Joachim abbatis de papis. fo. *88* [corr.][196]
8, fol. 41r]	Alia prophetia de papis. fo. *41*. [second figure corr.]
9, fol. 58r]	Prophetia Joachim de duobus ordinibus. fo. 52.[197]
10, fols. 44r–64v]	*Nota* [in margin] Liber Joachim de seminibus litterarum. fo. *44* [corr.]
11, fol. 65r–v]	*Nota* [in margin] De antichristo et de fine mundi. fo. *63*. [corr.]
12, fols. 65v–66r]	Henricus de Huntedon' in fine cronicorum de fine mundi. fo. *66*. [corr.]
13, fol. 67v]	Descripcio tabellarum et oraculi fratris Cirilli. *67*. [corr.]
14, fols. 68–87v]	*Nota* [in margin] Commentum Joachim super oraculum Cirilli. *68* [corr.]
15]	Prophetia de rege Anglie Ricardo ij°. fo. 106.[198]

196. Work 7, a self-contained quire (discussed below), has been displaced in subsequent binding, which has required the renumbering of the folios or, in some cases, the later provision of numbers that Kirkestede has not provided.
197. A paragraph of the *De seminibus* (work 10) that has its own marginal rubric on fol. 58r, reading *Ordo Cisterciensis et Premonstratensis incepit*. This, rather than a prophecy on the mendicants (Fleming, *Prophecies*, 45), seems to be what title 9 refers to. Its inconspicuous placement no doubt explains why its folio number was not altered.
198. Work 15 is now lacking, presumably lost when the last four folios were removed from the quire that contains the end of work 14. For the collation see James, *Corpus*, 2. 269, who describes the quire containing fols. 80–87 as '9^{12} (wants 9–12)'. Work 15 had evidently already been lost by the time the collection was rebound and the table of contents renumbered, and for that reason its folio number was not altered.

16, fols. 96r–99r]	Prophetie de regibus Anglorum. fo. *96*. [corr.]
17, fol. 99v]	Reuelacio facta sancto Thome martyri de quodam rege Anglie futuro post eum. *93*. [corr.]
18, fol. 100r]	Prophetia cuiusdam viri sancti de Danis, Scotis et Francis etc. *100*. [corr.]
19, fol. 100v]	Visio mirabilis in ciuitate Tripolis. fo. *100*. [corr.]
20, fols. 100v–102r]	Visio cuiusdam super statu ecclesie futuro. fo. *100*. [corr.]
21, fols. 102v–103r]	Visio cuiusdam matrone de iure regis Anglie ad regnum Francie. *103*. [corr.]
22, fol. 103r–v]	Prophetia cuiusdam fratris in carcere pape. *103*. [corr.]

It is readily apparent that Kirkestede worked on this collection over time, for one can see the changes when he added a new work with different ink and with a slightly different style of script, tighter or looser, larger or smaller, more or less formal. Besides the works listed in the table, he inserted in blank spots several other brief prophecies and prophetic extracts, usually without rubrics. There is no single *terminus post quem* applicable to all parts of the collection; some of the individual items, however, provide useful dates that suggest a time in the second half of his monastic career. The Blofeld prophecy on fol. 102r (added without rubric to work 20) is said to have been made in England in 1349; work 22 records a vision from 1356; the heading over a quatrain near the bottom of fol. 99r reads 1366. On fol. 97v Kirkestede recorded a solar eclipse that occurred on 25 May 1371, and discussed at some length its implications as interpreted 'in the books of the astrologers'; he inserted this on a blank half-page between two parts of the prophecies of the English kings (work 16).

Kirkestede probably kept his growing collection in loose quires, perhaps stitched but unbound, adding further texts as he found them. His insertion of more than a dozen lines on folio 97v (to take one example of many) could not have been written in a bound codex, because the script extends too far into the gutter. The table of contents on what is now the front flyleaf represents his final arrangement of the collection, unsystematic on the whole but containing some obvious groupings—the two works on papal prophecies (7 and 8), the Oracle of *ps*.-Cyril along with Joachim's commentary on it (13 and 14), three prophetic works pertaining to kings of England (15–17), three works that are called Visions (19–21). The table's appearance indicates that it was written in a single campaign, which is roughly datable; the title of work 15—the Prophecy of Richard II, King of England—even though the work itself is now lacking, implies that Kirkestede wrote the table after

Richard's coronation on 16 July 1377. Since the collection consisted of loose quires, it is not surprising that Kirkestede labelled it 'Quaternus monachorum sancti Edmundi' at the head of the table.

It was only at this point, with the quires all in order though probably still unbound, that Kirkestede foliated the contents of the collection. Later, however, when the quires were bound—or more likely, when they were rebound at a still later date—the old quire containing work 7 (Prophecies of the Popes) was displaced, and work 15 was lost or removed. An early modern hand has altered the original folio numbers on the table of contents to fit (with a few anomalies) the current location of the texts in the codex, and the same hand or another has replaced all of Kirkestede's foliation in the text after fol. 39.[199]

Of the works in this collection, the papal prophecies are the most important in dating Kirkestede's latest known activities. These are *pseudo*-Joachimite prophecies that situated the end of the world within the papacy itself, culminating in the Angelic Pope, who will have defeated the Antichrist and will rule over both the material and the spiritual world at the last days. This work (written *c*. 1304) traces the end through the supposedly final fifteen popes. The first of the sequence is Nicolas III (d. 1280), and it continues to describe historical personages down to the pope who reigned when the work was composed, Benedict XI (d. 1304), seventh in the line. The last eight popes were what Marjorie Reeves calls 'the prophetic series', that is, prophetic descriptions of nameless popes-to-be. But that was in 1304. By the end of Kirkestede's life the world, and the papacy, had moved on. He included two versions of this work in his book of prophecies. On fol. 41, a single parchment leaf that had already been used for another purpose,[200] Kirkestede copied a fragment of the second version called *Ascende calue* (*c*. 1328),[201] a list of the short-paragraph prophecies for the supposed last five popes of all time, beginning with the rubric 'Prophecy of the Lord Pope Clement VI' (1342–52), and followed by four others entitled 'The Pope after Him', 'Prophecy of the Pope

---

199. Fleming, *Prophecies*, has confused this issue by assuming that it was Kirkestede who made the changes, and she uses them as 'clues to Henry's methods'. Her 'distinctive earlier form' of arabic numerals are those written by Kirkestede; but the numbers in 'the modern style', forms that do not appear elsewhere in the numerous examples of Kirkestede's hand, are those of a later hand writing over readily visible erasures, probably long after Kirkestede's death. Unfortunately, therefore, the contrasting number styles do not reveal the stages in which Kirkestede assembled the codex. (Fleming's mention of an 'old style' reference to 'folio 42' should read 'folio 52'.)
200. James, *Corpus*, 2. 269, describes the quire containing folios 40–43 as '5⁴'; it comprises a bifolium (fols. 40 and 43) enclosing two singletons, fols. 41 and 42. For its prior use, see below.
201. The date is Fleming's (*Prophecies*, 5).

Next after That', 'Prophecy of the Penultimate Pope', and 'The Last Pope'.[202] His hand has numbered these five in the right-hand margin 1 through 5, implying that he had not seen the first ten paragraphs of the work.

The earlier version of the papal prophecies, the *Genus nequam*, was not copied by Kirkestede. It is contained in a separate quire, seven leaves of text and image and the final leaf blank, that was written around 1320, in East Anglia if not at Bury itself.[203] Kirkestede intended this quire to precede the paragraphs on fol. 41—which for that reason are simply called 'Other Papal Prophecies' in the table of contents; but in the process of binding or rebinding the early quire was displaced, accidentally or deliberately, and inserted toward the end of the manuscript on fols. 88–95. Well after this quire was written, someone added a pen-drawing of a beaver carefully shaded in dark brown, in the lower left quadrant of fol. 95r.[204] The image of the beaver was transferred to fol. 95 with the aid of a stencil or template made by pricking the outline through a sheet of parchment.[205] This was the sheet later reused by Kirkestede to copy the fragmentary *Ascende calue* (fol. 41r); the location of the pricks on fol. 41r shows that the stencil was made before Kirkestede wrote on that folio (Plate 8a).[206]

The *Genus nequam* prophecies are an illustrated earlier version of the *pseudo*-Joachimite prophecy containing (in this case) fourteen of the final fifteen popes.[207] The prophecies are illustrated with outline drawings of a pope and a symbolic animal, one pair of images per page, and each drawing is accompanied by the relevant paragraph of prophecy from *pseudo*-Joachim. As Fleming remarks, Kirkestede was not interested in the deeper themes of

202. Respectively, 'Prophetia de domino papa Clemente VIo', 'De papa futuro post eum', 'De papa tunc futuro prophetia', 'Prophetia de penultimo papa', 'De ultimo papa'.
203. The dating and localization, based on the illustrations, are those of L. Sandler, *A Survey of Manuscripts Illuminated in the British Isles* 5: *Gothic Manuscripts 1285–1385* (Oxford 1986), 2. 102–103.
204. The drawing of the beaver was not part of the *Genus nequam* written in the 1320s, and it is difficult to imagine how it might have any relevance to the papal prophecies. The drawing was presumably put there because the page was a usefully blank piece of parchment.
205. There are prick-marks clear through fol. 41, leaving faint prick-marks on the surface of fol. 95r to guide the artist. It seems that the transfer was made this way rather than by pouncing. Regarding pricking for transfer and pouncing, see J. J. G. Alexander, *Medieval Illuminators and their Methods of Work* (New Haven, CT, 1992), 50 and n. 94; Alexander notes that beasts in bestiaries seem to be the image most frequently transferred by pricking.
206. For this reason, Fleming's assumption (*Prophecies*, 44) that the *Ascende calue* fragment was written before 1352—logical though it may be—probably is too early by a number of years. The existence of the pricked stencil on fol. 41 seems to have escaped the notice of all who have hitherto examined this work.
207. Edited by Fleming, *Prophecies*, 148–200. Some versions have the fifteenth and final pope as well; Kirkestede's quire had only fourteen.

the 'angelic pope' or the *renouatio mundi*, but only in the approach of the Last Days.[208] All the popes were anonymous in this earlier quire, but Kirkestede added a headline annotation to each that gave them names, beginning with Nicolas III as the head of the sequence.[209] And beginning with Clement V (fol. 91v), whose death in 1313 must have fallen near the beginning of Kirkestede's life, he supplied at the bottom of each folio a brief word of identification (e.g., 'He was a Dominican') and the death date for each one as well. On the picture that Kirkestede took to represent Urban V (fol. 94r), instead of writing his annotation all at once, Kirkestede for the first time gave a name and an identification note, 'Iste fuit abbas in ordine nigrorum monachorum', but added the obit at a later time in a different ink, 'et obiit anno domini M CCC LXX et sedet in papatu annis VIII'. This suggests that Kirkestede obtained and began to annotate this quire during the papacy of Urban V, before 1370. The last illustration (fol. 94v) is the fourteenth, which Kirkestede labelled Gregory XI. At the bottom of that page he recorded Gregory's death in March 1378. The fifteenth page in the quire (fol. 95r), supposedly reserved for the final pope before the world's end, had been left blank—no text, no picture, save the later addition of the irrelevant beaver (see above).

On the otherwise blank fol. 95r, Kirkestede wrote the headnote for what was prophesied to be the last pope before the Day of Judgement, Urban VI, elected 8 April 1378. We have no hint of his thoughts, fears, or expectations as he wrote the name. This is the last dated evidence that Henry of Kirkestede was alive.

---

208. Fleming, *Prophecies*, 48.
209. For example, the rubric of the first prophecy (on fol. 88r) says simply 'Principium malorum' (beginning of the evil ones)—beside which Kirkestede's hand has added 'Prophetia de papa Nicolao III'; most have rubrics that identify them with abstractions, the bad popes and then the final good ones, things such as 'Occisio' or 'Sanguis' or (more positively) 'Confessio' or 'Penitentia' or (the angelic popes) 'Bona oratio'—to which the historical names were attached by Kirkestede.

APPENDIX TO CHAPTER 1

KIRKESTEDE'S HAND

N. R. Ker once remarked to us that Henry of Kirkestede has probably left more identifiable autographs than most other known 14th-cent. English monastic writers. Although much of Kirkestede's written work consists of the Bury St Edmunds *ex libris*, press-mark and contents of each Bury manuscript in his charge, he also copied individual treatises and documents[210] and most of Cambridge, Corpus Christi College, MS 404, as well as leaving numerous bibliographical notes. Together these provide a wide array of examples of his hand over thirty or more years engaged in very different tasks. As might be expected, the appearance of Kirkestede's script is influenced by what he is writing and where he is writing and when he is writing. Kirkestede usually wrote a rather splayed and uneven anglicana script with its carrot-topped ascenders, contrast between thick and thin strokes, long *r*'s in v form, abbreviation strokes swung upwards from the cross stroke of the *t*, looped carrot-topped *I*'s in *Item*, and frequent use of two forms of the same letter on the same page.[211] He uses two forms of the letter *a*, tear-drop and double-bowed, and two forms of the superscript *a*. He employs both a pointed majuscule *A* and a large minuscule, for a capital letter to mark the beginning of new sentences. He uses two forms of marginal paragraph mark, an *a* with a short, flat, horizontal stroke to the right and an *n* with the short, flat stroke curled back into a small pendule. Although he usually uses one or the other of these, both appear in the same text in Harley 1005 fol. 67v. His abbreviation for *-us* in long *9* form, crossed tironian *7* in *2* form that, like *u* or *v*, begins on or below the line, his split *r-e* ligature in *regula*, and his tall, narrow lower-case *h* seem distinctive, as are his long flowing superscript *a* and his *-ur* mark, so often seen in the abbreviations for *mon**a**chorum* and *continent**ur*** in the *ex libris* and table of contents.

---

210. See among others the extended example of his hand in London, College of Arms, MS Arundel 30 (plate 8b).
211. See also the discussion of his hand and the plates in Rouse, 'Bostonus Buriensis', 475, and the plates in Gransden, 'Some manuscripts'.

CHAPTER 2

COMPILING THE *CATALOGUS*

Henry of Kirkestede compiled, to the best of his ability, a list of all authoritative writers and their works, and some of the locations where these texts might be found. He named 674 authors in all, and assigned to them about 3,895 works, the exact number dependent upon one's definition of a 'work'. For a Benedictine monk working alone in the 14th cent., this was an enormous and unrivalled accomplishment. This chapter analyses the methods and identifies the great variety of sources that Kirkestede used to create the *Catalogus*.

The Context

A. *Roots and Purpose of the* Catalogus

Before we turn to details of compilation, it would be prudent to consider what it was that Kirkestede set out to create. Over the last 250 years and more, his catalogue has customarily been viewed through anachronistic spectacles, as successive students of this 14th-cent. monastic artefact have required it to conform to the expectations and practices of later centuries, and of divergent milieux.[1] And for the last hundred years, no consideration of Kirkestede's work has entirely freed itself from the influence of M. R. James's image of 'this excellent man [who] travelled all over England and part of Scotland, and examined the Libraries of one hundred and ninety-five religious houses'.[2] This was neither Kirkestede's method nor his intent.

The overriding literary tradition from which the *Catalogus* emerges is the genre of the *De uiris illustribus* of Jerome and his successors—but with added developments.[3] The *Catalogus* is first and foremost a bibliography. The original tracts *De uiris illustribus*, of course, were largely apologetic in intent, an element absent from the *Catalogus*: Kirkestede did not intend to emphasize

---

1. See chapter 4 below for the variety of motives that fuelled interest in the *Catalogus*.
2. James, *St Edmund*, 34.
3. For the *De uiris illustribus* as a genre see R. H. & M. A. Rouse, 'Bibliography before print,' in Rouse & Rouse, *Authentic Witnesses*, 469–94, and for its 9th-cent. influence, R. McKitterick, *The Carolingians and the Written Word* (Cambridge 1989), 200–210.

that England, for example, or the Benedictine Order had produced prominent writers. Rather, his purpose was to sort out, for himself and for his novices and colleagues, who wrote what: to provide a capsule biography, complete with date, and a full list of works. Given the time and place and the resources available to him, the goal was unattainable, but worth the effort. Amid 14th-cent. confusion, Kirkestede strove to impose bibliographic order.

Two of the *Catalogus*'s major refinements of the *De uiris illustribus* were the careful identification of works, and the location of copies of them. These ideas came directly from a quite different source, the *Registrum Anglie de libris doctorum et auctorum ueterum*, compiled by the Oxford Franciscans in or around the 1320s (between 1309/13 and 1331).[4] If the *De uiris illustribus* provided the *Catalogus* with its *raison d'être*, the *Registrum* furnished the practical elements of the structure: a list of numbered locations (of British abbeys and cathedral chapters), followed by a list of authors, titles of works, incipits for secure identification of the works, and a series of numbers corresponding to the list of locations. As we shall see, Kirkestede borrowed not only the *Registrum*'s structure but virtually every piece of information the *Registrum* had to offer. Acquaintance with the *Registrum* was the immediate impetus for Kirkestede's producing a bibliography on this model.

The Oxford Franciscans compiled the *Registrum* from the on-site reports of friars who visited the libraries of the old orders. As a region East Anglia was under-reported—forty-four titles from the Austin friars of Holy Trinity Ipswich, but after that very little: thirteen titles each from the Austin friars of St Peter's, Ipswich, and the Benedictines of St John's, Colchester, and no report at all of the books of Ramsey abbey, of the Augustinians of St Botulph's, Colchester, of the Cistercians of Coggeshall, of the Benedictines of Holme St Benets, nothing from the cathedral chapters of Ely or Norwich, nothing from the Cambridge schools. This sparse background makes it all the more striking that the *Registrum* reports 246 works from the library of Bury St Edmunds. The *Registrum*'s only appreciably larger reports from all of Britain are those for Christ Church, Canterbury, and St Albans. Clearly, the Franciscans who came to Bury must have been hospitably received by the abbey and been given free access to the Bury books, to search out the ones pertinent to their needs; and they may well have spent several days at the house.[5] Given that the *Registrum*'s reports seem to have been made by Franciscans on the journey between their home convents and the Oxford *studium*, it is probable that those who reported on the Bury library were

---

4. For the *Registrum*'s dates see Rouse & Rouse, *Registrum*, cxxix–cxxxiv.
5. Although in the event other titles were recorded, the obvious advance plan of the *Registrum* was to register the locations of books of *patristica et spiritualia*; see *Registrum*, lxxx–lxxxii.

Franciscans from the convent of Babwell on the outskirts of Bury—even though, on an official level, relations between abbey and convent were often far from cordial.

The *Registrum*'s compilers completed their duties before Kirkestede entered the monastery *c.* 1331, so he would presumably not have seen them at work himself; but on his entry to the order he must have found that the recent visit by the Franciscan book-hunters had marked the collective memory of the community.[6] He also found somewhere a text of the finished *Registrum*. He could possibly have obtained a copy at Oxford Greyfriars itself, the centre where the on-site reports were compiled and organized by author, but it is more likely that the Franciscans of nearby Babwell permitted him to borrow their copy of the *Registrum* and to use it over a long period.[7] Kirkestede's use of the *Registrum* as a bibliographical source is by far the earliest known.[8]

Another source affected the *Catalogus*'s structure, its influence less profound than the *De uiris illustribus* and the *Registrum*, but none the less pervasive in its effect. The *Manipulus florum*, like the *Registrum* an early 14th-cent. product, was compiled at the Sorbonne in Paris by Thomas of Ireland. It must have been the *Manipulus florum*'s list of authorities that taught Kirkestede to identify works by their closing words or explicits, not just with the incipits that were standard in the *Registrum*; and, as we shall see, Kirkestede incorporated into the *Catalogus* virtually all of Thomas's list of authors and works that he cited, and included quotations and paraphrases from the preface to the work.[9]

The final important influence shaping the outlines of the *Catalogus* came from Kirkestede himself. His most important contribution to the structure was also the most conspicuous, the arrangement of the list of authors alphabetically by the first letter of their names. The interior arrangement of two of the longer lists, the works of Augustine and of Ambrose, are also alphabetized by first letter of the titles. Such an arrangement confirms that he took for granted that the *Catalogus* would be used as a bibliographical tool

---

6. The dates are based on circumstantial evidence, the compilation of the *Registrum* (after 1309 and before 1331) and Kirkestede's own entry into the abbey.
7. The English province of the order presumably distributed copies to individual priories—but that is not demonstrable. Concerning the *Registrum*'s purpose and distribution, see *Registrum*, cxli–cxlviii.
8. He used it both for the *Catalogus* and for the list of writers in the *Speculum coenobitarum* (see chapter 3 below).
9. This is worth noting because the *Manipulus florum*'s list of authorities circulated independently; R. H. & M. A. Rouse, *Preachers, Florilegia, and Sermons: Studies on the* Manipulus Florum *of Thomas of Ireland* (Toronto 1979), 160 and 216 n. 61. Kirkestede evidently had a complete manuscript.

that should be searchable, and he included cross-references to facilitate the finding of a particular author.[10] No author-list among his sources was arranged alphabetically. Indeed, the only comparable contemporary scheme was Kirkestede's own classification of the Bury manuscripts, arranged alphabetically by content. Using his alphabetical structure, Kirkestede was able to organize and to integrate material gathered from an exceptionally wide range of sources.

Without question, however, the mainspring behind Kirkestede's creation of the *Catalogus* was his lifelong interest in books. We have no evidence that he was (or that he was not) a tireless and thoughtful reader, a thinker, or a writer. But, in contrast, there is a great variety of evidence documenting his concern for books, and his knowledge about books, and about the texts in books, as objects—evidence that he was determined to know and organize and record this information, for himself and for all like-minded others, in a lucid fashion that would permit the information to be found on demand and understood, 'retrievable' as we would now say.[11]

B. *The Date of Compilation*

The sum of evidence supplied by the text of the *Catalogus* and by Kirkestede's notes in Bury manuscripts indicates that he worked on the compilation, on and off, for most of his life as a Bury monk. A combination of internal and external evidence suggests the period of his life when he devoted much of his energy to it.

There is no fixed point at which we can say, at this time Kirkestede began work on his catalogue of writers. His bibliographical work in its broadest terms—including his revision of the *Speculum coenobitarum*, his organization of the large Bury book collection, and his extended flyleaf notes that were perhaps drafts of *Catalogus* entries[12]—we have assumed to date after his ordination, thus largely in the 1340s and 1350s, but surely before he took on the time-consuming office of prior in 1361. Kirkestede must have begun to compile the *Catalogus* in this same period. With respect to sequence, we

---

10. For example, under the letter M, between the entries for Martin of Braga (*364*) and Marcus Varro (*365*), is the entry, 'For Marcus Tullius see Tullius, under the letter T' (*Marcus Tullius: quaere literam T vocabulo Tullius*).
11. Aside from the obvious example of his classification of the Bury library, for other examples see his annotations concerning books in other libraries, his corrections of mistaken rubrics or attributions, or his identification of precise bibliographical citations, above in chapter 1, especially pp. li–lxiv.
12. See chapter 3 below and chapter 1 above, respectively.

assume that the *Catalogus* dates after the *Speculum coenobitarum*, with its related but very much simpler list of writers. Compiling the *Catalogus* and cataloguing the abbey's books may have gone hand in hand, however.

The years when Kirkestede worked most diligently on the *Catalogus* can be generally discerned from internal evidence. For example, he added a note in the text (apparently a memorandum to himself that he neglected to excise) just after the entry for Richardus Barre (*523*), 'Memorandum quod Dominus Ricardus de Bury quondam episcopus Dunelmensis edidit nuper tractatum quem intitulauit Philobiblon, id est amore librorum' ('Memorandum: Lord Richard de Bury, former bishop of Durham, recently wrote a treatise that he entitled *Philobiblon*, that is, The Love of Books'). The circumstances imply that Kirkestede had only just come across this information—or perhaps had only just remembered it. This in turn suggests that Kirkestede had all but finished the *Catalogus* entries under the letter R not long after 1345 (the date of Richard de Bury's death, when he became 'former bishop').[13] De Bury completed the *Philobiblon* in 1345 just before his death, and Kirkestede dated it even earlier, in 1342 (*527.1*); but the meaning of *nuper* ('recently') is flexible. Kirkestede's latest secondary source, a minor one, was the *Polychronicon* of Ranulf Higden (d. 1364); the *Polychronicon* circulated in several recensions, but Kirkestede seems to have used the latest version, chronicling events from the Creation to 1352.[14] Of the fifteen 14th-cent. authors listed in the *Catalogus*, few have death dates after mid-century. Five of these names came from a single source, a list of Dominican authors compiled by the English province of the order.[15] The others, with their death-dates, are these: John Maudith (*333*), d. after 1342; John Bromyard (*338*), d. 1352; [John] Ridewall (*520*), d. after 1340; Richard Fitzralph (*525*), d. 1360, but assigned by Kirkestede a *floruit* date of 1349; Richard de Bury (*527*), d. 1345, but given a *floruit* date of 1342; Richard Rolle (*528*), d. 1349; Simon of Boraston (*557*), d. after 1338; and Thomas Waleys (*586*), d. 1350. The latest date that Kirkestede specifically mentions in the *Catalogus* is 1366, as a *floruit* date for John of Tynemouth (*341*); Tynemouth's was a late entry: sixty-first of the sixty-two authors whose names begin with J. The most

---

13. First of the authors whose names begin with R is Rabanus, no. 492; after the position of the memorandum there are only five more author-entries under this letter of the alphabet, including that for Richard de Bury (no. 527).

14. Cf. Sharpe, *Latin Writers*, 454. Bale's *Index*, 336, cites a copy at Ramsey that ends in 1348; an early recension seems to have extended only to 1327.

15. Robertus de Oxford (*514*), d. *c*. 1340; Robertus de Holcote (*515*), d. *c*. 1349; Thomas de Sutton (*584*), d. *c*. 1315; Wilhelmus de Enkourt (*648*), d. after 1344; and Wilhelmus Brumyard (*650*), d. 1349. Kirkestede evidently came upon the Dominican list late in the game; see p. xcvii below.

recent author of all is Brigitta of Sweden (*110*), d. 1373. This incomplete entry, an evident afterthought, gives no date for her life and no works that she wrote, save a general 'scripsit diuersos libros' ('she wrote various books'), and Kirkestede's source for the name is not known.[16]

Nothing points to Kirkestede's doing major work on the *Catalogus* in the 1360s and '70s, therefore, even though sporadic efforts are visible. The energetic period of concentrated effort with which he began was followed by a period when he gave this project a lower priority, as his time available for it permitted. We assume that he continued to add and to insert here and there, and resisted until the very last admitting that his work on the catalogue was over. It may be significant that Kirkestede imposed a rational organization on only the three longest entries, those for Augustine, Ambrose, and Jerome. He left many anomalies and loose ends—the memorandum concerning Richard de Bury, or entries such as that for Brigitta without date or works, or even less satisfactory entries comprising only a name, such as that for Elizabeth (*174*). One should bear in mind, then, that along with what we shall describe in this chapter as deliberate actions and choices, a great deal of the *Catalogus*'s compilation was incidental and accidental, more nearly resembling organic growth.

Front-Matter to the Catalogus

A. *Title and Introduction*

The title of the *Catalogus* is taken from its opening words, 'Incipit Catalogus de libris autenticis et apocrifis'.[17] In the 16th cent., the antiquary John Bale, besides employing a version of this incipit, gave the work a more appropriate title, calling it the *Catalogus scriptorum ecclesiae*,[18] and since that time the two titles have been used almost interchangeably.[19] Despite the fact that Bale's coinage may more nearly reflect the contents, however, Kirkestede's own incipit is unquestionably the more authoritative. Thus, we use it for this edition.

16. Kirkestede copied an excerpt from her prophecies in Cambridge, Corpus Christi College, MS 404, fol. 102v (Bury P. 163), a manuscript that he compiled before 1378, but her name does not figure in the rubric or table of contents. This is the manuscript that contains the latest datable appearance of Kirkestede's hand; see p. lxxxii above.

17. Concerning medieval 'titles', see R. Sharpe, *Titulus: Identifying Medieval Latin Texts* (Turnhout 2003), 22–5.

18. Bale's reports of the *Catalogus* in his *Index* and *Scriptores* are cited below in chapter 4, p. clxxxii.

19. We have used both on occasion, Kirkestede's incipit in Richard Rouse's dissertation (1963) and Bale's more succinct title in Rouse, 'Bostonus Buriensis'.

The *Catalogus* opens with a disquisition on the related subjects of authenticity and orthodoxy. It provides an interesting clue, not to the 'what' but the 'why' of Kirkestede's project. The words and ideas of the introduction, composed almost entirely of quotations, seem on the surface not closely relevant to the purposes of the catalogue of authors and works. From Kirkestede's standpoint, however, this introduction was integral to the rest of the work in its concern with authority, and with texts that were authoritative.

The first half of Kirkestede's introductory discussion deals with the prime authority, the scriptures, considering the authentic and apocryphal books of the bible and the order in which these books are to appear. The second half, beginning with a brief description of the libraries of Eusebius, Origen, and Jerome, considers which authors and doctors are accepted by the church and which are not. The halves are separated by two tables that compare the books of the Old Testament with the New.

Hugh of Saint-Victor's *Didascalicon* Book IV serves as a major source for both sections of the introduction, supplemented (and often duplicated) by passages from Vincent's *Speculum historiale*, Gratian's *Decretum*, and several of the works from Bury's bibliographic collection (Bodl. MS e Musaeo 31), namely Isidore's *De ecclesiasticis officiis, Etymologiae, De ortu et obitu patrum*, and *Prooemium in libris ueteris et noui testamenti,* Jerome's *De uiris illustribus*, and the *pseudo*-Gelasian *De libris recipiendis et non recipiendis*.[20] In best Kirkestede fashion, the sources are cited in the text. There are few words of Kirkestede's own.

This deliberation over canonical versus apocryphal books of scripture serves to remind us that biblical commentary was the staple of the great majority of those whose writings are listed in the *Catalogus* proper. The introductory consideration of orthodox versus heterodox writings may seem strange alongside the fact that Kirkestede's catalogue includes ancient, Muslim, and Jewish writers without a murmur. Yet Kirkestede does on occasion, in the booklist itself, remark on the orthodoxy, or lapse from orthodoxy, or return to orthodoxy, of Christian writers—usually in quotations from patristic sources but occasionally with respect to medieval authors as well; see, for example, his comments on the subject in the *Catalogus* entries for Ambrosius (*37*), Berillus (*83*), Cirus (*132*), Hildegard (*249*), Macrobius (*369*), Origen (*404*), Papias (*419*), Peter Abelard (*433*), Pelagius (*478*), Robert Grosseteste (*505*), and Tertullian (*578*). An extensive discussion occurs in the entry for John Cassian (*285*), for whom Kirkestede had a special regard. A lengthy passage in support of Cassian's orthodoxy was copied by Kirkestede

---

20. Concerning e Musaeo 31 and this collection of patristic bibliographies, see p. xciv below.

on to the flyleaf of a Bury manuscript of the *Institutiones* and *Collationes* that Kirkestede himself had purchased for the abbey (Cambridge, Pembroke College, MS 92, fol. ii^r); this passage reappears at the head of the entry on Cassian in the *Catalogus*, and it forms the concluding paragraph of the *Catalogus*'s introduction, symbolic of the link between them in Kirkestede's thinking.

Orthodox writers who commented on scripture form, as we shall see, the substance of the *Catalogus*'s final element, the *Nomina doctorum*. It is tempting to see these two, the introduction and the concluding list of commentators, as a frame or a set of 'bookends' bracketing the bibliography, in order to situate the body of the *Catalogus* properly within the context of monastic learning.

B. *Preface to the Bibliography*

Following the introduction in Add. 3470 is a numbered list of monastic locations. We shall treat this list below in our discussion of the location numbers in the *Catalogus* entries, a subject with which it is inextricably linked. Kirkestede then prefaced the bibliography proper with a short paragraph, giving a concise practical explanation of its construction and its purpose. The *Registrum* had no similar introductory 'directions for use', and Kirkestede instead took the preface to Thomas of Ireland's list of authors to serve as a pattern for his own.[21] Most of Kirkestede's preface is a paraphrase of Thomas's, borrowing vocabulary, phrases, and concepts. Actual verbatim quotations are italicized here:

> Utilitati et expeditioni studentium et praedicatorum quidam S. Edmundi monachus ex informatione aliorum et eorum exemplaribus pro modulo suo volens proficere, nomina actorum, doctorum et librorum eorum originalium *secundum ordinem alphabeti ac partialium librorum numerum in unum colligere, principia pariter et fines,* locaque quibus hujusmodi libri poterint inveniri per numerum algorismi locorum nominibus correspondentem *hic scribere* et intitulare *curavit, ut quum alicui occurerint facilius possint ea cognoscere et securius allegare.* Quando quidem tamen multorum *librorum* principia non novit, *vidit neque fines* nec ubi potuerunt inveniri, *ideo si alicui occurrant poterit eos* in spatio vacuo ad hoc reservato *intitulare.* Primo

---

21. The preface to Thomas of Ireland's list of authors and works is edited, Rouse & Rouse *Preachers, Florilegia and Sermons,* 251. A modest share of the borrowed material is closer in its wording to Thomas's general prologue to the *Manipulus florum* (ib. 236–8, at 237), suggesting that Kirkestede had scanned at least the beginning and ending of the *Manipulus florum* in search of the phrases he wanted.

enim ponuntur *nomina doctorum* seu auctorum et anni quibus ipsi doctores floruerunt, secundo tituli et nomina librorum.

A certain monk of St Edmunds, following the example of others, wished to add his own small measure to their information, to be both useful and beneficial for students and preachers. So he has *collected together and recorded here, in a single alphabetical compilation, the names of the authors and doctors, the names of their books, the number of their parts, and their opening and closing words*; and he has indicated, by means of numbers corresponding to the place-names, the locations where these books might be found, *so that anyone who chanced upon them might easily recognize them and might confidently refer to them.* However, he did not know the opening words of many of the books, *nor did he see their closing words* nor know where the books might be found. Therefore, *anyone who chances upon this information should enter it* in the space reserved for it. First are placed the names of the doctors or authors and the years when they flourished, followed by the titles and names of the books.

To say that his compilation was made for the use of 'students and preachers' is unanticipated, and more appropriate to the schools (the community for which Thomas of Ireland wrote) than to the monastery; but in view of the large percentage of the monks who were ordained and the numbers who experienced at least some period of university training, the statement is not without relevance. Kirkestede's borrowing of someone else's phrases has the advantage of throwing his own words into relief, highlighting two things that were absent from his source: location, and the importance of authors' biographies. Location in particular is emphasized, for Kirkestede mentions it twice, once in detail ('locaque quibus hujusmodi libri . . . correspondentem') and again in summary ('nec ubi potuerunt inveniri'). And the importance of some sort of chronological setting for the authors is stressed in the last sentence. Overall, this paragraph says succinctly what is needed to permit a reader to use the catalogue of authors.

The Catalogue Entries

A. *Sources of the Information*

A respectable portion of the information in the *Catalogus* is derived from Kirkestede's first-hand acquaintance with manuscripts of the works that he lists; we shall consider these below. Most of the information, in contrast, is taken second-hand from other lists of authors and works. One of the principal goals of the present edition is to identify the *Catalogus*'s secondary sources, and to distinguish these from Kirkestede's own contribution as a primary source of bio-bibliographical knowledge in 14th-cent. England.[22]

Kirkestede's entry for each author is composed of different parts: author's name, date, titles, incipits and explicits, and library location numbers. This was an ambitious attempt, and for most entries not all of this information was available; as a result, often there is no date, a title but no incipit, an incipit but no explicit, incipit and explicit but no location numbers—and on rare occasions there is just an author's name and no title. Kirkestede gathered his information from a wide variety of bibliographical, biographical, and historical sources, some of them obvious and others little known, borrowing the information as he needed it. At times, especially for the briefest author-entries, all of the information comes from a single source. At times, instead, an entry represents a combination of information taken from more than one source. For the lengthy entries the combination of sources is often impressively large and complex. Identifying Kirkestede's secondary sources is essential; for unless an actual manuscript of a work was his source, an entry in the *Catalogus* does not reflect the state of texts available to Kirkestede at Bury and in and around East Anglia in the mid-14th cent. Such an entry reflects, rather, the time and the place in which the source was written; these range widely, from the patristic Middle East to Bede's England to the early 14th-cent. schools at Paris and Oxford. For this reason—to prevent the *Catalogus* from gravely misleading those who read and use it—we have tried to identify as precisely as we can Kirkestede's source for each part of each entry.

i. Registrum Anglie de libris doctorum et auctorum veterum

The *Registrum*, the principal model for the structure of the *Catalogus*, was also the most pervasive source of its contents. The text of the *Registrum* that Kirkestede used, no longer extant, shows no close affinity with either of the surviving *Registrum* manuscripts (both date from the 15th cent.), making the *Catalogus* an independent though indirect third witness to the *Registrum*'s text.[23] The *Registrum* provided Kirkestede with a catalogue of authors and their works, with the number of books or homilies they contained, often

---

22. In the edition we consider, with respect to information that is reported completely at second-hand, that our responsibility extends only so far as identifying the source of that information. See chapter 5 below, p. ccxii.
23. Indirect in that the *Catalogus* represents a use, not a copy. The *Registrum* survives in two independent witnesses, Bodl. MS Tanner 165 (*T*), and Cambridge, Peterhouse, MS 169 pt 1 (*P*), as well as in BL MS Royal 3 D. 1, which was copied from *P*.

with their incipits, and a list of locations where they might be found, in some forty British monastic and cathedral libraries. His most conspicuous use of the *Registrum* is the borrowing of its library numbers, which he applied in a complicated variety of ways that we shall discuss below. In compiling the *Catalogus* he tended to draw on the *Registrum* time and again, rather than all in a single campaign; this indicates that he had a copy at his disposal for much of the time that he worked on the *Catalogus*. Kirkestede used the *Registrum* in the entries for sixty-seven authors, and expressly named it as a source for four of them: Arnulfus (*31*), Baldwinus (*80*), Bacharius (*81*), and Gilbertus (*212*). The name that he employed, *Cathologus Anglie* or *Cathologus librorum Anglie*, does not appear as a rubric or colophon in either of the two surviving manuscripts.

Kirkestede's borrowings from the *Registrum* can be misleading, although no deception was intended. An entry taken wholesale from the *Registrum*, including the incipit and a location number, looks superficially as if it represents first-hand information supplied by Kirkestede. From his standpoint, the entry represented dependable information reported by the Oxford Franciscans earlier in the century, and its validity would not have changed in the interim (for example, a work seen by the Franciscans at Malmesbury *c.* 1320 was likely still to be at Malmesbury in 1350, and the work's incipit would not have changed). From a present-day standpoint, however, unless one is aware of its source such an entry would give the mistaken impression that Kirkestede himself travelled to Malmesbury in search of manuscripts.

ii. De uiris illustribus *and Cassiodorus*

The source for the greatest number of entries, some 246 authors, was a bibliographic corpus that circulated in England, containing the *De uiris illustribus* of Jerome, the two continuations by Gennadius and Isidore, and Cassiodorus's *Institutiones*, among other things.[24] Fortunately, the Bury manuscript of this corpus survives, Bodl. MS e Musaeo 31, with the class-mark (A. 31), table of contents, and occasional annotations all in Kirkestede's hand.[25] Kirkestede used the three *De uiris illustribus* sources exhaustively. He

---

24. The following editions of the works cited from this collection have been used: Jerome, *De uiris inlustribus*, and Gennadius, *De uiris inlustribus*, both ed. E. C. Richardson (Leipzig 1896); Isidore, *De uiris illustribus*, ed. C. Cordoñer Merino (Salamanca 1964); Cassiodorus, *Institutiones*, ed. R. A. B. Mynors, 2nd edn (Oxford 1963). The manuscript's other contents (see Mynors, xl and xliii) were not used in the list of authors and works, but were used in the introduction; see above.
25. For additional manuscripts containing this collection see Mynors, ibid. xxxix–xlvi.

omitted none of the authors contained in Isidore;[26] of those in Gennadius he omitted only seven (five of whom are heretics);[27] and from Jerome's *De uiris illustribus* he omitted nine biblical authors, four heretics, four authors for whom no works are named, and only four others.[28] He was equally thorough in reproducing the lists of titles, and he customarily cited the *De uiris illustribus* by name and by chapter. From Cassiodorus's *Institutiones diuinarum litterarum* Book I, he took all or parts of forty-four entries, again almost always citing his source.[29]

iii. Vincent of Beauvais

Kirkestede relied quite heavily on the *Speculum historiale* of Vincent of Beauvais, nearly always citing it by book and chapter. The *Speculum historiale* was used for approximately 105 authors, supplying names of writers, biographical information, and lists of their works. It seems to have been Kirkestede's habit, whenever he could, to draw his original list of titles from Vincent, and then to flesh this out with information from the *Registrum* (incipits, location numbers) or the *Manipulus florum* (incipits, explicits) or a Bury manuscript of the work—or, not infrequently, all three of these. Despite the overlay from other sources one can usually discern Vincent in the background, when the sequence of the titles in the *Speculum historiale* recurs in the *Catalogus*. As a rough comparison, we note that Vincent was the source of approximately 765 titles in the *Catalogus*, compared with a total of some 565 titles from a combination of the sources in Bodl. MS e Musaeo 31. Since the Bury manuscript of Vincent of Beauvais has not survived, and since there is no critical edition of this encyclopedia, it is impossible to make as careful an examination of Kirkestede's use of the *Speculum historiale* as can be made for his use of patristic sources.[30]

---

26. Bodl. MS e Musaeo 31, pp. 243–252, contains the shorter recension of Isidore's *De uiris illustribus* with thirty-three instead of forty-six chapters; see Cordoñer Merino, 20–26.
27. The following chapters are omitted: 3, 33, 36, 44, 46, 54, 73.
28. The following chapters are omitted: 1–9, New Testament authors; 93–4, 120, and 123, heretics; 64, 113, 122, and 130, no specific work named; and 14, 20, 93–4, 107, 123, 132.
29. It is unlikely that Kirkestede used Book II of the *Institutiones*, which does not appear in Bodl. e Musaeo 31.
30. We have cited the Mentelin edition of the *Speculum historiale* (Strasbourg 1473) throughout. While this edition is unfortunately rare, its text is closer to the manuscript that Kirkestede used than the more commonly cited edition of Douai 1624. See B. Ullman in *Speculum* 8 (1933) 325–6.

iv. Scriptores ordinis Praedicatorum

Entries for eighty-two authors in the *Catalogus*, identified by the words 'Frater Praedicator' in the biographical headings, come from a catalogue of Dominican writers that Kirkestede seems to have absorbed entirely. On only one occasion does he allude to this source, saying in the entry for Durandus (*146*) that 'he wrote, according to the Friars, . . .' ('scripsit secundum fratres . . .'). The version of the work that Kirkestede used has evidently not survived.[31] Several different lists of Dominican writers were composed during the 14th cent., based on a catalogue of Dominican masters compiled probably at Saint-Jacques in Paris. The core catalogue was widely disseminated, and enlarged individually in the order's provinces across western Europe with entries for more recent Dominicans and, especially, with entries for local Dominicans.[32] Kirkestede presumably used as his source the catalogue of Dominican writers compiled by the English province, which no longer survives. One can see, among the surviving Dominican lists, that Kirkestede's text resembled especially two similar catalogues, the *Catalogus Stamsensis* of 104 authors compiled at Stams in Bavaria in 1350, and the *Catalogus fratrum qui claruerunt doctrina* of 120 authors compiled by Laurent Pignon in France c. 1400.[33] For forty authors, all three lists (Stams, Pignon, *Catalogus*) are virtually identical in wording and in the sequence of the titles—see, for

---

31. M. R. James suggested that Philip Wolf of Seligenstadt used the same catalogue of Dominican writers as did Kirkestede (James, 'List of libraries', 45 n. 1). However, Wolf's catalogue survives only as an edition of excerpts from Bale's *Index* by R. L. Poole in *EHR* 33 (1918) 500–517, which makes comparison meaningless; the excerpts lack at least four of the Dominicans listed in the *Catalogus*.
32. Concerning medieval catalogues of Dominican writers see: H. Denifle, 'Quellen zur Gelehrtengeschichte des Predigerordens im 13. und 14. Jahrhundert', *Archiv für Litteratur- und Kirchengeschichte des Mittelalters* 2/2 (1886) 165–248; H. C. Scheeben, 'Die tabulae Ludwigs von Valladolid im Chor der Predigerbruder von St. Jakob in Paris', *AFP* 1 (1931), 223–63; P. Auer, *Ein neuaufgefundener Katalog der Dominikaner Schriftsteller*, Instituta historicum FF Praedicatorum Romae, Dissertationes historicae fasc. 2 (Paris 1933); G. Meersseman, *Laurentii Pignon catalogi et chronica*, Monumenta Ordinis Fratrum Praedicatorum historica 18 (Rome 1936) 1–135; H. D. Simonin, 'Notes de bibliographie dominicaine, pt 1: La tabula de Stams et la Chronique de Jacques de Soest', *AFP* 8 (1938) 193–214, and pt 2: 'Les ancien catalogues d'écrivains dominicains et la chronique de Bernard Gui', *AFP* 9 (1939) 192–213; R. Loenertz, 'Un catalogue d'écrivains et deux catalogues de martyrs dominicains', *AFP* 12 (1942) 279–303; R. Creytens, 'L'oeuvre bibliographique d'Echard, ses sources et leur valeur', *AFP* 14 (1944), 43–71; T. Kaeppeli, *Stephanus de Salanhaco et Bernardus Guidonis, De quatuor in quibus Deus praedicatorum ordinem insignivit*, Monumenta Ordinis Fratrum Praedicatorum historica 22 (Rome 1949) 1–206.
33. Both catalogues are edited by G. Meersseman. Concerning their textual relationship see Simonin pt 2, 210.

example, the long list of seventy-three titles for Albertus Magnus (*56*). Kirkestede's Dominican source contained seven authors not in the lists of Stams or Pignon, at least four of whom were singled out as English.[34] Because Stams and Pignon provide the nearest likeness to Kirkestede's list, we have collated the *Catalogus*'s entries for Dominican authors against them; but readers should bear in mind that Stams and Pignon themselves are neither sources (like the *Registrum*) nor witnesses (like Bale) to the text of the *Catalogus*.

Kirkestede did not make use of the Dominican list until much of his collecting from other sources was completed; either he did not know of it, or did not have a copy of it. Consistently, the Dominican authors occur late in the list of names under a given letter of the alphabet, to be followed only with random entries representing incidental finds, or oversights from sources already used.

v. Manipulus florum

Kirkestede relied on the explanatory prologues of Thomas of Ireland's *Manipulus florum* for the language he used in his own prologue. Thomas appended to his *florilegium*, completed in 1306, a list of nineteen authors and their works that were cited in his compilation, giving the incipit and explicit of nearly every one. Kirkestede borrowed heavily from this list. He took six complete author-entries from Thomas of Ireland's list of authorities, and he borrowed specific works attributed to each of the thirteen other authors in this source.[35] It is particularly important to distinguish those *Catalogus* entries that are borrowed from the *Manipulus* because such entries, with their plausible incipits and explicits, masquerade as first-hand knowledge of manuscripts; but they actually reflect the state of texts not at Bury or in England in the middle of the 14th cent., but at Paris in 1306. Kirkestede probably used the 14th-cent. Bury manuscript of the *Manipulus florum* now Cambridge, Peterhouse, MS 164, fols. 1r–147r; Kirkestede's hand entered the class-mark in this manuscript (M. 4), along with a few overlooked rubrics from the *florilegium* proper.[36]

---

34. Byardus (*103*), Jacobus de Vitriaco (*324*), Symon de Boraston Anglicus (*557*), Wilhelmus de Enkourt Anglicus (*648*), Wilhelmus de Kingesham Anglicus (*649*), Wilhelmus Bromyerd Anglicus (*650*), and Walterus Bokedene (*653*).
35. The *Manipulus florum* may have been used as a source in the following entries: *1–3, 7, 15, 85, 139, 203, 244, 281–282, 369, 462, 493, 498, 543, 582, 606, 666*.
36. See Kirkestede's headings in the margins of fols. 4v, 5r, 6r. James, *Pembroke*, 159–60, and Ker, *MLGB*, 19, have an incorrect shelf-mark (163) for this manuscript; James's descriptions of Pembroke MSS 163 and 164 refer to 164 and 163, respectively.

The foregoing are the major bibliographies, and the works containing bibliographies, which provided Kirkestede with the bulk of the material that comprises the *Catalogus*. In practice, though, Kirkestede drew further bibliographical information from a large number of minor sources. Any work in which an author recorded his own sources, or listed his own writings, might became a source of bibliographical data for Kirkestede, and seemingly no list was too small.

vi. Ranulf Higden, Ralph de Diceto, and the Mariale maius

These three sources together supplied Kirkestede with information for about fifty-five authors. Although Kirkestede did not include the name of Ranulf Higden as an author in the *Catalogus*, he made frequent use of the list of authorities prefixed to Higden's *Polychronicon*, and occasionally took information from the *Polychronicon* text as well. The *Catalogus* refers to the *Polychronicon* as a source only once, for Cassiodorus (*111*), 'secundum Polychronicon Cestrense', but Higden's list evidently provided data for fifteen entries in all, while another nine have relied on the body of Higden's work.[37] Kirkestede's manuscript of the *Polychronicon*, which does not survive, resembled the text of Oxford, Magdalen College, MS 181, and Cambridge, St John's College, MS A. 12, both of which preserve readings found in the *Catalogus* and not in other manuscripts of the *Polychronicon*.[38] For example, where the edition reads 'Suetonius de gestis Romanorum', the *Catalogus* reads (with Magdalen 181 and St John's A. 12) 'Erodotus, Quintillianus, Agellius, Suetonius de gestis Romanorum', treated by Kirkestede as one author with a very long name (*182*).

A similar list of authorities is prefixed to Ralph de Diceto's *Abbreuiationes chronicorum*—which itself is reported in the *Catalogus* (*500.1*). The list in the *Abbreuiationes chronicorum* supplied Kirkestede with material used in the entries for thirteen authors.[39]

An English compilation of historical and theological material concerning the Virgin Mary, perhaps to be dated to the mid 13th-cent., supplied

---

37. Ranulf Higden, *Polychronicon*, ed. C. Babington & J. R. Lumby, 9 vols, RS 41 (1865), I. 20–26 (list) and elsewhere. The *Polychronicon* may have been used as a source in the following *Catalogus* entries: *66, 74, 111, 163, 182, 217, 219, 232, 254, 344, 361, 367, 407, 464, 470, 506, 554, 558, 561, 579, 605, 659, 660, 674*.
38. Higden, I. l–li, 22 n.
39. Ralph de Diceto, *Abbreuiationes chronicorum*, ed. W. Stubbs, RS 68 (1876), I. 20–24. The *Abbreuiationes* may have been used as a source in the following entries: *163, 183, 210, 241, 297, 312, 357, 367, 500, 521–522, 565, 661*.

Kirkestede with authors and titles used in twenty entries.[40] He explicitly cites the source, 'librum qui dicitur Mariale maius', in the *Catalogus* entries for Absalon *(62)*, Crispinus *(127)*, Galfridus Vinsauf *(227)*, Proba *(472)* and Robertus de S. Victore *(519)*. The *Mariale* remains unedited and largely unstudied. The manuscript of this collection that Kirkestede presumably used, Cambridge, Pembroke College, MS 22 (Bury —), now begins imperfectly, but it contains on fol. 2r the prefatory list of the authors quoted in the text, and these authors and their works are further noted in the margins of the text itself.[41] Kirkestede went beyond the initial list, citing as well the works of authors whose names occur in the *Mariale* only as marginalia, such as Albumazor *(63)* or Crispinus *(127)*. In a few instances Kirkestede was able to supply both a title and its incipit from the marginalia—for example, Alexander Nequam *(4.16)* 'De nativitate B. Mariae serm. 1, *Egredietur* . . .', or the entire entry for 'Wido monachus Cartusiensis' *(652)*.

vii. Minor sources

At least twenty-two other sources were used from one to six times. Kirkestede borrowed from these unsystematically and no doubt incidentally, adding information from one or another when he happened to come across material of interest, presumably over an extended period of time. We simply list them and the *Catalogus* entries for which they were employed, as follows.

Aimoin de Fleury, Life of Abbo[42]—Abbo of Fleury *(9)*
Cassiodorus-Epiphanius, *Historia ecclesiastica tripartita*[43]—Didimus *(144)*, Palladius *(422)*
Decretum Gelasianum de libris recipiendis et non recipiendis[44]—the *Catalogus* introduction, and entries for Leo II *(343)*, Sedulius *(531)*.
Etienne de Bourbon, *Tractatus de diuersis materiis praedicabilibus*[45]—Gervaise

---

40. The *Mariale* may have been used as a source in the following entries: *1, 3–4, 62–64*, 119, *127, 170–171, 174, 227, 246, 371, 472, 505, 519, 531, 625, 652*.
41. Another Bury manuscript, Ipswich, Central Library, MS 4, was given to Bury by Abbot John Brinkley and bears Kirkestede's *ex dono* note and class-mark on fol. 1r; however, the Ipswich volume lacks the list of authors and the marginal citations. Only three other manuscripts of this text are known: Lambeth Palace Library, MS 52 (s. xiv); Salisbury Cathedral, MS 62 (s. xiii); and San Marino, Huntington Library, MS HM 26560 (s. xiv^{med}).
42. *PL* 139. 387–414.
43. Ed. R. Hanslik, *CSEL* 71 (1952).
44. Ed. E. von Dobschütz (Leipzig 1912).
45. The work is unedited. Portions were edited as theses at the École des Chartes in Paris and summarized in the school's *Position des thèses* in the year of the degree by J. Berlioz in 1977, D. Ogilvie-David in 1978, and J.-L. Eichenlaub in 1984. The greatest part (abridged, nevertheless) is still that of A. Lecoy de La Marche (Paris 1877), which we cite in the edition below.

(*221*), Geoffrey of Paris (*234*), Jacques de Vitry (*324*), Ado of Vienne (*408*), Turpin (*605*), Usuard (*663*)

Fulgentius[46]—Apuleius (*47*)

Gratian[47]—Theodorus (*591*)

Guido of St-Denis, *Sanctilogium*[48]—Odo (*405*), Usuard (*663*)

Guillelmus Durandus, *Rationale diuinorum officiorum*[49]—Hugh of Saint-Victor (*244*)

Hugh of Saint-Victor, *Didascalicon*[50]—Pamphilius (*438*)

'Ivo' (i.e. Hugh of Fleury), *Chronicon*[51]—Affricanus (*32*), Cassiodorus (*111*)

John of Salisbury, *Policraticus*[52]—Portumanus (*487*), Theofrastus (*602*)

John of Tynemouth, *Historia aurea*[53]—Peter Abelard (*433*)

Julian of Toledo, *Elogium*[54]—Ildefonsus (*246*)

Liber Florum[55]—Dorotheus (*151*), Excolio (*180*), Odo (*408*), Rufinus (*508*). Kirkestede cites this theological *florilegium* once, in the entry for Dorotheus (*151*), 'in libro florum'. Kirkestede's manuscript resembled Bodl. MS Lat. th. d. 30, which has a marginal gloss on fols. 3r and 33v that reads, 'Ex scolio super Dionisium'; from such a gloss in the Bury manuscript Kirkestede constructed the ghost-author 'Excolio, Super librum Dionisium'.

Liber Pontificalis[56]—Gelasius (*211*), perhaps cited indirectly through Vincent.

Martinus Polonus, *Chronicon pontificum et imperatorum*[57]—Rabanus (*492*), Theodorus papa (*590*), Theodorus archiepiscopus (*591*)

Ps. Miletus, *De actibus Johannis Apostoli*[58]—Lentius (*350*)

Nicholas Trevet, *Super Boetium de consolatione philosophiae*[59]—Frechulf (*198*)

---

46. Fulgentius, *Sermones antiqui*, ed. R. Helm (Leipzig 1898).
47. Ed. Friedberg, *Corpus iuris canonici* 1 (1879).
48. Unprinted; cited from BL Royal 13 D. ix, fol. 1r.
49. Ed. A. Davril & T. M. Thibodeau, *CCCM* 140 (1995).
50. Ed. C. Buttimer (Washington 1939).
51. Hugh of Fleury, *Historia ecclesiastica siue Chronicon*, in two redactions, of which there is no complete edition. First redaction ed. B. Rottendorff (Münster 1638); second part. ed. G. Waitz, MGH *Scriptores* 9. 337–64.
52. Ed. C. C. J. Webb (Oxford 1909).
53. Cited from Bodl. MS Bodley 240, the second half of which contains excerpts from the no longer extant Martyrology by the same author, which was used as a source for Papias (*419*).
54. *PL* 96. 43.
55. Not printed.
56. Ed. L. Duchesne, revised C. Vogel, 3 vols (Paris 1955–7).
57. Ed. L. Weiland, MGH *Scriptores* 22. 311–475.
58. *PG* 5. 1239–50.
59. Unprinted; cited here from Bodl. MS Rawlinson G. 187, fol. 1r.

Palladius, *Historia Lausiaca*⁶⁰—Didimus (*144*)
Paul the Deacon, *Historia Langobardorum*⁶¹—Dionysius (*141*), Fortunatus (*191*)
Ulric of Regensburg, *Consuetudines Cluniacenses*⁶²—Flavius (*196*)
Zacharias Chrysopolitanus, *Explanatio in unum ex quatuor*⁶³—Tatianus (*568*), Theophilus (*574*)

viii. Autobibliographies

For bibliographies of a few authors Kirkestede turned to lists made by the author himself. Strange to say, a conspicuous absence is perhaps the best known, Augustine's *Retractationes*, which Kirkestede did not use directly (his major sources, the *Registrum* and especially the *Manipulus florum*, had thoroughly absorbed the *Retractationes*). Kirkestede's sources of this type include the following.

Bede (*84*): *Historia ecclesiastica* V 24.⁶⁴
Hildegard of Bingen (*249*) [i.e. Gebeno of Eberbach]: *Pentachronon, siue speculum temporum futuorum*.⁶⁵
Iohannes de Deo (*309*): Kirkestede used a list of his writings that appears as an epilogue in several manuscripts of his works.
Peter of Blois (*444*): *Inuectiua in deprauatorem operum*.⁶⁶
Ralph Niger (*495*): *Chronicum*.⁶⁷

In addition to the sources we have identified, Kirkestede consulted some sort of tabular chronology that gave corresponding AD dates for the reigns of Roman emperors; perhaps it was something resembling an annotated copy of Martinus Polonus. With that in hand, Kirkestede whenever possible inserted AD dates in the headings for those authors whom Jerome or Gennadius dated only by reign. For the later authors, the dates were perhaps supplied from the chronicles of Paul the Deacon, William of Malmesbury, Florence of Worcester, and Ralph de Diceto or Ranulf Higden. When he could find no date, Kirkestede left a labelled space for a *floruit* date so that he could insert after the fact those he found belatedly; but ultimately he was able to find dates for only about one-third of the authors.

---

60. *PL* 74. 245–342.
61. Ed. L. Bethman & G. Waitz, MGH *Script. rer. Germ.* (1878).
62. *PL* 149. 663–778.
63. *PL* 186. 11–620.
64. Ed. B. Colgrave & R. A. B. Mynors, OMT (1969).
65. Partially printed, Pitra, *Analecta Sacra* 8. 484–8.
66. *PL* 207. 1115.
67. Ed. H. Krause (Frankfurt 1985).

The variety of secondary sources that Kirkestede used is extraordinary. The *Registrum* excepted, his sources are almost all either bibliographic compilations themselves, such as the *De uiris illustribus* texts and the catalogue of Dominican writers, or lists of authorities cited, such as those appended to the *Manipulus florum* or prefixed to Ranulf Higden and Ralph de Diceto, or autobibliographies such as Bede's. As is often the case, a bibliography finds its roots in other bibliographies.

B. *Method of Compilation*

Kirkestede compiled the *Catalogus* with material taken from these secondary sources, to which he added an appreciable amount of original information derived from manuscripts. He supplied the 674 authors in the *Catalogus* with biographical notes, and with from one title (or, very rarely, none at all) to the highest number of 511 titles for Augustine. He meant to supply each work with its identifying incipit and explicit, although the results fall far short of the intent. And he intended also to supply each work with a number, or a series of numbers, to designate the religious house(s) in which the work could be found. Although what he did provide by way of locating texts is notable, once again completion of the ambitious task was beyond his resources. For clarity's sake we shall discuss Kirkestede's methods according to these component parts—authors and works, incipits and explicits, and location numbers—before considering in general how he put the parts together.

i. *Arrangment of the authors*

The 674 authors are grouped alphabetically according to the first letter of their christian names, with occasional cross-references. Under the letter P, perhaps as an experiment, Kirkestede has grouped the first fifty-four authors by both first and second letter of the name, from Papias (*419*) to Proba (*472*). These fifty-four are followed by fifteen more names with first-initial P that are added at random, after the original scheme had been carried out. Other ventures into second-letter alphabetization were short-lived.[68]

Perhaps Kirkestede had a number of loose quires, each devoted to a single letter of the alphabet; some, such as the letter A, may have required more than one quire, while for other letters a bifolium would have sufficed.

---

68. For example, see the sequence of names beginning Jo- (*281–296*) followed by names beginning Ju- (*297–311*), with occasional lapses; these thirty-one are followed by a further thirty-one names beginning with J.

It might tell us something significant about the production of the *Catalogus* if we could explain the rationale of Kirkestede's sequence of names within the letter-group; but we see no overarching imperative at work, and it is quite likely that any original pattern has been obscured by repeated insertions made over the years. At the beginning of several of the letters he placed the author whom one would regard as the most important: e.g. A = Augustine (*1*), C = Cassiodorus (*111*), D = Dionisius (*139*), F = Fulgentius (*184*), G = Gregory (*203*), J = Jerome (*281*), O = Origen (*404*), R = Rabanus (*492*), T = Thomas Aquinas (*562*), Y = Isidore (Ysidorus, *666*). But this logic would not explain, for example, why Haimo of Auxerre (*240*) should be the first author beginning with H instead of the lengthy entry for Hugh of Saint-Victor (*244*), or why the derivative entry for Novatianus (*396*) copied from Jerome's *De uiris illustribus* should head the authors beginning with N, in place of the significant list for Nicholas Trevet (*398*) whose works Kirkestede knew first-hand in the libraries of Bury and of neighbouring Ramsey. Richard Sharpe argued plausibly that the sequence of the first four authors in the *Catalogus* was determined, or at least influenced, by the sequence of the classmarks in the Bury library: Augustine (1), Ambrose (2), Anselm (3), Alexander Nequam (4). But in subsequent cases, as he notes, 'there is no consistent correlation'.[69]

For most letter-groups no motive is apparent in the order, after the initial name. With one exception (see below), he did not start at the beginning of a source such as Jerome's *De uiris illustribus* and work systematically through to the end; his *Catalogus* was alphabetical, his sources were not. Nor did he exhaust his major sources all at once; rather, he appears to have returned to them time and again, so that entries from a given source ordinarily do not appear in clusters. Nevertheless, at times authors named in the Bury bibliographical codex (Bodl. MS e Musaeo 31: Jerome, Gennadius, Isidore, Cassiodorus) appear in batches; the largest encompasses entries numbered *33–45*, Adamantius to Adrianus. A revealing group taken from this manuscript is eight names beginning with P, *Catalogus* entries *473–480*, which immediately follow upon the sequence of names alphabetized by second letter. We can suppose that Kirkestede, after completing his two-letter alphabetical scheme, made one last sweep through e Musaeo 31 to pick up any stray authors whose names begin with P.

Only the names from the list of English Dominican writers are regularly entered in clusters: *56–61, 98–103, 172–173, 223–226, 261–270, 313–324, 376–379, 398–399, 509* (omit *511*)*–515, 555–557, 584–588, 637* (omit *652*)*–653,*

---

69. Sharpe, 'Reconstructing the medieval library', 207.

664–665;[70] and the authors' sequence in the *Catalogus* follows the sequence of comparable Dominican lists (Stams and Pignon), indicating that Kirkestede worked methodically through this source, entering each author in the appropriate alphabetical place. Only twice (at the points noted above) is the order disrupted by authors from other sources, quite possibly as a result of later insertions.

Along with Kirkestede's first-hand (manuscript-based) insertions, adding to and supplementing entries from secondary sources, there are numerous author-entries based entirely on first-hand information. Such authors, whose entries derive entirely from manuscripts of their works, tend to appear toward the end of a letter-group. The clearest example occurs under the letter I/J (entries *281–342*): of the fifteen authors at the end (*328–342*), all but two derive entirely from manuscripts of their works, rather than from secondary sources.[71] Kirkestede presumably compiled the basic lists of authors and works from secondary sources; but manuscripts, especially the Bury books, were the source from which he continually added information (including author entries) to the *Catalogus*, again and again over a long time, well after the initial search through his principal sources was concluded.[72]

ii. Arrangement of the entries for each author

After the author's name and a biographical note, however brief, came the titles of that author's works. The order in which the titles appear reflects not always strictly the sources from which they have been taken.[73]

a. Entries compiled wholly from secondary sources

The percentage of authors and works taken entirely from secondary sources is high. The survival in Bodl. MS e Musaeo 31 (Bury A. 31) of Kirkestede's manuscript of Jerome, Gennadius and Isidore, from which he furnished almost one-third of the author-entries in the *Catalogus*, provides an opportunity to examine closely his use of a source.

---

70. Three Dominican authors, Durandus (*146*), Ludoldus (*349*) and Oliverus (*413*), appear individually because no others from this source begin with those letters of the alphabet.
71. See the sequences (sometimes interrupted) of whole entries from manuscripts, at the end of letters B (*106–110*), C (*136–138*), G (*231–239*), H (*276–280*), M (*388–395*), P (*482–486*), and R (*525–528*).
72. The proportion of Bury's medieval library that survives is well above the average; see below, chapter 4 p. clxxx.
73. For three authors only, Augustine, Ambrose and Jerome, Kirkestede imposed specific principles of organization. See below, p. cviii.

While the sequence of authors' names is rarely methodical, the list of an author's works, in contrast, was often composed in straightforward fashion, especially those from the *De uiris* literature. At the end of the headnote Kirkestede cited his source with the formula 'et scripsit juxta . . .', or 'secundum . . .'; he neglected to credit Gennadius only twice and Jerome only once,[74] and he credited Isidore without exception. Thereafter he listed the author's works, usually following the sequence of his source; see, for example, the entry for Jacobus (*292*), where Kirkestede reproduced in sequence the list of twenty-one works found in Gennadius, chapter 1; or see Albertus Magnus (*56*), where Kirkestede's list of seventy-four titles varies only once from the (presumed) sequence in his catalogue of Dominican writers.

Anomalies abound, of course: titles were overlooked and added at the end, or the order was inverted, or the whole order was jumbled—reminding us that this is the work of a monk, who had differing and obligatory claims on his time every day, and who of course did not have the benefit of modern bibliographical handbooks.[75] One title might have been read as two: e.g. Philo, 'De victimis et repromissionibus' and 'De maledictis' (*452.16–17*) is 'De victimis et repromissionibus siue maledictis' in Jerome.[76] Or two titles became one; thus, Basil, 'De virginitate contra Marcellum' (*79.1*) was derived from Jerome's 'Contra Marcellum et De virginitate'.[77] Kirkestede was not always concerned to distinguish between composition and translation (see Sophronius *551.4* 'Vita Hilarionis', described in Jerome c. 134 as a work of Jerome's translated by Sophronius).

There are also deliberate alterations. Not knowing Greek, Kirkestede consistently omitted Greek titles or Greek words in his borrowings from Jerome, unless he found either a Latin gloss or a transliteration in Latin script in e Musaeo 31.[78] His changes usually were quite minor, standardizing discursive entries from the *De uiris illustribus* to suit the circumstances of a simple list. He sometimes shortened or reworded the title of a work; for example, for Anatholius, 'De decem libris arithmeticae institutionis' (Jerome c. 73), Kirkestede recorded simply, 'De arithmetica' (*24.2*).[79] He often moved the name of a work's recipient from the beginning to the end of the title,[80] and he usually substituted *contra* for *aduersus*.[81] When his sources described the

---

74. Leo (*343*), Prosper (*466*), and Theotimus (*596*) respectively.
75. For example, Alexander (*39*), Miltiades (*373*), Salmanus (*530*), Serapion (*548*).
76. See also Eusebius (*160*).
77. See also Basil *78.2*, Eustasius *177.2*, Methodius *361.4*.
78. See, for example, Miletus *371.19*.
79. See also, for example, Pachomius (*421.4*) and Sabbatius (*532.2*).
80. For example, Fastidius *190.1*.
81. For example, *28.1*, *29.1*, *34.1–2*, *129.1*, *132.1*.

type of work an author wrote without actually giving any titles, Kirkestede sometimes copied the description *in extenso*,[82] and at other times composed a suitable title himself, such as in the entry for Quadratus (*489*), where the *Catalogus* title 'De Christiana religione' was derived from Jerome c. 19, 'porrexit ei librum pro nostra religione conpositum'.[83] At times he evidently found the problem not readily soluble, for of the nineteen authors in the *De uiris illustribus* sources that Kirkestede omitted, eight have no specific titles assigned to them.[84]

b. Entries compiled from manuscripts

One hundred and forty-six author-entries in the *Catalogus* were composed entirely from manuscripts which Kirkestede saw in the Bury library and in the libraries of neighbouring monasteries. In contrast to the entries taken entirely from secondary sources, these entries—along with the much greater number of manuscript-based titles added to author-entries of mixed origin (for which, see below)—represent first-hand knowledge of English manuscripts of medieval texts as Kirkestede saw them in the third quarter of the 14th cent. Kirkestede tried to supplement these entries with biographical information and dates taken from chronicles or from extended rubrics, but often without success.

The lists of works occasionally represent the contents of codices that have survived. See, for example, Bodl. MS Rawlinson C. 697 (Bury A. 19), from which Kirkestede supplied the first three works of the Aldhelm entry (*8.1–3*). Eighteen of the works in the Anselm entry (*3.1–11, 14–17, 21–22* and *45*) are divided among three surviving Bury manuscripts, Bodl. MS e Musaeo 112 (Bury J. 13), BL MS Royal 7 B. ix (Bury D. 6), and Cambridge, Pembroke College, MS 1 (Bury A. 92). And although the titles of twenty-six of Jerome's scriptural commentaries (*281.15–40*) were copied in sequence from Vincent of Beauvais's *Speculum*, Kirkestede added their incipits and explicits from manuscripts J. 3 through J. 16 in the Bury library. Naturally, many manuscripts from which these entries were compiled have not survived. However, when Kirkestede's entry represents a peculiarity, or a particular collection of an author's works, we can at times refer to a similar manuscript that has survived from another English library. Kirkestede's misattributions of authorship (e.g. Anselm *3.13–14, 29–30, 32, 34, 43, 46, 57*) normally represent the opinion of the later middle ages, because he took his attributions from the manuscripts before him. Similarly, when the *Catalogus* lists an individual ser-

---

82. Compare Jerome c. 36 and Panthenus (*476*), Gennadius c. 9, and Oresiesis (*414*).
83. Compare also Jerome c. 84 and Juvencus (*310.1–2*), Gennadius c. 88 and Servus Dei (*539.1*).
84. See above p. xciv.

mon or letter (e.g. Anselm *3.54*), this indicates that that text had an independent manuscript existence, separate from the standard collection of the author's sermons or letters.

In many cases the *Catalogus* contains the earliest known list of works attributed to an English author. A good example is the Grosseteste entry (*505*); for this Kirkestede compiled a biography, partially derived from Trevet's chronicle, and then supplied a list of forty titles, all from manuscripts of Grosseteste's works. Other English authors for whom Kirkestede's list is the earliest, or one of the earliest, known are Alexander Nequam (*4*), Aelred of Rievaulx (*5*), Peter of Blois (*444*), Ralph Niger (*495*), Richard Rolle (*528*), Stephen Langton (*554*), William de Montibus (*625*), William of Peterborough (*626*), and William de Pagula (*629*).

Kirkestede saw manuscripts of works that have since disappeared. For examples, see Astulphus (*72*), Gregory of Bridlington (*208*), John of Tynemouth (*341*), Osbert of Clare (*417.1*), R. of Fressingfeld (*501*), and William of Peterborough (*626*).

c. Organizing entries of mixed origin

Many author-entries in the *Catalogus*—including the larger entries almost without exception—were compiled not from a single source but from a combination of sources, often including a large number of manuscripts. The entry for Fulgentius (*184*) is a straightforward example: the titles *184.1* and *13* came from Isidore and *184.2–12* from Vincent of Beauvais in sequence (both of these sources are cited in the headnote); *184.14–16* came from the *Registrum*; and the four sermons at the end of the entry (*184.17–20*) came from a Bury manuscript. It is sometimes difficult to distinguish which, of two or more possible sources, Kirkestede relied on. See, for example, the entry for Dionysius (*140*) which cites both Vincent and Jerome as sources, while the twenty works listed could come from either source alone. At times when he cited both sources Kirkestede clearly used Vincent alone, naming the second source only for greater authority; see, for example, the entry for Maximus (*359*), where Kirkestede names both Gennadius and Vincent, but reports from Gennadius only those titles that are available in the *Speculum historiale*.

Kirkestede's combining of sources can give unexpected results. For example, entry *324* was compiled from three different sources: the Dominican list, Vincent of Beauvais, and Étienne de Bourbon, with added information from a Bury manuscript. The *Catalogus* calls the author Jacobus de Vitriaco (Jacques de Vitry), but he has been conflated with Jacobus de Teriace (Jacobus de Cessolis) because of the similarity of names. Trying to make sense of his disparate sources, Kirkestede called this composite personage both Dominican (de Cessolis) and a cardinal (de Vitry), and attributed to him three works, the well-known 'De ludo scaccarii' written by Jacobus de Cessolis (*324.1*), and two other works (*324.2–3*) that are properly attributed to Jacques de Vitry.

Kirkestede imposed his own principle of organization on three large and significant author-entries. He organized the entries for the first two authors in the *Catalogus*, the 511 works of Augustine and the ninety-six works of Ambrose, by first-letter alphabetical order. The arrangement pertains to the keyword in each title, which is readily apparent for the most part. For the third example, the entry of 239 works of Jerome (*281*), Kirkestede unexpectedly employed a topical arrangement of sorts. The entry contains, in sequence, saints' lives, Marian material, scriptural commentary, questions and interpretations, anti-heretical tracts, translations, a dozen or more brief notes (mostly pseudonymous) that represent a single manuscript collection, eight or ten titles from the *Registrum*, and then an analysis of the Bury manuscript of Jerome's epistles—an analysis that begins with a topical grouping of four letters on the monastic or clerical life. At the end is the usual handful of afterthoughts.[85]

The task of discerning Kirkestede's sources is complicated by what seems on the surface to be a practice of taking information without method, first from one source and then another and then back again. For example, among the six works attributed to Priscian (*470*), the first three titles were taken from Vincent, the fourth from Ranulf Higden's *Polychronicon*, the fifth from a Bury manuscript, and the sixth from Vincent again. Or consider the entry for Athanasius (*6*), which appears superficially to have been compiled in alternation between works taken from manuscripts and titles from Jerome: specifically, works *1, 3, 7* and *9* come from Jerome and *2, 4–6, 8* and *10* from manuscripts.[86] The explanation for these seeming anomalies must surely be the simplest one: Kirkestede worked at compiling the *Catalogus* over a long time, perhaps as long as thirty-five years or more, and the frequent semblance of alternation or lack of method is simply the effect of repeated insertions, over years and years.

One cannot always discern whether a work has been taken from secondary sources or from a manuscript—and, thus, whether Kirkestede's record reflects the state of texts in East Anglia c. 1340–78, or their state in some quite different time and place. Ordinarily, the indication that a work represents a manuscript will be the incipit and explicit and the location numbers which follow the title; as we shall see, there are regular exceptions

---

85. For details see the headnote to Jerome (*281*).
86. The entry for Hilarius Pictavensis (*242*), for example, presents a similar interweaving of works taken from Jerome, Vincent, the *Registrum*, and manuscripts.

to this rule, and we have noted them. Conversely, Kirkestede did not always supply the incipit and explicit or the location numbers for those works which he did take from manuscripts. For example, the eleven titles assigned to Richard Rolle (*528*) have no incipits and explicits; but Rolle, Kirkestede's older contemporary (d. 1349), was not an author to be found in the secondary bibliographies, and the location number for Bury (**82**) is affixed to more than half of the works, strongly suggesting that the whole entry for this author was constructed from a manuscript or manuscripts at Bury St Edmunds.[87]

In compiling the longer entries for the patristic authors, in particular, Kirkestede mined as many sources as he could lay hands on. Inevitably, he did not always recognize duplication when the same work occurred with a different title. This is particularly true of the Augustine entry, with its unparalleled length. Thus, for example, Augustine's *De haeresibus* appears four separate times: *1.46*, 'De basibus, *Quid petis*', taken from a manuscript;[88] *1.114*, 'Ad [Quodvultdeum], *Quod petis*', taken from the *Registrum* 1. 195; *1.200*, 'De haeresibus diversis, *Quid petis*', taken from the *Manipulus florum*; and *1.204*, 'De omnibus haeresibus, *Cum Dominus*', from a different entry in the *Registrum* (1. 115) whose compilers obviously had similar problems.

Such duplication does not occur as often in lengthy entries for medieval authors, such as Anselm (*3*) or Hugh of Saint-Victor (*244*), which Kirkestede has compiled primarily from manuscripts, with only supplementary material from secondary sources; but even here there is combination of sources. Thus, the entry for Hugh was constructed initially from manuscripts of his works at Bury and at other libraries that Kirkestede knew, to which Kirkestede added in sequence eight titles from Vincent of Beauvais, two separate series of borrowings from the *Manipulus florum*, and more than a dozen works taken from the *Registrum*. And at the end of the entry, the titles are the usual mixture of oversights and afterthoughts.

iii. Incipits and explicits

When Kirkestede listed a work for which his source was a manuscript, he routinely added its incipit and explicit—with occasional lapses, of course.

---

87. See also, for example, Alcuin *7.12*, *14*, *27*, *32*, Aldhelm *8.4*, Abbo of Fleury *9.12* and *15*, Walter of Mortagne *607*, a list far from exhaustive.

88. 'basibus' is the result of a misreading of the abbreviated first syllable of 'heresibus'. Because this title with the word 'basibus' appears (in the alphabetized Augustine entry) among the titles whose keywords begin with B, clearly the error is not Tanner's mistake nor that of any hypothetical earlier copyist of the *Catalogus*. Either Kirkestede himself, or the rubricator of the manuscript from which he took the title, was responsible for the mistake.

Incipits are sometimes those of the prologue, sometimes those of the text proper. He tried, with fair success, to avoid quoting as the explicit any benediction that occurred at the end of a work, since its stock wording would not be useful as an identification. As a result, however, the *Catalogus*'s explicits sometimes seem to be chosen arbitrarily from anywhere within the final sentence or even final paragraph of a text. Thus, for Guitmund of Aversa, *De corpore et sanguine Christi* (*220.1*), an entry based on a Bury manuscript (Bodl. MS e Musaeo 33, p. 213), Kirkestede singled out as the explicit the word 'referamus' from the midst of the benediction, 'cui pro tanta caritate gracias *referamus* eternas regnanti cum Deo patre et Spiritu sancto per infinita secula seculorum amen'. There are scores of similar instances.[89]

Kirkestede attempted to supply incipits and explicits, as the only secure identification, for as many works in the *Catalogus* as he could, diligently adding them after the fact to lists of bare titles that had come from secondary sources. For example, while the sequence of works *2–12* in the entry for Fulgentius (*184*) reveals that these titles were taken from Vincent, Kirkestede has added from manuscripts the incipit and sometimes the explicit to nine of the eleven titles (*3–8* and *10–12*). Works *1–11, 13, 15–20* in the Cyprian entry (*112*), titles that were copied from Vincent, have likewise been supplied with incipits and explicits from manuscripts. The list of ninety-two titles attributed to Aquinas (*567*) were copied from the catalogue of Dominican writers, but at least a third of these titles have incipits and explicits supplied later from manuscripts of the works.[90] In general, Kirkestede succeeded very well; but, inevitably, errors ensued from the difficulty of matching works in his manuscripts with titles provided by secondary sources that ranged in date from the 4th cent to the 14th. In a few instances, the surviving Bury manuscript will explain the error (see examples at Anselm *3.9*, or at Isidore *666.16* and *666.19*). One must remember that, in numerous entries, the incipits represent manuscripts, while the titles to which they are attached and the order in which the titles appear depend on secondary sources and may not correspond to the medievaI codices that Kirkestede has seen.

In addition to manuscripts of the texts, Kirkestede supplied works with their incipits from three other sources. The *Registrum* was a frequent source

89. For (*pseudo-*) Augustine, *De igne purgatorio* (*1.228*), the manuscript on which the entry is based (again, Bodl. MS e Musaeo 33, p. 285) has more than two further full lines of benediction that occur after the word 'redimere', which Kirkestede settled on as the explicit. His explicit 'laus et' for Alexander Nequam on Canticles (*4.2*), an entry taken from another Bury manuscript, Bodl. MS Bodley 356, is a bizarre choice from the full benediction (fol. 257v) 'laus et honor et imperium per infinita secula seculorum amen'. And so on.

90. Seneca *543.1–13*, titles taken from Vincent, have incipits and explicits added for all but *543.7*; Jerome *281.14–40*, taken from Vincent, have incipits and explicits from manuscripts; see also Dionisius *140.3–4*, Didimus *144.4*, Effrem *155.1–8*, Josephus *296.1–2*, and so on.

of incipits, copied along with their titles.[91] And from the *Manipulus florum* Kirkestede added works with both incipits and explicits (usually shortened). Curiously, he never acknowledged having used this source, but unmistakable borrowings from the *Manipulus florum* appear in several entries, including Alanus *(15)*, Boethius *(94)*, Dionisius *(139)*, Hugh of Saint-Victor *(244)*, Macrobius *(369)*, Pliny *(462)*, Maimonides *(493)*, Richard of Saint-Victor *(498)*, Seneca *(543)*, and Cicero *(582)*. Entries derived from the *Manipulus florum* often betray themselves to the reader as titles with incipits and explicits but without location numbers; very frequently, however, Kirkestede combined location numbers taken from the *Registrum* with his borrowings from the *Manipulus florum*. He seldom exhausted the information available from this source, the only cases of thorough use being the entries in the *Manipulus* for Augustine *(1)*, Alanus *(15)* and Dionysius *(139)*. Kirkestede seems for the most part to have used the *Manipulus florum* as a supplementary source, supplying from it any titles (with their incipits and explicits) which he had not already found in his other sources for an author's works. It is important to identify the works that come from the *Manipulus florum*, because these entries in particular masquerade as actual manuscripts that Kirkestede saw. Finally, in addition to the major sources of *Registrum* and *Manipulus florum*, the *Mariale* provided a handful of incipits with its titles.[92]

iv. *Location numbers*

To titles with incipits and explicits, and to titles without, Kirkestede often assigned location numbers referring to the numbered list of 195 British monastic libraries that precedes the text of the *Catalogus*. Kirkestede took this list of locations and their numbers from the *Registrum*, and he added to it the names of several monastic libraries in East Anglia, which he numbered as well.[93]

Kirkestede's use of the location numbers has been a source of persistent misinterpretation, particularly during the last century or so of modern scholarly attention given to the *Catalogus*. We explain the principal problems in

---

91. See especially the large numbers of incipits from the *Registrum* in the entries for Augustine *(1)*, Ambrose *(2)*, Anselm *(3)*, Bede *(84)*, Bernard *(85)*, Gregory Nazianzenus *(204)*, Hugh of St Victor *(244)*, John Chrysostom *(282)*, Origen *(404)*, and Isidore *(666)*.
92. See Anselm *3.33*, Alexander Nequam *4.15, 16*, and Wido *652.1*.
93. See Rouse & Rouse, *Registrum*, lvi–lviii (discussion) and 2–6 (comparative edition in parallel columns of the lists in the two witnesses to the *Registrum* and in the *Catalogus*). *Registrum*'s use of the location numbers is analysed, ib. 246–322. Credit for the identification of the numbered locations of the *Registrum* and of those added by the *Catalogus* belongs to M. R. James, 'The list of libraries prefixed to the *Catalogus* of John Boston and the kindred documents', *Collectanea Franciscana* 2 (1922) 37–60.

detail below, but we wish to emphasize in advance that location numbers in *Catalogus* entries should never be taken at face value without pause for serious reflection. Although this chapter highlights the major difficulties, to understand fully the need for caution one would need also to understand Kirkestede's purposes, about which one can only surmise, and to recognize the severe limitation of Kirkestede's resources, which usually compelled him to deal in probabilities rather than certainties.

a. The list of libraries

A list of 186 libraries, grouped according to the Franciscan custodies of England, is prefaced to the *Registrum*; it consists of 167 locations numbered in arabic numerals, and nineteen in roman numerals distributed among the custodies and numbered in the following order: xiii–xxvii, v–vi, xi–xii. Building on this base Kirkestede compiled his own list of 195 libraries. He discarded the headings of the Franciscan custodies, irrelevant to a Benedictine, and he numbered all the locations consecutively in arabic numerals. He borrowed the list of 167 arabic-numbered libraries without change, he added eight new locations (libraries not in the *Registrum*), which he numbered 168–175, and then he renumbered as 176–194 the nineteen libraries designated in the *Registrum* list by roman numerals. At the end he added one more library not in the *Registrum*, presumably an afterthought, making a total of 195 libraries.[94]

There are textual problems at three points in the list of locations. One, at **103–106**, has no relevance to the *Catalogus*, since these numbers (representing locations on either side of the Welsh border) are simple borrowings from the *Registrum*.[95] However, the other two problems, at numbers **18–23** and **64–66**, involve monastic libraries that Kirkestede knew (or may have known) at first hand.

The comparative readings of the three witnesses to the list from **18** to **23**, in *K* (Kirkestede's *Catalogus*) and the two witnesses to the *Registrum*, *T* (Bodl. MS Tanner 165) and *P* (Cambridge, Peterhouse, MS 169.I), with their modern identifications, are as follows.

18, Nouus locus *T*   **18**, Nouus locus *P* **18**, Novus locus *K*
   Augustinians of Newark (Surrey)

19, Sancti Pauli London' *T* [see **22** below *P*]   **19**, London S. Pauli *K*
   Cathedral church of St Paul's, London

---

94. James, 'List of libraries', 40. Since Kirkestede, following his manuscript of the *Registrum*, leaves the location numbers **66** and **100** blank, there are in actuality 193 libraries on the list.
95. Discussed by Rouse & Rouse, *Registrum*, lvii–lviii.

COMPILING THE *CATALOGUS*

19, Wauerle *T*   **19**, Wauerlee *P*   **19**, Waverleye *K*
   Cistercians of Waverley (Surrey)

20, Lewys *T*   **20**, Lewes *P*   **20**, Lewes *K*
   Cluniac priory of St Pancras at Lewes (Sussex)

   21, Chicestre *P*[96]   **21**, [blank] *K*

22, Cicestr' *T*   **22**, Sancti Pauli Londonie *P*   **22**, Cicestria *K*
   Cathedral church of Holy Trinity, Chichester (Sussex)

23, Sowyk *T*   **23**, Suthwyk *P*   **23**, Suthwych *K*
   Augustinians of Southwick (Hants)

The only one of these numbers potentially used first-hand in the *Catalogus* is **19**. The error in Kirkestede's list—the number **19** assigned twice and the number **21** not used—was the *Registrum*'s original reading (*P* rationalized after the fact). That does not answer the question, however, of what Kirkestede meant by the number **19** on the several occasions when he added it to works in the *Catalogus* (as opposed to his simply copying it from the *Registrum*). The best that one can say is that if he took it to mean St Paul's, the information he seems to add may be genuine; he reported books from two other London-area collections, **10** Holy Trinity Aldgate and **11** Westminster. If instead he took **19** to mean Waverley, that 'information' is probably erroneous (copying errors or misinterpretation).

The comparison of the numbers from **61** to **67** is as follows.

61, Burgh' *T*   **61**, Burgh *P*   **61**, Burch *K*
   Benedictines of Peterborough (Northants)

62, Turney *T*   **62**, Thorneye *P*   **62**, Thorneye *K*
   Benedictines of Thorney (Cambs)

63, Crowland' *T*   **63**, Croulande *P*   **63**, Croylande *K*
   Benedictines of Crowland (Lincs)

[unnumbered] Burgus S. Petri *T*   **64**, Burgus S. Petri *P*   [blank] *K*
   A duplicate of **61**, perhaps a gloss that fell into the text (unnumbered in *T*, absent from *K*, but given a number in *P*)

64, Bernewelle *T*   **64**, Bernewell *K*
   Augustinian priory of Barnwell (Cambs)

65, Rammesey *T*   **65**, Bernewelle *P*   **65**, Ramesia *K*
   Benedictines of Ramsey (Hunts)

---

96. The number **21** is a correction of the typographical error that occurs ibid. p. 2 column 2 at 'Chichestre'.

| [**66** om. *T*] | **66**, Ramseye *P* | **66**, [blank] *K* |
| **67**, Ely *T* | **67**, Hely *P* | **67**, Ely *K* |

    Benedictine cathedral priory of Ely (Cambs)

Clearly the mistake at **66** in both *T*'s and Kirkestede's lists represents the reading of the original list in the *Registrum*, with both *T* and *K* as independent witnesses. More important, interpreting the meaning of these numbers for the *Catalogus* is made easier still by the fact that the Franciscans who compiled the *Registrum* included reports from almost none of these libraries (the only exception was Crowland, the meaning of whose location number **63** is not in dispute). When Kirkestede wrote one of the numbers **64** or **65**, then, there is no risk that he was importing confusion from the *Registrum*; he meant Barnwell and Ramsey, respectively. The use of **65** to localize the works of William of Peterborough monk of Ramsey (*626*)—one of which, moreover, appears in a surviving Ramsey manuscript—corroborates the assumption.

    The identification of libraries **168–175** and **195** added by Kirkestede presents few difficulties. With the exception of **168** Oxford Greyfriars and **195** Hinton Charterhouse in Somerset, they are monasteries in the vicinity of Bury: **169** is the Augustinian priory at Ixworth and **170**, the Blackfriars at Thetford. For **171** the text of the *Catalogus* is deficient—not simply in Tanner's transcript (Add. 3470), but also in two early modern (pre-Tanner) extracts from the medieval manuscript—reading only 'Fratrum . . .';[97] but because of its location on the list between two Thetford houses, we agree with M. R. James that **171** probably designates the Austin Friars in Thetford. Location number **172** is the Cluniac priory in Thetford, **173** the Franciscan convent of Babwell on the outskirts of Bury, **174** the Benedictine priory at Earls Colne in Essex, **175** the Benedictine nunnery at Barking, also in Essex, near London. Kirkestede's knowledge of the Greyfriars at Oxford (**168**) might either reflect his own first-hand knowledge or represent a report from other Bury monks studying at Oxford. He added **195** Hinton Charterhouse in Somerset at the end of the list, for reasons we cannot guess. Somerset was well outside the area that Kirkestede knew first-hand. Hinton (founded 1225–32) was the most important of the three Carthusian houses in England when Kirkestede began his work;[98] but we do not know how or why he proposed to report information in the *Catalogus* about its books and, in the event, he did not do so. We are hampered by the loss of Kirkestede's manu-

---

97. See note to the edition below, p. 20. Concerning the transmission of the *Catalogus* text, see chapter 4 below.

98. James, 'List of libraries', 44.

script of the *Registrum*: could Hinton have been present (as an addition to the list) in his *Registrum*?

b. Kirkestede's use of *Registrum* location numbers

More than half of the location numbers in the body of the *Catalogus* were simply imported directly from the *Registrum*, in company with the titles to which they are appended. It is clear, however, that Kirkestede has deliberately added many location numbers, from his own first-hand knowledge of certain monastic libraries. It is difficult to distinguish the two, but it is essential that we try. Kirkestede employed the *Registrum*'s location numbers in a variety of sometimes unusual ways, and it is often impossible to comprehend his motives. Moreover, we must keep in mind the possibility that what seem to be anomalies in Kirkestede's use of the numbers are in fact reflections of peculiarities in his copy of the *Registrum*. Even with respect to obvious copying errors, one can seldom be certain whether they should be attributed to corruptions in Add. 3470, to Kirkestede himself, or to his copy of the *Registrum*; common sense suggests some of each.

Often his borrowing was straightforward, as he copied from the *Registrum* a title and the complete sequence of location numbers that the *Registrum* offered for that title. However, Kirkestede seemingly had a self-imposed limit on location numbers, never recording more than ten per work and more commonly eight or fewer; thus the entire string of numbers available in a *Registrum* entry often exceeded his needs. In those instances he borrowed only part of the *Registrum*'s number-series, but his criteria for selection are elusive, given that we do not know his purposes: he might take the first half or last half of the series, or a segment in reverse order, or even a few apparently random numbers. For Hugh of Saint-Victor's *De archa Noe* (*244.17*), Kirkestede recorded only seven location numbers, selected on unknown grounds from the series of forty-two location numbers that the *Registrum* offers for the same work (*Registrum* 97. 4). At times he omitted the *Registrum* location numbers altogether.

Kirkestede's application of the numbers offered by the *Registrum* was often a good deal more complicated, however, than a simple borrowing or not-borrowing. Consider Kirkestede's treatment of the roman-numbered libraries cited by the *Registrum*. As we have seen, he swept aside these anomalies in the *Registrum*'s list, grouping these locations at the end of the *Catalogus*'s list of libraries and assigning them new arabic numerals in sequence (**176-194**). But when he was actually borrowing titles and numbers from the *Registrum* text, Kirkestede ignored his own renumbering, and simply transposed directly from roman to arabic numerals; for example, in all thirty-three instances when he copied the number **xii** (Buildwas) from the *Registrum*, it became

12 (Southwark) in the *Catalogus*. The same is true without exception for the other eighteen roman numerals.[99]

Frequently, Kirkestede took *Registrum* location numbers out of their original context, interpreting their meaning with good intentions but misleading results. It was his standard practice, when he copied into the *Catalogus* a title from a secondary source such as Vincent or Jerome, to search for what he took to be the same work in the *Registrum* and to enter any library numbers he might find there (along with incipits, as we have seen). Entries compiled from a combination of *Manipulus florum* and *Registrum* are especially common in the *Catalogus*. His manipulation of *Registrum* entries themselves was often problematic, combining two that he took to be identical, or identifying a *Registrum* title with a text that he found in Bury manuscripts. For example, on the basis of a manuscript, Kirkestede composed an entry for a corpus of twelve of Augustine's sermons 'De pascha', which he entered (*Catalogus 1.389*) with the incipit of the first sermon. In the *Registrum* list for Augustine, however, there are two individual entries of one sermon each, 'Sermo de die pasche' (*Registrum* 1. 232) and 'Sermo eius de pascha' (*Registrum* 1. 275); Kirkestede combined the location numbers from both these *Registrum* entries, and attached them to his corpus of twelve sermons. A striking example occurs in Kirkestede's entry for homilies of Origen, 'Super Lucam omel. 38' (*Catalogus 404.20*), a title taken from Vincent of Beauvais. The *Catalogus* gives five location numbers for this work: **20**, **63**, **35**, **105**, and **9**, although the *Registrum* lists just one number (**35**) for the same (*Registrum* 10. 26). The remaining location numbers—which a reader might assume to represent Kirkestede's first-hand information—are instead borrowings from elsewhere in the Origen entry in the *Registrum*: **20** and **63** come from 'Omelie eius' (*Registrum* 10. 29), and **105** and **9** from a sequence of six Origen sermons on individual verses from the gospels of Luke and Matthew (*Registrum* 10. 12–17). Conversely, Kirkestede sometimes applied location numbers from one *Registrum* entry to two or more entries in the *Catalogus*.[100] He also occasionally analysed the contents of a general title from the *Registrum*: for example, Jerome 'Super xii prophetas' (*Registrum* 6. 74), which has a series of thirty-one location numbers; the *Catalogus* lists the twelve commentaries

---

99. Though it is unlikely, one cannot be completely certain that his copy of the *Registrum* had not already made this 'improvement'—not in the initial list, but in the body of the *Registrum*. The new numbers **176** to **194** that Kirkestede added to the list do not appear in the text of the *Catalogus*.

100. For example, the *Registrum* entry for Augustine, 'Epistola ad Macedonium' (*Registrum 1.317*), has the location number **161**. The *Catalogus* has two such entries (*Catalogus 1.273* and *1.296*), the latter with an incipit not seen in the *Registrum*; but Kirkestede nevertheless gave to each entry the location number **161**.

individually, from Hosea to Malachi (*Catalogus 281.22–33*), and repeats for each the same six library numbers selected from among the *Registrum*'s thirty-one. Similarly, the *Registrum* has an entry for a sermon collection attributed to John Chrysostom (*Registrum 9. 13*), while the *Catalogus* lists no such collection under Chrysostom's name; but for each of ten individual items labelled as sermons, Kirkestede added a selection of between two and six of the seven library numbers from the *Registrum*'s 'Sermones eiusdem' (*Catalogus 282.16–18, 21–27*).

The letters of Jerome afford the most complex example of Kirkestede's use of the *Registrum* location numbers. The *Registrum* has a blanket entry, *Epistole Ieronimi* (6. 78), followed by a sequence of thirty-nine location numbers. The *Catalogus*, instead, itemizes ninety-nine individual epistles, near the end of the Jerome entry (*Catalogus 281.128–168, 170–207, 214–231, and 238*). The titles, incipits, and explicits of these letters came from a manuscript, presumably from the collection of Jerome letters in Bury's library. But almost all of these *Catalogus* entries (eighty-seven of the ninety-nine) are followed by an identical series of location numbers: **8**, **42**, **63**, **82**, **32**, **9**, **19**, **35** (**63** and **35** are often omitted), numbers that were selected from the entry in the *Registrum* for the Jerome letter-collection (*Registrum* 6. 78). The borrowing is further obscured by copying errors involving the numerals 32 and 35 —errors, it would seem, in Kirkestede's manuscript of the *Registrum* (for **32** read **23**, for **35** read **39**). Exceptionally, the location number for Crowland (**63**) is probably a genuine Kirkestede addition, since he did in fact have first-hand knowledge of the Crowland library and since the books at Crowland did include a collection of Jerome's epistles.

These eighty-seven *Catalogus* entries represent the most straightforward of the borrowings of *Registrum* location numbers for Jerome epistles. The locations assigned to another twelve *Catalogus* entries for Jerome epistles are peculiar, making us wish we understood Kirkestede's purpose: to *Catalogus* entry *281.142* Kirkestede assigned the first five library numbers from the *Registrum*'s entry for the collection (*Registrum 6. 78*); for *Catalogus 281.143*, Kirkestede borrowed the eighth to the thirteenth location numbers in the *Registrum* series; for *281.144*, Kirkestede borrowed the fifteenth to the twenty-first numbers in the *Registrum* entry (with one omission, **82** for Bury); for *281.146* and *281.150*, he gave a series, once of four and once of five numbers, identical with the thirty-first to the thirty-fourth or thirty-fifth numbers in the *Registrum* entry for Jerome's epistles; and for *281.152*, Kirkestede gave the single location number **15**, selected apparently at random from the *Registrum*'s entry, followed by the first three location numbers (again) in the *Registrum* sequence. One of the Jerome letters in the *Catalogus* (*281.151*) is recorded individually in the *Registrum* also (*Registrum 6. 100*); and so Kirkestede copied the location numbers from that entry, as well as adding two numbers from his base

(*Registrum* 6. 78) for good measure. The remaining five Jerome epistles listed in the *Catalogus* (*281.128, 130, 145, 147, 221*) each have from one to three location numbers taken without obvious pattern from *Registrum* 6. 78.

c. Criteria for distinguishing Kirkestede's added locations

Kirkestede's borrowing of *Registrum* location numbers was extensive, complex, often based on uncertain assumptions, and—it must be said—at times without discernible reason. Nevertheless, he did add information of his own, which is a valuable addition to our knowledge of the contents of English monastic and chapter libraries. Therefore, we need to establish criteria for distinguishing those location numbers that represent Kirkestede's first-hand knowledge of books and their locations. On rare occasions there is clear and unambiguous evidence;[101] much of the time, however, we simply face varying degrees of probability.

If a title in the *Catalogus* is followed by any or all of the location numbers supplied for this same title in the *Registrum*, we assume that the numbers were borrowed. Even if other evidence should suggest that a location number in the *Registrum* series, such as **15** (St Albans), represents a library that Kirkestede also knew at first hand, he has usually just copied the *Registrum*'s information; this was often the case even for Bury (**82**) itself. If a *Catalogus* title is copied from the *Registrum* but some or all of the location numbers are not found with that title in the *Registrum*, these additional numbers may represent Kirkestede's first-hand knowledge; but such numbers remain suspect. As the examples of the Origen homilies or of Augustine's 'De pascha' demonstrated, such seemingly 'added' location numbers may be the result of Kirkestede's misidentification of a title, or the result of a mistaken assumption, or the result of scribal error (by Kirkestede himself, or in his copy of *Registrum*, or in Tanner's transcript)—possibilities for inaccurate borrowings are many.[102]

The *Catalogus* is much larger than the *Registrum*, however. It contains 674 authors to the *Registrum*'s 99, and provides even for those authors like Augustine and Jerome who appear in both catalogues a much longer list of works, many of which are supplied with location numbers. Numbers that follow titles not found in the *Registrum* usually represent Kirkestede's first-hand knowledge—barring cases of mistaken identity, or of injudicious assumptions such as the example of Jerome's epistles (see above). Of course,

---

101. For example, the citation of a specific manuscript of Lawrence of Westminster (*358.1*) demonstrates beyond reasonable doubt that Kirkestede knew manuscripts from **11** Westminster at first hand.
102. See p. xvi above.

if the location number is one referred to only in the *Catalogus*, such as **61** Peterborough or **65** Ramsey, or if it represents one of the locations that Kirkestede added to the list, such as **173** Babwell, these indicate Kirkestede's first-hand knowledge of the library (barring, as always, copying errors).

The frequency of occurrence of a location number is one guide to its validity. A number used frequently by the *Registrum*, but scarcely ever with works that appear in the *Catalogus* alone, is suspicious. However, a few of the libraries that the Franciscans reported heavily in the *Registrum* were also reported generously by Kirkestede at first hand in the *Catalogus*, most notably St Albans (**15**) and Bury itself (**82**). Proportions should be weighed: for example, a location number may have been copied forty times into the *Catalogus* directly from the *Registrum*; if, moreover, the number should appear in the *Catalogus* three times as an addition to titles taken from the *Registrum*, and once more with a *Catalogus* work taken from elsewhere, the last four appearances are not above doubt. But if a number appears in the *Catalogus* only four times in all—three times added to a *Registrum* title and once with a non-*Registrum* title, these four appearances may well indicate that Kirkestede had first-hand and current information about this library.

Finally, two external factors must be taken into account in determining the import of each location number. The most obvious is the distance, or in some cases the accessibility, of a given library from Bury St Edmunds. There is no evidence to suggest that Kirkestede travelled across England, through Wales and Scotland, and to the Isle of Wight, recording books; even the Oxford Franciscans, with a good-sized group of surveyors and with greater mobility than Kirkestede, failed to visit more than half of the libraries on their list, which they had drawn up in advance.[103] As common sense would suggest, Kirkestede's first-hand information is restricted to East Anglian libraries, as well as two in London and one in Oxford. Aside from propinquity, one final external factor consists of notes in Kirkestede's hand in surviving Bury manuscripts that refer to specific book collections, in the neighbourhood of Bury, in London, or in Oxford. Although only seven of the libraries reported in the *Catalogus* are mentioned in surviving notes, the notes suffice to tip the balance for two of these, Walden (**68**) and Sibton (**77**), indicating that a location number used only three times in the *Catalogus* may represent valid first-hand information about the contents of a 14th-cent. monastic library.

If these criteria are applied in concert, it appears that the *Catalogus* contributes information concerning the following libraries, listed in descending

---

103. They visited, it seems, only ninety of the some 187 libraries on their list; the exact number on the list is variable, depending on interpretation of the number left blank and the numbers duplicated on the *Registrum* list.

order of the number of times each was cited (not borrowed) by Kirkestede.[104]

82 Bury *passim*
65 Ramsey (126)
83 Colchester St John's (124)
84 Colchester St Botulph's (45)
74 Holme St Benets (38)
15 St Albans (36)
61 Peterborough (32)
50 Pipewell (31)
63 Crowland (27)
10 Holy Trinity Aldgate (25)
170 Thetford Blackfriars (20)

173 Babwell (19)
168 Oxford Greyfriars (17)
86 Coggeshall (12)
73 Norwich Cathedral (12)
11 Westminster (10)
45 Warden (8)
147 Spalding (6)
175 Barking (4)
68 Walden (3)
77 Sibton (3)

In addition Kirkestede probably had knowledge of books at the following locations: **85** St Osyth's (11), **81** Ipswich St Peter's (10), **79** Butley (9), **169** Ixworth (1). And he possibly had knowledge of the following: **166** Hexham (29),[105] **42** Reading (23), **43** Woburn (22), **19** London St Paul's (11), **80** Ipswich Holy Trinity (8), **14** Stratford Langthorne (4), **64** Barnwell (3), **67** Ely (3), **44** Dunstable (2), **174** Earls Colne (2), **62** Thorney (1), and **78** Leiston (1).

d. Kirkestede's knowledge of East Anglian libraries

Kirkestede acquired his knowledge of the contents of these libraries by visiting them himself. No evidence suggests any more elaborate procedure, such as organized visits made by other monks under Kirkestede's direction. All the information about locations (save the borrowings from the *Registrum*) are the work of one man, possibly aided by the chance report of a fellow monk of a text seen at another house. Kirkestede travelled to other religious houses such as Ramsey or Norwich presumably on official business of the abbey, and he recorded the locations of various texts as he found them among the books of the monasteries that he visited.

Some convincing evidence supports this picture. Kirkestede recorded in the *Catalogus* a collection of sermons with the incipit 'Ut tota cum . . .', which he attributed to Lawrence of Durham (*Catalogus 358.1*) and located at

---

104. For an evaluation of the use of each individual location number, see appendix to the edition, p. 540 below.
105. Hexham is the most unlikely member of the group; see the appendix to the text, p. 572 below, under **166**.

Westminster.[106] A Westminster manuscript of these sermons survives as Oxford, Balliol College, MS 232; the proper incipit of the text, '*Dignum est, fratres*, ut tota cum . . .' is incomplete because the rubricator did not enter the first words (in italics here), making it almost certainly the very book that Kirkestede saw at Westminster.

He must also have been at Norwich cathedral, to enable him to note regarding the *Cantelarium* of Astulphus (*72.1*), 'and the work fills three folios, and is located at 73 [= Norwich cathedral priory] in the dormitory library'.[107] The quite circumstantial notes in his hand that appear at the end of several texts, referring to specific manuscripts at Sibton, Coggeshall, Babwell, Walden, and elsewhere also confirm that Kirkestede visited the libraries of these houses.[108] Corroboration that he visited other monasteries rests in the fact that all the libraries for which the *Catalogus* supplies additional location information (with the exception of the one at Oxford and the houses in and on the way to London) are within two or three days' journey from Bury, and most are closer still.

With the exceptions of St Albans (**15**), Crowland (**63**), and Bury itself (**82**),[109] Kirkestede presents information for libraries not cited in the *Registrum*. In some cases these are locations on the *Registrum* list that were not, in the event, reported in the *Registrum*, and in other cases they are houses whose names Kirkestede added. However, one must understand that he did not attempt to present anything like a catalogue of the contents of the libraries that he chanced to visit. The *Catalogus* is absolutely not, as it has sometimes been characterized, a union catalogue, not even of the neighbouring libraries that Kirkestede knew at first hand. He often referred to these locations only for the specific purpose of supplying additional authors and works, or supplying additional works for authors already on his list, or furnishing incipits and explicits for titles which he had already taken from other sources. Thus, for example, he added Ixworth (**169**) and Barking (**175**) to his list of locations solely in order to record unusual works that he found there: a codex of sermons of Richard of Ely (*526.1*) at Ixworth, and a codex with four unknown pastoral works attributed to Ralph of Flaix (*494.11–14*) at Barking. Conversely, his selections often strike one as arbitrary, reporting from a given location works that must have been available at others of the

---

106. A double error is involved here. The Lawrence in question was Lawrence of Westminster, not Lawrence of Durham; and the sermons were collected, not composed, by Lawrence of Westminster.
107. 'Et continet tria folia et est apud 73 in libraria dormitorii'; entry *72.1*.
108. See the text of these notes, p. lvi above.
109. And the possible exception of **42** Reading as well.

libraries he knew. Probably this is just one more indication (there are many) that the *Catalogus* was, and remained, a work in progress.

No method is perceptible in his procedure of collecting first-hand information—no standard 'Order of Entry' for the location numbers such as one sees in the *Registrum*. He seemingly visited the majority of these houses more than once, picking up additional information each time the opportunity arose. This would have been the case particularly for those houses closely related to Bury, such as Holme St Benets and Ramsey, or especially close geographically, such as Thetford or Babwell. He apparently inserted new location numbers wherever there was space for them on his draft entry, between the lines and between the previously-copied numbers, obscuring whatever pattern of work there might have been.

The majority of works for which manuscripts were his source Kirkestede found in the Bury library. The percentage of incipits and explicits that were derived from Bury manuscripts (even for titles provided by another source) is even greater. In 239 instances, location number **82** (Bury) is given as the source for works that Kirkestede has added; and in 189 other instances the incipit and explicit were added from Bury manuscripts to titles taken from the *Registrum* (along with the number **82**). Even when his *Registrum* source itself cited the location number **82**, Kirkestede customarily added the incipit and explicit from the Bury manuscript when the *Registrum* entry had none. In many instances, moreover, he did not add the Bury location number even though evidence shows that incipits and explicits have come from Bury manuscripts.[110] Because Kirkestede was writing at Bury, for the benefit of Bury novices and monks, perhaps he thought it redundant to be constantly recording Bury as the source of his information; but his motives are unknowable. However, we assume that on virtually every occasion when a work entered in the *Catalogus* has an incipit and explicit but no location number, the source was a Bury manuscript.

Entries supplied from manuscripts at locations that he knew at first hand, such as Colchester (**83**) or Ramsey (**65**), take their incipits and explicits from the manuscripts in those libraries. He did not always record them; for instance, of 126 works located at Ramsey, twenty-four are listed without incipits and explicits. The majority of location numbers added by Kirkestede

---

110. See, for example, Jerome *281.22–27*, where the location numbers are simply borrowings from the *Registrum* but the incipits and explicits have come from a Bury manuscript that survives (Bodl. MS e Musaeo 26). For a work clearly dependent on a Bury manuscript, without **82** for Bury nor indeed with any location at all, see Gildas *229.1*. Or see the series of titles all taken from the same Bury manuscript in the entry for Hugh, followed by one (*244.83*) to which he did not bother to add **82**.

appear individually, though they occasionally occur in series of three or even four.[111]

The location numbers that Kirkestede copied from the *Registrum* include a significant proportion of peculiarities, for a variety of reasons. It is in the nature of things that the location numbers added by Kirkestede (as transcribed in Add. 3470) must also include their share of mistakes. Within the category of works that Kirkestede added to the *Catalogus* from (apparently) first-hand information, the location numbers of fifty-five libraries that he almost certainly did not visit are recorded at least once. While some of these would doubtless be explained away if his working method were entirely understood, and while others may in some roundabout way have come from his text of the *Registrum*, at present one can only assume that most of these result from copying errors. A surprising proportion of the suspicious numbers congregate at certain titles, or after the works of certain authors. Perhaps the most conspicuous example is the entry of six works for the Roman poet and satirist Horace (*411.1–6*), whose biography Kirkestede took from Vincent of Beauvais and whose works he described from a single Bury volume ('Oratius totus in uno volumine', B13. 173) and from another codex at **63** Crowland; but to each of the six titles, along with the genuine locations at Bury and Crowland, have been added the location numbers of one or two other libraries that Kirkestede almost certainly did not know at first hand, for a total of six odd locations: **22** Chichester (Sussex), **27** Romsey (Hants), **37** Osney (Oxon), **53** Lenton (Notts), **75** Langley (Norf; the only appearance of this number in either the *Catalogus* or the *Registrum*), and **92** Dunkeswell (Devon).[112]

A final caveat to bear in mind is this: when Kirkestede added to a *Catalogus* entry a location number referring to a library that he knew at first hand, this in itself does not confirm that the work in question was available there. It means, rather, that in Kirkestede's judgement there was a work in that library identical with the work in the entry. When he added one of 'his' numbers to a series otherwise borrowed from the *Registrum*, or to a title taken from a secondary source, such a location number should not be treated as a precise identification, but as evidence that there was some work at that location which Kirkestede took to be the same, perhaps as a casual

---

111. Unusually long series of location numbers for 'Kirkestede' libraries appear in the entries for Eusebius Emissenus (*162.5*) **11**, **15**, **61**, **74**, **65**; Sibilla (*550.1*) **83**, **82**, **74**, **63**, **43**, **44**; and Smaragdus (*553.1*) **83**, **82**, **63**, **61**, **65**.
112. See also Gratian (*217*) with suspect numbers **53**, **14**; John of Tynmouth (*341.1*) with suspect numbers **162**, **147**; Paterius (*437*) with suspect numbers **16**, **105**, **13**, **139**; Robert Grosseteste (*505.35*) with suspect numbers **164**, **154**; and Robert Kilwardby (*510*) with suspect numbers **1**, **2**, **119**, **8**.

assumption, perhaps from memory—he would not have had his growing *Catalogus* with him at all times (maybe it never left the abbey), to compare with books he sought out or chanced upon at other places. For example, see the entry for the *De assumptione B. Mariae* of 'Anselm' (*3.33*, the work of Ambrose Autpert); Kirkestede took not only the title but also the incipit from one of his secondary sources, the *Mariale*, but he added the location numbers **73** Holy Trinity Norwich and **65** Ramsey, libraries that he knew at first hand. All that one can deduce with certainty from such an entry, though, is the fact that he saw, or remembered having seen, something at each of these places that he believed was probably the same as the work mentioned in the *Mariale*.

In our judgement, Kirkestede certainly supplied first-hand information concerning twenty-one 14th-cent. monastic libraries, probably concerning four others, and possibly concerning another eleven. But just as each library's status must be separately considered, so the individual appearance of each number is a separate case, and its potential validity must be individually weighed. Interpretation of the location numbers in the *Catalogus* demands serious efforts from readers.

The **Nomina doctorum**

Following the last title for the last author (Zoroastes, *674.1*), the *Catalogus* concludes with a section headed *Nomina doctorum qui scribunt super Bibliam*, 'Names of doctors who write on the bible', a list of commentators on the scriptures arranged according to the books of the bible. For each book the *Nomina doctorum* supplies the names of commentators taken from the *Catalogus* in the order of their appearance. Kirkestede included commentaries on whole books of the bible, citing merely the author's name, and expositions on shorter passages, for which he often supplied the title. In most cases this first alphabetical portion of the list is followed by a second group of from one to eleven commentators entered at random. The names not integrated into the alphabetical scheme indicate that the *Nomina doctorum* was created in the same fashion as the entries in the *Catalogus* itself—that is, by a concentrated effort that represents an initial search, followed by additional names as he came upon them.

As a record of biblical commentaries in the *Catalogus* the *Nomina doctorum* is incomplete. Kirkestede evidently overlooked some names,[113] and for other

---

113. For example, Ansbert (*21*), Hilduin (*279*), John of Tynemouth (*341*), and Etienne de Bourgogne (*555*). It is possible that he added these names to the *Catalogus* after having completed the *Nomina doctorum*.

authors he omitted one or two commentaries from a long list of their exegetical writings.[114] In one instance Kirkestede misread his own entry for Philo Judaeus 'In 5to libro Moysi' (*Catalogus 452.1*), treating it in the *Nomina doctorum* as if it read 'In 5 libris Moysi' and recording Philo's name under each book of the pentateuch. In perhaps two dozen cases, the lists in the *Nomina doctorum* include names not found in the text of the *Catalogus*.[115] These names may reflect Kirkestede's very broad interpretation of his own titles in the *Catalogus*. More likely, they are additions from other sources, included to make the list even more comprehensive.

This list of names is a revealing conclusion to the *Catalogus*, presenting in tabular form the authorities who interpret the central authoritative text of Christendom, the scriptures. The end, thus, harks back to the *Catalogus*'s introduction on 'authentic and apocryphal books,' which opens with a lengthy consideration of the bible's composition beginning, 'Omnis divina scriptura in duobus Testamentis continetur'.[116] The *Nomina doctorum* ties the biblical focus of the introduction and conclusion to the body of the *Catalogus*, Kirkestede's bibliography of 'Doctors who write'.

---

114. For example, Ambrose Super Cantica canticorum (*2.21*), Berengar Super Apocalipsin (*82.3*), Hillary of Poitiers Super Epistolas canonicas (*242.8*), or Stephen Langton Super Job and Super Ecclesiasten (*554.24, 25*).
115. For example, Andrew Super Tobiam, Claudius Super Johannem, Gilbert Super Deuteronomium, Maximus Super Evangelia, Origen Super Danielem, Robert Crikelade Super Ezechielem—not to mention a commentary on Ruth by 'quidam monachus'.
116. 'Omnis diuina scriptura—in eodem populo': excerpted from Hugh of Saint-Victor, *Didascalicon* IV 2, 3 and 8.

CHAPTER 3

KIRKESTEDE AND
THE *SPECULUM COENOBITARUM*

A short treatise on the history of monks and monasticism was printed in 1722, entitled *Speculum coenobitarum* and attributed to 'John Boston'.[1] The editor, Anthony Hall, transcribed the text from a manuscript at his own college, Oxford, The Queen's College, MS 304 (fols. 58r–66v), which had neither a title nor an author ascription. More than two centuries later, W. A. Pantin studied the *Speculum coenobitarum* and its versions as a group and sorted out the work's component parts, the only scholarly investigation of this text.[2] We wish to single out the evidence that points to Henry of Kirkestede as the author of the work's main revision.[3]

The Two Versions of the Speculum coenobitarum

The *Speculum coenobitarum* (*SC*), composed by an anonymous monk of Bury St Edmunds, served as textbook and reference work for novice monks, and would have proved a useful handbook for older monks as well. The *SC* consists of a brief history that traces the origins of monasticism back to the Old Testament, followed principally by lists of famous monks sorted by category: saints, authors, missionaries, and monks who wrote a rule or founded an order.[4] The text

1. A. Hall, *Nicolai Triveti Annalium continuatio, ut et Adami Murimuthensis Chronicon* . . . (Oxford 1722) 157–92. Hall silently classicized the manuscript's spelling, and added the profuse capitalization typical of his era.
2. W. A. Pantin, 'Some medieval English treatises on the origins of monasticism', in *Medieval Studies Presented to Rose Graham* (Oxford 1950), 189–215. Pantin belatedly reassigned his *sigla* for the manuscripts and overlooked some anomalies; therefore, Anthony Hall's base manuscript (Oxford, The Queen's College, MS 304, C in the introductory list of manuscripts on p. 190) is cited as Q throughout the text of the article; cf. p. 196. Pantin's history of the *Speculum coenobitarum* is restated by Knowles, *Religious Orders*, 2. 270–71.
3. This chapter is consciously confined to the question of Kirkestede's involvement. It is not the place for an edition of the versions of the *Speculum coenobitarum* with a full-scale study of the work in context.
4. The section on rules contains a certain amount of narrative prose in the unique manuscript of the original *Speculum coenobitarum*, but it is converted to just a list of names in the more widely-circulated revision.

survives wholly or in part in eight manuscripts ranging in date from the 1360s to the middle of the 15th cent.; none bears an author ascription or title.[5] The manuscripts reflect two stages in the text's development and the subsequent dispersal of its individual parts.[6]

The original version of the *SC* (not Hall's text) survives in a single manuscript, BAV MS Reg. lat. 127, with an unexpected provenance: it was copied for Hugh de Chiverey, abbot (1361–7) of the Benedictine abbey of Tournus in Burgundy. Considering the date and the place, we suggest that this small treatise may have been carried from Bury to Tournus in the baggage of Bury's abbot-elect Henry of Hunstanton in July 1361 as he was making his way to Avignon for papal confirmation.[7] Tournus on the Saône is a plausible stopping point for Hunstanton and his entourage on the journey south. BAV MS Reg. lat. 127 was compiled and written entirely at Tournus, as an effaced flyleaf note records: 'Hugh of Chiverey . . . caused this volume to be written to the edification of the monastic life . . . All these [works] were diligently collected by a monk of the aforesaid father, who says "Accept with favour, Father Hugh, the labour of your child"'.[8] The codex is primarily

---

5. We have examined the principal manuscripts at first hand, but we are also greatly indebted to Pantin, 'English treatises', who lists the following manuscripts. Original *SC*, BAV MS Reg. lat. 127, fols. 164v–179v (Tournus, *c.* 1361–7). Revised *SC*, Oxford, The Queen's College, MS 304, fols. 58r–66v (Glastonbury, *c.* 1401–20); the same, with an added part, in BL MS Cotton Vitellius E. xii, fols. 56r–70r (Durham, *c.* 1416–46). Excerpts from *SC*: Bodl. MS Bodley 240, pp. 765–769 (from original *SC*; Bury, *c.* 1377); BL MS Cotton Claudius E. iv, fols. 322v–331v (from the revised *SC*; St Albans, before 1394); BL MS Arundel 507, fol. 78v (from revised *SC*; Durham, *c.* 1396); Durham Cathedral, MS B. IV. 41, fol. 33r (from revised *SC*; Durham, *c.* 1431–55); and York Minster Library, MS XVI.K.5, fol. 223r (from revised *SC*; Cambridge Carmelites, s. xv).

6. Pantin described another six manuscripts, ranging in date from the early 15th cent. to the mid 16th, that may in part reflect the influence of *SC*: Durham Cathedral, MS B. III. 30, fols. 1r–55r, BL MS Harley 3775, BL MS Cotton Claudius A. xii, fol. 139ff., Cambridge, Gonville and Caius College, MS 230/116, fol. 42r, Bodl. MS Gough Essex 1, fol. 12r, and BL MS Harley 4843.

7. Concerning Hunstanton's journey to Avignon in 1361 see above, p. lxvi. There may well have been other Bury emissaries to and from Avignon in the course of these years.

8. 'Istud volumen ad edificacionem monastice vite . . . [*three effaced and largely illegible lines, in which one can read the following:*] conscribi fecit . . . Hugo de Chiueriaco . . . [*and the following, effaced but legible:*] Ista omnia collegit cum magna diligencia quidam monachus supradicti patris, qui sic dicit: Sume tui pueri, pater Hugo, benigne laborem . . .' [cf. Jdt 11:4]; BAV MS Reg. lat. 127, fol. ii^v, quoted from the description of A. Wilmart, *Codices Reginenses latini*, 2 vols (Vatican City 1937–45), i. 302–303. A note added on the back flyleaf, fol. 182v, recording that Duke Philip the Bold of Burgundy on 17 November 1366 rendered homage to Abbot Hugh for property held of the abbey, can have been added at any time on or after that date.

devoted to two works of Bernard Ayglier of Monte Cassino, his commentary on the Benedictine Rule (fols. 1r–117v) and his *Speculum monachorum* (fols. 120v–160r). Fols. 164v–179v contain the work from Bury, the original version of the *SC* (untitled), which is divided into three parts:[9]

> Pt 1 fols. 164v–173v. An explanation of the origins of monasticism in twelve chapters, written by 'a monk of the monastery of St Edmund in England'.[10] The text begins (fol. 165r), 'Tradunt philosophi naturales . . . Quidam etenim minus intelligentes . . .', and sets out monasticism's pre-Benedictine biblical and apostolic roots, the origins of the habit and the tonsure, the place of Benedict's rule (cc. 1–9), a consideration of hermits and anchorites, as well as a consideration of those whose example is to be avoided, the Sarabaites and the Girovagi. It concludes, 'Explicit generalis tractatus de cenobitis veteris et noui testamenti.'
>
> Pt 2 fols. 173v–175v. This is a list of 210 monks venerated as saints, from Longinus to Grimbard and Godefridus, once again said to have been compiled by 'a monk of St Edmund'.[11] The opening rubric names his sources in detail.[12] This is followed by an eight-line verse, notable because it repeatedly crops up in different guises throughout the subsequent tradition of the *SC*: 'Vates cunctorum sunt antiqui monachorum / Auctores dicti vatum natique relicti' etc.[13] The text proper begins 'Sanctus Longinus qui lancea latus Christi aperuit', and after the end a space is left blank, with the marginal heading, 'Space for inserting more names of monks that are saints'.[14] No names have been added.

9. The two works of Bernard of Monte Cassino were also available at Bury St Edmunds (see the notes to *Catalogus 86.1–2*), so it is possible that Hunstanton, or whoever it was who brought the *SC* text to Tournus, could in fact have brought a book from Bury containing all three of the texts that have been copied in BAV MS Reg. lat. 127. In that case, of course, Abbot Hugh's diligent monk was slightly exaggerating his own contribution to the collection.
10. 'Composuit quidam monachus monasterii sancti Edmundi de Bury in Anglia'; BAV MS Reg. lat. 127, fol. 164v.
11. 'Quidam monachus de sancto Edmundo'; ibid. fol. 174r.
12. 'Capitulacio breuis sanctorum monachorum quam quidam monachus de sancto Edmundo collegit ex pluribus locis scripturarum, videlicet ex opusculis Ieronimi et libris Cassiani de institutis patrum et collacionibus eorum .xxiiii., ex libro Ianuensis de Antichristo, historia tripartita et de historia ecclesiastica et historia Longobardorum et historia Anglorum, ex speculo historiali, ex libris Genadii et Ysidori de viris illustribus, ex libro Heraclidis qui dicitur paradisus, ex legenda aurea et legendis originalibus, ex libris dialogorum Gregorii et dialogorum Postumiani et Severi'; ibid.
13. The full verse is printed by Pantin, 'English treatises', 192.
14. 'Spacium pro pluribus nominibus sanctorum monachorum inserendis'; ibid. fol. 175r.

Pt 3 fols. 175v–179v. A discussion of twelve other religious orders, beginning, 'Sequitur de aliis ordinibus. Alii sunt ordines, ut canonici regulares, Grandemontenses, Cartusienses, Cistercienses . . .', and including the orders of friars. This section, not specifically attributed, was doubtless also compiled by a Bury monk as were parts 1 and 2.[15]

The date when this original version was compiled can be framed only by the latest works cited, the works of Thomas Aquinas (d. 1274) and the *Sext* (1300) on the one hand, and the date of the only surviving manuscript (1361–7) on the other.

Although someone carried off to Tournus a copy of this first version of *SC*, the continued presence of the original at Bury is betrayed by echoes and revisions. Presumably the earliest excerpt from *SC* occurred when most of part 1, the history of monasticism, was incorporated into a collection of tracts for novices, along with a short prologue created for the occasion. But we know of this collection for novices only because it, in turn, was later copied into a compendium written in 1377 at the expense of the Bury monk Roger of Huntingdon (Bodl. MS Bodley 240, Bury H. 55). Bodley 240 was compiled at Bury from earlier works and earlier collections available at the abbey—part 2 of the *Historia aurea* of John of Tynemouth,[16] followed by excerpts from his *Sanctilogium* and *Martyrologium*,[17] interspersed with other saints' lives, a long collection of St Edmund legends (pp. 623–677), and the compilation for the instruction of novices (pp. 765–848). Dating the earlier source material that went into the compilation is speculative. A date-frame for some of these materials occurs from the fact that Henry of Kirkestede has been associated with their origin,[18] including a collection of miracles of

---

15. Part 3 is immediately followed (BAV MS Reg. lat. 127, fols. 179v–181r) by a lengthy *quaestio* contrasting the relative merits of mendicants and possessioners; Pantin, 'English treatises', 194, treats this as part 4 of the *Speculum*, and he prints much of it on pp. 212–14. In its scholastic presentation ('Questio utrum perfeccior sit ordo mendicancium vel possessionatorum. Dicto breuiter . . . Primo. . . Secundo. . . Tercio. . . Quarto. . .') and in its apologetic or even polemic intent, this element seems completely out of place; we doubt it belongs to the *Speculum coenobitarum* or its author. Since there is no other copy of the original version for comparison, the matter cannot be settled. Whatever its origin, this tract does not persist in the tradition of the *Speculum*.

16. See V. H. Galbraith, 'The *Historia aurea* of John vicar of Tynemouth, and the sources of the St Albans chronicle 1327–1377', in *Essays in History presented to R. L. Poole* (Oxford 1927), 379–98.

17. Concerning both works see Sharpe, *Latin Writers*, 333–4. Bodl. MS Bodley 240 is described by C. Horstmann, *Nova legenda Anglie*, 2 vols (Oxford 1901), 1. lvii–lxv.

18. Both James, *St Edmund*, 69, and Pantin, 'English Treatises', 195–6, suggested that 'Boston of Bury' may have been involved in the compilation of Bodley 240. R. M. Thomson carried this a stage further, singling out the parts that he judged must surely have originated with Kirkestede; see his 'The Library and Archives of Bury St. Edmunds Abbey', PhD diss. (Sydney 1973), 1. 133–6.

St Edmund (complete with copious bibliographical citations).[19] Kirkestede himself figures in one of these accounts: in 1349 he and a younger monk, Thomas of Thakstede, vouched for a Bury man well known to them, John Langwood, when Langwood belatedly reported a miracle St Edmund had wrought years earlier.[20] As a boy, he said, he had carelessly broken his father's axe in two; but in response to his childish tears and prayers, St Edmund repaired the axe and spared him a severe beating. Langwood's narrative, with Thakstede's and Kirkestede's names as witnesses to Langwood's character, appears in the collection of Edmund legends copied into Bodley 240.[21] There would seem also to be a connexion to Kirkestede in this manuscript's numerous references that locate, physically, either the source of a given extract or another copy: references to Babwell (Bodley 240, p. 598), to Ramsey and Holme St Benets (p. 605), to a Bury book of the legends of English saints with the class-mark S. 146 (p. 621), to the priory of Thetford (p. 622–623), to a charter in the shrine of St Edmund kept in the chest with the indulgences and bulls (p. 648), to the charterhouse in London (pp. 708 and 719), and to the abbey at Saffron Walden (p. 820). Perhaps the location notes represent marginal annotations (presumably Kirkestede's) in an earlier copy, now incorporated into the text of Bodley 240.

The part of the material in Bodley 240 intended for the instruction of novices starts with the extract from *SC*, under the rubric *De origine monachorum tam veteris quam noui testamenti* (an echo of the colophon to part 1 of the *SC* quoted above).[22] The changes from the original version are these: a new

19. Sources cited, nearly always in the margin but sometimes in the rubric, include the bulls of translation, the Book of the Childhood of St Edmund by Geoffrey of Fountains (a monk of Bury), chronicles of Roger of Howden and Henry of Huntingdon, Abbo of Fleury, the chronicles of Westminster, Norwich, Ely, London, Marianus Scottus, and [John of] Wallingford, Abbot Sampson's book of the miracles of St Edmund, Book II of William of Malmesbury's *Gesta pontificum*, a book 'de Bliburgh', the Miracles of St Edmund in the collection of Archdeacon Herman, Book VIII of John of Salisbury's *Policraticus*, the chronicle of Jocelin of Brakelond, Osbert of Clare, prior of Westminster, a service book at the shrine of St Edmund, and the chronicles of the abbey—followed by records of more recent miracles as recounted by witnesses. Some of these sources are referred to several times, but the usual procedure was to exhaust one source before moving on to the next. Concerning Kirkestede's interest in the Edmund legends see chapter 1 above.
20. Thakstede was ordained some eleven or twelve years after Kirkestede's ordination, i.e. in December 1349 or perhaps 1350 (the record-keeping was momentarily disrupted by the Black Death); Lisle register, fol. 96vb.
21. Bodl. MS Bodley 240, p. 675, 'De securi fracto et miraculose reparato' ('The broken axe that was miraculously repaired'). The miracle is printed from this manuscript in Arnold, *Memorials*, 3. 339.
22. 'Explicit generalis tractatus de cenobitis veteris et noui testamenti'; BAV MS Reg. lat. 127, fol. 173v.

prologue aimed expressly at the instruction of novices was added; parts 2 and 3 were omitted; and only the first nine chapters of part 1 were retained, beginning 'Tradunt philosophi naturales . . . Quidam etenim minus intelligentes . . .'.[23] The result is a much simplified history of monasticism, from the time of the Old Testament until its culmination in the rule of Benedict. The creation of this condensed *SC* can be dated no more closely than after 1300 (the earliest possible date of the first version) and before 1377 (the date of Bodley 240); because it derived from the original version, however, it presumably antedated the popular reworking described below.

The principal revision of *SC* is the version that became most widespread. The compiler of version 2 restructured the original and enlarged it into five parts, for sharper definition and a change of emphasis. The first part was compressed, but its bibliographical citations were much increased in number. The second part (the list of 210 monastic saints) was subdivided and expanded into three separate categories: monastic saints, monastic authors, and monastic missionaries (parts 2–4); the original third part, the list and discussion of monastic orders, was replaced by a concise list of names and dates (pt 5). This expanded and restructured version was the form in which the *SC* spread from Bury to other houses in England. As with the previous versions, we cannot precisely date the making of the revision. Excerpts from it were made in places as distant from one another as St Albans and Durham before the end of the 14th cent., and early 15th-cent. copies and enlargements of the revision survive from St Albans and Durham as well. The revised *SC* was taken also to the Benedictine house at Glastonbury by the early 15th cent., where it was copied into an historical miscellany, now Oxford, The Queen's College, MS 304 (the chronicles of Peter of Ickham, Nicolas Trevet, and Adam of Merrymouth, with genealogies of the kings of England and lists of the abbots of Glastonbury) that was acquired for the abbey *c*. 1401–20 by the Glastonbury monk John Moorlinch.[24] These later manuscripts document a continuing interest in the early history of monasticism *c*. 1400. The principal St Albans and Durham manuscripts,

---

23. See above, the description of BAV MS Reg. lat. 127 pt 1, at p. cxxvii.
24. K. L. Scott, *Later Gothic Manuscripts, 1390–1490*, 2 vols (London 1996), 2. 125–7, discusses the illuminator of Queen's College 304, the Oriel Master, whose work (on Oxford, Oriel College, MS 75) she dates *c*. 1405–15; fig. 5 (vol. 1, after p. 64) shows Queen's College 304, fol. 1r. Moorlinch was a scribe himself, whose hand is seen in Bodl. MS Laud Lat. 4, dated 1406, and a table to William of Malmesbury dated 1411; see Sharpe, *Latin Writers*, 283. The dates known for the illuminator and for Moorlinch suggest that Pantin's proffered terminus of 1420 may be a little late. See also J. J. G. Alexander and E. Temple, *Illuminated Manuscripts in Oxford College Libraries* (Oxford 1985), 43 no. 431, and the catalogue of The Queen's College manuscripts by Peter Kidd, forthcoming.

respectively BL MSS Cotton Claudius E. IV and Cotton Vitellius E. XII, were severely damaged in the Cotton fire of 1731. Therefore one knows the text of the revised *SC* almost entirely through the undamaged Glastonbury manuscript, now Oxford, The Queen's College, MS 304, fols. 58r–66v, described as follows.[25]

Pt 1, fol. 58r: A tract on the origins and early history of monasticism. The first four lines of the verse 'Vates cunctorum sunt antiqui monachorum . . .' (see BAV MS Reg. lat. 127, fol. 174r) were prefixed in lieu of a title or rubric, followed by a shortened introduction taken from the introduction to pt 1 of version 1, beginning 'Quidam minus intelligentes . . .'.[26] Next is a compressed form of the original pt 1 cc. 1–9 (from the Old Testament to Benedict); cc. 10–12 (hermits, Sarabaites, and Girovagi) were dropped. The focus thus becomes strictly an exposition of the roots of Benedictine monasticism, not controversy.

Pt 2, fol. 59v: A list of 290 monastic saints, to which are prefixed the second four lines of the verse found on BAV MS Reg. lat. 127, fol. 174r ('Nomina sanctorum subscribuntur monachorum . . .'). The revision adds roughly eighty names to the list of saints found in pt 2 of the first version, comprising around twenty pre-Benedict and around sixty post-Benedict.

Pt 3, fol. 62r: A list of fifty-nine monastic authors and their works, almost every author being introduced with a biographical notice, however brief. The section opens with another quatrain, modelled after those borrowed from version 1 ('Nomina doctorum subscribuntur monachorum . . .', edited below). This list of writers is a new creation. Although the number of names is small compared to the list of saints that precedes it, the inclusion of a list of works for each monastic author readily makes this the dominant part of the revised version.

Pt 4, fol. 65v: A list of thirty-six early medieval missionaries, prefaced by one line of verse with the same metre as the verses previously quoted, 'Iam monachi restant fidei qui semina prestant'. This section also was new to the revision; it comprises little more than a list of names, with their dates and their mission fields.

Pt 5, fol. 66r: A list of twenty monks who wrote rules or founded orders. This section also is new. Compared with pt 3 of the first version, the number of names has been increased; but there is virtually no prose, merely a list of names and dates.

The revised *SC* took its inspiration and many of its words from the original treatise. But it explicitly refers to additional sources, and took new inform-

25. This is the manuscript that Hall printed in 1722.

ation from them. It ends (fol. 66v) with an extended colophon that attributes the revised work to a monk of Bury. In the process, it deftly recapitulates the various parts of this version (history, saints, authors, missionaries, founders), and emphasizes the common theme that present-day monks would do well to follow the example of their predecessors:

> A monk of the cloister of St Edmund, King and Martyr, excerpted the foregoing from various works and chronicles so that the monks of our day may see how glorious God made their fathers and founders, who —by their writings and teachings, signs and miracles, conversion of the nations, abundant preaching of the faith and the shedding of their blood —illuminate the world, and invigorate and strengthen the church. May Christ Jesus, Author and Lover of the monastic profession, now make monks glorious by their examples, and confirm them in the good by these most holy deeds. Amen.[27]

All later revisions, excerpts, and abridgments of *SC* are based on this revised version. The text of the revised *SC* that went to St Albans does not itself survive, but it was reworked there by Thomas Walsingham before 1394.[28]

---

26. Pantin, 'English treatises', 196. The first lines of text beside the historiated initial (a Benedictine seated by a book cupboard) are water-stained and smeared; Hall (157) therefore began his transcription at the middle of line 5, 'Religionis monastice', without troubling to mention the omission.

27. 'Ista prescripta de diuersis opusculis ac cronicis excerpsit quidam monachus de claustro sancti Edmundi regis et martiris, ut videant nostri temporis monachi quam gloriosos fecerit Deus illorum patres ac institutores qui scriptis suis et doctrinis, signis et miraculis, gentium conuersione, fidei crebra predicatione, ac sanguinis sui effusione mundum illuminant, ecclesiam roborant et confirmant. Horum exemplis iam monachos illustret, meritisque sanctissimis in bono confirmet Christus Jesus, monastice professionis auctor and amator. Amen'; Hall, 192, Pantin, 'English treatises', 197–8.

28. A manuscript of his *Gesta abbatum*, BL MS Cotton Claudius E. IV pt 1 (before 1394), fols. 322v–331v, contains a collection of short works of Walsingham's entitled *Defensio de prerogatiuis et dignitatibus ordinem monasticum concernentibus*. It incorporates verbatim excerpts from virtually all parts of the revised *Speculum coenobitarum*, and parts of the verse 'Vates cunctorum. . .' are interspersed at relevant places. For 'Vates cunctorum' see the descriptions above of BAV MS Reg. lat. 127 and Oxford, The Queen's College, MS 304. The date of Cotton Claudius E. IV is Pantin's ('English treatises', 202), based on V. H. Galbraith, *St. Albans Chronicle 1406–1420* (Oxford 1937), xxxviii, lxi. Ker, *MLGB*, dates Cotton Claudius E. IV to the 15th cent. (p. 166), but more recently, Sharpe, *Latin Writers*, 689, puts the date at the end of the 14th (before Walsingham left St Albans to become prior of Wymondham, rather than after his return). The *SC* portion of Claudius E. IV is described more fully by Pantin, 'English treatises', 202–206. The nature of Walsingham's changes to *SC* are considered by J. G. Clark, 'Thomas Walsingham reconsidered', *Speculum* 77 (2002) 832–60, at 851.

Other borrowings at St Albans survive from the 15th cent.[29] Another copy of the revised version, as we have seen, went north to Durham by *c.* 1396, when its list of the founders of monastic rules and orders was copied.[30] Further, a complete copy of the revised *SC* (BL MS Cotton Vitellius E. xii, fols. 56r–61v) was made at Durham late in the priorate of John Wessington (1416–46),[31] and the work continued to be quoted or at least echoed in Durham manuscripts until the eve of the Reformation.[32]

A sermon composed early in the 15th cent. for delivery at the General Chapter of the English Benedictines borrowed directly from *SC* for ideas, structure, and even verbatim quotation, in its opening historical survey of monasticism.[33] Regrettably, the author and the precise date are unknown. Last, we should note that three manuscripts from Bury and its surroundings, from the 15th and 16th cent., contain excerpts or echoes from the revised *Speculum coenobitarum*, attesting its continued vitality on its home ground.[34]

29. Pantin, 'English treatises', further reports borrowings from Walsingham's enlargement in BL MS Harley 3775 (before 1431) and in Cambridge, Gonville and Caius College, MS 230/116 (before 1465), both from St Albans.
30. The list appears in a miscellany of devotional extracts and texts, BL MS Arundel 507, fol. 78v, compiled by the Durham monk Richard of Segbroke. See W. A. Pantin, 'English monks before the suppression of the monasteries', *Dublin Review* 201 (1937) 250–70, at 256.
31. The manuscript, as we have noted, was damaged in the Cotton fire. Part 1 (fol. 56r–v), the history of monasticism, was reproduced from the manuscript in Dugdale's *Monasticon* before the fire. Despite its damaged state, therefore, the partially-printed Cotton Vitellius E. xii, in many places and in general shape, confirms the authenticity of the Glastonbury text.
32. Pantin, 'English treatises', 200–202, describes quotations or echoes in Durham Cathedral, MSS B. III. 30 and B. IV. 41, and BL MS Harley 4843.
33. Edited by W. A. Pantin, 'A sermon for a general chapter', *The Downside Review* 51 (1933) 291–308.
34. Pantin found the following excerpts/echoes. A manuscript from the Carmelites of Cambridge (York, Minster Library, MS XVI.K.5, fol. 223r) contains on fol. 223r in a 15th-cent. hand a copy of the quatrain 'Vates cunctorum. . .' that introduces part 1, followed by excerpts from part 5, the list of founders of rules and orders. The heading 'Mons gracie' suggests that this information was excerpted from an otherwise unknown manuscript of the *Speculum coenobitarum* at the Yorkshire charterhouse of Mount Grace. A manuscript written at Bury *c.* 1426 (BL MS Cotton Claudius A. xii; this is the *Collectanea* of Andrew Aston, hostillar of Bury) contains on fol. 139r a brief work entitled *De institucionibus ecclesiasticorum ordinum* that seems to draw widely on the revised *Speculum coenobitarum* parts 1–3 and 5; and an early 16th-cent. manuscript from the Benedictines of Colchester (Bodl. MS Gough Essex 1) contains on fol. 12r–v a list of monastic founders and rule-makers apparently influenced by the *Speculum coenobitarum* part 5.

Kirkestede as Potential Author

A. *Bale and the* Speculum

Overt attribution to Kirkestede of a work called *Speculum coenobitarum* derives from John Bale. In fact, two such works are ascribed to 'Bostonus Buriensis' in Bale's notebook:[35]

> De prima monachorum institutione, li. i. 'Primus institutor monachorum in.'
>   Nam operis collector coenobita Buriensis fuit.
>   *Ex collegio Magdalene Oxon.*
> Speculum coenobitarum, li. iij.

The first of these Bale found at Magdalen College, Oxford;[36] this same title is attached to a mid-15th-cent. copy of part 1 of the revised version in Durham Cathedral, MS B. IV. 41, fol. 33r, 'De prima institutione monachorum nigrorum'. It is worth noting that, although Bale listed it under 'Bostonus Buriensis', he implies that his manuscript merely said that its 'collector' came from the abbey at Bury, instead of bearing an attribution of authorship—and a second record in his notebook clearly treats the *Speculum coenobitarum* (again, without incipit) as anonymous. In neither entry did Bale record where he found the work entitled *Speculum coenobitarum*.

Subsequently, while Bale was in exile at Basel, he published a list of 'Boston's' writings in his *Scriptores*. The entry there offers a change:[37]

> Speculum coenobitarum, Lib. 3. *Primus institutor monachorum*
> De rebus sui coenobii, Lib. 1.
> [In opere *SC*,] prima ostendit monachorum initia ac progressus.

The *Scriptores* entry gives to the *SC* the incipit that the *Index* had assigned to *De prima monachorum institutione*, and it offers a new title, along with Bale's comment on the work.[38] Thus, in each list Bale provided two different titles, and three titles in all: *De prima institutione monachorum* ('On the first establishing of monks'), *Speculum coenobitarum* ('A mirror for monks'), and *De rebus*

---

35. Bale, *Index*, 49, 480.
36. It has left no other trace there; Magdalen's late medieval and renaissance booklists do not survive.
37. Bale, *Scriptores*, 541.
38. Bale's comment ('It shows the first beginnings and the progress of monks') is a reasonable summary of part 1 of either version of *SC*.

sui coenobi ('On matters concerning his monastery'). Their meanings are similar enough that we suppose all three to refer to the same text, especially in view of the fact that the three share only a single incipit. So we assume that Bale saw manuscripts of a treatise on monasticism, which were without attribution of authorship but were written by a monk of Bury, and were clearly reminiscent of the type of work done by the compiler of the *Catalogus*, 'Boston of Bury'. Because the various manuscripts gave it no fixed title, Bale (or his library sources) gave it a variety of descriptive names. We do not know whether he saw the original or the revised version, or perhaps a copy of each.[39]

In consideration of its subject matter and of the repeated internal statements that the compiler was a Bury monk, Anthony Hall identified the text in Oxford, The Queen's College, MS 304, fols. 58r–66v, with the *Speculum coenobitarum* that John Bale had reported under Boston's name; and Hall borrowed from the *Scriptores* both the title of the work and the attribution of authorship. Bale's incipit 'Primus institutor monachorum' does not fit the Queen's College copy nor any of the surviving manuscripts of this text, although the phrase 'primus institutor' recurs again and again in part 1 of the original version; and the phrase 'Primus institutor monachorum' appears as a marginal heading to the excerpt from part 1 in Bodl. MS Bodley 240 (p. 766), raising the possibility that these words elsewhere appeared in a rubric.

Clearly, evidence for Henry of Kirkestede's authorship of the *SC* cannot rest on Bale's attribution, much less Hall's. We must look to the work itself for evidence.

B. *The Original Version*

We are not convinced that Kirkestede compiled the original version. The intent of the work in general coincides with Kirkestede's interest in the instruction of novice monks. Certain aspects of it seem vaguely indicative, as well; for example, the extended bibliographic citation at the head of part 2 has an air of Kirkestede about it: 'Taken from the works of Jerome and the books of Cassian, *De institutis patrum* and his *XXIIII Collationes*, from Januensis' book on Antichrist, from the *Historia tripartita*, *Historia ecclesiastica*, *Historia Longobardorum* and *Historia Anglorum*, from the *Speculum historiale*, from

---

39. The fact that Bale says that *SC* contains 'three books' might seem to suggest that this was a manuscript of the first version, with its three parts; but in that case, what could one make of Bale's second title, which is said (in each entry) to contain only one book?

the books of Gennadius and Isidore, *De uiris illustribus*, from the book of Heraclidis called *Paradisus*, from the *Legenda aurea* and the complete legends, from Gregory's *Dialogi*, and from the *Dialogi* of Postumianus and Severus'.[40] Moreover, the initial emphasis here echoes Kirkestede's apparent interest in Cassian.[41] The wording of the prologue to this part, 'quidam monachus de sancto Edmundo collegit ex pluribus locis scripturarum', resembles wording in the prologue in the *Catalogus* that calls the list of authors and works an effort that 'quidam sancti Edmundi monachus ex informatione aliorum . . . in unum coll[egit]'.[42] But that formulation is not distinctive; the anonymous designation of 'quidam monachus' was common Benedictine practice, and use of the verb *colligere* to introduce compilations was routine in the 14th cent. The most serious stumbling block to the attribution is simply that no other extended prose of Kirkestede's survives for comparison. The lengthy introduction to the *Catalogus* consists of extracts from the works of others, linked together with virtually no intrusion of Kirkestede's own words. Save the one-paragraph prologue (itself derivative) in the *Catalogus*, we know Kirkestede only as an industrious compiler of lists and a writer of annotations. No evidence specifically excludes Kirkestede from consideration as author of the original *Speculum coenobitarum*; but nothing singles him out with conviction.

C. *The Revised* Speculum coenobitarum

The revised version of the *SC* found in Queen's 304 is a different matter. It seems to us probable that Kirkestede made this revision, and in particular that he was responsible for its list of monastic authors.

The multiplication and differentiation of lists in the revision, with their scores of added names, represent an interest in proper classification and distinction fitting to Kirkestede's bibliographical efforts. Parts 1 and 2, 4 and 5 of the revised *Speculum coenobitarum*, though not directly comparable with the *Catalogus*, are reminiscent of it, in the activity of meticulous list-making and in the diligent and insistent citation of sources. The sources include

---

40. 'Ex opusculis Ieronimi et libris Cassiani de institutis patrum et collacionibus eorum .xxiiii., ex libro Ianuensis de Antichristo, historia tripartita et de historia ecclesiastica et historia Longobardorum et historia Anglorum, ex speculo historiali, ex libris Genadii et Ysidori de viris illustribus, ex libro Heraclidis qui dicitur paradisus, ex legenda aurea et legendis originalibus, ex libris dialogorum Gregorii et dialogorum Postumiani et Severi'; BAV MS Reg. lat. 127, fol. 173v, rubric.
41. See above, p. xxxvii, and see the *Catalogus* entry, Cassianus *285* headnote.
42. BAV MS Reg. lat. 127, fol. 173v, and p. 20 below.

many of the most important sources of information for the *Catalogus* (Jerome, Gennadius, Isidore, John Cassian, Vincent of Beauvais), and an occasional oddity common to both compilations. *SC* frequently treats sources as not just words on a page, but physical objects one can hold and see, typical of Kirkestede as librarian; and the citation of sources is repeatedly formulated as 'Suggestions for further readings', representative of Kirkestede as novice-master: for example, 'See the rest of this there, [in Josephus]; and there is much also that is relevant in the *Historia scholastica* on the Gospels, and in the *Speculum historiale* . . . but best and most fully in Josephus' (Bury owned a two-volume Latin Josephus).[43] Or, after quotation of 'Jerome in his letter to Eustochium' comes the invitation, 'See this in the book of Jerome's letters' (Bury owned a large collection, listed in the late 12th-cent. catalogue simply as 'Jerome's letters' and partially analysed in the *Catalogus* under Jerome's name).[44] 'Anyone who wants to examine further the manners and practices of the monks of the early church should read Cassian, *De institutis monachorum*, and the *24 Collationes*, and Philo, *De uita theoretica*'; the two Cassian works appear together in a Bury manuscript that Kirkestede himself paid for, and appear in the *Catalogus*; moreover, the obscure work attributed here to Philo is also attributed to him in the *Catalogus*.[45] In part 2 of *SC*, which is the list of monastic saints with St Benedict as its high point, comes this advice: 'Concerning St Benedict, look in the second book of the blessed Gregory's Dialogues, and in four places in the History of the Lombards, and in Sigebert's Chronicle'.[46]

These aspects of the treatise on monastic history seem to us significant links with the *Catalogus* and its author. Moreover, the fact that the revised part 1 retained (from the original) the Joachimite tripartite structure of salvation history assumes greater importance, when viewed in the context of Kirkestede's (*pseudo-*) Joachimite interests in his later years.[47] In addition, a reference to Abbot Eugippius and Johannes Gerundensis, whose names appear in the list of writers of monastic rules in part 5 of the revised

---

43. Hall, 159; see the catalogue in Sharpe & others, *Benedictines*, B13. 10 and 236–7.
44. Quotation from the *Speculum coenobitarum*; Hall, 162. For the Bury catalogue, see Sharpe & others, *Benedictines*, B13. 193. For Jerome's letters in the *Catalogus* see *281.128–231*.
45. For Cassian's *Institutes* and *Collations* see Sharpe & others, *Benedictines*, B13. 257–9; *Catalogus 285.1, 3–5*; and the 14th-cent. Bury manuscript that Kirkestede purchased, Cambridge, Pembroke College, MS 92 (Bury J. 35). The unidentified *De uita theoretica, quem Supplicium attitulauit*, attributed to Philo Judeus more than once in part 1 of the *Speculum coenobitarum* (cf. Hall, 162 and 163), also appears in the *Catalogus* entry for Philo (*452.10*), intruded among a list of some two dozen other titles simply copied from Jerome's *De uiris illustribus*.
46. Hall, 169.
47. See chapter 1 above, p. lxxvii.

SC, was inserted by Kirkestede in the margin of a similar list in a mid-14th-cent. Bury chronology.[48] The facts come second-hand from Isidore's *De uiris illustribus*, but Isidore made no link between the two names; they are combined by Kirkestede's note in the chronology, and in the revised *SC* part 5. [49]

Not surprisingly, the most persuasive connexion with Kirkestede and the *Catalogus* is part 3 of the revised *SC*, the list of monastic authors and their writings (edited below). The *SC*'s list of authors and works differs from the *Catalogus* in many respects: in purpose (to emphasize the importance of monks, *vs.* to locate the works one should read); in organizing principle (rough chronological order, *vs.* rough alphabetical order); in scope (monastic authors only, *vs.* all authoritative writers); and in scale (fifty-nine authors and their works, *vs.* 674 authors, their works, their incipits and explicits, and their locations).[50] But these considerations do not obscure the fact that a single personality lies behind both lists: the same mind, the same sources, the same working methods, the same bibliographical interests.

To begin with the surface resemblance, we note that only five of the fifty-nine monastic writers named in the *SC* do not appear in the *Catalogus* as well. (Of the five, four are insignificant; the fifth is Benedict, whose omission from the *Catalogus* is puzzling any way one looks at it.[51]) And in the *SC* as in the *Catalogus*, the authors are introduced with a biographical notice (often exceedingly brief, and sometimes lacking—as in the *Catalogus*).

Three features deserve emphasis. First, the list of an author's works in *SC* may match the contents, but it seldom matches the sequence of the corresponding list in the *Catalogus*. This confirms that *SC* was not simply copied from the *Catalogus* (or vice versa). Second, on several occasions the contents of a list of works in the *SC* corresponds to a list in the *Catalogus* that was compiled from two or more different sources, showing that the *SC* entry as well was drawn from the same combination of sources. Third, a list in *SC* often lacks the final several titles from the corresponding entry in the *Catalogus*.

---

48. See Hall, 191, and BL MS Campbell Roll XXI.1; we thank Rod Thomson for calling this note to our attention. Both rules are reported as well in the *Catalogus* (Eugipius *167.2* and Johannes Gerundinensis *289.1*), and in part 3 of the *Speculum coenobitarum*.
49. Perhaps the entire list of monastic founders in BL MS Campbell Roll XXI.1 had been copied from the same source that provided part 5 of the *Speculum*—with the omissions that Kirkestede later supplied.
50. Unexpectedly, two works of Odo of Cluny (no. 47) in *SC* have incipits: works 3 and 9. Why these, or why only these, have incipits is a puzzle.
51. *SC* 6 Moses monachus, 11 Sanctus Isaac, 30 Fructuosus monachus, 39 Sanctus Benedictus, 52 Robertus monachus. Benedict wrote only the Rule; but having composed a single work did not disqualify many other *SC* authors who do appear in the *Catalogus*.

This reflects, first, that work on the *Catalogus* extended over time, with further titles added to existing lists as Kirkestede found them;[52] and second, that the list in the *SC* was finished and done with before Kirkestede ceased work on the *Catalogus*.

The entries for Anselm in the *SC* (49) and the *Catalogus* (3) exemplify all three features. The *Catalogus* entry attributes fifty-nine titles to Anselm, *SC* twenty-eight. These twenty-eight titles are near-exact counterparts of the first thirty-five titles in the *Catalogus* list.[53] The *SC*'s sequence, however, is not that of the *Catalogus*; if anything, it is closer (but not very close) to the sequence of titles in a major source for both lists, Vincent of Beauvais's *Speculum historiale* (e.g. *SC* 1 = Vincent [1], *SC* 2 = V[3], *SC* 3 = V[3bis], *SC* 4 = V[7], *SC* 5 = V[4], *SC* 6 = V[5], *SC* 7 not in Vincent, *SC* 8 = V[11], *SC* 9 not in Vincent, *SC* 10 = V[13], *SC* 11 = V[6], *SC* 12 = V[8], *SC* 13 = V[9], *SC* 14 = V[10], etc.). The first thirty-five titles in the *Catalogus* derive primarily from Bury manuscripts, confirmed and supplemented by Vincent of Beauvais and by bibliographical references in the Bury copy of the *Mariale*.[54] The *SC* list, despite the variations in sequence, shows by the phrasing of its titles that Vincent was its main source. But at least one of its titles came from the *Mariale* (*SC* 26, corresponding to *Catalogus* 3.33); and those titles not available in either Vincent or the *Mariale* surely must have been taken from Bury manuscripts of Anselm's works, which Kirkestede also relied on for the list of Anselm's works in the *Catalogus*. The *SC* list, thus, reflects the same combination of sources used for the first thirty-five titles of the *Catalogus* list. However, the titles at the end of the *Catalogus* entry for Anselm, *3.36–59*, constitute the sort of bottom-of-the-barrel conclusion typical of many of the longer lists in the *Catalogus*, where one can observe Kirkestede adding items one or two at a time—an isolated letter or sermon circulating separately from the major collections, individual works of doubtful attribution, records from secondary sources of titles not recognized as repetitions. Half of these final items in the *Catalogus* (twelve of the twenty-four titles), one can readily see, represent Kirkestede's decision to scrutinize once more the Anselm entry in the *Registrum*, in order to collect from there any titles not yet included from other sources. All of these final titles, *3.36–59*, are absent from the *SC*'s entry for Anselm, doubtless because *SC* was finished long before Kirkestede had abandoned his lifetime of tinkering with the *Catalogus*. Many of the shorter entries also exemplify one or other of the

---

52. See chapter 2 above.
53. There are six exceptions in the *SC* list (*Catalogus 3.13, 18, 19, 29, 30, 32*), and the *Catalogus* analyses the *Meditationes* to which *SC* gives a single title. See the editions of the respective lists below.
54. See chapter 2 p. xcviii above.

features we have singled out, although none is as obvious as the lengthy Anselm entry in its correspondence to the compiling of the *Catalogus*.⁵⁵

For some authors, it is not just the content of an entry but its very presence (or absence) that links part 3 of *SC* with the *Catalogus*. The two lists concur, for example, in their disregard for Anglo-Saxon (i.e. pre-Conquest) authors. Among the 674 authors in the *Catalogus*, at most six can be called Anglo-Saxon, but only by stretching the category from Aldhelm (*8*), King Alfred (*76*), Bede (*84*), and Byrhtferth of Ramsey (*90*) to include the Carolingian Alcuin (*7*) and the archbishop of Canterbury Theodore of Tarsus (*591*). The *SC* among its fifty-nine authors includes only three Anglo-Saxons (Aldhelm, Bede, and Byrhtferth), all found among the handful in the *Catalogus*.⁵⁶ The Commentary on Canticles by the 12th-cent. Ramsey monk William of Peterborough is so rare that only one surviving manuscript is known, in Prague; yet it appears in both the *Catalogus* and the revised *SC* part 3.

Parallels link the sources cited by *SC* with those cited in the *Catalogus*, and they range from the obvious to the unique. That both compilations took the names of authors and titles from the standard *De uiris illustribus* literature (Jerome, Gennadius, Isidore) and from Vincent of Beauvais is not surprising. It is less of a given that both should treat the collection of Marian material in the *Mariale* as a bibliographical source. The truly unique parallel source, however, is the *Registrum*—a work that Kirkestede plundered thoroughly in making the *Catalogus*, and the direct model for his attempt to provide locations of the works that he listed. The *SC*'s list of authors and works also borrowed repeatedly from the *Registrum*; but it was usually employed as a complement to other sources, so that its presence is not always conspicuous.⁵⁷ As a visible and unmistakable example, however, one could not surpass the *SC* entry for St Bernard (*50*): all thirty-nine titles attributed to this author have been taken, in sequence, from the *Registrum*'s list of Bernard's works. The *SC*'s faithfulness to the *Registrum*'s order is remarkable, for such a lengthy medieval sequence.⁵⁸ (As usual, the sequence is unrelated to the sequence of the corresponding list in the *Catalogus*.) The *SC* therefore joins the *Catalogus* as the only direct borrowers from the *Registrum* in the 14th cent.; the two of them constitute the only known use of the

---

55. See, for example, *SC* 14 (Ephraem), *SC* 16 (Gregory of Nazianzus), *SC* 36 (Cassiodorus), *SC* 43 (Aldhelm), *SC* 51 (Aelred), *SC* 54 (Haimo), and the corresponding lists in the *Catalogus*.
56. *SC* 43 (Aldhelm), 44 (Bede), and 57 (Byrhtferth). Alfred and Theodore were omitted because they were not monks. The omission of Alcuin is curious.
57. See, for example, *SC* 22 (Jerome) or *SC* 45 (Hrabanus), where titles from Vincent are followed by a series taken from the *Registrum*.
58. The only anomalies are the inversion of *Speculum* works 12 and 13, and the fact that work 14 should follow 16.

Registrum as a bibliographical source until the time of John Bale in the 16th cent.

*
* *

We assume that John Bale knew a history of monasticism similar to or identical with the text later printed by Hall, and that his familiarity with the *Catalogus* led Bale to conclude that *SC* must have been produced by the same Bury bibliographer. Our conclusions agree with Bale's.

Ironically, besides the attributions to 'Boston', Bale's *Index* reproduces a mid-15th-cent. booklist that attributes to Henry of Kirkestede, under his own name, what may in fact be the *SC* in yet another guise. Bale did not himself see the work, but copied title and attribution into his notebook from a list of books that had belonged to John Whethamstede, twice abbot of St Albans (1420–40 and 1452–65).[59]

> Henricus Crixstede,[60] Benedictinensis monachus, scripsit,
> In regulam monachorum, li. i.
> Atque alia nonnulla   Claruisse fertur A.D. <*blank*>
> Ex actis Ioannis Whitamstede[61]

Bale apparently took his extracts from the list of Whethamstede books in BL MS Cotton Otho B. IV, fols. 12v–16r, now badly burned; Tanner cited the name Crixstede from the same list, which he saw before the Cotton fire.[62]

The text that Whethamstede had must have borne a specific attribution to Henry of Kirkestede. But was 'in regulam monachorum' just one more

59. Concerning John Whethamstede or Wheathampstead (d. 1465), see Sharpe, *Latin Writers*, 344–5, and D. R. Howlett, 'Studies on the Latin Writings of John Whethamstede', DPhil. diss. (Oxford 1975).
60. There is no village or town named 'Crixstede' in E. Ekwall, *The Concise Oxford Dictionary of English Place-names*, 4th edn (Oxford 1960), nor anything resembling it except 'Kirkestede'.
61. Bale, *Index*, 161, entry under the author's name, and see ibid. 516, in Bale's extract from Whethamstede's list (there as 'Henricus Crixstede super regulam monachorum'). Bale's extract from the booklist is edited with annotations, B90; a list of books paid for by Whethamstede (in BL MS Arundel 34) is edited, B88.
62. Tanner, *Bibliotheca*, 209: 'Crixtedus, Henricus, monachus Benedictinus scripsit *In regulam S. Benedicti* lib. i', transcribed from Whethamstede, citing as a source Cotton Otho B. IV (the readable portions of which are edited, B89). Tanner classed Crixstede as an 'incertae aetatis scriptor'. The booklist in Arundel 34 refers to 'an excellent gloss of Benedict's Rule' for the making of which Whethamstede paid 40 shillings ('In factura unius libri cum glosa nobili super regulam beati Benedicti: xl s.'); Sharpe & others, *Benedictines*, at B88. 24, tentatively identify this entry with the 'Crixstede' entry copied by Bale.

description of the untitled *SC*, on a par with 'de rebus sui coenobii' or 'de prima institutione monachorum'? We know that a manuscript of the revised *SC*, as well as reworkings of it, had been available at St Albans since before the end of the 14th cent. More significant is the fact that Whethamstede himself demonstrably knew the work, and borrowed from *SC* virtually all of its information on monastic history to incorporate into his own lengthy *Granarium*.[63] The peroration of part 1 of the revised *SC* proclaims that the age-old history of monks, with its roots in the old and new testaments 'in the time of . . . the blessed Elijah and Elisha and the Sons of the Prophets . . . of John the Baptist, Christ and the Apostles', to the Desert Fathers and others, achieved its culmination in the Rule of 'the blessed Benedict, the ultimate law-giver of their institution'—which might suggest a title such as 'in regulam monachorum'.[64] It may, instead, be relevant that the only surviving manuscript of the original *SC*, BAV MS Reg. lat. 127, is preceded by both a commentary on the Benedictine Rule and a *Speculum monachorum*; perhaps a manuscript with similar contents gave rise to the title in Whethamstede's list.[65] Our summary remains inconclusive: what Whethamstede referred to may well have been a copy of the *SC*, or it may, instead, have been a commentary on the Rule; in either case, it was a text attributed to Henry of Kirkestede.

Regardless of how one interprets Whethamstede's booklist, and regardless of what works Bale may have seen, the textual evidence makes it a near certainty that Henry of Kirkestede compiled the revised *SC*; it is possible that he compiled the original version as well, but the evidence is not compelling. The experience of constructing the list of authors and works for the revised *SC* may have served as groundwork for that much more ambitious undertaking, the *Catalogus de libris autenticis et apocrifis*. The two compilations, in any event, clearly fit into the life of one person.

---

63. Knowles, *Religious Orders*, 2. 268.
64. Hall, 164.
65. See note 9 above. Aside from this list, there is no other hint that Kirkestede commented on the Rule; but there is equally no hint, beyond the evidence of the surviving work itself, that Kirkestede compiled a *Catalogus*.

APPENDIX TO CHAPTER 3

THE LIST OF MONASTIC AUTHORS IN THE REVISED
SPECULUM COENOBITARUM
(OXFORD, THE QUEEN'S COLLEGE, MS 304)

The following is a transcription of Oxford, The Queen's College, MS 304, fols. 62r–65v (Glastonbury, *c*. 1401–20); it was previously printed by A. Hall, 'Joannis Bostoni Speculum coenobitarum', in his *Nicolai Triveti Annalium continuatio, ut et Adami Murimuthensis Chronicon cum ejusdem continuatione, quibus accedunt Joannis Bostoni Speculum coenobitarum et Edmundi Bottoni Hypercritica* (Oxford 1722), 157–92, at 174–89. The text (in continuous paragraphs in the manuscript and in Hall's edition) is presented here as a numbered list to facilitate reference. The minimal apparatus comprises (1) a cross-reference to the corresponding entry in the *Catalogus* (abbreviated K), where bibliographical information can be found; and (2) a reference to the source of the title, followed when appropriate by numbers in brackets [1, 2, etc.] that indicate the sequence of titles in the source, which often governs the *Speculum* sequence.

NB. In editing entries in the *Catalogus* (see below) we list all plausible sources, because Kirkestede often combined information from different sources to construct a single entry; here, in contrast, we cite for each title the single most plausible source.

Oxford, The Queen's College, MS 304 fol. 62r]

Nomina doctorum subscribuntur monachorum
De scriptis quorum laus lucet theologorum
Horum scripturis sapientes sunt modo fulti
Ecclesie puris clarent studiis quia multi.

1. ORIGENES monachus floruit circa annum Domini .ccclxxii. iuxta Vincencium in Speculo historiali libro .xii. ca. .xi. Hic .vi.^{ml} et amplius tractatuum scripsit. licet enim in multis erravit, multa tamen utilia reliquit, quorum quedam ecclesia recipit. Nam papa Gelasius in decretis suis illa opuscula Origenis approbat que beatus Ieronymus non reprobat. Scribitur in historia Mariani Scoti quod Origenes in scribendo tam sedulus fuit ut Ieronymus dicat se legisse .vi.^{ml} librorum eius. Scripsit enim

Vincent XII 11–14; paragraph at the end of the entry (below) comes from Jerome c. 54.

1. Super Genesin omelias xvii

    (K404. 1) Vincent XII 11 [1].

2. Super Exodum omelias xiii

    (K404. 2) Vincent XII 11 [2].

3. Super Leviticum omelias xvi

    (K404. 3) Vincent XII 11 [3].

4. Super librum Numeri omelias xviii
   (K404. 4) Vincent XII 11 [4].

5. Super Iosue omelias xxvi
   (K404. 6) Vincent XII 11 [6].

6. Super Iudicum omelias ix
   (K404. 7) Vincent XII 11 [7].

7. De Elchana tractatum
   (K404. 8) Vincent XII 11 [8].

8. Super Iob libros iii
   (K404. 10) Vincent XII 11 [9].

9. Super Psalmum .xxxvi. omelias v
   (K404. 11) Vincent XII 11 [10].

10. Super Psalmum .xxxvii. omelias ii
    (K404. 12) Vincent XII 11 [11].

11. Super Psalmum .xxxviii. omelias ii
    (K404. 13) Vincent XII 11 [12].

12. Super ceteris libros v
    Source unidentified.

13. Super Ysaiam omelias ix
    (K404. 16) Vincent XII 11 [15].

14. Super Ieremiam omelias xiiii
    (K404. 17) Vincent XII 11 [16].

15. Super Ezechielem omelias xiiii
    (K404. 18) Vincent XII 11 [17].

16. Super Matheum libros .xxvi. quorum .xii. primi raro inveniuntur
    (K404. 19) Vincent XII 11 [18].

17. Super Lucam omelias xxxviii
    (K404. 20) Vincent XII 11 [19].

18. Super principium Ioannis tractatum i
    (K404. 21) Vincent XII 11 [20].

19. Super epistolam ad Romanos libros x
    (K404. 22) Vincent XII 11 [21].

20. Scripsit et Pariarcon in quibus eius hereses inveniuntur
    (K404. 26) Vincent XII 12.

21. Extat eciam libellus qui Planctus Origenis dicitur et a beato Ieronymo translatus inscribitur
    (K404. 27) Vincent XII 13.

22. De tunicis et pelliciis Ade et Eve exposicionem
    Source unidentified.

23. Super Ysaiam comentarios libros xxx
    (K404. 16) Vincent XII 11 intro. [1].

24. Super Ezechielem comentarios libros xxv
    (K404. 18) Vincent XII 11 intro. [2].

25. De martiribus ad Ambrosium librum i
    Vincent XII 11 intro. [4].

26. De singularitate clericorum et cohabitacione mulierum librum i
    (K404. 23). Source unidentified.

27. Item pro seipso librum Apologiticum i.e. excusatorium
    Vincent XII 14.

Propterea quintam, sextam, et septimam edicionem, quas eciam Ieronymus de eius bibliotheca habet, miro labore repperit, et cum ceteris edicionibus comparavit. Diale[c]dicam et geometriam, arsmetricam, musicam, gramaticam, rethoricam, omnesque philosphorum sciencias didicit; et obiit anno etatis sue lxix.

>Jerome c. 54.

2. SANCTUS ANTONIUS abbas floruit circa annum Domini .cclxv. et scripsit

1. Egypciace ad diversa monasteria epistolas que in Grecam linguam translate sunt, quarum precipua est ad Arseonitas monachos

   >(K12) Jerome c. 88; source of the date unidentified.

3. SANCTUS MACHARIUS Egypcius unam scripsit

1. Epistolam ad monachos iuniores in qua dicit inter alia illum perfecte posse servire Deo qui condicionem creacionis sue cognoscens ad omnes seipsum inclinaverit labores

   >(K362) Gennadius c. 10.

4. SANCTUS MACHARIUS Alexandrinus scripsit iuxta Genadium

1. Adversus mathematicos librum i in quo labore orientalium quesivit solacia scripturarum

   >(K363) Gennadius c. 28.

5. SANCTUS EVAGRIUS abbas, discipulus Macharii, scripsit iuxta Genadium

   >Gennadius c. 11, with an addition from Jerome c. 125.

1. Vitas patrum

   >(K156. 1) Gennadius c. 11 [1].

2. Item adversus septem principalium viciorum suggestiones librum i

   >(K156. 2) Gennadius c. 11 [2].

3. Item cenobitis et synodochis doctrinam vite communis

   >(K156. 4) Gennadius c. 11 [5].

4. Item anachoritis simpliciter viventibus librum .c. sentenciarum per capitula degestum

   >(K156. 3) Gennadius c. 11 [3].

5. Item eruditis et studiosis anachoritis librum .l. sentenciarum

   >Gennadius c. 11 [4].

6. Item ad virginem Deo sacratam librum compe [fol. 62v] tentem religioni et sexui

   >(K156. 6) Gennadius c. 11 [6].

7. Item paucas sentenciolas valde obscuras solis monachis cognoscibiles

   >(K156. 7) Gennadius c. 11 [7].

8. Item vitam sancti Antonii de greco Athanasii transtulit in latinum

   >(K156. 8) Jerome c. 125.

6. SANCTUS MOYSES monachus et episcopus fecit

1. De discrecione et de monachi destinacione vel fine collaciones .ii. quas Cassianus scripsit in libro collacionum patrum

Cassian, *Collationes* I–II (*CSEL* 13. 6–65).

7. SANCTUS SERAPION peritissimus erat sciencia litterarum scripturasque omnes memoriter recolebat, et scripsit

> Jerome c. 99, with an addition from Cassian, *Collatio* V (*CSEL* 13. 119–51).

1. Adversus Manicheos egregium librum

   (K547. 1) Jerome c. 99 [1].

2. Et de psalmorum titulis alium

   (K547. 2) Jerome c. 99 [2].

3. Item ad diversos utiles epistolas

   (K547. 3) Jerome c. 99 [3].

4. Item ad monachos de viciis principalibus collacionem unam

   Cassian, *Collatio* V.

8. SANCTUS PACHOMIUS scripsit

> Gennadius c. 7.

1. Regulam utrique generi monachorum aptam quam angelo dictante didicerat

   (K421. 1) Gennadius c. 7 [1].

2. Item ad abbatem Sirum epistolam unam

   (K421. 2) Gennadius c. 7 [3].

3. Ad abbatem Cornelium epistolam unam

   (K421. 3) Gennadius c. 7 [2].

4. De Pasca epistolam unam

   (K421. 4) Gennadius c. 7 [4].

5. De die remissionis epistolam

   (K421. 5) Gennadius c. 7 [5].

6. De fratribus extra monasterium laborantibus unam epistolam

   (K421. 6) Gennadius c. 7 [6].

9. SANCTUS THEODORUS successor beati Pachomii scripsit

> Gennadius c. 8 and Cassian, *Collatio* VI (*CSEL* 13. 152–76).

1. Ad alia monasteria .iii. epistolas sanctarum scripturarum in quibus frequenter meminit magistri sui sancti Pachomii et doctrine eius ac vite proponit exempla que ut doceret angelo administrante didicerat

   (K573. 1) Gennadius c. 8.

2. Fecit eciam .i. collacionem de nece sanctorum monachorum a saracenis occisorum in partibus Palestine iuxta Thecue civitatem ubi Amos propheta ortus fuit. Hanc collacionem scripsit Cassianus in libro collacionum patrum

   Cassian, *Collatio* VI.

10. SANCTUS ORESIESIS monachus et Pachomii discipulus composuit

1. Librum tocius monastice discipline instrumentis constructum et ut simpliciter dicam in totum pene vetus et novum testamentum in compendiosis distinccionibus iuxta monachorum dumtaxat necessitatem invenitur expositum quem vice testamenti prope diem obitus sui fratribus obtulit

   (K414) Gennadius c. 9.

APPENDIX TO CHAPTER 3

11. SANCTUS YSAAC fecit

1. II collaciones de oracione et cetera

    Cassian, *Collationes* IX–X (*CSEL* 13. 248–308).

12. SANCTUS AMMONIUS monachus vir discretus et valde eruditus in philosophia inter multa ingenii sui monumenta

    Jerome c. 55.

1. De constancia monachi et Iesu opus elegans composuit et

    (K30. 1) Jerome c. 55 [1].

2. Ewangelicos canones primus excogitavit

    (K30. 2) Jerome c. 55 [2].

13. DIDYMUS monachus ab anno etatis sue quarto oculorum lumine privatus, sed nec magistris litterarum traditus nec umquam elementa prima cognoscens, testamentum vetus et novum de verbo ad verbum interpretatus est. Gramaticam enim rethoricam, musicam, geometriam, et astronomiam et silogismos Aristotelis et eloquenciam Philonis auditu didicit

    The entry was based on Jerome c. 109, with insertions at the beginning from *Registrum* 16 and an unknown source. The headnote is quoted from *Historia tripartita* VIII 8.

1. De Trinitate fecit libros iii

    (K144. 9) *Registrum* 16. 2.

2. Item Origenis opus de principibus i.e. Periarchon interpretatus est et in eis explanaciones reliquit eximias

    (K144. 10). Source unidentified.

3. Item comentarium in psalmos omnes

    (K144. 1) Jerome c. 109 [1].

4. Item comentarium in ewangelium Mathei et Iohannis et [de] dogmatibus

    (K144. 2) Jerome c. 109 [2].

5. Item contra Arrianos libros ii

    (K144. 3) Jerome c. 109 [3].

6. Item de Spiritu sancto librum i

    (K144. 4) Jerome c. 109 [4].

7. Item in Ysaiam thomos xviii

    (K144. 5) Jerome c. 109 [5].

8. In Osee libros iii

    (K144. 6) Jerome c. 109 [6].

9. In Zachariam libros v

    (K144. 7) Jerome c. 109 [7].

10. Comentarios in Iob

    (K144. 8) Jerome c. 109 [8].

14. SANCTUS EFFREM monachus scripsit

    The entry was based on Vincent XV 87, with insertions at the beginning from Jerome c. 115 and a Bury manuscript.

1. De Spiritus sancto librum i

    (K155. 1) Jerome c. 115.

2. De transfiguracione Domini sermonem i

    (K155. 2). The source may have been a Bury manuscript.

3. De penitencia omeliam i
   (K155. 3) Vincent XV 87 [1].

4. De luctantibus seculi librum i
   (K155. 4) Vincent XV 87 [2].

5. De compunctione librum i
   (K155. 5) Vincent XV 87 [3].

6. De beatitudine anime librum i
   (K155. 6) Vincent XV 87 [4].

7. De resurrectione et iudicio librum i
   (K155. 7) Vincent XV 87 [5].

8. De die iudicii omeliam unam
   (K155. 8) Vincent XV 87 [6].

15. SANCTUS BASILIUS monachus et archiepiscopus Capadocie scripsit
   Vincent XV 81.

1. In Exameron libros ix
   (K78. 1) Vincent XV 81 [1].

2. Item regulam de institucione monachorum in libro i
   (K78. 3) Vincent XV 81 [2].

3. Item de doctrina et institucione novicii tractatum i
   Vincent XV 81 [3].

4. De triplici pungna monachi epistolam i
   (K78. 6). The source may have been a Bury manuscript.

5. Contra Eunomium de Spiritu sancto librum i
   (K78. 2) Vincent XV 81 intro. [1].

6. Item breves et plures tractatus ad monachos
   (K78. 7) Vincent XV 81 intro. [2].

16. SANCTUS GREGORIUS NAZENZENUS monachus et episcopus scripsit
   Vincent XV 90 (works *1–9*), followed by *Registrum* 18 (works *10–13*).

1. De morte fratris Cesarii
   (K204. 1) Vincent XV 90 [1].

2. Item laudes Maximi philosophi
   (K204. 3) Vincent XV 90 [5].

3. Item laudes Machabeorum
   (K204. 2) Vincent XV 90 [2].

4. Laudes Cipriani
   (K204. 4) Vincent XV 90 [3].

5. Laudes Athanasii
   (K204. 15) Vincent XV 90 [5].

6. De nupciis et virginitate contra Eunomium libros ii
   (K204. 5) Vincent XV 90 [6].

7. De spiritu librum i
   (K204. 6) Vincent XV 90 [7].

8. Item contra Iulianum imperatorum librum i
   (K204. 7) Vincent XV 90 [8].

9. Liber appolligiticus libros iii
   (K204. 8) Vincent XV 90 [9]; R18. 1–2.

10. Sermonem de nativitate

> (K204. 9) R18. 3.

11. Item sermonem de monachis

> (K204. 10) R18. 8.

12. Item de luminibus sive de secundis Epipha [fol. 63r] niis tractatum i

> (K204. 11) R18. 4.

13. Item de agro regresso sive de semetipso librum i

> (K204. 12) R18. 6.

17. PETRONIUS monachus et episcopus Bononiensis scripsit

> Gennadius c. 42.

1. Vitas patrum Egipti monachorum

> (K447. 1) Gennadius c. 42 [1].

2. Item de ordinacione episcopi Rome et humilitate librum i

> (K447. 2) Gennadius c. 42 [2].

18. VIGILIUS diaconus et monachus composuit ex tradicione patrum

1. Regulam monachorum iuxta Genadium.

> (K623) Gennadius c. 52.

19. LEANDER monachus Spalensis et episcopus scripsit

> Isidore c. 28.

1. Adversus hereticorum dogmata libros ii

> (K346. 1) Isidore c. 28 [1].

2. Item adversus Arrianos libros ii

> (K346. 2) Isidore c. 28 [2].

3. Ad Florentinam sororem de institucione virginum et de contemptu mundi librum i

> (K346. 3) Isidore c. 28 [3].

4. In toto psalterio duplici edicione oraciones conscripsit

> (K346. 6) Isidore c. 28 [4].

5. Item ad episcopos alios epistolas multas

> (K346. 8) Isidore c. 28 [5].

6. Item de morte non timenda epistolam i

> (K346. 5) Isidore c. 28 [6].

20. IOHANNES GERUNDINENSIS monachus et episcopus scripsit

> Isidore c. 31. Kirkestede added this monk's name to BL MS Campbell Roll XXI.1 (see above p. cxxxviii).

1. Unam regulam monachis

> (K289. 1) Isidore c. 31 [1].

2. Item cronicon et alia multa scripsisse dicitur

> (K289. 2) Isidore c. 31 [2].

21. EUTROPIUS monachus scripsit

> Isidore c. 32.

1. Ad papam epistolam i, et

> (K176. 1) Isidore c. 32 [1].

2. Ad episcopum Hircanensem de distrinctione (*sic*) monachorum librum unum

(K176. 2) Isidore c. 32 [2].

22. SANCTUS IERONYMUS monachus et presbyter cardinalis floruit circa annum Domini .ccclxxxix.

> Vincent XVII 19 provided the first eighty-five titles in sequence; thereafter the titles come in small groups from other sources (and an occasional oversight from Vincent), followed by a significant group of titles from the *Registrum* including two series in sequence (97–126 and 129–133), with another assortment of miscellaneous sources at the end.

Hic litteris grecis latinis et hebraicis sufficienter edoctus omnes Veteris Testamenti libros ex hebreo in latinum convertit eosque comentatus est et Novum grece fidei reddidit. Solus ex antiquis doctoribus omnes xvi prophecies (*sic*) exposuit et lxiiii libris editis comentatus est. Danielem quoque caldaico stilo locutum et Iob <ex> arabico in romanam linguam mutavit. Ewangelium eciam Mathei ex hebreo fecit esse romanum. Psalterium ex hebreo latina modulacione composuit. Duos libros Salamonis inplantavit. Cantica canticorum ex Origenis interpretacione transtulit in latinum. Epistolas Pauli et Iohannis revelacionem disseruit.

1. Exposicionis sue fidei librum i

   (K281. 150) Vincent XVII 19 [1].

2. De simbolo Niseno tractatum i

   (K281. 233) Vincent XVII 19 [2].

3. Ex regulis diffinicionum contra hereticos tractatum i

   (K281. 87) Vincent XVII 19 [3].

4. Contra Pelagianos libros iii

   (K281. 74) Vincent XVII 19 [4].

5. Contra Iovinianum libros ii

   (K281. 67) Vincent XVII 19 [5].

6. Contra Luciferianum librum i

   (K281. 68) Vincent XVII 19 [6].

7. Contra Helvidium de virginitate beate Marie librum i

   (K281. 11) Vincent XVII 19 [7].

8. Contra Vigilancium librum i

   (K281. 69) Vincent XVII 19 [8].

9. Contra Origenem de resurexione carnis librum i

   (K281. 70) Vincent XVII 19 [9].

10. Ad Avitum presbyterum de erroribus Origenis librum i

    (K281. 72) Vincent XVII 19 [10].

11. Ad Pammacheum et Occeanum librum i

    (K281. 88) Vincent XVII 19 [11].

12. Contra Ruffinum presbyterum librum i

    (K281. 82) Vincent XVII 19 [12].

13. Apologeticus et Augustini librum i

    Source unidentified.

14. Exortatorium ad Iulianum librum i
    (K281. 161) Vincent XVII 19 [13].

15. De penitencia ad Rusticum monachum librum i
    (K281. 133) Vincent XVII 19 [14].

16. Ad papam Damasum librum i
    (K281. 125) Vincent XVII 19 [15].

17. Ad Occeanum librum i
    (K281. 136) Vincent XVII 19 [16].

18. Ad Hebidiam librum i
    (K281. 59) Vincent XVII 19 [17].

19. Ad Alganciam librum i
    (K281. 52) Vincent XVII 19 [18].

20. Ad Silviam et Fretelam librum i
    (K281. 205) Vincent XVII 19 [19].

21. De homine perfecto librum i
    (K281. 126) Vincent XVII 19 [21].

22. De Ioachim et Anna librum i
    (K281. 9) Vincent XVII 19 [22].

23. De .xv. signis tractatus i
    (K281. 127) Vincent XVII 19 [23].

24. De viris illustribus librum i
    (K281. 90) Vincent XVII 19 [24].

25. De distancia locorum
    (K281. 89) Vincent XVII 19 [25].

26. De interpretacionibus hebraycorum librum i
    (K281. 61) Vincent XVII 19 [26].

27. De optimo genere interpretandi librum i
    (K281. 63) Vincent XVII 19 [27].

28. De studio scripturarum librum i
    (K281. 13) Vincent XVII 19 [28].

29. De questionibus hebraicis in Genesi librum i
    (K281. 56) Vincent XVII 19 [29].

30. De .iii. questionibus ad Damasum papam librum i
    (K281. 236) Vincent XVII 19 [30].

31. De veste sacerdotali librum i
    (K281. 139) Vincent XVII 19 [31].

32. De xlii mansionius filiorum Israel librum i
    (K281. 97) Vincent XVII 19 [32].

33. De .vii. gradibus ecclesie librum i
    (K281. 152) Vincent XVII 19 [33].

34. De questionibus hebraicis libri Regum libros ii
    (K281. 57) Vincent XVII 19 [34].

35. De questionibus Paralepomenon libros ii
    (K281. 58) Vincent XVII 19 [35].

36. Braviarii (*sic*) super psalterium librum unum
    (K281. 14–15) Vincent XVII 19 [36].

37. Comentarium super Ecclesiasticum [Ecclesiasten] librum i
    (K281. 16) Vincent XVII 19 [37].

38. Super Ysaiam libros xviii
    (K281. 18) Vincent XVII 19 [38].

39. Super Ieremiam libros xi
    (K281. 19) Vincent XVII 19 [39].

40. Super Ezechielem libros xiiii
    (K281. 20) Vincent XVII 19 [40].

41. Super Danielem librum i
    (K281. 21) Vincent XVII 19 [41].

42. Super Osee libros iii
    (K281. 22) Vincent XVII 19 [42].

43. Super Iohelem librum i
    (K281. 23) Vincent XVII 19 [43].

44. Super Amos libros tres
    (K281. 24) Vincent XVII 19 [44].

45. Super Abdiam librum i
    (K281. 25) Vincent XVII 19 [45].

46. Super Ionam librum i
    (K281. 26) Vincent XVII 19 [46].

47. Super Micheam libros ii
    (K281. 27) Vincent XVII 19 [47].

48. Super Naum librum i
    (K281. 28) Vincent XVII 19 [48].

49. Super Abacuc libros ii
    (K281. 29) Vincent XVII 19 [49].

50. Super Sephoniam librum i
    (K281. 30) Vincent XVII 19 [50].

51. Super Aggeum librum i
    (K281. 31) Vincent XVII 19 [51].

52. Super Zachariam libros iii
    (K281. 32) Vincent c. 29 [52].

53. Super Malachiam librum i
    (K281. 33) Vincent XVII 19 [53].

54. Super Matheum libros iiii
    (K281. 35) Vincent XVII 19 [54].

55. Super Marcum librum i
    (K281. 36) Vincent XVII 19 [55].

56. Super epistolam ad Ephesios libros iii
    (K281. 37) Vincent XVII 19 [56].

57. Super epistolam ad Titum librum i
    (K281. 39) Vincent XVII 19 [58].

58. Super epistolam ad Galathas libros iii
    (K281. 38) Vincent XVII 19 [57].

59. Super epistolam ad Philemonem librum i
    (K281. 40) Vincent XVII 19 [59].

60. De vita clericorum librum i
    (K281. 129) Vincent XVII 19 [60].

61. Epitaphium ad Heliodorum episcopum
    (K281. 134) Vincent XVII 19 [61].

62. De institucione clerici vel monachi librum i
    (K281. 128) Vincent XVII 19 [62].

63. De vita monachi ad Rusticum librum i

   (K281. 130) Vincent XVII 19 [63].

64. De vita clerici librum i

   (K281. 131) Vincent XVII 19 [64].

65. De virginitate librum i

   (K281. 170) Vincent XVII 19 [65].

66. Ad Demetriadem virginem [fol. 63v] librum i

   (K281. 203–204) Vincent XVII 19 [66].

67. De institucione Paule librum i

   (K281. 174) Vincent XVII 19 [67].

68. Ad matrem et filiam in Gallia librum i

   (K281. 175) Vincent XVII 19 [68].

69. De lapsu virginis Susanne librum i

   (K281. 206) Vincent XVII 19 [69].

70. De lapsu Fabiani librum i

   (K281. 140) Vincent XVII 19 [70].

71. De monogamia librum i

   (K281. 173) Vincent XVII 19 [71].

72. De viduitate servanda librum i

   (K281. 171) Vincent XVII 19 [72].

73. De morte Nebridii librum i

   (K281. 172) Vincent XVII 19 [73].

74. De dormicione Pa[u]line librum i

   (K281. 176–77) Vincent XVII 19 [74–5].

75. De morte Fabiole librum i

   (K281. 178) Vincent XVII 19 [76].

76. Epitaphii sancte Paule librum i

   (K281. 179) Vincent XVII 19 [77].

77. Ad Tirasium librum consolatorium

   (K281. 180) Vincent XVII 19 [78].

78. De resurexione ad Mimervium (sic) et Alexandrum librum i

   (K281. 71) Vincent XVII 19 [79].

79. Apolegiticum ad Pammachium

   (K281. 84) Vincent XVII 19 [80].

80. De contemptu seculi librum i

   (K281. 132) Vincent XVII 19 [81].

81. Ad Thespontem librum i

   (Cf. K281. 74) Vincent XVII 19 [82].

82. Ad Demmonem librum i

   (K281. 224) Vincent XVII 19 [83].

83. De .iii. virtutibus librum i

   (K281. 137) Vincent XVII 19 [84].

84. De morte Osee et seraphin et calculo librum i

   (K281. 149) Vincent XVII 19 [85].

85. Super Psalmum .xliiii. librum i

   (K281. 168) Vincent XVII 19 [86].

86. Altercacionis Lucifariani et orthodoxi librum i

   (K281. 91) R6. 9; Jerome c. 135 [4].

87. Super Parabolas librum i

(K281. 49) R6. 113.

88. Super Cantica omelias ii

(K281. 50) R6. 114.

89. Super Lucam omelias xxxix

(K281. 36) Jerome c. 135 [25].

90. De Psalmis a decimo usque ad xvi^m tractatus vii

(K281. 54) Jerome c. 135 [26].

91. De libris historie dieni [divine] epistolam i

(K281. 13) Vincent XVII 19 [28].

92. De .iii. naturis anime librum i

(K281. 237). Source unidentified (*MF* IV 17 was probably not used).

93. Ad Marcellam de urbe secedenda librum i

(K281. 191). The source may have been the Bury manuscript of Jerome's letters.

94. De egrotacione Brisille librum i

(K281. 181) Jerome c. 135 [14], or perhaps the Bury manuscript of Jerome's letters.

95. Ad Silvinam librum i

(K281. 207). The source may have been the Bury manuscript of Jerome's letters.

96. Ad Lucinum h[er]eticum librum i

(K281. 167). The source may have been the Bury manuscript of Jerome's letters.

97. De .vii. mirabilibus librum i

(K281. 117) R6. 8.

98. De persecucione Christianorum librum i

(K281. 116) R6. 3.

99. Super edificium Prudencii librum i

(K281. 92) R6. 5.

100. Glose .vii. ebdomade librum i

(K281. 114) R6. 6.

101. De usu psallendi librum i

(K281. 115) R6. 7.

102. De tribus diebus librum i

R6. 12.

103. De fide eius apud Bethleem

(K281. 235) R6. 15.

104. Ad Pammachium et Marcellum libros ii

(K281. 76) R6. 16.

105. De vita Hildefonsis librum i

R6. 20.

106. Commentum super alphabetum grecum et hebreum

(K281. 64) R6. 24.

107. De quibusdam capitulis .iiii. ewangeliorum

(K281. 112) R6. 26.

108. De naturis quorundam animalium et avium allegatorum (*sic*)

(K281. 113) R6. 27.

APPENDIX TO CHAPTER 3

109. De litteris

　　(K281. 122) R6. 30.

110. De accentibus

　　(K281. 123) R6. 31.

111. De terra promissionis ad Dardanum

　　(K281. 138). The source may have been the Bury manuscript of Jerome's letters.

112. De verbo vite

　　(K281. 124). The work and its source are unidentified; like the *Speculum*, the *Catalogus* offers only the title, without incipit and explicit.

113. Super Actus apostolorum

　　(K281. 41) R6. 32.

114. Super epistolas Iohannis, Iacobi, Petri, Iude

　　(K281. 42–45) R6. 34–36, 61.

115. De iudicio Salomonis

　　(K281. 154) R6. 39.

116. De assumpcione beate Marie

　　(K281. 12) R6. 43.

117. De infancia Christi

　　(K281. 9?) R6. 46.

118. Ysagogas ad epistolas componendas R6. 48.

119. De membris et motibus Domini

　　(K281. 101) R6. 51.

120. De spera celi et diversis scripturas

　　(K281. 102) R6. 57.

121. De mensura spere celi et .xii. lapidibus preciosis

　　(K281. 103 and 105) R6. 58.

122. De .xii. mensuris pondere et mensura corporum altitudinis

　　(K281. 104 and 106) R6. 60.

123. De musicis instrumentis

　　(K281. 99) R6. 88.

124. De partibus minus notis Veteris Testamenti

　　(K281. 100) R6. 89.

125. De proverbiis Enei Senece R6. 103.

126. De gradibus Romanorum

　　(K281. 110) R6. 105.

127. De romanis pontificibus

　　(K281. 107) R6. 69.

128. De disciplina et habitu virginali

　　(K281. 215) R6. 64.

129. De essencia et immensitate Dei

　　(K281. 93) R6. 90.

130. De essencia Trinitatis R6. 94.

131. De .vi. civitatibus fugitivorum

　　(K281. 109) R6. 95.

132. Diologus contra Pelagium R6. 97.

133. De racione anime

　　(K281. 85) R6. 110.

134. De habitacione clericorum et mulierum

> (K281. 214). Source unidentified (*MF* IV 8 was probably not used).

135. De Melchisedech

> (K281. 151) R6. 100.

136. De quorundam hereticorum sententiis

> Source unidentified.

137. De Spiritu sancto librum Didimi transtulit in latinum

> (K281. 94) R6. 98, 107.

138. De Malco captivo monacho

> (K281. 2) Jerome c. 135 [27].

139. Vitam sancti Frontonii monachi et episcopi

> (K281. 4). The source may have been a Bury manuscript.

140. Vitam sancti Hillarionis

> (K281. 3) Jerome c. 135 [28].

141. Vitam sancti Pauli heremite

> (K281. 1) Jerome c. 135 [1].

142. Plerasque patrum monachorum heremitarumque vitas veracissime textuit historiis

> Source unidentified.

143. Adortaciones et dicta eorundem de greco transtulit in latinum

> (K281. 6). The source may have been a Bury manuscript.

144. Epistolas breves ad diversos lxx

(K281. 128ff.) R6. 78, but the number of epistles may come from the Bury manuscript of Jerome's letters.

145. Sermones x

> (K281. 120) Vincent XVII 19 [88].

146. Omelias Origenis .xxxviii. transtulit et correxit

> (K281. 96) Jerome c. 135 [6].

23. IOHANNES DAMASCENUS presbyter et monachus floruit circa annum Domini .xc. scripsit

1. Librum sentenciarum in quo continetur orthodoxe fidei tradicio quem quidem librum Bur[gun]dio transtulit de greco in latinum

> (K286) This title, complete with the note about Burgundio, may have come from a Bury manuscript.

24. SANCTUS HERACLIDES monachus scripsit

1. Librum qui dicitur Paradisus de vitis patrum

> (K256) Vincent XVIII 64.

25. SANCTUS CASSIANUS monachus qui et Iohannes heremita scripsit

Vincent XX 14–15.

1. Vitas patrum compertas in Egypto doctrinasque et regulas datas et alios plures composuit

Vincent XX 14 [1].

2. Scripsit enim de institutis et regulis patrum libros iiii

> (K285. 1) Vincent XX 14 [2].

APPENDIX TO CHAPTER 3

3. Item de remediis octo principalium viciorum libros viii

   (K285. 2) Vincent XX 14 [3].

4. Item xxiiii collaciones patrum

   (K285. 3) Vincent XX 14 [4].

5. Item de incarnacione Domini adversus Nestorium

   (K285. 8) Vincent XX 15 [2].

6. Item scripsit quatuor regulas omnium monachorum professioni necessaria continentes

   (K285. 7) Vincent XX 15 [1].

26. SANCTUS EUCHERIUS monachus et episcopus Lugdunensis scripsit

   Gennadius c. 64.

1. De contemptu mundi librum i

   (K164. 1) Gennadius c. 64 [1].

2. Item ad Salenem et Veranem episcopos librum i

   Gennadius c. 64 [2].

3. Item opuscula Cassiani in uno collegit volumine tam clericis quam monachis necessaria

   (K164. 3) Gennadius c. 64 [3].

27. EGIPCIUS abbas floruit circa annum Christi .cccclxxx. et scripsit

   Isidore c. 13 (works *1–2*), followed by Cassiodorus I.23.1 (works *3–4*).

1. Vitam sancti Severini

   (K167. 1) Isidore c. 13 [1].

2. Item [fol. 64r] regulam monachorum

   (K167. 2) Isidore c. 13 [2].

3. Item ad Probam virginem

   (K167. 3) Cassiodorus I.23.1 [1].

4. Ex operibus Augustini altissimas questiones ac sentencias diversas in uno libro .ccc. et .xxxviii. capitula continentes

   (K167. 4) Cassiodorus I.23.1 [2].

28. SANCTUS FULGENCIUS monachus et episcopus scripsit

   The basis of the entry was Vincent XXI 108 (works *1–10*), followed by Isidore c. 14 (works *11–13*) and the oversight from Vincent (*14*).

1. De remissione peccatorum libros ii

   (K184. 2) Vincent XXI 108 [1].

2. Ad Donatum de fide librum i

   (K184. 3) Vincent XXI 108 [2].

3. De misterio mediatoris libros iii

   (K184. 4) Vincent XXI 108 [3].

4. Contra obiectiones Trasamundi regis Arriani librum i

   (K184. 6) Vincent XXI 108 [5].

5. De continencia coniugatorum librum i

   (K184. 7) Vincent XXI 108 [6].

6. Ad Probam de virginitate et humilitate librum i

   (K184. 8) Vincent XXI 108 [7].

APPENDIX TO CHAPTER 3

7. Ad eandem de oracione et compunctione librum unum

    (K184. 9) Vincent XXI 108 [8].

8. Ad Eugippium de caritate librum i

    (K184. 10) Vincent XXI 108 [9].

9. Ad Theodorum senatorum librum i

    (K184. 11) Vincent XXI 108 [10].

10. De penitencia et indulgencia librum i

    (K184. 12) Vincent XXI 108 [11].

11. De libero arbitrio librum i

    (K184. 13) Isidore c. 14 [1].

12. De Trinitate librum i

    (K184. 1) Isidore c. 14 [2].

13. De incarnacione Domini librum i

    Isidore c. 14 [3].

14. Item sermones pulcherimos precipue de nativitate Domini et de beato Stephano qui in ecclesiis leguntur

    (Cf. K184. 17–18, 20) Vincent XXI 108 [12].

29. FAUSTUS abbas Lirinensis et episcopus Gallie scripsit iuxta Gennadium de viris illustribus

  Gennadius c. 86.

1. De Spiritu sancto librum i

    (K187. 6) Gennadius c. 86 [1].

2. De gracia Dei librum i

    (K187. 1) Gennadius c. 86 [2].

3. Adversus Arrianos et Macedonios librum i

    (K187. 3) Gennadius c. 86 [3].

4. Ad diaconum grecum epistolam in modum libelli

    (K187. 4) Gennadius c. 86 [4].

5. Ad Felicem prefectum epistolam i

    (K187. 5) Gennadius c. 86 [6].

6. De timore Domini librum i

    (K187. 2) Gennadius c. 86 [7].

7. Et alia multa scripsisse dicitur et egregius doctor creditur et probatur

    Gennadius c. 86 [5*bis*].

8. Fuit alius Faustus monachus et hereticus contra quem scripsit sanctus Augustinus

    This observation is perhaps based on *Registrum* 1. 34–5.

30. FRUCTUOSUS monachus et episcopus scripsit

1. Regulam monachorum de qua Gracianus facit mencionem de Con. di. 5 Carnem

    Decretum pt 3, D. 5 de cons. c. 32.

31. SANCTUS HILLARIUS monachus sancti Honorati et postea episcopus Arelatensis vir erat in scripturis doctus et ingenio morali aliqua edidit que erudite anime et fidelis lingue indicio sunt in quibus ad multorum utilitatem vitam sancti Honorati composuit.

    (K243) Gennadius c. 70.

32. SANCTUS SOFRONIUS monachus scripsit

> Jerome c. 134.

1. De laude Bethleem librum i

    (K551. 1) Jerome c. 134 [1].

2. De virginitate ad Eustochium librum i

    (K551. 3) Jerome c. 134 [3].

3. Item vitam Hillarionis monachi et alia opuscula Ieronymi in grecum sermonem transtulit

    (K551. 4–5) Jerome c. 134 [4].

4. Psalterium quoque et Prophetas quos Ieronimus de hebreo sermone in latinum vertit in grecum sermonem transtulit

    (K551. 6) Jerome c. 134 [5].

33. IACOBUS monachus cognomento sapiens episcopus Persarum floruit circa annum Christi .cccxxxvi. et scripsit iuxta Genadium

> Gennadius c. 1.

1. De fide contra omnes hereses

    (K292. 1) Gennadius c. 1 [1].

2. De caritate generali

    (K292. 2) Gennadius c. 1 [2].

3. De ieiunio

    (K292. 3) Gennadius c. 1 [3].

4. De oracione

    (K292. 4) Gennadius c. 1 [4].

5. De dilexione erga proximum speciali

    (K292. 5) Gennadius c. 1 [5].

6. De resurexione

    (K292. 6) Gennadius c. 1 [6].

7. De vita post mortem

    (K292. 7) Gennadius c. 1 [7].

8. De humilitate

    (K292. 8) Gennadius c. 1 [8].

6. De penitencia

    (K292. 9) Gennadius c. 1 [9].

7. De satisfactione

    (K292. 10) Gennadius c. 1 [10].

8. De virginitate

    (K292. 11) Gennadius c. 1 [11].

9. De sensu anime

    (K292. 12) Gennadius c. 1 [12].

10. De circumcisione

    (K292. 13) Gennadius c. 1 [13].

11. De acino benedicto pro quo in Ysaia legitur, Non est exterminatus botrus

    (K292. 14) Gennadius c. 1 [14].

12. De Christo quod filius Dei sit et consubstancialis patri

    (K292. 15) Gennadius c. 1 [15].

13. De castitate adversus gentes

    (K292. 16) Gennadius c. 1 [16].

14. De constructione tabernaculi

>(K292. 17) Gennadius c. 1 [17].

15. De gencium conversione

>(K292. 18) Gennadius c. 1 [18].

16. De regno Persarum

>(K292. 19) Gennadius c. 1 [19].

17. De persecucione Christianorum

>(K292. 20) Gennadius c. 1 [20].

34. PALLADIUS monachus et discipulus sancti Evagrii scripsit iuxta Historiam tripartitam

>The *Historia tripartita* has only the name, without titles of works.

1. De vitis patrum librum i

>(K422). Source unidentified; a variant name for *24.1* above.

2. Item de agricultura

>(K423). The source may have been a Bury manuscript.

35. SANCTUS CESARIUS monachus et episcopus Arelatensis

1. X omelias morales utiles ad monachos edidit

>(K135) Vincent XXIV 141.

36. CASSIODORUS senator et postea monachus floruit circa annum Domini .dx. scripsit

>The sources were perhaps a combination of Vincent XXII 49 and *Registrum* 14. This entry follows the sequence in the *Catalogus* (K111) more closely than that of the sources.

1. Super Psalmos commentarios[?] .cl. tractatus

>(K111. 2) Vincent XXII 49 [2]; R14. 2.

2. Item de racione anime librum i

>(K111. 3) Vincent XXII 49 [3].

3. De institucione scripturarum librum i

>(K111. 4) R14. 5.

4. De tropis librum i

>(K111. 5). Source unidentified.

5. De orthographia librum i

>(K111. 6) R14. 10.

6. Super Cantica canticorum librum i

>(K111. 8) R14. 4.

7. Item epistolas multas ad diversos

>(K111. 10) R14. 6; Vincent XXII 49 [1].

37. ATHANASIUS monachus et episcopus Alexandrie floruit anno Christi circa .ccccxl. et scripsit

>Jerome c. 87, supplemented by *Registrum* 17.

1. Contra gentes librum i

>(K6. 1) Jerome c. 87 [1].

2. De Trinitate libros viii

>(K6. 2) R17. 2.

3. Ad monachos librum i

>(K6. 8) R17. 19.

4. De virginitate et Arrianis libros plures

> (K6. 3) Jerome c. 87 [3–4].

5. De Spiritu sancto librum i

> (K6. 4). Cf. R17. 12.

6. Contra Arrium, Sabellinum et Fotinum libros iii

> (K6. 10) R17. 13.

7. De fide librum i

> (K6. 6) R17. 9–11.

8. De titulis Psalmorum librum i

> (K6. 9) Jerome c. 87 [5].

9. Symbolum Quicunque vult et alia

> (K6. 5) R17. 1.

38. PROSPER monachus Aquitanitus floruit anno Domini .ccccl. et scripsit

> Perhaps based on *Registrum* 23, but the likeness is slight; the source may have been a Bury manuscript.

1. De vita contemplativa libros iii

> (K466. 4) R23. 6.

2. Item sentenciarum sive epigramatum [fol. 64v] libros .iii., alio nomine dicitur liber de vera innocencia

> (K466. 3) R23. 10. The alternate title, identically phrased in the *Catalolgus*, may have been taken from a Bury manuscript.

3. Item epistolas et multa alia

> (K466. 6) R23. 2.

39. SANCTUS BENEDICTUS abbas circa annum Christi .dxvi. scripsit

1. Regulam monachorum iuxta sanctum Gregorium secundo Dialogorum

> Gregory *Dialogi* II 36 (ed. A. de Vogüe, SChr 260 (Paris 1979), 2. 242).

40. SANCTUS GREGORIUS monachus et papa scripsit

> *Registrum* 2, perhaps supplemented by Bury manuscripts.

1. Super Iob libros xxxv

> (K203. 1) R2. 5.

2. Item ad prelatos et pastores libros iiii

> (K203. 2) R2. 3.

3. Item dialogorum libros iiii

> (K203. 3) R2. 4.

4. Super Evangelia omelias xl

> (K203. 4) R2. 2.

5. Item commentariolum super Cantica

> (K203. 6) R2. 10.

6. De conflictu viciorum et virtutum

> (K203. 12) R2. 9.

7. Item registrum continens libros xiiii

> (K203. 5) R2. 7.

8. Item super Genesim librum i

> (K203. 15) R2. 15.

9. De sacramento altaris librum i

> (K203. 8) R2. 18.

10. Super primam et ultimam partem Ezechielis omelias xxii

> (K203. 7) R2. 6.

APPENDIX TO CHAPTER 3

11. Ad Augustinum Cantuariensem de pollucione nocturna epistolam unam

    (K203. 9) R2. 8.

12. Item de reconsiliacione monachorum librum i

    (Cf. K203. 10) R2. 12.

13. Item ad Augustinum Cantuariensem et alios multos epistolas quamplures

    (Cf. K203. 10–11). The source may have been a Bury manuscript.

41. ANGELONIUS monachus floruit circa annum Domini .dcccxxx. iuxta Vincencium in Speculo et scripsit

1. Ad Lodovicum imperatorem super libros Regum librum i

    (K10) Vincent XXV 33.

42. AMALARIUS monachus scripsit

1. Ad Lodovicum imperatorem de officiis ecclesie libros iiii

    (K14) Vincent XXV 33.

43. SANCTUS ALDELMUS abbas Malmesburie et episcopus Schirbornie floruit circa annum Domini .dclxvi. et scripsit

> The sequence of works (identical with *Catalogus*, K8) repeats that of a Bury manuscript, Bodl. MS Rawlinson C. 697 (Bury A. 119), the probable source of this entry.

1. Enigmata in quibus continentur versus mille

    (K8. 1) Rawlinson C. 697, fol. 1v.

2. Item de virginitate et laude sanctorum ad abbatissam de Berkynge librum i

    (K8. 2) Rawlinson C. 697, fol. 17r.

3. De .viii. viciis principalibus librum i

    (K8. 3) Rawlinson C. 697, fol. 56r.

44. SANCTUS BEDA monachus Gyrwynensis et prebyter venerabilis floruit circa annum Domini .dccvi. et scripsit iuxta Vincencium et alios

> Three successive sources, Vincent XXIV 133 (works *1–15*), Bede's own list at the end of the *Historia ecclesiastica* (works *16–36*, except *28* and *30*), and *Registrum* 7 (works *37–42*).

1. Super Genesim libros iiii

    (K84. 1) Vincent XXIV 133 [1].

2. De tabernaculo Moysi libros iii

    (K84. 2) Vincent XXIV 133 [2].

3. Super Samuelem libros iiii

    (K84. 3) Vincent XXIV 133 [3].

4. De templo Salomonis libros ii

    (K84. 4) Vincent XXIV 133 [4].

5. Super Esdram et Neemiam libros iii

    (K84. 12) Vincent XXIV 133 [5].

6. Super Tobiam librum i

    (K84. 14) Vincent XXIV 133 [6].

7. Super Psalmos librum i

    (K84. 63) Vincent XXIV 133 [7].

8. Super Parabolas Salomonis libros iii

    (K84. 6) Vincent XXIV 133 [8].

APPENDIX TO CHAPTER 3

9. Super Cantica canticorum libros vi
   (K84. 7) Vincent XXIV 133 [9].

10. Super Marcum omelias iiii
    (K84. 22) Vincent XXIV 133 [10].

11. Super Lucam omelias vi
    (K84. 23) Vincent XXIV 133 [11].

12. Super epistolas canonicas libros vii
    (K84. 27) Vincent XXIV 133 [12].

13. Super Actus apostolorum libros ii
    (K84. 26) Vincent XXIV 133 [13].

14. Super Apocalipsim libros iii
    (K84. 28) Vincent XXIV 133 [14].

15. De questionibus libri Regum librum i
    (K84. 5) Vincent XXIV 133 [15].

16. Super Abacuc librum i
    (K84. 13) *HE* [24].

17. Super Iob librum i
    (K84. 19) *HE* [28].

18. Super Ecclesiastem librum i
    (K84. 20) *HE* [29].

19. De .vi. etatibus seculi epistolam i
    (K84. 30) *HE* [42].

20. De mansionibus filiorum Israel tractatum i
    (K84. 31) *HE* [43].

21. De illo Ysaie, Et claudentur ibi in carcerem tractatum i
    (K84. 32) *HE* [44].

22. De bisexto et equinoxio epistolam i
    (K84. 33) *HE* [45].

23. De naturis rerum librum i
    (K84. 42) *HE* [56].

24. De neupmatibus et tropis librum i
    (K84. 47) *HE* [61].

25. De temporibus, horis et momentis
    (K84. 44) *HE* [57].

26. De arte metrica librum i
    (K84. 46) *HE* [60].

27. De gestis Anglorum libros v
    (K84. 38) *HE* [52].

28. De locis sanctis et situ Ierusalem epistolam i
    (K84. 56) R7. 3.

29. De orthographia librum i
    (K84. 45) *HE* [59].

30. Lamentacionis in die iudicii
    (K84. 53) R7. 31.

31. Epigramatum librum i
    HE [55].

32. Ympnorum librum i
    (K84. 40) *HE* [54].

33. Martilogium de nataliciis sanctorum
    (K84. 39) *HE* [53].

34. Vitam sancti Felicis confessoris
    (K84. 34) *HE* [48].

35. Vitam sancti Cuthberti

    (K84. 36) *HE* [50].

36. Vitam et passionem sancti Anastasii transtulit in latinum

    (K84. 35) *HE* [49].

37. De divinis officiis librum i

    (K84. 48) R7. 36.

38. Exameron libros vi

    R7. 42.

39. Super mulierum fortem tractatum i

    (K84. 58) R7. 47.

40. De figuris gramaticorum

    R7. 50.

41. De compoto

    (K84. 51) R7. 51.

42. De ponderibus et mensuris librum i

    R7. 54.

43. Super epistolas Pauli ex operibus sancti Augustini collecta

    (K84. 61) R7. 53.

45. RABANUS abbas Fuldensis et postea archiepiscopus Magundensis floruit circa annum Domini .dcccxiiii. et scripsit

> Vincent XXV 28 (works *1–17*, with 2 exceptions), followed by *Registrum* 11 (works *18–26*)

1. De laude crucis libros ii

    (K492. 1) Vincent XXV 28 [1].

2. De institucione clericorum librum i

    (K492. 2) Vincent XXV 28 [2].

3. Super Genesim libros iiii

    (K492. 3) Vincent XXV 28 [3].

4. Super Exodum libros iiii

    (K492. 4) Vincent XXV 28 [4].

5. Super Numerum librum i

    (K492. 5) Vincent XXV 28 [5].

6. Super Leviticum librum i

    (K492. 7) R11. 17.

7. Super Deuteronomium librum i

    (K492. 8) R11. 19.

8. Super Regum librum i

    (K492. 6) Vincent XXV 28 [6].

9. Super Paralipomenon libros iiii

    (K492. 9) Vincent XXV 28 [7].

10. Super Iudith libros vii

    (K492. 10) Vincent XXV 28 [8].

11. Super Hester librum i

    (K492. 11) Vincent XXV 28 [9].

12. Super librum Sapiencie libros iii

    (K492. 12) Vincent XXV 28 [10].

13. Super Ecclesiasticum libros x

    (K492. 13) Vincent XXV 28 [11].

14. Super Ieremiam librum i

    (K492. 14) Vincent XXV 28 [12].

15. Super Machabeorum librum i

(K492. 15) Vincent XXV 28 [13].

16. De naturis rerum libros xxii

(K492. 20) Vincent XXV 28 [16].

17. Super Matheum omeliam i

(K492. 16) Vincent XXV 28 [14].

18. Ethimologiarum librum i

(Cf. K492. 20) R11. 3.

19. Super Parabolas librum i

(K492. 17) R11. 8.

20. De compoto

(K492. 22) R11. 9.

21. De significacionibus verborum

(K492. 21) R11. 13.

22. Liber qui [fol. 65r] dicitur Dominus vobiscum

R11. 15.

23. Super epistolas Pauli ad Corinthios, Galathas, et Ephesios

(K492. 18) R11. 20.

24. De officiis ecclesiasticis

(K492. 23) R11. 21.

25. De predestinacione

(K492. 24) R11. 22.

26. Super Apocalipsin

(K492. 19) R11. 23.

46. RADULPHUS FLAVIACENSIS monachus scripsit

Registrum 37; all of these titles but work *2* appear in a list written by Kirkestede on the flyleaf of a Bury manuscript, Cambridge, Pembroke College, MS 29 (Bury R. 14).

1. Super Leviticum libros xx

(K494. 1) R37. 1.

2. Super Regum libros 4

(K494. 5) R37. 5.

3. Super epistolas Pauli

(K494. 2) R37. 2.

4. Super Apocalipsim

(K494. 3) R37. 3.

5. Super Parabolas

(K494. 4) R37. 4.

6. De re militari librum i

R37. 6.

7. De sanctuario, quod est sancta Maria

(K494. 15) R37. 7.

8. De abbate et monacho librum i

(K494. 14) R37. 8.

9. Super Matheum librum i

(K494. 8) R37. 11.

10. De .vi. etatibus et de hiis que futura sunt

(K494. 9) R37. 9.

11. De diversis miraculis et meditacionibus

(K494. 10) R37. 10.

47. SANCTUS ODO primus abbas Cluniacensis floruit circa annum Christi .dcccx. et scripsit

> *Registrum* 50; the works do not follow the sequence of either *Catalogus* (K405) or *Registrum*. Works *8–9* are not in R, and the wording of the title of *9* is much different from K's; they may reflect the rubrics of a Bury manuscript.

1. Super quinque libros Moysi libros iii

   (K405. 2) R50. 1.

2. De onere Philistiim librum i

   (K405. 4) R50. 5.

3. De viciis et virtutibus anime libros .iii., principium *Auctor*

   (K405. 6) R50. 8 (without the incipit).

4. Item librum vite

   (K405. 3) R50. 4.

5. Item de ternario librum i

   (K405. 8) R50. 2.

6. Item librum parcium compositarum

   (K405. 5) R50. 6.

7. Item librum chronicarum

   (K405. 7) R50. 7.

8. Item medullam moraliam Gregorii collegit in uno volumine

   (K405. 9). Source unidentified.

9. Item sermonem de sancto Benedicto qui legitur in eius translacione, principium *Festiva beatissimi*

   (K405. 10). Source unidentified; the source may have been a Bury manuscript.

10. Item sermones et epistolas quamplures

    (K405. 11–12) R50. 3 (sermons only).

48. SANCTUS LANFRANCUS monachus Beccensis et archiepiscopus Cantuarie floruit circa annum Christi .mlxxiiii. et scripsit

> *Registrum* 51.

1. Contra Berengarnium (*sic*) librum i

   (K344. 1) R51. 2.

2. Item de corpore et sanguine Domini librum i

   (K344. 1*bis*) R51. 5.

3. De consuetudinibus monachorum librum i

   R51. 4.

4. Item epistolas quam plures ad diversos

   (K344. 4) R51. 1.

49. SANCTUS ANSELMUS monachus Beccensis et archiepiscopus Cantuarie floruit circa annum Christi .mcii. et scripsit

> Vincent XXVI 71 was the basis for the entry (works *1–16* except *7* and *15*, and scattered additions later), with other titles probably derived from the same Bury manuscripts that were used for the corresponding *Catalogus* entry (K3); *Registrum* 33 was probably not used.

1. Prosologion

   (K3. 22) Vincent XXVI 71 [1].

2. Item monologion

   (K3. 21) Vincent XXVI 71 [3].

3. Item de Trinitate

> (K3. 20) Vincent XXVI 71 [3 again, the same misreading that occurs at K3. 20].

4. Item de conceptu virginali et peccato origenali (*sic*)

> (K3. 1) Vincent XXVI 71 [7].

5. Item de veritate et libero arbitrio et casu diaboli

> (K3. 2) Vincent XXVI 71 [4].

6. Item de concordia liberi arbitrii et presciencia divine predestinacionis et gracie

> (K3. 3) Vincent XXVI 71 [5].

7. Item de libero arbitrio librum i

> (K3. 4). Cf. R33. 16; the source may have been a Bury manuscript.

8. Cur deus homo libros ii

> (K3. 5) Vincent XXVI 71 [11].

9. Meditacionum et oracionum librum i

> (Cf. K3. 23–27) Vincent XXVI 71 [12].

10. De gramatico librum i

> (K3. 6) Vincent XXVI 71 [13].

11. De casu diaboli librum i

> (K3. 7) Vincent XXVI 71 [6].

12. De incarnacione verbi librum i

> (K3. 15) Vincent XXVI 71 [7].

13. De sacramento altaris epistolam i

> (K3. 16) Vincent XXVI 71 [8].

14. De azimo epistolam i

> (K3. 17) Vincent XXVI 71 [10].

15. De beatitudine et miseria libros xxv

> (K3. 18). The source may have been a Bury manuscript.

16. Super Cantica canticorum

> (K3. 31) Vincent XXVI 71 [15].

17. De similitudinibus librum i

> (K3. 14). Cf. R33. 20; the source may have been a Bury manuscript.

18. De processione Spiritus sancti librum i

> (K3. 8) Vincent XXVI 71 [17].

19. Contra insipientem librum i

> (K3. 9). The source may have been a Bury manuscript.

20. Contra respondentem pro insipiente librum i

> (K3. 10) Vincent XXVI 71 [2].

21. Dispu[ta]cio Iudei cum Christiano de fide catholica

> (K3. 12). The source may have been a Bury manuscript.

22. De predestinacione et libero arbitrio

> (Cf. K3. 3). Cf. Vincent XXVI 71 [5] and R33. 5.

23. Disputacio pro insipiente librum i

> (K3. 11). The source may have been a Bury manuscript.

24. Tractatus de excellencia beate Virginis

(K3. 28). The source may have been a Bury manuscript.

25. Item Parabolarum sive Proverbiorum librum i

(K3. 34) Vincent XXVI 71 [14].

26. Item sermones de assumpcione beate Marie

(K3. 33). The source may have been a Bury manuscript.

27. Item sigillum sancta Marie

(K3. 30). The source may have been a Bury manuscript.

28. Item de gracia et libero arbitrio librum i

(Cf. K3. 3). Cf. Vincent XXVI 71 [5] or R33. 5.

29. Item epistolas ccxvi

(K3. 35) Vincent XXVI 71 [16], or perhaps a Bury manuscript.

50. SANCTUS BERNARDUS scripsit

Registrum 34 provided the entire list of forty-seven titles, save two inserted near the end; this entry establishes the *Speculum coenobitarum* (along with the *Catalogus*) as by far the earliest indisputable use of the *Registrum* as a bibliographical resource. The two *pseudepigrapha* inserted at *45–46* may have been taken from a Bury manuscript.

1. Ad Senonensem archiepiscopum de .iii. virtutibus

(K85. 19) R34. 1.

2. De cohabitacione fratrum

(K85. 27) R34. 2.

3. Item oraciones eiusdem quomodo imitetur Christus

(K85. 36) R34. 4.

4. Exhortaciones Bernardi

(K85. 22) R34. 5.

5. Ad Davidem nepotem suum de operibus .vi. dierum

(K85. 25) R34. 6.

6. Ad clericos de conversacione

R34. 8.

7. De colloquio Symonis et Iesu

(K85. 24) R34. 9.

8. Super illud Intravit Iesus

(K85. 28) R34. 10.

9. Super illud Cum esset desponsata

(K85. 30) R34. 11.

10. Super Ysayam

(K85. 31) R34. 12.

11. De .vi. verbis Domini in cruce

R34. 13.

12. Sentencie contemplative eius

R34. 14.

13. Super regulam

R34. 18.

14. Omelie eius super epistolam Iacobi

(K85. 32) R34. 16.

15. Planctus eius super mortem fratris sui

(K85. 34) R34. 15.

16. Ad A[dam] Romane ecclesie diaconum

    (K85. 26) R34. 20.

17. Ad fratres de monte Dei

    (K85. 17) R34. 23.

18. Sermones eiusdem super Cantica canticorum

    (K85. 12) R34. 21.

19. Epistolas multas

    (K85. 38) R34. 24.

20. De consideracione libros v

    (K85. 9) R34. 25.

21. De precepto et dispensacione etc.

    (K85. 7) R34. 26.

22. Super Missus est librum i

    (K85. 13) R34. 27.

23. De .xii. gradibus humilitatus librum i

    (K85. 5) R34. 28.

24. De gracia et libero arbitrio librum i

    (K85. 6) R34. 29.

25. De diligendo Deo librum i

    (K85. 2) R34. 30.

26. De amore Dei

    (K85. 3) R34. 31.

27. De videndo Deo

    R34. 32.

28. Super Psalmum Qui habitat

    (K85. 11) R34. 33.

29. Ad quendam monachum de superfluitatibus

    R34. 34.

30. Ad Eugenium papam libros v

    R34. 35.

31. De virtutibus et viciis

    R34. 36.

32. Exposiciones ecclesiasticarum regularum

    R34. 38.

33. Super illud, Dixit Symon Petrus ad Iesum

    R34. 39.

34. Ad Robertum [fol. 65v] monachum fugientem

    R34. 40.

35. Ad milites templi

    R34. 41.

36. Ad Willelmum abbatem

    R34. 42.

37. Sermonem in nativitatem beate Marie

    R34. 43.

38. Sermonem de Ieppte

    R34. 44.

39. Epitalamium

    R34. 45.

40. Meditaciones

    (K85. 21) R34. 46.

APPENDIX TO CHAPTER 3

41. De concepcione beate Marie
    (K85. 42) R34. 47.

42. De varietate ordinis monastici
    R34. 48.

43. De caritate ad fratres Cartusie
    R34. 49.

44. Apologiticum eiusdem
    (K85. 8) R34. 50.

45. Speculum eiusdem
    The source may have been a Bury manuscript.

46. De caritate
    The source may have been a Bury manuscript.

47. De visitacione infirmorum
    R34. 51.

51. SANCTUS ELREDUS abbas Ryvallensis scripsit

Registrum 39 may have been used and perhaps Bury manuscripts were consulted, but the principal source of this entry remains unidentified.

1. Speculum caritatis libros ii
   (K5. 2) R39. 9.

2. De spirituali amicicia libros iii
   (K5. 3) R39. 6.

3. De anima librum i
   (K5. 7) R39. 11.

4. De institucione inclusarum libros ii
   (K5. 5) R39. 7.

5. Vitam sancti Edwardi regis Anglorum
   (K5. 14) R39. 13.

6. Vitam sancti Niniani
   (K5. 15). Source unidentified.

7. Miracula ecclesie de Extildesham (*K*: Augustaldensis)
   (K5. 12). Source unidentified.

8. Relacionem eiusdem de standardo
   (K5. 13). Source unidentified.

9. Chronicam eiusdem
   (K5. 11). Source unidentified.

10. Lamentacionem eius de morte regis David
    (K5. 16). Source unidentified.

11. Geneologiam regum Anglie
    (K5. 16*bis*). Source unidentified.

12. Liber qui dicitur sagitta Ionathe
    (Cf. K5. 10). Source unidentified.

13. De diversis virtutibus
    (K5. 10). Source unidentified.

14. Sermones eius de omnibus solempnitatibus anni et plures in synodis
    (K5. 18). Source unidentified.

15. Epistole eiusdem cc
    (K5. 19) R39. 12

16. Item de omnibus in Ysaya omelias xxx
    Source unidentified.

17. Oracio illius pastoralis, O pastor bone etc.

> Source unidentified.

52. ROBERTUS monachus scripsit

1. Super librum Trenorum libros v

> Source unidentified.

53. BERNARDUS abbas Cassinensis et cardinalis floruit circa annum Christi .mcxl. et scripsit

> The source of this whole entry may have been a Bury manuscript.

1. Quendam tractatum de professione monachorum et intitulatur Speculum monachorum

> (K86. 1).

2. Item scripsit notabilem exposicionem super regulam sancti Benedicti

> (K86. 2).

3. Item de monacho bestialiter vivente tractatum i

54. HAYMO monachus et doctor modernus scripsit

> *Registrum* 27 may have been used, but a more likely source for most if not all of the titles is a Bury manuscript.

1. Super Ysaiam libros ii

> (K240. 2) R27. 3.

2. Super epistolas Pauli

> (K240. 3) R27. 2.

3. Super Apocalipsim

> (K240. 4) R27. 5.

4. Super .v. libros Moisi

> (K240. 1). Source unidentified.

5. Super epistolas et Ewangelia tocius anni omelias notabiles et sermones

> (K240. 5) R27. 6.

6. Item in Christianarum rerum memoria

> (K240. 6). Source unidentified.

55. IOACHIM abbas de Calabria floruit circa annum Domini .mcxlii. et scripsit

> Like the corresponding *Catalogus* list (K293), this entry is presumably based on Bury manuscripts.

1. Super Apocalipsim libros iii

> (K293. 1).

2. Comentarios super libros prophetarum

> (K293. 2).

3. De moribus paparum qui post eum futuri erant librum i

> (K293. 4).

Hic libros suos corrigendos domino pape optulit.

56. WILLELMUS monachus de Rameseya scripsit

1. Super Cantica canticorum omelias xxx

> (K626. 1) The source must have been a manuscript. That this rare work was known to the compiler of the *Speculum coenobitarum* list and to the compiler of the *Catalogus* is a persuasive link between the two.

57. BRITHFERTHUS monachus de Ramesia scripsit

1. Super Bedam de temporibus libros iiii

    (K90). The source may have been a Bury manuscript.

58. SMARAGDUS abbas scripsit

    The source of this whole entry may have been a Bury manuscript.

1. Exposicionem super regulam sancti Benedicti

    (K553. 2).

2. Item diadema monachorum

    (K553. 1).

59. GRACIANUS monachus compilavit

1. Decreta

    (K217) The source was presumably a Bury *Decretum*.

CHAPTER 4

THE HISTORY OF THE TEXT OF THE *CATALOGUS*

The text of Henry of Kirkestede's *Catalogus* survives only as a late 17th-cent. transcript, CUL MS Add. 3470.[1] We set forth here what can be known or sensibly assumed about the transmission of the text, from Kirkestede to the surviving transcript in Cambridge University Library. We shall consider early copies of the *Catalogus*, early excerpts, and early echoes and mentions of it. In the 17th and 18th cent. Kirkestede's booklist came to be regarded as the progenitor of English bibliography. Particular and near-constant interest in the *Catalogus* persisted in England, from the Dissolution in the 16th cent. to the reign of George II when parts of the text were printed. Motives governing early modern interest in the *Catalogus* encompassed humanism and, especially, polemical protestantism, and the work was quoted in support of major shifts in the political and religious purposes of the English antiquaries. The flurry of early modern attention in the *Catalogus* invested it with elements of factional bias that would have surprised its author; but its partisan usefulness accounted in large measure for the text's survival.

Virtually every piece of evidence about the *Catalogus* has reached us by way of John Bale. We know of the Norwich copy of the *Catalogus*, no longer extant, only through Bale's report of it. And the Bury copy of the *Catalogus*, also no longer extant, was acquired, quoted, and publicized by Bale, passing from him to the 17th- and 18th-cent. antiquaries who quoted, excerpted, transcribed, and ultimately lost it.

Two Medieval Copies of the Catalogus

Two copies of the *Catalogus*, almost certainly medieval, were known in the mid-16th cent. Neither survives. The copy made at Bury by the scribe Boston is the more important to us, because this manuscript engendered the transcript on which the present edition depends. Knowledge about Boston comes

---

1. Much of the following discussion of Bale's use of the *Catalogus*, the Norwich catalogue, and the provenance of the text is indebted to an unpublished typescript generously shared, years ago, by the late R. W. Hunt.

from his colophon to the *Catalogus*, which tells us only his name and the fact that he was the scribe:

> Thou O King who readest this book, have mercy on the scribe.
> For in truth when he wrote it, he did not do so carelessly, in my opinion.
> Should it displease Thee, may Thy measureless grace appear
> Which Thou extendest to all things, and may it suffice for the purpose.
> The scribe, whose name is called after the town of Boston,
> Will be doomed, unless God give a sign of His grace.[2]

Because we do not know the date of this non-extant manuscript, we cannot argue whether Boston made his copy in Kirkestede's lifetime—potentially as Kirkestede's amanuensis creating a fair copy from Kirkestede's draft notes and at Kirkestede's direction—or whether Boston's copy was made after Kirkestede's death from Kirkestede's draft or fair copy.[3] In contrast to its speculative origins, Boston's copy of the *Catalogus* left substantial evidence about its early modern existence, after it was acquired by John Bale. We shall trace later the details of this manuscript's transmission in the early modern era.

A second medieval copy of the *Catalogus* belonged to the Benedictine cathedral chapter in Norwich, and was seen there by John Bale in the 16th cent. The manuscript was not cited by any other writer, so (as with the scribe Boston's copy) our only sure knowledge of its age is that it predated Bale; and our knowledge of its contents depends on the extracts from it in Bale's *Index*. He described it thus in a separate entry: 'Catalogus doctorum ac librorum diversorum quorum nomina ponuntur secundum ordinem alphabeti li. 1: *Abbas Ioachim, require vocabulum Ioachim, etc*. Ex Bibliotheca Nordouicensis monasterii'.[4] The manuscript was obviously anonymous, for Bale recorded it in his notebook under its title, among the authors whose names begin with the letter C; and the manuscript obviously did not mention the scribe Boston's name. The title Bale recorded, which he presumably found on the Norwich manuscript, is a pastiche assembled from

---

2. Add. 3470, p. 152: 'Qui legis hunc librum, scriptoris, Rex, miserere, / Dum scripsit vere, non fecit ut æstimo pigrum. / Si tibi displiciat, veniat tua gratia grandis / Quam cunctis pandis, hæc sibi sufficiat. / Scriptoris nomen Botulphi villa vocatur, / Qui condempnatur, nisi gratum det Deus omen'. We are grateful to Blair Sullivan for help with this translation.
3. The notes, draft, or exemplar which the scribe Boston copied has left no trace.
4. Bale, *Index*, Appendix II, 'Libri Anonymi' (p. 472). Note that the list of anonymous books is a creation of Poole & Bateson's, the *Index*'s original editors, whereas Bale himself recorded such works alphabetically according to the initial letter of the title.

Kirkestede's introduction ('Incipit catalogus') and from Kirkestede's explanatory paragraph immediately preceding the booklist proper.

The incipit that Bale cites for the Norwich manuscript does not correspond with the incipit of Add. 3470. It is, instead, a cross-reference (to the entry for Joachim of Fiore, *Catalogus 293*). This suggests that the Norwich Benedictines had created, and bound at the head of the text, a list of the authors' names alphabetized by at least the first and second letters, to increase the catalogue's 'searchability'. As we shall see, they made other minor additions to the text.

Bale cited the Norwich catalogue as a source of information for twenty-four authors in his notebook or *Index*.[5] Curiously, Bale did not recognize it as a version of the work that he had elsewhere attributed to the authorship of Bostonus Buriensis. He was conscious of its close similarity to the Bury *Catalogus*, however, and in twelve instances when it either duplicated the wording of the Bury *Catalogus* or varied from it only slightly he cited the two jointly, with the formula 'Ex utroque catalogo Nordouicensi et Buriensi', or, more frequently, just 'Ex utroque Anglorum catalogo'.[6]

Entries of this sort in Bale's *Index*—ones that purport to come from both catalogues—seldom differ in wording from the text of Add. 3470, occasionally by the addition of a title or the lengthening of an incipit, and by a note (not in Add. 3470) in the entry for Ioannes Scotus concerning the condemnation of his *De eucharistia* at the Council of Vercelli. It is impossible to determine whether such minor variations reflect the text of the Norwich manuscript or were merely Bale's own additions, since, as we shall see, he did alter his excerpts when he had additional information at hand.

On fourteen occasions Bale cited the Norwich catalogue independently.[7]

---

5. Cited by page numbers of Bale's *Index*: *ex bibliotheca et catalogo Nordovicensi*, p. 287 Mattheus Florilegus; *ex Nordovicensi scriptorum catalogo* (or *ex catalogo scriptorum Nordovicensi*), p. 48 Bernardus Siluestris, p. 53 Caradocus, p. 93 Gildas, p. 147 Guilhelmus Rubrouke, p. 164 Henricus Huntyngdon (a secondary entry; see *ex utroq. Angl. cat.*), p. 170 Hugo de Hibernia, p. 288 Mattheus [Florilegus], p. 297 Nennius Brito, p. 331 Radulfus Niger, pp. 384–5 Robertus S. Michaelis, p. 398 Rogerus Cestriensis (entered twice in the edition and twice on fol. 155r of Bale's notebook, *ex cat. script. Nord.* and *ex Nord. script. cat.* respectively); *ex catalogo antiquo Nordovicensi*, pp. 375–6 Robertus Grostede; *ex catalogo Nordovicensi*, p. 405 Rogerus de Wyndore; *ex utroque Catalogo Nordovicensi et Buriensi*, p. 1 Abbo, p. 12 Adelredus, pp. 15–16 Albinus, pp. 24–5 Alexander Nequam; *ex utroque Anglorum Catalogo*, p. 8 Adelardus, p. 31 Anselmus, p. 34 Arnulfus, pp. 43–4 Bedas, p. 160 Henricus Cossey, p. 164 Henricus Huntyngdon (and see *ex Nord. script. Cat.*), p. 247 Ioannes Scotus, p. 369 Robertus Crikeladensis.
6. ibid. 1, 8, 12, 15–16, 24–5, 31, 34, 43–4, 160, 164, 247, 369.
7. ibid. 48, 53, 93, 147, 164, 170, 287, 288, 297, 331, 376, 384–5, 398, 405. (The figures that we cite for Bale's notes will not tally precisely, because Bale sometimes cited the Norwich manuscript twice, once jointly with the *Catalogus* and once independently, for the same author.)

In seven of the fourteen, material from the Norwich catalogue immediately follows an entry from the Bury *Catalogus* for the same author.[8] In the other seven, Bale cited the Norwich catalogue for authors whose names do not appear in the *Catalogus*.[9] It must have been these additions that caused Bale to consider the Norwich catalogue as a separate source. However, its supplementary material—rather than being information that has dropped out of the *Catalogus* text—seems to have comprised additions to the text made at Norwich itself from manuscripts in the Norwich library. For example, the names 'Mattheus Florilegus' (p. 287) for Matthew Paris and 'Rogerus Cestriensis' (p. 398) for Ranulf Higden both come specifically from Norwich manuscripts, as can be seen elsewhere in the *Index*. It would seem also that *floruit* dates were occasionally added to the Norwich *Catalogus* manuscript. Thus, in the entry for Henricus Cossey (p. 160), cited 'ex utroque Anglorum catalogo', the date and place of his death (not found in Add. 3470) were available in the Norwich manuscript described in Bale's notebook.[10] Dates were supplied in the Norwich *Catalogus* for at least two other authors (Gildas and Henry of Huntingdon).[11]

Judging from Bale's evidence, then, we suppose that the Norwich catalogue was a text of Kirkestede's *Catalogus*, with additions based on books at Norwich; there is no proof that the Norwich manuscript contained those parts of the *Catalogus* not quoted by Bale, but it is a reasonable assumption. Perhaps Kirkestede gave a copy of the *Catalogus* to the Norwich Benedictines, or lent them an exemplar from which to make a copy. Despite Bury's sometimes rancorous relations with the bishop of Norwich,[12] we know that Kirkestede had been permitted access to the Norwich books; he reported in the *Catalogus* twelve works from the cathedral library and even supplied specific information about the location of one of them, a *Cantelarium* of Astulphus: 'It contains three folios, and is housed in the library of the dormitory'.[13]

Probably the Norwich *Catalogus* was made during or shortly after Kirkestede's lifetime (though it may have been made later). Thereafter, the

---

8. ibid. 47–8, 93, 164, 297, 331–2, 375–6, 384–5.
9. ibid. 53 Caradocus, 147 Guilhelmus Rubrouke, 170 Hugo de Hibernia, 287 Mattheus Florilegus, 288 Mattheus [Florilegus], 398 Rogerus Cestriensis, 405 Rogerus de Wyndore.
10. The citation for Henricus Costesey *ex biblioteca Nordouicensi* (Bale, *Index*, 160) is on the same page of the edition as the citation for this author *ex utroque Anglorum catalogo*, but the two are not together in the manuscript of Bale's notebook (Bodl. MS Selden supra 64, on fols. 20r and 63r, respectively).
11. Pages 93 and 164 of the *Index* edition, respectively.
12. See p. xxxv above.
13. *Catalogus* 72.1, 'et continet tria folia et est . . . in libraria dormitorii'.

Norwich copy was enlarged, probably by means of annotation and insertion over time from sources and manuscripts in the Norwich library. The nature of the *Catalogus* invites such revision, and Kirkestede explicitly requested that his work be enlarged.[14] The Norwich *Catalogus* was seen, evidently *in situ*, by Bale between 1548 and 1553; its fate thereafter is unknown.[15]

The Ely Extracts

A late 15th-cent. composite manuscript from Ely Cathedral (Lambeth Palace Library, MS 448) contains three pages of extracts from the *Catalogus*;[16] these constitute the only witness to the *Catalogus* that has not reached us through the mediation of John Bale. The individual parts of Lambeth 448 were written at and pertain to Ely, at and after the middle of the 15th cent.; this includes an Ely chronicle in the first ten quires. The final segment of the book, fols. 117r–153r, is a paper booklet in which are found the extracts from the *Catalogus*, along with miscellaneous excerpts from chronicles, saints' lives, and lists of popes, kings, and bishops. The inclusion of several first-hand descriptions of events surrounding the accession of Edward IV suggests that this part may have been compiled during the period 1456–64.[17] Its compiler shows an interest in and knowledge of Bury St Edmunds. Notice of a great fire at Bury in 1140 has been added in the upper margin of the first page (of this segment = fol. 117r); and there is also what appears to be an eye-witness account of the parliament of 1446–7 held at Bury, and a report of the suspected murder of the duke of Gloucester (d. 1447).[18] The com-

---

14. *Catalogus*, preface, p. 20 below; Kirkestede, referring specifically to incipits, explicits, and locations that he had not seen, adds, 'si alicui occurrant poterit eos in spatio vacuo ad hoc reservato intitulare'.
15. The dates are those of Bale's return from his first continental exile and his departure on his second and final exile. The medieval library of the Norwich cathedral priory has been well studied. See especially N. R. Ker, 'Mediaeval manuscripts from Norwich cathedral priory', *Transactions of the Cambridge Bibliographical Society* 1 (1949–53) 1–28; and the survey by Sharpe, *Benedictines* 288–92.
16. See the description by James, *Lambeth*, 619–23. James recognized that these notes might have been taken from the *Catalogus*.
17. Lambeth Palace Library, MS 448, fols. 143v–146r. The notes are printed by J. Gairdner, *Three Fifteenth-Century Chronicles*, Camd. NS 28 (1880), xv–xx, 148–163. Strictly speaking, we cannot be certain that the two copies of the *Catalogus*, Boston's and the one at Norwich, predate the Ely extracts. We think it likely, however.
18. The presence of these Bury materials in this segment of the manuscript makes it probable that the Ely extracts were taken from the Bury copy of the *Catalogus*, rather than from the copy at Norwich.

piler could easily have visited Bury, only thirty miles from Ely, carrying his paper booklet of notes in his satchel and copying entries from the *Catalogus*, and from other Bury records, on to blank pages when it pleased him.

Extracts from the *Catalogus* appear on scattered pages, fols. 118v, 119v, and 149v, having been added on to whatever white space remained available; there are notes from other sources at the top of each of the three pages. The extracts comprise notes taken from the *Catalogus* entries for twenty-two authors.[19] The choice of author-entries to excerpt was narrowly selective, but the criteria for selection are not self-evident. The names include both English and non-English authors, patristic and medieval, important names and virtual unknowns. But whatever the grounds for inclusion may have been, we probably have in this codex only a portion of the excerpts that were originally made; there are eleven authors whose names begin with the letters A–B on fol. 118v and eleven beginning R–Y on fols. 149v and 119v (in that order). One would suppose that the Ely excerptor made extracts from the central portion of the *Catalogus* as well (comprising 404 authors), but if so, they have not been found.

The Ely excerpts seldom contain all or most of the corresponding *Catalogus* entries—for only eight of the twenty-two authors cited. For all but two, Berillus (*83*) and Vigilius diaconus (*623*), Kirkestede's reference to the source of the entry has been omitted. Few incipits and even fewer explicits are given, for various works in only nine of the twenty-two entries. The extracts include no locations, either as numbers or spelled out as place-names. Extracts from the longer *Catalogus* entries are severely curtailed; the most extreme example is the selection of just five of the forty-nine titles that the *Catalogus* lists for Isidore of Seville (*666.20–21, 33, 34,* and part of *48*).[20] Perhaps the excerptor was interested more in biographies than in lists of works; his extracts from the Grosseteste, Sedulius, and Ptolemy entries consist primarily of excerpts from the *Catalogus*'s headnotes for these authors.

In a few instances the readings of the Ely excerpts differ from the surviving text of the *Catalogus*. For four works the excerpts offer longer incipits, and for two they preserve entirely different incipits from the corresponding

---

19. Fol. 118v, Albertus Lumbardus (*58*), Aquila (*66*), Aluredus Rex (*76*), Basilius (*78*), Berillus (*83*), Bernardus (*85*), Bernardus Cassinensis (*86*), Bonaventura (*89*), Bartholomaeus (*93*), Boetius (*94*), Bartholomeus Pisanus (*100*); fol. 149v, Robertus Grosted (*505*), Sedulius (*531*), Sulphius [= Sulpicius] (*535*), Tholomeus (*579*); fol. 119v, Thomas de Aquino (*567*), Vigilius diaconus (*623*), Wilhelmus de Montibus (*625*), Wilhelmus de Pagula (*629*), Wilhelmus Durandi (*633*), Usuardus (*663*), Ysidorus (*666*).
20. Other examples: for Bernard (*85*), of forty-four titles in the *Catalogus* the Ely excerptor copied only sixteen, works *1–6, 14, 18, 22, 23, 27, 42, 41, 43, 44*, and *37*, in that order; for Boethius (*94*), works *1–5, 7, 15,* and *17*—only eight of a possible eighteen.

works in the *Catalogus*.²¹ Two other minor additions also occur in the Ely extracts, probably scribal (additions shown here in italics): in the headnote to Thomas Aquinas (*567*), 'scripsit multa *excellencia*', and in the description of the alphabetical *carmina* of Sedulius (*531.5*), '*et incipit* ab H usque *ad Z*'. All other differences, in spelling, in the addition of an initial 'item' and a final 'etc.' to many of the titles, and in condensation, simply reflect the standards of the Ely excerptor. While the Ely extracts may imply that some words have been lost from the medieval text of the *Catalogus*, on the whole they support the good faith of the text in Add. 3470.

No other medieval witnesses to the *Catalogus* have been found, neither extracts nor references, and nothing more is heard of the *Catalogus* until after the dissolution of the monastery of Bury in 1539.²² When John Leland visited Bury (between 1536 and 1542) he recorded only twenty-two works that he considered noteworthy, and the *Catalogus* is not among them.²³ A large number of identifiable Bury manuscripts survive, about 250. More than half of these were saved through the actions of William Smarte or Smart (d. 1599), who held a succession of important posts in the government of the port city of Ipswich (treasurer, coroner, portman, five times bailiff). It has been suggested that the manuscripts had been saved from dispersal or destruction at the Dissolution by his father, Richard Smarte (d. 1560)—a fervent Protestant-burning Catholic during Mary's reign—but there is no evidence to support the conjecture. At William Smarte's death in 1599, he bequeathed at least three Bury manuscripts to the town of Ipswich (they are now Ipswich Town Library at Ipswich School, MSS 4, 6, and 8, and possibly MS 2); and an unknown number, perhaps 150, he left to Pembroke College, Cambridge, at the behest of Richard Buckenham (d. 1628), a neigh-

---

21. Longer incipits: Bernard of Casino (*86.2*), Willelmus de Pagula (*629.3*), Durandus (*633.6*), and Isidore (*666.20*). Different incipits: Bonaventure (*89.6*) and Durandus (*633.3*).

22. Tanner (*Bibliotheca*, 114) noted an additional 16th-cent. reference, saying that MS Ashmole 770, containing the Lichfield Chronicle continued to 1559, cites the history of Thomas Rudbourne 'ex libro Ioannis Bostoni de scriptoribus Britannicis'. The original reference, Ashmole 770, fol. 19v, was to 'Iohann. Ballano in libro suo de scriptoribus Britann.' which was altered to read 'Iohann. Bostono. . .', which is puzzling, since Rudbourne does not appear either in Bale's excerpts from the *Catalogus* or in Add. 3470.

23. Leland's letter of introduction from Thomas Cromwell suggests that some of the library had been scattered before his arrival, and the *Catalogus* may already have been in Ailot Holt's possession by then; however, it was not the sort of work likely to attract Leland's notice. The letter appears in *The Itinerary of John Leland in or about the Years 1535–1543*, ed. L. Toulmin Smith, pts 4–5 (London 1908), 148; and the list of manuscripts seen at Bury appears in J. Leland, *De rebus Britannicis collectanea*, ed. T. Hearne (Oxford 1715), 3. 162–3. Both are reprinted in James, *St Edmund*, 9–11. An annotated edition of Leland's list for Bury is Sharpe & others, *Benedictines*, B16.

bour, close family friend, and master of that college.[24] Most of these have survived, though not all.[25]

The Catalogus *in the Early Modern Era*

The rapid dispersal of England's monastic libraries soon evoked, in reaction, signs of an effort to find what these books had been and where they had gone, and especially to investigate England's medieval authors, what they wrote, and where manuscripts of their works might be located.[26] The *Catalogus* of 'Boston of Bury,' as Kirkestede was known then, performed an important function in this process.

A. *John Bale's Manuscript*

A manuscript of the *Catalogus*, along with a number of other Bury books, was taken from the Bury library by Ailot Holt, a monk of the abbey pensioned at the dissolution of the house in 1539.[27] Holt's copy, with its colophon

---

24. Concerning Smarte and the transferral of the Bury manuscripts to Ipswich and Pembroke College see J. Blatchly, *The Town Library of Ipswich provided for the use of the Town Preachers in 1599* (Woodbridge 1989), 1–8.
25. For the Pembroke College manuscripts one has the list of Pembroke manuscripts published in 1600 by Thomas James, librarian of Thomas Bodley's library in Oxford. Items numbered 74–231 (no. 231 is a group of thirty-five volumes) on the list purport to belong to Smarte's gift, excerpted by James, *St Edmund*, 12–19. A second list appears in the *Register of Benefactors to the College Library* compiled by Matthew Wren (d. 1667), which lists eighty items from the Smarte bequest; James, *St Edmund*, 20–22, and see also James, *Pembroke*, xx–xxiii ('Manuscripts entered in Thomas James's catalogue, now missing'). A significant number of the items on Thomas James's list were demonstrably not part of the Smarte bequest, while Wren has markedly understated the size of the bequest. The suggested number of 150 may itself be an understatement.
26. D. C. Douglas, *English Scholars 1660–1730*, 2nd edn (London 1951), 156–7; C. E. Wright, 'The dispersal of the libraries in the sixteenth century', in F. Wormald & C. E. Wright, *The English Library before 1700* (London 1958), 148–75. Concerning the dispersal of monastic books in England see N. R. Ker, 'The migration of manuscripts from the English medieval libraries', in his *Books, Collectors and Libraries: Studies in the Medieval Heritage*, ed. A. G. Watson (London 1985), 459–70.
27. Bressie, 'Textual corruption', 249. 'Pensions assigned 4 Nov. . . . to the abbot and monks of St Edmund's Bury . . . Ailot Halstede *alias* Holte . . . £6 13s. 8d. [i.e. £13s. 4d.]'; J. Gairdner & R. H. Brodie, *Letters and Papers, Foreign and Domestic, of the Reign of Henry VIII*, 14/2 (1895), 168 no. 462. Perhaps Jeremiah Holt, rector of Stonham Aspel (some 18 or 20 miles from Bury), who gave several Bury manuscripts to St John's College in 1634, was a later kinsman. See James, *St John's*, for descriptions of MSS 35, 92, 94, 138, 140, 149, and 170.

by the scribe Boston, belonged c. 1548 to the author, bibliographer, and polemicist John Bale (1495–1563).[28] Bale, a native of Suffolk, acquired the *Catalogus* from Holt along with information concerning several other Bury manuscripts.[29] Bale had been in exile from about August 1540 (after the fall of his patron Thomas Cromwell) to shortly after the appearance of the first edition of his *Scriptores* or *Summarium* (Ipswich [*recte* Wesel] 1548) and the accession of Edward VI. Since 'Boston of Bury' was not used in the *Summarium*, Bale presumably acquired the manuscript shortly after his return from exile in early August 1548.[30] He recorded 'Boston' thus in his notebook or *Index*: [31]

> Bostonus Buriensis, seu ad fanum Eadmundi, in Sudouolgia monachus, scripsit ex Burcardo libro tertio, Hugone de sancto Victore, Vincentio, Graciano, Isidoro, et Cassiodoro, Catalogum de libris et autoribus tam autenticis quam apocriphis, li. i.
> 'Omnis diuina scriptura in duobus'   *Ex Ayloto Holte, Buriensi.*
> De prima monachorum institutione, li. i. 'Primus institutor monachorum in.'
>   Nam operis collector coenobita Buriensis fuit.
>   *Ex collegio Magdalene Oxon.*
> Speculum coenobitarum, li. iij.
> Bibliothecarum Angliae fructus, li. i.

Bale first mentioned 'Boston' in print in his edition of Leland's *Laboryouse Journey and Serche* (1549), describing him as the only collector 'of the names and workes of lerned writers' that England had had before Leland, and describing his catalogue as 'verye copyouse'. 'Bostonus Buryensis' is also cited in Bale's list, appended to the *Laboryouse Journey*, of additional writers

---

28. Concerning Bale see H. McCusker, *John Bale, Dramatist and Antiquary* (Bryn Mawr 1942); J. W. Harris, *John Bale. A Study in the Minor Literature of the Reformation*, Illinois Studies in Language and Literature 25/4 (Urbana, IL, 1940); W. T. Davies, *A Bibliography of John Bale*, Oxford Bibliographical Society. Proceedings and Papers 5/4 (1939) 201–279 (Additions and corrections, Oxford Bibl. Soc. NS 1 (1947) 44–5); L. P. Fairfield, *John Bale, Mythmaker for the English Reformation* (West Lafayette, IN, 1976); and C. Brett & J. P. Carley's introduction to the reissue of Bale's *Index* (Woodbridge 1990), xi–xviii. See also J. P. Carley, *The Libraries of King Henry VIII* (London 2000) 250–51.
29. Bale quotes Holt as source for Anselm, p. 31, 'Boston', p. 49, W. Hilton, pp. 105–106, Peter of Blois, p. 319, and Richard Rolle, p. 351.
30. It would be helpful if we knew precisely where Bale was when he met Holt, but we do not. See Davies, *Bibliography*, 219–20, McCusker, *John Bale*, 14–17. Bale mentions the *Catalogus* in print in 1549; see below.
31. Bale, *Index*, 49 (= Bodl. MS Selden supra 64, fol. 17v).

destined to be included in the second edition of his *Scriptores*.[32] Bale found the *Catalogus* to be a mine of information on medieval English authors, and he quoted 'Boston' frequently in the notebook that he compiled during the years 1549–57 in preparation for the revision of his *Scriptores*. His manifestly embellished account of 'Boston' and the *Catalogus* in this second edition has formed the basis for all succeeding biographies of 'Boston' until the 20th cent.:

> BOSTONUS BURIENSIS.
> Bostonus Buriensis, in magno illo Sudouolgiorum comitatus coenobio, ad Eadmundi fanum monachus, omnes ingenii neruos & industriam ad id intendebat, ut rem literariam promoueret. Magnis enim laboribus hic Angliam circuiuit uniuersam, & mira sedulitate ac diligentia omnes omnium regni monasteriorum bibliothecas inuisit. Librorum collegit titulos, & authorum eorum nomina: quae omnia alphabetico disposuit ordine, & quasi unam omnium Bibliothecam fecit. Ipsorum etiam aetates ac uitas, cum operum initiis curiose adiunxit, & in quibus essent ea opera inuenienda coenobiis calendarii uice per numeros demonstrauit. Addidit eidem quoque labori, ex Burcardo Vuormaciensi, Hugone de S. Victore, Cassiodoro, Isidoro, Gratiano, Vincentio, & aliis scriptoribus multa, de libris & authoribus tam authenticis quam apocryphis. & id opus uocabat
> *Catalogum scriptorum Ecclesiae*, Lib. 1. *Omnis diuina Scriptura in duobus*.
> *Speculum coenobitarum*, Lib. 3. *Primus institutor monachorum*.
> *De rebus sui coenobij*, Lib. 1.
> *Atque alia nonulla edidit*. In primo opere, solenniorum Angliae bibliothecarum libros & authores prodit: in secundo, prima ostendit monachorum initia ac progressus. Et claruit anno nati Seruatoris 1410, Henrico quarto regnante.[33]

Presumably, Bale's only source of information about the *Catalogus* and its compiler was the manuscript of the work itself. He reported the list of sources from the rubric, and the opening words of the text, just as they appear in Add. 3470. He also described the text and added comments of his own concerning 'Boston's' monastery, his learning, industry, and purpose. It was Bale whose conjecture, based on the presence of the location numbers in the *Catalogus*, gave rise to the story that 'Boston' visited all the monastic libraries of England. In addition to the *Catalogus*, Bale attributed two other titles to 'Boston' in the *Scriptores*, and two different ones in the *Index*, all four of which

---

32. J. Leland, *The Laboryouse Iourney & Serche of Johan Leylande, for Englande's Antiquitees, geuen of hym as a newe yeares gyfte to Kynge Henry the viii.*, ed. J. Bale (London 1549), signatures C8ᵛ, D1ᵛ, G4ᵛ; repr. in *Bibliographiana* 1, ed. W. A. Copinger (Manchester 1895) 52, 54.

33. Bale, *Scriptores*, 1. 541.

are probably confused references to the *Speculum coenobitarum*.³⁴ Bale's source for the *floruit* date of 1410 is a mystery; no date of any sort appears in Bale's notebook, presumptive source of this *Scriptores* entry. With the exception of the date, Bale displays no more information about the *Catalogus* and its compiler than can be deduced today from Add. 3470.

In preparation for the second edition of the *Scriptores*, Bale made extracts in his notebook from more than one hundred author-entries in the *Catalogus*. Extracts from the *Catalogus* are variously cited as 'ex Bostoni Buriensi catalogo', 'ex Bostono Buriensi monacho', 'ex catalogo Bostoni Buriensi', 'ex Bostono Buriensi', or merely 'ex Bostono'—not to mention the dozen excerpts cited jointly with the Norwich *Catalogus*.³⁵ Bale made extracts from all the *Catalogus* entries for English writers (and from some mistakenly thought to be English), with the exceptions of John of Salisbury (*288*), Richard Fitzralph (*525*), and Richard de Bury (*527*).³⁶

Bale's extracts in the *Index* potentially add to and improve several readings in the surviving text of the *Catalogus*, and serve as a possible gauge against which to assess the accuracy of Add. 3470; but one must exercise caution. The editors of the *Index* observe that Bale in his published works permitted his bias to twist his results and distort the manuscript evidence while, in marked contrast,

> there is a great difference, in this regard, between the *Index* . . . and Bale's other bibliographical works. In the [*Index*] (a private notebook never meant for publication) Bale records the source for each title, giving precise information about where he saw the text; there are no elucidations or editorial additions.³⁷

To this we would add, 'relatively speaking'. For demonstrably there are changes, and additions, in Bale's notes, some of them minor and some the basis for later confusion.

In general, Bale identified the *Catalogus* as his source, and he copied it accurately enough, though selectively. Because this is commonly the case, it has been assumed that the extracts in the *Index* represent Bale's manuscript of the *Catalogus* exactly. However, Bale's purpose was simply to compile a working notebook for the second edition of the *Scriptores*; and in making

---

34. See above, chapter 3 p. cxxxv.
35. See above, p. clxxvi.
36. It may be relevant that Bale had assembled a substantial list of John of Salisbury's works from Cambridge college libraries; and that *Catalogus* lists only a single work for Fitzralph, which Bale recorded (along with much else) at Oriel College, Oxford.
37. Brett & Carley, in their introduction to Poole & Bateson's edition of John Bale's *Index*, xiv.

notes from various bibliographical sources, he naturally made these conform to his needs, selecting only what he wanted from each source, adding to it, and, if necessary, correcting it from his own knowledge without acknowledging that he did so—precisely because it was a private notebook not meant for publication. If Bale's notes from the *Catalogus* are to be useful in establishing the text of the *Catalogus*, then we must understand Bale's alterations that are incorporated into the text as it appears in the *Index*.

Bale consistently standardized the language of all of his sources, including the *Catalogus*. Thus, Kirkestede's 'floruit A.C.' became 'claruit A.C.', 'Frater predicator' was changed to 'Dominicanus', 'Wilhelmus' and 'Walterus' to 'Guilhelmus' and 'Gualtherus'. Bale betrayed his Neo-Latin training by regularly substituting 'divus' and 'fanum' for 'sanctus' and 'monasterium'. In the entries for the more common authors, Bale took from the *Catalogus* only the works not already supplied from other sources. The sequence in which the works appear was often scrambled, for unknown reasons. Bale uniformly omitted Kirkestede's explicits; and he ignored the location numbers as well, save in rare instances where he converted the numbers into place-names.[38] At the end of the list of titles Bale commonly added 'Atque alia nonnulla' or a similar blanket phrase, followed by the writer's dates, having transplanted it from the head of the entry in the *Catalogus*. There are also occasional variations in syntax and word order in the biographical notes.

Beyond such routine standardizations, however, Bale also inserted additional information, from his own knowledge or from unacknowledged sources. When his editors recognized the *Index* as 'a private notebook never meant for publication', to them this meant 'no elucidations or editorial additions'. But in fact the notebook aspect is a blade with two edges: Bale's aim was never to produce an accurate transcription of 'Boston's' *Catalogus*—or of the *Nordovicensis scriptorum catalogus*, or of any other of his sources—but to collect and record from them reliable information about (presumed) English authors and their works. If he could improve on the information in the course of recording it, he quite naturally made what he considered to be appropriate changes or additions. He can be demonstrated to have done this frequently enough that it raises a major question for editors, each time the extracts in the *Index* differ from the surviving text in Add. 3470: are these added materials in the *Index* simply Bale's own contribution, or do they represent losses to the text that occurred in the transcription of the *Catalogus*?

These are the sorts of silent change Bale made. In the brief biographies, he added authors' dates when they were not supplied, he corrected dates that he thought wrong, and from his extensive knowledge of medieval English

---

38. For example, *Index*, p. 56 Columbanus, p. 318 Petrus Babion, p. 468 Dares Frigius.

bio-bibliography he corrected errors he recognized in the *Catalogus*. As an example of this last, he combined under the name Robertus Holcoth (p. 381) the material found in the *Catalogus* under Holcote (*277*) and Robertus de Holcote (*515*). Clearly Kirkestede had thought these were two different people, for in alphabetizing his authors he entered the first under the letter H and the second under R; so Bale's version does not represent the original text, but is his own correction. Bale correctly made one entry (p. 98) of the titles found in the *Catalogus* under Gregorius alius (*205*) and Gregorius de Bridelington (*208*). To his extract for Guido de Columpna (pp. 111–12) he added a pertinent explanatory sentence from the *Catalogus* entry for Dares Frigius (*152*). In the *Index* under 'Guilhelmus Paruus, Neuburgensis ecclesiae canonicus' (p. 144) he correctly combined the titles found in the separate *Catalogus* entries for Wilhelmus Parvus (*627*) and Wilhelmus Neubrigensis (*658*). Conversely, Bale took the entry for Robertus Molendinensis in the *Catalogus* (*506*), itself a muddle (derived from a muddle in its source, the *Registrum*), and increased the confusion by dispensing with Robert of Melun entirely and, instead, distributing the titles between Robertus Crikeladensis (p. 369) and Robertus Lorayn (p. 384).

In a number of instances Bale's extracts in the *Index* contain longer incipits than are found in Add. 3470, which suggests that some of the incipits in the *Catalogus* were originally longer than they are in the surviving text. In addition, the extracts in Lambeth 448 (Ely cathedral) discussed above contain four longer and two additional incipits, as well as two minor additions in the text.[39] Unfortunately, these two witnesses, potentially useful as corroboration for one another, do not report the same *Catalogus* entries—save in one work of William of Pagula (*629.3*), for which the Ely extracts report a three-word incipit; but Bale's *Index* (p. 143) in this case confirms the single-word incipit found in Add. 3470.[40]

It is impossible to discern how much of the surplus material in the *Index* was added by Bale, and how much instead legitimately represents the reading of his text of the *Catalogus*. One may safely discount those of his additions that are written in a different ink at a later time.[41] In other cases, the circumstantial evidence of Bale's silent addition is inescapable. For example, for a work of Stephen Langton ostensibly copied from the *Catalogus*

---

39. See above, p. lxxix.
40. Also, in a note added to the last work in the *Catalogus* entry for Sedulius (*531.5*), both Bale and the Ely extracts have expanded the title of a hymn given as 'Hostis Herodes' (Add. 3470) to read 'Hostis Herodes impie'; we suppose that this word has dropped from the surviving text of the *Catalogus* and have emended accordingly, although it is possible that Bale and the anonymous Ely recorder independently completed the hymn's opening phrase.
41. These are carefully noted in the edition of the *Index*.

(554.16), Bale provided a four-word incipit (p. 417) while Add. 3470 has none; but this is an entry that Kirkestede had borrowed wholesale, location numbers and all, from *Registrum* 57. 5, which has no incipit (Bale probably took the incipit from his immediately preceding notes on Langton based on a book in Cambridge University Library, copied onto the same folio with the *Catalogus* extracts).[42] Throughout, Bale consistently extended any incipit that was the first word of an obvious and familiar biblical quotation ('Ductus est' becomes 'Ductus est Iesu in desertum'; 'Erunt signa' becomes 'Erunt signa in sole et luna', and so on).[43] Bale's incipits in his notebook are uniformly long, and they do not in general vary with the character of his sources, whereas the incipits in the *Catalogus* are uniformly short; thus, Bale would have been predisposed to lengthen Kirkestede's incipits if at all possible. See, for example, the extracts (pp. 131–2) supposedly from the *Catalogus* entry for William de Montibus (*625*), where Bale's incipits are consistently longer than those in Add. 3470, resulting in one as long as seven words—completely out of pattern for the *Catalogus*. It is doubtful that the *Catalogus* would have contained just a handful of long incipits now and then, and unlikely that all the incipits throughout would have been uniformly shortened by a copyist.

There is in the *Index* considerable, and not always understandable, variation in the number of works that Bale extracted from the *Catalogus*. Thus, in the entry for Richard of Saint-Victor (pp. 361–2), for which the *Catalogus* (*498*) is Bale's only stated source, Bale listed only sixteen of the *Catalogus*' thirty-eight titles. More perplexing than his omissions, however, are Bale's additions to the titles. As with the incipits, some of these Bale unmistakably supplied from other sources. In excerpts supposedly from the *Catalogus* entry for Gilbert of Hoyland (*212*), for example, Bale lengthened the titles of works 2 and 7 with the addition of words that are not found in the *Registrum*, Kirkestede's source for the whole entry. Bale also occasionally added, usually at the end of a given 'extract', one or more works that do not appear in Add. 3470. In some of these instances, again, it is evident that these represent Bale's own additions, rather than representing titles that have been lost from the text of the *Catalogus*. For example, Add. 3470 lists three works for Wilhelmus de Altona (*638*), and it is confirmed in this by the list of Dominican writers from which the entry came. The extract in the *Index* (p. 113) gives an additional title, which must have been added by Bale from elsewhere. A title that the *Index* (p. 87) attributes to Gervase of Tilbury (*221*)

---

42. Both entries are on the same folio of his notebook, Bodl. MS Selden supra 64, fol. 167r.
43. Respectively *Catalogus* 71.1 (*Index*, p. 2) and 505.38 (p. 375); see also *107.1* (p. 318), *399.7* and *9* (p. 301), *444.9* (p. 319), *498.17* and *23* (p. 362), and so on.

not found in Add. 3470 is likewise not found in Kirkestede's source, Étienne de Bourbon; therefore this, again, is Bale's own addition.

One must set against this background, of repeated and demonstrable silent additions by Bale, those additions whose source cannot be verified. A title not found in Add. 3470 appears in each of these five *Index* entries supposedly taken from the *Catalogus*: Gualtherus Bokedene (p. 100 = *Catalogus 653*), Ioannes Cornubiensis (p. 196 = *328*), Lanfrancus (p. 278 = *344*), Osbernus (p. 315 = *418*), and Warnerius (p. 465 = *608*). We cannot accept without question the judgement of an earlier scholar, 'The many . . . additional titles . . . in [Bale's] excerpts from Boston are all presumably authentic though now lost from the text'.[44] Conversely, the possibility that these additional works were originally in the text of the *Catalogus* cannot be discounted. Because some of Bale's supplementary material could represent loss from the text of the *Catalogus*, we have recorded all of his additions in the *apparatus criticus*.[45]

However, it is not just a majority, but the overwhelming majority of the extracts in Bale's *Index* (as was true of the Ely extracts) that confirm the bona fides of the titles and incipits given in Add. 3470.

B. *The Subsequent Fortunes of Bale's Manuscript*

After the accession of Mary Tudor, Bale, now bishop of Ossory, was forced to flee Ireland in early September 1553. He had to leave his large library of over 400 manuscripts behind, probably at his residence in Kilkenny which was ransacked a few days after he left, or possibly he left it in Dublin with his friend William Williams, who himself soon fled.[46] The *Catalogus* was among the books Bale left behind. It appears in a list of manuscripts lost in Ireland that Bale compiled from memory and published in the second edition of his *Scriptores*: 'Bostoni Buriensis Catalogus scriptorum ecclesiae, opus valde laboriosum & utile'.[47] The immediate fate of the manuscript is not known. However, it probably remained in Ireland as did most of the collection, the bulk of which Bale conjectured had come into the

---

44. Bressie, 'Textual corruption', 251.
45. Obviously, this does not include the reports that Bale ascribes jointly to the *Catalogus* and another source, such as the Norwich catalogue (see above), the collection of Nicolas Brigham (p. 90), or the annals of Nicolas Trevet (p. 81).
46. McCusker, *John Bale*, 22–4, 30–31; and Davies, *Bibliography*, 223–5.
47. No. 61 in the list as printed and discussed by H. McCusker, 'Books and manuscripts formerly in the possession of John Bale', *The Library*, 4th ser. 16 (1935) 144–65; and id. *John Bale*, 29–54; see also Davies, *Bibliography*, 224–5, 229.

possession of Sir Anthony St Ledger, Deputy for Ireland, and his son, Sir Warham.[48]

Many references to 'Boston' and the *Catalogus* during the late 16th and early 17th cent. were based on the information in Bale's *Scriptores*, rather than reflecting knowledge of an actual manuscript.[49] Soon after Bale's death, 'Boston's' name appeared as an authority in the debate concerning the relative antiquity of Oxford and Cambridge. The initial pamphlet, without reference to 'Boston', was written by Thomas Caius in 1566.[50] John Caius, in a reply published in London in 1568, said that according to 'Boston' the ancient Oxford schools closed by Harold were not restored before the reign of Stephen, when Robert Pullen moved all the learned of the realm to assemble at Oxford.[51] This information was taken, unattributed, from Bale, who mistakenly cited 'Boston' as his source for this statement.[52] John Caius appended a list of the authorities upon which he based his argument, and among them is 'Io. Bostonus Buriensis', the first mention of a christian name for 'Boston'. John Caius's source for the name is unknown, and it is reasonable to suppose that he created it himself, perhaps through some misinterpretation.[53] Thomas Caius wrote a reply to this pamphlet, countering that 'Boston' was a poor authority on this topic since he did not flourish before the reign of Henry IV—information he derived jointly from Bale and John Caius.[54] A brief notice on 'Boston of Burie' appeared in Holinshed's *Chronicles* (1577), wholly dependent on Bale's

---

48. McCusker, *John Bale*, 30–31.
49. These references occur in controversial literature, whose writers deliberately obscured or falsified their bibliographical sources to disguise the fact that they borrowed copiously, and without acknowledgment, from their opponents. See, for example, Douglas's remarks on John Pits (*English Scholars*, 157).
50. Thomas Caius, *Assertio antiquitatis Oxoniensis academiae*, pr. in John Caius, *De antiquitate Cantabrigiensis academiae libri duo* (London 1568); ed. Thomas Hearne in *Vindiciae antiquitatis academiae Oxoniensis* . . . 1 (Oxford 1730) 273–310.
51. John Caius [336] and [362]; also in Hearne, *Vindiciae*, 1. 1–272, and Caius *Opera*, ed. E. S. Roberts (Cambridge 1912).
52. Bale, *Scriptores*, 1. 191–2: 'Robertus Polenus . . . Vixit anno incarnati ueri Messiae 1146 regnante Stephano Anglorum rege, ut Bostonus Buriensis ostendit'. Neither the entry from the *Catalogus* in Bale's *Index* (p. 386) nor that in Add. 3470 (507) bears a date.
53. In a booklist or list of authors the palaeographical distance is short between the abbreviation for 'Item' and that for 'Iohannes'.
54. Thomas Caius, *Anima adversiones aliquot in Londinensis de antiquitate Cantabrigiensis academiae libros duos*. This appears as a manuscript appended to a copy of John Caius's *De antiquitate*, Bodl. 8° Rawlinson 470, pp. 427–585 at 577; ed. Hearne, *Vindiciae*, 2. 315–437, at 429.

THE HISTORY OF THE TEXT OF THE CATALOGUS

Scriptores.⁵⁵ And John Pits cited 'Boston' a number of times in his *De illustribus Angliae scriptoribus* (1619),⁵⁶ with a laudatory description of 'Boston' himself. Like his predecessors, however, Pits took his information from Bale, and he was sufficiently candid to state that he had not been able to see the manuscript or locate where it might be found. Pits made a significant change in the story, however, when he referred to Boston 'in suo *maiore* catalogo',⁵⁷ instead of Bale's customary 'in *magno* suo catalogo'.⁵⁸ This slight alteration, from 'his large catalogue' to 'his larger catalogue', created a long-lived and near-indestructible confusion of the *Catalogus* with the Franciscan *Registrum*.

Fifty-three years after Bale had abandoned his manuscript of the *Catalogus* in Ireland, James Ussher (1581–1656), then a young scholar and ecclesiastic in Dublin, owned a manuscript of the *Catalogus*. This must surely have been the one abandoned by Bale in 1553; the odds are clearly against there having been a second medieval manuscript of the *Catalogus* in Ireland at the time.⁵⁹ Ussher first mentioned the manuscript in a letter to William Camden (1551–1623), written on 30 October 1606 from his college in Dublin: 'When I shall hear further from you both [Camden and Sir Robert Cotton (1571–1631)], I propose to take some order for the conveyance of my Boston unto you'.⁶⁰ Ussher may have acquired the manuscript not long before he wrote this letter. He was only twenty-five years old in 1606, although he was already an active scholar. He wrote the letter just after his return from England on a book-buying trip, during which he had made the acquaintance of Camden and Cotton.

Ussher made use of the *Catalogus* in a number of his writings. In the *Historia dogmatica* he quoted the *Catalogus* concerning Alfred's translation of the scriptures, citing it as 'Bostonus Buriensis in suo scriptorum catalogo

---

55. Raphael Holinshed, *Chronicles of England, Scotlande, and Irelande* (London 1577), 2. 1164. It reads in full, 'Boston of Burie, a monke of the abbey of Burie in Suffolke, wrote a cataloge of all the writers of the churche, and other treatises'.
56. John Pits, *De illustribus Angliae scriptoribus* (Paris 1619), 52, 210–11, 301, 351–2, 593.
57. ibid. 352; see for example Bale, *Scriptores*, 1. 182, 'in magno scriptorum suorum Catalogo', in the entry for Achardus.
58. ibid. 352, Alfredus/Aluredus; Bale, *Scriptores*, 1. 322–3 (Alphredus Anglicus).
59. Ussher acquired another of Bale's manuscripts in Ireland, now Lambeth Palace Library, MS 61. Yet another manuscript, Bodl. MS e Musaeo 86, which was no. 47 on Bale's list of lost books, was annotated by Ussher but not owned by him. See McCusker, *John Bale*, 35–6, 48, and id. 'Books and manuscripts', 151, 163.
60. *V. Cl. Gulielmi Camdeni et Illustrorum Virorum ad G. Camdenum Epistolae* (London 1691), 86, and in the collected works of James Ussher, ed. C. R. Elrington, 15 (Dublin 1847), 18. For background see C. E. Wright, 'The Elizabethan Society of Antiquaries and the formation of the Cottonian Library', in F. Wormald & C. E. Wright, *The English Library before 1700* (London 1958), 176–212.

(quem MS. penes me habeo)'.[61] Notes Ussher had copied from the *Catalogus* concerning Alfred's commentaries on the old and new testaments, doubtless in connexion with this publication, were later used by Thomas Hearne (1678–1735), who found them in a collection of papers in the possession of Ussher's nephew, James Tyrrell.[62] Ussher referred to 'Boston' again in his *Gotteschalci et praedestinatianae historia*, published in 1631.[63]

Early on, still in Ussher's lifetime, an element of uncertainty was introduced to the history of his manuscript. Sometime between 1610 and 1625, Richard James (1592–1638), Robert Cotton's librarian, made excerpts from a manuscript of the *Catalogus* that he called in his notebook 'Bostonus Buriensis, MS Reg. Bib.';[64] the notes comprise extracts from Kirkestede's introduction and from seventeen author-entries in the *Catalogus*.[65] In addition to James's notes, the Oxford antiquary Brian Twyne (1579–1664) made notes from the same manuscript (shown to him by Thomas Allen [1542–1632] who in turn had borrowed it from Richard James).[66] Twyne's extracts include the *Catalogus*'s incipit 'Omnis divina scriptura . . .', the list of 195 libraries, and parts of the entries relating to Alcuin (*7*) and Alfred (*76*). Twyne probably compiled the volume in which these notes appear during the years 1610–15,[67] a fact that gives a rough *terminus ante quem* to James's excerpts.

Only incidental variants from Add. 3470 appear in either James's or Twyne's extracts, and it is obvious that they had in their hands a manuscript of the *Catalogus* attributed to Boston. But can this have come from the Royal Library? Although it is difficult to explain this away as a

---

61. Published posthumously: James Ussher, *Historia dogmatica controversiae inter orthodoxos et pontificios de scripturis et sacris vernaculis*, ed. H. Wharton (London 1690), 124; also ed. Elrington, 12. 305.
62. John Spelman, *The Life of Ælfred the Great*, ed. Thomas Hearne (Oxford 1709), 213 n. 1.
63. James Ussher, *Gotteschalci et praedestinatianae controversiae ab eo motae historia* (Dublin 1631), 3; also ed. Elrington, 4. 3.
64. Bodl. MS James 11, p. 195 (old pagination 240).
65. Excerpts from the introduction, ibid. pp. 195–197 (240–242); extracts in sequence from *Catalogus* entries *7, 50, 76, 90, 106, 112, 179, 217, 248, 426, 570, 579, 591, 639, 666*, and two afterthoughts *288* and *433*, on pp. 197–200 (242–245). There are also casual allusions to the *Catalogus* added marginally to texts James had copied from elsewhere, ibid. 89 (134), 90 (135), and 145 (190), concerning Johannes Scotus, Lanfranc, and Alanus respectively. James used two of these incidental notes, concerning the commentaries of Lanfranc and the *De eucharistia* of Johannes Scotus, in a pamphlet: Richard James, *Anti-Possevinus, sive Concio habita ad clerum in Academia Oxoniensi A.D. 1625* (Oxford 1625) 12–13.
66. Bodl. MS Twyne 22, pp. 403 (excerpts) and 406: 'Hactenus ex Bostono in Catalogo suo minore quem Mr° Tho. Allen mutuo accepit a Mr° Ric. James et mihi ostendebat'. Thomas Tanner copied this note (and one referring to Pits and the 'greater' *Catalogus*) onto Add. 3470, fol. i^v.
67. This was the conclusion of Richard Hunt, whose judgement we respect but whose evidence we have been unable to identify.

misstatement,[68] it would be even more difficult to accept James's indication that the manuscript he saw was a *Catalogus* in the royal collection.[69] No such work is listed in the catalogues of the Royal Library. The most persuasive argument, though, is the lack of any other reference by the antiquaries to a second manuscript of the *Catalogus*, available in the Royal Library. Circumstantial evidence indicates instead that the manuscript used by James and Twyne must have been Ussher's manuscript, which Ussher had shortly before (in 1606) promised to send to James's employer, Robert Cotton. Perhaps James misunderstood his patron's explanation of the source of the *Catalogus*. The *Catalogus* was a document which aroused a great deal of interest among the antiquaries for an extended period, but the only tangible manuscript to which they refer is the Ussher copy.

Brian Twyne did remark more than once in his notes that he was citing the 'lesser' *Catalogus*, but this, also, was not an echo of a second manuscript in circulation, for Twyne specifically attributed this information to the statement of John Pits—saying, for example, 'This is his [Boston's] lesser catalogue, for he produced another that was much fuller; Pits mentioned that larger catalogue of Boston of Bury in his Life of Alfred'.[70] Twyne did not recognize that Pits was in turn citing the entry from Bale's *Scriptores*.[71]

Ussher's manuscript of the *Catalogus* became well known to 17th-cent. scholars and was often cited by them, since he allowed them to consult it and to borrow it upon request. Thomas James (d. 1629), Thomas Bodley's first librarian and Richard James's uncle, cited 'Boston of Bury, the painefull but vniudicious Monke', to add authority to a canon of apocryphal books of the

---

68. Since at least 1542 the royal library had possessed a manuscript of the *Registrum*, BL MS Royal 3 D. 1 (Cambridge, 1452)—see the description in BM *Cat. Royal*, 1. 76—and confusions between *Catalogus* and *Registrum* were not unusual. But it is difficult to imagine how such a confusion could have affected James's statement, especially since his extracts include Kirkestede's introduction, for which the *Registrum* has nothing remotely similar.
69. Almost a century later, Thomas Hearne saw James's note and speculated on the possible fate of the manuscript; see below at n. 117.
70. Bodl. MS Twyne 22, p. 406: 'Iste est catalogus illius minor, alium enim edidit multo copiosiorem, ex quo plurima citantur ad auctoribus quae hic non occurunt in hoc catalogo; et illius maioris catalogi Bostoni Buriensis meminit Pitseus in uita Aluredi seu Alfredi Anglici'. And next to his excerpt from the list of libraries (p. 406) he says, 'Notandum quod Bostonus duorum catalogorum maioris scilicet cuius meminit Pitseus in Gul: Sherwode et alibi, et minoris cuiusmodi fuit iste unde haec excerpsimus author extitit'.
71. Brian Twyne also mentioned 'Boston' in his *Antiquitatis Academiae Oxoniensis apologia* (Oxford 1608), 225, in the chapter concerning Robert Pullen, and (unpaginated, Ddd2v) in the list of authorities at the end. He gave no evidence at this early date of having seen a manuscript of the *Catalogus*, citing 'Boston' jointly with Leland and Bale.

bible in his *Manuduction* (1625);[72] and at the head of his list of sources cited he placed 'Boston of Burie, his Alphabeticall Catalogue of Manuscript bookes, gathered out of 195 seuerall places, lent me by the most Reuerend, my Lord of Armagh'.[73] Late in life Ussher lent the *Catalogus* to Roger Twysden (1597–1672), who used it in his *Scriptores X* (1652) to substantiate the attribution of several works to Serlo (*Catalogus 562*) and Ralph of Diceto (*500*), and he noted its omission of the writer John Brompton; Twysden cited the manuscript as 'penes Jacobum Usserium Armachanum'—but by this he meant only that Ussher had title, while he himself actually had use of the book.[74] It was still in Twysden's hands when Ussher died in 1656.

An indirect and posthumously-printed report about Ussher's manuscript comes from Thomas Fuller (1608–61): '[Boston's] manuscript was never printed, nor was it my happiness to see it, but I have often heard the late Reverend Arch-Bishop of Armagh [Ussher] rejoyce in this, that he had, if not the first, the best Copie thereof in Europe'.[75] Confirmation that this was the *Catalogus* rests in Fuller's quotation of James Ware's transcription of the verse colophon from Ussher's manuscript. Ware (1594–1666) had also made notes concerning the Irish writers and the list of monasteries; these notes survive and, save for minor variants, they are identical with Add. 3470.[76]

During the years that the Ussher manuscript was in Twysden's possession, several references to the *Catalogus* appear in the books and manuscripts of Anthony Wood (1632–95), the Oxford antiquary; but it seems that he did not actually see the manuscript. Wood instead cited the *Catalogus* through Brian Twyne's extracts with which he was quite familiar, and on that basis he perpetuated Twyne's notion of a *Catalogus minor*: 'Boston's little catalogue or imperfect; vide Notas ad Pits p. 352'.[77] Again in his *Historia et antiquitatis universitatis Oxoniensis*, Wood cites 'Boston' *in catalogo suo minore.*[78]

---

72. 'Painefull' meaning 'painstaking'; Thomas James, *A Manuduction, or Introduction unto Divinitie: Containing a Confutation of Papists by Papists, throughout the important Articles of our Religion* (Oxford 1625), 3–4; his footnote identifies the source thus: 'Boston of Burie in his Catalogue of Manuscript books ouer all England in his time'.
73. ibid. [138].
74. Roger Twysden, *Historiae Anglicanae scriptores X* (London 1652), xxvii, xxix, xxxix.
75. Thomas Fuller, *A History of the Worthies of England* (London 1662), 'Lincolne-shire', 165–6; ed. J. Freeman (London 1952) 331.
76. BL MS Add. 4787, fols. 132r–133v. This was MS Clarendon 36 in Edward Bernard, *Catalogi librorum manuscriptorum Angliae et Hiberniae* (Oxford 1697), *pars altera* 6–7.
77. Bodl. MS Wood E. 4 (no. 99), p. 11. The note is printed in *The Life and Times of Anthony Wood*, ed. A. Clark, Oxford Historical Society 30 (1895), 4. 260.
78. Anthony Wood, *Historia et antiquitates universitatis Oxoniensis* (Oxford 1674), 1. 57–8 note a. Wood's notes for this comment appear in Bodl. MS Wood E. 4, p. 99. Another reference by him to

Roger Twysden retained Ussher's manuscript of the *Catalogus*, and on Twysden's death in 1672 it remained in his family. From the Twysdens the Ussher manuscript was next acquired by Thomas Gale (1635–1702), who had long been interested in the *Catalogus*—although it is not clear from which Twysden he acquired it, nor precisely when. Anthony Wood, whose narrative (in common with many other antiquaries' remarks on the subject) includes a good measure of hearsay, noted, 'In 1684 Dr. Thomas Gale did obtain from the study of Twysden in Kent, then lately deceased, an original copie of Johannes Bostonus Buriensis'.[79] At that date Roger Twysden had been dead a dozen years—although his younger brother Thomas was indeed late deceased (in 1683). But Wood was probably mistaken about the date. Thomas Gale's own notes, on the flyleaf of a copy of Bale's *Scriptores*, place the book still in Twysden hands a year later, saying, 'Boston, in the year 1685, is in the hands of Sir William Twysden of Kent' ('Bostonus anno 1685 est penes Wm. Twysden eq. auratum de Cantia'), i.e. in the hands of Roger's eldest son and heir William (d. 1697).[80] Gale acquired the Ussher

the *Catalogus*, based on Twyne's extracts, occurs in Wood, *Survey of the Antiquities of the City of Oxford*, ed. A. Clark, Oxford Historical Society 17 (Oxford 1890), 2. 379.

79. Wood's note continues, 'A copie of this Dr. Barlow [1607–91] is supposed to have from the library of [James] Usher which he conceals, as Br[ian] Tw[yne's] interleaved copie. I saw this when I was at London, in Nov. 1691, quaere' (*Life and Times*, 3. 35). In Bodl. MS Wood E. 4, p. 38, Wood again speaks of Barlow, 'Dr. Thomas Marshall [1621–85] concludes that Dr. Thomas Barlow must needs have this book' (*Life and Times*, 4. 260). There is no other evidence that Barlow ever had a text of the *Catalogus*. The comments on Barlow and Twyne's interleaved copy are apparently based on hearsay; however, the latter reference is peculiar since Wood was familiar with Twyne's manuscripts. What Wood saw in London must have been the Ussher-Twysden manuscript; it is known from other evidence to have been there on 30 January 1694 (see below).

80. CUL F.156.a.3.1, formerly the property of Archbishop Matthew Parker (1504–75), whose signature appears at the top of the (unpaginated) first page of the preface, 'Matthaeus Cantuar. 1574'. There are notes by several hands, apparently including Parker's. Gale's hand, suggested by the sale catalogue, was confirmed by comparison with Gale's notes on the front flyleaves of a volume of Herodotus (Frankfurt 1608) = CUL Adv.a.32.2 (concerning which see [H. R. Luard], *A Catalogue of Adversaria and Printed Books containing MS. Notes preserved in the Library of the University of Cambridge* (Cambridge 1864), 4, numbered Nn.1.7). The *Scriptores* volume (two parts in one) is described in the catalogue of the Conybeare sale of 1758: 'A Catalogue of the Libraries of the late Right Reverend Dr. John Conybeare, Late Bishop of Bristol, and Dean of Christ-Church, Oxford; The Rev. Dr. Thomas Gale, Dean of York; Roger Gale [Thos.' eldest son], Esq., the great Antiquarian. To which will be added, the Valuable Library of the late Reverend Mr. Walmsley, of Litchfield; and Many Others*: vol II . . . Containing near two hundred thousand volumes . . . at T. Osborne's and J. Shipton's in Gray's-Inn'; on p. 12 as lot 16702, 'Balei Scriptorum Britanniae Centuriae IX cum Observationibus MSS. a D. Galeo, £1 1s, Basil. 1559'.

Catalogus, therefore, in or after 1685; and Henry Wharton in 1689 confirmed that Gale owned the manuscript at that date.[81] As to how Gale acquired it, Awnsham Churchill, evidently the next owner of the manuscript, said in 1695 that Gale 'stole [it] of Sir W. Twysden'—ignoring the fact that Twysden's own title to the manuscript had been shaky enough.[82]

C. *Efforts to Publish the* Catalogus

Beginning with Gale, interest in the *Catalogus* turned to the publication of the work. William Oldys noted that Gale intended to publish the *Catalogus* and Leland's *Itinerary* together: 'Dr. Thomas Gale had also thoughts of publishing Boston not long after the fire of London [1666], with copious illustrations, but his industry in this service to the learned is said to have been dampened by his preferment in the Church'.[83] Gale indeed moved up the ladder of appointment, from Regius Professor of Greek at Cambridge to canon and head of the cathedral school at St Paul's, eventually to be named dean of York. Among the notes Gale copied into his *Scriptores* from the Bale/Ussher/Twysden manuscript of the *Catalogus* are incidental clarifications of two entries in Add. 3470, Alanus (*16*) and Columbanus (*138*). Though Gale did not succeed (if such was his intent) in publishing the *Catalogus*, he described it in the introduction to his *Historiae Britannicae . . . scriptores* (1691), differing from his predecessors only in that he surprisingly placed 'Boston' in the reign of Henry VII (1485–1509).[84] He was the first, at least in print, to observe that the *Catalogus* is a key to what was once in the monastic libraries—although he concluded that the Dissolution had essentially invalidated 'Boston's' work: 'He surveyed all the libraries of all the English monasteries, and collected in a substantial catalogue whichever of their historiographers (and other authors as well) might be of use to learned men;

---

81. Henry Wharton, *Appendix ad Historiam literariam Cl. V. Gulielmi Cave . . . De scriptoribus ecclesiasticis* (London 1689), 90: 'MS olim penès Cl. Usserium, nunc verò penès doctissimum virum Thomam Gale, S. Theol. Profess. qui illum suo tempore, ita vovemus, publici juris faciet'. Hearne presented a contradictory statement based on double hearsay, in a letter of 20 January 1709: 'Dr. Thomas Smith has heard that Gale received his manuscript from Sir William Dugdale, from whom it later passed to Thomas Tanner'; *Remarks and Collections of Thomas Hearne*, ed. C. E. Doble, Oxford Historical Society 7 (Oxford 1886), 2. 164.
82. A letter from Churchill in reply to Thomas Tanner, 30 July 1695 (Bodl. MS Tanner 24, fol. 47r); cited by Richard Hunt.
83. This is quoted from a marginal note by William Oldys transcribed into Edward Malone's copy of Fuller's *Worthies*, 'Lincolne-Shire', 166 (now Bodl. MS Malone 3).
84. Thomas Gale, *Historiae Britannicae, Saxonicae, Anglo-Danicae scriptores XV* (Oxford 1691), 1. 1–2.

but there is no concealing the fact that the overthrow of the monasteries, which followed soon thereafter, dispersed all these books and rendered useless Boston's careful diligence, for the most part'.[85]

Roughly contemporary with the complex passage of the actual manuscript from Ussher through various Twysdens to Gale, the second half of the 17th cent. saw the publication of three biographical dictionaries, each with an entry for the compiler 'Boston of Bury' based on second-hand information, primarily upon Bale's *Scriptores*. Thomas Fuller in his *Worthies* (1662) described 'Boston' as the precursor of Leland, Bale, and Pits.[86] He discussed 'Boston' in the chapter on Lincolnshire, as a native of the town of Boston. Misinterpreting the colophon in which the monastic scribe addressed his heavenly King, Fuller concluded that Boston had dedicated the work to Henry IV.[87] The short biography of 'Boston' in Henry Wharton's appendix to Cave's *Historia literaria* (1689) presented no new information.[88] Wharton's reference in the *Historia* proper (p. 601) to the writings of Berengar 'according to Boston of Bury' ('testatur Bostonus Buriensis') in fact came from the *Registrum*—a fresh source of confusion; Wharton was chaplain and librarian to Archbishop Sancroft, owner of a manuscript of the *Registrum* (now Bodl. MS Tanner 165);[89] and Wharton regarded the *Registrum* as an imperfect version of the *Catalogus*.[90] William Nicolson's *English Historical Library* (1697) also presented a biographical discussion of 'Boston', differing from the previous accounts only in an error, asking whether the Carmelite writer Alan of Lynn enlarged the smaller or the

---

85. 'Omnes omnium Angliae monasteriorum bibliothecas perlustravit, et quos historiographos (necnon et alios auctores) earum quaelibet subministrare ad usus doctorum hominum valerent, locupleti catalogo complexus est. Non est tamen dissimulanda monasteriorum subversio, quae brevi subsecuta est, haec libros omnes dispersit, et Bostoni providam diligentiam, maxima ex parte, inutilem reddidit'; ibid. We are grateful to Blair Sullivan for advice on this translation.
86. Fuller, as n. 83.
87. Fuller may have been further persuaded by Bale's statement in the *Scriptores* (1. 541) that 'Boston' wrote in 1410 'in the reign of Henry IV'.
88. Wharton, as n. 81.
89. See Rouse & Rouse, *Registrum*, xxxvii–xxxviii and clxii. Wharton made extracts (Lambeth Palace Library, MS 594, p. 40) from Sancroft's manuscript that he labelled, 'Excerpta ex libro Bostoni Buriensis de Scriptoribus ecclesiasticis'.
90. It was at this same time that Gale added a note, to his already extensive annotations on the flyleaf of his copy of Bale's *Scriptores*: 'Quamdam epitomen Bostoni habet Archp. Cant. anno 1689'—either from having seen Sancroft's *Registrum* or—more likely, in view of the timing—from having seen Wharton's printed reference to it.

larger catalogue of 'Boston' (a task not elsewhere associated with Alan of Lynn before or since).[91]

By early 1694, presumably through purchase, the Ussher manuscript of the *Catalogus* had left Gale's hands and belonged to John and Awnsham Churchill, London booksellers at the sign of the Black Swan.[92] Awnsham Churchill had access also to the autograph manuscript of Leland's *Itinerary*, and he wanted to publish Leland and 'Boston' together. He let it be known that he was looking for an editor. Edmund Gibson, who was producing an English edition of Camden's *Britannia* for Churchill with the aid of Thomas Tanner (1674–1735),[93] informed Tanner of Churchill's plan in a letter dated 30 January 1694 (Tanner, it should be noted, had just completed his own *Notitia monastica* and was looking for a publisher):

> The book [*Notitia monastica*] must be printed at London (for they cannot endure the slowness of our Oxford-press which makes their money lye too long dead;) and if you can have some other employment to bring in money, it might be noe ill peice of husbandrie to attend the Press. Now here's a gentleman (I mean a bookseller) designs to publish Leland *De viris illustribus* and *Boston of Bury* along with it. The latter is Sir Roger Twisden's book, and perhaps the onely one in the world; and while your book is printing, if you could be well pay'd for transcribing that, and contrive to get money both ways, I am of opinion you could not employ your time better.[94]

Interested in the proposition, Tanner drafted the following reply on a blank page of the letter:

> As for *Leland* and *Boston of Bury* I do not know what digestion or what manner they intend to print them, so that I can only tell you (that if you think I am fit to be the Editor of them) I shall be heartily glad of an opportunity to live at London for a quarter or half a year and that

---

91. William Nicolson, *English Historical Library* 2 (London 1697), 225–6, and see his attribution of the *Speculum coenobitarum* to 'Boston', ib. 182. It is difficult to imagine how Nicolson derived this mistaken notion from Bale's entry for Alan of Lynn (*Scriptores*, 1. 551–3), which was probably his source.

92. H. R. Plomer, *A Dictionary of the Printers and Booksellers who were at work in England, Scotland and Ireland from 1688 to 1725* (London 1922), 69–70.

93. Tanner's work on the *Catalogus* is very closely connected with the publication of his *Bibliotheca Britannico-Hibernica*, which is thoroughly discussed in W. T. Davies, 'Thomas Tanner and his *Bibliotheca*', *The Times Literary Supplement* (14 December 1935) 856; and by R. W. Hunt, 'Tanner's *Bibliotheca Britannico-Hibernica*', *Bodleian Library Record* 2 (1949) 249–56. Richard Sharpe has in hand a new study of Tanner's work.

94. Bodl. MS Tanner 25, fol. 116v, printed in Hunt, 'Tanner's *Bibliotheca*', 250.

if for the Transcribing and Edition of them (with my History of Monasteries) the Bookseller can afford to make me a handsome allowance to defray my charges and the loss of my time, I shall stand to any bargain you shall make.[95]

Awnsham Churchill himself had made inquiries and received Tanner's name from Dr. Charlett, master of University College, Oxford. Captain Charles Hatton, the antiquary who lent manuscripts of Leland's *Itinerary* and his *Collectanea* for the intended publication, commented perceptively on the proposed printing of 'Boston of Bury', in a letter to Charlett of 10 May 1694:

> Mr. Churchill hath in his hands the famed Catalogue of Bostonus Buriensis which hath by learned men been cited with such high encomiums that I verily believe the publication thereof would generally be very acceptable to most lovers of learning. But yet tho I am of opinion it will not answer (at all) expectation, I thinke it much more advisable to publish it entire then to strike out or omit any part thereof. For most readers will be inclinable to apprehend, if anything be, it was either by want of judgement in or by partiality of the editor.[96]

In mid-May of 1694, Awnsham Churchill came to Oxford and sealed the agreement with Tanner for forty pounds,[97] and on 26 May asked him for 'another account of the designe'.[98] At this time Tanner envisaged printing all of Leland and 'Boston' and supplementing them with material from Bale and Pits where the former were deficient.[99] Early in the summer of 1694 Tanner went to London as planned. He finished transcribing the *Catalogus* by mid-July and returned the manuscript to Churchill in October.[100] Churchill prematurely included the work in an advertisement of books 'In

---

95. Bodl. MS Tanner 25, fol. 117v, printed in Hunt, 'Tanner's *Bibliotheca*', 250.
96. Bodl. MS Ballard 33, fol. 10v; another portion of the letter is printed by Hunt, 'Tanner's *Bibliotheca*', 250.
97. See the letter from Gibson to Tanner dated 18 May 1694, printed by Hunt, 'Tanner's *Bibliotheca*', 251, from Bodl. MS Tanner 25, fol. 152r.
98. Portions of Churchill's letter are printed by Hunt, 'Tanner's *Bibliotheca*', 251–2, from Bodl. MS Tanner 25, fol. 160r.
99. Tanner describes his plans in a letter to Dr. Charlett in Bodl. MS Ballard 4, fol. 84r, as 'the bare printing of Leland and Boston of Bury and supplying what was wanting by wholesale out of Bale and Pits within a twelvemonth', cited in Davies, 'Thomas Tanner', and Hunt, 'Tanner's *Bibliotheca*', 252. Tanner's achievement is clearly placed in the larger picture of English historiography by D. C. Douglas, *English Scholars 1660–1730*, 2nd edn (London 1951), 157–64.
100. Hunt, 'Tanner's *Bibliotheca*', 252. Tanner's transcript is now CUL MS Add. 3470.

the Press' which he added following the preface of Sir Richard Blackmore's *Prince Arthur, an Heroick Poem* that he published in February 1695.[101]

Tanner's book, however, would not be printed for several decades. As Tanner progressed, the scope of his work increased. The extent of the increase can be seen in a draft prospectus for the book which he drew up in June 1696. The book was to be entitled *Bibliotheca Britannica*,[102] and instead of being a mere printing of Leland and 'Boston' Tanner envisaged a great biographical dictionary of English writers containing his and Leland's authors arranged by century, and 'At the end will be printed entire *Boston* monk of *Bury* his Catalogue of Ecclesiastical Writers'.[103]

Eventually the scale of the work became unmanageable. In the following years Tanner's appointment as chancellor of Norwich cathedral, his marriage, and the burden of additional commitments interrupted his efforts to finish the great biographical dictionary. Although he periodically resumed the work, he never completed the *Bibliotheca*.

Even though Tanner never saw the *Catalogus* in print, it is crucial to the history of the text that he intended to do so, that he planned for it to 'be printed entire'. Tanner's careful transcription preserves the only surviving text of the *Catalogus*.[104] Because Tanner made the transcript for publication—as copy ready to hand to the printer, it seems—the text is carefully, neatly, and legibly written and laid out.[105] Most entries have separate vertically-ruled columns devoted respectively to titles (which are underlined), to incipits and explicits, and to library numbers (see our frontispiece).[106] Tanner took care to correct his own errors in spelling and word order. In general, however, he did not adhere to the punctuation or capitalization of his manuscript. Further, he standardized the spelling to conform to the practice of his day in the use of the letters *v*, *j*, and *w*, and he resolutely replaced Kirkestede's 14th-cent. *e* with a neoclassical *æ*.

101. Thomas Hearne was quick to notice this and recorded it in his diary; *Collections*, ed. Doble, 9. 33; and Hunt, 'Tanner's *Bibliotheca*', 252.
102. The earliest known mention of this new title to designate the enlarged catalogue occurs in a letter from Tanner to Peter Le Neve on June 13, 1696; printed in John Nichols, *Illustrations of the Literary History of the Eighteenth Century* (London 1818), 3. 408. See Davies, 'Thomas Tanner', and Hunt, 'Tanner's *Bibliotheca*', 252–3.
103. The enlarged plans for the *Bibliotheca* are printed by Hunt, 'Tanner's *Bibliotheca*', 257–8, from a draft written by Tanner in 1696 in Bodl. MS Tanner 469, fol. 1r.
104. See below for a description of CUL MS Add. 3470.
105. Its readiness for the printer is indicated by, for example, a note in Add. 3470, p. 103, at the end of the entry for Laurentius (*358*), directed by Tanner to the printer, 'Mem. this to [be] printed as verses'.
106. The top of CUL Add. 3470, p. 19, is reproduced by Gransden, 'Some manuscripts', pl. LXXXIIIA.

Tanner scrupulously expunged (i.e. underscored with dotted lines) readings that he questioned, and called attention to them by question marks in the left margin (or perhaps the latter are the work of a later hand). When he could not read the Ussher manuscript he left spaces for the words omitted. Most blank spaces, however, such as those that often follow the word 'floruit' in the headings, clearly represent blanks in his manuscript source. Tanner also distinguished more than a dozen modern annotations or additions to the Ussher text by underlining these in pale red ink.[107]

A capital N appears in the margins to the left of the names of some eighty-nine English authors; as a group they correspond closely to those *Catalogus* entries that were eventually published in full in Tanner's *Bibliotheca* (see below). Perhaps Tanner himself entered the letters against most of these names, and one would assume that this was his way of singling out entries to be printed; however, it looks as though a different hand has written some of the Ns, leaving one to wonder when and why.[108] In addition, there are conspicuous dots in the margins beside certain works of some authors such as Anselm and Bede; the purpose of the marks is not self-evident, but they are probably vestiges of Tanner's evolving plans for the *Catalogus* and the *Bibliotheca*.

After the death of William Sancroft (1693), Tanner acquired the archbishop's manuscript of the *Registrum* (T) which he collated against his own transcript of the *Catalogus*.[109] Unlike Wharton, Tanner seems to have recognized that the *Registrum* was not just a shortened version of the *Catalogus*.[110] He annotated Add. 3470 with variant or additional information that the *Registrum* provided, placing the additions in square brackets labelled 'MS S' or just 'S', for Sancroft. The majority of his additions consist of series of location numbers for the works of patristic authors (certainly not all such numbers), although Tanner also added occasional works and incipits, as well

---

107. At the first such instance, following an addition to the Arnulfus entry (*31*) that he underlined in pale red ink, Tanner adds, 'N. B. Quae hic minio subnotantur manu recenti inseruntur' (Add. 3470 p. 35 bottom). See also *97.11* Bernardus de Trilia, *168.2* Ernaldus, *213* Gilbertus, *216* Galfridus, *221* Gervasius, *227* Galfridus Vinsauf, *241.1* Haimo of Fleury, *280.1* Houden, *334* Johannes de Alba Villa, *413* oliverus, *506.12* Robertus Molendinensis, and the notice following *523* Ricardus Barre. Tanner's faded red ink does not reproduce in photographs or microfilm.
108. These annotations in Add. 3470 only start with authors whose names begin with B; the device evidently had not occurred to Tanner until he had already copied out the *Catalogus*'s English authors beginning with A (Anselm, Alexander Nequam, Ailred, Alcuin, Aldhelm, etc.). There are occasional omissions and anomalies, as one might expect.
109. See above, and see Rouse & Rouse *Registrum*, xxxviii.
110. See his slightly ambivalent characterization of Sancroft's manuscript in the biography of 'Boston' in Tanner's *Bibliotheca*, 114.

as one author, Amazor, from the *Registrum*. He wrote his annotations from this source in a slanting cursive hand, making them readily and no doubt deliberately distinguishable from the text of the *Catalogus*.

On the blank side of an envelope now bound in at the head of Add. 3470 as fol. ii^r, Tanner copied from the *Registrum*'s list of libraries any anomalies (such as the libraries with roman numerals), with the marginal note, 'The rest exactly as numbered in my transcript'.[111] Tanner had also seen Brian Twyne's notes, made when the *Catalogus* manuscript had belonged to Ussher, and he noted on fol. ii^v that Twyne's transcript of the list of libraries 'agrees with my transcript' ('concordat cum transcripto meo'). In his own transcript of the list Tanner queried the reading '173. Babewelle *monachorum*' (Add. 3470, p. 12) and added the correction from Twyne's extracts, 'minorum (ex MS Twine)'. He also jotted down on fol. ii^v Twyne's note (from Pits) about 'Boston's' supposed two catalogues, greater and lesser.

Tanner added no new information about the author or his catalogue in his biography of 'Boston' in the *Bibliotheca*.[112] The contribution of the *Bibliotheca* lies instead in the thorough search it prompted Tanner to make for Bale's manuscript and for references to it, through both manuscript and printed materials in 17th-cent. English libraries. Had another manuscript of the *Catalogus* existed, it is reasonable to suppose that Tanner would either have found it or have had it called to his notice by the energetic antiquaries of his acquaintance. We assume he would have heard echoes or picked up traces, had another manuscript existed in his time. The accumulated references to 'Boston' which he presented in the *Bibliotheca* were the most extensive to date, and have not been much expanded since.

While Tanner was working on his *Bibliotheca*, early 18th-cent. interest in 'Boston' continued among the circle of Oxford antiquaries, but none of them seems to have seen a manuscript of the *Catalogus*. They anticipated an early publication of Leland and 'Boston'. When Tanner had assumed the task, Camden's editor Edmund Gibson had even said hopefully that the same job in Gale's hands would have been seven years' work.[113] When an edition did not appear, they became impatient. Among contemporary scholars Thomas Hearne and Anthony Hall showed particular interest in the *Catalogus*.[114] Hearne was eager to see Leland and 'Boston' in print, and ready to publish them himself. His interest in the *Catalogus* appeared in his correspondence and diaries beginning in 1705. In that year Hearne wrote,

---

111. See the discussion of the location numbers above, chap. 2 p. cxi.
112. Tanner, *Bibliotheca*, 114.
113. Bodl. MS Ballard 5, fol. 23v, cited by Davies, 'Thomas Tanner'.
114. Regarding Hearne, see the portrait by D. C. Douglas, *English Scholars 1660–1730*, 2nd edn (London 1951), 178–94; and concerning Hall, ib. 162, 177, and see above, pp. cxxi and cxxxvi.

'He [Tanner] has promised an edition of Boston and Leland . . . but I am afraid he will not make good his promise, though in a letter he sent lately to Dr. Charlett he told him he was continually drudging at it and wondered if anyone should be so uncivil as to take the work out of his hands, the Dr. having told him that I had a design of printing Leland by itself'.[115] Again in September 1707, Hearne complained to Thomas Smith that Tanner was hindering other scholars from publishing the two manuscripts.[116] Two years later, in September 1709, Hearne began to note down references to the *Catalogus*, toward the end of producing an edition if he could find a copy of the text. A passage in Hearne's diary presents a good illustration of the rumour and hearsay about the *Catalogus* that circulated in early 18th-cent. Oxford:

> The Most Reverend Dr Ussher formerly possessed John Boston's Catalogue of British Writers. Voss seems to have borrowed it, for he cites it in many places. Anthony Wood alluded to another and much briefer catalogue of this same author, but Ussher's copy was the best and to be preferred before all others, according to Nicolson. I found mention of it in the Ussher papers now in the possession of Tyrell. But where it might be now cannot be said. There was a copy of this in the library at St James's Palace many years ago, but it is missing now. Doubtless someone took it. There is no lack of those who speculate that Anthony Wood stole it—a baseless and unjust accusation, I should think. It is absolutely certain that Thomas Tanner has a copy; but it is not confirmed whether this is a recent transcription or a little older; we anticipate an edition from him.[117]

---

115. *Reliquiae Hearnianae: the Remains of Thomas Hearne M. A.*, ed. P. Bliss, 2nd edn (London 1869), 1. 17.
116. Hearne's *Collections*, ed. Doble, 2. 53.
117. ibid. 267: 'Joannis Bostoni Catalogus Scriptorum Britannorum olim possidebat Reverendissimus Usserius. A quo forte mutuo accepit Io. Ger. Vossius, qui multis locis citavit. Alium ejusdam auctoris multo minorem brevioremque catalogum adduxit Antonius a Wood. Sed prior praeferendus. Usserij apographum fuit omnium optimum, notante Nicholsono. Hujus mentionem factam reperio in Collectaneis Usserianis MSS. penes cl. Tyrrellum. Ubinam autem nunc exstet non liquet. In Bibliotheca Jacobaea ante aliquot annos custodiebatur exemplar quoddam; verum nunc desideratur. Surripuit nempe quispiam. Id Antonium a Wood abstullisse non desunt qui conjiciant. Absque causa et iniuste, ut censeo. Hoc tam certum quam quod certissimum Thomam Tannerum exemplar habere; sed neque illud constat an sit transcriptum recentius vel paullo antiquius. Ab eo Editionem expectamus'. The citations from 'Bostonus Buriensis' in Vossius *De historicis latinis* (Leyden 1627), 349, 382, etc., are taken wholly from Bale's *Scriptores*. The reference to a supposed royal manuscript is based on Richard James's extracts mentioned above; but the rumour that Anthony Wood stole it from the royal collection is indicative of Wood's reputation in early 18th-cent. Oxford. See also William Nicolson, *English Historical Library* 2 (London 1697), 225–6.

Anthony Hall (d. 1723) published Leland's *Scriptores* in 1709, and he went on to concern himself with 'Boston of Bury'. In 1722 he published the work that he identified with the *Speculum coenobitarum* of Bostonus Buriensis reported by Bale's *Scriptores*.[118] In a footnote to the introduction he gave the opening words of the *Catalogus*, 'Omnis summa scripturarum in duobus Testamentis continetur', which he says John Bridges copied for him from Twysden's manuscript. In this introduction, Hall stated that there were at least three manuscripts of the *Catalogus* in England and that he wished their owners would commit them to print.[119] It is impossible to tell which of the rumoured copies Hall had in mind, and he actually saw not a one.

Hearne likewise never saw the manuscript of the *Catalogus* that he sought, although he did publish Leland's *Itinerary* and his *Collectanea*. But his continuing interest in the *Catalogus* provides us with further information of a sort. On 29 June 1719 John Bridges told Hearne that 'Boston of Bury whence Dr. Tanner took his Transcript, is now in the Hands of Mr. John [i.e. Awnsham] Churchill'.[120] And six years later, on 11 September 1725, Hearne noted, 'We happened to talk of Boston of Bury, and of Dr. Tanner, who had (many Years ago) promised to print Boston, but, 'tis thought, hath now laid aside that design. I promised to publish this Book, if I could have a Copy of it; but I could never yet see one. Mr. Anstis hinted as if he knew where there is a Copy. I think he said in the hands of Mr. Awnsham Churchill, a Bookseller'.[121]

This is the last reference to Ussher's manuscript, from which Tanner had taken his transcript. And indeed, Tanner in 1694 seems to have been the latest person one can demonstrate to have laid eyes on the manuscript. When Churchill died in 1728, his stock of books went to his nephews William,

---

118. See chapter 3 above.
119. A. Hall, *Nicolai Triveti Annalium continuatio, ut et Adami Murimuthensis Chronicon* . . . (Oxford 1722), vi–vii, xi–xii.
120. Hearne's *Collections*, ed. Doble, 7. 24. Bridges presumably means Awnsham Churchill, since John Churchill had died soon after 1714.
121. Hearne's *Collections* 9, ed. H. E. Salter, Oxford Historical Society 65 (1914), 24. To the statement 'I think he said . . .' Hearne added a later note, 'He did say so'; he identifies Anstis as Garter King of Arms. On 24 September 1725 Hearne again comments, 'I was afraid that he [Tanner] had laid aside this worthy Design. And, upon that supposition, I had some thoughts my self of publishing Boston of Bury, if I could procure a Copy, and this I told lately to Mr Anstis, who said he would mention it to the Dr [Tanner] but whether he hath or no, I cannot say'; ibid. 31. Whether Anstis, and Bridges earlier, had actually seen the manuscript in Awnsham Churchill's hands is not known. Otherwise, the last time one can be certain that Ussher's manuscript was still in existence was October 1694, when Tanner had returned it after completing his transcript.

Awnsham, and Joshua Churchill, the latter two also booksellers.[122] Nothing is known of the subsequent fate of the manuscript.

Cambridge University Library Add. 3470

To accompany the external evidence that Tanner's transcript (Add. 3470) preserves a text of the *Catalogus* at only one remove from the Bury manuscript owned by John Bale, there are further indications, both historical and textual, that Tanner made his transcript from a medieval manuscript. A gap in our knowledge of the transmission occurs during the half-century that separates Bale's loss of his manuscript (1553) and Ussher's first mention of it (1606); but it is improbable that Ussher's manuscript was itself merely a transcript. His manuscript was greatly esteemed by those scholars and collectors to whom he lent it, William Camden, Robert Cotton, Thomas James, Roger Twysden, and others readily familiar with the difference between a medieval and a 17th-cent. book. It was highly valued as well among those who knew it only by reputation: Thomas Fuller reported the manuscript's renown in saying that Ussher had 'the best copy thereof in Europe', and Anthony Wood, speaking of the same manuscript, called it 'an original copy of Johannes Bostonus Buriensis'. That Awnsham Churchill considered his, formerly Ussher's, manuscript worthy of publication in the same volume with Leland's autograph *De scriptoribus Britannicis* implies that he considered the Ussher manuscript also to be uniquely authentic. Churchill's friend Edmund Gibson described this manuscript of the *Catalogus* as formerly 'Sir Roger Twisden's book, and perhaps the onely one in the world'.

Textual evidence from Add. 3470 reinforces the supposition that it was copied from a medieval manuscript. The fact that Tanner labelled a number of additions to the text 'in manu recenti inseruntur' implies at the very least that the text hand was earlier than the 17th cent. Tanner found Ussher's manuscript difficult to read in places; he queried numerous readings and even left a blank in his transcript on more than one occasion. Furthermore, Add. 3470 preserves abbreviations from Ussher's manuscript that Tanner was unable to extend. In such cases he attempted to reproduce the graphic form before him, with a series of dots underneath to indicate his uncertainty. Examples include the following (with the numbers of the corresponding *Catalogus* entry): ambo$\mathrm{2\!\!\!\!\perp}$ for 'amborum' (*414*), A$\mathrm{2\!\!\!\!\perp}$ for 'Aristotelis' (*46.26*), Cc$^\mathrm{a}$ for 'Cantica' (*281.213*), dīne for 'divine' (*667.10*), Ed$^\mathrm{ius}$, Ed$^\mathrm{i}$ for 'Edmundus', 'Edmundi' (*171.1*), ex$^\mathrm{m}$ for 'exemplum' (*283.7*), m$^\mathrm{a}$ for 'materia'

---

122. H. R. Plomer, *A Dictionary of the Printers and Booksellers who were at work in England, Scotland and Ireland from 1688 to 1725* (London 1922), 69–70.

(*275.2*), M^t for 'Matthei' (*282.42*), nuo perhaps for 'numero' (*53.1*), p̄dentis for 'prudentis' (*392.1*), p̄icis for 'pincis' (*425.8*), R^m for 'Responsorium' (*524*), Sithi for 'Scithiotica' (*285.3*), Sp̄c̄ for 'Spiritus' (*247.1*), Ut^m for 'Utrum' (*46.43*).

In addition, several errors in transcription seem to stem from misinterpretation of abbreviations in Ussher's manuscript. In several cases (e.g. *56.6, 70*) Tanner was puzzled by the abbreviation for *dupliciter*; he queried it each time it appeared, usually writing *dupliciter* as a superscript query, and twice rendering it instead as *duntaxat* (*528.8, 567.55*). In the headnotes to a number of entries (see *38, 39, 40, 42, 43*) Tanner copied as the source 'Jeronimum vita sua' (with the italicized words queried), and then supplied the variant reading *ubi supra* above the last two words.[123] *Quoniam* Tanner nearly always rendered as *Quum*. His struggles with the abbreviations in Ussher's manuscript imply that Tanner was reading a medieval script.

The combination of external and internal evidence allows one to postulate the following transmission of the text: a manuscript of the *Catalogus* was written at Bury, either composed under Kirkestede's direction or copied from Kirkestede's fair copy, by the scribe Boston; Boston's copy was conveyed by a pensioned Bury monk, Ailot Holt, to John Bale from whom it passed through unknown hands to James Ussher. From Ussher the manuscript passed to Roger Twysden and then to his son William, from whom it was procured by Thomas Gale. From Gale the manuscript was acquired by Awnsham Churchill, who commissioned Tanner to transcribe it. Thereafter the medieval manuscript disappeared and the transcript survived.

When Tanner died in 1735, his transcript of the *Catalogus* and the unfinished manuscript of the *Bibliotheca* were left in the hands of his brother, Joseph Tanner. David Wilkins was chosen as Tanner's literary executor to prepare the *Bibliotheca* for the press, and he received the manuscripts.[124] He did not follow Tanner's plan for publishing the whole *Catalogus* as an appendix, however, because it included a great number of foreign authors and because he thought location numbers for those authors were pointless, since they referred to libraries no longer extant. Therefore, Wilkins printed only extracts from the *Catalogus* which he confined to the preface of the *Bibliotheca* (pp. xvii–xliii), consisting of Kirkestede's introduction, the table of libraries, the names of all authors included, full entries (including locations) for the British authors, the *Nomina doctorum* at the end, and the scribal colophon, all of this printed from Tanner's transcript. Tanner's annotations from the *Registrum* were also printed, in square brackets, and in some cases they slipped into the printed

---

123. Tanner in several instances cites Jerome, 'De claris scriptoribus [queried]', and then corrects this to 'De catholicis scriptoribus'; again the confusion in all probablility results from an abbreviation in Ussher's manuscript.

124. Tanner, *Bibliotheca*, xiv–xv.

text.¹²⁵ In general, however, there are only minor variants, mostly typographical errors, between the printed excerpts and the portions of Add. 3470 from which they were taken.

The *Bibliotheca Britannico-Hibernica* was published in 1748, three years after Wilkins himself had died. Between Bale's publicizing of 'Boston' in 1549 and Thomas Tanner's death in 1735 English antiquaries pursued the *Catalogus*, and anticipated its appearance in print, with fervour. But thereafter it seems that academics were satisfied with its abridged and somewhat off-hand publication in the *Bibliotheca* (as a 27-page segment in the 47-page preface). Bibliography—like other fields of study, each in its own time and at its own pace—had evidently undergone the Enlightenment transformation, from passive dependence on traditional and received wisdom to active and rational investigation. Even before Tanner's death, the scholarly world had made a beginning at the systematic study of books and charters based on a reasoned and integrated examination of the language, the handwriting, and the physical materials. A medieval booklist might play a role in such study, but the role was unquestionably auxiliary. Indeed, Tanner's diminishing investment of time and energy in this document may reflect his own growing perception that what had seemed so vitally important in 1694 no longer did so in the 1720s and '30s. And by the time we shall next see interest in publishing the *Catalogus*, at the close of the 19th cent., it will no longer be as a crucial key to the authorship of works but as a cultural artefact in its own right.

Most of Wilkins's manuscripts, the *Catalogus* among them, were purchased after the death of his widow Margaret (d. 1750) by her brother Robert, later seventh Lord Fairfax of Cameron, and were kept at Leeds Castle in Kent.¹²⁶ The Fairfax Library was sold at Christie's on 10 January 1831, with the *Catalogus* transcription as lot 113, 'List of Theological Writers with a Catalogue of their Works . . . unbound'.¹²⁷ It was purchased probably by the London bookdealer Thomas Thorpe, who sold it to Sir Thomas Phillipps, in whose library it was given the number 10428.¹²⁸ At the suggestion of M. R. James

---

125. See Bressie, 'Textual corruption', 249–51. For example, see *Bibliotheca*, xxxiv, 'Lanfrancus Librum consuetudinarium', which has slipped into the text from Tanner's annotations.
126. Add. 3470, fol. iʳ, in ink, 'Fairfax MSS. Leeds Castle'. See also E. F. Jacob, 'Wilkins's Concilia and the fifteenth century', *Transactions of the Royal Historical Society*, 4th ser. 15 (1932) 103–104.
127. *A Catalogue of the . . . Library . . . Removed from Leeds Castle, in Kent . . . collected by the Lords Fairfax and added to by the Rev. Dr. Wilkins . . .* (Sale Catalogue of 10 January 1831, Christie), p. 11 no. 113.
128. Add. 3470 inside front cover: in ink '10428', printed on a slip '10428'; p. 1 in ink, 'Phillipps MS 10428'. See *Catalogus librorum manuscriptorum*, Middle Hill Press (1837) no. 10428: and A. N. L. Munby, *The Formation of the Phillipps Library up to the Year 1840*, Phillipps Studies 3 (Cambridge 1954), 44–7, 167.

it was bought at Sotheby's in the tenth Phillipps sale, 8 June 1898 (lot 500), by Cambridge University Library,[129] where it was catalogued as Additional Manuscript 3470.

A Description of CUL MS Add. 3470

Contents

1. fol. ii. Envelope unfolded, with notes primarily in Tanner's hand: fol. ii^r, excerpts from the list of libraries copied from Sancroft's manuscript of the *Registrum*, Bodl. MS Tanner 165 (*T*); fol. ii^v, address to 'The Revd Dr Tanner/ Chancellor in Norwich' and notes including one that cites Brian Twyne's reference to the *Catalogus*.

2. pp. 1–152, Henry of Kirkestede, *Catalogus*. pp. 1–12, *Bostonus Buriensis* [centered heading] and Kirkestede's introduction; pp. 10–12, *Nomina locorum* . . . [list of libraries]; pp. 13–149, the list of authors and works; pp. 149–151, *Nomina doctorum* . . . [list of biblical commentators]; p. 152, Boston's colophon.

Paper (foolscap). i (18th cent., blank) + i (18th cent.) + 152 pp. + i (18th cent., blank), 325 × 212 mm. Too tightly bound to permit collation; catchwords for each page. Vertical rules in red ink, 2 to mark the margins (pp. 1–12) or usually 6 to mark columns (pp. 13–152), otherwise unruled. Paginated in upper left corner. New letters of the alphabet normally begin at the top of a verso or recto page with a capital letter in red ink. Modern notes in pencil on the list of libraries (pp. 10–12).

Bound in quarter brown binder's cloth over brown cardboard sides, by Cambridge University Library.

Written by Thomas Tanner in London, June–July 1694. Belonged to the Fairfax family, Leeds Castle, Kent: p. i, 'Fairfax MSS/ Leeds Castle'. Acquired by Sir Thomas Phillipps, Bart., no. 10428 in his library. Printed label remounted on lower front pastedown, also written there in ink and on p. 1 top. Sotheby's paper label '500'. Purchased by Cambridge University Library at the Phillipps Sale, Sotheby's, 6 June 1898, lot 500.

---

129. Add. 3470 inside front cover: printed on a paper disc, '500'. *Bibliotheca Phillippica* (Sale Catalogue of June, 1898, Sotheby & Co.), 67. Concerning James's role see Rouse & Rouse, *Registrum*, xxi–xxiv.

Modern Interest in Editing the Catalogus

As we have seen, the only early plan to print the text of the *Catalogus*, jointly Awnsham Churchill's and Thomas Tanner's, was ultimately replaced by a more spartan presentation in the early 18th cent. In the same years Thomas Hearne expressed his eagerness to publish the text, but he was unable to lay hands on the manuscript. After the posthumous appearance of Tanner's *Bibliotheca Britannico-Hibernica* in 1748, interest in publishing the *Catalogus* seems to have vanished as completely as did the Bale/Ussher/Churchill manuscript.

It was Montague Rhodes James at Cambridge who, in the 1890s, revived interest in the *Catalogus* and thereafter steadily pressed for an edition of the text.[130] By the time he wrote the article 'John Boston of Bury and his predecessors' in 1898, James was already aware that the *Catalogus* depended in many fundamental respects upon the *Registrum*; he announced in 1900 that he would gladly edit the works himself if he received any encouragement, and he concluded, 'If anyone has progressed further in the study of Boston, I would ask him to communicate with me. Only, whoever does the work, let Boston be printed'.[131] In 1913, on the eve of the Great War, he gave the work of editing the *Catalogus* and the related catalogue, the *Registrum Anglie de libris doctorum et auctorum veterum*, to the nuns of Stanbrook abbey, where Sister Josephine Chichester began the task of transcribing, collating, and identifying the authors and works.[132] A. G. Little mentioned the forthcoming edition in print, in 1917.[133] In 1920 an agreement was reached with Father Joseph de Ghellinck at Louvain to publish the work in the newly-founded *Spicilegium sacrum Lovaniense*, with James to write the introduction. In 1922, James established the identifications of the 195 libraries in the list prefixed to the *Catalogus* and the *Registrum*.[134] Father de Ghellinck paid several visits to Stanbrook Abbey, and announced the forthcoming publication of the text in 1923 at the Congrès International des Bibliothécaires et des

---

130. This history has been recounted in greater detail, from the standpoint of the project to edit the *Registrum*, by Rouse & Rouse, *Registrum*, xxi–xxix, and as a part of James's biography by R. Pfaff, *Montague Rhodes James* (London 1980), 200–202.
131. *The Guardian* 66 (7 February 1900), 199.
132. The history of modern work on the *Catalogus* is inextricably bound up with that of its main source, the Franciscan *Registrum*.
133. A. G. Little, *Studies in English Franciscan History* (Manchester 1917), 164 n. 4.
134. M. R. James, 'The list of libraries prefixed to the catalogue of John Boston and the kindred documents', *Collectanea Franciscana* 2 (1922) 37–60.

Bibliophiles.[135] Meanwhile, another scholar, Ernest A. Savage, in 1925 published the first general discussion of the *Catalogus* and the *Registrum*, in an effort to determine what light the two catalogues shed on Scottish libraries.[136]

In 1934, Sister Josephine gave her texts of the *Catalogus* and the *Registrum* to W. A. Pantin to make them ready for the press. Pantin, now joined by Dr. R. W. Hunt and Sir Roger Mynors, examined the text and realized that considerably more work was still necessary before a critical edition of the two catalogues could be published. They recognized as well that the *Registrum*, as a major source of the *Catalogus*, took precedence, and the project to edit the *Catalogus* was set aside for a time.

The most important general decision taken by Hunt and Mynors pertained to the type of apparatus required by editions of these two compilations. They concluded that to print off the texts without annotation, and specifically without reference to the manuscripts on which they were based, would be a disservice to scholarship and actively misleading. They adopted this as their rule for editing the two texts in the 1930s, and since that time it has become firmly fixed as the fundamental principle for these editions.

World War II interrupted work on both documents. In 1945 an American scholar, Ramona Bressie, established that John Bale had acquired his manuscript of the *Catalogus* from a pensioned Bury monk, and attempted to demonstrate the existence of modern textual corruption in the Cambridge manuscript by pointing out variant readings between it and the extracts in Bale's notebook.[137] Mynors in 1955 edited a number of the *Catalogus* entries for classical authors.[138] In 1959 Richard Rouse, then a doctoral student at Cornell University, began work on 'Boston of Bury'. He and his wife Mary spent 1961–2 in Oxford, under the direction of Hunt and Mynors, completing the preliminary work necessary for an edition of the *Catalogus*. This preliminary edition became Richard's doctoral dissertation in 1963. Extensive research on the abbey at Bury, its officers, manuscripts, and archives, by Antonia Gransden, Rod Thomson, and others, has clarified the setting

---

135. J. de Ghellinck, 'Le Catalogue des bibliothèques Anglaises en 1410', *Congrès International des Bibliothécaires et des Bibliophiles* (Paris 1925) 454–5.

136. E. A. Savage, 'Notes on the early monastic libraries of Scotland with an account of the *Registrum librorum Angliae* and of the *Catalogus scriptorum ecclesiae* of John Boston of the abbey of Bury St. Edmunds', *Edinburgh Bibliographic Society* 14 (1926) 1–46; repr. in his *Special Librarianship in General Libraries* (London 1939) 285–310.

137. R. Bressie, 'Modern textual corruption in MS. Cambridge Additional 3470', *Modern Language Notes* 60 (1945) 248–54.

138. R. A. B. Mynors, 'The Latin classics known to Boston of Bury', in *Fritz Saxl 1890–1948, A Volume of Memorial Essays* (London 1957), 199–217.

in which Kirkstede worked. The editing of the *Registrum* for the Corpus of British Medieval Library Catalogues in 1991 cleared a major obstacle to this present edition, and the process illuminated several aspects of the history of the *Catalogus*.[139] Finally, the subsequent publication of the other volumes in the Corpus has greatly facilitated the identification both of the titles in the *Catalogus* and of the now-lost manuscripts in the libraries whose books Kirkestede selectively reported.

---

139. R. H. Rouse, M. A. Rouse, & R. A. B. Mynors, *Registrum Anglie de libris doctorum et auctorum veterum* (London 1991).

CHAPTER 5

THE EDITION OF THE *CATALOGUS*

This edition reproduces the only known text of the *Catalogus*, CUL MS Add. 3470, with the following editorial changes made silently. Numbers have been assigned to the authors and to their works to facilitate reference. The capitalization and punctuation in Add. 3470, which reflect Tanner's conventions rather than the medieval text of the *Catalogus*, have been standardized and reduced to a minimum. We have abandoned Tanner's common division of the text into five vertical columns with headings (*Tituli librorum*, *Num. librorum*, *Princ. librorum*, etc.), just as he often abandoned it himself. Abbreviations have been extended, with the use of brackets for proper nouns when the precise form is questionable.

One pervasive editorial change is a form of annotation in the text itself: location numbers that were simply copied from corresponding entries in the *Registrum* are indicated by underlining, to distinguish them visually from numbers that Kirkestede has, or may have, provided from first-hand knowledge.

Our annotations observe the customary distinction between critical apparatus and apparatus of sources. The former includes two types of emendation encouraged by the manuscript itself. Those passages in Add. 3470 which Tanner indicated were written in his exemplar by a recent hand, we have moved from the text to the critical notes. Moreover, Tanner frequently indicated that he was uncertain of readings in Ussher's manuscript. We note such instances in the critical apparatus; and when comparison with an entry's source, or with corresponding passages in the *Speculum coenobitarum*, the Ely extracts, Bale's *Index*, or extracts left by other early modern readers of the medieval manuscript, permits us to determine the original reading with reasonable certainty, we have emended the text and have moved the questionable readings to the critical notes. Overall, we have seldom altered Tanner's text.

We include in the critical apparatus the variant readings between Add. 3470 and its sources, and those between Add. 3470 and its witnesses (the Ely extracts, the extracts in Bale's *Index*, and the incidental extracts of the antiquaries). Principal among the variants of Add. 3470's sources are location numbers derived from the *Registrum*. Because numbers are more prone to corruption than words, we considered the possibility of emending

Kirkestede's borrowed location numbers on the basis of the edited text of the *Registrum*. On balance, however, because Kirkestede's copy of the *Registrum* has not itself survived, it seemed more prudent to place variant location numbers from the *Registrum* in the critical apparatus;[1] there is no way to determine whether corrupt numbers stem from Kirkestede's *Registrum*, from Kirkestede's errors, or from mistranscription by either of the copyists, Boston or Tanner—and no way, in fact, to determine whether Kirkestede's reading may not preserve the correct number.[2] Among Add. 3470's variations from the early witnesses, for obvious reasons we have not included those entries in Bale's notebook that cite as joint sources the *Catalogus* and something else. And as we have explained, the testimony of Bale's notes is not sufficiently unambiguous to warrant emending the text when the notes vary from Add. 3470.[3]

The source annotations can be complex. For the large number of author-entries that consist entirely of information copied from an intermediate source—including the author's name, identifying information about him, and titles of his works—we have simply identified the source and nothing more, because this was the extent of Kirkestede's knowledge. Authors who represent first-hand knowledge on Kirkestede's part require more, by way of identification. It has occasionally been necessary to add in brackets the name by which the author is more commonly known. Immediately under the author's name are notes that pertain to the entry as a whole: necessary cross-references to other authors in the *Catalogus*; discussion concerning the identity of the author; the sources used by Kirkestede in compiling the entry; references to places where portions of the entry may appear—in Bury manuscripts, in the *Speculum coenobitarum*, in the Ely extracts, in Bale's *Index*, in the extracts of the antiquaries (i.e. witnesses roughly in chronological order); references to manuscripts which contain a similar collection of works and may thus explain sequence or attribution or the like; and, when appropriate, a notation of modern studies that have been of particular use in editing the entry as a whole, including handbooks such as Richard Sharpe's *Handlist of the Latin Writers of Great Britain and Ireland*.

1. The exception to this rule is the change in the entry for Jerome (*281.235*), where location number **182**, a number never used by Kirkestede, has been emended to read **1** (taken from the *Registrum*) and **82** (Bury, representing the manuscript from which Kirkestede derived the incipit and explicit of this work); the change was made because in this instance one can be reasonably assured that the corruption has occurred since Kirkestede's day.
2. Moreover, the text of the *Catalogus* was one of the three independent witnesses used to establish the text of the *Registrum*; cf. Rouse & Rouse, *Registrum*, xxx–lv. To emend the *Catalogus* on the basis of the edited *Registrum* would risk circular arguments.
3. See chapter 4 p. clxxxiv above.

THE EDITION OF THE CATALOGUS

An effort has been made to identify the source of every work entered in the *Catalogus*. Source-notes for the works begin with a reference to the same work in the *Registrum*—e.g. R1. 1; and, in similar abbreviated form, the references to other sources in which the work appears, e.g. Vincent XXIV 19 (Vincent of Beauvais, *Speculum historiale*, Book XXIV c. 19), etc., as identified in the list of sources at the head of each author-entry. In cases when the entry is long, such that finding the corresponding title in the source might be difficult, or when the sequence in the source influences the sequence in the *Catalogus*, the title's relative position in the source is indicated by a number in brackets (e.g. Vincent XXIV 19 [1], Vincent XXIV 19 [2], etc.). In many instances more than one source is listed for a given work since, for example, the title may derive from Vincent, the incipit and explicit from the *Manipulus florum*, and the location numbers from the *Registrum*.

For works which consist entirely of information copied from a secondary source or a combination of such sources, we have gone no further in identification than to refer readers to those sources—because they comprised the extent of Kirkestede's knowledge. Such titles do not represent manuscripts that Kirkestede actually saw, thus reflecting the state of these texts in 14th-cent. England; they are instead derivative entries, providing information pertinent only to the period and area in which the secondary source was compiled. We made two exceptions to this rule: works which appear to come from sources but for which no source has been found, are identified, since this is the first step to locating the source; likewise, we have identified titles even if they have no incipit and explicit, when the entry appears to derive from Bury manuscripts—works for which one has a surviving Bury manuscript, or a reference in one of the Bury booklists, or for which the location number **82** is cited.

For titles that appear to represent actual manuscripts, we have given as much information as may be necessary for the identification of the entry. The incipit and explicit are considered the basic part of an entry, since they represent the text which Kirkestede saw in manuscript. Thus, when the incipit and explicit are not those of the title given, the title is corrected in the notes and the printed reference is that of the work whose incipit and explicit appear. If a work is incorrectly attributed in the *Catalogus* the correct author is given, along with the authority upon which the correction is based; a correct or better-known title is supplied when needed. For a few authors, whose writings and *pseudepigrapha* have been comprehensively catalogued in a modern study such as *Aristoteles Latinus* or S. H. Thomson's study of Robert Grosseteste, reference to such a study has been used as the most efficient means of identification. Since the *Catalogus* was heavily based upon manuscripts at Bury St Edmunds—including, on many occasions, entries for which Kirkestede did not bother to add the number **82** for his own library—cross-references are given to all evidence corroborating the existence of a Bury manuscript, such as the appearance of a work in the late 12th- and early 13th-cent. catalogue of Bury books, the extant Bury manuscript or manuscripts which may have been a source for the entry, and the appearance of a work in the list of manuscripts seen at Bury by Leland. Such references are noted in brackets when there is no **82** in the entry. Where no surviving Bury manuscripts provide the key, peculiarities in a work's attribution, its title, or its incipit and explicit have been explained wherever possible by identifying a contemporary manuscript (preferably English) which contains the same peculiarity. References to authoritative handlists, such as *Clavis patrum latinorum* and Sharpe's *Latin Writers*, and to modern editions have been given wherever possible, for positive identification.

Any necessary correction of incipit and explicit is given, for the purpose of identification. Likewise, it has frequently been necessary to note where the incipit and explicit can be found in an edition, if these do not occur at the exact beginning and end of the printed text. We note when an incipit or explicit remains unidentified; in a few such instances, a longer incipit taken from Bale's *Scriptores* has been supplied in the hope that it may enable someone to identify an elusive text.

Cross-references to any other work in the *Catalogus* stand last in each entry. When the same work appears more than once, customarily the full identification notes are given only once, either the first time the work appears or, in cases where a work is attributed to several authors, under the name of the real author.

With the exception of two or three lengthy entries (Augustine, Ambrose, Jerome), no author and his works require all the possible types of notes described above, since only those which are pertinent will appear in a given instance.

The notes for the two remaining parts of the *Catalogus*, Kirkestede's introduction and the *Nomina doctorum*, are largely self-explanatory. Those for the introduction identify the sources employed. Since the source for the information contained in the *Nomina doctorum* is the *Catalogus* itself, annotations consist only of cross-references to the *Catalogus* text and any requisite critical apparatus.

THE PLATES

Left: Plate 1a. Cambridge, Pembroke College, MS 28 (Bury P. 64), fol. [69]. Peter the Lombard's *Sentences*, with notes, including Kirkestede's, in the margin.

Below: Plate 1b. Bodl. MS Bodley 297 (Bury C. 53), p. 345 top. A copy of the Chronicle of John of Worcester, here showing Kirkestede's note about the dating of Sweyn's death.

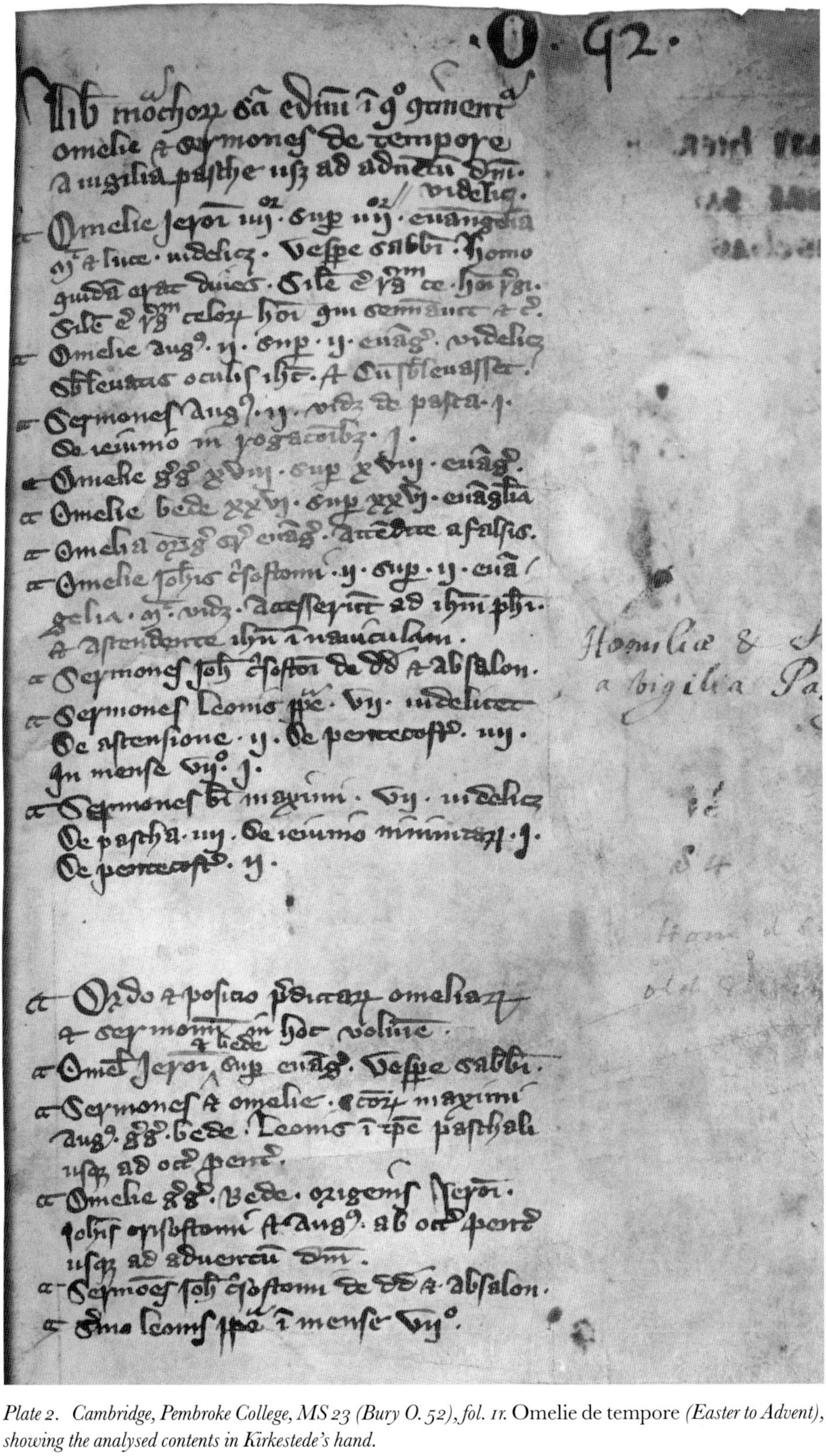

Plate 2. Cambridge, Pembroke College, MS 23 (Bury O. 52), fol. 1r. Omelie de tempore (Easter to Advent), showing the analysed contents in Kirkestede's hand.

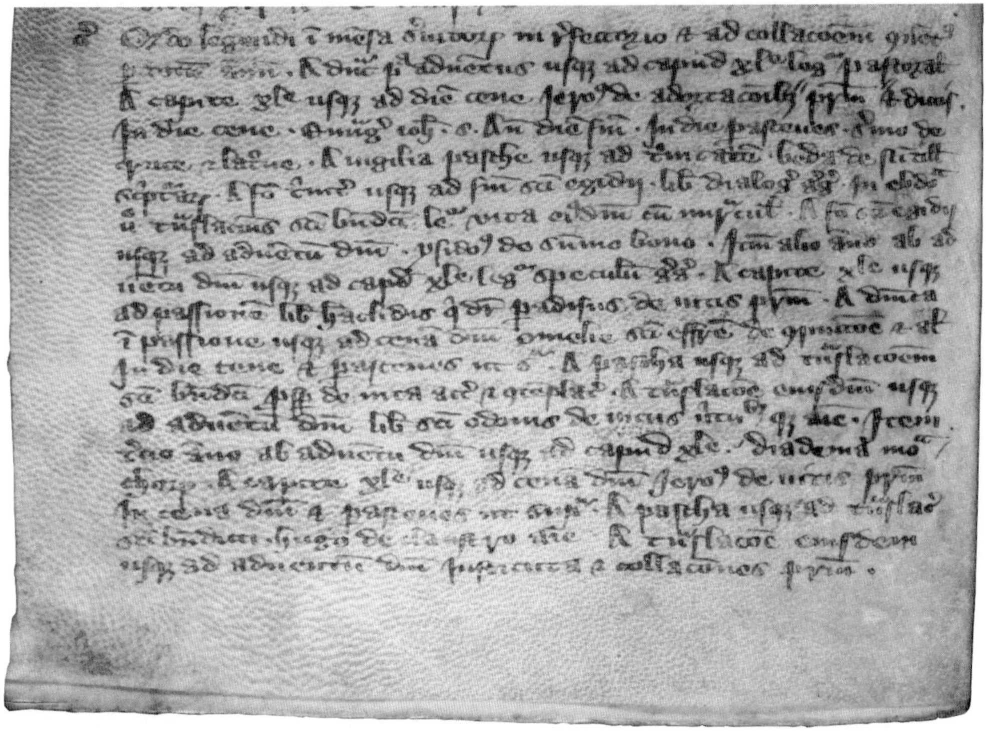

Plate 3a. BL MS Harley 1005 (Bury C. 68), fol. 35v. The Liber albus, *showing a list in Kirkestede's hand of the refectory reading for a three-year cycle (beginning 'Ordo legendi in mensa').*

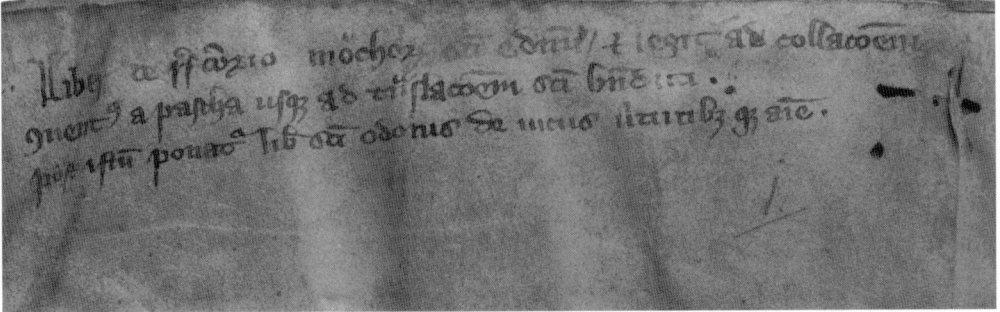

Plate 3b. Wisbech & Fenland Museum, Town Library, MS 1 (Bury P. 119), fol. i^r. A copy of Prosper of Aquitaine, showing a note in Kirkestede's hand detailing when this manuscript was to be read in the refectory.

Plate 4a. Cambridge, Pembroke College, MS 25 (Bury O. 55), fol. 3r. A homiliary, to whose early 13th-cent. ex libris Kirkestede has added a note of the contents and (at a slightly later time) a note that the Ars praedicandi *of Alanus Porretanus appears at the end.*

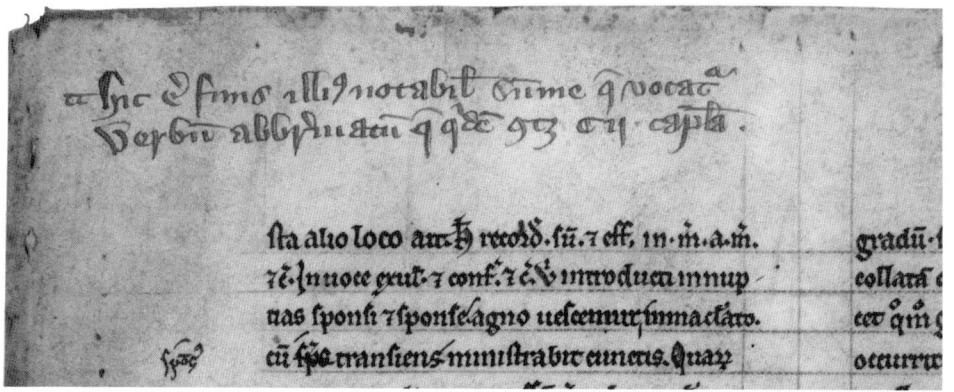

Plate 4b. Cambridge, Pembroke College, MS 313, fol. 1r. A collection of binding fragments from Pembroke College manuscripts including a quire that in Kirkestede's day was bound at the end of Pembroke College 25. This plate shows the beginning of the quire, with Kirkestede's note identifying the fragmentary text (the Verbum abbreuiatum*) that precedes the* Ars praedicandi *noted above.*

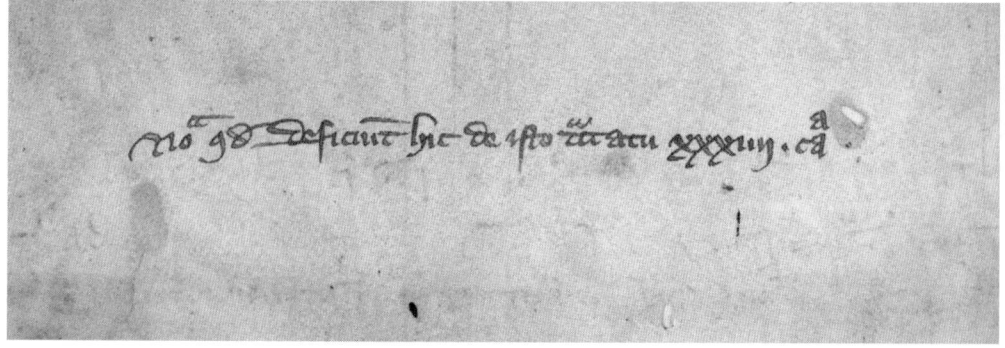

Plate 4c. Cambridge, Pembroke College, MS 313, fol. 8v. The end of this quire (formerly bound at the end of Pembroke College MS 25), showing Kirkestede's note at the end of the fragmentary text by Alanus, recording the missing chapters.

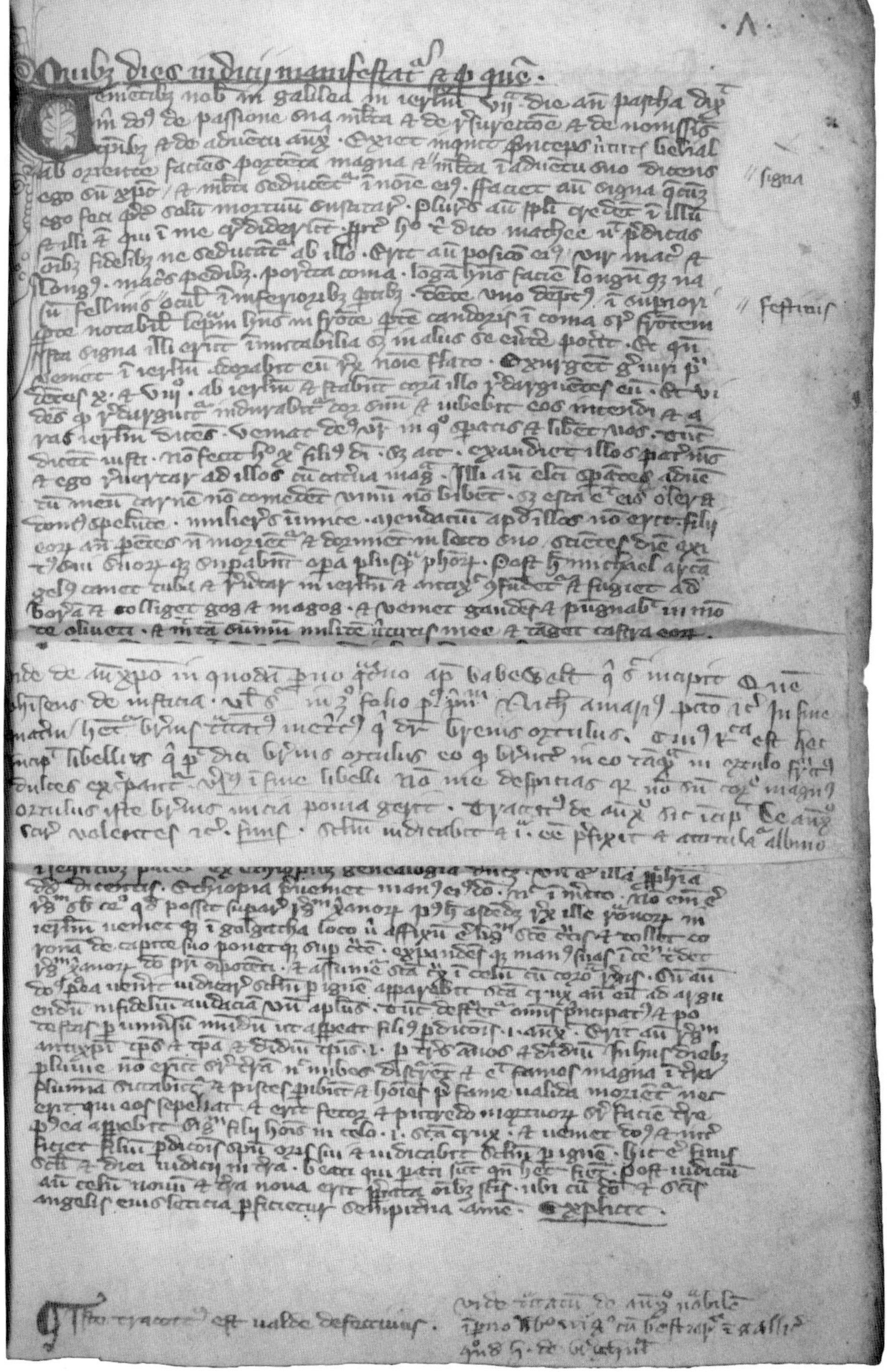

Plate 5. Cambridge, Corpus Christi College, MS 404 (Bury P. 163), fol. 7r. A collection of prophetical texts, here showing also a tipped-in note that precedes it, both in Kirkestede's hand, documenting Kirkestede's interest in the Antichrist as well as his knowledge of books at the Franciscan house of Babwell.

Plate 6a. Bodl. MS Bodley 833, fol. 1r. The Euphrastica *of William of Peterborough. This plate shows an* ex libris *for Ramsey abbey, written by Kirkestede.*

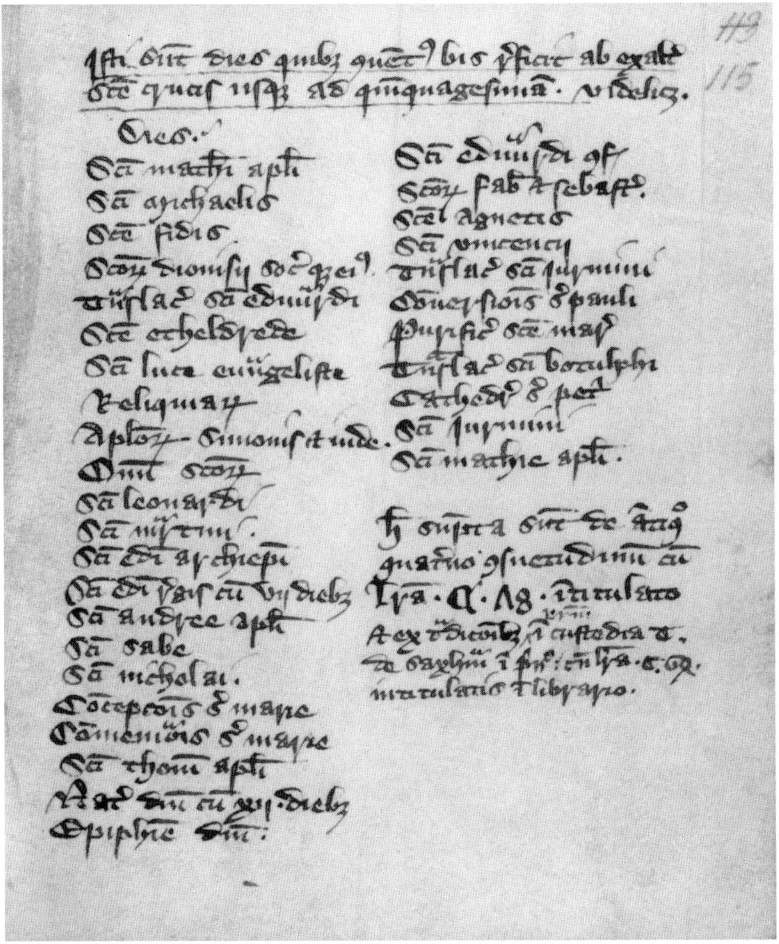

Plate 6b. BL MS Harley 1005 (Bury C. 68), fol. 115r. The Liber albus. *This plate shows a list of days when the monks are permitted two meals, which Kirkestede has copied from an abbey custumal for which he cites the shelf-mark, and he records a second copy.*

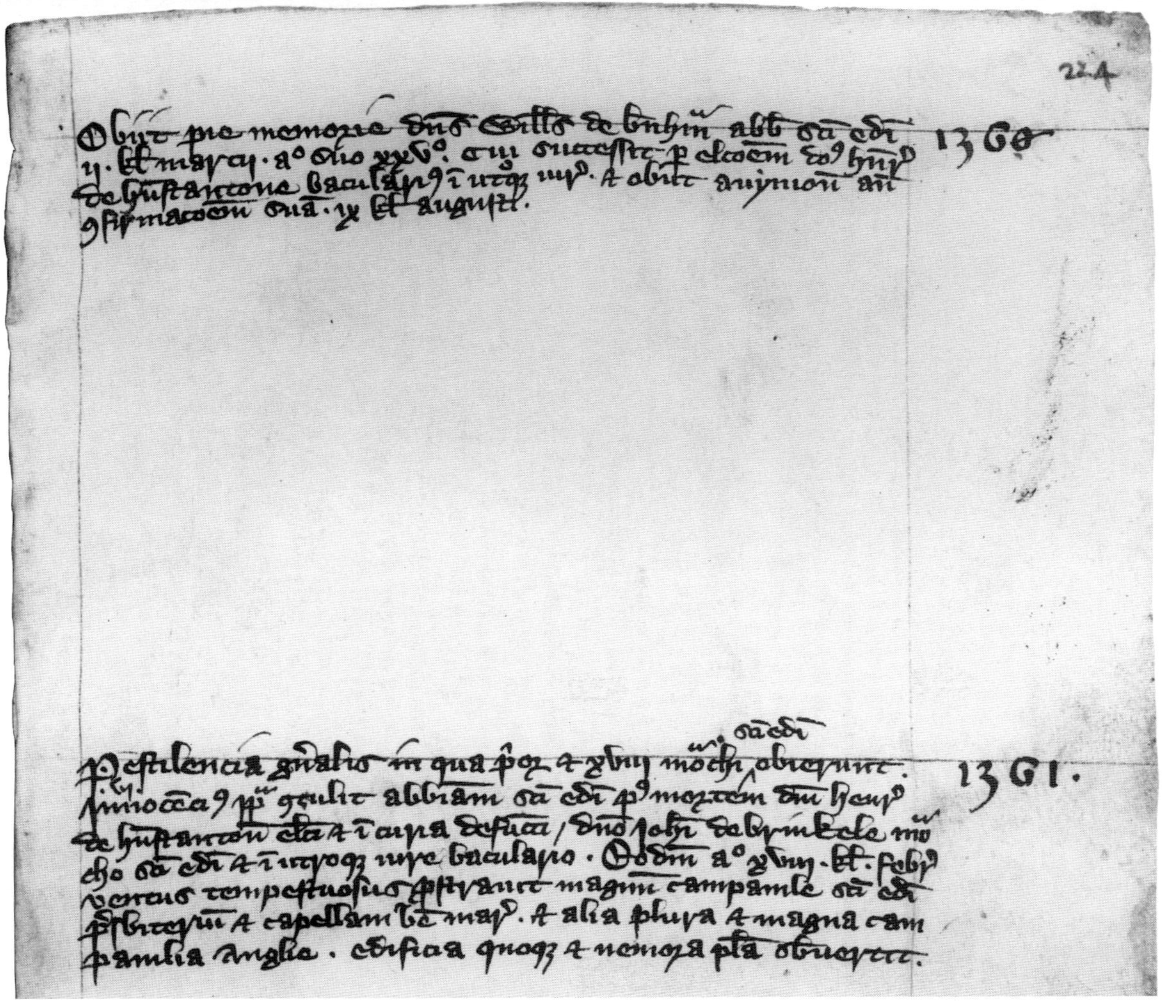

Plate 7. Bodl. MS Lat. hist. d. 4 (Bury C. 59), fol. 224r. A book of histories, showing here Kirkestede's informal annals for 1360–61, in which he records the deaths of two abbots, the return of virulent plague to the abbey, and the destruction of Bury's bell tower.

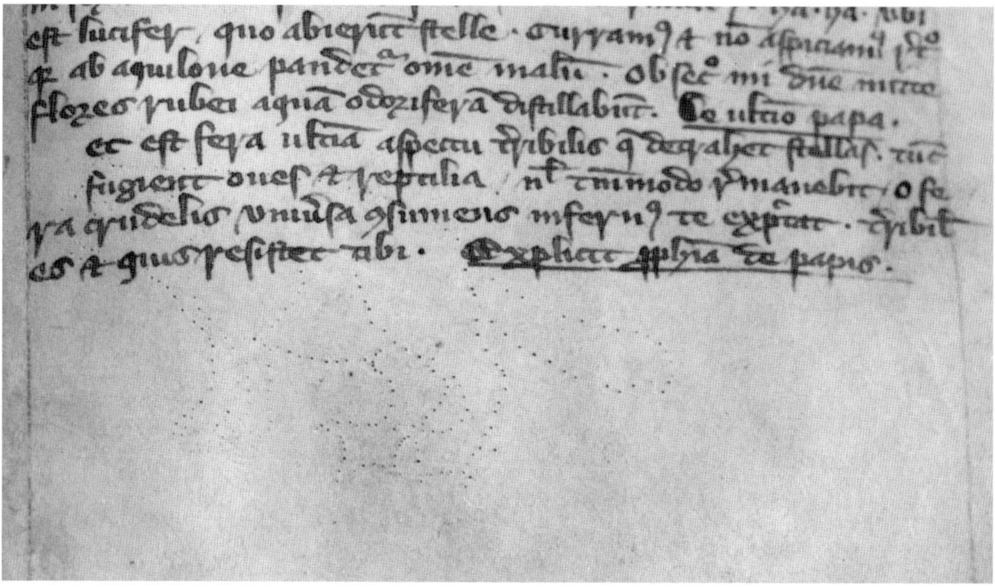

Plate 8a. Cambridge, Corpus Christi College, MS 404 (Bury P. 163), fol. 41r. A collection of prophetical texts, showing here a former piece of scrap parchment containing a pin-prick template for the picture of a beaver (transferred to what is now fol. 95r in this manuscript), partly visible, partly written over by the papal prophecies copied in Kirkestede's hand.

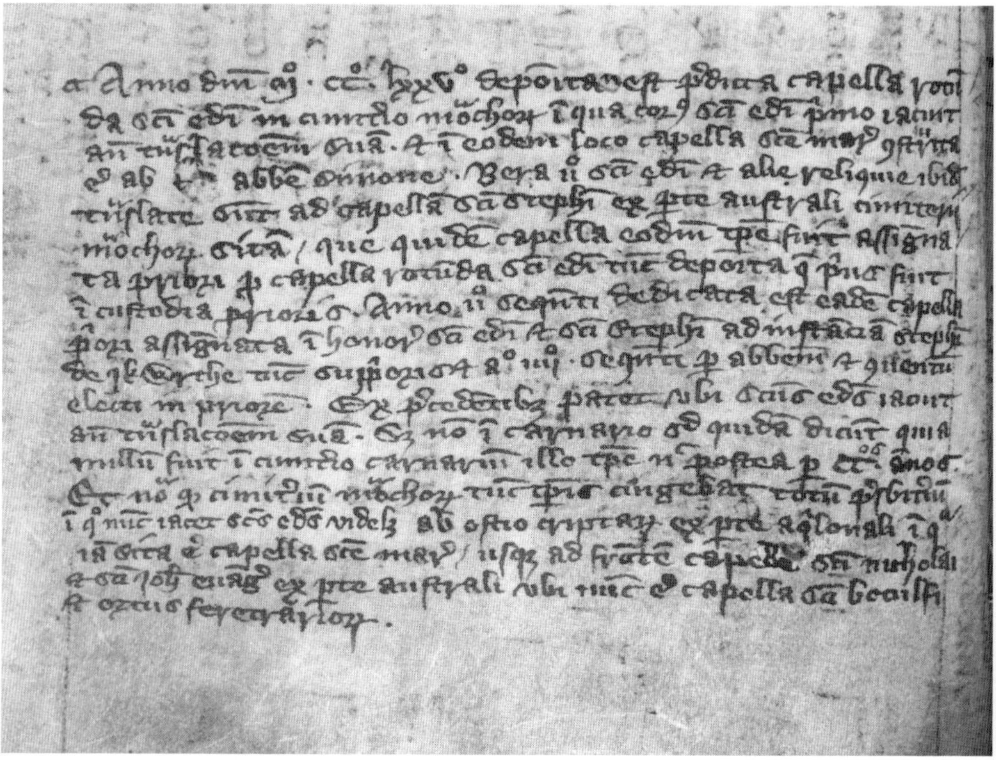

Plate 8b. College of Arms, MS Arundel 30 (Bury —), fol. 8v. The Bury Chronicle etc., showing here Kirkestede's history of the Round Chapel in the abbey cemetery.

*CATALOGUS DE LIBRIS
AUTENTICIS ET APOCRIFIS*

[CATALOGUS DE LIBRIS AUTENTICIS ET APOCRIFIS]

Incipit Cathologus de libris autenticis et apocrifis juxta Burcardum lib. iii[1] et Hugonem de Sancto Victore in suo Didascalicon libro iv et Vincentium in Speculo historiali libro primo et Gratianum Di. 15a *Sancta Romana* et Di. xxxvii *Legimus*[2] et in glossa et juxta Ysidorum et Cassiodorum.

Omnis divina scriptura[3] in duobus Testamentis continetur, in Veteri scilicet et in Novo. Utrumque Testamentum tribus ordinibus distinguitur: Vetus Testamentum continet Legem, Prophetas et Agiografos, id est Sancta scribentes, Novum autem continet Evangelium, Apostolos, Patres et Doctores. Primus ordo Veteris Testamenti, id est Lex, Pentateuchum habet, id est quinque libros Moysy, quos idem Moyses scripsisse perhibetur. In hoc ordine primus est Bresith qui est Genesis, et dicitur Genesis eo quod generatio seculi in eo contineatur. Secundus est Elesinoth qui est Exodus, ab exitu filiorum Israel de Aegypto dictus. Tertius Vegecra, id est Leviticus, qui Levitarum ministeria et diversitatem victimarum exequitur. Quartus Vegedebar qui est Numeri, et vocatur liber Numerorum quia in eo egressae de Egipto tribus enumerantur et 42ae per heremum mansiones. Quintus Adabarim qui est Deuteronomius. Deuteros Graecum verbum est et interpretatur secundus, nomia interpretatur lex; inde dictus est Deuteronomius, quasi Secunda Lex, quia in eo replicantur ea quae in praecedentibus diffusius dicta sunt. Secundus ordo Veteris Testamenti est Prophetarum et continet octo volumina. Primum Josuae benin, id est filium Nun, qui et Josue et Jesus et Jehu Navae nuncupatur; hujus libri idem Josue, cujus nomine inscribitur, autor fuisse creditur, in quo terra promissionis populo dividitur. Secundum Sophim, qui est liber Judicum, a principibus dictus qui judicabant populum Israel antequam reges essent in eodem populo;[4] quem a Gedeone et Samuele editum dicunt. Huic quidam compingunt historiam Ruth sub uno volumine,[5] eo quod tempore judicum facta fuisse narratur, quam Gedeon et Samuel scripserunt. Tertium Samuel[6] qui est primus et

1. Cited indirectly through Gratian Di. 15 c. 1.
2. Not used below.
3. 'Omnis divina scriptura – in eodem populo': excerpted from Hugh of Saint Victor, *Didascalicon* IV 2, 3 and 8.
4. See note 3.
5. 'Huic – volumine': *Didascalicon* IV 8.
6. 'Tertium Samuel – historias': excerpts from *Didascalicon* IV 2, 3 and 8.

secundus Regum, et dicitur Samuel quia Samuel autor ejus extitit et quia ejus et sacerdotium et gesta describit; qui licet historiam Saul et David contineat, utrique tamen ad Samuel referuntur, quia unxit utrumque. Quartum Malachim, id est Regum, qui est tertius et quartus Regum, et dictus est Malachim pro eo quod reges Judae et Israeliticae gentis gestaque eorum per ordinem narrat. Hunc Jeremias primum in unum volumen collegit, nam antea sparsus erat per singulorum regum historias;[7] et hoc patet quia idem est finis hujus libri et Jeremiae. Liber autem Regum in quatuor voluminibus distinguitur apud nos, sed secundum Hebraeos in duobus voluminibus. Quintum Ysaiam[8] qui potius evangelista quam propheta, dicitur edidisse librum suum. Sextum Jeremiam, quem librum similiter Jeremias edidit cum Trenis, quos nos Lamenta vocamus, eo quod in tristioribus rebus funeribusque adhibeantur, in quibus quadruplex diverso metro composuit alphabetum.[9] De Baruch non fit mentio in libris Cassiodori, Ysidori, Hugonis in Didascalicon nec Jeronimi cum aliis libris Veteris Testamenti. Septimum Ezechielem[10] ab Ezechiele similiter scriptum, qui principium et finem obscuriora habet. Octavum Thareasra qui est .xii. Prophetarum. Hic liber auctorum suorum nominibus praenotatur, quorum nomina sunt Osee, Johel, Amos, Abdias, Jonas, Micheas, Naum, Abacuch, Sophonias, Aggeus, Zacharias et Malachias; qui propterea Minores dicuntur quia sermones eorum breves sunt, unde et uno volumine comprehenduntur. Ysaias autem et Jeremias, Ezechiel et Daniel Majores sunt, singuli suis voluminibus distincti. Tertius ordo librorum de Veteri Testamento .ix. habet libros. Primus est Job, quem quidam Moysen, alii unum ex Propetis, nonnulli ipsum Job scripsisse credunt. Secundus David, [p. 2] id est liber Psalmorum, quem Graeci et Hebraei quinque incisionibus[11] et uno Psalmorum volumine comprehendunt. Psalmos autem David composuit, sed Esdras postea Psalmos ita ut nunc sunt ordinavit et titulos addidit. Tertius liber est Masloth, quod Graece Parabolae, Latine Proverbia sonat, videlicet Salomonis. Quartus Celeth qui est Ecclesiastes. Quintus Sirarsim, id est Cantica Canticorum.[12] Tribus nominibus[13] vocatum esse Salamonem Scriptura docet: Idida, id est Dilectum Domini, quia eum dilexit Dominus, et Celeth, id est Ecclesiasten; ecclesiastes autem Graeco sermone appellatur qui coetum vel ecclesiam congregat, quem nos nuncupare possumus concionatorem, qui loquitur non ad unum specialiter sed ad totam concionem populi; porro Pacificus vocatus

7. See note 6.
8. 'Quintum Ysaiam – alphabetum': excerpts from *Didascalicon* IV 2 and 8.
9. See note 8.
10. 'Septimum Ezechielem – Canticorum': excerpts from *Didascalicon* IV 2, 3 and 8.
11. incisionibus: queried by Tanner.
12. See note 10.
13. 'Tribus nominibus – amplexibus': *Didascalicon* IV 8.

est, eo quod in regno ejus pax fuit. Juxta numerum igitur vocabulorum suorum tria edidit volumina: primum Masloth, id est Parabolas sive Proverbia; secundum quod Hebraice Celeth, Graece Ecclesiastes, Latine Concionator dicitur, eo quod sermo ejus non ad unum sicut in Proverbiis sed ad universos generaliter quasi ad totam concionem et ecclesiam dirigatur; tertium Sirarisim, id est Cantica Canticorum, quod est quasi epithalamium, id est carmen nuptiale Christi et ecclesiae. In Proverbiis parvulum docet et quasi de officiis per sententias erudit, unde ut ad filium ei crebro sermo repetitur. In Ecclesiaste vero maturum virum aetatis instruit, ne quicquam in mundi rebus putet esse perpetuum sed caduca et brevia universa quae cernimus. Ad extremum[14] iam consummatum virum et calcato seculo praeparatum in Cantica Canticorum sponsi jungit amplexibus.[15] Sextus liber[16] de tertio ordine Veteris Testamenti est liber Danielis ab eodem editus. Hunc secundum LXX interpretes catholica ecclesia non legit, eo quod multum a veritate discordet; nec apud Hebraeos Susannae habet historiam nec Ympnum trium puerorum nec Belis draconisque fabulas. Daniel etiam apud Hebraeos non inter Prophetas sed inter Agiographos habetur. Septimus Dabreiamin qui est Paralipomenon, et dicitur Paralipomenon Graece quod nos praetermissorum vel reliquorum dicere possumus, quia ea quae in Lege vel Regum libris [a]ut omissa vel non plene prolata sunt in isto summatim ac breviter replicantur. Hunc librum sapientes Synagogae scripserunt. Octavus Esdras, et est liber unus ab eodem Esdra compositus, in cujus textu ejusdem Esdrae Neemiaeque sermones sub uno volumine continentur. Secundus, tertius et quartus liber Esdrae apocriphi sunt. Nonus Hester. Hunc librum Esdras creditur conscripsisse. Omnes ergo fiunt[17] numero .xxii. Quidam historiam Ruth et Lamentationes Jeremiae seorsum per se inter Agiographa computantes et .xxii. praecedentibus libris addentes, .xxiv. Veteris Legis numerant sub figura et numero .xxiv. seniorum qui in Apocalypsi Agnum adorant. Sunt praeterea alii quidam libri, ut Sapientia Salomonis, liber Jehu filii Sirach qui dicitur Ecclesiasticus, liber Judith, Thobias et libri Machabeorum, qui leguntur quidem sed non scribuntur in canone. Liber Sapientiae apud Hebraeos nusquam est, unde et ipse stylus Graecam magis eloquentiam redolet; hunc nonnulli scriptorum veterum Judaei Filonis esse,[18] quidam ipsius Salomonis affirmant, et vocatur[19] liber Sapientiae quia in eo Christi adventus, qui est Sapientia Patris, et passio ejus evidenter

14. extremum: queried by Tanner.
15. See note 13.
16. 'Sextus liber – esse': excerpts from *Didascalicon* IV 2, 3 and 8
17. fiunt: sunt Add. 3470; Tanner, uncertain of this reading, has added 'fuerint' as a variant reading.
18. See note 16.
19. 'et vocatur – constat': excerpts from *Didascalicon* IV 3 and 8

exprimitur. Librum Ecclesiasticum certissime Jesus filius Sirach Jerosolomita, nepos Jehu sacerdotis magni cujus meminit Zacharias, composuit, et dicitur Ecclesiasticus quia de totius ecclesiae disciplina religiosae conversationis magna cura et ratione sit editus. Hic apud Hebraeos reperitur sed inter apocrifos habetur. De hiis duobus Jeronimus sic dicit: Fertur panarethos Jesu filii Sirach liber et alius pseudographus qui Sapientia Salomonis inscribitur; quorum priorem Hebraicum reperi non Ecclesiasticum, ut apud Latinos, sed Parabolas praenotatum, cui juncti erant Ecclesiastes et Cantica Canticorum, ut similitudinem Salomonis non solum librorum numero sed et materiarum genere coequaret. Secundus apud Hebraeos nusquam est. Sicut ergo Judith et Tobiae et Machabeorum libros legit ecclesia, sed non inter canonicas scripturas recipit,[20] sic et haec duo volumina legat ad aedificationem plebis, non ad autoritatem ecclesiasticorum dogmatum confirmandam. Judith vero et Tobias et libri Machabeorum, quorum, ut testatur Jeronimus, stilus [p. 3] magis Graecus esse probatur, quibus autoribus scripti sunt minime constat.[21] Item secundum quosdam[22] historiam Judith ipsa vel Achior scripsit; primum Machabeorum scripsit Symon pontifex, ultimam ejus partem Johannes filius ejus; posteriorem quidam Judeus a Graecis eruditus edidisse cognoscitur. Istos autem quinque libros Judei inter apocrifos separant, ecclesia tamen Christi inter divinos honorat et praedicat. Vetus Testamentum Esdras scriba post incensam Legem a Caldeis, dum Judei regressi sunt in Jerosolumam, divino afflatus spiritu reparavit cunctaque Legis ac Prophetarum volumina quae fuerant a gentibus corrupta correxit et in .xxii. libros constituit.[23]

Interpretes[24] autem Veteris Testamenti primum LXX interpretes, quos Phtolomeus cognomento Philadelphus rex Aegypti omnis literaturae sagacissimus, cum Pisistratum Atheniensem tirannum, qui primus apud Graecos bibliotecam instituit, et Seleuchum Nichanorem et Alexandrum[25] et caeteros priores qui sapientiae operam dederant in studio bibliotecarum aemularetur, non solum gentium scripturas sed et divinas literas in suam bibliotecam conferens, ita ut .lxx. millia librorum in tempore ejus Alexandriae invenirentur, ab Eleasaro pontifice petens, scripturas Veteris Testamenti in Graecam vocem ex Hebrea lingua per LXX interpretes interpretari fecit. Siquidem singuli in singulis cellis separati ita omnia per Spiritum Sanctum interpretati sunt, ut nichil in alicujus eorum codice inventum esset, quod in caeteris vel in verborum ordine discreparet, propter quod una est eorum interpretatio. Et haec

---

20. Scripturas non recipit: Add. 3470.
21. See note 19.
22. 'Item secundum quosdam – constituit': source unidentified.
23. See note 22.
24. 'Interpretes – in suo Didascalicon': *Didascalicon* IV 5; 'Et haec fuit prima interpretatio' is added in Add. 3470.
25. Alexandrum: queried by Tanner.

fuit prima interpretatio. Sed Jeronimus dicit huic rei non esse adhibendam fidem. Secundam, tertiam et quartam interpretationem faciunt Aquila, Symmachus et Theodocion; quorum primus, id est Aquila, Judaeus fuit, Symachus vero et Theodocion Hebionitae haeretici. Obtinuit tamen usus ut post LXX interpretes ecclesiae Graecorum eorum reciperent exemplaria et legerent. Quinta est Vulgaris, cujus auctor ignoratur. Sexta et septima est Origenis, cujus codices Eusebius et Pamphilius vulgaverunt. Octava est Jeronimi, quae merito ceteris antefertur, nam et verborum tenacior et perspicuitate sententiae clarior. Haec Hugo in suo Didascalicon.[26]

Item alio modo de interpretibus secundum Ysidorum libro de Libris Veteris et Novi Testamenti[27] et libro Etymologiarum 6to.[28] Primam[29] post Esdram interpretationem de Hebraeo LXX interpretes ediderunt sub Phtolomaeo Egiptiorum rege, successore Alexandri, qui in legendo studiosus fuit omniumque libros gentium congregavit. Iste enim ab Eleazaro, qui erat princeps sacerdotum, multa dona mittens ad Templum petiit, ut senes de xii tribubus Israel transmitterentur, qui interpretarentur omnes libros in Graecum ex Hebraico. Haec fuit prima interpretatio vera et divina. Fuerunt et alii interpretes qui ex Hebraica lingua in Graecum sacra eloquia transtulerunt; nam secundam editionem Aquila, tertiam et quartam Theodocion et Symachus ediderunt, ambo Judaei proseliti. Quinta est Vulgaris, cujus auctor non apparet, et ob hoc sine nomine interpretis quinta editio nuncupatur. Sextam et septimam editionem Origines miro labore repperit et cum caeteris editionibus comparavit. Hii sunt itaque tantum qui sacras Scripturas. . . .[30] Nam Latinorum interpretum, qui de Graeco in nostro eloquio transtulerunt, ut meminit S. Augustinus, infinitus numerus est. De Hebraeo autem in Latinum eloquium tantummodo B. Jeronimus, trium linguarum peritus, sacras Scripturas convertit eloquenterque transfudit; cujus editione generaliter omnes ecclesiae usquequaque utuntur, pro eo quod veneracior sit in sententiis et clarior in verbis.[31]

26. See note 24.
27. The actual source is Isidore's *De ecclesiasticis officiis* (I 12), which (with I 11) is attached without rubric to the *Proemium in libris Veteris et Noui Testamenti* in Bodl. MS e Musaeo 31 (Bury A. 31). This excerpt begins there on p. 139. See the discription of the contents of e Musaeo 31 and similar bibliographical collections in R. A. B. Mynors, *Cassiodori Senatoris Institutiones* (Oxford 1961), xl, xliii.
28. 6to: 5to Add. 3470, queried by Tanner.
29. 'Primam post – in verbis': Isidore's *De ecclesiasticis officiis* I 12, with four interpolations from his *Etymologiarum* VI 4. The sentence 'Haec fuit prima interpretatio vera et divina' is added in Add. 3470.
30. 'Scripturas de Hebraeo in Graecum verterunt. Qui etiam et numerantur' is added in Isididore *De officiis*.
31. See note 29.

Primus ordo Novi Testamenti quatuor volumina habet, videlicet quatuor evangelia Matthei, Marci, Lucae et Johannis.[32] Plures evangelia[33] conscripserunt, sed quidam sine Spiritu Sancto magis conati sunt ordinare narrationem suam quam historiae texere veritatem. Unde sancti patres per Spiritum Sanctum docti quatuor tantum in auctoritatem receperunt, id est Matthei, Marci, Lucae et Johannis, ad similitudinem quatuor animalium in [p. 4] Ezechiele. Primus, id est Matheus, evangelium suum scripsit Hebraice; secundus Marcus Graece scripsit; tertius Lucas inter omnes evangelistas Graeci sermonis peritissimus quippe ut medicus, in Graecia evangelium suum scripsit Theophilo episcopo, ad quem etiam Actus Apostolorum idem scripsit; quartus et ultimus Johannes evangelium suum scripsit.[34] Canones evangeliorum[35] S. Ammonius Alexandriae monachus et episcopus primus excogitavit, quem postea Caesariensis Eusebius secutus plenius exposuit. Qui ideo facti sunt, ut per eos invenire et scire possimus, qui reliquorum evangelistarum similia aut propria dixerunt. Sunt autem numero decem, quorum primus continet numeros in quibus quatuor eadem dixerunt Mattheus, Marcus, Lucas, Johannes; secundus in quibus tres, Matheus, Marcus, Lucas; tertius in quibus tres Matheus, Lucas, Johannes; quartus in quibus tres Mattheus, Marcus, Johannes; quintus in quibus duo Marcus, Lucas; sextus in quibus duo Mattheus, Marcus; septimus in quibus duo Mattheus, Johannes; octavus in quibus duo Lucas, Marcus; nonus in quibus duo Lucas, Johannes; decimus in quibus singuli eorum propria quaedam dixerunt. Quorum expositio haec est: per singulos enim evangelistas numeris quidam capitulis affixis adjacet, quibus numeris subdita est area quaedam minio notata,[36] quae indicat in quoto canone positus sit numerus cui subjecta est area. Verbi gratia, si est area prima in primo canone, si secunda in secundo, si tertia in tertio, et sic per ordinem usque ad decimum pervenies. Si igitur aperto quolibet evangelio placuerit scire, qui reliquorum evangelistarum similia dixerint, assumas adjacentem numerum capituli et requiras ipsum numerum in suo canone quem indicat; ibique invenies quot et quid dixerunt; et ita demum in corpore inquisita loca, quae ex ipsis numeris indicantur, per singula evangelia de eisdem dixisse invenies.[37]

Alius modus[38] inveniendi concordantias evangeliorum. Sume aliquem numerum contentum sub aliquo evangelio, utpote in primo canone scilicet

---

32. 'Primus ordo – Johannis': *Didascalicon* IV 2.
33. 'Plures evangelia – scripsit': *Didascalicon* IV 6.
34. See note 33.
35. 'Canones evangeliorum – invenies': *Didascalicon* IV 10.
36. notata vocata: Add. 3470
37. See note 35.
38. 'Alius modus – evangeliis': source unidentified.

qui continetur sub Matheo in principio³⁹ tabulae, et in eadem linea 2 sub Marco, 7 sub Luca, 10 sub Johanne, quia per istos numeros inveniendae sunt concordantiae; et quali modo inveneris 8⁴⁰ in Matheo, tali modo inveniendi sunt caeteri numeri in caeteris evangelistis. Verte igitur ad Matheum, et incipe numerare a primo numero rubeo contento in margine Matthei per omnes numeros rubeos usque compleveris numerum octonarium. Autoritas autem opposita illi numero est autoritas quam quaeris, et numerus rubeus eidem autoritati oppositus docet in quo canone est illa autoritas. Unitas enim erit qui numerus appropriatur primo canoni. Pari modo quaere 2 in Marco, 7 in Luca, 10 in Johanne, et invenies literam concordantem in omnibus evangelistis in primo canone, et per consequens capitula. Si autem fuerit magnus numerus, ut 320 vel 230 vel plus vel minus, verte ad evangelium sub quo ille numerus ponitur, et quaere simile de nigris numeris in margine illius evangelii vel propinquiorem, minorem tamen, et tunc ab illo nigro numero minori computa per rubeos numeros usque dum compleveris numerum quem quaeris, et in opposito ejus erit auctoritas quam dictus numerus contentus in tabula docet quaerendam, et quoto capitulo et quoto canone; quia si numerus rubeus oppositus sit 1 est in primo canone, si 2 in secundo, si 3 in tertio, si 4 in quarto, si 5 in quinto, si 6 in sexto, si 7 in septimo, si 8 in octavo, si 9 in nono, si 10 in decimo canone, in quo nullus alteri concordat sed unusquisque sua propria verba dicit, nec rubeus numerus 10 excedit, scilicet numerus rubeus scriptus in evangeliis.⁴¹

Item Hieronymus libro De catholicis scriptoribus et Ysidorus in libro Ethimologiarum et De libris Veteris et Novi Testamenti de evangelistis.⁴² Matheus apostolus et evangelista ex tribu Levi sumpsit cognomen, ex pupplicano a Christo electus, ex peccante translatus. Hic scripsit evangelium litteris [p. 5] Hebraicis, et ea quae ex ore Christi audivit vel quae ab illo facta vel gesta vidit primum in Judea, postmodum in Macedonia praedicavit.⁴³

Marcus⁴⁴ discipulus et interpres Petri ejusque in baptismate filius, juxta quod Petrum referentem audierat, rogatus a fratribus Romae, breve scripsit evangelium in Graeca lingua; quod cum Petrus audisset, approbavit et ecclesiis legendum sua autoritate adidit. Istud evangelium nonnulli dictatum

---

39. principio: queried by Tanner.
40. 8: queried by Tanner.
41. See note 38.
42. This paragraph is composed of excerpts from Isidore's *De ortu et obitu patrum* c. 76, *Etymologiarum* VI 1 paragraph 35, and *Proemium in libris Vet. et Nou. Test.* c. 91, probably taken from Bodl. MS e Musaeo 31 (Bury A. 31).
43. See note 42.
44. This paragraph is quoted from Jerome's *De uiris illustribus* c. 8, with two brief interpolations from Isidore's *De ortu* c. 83. The phrase 'in Graeca lingua' is probably taken from *Etym*. VI 1 paragraph 35.

a Petro Romae ferunt. Assumpto itaque evangelio Marcus perrexit ad Egiptum, et primus Alexandriae cathedram tenuit primusque ecclesias Egiptiorum fundavit. Denique Philo disertissimus Judeorum, videns Alexandriae primam ecclesiam adhuc judaizantem, quasi in laudem gentis suae librum super eorum conversatione scripsit, et quoniam Lucas narrat Jerosolymis credentes omnia habuisse communia, sic ille quod Alexandriae sub Marco fieri doctore cernebat memoriae tradidit. Passus est apud Alexandriam sub Nerone.[45]

Lucas Sirus,[46] natione Antiochenus arte medicus, unusque secundum quosdam de lxxii discipulis, postea discipulus S. Pauli ac omnis peregrinationis ejus comes individuus, scripsit evangelium Graeco sermone et historiam de Actibus Apostolorum.[47] Igitur Visionem[48] Pauli et Teclae et totam baptizati leonis fabulam inter scripturas apocrifas computamus. Quale est, ut individuus comes apostoli inter caeteras ejus res hoc solum ignoraverit? Sed et Tertullianus vicinus illorum temporum refert presbyterum quendam in Asia amatorem apostoli Pauli convictum[49] apud Johannem, qui auctor esset libri et confessum se hoc Pauli amore fecisse et de loco excidisse. Quidam suspicantur, quotienscunque Paulus in Epistolis suis dicat juxta evangelium meum, de Lucae significare evangelio, et Lucam non solum ab apostolo Paulo didicisse evangelium sed a caeteris omnibus. Igitur Lucas evangelium sicut audierat scripsit, sed Acta Apostolorum sicut viderat ipse composuit.[50]

Johannes apostolus et evangelista, morem aquilae affectans, coelum et terram avidus transvolat, atque Nativitatem Verbi occulta misterii intelligentia penetrat. Scripsit enim . . .[51] et ea quae ab ore Christi audivit et vidit ab eo fieri praedicavit. Haec Hieronimus et Ysidorus ubi supra.[52]

Secundus ordo librorum de Novo Testamento quatuor similiter habet volumina. Primum continet epistolas Pauli numero xiv, quas idem apostolus scripsit: decem scilicet ad ecclesias et quatuor ad personas, Thimotheo 2, Tito 1 et Philemoni 1. Ultimam tamen ad Hebraeos plerique dicunt non Pauli esse propter dissonantiam sermonis, eandemque alii Lucam vel

---

45. See note 44.
46. 'Lucas Sirus – Apostolorum'. The majority of this section is adapted from *De ortu* c. 82. The phrase concerning which two works were written by Luke is not quoted from any source, but may be adapted from *Didascalicon* IV 6, *Etym.* VI 1, or Jerome's *De viris* c. 7. The phrase 'unusque secundum quosdam de lxxii discipulis' is added in Add. 3470.
47. See note 46.
48. 'Igitur Visionem – composuit': Jerome *De viris* c. 7.
49. convictum: queried by Tanner.
50. See note 48.
51. This may once have contained material from *Etym.* VI 2 paragraph 39: 'Scripsit enim . . . evangelium ultimum in Asia . . .'.
52. This paragraph is composed of extracts from *Proemium in libris Vet. et Nou. Test.* cc. 88, 91.

Barnabam scripsisse, alii Clementem suspicantur. Scripsit enim Paulus ad Romanos epistolam 1, ad Corinthios 2, ad Galathas 1, ad Ephesios 1, ad Philippenses 1, ad Colosenses 1, ad Thessalonicenses 2, ad Thimotheum 2, ad Titum 1, ad Philemonem 1, ad Hebraeos 1. Quidam dicunt eum scripsisse 15mam epistolam ad Leodicenses, sed haec in canone non habetur, sed ab omnibus exploditur.[53]

Secundum volumen de secundo ordine librorum Novi Testamenti continet vii epistolas canonicas, auctorum suorum nominibus intitulatas. Est enim prima earum una Jacobi, Petri duo, Johannis tres et Judae una. Epistola tamen Jacobi a nonnuliis ejus esse negatur, sed sub nomine ejus aestimatur ab alio forte dictata. Item secunda epistola Petri a quibusdam ejus esse non creditur[54] propter styli sermonisque cum priore dissonantium. Sed et evangelium juxta Marcum Petri esse dicitur; libri autem Petri, e quibus unus Actorum ejus inscribitur, alius Evangelii, tertius Praedicationis, quartus Apocalipseos, quintus Judicii, inter apocrifa repudiantur.[55] Prima epistola Johannis ejus esse asseritur, reliquae duae cujusdam Johannis Presbyteri aestimantur, cujus juxta Jeronimum alterum sepulcrum apud Ephesum [p. 6] demonstratur. Judas epistolam suam edidit.[56] Haec Jeronimus et Ysidorus.

Tertium volumen[57] continet Actus Apostolorum, in quibus primordia fidei Christianae in gentibus et nascentis ecclesiae historia digeruntur, et apostolorum gesta narrantur. Hunc librum scripsit Lucas evangelista.

Quartum volumen continet Apocalipsim, quem scripsit Johannes apostolus in Pathmos insula exilio relegatus. Apocalipsis ergo Latine interpretatur Revelatio,[58] quia in hoc libro continentur quae revelavit Deus Johanni et Johannes ecclesiae.

In tertio ordine primum locum habent Decreta et Decretalia, quae canones, id est regulares, appellantur; canon enim Graece, Latine regula nuncupatur. Canones autem generalium conciliorum a temporibus Constantini coeperunt. In praecedentibus enim annis persecutione fervente, docendarum plebem non dabatur facultas, nec licentia episcopis in unum convenire. Inde Christianitas in diversas haereses scissa est. Tempore autem Constantini imperatoris sancti patres, de omni orbe terrarum convenientes, in Concilio Niceno juxta apostolicam et evangelicam fidem secundum post

---

53. This paragraph is composed of extracts adapted from *Didascalicon* IV 2 and 6, and Jerome, *De uiris*, c. 5. The phrase 'sed haec in canone non habetur' is added in Add. 3470.
54. The source for this sectlon is unidentified.
55. 'propter styli – repudiantur': Jerome, *De viris*, c. 1.
56. 'Prima epistola – edidit': source unidentified.
57. 'Tertium volumen – Revelatio'. This section is composed of extracts from *Didascalicon* IV 2, 6 and 12. Add. 3470 inverts the order in which these two volumes appear in *Didascalicon*.
58. See note 57.

apostolos symbolum tradiderunt.[59] Post illas[60] igitur Veteris et Novi Testamenti scripturas, quas canonice recipit et approbat ecclesia catholica, etiam has suscipi statuit scripturas, sanctam videlicet synodum Nicaenam cccxviii episcoporum, mediante S. Constantino imperatore, in qua Arrius haereticus condempnatus est; item sanctam synodum Constantinopolitanam cl episcoporum, mediante Theodosio seniore Augusto, in qua Macedonius haereticus debitam excepit dampnationem; tertiam sanctam synodum Ephesinam cc episcoporum cum consensu beati[61] papae Caelestini, mediante juniore Theodosio Augusto, in qua Nestorius dampnatur est; quartam sanctam synodum. Calcedonensem dcxxx episcoporum, mediante Marciano Augusto, in qua Eutices abbas Constantinopolitanus et Dioscorus quondam Alexandriae episcopus et Nestorius cum omnibus suis complicibus damnati sunt. Sed et siqua sunt concilia, quae sancti patres sanxerunt post istarum quatuor auctoritatem, sancta ecclesia decrevit recipienda et inviolabiliter custodienda.[62]

Secundum locum[63] habent in tertio ordine librorum de Novo Testamento sanctorum patrum et doctorum ecclesiae scripta, videlicet Jeronimi, Ambrosii, Augustini, Gregorii, Basilii, Origenis, Ysidori, Bedae et aliorum multorum orthodoxorum, quae tam infinita sunt ut numerari non possint. Ex quo profecto apparet quantum in fide Christian[a] fervorem habuerint, pro cujus assertione tot et tanta opera memoranda posteris reliquerunt. In hiis autem ordinibus maxime apparet utriusque Testamenti convenientia, quod, sicut post Legem Prophetae et post Prophetas Hagiographi, ita post Evangelium Apostoli, post Apostolos Patres et Doctores ordine successerunt.[64] Haec Hugo in suo Didascalicon et Gelasius notat Di. 15ma ut supra.

---

59. 'In tertio – tradiderunt'. This section is composed of extracts from *Didascalicon* IV 2 and 11.
60. 'post illas – custodienda'. This section is quoted from the *Decretum Gelasianum* IV intro. and 1, with five interpolations from *Didascalicon* IV 12. The phrase 'quas canonice recipit et approbat ecclesia catholica' is added in Add. 3470.
61. beati] beatae *Add. 3470*.
62. See note 60.
63. *Didascalicon* IV 2. The names of Ambrose and Origen are out of sequence in Add. 3470; and the name of Basil has been added.
64. See note 63.

Vetus Testamentum dividitur in libros
- Legales
  - Genesin[65]
  - Exodum
  - Leviticum
  - Numeros
  - Deuteronomium
- Prophetales
  - Josuae
  - Judicum
  - Ruth
  - Regum
  - Ysaiam
  - Jeremiam
  - Ezechielem
  - XII Prophetas
- Agiographos
  - Job
  - Psalterium
  - Proverbium
  - Ecclesiasten
  - Cantica Canticorum
  - Danielem
  - Paralipomenon
  - Esdram
  - Hester
- < >
  - Librum Sapientiae
  - Ecclesiasticum
  - Judith
  - Tobiam
  - Machabeorum

Novum Testamentum dividitur in
- Evangelistas
  - Matheum
  - Marcum
  - Lucam
  - Johannem
- Apostolos
  - Ad Romanos 1
  - Ad Corinthios 2
  - Ad Galatas 1
  - Ad Ephesios 1
  - Ad Philippenses 1
  - Ad Colosenses 1
  - Ad Thesalonicenses 2
  - Ad Thimotheum 2
  - Ad Titum 1
  - Ad Philemonem 1

65. This is a diagram of the scheme of division of the books of the bible expounded by Hugh of Saint-Victor in *Didascalicon* IV 2.

p. 7]
Alia divisio:[66]

Vetus Testamentum dividitur in libros
- Doctores
  - Ad Hebraeos 1
  - Jacobi 1
  - Petri 2
  - Johannis 3
  - Judas 1
  - Actus Apostolorum
  - Apocalipsim
  - Decreta et Decretalia
  - Originalia Doctorum
- Legales
  - Genesim 1
  - Exodum 1
  - Leviticum 1
  - Numeros 1
  - Deuteronomium 1
- Historiales
  - Josuae vel Jehu Navae 1
  - Judicum 1
  - Ruth 1
  - Regum 4
  - Paralipomenon 2
  - Esdram 2
  - Hester 1
  - Judith 1
  - Tobiam 1
  - Machabaeorum 2
  - Job 1
- Sapientiales
  - Proverbiorum 1
  - Ecclesiasten 1
  - Cantica Canticorum 1
  - Ecclesiasticum 1
  - Librum Sapientiae 1
- Prophetales
  - Psalterium 1
  - Ysayam 1
  - Jeremiam 1
  - Ezechielem 1
  - Danielem
  - XII Prophetas 12

66. The source for this diagram and the scheme it represents is unidentified.

In Novo Testamento	Legalibus correspondent 4 Evangelistae	Matheus 1 Marcus 1 Lucas 1 Johannes 1
	Historialibus correspondent	Actus Apostolorum 1 Epistola Jacobi 1 Epistolae Petri 1 Epistola Johannis 3 Epistolae Judae 1
	Sapientialibus correspondent Epistolas Pauli	Ad Romanos 1 Ad Corinthiosos 2 Ad Galatas 1 Ad Ephesios 1 Ad Philippenses 1 Ad Colosenses 1 Ad Thessalonicenses 2 Ad Thimotheum 2 Ad Titum 1 Ad Philemonem 1 Ad Hebraeos 1
	Prophetalibus correspondet	Apocalipsim 1

Dicto breviter de ordine et numero librorum Veteris et Novi Testamenti secundem Burcardum, Jeronimum, Ysidorum, Cassiodorum et Hugonem in Didascalicon, jam nunc subjiciendum est de opusculis sanctorum patrum et doctorum, quae in ecclesia catholica recipiuntur. Apud nos S. Pamphilus martir, cujus vitam Eusebius Caesariensis conscripsit, Pisistratum in sacro bibliotecae studio adaequare contendit. Hic enim in bibliotheca sua prope .xxx. milia voluminum habuit.[67] Origenes apud Graecos in Scripturarum labore tam Graecos quam Latinos operum suorum numero superavit. Denique S. Jeronimus sex milia librorum ejus elegisse fatetur. Horum tamen omnium studia Augustinus ingenio vel scientia sua vicit.[68] Origenis tamen scripta recipit ecclesia quae Jeronimus non repudiat; verumptamen quando omeliae ejus leguntur in ecclesia, nomen ejus propter haeresis infamiam subticetur. Volunt tamen quidam doctores ut in principio omelia ejus dicatur omelia Origenis correcta et approbata a Jeronimo; sed secundum Willelmum Durandum in suo Rationali dici debet omelia lectionis ejusdem.[69]

---

67. 'Apud nos – habuit': *Didascalicon* IV 13.
68. 'Origenes apud – vicit': *Didascalicon* IV 14.
69. 'Origenis tamen – ejusdem'. The reference to Durandus is unidentified.

Scripserunt[70] et alii viri catholici quamplures, scilicet S. Dionisius Areopagita, episcopus et martir, S. Ignatius, S. Ciprianus episcopus et martir, S. Eusebius Caesariensis, S. Basilius episcopus Cappadociae, S. Gregorius Nazianzenus, S. Gregorius Theologus, Didimus Alexandrinus. Rufinus presbyter Aquilinensis vir religiosus multa scripsit et interpretatus est; sed quum B. Jeronimus in aliquibus eum de arbitrii libertate notavit, illa sentire debemus quae secundum Jeronimum sentire cognoscimus, et non solum de Rufino et Origene sed et de universis quos idem Jeronimus zelo Dei et fidei religione reprehendit. Item scripserunt S. Jeronimus, S. Athanasius Alexandrinus episcopus, Sanctus Hillarius Pictavensis episcopus; Sedulius presbyter et vir religiosus scripsit Opus Paschale; S. Ambrosius Mediolanensis episcopus, S. Johannes Chrysostomus episcopus Constantinopolitanus, S.Theophilus episcopus [p. 8] Alexandriae, S. Cyrillus episcopus Alexandriae, S. doctor Augustinus episcopus Ypon[ensis], Orosius, Sanctus Prosper vir religiosissimus, Cassiodorus, S. Gregorius papa, Proculus, Prudentius, Arator, Juvencus,[71] Leo papa sanctus, cujus scripta ad Flavianum si quispiam usque ad unum iota disputaverit et non ea in omnibus venerabiliter receperit, anathema sit.[72] Item scripserunt Ysidorus, S. Beda, Anselmus, Albinus vel Alcuinus, Alexander Nequam, Fulgentius, Johannes Damascenus, Bernardus, Innocentius papa, Yvo Carnotensis, Haymo monachus, Hildefonsus, Petrus Comestor, Petrus Lumbardus, Petrus Pictavensis, Rabanus.[73] Item vitas[74] patrum Antonii, Pauli, Hilarionis et omnium monachorum et heremitarum, quas scripsit B. Jeronimus, recepit et legit ecclesia cum omni veneratione. Item Actus B. Silvestri papae, licet ejus qui conscripsit no[me]n ignoretur, a multis in urbe Roma catholicis legi cognovimus. Item scripta De inventione Sanctae Crucis et De inventione capitis S. Johannis Baptistae. Item opuscula atque tractatus omnium patrum ortodoxorum, qui in nullo a[75] sanctae Romanae ecclesiae fide deviarunt. Item recipit et approbat sancta Romana ecclesia Decretales epistolas, quas beatissimi papae diversis temporibus ediderunt. Item Gesta sanctorum martirum, exceptis quibusdam paucis qui singulari cautela in sancta Romana ecclesia secundum antiquam consuetudinem non leguntur, quia eorum qui scripserunt nomina penitus

70. 'Scripserunt et – Juvencus'. This list is compiled, with rearrangements and with three additions, from *Didascalicon* IV 14; the discussion of Rufinus may also be based on the *Decretum Gelasianum* IV 5.
71. See note 70.
72. 'Leo papa – sit': *Decretum Gelasianum* IV 3. This extract appears again in the *Catalogus* entry for Pope Leo, *343*.
73. 'Item scripserunt – Rabanus'. The source for this list is unidentified; only the first two, Isidore and Bede, appear in the *Didascalicon*.
74. 'Item vitas – celebrat'. This section is adapted from *Decretum Gelasianum* IV 3 and 4.
75. a] ad *Add. 3470*.

ignorantur, et ab infidelibus aut superflua aut minus apta quam rei ordo fuerit scripta esse putantur; sicut cujusdam Cirici et Julittae, sicut Georgii aliorumque hujusmodi passiones, quae ab haereticis perhibentur conscriptae, sancta Romana ecclesia veneratur et celebrat.[76] Sunt praeterea quamplurima alia opuscula a viris religiosis et sapientibus diversis temporibus conscripta, quae licet autoritate universalis ecclesiae probata non sint, tamen quia a fide catholica non discrepant et nonnulla etiam utilia docent, inter divina computantur eloquia.

Praeter haec etiam alia volumina apocripha nuncupantur, in quibus et si inveniatur aliqua veritas, tamen nulla est in eis canonica auctoritas, quia multa in hiis voluminibus sub nominibus prophetarum et recentiora sub nominibus apostolorum ab haereticis proferuntur;[77] e quibus[78] pauca quae ad memoriam venerunt subdenda sunt. Imprimis Arminensem synodum a Constantio Caesare Constantini filio congregatam, mediante Tauro praefecto, in aeternum Romana dampnat ecclesia; item Itinerarium nomine Petri apostoli, quod appellatur S. Clementis libros x; Actus nomine Andreae apostoli; Actus nomine Thomae apostoli; Actus nomine Petri apostoli; Actus nomine Philippi apostoli; Evangelium Thadaei; Evangelium Bernabae; Evangelium Petri;[79] Evangelium Thomae quibus ut dicitur Manichaei utuntur; Evangelium Bartholomaei; Evangelium Andreae; Evangelia quae falsavit quidam Lucianus; Evangelia quae falsavit Ysicius; liber De infantia Salvatoris, et de S. Maria, et de obstetrice Salvatoris; liber qui vocatur Pastor; libri omnes quos fecit Lentius discipulus diaboli; liber qui appellatur Fundamentum; liber qui appellatur Thesaurus; liber De filiabus Adae; Centimetrum de Christo Virgilianis compaginatum versibus; liber qui appellatur Actus Pauli et Teclae; liber qui appellatur Nepotis; liber Proverbiorum ab haereticis conscriptus et S. Sixti nomine signatus; revelatio vel visio quae appellatur Pauli Revelatio; Thomae Revelatio; Stephani; liber qui appellatur Transitus S. Mariae; liber qui appellatur Assumptio S. Mariae; liber qui appellatur Poenitentia Adae; liber qui appellatur Poenitentia Originis; liber qui appellatur Testamentum Job; liber qui appellatur Poenitentia[80] Cipriani; liber Diogiae[81] nomine Gigantis, qui post diluvium cum dracone ab haereticis pugnasse perhibetur;[82] liber qui appellatur Jamne et Mambre; liber qui appellatur Sors Apostolorum; [p. 9] liber Lusan;[83] liber qui appellatur

---

76. See note 74.
77. 'Sunt praeterea – proferuntur': source unidentified.
78. 'e quibus – dampnata': *Decretum Gelasianum* V.
79. Evangelium Petri: Evangelium Iacobi minoris; Evangelium Petri, *Decretum Gelasianum*.
80. Poenitentia: queried by Tanner.
81. Diogiae: queried by Tanner.
82. 'Poenitentia Originis – perhibetur'. The order of these works is rearranged in Add. 3470.
83. Lusan: queried by Tanner.

Canones Apostolorum; liber qui appellatur Laus Apostolorum;[84] liber Physiologus ab haereticis conscriptus et B. Ambrosii nomine praesignatus; Historia Eusebii Pamphili; opuscula Tertulliani sive Affricani; opuscula Posthumiani et Galli; opuscula Montani, Priscillae et Maximillae; opuscula Faustini Manichaei; opuscula alterius Clementis Alexandrini; opuscula Cassiani presbiteri Galliarum; opuscula Victorini Pictavensis; opuscula Fausti Remensis Galliarum; opuscula Frumentii; Epistola Jesu ad Abagarum regem, Epistola Abagari ad Jesum; opuscula Lactantii; opuscula Comodiani; opuscula Tharsi Cipriani; opuscula Arnobii; opuscula Tyconii;[85] Passio Cirici et Julittae; Passio Georgii; scripta quae appellantur Salomonis Contradictio; Philacteria omnia, quae non ab angelo, ut illi confingunt, sed magis a daemone conscripta sunt. Haec et hiis similia, quae Simon Magus, Cherinthus, Martion, Basilides, Ebion, Paulus Samosatenus, Fotinus et Bonosus[86] qui simili errore defecerunt, Montanus quoque cum suis sequacibus, Apollinaris, Valentinus, Apollinaris[87] sive Manichaeus, Faustus, Sabellius, Arrius, Macedonius, Eunomius, Novatus, Sabatius, Calixtus, Donatus, Eustachius, Novianus,[88] Pelagius, Julianus, Caelestinus, Maximianus, Priscillianus, Persilianus[89] ab Hispania, Lampadius, Dioscorus, Euticius, Petrus et alius Petrus, e quibus unus Alexandriam, alius Antiochiam maculavit, Jovinianus, Nestorius, [90] Achatius Constantinopolitanus cum suis consortibus, nec non et omnes haereses quas ipsi eorumque discipuli docuerunt vel conscripserunt, quorum nomina minime retinemus, non solum repudiata verum etiam ab omni catholica et Romana ecclesia eliminata atque cum suis auctoribus auctorumque sequacibus sub anathematis vinculo in aeternum confitemur esse dampnata.[91] Haec Gelasius papa in Decretis suis et Gracianus Di. 15 *Sancta Romana* et Di. 37 c. *Legimus* et Hugo in Didascalicon. Sed notandum quod quidam libri reputantur[92] apocrifi quia veritati adversantur, ut sunt libri haereticorum; quidam vero apocrifi quia eorum auctores ignorantur, licet veritatem puram contineant, ut est Evangelium Nazareorum; quidam etiam quia de veritate dubitatur, ut est liber De ortu et infantia S. Mariae et liber De infantia Salvatoris librique De Assumptione S. Mariae, quorum primum Jeronimus ad petitionem Heliodori episcopi scripsit, prout ipsam narra-

---

84. 'Liber qui appellatur Laus Apostolorum' is another version of the name 'Liber Lusan' just mentioned.
85. 'opuscula Lactantii – Tyconii'. This block of five works is out of place.
86. Bonosus] Donosius *Add. 3470, queried by Tanner.*
87. Valentinus, Apollinaris sive: Valentinus sive, *Decretum Gelasianum.*
88. Novianus: Iovinianus, *Decretum Gelasianum*
89. Persilianus: queried by Tanner.
90. Jovinianus is the same as Novianus; see note 88. Nestorius should precede Lampadius.
91. See note 78.
92. 'reputantur apocrifi – electurus': Vincent I 9.

tionem de Joachim et Anna et de ortu B. Mariae Virginis se quondam adhuc adolescentulum in quodam libello legisse meminit. Haec ipsa tamen quae scribit nec vera nec falsa esse asserit, sed tantummodo, sive vera sive falsa sint, ea salva fide ac sine piaculo animi credi et legi posse ab hiis qui credunt Deum haec omnia facere potuisse. Neque aliter a quoquam Christiano libri apocriphi sive etiam phisici vel poetici legendi, nisi in mente jugiter servando quod dicit apostolus: Omnia probate, quod bonum est tenete. Unde idem Jeronimus contra Vigilantium: Operis, inquit, ac studii mei est multos libros legere, ut ex plurimis diversos carpam flores, non tam omnia probaturus quam quae bona sunt electurus.[93] Illa autem apocripha[94] quae non sunt contra fidem catholicam, quorum scilicet et author penitus ignoratur et de veritate dubitatur, si quando legantur a quoquam vel enarrentur, utrum credi vel non credi debeant, ipsius legentis vel audientis judicio vel voluntati relinquitur, sicut cum juniores aliqui vel narrationes ignotae ab illis plerumque qui viderint vel audierint, ut assolet, referuntur. Apostoli namque de libris gentilium et apocrifis nonnulla in epistolis suis sibi testimonia usurparunt.[95] Judas enim apostolus in canonica sua de malis hominibus loquens ita scribit: Prophetavit autem de hiis unus ab Adam Enoch etc. Qui tamen liber Enoch inter apocripha computatur.[96] In libris quoque Moysy et in prophetarum voluminibus quaedam de libris gentilium assumpta sunt. Necque haec dico quia [p. 10] velim apocriphis, quod absit, auctoritatem dare, sed quod licet ea legere et etiam credere quae non sunt contra catholicam fidem, licet non habeant veritatis certitudinem.[97] Haec Vincentius in Speculo Historiali lib. 1° cap. 9°. Similiter quoad[98] sanctos non canonizatos dicit Hostiensis in Lectura sua super c.[99] *Audivimus* Extra. de religione et veneratione sanctorum, quod licitum esse[t] cuilibet in secreto preces porrigere alicui defuncto quam sanctum credit, ut pro ipso ad Deum intercedat, non tamen licet pro tali officium solemne facere vel preces solemnes publice emittere, donec canonizatus fuerit. Et idem dicit Innocentius. Et hoc de novo statutum est in Concilio Turonensi celebrato per dominum papam Alexandrum III AD 1163°. Ante vero solebant metropolitani et diocesani cum populo sanctos miraculis coruscantes in publico venerari et in scriniis honorifice collocare. Libros etiam gentiles et

---

93. See note 92.
94. 'Illa autem apocripha – usurparent': source unidentified.
95. See note 94.
96. 'Judas enim – computatur': Vincent I 9.
97. 'Neque haec – certitudinem': ibid.
98. 'Similiter quoad – *Hinc etiam*': source unidentified. The last half of this section, 'Beatus tamen Benedictus – debeatis', reappears in the *Catalogus* entry for John Cassian, *285*. Virtually the same portion also appears in Kirkestede's hand in Cambridge, Pembroke College, MS 92, fol. ii^(r–v).
99. c.: Tanner, uncertain of this reading, has added 'caput' as a variant.

apocriphos ante Decretum Gelasii papae indifferenter legere licuit et habere. Hinc cavendum est cuilibet lectori, cum reppererit aliquem sanctum nominatum post tempora papae Alexandri III, ne publice talem ut sanctum honoretur, quousque fuerit ab ecclesia Romana canonizatus. Et quamvis opuscula Cassiani superius inter apocripha computentur juxta Decretum papae Gelasii I, beatus tamen Benedictus postea statuit quaedam illius opuscula in capitulo monachorum legenda, videlicet Instituta patrum et Collationes eorum, ut habetur in Regula sua cap. 42° et cap. 73°; quae quidam Regula a B. Gregorio papa et ab universali ecclesia est approbata, ut habetur in 2do Dialogorum et 18 q. 2 c. *Perniciosam*. Et scienduum quod B. Benedictus nichil in Regulam suam praecepit sacris canonibus obvians vel repugnans; probatur enim in canone monachorum esse licita quae in regula conceduntur vel etiam inducuntur, sicut patet 16 q. 1 *Superiori auctoritate* et Extra. *Ne clerici vel monachi*, c. i. Decretum etiam Gelasii non obviat supradictis; licet enim opuscula Cassiani, de quibus loquitur Decretum,[100] publice in ecclesia legi non debeant, in capitulo tamen monachorum secundum Regulam S. Benedicti sine periculo legi possunt, unde Cassiodorus in libro De institutione divinarum literarum sic ait ad monachos suos: Cassianus de libero arbitrio suo a B. Prospero jure culpatus est; ejus tamen opuscula sedule legite et libenter audite, si in rebus talibus excedentem monemus, ut sub cautela legere debeatis.[101] Item quidam doctor modernus scribit quod firmissime tenendum est B. Benedictum nihil contra sacros canones in sua regula statuisse, sicut in canone satis patet 16 q. 1 *Hinc etiam*.[102]

Nomina locorum in quibus infra scripti libri reperientur, ut patet per numerum algorismi:

Registrum, pp. 2–6; Twyne extracts, p. 406; Ware extracts, fols. 132v–133r.

1. Cantuariae Trinitatis	10. London. Trinitatis	18. Novus Locus
2. Cantuariae Augustini	11. Westmonasterium	19. London. S. Pauli
3. Cantuariae Gregorii	12. S. Maria ultra pontem	19. Waverleye
4. Faveresham		20. Lewes
5. Ledes	13. Waltham	21.
6. Boxleye	14. Stratfordia	22. Cicestria
7. Rofa	15. S. Albanus	23. Suthwych
8. Batalie	16. Prioratus Roberti	24. Tichefeld
9. Merthone	17. Bokenham	25. Quareria

---

100. Gregory IX, *Decretales*, III.45.1, De reliquiis et veneratione sanctorum.
101. See note 98.
102. See note 98.

26. Bellus Locus
27. Rumesia
28. Modesfonte
29. Christi Ecclesia
30. S. Swithini
31. S. Barnabae

p. 11]

32. S. Mariae Winton.
33. S. Dionisii
34. Werewell
35. Saresbiria
36. Herles
37. Oseneya
38. S. Frideswita
39. Eynesham
40. Abendonia
41. Thame
42. Radingia
43. Woburne
44. Dunstable
45. Wardona
46. S. Neotus
47. Bittlesdene
48. Northampton S. Andreae
49. Northampton S. Jacobi
50. Pipewelle
51. Leycestria
52. Gerondona
53. Lentona
54. Chelefordia
55. Thurgertone
56. Novus Locus
57. Rucheforde
58. Crokestone
59. Ladale
60. Blanchewell
61. Burch
62. Thorneye
63. Croylande
64. Bernewell
65. Ramesia
66.

67. Ely
68. Walden
69. Huntyngdon
70. Westacre
71. Castelacre
72. Derham
73. Norwic. S. Trinitatis
74. S. Benedictus de Holm
75. Langeley
76. Bliburgh
77. Sibbetone
78. Leystone
79. Buteleye
80. Gypewic Tirinitatis
81. Gypewic Petri
82. S. Edmundus de Bury
83. Colcestriae S. Johannis
84. Colcestriae Botulphi
85. S. Ositha
86. Coggeshale
87. Tilteya
88. Dummowe
89. Bomeneye
90. Lancenetone
91. Plomtone
92. Duncawile
93. Buckfestar
94. Forda
95. Exonia
96. Tantonia
97 Alingeleya
98. Glastonia
99. Totonia
100.
101. Tore
102. Bristollia S. Augustini
103. Malmesbira
104. Cirencestria
105. Clammorgan
106. Dore

107. Wigemore
108. Glovernia S. Petri
109. Lantonia
110. Teukesbiria
111. Evesham
112. Wigornia Wlstani
113. Persover
114. Bordesle
115. Wenelach
116. Salopia
117. Lilleshulle
118. Cestriae abbatia
119. Basingwerch
120. Planagustel
121. Aberkunewon
122. Deulacresse
123. Crokesden
124. Mirevallis
125. Coventria
126. Cumbe
127. Stanle
128. Kelineworthe
129. Burtonia
130. Lincolnia
131. Hospitalis Lincoln.
132. Semplyngham
133. Revesby
134. Kyrkestede
135. Torkeseye
136. Luya
137. Grymesby

p. 12]

138. Toringtone
139. Eborac. S. Mariae
140. Funteygnes
141. S. Oswaldi
142. Ryvallis
143. Bridelington
144. Whiteby
145. Meltone
146. Kirkeham
147. Spaldinges
148. Thornhom
149. Karleolum

150. Holmcoltram
151. Fornayse
152. Gedesworth
153. Kelcom
154. Melros
155. Neubotle
156. De S. Andrea
157. De S. Cruce
158. Dumfermyn
159. S. Agathae
160. Jorevallis
161. Giseborne
162. Tynemutha
163. Novum Monasterium
164. Dunelmia
165. Bringeborne
166. Hemldesham vel Heclesham
167. Cern. S. Mariae
168. Fratrum Minorum Oxon.
169. Yxworth
170. Fratrum Praedic. Theffordiae
171. Fratrum . . .
172. Thefordia monachorum
173. Babewelle minorum
174. Colne
175. Berkynge
176. Flexleya
177. Welles
178. Nortone
179. Bildewas
180. Bathonia
181. Herefordia Cutlaci
182. Herefordia cathedr. ecclesia
183. Leministria
184. Wermeleya
185. Brekennow
186. Clifordia
187. Witham Cartusie veteris
188. Schireburna
189. De Monte Acuto
190. Muchelnie
191. Goltclive
192. Bradenstok
193. Stanlie
194. Farleya
195. Hentonae Cartusiae

66.] 66 omittitur illic *add. Twyne extracts, interlinear note*   100.] 100 omittitur hic *add. Twyne extracts, interlinear note*   120. Planagustel *queried by Tanner, confirmed by Twyne extracts, Ware extracts*   136. Luya *queried by Tanner, confirmed by Twyne extracts, Ware extracts*   171. Fratrum . . . *thus also Twyne extracts and Ware extracts* 173. Babewelle minorum] 173. Babewelle monachorum *Add. 3470; Tanner, uncertain of this reading, has added Twyne's reading as a variant*: minorum (MS Twine) *i.e. Twyne extracts, reading confirmed by Ware extracts*

UTILITATI et expeditioni studentium et praedicatorum quidam S. Edmundi monachus ex informatione aliorum et eorum exemplaribus pro modulo suo volens proficere, nomina actorum, doctorum et librorum eorum originalium secundum ordinem alphabeti ac partialium librorum numerum in unum colligere, principia pariter et fines, locaque quibus hujusmodi libri poterint inveniri per numerum algorismi locorum nominibus correspondentem hic scribere et intitulare curavit, ut quum alicui occurerint facilius possint ea cognoscere et securius allegare. Quando quidem tamen . . . multorum librorum principia non novit, vidit neque fines nec ubi potuerunt inveniri, ideo si alicui occurrant poterit eos in spatio vacuo ad hoc reservato intitulare. Primo enim ponuntur nomina doctorum seu auctorum et anni quibus ipsi doctores floruerunt, secundo tituli et nomina librorum.

Quando quidem tamen] numero *added above the line in Add. 3470, queried by Tanner*

For the source of this paragraph see p. xci above.

Augustinus *1. 6*

p. 13]

1 AUGUSTINUS doctor et episcopus Ypponensis in Lumbardia anno ab incarnatione Domini 385 baptizatus ab Ambrosio scripsit

Registrum 1, Vincent XIX 54 (references are followed by numbers in brackets [1, 2, etc.] that indicate the sequence of titles in the chapter), *Manipulus florum* II, Cassiodorus I. l. 4, 2. 5, *Mariale*.
This, much the longest entry in the *Catalogus*, is alphabetized by keyword. Greek X, transliterated (by Tanner?) as Ch, is alphabetized as Latin X.
Ware extracts, fol. 132r, headed 'Inter August. opera' (*206* below only).

1 De Achademicis lib. 3   *O utinam ratione . . . quam speramus*   1.15.65.85.83. 42.152.103

R1. 1, Vincent XIX 54 [6], *MF* II 40. *CPL* 253. *CCSL* 29. 3; incipit 'O utinam Romaniane'.

2 De Ada serm. 1   *Nemo qui . . . coaeternum filium*

Ps. Chrysostom; *CPL* 922. *De lapsu primi hominis*. Attributed to Augustine with the title *De Adam* in English manuscripts (e.g. CUL MS Kk. 4. 11, fol. 234r (Norwich, s. xiv)). *PL* 95. 1208. Explicit unidentified.

3 Contra adversarium legis et prophetarum lib. 2   *Librum quem . . . curabo* 84.1.105.152.9.43.35.15

84 *may be* 82 *R*

R1. 87, Vincent XIX 54 [57], *MF* II 96. *CPL* 326. *CCSL* 49. 35. [**82** Bury = San Marino, Huntington Library, MS HM 31151, fol. 70r (Bury A. 10), B13. 42b.]

4 De adulterinis conjugiis lib. 2   *Prima quaestio est . . . suasio castitatis* 84.85. 20.26.15.13.35.19

R1. 86, Vincent XIX 54 [63], *MF* II 61. *CPL* 302. *CSEL* 41. 347. See also *92* below. [**82** Bury = B13. 31b.]

5 De adventu Domini serm. 1   *Sanctam ac . . . pervenire*

CPPM 1. 146, 901. Caesarius Arelatensis, *serm.* 188. *CCSL* 104. 767–70, inc. 'Sanctam et'.

6 De agone Christiano lib. 1   *Corona . . . mereamur*   84.2.20.10.12.15.13. 35

20.10.12] xii.x.xx *R*

R1. 30, Vincent XIX 54 [22], *MF* II 83. *CPL* 296. *CSEL* 41. 101.

Augustinus   *1. 7*

7   De altercatione cum Maximo lib. 1   *Cum Augustinus* . . .

Whole entry from R1. 110 and Vincent XIX 54 [33].

8   Contra Adimantium Manichaeum lib. 1   *De eo quod scripsit* . . . *vincuntur*   20.152

Whole entry from R1. 22, Vincent XIX 54 [35], and *MF* II 27.

9   De anima et ejus origine ad Jeronimum lib. 2   *Deum nostrum* . . . *liberari*   1.89.152.154.43

Whole entry from R1. 72, Vincent XIX 54 [12, 54], and *MF* II 75.

10   De natura animae ad Renatum lib. 1   *Sinceritate* . . . *conscripsi*   84.1.71.90. 9.43.19.35.49

84 *may be* 82 *R* 1.71] 111 *R*

R1. 85 and 139, *MF* II 62. *CPL* 345. *CSEL* 60. 303. [**82** Bury = Cambridge, King's College, MS 3 pt 2, fols. 1r–9v (Bury —), B13. 29c.] Location number **9** is taken from R1. 139, and the others with the exception of **84** from R1. 85.

11   De natura animae ad Petrum lib. 1   *Domino dilectissimo* . . . *fecerit*   84.42. 161.95.103.15.1.139

84 *may be* 82 *R*

R1. 140, *MF* II 63. *CPL* 345. Book II. *CSEL* 60. 336. [**82** Bury = Cambridge, King's College, MS 3 pt 2, fol. 9v (Bury —), B13. 29c.]

12   De animae quantitate lib. 1   *Quum in Deo* . . . *observabo*   81.84.13.15.35.9. 108.90.156

R1. 8, Vincent XIX 54 [77], *MF* II 60. *CPL* 257. *PL* 32. 1035. [**82** Bury = Cambridge, King's College, MS 3 pt 3, fol. 1r (Bury —), incipit 'Quoniam video', explicit (fol. 18r) 'reservabo'; B13. 29d.]

13   De immortalitate animae lib. 1   *Si alicubi* . . . *probatur*   1.84.13.15.35.9. 90. 43.42.81

84 *may be* 82 *R*

R1. 5, Vincent XIX 54 [2], *MF* II 20. *CPL* 256. *CSEL* 89. 99. [**82** Bury =

B13. 50b = BL MS Harley 3027, fol. 21r, explicit (fol. 27v) does not correspond.]

14 De 2 animabus contra Manichaeos lib. 1   *Opitulante . . . longitudo* 84.1.94.95.35.13.15.19.9.103

> 84 *may be* 82 *R*

> R1. 15, Vincent XIX 54 [70], *MF* II 39. *CPL* 317. *CSEL* 25. 51. [**82** Bury = B13. 81f.]

15 De natura et origine animae ad Vincentium lib. 2   *Quod mihi . . . plausibus*   84.42.16.1.95.103.151.135

> 84 *may be* 82 *R* 16.1] 161 *R* 151] 15.1 *R* 135] 139 *R*

> R1. 141, *MF* II 31. *CPL* 345. Book III. *CSEL* 60. 359. [**82** Bury = Cambridge, King's College, MS 3 pt 2, fols. 16v–32v (Bury —), B13. 29c.]

16 De pugna animae lib. 1   *Quotquot spiritu . . .*   153.154

> R1. 238 (whole entry).

17 Annotationum in Job lib. 1   *Et opera magna . . .*   8.116.152

> Whole entry from R1. 40 (numbers have been lost), Vincent XIX 54 [110], and *MF* II 117. Same as *255* below.

18 De libero arbitrio lib. 3   *Dic mihi quaeso . . . compellit*   1.161.156.105.82. 43.152

> R1. 9, Vincent XIX 54 [69], *MF* II 5. *CPL* 260. *CCSL* 29. 211. See also *276* below. **82** Bury = BL MS Royal 7 B. ix, fol. 46v (Bury D. 6).

19 De libero arbitrio tract. 1   *Necessaria valde res . . . sed Christo*   61

> *Ps.* Augustine, *De pace et concordia. PL* 158. 1015, incipit 'Necessaria valde est' explicit unidentified. **61** Peterborough = BP21. 283f, 'Tractatus sic incipiens *Necessarium valde est*', unattributed.

20 De gratia et libero arbitrio lib. 1   *Propter eos . . . quam doceri*   1.163.161.82. 16.63.12.15

> 12] xii *R*

Augustinus *1. 20*

21. R1. 95, Vincent XIX 54 [99], *MF* II 70. *CPL* 352. *PL* 44. 881. Explicit is that of the *De octo quaestionibus Dulcitii* (*402* below), *PL* 40. 147–70. Same as *192* below. **82** Bury = B13. 50h = BL MS Harley 3027, fol. 123r; explicit (fol. 140r) does not correspond.

21 De actione triplici poenitentiae

poenitentiae] penitus *Add. 3470; Tanner, uncertain of the reading, has added the correction as a variant*

R1. 77 (whole entry).

22 Contra Arrianorum sermones lib. 1   *Eorum praecedenti . . . conclusimus*
    1.166.161.82.8.80.9.35

R1. 81, Vincent XIX 54 [55], *MF* II 93. *CPL* 702. *PL* 42. 683. Same as *385* below. **82** Bury = San Marino, Huntington Library, MS HM 31151, fol. 55v (Bury A. 10), explicit (fol. 70r) 'concludimus'; B13. 42d.

23 Super Apocalypsin omeliae vel sermones 18   *In lectione revelationis . . . in Deo*   1.94.160

R1. 174. Caesarius Arelatensis; *CPL* 1016. *PL* 35. 2417, explicit 29 lines from the end of the text. Location number **160** was taken from R1. 151, 'Omelie eius'.

24 De assumptione S. Mariae tract. 1   Prologus: *Ad interrogata . . . ignosce tu et tui*   161.82.133

tu et tui] tamen tu *Add. 3470, queried by Tanner*

R1. 176. *CPPM* 2. 161. *PL* 40. 1141. Probably the same as *25* below, and see also Anselm *3.33* and Ansbertus *21.1* below. **82** Bury = Cambridge, Pembroke College, MS 1, fols. 25v–27r (Bury A. 92) without the prologue, attributed to Augustine in the margin and in the flyleaf table of contents.

25 Item de assumptione S. Mariae serm. 1

Mariale fol. 190v (whole entry). Probably the same as *24* above, and see also Anselm *3.33* and Ansbertus *21.1*.

26 De temptatione Abrahae   95.158.156.149

R1. 178 (whole entry save three suspect location numbers).

27 Ad Auxilium   8.95.163.155

R1. 198 and 1.147 (whole entry). Location number **163** is taken from R1. 147, 'Epistole eius' and **155** is copied in error from the next title in the *Registrum*, R1. 199.

Augustinus *1. 36*

28 De altercatione cum Pascentio lib.   *Laurentius judex* . . .   105.35.167

   R1. 112 (whole entry save the suspect **167**).

29 De 12 abusivis saeculi lib. 1   *Primo si sum operibus* . . . *in futuro*   84.81.43.9. 19.35.13.15

   R1. 203, *MF* II 54. *Ps*. Augustine; *CPL* 1106. *CSEL* 3/3. 152. Cf. James extracts, p. 197. Same as Ciprianus *112.1*. [**82** Bury = B13. 50f = BL MS Harley 3027, fols. 99v–105v, incipit 'Primo si sine operibus'.]

30 Ad Arnitarium et Paulinam de voto ep. 1   *Vir egregius* . . . *filii*   84.1.15.23

   23] xxiii *R*

   R1. 282. *Ad Armentarium et Paulinam de voto reddendo*; *CPL* 262 *ep*. 127. *CSEL* 44. 19. Same as *489* below.

31 Ad Asellicum episcopum ep. 1   *Literas sanctitatis* . . . *ventilamus*   84

   CPL 262 *ep*. 196. *CSEL* 57. 216.

32 Ad Apringium episcopum ep. 1   *Non dubito* . . . *praestantissime*   84

   CPL 262 *ep*. 134. *CSEL* 44. 84.

33 De adventu Domini secundo serm. 1   *Vos inquam* . . . *quaerere debetis*   84

   Vincent XIX 54 [79]. Quodvultdeus; *CPL* 404. This is an extract comprising cc. 11–16 and the beginning of c. 17 of the *De symbolo contra Iudaeos* (*444* and *447* below). Printed as a separate work, with this title, in *PL* 95. 1470.

34 De baptismo contra Donasticos lib. 7   *In libris* . . . *in Petrum*   84.94.9.43.35

   R1. 45, Vincent XIX 54 [39], *MF* II 24. *CPL* 332. *CSEL* 51. 145. [**82** Bury = Harvard, Houghton Library, MS Richardson 26, fol. 23r (Bury A. 6), B13. 67a.]

35 De baptismo parvulorum lib. 2   *Quamvis* . . . *tandem alii*   97.46.20.1.15

   R1. 60, Vincent XIX 54 [40], *MF* II 32. *CPL* 342. *CSEL* 60. 3. Explicit 'tandem aliquando finitus'. Same as *414* below. [**82** Bury = Harvard, Houghton Library, MS Richardson 26, fol. 83r (Bury A. 6).]

36 De unico baptismo lib. 1   *Respondere* . . . *sacramentum*   84.85.97.20

   R1. 61, Vincent XIX 54 [41], *MF* II 11. *CPL* 336. *CSEL* 53. 3. Same as *73* below. [**82** Bury = Harvard, Houghton Library, MS Richardson 26, fol. 121r (Bury A. 6).]

Augustinus *1. 37*

37 De benedictionibus Jacob et Esau   *Quid est quod . . . superaveris*

   CPL 284 *serm.* 4. CCSL 41. 20–48 (the version in Collection D; ib. 18–19).

38 De boni perfectione

   Possibly CPL 347 (= *227* and *370* below). Source unidentified.

39 De boni natura lib. 1   *Summum bonum . . . reponant*   50.46.39.139

   R1. 36, Vincent XIX 54 [46], *MF* II 7. CPL 323. CSEL 25. 855. [**82** Bury = BL MS Royal 7 B. ix, fol. 65r (Bury D. 6).]

40 Breviculus collationum cum Donatistis lib. 3   *Cum catholici . . . in futurum*   127.105.151

   R1. 66 (location numbers lost), Vincent XIX 54 [141], *MF* II 125. CPL 337. CSEL 53. 39. Explicit unidentified. The location numbers (**151** = **15.1**) probably came from the *Registrum*, which is corrupt at this point.

p. 14]

41 De tempore barbarico vel de barbarorum incursu in Africam lib. 1   *Admonet Deus . . . recipiant*   84.89.94.95

   84 may be 82 R

   R1. 173, Vincent XIX 54 [105], *MF* II 140. Quodvultdeus; CPL 411. CCSL 60. 423. Same as *457* below. [**82** Bury = B13. 43g.]

42 De blasphemia in Spiritum Sanctum lib. 1   *Magna quaestio est . . .*   8.89.90.1.139

   R1. 210. CPL 284 *serm.* 71. Ed. P. Verbraken, *RB* 75 (1965) 65.

43 Super Beati immaculati   43.85.166

   R1. 224.

44 Ad Bonefacium ep. 1   *Quaeris a me . . . rationem*   83

   CPL 262 *ep.* 98. CSEL 34/2. 520 *ep.* 98.

45 Item ad eundem ep. 9   *Ornet mores . . . honorabiliter*   83

   Ps. Augustine; CPL 367. PL 33. 1095 (16 epistles). Explicit unidentified.

46 De basibus lib. 1   *Quid petis . . . adjunctis*

   De haeresibus, probably taken from a manuscript. Same as *114, 200,* and *204* below.

Augustinus   *1. 55*

47 De catezizandis rudibus lib. 1   *Petisti a me . . . sustinere*   94.152

> Whole entry from R1. 41, Vincent XIX 54 [49], and *MF* II 59.

48 De cantico Exodi serm. 1   *Sensum vestrum . . . in mare*

> *CPL* 284. *PL* 39. 1634 *serm.* 363.

49 De cantico novo   *Omnes qui baptismum . . . omnibus vestris*   83.90.95.32.80

> 83 *may be* 82 *R*
>
> R1. 175, *MF* II 137. Quodvultdeus; *CPL* 405. *CSEL* 60. 381. [**82** Bury = B13. 43c.]

50 De catechumenis lib. 1   *Quum in proximo . . . saltem vestris*

> *MF* II 139. Quodvultdeus; *CPL* 407, incipit 'Quoniam'. *De cataclysmo, sermo ad catechumenos. PL* 40. 693.

51 De civitate Dei lib. 22   *Gloriosissimam . . . nullus*   83.1.164.126

> 126] 125 *or* 128 *R*
>
> R1. 70, Vincent XIX 54 [96], *MF* II 1. *CPL* 313. *CCSL* 47–48. [**82** Bury = B13. 182.]

52 De laude caritatis serm. 1   *Divinarum scripturarum . . . sit gravis*   83.103.9.15.97

> 83 *may be* 82 *R*
>
> R1. 166. *CPL* 284 *serm.* 350. *PL* 39. 1533–5.

53 De caritate Dei vel Christi lib. 1   *Solo corde . . . remanent*   1.16.2.154.25

> 16.2] 162 *R* 25] xxv *R*
>
> R1. 143. *CPL* 279. *PL* 35. 1977, incipit 'Solo corde' at col. 1979; explicit is probably that of tract II (col. 1997), 'manet in aeternum'.

54 De quatuor virtutibus caritatis serm. 1   *Desiderium . . . folia laudis*   95.105.89.153

> 105] 15 *R*
>
> Whole entry from R1. 206 and *MF* II 136.

55 Commonitorium ad fortitudinem lib. 1   *Cum Manichei . . . desiderant*

> Whole entry from Vincent XIX 54 [95] and *MF* II 66, explicit 'deserant'. Same as *309* below.

Augustinus   *1. 56*

56   De confessionibus lib. 13   *Magnus es Domine . . . aperietur*   83.1.92.93.95. 43

   R1. 33, Vincent XIX 54 [7], *MF* II 4. *CPL* 251. *CCSL* 27. [**82** Bury = B13. 43a.]

57   De concupiscentia carnis versus spiritum serm. 1.

   Vincent XIX 54 [43] (whole entry).

58   De continentia lib. 1   *De virtute . . . agitur ut qui gloriatur*   163.166.95.158. 156.20

   R1. 149, Vincent XIX 54 [76]. *CPL* 298. *CSEL* 41. 141.

59   De conjugio bono lib. 1   *Quum unusquisque . . . fuerunt*   82.1.95.42.43.9. 19.13

   R1. 49, Vincent XIX 54 [62], *MF* II 79. *CPL* 299, incipit 'Quoniam'. *CSEL* 41. 187. **82** Bury = B13. 22b. / **42** Reading = B71. 123d, perhaps equivalent of Bodl. MS Laud Misc. 578, fol. 99r.

60   De clericorum singularitate lib. 1   *Promiseram . . . evenire*   166.161.156. 105. 43.152

   R1. 130. *Ps.* Cyprian; *CPL* 62. *CSEL* 3/3. 173. Explicit unidentified. Same as Jeronimus *281.214* and Origines *404.23*.

61   De confutatione quorundam capitulorum lib. 1   *Quum Christiano . . . vindemiantem*   161.152.8.9.43.120.63

   120] 1.20 *R* 120] *Tanner 165*

   R1. 122, incipit 'Quidam Christiane'. Prosper of Aquitaine; *CPL* 521. *PL* 45. 1843.

62   De consuetudinibus ecclesiae lib. 2   *Dilectissimo filio . . . lectura*

   Vincent XIX 54 [27]. *CPL 262 epp. 54–5. Ad inquisitiones Januarii. CSEL* 34/2. 158–213. Same as *69* and *242* below.

63   De 10 cordis psalterii serm. 1   *Dominus et Deus noster . . . inveniemus*   164.95. 89.90.124.32.9

   R1. 160, Vincent XIX 54 [66], *MF* II 36. *CPL* 284 *serm.* 9. *CCSL* 41. 105. Location number **89** is taken from R1. 151, 'Omelie eius'.

Augustinus *1. 71*

64 De correptione et gratia lib. 1   *Lectis literis . . . peccatorum*   82.42.43.1. 165.166.161

> R1. 96, Vincent XIX 54 [100]. *CPL* 353. *CSEL* 92. 219. **82** Bury = B13. 81c.

65 De correctione Donatistarum lib. 1   *Laudo et . . . commendat*   83.152

> R1. 75 (title), Vincent XIX 54 [85], *MF* II 35 (incipit and explicit). *CPL* 262 *ep.* 185. *CSEL* 57. 1.

66 De credendi utilitate lib. 1   *Si mihi honor . . . promtior*   84.1.161.43.13. 9.32.103

> 84 *may be* 82 *R*

> R1. 14, Vincent XIX 54 [23], *MF* II 57. *CPL* 316. *CSEL* 25. 3. Incipit 'Si mihi Honorate'.

67 De cura pro mortuis gerenda lib. 1   *Sanctitati . . . defuisset*   84.1.161. 42.153. 154.8

> 153] *illeg. in Add. 3470; perhaps* 159

> R1. 93, Vincent XIX 54 [26], *MF* II 45. *CPL* 307. *CSEL* 41. 621. [**82** Bury = B13. 31e.]

68 Super Cantica Canticorum lib. 1

> R1. 132 (whole entry).

69 De coena Domini ad Januarium   *Dilectissimo . . .*   163.166.158.156.152

> R1. 150 (title and location numbers). Source of the incipit may have been a manuscript. Same as *62* above and *242* below.

70 Ad clericos ep. 1   161.1.165.16

> R1. 165 (probably whole entry). Kirkestede presumably took location numbers **1** to **16** from the *Registrum*, which is corrupt here; see the note to R1. 165.

71 Ad Celestinum papam   95.159.153.148

> R1. 197 (whole entry save three suspect location numbers).

29

Augustinus   *1. 72*

72   De compunctione cordis   <u>89</u>.102.120

   89] 83 *R*

   R1. 209 (whole entry save two suspect location numbers).

73   Ad Constantium   <u>152</u>.<u>97</u>.<u>27</u>

   27] 20 *R*

   R1. 236, 61 (whole entry). Location number **152** comes from R1. 236, **97** and **27** (**20**) from R1. 61 Same as *36* above.

74   Cathegorias   <u>84</u>.<u>42</u>.<u>1</u>.<u>20</u>.9.<u>39</u>

   84] 82 *R*

   R1. 220 (whole entry save suspect **9**). Same as *383* below.

75   De corpore Christi revelatio   *Sicut autem vos . . . curiosus*   <u>154</u>.<u>139</u>

   Whole entry from R1. 244 (title and location numbers) and *MF* II 23 (incipit 'Sicut ante nos' and explicit).

76   De Crucis misterio   <u>35</u>.<u>95</u>.96.117.<u>8</u>

   R1. 248, 269 (whole entry save two suspect location numbers). Location numbers **35** and **95** are taken from R1. 248, **8** from R1. 269.

77   De vera credulitate   <u>103</u>

   R1. 260 (whole entry).

78   Ut res commodatae reddantur   <u>9</u>

   R1. 276 (whole entry).

79   De laude et utilitate spirtualium canticorum   *Oculum fidei* . . .   <u>15</u>

   Whole entry from R1. 283 (incipit 'Oculis fidei' and location number, same as *490* below) and R1. 285 (title and location number). These are two separate works in the *Registrum* and it is not apparent why Kirkestede joined them.

80   De conceptu virginali et originali peccato   *Cum omnibus* . . .

   R1. 293 (whole entry, incipit 'Cum in omnibus'). Same as Anselmus *3.1*.

Augustinus *1. 89*

81 Ad Cresconium grammaticum lib. 4   *Quum ad te . . . dampnatos*   <u>152</u>

   Whole entry from R1. 53 (title, incipit, location number), Vincent XIX 54 [74], and *MF* II 92 (title, incipit, explicit). Incipit 'Quando ad te'.

82 De correctione et moribus Donatistarum ad Vincentium ep. 1   *Accepi . . . curaverunt*   82

   MF II 34. *CPL* 262 *ep.* 93. *CSEL* 34/2. 445. Same as *484* below. **82** Bury = B13. 32, 'Epistole Augustini'.

83 De concordia evangeliorum sive de consensu evangelistarum lib. 4   *Inter omnes . . . lavat*   <u>82</u>.<u>89</u>.<u>161</u>.<u>118</u>.<u>126</u>.1

   R1. 43, Vincent XIX 54 [115], *MF* II 89. *CPL* 273. *CSEL* 43. **82** Bury = Bodl. MS e Musaeo 33, p. 1 (Bury A. 25), B13. 13a.

84 De contemplatione Domini nostri Jesu Christi   *Quum in medio . . . Deum meum*

   MF II 102 (whole entry), incipit 'Quoniam in medio'.

85 De consonantia Mathaei et Lucae in omnibus generibus Christi   *Expectationem . . . cum caritate teneatis*

   CPL 284 *serm*. 51. Ed. P. Verbraken, *RB* 91 (1981) 23.

86 De cognitione verae vitae ad fratres heremitas   *Sapientia Dei . . .*

   R1. 108, neither title nor incipit match exactly. Same as *487* below.

p. 15]

87 De vera caritate   *Karissimi fratres . . . mereamur*

   Unidentified.

88 De civibus   <u>166</u>.60

   R1. 302 (whole entry save the suspect **60**).

89 Contra quod attulit centurius ad Donatum lib. 1   *Dicis de eo . . .*   149. 150.152.158

   centurius] centur *Add. 3470, queried by Tanner*

Augustinus *1. 89*

The title and incipit come from R1. 46, Vincent XIX 54 [135], and *MF* II 118. Not extant (*Retractationes* II 19). The location numbers represent a thorough muddle: **149** Carlisle and **150** Holme Cultram, both in Cumberland, are not genuinely reported by either the *Registrum* or the *Catalogus*; **152** Jedburgh and **158** Dunfermline, along the Scottish border, are far outside the range of Kirkestede's acquaintance; and of course since this work did not survive from the patristic era into the middle ages, there should be no location numbers at all.

90 De cataclysmo serm. 2   *Vos fratres* . . .   83.<u>89</u>.<u>95</u>.<u>94</u>.<u>90</u>

83 *may be* 82 *R*

R1. 172, *MF* II 139. The incipit, not in *Registrum* or *Manipulus florum*, may be that of an unedited sermon of Geoffrey Babion which is attributed to Augustine in BNF MS lat. 3833, fol. 64r; see J. P. Bonnes in *RB* 56 (1945), 203 no. 58. [**82** Bury = B13. 43f.]

91 Contra cartulam Valerio comiti missam   15.<u>43</u>.85.129

R1. 208.

92 De adulterinis conjugiis ad Pollentium   *Sanctis fratribus* . . .

R1. 86. The title is the same as *4* above. Incipit is perhaps that of *De perfectione justitiae hominis*, *370* below. Source of this combination is unknown.

93 Ad Consentium ep. 1   *Quantum ad oculos* . . . *veniam*   83

CPL 262 *ep*. 205. *CSEL* 57. 323.

94 De non cogitando de crastino serm. 1   *Cultores Dei* . . .

Ps. Augustine; not in *CPPM*. Attributed to Augustine in BNF MS lat. 2152, fols. 123v–125r.

95 De consolatione mortuorum serm. 2   *Praebete silentium* . . . *ita factum est*

CPPM 1. 1111–12. *PL* 40. 1159.

96 De contemptu mundi serm. 1   *Audite fratres* . . . *salutetis*

CPPM 1. 1121, 1186. *PL* 40. 1215, the explicit ('salutis') occurs 16 lines from the end of the text.

Augustinus *1. 104*

97 Cur quando et quomodo Deus homo lib. 1   *Cur quando et quomodo ... omnes invitat*

    Unidentified.

98 Ad quendam comitem de salutaribus documentis   *O mi fratres ... regnare concedis*   83

    Paulinus Aquileiensis; see E. Portalié in *DTC* 1. 2309. *PL* 40. 1047. Incipit 'O mi frater'; explicit does not correspond. Same as *136* below. [**82** Bury = BL MS Harley 3027, fols. 170r–192r, explicit 'regnare concedis'.]

99 De vita et moribus clericorum   *Propter quod nolumus ... nobis*

    CPL 284 *serm.* 355. Ed. C. Lambot, *Stromata patristica et mediaevalia* 1 (Utrecht 1950) 123. Same as *377* below.

100 Item de vita et moribus clericorum   *Caritati vestrae ... ibi regnemus*

    CPL 284 *serm.* 356. Ed. C. Lambot, *Stromata patristica et mediaevalia* 1 (Utrecht 1950) 132. Same as *378* below.

101 De doctrina et disciplina Christianorum serm. 1   *Locutus est ... ad Dominum*   <u>163</u>.<u>161</u>.<u>94</u>.<u>95</u>.<u>158</u>

    Whole entry probably from R1. 153 (title and location numbers), Vincent XIX 54 [103], and *MF* II 29 (title, incipit, and explicit 'ad Deum'), in all of which the title reads 'De disciplina Christianorum'. *CPL* 310. *CCSL* 46. 207. Same as *503* below.

102 Ad Deogratias presbyterum de V quaestionibus contra paganos   *Monet quosdam ... tollerandum*   83.<u>94</u>.<u>105</u>.<u>152</u>.8

    83 *may be* 82 *R*

    R1. 58, Vincent XIX 54 [84]. *CPL* 262 *ep.* 102. *CSEL* 34/2. 545. Incipit 'Mouet quosdam' is that of *quaestio* 1. Same as *401* below.

103 De disciplinis liberalibus   <u>19</u>

    Whole entry from R1. 6 and Vincent XIX 54 [6]. Not extant (*Retractationes* I 6).

104 De divinatione daemonum lib. 1   *Quodam die ... respondebimus*   <u>1</u>.<u>9</u>.<u>152</u>

    Whole entry from R1. 57 (title, incipit, location numbers), Vincent XIX 54 [17], and *MF* II 76 (incipit, explicit).

Augustinus *1. 105*

105 De doctrina Christiana lib. 4   Prologus: *Sunt praecepta* . . .   Liber: *Duae sunt . . . adjuvante Deo*   82.42.43.19

> R1. 31, Vincent XIX 54 [51], *MF* II 12. *CPL* 263. *CCSL* 32. 1. Same as *506* below. See also *176* below. **82** Bury = B13. 185, and Cambridge, Pembroke College, MS 1, fols. 92r and 92v (Bury A. 92); explicit does not correspond (fol. 112v). **42** Reading = Chicago, Newberry Library, MS 12. 1, fol. 34v = B71. 53b.

106 Ut Deus non tantum in lingua sed opere laudetur lib. 1   *Resurrectio . . . comparemus* 82.15

> R1. 281. Caesarius Arelatensis; *CPL* 368 spurious *serm.* 252. *CCSL* 104. 824 (*serm.* 206).

107 De definitionibus fidei rectae et de dogmate ecclesiastico lib. 1   *Credimus . . . inveniri*   83.8.9.15.105.115

> 15] xv *R* 105] 165 *R*

> R1. 127, *MF* II 15. Gennadius; *CPL* 958. *De ecclesiasticis dogmatibus*. Same as Gennadius *210.4*. See also *174* below. [**82** Bury = Cambridge, Pembroke College, MS 20, fol. 43r (Bury J. 57), attributed to Augustine in Kirkestede's table of contents; Cambridge, Pembroke College, MS 34, fol. 256v (Bury T. 7), with Kirkestede's marginal note of the incipit and explicit.]

108 Contra Donatistas post collationem lib. 1   *Silvanus senex . . . o homo*   161.108

> R1. 67 (title, location numbers), Vincent XIX 54 [53], *MF* II 126 (title and incipit from the *Retractationes* passage prefixed to this work). *CPL* 338. *CSEL* 53. 97, and concerning the incipit see ib. 163. Explicit, and source of the explicit, unidentified.

109 Contra Donatistam quendam lib. 1   *Probationes* . . .

> Whole entry from R1. 55, Vincent XIX 54 [137], and *MF* II 120. Not extant (*Retractationes* II 28).

110 Disputatio contra Julianum   *Extorsisti* . . .

> Source unidentified (cf. R1. 91, 114). The incipit is that of the *De unitate contra Felicianum, 165* below.

111 De casu diaboli lib. 1   *Quid habes* . . .   162

> 162] 161 *R*

> R1. 144 (whole entry). Same as Anselmus *3.7*.

Augustinus *I. 122*

112 Ad Quod vult Deus diaconem   *Acceptis* . . .   90.95.80.15

    R1. 193 (whole entry).

113 Ad eundem   *Cum in hoc* . . .

    R1. 194 (whole entry); incipit 'Cum mihi haec'.

114 Ad eundem   *Quod petis* . . .

    R1. 195 (whole entry). Same as *46* above and *200, 204* below.

115 De dedicatione ecclesiae   1.90.92

    R1. 289 (whole entry save two suspect location numbers).

116 Dialogus ejus et Jeronimi de ratione animae lib. 2 . . . *fluenta sanctorum* 82.157.166.126.154

    R1. 200 (location numbers **157–154**). *CPL* 633 *ep*. 37. *PL* 30. 261, explicit (col. 271) 'fluentis sanctorum'. Same as Jeronimus *281.85–86*. **82** Bury = B13. 32, 'Epistole Augustini'.

117 Ad Deodatum discipulum   153.165.145

    R1. 229 (whole entry save two suspect location numbers).

118 Disputatio cum Deodato   128

    R1. 230 (probably the whole entry, though the *Registrum* text is corrupt at this point).

119 De duobus divitibus et avaris   9.135

    R1. 278 (whole entry save the suspect **135**).

120 Ad Donatum et Donatistam ep. 1   *Quod te* . . . *conservet*   82.156.139

    CPL 262 *ep*. 112. *CSEL* 34/2. 657. **82** Bury = B13. 32, 'Epistole Augustini'.

121 Ad eundem ep. 1   *Si posses* . . . *communium*   83.97.93

    CPL 262 *ep*. 173. *CSEL* 44. 640, explicit 'convivium'.

122 De dialectica Augustini   164.95.156.152

    R1. 159 (whole entry).

Augustinus   *1. 123*

123   De detractione   *Quisquis regni* . . .   <u>163</u>

   R1. 156 (whole entry).

124   Contra epistolam Donati lib. 1   *Abs te ipso* . . .   <u>165</u>

   165] 166 *R*

   Whole entry from R1. 21, Vincent XIX 54 [129], and *MF* II 111. Not extant (*Retractationes* I 21).

125   Contra partem Donati lib. 1   *Omnes qui* . . .

   Whole entry from R1. 20, Vincent XIX 54 [128], and *MF* II 110. Same as *397* below.

126   Item contra partem Donati lib. 2   *Quum Donatistae* . . .   <u>95</u>.<u>43</u>.<u>35</u>.15

   Whole entry from R1. 32, Vincent XIX 54 [131], and *MF* II 113. Not extant (*Retractationes* II 5, incipit 'Quoniam'). Location numbers **95** (= 9 R), **43**, and **35** are taken from *34* above, 'De baptismo contra Donatistas'; source of **15** is unknown.

127   Probationes et testimonia contra Donatum lib. 1   *Qui timetis* . . .   <u>164</u>. <u>165</u>.<u>103</u>.<u>35</u>

   165] 105 *R* 35] 53 *R*

   Whole entry from R1. 54, Vincent XIX 54 [136], and *MF* II 119. Not extant (*Retractationes* II 27).

128   Admonitio Donatistarum lib. 1   *Quicunque* . . .

   Whole entry from R1. 56 and *MF* II 121. Not extant (*Retractationes* II 29).

129   Ad Dioscorum ep. 1   *Tu me . . . flagito*   84

   Vincent XIX 54 [87]. *CPL* 262 *ep.* 118. *CSEL* 34/2. 665.

130   Ad Dardanum ep. 1   *Fateor . . . veniam*   82

   CPL 262 *ep.* 187. *CSEL* 57. 81. Same as *358, 364* and *390* below. **82** Bury = B13. 32, 'Epistole Augustini'.

131   Ad Donatistas ep. 1   *Cum in auribus . . . pervenirent*   84

   CPL 262 *ep.* 141. *CSEL* 44. 235. [**82** Bury = B13. 32, 'Epistole Augustini'.]

p. 16]

132 Ad eosdem ep. 1   *Caritas . . . gaudeatis*   84

    CPL 262 *ep.* 105. CSEL 34/2. 595.

133 De die novissimo ad Desichium epistolam   *Accepi . . . delectant*   82

    CPL 262 *ep.* 199. *Ad Hesychium.* CSEL 57. 243, explicit 'delectavit'. **82** Bury = B13. 32, 'Epistole Augustini'.

134 De <substantia> dilectionis serm. 1   *Cotidianum . . . universorum*

    substantia *lacking in Add. 3470, a query by Tanner*

    Ps. Augustine, composed of excerpts from works of Hugh of St Victor; CPPM 2. 3069. PL 40. 843.

135 De bono disciplinae serm. 2   *Multi . . .*

    Valerianus Cemeliensis; CPL 1002 *hom.* 1. PL 40. 1219.

136 De documentis salutaribus   *O mi frater . . . regnare*

    Same as *98* above.

137 Epistolae Augustini 188   *Domino illustri . . . reperias*   82.83.42.43.152.<u>9</u>. 108

    R1. 147, Vincent XIX 54 [125]. CPL 262. CSEL 34/1, 34/2, 44, 57, and 58. The incipit is that of *ep.* 132, which stands first in a number of collections of Augustine letters; see, for example, BL MS Royal 5 D. VI, and the manuscripts listed in CSEL 58. xi–xvi. **82** Bury = B13. 32, 183. / **42** Reading = B71. 45a and 47, and B72. 5 (the latter the receipt for books delivered to King John in 1208 by Reading abbey).

138 Super Ezechielem

    This work and its source are unidentified.

139 Super epistolam Johannis serm. 10   *Meminit sanctitas . . . praedicanti*   83.<u>1</u>.<u>163</u>.<u>94</u>.92.<u>99</u>.<u>95</u>

    99.95 *om. R, habet Peterhouse 169*

    R1. 106, *MF* II 106. CPL 279. PL 35. 1977. Same as *216* below. [**82** Bury = B13. 184.]

Augustinus   *1. 140*

140   Super epistolam Jacobi lib. 1   *Si vel nunc . . .*

   Vincent XIX 54 [139]. The title comes from Vincent; for reasons not apparent, however, the incipit is that of the *Ad Emeritum Donatistarum episcopum post collationem, 161* below.

141   De ecclesiae facultatibus lib. 1   *Utinam inquit . . . honor et gloria*

   A sermon that survives largely in 15th-cent. manuscripts, for example, CUL MS Ii. 1. 29, fols. 239r–241v (England, s. xv), incipit 'Utrum inquis congregandis fratribus'.

142   Encheridion ad Laurentium lib. 1   *Dici non potest . . . conscripsi*   83.41.81. 89.42.43.63

   89 *may be* 8.9 *R (R1. 134)*

   R1. 92, 134, Vincent XIX 54 [11], *MF* II 16. *CPL* 295. *CCSL* 46. 49. **42** Reading = B71. 101b and 123c. / [**82** Bury = B13. 149b, 186, 202b; Cambridge, Pembroke College, MS 41, fol. 11r latest foliation (Bury A. 31), without rubric, title added by Kirkstede in upper margin; BL MS Royal 7 B. ix, fol. 29vb (Bury D. 6); Cambridge, Pembroke College, MS 1, fol. 113r (Bury A. 92).]

143   Expositio quarundam propositionum ex epistola Pauli ad Romanos lib. 1   *Sensus hii sunt . . . quorum deus venter est*

   R1. 23 (title), *MF* II 144 (incipit, explicit). *CPL* 280. *CSEL* 84. 3. Though it appears the whole entry may come from the *Registrum* and the *Manipulus florum,* Bury possessed a copy of this work: **82** Bury = B13. 50e ('Augustinus de epistolis Pauli') = BL MS Harley 3027, fol. 87v (incipit comes from the paragraph of the *Retractationes* that precedes the text, fol. 87va); explicit (fol. 99r) does not correspond.

144   Super epistolam Jacobi ad duodecim tribus lib. 1   *Duodecim tribubus . . .*

   Whole entry from R1. 59 and *MF* II 122. Not extant (*Retractationes* II 32).

145   Super epistolam ad Galathas lib. 1   *Causa propter quam . . . Jesu Christi* 82.99.156.152.90

   R1. 24, Vincent XIX 54 [120], and *MF* II 145. *CPL* 282. *CSEL* 84. 55.

146   De exidio urbis Romae serm. 1   *Intueamur . . . possitis*   103.128.151.20

   151] 15.1 *R*

   R1. 251. *CPL* 312. *CCSL* 46. 249.

Augustinus *1. 156*

147 De ebrietate   *Licet populo . . . refectiones*   97.<u>139</u>.<u>156</u>.<u>9</u>

   97 *perhaps read* 79

   R1. 154. Caesarius Arelatensis. *CPL* 368 spurious *serm.* 294. *CCSL* 103. 205, incipit 'Licet propitio' explicit 'refectionem'. Location numbers **139** to **9** are taken from R1. 155.

148 Elucidarium Augustini   <u>155</u>

   R1. 199 (whole entry).

149 Exameron Augustini serm. 7   <u>156</u>.<u>129</u>.<u>108</u>.<u>167</u>

   R1. 202 (whole entry).

150 De elemosina danda lib. 1   *Multa et magna . . . geminabit*

   MF II 133 (whole entry). Same as *211* below and Cyprianus *112.8*.

151 De epiphania Domini serm. 5   *Nuper . . .*   8.<u>15</u>.<u>1</u>

   R1. 264–268 (whole entry).

152 Exortationum lib. 1   94.<u>42</u>.<u>80</u>.<u>19</u>

   R1. 167 (whole entry).

153 Item de elemosina serm. 1   *Admonet . . . dabitur*   <u>153</u>.<u>154</u>.<u>103</u>.<u>13</u>

   R1. 237. *CPL* 285 *serm.* 389. Ed. C. Lambot, *RB* 58 (1948) 43. [**82** Bury = B13. 43d.]

154 Enucleationes de videndo Deo lib. 1   83.<u>8</u>.<u>80</u>.<u>9</u>.<u>15</u>

   83 *may be* 82 R

   R1. 218. [**82** Bury = B13. 50i–j = BL MS Harley 3027, fol. 140v has *Enucleationes* in the rubric and the running head, but the text is *De 8 questionibus Dulcitii*, *402* below]

155 Ad Ennodium episcopum ep. 1   *Quaestio . . . ne graveris*   83

   Vincent XIX 54 [89]. *CPL* 262 *ep.* 164. *CSEL* 44. 521, ad Evodium.

156 Ad Emeritum ep. 1   *Ego cum . . . dilecte*   83

   CPL 262 *ep.* 87. *CSEL* 34/2. 397.

Augustinus *I. 157*

157 Ad Eleusium et Glorium ep. 1   *Fortunium . . . videatur*   83

   CPL 262 *ep.* 44. CSEL 34/2. 109.

158 Ad Edicciam ep. 1   *Lectis . . . concordia*   83.<u>139</u>.<u>156</u>.<u>166</u>

   R1. 298. CPL 262 *ep.* 262. CSEL 57. 621.

159 Epistolae ad Romanos inchoatam expositionem lib. 1   *In epistola qua*
   . . .   83.<u>81</u>.<u>152</u>.<u>103</u>.<u>15</u>

   83 *may be* 82 *R*

   R1. 25, Vincent XIX 54 [130]. CPL 281. CSEL 84. 145.

160 Super evangelia Mathaei et Lucae expositio

   Vincent XIX 54 [114]. Same as *407* and *410* below.

161 Ad Emeritum post collationem cum Donatistis lib. 1   *Si vel nunc. . .*

   Whole entry from R1. 73 and *MF* II 128. Not extant (*Retractationes* II 46).
   See also *140* above.

162 De essentia divinitatis Dei, secundum quosdam   *Omnipotens Deus . . .
   sicut ymago*

   An extract of the *De formulis spiritualis intelligentiae* of Eucherius of Lyon; *CPL*
   488n; see E. Portalié in *DTC* 1. 2309. *PL* 42. 1199. Same as Jeronimus
   281.93.

163 Contra Faustum Manicheum lib. 23   *Faustus . . . possint*   83.<u>43</u>.<u>8</u>.<u>9</u>.<u>35</u>.
   <u>13</u>.<u>15</u>

   R1. 34 (title, location numbers), Vincent XIX 54 [10], *MF* II 68 (number
   of books, incipit, explicit 'possitis'). *CPL* 321. *CSEL* 25. 251. [**82** Bury = B13.
   37 = Bodl. MS e Musaeo 32, fol. 1r (Bury A. 24), expl. 'possitis' (fol. 362v).]

164 Expositio fidei Augustini   *Omnes quos . . .*

   Augustini] Augustinus *Add. 3470*

   De summa trinitate deoque vero sermo, apparently a series of extracts from
   Augustine's *De trinitate*. Found in Cambridge, Corpus Christi College, MS
   19, fol. 6r, Zurich Centralbibliothek, MS S.2040, fol. 117r, Vatican Library,
   MS Reg. lat. 125, fol. 7r, etc.

Augustinus   *1. 172*

165   Contra Felicianum de unitate lib. 1   *Extorsisti . . . mercedem*   83.1.95.42. 43

83 *may be* 82 *R*

R1. 98, Vincent XIX 54 [28], *MF* II 81. Vigilius Thapsensis; *CPL* 808. *PL* 42. 1157. See also *110* above. [**82** Bury = San Marino, Huntington Library, MS HM 31151, fol. 162r (Bury A. 10) = B13. 42f.]

166   De feria quarta   *Celesti . . . cum sancto*   83.95.90.32.80

83 *may be* 82 *R*

R1. 258, *MF* II 138. Quodvultdeus; *CPL* 406. *CCSL* 60. 395. [**82** Bury = B13. 43e.]

167   Contra Felicem Manichaeum lib. 1   *Honorio . . . gestis*   10.152

R1. 35, Vincent XIX 54 [132], *MF* II 114. *CPL* 322. *CSEL* 25. 801.

168   De fide vel symbolo lib. 1   *Quoniam scriptum . . . et intelligant*   83.8.90.32

83 *may be* 82 *R*

R1. 17, Vincent XIX 54 [29], *MF* II 109. *CPL* 293. *CSEL* 41. 3.

169   De fide et operibus lib. 1   *Quibusdam . . . redargui*   116.152.43.35

Whole entry from R1. 65 (title, incipit, location numbers), Vincent XIX 54 [103], *MF* II 65 (title, incipit, explicit 'redargui posset').

170   De fide ad Petrum lib. 2   *Epistolam . . . revelabit*   9.43.19.13.15

R1. 126, Vincent XIX 54 [48], *MF* II 84. Fulgentius Ruspensis; *CPL* 826. *CCSL* 91. 711; explicit is that of c. 44. See also *250* below.

171   De fide sancti Trinitatis ad Donatum lib. 1

Donatum *Add. 3470, queried by Tanner*

Source unidentified. Fulgentius Ruspensis. Attributed to Augustine in Bodl. MS Bodley 136, fol. 69r (England, s. xiii^ex). Same as Fulgentius *184.3*.

172   Contra Fortunatum Manichaeum lib. 1   *Ego iam . . . Deo gratias*   15

Whole entry from R1. 16 (location number) and *MF* II 38 (title, incipit, explicit). Same as *270* below.

Augustinus   *1. 173*

173   Contra epistolam Manichaei quod dicitur Fundamentum lib. 1   *Unum verum . . . arguatur*   83.9.43.15.20

   R1. 29, Vincent XIX 54 [69], *MF* II 26. *CPL* 320. *CSEL* 25. 193.

p. 17]

174   De fide Augustini exemplar   *Credimus . . .*

   Augustini] Augustinus Add. *3470*

   R1. 288 (whole entry). See also *107* above.

175   De fide rerum invisibilium lib. 1   *Sunt qui . . . cum coeperint*

   MF II 14 (whole entry).

176   Item de fide serm. 1   *Haec dicimus . . . faciamus*

   This work appears in Bodl. MS Bodley 204, fols. 101v–102r. According to its rubric, this is an extract from the *De doctrina christiana* (*105* above and *506* below); reference unidentified.

177   Flores Augustini   166.117.163.43.15.104

   R1. 295 (whole entry).

178   Ad Fortunatianum ep. 1   *Commonitorium . . . laetifices*   83

   CPL 262 *ep.* 148. *CSEL* 44. 332. Same as *501* below.

179   Ad Festum epistolam 1   *Si pro errore . . . misericordia Dei*   83

   CPL 262 *ep.* 89. *CSEL* 34/2. 419.

180   De eo: Fundamentum aliud   83.15

   R1. 234. Caesarius of Arelatenis; *CPPM* 1. 889. *CCSL* 104. 724–9. Same as *228, 360,* and *486* below.

181   Item de fide serm. 1   *Recordamur . . .*

   CPL 284 *serm.* 346. *PL* 39. 1522 *serm.* 346. Same as *460* and *475* below. See also *456* below.

Augustinus 1. 188

182 Extrema verba Augustini de fide   *Da nobis . . . reputare*   83.60.10

> *CPL* 328. *CCSL* 50A. 551–5. [**82** Bury = Cambridge, Pembroke College, MS 108, fol. 54v (Bury F. 12); the title matches Kirkestede's table of contents rather than the rubric on 54v.]

183 De concordia fratrum serm. 1   *Dies isti . . . reddatur*   83.82.9

> *CPL* 284 *serm.* 211. Ed. S. Poque, SChr 116 (1966) 154.

184 Super Genesin ad literam lib. 12   *Omnis divina . . . concludamus*   83.<u>1</u>.<u>166</u>.<u>161</u>.<u>152</u>.<u>103</u>

> 83 *may be* 82 *R* 166] 164 *R*
>
> R1. 51 (title, incipit, location numbers), Vincent XIX 54 [108], *MF* II 3 (title, incipit, explicit). *CPL* 266. *CSEL* 28/1. 3. [**82** Bury = B13. 26.]

185 De gaudiis electorum et de poenis dampnatorum lib. 1   *Tria . . . misericordem*   166.<u>158</u>.<u>154</u>   Iste liber ascribitur Patricio et intitulatur De tribus habitaculis.

> R1. 300. Patrick, bishop of Dublin (1074–84). Same as *206* below; for edition and discussion of this work see Patricius *434.1*.

186 De Genesi contra Manicheos lib. 2   *Primum ergo si elegerint . . . exposui*   <u>1</u>.<u>165</u>.<u>161</u>.<u>94</u>.<u>9</u>.<u>43</u>

> R1. 10 (title, location numbers), Vincent XIX 54 [107], *MF* II 42 (title, incipit, explicit). *CPL* 265. *PL* 34. 173. Same as *304* below. [**82** Bury = B13. 42c = San Marino, Huntington Library, MS HM 31151, fol. 108r (Bury A. 10).]

187 Item de Genesi ad literam lib. 1   *Imperfectum . . . ad similitudinem*

> R1. 18, Vincent XIX 54 [127], *MF* II 86. *CPL* 268. *CSEL* 28/1. 459. The word 'imperfectum' rightly belongs with the title, because it is descriptive of the work itself. Kirkestede has confused it with the incipit because of the reading in the *Manipulus florum*, where this word follows the number of books and precedes the real incipit. The explicit is presumably supplied from a manuscript.

188 De gestis Pelagii lib. 1   *Postquam . . .*   <u>161</u>

> Whole entry from R1. 74 (title, location number) and *MF* II 129 (title, incipit). Same as *379* below.

Augustinus   *1. 189*

189   Contra Gaudentium episcopum lib. 2   *Gaudentius* . . .

   Whole entry from R1. 88 and *MF* II 97.

190   Ad Glorium et Eleusinum ep. 1   *Dixit quidam* . . . *si nolitis*   83

   Vincent XIX 54 [92]. *CPL* 262 *ep.* 43. *CSEL* 34/2. 85.

191   De gratia ad Vitalem

   Vincent XIX 54 [60] (whole entry).

192   De gratia et libero arbitrio, in A.

   Vincent XIX 54 [99] (whole entry). Same as *20* above.

193   De gratia Novi Testamenti lib. 1   *Quinque mihi* . . . *testamur*   82.9.43.13. 15.115

   R1. 63 (location numbers), Vincent XIX 54 [24], *MF* II 58 (title, incipit, explicit). *CPL* 262 *ep.* 140. *CSEL* 44. 155.

194   Gesta cum Emerito episcopo Donatistarum lib. 1   *Gloriosissimo* . . . *manet in aeternum*

   R1. 80 (title, incipit), *MF* II 132 (incipit). *CPL* 340. *CSEL* 53. 181.

195   De gratia Christi contra Pelagios et Celestium et de originali peccato lib. 2   *Quantum* . . .   161.43.153.152.80

   R1. 78 (whole entry), *MF* II 131. Same as *372* below.

196   Quod nulla est gloria mundi   *Apostolica* . . . *consequuntur*   166.95.158. 105.115

   R1. 299. *CPPM* I. 1185, explicit 'consequamini'; *CPL* 368 *serm.* 58. *PL* 40. 1341.

197   De eo: Semper gaudete serm.   *Audistis* . . . *societatem*   1.28.15

   1.28] 128 *R*

   R1. 270. *CPL* 284 *serm.* 171. *PL* 38. 933.

198   De 7 diebus Geneseos serm. 7

   Cassiodorus I. 1. 4 (whole entry).

Augustinus *1. 207*

199 Contra quinque haereses lib. 1   *Debitor . . . custodit*   83.<u>43</u>.42.8.90.80

> R1. 99 (title, incipit), *MF* II 13 (title, incipit, explicit). Quodvultdeus; *CPL* 410. *PL* 42. 1101. **42** Reading = B71. 43d = Chicago, Newberry Library, MS 12. 6, fol. 63r. / [**82** Bury = B13. 22d.]

200 De haeresibus diversis lib. 1   *Quid petis . . . adjunctis*

> *MF* II 71 (whole entry), explicit 'adiuvetis'. Same as *46* and *114* above, and *204* below.

201 Item ad consulta Hillarii

> R1. 125 (whole entry).

202 Contra Hillarium lib. 1   *Qui dicunt . . .*

> R1. 38 (whole entry). Not extant (*Retractationes* II 11).

203 Summa Augustini et Jeronimi de Hillario

> R4. 8 (whole entry), *s.n.* Hilary.

204 De omnibus haeresibus lib. 1   *Cum Dominus . . .*   1.<u>94</u>.<u>95</u>.<u>43</u>.<u>90</u>.80

> R1. 115 (whole entry). Same as *46*, *114*, and *200* above.

205 Contra quinque hostium genera

> Vincent XIX 54 [44].

206 De tribus habitaculis lib.   *Tria sunt . . . misericordem*   <u>153</u>.174   Iste liber intitulatur a quibusdam De gaudiis electorum et poenis dampnatorum, ut supra in G. A quibusdam autem ascribitur Patricio archiepiscopo Hiberniae et intitulatur hic, De tribus habitaculis coeli, mundi et inferni, ut patet in litera P.

> archiepiscopo] archiepiscopae *Add. 3470*; archiepiscopo *Ware extracts fol. 132r*

> R1. 239. Same as *185* above; for a discussion of the work see Patricius *434.1*.

207 Quod homo factus est ad imaginem Dei serm .1   *Tanta . . . reformant*   <u>163</u>.<u>166</u>.<u>156</u>.<u>161</u>

> 156] 126 *R*

Augustinus   *1. 207*

    R1. 152. *Ps.* Augustine, c. 35 of *De spiritu et anima*. *PL* 40. 1213 (cf. *PL* 40. 805). Same as *212* below.

208 De humilitate   95.105.89.153

    R1. 320 (whole entry).

209 Ad Honoratum episcopum ep. 2   *Caritati . . . defecerunt* 83

    CPL 262 *ep.* 228. *CSEL* 57. 484.

210 De S. Helya   serm. 1   Dominus Deus . . .

    CPL 284 *serm.* 11. *CCSL* 41. 161.

211 De eodem   sermo 1   *Multa . . . germinabit*

    Probably whole entry from *MF* II 133 (title *De elemosina*, explicit 'geminabit'). Evidently the same as *150* above.

212 De imagine, ut supra   lib. 1   *Tanta . . . reformant*

    Same as *207* above.

213 De jejunio sabbati ad Casulanum   *Nescio* . . .   9.103

    R1. 263 (whole entry).

214 De incarnatione Christi lib. 1   *Species vero . . . recipiantur* 42.46.90

    Whole entry from R1. 228 (title, location numbers), Vincent XIX 54 [102], and *MF* II 18 (incipit, explicit).

[p. 18]

215 Super evangelium Johannis omel. 124   *Intuentes . . . sermonem* 83.81.63.80.85

    R1. 105, Vincent XIX 54 [116], *MF* II 25. *CPL* 278. *CCSL* 36. [**82** = B13. 188; Bodl. MS e Musaeo 6, fol. 1r (Bury A. 8), with title including the number of homilies noted by Kirkestede on the flyleaf.] / **63** Crowland = B24. 3.

216 Super epistolam Johannis et vocatur Liber de caritate, supra in E   lib. 10   *Meminit . . . praedicanti* 83.1.163.94.92

    R1. 106. Same as *139* above.

Augustinus   *1. 225*

217 Ad Januarium de divinis observantiis   *Laetos . . . Deo gratias*

Perhaps *Ad Januarium de Pascha*, incipit 'Lectis. . .'. *CSEL* 34/2. 169, *ep.* 55.

218 Ad Julianum ep. 1   *Grate . . . certiores*   83

CPL 262 *ep.* 188. *CSEL* 57. 119.

219 De die judicii serm. 1   *O fratres . . .*

Ps. Augustine; *CPPM* 1. 1036. *PL* 39. 2210.

220 De jejunio quadragesimae serm. 1   *Quadragenarius . . .*

Unidentified.

221 De S. Joseph serm. 1   *Quotiens . . . corecta*

Caesarius Arelatensis; *CPPM* 1. 798. *CCSL* 103. 365.

222 De verbo Jacobi: Quicunque etc.   *Quod ad te . . . digneris*

Vincent XIX 54 [13]. *CPL* 262 *ep.* 167. *CSEL* 44. 586. Same as *266* below.

223 De innocentia vera lib. 1   *Innocentia . . . respexeris*   82.<u>161</u>.<u>152</u>.<u>103</u>.<u>35</u>
Hic liber appellatur a quibusdam Liber sententiarum Prosperi, ut patet in P litera.

R1. 123, *MF* II 108. Prosper of Aquitaine; *CPL* 525. *CCSL* 68. 219. Same as Prosper *466.3*.

224 De judicio Domini ad pan

pan *Add. 3470, queried by Tanner; perhaps the title originally read* 'De iudicio Domini et ad poenitentiam'

Source unidentified. *Ps.* Augustine; *CPPM* 1. 1035. *PL* 39. 2209.

225 Contra Julianum Pelagianum lib. 6   *Contumelias . . . qua vinceris*   82.<u>152</u>.<u>154</u>.<u>103</u>.9.<u>43</u>

43 om. R, habet Peterhouse 169

R1. 91, Vincent XIX 54 [37, 71], *MF* II 99. *CPL* 351. *PL* 44. 641. **82** Bury = Bodl. MS Add. C. 181, fols. 37v–173v (Bury A. 27), with correct rubric but with running headline *De nuptiis et concupiscentia*; the entry in B13. 42a,

Augustinus *1. 225*

'Contra Iulianum hereticum', refers instead to *CPL* 346 (*373* below), as is confirmed by the manuscript equivalent to B13. 42 (San Marino, Huntington Library, MS HM 31151, fol. 5r).

226 Yponosticon Augustini contra Pelagianos lib. 1   *Adversarii . . . salutaris* 82.1.105.42.152.95

R1. 100, *MF* II 72. *Ps.* Augustine; *CPL* 381. Ed. J. E. Cisholm *Ps.-Augustinian Hypomnesticon* (Freiburg 1980) vol. 2. See also *366* below. **82** Bury = B13. 42e = San Marino, Huntington Library, MS HM 31151, fol. 139r (Bury A. 10); B13. 187.

227 De justitiae perfectione lib. 1   *Sanctis fratribus . . . non dubito*   82.1.94.83. 63.98.50

R1. 113, *MF* II 67. *CPL* 347. *CSEL* 42. 3. Same as *370* below, and see *38* above. **82** Bury = B13. 81d.

228 De igne purgatorio serm. 1   *In lectione . . . redimere*   82.94.154.103.80.35

R1. 168. Same as *180* above and *360* and *486* below. **82** Bury = Bodl. MS e Musaeo 33, p. 285 (Bury A. —), with Kirkestede's title and attribution in the table of contents and at the top of p. 285, which has no rubric.

229 Contra Januarium   *Dominis sanctis . . . prudentiae*

Unidentified.

230 De Johanne evangelista   1.161

R1. 177 (whole entry).

231 Quomodo Jesus sit filius Dei   95

R1. 181 (whole entry).

232 Quomodo Jesus tribus nominibus nominatur   95.96

95.96] 96 *R*; 95.96 *Tanner 165*.

R1. 182 (whole entry).

233 Quid sit judicare terram   95

R1. 183 (whole entry).

Augustinus   1. 244

234 De judicio et justitia   95

> R1. 186 (probably whole entry, *Registrum* text corrupt at this point).

235 Contra incestos   103.163

> R1. 249 (whole entry save the suspect number **163**).

236 De libro Jesu Navae   15.95

> R1. 138 (whole entry).

237 De libro Judicum   15.163.166

> R1. 142 (whole entry save the suspect numbers **163** and **166**).

238 Ad juvenes sermo 1   *Ad vos . . . sapientiam*   103.15

> R1. 250. Dubious; *CPL* 285 *serm.* 391. *PL* 39. 1706.

239 De justis qui in vita misericordiam faciunt   *Cum petivisses . . .*   166.158.154

> R1. 301. The incipit, for reasons not apparent, is that of *248* below.

240 De connubio Jacob   127

> R1. 313 (whole entry).

241 De non jurando   50

> Source unidentified. Presumably this is *PL* 38. 1406 (*CPL* 284 *serm.* 307), which is called *De non jurando* in CUL MS Ii. 4. 23, fol. 127v.

242 Ad inquisitiones Januarii lib. 2   *Ad ea . . . lecturam*   82.1.95.156.152

> Whole entry from R1. 47 (title, incipit, location numbers), Vincent XIX 54 [27], and *MF* II 85 (title, number of books, incipit, explicit).

243 Contra Julianum sermo   82

> R1. 114 (whole entry).

244 Contra Judaeos et Paganos in P.

> See *380* below.

49

Augustinus *1. 245*

245 Ad Jeronimum ep. 1   *Jam pridem . . . quam nulla*   82

> *CPL* 262 *ep.* 82. *CSEL* 34/2. 351. **82** Bury = B13. 32, 'Epistole Augustini'.

246 Ad Italicam ep. 1   *Epistolas . . . de qua*   82

> R1. 253. *CPL* 262 *ep.* 99. *CSEL* 34/2. 533. **82** Bury = B13. 32, 'Epistole Augustini'.

247 Ad Januarium episcopum ep. 1   *Clerici et . . . poeniteat*   82

> *CPL* 262 *ep.* 88. *CSEL* 34/2. 407. **82** Bury = B13. 32, 'Epistole Augustini'.

248 Ad Italicam ep. 1   *Cum petivisses . . . valeamus*   82

> R1. 254. An epitome of the *De videndo Deo ad Paulinam*, *495* below; source of the confusion with *Ad Italicam* unknown. F. Römer, *Die handschriftliche Überlieferung der Werke des heiligen Augustinus* (Vienna 1972) 2/1. 281 lists nineteen surviving manuscripts in British libraries. See also *239* above. **82** Bury = B13. 32, 'Epistole Augustini'.

249 Ad Innocentium papam ep. 1   *Quia te . . . comperimus*   82

> The *Acta Concilii Milevitani*; *CPL* 262 *ep.* 176. *CSEL* 44. 663. **82** Bury = B13. 32, 'Epistole Augustini'.

250 De Xalendis Januarii lib. 1   *Epistolam fili . . .*   1

> R1. 124 (whole entry); through a copying error, the incipit is derived from R1. 126, *De fide ad Petrum* (*170* above).

251 Ad Jeronimum ep. 1   *Audivi . . . gloriantur*

> *251–254*: These four letters to Jerome appear in this same sequence in the codex of Jerome letters that Kirkestede used in compiling the Jerome entry; see Jeronimus *281.128–232*. For another Augustine letter from this corpus see *398* below.
>
> *CPL* 262 *ep.* 67. *CSEL* 34/2. 237.

252 Ad Jeronimum ep. 1   *Nunquam . . . sententia*

> *CPL* 262 *ep.* 28. *CSEL* 34/1. 103.

253 Ad Jeronimum ep. 1   *Habeo gratias . . . praesumentis*

> *CPL* 262 *ep.* 40. *CSEL* 34/2. 69.

Augustinus 1. 263

254 Ad Jeronimum ep. 1   *Ex quo . . . praesentiam*

> *CPL* 262 *ep.* 71. *CSEL* 34/2. 248.

255 Super Job annotationes lib. 1   *Opera magna . . . ne recedat*

> R1. 40, *MF* II 117. *CPL* 271. *CSEL* 28/2. 509. Same as *17* above.

256 De latrone beato serm. 1   *Deus erat . . . in regnum*   82.<u>166</u>.<u>158</u>.<u>154</u>

> R1. 303. Eusebius Gallicanus; *CPL* 368 spurious *serm.* 154. *CCSL* 101. 279.

257 Alius sermo de latrone et cruce   *Quum hesterna . . . placatus*   45

> *Ps.* Augustine (Maximus Taurinensis); *CPPM* 1. 2085, and cf. 1. 91. *CCSL* 23. 309 *ep.* 74, incipit 'Quoniam hesterna'. Explicit unidentified.

258 Locutiones in Eptaticum lib. 7   *Locutiones . . . super eos*   82.<u>1</u>.<u>15</u>.<u>20</u>

> R1. 83, Vincent XIX 54 [109], *MF* II 94. *CPL* 269. *CCSL* 33. 381. Probably the same as *305* below.

259 De luctatione Jacob lib. 1   *Hoc maxime . . . angelus eius*

> *CPL* 284 *serm.* 5. *CCSL* 41. 50, incipit 'Haec maxime', explicit 'angelis eius'.

260 De lapsu et reparatione hominis   <u>162</u>.<u>154</u>.<u>97</u>

> R1. 145 (whole entry). Same as Johannes Crisostomus *282.2*.

p. 19]

261 Ad Licentium   *Vix reperio . . . putavi*   82.<u>166</u>.<u>156</u>.<u>139</u>

> R1. 296. *CPL* 262 *ep.* 26 pt 1. *CSEL* 34/1. 83. **139** is taken from R1. 297. / **82** Bury = B13. 32, 'Epistole Augustini'.

262 Item ad eundem   *Si versus tuus . . . viluisti*   82

> R1. 297. *CPL* 262 *ep.* 26 pt 2. *CSEL* 34/1. 86. **82** Bury = B13. 32, 'Epistole Augustini'.

263 Ad Longinianum ep. 1   *Longiniano . . . beati*   82

> *CPL* 262 *ep.* 233. *CSEL* 57. 517, explicit 'beatique simus'. **82** Bury = B13. 32, 'Epistole Augustini'.

Augustinus *1. 264*

264 Item ad Longinianum ep. 1   *Longiniano . . . contexamus*   82

  CPL 262 *ep*. 235. CSEL 57. 521. **82** Bury = B13. 32, 'Epistole Augustini'.

265 Item ad Laetum ep. 1   *Legi . . . voluisset*   82

  CPL 262 *ep*. 243. CSEL 57. 568. **82** Bury = B13. 32, 'Epistole Augustini'.

266 De eo quod scriptum est: Qui totam legem servaverit, offendat autem in uno, factus est omnium reus   *Quod ad te . . . digneris*   82

  MF II 134. Same as *222* above.

267 Super libros Machabeorum lib. 2

  This work and its source are unidentified.

268 Contra mendacium lib. 1   *Multa . . . veniremus*   84.<u>95</u>.<u>1</u>.<u>42</u>.<u>114</u>

  84 *may be* 82 *R*

  R1. 89, Vincent XIX 54 [59], MF II 44. CPL 304. CSEL 41. 469. [**82** Bury = B13. 31d.]

269 Item de mendacio lib. 1   *Magna . . . sustinere*   84.<u>1</u>.<u>94</u>.19.15

  R1. 27, MF II 53. CPL 303. CSEL 41. 413. [**82** Bury = B13. 31c.]

270 Unde malum contra Fortunatum lib. 1   *Quinto . . . ostensurus*   84.<u>89</u>.<u>1</u>.<u>95</u>.<u>42</u>

  84 *may be* 82 *R*

  R1. 16. CPL 318. CSEL 25. 83–112, *Contra Fortunatum disputatio*; the explicit is that of Fortunatus's last speech. Same as *172* above.

271 Item Unde malum, ut supra in A.

  This is a common title for the first part of *De libero arbitrio*, *18* above, which circulated independently. [**82** Bury = B13. 81g].

272 De Maximianistis lib. 1   *Multa iam . . .*

  Whole entry from R1. 62 and MF II 123. Not extant (*Retractationes* II 35).

273 Ad Macedonium ep. 1   *Quamvis . . . occuperis*   84.<u>161</u>

  R1. 317, Vincent XIX 54 [86]. CPL 262 *ep*. 155. CSEL 44. 430.

52

Augustinus 1. 280

274 De magistro lib. 1   *Quid tibi ... asserebatur*   9.93.<u>94</u>.<u>35</u>

> Whole entry from R1. 12 (title, incipit, location numbers **94** and **35**), R1. 11 (location number **9** by mistake), Vincent XIX 54 [25], and *MF* II 21 (title, incipit, explicit).

275 Contra Maximinum haereticum lib. 3   *Cum Augustinus ... gaudeamus*   95.<u>103</u>.<u>32</u>.<u>43</u>

> Whole entry from R1. 110–111 (title, incipit from R1. 110, location numbers from R1. 111) and *MF* II 74 (incipit) and II 73 (explicit). Same as 277 below. See also 7 above and 292 below.

276 De musica lib. 6   *Modus ... videremus*   84.19.50.<u>103</u>

> R1. 11, Vincent XIX 54 [16], *MF* II 107. *CPL* 258. *PL* 32. 1081.

277 Item contra Maximinum lib. 3   *Cum Augustinus ... gaudeamus*   161.<u>105</u>.<u>152</u>

> Whole entry from R1. 110–111 and *MF* II 74, II 73 (same as 275 above), with the location numbers from R1. 110. See also 7 above and 292 below.

278 De mirabilibus sanctae Scripturae lib. 3   *Cum omnipotentis ... castigaretur*   84.<u>1</u>.<u>127</u>.<u>105</u>

> 84 *may be* 82 *R* 127] 157 *R*

> R1. 109, *MF* II 9. 'Augustinus Hibernicus'; *CPL* 1123. *PL* 35. 2151. [**82** Bury = B13. 101d = Bodl. MS Lat. th. c. 26, fol. 60v (Bury J. 16), whose incipit does not correspond; Cambridge, Pembroke College, MS 20, fol. 28v (Bury J. 57) – a marginal note on fol. 42v says that the last two chapters are lacking from this manuscript, but the explicit (fol. 42v, 'castigarentur') corresponds, as does the incipit; Cambridge, Pembroke College, MS 34, fol. 259r (Bury T. 4), both incipit and explicit (fol. 272v, 'castigarentur') match and Kirkestede has noted them in the margin (fol. 258v); and Cambridge, Pembroke College, MS 87, fol. 121r (Bury E. 11), whose explicit tallies (fol. 131r) though the incipit does not.]

279 Super Mulierem fortem sermonem   *Praestabitur ... habitant*   84.83.<u>1</u>.<u>12</u>

> 12] xii *R*

> R1. 305, Vincent XIX 54 [112], *MF* II 143. *CPL* 284 *serm.* 37. *CCSL* 41. 446.

280 De misericordia   *Misericordia ... querebatur*

> *Ps.* Augustine; *CPPM* 1. 1095, incipit varies. *CPL* 368 spurious *serm.* 310. A version of this is printed, *PL* 39. 2340.

Augustinus *1. 281*

281 De mulierum consortio fugiendo

 Source unidentified. Same as *286* below.

282 De moribus ecclesiae et moribus Manicheorum lib. 2 *In aliis . . . velitis*
8̲2̲.43.1̲3̲.1̲5̲.9̲5̲.9̲4̲

 R1. 7, Vincent XIX 54 [8], *MF* II 43. *CPL* 261. *CSEL* 90. 3. **82** Bury = BL MS Royal 7 B. IX, fol. 73v (Bury D. 6); explicit, fol. 76v, does not correspond.

283 De tribus Mariis 1̲6̲3̲

 R1. 146 (whole entry).

284 De monachis fugitivis 1̲6̲1̲

 R1. 163 (whole entry).

285 De Magdalenae poenitentia 1̲6̲1̲

 R1. 164 (whole entry).

286 De inhonestate mulierum serm. *Nemo dicat . . . oculi mei*

 inhonestate] honestate *R;* inhonestate *Peterhouse 169*

 R1. 169. Caesarius Arelatensis; *CPL* 368 spurious *serm.* 293. *CCSL* 103. 180. Same as *281* above.

287 De mundi lapsu et anarcia 95.3̲2̲.3̲5̲.1̲1̲5̲.1̲0̲4̲

 anarcia] avaricia *R*

 R1. 191 (whole entry).

288 De maledictis 1̲5̲4̲

 R1. 245 (whole entry).

289 De molendino 1̲5̲4̲

 R1. 246 (whole entry).

290 De muliere curva *Apostolum . . . seperandus*

 CPL 285 *serm.* 392. *PL* 39. 1709.

Augustinus *1. 300*

291 De mirabilibus mundi   124

   R1. 272 (whole entry).

292 Contra Maximum episcopum Arrianum   9.20.104

   Whole entry from R1. 279 and Vincent XIX 54 [33]. See also *275* and *277* above.

293 Meditationes   *Domine Deus . . . miserationem*   82.15.35.9.20

   20] xx *R*

   R1. 280. *Ps.* Augustine; *CPL* 386n. *PL* 40. 901. For a discussion of the meditations attributed to Augustine see M. Martins in *Broteria* 60 (1955), 520. This entry represents a manuscript similar to Oxford, Trinity College, MS B 89, fols. 82v–90v, containing 29 homilies with the same incipit and explicit.

294 Item ad Maximum ep. 1   *Serium ne aliquid . . . cognovero*   82.63.64

   CPL 262 *ep.* 17. *CSEL* 34/1. 39. **82** Bury = B13. 32, 'Epistole Augustini'. / **63** Crowland = B24. 6, 'epistole sue [Augustini]'.

295 De motu corporalium et spiritualium   166.161

   R1. 312 (whole entry save the suspect **161**).

296 Ad Macedonium   *Quantum desperavi . . .*   161

   R1. 317 (title and location number). Incipit unidentified. See *273* above.

297 Ad eundem ep. 1   *Negotiosissimum . . . fili karissime*   82

   R1. 318. *CPL* 262 *ep.* 153. *CSEL* 44. 395. **82** Bury = B13. 32, 'Epistole Augustini'.

298 Ad monachos   94

   R1. 319 (whole entry).

299 De institutione monachorum serm. 1

   Source unidentified. Presumably the same as *417* below.

300 Item de monachis ad Sammatum monachum serm. 2

   This work and its source are unidentified.

55

Augustinus   *1. 301*

301   Item super psalmum: Ecce quam bonum

   Source unidentified. *Enarratio in psalmum cxxxii. CCSL* 40. 1926.

302   De mensura, numero et pondere   166.161.116.35.50

   R1. 309. The whole entry came from the *Registrum* save the addition of **50** Pipewell, a library that Kirkestede evidently knew. Perhaps he saw there *ps.* Bede *De ponderibus et mensuris*; see R1. 309 for bibliography.

303   Ad Memorum episcopum patrem Juliani ep. 1   *Nullas . . . memores*   83.103.166.163

   R1. 262. *CPL* 262 *ep.* 101. *CSEL* 34/2. 539. Location numbers **166** and **163** are taken from R1. 147 *Epistole Augustini.*

304   Contra Manicheos   83.80

   R1. 213, Vincent XIX 54 [34]. Same as *186* above.

305   De modis locutionum lib. 7   83.43

   83 *may be* 82 *R*

   R1. 221, and cf. R1. 83. Probably the same as *258* above.

p. 20]

306   Ad Marcellinum ep. 1   *Illustri . . . desideratissime*   83

   CPL 262 *ep.* 138. *CSEL* 44. 126.

307   Ad eundem ep. 1   *Epistolam . . . soluta est*   83

   CPL 262 *ep.* 143. *CSEL* 44. 250.

308   Ad eundem. ep. 1   *Circumcelliones . . . karissime*   83

   CPL 262 *ep.* 133. *CSEL* 44. 80.

309   Commonitorium ad ecclesias sub qua cautela Manichei si conversi fuerint suscipi debeant   *Manichei . . . deserunt*

   Probably the whole entry from *MF* II 66, although the wording of the title varies somewhat. Same as *55* above.

56

Augustinus *1. 318*

310 De nuptiis et concupiscentia ad Valerium comitem lib. 2   lib. 1: *Haeretici . . . impendas*; lib. 2: *Inter militiae . . . posset*   83.42.9.43.19

> 83 *may be* 82 *R*
>
> R1. 82, Vincent XIX 54 [36], *MF* II 80. *CPL* 350. *CSEL* 42. 211. See also *431* and *498* below. [**82** Bury = B13. 60 = Bodl. MS Add. C. 181 (Bury A. 27), fols. 1v and 14v respectively, explicit (fol. 36v) 'possit esse et ipsorum'.]

311 De natura et gratia lib. 1   *Liber . . . bonitas*   83.42.9.43.19

> R1. 69, Vincent XIX 54 [98], *MF* II 69. *CPL* 344. *CSEL* 60. 233. Location numbers are repeated from *310* above.

312 De natura et voluntate lib. 1   *Spiritus . . . delectatur*   43

> R1. 225 (title and location number). Incipit and explicit unidentified.

313 De natali Domini serm. 1   *Rogo vos . . . intromittat*   83.8.1.15

> 83] 82 *R*
>
> R1. 219. Possibly the work of Sedatus Nemausensis; *CPL* 1006. *PL* 39. 1977 spurious *serm.* 117.

314 Ad Nebridium ep. 1   *Utrum . . . legere te*   82.156.153.154

> R1. 205. *CSEL* 34/1. 4 *ep.* 3. **82** Bury = B13. 32, 'Epistole Augustini'.

315 Ad eundem ep. 1   *Prohemio . . . blandimur*   82

> *CSEL* 34/1. 13 *ep.* 7. **82** Bury = B13. 32, 'Epistole Augustini'.

316 Ad eundem ep. 1   *Quia mei . . . excesserim*   82

> A combination of *ep.* 9 (*CSEL* 34/1. 20) and most of *ep.* 14 (*CSEL* 34/1. 32) which circulated as one letter; see *CSEL* 34/1. 32n. **82** Bury = B13. 32, 'Epistole Augustini'.

317 Ad eundem ep. 1   *Nunquam . . . verterem*   82

> *CSEL* 34/1. 22 *ep.* 10. **82** Bury = B13. 32, 'Epistole Augustini'.

318 Ad eundem ep. 1   *Mirum . . .non habeo*   82

> *CSEL* 34/1. 9 *ep.* 4. **82** Bury = B13. 32, 'Epistole Augustini'.

Augustinus 1. 319

319 Ad Nectarium ep. 1   *Jam senio ... gaudere*   82

> *CPL* 262 *ep.* 91. *CSEL* 34/2. 427. **82** Bury = B13. 32, 'Epistole Augustini'.

320 De duobus nativitatibus Christi   *Quare Filius ...*

> *CPPM* 1. 903, 6445. *CPL* 809. *PL* 39. 1981 spurious *serm.* 118, incipit '*Filius Dei ...* Hodie fratres'.

321 De operibus monachorum lib. 1   *Jussioni tuae ... noverim*   82.1.163. 105.153

> R1. 48 (title, incipit, location numbers), Vincent XIX 54 [30], *MF* II 19 (title, incipit, explicit). *CPL* 305. *CSEL* 41. 531.

322 De ordine rerum lib. 2   *De ordine ... allatum*   83.152.103.43.13

> 83] 82 *R*
>
> R1. 3 (title, incipit, location numbers), Vincent XIX 54 [4], *MF* II 41 (explicit 'illatum'). *CPL* 255. *CCSL* 29. 89.

323 De ovibus lib. 1   *Verba quae ... Deus noster*   82.89.9.13.15.1

> 89 *may be* 139 *R*
>
> R1. 316, *MF* II 50. *CPL* 284 *serm.* 47. *CCSL* 41. 572. **82** Bury = Harvard University, Houghton Library, MS Richardson 26, fols. 13v–23r (Bury A. 6); see note to *340* below.

324 Ad Orosium presbyterum de errore Priscillianistarum   lib. 1   *Respondere tibi ... non eget*   43.152

> R1. 71. *CPL* 327. *CCSL* 49. 165. Explicit unidentified. Same as *400* below.

325 De quaestionibus Orosii lib. 1   *Licet ... non prodesse*   82.1.83.42.8. 80

> R1. 120 (location numbers), Vincent XIX 54 [47], *MF* II 8 (title, incipit, explicit). Same as *405* below, and Orosius *407.2*. **82** Bury = B13. 50g = BL MS Harley 3027, fols. 106r–118v.

326 De oratione Dominica serm. 1   *Beatus ... permanebit*   95.89.8.90.9. 35

> R1. 314. *CPL* 284 *serm.* 56. Ed. P. Verbraken in *RB* 68 (1958) 26.

327 De oratione Dominica serm. 1   *Symbolum . . . merces est*

   CPL 284 *serm.* 58. Ed. P. Verbraken in *Ecclesia orans* 1 (1984) 119.

328 De oratione Dominica serm. 1   *Ascultate . . .*

   Unidentified.

329 De oratione Dominica tract. 1   *Evangelica . . .*

   Cyprian; *CPL* 43. Attributed to Augustine in CUL MS Ii. 4. 23, fol. 79r. Same as Ciprianus *112.6*.

330 De obedientia et humilitate serm. 1   *Nihil sic . . . audiat*   82.<u>104.63</u>.9.83

   R1. 315. Jerome; *CPL* 605. *CCSL* 78. 552.

331 Ad Optatum episcopum ep. 1   *Quamvis . . . desiderabile*   82

   Vincent XIX 54 [91]. *CPL* 262 *ep.* 190. *CSEL* 57. 137, explicit 'desiderabilis frater'. **82** Bury = B13. 32, 'Epistole Augustini'.

332 De officiis   *Quaeris a me . . .*

   Isidore; *CPL* 1207. Incipit is that of the *Epistola missoria*. Same as Ysidorus *666.22*.

333 De orando Deo ad Probam ep. 1   *Et petisse te . . . intelligimus*   82

   R1. 223. *CPL* 262 *ep.* 130. *CSEL* 44. 40. **82** Bury = B13. 32, 'Epistole Augustini'.

334 Ad Olimpium ep. 1   *Quicquid . . . Domine*   82

   CPL 262 *ep.* 96. *CSEL* 34/2. 514. **82** Bury = B13. 32, 'Epistole Augustini'.

335 Ad eundem ep. 1   *Quamvis . . . participem*   82

   CPL 262 *ep.* 97. *CSEL* 34/2. 516. **82** Bury = B13. 32, 'Epistole Augustini'.

336 Ad Orontium ep. 1   *Ago gratias . . . suscipiende*   82

   CPL 262 *ep.* 257. *CSEL* 57. 604, explicit 'suscipiende fili'. **82** Bury = B13. 32, 'Epistole Augustini'.

337 Omeliae 50   89.<u>63</u>.<u>104</u>.<u>123</u>.<u>152</u>.<u>160</u>

   R1. 151 (whole entry save the number of homilies).

Augustinus *1. 338*

338 De die ordinationis suae   95.35.1.166.157

    R1. 196. Same as *430* below.

339 De orando Deo ad Probam aliam ep.   *Est quidem* . . .   43.9.15.109.23

    23] xxiii *R*

    R1. 222 (whole entry).

340 De pastoribus et ovibus lib. 2   *Spes tota* . . . *ad unitatem*   82.89.103.97.104.139

    97] 95 *R*

    R1. 155 (location numbers **82** to **103**), R1. 316 (location numbers **97** to **139**), Vincent XIX 54 [38], *MF* II 49–50. *CPL* 284 *serm.* 46–7 (title). *CCSL* 41. 529. The incipit and explicit, which are those of the *De pastoribus* alone (*serm.* 46), derive from *MF* II 49. See also **82** Bury = Harvard University, Houghton Library, MS Richardson 26, fols. 3r–13v (*De pastoribus*, followed on fols. 13v–23r by *De ouibus, 323* above: Bury A. 6).

341 De patientia lib. 1   *Virtus autem* . . . *caritati*   89

    Whole entry from R1. 212A (title, location number), Vincent XIX 54 [68], and *MF* II 56 (title, incipit 'Virtus animi', explicit).

342 De poenitentia lib. 1   *Quum sit* . . . *mors aeterna*   82.42.43.49.50.94

    R1. 116, Vincent XIX 54 [67], *MF* II 48. Dubious; *CPL* 284 *serm.* 351, incipit 'Quoniam'. *PL* 39. 1535. **42** Reading = Bodl. MS Auct. F. inf. 1. 2, fol. 159v, incipit 'Quam sit', explicit does not correspond.

343 Item de poenitentia lib. 1   *Vox poenitentis* . . . *correctis*

    MF II 51 (whole entry, explicit 'correctus'). Same as *353* below.

344 Item de poenitentia serm. 1   *Poenitentes* . . . *tene*

    CPL 285 *serm.* 393. Probably Geoffrey Babion; see J. Bonnes in *RB* 56 (1945–6), 204. *PL* 39. 1713. Same as *346* below.

345 De vera et falsa poenitentia lib. 1   *Quum sit* . . . *suavitatis*   13.16.10

    10] x *R*

    R1. 79. *Ps.* Augustine; *CPL* 386n. For a discussion of the authorship see C. Fantini in *Ricerche di storia religiosa* 1 (1954) 200–209. *PL* 40. 1113.

Augustinus *1. 354*

346 Quam sit fructuosa poenitentia ante ultimam necessitatem   *Poenitentes
. . .*   95.9.35.104.46

> R1. 137 (whole entry). Same as *344* above.

347 Super psalterium tractatus vel omeliae 150   *De Domino . . . secundum carnem*   83.1.94.43.15.35.53

> R1. 104, Vincent XIX 54 [17]. *CPL* 283. *CCSL* 38, 39, 40. [**82** Bury = B13. 179–181 = Bodl. MSS e Musaeo 8 (Bury A. 2) and e Musaeo 7 (Bury A. 3), on Psalms 51–99 and 100–150 respectively, explicit 'secundum carnem mors est'; the first volume (Bury A. 1) on Psalms 1–50 is missing.] Location number **94** is taken from *Registrum* 1.151, 'Omelie eius'.

[p. 21]

348 Praeterea scripsit super psalmos   *Psalmum vobis . . . Jesus Christus*

> *CPPM* 1. 733. *CPL* 285 *serm.* 366. *PL* 39. 1646.

349 Super versum psalmi 26: Sustine Domine   *Frequenter . . . vincentes*

> *349–357*: These nine sermons appear in this sequence in Bodl. MS Bodley 204, fols. 26v–39r (*Collectio tripartita*). *PL* 38. 244, and cf. *CCSL* 41. 493 (*serm.* 40).

350 Super versum psalmi: Quis est homo   *Vocans . . . pacem*

> *CCSL* 41. 213 (*serm.* 16). See note to *349* above.

351 Super versum psalmi 49: Deus manifeste   *Ad exortandum . . . ad Dominum*

> *CCSL* 41. 245 (*serm.* 18). See note to *349* above.

352 Item de eodem   *Cantavimus . . . bona vita*

> *CCSL* 41.237 (*serm.* 17). See note to *349* above.

353 De versu psalmi 50: Cor mundum   *Vox poenitentis . . . dies mortis*

> The biblical text for this sermon is not *Cor mundum* (verse 12) but *Auerte faciem tuam* (verse 11). *PL* 39. 1549 (*serm.* 352). See note to *349* above. Same as *343* above.

354 Item de eodem serm. 1   *Voce . . . ex amore*

> *CCSL* 41. 261 (*serm.* 20). See note to *349* above.

Augustinus *1. 355*

355 De versu psalmi: Laetabitur justus in   *Jocundabitur . . . redemptoris*

> CCSL 41. 276 (*serm.* 21). See note to *349* above.

356 De versu psalmi 67: Sicut deficit fumus   *Audivimus . . . timeamus*

> R1. 179. CCSL 41. 289 (*serm.* 22). See note to *349* above. Same as *446* below.

357 De versu psalmi 72: Tenuisti manum   *Quod cantavimus . . . desideramus*

> manum] via *Add. 3470*
>
> CCSL 41. 309 (*serm.* 23). See note to *349* above.

358 De praesentia Dei lib. 1   *Fateor . . . et veniam*   83.152.154.35.15

> 83.152] 82.153 *R*
>
> R1. 217. Same as *130* above, and *364* and *390* below. [**82** Bury = B13. 50c = BL MS Harley 3027, fols. 28r–36v.]

359 De decem praeceptis et decem plagis Aegypti serm. 1   *Non est . . . illaesi*
89.43.116.152.8

> R1. 211, *MF* II 104 (explicit does not correspond). Caesarius Arelatensis; *CPL* 368 spurious *serm.* 21. CCSL 103. 413, explicit unidentified.

360 De poenis purgatorii   *In lectione . . . redimamus*

> Same as *180* and *228* above and *486* below.

361 De pulcro et apto lib. 3

> Source unidentified. Not extant; for references to this work see Schanz, 4/2. 412.

362 Quod Paulus reprehendit Petrum

> Vincent XIX 54 [14] (whole entry).

363 De praedestinatione divina et gratia Dei lib. 1   *Dum sacrarum . . . voragine*

> *MF* II 6 (probably the whole entry). The end of the title 'et gratia Dei', which is not found in the *Manipulus florum*, is correct, and perhaps represents an annotation in a Bury copy of the *MF*; the remainder of the entry, including its faulty incipit, came from *MF* II 6.

364 De praescientia Dei ad Dardanum lib. 1   *Dilectissime . . . concedis*

> Vincent XIX 54 [50], *MF* II 130. *De praesentia Dei. CPL* 262 *ep.* 187. *CSEL* 57. 81, explicit 'concedis et venia'. Same as *130* and *358* above, and *390* below. [**82** Bury = B13. 50c = BL MS Harley 3027, fols. 28r–36r, incipit 'Fateor me frater dilectissime', explicit 'concedis et veniam'.]

365 De praedestinatione et praeseverantia sanctorum ad Prosperum et Hillarium lib. 2   *Dixisse . . . longitudo*   82.1.94.43.8.80

> R1. 101, Vincent XIX 54 [32], *MF* II 10. *CPL* 354. *PL* 44. 959. **82** Bury = B13. 81a.

366 De praedestinatione contra Pelagium   *Addendum est etiam . . . prorogare*   83

> *Ps.* Augustine; *CPL* 381. Book VI of the *Hypomnesticon*, which often occurs with the rubric 'Augustinus contra Pelagianos de praedestinatione divina' (e.g. *PL* 45. 1657, and the Huntington manuscript). See also *226* above. [**82** Bury = B13. 42e = San Marino, Huntington Library, MS HM 31151, fol. 157v (Bury A. 10), incipit 'Addere etiam'.]

367 Contra literas Petiliani lib. 3   *Noster . . . revertetur*   152

> R1. 52, Vincent XIX 54 [73], *MF* II 91. *CPL* 333. *CSEL* 52. 3.

368 Contra epistolam Parmeniani lib. 3   *Multa . . . gloriari*   83.1.9.43.15. 20

> 83] 82 *R*

> R1. 44, Vincent XIX 54 [72], *MF* II 90. *CPL* 331. *CSEL* 51.

369 Ad Pascentium comitem ep. 1   *Volueram . . . scripturae*   83

> Vincent XIX 54 [93]. *CPL* 262 *ep.* 238. *CSEL* 57. 533.

370 De perfectione justitiae vel hominis   *Sanctis . . . non dubito*   83.1.94. 63.163

> R1. 113, Vincent XIX 54 [97], *MF* II 67. Same as *227* above, and see *38* and *92* above.

371 De perjurio serm. 1   *Prima . . . ad Dominum*   103.128.80.13.15

> R1. 247. *CPL* 284 *serm.* 180. *PL* 38. 912.

Augustinus *I. 372*

372 Contra Pelagium et Celestium, supra in G.   *Quantum . . . veruntamen*

R1. 78, Vincent XIX 54 [144]. *CPL* 349. *CSEL* 42. 125. Same as *195* above.

373 Contra epistolas Pelagianorum lib. 4   *Noveram . . . sine Domino*   1.152. 154.9.13

R1. 90, Vincent XIX 54 [147], *MF* II 98. *CPL* 346. *CSEL* 60. 423; explicit is that of Book II (ib. 485). [**82** Bury = San Marino, Huntington Library, MS HM 31151, fol. 5r (Bury A. 10).]

374 De bono perseverantiae lib. 1   *Iam de perseverantia . . . quod scribo*   83.1. 94.165.158

83 *may be* 82 *R*

R1. 102. *CPL* 355. *PL* 45. 993. [**82** Bury = B13. 81b.]

375 De persecutione Christiana lib. 1   *Deus hoc est . . . posse*

Unidentified.

376 De pugna David et Goliae

Cassiodorus I. 2. 5 (whole entry).

377 Quod non licet habere proprium serm. 1   *Propter quod . . .*

De uita et moribus clericorum suorum I. Same as *99* above.

378 Item de eodem serm. 1   *Caritati . . .*

De uita et moribus clericorum suorum II. Same as *100* above.

379 Pellagii gesta supra in G. lib. 1   *Postquam . . .*   161

Whole entry from R1. 74 (title, location number) and *MF* II 129 (title, incipit). Same as *188* above.

380 Contra paganos et Judaeos   *Beatus . . .*   94.1.166

R1. 117 (title, incipit, location numbers save the suspect **166**).

381 Super psalmos 15 graduum   *Brevis . . .*   42.43.154

42.43] 42.42 *Tanner 165*; 42 *R*

R1. 133 (whole entry).

Augustinus *1. 389*

382 Super id: Petre amas me   95

> R1. 188 (whole entry).

383 Super praedicamenta ejus   43.152.65

> R1. 235. *CPL* 362. Ed. L. Minio-Paluello, *Ps.-Augustini Paraphrasis Themistiana* (Bruges 1961) 133. Same as *74* above. See also Alcuin *7.2* and *7.12* below.

384 De phitonissa   90.9

> R1. 231 (whole entry).

385 Contra perfidiam Arrianorum super in A.   *Eorum praecedenti* . . .

> R1. 273 (whole entry). Same as *22* above.

386 Summa de peccato quid sit   80.90.166

> Summa] Sermo *R*

> R1. 274 (title and location number **80**), R1. 151 (*Omelie eius*, location number **166**); source of **90** is unknown.

387 De paradiso   166

> R1. 308 (whole entry).

388 Pronosticon Augustini   22.152.164

> R1. 158 (whole entry save suspect **22**).

389 De Pascha serm. 12   *Admonet* . . .   1.90.3.15.20.13.9

> 13.9] 139 *R*

> R1. 232 (location numbers **1, 90**) and R1. 275 (location numbers **3** to **9**). A series of twelve sermons on Easter attributed to Augustine (numbered 1–2 and 1–10) in CUL MS Ii. 1. 35 begins on fol. 85v, 'Admonet nos dilectissimi tanta ista et tam (?) sancta sollempnitas, exhortari uos ad uigilandum et orandum. Dimicat (?) enim fides nostra contra huius seculi noctem, ne interiores oculi nostri in noctem cordis obdormiant. In quod malum ne incidamus. oremus illa uoce qua legimus, et dicamus domino deo nostro. Illumina oculos meos ne unquam obdormiam in morte, ne quando dicat inimicus meus preualui aduersus eum. Hic ille inimicus, qui aduersus dominum nostrum Iesum Christum insanos iudeos uelut propria uasa et arma'.

Augustinus   *1. 390*

390 De praesentia Dei ad Dardanum lib. 1   *Quaeris* . . .   81.43.152.103.8

   8] 80 R

   R1. 76 (whole entry). Same as *130*, *358*, and *364* above.

p. 22]

391 Ad Paulinum ep. 1   *O bone . . . sentiat*   83

   Vincent XIX 54 [88]. *CPL* 262 *ep.* 27. *CSEL* 34/1. 95.

392 Ad Paulinum et Therasiam ep. 1   *Cum literas . . . fratres*   84

   CPL 262 *ep.* 31. *CSEL* 34/2. 1.

393 Item ad Paulinum ep. 1   *Quod de tam . . . affectum*   84

   CPL 262 *ep.* 149. *CSEL* 44. 348.

394 Ad Pammachium ep. 1   *Bona . . . metueres*   84

   CPL 262 *ep.* 58. *CSEL* 34/2. 216.

395 Ad Possidium ep. 1   *Magis . . . ut facias*   84

   CPL 262 *ep.* 245. *CSEL* 57. 581.

396 Super illud: Tibi derelictus est pauper   95

   R1. 184 (whole entry). Same as *458* below.

397 Psalmus contra partem Donati lib. 1   *Omnes qui* . . .

   Whole entry from R1. 20 and *MF* II 110. Same as *125* above.

398 Ad Praesidium ep. 1   *Sicut praesens . . . cognovero*

   CPL 262 *ep.* 74. *CSEL* 34/2. 279. See note to *251–254* above. [**82** Bury = B13. 32, 'Épistole Augustini'.]

399 Contra Pelagium ad papam Sixtum   *Tres eramus* . . .

   Vincent XIX 54 [101]. *CPL* 262 *ep.* 194. *CSEL* 57. 176, incipit 'Tristes eramus' (line 11). [**82** Bury = B13. 32, 'Épistole Augustini'.]

Augustinus   *1. 406*

400 Contra Priscillianistas et Origenistas ad Orosium   *Responderi tibi . . . dignatus est*

> Vincent XIX 54 [15], *MF* II 127. *CCSL* 49. 165, incipit 'Respondere tibi', explicit (ib. 178) 'dignatus est caritatem'. Same as *324* above.

401 Quaestiones 6 contra paganos   *Monet quosdam . . . toleravit*   83.<u>94</u>.<u>8</u>.<u>43</u>. <u>1</u>.<u>152</u>

> 83] 82 *R*

> Whole entry from R1. 58 (incipit 'Mouet quosdam', location numbers) and *MF* II 135 (title, incipit 'Mouet quosdam', explicit 'tolerandum'). Same as *102* above.

402 De 8 quaestionibus Dulsinii lib. 1   *Quantum mihi . . . discere quam*   <u>1</u>.<u>9</u>.43. <u>35</u>.<u>20</u>.57

> R1. 94, Vincent XIX 54 [31], *MF* II 100. *CPL* 291. *CCSL* 44A. 253. Location numbers **9**, **35**, and **20** are taken from R1. 147, 'Epistole eius'. See also *20* and *154* above. [**82** Bury = BL MS Harley 3027, fols. 140v–152v, explicit 'discere quam docere'.]

403 De 56 quaestionibus Veteris et Novi Testamenti   *De hoc est quod . . . persuaderi*

> *MF* II 33 (whole entry).

404 De 83 quaestionibus lib. 1   *Omne verum . . . fideles*   82.<u>1</u>.<u>42</u>.<u>43</u>.<u>15</u>.<u>20</u>

> R1. 26, Vincent XIX 54 [106], *MF* II 22. *CPL* 289. *CCSL* 44A. 11, explicit 'fideles ambo essent'. See also *500* below. **82** Bury = B13. 66, 'Quaestiones Augustini octoginta'; Cambridge, Pembroke College, MS 34, fol. 239r (Bury T. 7), with the end of this work and the beginning of the next noted in the margin by Kirkestede, fol. 256v; extracts from this work are contained in BL MS Royal 7 B. ix, fol. 77r (Bury D. 6).

405 De quaestionibus Orosii   *Licet multi . . . desiderant*

> Whole entry from R1. 120 (incipit), Vincent XIX 54 [47], and *MF* II 8 (title, incipit, explicit 'desiderat non prodesse'). Same as *325* above and Orosius *407.2*.

406 Quaestiones de Eptatico Arrianorum lib. 7   *Cum scripturas . . . piscantur*   <u>9</u>.<u>43</u>.<u>19</u>.<u>15</u>.<u>1</u>.50

> R1. 84, Vincent XIX 54 [108], *MF* II 95. *CPL* 270. *CCSL* 33. 1.

Augustinus   *1. 407*

407 Quaestiones evangelicae lib. 3   *Hoc opus . . . Patrem Dominum*   43.1.20

  R1. 39, *MF* II 88. *CPL* 275. *CCSL* 44B. 1. Same as *160* above and *410* below.

408 De quaestionibus Hebraicis   163

  R1. 157 (whole entry).

409 Ad Quod vult Deus, supra in D.

  See *112–114* above.

410 Super evangelium Matthei et Lucae   *Cum diceret . . .*

  Vincent XIX 54 [114]. The incipit is that of Book I. Same as *160* and *407* above.

411 De quaestionibus contra Manicheos   *Unus Deus . . . toto desiderio*

  Evodius Uzaliensis; *CPL* 390. *CSEL* 25/2. 951, explicit 'toto desiderio convolate'.

412 De vera religione lib. 1   *Cum omnis . . . ex quo omnia*   83.42.43.1.93. 95

  83] 82 *R*

  R1. 13 (title, incipit, location numbers), Vincent XIX 54 [20], *MF* II 17 (title, incipit, explicit). *CPL* 264. *CCSL* 32. 187. [**82** Bury = B13. 22c.]

413 De resurrectione serm. 1   *Ferunt . . . resuscitant*   79

  CPPM 1. 1363. *PLS* 2. 1202 para. 2. A number of manuscripts begin at this point, including BL MS Royal 5 B. 1, fol. 94r–v (see the list in *CPPM*). Explicit unidentified; the explicit in Royal 5 B. 1 does not correspond.

414 Responsiones ad Marcellum   *Quamvis . . .*

  Vincent XIX 54 [82]. Same as *35* above.

415 De resurrectione lib. 1   *Quodam loco . . . portari*   166.116.103.1.139

  R1. 306 (title, location numbers). *Ps.* Eusebius Emesenus Gallicanus; *CPL* 966 *serm.* 19. *CCSL* 101. 223, explicit 'portaret in caelum'. Attributed to Augustine in BL MS Royal 5 C. v, fol. 102v.

Augustinus 1. 423

416 Retractationum lib. 2   *Jam diu . . . cepissem*   83.43.1.94.95.42.90

    83] 82 *R*

    R1. 97, Vincent XIX 54 [124], *MF* II 82. *CPL* 250. *CCSL* 57. Location number **94** comes from R1. 97, and the others by error from R1. 98. **82** Bury = B13. 62a = Bodl. MS e Musaeo 31, p. 1 (Bury A. 31).

417 De institutione monachorum regulam unam   163.95.103

    R1. 148 (whole entry). Presumably the same as *299* above.

418 De institutione canonicorum regulam 1   *Ante omnia . . . non inducatur*   83.1.163.82.89.153

    89] 9 *R*

    R1. 128, Vincent XIX 54 [123], *MF* II 47, 46. *CPL* 1839a, 1839b. The 'Regula secunda' and 'Regula tertia'. Ed. D. de Bruyne in *RB* 42 (1930) 318–26. Location number **163** should perhaps read **63**. See also *440* below.

419 De heremitis regulam <lib.> 2   *Cum diffinitione . . .*

    CPPM 2. 3591, incipit 'Communi definitione'. Ed. W. Hümpfner, *Iordani de Saxonia Liber Vitasfratrum* (New York, NY, 1943) 485.

420 Item aliam regulam ad sanctimoniales

    Source unidentified. This is perhaps the *Obiurgatio contra sanctimonialium dissensionem*, *CPL* 1838; or the *Transcriptio 'Comentarii' pro sanctimonialibus*, *CPL* 1839c.

421 De eo quod scriptum est in lege: Respice testamentum   103.97

    testamentum] te ipsum *R*

    R1. 255 (whole entry).

422 Ad Rominianum ep. 1   *Non haec . . . haerentem*   82

    CPL 262 *ep.* 15. *CSEL* 34/1. 35. **82** Bury = B13. 32, 'Epistole Augustini'.

423 De illo proverbio: Redemptio animae viri   95

    R1. 192 (whole entry).

Augustinus   *1. 424*

424   De processione Sancti Spiritus   <u>67</u>

>   R1. 136 (whole entry).

425   Soliloquiorum lib. 2   *Volventi . . . ut speramus*   <u>83</u>.<u>1</u>.<u>81</u>.<u>8</u>.<u>9</u>.<u>19</u>

>   83] 82 *R*

>   R1. 4 (title, incipit, location numbers), Vincent XIX 54 [1], *MF* II 28 (explicit). *CPL* 252. *CSEL* 89. 1. [**82** Bury = B13. 50a = BL MS Harley 3027, fols. 1r–20v, begins incomplete; BL MS Royal 7 B. IX, fol. 39v (Bury D. 6).]

426   Sermones numero 200   <u>117</u>.<u>103</u>.<u>1</u>.<u>95</u>.<u>94</u>

>   Whole entry from R1. 294 and Vincent XIX 54 [126], save the number of sermons.

427   De sermone Domini in monte lib. 2   *Sermonem . . . quod ortares*   <u>83</u>.<u>42</u>.<u>43</u>.<u>1</u>.<u>8</u>.<u>9</u>.<u>90</u>

>   83] 82 *R*

>   R1. 19 (title, incipit, location numbers), Vincent XIX 54 [113], *MF* II 87 (title, incipit, explicit). [**82** Bury = B13. 50d = BL MS Harley 3027, fols. 38v–86r; explicit does not correspond.]

428   De spe

>   spe] sper° *Add. 3470, queried by Tanner*

>   Source unidentified. This is probably *CPL* 284 *serm* 157 (*PL* 38. 859).

429   Speculum ecclesiae sive manuale   *Adesto mihi . . . sempiternaliter*

>   *MF* II 105 (whole entry).

430   Ut silentium habeatur in ecclesia   <u>95</u>

>   R1. 196 (whole entry). Same as *338* above.

p. 23]

431   De sacramento altaris   *Haeretici . . . impendas*   <u>43</u>.<u>12</u>

>   12] xii *R*

R1. 226 (title and numbers). The incipit and explicit, inexplicably, are those of *De nuptiis et concupiscentia* Book I, *310* above.

432 De sacerdotis periculo   *Si diligenter* . . .   <u>9</u>

     R1. 277 (whole entry).

433 De Salamonis praevaricatione   <u>166</u>

     R1. 304 (whole entry).

434 De spiritu et anima secundum quosdam lib. 1   *Quoniam dictum* . . . *aliud non*   65.63.82.83.15

     MF II 103. *Ps.* Augustine. *CPPM* 2. 153. **65** Ramsey = B68. 432a = BL MS Royal 5 F. xv, fols. 36r–50r, a codex that also includes Bernardus *85.21*; for other copies at Ramsey see B68. 304, 346, 386, and 483. / **82** Bury = BL MSS Royal 5 A. VIII, fol. 1r (Bury A. 52), and 7 B. IX, fol. 69r (Bury D. 6), both with explicit 'aliud non est quam ratio'.

435 Ad Simplicianum de diversis quaestionibus lib. 2   *Gratissimam* . . . *non recuso*   <u>152</u>

     R1. 28, Vincent XIX 54 [75], *MF* II 112. *CPL* 290. *CCSL* 44.

436 Disputationum lib. 4   *Te patrem* . . . *certissimum*

     Unidentified.

437 Alius liber soliloquiorum devotus stilum habens libri Confessionum; vocatur etiam ab aliquibus liber Meditationum. Secundus liber istius libri sic incipit: *Agnoscam te cognitor etc.* Finis: *Et reminiscere facis etc.*

     Ps. Augustine, *Soliloquia animae ad Deum*; *CPPM* 2. 3071. *PL* 40. 863.

438 Speculum   *Quis ignoret* . . .   <u>161</u>.<u>152</u>.<u>35</u>.<u>13</u>.<u>12</u>

     R1. 121 (whole entry).

439 Contra Secundinum Manichaeum lib. 1   *Benevolentia* . . .

     Whole entry from R1. 37, Vincent XIX 54 [133], and *MF* II 115.

440 Ad servos Dei   <u>15</u>

     R1. 287 (whole entry). See also *418* above.

Augustinus   *1. 441*

441 De judicio Salomonis inter 2 mulieres   *Inter duas . . .*

> *CPL* 284 *serm.* 10. *CCSL* 41. 153.

442 De spiritu et litera   *Lectis . . . quam ex ipso*   82.1.152.154

> R1. 64, 161, Vincent XIX 54 [42], *MF* II 124. *CPL* 343. *CSEL* 60. 155. **82** Bury = B13. 67b = Harvard, Houghton Library, MS Richardson 26, fol. 129r (Bury A. 6).

443 De symbolo ad catechumenos lib. 4   *Accipite . . . properavit*

> Vincent XIX 54 [104]. *CPL* 309 followed by *CPL* 401–403 (Quodvultdeus). *CCSL* 46. 185 followed by *CCSL* 60. 305, explicit (ib. 363) 'praeparauit'.

444 De symbolo contra Judaeos lib. 1   *Inter pressuras . . . optinet*   82.90.9.13.1.32

> R1. 240. Quodvultdeus; *CPL* 404. *CCSL* 60. 227. Same as *447* below. See also *33* above.

445 Item de symbolo serm. 1   *Sacrosancti . . . unus Deus*   82

> *CPL* 284 *serm.* 215. Ed. P. Verbraken in *RB* 68 (1958) 18–25. **82** Bury = B13. 43b; London, Wellcome Historical Medical Library, MS 801A, fol. 72r (Bury M. 27).

446 Super illud: Sicut deficit fumus   95

> R1. 179 (whole entry). Same as *356* above.

447 Expositio symboli contra Judaeos, paganos, Arrianos   *Inter pressuras . . . optinet*

> *MF* II 142 (whole entry). Same as *444* above. See also *33* above.

448 De symbolo   *Pro modulo . . . agnoscitur*

> Vincent XIX 54 [104]. *CPL* 284 *serm.* 214. Ed. P. Verbraken in *RB* 72 (1962) 14–21.

449 De symbolo ad Laurentium   *Quod quidem . . . fidelissime*

> Unidentified.

Augustinus *1. 458*

450 De Trinitate lib. 15 *Lecturus . . . concludam* 82.89.94.95.1.63.98

R1. 42, Vincent XIX 54 [9], *MF* II 2. *CPL* 329. *CCSL* 50–50A. **82** Bury = B13. 29a = Cambridge, King's College, MS 3 pt 1, fols. 6r–126r (Bury —).

451 De Trinitate et Trinitatis unitate serm. 1 *Legimus . . . et contra vitare* 82.103.15.42

R1. 215 (title, incipit, location numbers **82** to **15**), R1. 227 (location number **42**). *Ps.* Augustine; *CPPM* 1. 1030, 5563. *PL* 39. 2196. Explicit unidentified. **42** Reading = B71. 111c.

452 Item de Trinitatis unitate et trinitate tract. 1 *Catholicae . . . non intelligentes*

Whole entry from R1. 216 (title, incipit) and *MF* II 141 (title, incipit, explicit 'non intelligetis').

453 De theologia mistica

This work and its source are unidentified.

454 De Testamento Veteri 103

R1. 261 (whole entry).

455 De Trinitate et columba lib. 1

R1. 119 (whole entry).

456 De timore Dei serm. 3 *Recordare . . . cogeret* 95.15.1.25

25] xxv *R*

R1. 256–257. *CPL* 284 *serm.* 346–8. *PL* 39. 1522–9. Same as *459–461* below. See also *181* above and *475* below.

457 De tempore barbarico, ut supra in B. *Admonet . . .*

Vincent XIX 54 [105]. Same as *41* above.

458 Super id: Tibi derelictus est pauper 95

R1. 184 (whole entry). Same as *396* above.

Augustinus   *1. 459*

459   De timore Dei serm. 1   *Multa . . . regnum coelorum*   82.<u>95</u>.<u>15</u>.1.<u>25</u>

   25] xxv *R*

   R1. 256. *CPL* 284 *serm.* 347. *PL* 39. 1524. The location numbers (save **82** Bury) have been repeated from *456* above.

460   De eodem serm. 1   *Recordare . . . sanentur*   82

   CPL 284 *serm.* 346. Same as *181* above and *475* below. See *456* above.

461   De eodem serm. 1   *Non dubito . . . cogeret*   82

   R1. 257. *CPL* 284 *serm.* 348. *PL* 39. 1526. See *456* above.

462   De quantitate temporis tract. 1   *Temporis . . .*

   Tyconius, *Liber regularum* rule 5: *De temporibus*, incipit 'Temporis quantitas in scripturis'. *CPL* 709. Ed. F. Burkitt, *Texts and Studies: Contributions to Biblical and Patristic Literature* 3/1 (Cambridge 1895) 55.

463   Collatio de Trinitate per modum dialogi   *Cum me . . . nanciscantur*

   Ps. Augustine; *CPL* 379. *PL* 42. 1207.

464   Liber qui dicitur Inquisitio de Trinitate   *Quomodo Deus . . . fideliter*

   Quaestiones de trinitate et de Genesi; CPPM 2. 169. *PL* 42. 1171–6, followed (it seems) by the *Interrogationes et responsiones in Genesim, PL* 100. 516–66, explicit 'credo fideliter Christum'.

465   De vita beata lib. 1   *Si philosophiae . . . discessimus*   82.<u>152</u>.<u>153</u>.<u>159</u>.<u>103</u>.<u>13</u>

   159] 154 *R*

   R1. 2, Vincent XIX 54 [3], *MF* II 37. *CPL* 254. *CCSL* 29. 65. **82** Bury = B13. 81e.

466   De bono viduitatis   *Augustinus . . . in gratia Dei*   <u>95</u>.<u>152</u>

   Whole entry from R1. 118 (title, location numbers), Vincent XIX 54 [64], and *MF* II 78 (incipit, explicit).

Augustinus *1. 475*

467 De vita Christiana lib. 1   *Ut ego ... absentes*   <u>161</u>.<u>153</u>.<u>154</u>.<u>114</u>.<u>9</u>.<u>35</u>.<u>20</u>

 Whole entry from R1. 129 (incipit, location numbers), Vincent XIX 54 [21], and *MF* II 30 (title, incipit, explicit 'absentes conferamus'). Same as *504* below.

468 De veritate   *Quoniam dictum . . .*

 dictum] domini *R*

 R1. 321 (whole entry). Same as Anselmus *3.2*.

p. 24]

469 Ad Valerium episcopum ep. 1   *Ante omnia ... instructum*   82.<u>90</u>

 R1. 241. *CPL* 262 *ep*. 21. *CSEL* 34/1. 49. **82** Bury = B13. 32, 'Epistole Augustini'.

470 Ad Valentinum monachum ep.   *Venerunt ... vobiscum Dominus*   82.<u>94</u>. <u>105</u>.<u>9</u>.<u>15</u>.<u>1</u>.<u>139</u>

 R1. 323. *CPL* 262 *ep*. 214. *CSEL* 57. 380. **82** Bury = B13. 32, 'Epistole Augustini'.

471 Ad eundem   *Cresconium . . .*   <u>94</u>.<u>105</u>.<u>9</u>.<u>15</u>.<u>1</u>.<u>139</u>

 Whole entry from R1. 324 (title, incipit) and R1. 323 (location numbers).

472 De conductis ad vineam   <u>95</u>

 R1. 187 (whole entry).

473 De eo: Quod non volo facio   <u>95</u>

 R1. 189 (whole entry).

474 De eo: Si vis venire ad vitam, serva mandata   <u>95</u>

 R1. 190 (whole entry).

475 De vita aeterna serm. 1   *Recordamini ... ante sanentur*

 Same as *181* and *460* above. See also *456* above.

Augustinus *1. 476*

476 De sancta virginitate lib. 1   *Librum de . . . super exaltate*   82.42.1.32.9.43

   R1. 50 (title, location numbers), Vincent XIX 54 [65], *MF* II 77 (title, incipit, explicit). *CPL* 300. *CSEL* 41. 235.

477 Ad Volusianum de quibusdam quaestionibus ep. 1   *Bis legi . . . multum* 82.166

   R1. 310, Vincent XIX 54 [80]. *CPL* 262 *ep.* 137. *CSEL* 44. 96. **82** Bury = B13. 32, 'Epistole Augustini'.

478 Item ad Volusianum ep. 1   *De salute . . . ponitur*   82

   R1. 311. *CSEL* 262 *ep.* 132. *CSEL* 44. 79. **82** Bury = B13. 32, 'Epistole Augustini'.

479 De verbis Domini serm. 86   *Evangelium . . . conversi*   82.1.92.99.93

   99] 95 *R*

   R1. 103, Vincent XIX 54 [117]. The number of the sermons indicates this to be a collection *De uerbis Domini et de uerbis apostoli*, the two groups frequently appearing together with consecutive numbering; typical collections are in Bodl. MS Bodley 159 (89 sermons) and CUL MS Gg. 1. 25 (88 sermons). The incipit is that of *De uerbis Domini serm.* 1 (*PL* 38. 636). The explicit is that of the benediction common to most of these sermons, 'conuersi ad Dominum etc.'. **82** Bury = B13. 19.

480 De verbis apostoli serm. 24   *Audivimus . . . exigat*   82.1.92.99.93

   99] 95 *R*

   R1. 103, Vincent XIX 54 [118]. The incipit is that of *De uerbis apostoli serm.* 2 (*PL* 38. 729); the explicit is that of *De uerbis apostoli serm.* 24 (*PL* 38. 909). A similar collection of 24 sermons may be found, for example, in CUL MSS Ii. 3. 23, fol. 152r, and Ii. 1. 28, fol. 123v.

481 De verbis apostoli serm. 33   *Audivimus . . . et vivere*

   The incipit is that of *De uerbis apostoli serm.* 2 (*PL* 38. 729); the explicit is that of *De uerbis apostoli serm.* 34 (*PL* 39. 1962). A similar collection, containing 34 sermons and beginning with *De uerbis apostoli serm.* 1, may be seen in Bodl. MS Laud Misc. 136, fol. 77r.

482 De verbis Jacobi: An omnia etc.

   Vincent XIX 54 [121] (whole entry).

Augustinus   *1. 491*

483 De verbis Jacobi: Qui tota etc.

> Vincent XIX 54 [13] (whole entry).

484 Ad Vincentium ep. 1   *Accepi . . . curaverint*   82

> Vincent XIX 54 [83]. Same as *82* above. **82** Bury = B13. 32, 'Epistole Augustini'.

485 De communi vita clericorum serm. 2

> Source unidentified. *CPL* 284 *serm.* 355–6. Ed. C. Lambot, *Stromata patristica et mediaevalia* 1 (Utrecht 1950) 123–43.

486 De 7 vitiis capitalibus   *In lectione . . . redimere*

> Same as *180, 228,* and *360* above.

487 De verae vitae cognitione lib. 1   *Sapientia . . . condidit*   82.55.46.152. 60

> 60] 160 *R*
>
> R1. 108. Honorius Augustodunensis; see E. Portalié in *DTC* 1. 2309. *PL* 40. 1005. Explicit unidentified. Same as *86* above. **82** Bury = Cambridge, Pembroke College, MS 87, fol. 139v (Bury E. 11); explicit does not correspond.

488 De 4 virtutibus cardinalibus   *Quatuor . . .*   15.50.154

> R1. 243. Martin of Braga; *CPL* 1080. Same as Martinus *364.1,* Seneca *543.18.*

489 De voto reddendo   *Dominis eximiis . . . honoratur*

> The incipit is that of the salutation; explicit 'honorabiles et desiderabiles filii'. Same as *30* above.

490 De S. Vincentio serm. 1   *Oculis . . . Deum*   15

> R1. 283. *CPL* 284 *serm.* 277. *PL* 38. 1257. See *79* above.

491 Item de eodem serm. 1   *Vincentii . . . in nobis*

> *CPL* 284 *serm.* 277A. Ed. G. Morin, *Miscellanea Agostiniana* 1 (Rome 1930) 243.

Augustinus   *1. 492*

492 Item de eodem serm. 1   *In passione . . . sanctorum ejus*

R1. 284. Dubious; *CPL* 284 *serm.* 276. *PL* 38. 1255 (and see also *CSEL* 21. 273).

493 De utilitate psalmorum   *Quoniam grata . . . laudabit*

Nicetas of Remesiana, *De utilitate hymnorum*; *CPL* 649. Ed. C. Turner, *JTS* 24 (1923) 234, incipit (near the beginning of c. 3; Turner's B family of manuscripts omit cc. 1 and 2) 'Quam sint grata', explicit (p. 241) 'laudabunt Dominum'. Attributed to Augustine in, for example, Bodl. MS Rawlinson C. 531, fol. 183r, incipit 'Quam grata sit'.

494 De videndo Deo ad Ytalicam   *Non solum . . . explicare*   82.<u>103</u>.<u>109</u>

R1. 252. *CPL* 262 *ep.* 92. *CSEL* 34/2. 436. **82** Bury = B13. 32, 'Epistole Augustini'.

495 De videndo Deo ad Paulinam lib.   *Memor . . . valeamus*   82.<u>81</u>.<u>1</u>.<u>95</u>

R1. 68, Vincent XIX 54 [78], *MF* II 64. *CPL* 262 *ep.* 147. *CSEL* 44. 274. See also *248* above. **82** Bury = B13. 50j = BL MS Harley 3027, fol. 192v, ends incomplete; and B13. 32, 'Epistole Augustini'.

496 De visitatione infirmorum lib. 2   *Visitationis . . . justificatis*   82.<u>160</u>

R1. 107. *Ps.* Augustine; see E. Portalié in *DTC* 1. 2310. *PL* 40. 1147. **82** Bury = Cambridge, Pembroke College, MS 87, fol. 130v (Bury E. 11).

497 De conflictu vitiorum et virtutum secundum quosdam lib. 1   *Apostolica . . . fidem*   82.81.43.19.35

R1. 204, *MF* II 55. Ambrose Autpert; see E. Portalié in *DTC* 1. 2310. *CCCM* 27B. 909, explicit 'fidem praebeto'; these words, the end of c. 26 (p. 929), sometimes conclude this text, in the tradition that attributes it to Augustine. Same as Gregorius *203.12* and Leo *343.3*. **82** Bury = Cambridge, Pembroke College, MS 87, fol. 134v (Bury E. 11), explicit does not match.

498 Ad Valerium comitem de institutione vitae   82.<u>81</u>.<u>89</u>.<u>90</u>.<u>32</u>

81] 1 *R*

R1. 207. Probably Book I of *De nuptiis et concupiscentia ad Valerium* (*310* above), *CPL* 350.

499 De voto reddendo ad Armentarium, in A.

See *30* above.

Augustinus *1. 509*

500 De decem virginibus serm. 1   *Inter parabolas* . . .

   CPL 289 *quaestio* 59. *CCSL* 44A. 110. See *404* above.

501 Commonitorium de videndo Deo   *Sicut prius* . . .

   This entry may be taken from the *Retractationes*, in which the incipit reads 'Sicut praesens rogaui'; however, there is no other evidence that this source was used directly. Same as *178* above.

502 De Christianis bonis et malis   1

   R1. 290 (whole entrry).

503 De doctrina Christianorum   *Locutus est* . . . *ad Dominum*   163.161

   doctrina] disciplina *R MF*

   Whole entry from R1. 153 (title, incipit, location numbers) and *MF* II 29 (title, incipit, explicit). Same as *101* above.

504 De vita Christiana   *Ut ego peccator* . . . *absentes*   82

   R1. 129, *MF* II 30. Pelagius; *CPL* 730. *PL* 40. 1031. Same as *467* above.

505 De persecutione Christiana   *Frequenter* . . . *insidiis*   82

   R1. 131. Jerome; *CPL* 606. *CCSL* 78. 556. Same as Jeronimus *281.116*.

506 De doctrina Christiana lib. 4   *Duae sunt* . . .   65

   R1. 31, Vincent XIX 54 [51]. The incipit is that of Book I. Same as *105* above. See also *176* above.

507 De militia Christiana

   Source unidentified. Same as Basil *78.5* below. Attributed to Augustine with the title *De militia spirituali* in, for example, CUL MS Ff. 1. 14, fols. 90v–101v.

508 Yponosticon, supra in J.

   See *226* above.

509 Ad Ypponensem ecclesiam ep. 1   *Utinam* . . . *fratres*   82

   CPL 262 *ep.* 78. *CSEL* 34/2. 331. **82** Bury = B13. 32, 'Epistole Augustini'.

79

Augustinus *1. 510*

510 Ad cives Ypponenses ep. 1   *Imprimis . . . orate*   82

> Imprimis *queried by Tanner*
>
> CPL 262 *ep.* 122. *CSEL* 34/2. 742. **82** Bury = B13. 32, 'Epistole Augustini'.

511 Super illud Ysaiae: Vinea facta est   *Dei organa . . . laudes*

> organa *queried by Tanner*
>
> Dubious; CPL 417a. Ed. M. Bogaert in *RB* 75 (1965) 109.

p. 25]

> Horum omnium in libro Retractationum reperiuntur 93 tantum volumina, quae continent libros 232; caeteros enim nondum fecerat quando istos retractavit. Inveniuntur autem ejus libri cum epistolis et tractatibus circiter 1030, exceptis sermonibus et aliis parvis, quorum non est numerus. Fertur autem scripsisse libellum De spiritu et anima, qui apud scolasticos praecipue habetur, sed non videtur liber ille stilum Augustini sapere nec inter Augustini libros in armariis publicis et antiquis invenitur. E[s]t autem liber ille procul dubio utilissimus et eleganter, diserte atque compendiose compositus. Et quibusdam videtur ex diversis libris Augustini ad compendium extractus per Magistrum Hugonem de S. Victore. Haec Vincentius in Speculo historiali lib. 19 c. 54.[a]
>
> Et sciendum quod B. Augustinus ante conversionem suam scripsit De pulcro et apto libros tres. Post conversionem vero suam ad huc cathecumenus scripsit libros Soliloquiorum, De immortalitate animae, De vita beata, De ordine rerum, De achademicis, De disciplinis liberalibus.[b] Post baptismum vero scripsit De confessionibus, De moribus, De Trinitate, et alia quae superius recitantur.[c]

> habetur] non habetur *Add. 3470*
>
> [a] Vincent XIX 55. [b] ibid. XIX 50. [c] ibid. XIX 54.

2 AMBROSIUS   sanctus doctor archiepiscopus Mediolanensis in Lumbardia floruit tempore Valentis, Gratiani et Theodosii imperatorum circa anno Christi 385.

> *Registrum* 3, Vincent XVIII 32 (references are followed by numbers in brackets [1, 2, etc.] that indicate the sequence of titles in the chapter), *Manipulus*

florum III, Cassiodorus I. 1. 5, 3. 1, 3. 6, 8. 10. This entry is alphabetized by keyword.

1 De archa Noae lib. 1   <u>99</u>

   Whole entry from R3. 4 and Vincent XVIII 32 [17].

2 De S. Abrahamo lib. 2   *Abraham . . . vitiorum est*   13.<u>139</u>.<u>63</u>.161

   Whole entry from R3. 38 (location numbers), Vincent XVIII 32 [18], and *MF* III 34 (title, incipit, explicit).

3 De Abel et Caym lib. 2   <u>99</u>

   R3. 5 (whole entry).

4 De Assenech filia Pontifaris   *Et factum . . . in terra Egiptii*   82.<u>1</u>.<u>8</u>.167

   R3. 69. Anonymous. Ed. P. Batiffol, *Livre de la prière d'Aseneth*, Studia patristica 2 (Paris 1890) 88–115.

5 De passione S. Agnetis   82

   Vincent XVIII 32 [2]. *Ps.* Ambrose. *CPL* 2159. *BHL* 156.

6 De aquis coelestibus   <u>161</u>

   R3. 28 (whole entry).

7 Super Apocalipsin   <u>1</u>.<u>43</u>.<u>111</u>

   R3. 68 (whole entry).

8 Contra Auxentium lib. 3   <u>94</u>

   R3. 54 (whole entry).

9 De bono animae   <u>94</u>.97

   R3. 52 (whole entry save the suspect **97**).

10 De passione Agricolae   <u>163</u>

   R3. 44 (whole entry). Same as *88* below.

Ambrosius 2. 11

11 Contra Auxentium Valentiniano lib. 1   *Dalmatius . . . novi*   82.163.165

> CPL 160 *ep.* 75 (*al.* 21). CSEL 82/3. 74.

12 De benedictionibus patriarcharum lib. 1   *Primum . . . Apollo*   82.94.95. 19.35.13.63

> R3. 34, Vincent XVIII 32 [23], *MF* III 23. CPL 132. CSEL 32/2. 125, explicit (160) 'Apollo rigauit'. Same as *17* and *64* below. **82** Bury = B13. 33a.

13 Super Beati immaculati lib. 1   *Licet . . . passus est*   82.42.39.153.154.9.43

> R3. 26, Vincent XVIII 32 [30]. CPL 141. CSEL 62. Same as *55* and *65* below. **82** Bury = B13. 150.

14 De traditione basilicae ep. 1   *Quoniam in . . . expleant*   82

> CPL 160 *ep.* 76 (*al.* 20). CSEL 82/3. 108. **82** Bury = Cambridge, Pembroke College, MS 42, fol. 144r (Bury A. 61).

15 De beatitudinibus   20

> 20] xx *R*
>
> R3. 82 (whole entry).

16 Item de basilicis tradendis contra Auxentium ep. 1   *Video vos . . . donavit*   82

> Vincent XVIII 32 [33]. CPL 160 *ep.* 75a (*al.* 21a). CSEL 82/3. 82.

17 De patriarchis secundum Cassiodorum lib. 7

> Cassiodorus I. 1. 5 (whole entry). Same as *12* above and *64* below.

18 De consolatione Valentiniani lib. 1   *Et si incrementum . . . recompenses*   161. 163.95.105.89.43

> Whole entry from R3. 37 (title, location numbers) and *MF* III 32 (title, incipit, explicit). Same as *89* and *90* below.

19 De corpore et sanguine Domini   *Hiis abluta . . .*

> This is a compilation of excerpts from the *De mysteriis* (CPL 155) nos. 43–51, 52–4, 57 (CSEL 73. 107–115) and the *De sacramentis* (CPL 154) IV nos. 13–16, 19–28, and V nos. 5–8 (CSEL 73. 51–62), attributed to Heriger of Lobbes. It survives, for example, in Troyes BM MS 1961, fols. 121v–128r.

Ambrosius 2. 26

20 De diversitate et pluralitate coelorum <u>161</u>

>   R3. 27. This brief work, made of excerpts from the *Hexaemeron*, travelled with two similar compositions, *6* above and *66* below; see the discussion at R3. 27. [**82** Bury = this work appears in the table of contents of Cambridge, Pembroke College, MS 42, fol. 19r (Bury A. 61).]

21 Super Cantica Canticorum

>   Source unidentified. Probably this is one of the several collections of excerpts concerning the Canticles from Ambrose's various writings which circulated in the middle ages. The commonest is that of William of St Thierry, *Excerpta de libris beati Ambrosii super Cantica canticorum*, CCCM 87. 207–384.

p. 26]

22 De S. David apologia lib. 1   *Apologiam . . . mercarentur*   82.<u>94</u>.<u>95</u>.<u>105</u>.<u>89</u>. 43

>   R3. 25, Vincent XVIII 32 [24], *MF* III 18. *CPL* 135. *CSEL* 32/2. 299. **82** Bury = B13. 84f; Cambridge, Pembroke College, MS 42, fol. 158rb (Bury A. 61).

23 Exameron, id est de 6 diebus lib. 6   *Tantum opinionis . . . perpetuitas*   82.<u>43</u>.94.95.89.81.85

>   89 *may be* 39 *R*

>   R3. 7, Vincent XVIII 32 [16], *MF* III 2. *CPL* 123. *CSEL* 32/1. 1. **82** Bury = B13. 206.

24 De excessu fratris sui lib. 2   *Deduximus . . . timere*   82.<u>94</u>.<u>95</u>.<u>48</u>.<u>32</u>.<u>19</u>

>   48] 43 *R*

>   R3. 35, Vincent XVIII 32 [13], *MF* III 3. *CPL* 157. *CSEL* 73. 209.

25 De vita et ordinatione episcoporum   35.<u>43</u>.<u>104</u>

>   104] 164 *R*

>   R3. 46 (whole entry). Same as *26* below.

26 De observantia episcoporum lib.   *Audite . . . promisisti*   82.<u>9</u>.<u>1</u>.<u>104</u>.15.58

>   R3. 1. *Ps*. Ambrose; *CPL* 171a. *PL* 17. 567. Same as *25* above and *75* below, and see also *59* below. **82** Bury = Cambridge, Pembroke College, MS 42, fol. 15r (Bury A. 61); incipit is that of c. 2, which has its own three-line initial.

Ambrosius   2. 27

27 Egesippum ab eo translatum historiam   *Historiae* . . .   *Parthico* . . .   82. 164.118.161.95

> R3. 47. *Ps.* Ambrose; see the note before *CPL* 170. Concerning this translation see *CSEL* 66/2. xxv–xxxi. *PL* 15. 1961. Incipit 'Historiae' is that of the prologue, 'Parthico' that of Book I. Same as Egesippus *163.1*. See also Josephus *296.1*.

28 De consecratione ecclesiarum lib. 1   *Morem* . . . *erit*   82.35.105

> R3. 62. Author uncertain (*ps.* Remigius, *ps.* Ambrose, *ps.* Ivo); attributed to Ambrose in Oxford, Merton College, MS 118, fol. 219v. *PL* 131. 845. **82** Bury = B13. 84e. Same as Yvo *667.7*.

29 Epistolarum ad diversos 78   lib. 8   *Pulcrum* . . .   82.94.95.9.19.35

> R3. 13, Vincent XVIII 32 [38]. *CPL* 160. *CSEL* 82 pts. 1–3. Incipit 'Pulchre' is that of *ep.* 1 (*CSEL* 82/1. 3). **82** Bury = B13. 46b = Cambridge, Pembroke College, MS 42, fol. 20v (Bury A. 61) containing a collection of 79 letters (but Kirkestede's table of contents on fol. i^r says 78 letters) in 8 books.

30 De passione S. Emerencianae ecclesiae Vercellensi ep. 1   *Conficior* . . . *temulentia*

> Vincent XVIII 32 [2]. *CPL* 160 *ep.* 63 extra coll. 14 (*al. ep.* 63). *CSEL* 82/3. 235. Same as *60* below.

31 De fuga saeculi lib. 1   *Frequens* . . . *hauserunt*   82.89.94.95.42

> R3. 21, Vincent XVIII 32 [5], *MF* III 26. *CPL* 133. *CSEL* 32/2. 163. **82** Bury = B13. 84b.

32 De fide expositionem   *Abraham* . . . *non poterit*   82.42.43.1.20

> R3. 66. Perhaps the same as *33* and *82* below, or perhaps *CPL* 150–51 together; incipit and explicit unidentified. (The incipit is conceivably that of *De Abraham*, inc. 'Abraham libri huius titulus est', but a connection with this title is not evident and the explicit does not correspond.)

33 De fide Trinitatis lib. 5   *Regina* . . . *metitur*   82.95.105.8.43

> R3. 3. *CPL* 150. *CSEL* 78. Same as *82* below. **82** Bury = B13. 59, 204.

34 De Gedeon   *Jerobaal* . . . *scrutatur*   166

> R3. 48, *MF* III 20. *CPL* 151. *CSEL* 79. 1, explicit 'scrutatur dei'. Same as *73* below.

35 De inventione sanctorum Gervasii et Protasii tract. 2   *Domine . . . reliquias*
   82.94

   R3. 6, Vincent XVIII 32 [1]. *CPL* 160 *ep.* 77 (*al.* 22). *CSEL* 82/3. 126. **82**
   Bury = Cambridge, Pembroke College, MS 42, fol. 155r (Bury A. 61).

36 De Helia et jejunio lib. 1   *Divinum ad . . . pietatis*   94

   Whole entry from R3. 51 (title, location number), Vincent XVIII 32 [25],
   and *MF* III 12 (title, incipit, explicit). Same as *37* below.

37 De utilitate et laude jejunii   43.161.163

   R3. 30 (whole entry). Same as *36* above.

38 De incarnatione Christi lib. 1   *Debitum . . . intelligibilium*   94.105.9.104.25

   Whole entry (save the three suspect location numbers) from R3. 50 (title and
   location numbers), Vincent XVIII 32 [8], and *MF* III 25 (title, incipit, explicit).
   See also *59* below.

39 De Jacob et vita beata lib. 2   *Necessarius . . . peremptus*   82.95.105.8.1

   R3. 24 (title, incipit, location numbers), Vincent XVIII 32 [21], *MF* III 27
   (title, incipit, explicit). *CPL* 130. *CSEL* 32/2. 3. **82** Bury = B13. 84c.

40 De S. Joseph lib. 1   *Sanctorum . . . patrem*   82.94.95.105.111

   R3. 33, Vincent XVIII 32 [22]. *CPL* 131. *CSEL* 32/2. 73.

41 De S. Johanne Baptista serm. 1   *Hodie . . . non sufficit*

   Petrus Chrysologus; *CPL* 227 *serm.* 127, and cf. 930. *CCSL* 24B. 782; explicit
   unidentified.

42 De infirmitate hominis cum interpellationibus Job et David

   Vincent XVIII 32 [37] (whole entry).

43 De interpellatione Job lib. 2   *Multas . . . intellectum*

   MF III 14 and 16 (whole entry).

44 De interpellatione David et psalmi 72   lib. 2   *Multi . . . saecula saeculorum*

   MF III 15 and 17 (whole entry).

Ambrosius   2. 45

45 Ad Irenaeum   <u>162</u>

   R3. 39 (whole entry).

46 De vera innocentia   <u>20</u>

   R3. 79 (whole entry).

47 Super Lucam omelia vel lib. 10   *Scripturi . . . quamplures*   82.<u>118</u>.<u>43</u>.<u>42</u>. <u>154.119</u>

   154.119] 114.159 *R*

   R3. 11, Vincent XVIII 32 [31]. *CPL* 143. *CCSL* 14. 1. **82** Bury = B13. 25 = Bodl. MS e Musaeo 27, p. viii (Bury A. 67), explicit 'complures fuisse' (p. 229).

48 De ligno vitae   <u>15</u>

   R3. 77 (whole entry).

49 De musica lib. 1

   This work and its source are unidentified.

50 De misteriis lib. 1   *De moralibus . . . operetur*   82.<u>105</u>.<u>116</u>.<u>42</u>.43.19

   R3. 9, Vincent XVIII 32 [9]. *CPL* 155. *CSEL* 73. 87. For **82** Bury see B13. 187, 195.

51 De media nocte   <u>35.161.163</u>

   R3. 74 (whole entry save two suspect location numbers).

52 De bono mortis lib. 1   *Quoniam superiori . . . a saeculis*   82.<u>163</u>.<u>161</u>.<u>105</u>.<u>89</u>

   R3. 36, Vincent XVIII 32 [20]. *CPL* 129. *CSEL* 32/1. 703. **82** Bury = B13. 46a = Cambridge, Pembroke College, MS 42, fol. 1r (Bury A. 61); Cambridge, Pembroke College, MS 1, fol. 17v (Bury A. 92), in the rubric 'Liber beati *Anselmi* de bono mortis' Kirkestede has corrected the author to 'Ambrosii'.

53 De vinea Nabuthae lib. 1   *Nabuthae . . . mereamur*   82.<u>1</u>.<u>22</u>.<u>63</u>.<u>139</u>.<u>128</u>

   R3. 14 (title, incipit, location numbers **1** to **128**), R3. 42 (location number **82**), Vincent XVIII 32 [28], *MF* III 11 (incipit, explicit). *CPL* 138. *CSEL* 32/2. 469. **82** Bury = B13. 46c = Cambridge, Pembroke College, MS 42, fol. 173r

Ambrosius   2. 61

(Bury A. 61), with this title one of the handful that is singled out in Kirkestede's table of contents.

54   De officiis ministrorum lib. 3   *Non arrogans . . . conferant*   82.<u>163</u>.118. <u>93</u>.<u>94</u>

R3. 12, Vincent XVIII 32 [12], *MF* III 1. *CPL* 144. *CCSL* 15. **82** Bury = B13. 205.

55   Super Octonarium, supra in B. lib. 1   *Licet . . .*   82.<u>42</u>.<u>39</u>.<u>153</u>.<u>154</u>.<u>9</u>

R3. 26 (whole entry). Same as *13* above and *65* below.

56   Super prophetas commentarios, per Cassiodorum

Cassiodorus I. 3. 6 (whole entry).

p. 27]

57   De paradiso lib. 1   *De paradiso . . . spiritualia*   82.<u>94</u>.<u>89</u>.<u>114</u>.<u>8</u>.<u>19</u>

94] 95 *R*

R3. 22 (title, location numbers), Vincent XVIII 32 [3], *MF* III 29 (title, incipit, explicit). *CPL* 124. *CSEL* 32/1. 265. **82** Bury = B13. 84d.

58   De poenitentia unica lib. 2   *Poenitentia . . . absolvere*   42.43.111.<u>9</u>.<u>19</u>.<u>13</u>.<u>15</u>

R3. 8, Vincent XVIII 32 [4]. The incipit is that of the *pseudo*-Ambrosian *De poenitentia* of Victor Cartennensis (*CPL* 854) and the explicit is that of Ambrose's *De poenitentia* (*CPL* 156), here treated as Books I and II. **42** Reading = B71. 103a.

59   De cura pastorali lib. 1   *Debitum . . . intelligibilium*

R3. 31, Vincent XVIII 32 [11]. The title refers to *CPL* 171a, *ps*. Ambrose. The incipit and explicit, however, are those of the *De incarnationis dominicae sacramento* (*CPL* 152), *38* above. (Title) same as *25–26* above and *75* below.

60   De eligendo pontifice ad Vercellenses lib. 1   82.<u>95</u>.<u>89</u>.<u>116</u>.<u>8</u>.<u>1</u>.<u>115</u>

R3. 23, Vincent XVIII 32 [15]. *CPL* 160 *ep*. 63. Same as *30* above.

61   Super epistolas Pauli secundum Cassiodorum lib. 14   <u>95</u>.<u>111</u>.<u>108</u>.<u>35</u>.<u>98</u>

Whole entry from R3. 2, Vincent XVIII 32 [32], and Cassiodorus I. 8. 10.

Ambrosius   2. 62

62 De paschali misterio   <u>161</u>.<u>163</u>

   R3. 32 (whole entry).

63 De poenitentia ep. 4

   MF III 24 (whole entry).

64 De patriarchis supra in B.   *Primum omnium . . . rigavit*   <u>82</u>.<u>9</u>.<u>4</u>.<u>95</u>.<u>116</u>.<u>19</u>.<u>35</u>

   9.4] 94 *R*

   R3. 34, *MF* III 23. Same as *12* and *17* above.

65 Super psalterium, secundum Cassiodorum, et specialiter super Beati immaculati   <u>43</u>

   Whole entry from R3. 65 (title, location number) and Cassiodorus I. 3. 1 (title). Same as *13* and *55* above.

66 De quantitate solis et lunae   <u>161</u>

   R3. 29 (whole entry).

67 Quaestiones de Veteri et Novo Testamento   <u>108</u>.<u>167</u>

   R3. 73 (whole entry).

68 De tribus quaestionibus Salomonis   <u>43</u>.50

   R3. 64. Spurious; *CPL* 555. *CCSL* 69. 253. Same as *80* below.

69 Librum quid dicitur Recapitulatio   <u>154</u>.<u>22</u>.163

   R3. 57 (whole entry save the suspect **163**).

70 De sacramento regenerationis

   Source unidentified. Only fragments of this work survive; *CPL* 161.

71 Sermones declamatorii 75   <u>139</u>

   R3. 80, Vincent XVIII 32 [39]. See *CPL* 180–83.

Ambrosius 2. 81

72 Contra relationem Symmachi ep. *Cum vir . . . convenire* 82.<u>94</u>

   R3. 53. *CPL* 160 *ep.* 73 (*al.*18). *CSEL* 82/3. 34. **82** Bury = Cambridge, Pembroke College, MS 42, fol. 128r (Bury A. 61).

73 De Spiritu Sancto ad Gratianum lib. 3 *Jeroboal . . . scrutatur* 9.<u>35</u>.<u>15</u>.<u>20</u>

   20] 23 *R*

   Whole entry from R3. 70 and Vincent XVIII 32 [7]. Same as *34* above.

74 De sacramentis lib. 6 *De sacramentis . . . in omnia* 82.<u>1</u>.<u>42</u>.<u>20</u>.139

   R3. 10, Vincent XVIII 32 [10], *MF* III 10. *CPL* 154. *CSEL* 73. 13.

75 De dignitate sacerdotali lib. 1 *Si quis . . . promeruisti* <u>161</u>.<u>153</u>.<u>154</u>.15

   R3. 31 (location numbers), *MF* III 19 (title, incipit, explicit). *Ps.* Ambrose; *CPL* 171a. *PL* 17. 567. Same as *25* and *26* above, and see *59* above. [**82** Bury = Cambridge, Pembroke College, MS 42, fol. 14v (Bury A. 61), with rubric *De obseruancia episcoporum*.]

76 De simbolo ad Neophitos lib. 1

   Vincent XVIII 32 [35] (whole entry).

77 Ad Susannam virginem coruptam <u>163</u>.43.153

   R3. 41. Same as *91* below.

78 De judicio Salomonis de duabus mulieribus <u>163</u>

   R3. 43 (whole entry).

79 De poenitentia Salomonis <u>63</u>

   R3. 81 (whole entry).

80 De 3^{bus} quaestionibus Salomonis <u>43</u>.50

   R3. 64. Same as *68* above.

81 De silentio triplici primum tractatum *Tria sunt . . . praeparatum est* 168

   Hugh of Saint-Victor, *De uerbo incarnato*, collation I. *PL* 177. 315–18, explicit 'praeparatum est ab initio saeculi'. Same as Hugo *244.27*.

Ambrosius   2. 82

82 De Trinitate ad Gratianum lib. 5   *Regina . . . metitur*   82.<u>95</u>.<u>105</u>.<u>8</u>.<u>43</u>

>   R3. 3, *MF* III 30. Same as *33* above.

83 De S. Thobia lib. 1   *Lecto . . . perpetua*

>   Whole entry from Vincent XVIII 32 [26] and *MF* III 13.

84 De obitu Theodosii ep. 1   *Hoc nobis . . . hospicio*   82.<u>94</u>.<u>35</u>

>   R3. 55, Vincent XVIII 32 [34]. *CPL* 159. *CSEL* 73. 371. **82** Bury = Cambridge, Pembroke College, MS 42, fol. 147v (Bury A. 61).

85 De thema

>   This work and its source are unidentified.

86 De laude virginum lib. 3   *Si juxta . . . invenit*   82.<u>95</u>.<u>89</u>.42.43

>   R3. 15, Vincent XVIII 32 [27]. *CPL* 145. Ed. F. Gori, S. Ambrosii opera 14/1 (Milan 1989) 100. **82** Bury = B13. 33b. **42** Reading = Bodl. MS Rawlinson A. 376, fol. 1r.

87 De viduis lib. 3   *Bene . . . augeatis*   82.95.<u>89</u>.<u>9</u>.<u>19</u>

>   19] xix *R*

>   R3. 16. *CPL* 146. Ed. F. Gori, S. Ambrosii opera 14/1 (Milan 1989) 244. **82** Bury = B13. 33c.

88 De passione Vitalis et Agricolae   <u>163</u>

>   R3. 44 (whole entry). Same as *10* above.

89 De morte Valentiniani   <u>35</u>.<u>43</u>.166.167

>   R3. 63 (whole entry save two suspect numbers). Same as *18* above and *90* below.

90 De consolatione Valentiniani   *Et si incrementum . . . recompenses*   <u>161</u>.<u>163</u>.<u>95</u>.<u>105</u>.<u>89</u>

>   Whole entry from R3. 37 (title, location numbers), Vincent XVIII 32 [14], and *MF* III 32 (title, incipit, explicit). Entry identical with *18* above. Same as *89* above.

Anselmus   3.

91 De lapsu virginis consecratae lib. 1   *Audite . . . remedium*   82.89.42.43. 9.15.1

> R3. 17. *Ps.* Ambrose; *CPL* 651. Ed. E. Cazzaniga (Turin 1948). Works *91–93* often appear together; see, for example, BL MS Royal 5 F. IV, fol. 51r, in which this work (*91*) begins 'Audite' and in which cc. 9 and 10 (= *92* and *93*) are given separate rubrics. *PL* 16. 361 cc. 1–8. Same as 77 above and Jeronimus *281.206*. See also *92*, *93* below. **42** Reading = B71. 104b = Bodl. MS Rawlinson A. 376, fol. 95r.

92 Ad violatorem virginis ep. 1   *De te . . . sine malum*   82.15.1.39.20.19

> 20.19] xx.xix *R*

> R3. 18. Chapter 9 of the *De lapsu uirginis* (*91* above). See also 77 above and *93* below.

93 Ad virginem lapsam   *Quis consoletur . . . praestari cupio*

> R3. 19. Chapter 10 of *De lapsu uirginis* (*91* above). See also 77 and *92* above.

94 De virginitate lib. 2   *Nobile . . . servare*   161.82.1.15.83

> R3. 59. The incipit and explicit indicate that this entry contains both the *De uirginitate* (*CPL* 147) and the *Exhortatio ad virginitatem* (*CPL* 149). Ed. F. Gori, S. Ambrosii opera 14 (Milan 1989), 2. 12 and 198 respectively. Location numbers **161, 1, 15** are probably repeated from R3. 18 *De corrupcione uirginum* (*92* above).

95 De Ysaac et anima lib. 1   *In patre . . . custodire*   82.89.32.19.35.13.15

> R3. 20 (title, location numbers), Vincent 19, *MF* III 28 (title, incipit, explicit). *CPL* 128. *CSEL* 32/1. 641. **82** Bury = B13. 84a.

96 Super Ysaiam prophetam

> Source unidentified. Only fragments of this commentary survive; *CPL* 142.

p. 28]

3 ANSELMUS monachus et abbas de Becco et postea Cantuariensis archiepiscopus floruit circa A.D. 1094 et scripsit ea quae sequuntur.

> *Registrum* 33, *Manipulus florum* XII, *Mariale*; Vincent XXVI 71 was perhaps not used.

Anselmus *3*.

> For such a long entry, an unusually high percentage of its titles were based on manuscripts, most or all of them at Bury, and a large amount of corroborating evidence survives in the form of a general entry in the Bury catalogue (**82** Bury = B13. 18, 'Libri Anselmi archiepiscopi') and in the surviving Bury collections cited below (see esp. BL MS Royal 7 B. IX and Cambridge, Pembroke College, MS 1). Specifically, forty-two of the fifty-nine titles have accompanying incipits, or incipits and explicits, and most have an accompanying number **82** for Bury as well. These include the first thirty-seven titles in a row, with only four interruptions (*20, 30–31, 33*). The remaining titles are mostly scattered *Registrum* entries that Kirkestede had not already duplicated from Bury manuscripts.
> *Speculum coenobitarum* 49.
> Bale, *Index*, 31, 'ex utroque anglorum catalogo' (works *18–20, 24, 27–28, 34, 37, 39, 45, 47–54, 56, 59, 58*).
> Sharpe, *Latin Writers*, 59–61.

1 De conceptu virginali et originali peccato lib. 1   *Cum in omnibus . . . probari poterit*   82.42.94.9.19.1

> R33. 2, *MF* XII 6, and cf. Vincent XXVI 71. Sharpe, *Latin Writers*, 59. *SAO* 2. 139. Same as Augustinus *1.80*. **82** Bury = Bodl. MS e Musaeo 112, p. 306 (Bury J. 13); BL MS Royal 7 B. IX, fol. 133vb (Bury D. 6); Cambridge, Pembroke College, MS 1, fol. 69r (Bury A. 92). / **42** Reading = B71. 117b = Edinburgh UL MS 104 pt 2, fol. 40r.

2 De veritate et libero arbitrio et casu diaboli lib. 1   *Quoniam dictum . . . rectitudo*   82.163.94.42.153.8

> 153] 139 *R*

> R33. 8, *MF* XII 2, and cf. Vincent XXVI 71. Sharpe, *Latin Writers*, 60. *SAO* 1. 173. Incipit and explicit (probably taken from the *Manipulus florum*) are those of the *De ueritate* only; the location numbers are taken from the *Registrum*. This is a conflation of three titles, which appear in this sequence both in *MF* XII 2–4 and on the table of contents in Cambridge, Pembroke College, MS 1, as well as in the text of that manuscript (fols. 37r–46v, with a single preface to the three on fol. 37ra, 'Incipit prefacio in subditos tractatus'). Same as Augustinus *1.468*. See also *4* and *7* below. **82** Bury = BL MS Royal 7 B. IX, fol. 151ra–153rb (Bury D. 6); Cambridge, Pembroke College, MS 1, fol. 37r (Bury A. 92).

3 De concordia praescientiae divinae, praedestinationis et gratiae cum libero arbitrio lib. 1   *De tribus illis . . . impendere*   82.161.95.158.116

> R33. 5 (location numbers), *MF* XII 14 (title, incipit, explicit), and cf. Vincent XXVI 71. Sharpe, *Latin Writers*, 59. *SAO* 2. 245. The whole entry could come from the *Registrum* and the *Manipulus florum*, but Bury possessed several copies of this work. **82** Bury = Bodl. MS e Musaeo 112, pp. 262–304 (Bury J. 13);

Anselmus 3. 9

BL MS Royal 7 B. ix, fol. 121r–126v (Bury D. 6); Cambridge, Pembroke College, MS 1, fol. 63r (Bury A. 92).

4 De libero arbitrio lib. 1   *Quum liberum . . . interrogare*   82.<u>114</u>.<u>94</u>.42.<u>153</u>

    114] 118 *R*

R33. 16, *MF* XII 3. Sharpe, *Latin Writers*, 59. *SAO* 1. 207. **82** Bury = Bodl. MS e Musaeo 112, pp. 243–262 (Bury J. 13); BL MS Royal 7 B. ix, fol. 137r (Bury D. 6); Cambridge, Pembroke College, MS 1, fol. 40r (Bury A. 92). / **42** Reading = B71. 118f = Edinburgh UL MS 104, fol. 174r.

5 Cur Deus homo lib. 2   *Saepe et studiose . . . debemus*   82.94.43.<u>8</u>.80.<u>9</u>.1

R33. 6, *MF* XII 1, and cf. Vincent XXVI 71. Sharpe, *Latin Writers*, 59. *SAO* 2. 47. **82** Bury = Cambridge, Pembroke College, MS 1, fol. 47r (Bury A. 92).

6 De grammatico lib. 1   *De grammatico . . . non negabis*   82.<u>161</u>.<u>94</u>.<u>160</u>.1

R33. 21, and cf. Vincent XXVI 71. Sharpe, *Latin Writers*, 59. *SAO* 1. 145. **82** Bury = Cambridge, Pembroke College, MS 1, fol. 27r (Bury A. 92).

7 Item de casu diaboli lib. 1   *Illud apostoli . . . loquendi*   82.<u>94</u>.<u>116</u>.42.<u>153</u>

R33. 24 (title, location numbers), *MF* XII 4 (title, incipit, explicit), and cf. Vincent XXVI 71. Sharpe, *Latin Writers*, 59. *SAO* 1. 233. Same as Augustinus *1.111*. **82** Bury = Cambridge, Pembroke College, MS 1 fol. 42r (Bury A. 92).

8 De processione Spiritus Sancti lib. 1   *Negatur . . . latinitatis*   82.<u>42</u>.<u>8</u>.<u>129</u>.32

    129] 9.1 *R*

R33. 14, *MF* XII 7. Sharpe, *Latin Writers*, 59. *SAO* 2. 175. **82** Bury = BL MS Royal 7 B. ix, fol. 114v (Bury D. 6); Cambridge, Pembroke College, MS 1, fol. 56v (Bury A. 92).

9 Contra insipientem lib. 1   *Ergo Domine . . . benevolentia*   82

The incipit is that of an excerpt (cc. 2–4) from the *Proslogion* (*22* below); the explicit is that of the *Contra respondentem pro insipiente* (*10* below, ends 'beneuolentia, non maleuolentia, reprehendisti'). **82** Bury = BL MS Royal 7 B. ix, fols. 126v–128v (Bury D. 6), where three works follow one another with space left but no rubric for works *9* (fol. 126v), *10* (fol. 127), or *11* (fol. 127v); and Cambridge, Pembroke College, MS 1, fols. 34r–36r (Bury A. 92), where they were copied as one work (with internal rubrics, but with a single formal incipit and explicit).

Anselmus *3. 10*

10 Contra respondentem pro insipiente lib. 1   *Quoniam non . . . reprehendisti*
   82

   MF XII 12, and cf. Vincent XXVI 71. Sharpe, *Latin Writers*, 60. *SAO* 1. 130.
   See also *9* above. **82** Bury = BL MS Royal 7 B. ix, fols. 127v–128v (Bury
   D. 6); Cambridge, Pembroke College, MS 1, fol. 35r (Bury A. 92).

11 Disputationum pro insipiente lib. 1   *Dubitanti . . . suscipienda*   **82**

   MF XII 11. Gaunilo. *Liber pro insipiente aduersus S. Anselmum. SAO* 1. 125. See
   also *9* above. **82** Bury = BL MS Royal 7 B. ix, fol. 127r–v (Bury D. 6);
   Cambridge, Pembroke College, MS 1, fol. 34r (Bury A. 92).

12 Disputationis Judaei cum Christiano lib. 1   *Reverendo . . . pronunciabatur*
   82

   MF XII 15. Gilbert Crispin. Ed. B. Blumenkranz, Stromata patristica et
   mediaevalia 3 (Utrecht 1956). The incipit is that of the prefatory letter
   addressed to Anselm.

13 Disputatio inter Christianum et gentilem lib. 1   *Majestas . . . facientes*   **82**

   Ps. Anselm. Attributed to Anselm in, for example, BL MS Royal 5 E. xiv,
   fol. 70r, CUL MSS Dd. 1. 21, fol. 178r, and Gg. 5. 34, fol. 118r.

14 De similitudinibus lib. 1   *Voluntas tripliciter . . . in qua voluit*   82.<u>161</u>.
   83.<u>123</u>.<u>39</u>

   R33. 20, *MF* XII 16. *Ps.* Anselm (Alexander of Canterbury); Sharpe, *Latin
   Writers*, 61. See R. W. Southern and F. S. Schmitt, *Memorials of St. Anselm*
   (London 1969), 51. *PL* 159. 605. **82** Bury = Cambridge, Pembroke College,
   MS 1, fol. 1r (Bury A. 92), attributed to Anselm, and Pembroke College, MS
   20, fol. 50v (Bury J. 57), attributed to Anselm.

15 De incarnatione Verbi lib. 1   *Domino patri . . . inveniet*   <u>82</u>.94.<u>42</u>.8.<u>32</u>.<u>9</u>

   R33. 19, *MF* XII 5, and cf. Vincent XXVI 71. Sharpe, *Latin Writers*, 59. *SAO*
   2. 3. **82** Bury = BL MS Royal 7 B. ix, fol. 129r–131v (Bury D. 6); Cambridge,
   Pembroke College, MS 1, fol. 87v (Bury A. 92).

16 De sacramento altaris lib. 1   *Domino et amico . . . epistolam*   **82**

   Cf. Vincent XXVI 71. Sharpe, *Latin Writers*, 60 (*Ep. ad Waleramnum de sacramentorum diuersitate*). *SAO* 2. 239. Same as *42* below. **82** Bury = Cambridge,
   Corpus Christi College, MS 135, fol. 133r (Bury A. 83), in which this epistle is singled out from the collection by Kirkestede's table of contents;
   Cambridge, Pembroke College, MS 1, fol. 68v (Bury A. 92).

17 De fermentato et azimo ep. 1   *Anselmus ... repudiendum*   82.1.9.42.94.
161

> R33. 22, *MF* XII 8, and cf. Vincent XXVI 71. Sharpe, *Latin Writers*, 59. *SAO* 2. 223. **82** Bury = BL MS Royal 7 B. ix, fol. 120r (Bury D. 6); Cambridge, Pembroke College, MS 1, fol. 62r (Bury A. 92); and Cambridge, Corpus Christi College, MS 135, fol. 129r (Bury A. 83), in which this epistle is singled out from the collection in Kirkestede's table of contents.

18 De beatitudine et miseria lib. 1   *Notandum est ... diligunt*   73.83

> J. Déchanet, *Guillaume de Saint-Thierry: Lettre aux frères du Mont-Dieu*, SChr 223 (Paris 1975) 53ff, considers that a genuine sermon of Anselm underlies this work, though its surviving state – the state in which Kirkestede knew it – is not thought to be Anselm's direct handiwork. *PL* 184. 353–64.

19 De eterna beatitudine tract. 1   *Multi homines ... depereunt*   82.9.32

> R33. 35. Eadmer; ed. R. W. Southern & F. S. Schmitt, *Memorials of St Anselm* (London 1969), 274–88. **82** Bury = Cambridge, Corpus Christi College, MS 135, fol. 147r (Bury A. 83), where Kirkestede has provided the missing title in the upper margin.

20 Soliloquiorum de Trinitate lib. 3

> The source for this entry is perhaps a misreading of the title of *21* below in Vincent of Beauvais, 'Scripsit et monologion id est soliloquium de sancta Trinitate'. However, the *Catalogus*'s list of Anselm's works does not otherwise seem to have relied on Vincent.

21 Monologion, id est soliloquium lib. 1   *Si quis ... trinus et unus*   82.15.35.
166.97

> 166.97] 164.94 *R*

> R33. 9, *MF* XII 9, and cf. Vincent XXVI 71. Sharpe, *Latin Writers*, 60. *SAO* 1. 13. **82** Bury = BL MS Royal 7 B. ix, fol. 105r (Bury D. 6); Cambridge, Pembroke College, MS 1, fol. 74v (Bury A. 92). / **15** (St Albans) = Bodl. MS Laud Misc. 264, fol. 45r.

22 Prosologion, id est alloquium de Deo lib. 1   *Eya ... benedictus*   82.151.36.
13.39.20

> R33. 7, *MF* XII 10, and cf. Vincent XXVI 71. Sharpe, *Latin Writers*, 60. *SAO* 1. 97. See also *9* above. **82** Bury = BL MS Royal 7 B. ix, fol. 126v (Bury D. 6); Cambridge, Pembroke College, MS 1, fol. 84r (Bury A. 92).

Anselmus *3. 23*

23 De redemptione humana meditatio   *Anima Christiana . . . possideat*   82. 92.94.155.157

> R33. 38, and cf. R33. 18. Sharpe, *Latin Writers*, 60 (*Meditationes* and *Orationes*). *SAO* 3. 84 (*meditatio* 3).

24 De planctu virginitatis amissae meditatio   *Anima mea . . . misericordia tua*   82.92.94.155.157

> Cf. R33. 18. *SAO* 3. 80 (*meditatio* 2). The location numbers are repeated from *23* above.

25 Ad concitandum timorem meditatio   *Terret me . . . interminata*   82.92.94. 155.157

> Cf. R33. 18. *SAO* 3. 76 (*meditatio* 1). The location numbers are repeated from *23* above.

26 De passione Christi meditatio   *Domine Jesu . . . quia pius*   82.92.94.155. 157

> *SAO* 3. 6 (*oratio* 2). The location numbers are repeated from *23* above.

27 Item orationes de sancto cruce, de S. Maria, de S. Johanne Baptista, de sanctis Petro et Paulo, de S. Johanne evangelista, de S. Stephano, de S. Martino, de S. Nicholao, de S. Benedicto, de S. Maria Magdal[ena], pro amicis et inimicis, ad corpus Domini suscipiendum. Item orationem cotidianam, principium: Omnipotens Deus. Item orationem Sub cujus nomine regitur ecclesia.

> For bibliography concerning the authorship of the orations attributed to Anselm, see Sharpe, *Latin Writers*, 60. The following orations are named here in sequence: *or.* 4, 5–6, 8, 9–10, 11, 13, *De S. Martino*, 14, 15, 16, 18–19, 3, 1, 17.

28 De excellentia B. Virginis lib. 1   *Supereminentiam . . . famulemur*   82

> *Ps.* Anselm; perhaps Eadmer according to Sharpe, *Latin Writers*, 104. *PL* 159. 557–80.

29 Super illud evangelii: Intravit Jesus expositio   *Intravit . . . haec est pars optima*   82.<u>165</u>.4<u>2</u>.<u>126</u>

> 42] 43 *R*

> R33. 11. Ralph d'Escures; Sharpe, *Latin Writers*, 60; R. W. Southern & F. S. Schmitt, *Memorials of St Anselm* (London 1969), 17. *PL* 158. 644 (*hom.* 9).

Anselmus 3. 35

30 Sigillum S. Mariae 73.<u>42</u>.<u>15</u>.<u>126</u>.<u>139</u>

    42] 43 *R*

    Honorius Augustodunensis. The source for this title was probably a manuscript; attribution to Anselm was common. It appears among the works of Anselm in Cambridge, Peterhouse, MS 245, fol. 96r, and see the entry in the York catalogue, B120. 349. Location numbers **42** to **139** are taken through copying error from R33. 11 (i.e. the preceding work, *29* above).

31 Super Cantica Canticorum <u>8</u>

    R33. 33 (whole entry), and cf. Vincent XXVI 71.

32 De conceptione S. Mariae serm. 1 *Principium quo salus . . . genuisse* 82

    Eadmer; Sharpe, *Latin Writers*, 104. Ed. H. Thurston & T. Slater, *Eadmeri tractatus de conceptione Sanctae Mariae* (Freiburg im Br. 1904) 1–52. **82** Bury = BL MS Royal 6 B. x, fol. 2r (Bury A. 88), attributed to Anselm in Kirkestede's rubric in the upper margin, and in his table of contents, fol. 1r.

33 De assumptione B. Mariae serm. 1 *Ades nobis . . .* 73.65

    Mariale fol. 12r. Ambrose Autpert; *CPL* 368 *serm*. 208. *CCCM* 27B. 1027. The title and incipit are probably taken from the *Mariale*. Same as Ansbertus *21.1*, and see also Augustinus *1.24* and *1.25*.

p. 29]

34 Parabolarum sive proverbiorum lib. 1 *Ante prandium . . . nomen tuum* 82

    Cf. Vincent XXVI 71. Galandus Regniacensis. Ed. J. Châtillon & M. Dumontier, *Revue du moyen–âge latin* 9 (1953) 1–152. A manuscript of this work attributed to Anselm was seen at the Cistercian abbey of Lannois in the 18th cent.; Edmond Martène and Ursin Durand, *Voyage littéraire de deux religieux bénédictins* (Paris 1717–24), 2. 169.

35 Epistolas 366 *Gloria in . . . latus amen* 83.<u>94</u>.<u>116</u>.<u>1</u>.<u>24</u>.<u>27</u>

    83] 82 *R* 24.27] xxiiii.xxvii *R*

    R33. 23, and cf. Vincent XXVI 71. Sharpe, *Latin Writers*, 60. *SAO* vols. 3–5. Incipit is that of *ep*. 1 (ib. 3. 97); explicit unidentified. [**82** Bury = B13. 28 = Cambridge, Corpus Christi College, MS 135, fol. 1r (Bury A. 83); Kirkestede's table of contents states that this manuscript contains 367 letters.]

Anselmus *3. 36*

36   Si malum nichil est ep. 1   *Frater . . . bonum esse*   <u>165</u>

    R33. 10. *SAO* 3. 224 *ep.* 97. Explicit 'bonum est quod fecit'. [**82** Bury = B13. 28, 'Epistole Anselmi archiepiscopi' = Cambridge, Corpus Christi College, MS 135, fol. 29v (Bury A. 83), explicit 'bonum est fecit'; this epistle is singled out from the collection in Kirkestede's table of contents.]

37   Super psalterium Beatus vir   *Hic triplex . . .*   <u>118</u>.<u>126</u>.<u>161</u>.<u>95</u>.<u>23</u>.<u>20</u>

    R33. 17. Incipit unidentified.

38   Super epistolas Pauli   <u>161</u>.<u>95</u>.<u>156</u>.<u>160</u>.<u>42</u>

    R33. 15 (whole entry).

39   De septem virtutibus   <u>19</u>.<u>153</u>.<u>166</u>

    R33. 13 (whole entry).

40   De ymaginibus   <u>123</u>

    R33. 34 (whole entry).

41   Sermones   <u>89</u>.<u>43</u>.<u>19</u>.<u>116</u>.<u>166</u>.65

    R33. 12. *Ps.* Anselm; Sharpe, *Latin Writers*, 60, and see A. Wilmart in *AHDLMA* 2 (1927) 5–29 and *PL* 158. 585.

42   De sacramentis ecclesiae ep. 1   *Domino Valeriano . . . haec sapientiae*   <u>1</u>

    R33. 37. Same as *16* above; explicit does not correspond.

43   De dedicatione ecclesiae sermo   *Quia sancta . . . consecuti*

    Ps. Anselm; see *41* above. Attributed to Anselm in Cambridge, Corpus Christi College, MS 316, fol. 194v.

44   Super illud: Dum medium silentium   *Omnipotens sermo . . . durus bellator*

    Omnipotens *queried by Tanner*

    Ps. Anselm; see the bibliography at *41* above. This sermon is attributed to Anselm in BL MS Royal 8 D. VIII, fol. 170v (England), explicit (fol. 180v) does not correspond; and it appears, unattributed, in a collection of largely Anselmian works in Royal MS 5 E. XIV, fol. 30r (England), end missing.

45 De corpore Christi lib. 1   *Primum . . . animam*   82

> **82** Bury = Cambridge, Pembroke College, MS 1, fol. 30r (Bury A. 92); attributed to Anselm in the running headline and in Kirkestede's table of contents.

46 De Antichristo, secundum quosdam tract. 1   *De Antichristo . . . praefixit*

> Ps. Anselm. *CCCM* 45. 161–6. [**82** Bury = Cambridge, Pembroke College, MS 1, fol. 25r (Bury A. 92), attributed to Anselm there and in Kirkestede's table of contents (fol. i^v).]

47 De humanis moribus lib. 1   <u>21</u>.<u>24</u>

> 21.24] xxi.xxiiii *R*
>
> R33. 40 (whole entry).

48 De timore mortis   <u>24</u>

> 24] xxiiii *R*
>
> R33. 41 (whole entry).

49 De voluntate Dei tract. 1   *Cum de voluntate . . . ad modum*   82

> *PL* 158. 487.

50 De propria voluntate   <u>163</u>.<u>114</u>.<u>12</u>

> 12] xii *R*
>
> R33. 4 (whole entry).

51 Super Matthaeum et Johannem lib. 2   *Omnibus . . .*   <u>160</u>.<u>42</u>

> R33. 28, 29 (whole entry).

52 Super Apocalypsin   <u>160</u>

> R33. 31 (whole entry).

53 De scientia animae Christi   *Hugoni . . . impetrare*   82

> *Epistola ad Hugonem de S. Victore.* Walter of Mortagne. *PL* 186. 1052. The explicit, a variant, is identical with that in Bodl. MS Laud Misc. 277, fol. 86r–v.

Anselmus *3. 54*

54 De motione altaris tract. 1   *Quod de altari* . . .   82

> R. W. Southern & F. S. Schmitt, *Memorials of St Anselm* (London 1969) 321. This letter circulated by itself in certain manuscripts, with the incipit given here; cf. Bodl. MS Lat. th. d. 29, fol. 60v, 'Sententia Anselmi archiepiscopi de consecratione altaris'.

55 Item omeliae   94

> R33. 1 (whole entry).

56 De fide Christiana   24

> 24] xxiiii *R*

> R33. 39 (whole entry).

57 De 14 beatitudinibus   *Superius annunciatur . . . contempserunt*   32.108.19.139.49

> R33. 36. *Ps.* Anselm; Sharpe, *Latin Writers*, 60. This work exists in several versions; one version with the incipit given here appears in Cambridge, Corpus Christi College, MS 316, fol. 198v; another version was printed by Plantin (Antwerp 1602) 315-45.

58 De versibus heroicis   105

> R33. 32 (whole entry).

59 De 7 gradibus humilitatis   19.94

> R33. 25 (whole entry, with location number **94** taken by error from R33. 26).

4 ALEXANDER NEQUAM de territorio S. Albani natus, Cirencestrensis ecclesiae canonicus regularis, abbas ibidem, floruit circa A.D. <*blank*> et obit A.C. 1270 et sepultus est apud Wigorniam in claustro monachorum cujus tumuli superscriptio talis est:

> Ecclipsim patitur Sapientia, Sol sepelitur;
> Cui si par unus, minus esset flebile funus,
> Vir bene discretus et in omni more facetus.
> Dictus erat Nequam, vitam duxit tamen aequam.

Hic semel petiit monachatum apud S. Albanum, et scripsit abbati sic: Si vis, veniam. [Sin autem, tu autem.] Respondit abbas: Si bonus es, venias; si nequam, nequaquam. Et ille indignatus propter cognomen suum transtulit se ad Cirenstriam.

> Sin autem, tu autem add. Bale; Tanner, unable to read his manuscript, adds these words as a possible reading in Add. 3470

> Registrum 42, Mariale.
> Roughly half of the titles come from Bury manuscripts; most of the remainder come from the Mariale, the Registrum, and a manuscript at Ramsey (**65**). Bale, Index, 24–5, 'ex utroque catalogo Nordovicensi ac Buriensi'.
> Sharpe, Latin Writers, 51–3.
> See R. W. Hunt, The Schools and the Cloister: The Life and Writings of Alexander Nequam (1157–1217), ed. M. T. Gibson (Oxford 1984).

1 De naturis rerum lib. 5   Forma decens . . . largitori   82.<u>114</u>.<u>1</u>.<u>10</u>.<u>12</u>

> 10.12] xii.x *R*

> R42. 6. Sharpe, Latin Writers, 52; Hunt, Nequam, 134–6. De naturis rerum et in Ecclesiasten. Books I–II are ed. T. Wright, RS 34 (1863) 1–354.

2 Super Cantica lib. 6   Humilitas . . . laus et   82.<u>1</u>.<u>42</u>.<u>108</u>.<u>15</u>

> R42. 1. Sharpe, Latin Writers, 52; Hunt, Nequam, 137. **82** Bury = Bodl. MS Bodley 356 (Bury A. 162), beginning lost; explicit (fol. 257v), 'laus et honor et imperium per infinita secula seculorum amen'; this work was seen by Leland at Bury, B16. 13.

3 Super psalterium   De orto deli<ciarum> . . .   82.<u>15</u>.<u>153</u>.<u>10</u>

> deli *queried by Tanner* deliciarum paradysi quatuor *add. Bale* 'ex utroque catalogo Nordouicensi ac Buriensi' 10] x *R*

> R42. 5. Sharpe, Latin Writers, 52; Hunt, Nequam, 134. The incipit is that of the prologue.

4 De difficilibus verbis Bibliae lib. 1   Ferrum . . . angelica   82

> Corrogationes Promethei. Sharpe, Latin Writers, 52; Hunt, Nequam, 131–3. Extracts have been edited: P. Meyer, Notices et extraits 35/2. 641–82; H. H. Glunz, History of the Vulgate in England (Cambridge 1933) 351; and Appendix to W. Cave, Historia Literaria (London 1688) 708.

5 Super mulierem fortem lib. 3   Splendor . . . opus   82.<u>42</u>.<u>20</u>.28

> 20] xx *R*

> R42. 3. Sharpe, Latin Writers, 53; Hunt, Nequam, 139.

Alexander Nequam   4. 6

  6 De conversione B. Mariae Magdalenae meditatio   *Ad mensam* . . .   82

      Meditatio de Magdalena; Sharpe, *Latin Writers*, 52; Hunt, *Nequam*, 146. **82** Bury = B16. 4.

  7 Super Ecclesiasten lib. 3   *Superfluo . . . largitori*   42.114.1.108.15

      R42. 2. Books III–V of *1* above.

  8 De fide, spe et caritate tract. 1   42

      R42. 4 (whole entry).

p. 30]

  9 Super Vetus Testamentum et Novum   108

      R42. 8 (whole entry).

10 Super symbolum Athanasii   *Caput aquilae . . . cui personae*   82.166.115.65

      aquilae *queried by Tanner* 115] 1.15 *R*

      R42. 10. Sharpe, *Latin Writers*, 52; Hunt, *Nequam*, 129–30.

11 Ysagogarum lib. 1

      R42. 11 (whole entry).

12 Quaestionum lib. 1   20.65

      20] xx *R*

      R42. 12. Sharpe, *Latin Writers*, 53; Hunt, *Nequam*, 130.

13 Sermones ab adventu Domini   *Post susceptam* . . .   15.65

      R42. 9. Sharpe, *Latin Writers*, 53; Hunt, *Nequam*, 21–4, 150–53. Incipit unidentified.

14 Regulas super theologiam   124.115.12.65

      12] xii *R*

      R42. 7. Alan of Lille. *PL* 20. 621.

15 Cur Deus homo, vel cur Filius incarnatus tract. 1   *Operis* . . .

> *Mariale* fol. 23r, and cf. fols. 19v, 40r (whole entry)

16 De nativitate B. Mariae serm. 1   *Egredietur* . . .

> *Mariale* fol. 189r (whole entry).

17 De annunciatione serm. 6   *In hoc versu . . . collecemur*   82

> collecemur *queried by Tanner*
>
> These six sermons appear attributed to Nequam in Durham Cathedral Library, MS B. IV. 30, fol. 1r. Of doubtful authenticity; Hunt, *Nequam*, 150.

18 De desponsatione B. Mariae tract. 1

> *Mariale* fol. 16v (whole entry).

19 Liber qui dicitur Festivale

> *Mariale* fol. 2r (whole entry).

20 De utensilibus necessariis lib. 1   *Quam bene . . . animarum fidelium*

> *De nominibus utensilium*. Sharpe, *Latin Writers*, 52. Ed. Hunt, *Teaching Latin*, 1. 181, incipit 'Qui bene', explicit unidentified. [**82** Bury = London, Wellcome Historical Medical Library, MS 801, fols. 104r–119v (Bury M. 27).]

21 Scintillarium poetarum vel methologias

> Source unidentified. Alberic of London; Sharpe, *Latin Writers*, 53; E. Rathbone in *MARS* 1 (1941) 35–8. Attributed to Nequam in Cambridge, Trinity College, MS R. 14. 9, fols. 38r–63r: 'Incipiunt mithologie Alexandri Nequam et alio nomine scintillarium appellatur'.

5 ADELREDUS sanctus primo monachus et tandem abbas Rievallensis de ordine Cisterciensi floruit circa A.D. 1160 et scripsit ea quae sequuntur.

> (Aelred of Rievaulx.)
> *Registrum* 39; *Vita Aelredi* (*VA*, summary of Walter Daniel's Life excerpted from John of Tynemouth's *Sanctilogium* in Bodl. MS Bodley 240, p. 594 (Bury H. 55) [we cite the version edited by C. Horstmann, *Nova legenda Anglie* (Oxford 1901), 2. 544–53], which provided the titles for works *1–3, 5–7, 14, 16–18*. One or more Bury manuscripts supplemented or (work *4*) provided the first six works. The remainder of the entry is an unsystematic series from secondary sources and another manuscript (*10*).

Adelredus *5.*

> *Speculum coenobitarum* 51.
> Bale, *Index*, 11–12, 'ex utroque catalogo Nordovicensi et Buriensi'.
> Sharpe, *Latin Writers*, 28–30.
> See A. Hoste, *Bibliotheca Aelrediana*, Instrumenta patristica 2 (Steenbrugge 1962).

1 Super evangelium: Cum esset Jesus annorum xii tract. 3   *Petis a me . . . curavimus*   82.<u>160</u>

> R39. 8, *VA. De Iesu puero duodenni.* Sharpe, *Latin Writers*, 28; Hoste, 51. *CCCM* 1. 249.

2 Speculum caritatis continens lib. 3   *Extendisti . . . intercedat*   82.<u>105</u>

> R39. 9, *VA.* Sharpe, *Latin Writers*, 30; Hoste, 41. *CCCM* 1. 5.

3 De spirituali amicitia sub dialogo lib. 3   *Ecce ego . . . omnia in omnibus*   82.<u>43</u>.<u>160</u>

> R39. 6, *VA.* Sharpe, *Latin Writers*, 29; Hoste, 63. *CCCM* 1. 287.

4 Soliloquiorum lib. 1   *Quare tristis . . . aucupemus*   82.105

> Cf. R39. 10 ('Dialogus eius'). Incipit is that of the *Dialogus inter hominem et rationem*, not extant; Sharpe, *Latin Writers*, 29; Hoste, 82. Explicit unidentified.

5 De institutis inclusarum lib. 1   *Jam pluribus . . . intercedat*   82.<u>43</u>.<u>124</u>

> R39. 7, *VA.* Sharpe, *Latin Writers*, 28; Hoste, 75. *CCCM* 1. 637.

6 De oneribus Babilonis omeliae 33   *Tempus est . . .*   163.<u>105</u>.<u>127</u>.<u>126</u>.<u>114</u>

> R39. 4, *VA.* Sharpe, *Latin Writers*, 29; Hoste, 55. *PL* 195. 363. Location numbers **163** and **105** come from R39. 4, **127** and **126** from R39. 3 (by copying error), and **114,** again by copying error, from R39. 5 (*18* below). Neither the incipit nor the wording of the title come from *Registrum*. [**82** Bury = perhaps Cambridge, St John's College, MS F. 3, fols. 173r–178v (Bury E. 24), beginning of the text only; neither title nor incipit corresponds with this entry.]

7 De anima lib. 2   105

> Whole entry from R39. 11 and *VA.*

8 Super Cantica   43

> R39. 2 (whole entry).

9 De virginitate B. Mariae   43

> R39. 1 (whole entry).

10 De diversis virtutibus et militia Christiana tract. 1   *Sagitta . . . abissi*
   82.166.157

> Unidentified. The supposed incipit and explicit may rather be a corruption of a biblical lemma, 'Sagitta Jonatae numquam abiit'.

11 Cronica ab Adam usque ad Henricum I regem Angliae lib. 1

> This may stem from a confusion with *16* below, *Genealogia regum Angliae*; a chronicle is attributed to Aelred in *Chronicon Angliae Petriburgense*, ed. J. A. Giles (London 1845) 95, 'A.D. 1153. Hic finit chronica Alredi.'

12 De miraculis ecclesiae Augustaldensis lib. 1

> Source unidentified. Sharpe, *Latin Writers*, 29; Hoste, 127.

13 De standardo tract. 1

> Source unidentified. Sharpe, *Latin Writers*, 29; Hoste, 119.

14 Vitam S. Edwardi confessoris   92.82.11

> R39. 13, *VA*. Sharpe, *Latin Writers*, 30; Hoste, 123. *PL* 195. 737.

15 Vitam S. Niniani confessoris

> Source unidentified. Sharpe, *Latin Writers*, 30; Hoste, 115.

16 Vitam Davidis regis Scotiae cum lamentatione de morte ejus in genealogia regum Angliae lib. 1   82

> *VA*. Sharpe, *Latin Writers*, 30; Hoste, 113. *PL* 195. 711.

17 Super evangelium: Nemo accendit expositio   93.82

> *VA*. Unidentified; said to have been written at the request of his kinsman Lawrence, abbot of Westminster.

18 Sermones in causis et synodis 100   163.105.160.114

> *VA*. Sharpe, *Latin Writers*, 29. *CCCM* 2A.

Adelredus 5. *19*

19 Epistolas ad diversos 300   **105**

> R39. 12 (whole entry save the number of epistles).

6 ATHANASIUS doctor et episcopus Alexandriae tempore Theodosii imperatoris floruit circa A.D. 340 et scripsit secundum Jeronimum

> Jerome c. 87 (all of entries *1, 3, 7, 9, 11–12*); *Registrum* 17 not used.
> The entry for Athanasius is constructed in a curious alternation between Jerome and the contents of one or more Bury manuscripts.
> *Speculum coenobitarum* 37.

1 Contra gentes lib. 2

2 De Trinitate lib. 8   *Unus Deus ... Trinitatis*   82

> Concerning the authorship of this work, *CPL* 105. *CCSL* 9. 1. **82** Bury = B13. 100c.

3 De virginitate lib. 1

4 De Spiritu Sancto lib. 1   *Hiis qui Filium ... potuerimus*   82

> *CCSL* 9.165. **82** Bury = B13. 100e.

5 De fide catholica symbolum 1   *Quicunque vult ... non poterit*   82, et ubique inter Christianos

> The Athanasian Creed. Concerning this work and commentaries upon it see *CPL* 167, 1052, 1747, 1762. **82** Bury = B13. 100d.

p. 31]

6 De fide Athanasii lib. 1   *Credo in Deum ... placuit*   82

> *CPL* 552. *CCSL* 9. 129–32.

7 De persecutionibus Arrianorum plures tractatus

8 Exortatorium ad monachos   *Ut quid ... erit vobiscum*

> *CPL* 1155. *PL* 103. 665, incipit 'Etsi quod'.

9 De titulis psalmorum lib. 1

Alcuinus 7. 1

10 Contra Arrium, Sabellium et Fortunium lib. 1   *Cum apud . . .*   82

> Cf. R17. 13. Title is that of *CPL* 807 (Vigilius Thapsensis), but the incipit is that of a pseudonymous anti-Arrian tract. Same as Vigillius *635.2*. **82** Bury = B13. 100f; Cambridge, Pembroke College, MS 108, fol. 59r (Bury F. 12).

11 Historiam de vita S. Antonii, secundum Jeronimum

12 Epistolas plures ad diversos

7 ALCUINUS qui et ALBINUS genere Anglicus, S. Adriani abbatis discipulus et monachus et post Adrianum abbas S. Augustini Cantuariensis, in philosophia excellentissimus, in Graeca lingua peritus et in Latina sicut in Anglica sibi naturali pleniter instructus, secundum Bedam 5. libro De gestis Anglorum, floruit circa A.D. 723. Hic a regibus Anglorum pro pace missus ad Franciam a rege Carolo fotus est hospitio, cujus praecipue magisterio ipse rex omnes artes didicit liberales. Huic etiam rex Karolus dedit abbatiam S. Martini Turonensis regendam. Iste Alcuinus studium de Roma Parisiis transtulit, quod illuc quondam a Graecia translatum fuerat a Romanis. Nam fundatores Parisiensis studii fuerunt quatuor monachi Bedae discipuli, scilicet Alcuinus praecipue, Rabanus, Claudius et Johannes Scotus. Haec Martinus in Cronicis papae et Wilhelmus Malmesburiensis et Vincentius in Speculo historiali libr. 24 cap. 173. Scripsit autem Alcuinus qui et Albinus ea quae sequuntur, et jussu ipsius regis divinam correxit historiam.

> fuerat] fuerunt *Add. 3470*, fuerat *James extracts, Twyne extracts* 173] 17 *Twyne extracts, in error*

> *Registrum* 26 ('Opera Albini') and 38 ('Opera Alquini'), Vincent XXIV 173–4, *Manipulus florum* XV ('Libri Alquini et Alani'); Martinus Polonus (MGH *Scriptores* 22 (1872), 426–7); William of Malmesbury's *Gesta Regum* (RS 90 (1887–9), I. 68, 72); Bede's *Historia Anglorum* V 20 (OMT (1969) 530–32; concerns Albinus, abbot of St Peter's, Canterbury).
> Vincent of Beauvais provided in sequence works *1–11*, with the exception of work *2* (titles only; Kirkestede adds information from other sources). Works *20–25* are taken, in strict inverted sequence, from *Registrum* 26. The rest of the entry (works *12–19* and *26–32*) is the usual unsystematic assortment.
> Bale, *Index*, 15–16, 'ex utroque catalogo Nordovicensi et Buriensi'.
> James extracts, p. 197; Twyne extracts, p. 403.
> *CMA Gallia* 2 *Alcuin* (Turnhout 1999), and Sharpe, *Latin Writers*, 36–46, both with lists of manuscripts.

1 De Trinitate ad Karolum lib. 3   *Domino glorioso . . . nullus est*   82.<u>95</u>.<u>8</u>.<u>128</u>.<u>32</u>.80

> R38. 2 (same as R38. 7), Vincent XXIV 173, *MF* XV 1. *De fide sanctae et indiuiduae Trinitatis*; *CMA Gallia* ALC28; Sharpe, *Latin Writers*, 39. *PL* 101. 11.

Alcuinus 7. *1*

> The incipit is that of the *epistola nuncupatoria*; explicit is that of Book III c. 22. Same as *27* below.

2 Dialogorum de Trinitate lib. 1   *Cum omnis* . . .   82.<u>9</u>.<u>15</u>.<u>139</u>.<u>63</u>

> Ad Fredegisum dialogus.   Cum omnis scientia disciplina sit . . . Bale '*ex utroque catalogo Nordovicensi et Buriensi*'
>
> Cf. R38. 6 and Sharpe, *Latin Writers*, 40. The incipit is that of the *pseudo-*Augustinian *Categoriae decem*; cf. *CPL* 362, and *12* below. Ed. L. Minio-Paluello, *Ps.-Augustini Paraphrasis Themistiana* (Bruges 1961) 133. Location numbers **9** to **63** are taken from R38. 6, but the source of the title is unknown.

3 Dialogorum inter ipsum et Karolum lib. 1   *Natura* . . . *litera*   83

> Vincent XXIV 173. Incipit and explicit unidentified; a longer incipit 'Natura enim ipsa summus' is given by Bale, *Scriptores*, 111.

4 Sententiarum lib. 1

> Vincent XXIV 173 (whole entry).

5 Quaestiones super Genesin ad literam   *Quis individuus* . . .   82

> Vincent XXIV 173. *CMA Gallia* ALC76, inc. 'Quia indiuiduus'; Sharpe, *Latin Writers*, 43. *PL* 100. 516.

6 Super Cantica Canticorum lib.

> Vincent XXIV 173 (whole entry).

7 Super epistolam ad Hebraeos

> Vincent XXIV 173 (whole entry).

8 Super Ecclesiasten   <u>163</u>

> R26. 1 and Vincent XXIV 173 (whole entry).

9 Super evangelium Johannis lib. 1   *Quantum* . . . *promisit*   82

> Vincent XXIV 173. *CMA Gallia* ALC51 and cf. ALC45. 213; Sharpe, *Latin Writers*, 37. *PL* 100. 740. **82** Bury = B13. 70.

10 De ratione animae lib. 1   *Sanctae solicitudini* . . . *meritorum claritate*   74

> Vincent XXIV 173 and *MF* XV 3. *CMA Gallia* ALC17; Sharpe, *Latin Writers*, 38. MGH *Epistulae* 4. 473.

Alcuinus 7. 19

11 Quaestionum et responsionum Albini et Fridegisi de Trinitate lib. 1
Desideratissimo . . . in cruce 82.<u>15</u>

> R38. 9, Vincent XXIV 173, *MF* XV 2. *De Trinitate ad Fredegisum quaestiones*, *CMA Gallia* ALC36, Sharpe, *Latin Writers*, 40. *PL* 101. 57.

12 Categoriarum ad Karolum lib. 1

> Source unidentified; this is Alcuin's *carmen* 73, a verse 'prologus' to the Augustinian *Categoriae* that he sent to Charlemagne. *CMA Gallia* ALC11. 73. MGH *Poet. lat. med. aev.* 1. 295.

13 De ecclesiasticis dogmatibus lib. 1

> *MF* XV 5 (whole entry).

14 Super Vetus et Novum Testamentum

> Unidentified.

15 De fide catholica lib. 1 *Quotiens . . .* 82.<u>98</u>

> R26. 8. The title may refer to the *Confessio fidei*, *CMA Gallia* ALCPs4, but the incipit is unidentified; a longer incipit 'Quotiens occurrit animo' appears in Bale, *Scriptores*, 112. According to Tanner, *Bibliotheca*, 22, this work is printed in H. Canisius, *Antiquae lectionis*, vol. 6 p. 520 (unidentified).

16 De Antichristo ad Carolum lib. 1 *In primis . . . documenta* 82

> *Ps.* Alcuin. *CMA Gallia* ALCPs30. *PL* 101. 1291.

17 De proprietate nominum Deo convenientium lib. 1 *Domino David . . . dulcedinem*

> *MF* XV 4 (whole entry).

18 Speculum parvulorum lib. 1 *In scriptura . . . aperte nunc* <u>159</u>

> Whole entry from R38. 5 (location number) and *MF* XV 6 (title, incipit, explicit 'apte nunc dicitur').

19 Ad Carolum orationem 1 *Dominus . . . admitte* 82

> Unidentified. A longer incipit 'Dominus et magister noster' appears in Bale, *Scriptores*, 111. Tanner (*Bibliotheca*, 22) reported that this work was printed by Baluze (S. Baluzius, *Miscellanorum libri 1–7* (Paris 1678–1757), 1. 365–74) but

Alcuinus   7. *19*

> there is no correspondence of title ('Alcuini epistola ad Karolum Magnum'), incipit, or explicit.

20 De confessione tract. 1   <u>15</u>

> R26. 7 (whole entry).

21 De proprietate sermonum vel rerum lib. 1   <u>8</u>

> R26. 6 (whole entry).

p. 32]

22 Disputationis cum Pipino lib. 1   *Quid est litera . . . exul*   <u>8</u>.82

> R26. 5. Sharpe, *Latin Writers*, 42. *PL* 101. 975; the explicit appears at *PL* 101. 977 line 43.

23 De manifestatione Trinitatis lib. 1   <u>8</u>

> R26. 4 (whole entry).

24 Didascalicon lib. 1   <u>126</u>

> R26. 3 (whole entry).

25 Cronicarum lib. 1   <u>126</u>

> R26. 2 (whole entry).

26 De sapientia lib. 1   <u>46</u>

> R38. 10 (whole entry).

27 De Trinitate ad Karolum

> Source unidentified; R38. 7 ('Ad eundem [sc. Karolum] de fide sancte trinitatis et incarnacionis') is not a good match, and the *Registrum*'s location number there was not borrowed. See *1* and *2* above.

28 Historiam quae canitur in ecclesia Anglicana

> Source unidentified. This is presumably the *Versus de patribus regibus et sanctis Eboracensis ecclesiae*, CMA Gallia ALC87, Sharpe, *Latin Writers*, 44.

29 Item vitam S. Martini a Severo Sulpitio descriptam dictis planioribus elucidavit

> Source unidentified. *CMA Gallia* ALC89, Sharpe, *Latin Writers*, 42 (*PL* 101. 657).

30 De doctrina B. Basilii lib. 1   98

> 98] 94 *R*
>
> R38. 11 (whole entry).

31 De virtutibus et vitiis et utilitate animae lib. 1   *Primo omni . . . coronabitur*   15.20.50.82.95.

> R38. 1. *CMA Gallia* ALC37 (inc. 'Primum omnium'), Sharpe, *Latin Writers*, 41. *PL* 101. 614.

32 Epistolarum ad diversos lib. 1   163.164

> *CMA Gallia* ALC45; Sharpe, *Latin Writers*, 42. [**82** Bury = Lambeth Palace Library, MS 218, fol. 131r (Bury E. 43); seen by Leland at Bury, B16. 5.]

8 ALDHELMUS monachus et abbas Meldunensis monasterii et postea Shirburnensis ecclesiae episcopus, in Graeca lingua et Latina sufficienter eruditus, floruit circa An. Dom. 668 et scripsit

> A Bury manuscript (Bodl. MS Rawlinson C. 697) was the main source of this entry.
> *Speculum coenobitarum* 43.
> Bale, *Index*, 18.
> Sharpe, *Latin Writers*, 46.

1 Enigmata in quibus continentur versus mille   *Altrix cunctorum . . . sophos*   82.65

> *CPL* 1335. See Sharpe, *Latin Writers*, 46 sub *Epistola ad Acircium*. *CCSL* 133. 367. **82** Bury = Bodl. MS Rawlinson C. 697, fol. 1v (Bury A. 119); seen by Leland at Bury, B16. 17.

2 De virginitate et laude sanctorum et sanctarum ad Shildelittiam abbatissam de Berking lib. 1   *Metrica . . . coronam*   82.65

> *CPL* 1333. Sharpe, *Latin Writers*, 46. MGH *Auct. Antiq.* 15. 350. **82** Bury = Bodl. MS Rawlinson C. 697, fol. 17r (Bury A. 119); seen by Leland at Bury, B16. 16.

Aldhelmus *8. 3*

3 De 8 vitiis principalibus lib. 1   *Digestis . . . per ethram*   82

> ethram *queried by Tanner*

> CPL 1333. See Sharpe, *Latin Writers*, 46 sub *De uirginitate*. MGH *Auct. Antiq.* 15. 452. **82** Bury = Bodl. MS Rawlinson C. 697, fol. 56r (Bury A. 119).

4 De Pascha contra errorem Britonum lib. 1

> Source unidentified. *Ad Gerontium*. MGH *Auct. Antiq.* 15. 480 (*ep.* 4).

9 ABBO Floriacensis monachus et abbas et postea pro fide Christi martirizatus floruit circa A.D. <*blank*> et scripsit multa.

> Many of the titles are paraphrased from Aimoin of Fleury's *Vita S. Abbonis*, *PL* 139. 387–414. Kirkestede also drew on manuscripts of Abbo's works, found especially at **65** Ramsey where Abbo spent a short time as a monk. The attribution to Abbo of *12* and *15* below rests on the *Catalogus* alone.
> Bale, *Index*, 1, 'ex utroque catalogo Nordovicensi et Buriensi'.
> Sharpe, *Latin Writers*, 1–4.

1 De solis et lunae ac planetarum cursu lib. 1

> Aimoin of Fleury, *Vita S. Abbonis*, c. 3, *PL* 139. 390 (whole entry).

2 Contra episcopum Aurilianensem lib. 1

> Aimoin of Fleury, *Vita S. Abbonis*, c. 7, *PL* 139. 394 (whole entry).

3 De vita et passione S. Edmundi regis ad S. Dunstanum lib. 1

> Sharpe, *Latin Writers*, 3. Ed. M. Winterbottom, *Three Lives of English Saints* (Toronto 1972) 67–87. [**82** Bury = BL MS Cotton Titus A. VIII, fols. 65r–78r (Bury S. 153); the manuscript's rubric does not correspond with the title here, but Kirkestede's note on fol. 67r ('deficit hic multum') indicates that he has seen another text; a text was seen at Bury by Leland, B16. 1.]

4 De compoto lib. 1

> Sharpe, *Latin Writers*, 2, either the *Computus* (not printed) or the *Epistolae de computo* (part. ed. P. Varin, *Bulletin des Comités historiques des monuments écrits de l'histoire de France* 1 (1849) 117–127). Cf. Aimoin's Life, c. 3, *PL* 139. 390.

5 Categoriarum spiritualium de evangeliis lib. 1   65

> Not known to survive; Sharpe, *Latin Writers*, 1. See also *14* below. **65** Ramsey = B67. 180.

6 Ad Hugonem regem Franciae et filium ejus Robertum apologeticum lib. 1

> Aimoin of Fleury, *Vita S. Abbonis*, c. 8, *PL* 139. 394. *Liber apologeticus*, Sharpe, *Latin Writers*, 3. *PL* 139. 461.

7 Ad Robertum regem Franciae ep. 1

> Aimoin of Fleury, *Vita S. Abbonis*, c. 9, *PL* 139. 397 (whole entry).

8 Ad Bernardum Bellilocum ep. 2

> Aimoin of Fleury, *Vita S. Abbonis*, c. 10, *PL* 139. 397 (whole entry).

9 Ad papam Gregorium V ep. 1

> Aimoin of Fleury, *Vita S. Abbonis*, c. 12, *PL* 139. 403 (whole entry).

10 Ad Othonem imperatorem ep. 1

> Aimoin of Fleury, *Vita S. Abbonis*, c. 13, *PL* 139. 403 *Carmen acrostichum ad Ottonem imperatorem*, Sharpe, *Latin Writers*, 1.

11 Ad S. Odilonem Cluniacensem ep. 1

> Aimoin of Fleury, *Vita S. Abbonis*, c. 13, *PL* 139. 404 (whole entry).

12 De S. Stephano sequentiam 1

> sequentiam *queried by Tanner* unam ac responsoria *add. Bale 'ex utroque catalogo'*
>
> Unidentified.

13 Item circulos annorum incarnationis Dominicae ab ipso Verbi incarnati primo usque ad sua tempora juxta veram evangelii fidem correxit atque ad annos circiter 1295 Christi dilatavit, in quo opere mentionem facit de anno transitus S. Benedicti. Extant et alia quamplurima ad alios ejusdem scripta.

> Aimoin of Fleury, *Vita S. Abbonis*, c. 13, *PL* 139. 404 (whole entry).

14 Super evangelium omelia   *Erunt signa . . .*

> Perhaps the same as 5 above.

Abbo *9. 15*

   15 Sermo in coena Domini   65

      Unidentified.

p. 33]

10 ANGELONIUS monachus floruit circa A.D. 830 et scripsit juxta Vincentium in Speculo historiali lib. 25 cap. 33 ad Lodovycum imperatorem

    (Angelomus of Luxeuil)
    Registrum 45, Vincent XXV 33.
    Speculum coenobitarum 41.

  1 Super libros Regum lib. 4   *Viginti et . . . absconditi*   82.43.108.151

    151] 15.1 *R*

    R45. 1. Stegmüller *Bibl.* 1335–8. *PL* 115. 247.

11 AVITUS episcopus Hispanus floruit tempore Orosii circa A.D. 496 et scripsit multa secundum Ysidorum De viris illustribus et secundum Genadium in libro De viris illustribus

    Whole entry from Isidore c. 23 (works *1–6*) and Gennadius c. 48 (work *7*).

  1 De origine mundi lib. 1

  2 De originali peccato lib. 1

  3 De sententia Dei lib. 1

  4 De diluvio mundi lib. .1

  5 De transitu maris rubri lib. 1

  6 De laude virginitatis lib. 1

  7 Item scripturam Luciani presbyteri de inventione sanctorum Stephani, Gamalielis, Nichodemi et Abibonis de Graeco transtulit in Latinum secundum Genadium

    Stephen's name comes from the preceding chapter of Gennadius (c. 47, Lucianus); the source for the other three names is not known. See Lucianus *347.1*.

12 ANTONIUS monachus et abbas floruit tempore Constantini circa A.D. <blank> et scripsit juxta Jeronimum libro De viris illustribus ad diversa monasteria Egiptae epistolas septem, quae in Graecam linguam translatae sunt, quarum praecipua est illa ad Arseonitas.

> Jerome c. 88 (whole entry).
> *Speculum coenobitarum* 2.

13 ANDREAS canonicus S. Victoris et auditor Magistri Hugonis floruit circa A.D. <blank> et scripsit multa

> *Registrum* 43.
> The main source for this entry was a Bury manuscript of Andrew on the Heptateuch (works *1–7*, Sharpe, *Latin Writers*, 58), which must have been similar to Cambridge, Corpus Christi College, MS 30.
> Sharpe, *Latin Writers*, 58–9.

1 Super Genesin ad literam lib. 1   *Difficile* . . .   <u>161</u>

> R43. 4. Stegmüller *Bibl.* 1295. CCCM 53. 4 (*Prologus ad Heptateuchum* preceding the Genesis commentary).

2 Super Exodum lib. 1   *Iste secundus* . . .   <u>161</u>.<u>108</u>.163

> *2–8*: R43. 1, 'Super Vetus Testamentum', with the location numbers **161**, **108** repeated from R43. 1 and R43. 2 ('Super Exodum').

> R43. 2. Stegmüller *Bibl.* 1296. CCCM 53. 96.

3 Super Leviticum lib. 1   *Liber Leviticus* . . .   <u>161</u>.<u>108</u>.163

> Stegmüller *Bibl.* 1297. CCCM 53. 158.

4 Super Numerum lib. 1   *Quam multitudini* . . .   <u>161</u>.<u>108</u>.163

> Stegmüller *Bibl.* 1298. CCCM 53. 180, incipit 'Quoniam multitudinis'.

5 Super Deuteronomium lib. 1   *Deuteronomii . . . facie ad faciem*   <u>161</u>.<u>108</u>

> Stegmüller *Bibl.* 1299. CCCM 53. 195.

6 Super Josue lib. 1   *A nomine* . . .   <u>161</u>.<u>108</u>

> Stegmüller *Bibl.* 1300. CCCM 53. 215.

7 Super Judicum lib. 1   *Primum tempora* . . .   <u>161</u>.<u>108</u>

> Stegmüller *Bibl.* 1301. CCCM 53. 220, incipit 'Tempora iudicum'.

Andreas *13. 8*

   8 Super libros Regum lib. 1   <u>161</u>.<u>108</u>

       Source unidentified; location numbers repeated from R43. 1–2. Stegmüller *Bibl.* 1302–1305. Sharpe, *Latin Writers*, 58.

   9 Super Paralipomenon lib. 1   *In hac ultima* . . .

       Stegmüller *Bibl.* 1306. Sharpe, *Latin Writers*, 58. CCCM 53A. 118.

  10 Super Ecclesiasten lib. 1   <u>161</u>

       R43. 2 (whole entry).

  11 Super Parabola\<s\> Salomonis lib. 1   <u>161</u>

       R43. 3 (whole entry).

  12 Super Ysayam lib. 1   *In explanando . . . eligat*   **82**

       Stegmüller *Bibl.* 1312. Sharpe, *Latin Writers*, 58. **82** Bury = Cambridge, Pembroke College, MS 45, fol. 1r (Bury A. 124).

  13 Super Jeremiam lib. 1   *Frequens . . . hominibus*   **82**

       Stegmüller *Bibl.* 1313. Sharpe, *Latin Writers*, 58. **82** Bury = Cambridge, Pembroke College, MS 45, fol. 76r (Bury A. 124); Kirkestede entered the title in place of an omitted rubric.

  14 Super Danielem lib. 1   *Ad commendationem . . . apponere*   **82**

       Stegmüller *Bibl.* 1315. Sharpe, *Latin Writers*, 58. CCCM 53F. 5. **82** Bury = Cambridge, Pembroke College, MS 45, fol. 111r (Bury A. 124); Kirkestede entered the title in place of an omitted rubric.

  15 Super Johelem lib. 1

       Source unidentified. Sharpe, *Latin Writers*, 59 (Comm. on Minor Prophets).

14 AMALARIUS monachus floruit circa A.D. 830 juxta Vincentium in Speculo historiali lib. 25 cap. 33 et scripsit

    Vincent XXV 33.
    Speculum coenobitarum 42.

Alanus 15. 4

1 Ad Ludovicum de officiis ecclesiasticis lib. 4   *Gloriosissime . . . orationes*   82

> *PL* 105. 985. **82** Bury = B13. 248, 'Exceptiones de Amalario cum plerisque sententiis'; B13. 244, 'Amalarius' = Cambridge, Pembroke College, MS 44 (Bury A. 121); Book IV cc. 46–7 are omitted from this manuscript which ends (fol. 105v) '. . . orationes'.

p. 34]

15 ALANUS floruit circa A.D. <*blank*> et scripsit multa

> (Alain de Lille)
> Same as Alanus Porrens *16*; see also Anti–Claudianus *64*.
> Works *1–5* with their incipits and explicits are taken from *Manipulus florum* XV ('Libri Alquini et Alani'). Location numbers added to this second-hand information are those of Babwell (**173**) and St Benet Hulme (**74**), houses with whose libraries Kirkestede was acquainted.
> Gale extracts, antepenultimate back flyleaf, verso.

1 De maximis theologicis lib. 1   *Communis animi . . . possideatur*   173

> *Gale extracts inexplicably note, 'Incipit desinit'*
>
> *MF* XV 7. *PL* 210. 617. [**82** Bury = Cambridge, Pembroke College, MS 87, fol. 178r (Bury E. 11), inc. 'Omnis scientia'; Kirkestede noted in the margin 'Hic incipit liber' two thirds of the way down the page beside the words 'Communis animi', and at the end (fol. 192v), which does not match this explicit, he noted 'Finis deficit'; the manuscript at **173** Babwell, used for this entry, was no doubt the basis for the notes in Pembroke 87.]

2 De fide catholica lib. 1   *Quicquid est . . . judicabunt*

> judicabit *Gale extracts*
>
> *MF* XV 8 (whole entry). See also *5* below.

3 De planctu sive de conquestione naturae lib. 1   *In lacrimas . . . aspectus*   74

> *MF* XV 9. Ed. N. M. Häring in *Studi medievali* ser. 3, 19 (1978) 797–879.

4 Principium commenti   *Omnis scientia . . . crisma*   173

> Principium] Primum *Gale extracts; MF confirms Tanner's reading*
>
> *MF* XV. 7a. *PL* 210. 622, explicit (col. 680) 'chrisma quo confirmatur'; the explicit is taken from the *Manipulus florum*.

Alanus *15. 5*

    5 Item ad principium commenti   *Clemens . . . homo judex*

        ad principium] aliud primum *Gale extracts; MF confirms Tanner's reading*

        MF XV. 8a (whole entry), the commentary to *2* above.

    6 Anticlaudianum de Antirufino   *Cum f<u>l<m>inis . . . post fata*   83

        flinis *Add. 3470*, queried by Tanner; fullimis *Gale extracts*

        Ed. R. Bossuat (Paris 1955) 55–198, explicit 'post fata silebit'.

16 ALANUS PORRENS floruit circa A.D. *<blank>* et scripsit ad episcopum Nomonensem

    (Alain de Lille)
    Same as Alanus *15*.
    These works constitute part of a collection of Alain's works similar to BAV MS Reg. lat. 424 pt 1 (i.e. fols. 1r–76r), a 13th-cent. Parisian manuscript.

    1 De modo et arte praedicandi lib. 1   *Vidit Jacobus . . . de virginibus*   82. 173.74

        PL 210. 110; the incipit is that of the preface. **82** Bury = BL MS Royal 7 C. XI, fol. 98r (Bury V. 21), explicit (fol. 126v) does not correspond but virgins are the subject of the final chapter; Kirkestede's contents note in Cambridge, Pembroke College, MS 25, fol. 3r (Bury O. 55), 'in quo continentur . . . tractatus Alani Porrei de arte predicandi', refers to a fragment once bound at the end of that manuscript (cf. above, p. lii and plate 4a), a fragment now kept in a collection of binding scraps, Pembroke College, MS 313, with Kirkestede's marginal identification note.

    2 Sermones de tempore   *Scientes . . .*

        The incipit is that of a collection of Alain's sermons *De aduentu Domini*; cf. BAV MS Reg. lat. 424 fol. 46r. The first sermon appears in *PL* 210. 195.

    3 Sermones de 70 et aliis   *Circumdederunt . . .*

        The incipit is that of a collection of Alain's sermons *In dominica quinquagesime*; cf. BAV MS Reg. lat. 424 fol. 59. The first sermon appears in *PL* 210. 237.

17 APOLLINARIS Asiae Jeropolitanus episcopus floruit circa A.D. 158 juxta Vincentium lib. 11mo cap. 112 et scripsit juxta Jeronimum libro De viris illustribus

    Whole entry (save the date) jointly from Vincent XI 112 and Jerome c. 26.

Ansbertus 21.

1 De fide Christianorum lib. 1

2 De veritate lib. 2

3 Adversus gentes lib. 1

4 Adversus Cathafrigas lib. 2

18 APRINGIUS ecclesiae Patensis Spaniarum episcopus floruit circa A.D. \<blank\> et scripsit juxta Ysidorum libro De viris illustribus

> Isidore c. 17 (whole entry).

1 Super Apocalipsin expositionem 1

19 ACHACIUS Caesariensis episcopus floruit circa A.D. \<blank\> tempore Constantini et scripsit juxta Jeronimum

> Jerome c. 98 (whole entry).

1 Super Ecclesiasten volumina 17, et multos alios et diversos tractatus composuit

20 AMBROSIUS Alexandrinus auditor Didimi floruit circa A.D. \<blank\> et scripsit juxta Jeronimum

> Jerome c. 126 (whole entry).

1 Adversus Apollinaristas lib. 1

2 Super librum Job commentarium

21 ANSBERTUS monachus et abbas Fontanell[ae] et postea episcopus Rotomagensis floruit circa A.D. 660 et scripsit

> Ausbertus] *Add. 3470; Tanner, uncertain of this reading, has added the correction as a variant reading*

> Ansbert is discussed in Vincent XXIV 100 but without mention of these works. Kirkestede has combined the biography of Ansbert of Rouen with works of Ambrose Autpert, taken presumably from a manuscript.
> See J. Winandy, 'L'oeuvre littéraire d'Ambroise Autpert,' *RB* 60 (1950) 93; and concerning Ansbert see *CPL* 2089.

Ansbertus *21. 1*

1 De assumptione Beatae Mariae serm. 5   *Adest nobis . . . inter praecipuas sanctorum solemnitates*   168

> Ambrose Autpert; *CPL* 368 *serm.* 208. *CCCM* 27B. 1027; this is just a single sermon, and the explicit does not correspond. Same as Anselmus *3.33*, and see also Augustine *1.24* and *1.25*.

2 Super Apocalipsim

> Source unidentified. Ambrose Autpert.

22 ARATOR poeta et Romanae ecclesiae subdiaconus floruit circa A.C. 542, qui libros metricos duos eleganter de historia Actum Apostolorum composuit. Principium: *Qui meriti florem manibus undosis.* Finis: *Gratia palmam.*

> Vincent XXII 51 (whole entry save the date).

[p. 35]

23 APYON floruit circa A.D. 213 et scripsit juxta Vincentium in Speculo historiali lib. 12 cap. 16 et juxta Jeronimum libro De viris illustribus

> Vincent XII 16 (whole entry save work *3*); Jerome c. 49 is perhaps cited through Vincent.

1 Exameron lib. 1

2 De resurrectione lib. 6

3 De mirabilibus Egypti lib. 1

> This work and its source are unidentified.

24 ANATHOLIUS Alexandrinus Laodociae Siriae episcopus floruit circa A.D. 285 tempore Probi et Cari imperatorum, et scripsit juxta Jeronimum libro De viris illustribus

> Jerome c. 73 (whole entry save the date).

1 De Pascha lib. 1

2 De arithmetica lib. 1

25 AMPHILOCIUS Siconi episcopus floruit circa A.D. <*blank*> et scripsit juxta Jeronimum libro De viris illustribus

> Whole entry from Jerome c. 133 (work *1*) and Vincent XVII 94 (work *2*).

1 De Sancto Spiritu lib. 1

2 Vitam S. Basilii archiepiscopi lib. 1

26 ARNOBIUS rethor floruit circa A.C. <*blank*> tempore Diocletiani et scripsit juxta Jeronimum libro De viris illustribus

> Jerome c. 79 (whole entry)

1 Adversus gentes volumina quae vulgo extant

27 ATTICUS Constantinopolitanus episcopus floruit tempore Archadii circa A.C. <*blank*> et scripsit juxta Genadium libro De illustribus viris ad filias Achadii imperatoris

> Gennadius c. 53 (whole entry).

1 De fide et virginitate lib. 1

28 ANTHIOCHUS episcopus floruit circa A.D. <*blank*> et scripsit juxta Genadium libro De viris illustribus tempore Archadii

> Gennadius c. 20 (whole entry).

1 Contra avaritiam 1 longum volumen

2 De caeco illuminato a Salvatore omeliam 1

29 AUDENTIUS episcopus Hispanus floruit circa A.C. <*blank*> et scripsit juxta Genadium libro De viris illustribus

> Gennadius c. 14 (whole entry).

1 Adversus Manicheos et Arrianos quae praetitulavit De fide contra haereticos lib. 1

Ammonius   *30*.

30 AMMONIUS monachus et episcopus Alexandrinus floruit circa A.D. 370 et scripsit secundum Jeronimum De catholicis scriptoribus

> Jerome c. 55 (whole entry save the date).
> *Speculum coenobitarum* 12.

1 De constantia Moysis et Jesus lib. 1

2 Item canones evangeliorum

31 ARNULPHUS vel **ARNALDUS** monachus et abbas floruit circa A.C. 1120 et scripsit juxta Cathologum Angliae

> Gallus Belvacensis, Cantuariae mansit sub Lanfranco, post sub Anselmo, atque Abbas Burgi Petri, a Radulfo episcopus fit Roffensis   *add. Add. 3470; according to Tanner this was added in a recent hand*

> See also Ernaldus *168*.
> *Registrum* 36 (the 'Cathologum Angliae').
> Bale, *Index*, 34, 'ex utroque Anglorum catalogo'.

1 De operibus sex dierum lib. 1   94

> R36. 1 (whole entry).

2 De corpore et sanguine Domini lib. 1   *Faciem . . . non peribimus*   166

> Ernulf, bishop of Rochester (1040–1124); Sharpe, *Latin Writers*, 113. Ed. P. J. Cramer in *St Anselm and St. Augustine: Episcopi ad saecula*, ed. J. C. Schnaubelt, Anselm Studies 2 (New York 1988) 143–63.

3 De 6 verbis Domini in cruce   *Ultima Christi . . .*   94

> R36. 2. Ernaldus Bonaevallis; Stegmüller *Bibl.* 2254. *PL* 189. 1677. Same as Ernaldus *168.1*.

> Solutiones ad Lambertum lib. 1   Venerabili in . . . in zenio charitatis. Vide infra verbum Ernaldus   *added entry in Add. 3470; according to Tanner this was added in a recent hand*

p. 36]

32 AFFRICANUS inter scriptores ecclesiasticos nominatissimus floruit juxta Yvonem in Cronicis A.C. 239 et scripsit

> See also Julius Affricanus *302*.

'Yvo' = Hugh of Fleury, *Historia ecclesiastica siue Chronicon*, ed. B. Rottendorff (Münster 1638) 78, *s.a.* 239.

33 ADAMANTIUS floruit circa A.C. <*blank*> et scripsit juxta Cassiodorum

Another name for Origen *404*. Cassiodorus I. 30. 2 (work *2*, whole entry). The source from which Kirkestede derived titles *1* (see *404.24* below) and *3* (see *404.6* below) under the name Adamantius is unidentified.

1 De adventu Domini

2 De ortographia lib. 1

3 Super Josue et Judicum

34 ASCLEPIUS Vagensis episcopus floruit A. Ch. 495 et scripsit juxta Genadium libro De viris illustribus

Gennadius c. 74 (whole entry save the date).

1 Contra Arrianos lib. 1

2 Item contra Donatistas lib. 1

35 APOLLINARIS Laodicensis Siriae presbiter floruit circa A.D. 388 et scripsit secundum Jeronimum libro De catholicis scriptoribus

Jerome c. 104 (whole entry save the date).

1 Adversus Porphyrium lib. 30

2 Item alia volumina innumerabilia

36 APOLLONIUS vir disertissimus floruit circa A.C. 194 et scripsit juxta Jeronimum libro De catholicis scriptoribus

Jerome c. 40 (whole entry save the date).

1 Contra Montanum haereticum Priscam et Maximillam volumen insigne

37 AMBROSIUS primum Marcionites, deinde ab Origine correctus, ecclesiae sanctae diaconus, cui liber Origenis de martirio scribitur, floruit A.C. 222. Hujus industria, sumptu et instantia Origenes infinita volumina dictavit. Ad Origenem vero plures scripsit epistolas, et obiit ante mortem Origenis, et in hoc a plerisque reprehenditur quod ipse vir locuples amici sui scilicet Origenis senis et pauperis moriens non recordatus est. Haec Jeronimus.

> Jerome c. 56 (whole entry save the date).

38 APOLLONIUS Romanae urbis senator et martir floruit A. Ch. 186 et scripsit secundum Jeronimum ubi supra

> Jerome c. 42 (whole entry save the date).

1 De ratione fidei suae volumen insigne

39 ALEXANDER episcopus Cappadociae et martir floruit circa A. Ch. 250 et scripsit secundum Jeronimum ubi supra

> ubi supra *corr. by Tanner from* vita sua *in Add. 3470*

> Jerome c. 62 (whole entry save the date).

1 Ad Marciscum episcopum Hierosolym[ae] ep. 1

2 Ad Antiochenses ep. 2

3 De pace ecclesiae ep. 1

4 Ad Originem ep. 1

5 Contra Demetrium pro Origene lib. 1

6 Item epistolae aliae ad diversos

p. 37]

40 ARABIANUS floruit circa A. Ch. 200 et scripsit secundum Jeronimum ubi supra

> ubi supra *corr. by Tanner from* vita sua *in Add. 3470*

> Jerome c. 51 (whole entry save the date).

1 Quaedam opuscula ad Christianum dogma pertinentia

41 AGRIPPA cognomento Castoris vir valde doctus floruit A. Ch. 119 et scripsit secundum Jeronimum adversum 34 volumina Basilidis haeretici

> 34] Viginti quattuor *Jerome*

> Jerome c. 21 (whole entry save the date).

42 ARCHELAUS episcopus Mesapotamiae floruit circa A. Ch. 279 et scripsit juxta Jeronimum ubi supra

> ubi supra *corr. by Tanner from* vita sua *in Add. 3470*

> Jerome c. 72 (whole entry save the date).

1 Adversum Manichaeum lib. 1

43 ACHILLIUS SEVERUS Hispanus obiit A.D. 365 et scripsit secundum Jeronimum ubi supra volumen quasi Odiporicum, totius vitae suae statum continens tam prosa quam versibus quod vocatur Pera. Ad istum duo libri epistolarum Lactantii scripti sunt.

> ubi supra *corr. by Tanner from* vita sua *in Add. 3470*

> Jerome c. 111 (whole entry save the date)

44 APTATUS vel OPTATUS episcopus Afer Melivitanus floruit circa A. Ch. 367 et scripsit secundum Jeronimum et Cassiodorum libro De institutione divinarum literarum

> Jerome c. 110; Cassiodorus I. 28. 4 (author's name only).

1 Contra Donatianos lib. 6

> Jerome (whole entry).

2 Super Vetus Testamentum et Novum commentarios

> This work and its source are unidentified.

45 ADRIANUS floruit circa A. Ch. <*blank*> et scripsit juxta Cassiodorum ubi supra

> Cassiodorus I. 10. 1 (whole entry).

Adrianus 45. 1

1 Super Vetus et Novum Testamentum commentarios

46 ARISTOTILES philosophus floruit anno <blank>

> Vincent IV 84 (references are followed by numbers in brackets [1, 2, etc.] that indicate the sequence of titles in the chapter).
> The initial sequence of titles was governed, loosely, by the sequence in Vincent of Beauvais. Most of the entries were completed, or (after work *32*) taken entirely, from manuscripts at Bury and at neighbouring houses in Colchester (**83**, **84**), with a handful of titles taken from unidentified sources.
> See *Aristoteles latinus pars prior* (cited *AL*), ed. G. Lacombe & others (Rome 1939); and A. Birkenmajer, *Classement des ouvrages attribués à Aristote par le Moyen-Age latin* (Krakow 1932).

1 Periarmeniarum lib. 2   *Oportet . . . inesse contraria*   83

> Vincent IV 84 [3]. *AL* (7). Incipit 'Primum oportet'.

2 Topicorum lib. 8   *Propositum . . . continuo*   84

> Vincent IV 84 [4]. *AL* (8).

3 Elencorum lib. 2   *De sophisticis . . . habere gratas*   83

> Vincent IV 84 [5]. *AL* (9).

4 Priorum analeticorum lib. 2   *Primum . . . unius signi*   83

> *AL* (10). Explicit 'unius signum'.

5 Posteriorum analeticorum lib. 2   *Omnis . . . ad omnem*   84

> *AL* (11). Explicit 'ad omne rerum'.

6 De physica et naturali scientia lib. 8   *Quum intelligitur . . . magnitudinem*   83

> Vincent IV 84 [6]. *AL* (16), (17), or (16a). Incipit 'Quoniam quidam intelligere'.

7 Ethicorum lib. 10   *Omnis ars . . . consuetudinibus*

> Vincent IV 84 [20]. *AL* (47) , *Summa Alexandrinorum*. Explicit 'consuetudinibus similantur'.

8 De generatione et corruptione lib. 2   *De generatione . . . non esse*   84

> Vincent IV 84 [7]. *AL* (20) or (22).

Aristotiles 46. 18

9 De anima lib. 3   *Bonorum . . . aliquid alteri*   83

   AL (26) or (27).

10 De sensu et sensato lib. 1   *Quoniam autem . . . dictum est*   83

   Vincent IV 84 [8]. *AL* (28) or (33).

11 Poleticorum lib. 1

   Source unidentified. *AL* (54) or (55).

12 De memoria et reminiscentia lib. 1   *Reliquorum . . . causas dictum est*   83

   Vincent IV 84 [9]. *AL* (29).

13 De sompno et vigilia lib. 3   *De sompno . . . divinationem*   83

   Vincent IV 84 [10]. *AL* (30) or (35).

14 De morte et vita lib. 1   *De eo autem . . . longioris vitae*   83

   Vincent IV 84 [11]. *De longitudine. AL* (31). Same as *34* below.

15 De vegetabilibus et plantis lib. 2   *Tria ut . . . fructus amarus*   83

   Vincent IV 84 [12]. Nicolaus Damascenus. *AL* (84).

16 De animalibus lib. 21   *Quaedam . . . causam moventem*   83

   Vincent IV 84 [13]. *AL* (64). The incipit is that of the text.

17 De differentia spiritus et animae lib. 1   *Interrogasti . . . in futuro*   83

   Costa ben Luca. *AL* Append. VI.

18 Metheororum lib. 4   *Postquam . . . extranee;*   Aliter: *De primis,* Finis : *plantam*   83

   extranee] exuee Add. *3470, queried by Tanner*

   Vincent IV 84 [15]. *AL* (23) and *AL* (25).

Aristotiles   *46. 19*

p. 38]

19 Methafisicorum lib. 14   *Omnes . . . principia*   Alia translatio continet lib. xi. Principium: *Consideratio*. Finis: *intellectus*

> Vincent IV 84 [16]. *AL* (39) or (42), *Metaphysica medie translationis* or *Metaphysica noue translationis*; the second incipit and explicit are those of the *Metaphysica noua*, *AL* (41).

20 De regimine principum vel dominorum ad Alexandrum qui intitulatur Secreta secretorum lib. 1   *O fili . . . probabiliorem*   Prologus: *Domino suo . . .* 83

> Ps. Aristotle. *AL* Append. I. Explicit 'probabiliorem partem'. See *30* and *41* below.

21 De rethorica lib. 1

> Vincent IV 84 [18].

22 De perspectiva lib. 1

> Vincent IV 84 [17].

23 De coelo et mundo lib. 4   *Summa . . . intentionem*   Alium principium: *De natura*. Finis: *hoc modo*   84

> *AL* (18), *De celo ueteris translationis*, explicit 'intentionem nostram in eo'; and *AL* (19), *De celo noue translationis*.

24 Item de mundo lib. 1   *Multotiens . . .*   Alium principium : *Est igitur*. Finis: *confestim*

> Ps. Aristotle. *AL* (80). The translation is that of Nicholaus Siculus; the second incipit is that of the second paragraph. Explicit 'confestim particeps esset'. Ed. W. L. Lorimer & L. Minio-Paluello, *AL* 11/1–2 (1965²) 29–49.

25 Item de mundo ad Alexandrum ep. 1   *Aristotiles . . . assumentes*   84

> Vincent IV 84 [11]. Ps. Aristotle. *AL* (60). *Epistola ad Alexandrum*.

26 De pomo vel de morte Aristotilis lib. 1   *Cum homo . . .*   Aliter: *Cum clausa . . . sicut tu es*

> A2̶] *Add. 3470; Tanner adds* Aristotilis *above the line as a possible reading*

> Ps. Aristotle. *AL* Append. III. The incipits are those of prologue and text, respectively.

Aristotiles *46. 36*

27 De problematibus partes vel lib. 35   *Propter quid . . . propter quod non oportet*

   Ps. Aristotle. *AL* (73).

28 De mineris   *De commixtione . . . constans*   84

   Albertus Magnus. Ed. *Doctoris angelici diui Thomae Aquinatis . . . Opera omnia*, ed. S. E. Frette & others, 34 vols. (L. Vives: Paris, 1871–1880), 5. 1–103. Explicit unidentified.

29 De coloribus lib. 1   *Simplices . . . naturae et scientiae*   84.3.15

   Ps. Aristotle. *AL* (82). Explicit unidentified.

30 De sanitate regenda ad Alexandrum lib. 1

   Ps. Aristotle. *AL* Append. II. This is an excerpt of the *Secretum secretorum, 20* above. [**82** Bury = Cambridge, Gonville and Caius College, MS 225/240 (Bury V. 12) which contained a copy of this, according to Kirkestede's table of contents 'Aristotelis ad Alexandrum de sanitate regenda'; only the final page survives (p. 177).]

31 Cathegoriarum, id est praedicamentorum lib. 1   *Equivoca . . . enumerati sunt*

   Vincent IV 84 [1]. *AL* (6).

32 Sex principiorum lib. 1   *Formae est . . . ut ignis*

   Vincent IV 84 [2]. Possibly the work of Gilbertus Porretanus. *AL* Append. VIII. Incipit 'Forma uero est'.

33 De inundatione Nili lib. 1   *Propterea quidem . . . de Nilo quidem*   84

   Ps. Aristotle. *AL* (83). Incipit 'Propter quid'.

34 De morte et vita

   Source unidentified. Same as *14* above, *De longitudine*.

35 De juventute et senectute lib. 1   *De juventute . . . dictum est de*   84

   AL (32). Explicit 'dicendum est'.

36 De intelligentia lib. 1   *Cum rerum . . . prologum fecit*   83

   Attributed to an anonymous neo-Platonist. *AL* (88). Explicit 'prologum fecit Aristotilis'.

Aristotiles *46. 37*

37 De progressu animalium lib. 1   *De partibus . . . contemplari*   83

AL (67).

38 De causis lib. 1   83

Probably the same as Proculus *486.1*.

39 De motu animalium lib. 1   *De motu . . . de generatione dicere*   83

AL (68).

40 De proprietatibus elementorum lib. 1   *Postquam . . . declarationem*   84

Ps. Aristotle. AL (85).

41 De phisonogmia lib. 1   *Quoniam et animae . . . apparentia*   84

Ps. Aristotle. AL (74). This is an excerpt of the *Secretum Secretorum*, *20* above. [**82** Bury = BL MS Royal 12 C. VI, fol. 43r (Bury M. 83), a manuscript procured for the abbey by Kirkestede; explicit 'superapparentia fit'.]

42 De bona fortuna lib. 1   *Quoniam autem . . . kalokagathiam*

AL (50) or (51).

43 De lineis lib. 1   *Utrum sunt . . . puncta autem*

Utrum] Ut^m Add. *3470, queried by Tanner*

Ps. Aristotle. AL (78). Explicit 'puncta autem habet'.

44 De vita Aristotelis   *Aristotiles . . . ultimum intellectum*

Concerning the authorship of this work see Birkenmajer, 17–18. AL (87). Explicit 'ultra intellectum'.

45 De lapidibus

Source unidentified. *Ps.* Aristotle; see Birkenmajer, 12.

47 APULEIUS Platonicus philosophus Maudarensis floruit ante incarnationem et scripsit secundum Augustinum libro De civitate Dei

See also Hermes *259* and Tremegistus *592*.
Vincent V 6–7; Augustine, *De ciuitate Dei* VIII 14 (probably cited through Vincent); Fulgentius.

Apuleius 47. 8

1 De deo Socratis lib. 1   *Quoniam me . . . nec accessit*   83

   Vincent V 6, Aug. Ed. P. Thomas, *Apulei Platonici Madaurensis De philosophia libri* (Leipzig 1908). [**82** Bury = CUL MS Ff. 3. 5, fol. 1r (Bury A. 130), incipit 'Qui me'.]

2 De vita et moribus Platonis lib. 1

   Vincent V 6 (whole entry).

3 Cosmographiam

   Quidam tamen dicunt quod hii tres libri sunt unum volumen intitulatum De deo Socratis; quod puto verum. Edidit etiam librum Peryermenias, cujus libri commentator Apulei annumerat librum Mercurii Trismegisti De divinitate etc. Forte Apuleius hunc librum transtulit de Graeco in Latinum et scribitur ei.

   Source unidentified.

4 Item composuit Phedronem

   Source unidentified.

5 Item de republica, secundum Fulgentium libro de rebus signatis ad Calcidium

   signatis *queried by Tanner*

   The reference is to Fulgentius, *Sermones antiqui*, ed. R. Helm (Leipzig 1898) 123.

6 Item librum qui dicitur Hermogoras

   Source unidentified.

7 Item librum medicinalem

   Source unidentified.

8 Item ephitomen sanctorum patrum in [   ] 6°

   in [   ] 6° *the illegible portion is queried by Tanner*

   Source unidentified.

Apuleius   47. 9

   9 Item de asino aureo, secundum Fulgentium ubi supra

      Fulgentius, 117.

  10 Item de ponderibus et numeris

      Work and source unidentified.

  11 Item librum ludicrorum

      Unidentified.

48 AGELLIUS in Actica regione floruit A. Ch. 105 et scripsit libros

    (Aulus Gellius)
    Although no source has been identified for this entry and no incipits are given, both of these works were read in the 14th cent. and were probably to be found in the Bury library, since Gellius is cited in the Bury chronicle; A. Gransden, *The Chronicle of Bury St. Edmunds* (London 1964), xviii.

   1 Noctium Atticarum lib. 1

      Ed. P.K. Marshall, 2 vols. (Oxford 1968).

   2 De bellis Armeniae lib. 3

      Ps. Aulus Gellius. See B. Smalley, *English Friars and Antiquity* (Oxford 1960), 332–3.

p. 39]

49 ARISTIDES Atheniensis philosophus floruit circa A.D. 162 et scripsit juxta Jeronimum et Vincentium in Speculo historiali lib. 10 cap. 72

    Jerome c. 20 (whole entry save the date); this author does not appear in Vincent.

   1 Pro Christianis apolegiticum lib. 1

50 ANSEGISUS monachus et abbas Bobiensis floruit circa A.D. 830 juxta Vincentium in Speculo historiali lib. 25 cap. 33 et scripsit

    Vincent XXV 33.
    James extracts, p. 197.

1 Edita imperatoris magni Karoli et Ludovici filii ejus ad ecclesiasticam legem pertinentia lib. 2   Finis 1^{mi}: *dominatile*; 2^{di}: *constituta est*   82

> Ludowici *James extracts*
>
> Vincent XXV 33. MGH *Leges* 1. 271–99; explicit of Book I unidentified.

2 Item dicta eorundem ad mundanam legem pertinentia lib. 2   Finis 1^{mi}: *de pace*; 2^{di}: *ad caballum*

> Vincent XXV 33. MGH *Leges* 1. 301–320; 'explicit' of Book I (edition Book III) is in fact the incipit; the second explicit is that of IV 70.

51 ADELARDUS Bathoniensis philosophus

> Bale, *Index*, 8, 'ex utroque catalogo Anglorum'.
> Sharpe, *Latin Writers*, 23–4.

1 De naturis rerum Ricardo episcopo Bathoniensi lib. 1   *Meministi . . . veniamus*   82

> *Quaestiones naturales*; Sharpe, *Latin Writers*, 23. Ed. M. Müller, *Beiträge* 31/ 2 (1934) 1.

2 Item librum qui dicitur Sic et non

> Peter Abelard. Same as Petrus Abelardi *433.1*.

3 De septem artibus liberalibus lib. 1   *Saepe numero . . . diiudica*   82   Iste liber est partim prosaicus et partim metricus

> diiudica] dumdica *Add. 3470, queried by Tanner*
>
> *De eodem et diuerso*; Sharpe, *Latin Writers*, 23. Ed. H. Willner, *BGPM* 4/1 (1903) 1; the incipit is that of c. 1.

4 Item librum Ezichiafaris transtulit de Arabico in Latinum   *Liber iste 7 planetarum . . .*

> Translation of al-Khwarizmi's *Zij*; Sharpe, *Latin Writers*, 24. Ed. A. Børnbo & others, *Det Kongelige Danske Videnskabernes Selskabs Skrifter*, Danske Videnskabernes Selskabs Skrifter, historisk og filosofisk afdeling, 7th ser. 3 (Copenhagen 1914) 1–31.

Alexander 52.

52 ALEXANDER Altisiodorensis

(Guilielmus Altissiodorensis)
This entry came from a Bury manuscript. The name 'Allexder Altisiodori' appears in Cambridge, Pembroke College, MS 4, fol. 111v (Bury —) in a late 14th-cent. contents note and may be the source for the name here, even though the contents notes in Pembroke MSS 2 and 3 (also used here) give the correct name, Gulielmus.

1 Super 1^{mum} librum sententiarum lib. 1   *Fides est* . . .

Printed, *Gulielmus Altissiodorensis Summa super libros sententiarum* (Paris 1500/1). [**82** Bury = Cambridge, Pembroke College, MS 2, fol. 1r (Bury A. 109).]

2 Super 2^{dum} librum sententiarum lib. 1

ibid. [**82** Bury = Cambridge, Pembroke College, MS 2, fol. 38r (Bury A. 109).]

3 Super 3^{ium} librum sententiarum lib. 1

ibid. [**82** Bury = Cambridge, Pembroke College, MS 3 (Bury A. 110).]

4 Super 4^{tum} librum sententiarum lib. 1   *Dicto de . . . illa gaudia*

ibid. [**82** Bury = Cambridge, Pembroke College, MS 4 (Bury —).]

53 ADALBERTUS diaconus floruit <*blank*> et scripsit . . . excerpsit

et scripsit . . . *Tanner has added* nuo *in superscript above the ellipsis*

(Adalbert of Metz)
Bale, *Index*, 2, 'Adalbertus Diaconus, Spaldingensis monasterii'; probably Bale misinterpreted his own notes (a reference to location number **147** = Spalding) when he created this ghost.
Concerning the author's identity see Sharpe, *Latin Writers*, 5.

1 De Moralibus Gregorii lib.   *Nonnulli . . . amore justitiae*   147.82   Iste liber vocatur Speculum et continet 155 capita.

Nonnulli] namque ita sunt simplices . . . *add. Bale*

Stegmüller *Bibl.* 859. **147** Spalding = seen by Leland at Spalding, B96. 1. / **82** Bury = B13. 48a.

54 ALEXANDER DE HALES Frater Minor floruit <blank> et scripsit

Bale, *Index*, 22 (works 3–4).
Sharpe, *Latin Writers*, 49–51.

1 Super 4^{or} libros sententiarum

 The source for this entry was probably a manuscript. Sharpe, *Latin Writers*, 49; Stegmüller *Sent.* 59. Ed. *Bibliotheca Franciscana scholastica medii aevi* 12–15 (Quaracchi 1951–7). [**82** Bury = Cambridge, Pembroke College, MS 43 (Bury A. 114), excerpts, identical with *2* below.]

2 Item quaestionum lib. 1

 Sharpe, *Latin Writers*, 50. Ed. *Bibliotheca Franciscana scholastica medii aevi* 19–21 (Quarrachi 1960). See also *1* above. [**82** Bury = Cambridge, Pembroke College, MS 43 (Bury A. 114), with Kirkestede's contents note at the top of fol. 1r, 'Questiones excerpte de summa Alexandri de Hales super 4^{or} libros sententiarum'; his notes also straighten out a textual muddle on fols. 60r and 110v.]

3 De mysteriis ecclesiae metrice lib. 1 *Anglia quo . . .*

 John of Garland; Sharpe, *Latin Writers*, 254. Same as Johannes de Garlandia *331.3*.

4 Exoticon de expositione verborum Graecorum et Hebraicorum lib. 1 *Chere theoren . . .*

 Chere theoren] Ther. theor. *Add. 3470, queried by Tanner* De verbis exoticis lib. 1 There theorem . . . *Bale*

 Sharpe, *Latin Writers*, 49. Ed. Hunt, *Teaching Latin*, 1. 304.

55 ALEXANDER Magnus floruit <blank>

This entry is based entirely on manuscripts, at Bury and at nearby Saffron Walden (**68**). Kirkestede mentions the Walden manuscript in a note in Cambridge, Gonville and Caius College, MS 154/204, fol. 150r (Bury P. 162).

1 Gesta Alexandri Magni *Interea rex . . . vel Nectanabus . . . spiritum exalavit, vel . . . occubuit*

 It is unclear just what Kirkestede's manuscript contained. 'Interea rex' is the incipit of the *Historia de Proeliis*, versions I.1 and I.2 c. 2; ed. O. Zingerle, *Germanistische Abhandlungen* 4 (Breslau 1885), 129–265 ('Interea Philippus rex Macedonum'). 'Nectanabus . . . exalauit', however, are the incipit and explicit

Alexander 55. *1*

>   of a common chapter list to *3* below; cf. BL MS Royal 15 C. VI, fols. 102v–103r. And the second explicit belongs to the text of *3* below.

2 Gesta Alexandri Magni metrice lib. 10 *Gesta ducis . . .*

>   Walter of Châtillon. *PL* 209. 463.

3 Item gesta Alexandri Magni *Egipti sapientes . . . extinctus* 68

>   The medieval abridgement of Julius Valerius; ed. J. Zacher, *Julii Valerii Epitome* (Halle 1867), explicit 'extinctus occubit'. See *1* above.

p. 40]

4 De ortu et vita et obitu Alexandri *Quoniam non est . . . armasset* 68

>   An extract from the Epitome of Trogus Pompeius. It is found with this title in London, College of Arms, MS Arundel 1 (Canterbury Franciscans, s. xiv), fol. 206v, immediately following *3* above.

5 Epistola Alexandri ad Aristotilem de situ Indiae *Semper memor . . . de nobis*

>   Ed. W. W. Boer, *Epistola Alexandri ad Aristotilem ad codicum fide edita et commentario critico instructa* (The Hague 1953); the explicit appears on p. 53 line 4. This short work often travelled with *3* above; cf. BL MS Royal 13 A. 1.

56 ALBERTUS Teutonicus Frater Praedicatorum et doctor theologiae et episcopus Ratisponensis floruit A. Ch. <*blank*> et scripsit quae sequuntur

>   *Registrum* 61, *Script. Ord. Praed.*, cf. Stams, 7.
>   The first seventy-three titles come from the catalogue of Dominican writers, with additions from one actual codex (work *67*) and from the *Registrum* (work *74* below, with location numbers carelessly borrowed). Seventy-two of the titles here recur in Stams, with minor variations in the sequence: *31–53* appear after *54–73*, and the Stams list ends with *51, 30, 52, 53*.

1 Super Porphyrium comment. 1

2 Super Praedicamenta comm. 1

3 Super Peryermenia comment.

4 Super 6 principia commentarium

Albertus 56. 21

5 Super librum Priorum comm. 1

6 Super Posteriorum dupliciter

    dupliciter *queried by Tanner*

7 Super libros Naturales introductorium

8 De 4^{or} coaequaevis lib. 1

    coaequis *Add. 3470, queried by Tanner*

9 De origine animae lib. 1

10 De potentiis animae lib. 1

11 De intellectu et intelligibilitate lib. 1

12 Contra unitatem intellectus lib. 1

13 De unitate formae lib. 1

14 De homine lib. 1

15 De bono lib. 1

16 De lapidibus lib. 1

17 De herbis lib. 1

18 De alchimia lib. 1

    alignomia *Add. 3470, queried by Tanner*

19 Contra libros nigromanticorum lib. 1

    grammaticorum *Add. 3470, queried by Tanner*

20 Problemata

    Works *20–22* refer to one work in Stams.

21 Contra Averroistas quaestiones 15

    Ancroistas *Add. 3470, queried by Tanner*

Albertus 56. 22

22 Ad clerum Paris. quarundam quaestionum determinationes

23 Super speram lib. 1

24 De natura locorum lib. 1

25 Speculum astrolabium

26 De nutrimento et nutribili lib. 1

27 De proprietatibus elementorum lib. 1

28 De muliere forti lib. 1

29 De partu hominis lib. 1

30 De perfectione vitae spiritualis lib. 1

31 Super Job

32 Super Cantica

33 Super Ysaiam

34 Super Jeremiam

35 Super Ezechielem

36 Super Danielem

37 Super xii prophetas minores

p. 41]

38 Super Matthaeum et Marcum

39 Super Lucam et Johannem

40 Super epistolas Pauli

41 Super Dionisium de divinis nominibus

42 Super Dionisium de coelesti jerarchia

43 Super Dionisium de simbolica jerarchia

44 Super Dionisium de ecclesiastica jerarchia

45 Super libros sententiarum Petri Lombardi

46 De theologia summam l<ib. 2>

> *The number of books is illegible in Add. 3470*

47 De ministerio missae tract. 1

48 De corpore Domini tract. 1

49 De laudibus B. Virginis

50 De sancto amore contra Wilhelmum

51 Secretum secretorum

52 Super Eucliden expositio 1

53 Super perspectivam Almagesti et quosdam alios libros mathe<matic>os

> mathematicos] matheseos *Add. 3470*

Item sequentes plures composuit:

54 Super libros Phisicorum

55 Super librum de Coelo et mundo

56 Super libros Metheororum

57 Super librum de Generatione et corruptione

58 Super librum de Anima

59 Super librum de Sensu et sensato

60 Super librum de Memoria et reminiscentia

Albertus *56. 61*

   61 Super librum de Inspiratione et respiratione

   62 Super librum de Sompno et vigiliis

   63 Super librum de Morte et vita

   64 De longitudine et brevitate vitae

   65 Super librum de plantis et vegetabilibus

   66 Super librum de Mineralibus

   67 Super librum de Animalibus lib. 6   *Scientiam . . . reprehensiones*   73.147

> *De animalibus lib. xxvi*; ed. H. Stadler in *BGPM* 15–16 (1920).

   68 Super librum de Causis

   69 Super Methaphisicam

   70 Super librum Ethicorum dupliciter commentarium

> dupliciter *queried by Tanner*

   71 Super Poleticam

   72 Super Rethoricam

   73 Super librum Ethicorum quaestiones   9̲3.101

> Location number **93** is taken from the *Registrum*, copied here by mistake from R61. 1 (74 below). The source of the number **101** is not evident; this is its only appearance in the *Catalogus*, and the authenticity of its three appearances in the *Registrum* is doubtful.

   74 Super Apocalypsim

> R61. 1 (whole entry).

57 ALBERTUS Erfordensis Frater Praedicator floruit A Ch. <*blank*> et scripsit

> *Script. Ord. Praed.* (whole entry), cf. Stams, 55.

1 Super Porphirium

2 Super Praedicamenta

3 Super Peryarmenias

4 Super Sex principia

58 ALBERTUS Lumbardus Frater Praedicator floruit A. Ch.   <blank> et scripsit

> *Script. Ord. Praed.* (whole entry), cf. Stams, 104.
> Ely extracts, fol. 118v; the compiler has mistakenly copied the identification of Albertus (*58*) with the titles ascribed to Arnaldus (*59*); the reading of Add. 3470 is confirmed by Stams.

1 Super totam Bibliam lectur. 1

p. 42]

59 ARNALDUS Laudiensis Frater Praedicator floruit A. Ch. <blank> et scripsit

> Laudiensis] Leodinensis *Stams*

> *Script. Ord. Praed.* (whole entry), cf. Stams, 83.
> Ely extracts: see headnote to Albertus *58*.

1 Librum qui dicitur Narratorium

2 De mirabilibus mundi lib. 1

60 ALBRANDINUS Lumbardus Frater Praedicator floruit A. Ch. <blank> et scripsit

> *Script. Ord. Praed.* (whole entry), cf. Stams, 98.

1 Sermones de tempore et sanctis

2 Librum qui dicitur Scala fidei

Augustinus *61*.

61 AUGUSTINUS Dacus Frater Praedicator floruit A. Ch.   <*blank*> et scripsit

> *Script. Ord. Praed.* (whole entry), cf. Stams, 100.

1 Libellum pro informatione praedicantium, quem Pugillarem nominant

> informatione] informationem *Add. 3470*

62 ABSOLON floruit A Ch. <*blank*> et scripsit juxta librum qui dicitur *Mariale* majus

> *Mariale* fol. 2r.

63 ALBUMASAR floruit<*blank*> et scripsit

> The name alone appears in *Mariale* fol. 2r.

1 Introductorium judiciorum astrorum

> Source unidentified.

64 ANTICLAUDIANUS   65

> See Alanus *15*.
> *Mariale* fol. 2r.
> **65** Ramsey = B68. 197.

65 ALUREDUS Anglicus et domini Octoboni cardinalis capellanus commensalis floruit A.Ch.   <*blank*>   et scripsit

> commensalis] commessalis *Add. 3470, queried by Tanner;* commensalis *Bale*

> See also Aluredus *76*.
> A similar biographical notice appears in the prologue in Bodl. MS Bodley 77, fol. 138r.
> Bale, *Index*, 28.
> Sharpe, *Latin Writers*, 55, 'Alfred the Priest'.

1 De musica lib. 1 *Licet mihi . . . et submissa*

> Sharpe, *Latin Writers*, 55. See D. P. Blanchard, 'Alfred le musicien et Alfred le philosophe', *Rassegna Gregoriana* 8 (1909) 419–32. Not printed.

2 Super Boetium de Consolatione philosophiae

> Alfred the Great. This entry could have been supplied from a number of sources known to Kirkestede, such as the *Gesta regum* or the *Gesta pontificum* of William of Malmesbury.

66 AQUILA Ponticus, secundus interpres post LXX, floruit circa A.D. 129 et transtulit Vetus Testamentum de Hebraeo in Graecum.

> Whole entry from Vincent XI 90 and Higden, 5. 20.
> Ely extracts, fol. 118v.

67 ALBERTANUS Causidicus Brixiensis floruit circa A. Ch. 1238 tempore Frederici imperatoris et scripsit

> (Albert of Brescia)
> This entry was compiled from a Bury manuscript that must have been similar to Oxford, Magdalen College, MS 7 (s. xv), which comprises these three works.

1 De dilectione Dei et proximi et aliarum rerum et de forma vitae lib. 4
   Initium mei . . . satago pervenire   82

> forma *queried by Tanner*

> Printed, Cuneo 1507. This rare printing also contains works *2* and *3* below.

2 De consolatione et consilio lib. 1   *Quoniam multi . . . cum gaudio*

> Ed. T. Sundby, Chaucer Society (London 1873). Explicit 'cum gaudio et laetitia recesserunt'.

3 De doctrina dicendi et tacendi et faciendi lib. 1   *Initio et medio . . . praedicta tibi*

> Printed in *Brunetto Latinos Levnet og Skrifter*, ed. T. Sundby (Copenhagen 1869), xciii–cxix. Explicit 'praedicta tibi narrare'.

68 AVICENNA floruit anno <blank> et scripsit

> This entry, including works *1* and *9* without incipits, was presumably taken from manuscripts.

1 De motu cordis lib. 1

> Either the *De motu cordis* of Aluredus Anglicus or the *De motu cordis* of Thomas Aquinas; BNF MS lat. 6443, fols. 182v–184v (s. xiii^{ex}, N. France; heavily

Avicenna 68. 1

    annotated with English hands) contains both works along with several works of Avicenna.

2 De medicina lib. 5   *In primis . . . tinnitum*

    Canon medicinae. Printed Passau: Johann Herbort, 1479. [**82** Bury = Cambridge, Gonville and Caius College, MS 480/476, fol. 1r (Bury A. 200), explicit (fol. 305v) does not correspond.]

3 De logica   *Dicemus quod . . . infinito*

    Avicenne . . . opera in lucem redacta (Venice 1508) 2–12 (the numbers refer to the two facing pages of an opening, rather than to folios); explicit 'sint gratie infinite' appears at the end of what is called part II, in the first column of opening no. 12.

4 De coelo et mundo   *Collectiones . . . benigne*

    ibid. 37–42; explicit not found.

5 De phisica   *Postquam . . . per se notae*

    ibid. 13–36 under the title *Sufficientia*, explicit 'per se notae sunt'.

6 De anima   *Reverendissimo . . . de animalibus*

    Printed Venice 1508, openings 1–28 (of the second sequence, beginning after fol. 42r of the initial numbered sequence in this edition).

7 De methaphisica lib. 4   *Postquam autem . . . rex terreni*

    terreni] terrorem *Add. 3470, queried by Tanner*

    ibid. 70–109 (second sequence), explicit 'rex terreni mundi et est vicarius dei in illo'.

8 De ortu et divisione scientiarum   *Scientia vel . . . omnes deos*

    Alpharabius. This work is attributed to Avicenna in BNF MS lat. 6443, fol. 185v (cf. *1* above). Ed. Clemens Baeumker in *BGPM* 19/3 (1916) 17–24, incipit 'Scias nihil'.

9 De alkimia lib. 1

    The source of this entry was probably a manuscript. Several anonymous alchemical works circulated under Avicenna's name; cf. Glasgow UL MS Hunterian 110, fols. 1r–9r, and BL MS Sloane 1128, fols. 100v–152r.

[p. 43]

69 ALGAZEL floruit <*blank*> et scripsit

The name and the work must derive from a manuscript.

1 De metaphisica   *Usus fuit . . . naturalibus*

70 ALKINDUS

1 De aeribus et pluviis

Source and work unidentified.

71 ACHARDUS floruit A. Ch. <*blank*> et scripsit

Achardus] Anglus *add. Bale*

(Achard, abbot of Saint-Victor of Paris, 1155)
Bale, *Index*, 2.
Sharpe, *Latin Writers*, 4.

1 Super evangelium Ductus est   *Ductus est . . . plenitudinem*

De Christi tentatione lib. 1 Ductus est Iesu in desertum . . . *Bale*

Sharpe, *Latin Writers*, 4. Ed. J. Châtillon, *Textes philosophiques du moyen âge* 17 (1970), serm. 25.

2 Item

Nothing has been lost here, apparently; Bale adds nothing further to Add. 3470

72 ASTULPHUS floruit <*blank*> et scripsit

Astulphus] conversus *add. Bale*

Bale, *Index*, 35.
Sharpe, *Latin Writers*, 64; Kirkestede and Bale are the only sources of information about this author, whose work does not survive.

1 Cantelarium sive dialogum inter ipsum Astulphum et novicium et continet tria folia et est apud 73 in libraria dormitorii.

dormitorii et est Nordovici in monasterio trinitatis. *Bale*

Astulphus 72. 1

> 73 = Holy Trinity, Norwich. Bale saw this work at Norwich and supplied from there the incipit 'Miser Astulphus claustrorum noviciis salutem'.

73 ALBERICUS floruit A.M. <blank> et scripsit juxta Vincentium lib. 3 cap. 96

> Vincent III 96 (whole entry).

1 Poetarium

74 ALFRIDUS Beverlacensis thesaurarius floruit A. Ch. <blank> et scripsit

> Higden, 1. 24.
> Sharpe, *Latin Writers*, 54.

75 ALPHARABIUS

1 Super librum Proculi de Causis   *Cum ergo removet . . . non adquisitum*

> Same as Proculus *486.3*.

76 ALUREDUS rex Anglorum floruit circa A.D. <blank> et scripsit multa; in philosophiae namque studiis perfecte usque ad unguem disertus orator extitit, et facundus interpres totum fere testamentum in linguam Anglicam transtulit.

> See also Aluredus *65*.
> Source unidentified.
> Ely extracts, fol. 118v.
> Bale, *Index*, 28.
> James extracts, p. 197; James Ussher, *Historia dogmatica*, ed. H. Wharton (London 1690), 124.
> Sharpe, *Latin Writers*, 55.

77 ALVARUS Pelagii Frater Minor natione Hispanus, domini papae poenitentiarius, et doctor decretorum floruit circa A. Ch. <blank> et scripsit De planctu ecclesiae, in quo vitia et defectus omnium statuum declarantur et eorum contrariae virtutes.

> poenitentiarius] primarius *Add. 3470; Tanner, uncertain of this reading, has added* poenitentiarius *as a variant reading*

> The source of this entry was probably a manuscript.

[p. 44]

78 BASILIUS archiepiscopus Cappadociae floruit circa A. Ch. 366 et Graecae scripsit juxta Jeronimum libro De viris illustribus et Ysydorum et juxta Vincentium in Speculo historiali lib. 15 cap. 81

> Vincent XV 81, Jerome c. 116, Cassiodorus I. *praef.* 4; this author does not appear in Isidore, and *Registrum* 15 was apparently not used.
> *Speculum coenobitarum* 15.
> Ely extracts, fol. 118v.

1 In exameron Attico sermone omelias 8   *Conveniens* . . .   65

> Vincent XV 81 and Jerome 116. *PG* 30. 869.

2 De Spiritu sancto contra Ennomium lib. 1

> Whole entry from Vincent XV 81 and Jerome 116.

3 De institutione monachorum lib. 1   *Satis libenter . . . ex Deo est*   82. 83. 86

> Vincent XV 81. *PL* 103. 483. Incipit is that of the *Praefatio Rufini in regulam sancti Basilii*.

4 De vita communi monachorum regulam 1   *Misericors . . . spiritu*   83

> Incipit and explicit unidentified.

5 De vita solitaria monachorum regulam 1   *Audi fili . . . diligentibus eum*   83

> Ps. Basil, *Admonitio ad filium spiritalem*; *CPL* 1155a. *PL* 103. 683. [**82** Bury = BL MS Royal 8 F. XIV, fol. 157r (Bury G. 15).]

6 De triplici pugna monachorum ep. 1   *Gravem quidem . . . locatur cui*

> Unidentified.

7 Item alios breves, pluresque tractatus composuit

> Whole entry from Vincent XV 81 and Jerome 116.

8 Sermones plures   *Melior est . . . ad dextram*   74

> See *PG* 31. 1723; incipit and explicit unidentified.

Basilius *78. 8*

9 Vetus et Novum Testamentum a primo usque ad finem Graeco sermone declaravit secundum Cassiodorum libro De institutione divinarum literarum

 Cassiodorus I. *praef.* 4 (whole entry).

79 BASILIUS Anchiranus episcopus floruit tempore Constantini A.D. <blank> et scripsit secundum Jeronimum

 Jerome c. 89 (whole entry).

1 De virginitate contra Marcellum lib. 1

2 Item multa alia

80 BALDWINUS archiepiscopus Cantuariensis floruit circa A.D. 1120 et scripsit juxta Cathalogum librorum Angliae

 Registrum 64.
 Bale, *Index*, 36–7.
 Sharpe, *Latin Writers*, 66–7.

1 De sacramentis et specialiter altaris lib. 1 <u>105</u>.65

 De sacramentis *Bale*

 R64. 2 ('De sacramentis'). *De sacramento altaris*; Sharpe, *Latin Writers*, 67. Kirkestede's correction of the *Registrum* title presumably came from the manuscript at **65** Ramsey.

2 De commendatione fidei lib. 1 <u>105</u>

 R64. 1 (whole entry).

3 Item sermones quamplures 14 *Candidiores . . . ad praelatos* 74.<u>105</u>.65

 R64. 3. Sharpe, *Latin Writers*, 67, for the division into 14 sermons. *PL* 204. 403. The incipit is that of *tract.* 16 (*PL* 204. 561), which stands first in some collections such as BNF MS lat. 2601 (s. xii[ex]); P. Guebin, in *JTS* 13 (1911–12), 571–4. Explicit unidentified.

81 BACHARIUS floruit circa A. Ch. <blank> et scripsit juxta Cathologum librorum Angliae et juxta Gennadium (Hic vacare Deo

Berengarius 82. 4

disponens elegit peregrinationem propter servandam castitatem, secundum Gennadium.)

Registrum 75 ('Cathologum librorum Angliae'), Gennadius c. 24 (work *2*).
Bale, *Index*, 285 (*s. n.* 'Macceus').

1 De reparatione lapsi et fructu poenitentiae lib. 1   *Nisi vererer . . . intervenire*
82.65

R75. 1. *CPL* 569. *PL* 20. 1037. **82** Bury = B13. 21b.

2 De fide lib. 1

Gennadius (whole entry)

82 BERENGARIUS floruit circa A. Ch. <*blank*> et scripsit

al. ridus *Add. 3470, written in the margin for addition after the letter a in Berengarius; this may be a corruption of an attempt to change the author's name to Berengaudus*

(Berengaudus)
Registrum 49, supplemented by a Bury manuscript of the Apocalypse commentary.

1 De incarnatione Verbi lib. 1   <u>126.19</u>

R49. 1 (whole entry).

2 Super Cantica Canticorum lib. 1   <u>98</u>

R49. 4 (whole entry).

3 Super Apocalipsim lib. 1   *Beatum Johannem . . . defendamus*   99.<u>166</u>.<u>114</u>.
<u>105</u>.<u>8</u>.<u>19</u> Huic libro praeponitur vel postponitur prologus qui sic incipit: *Quisquis*. Finis: *commutandum*.

R49. 2. Stegmüller *Bibl.* 1711. *PL* 17. 765. See also Berengarius *96*. Cambridge, Pembroke College, MS 85 pt 3, fol. 1r (Bury B. 340) was not the manuscript used here, because this text was already imperfect; Kirkestede noted in the margin of fol. 16v (on the basis of a complete manuscript) 'Deficit hic .i. quaternus'.

4 Item epistolas quamplures

R49. 3 (whole entry).

Berillus   *83.*

p. 45]

83 BERILLUS episcopus Arabiae floruit circa A. Ch. 240 et scripsit juxta Vincentium in Speculo historiali lib. 12 cap. 30 varia opuscula et maxime epistolas, in quibus Origeni gratias agit. Extat Dialogus Origenis et Berilli, in quo haereseos coarguitur secundum Jeronimum. Hic cum aliquanto tempore gloriose rexisset ecclesiam, ad extremum lapsus est in haeresin quae Christum ante incarnationem fuisse negat; ab Origine correctus, scripsit opuscula supradicta.

>Whole entry (save date) from Vincent XII 30 and Jerome c. 60.
>Ely extracts, fol. 118v.

84 BEDA monachus et presbiter, venerabilis monasterii ad Wyremutham in Gyrvum in provincia scilicet Northanhunbrorum, floruit A.D. 706 et scripsit

>*Registrum* 7 and Bede, *Historia ecclesiastica* V 24 (B. Colgrave and R. A. B. Mynors, OMT (1969) 566–71). (Vincent XXIV 133 not used.)
>Works *1–47* appear in this sequence in *Historia ecclesiastica* (*HE*); Kirkestede copied that passage, with its list of titles, onto fol. 1^r of Bodl. MS e Musaeo 9 (Bury B. 290). Bede's list has been supplemented here with (mostly Bury) manuscripts. The remainder of the entry is a combination of *Registrum* titles not duplicated (or not recognized) in *HE*, attributions in manuscripts, and unidentified sources.
>*Speculum coenobitarum* 44.
>Bale, *Index*, 43–4, 'ex utroque catalogo Anglorum' (works *18, 24, 32–33, 37, 45, 48–56, 58–60, 64–71*).
>Sharpe, *Latin Writers*, 70–76.
>See M. L. W. Laistner, *A Handlist of Bede Manuscripts* (Ithaca, NY, 1943), and C. W. Jones, *Bedae pseudepigrapha: Scientific Writings Falsely Attributed to Bede* (Ithaca, NY, 1939).

1   Super Genesin, Exodum, Leviticum, Numerum et Deuteronomium lib. 4
    In principio . . . uniebant   82.<u>166</u>.<u>108</u>.<u>15</u>.<u>139</u>.50

>Bede on Genesis (*CPL* 1344; Sharpe, *Latin Writers*, 71; *CCSL* 118A) and *ps.* Bede on the rest of the Pentateuch (Stegmüller *Bibl.* 1648–51; *PL* 91. 285). **82** Bury = B13. 6 = Bodl. MS e Musaeo 36, fol. 1r (Bury B. 280), which contains the five commentaries. / Location numbers **166** to **139** are taken from R7. 35, 'Super Genesim'.

2   De tabernaculo Moysi lib. 3   *Locuturi . . . dum dixit*   82.<u>94</u>.<u>95</u>.42.43.<u>35</u>

>R7. 17. *CPL* 1345. Sharpe, *Latin Writers*, 72. *CCSL* 119A. 5. Explicit 'benedixit Dominus'. **82** Bury = B13. 208. **42** Reading = B71. 92a.

3 Super Samuelem lib. 4   *Studium . . . gaudebunt*   82.35.10.104.27.154

    10] x *R*   27] xxvii *R*

    R7. 12. *CPL* 1346. Sharpe, *Latin Writers*, 71. *CCSL* 119. 5. **82** Bury = B13. 207.

4 De templo Salomonis lib. 2 *Hortatur nos . . . cum majoribus* 82.94.43.105.1.10.104

    R7. 19. *CPL* 1348. Sharpe, *Latin Writers*, 73. *CCSL* 119A. 143. **82** Bury = B13. 151a = Cambridge, Pembroke College, MS 81, fol. 1r (Bury B. 282).

5 In librum Regum quaestiones 30   *Dilectissimo . . . gaudium Domini* 82.1.35.104.139.105

    R7. 18. *CPL* 1347. Sharpe, *Latin Writers*, 73. *CCSL* 119. 293. **82** Bury = B13. 151b = Cambridge, Pembroke College, MS 81, fol. 102v (Bury B. 282); explicit 'gaudium Domini uestri' (fol. 131v) has a blank space (erasure of three or four letters) separating the last two words.

6 Super Proverbia Salomonis lib. 3 *Parabolae . . . serviciis* 82.93.42.8.9.10.96

    R7. 13. *CPL* 1351. Sharpe, *Latin Writers*, 72. *CCSL* 119B. 23. **82** Bury = B13. 7 = Oxford, Balliol College, MS 175, fol. 1r (Bury B. 283), explicit 'seruitus' (fol. 93v).

7 Super Cantica Canticorum lib. 6 *Cantica . . . permane* 82.42.9.35.15.1.23

    R7. 25. *CPL* 1353. Sharpe, *Latin Writers*, 72. *CCSL* 119B. 185; incipit is that of the rubric ('Incipiunt Cantica Canticorum'). See also *60* below. **82** Bury = B13. 99.

Distinctiones capitulorum ex tractatu Jeronimi excerptae:

    ex tractatu *queried by Tanner; this is a side-heading that brackets titles 8–11 in Add. 3470*

8 Super Ysaiam

9 Super Danielem

10 Super partem Jeremiae

11 Super XII Prophetas

Beda   *84. 12*

12   Super Esdram et Neemiam lib. 3   *Cunctis . . . in bonum*   8.<u>82</u>.<u>15</u>.<u>1</u>.<u>139</u>. <u>104</u>.<u>161</u>

> R7. 21. *CPL* 1349. Sharpe, *Latin Writers*, 72. *CCSL* 119A. 241. **82** Bury = B13. 41b.

13   Super canticum Abacuch lib. 1   <u>105</u>.<u>1</u>

> R7. 16. [**82** Bury = a fragment of this work appears in Cambridge, Pembroke College, MS 81, fols. 132v–149v (Bury B. 282).]

14   Super Thobiam lib. 1   *Liber sancti . . . viventium*   <u>82</u>.<u>94</u>.49.<u>89</u>.<u>42</u>.<u>8</u>

> 49 *may be* 39 R
>
> R7. 7. *CPL* 1350. Sharpe, *Latin Writers*, 72. *CCSL* 119B. 3. **82** Bury = Oxford, Balliol College, MS 175, fol. 94r (Bury B. 283).

Capita lectionum:

> This is a side-heading that brackets titles 15–21 in Add. 3470.

15   Super Pentateucum

16   Super Josue

17   Super Judicum

18   Super libros Regum et verba dierum

> verba dierum *queried by Tanner*

19   Super librum Job

20   Super Ecclesiasten et Cantica Canticorum   <u>161</u>

> Whole entry from R7. 37 and *HE*.

21   Super Ysaiam, Esdram et Neemiam

22   Super evangelium Marci commentarium lib. 4   *Conferendum . . . formam Domini*   82.42.<u>15</u>.111.<u>9</u>.<u>1</u>.<u>20</u>

> R7. 10. *CPL* 1355. Sharpe, *Latin Writers*, 72. *CCSL* 120. 437. **82** Bury = B13. 210. **42** Reading = B71. 93.

Beda *84. 29*

23 Super evangelium Lucae lib. 6   *Quoniam quidem . . . conclusit*   82.42.<u>8</u>.<u>9</u>. <u>35</u>.<u>13</u>.<u>1</u>

> R7. 11. *CPL* 1356. Sharpe, *Latin Writers*, 72. *CCSL* 120. 19. **82** Bury = B13. 209; Cambridge, Pembroke College, MS 83, fol. 7v (Bury B. 287), 'Explicit exposicio uenerabilis Bede super Lucam' added (fol. 229v) by Kirkestede. **42** Reading = B71. 89 = BL MS Egerton 2204.

24 Omeliae 50 super evangelia lib. 1   *Fuit Johannes . . . adventu*   94.<u>13</u>.<u>15</u>.<u>25</u>. 53.<u>57</u>

> R7. 26. *CPL* 1367. Sharpe, *Latin Writers*, 73. *CCSL* 122. 1; the incipit is the biblical *lemma* for *hom.* 1, and the 'explicit' is, rather, the incipit of that homily ('Aduentum dominice. . .').

25 In apostolum quaecunque in opusculis S. Augustini exposita inveni, cuncta per ordinem scribere curavi lib. 14   *Paulus apostolus . . .*   82.<u>95</u>.<u>1</u>

> R7. 41, 53. Florus of Lyon; see Sharpe, *Latin Writers*, 75. Same as *61* and *65* below; see also Petrus Tripolitanus *480.1*. **82** Bury = cf. B13. 57–58 = Bodl. MS e Musaeo 9 (Bury B. 290), which contains *ps.*-Bede (Romans and I Corinthians), rubricated on p. 1, 'Liber uenerabilis Bede monachi et presbiteri super epistolas Pauli siue Liber florum eiusdem'. **95** is taken from R7. 41, and **1** from R7. 53.

26 In Actus Apostolorum lib. 2   *Domino in Christo . . . servavi*   82.<u>94</u>.<u>42</u>.<u>9</u>.<u>19</u>

> R7. 5. *CPL* 1357. Sharpe, *Latin Writers*, 72. *CCSL* 121. 1–99. **82** Bury = B13. 41a.

27 In septem epistolas canonicas lib. 7   *Jacobus . . . omne saeculum*   82.<u>94</u>.42. <u>9</u>.<u>19</u>.<u>13</u>

> R7. 15. *CPL* 1362. Sharpe, *Latin Writers*, 72. *CCSL* 121. 181. Location numbers **82** to **19** may be repeated from *26* above, but Bury did possess a copy. **82** Bury = B13. 40b = Cambridge, King's College, MS 7, fols. 77r–147r, modern foliation (Bury B. 292).

28 Super Apocalipsin lib. 3   *Apocalipsis . . . pietate*   82.42.<u>35</u>.<u>13</u>.<u>15</u>.<u>1</u>.<u>139</u>

> R7. 14. *CPL* 1363. Sharpe, *Latin Writers*, 72. *PL* 93. 129. **82** Bury = B13. 40a = Cambridge, King's College, MS 7, fols. 1r–76v, modern foliation (Bury B. 292), with title added in upper margin by Kirkestede.

29 Item capitula lectionum in totum Novum Testamentum excepto evangelio

Beda *84. 30*

30 De sex aetatibus saeculi ep. 1   82.43.13

    R7. 46. Same as *71* below.

31 De mansionibus filiorum Israel ep. 1

32 De eo quod ait Ysaias: Et claudentur ibi in carcerem, et post multos dies visitabuntur ep. 1

33 De aequinoctio juxta Anatholinum ep. 1   15.1

    Whole entry from R7. 52 and *HE*.

34 Item librum vitae et passionis S. Felicis de metrico Paulini opere in prosam transtuli

p. 46]

35 Item librum vitae et passionis S. Anastasii de Graeco translatum et pejus a quodam imperito emendatum prout potui ad sensum correxi

36 Item vitam S. patris, monachi simul et antistitis Cuthberti prius heroico metro et postmodum paulo sermone descripsi   *Nobis scribendi . . . caruit*   82.95

    R7. 40. *CPL* 1381. Ed. B. Colgrave, *Two Lives of St. Cuthbert* (Cambridge 1940) 154–306, incipit 'Principium nobis scribendi', explicit 'coronat'.

37 Item historiam abbatum monasterii hujus in quo supernae pietati servire gaudeo, Benedicti, Ceolfridi et Huaethberti in lib. 2   *Religiosus . . . impendant*   82.163.15

    R7. 29. *CPL* 1378. Sharpe, *Latin Writers*, 73. Ed. C. Plummer, *Venerabilis Baedae opera historica* (Oxford 1896) 1. 364–87.

38 Historiam ecclesiasticam nostrae insulae ac gentis in lib. 5   *Gloriosissimo . . . inveniam amen*   82.94.9.19.35.13.15

    R7. 23. *CPL* 1375. Sharpe, *Latin Writers*, 73. Ed. B. Colgrave & R. A. B. Mynors, OMT (1969) 2; explicit is that of the preface, whose last paragraph is attached to the end of the book in the English manuscripts (ib. xl–xli, lvii–lviii, and 570n). **82** Bury = B13. 211 = Dublin, Trinity College, MS 492, fol. 1r (Bury B. 296).

Beda *84. 47*

39 Martilogium de natalitiis sanctorum martirum diebus, in quo omnes quos invenire potui non solum qua die, verum etiam quo genere certaminis vel sub quo judice mundum vicerunt, diligenter annotare curavi   *Octave . . . hermetis*

> The lengthy title was taken from *HE*, but no English copies of Bede's *Martyrologium* are known to survive; Sharpe, *Latin Writers*, 73. The incipit 'Octaue Domini' would be the same for 1 January in any number of martyrologies; explicit unidentified.

40 Ympnorum diverso metro sive rithmo lib. 1

41 Epigramatum heroico metro sive elegiaco lib. 1

42 De natura rerum lib. 1   *Operatio . . . extenditur*   82.94.95.43.19.127.128

> R7. 2. *CPL* 1343. Sharpe, *Latin Writers*, 72. *CCSL* 123A. 192.

43 De temporibus et luna lib. 1   *De temporum . . . palmam*   82.65

> *De temporum ratione. CPL* 2320. Sharpe, *Latin Writers*, 73. *CCSL* 123B. 268. **82** Bury = B13. 64.

44 Item de temporibus, horis et momentis lib. 1   *Tempore . . . patet*   82.95.42.80.9.19.15

> R7. 8. *De temporibus. CPL* 2318. Sharpe, *Latin Writers*, 73. *CCSL* 123C. 585. **82** Bury = B13. 64.

45 De orthographia alphabeti ordine distinctum lib. 1   *A aeternus . . .*   163. 126.124

> Whole entry from R7. 27 (incipit and location numbers) and *HE* (title).

46 De metrica arte lib. 1   *Qui notitiam . . . sempiternam*   82.163.166.43.1.139

> R7. 32. *CPL* 1565. Sharpe, *Latin Writers*, 72. *CCSL* 123A. 81.

47 De scematibus et tropis, id est de figuris et modis locutionum quibus scientia Scriptura contexta est lib. 1   *Solet . . . uxoris Loth*   82.1.166.126.43.124

> R7. 4. *CPL* 1567. Sharpe, *Latin Writers*, 72. *CCSL* 123A. 142. Same as Cassiodorus *III.5*; probably the same as *52* below. **82** Bury = Cambridge, Pembroke College, MS 1, fol. 23r (Bury A. 92).

Haec Beda in fine Historiae Anglorum, et obiit An. Christi 734 anno aetatis suo 59°. Dicitur autem et alia scripsisse, videlicet

Beda   *84. 48*

48 De divinis officiis lib. 1

>   R7. 36 (whole entry).

49 De mensibus cum tabulis lib. 1   *Januarius* . . .   82

>   R7. 44. *Ps.* Bede; Sharpe, *Latin Writers*, 75, and see Jones, *Bedae pseudepigrapha*, 68–9. Cf. *PL* 90. 759.

50 De formationibus signorum lib. 1   *Igitur* . . .   82

>   R7. 45. Probably *ps.* Bede, *De constellationibus.* Cf. Thorndike/Kibre 656.

51 De compoto lib. 1   *Romulus* . . .   82.15.115

>   R7. 51. Incipit is evidently that of a section called 'On the Roman Months', either *De temporum ratione* c. 12 (*CCSL* 123B. 319) or the *pseudo*-Bedan *De ratione computi* c. 7 (*PL* 90. 585); cf. Jones, *Bedae pseudepigrapha*, 40. We are not aware that either text had an independent existence in manuscript.

52 De tropographia lib. 1   9.115

>   R7. 49 (whole entry). Probably the same as *47* above.

53 Lamentationum in diem judicii lib. 1   *Inter . . . fratribus almis*   82.1.163.65

>   R7. 31. *CPL* 1370. *CCSL* 122. 439 (explicit at line 161).

54 Super librum Donati expositio 1   *Iste titulus . . . accentum*   82

>   Remigius of Auxerre; ed. W. Fox, Teubner (1902), explicit 'nullus certus accentus' (p. 91 line 5) is followed by six additional lines in the edition.

55 Super Mattheum commentarium lib. 1   35.85.167

>   R7. 9. *Ps.* Bede. Sharpe, *Latin Writers*, 75. *PL* 92. 9.

56 De locis sanctis et situ Jerusalem lib. 1   *Situs in . . . satagas*   128.95.129.19.35

>   128] 126 *R*
>
>   R7. 3. *CPL* 2333. Sharpe, *Latin Writers*, 72. *CCSL* 175. 251.

57 Descriptionis situs terrae, provinciarum et civitatum lib. 1   8.94.95.164. 90.1

> 164] 154 R
>
> Cf. R7. 39 (*Nomina regionum et locorum de Actibus Apostolorum*, *CPL* 1359), the source of the location numbers. The source of Kirkestede's title is unidentified.

58 Super mulierem fortem expositio 1   *Mulier . . . serviciis*   82.42.15

> R7. 47. *CPL* 1351, on Proverbs 31:10–31. *CCSL* 119B. 149–63.

59 De quatuor difficilibus lib. 1   42

> R7. 48 (whole entry).

60 Contra Julianum episcopum Eclanensem de Campania lib. 1   *Primo admonendum . . . valemus*   82

> Eclanensem] Eccanensem *Add. 3470, queried by Tanner*
>
> This is Book I of *In Cantica Canticorum* (*CPL* 1353; see 7 above), which circulated alone in certain manuscripts; see Laistner, 66–70. *CCSL* 119B. 167–80, which treats 'Contra Julianum' as an unnumbered introductory letter preceding Book I.

61 Super epistolas Pauli ex operibus Augustini collectionem lib. 4 supra est, In apostolum

> Same as 25 above.

62 De temporibus et variis temporum spaciis sub interrogatione et responsione lib. 1   *Tempora . . .*   82

> sub *queried by Tanner*
>
> Spurious; Jones, *Bedae pseudepigrapha*, 38. *De ratione computi*. *PL* 90. 579.

63 Super psalmos vel psalterium lib. 1   20.65

> R7. 56. Unidentified.

64 In defensione gratiae Dei lib. 7   161

> R7. 24 (whole entry).

Beda *84. 65*

65 Florum, secundum quosdam lib. 1   164.154   supra, In apostolum

    R7. 34 (whole entry). Same as *25* above.

66 Qualiter contigit quod memoria Andreae sit in Scotia   163

    R7. 28 (whole entry).

p. 47]

67 Passionarium   128

    R7. 38 (whole entry).

68 Quod episcopi Candidae Casae debent esse subjecti archiepiscopo Eboracensi   163

    R7. 33 (whole entry).

69 De veritate annorum divinorum lib. 1   *Ad veritatem* . . .   82

    Unidentified.

70 Denotationes circulorum lib. 1   *Quae ad* . . .

    Unidentified.

71 Cronica de 6 aetatibus   *Adam annorum* . . .

    R7. 6. *Chronica minora et maiora*, CPL 2273. Cf. Sharpe, *Latin Writers*, 71. MGH *Auct. Antiq.* 13 = *Chronica minora* 3. 247–327; the incipit is that of c. 10, p. 249. Same as *30* above.

72 De ratione bisexti ep. 1

    From Bede's list in *HE*, overlooked above (it occurs in *HE* between *32* and *33* above).

85 BERNARDUS Albus monachus et abbas Clarevallensis de ordine Cisterciensi, floruit circa A. Ch. 1140 et scripsit multa juxta Vincentium in Speculo historiali lib. 29 cap. 2

    Registrum 34, Vincent XXIX 2 (references are followed by numbers in brackets [1, 2, etc.] that indicate the sequence of titles in the chapter), *Manipulus florum* VI.

Bernardus *85. 6*

Most (twenty-nine) of these forty-four works are reported from manuscripts, from Bury and nearby houses. With two exceptions, the other fifteen titles come in a haphazard order from the *Registrum*.
Speculum coenobitarum 50.
Ely extracts, fol. 118v.
Sancti Bernardi Opera, ed. J. Leclercq & others, 8 vols. (Rome 1957–77).

1 De contemptu mundi ad clericos lib. 1   <u>94</u>

    Whole entry from R34. 8 (location number) and Vincent XXIX 2 [1] (title).

2 De diligendo Deo lib. 1   *Illustri . . . praedicant*   82.<u>94</u>.<u>8</u>.<u>9</u>.<u>19</u>.<u>63</u>.<u>46</u>

    R34. 30, Vincent XXIX 2 [4], *MF* VI 9 (incipit, explicit). *SBO* 3. 119. Same as Hugo *244.12*.

3 De amore Dei lib. 1   *Venite . . . benedicimus*   82.<u>94</u>.<u>89</u>.<u>42</u>.<u>80</u>.<u>13</u>.<u>63</u>

    R34. 31, *MF* VI 10. William of Saint-Thierry. *De contemplando Deo. PL* 184. 367.

4 De xii gradibus humilitatis lib. 1   *Rogasti . . . humilitatis*   82.<u>94</u>.<u>92</u>.<u>41</u>.<u>8</u>.<u>9</u>. <u>19</u>.<u>13</u>

    41] 43 *R*

    R34. 28, Vincent XXIX 2 [5], *MF* VI 6 (incipit, explicit). *SBO* 3. 16. **82** Bury = Cambridge, Pembroke College, MS 118, fols. 12r–16v (Bury Y. 12), incipit (not at the beginning) marked with a red initial, explicit tallies.

5 De xii gradibus superbiae lib. 1   *Primus . . . in nostro*   82 <u>94</u> <u>92</u> <u>41</u> <u>8</u> <u>9</u> <u>19</u> <u>13</u>

    41] 43 *R*

    R34. 28, *MF* VI 7. *SBO* 3. 38. **82** Bury = Cambridge, Pembroke College, MS 118, fol. 16v (Bury Y. 12), explicit (fol. 20ra) 'in nostro cadite leges'.

6 De gratia et libero arbitrio lib. 1   *Loquente . . . magnificavit*   82.<u>94</u>.<u>43</u>.<u>9</u>.<u>19</u>. <u>13</u>.115

    43] 93 *R*

    R34. 29, Vincent XXIX 2 [6], *MF* VI 5. *SBO* 3. 165.

Bernardus *85. 7*

7 De praecepto et dispensatione lib. 1 *Quum mente . . . voluntati* 82.94.92.
43.153.105.1

   153] 163 *R*   105] 15 *R*

   R34. 26, Vincent XXIX 2 [7], *MF* VI 3 (incipit, explicit). *SBO* 3. 254, incipit 'Qua mente'. **82** Bury = BL MS Royal 8 F. xiv, fols. 141v–149r (Bury G. 15), incipit 'Qua mente'; manuscript procured by, and this segment copied by, Kirkestede.

8 Ad Cistertienses et Cluniacenses apolegiticum lib. 1 *Venerabili . . . precor et supplico* 82.153.1.74.77.79

   R34. 50, Vincent XXIX 2 [8]. *SBO* 3. 81.

9 De consideratione ad Eugenium lib. 5 *Subit . . . quaerendi* 82.92.94.93.
19.39.63

   93] 13 *R*

   R34. 25, Vincent XXIX 2 [11], *MF* VI 1. *SBO* 3. 393.

10 De laude novae militiae lib. 1 *Novuum . . . digitos nostros* 74.82

   R34. 41, Vincent XXIX 2 [16], *MF* VI 8. *SBO* 3. 214, explicit (p. 239) 'digitos uestros ad bellum'.

11 Super psalmum Qui habitat omelias 18 *Considero . . . in saecula* 82

   R34. 33, Vincent XXIX 2 [13], *MF* VI 12. *SBO* 4. 383 (17 homilies), explicit 'in saecula' *hom.* 17 (p. 492).

12 Super Cantica Canticorum omel. 84 *Vos fratres . . . super omnia* 82.94.
92.9.19.35.2

   94 *may be* 49 *R*   92 *may be* 97 *R*   2 *may be* 20 *R*

   R34. 21, Vincent XXIX 2 [24], *MF* VI 2 (incipit, explicit). *SBO* vols. 1–2 (86 homilies); incipit of *hom.* 1 (*SBO* 1. 3) 'Vobis fratres'; explicit of both *hom.* 84 and 85 (and others), 'super omnia Deus benedictus in secula'. **82** Bury = Cambridge, Pembroke College, MS 9, fol. 1r (Bury B. 309), where both *hom.* 84 (fol. 153v) and *hom.* 85 (fol. 156r) end with this explicit; BL MS Royal 7 C. II, fols. 132r–165r (Bury R. 40) contains only twenty-four sermons, begins incomplete.

Bernardus *85. 20*

13 Super Missus est omel. 4   *Quid sibi . . . destinavi*   82.156.<u>9</u>.<u>12</u>.50.<u>19</u>.<u>15</u>

   12] xii *R*

   R34. 27, Vincent XXIX 2 [15], *MF* VI 4. *SBO* 4. 13. **82** Bury = Cambridge, Pembroke College, MS 118, fol. 20r (Bury Y. 12), ends imperfectly.

14 Super Magnificat tract. 1   *Si circumstantiam . . . dolo exhibuit*   <u>161</u>.<u>43</u>.<u>57</u>. 82.63.65

   Vincent XXIX 2 [17]. Hugh of Saint-Victor; Goy, 383. *PL* 175. 413. Location numbers **161** to **57** seem to be taken, for reasons not apparent, from R34. 33 (= *11* above).

15 Ad Hugonem de S. Victore ep. 1   *Si tibi . . . electione*

   Vincent XXIX 2 [9]. *SBO* 7. 184 (*ep*. 77).

16 Contra haereses Petri Adelardi ad Innocentium papam ep. 1   *Amantissimo . . . transmisi*

   Vincent XXIX 2 [12]. *SBO* 8. 17–38 (*ep*. 190).

17 Ad fratres de monte lib. 1   *Misericors . . . secretum meum*   82.63.65

   R34. 23. The incipit is that of a short extract from *De uia miserationis* that appears in a British manuscript, BL Royal 6 B. XI, fol. 35r, labelled 'B[ernardus] ad fratres de monte'; the extract is followed (fol. 35v) without break by William of St-Thierry (*ps*. Bernard), *Epistola ad fratres de monte Dei* (ed. J.-M. Déchanet, SChr 223 (1975) 130). Same as Wilhelmus *632.2*.

18 De 6 alis seraphim tract. 1   *Prima ala . . . beatudinem*   82.65

   Alain de Lille. *PL* 210. 269. **82** Bury = London, Wellcome Historical Medical Library, MS 801A, fol. 124r (Bury B. 357), attributed to Bernard in the contents list.

19 De tribus virtutibus, caritate, castitate et humilitate lib. 1   *Placuit . . . nescirem*   82.<u>13</u>.<u>43</u>

   R34. 1. *SBO* 7. 100 (*ep*. 42).

20 De quinque partibus dilectionis lib. 1   *Ars est . . . novissimi*   82

   dilectionis] dilectione *Add. 3470*

   William of Saint-Thierry, *De natura et dignitate amoris*. Ed. R. Thomas, Pain de Cîteaux 24 (Chambarand 1965) 11–166, explicit 'nouissimi primi'.

Bernardus *85. 21*

21 Meditationum lib. 1   *Multi . . .*   82.63.65.61.1.69.83

> R34. 46, Vincent XXIX 2 [2], *MF* VI 14. *PL* 184. 485. **82** Bury = BL MS Royal 5 A. VIII, fol. 108v (Bury A. 52); BL MS Royal 10 B. XII, fol. 20r (Bury D. —). / **61** Peterborough = Peterborough Cathedral, MS 3, fol. 181r = BP21. 190b, and a score of other entries in the same catalogue.

22 Exortationum de passione Christi lib. 1   *Dominus noster . . .*   154.42.153.139.20.82

> 20] xx *R*

> R34. 5 and 34. 14, Vincent XXIX 2 [3]. This entry illuminates the two *Registrum* entries and alters their identification in the edition; the title *Exortationes Bernardum* (often a variant title of the *De consideratione*) and the location number **154** come from R34. 5, while the incipit 'Dominus noster Jesus Christus in die palmarum' belongs to a work entitled *Sententie contemplatiue* in Utrecht, UL MS 158, fols. 33r–61r, the title that appears at R34. 14 with the sequence of location numbers **42** to **20**. Kirkestede's combining of these elements presumably depended on the work that he saw in a Bury manuscript [**82**] which has not been identified.

23 De passione B. Mariae et passione filii sui lib. 1   *Quis dabit . . . benedictus*   82.153.42.154

> Ps. Bernard, an extract from Ogier de Locedio's *De laudibus sanctae Dei genetricis*, inc. 'Quis dabit capiti meo aquam'; see H. Barré in *Revue d'ascétique et de mystique* 28 (1952) 243–66. The location numbers **153** to **154** are copied from *22* above.

24 De colloquio Simonis et Jesus capitula 61   *Ut tibi dilectissime . . . habeamus*   94.83

> R34. 9, *MF* VI 11. Geoffrey of Auxerre. *PL* 184. 437–76 prints sixty chapters, with this incipit and explicit.

25 Ad Davidem nepotem suum ep. 1   114

> 114] 154 *R*

> R34. 6 (whole entry).

p. 48]

26 Ad Adam monachum ep. 1

> Source unidentified; cf. R34. 20. *SBO* 7. 31 (*ep.* 7).

27 De cohabitatione fratrum lib. 1   126

   R34. 2 (whole entry).

28 Super illud: Intravit Jesus

   R34. 10 (whole entry).

29 De assumptione   *Quid est, fratres* . . .   63

   SBO 5. 238, *In Assumptione* (*serm.* 3). **63** was copied by mistake from R34. 10 (*28* above).

30 Super illud: Cum esset desponsata   63

   R34. 11 (whole entry).

31 Super Ysaiam lib. 1   *Memor* . . .   166.163

   R34. 12; this erroneous combination of title and incipit comes from the *Registrum*. Source of the location numbers is unknown.

32 Super epistolam Jacobi lib. 1   111.166

   R34. 16 (whole entry save the suspect **166**).

33 Super 5 libros Moysy

   This work and its source are unidentified.

34 Planctum super mortem fratris sui   153   Vide etiam in omeliis super Cantica

   R34. 15 (whole entry).

35 Quaestionum quatuor lib. 1   156.65

   R34. 3. Unidentified.

36 Quomodo Christus imitetur lib. 1   154

   R34. 4 (whole entry).

37 De operibus 6 dierum, secundum quosdam lib. 1   105

   R34. 7 (whole entry).

Bernardus   *85. 38*

38 Epistolarum ad diversos 245 lib. 1   77.86.<u>93</u>.94.<u>8</u>.<u>9</u>.<u>19</u>

   93] 13 *R*

   R34. 24, Vincent XXIX 2 [18]. *SBO* vols. 7–8.

39 Sermones pene innumerabiles   8<u>2</u>.83.86.79.<u>94</u>.<u>9</u>.<u>13</u>

   R34. 22, Vincent XXIX 2 [19]. *SBO* vols. 4–6/1.

40 De viis vitae, scilicet confessione et poenitentia serm. 1   *Notas mihi . . . salvatoris*   86

   SBO 6/1. 234 (*serm.* 40).

41 De 7 gradibus obedientiae serm. 1   *Non possumus . . . sponsus ecclesiae*   86

   SBO 6/1. 243 (*serm.* 41).

42 De conceptione B. Mariae ep. 1   *Inter ecclesias . . . emendare*

   R34. 47. *SBO* 7. 388 (*ep.* 174).

43 De gemitu animae   *Primum quidem . . . in epistolis Pauli prae occisione*   74

   animae *queried by Tanner*

   Unidentified.

44 De xii gradibus scalae Jacob serm.   *Omnium tempore . . . in gloria vitae*

   Unidentified.

86 BERNARDUS monachus et abbas Cassinensis et postea cardinalis floruit circa A.D. 1255 et scripsit quendam tractatum de professione monachorum qui intitulatur

   Speculum coenobitarum 53.
   Ely extracts, fol. 118v.

 1 Speculum monachorum continet partes 3   *Praecordialissimo . . . ad faciem*   82.73.20

   Ed. H. Walter (Venice 1901). **82** Bury = the text in BL MS Harley 1206, fol. 1r (Bury S[?] 23), was procured for Bury at the beginning of the 16th cent., too late to have been used for this entry and the next; but works 1–2 occur there in this sequence with these incipits and explicits, and the Bury manuscript Kirkestede cites must have done the same. / **73** Norwich, cathedral priory = B58. 16.

2 Super regulam S. Benedicti expositionem 1   *Legitur in . . . aeternam*   82. 73.30

> Legitur in] proverbiis *add. Ely extracts fol. 118v*

> Ed. A. M. Caplet (Monte Cassino 1894); Kirkestede quoted a paragraph from this work in the headnote to the entry for John Cassian (*285*). **82** Bury = the text in BL MS Harley 1206, fol. 59r (Bury S[?] 23) was evidently not used; see note to *1* above. / **73** Norwich, cathedral priory = CUL MS Kk. 2. 21, fol. 1r = B58. 12.

87 BERNARDUS Silvestris floruit circa A. Ch. <*blank*> et scripsit

> Bale, *Index*, 47–8.
> Gale extracts, verso of penultimate back flyleaf.

1 Librum partim metricum partim prosaicum   *Congeries . . . manus*   82

> *Cosmographia*. Ed. C. S. Barach & J. Wrobel, Bibliotheca philosophorum mediae aetatis 1 (Innsbruck 1876) 7.

2 De vita parricidae imperatoris lib. 1   *Semper ut . . . liber et explicit*

> parricidae *queried by Tanner, omitted with ellipsis by Gale extracts*

> Ed. B. Hauréau, *Le Mathematicus de Bernard Silvestris et la Passio Sanctae Agnetis de Pierre Riga* (Paris 1895) 15; explicit (37), 'Liber et explicitus ad mea uota meus'.

88 BERNARDUS Morlanensis monachus de Cluniaco floruit circa A. Ch. <*blank*> et scripsit ad Petrum abbatem suum Cluniacensem

> Bale, *Index*, 47.

1 De contemptu mundi, metrice lib. 3   *Hora . . . ne pereamus*   61.45.82

> Hora] novissima tempora pessima sunt vigilemus *add. Bale; atypically, Bale reports Kirkestede's three locations, converted from numbers into names*

> Ed. H. C. Hoskier (London 1929).

89 BONAVENTURA Frater Minor et successor B. Francisci floruit A. Ch. 1269 et scripsit multa

> This entry was composed from manuscripts, most of them at Bury. Ely extracts, fol. 118v.

1 Itinerarium mentis in Dominum, continet lib. 1   *In primo . . . fiat, fiat*   82

> *SBonO* 5. 295.

2 Super libros sententiarum Petri lib. 4

> *SBonO* 1–4. [**82** Bury = Cambridge, Pembroke College, MS 10 (Bury B. 385), contains two manuscripts bound together of, respectively, Bonaventure on the fourth book of the *Sentences* and on the second, both ending incomplete.]

3 Breviloquium de veritate theologiae et de sacramentis lib. 7   *Flecto jenua . . . qui est trinus*   82.65   et vocatur a quibusdam Breviloquium pauperis

> *SBonO* 6. 537. **82** Bury = Cambridge, Pembroke College, MS 80, fol. 85r (Bury B. 225), with Kirkestede supplying the missing title; Cambridge, Pembroke College, MS 107 (Bury B. 328), with this exact title in full in Kirkestede's table of contents.

4 Summa quae vocatur Pharetra et continet lib. 4   *Gregorius . . .*

> Spurious; this may be the work of William de la Furmenterie or Guibert of Tournai. Ed. *S. Bonaventura Opera omnia* (Rome 1588–96), 6. 102.

5 Meditationes et contemplationes lib. 1   *Ecce descripsi . . . 2^{dum} cherubim et 3^{ium}*   10.61.147

> *SBonO* 8. 3. **61** Peterborough = six entries in the Peterborough catalogue (BP21. 193b, 195a, 199b, 222c, 247b, and 298b) of works that Kirkestede may have considered, correctly or not, to be identical with this.

6 Vitam Christi ab annunciatione ad ascensionem   *Cum per . . . ergo iteratio*   82

> Cum per] Inter alia virtutem *Ely extracts fol. 118v; this latter reading is the incipit of the prologue*

> *Meditationes uitae Christi*; Ioannes de Caulibus (de S. Geminiano). *CCCM* 153. 11; incipit is that of c. 1; explicit (p. 353) 'ergo iteratio utriusque decorem substantie designauit.'

p. 49]

90 BRIDFERTHUS monachus Ramesiae floruit A. Ch. *<blank>* et scripsit

> *Speculum coenobitarum* 57.
> Bale, *Index*, 50.
> Sharpe, *Latin Writers*, 81.

1 Super librum Bedae de temporibus lib. 1   *Spiraculo* . . .   82

> Concerning identification and attribution see Sharpe, *Latin Writers*, 81.

91 BRUNO Sigiensis episcopus floruit A.C. *<blank>* et scripsit

> *Registrum* 63.

1 Super 5 libros Moysy lib. 1   <u>154</u>.<u>105</u>

> R63. 1 (whole entry).

2 Super epistolas Pauli lib. 1   *Hoc non* . . . *id est veritas*   <u>82</u>.<u>15</u> vel Principium: *Primum*. Finis: *in quibus*

> non *queried by Tanner*

> R63. 2. Bruno Carthusiensis; Stegmüller *Bibl.* 1817–30. *PL* 153. 11, incipit 'Primum'. Neither the first incipit nor the two explicits have been identified.
> **82** Bury = B13. 117.

92 BUCONIUS Mauritaniae Castellani opidi episcopus floruit A. Ch. *<blank>* et scripsit juxta Genadium

> Buconius] Voconius *Gennadius*

> Gennadius c. 79 (whole entry).

1 Adversus Judaeos lib. 1

2 Adversus Arrianos vel haereticos lib. 1

3 De sacramentis lib. 1

Bartholomaeus 93.

93 BARTHOLOMAEUS Frater Minor floruit circa A.C. 1209 et scripsit

(Bartholomaeus Anglicus)
Ely extracts, fol. 118v.
Sharpe, *Latin Writers*, 69.

1 De proprietatibus rerum lib. 19   *Cum proprietates . . . vivens*   82

> Printed, Basel *c.* 1470 (*GW* 3402). **82** Bury = Glasgow UL MS Hunterian 209 (Bury B. 332).

94 BOETIUS philosophus floruit circa A. Ch. 512 et scripsit multa secundum Vincentium in Speculo historiali lib. 220 cap. 15

> *Registrum* 58, Vincent XXII 15 (references are followed by numbers in brackets [1, 2, etc.] that indicate the sequence of titles in the chapter), *Manipulus florum* XVIII.
> At least ten and perhaps thirteen of the seventeen titles come from Bury manuscripts; the other titles have been inserted seemingly at random from Kirkestede's secondary sources.
> Kirkestede recorded portions of this entry on Lambeth Palace Library, MS 67, fol. i^v (Bury B. 318), including the first half of the heading, 'Boetius — et scripsit' with the date, and ten titles usually with incipit and explicit (in the sequence *1, 2, 4, 6, 7* [without incipit and explicit], *9, 10* [without incipit and explicit], *14, 12, 5*).
> Ely extracts, fol. 118v.

1 De Trinitate lib. 3   *Investigatio . . . bonorum causa*   82.163.164.94.82.15

> *The second* 82] 42 *R*

> R58. 1, Vincent XXII 15 [1], *MF* XVIII 1. *CPL* 890. Ed. H. F. Stewart & others, *Boethius: the Theological Tractates* (London 1973) 2, incipit 'Inuestigatam'; explicit (p. 30) does not correspond. Incipit and explicit were taken from the *Manipulus florum*. **82** Bury = B13. 29b = Cambridge, Pembroke College, MS 84, fol. 1r (Bury B. 319); B13. 175; Cambridge, King's College, MS 3 pt 4, fol. 1r (Bury —), incipit 'Inuestigatam', explicit 'bonorum causa prescribit'.

2 De disciplina scolarium lib. 3   *Vestram novit . . . permanebunt*   82

> Vincent XXII 15 [3], *MF* XVIII 4. *Ps.* Boethius. Ed. O. Weijers (Leiden 1976) 93. **82** Bury = the title is still legible on an erased table of contents in BL MS Royal 8 C. IV, fol. 41r (Bury R. 42), but the work itself is missing.

3 De persona Christi lib. 2   *Christianam . . . praescribit*   82.15

> R58. 6. *Contra Eutychen et Nestorium*; *CPL* 894. Ed. H. F. Stewart & others, *Boethius: the Theological Tractates* (London 1973) 72, incipit does not correspond.

82 Bury = Cambridge, Pembroke College, MS 84, fol. 13r (Bury B. 319), with marginal rubric (fol. 13) and colophon (fol. 31v), 'Boecii de persona Christi' both written by Kirkestede.

4 De consolationibus philosophiae lib. 5   *Carmina . . . cuncta cernentis*   82. 162.163.94.42.9.15.1

Carmina] Carissimam *Add. 3470; Tanner, uncertain of this reading, has added* Carmina *as a variant reading*   163] 164 *R*   42] 43 *R*

R58. 2 (title, location numbers), Vincent XXII 15 [2], *MF* XVIII 3 (title, incipit, explicit). *CPL* 878. *CCSL* 94. **82** = B13. 176; BL MS Royal 8 B. IV, fol. 102r (Bury S. 184), incomplete; Cambridge, Pembroke College, MS 84, fol. 32r (Bury B. 319), contains a commentary on the *Consolatio*.

5 De providentia Dei lib. 1

R58. 5 (whole entry).

6 De diffinitionibus Tullii lib. 1   *Dicendi . . . satis esse*

MF XVIII 2 (whole entry; explicit 'satis esse dixi').

7 De musica lib. 5   *Omnem . . . nusquam una*   82.166.43.1

omnem *queried by Tanner*   una] un *Add. 3470, queried by Tanner*   166] 161 *R*

R58. 4, Vincent XXII 15 [4]. *CPL* 880. Ed. G. Friedlein (Leipzig 1867) 178, incipit 'Omnem'. **82** Bury = B13. 177b and cf. B13. 65b; Lambeth Palace Library, MS 67, fol. 96r (Bury B. 318).

8 De arithmetica lib. 1   *In dandis . . .*   164.166.79.1.43

166] 161 *R*

R58. 3. *CPL* 879. *CCSL* 94A. 3, incipit is that of the prologue. [**82** Bury = B13. 177a and cf. B13. 65a; Lambeth Palace Library, MS 67, fol. 1r (Bury B. 318).]

9 De logica lib.1

Vincent XXII 15 [5] (whole entry).

10 Topicorum lib. 3   *Omnis ratio . . . reservemus*

Vincent XXII 15 [6]. *CPL* 889. *PL* 64. 1173; explicit is that of Book III.

Boetius *94. 11*

11 De divisionibus lib. 1   *Quoniam magnos . . . expressimus*

   Vincent XXII 15 [7]. *CPL* 887. *PL* 64. 875.

12 De geometria practica

   R58. 7 (whole entry).

13 Super Porphyrium lib. 5   *Secundus . . . ad praedicamenta*

   CPL 881. *CSEL* 48.

14 Item libros cathegoriorum, siligismorum ypoteticorum et comenta super Aristotilem

   Vincent XXII 15 [8] (whole entry).

15 Comicos quinquaginta, in quos praecellit ille qui sic incipit: *O amor deus, deitas . . .* Sed et uxor ejus Elpes nomine, filia regis Ciciliae, ympnum in laudem apostolorum Petri et Pauli edidit, qui sic incipit: *Felix per omnes festum mundi . . .*

   Source unidentified. *O amor deus, deitas* i.e. *De S. Trinitate.* ed. G. K. Dreves, *Cantiones et muteti* 2, *AH* 21 (1895) 11–13. *Felix per omnes festum mundi*, attributed to Paulinus Aquileiensis, MGH *Poetae latini* 1. 136–7; ed. C. Blume, *AH* 50 (1907) 141–2, repr. *PLS* 3. 1278–9.

16 Item de modo praedicandi de Trinitate lib. 1

   praedicandi *queried by Tanner*

   The three works *16–18* appear in Cambridge, Pembroke College, MS 84, fols. 8v–31v (Bury B. 319), but not with these titles.

   CPL 891. Ed. H. F. Stewart & others, *Boethius: the Theological Tractates* (London 1973) 32.

17 De ebdomadibus lib. 1

   CPL 892. Ed. Stewart (as *16*) 38. See note to *16* above.

18 De fide Christiana lib. 1

   CPL 893. Ed. Stewart (as *16*) 52. See note to *16* above.

95 BARDESANES Sirus floruit circa A. Ch. <*blank*> et scripsit juxta Jeronimum libro De viris illustribus

> Jerome c. 33 (whole entry).

1 Contra haereticos infinita volumina

2 Item de fato lib. 1

3 Et multa alia.

p. 50]

96 BERENGARIUS floruit circa A. Ch. 1069 et scripsit secundum quosdam

1 Super Apocalipsim lib. 1   *Planior est si dixisset* . . .   45

> Haimo of Auxerre; Stegmüller *Bibl.* 3072, 3122. *PL* 117. 939. See also Berengarius *82.3*.

97 BERNARDUS de Trilia Hispanus floruit A. Ch. <*blank*> et scripsit postillas

> *Script. Ord. Praed.* (whole entry), cf. Stams, 20.

1 Super Proverbia

2 Super Cantica Canticorum

3 Super Ecclesiasten

4 Super librum Sapientiae

5 Super Johannem

6 Tria quodlibet

7 De spiritualibus creaturis quaestiones

8 De potentia Dei

9 De anima conjuncta et separata quaestiones

Bernardus   97. 10

   10 De differentia esse et essentiae quaestiones

   11 Super totam astrologiam quaestiones

   > In Apocalypsim Johannis *an additional entry in Add. 3470; according to Tanner this title was added in a recent hand*

98 BERNARDUS Claremontensis episcopus et Frater Praedicator floruit A. Ch. <*blank*> et scripsit

> *Script. Ord. Praed.* (whole entry), cf. Stams, 37.

   1 Super librum sententiarum lecturam 1

   2 Contra Henricum de Gandavo ubi impugnat Thomae de Aquino

   3 Contra Godefridum de Fontibus eadem causa

   4 Contra Jacobum Neapolitanum heremitam Augustinensem eadem causa

   > *om. Stams*

99 BOCHARDUS Theutonicus Frater Praedicator floruit A. Ch. <*blank*> et scripsit

> Bochardus] Burchardus *Stams*

> *Script. Ord. Praed.* (whole entry), cf. Stams, 52.
> James extracts, p. 197.

   1 Summam juris

100 BARTHOLOMEUS Pisanus Frater Praedicator floruit A. Ch. <*blank*> et scripsit

> *Script. Ord. Praed.* (whole entry), cf. Stams, 59.
> Ely extracts, fol. 118v.

   1 Summam de virtutibus

   2 Summam de vitiis

   3 Tabulam ad inveniendum Pascha

101 BOETIUS Dacus Frater Praedicator floruit A. Ch. <*blank*> et scripsit

Script. Ord. Praed. (whole entry), cf. Stams, 63.

1 De modis sign[ific]andi lib. 1

significandi] signandi *Add. 3470, queried by Tanner*

2 Quaestiones super libros Aristotelis

This title represents eleven commentaries on the works of Aristotle listed in Stams and in Pign. 64.

3 De eternitate mundi

102 BUMBALONIUS Bononiensis Frater Praedicator floruit A. Ch. <*blank*> et scripsit

Script. Ord. Praed. (whole entry), cf. Stams, 64.

1 Super veterem logicam

Stams lists four commentaries on Aristotle.

2 Super librum sententiarum

[p. 51]

103 BYARDUS Frater Praedicator floruit A. Ch. <*blank*> et scripsit

Byardus] Nicolaus Bayarde *Bale*

Script. Ord. Praed. (whole entry). The author is omitted by Stams and Pign.; but 'Nicholaus de Byardo, Gallicus', is included, attributed with additional works, in the list of Dominican writers compiled by Stephen de Salanhac and Bernard Gui upon which Stams, Pign., and the Bury source are based. Bale, *Index*, 299.

1 Distinctiones notabiles

Absconditur malum a diabolo sub dilectatione *add. Bale as incipit*

104 BACHILLUS Corinthiorum episcopus floruit circa A. Ch. 197 et scripsit juxta Jeronimum libro De catholicis scriptoribus

Jerome c. 44 (whole entry save the date).

Bachillus *104. 1*

   1 De Pascha librum elegantem unum

105 BELLATOR presbyter vir religiosissimus floruit circa A. Ch. <*blank*> et scripsit juxta Cassiodorum libro De institutione divinarum literarum

      Cassiodorus I. 1. 9 etc. (whole entry).

   1 Super Ruth lib. 2

      Cassiodorus I. 1. 9 (whole entry).

   2 Super librum Sapientiae lib. 8

      Cassiodorus I. 5. 5 (whole entry).

   3 Super Esdram lib. 2

      Cassiodorus I. 6. 6 (whole entry).

   4 Super Tobiam lib. 5

      Cassiodorus I. 6. 4 (whole entry).

   5 Super Hester lib. 6

      Cassiodorus I. 6. 4 (whole entry).

   6 Super Judith lib. 19

      Cassiodorus I. 6. 4 (whole entry).

   7 Super librum Machabeorum lib. 10

      Cassiodorus I. 6. 4 (whole entry).

106 BURCARDUS Warmaciensis episcopus floruit A. Ch. 1012 secundum eundem in quadam epistola et scripsit

      Source unidentified.

   1 De consiliis et decretis paparum lib. 20   *Burcardus* . . .

      PL 140. 537.

107 BABIO floruit <blank> et scripsit

> Babio] Petrus Babion *Bale*

> (Geoffrey Babio)
> Bale, *Index*, 318.

1 Super Mattheum expositionem   *Dominus ac redemptor . . . meruerunt*   43.74.63

> Dominus ac redemptor] noster *add. Bale*

> *PL* 162. 1227, among the works of Anselm of Laon. The incipit is that of the prologue; see Stegmüller *Bibl.* 2604. Explicit unidentified.

2 Item sermones 70   *Dicite pusill[an]i[mes] . . . Ante adventum . . .*   74.43

> pusillanimes] pusilli *Add. 3470, queried by Tanner*; pusillanimes *Bale*

> The incipit of *serm.* 1 is 'Dicite pusillanimes . . . [Is 35:4–6]. Ante adventum . . .'. See J. P. Bonnes in *RB* 56 (1945–6) 174–215.

108 BERNARDUS Papiensis praepositus floruit circa A. Ch. <blank> et scripsit

1 Breviarium in quo continentur extravagantia Romanorum pontificum et auctoritates Veteris et Novi Testamenti et sanctorum ecclesiae doctorum lib. 5   Principium: *Juste judicate . . .*

> The *Compilatio prima.* Ed. E. Friedberg, *Quinque compilationes antiquae* (Leipzig 1882; repr. Graz 1956) 1. [The *Breuiarium* appears in Lambeth Palace Library, MS 105, fol. 137r, but this part of the manuscript is not from **82** Bury.]

109 BARTHOLOMEUS Brixiensis floruit circa A. Ch. <blank> et scripsit

> See J. F. von Schulte, *Die Geschichte der Quellen und Literatur des canonischen Rechts von Gratian bis auf die Gegenwart*, 3 vols. (Stuttgart 1875–80), 2. 83–8.

1 Summam super toto corpore decretorum

> Source unidentified. Perhaps the *Casus decretorum*, Schulte, 2. 84.

2 Item quaestiones   *Ad honorem . . . allegata*

> Schulte 2. 86. Printed, *Primum volumen tractatum ex variis juris interpretibus collectorum*, vol. 17 (Lyon 1549).

Bartholomeus   *109. 3*

3 Brocarda juris canonici   *Quoniam secundum juris . . . aliter probari*

> Brocarda queried by Tanner
>
> Schulte 2. 84. Printed, *Tractatus universi juris duce et auspice Gregorio XIII*, vol. 18 (Venice 1584)

110 BRIDA sancta principissa Sueciae scripsit diversos libros

> (St Birgitta of Sweden)
> Source unidentified. A brief excerpt from St Birgitta's visions, containing the internal date 1348, appears in Cambridge, Corpus Christi College, MS 404, fol. 102v (Bury P. 163), transcribed by Kirkestede. Her name does not figure in either the excerpt's heading or the table of contents.

p. 52]

111 CASSIODORUS prius consul, deinde senator et tandem monachus, floruit A. Ch. 536 et scripsit juxta Yvonem et juxta Vincentium in Speculo historiali lib. 22° cap. 49° ea quae sequuntur

> *Registrum* 14, Vincent XXII 49, Cassiodorus I. 6. 4 and I. 8. 1, Higden, I. 22; 'Ivo' = Hugh of Fleury, *Chronicon* (Münster 1638) 124.
> To construct this entry Kirkestede used each of these sources, in conjunction with Bury manuscripts of works attributed to Cassiodorus.
> *Speculum coenobitarum* 36.

1 Cronica de gestis pontificum et imperatorum secundum Polycronicon Cestrense lib. 1

> Higden, 1. 22 (whole entry)

2 Super psalterium tract. 150   *Beatus vir. Nimis pulcrum . . .*   65.82

> R14. 2, Vincent XXII 49. *CPL* 900. *CCSL* 97–98. **82** Bury = B13. 20, 55, and 30 (vols. 1, 2, 3 respectively); and Bury fragments: CUL MS Add. 4406/1 (2 leaves), and Columbia, MO, University of Missouri Library, MS Rare-L/PA/3381.A1/F7 no. 14 (1 leaf).

3 De ratione animae lib. 1

> Vincent XXII 49 (whole entry). Same as 7 below.

4 De institutione divinarum literarum vel scripturarum lib. 2   *Dum studia . . .*

R14. 5. *CPL* 906. Ed. R. A. B. Mynors (Oxford 1961²). [**82** Bury = B13. 62b = Bodl. MS e Musaeo 31, p. 79 (Bury A. 31), incipit 'Cum studia'.]

5 De tropis lib. 1

Source unidentified. Bede, *De schematibus et tropis*, not infrequently attributed to Cassiodorus in the Middle Ages. Same as Beda *84.47*.

6 De ortographia lib. 1

Whole entry from R14. 10 and Vincent XXII 49.

7 Item de anima lib. 1   *Cum jam . . . tractari*   82.15.83

CPL 897. *CCSL* 96. 533. Same as *3* above.

8 Super Cantica canticorum lib. 1   *Salamon . . . diligentibus*   82.<u>15</u>

R14. 4. Spurious; *CPL* 910. *PL* 70. 1056. **82** Bury = B13. 100a.

9 Super Lamentationes Jeremiae lib. 1   *Habes . . . comprehenduntur*

R14. 7. An unidentified work with this incipit and explicit appears in the library of the Cistercians at Wilhering, MS IX.128 fols. 1r–141r, inc. 'Habes in Lamentationibus Jeremiae quatuor alfabeta . . .', attributed to Jerome, and in Douai, Bibliothèque municipale, MS 398, attributed to Bede; there are a number of other Continental manuscripts, especially Austrian, but we know of no English examples nor of any attribution to Cassiodorus.

10 Epistolarum 341 ad diversos lib. 9   *Oportet . . .*

R14. 6, Vincent XXII 49. *Variae*; *CPL* 896. *CCSL* 96. 9.

11 Super Tobiam

Cassiodorus I. 6. 4 (whole entry).

12 Super Hester

Cassiodorus I. 6. 4 (whole entry).

13 Super Judith

Cassiodorus I. 6. 4 (whole entry).

Cassiodorus *III. 14*

14 Super libros Machabeorum

 Cassiodorus I. 6. 4 (whole entry).

15 Super epistolam ad Romanos

 Cassiodorus I. 8. 1 (whole entry).

16 Super epistolas canonicas

 Cassiodorus I. 8. 1 (whole entry).

17 Item historiam tripartitam de Graeco transtulit in Latinum

 R14. 1. Neither *Registrum* nor the Bury catalogue entry provides the information about translation. [**82** Bury = B13. 240.]

18 Diversarum formularum lib. 1

 R14. 11 (whole entry).

112 CIPRIANUS Afer Caecilius episcopus Carthaginis et martir floruit circa A. Ch. 258 et scripsit multa secundum Vincentium in Speculo libro 12° cap. 62

 Registrum 21, Vincent XII 62, Jerome cc. 66–7. The first twenty-two titles, with three interruptions (*12, 14, 21*), come in sequence from Vincent with incipits and explicits from Bury manuscripts and locations from *Registrum*.

1 De 12 abusionibus seculi lib. 1 82

 R21. 18, Vincent XII 62. Spurious; *CPL* 1106. Cf. James extracts, p. 197. Same as Augustinus *1.29*. **82** Bury = BL MS Royal 8 F. xiv, fol. 162v (Bury G. 15); this manuscript was procured, and this segment was copied, by Kirkestede.

2 De gratia Dei ad Donatum lib. 1 *Dum admones . . . mulcedo* 82

 mulcedo *queried by Tanner*

 R21. 30, Vincent XII 62. *CPL* 38. *CCSL* 3A. 3, incipit 'Bene admones'.

3 De lapsis lib. 1 *Pax ecce . . . sed coronam* 82

 R21. 29, Vincent XII 62. *CPL* 42. *CCSL* 3. 221.

Ciprianus *112. 14*

4 De aleatoribus lib. 1   *Magna nobis* . . .

    Vincent XII 62. Spurious; *CPL* 60. *CSEL* 3/3. 92.

5 De unitate ecclesiae catholicae lib. 1   *Cum moneat . . . regnabimus*   82

    R21. 13, Vincent XII 62. *CPL* 41. *CCSL* 3. 249.

6 De oratione Dominica lib. 1   *Evangelica . . . non desinamus*   82

    R21. 5, Vincent XII 62. *CPL* 43. *CCSL* 3A. 90. Same as Augustinus *1.329*.

7 De mortalitate lib. 1   *Et si apud . . . majorum*   82

    R21. 6, Vincent XII 62. *CPL* 44. *CCSL* 3A. 17, explicit 'maiora'.

8 De opere et eleemosynis lib. 1   *Multa et . . . geminabit*   82

    R21. 17, Vincent XII 62. *CPL* 47. *CCSL* 3A. 55. Same as Augustinus *1.150*.

9 De bono patientiae lib. 1   *De patientia . . . honoremus*   82

    R21. 9, Vincent XII 62. *CPL* 48. *CCSL* 3A. 118, explicit 'honoremur'.

10 De zelo et livore lib. 1   *Zelarum quidem . . . coronatur*   82

    R21. 21, Vincent XII 62. *CPL* 49. *CCSL* 3A. 75, incipit 'Zelare quod'; but the explicit is that of *Ad Fortunatum, 12* below (*CCSL* 3. 216).

11 Ad Demetrium lib. 1   *Oblatrantem . . . securus*   82

    R21. 8, Vincent XII 62. *CPL* 46, *Ad Demetrianum*. *CCSL* 3A. 35.

12 Ad Fortunatum lib. 1   *Desiderasti* . . .

    R21. 11. *CPL* 45. *CCSL* 3. 183. See also *10* above.

13 De sacramento Christi ad Quirinum lib. 3   *Judeos . . . ac nocte*   82

    R21. 14, Vincent XII 62. *CPL* 39. *CCSL* 3. 6.

14 De disciplina et habitu virginum lib. 1   *Disciplina . . . honorare*   82

    R21. 19. *CPL* 40. *CSEL* 3/1. 187. Same as Jeronimus *281.215*.

Ciprianus   *112. 15*

15   De laude martirii lib. 1   *Etsi incongruens . . . non negare*   <u>82</u>

   R21. 23, Vincent XII 62. Spurious; *CPL* 58. *CSEL* 3/3. 26–52.

16   Ad Antonianum lib. 1   *Accepi . . .*

   Vincent XII 62. *CPL* 50 *ep.* 55. *CSEL* 3/2. 624.

17   Ad Julianum lib. 1   *Scripsisti . . .*

   Vincent XII 62. *CPL* 50 *ep.* 73. *CSEL* 3/2. 778.

p. 53]

18   De sacramento calicis ad Caecilium lib. 1   *Quanquam sciam . . .*

   R21. 22, Vincent XII 62. *CPL* 50 *ep.* 63. *CSEL* 3/2. 701.

19   Ad Cornelium lib. 1   *Et religiosum . . .*

   Vincent XII 62. *CPL* 50 *ep.* 47. *CSEL* 3/2. 605.

20   De duobus montibus lib. 1   *Probatio . . .*

   Vincent XII 62. Spurious; *CPL* 61. *CSEL* 3/3. 104.

21   De elementis lib. 1

   R21. 24 (whole entry).

22   Epistolas 619 parvas ad diversos

   R21. 1, Vincent XII 62. *CPL* 50. *CCSL* 3B–3C. [**82** Bury = B13. 21a.]

23   Sermones ad diversos

   Cf. R21. 32.

24   Ad Cornelium papam ep. 7

   Iste Ciprianus suadente presbytero Caecilio, a quo et cognomen sortitus est, et Christianus factus est. Haec Jeronimus libro De catholicis scriptoribus.

   Jerome cc. 66–7 (whole entry). Same as Cornelius *118.5* below.

25 Coena Caecilii Cipriani episcopi   *Quidam rex . . . domos suas*

> R21. 31. *Ps.* Cyprianus Gallus; *CPL* 1430. MGH *Poet. lat.* 4/2. 872–98, explicit 'domos suas repetierunt'.

113 CLEMENS papa floruit circa A. Ch. 93 et scripsit juxta Vincentium in Speculo historiali lib. xi cap. 12 et juxta Jeronimum

> *Registrum* 99, Vincent XI 12, Jerome c. 15.

1 Ad ecclesiam Corinthiorum ep. 1

> Whole entry from Vincent XI 12 and Jerome.

2 Ad S. Jacobum Hierosolymitanum episcopum ep. 1   95.82
De ista epistola sumpsit B. Benedictus quartum capitulum regulae suae de instrumentis bonorum operum et quaedam alia, quae posuit in prologo regulae suae, ut patet ibidem plenius, et est nobilis epistola pro praelatis.

> R99. 3, Vincent XI 12.

3 Item ad S. Jacobum aliam epistolam   95.82

> R99. 4 (whole entry). The location numbers are repeated from *2* above.

4 Ad universos ep. 1   82

> This work and its source are unidentified.

5 Item aliam epistolam quae a veteribus reprobatur   82

> Jerome. Work unidentified.

6 Item aliam epistolam doctrinam Petri continentem   82

> This work and its source are unidentified.

7 Itinerarium continens lib. 10   *Tibi quidem . . . exhiberet*   82.43.126.156. 155

> R99. 1 (location number **43** and the number of books) and R99. 2 (title and the last three location numbers). *Ps.* Clement, *Recognitiones. GCS* 51. 3; incipit is that of the translator's prefatory letter. **82** Bury = B13. 178.

Clemens 113. 8

8 Dispositionum secundum Bedam lib. 6

> This work and its source are unidentified. Possibly a corruption of 'Disputationum' and, thus, another reference to 7 above.

9 De disceptationibus Petri et Symonis Magi lib. 1   *Ego Clemens . . . a Laodicia*

> Same as 7 above; the incipit is that of Book I (*GCS* 51. 6), and the explicit (*GCS* 51. 366) is that of the 'English family' of manuscripts; see *GCS* 51. lxxii–lxxx, and 366n.

114 CLEMENS Alexandriae presbyter cognomento Stromates et auditor Pothemii floruit A. Ch. 211 et scripsit multa juxta Jeronimum et juxta Vincentium libro undecimo, capite ultimo

> Vincent XI 126, Jerome c. 38, Cassiodorus I. *praef.* 4 and I. 8. 4.

1 De paradoxis lib. 1

> Source unidentified.

2 Adversus gentes lib. 1

> Vincent XI 126 and Jerome 38 (whole entry).

3 Stromatum lib. 8

> Vincent XI 126 and Jerome 38 (whole entry).

4 Paedagogi lib. 4

> Jerome 38 (whole entry).

5 De jejunio lib. 1

> Vincent XI 126 and Jerome 38 (whole entry).

6 De obtrectatione lib. 1

> Vincent XI 126 and Jerome 38 (whole entry).

7 De canonibus ecclesiasticis et adversus eos qui sequuntur Judaeorum errorem lib. 4

> Vincent XI 126 and Jerome 38 (whole entry).

Clemens *115. 1*

8 Item alium librum qui inscribitur Dives ille et continet lib. 1

> Jerome 38 (whole entry).

9 Vetus et Novum Testamentum a principio usque ad finem Graeco sermone declaravit secundum Cassiodorum libro De institutione divinarum literarum

> Cassiodorus I. *praef.* 4 (whole entry).

10 De Pascha, juxta Jeronimum lib. 1

> Jerome 38 (whole entry).

11 Varietatum et disputationum lib. 7
Constat Originem hujus fuisse discipulum secundum Jeronimum libro De claris scriptoribus

> claris *Tanner has corrected this in most other instances to* catholicis

> Jerome 38 (whole entry). This title represents two Greek titles in Jerome that have interlinear Latin translations in the Bury bibliographic codex, Bodl. MS e Musaeo 31, pp. 196–197 (Bury A. 31).

12 Super epistolas canonicas, secundum Cassiodorum

> Cassiodorus I. 8. 4 (whole entry).

p. 54]

115 CLEMENS Lantoniensis ecclesiae presbiter floruit A. Ch. <*blank*> et scripsit

> This entry probably came from the *Registrum*, but the extant text of the *Registrum* is corrupt at this point. There is no entry for Clement in Tanner 165, and in Peterhouse 169 there is an entry for Pope Clement to which Clement of Lanthony's *De concordia euangelistarum* has been added; see *Registrum* 99 and notes. Perhaps Kirkestede saw a manuscript of the work as well.
> Bale, *Index*, 55.
> Sharpe, *Latin Writers*, 86–9.

1 De concordia quatuor evangeliorum   *Clemens* . . .   128

> R99. 5 (title, location number). Stegmüller *Bibl.* 1981.

Columella   *116*.

116 COLUMELLA floruit circa annum <*blank*> et scripsit juxta Cassiodorum ubi supra

> Cassiodorus I. 28. 6 (whole entry).

1 De agricultura lib. 16

117 CURTIUS floruit circa A. Ch. <*blank*> et scripsit juxta Cassiodorum

> Same as Valeranus *628*.
> Cassiodorus I. 30. 2 (whole entry).

1 De ortographia lib. 1

118 CORNELIUS urbis Romae episcopus floruit circa A. Ch. 255 et scripsit juxta Vincentium lib. xii° cap. 54° et secundum Jeronimum libro De viris illustribus

> Whole entry from Vincent XII 54 and Jerome c. 66.

1 De synodo Romanorum ad Flavianum ep. 1

2 De Novatiano et lapsis ep. 1

3 De gestis synodi ep. 1

4 Ad Flavianum epistolam aliam haereseos causas et anathema continentem

> ad Flavianum] ad Fabium *Jerome edition;* ad Flauianum *Jerome in Bodl. MS e Musaeo 31 p. 204*

5 Huic etiam scripsit Ciprianus epistolas septem.

> septem] octo *Jerome edition;* septem *Jerome in Bodl. MS e Musaeo 31 p. 204*

> Same as Cyprian *112.24*.

119 CLAUDIUS monachus et discipulus S. Bedae secundum quosdam floruit circa A. Ch. 815 et scripsit ex opusculis Origenis, Jeronimi, Ambrosii, Hillarii, Augustini, Rufini, Johannis, Fulgentii, Leonis Maximi, Gregorii et Bedae

> (Claudius of Turin)

Mariale fol. 2r; *Registrum* 68 probably not used.
Bale, *Index*, 55.
Sharpe, *Latin Writers*, 85–6, for the erroneous association with Bede.

1 Super evangelium Mathaei lib. 3   *Domino sancto* . . .

> Cf. R68. 1. Stegmüller *Bibl.* 1958. [**82** Bury = B13. 69 = Cambridge, Pembroke College, MS 12 (Bury C. 16).]

120 CLAUDIUS vel CLAUDIANUS gentilis poeta, Romae claruit A. Ch. 387 et scripsit juxta Vincentium in Speculo lib. 18 cap. 101

> See also Maximianus *395*.
>
> Vincent XVIII 101. The addition of **82** Bury (without incipits and explicits) to the two titles taken from Vincent may simply represent Kirkestede's knowledge that these works existed in the abbey library.

1 Claudianum majorem lib. 1   82

2 Claudianum minorem lib. 1   82

> In quibus duobus libris sunt multa proverbia notabilia

121 CLAUDIANUS Viennensis ecclesiae presbyter floruit <*blank*> et scripsit juxta Genadium libro De viris illustribus

> Gennadius c. 84.

1 De statu et substantia animae lib. 1   *Praecipis ut* . . .   45

> This is the incipit of the letter of Faustus Reiensis (*CPL* 963 *ep.* 3) that precedes the *De statu anime* in manuscripts (*CPL* 983). *CSEL* 11. 8, and 18.

CASSIANUS Vide vocabulum in litera J.

> See Johannes Cassianus *285*.

CRISOSTOMUS Vide vocabulum in litera J.

> See Johannes Crisostomus *282*.

CITHERO Vide vocabulum TULLIUS in litera T.

> See Tullius Marcus *582*.

122 CATO Stoicus et philosophus floruit tempore Tholomaei Caesaris et scripsit juxta Vincentium in Speculo lib. 6

> Vincent VI 107, Higden, 4. 204.

1 De moribus, partim metricum   *Si Deus est . . .*   et partim prosaicum *Cum animadverto . . .*   lib. 1

> Vincent VI 107. *Disticha Catonis*. Ed. M. Boas & H. J. Botschuyver (Amsterdam 1952).

Ex Policronica Cestriae libro 3^{io}: Iste Cato fecit unum magnum librum moralem, qui dicitur Ethica Catonis, de qua extractus ille parvus liber metricus, qui legitur primus in scolis.

> Per Rob. Grosthed *added in red ink in the margin of Add. 3470 next to the Higden excerpt.*

p. 55]

123 CANDIDUS floruit circa A.D. 189 et scripsit

> Jerome c. 48.

1 De concordia 4 evangeliorum in passione Domini lib. 1   *Quia longum . . . positum fuit*

> Unidentified.

2 Item in Exameron pulcherrimum tractatum, secundum Jeronimum

> Jerome 48 (whole entry).

124 CONSTANTIUS episcopus floruit A. Ch. <*blank*> et scripsit juxta Ysidorum libro De viris illustribus

> Isidore c. 4 (whole entry).

1 Vitam S. Germani episcopi

125 CELIUS AURELIUS floruit circa annum <*blank*> et scripsit juxta Cassiodorum ubi supra

> Cassiodorus I. 31. 2 (whole entry).

1 De medicina lib. 1

126 CIRILLUS Alexandriae episcopus floruit circa A. Ch. <blank> et scripsit multa juxta Genadium

    Gennadius c. 58, Cassiodorus I. *praef.* 4.

1 De defectu synagogae lib. 1

    Gennadius 58 (whole entry).

2 De fide lib. 1

    Gennadius 58 (whole entry).

3 Adversus Nestorium lib. 1

    Gennadius 58 (whole entry).

4 Omeliarum lib. 1

    Gennadius 58 (whole entry).

5 Sermonum lib. 1   *Dives est* . . .   83.82

    Incipit unidentified. **82** Bury = B13. 256, 'Cirillus'.

6 Item presbyteris diaconibus et conventibus monachorum et aliis personis ep. 26   *Venerunt* . . .

    A collection of letters attributed to Cyril with this incipit comprises pt C of Paris, Bibliothèque de l'Arsenal, MS 903, a composite manuscript.

7 Vetus et Novum Testamentum a principio usque ad finem Graeco sermone declaravit, secundum Cassiodorum libro De institutione divinarum literarum

    Cassiodorus I. *praef.* 4 (whole entry).

8 Item librum qui dicitur Golia, secundum Leonem papam

    Source unidentified. *Scolia de incarnatione Unigeniti.*

127 CRISPINUS monachus floruit A. Ch. <blank> et scripsit juxta *Mariale*

    Source unidentified. Only the name appears in *Mariale* fol. 2r.

1 De incarnatione Domini lib. 2

Celestius *128.*

128 CELESTIUS floruit A. Ch. 365 et scripsit juxta Genadium De viris illustribus

> Gennadius c. 45 (whole entry save date).

1 De monasterio ep. 1 in modum libelli omnibus Deum desiderantibus necessariam

129 COMODIANUS floruit A. Ch. <blank> et scripsit juxta Genadium ubi supra

> Gennadius c. 15 (whole entry).

1 Contra Paganos lib. 1

> Tertullianum, Lactantium et Papiam auctores est secutus; moralem sane doctrinam et maxime paupertatis voluntariae amorem optime prosecutus est.

130 CIRILLUS Jerosolymitanus episcopus floruit A.D. 349 et scripsit secundum Jeronimum De catholicis scriptoribus in adolescentia sua opuscula

> Jerome c. 112 (whole entry save the date); because the Greek title of Cyril's work is neither translated nor transliterated in the Bury Jerome (Bodl. MS e Musaeo 31, p. 212), Kirkestede omitted it here.

131 CELESTIUS papa floruit A. Ch. 429 et scripsit juxta Genadium

> Celestinus *Gennadius*
>
> Gennadius c. 55 (whole entry save the date).

1 Contra Nestorium decretorum lib. 1

132 CIRUS genere Alexandrinus medicus et monachus floruit A. Ch. 495 et scripsit ante lapsum secundum Genadium

> Gennadius c. 82 (whole entry save the date).

1 Contra Nestorium libros elegantes

133 CAECILIUS floruit A. Ch. 258 quo suadente Ciprianus factus est Christianus secundum Jeronimum ubi supra

> Jerome c. 67 (whole entry save the date).

[p. 56]

134 CHEREALIS episcopus natione Afer interrogatus est a Maximiano Affricanorum episcopo si possit vel paucis divinae Scripturae testimoniis absque dubitationis assertione fidem catholicam assignare; de qua ille, in nomine Domini, suffragante sibi veritate, non paucis testimoniis sed copiosis Veteris et Novi Testamenti indicibus approbavit et libello edidit.

Gennadius c. 97 (whole entry).

135 Sanctus CESARIUS monachus et Arelatensis episcopus floruit A. Ch. 781 et scripsit juxta Vincentium lib. 24 cap. 141

Vincent XXIV 141; *Registrum* 20 not used.
A manuscript, or at most two, at each of the locations listed provided this entry. The entry is similar to the material listed in the catalogue of **61**, Peterborough abbey (BP21), listed below.
Speculum coenobitarum 35.

1 Omelias ad monachos 10   *Dominis sanctis et in . . . durarent*   74.15.61.65

Vincent XXIV 141. This title should refer to the sermons *Ad monachos* of ps. Eusebius Emesenus 'Gallicanus'; *CPL* 966. 35–44 (numbered 36–45 in *CCSL* 101A. 419–542), but the incipit does not correspond. Various collections mingling sermons of Caesarius of Arles and those of Eusebius 'Gallicanus' (attributed to Caesarius) circulated in England; see for example the collection of eleven sermons labelled 'Omelie beati Cesarii episcopi ad monachos' in BL MS Royal 5 F. x, fols. 2r–37r (Wallingford Priory, s. xii), which begins with Caesarius *serm.* 233, incipit 'Dominis sanctis et in Christo desiderandis fratribus' (*CCSL* 104. 925) and ends with the tenth homily *Ad monachos* of Eusebius Emesenus 'Gallicanus', explicit 'sine fine durarent' (*3* below). **61** Peterborough = BP21. 28a along with *2* below, in the same codex cited for Eusebius *162.5* (BP21. 28b), and see also BP21. 258b (followed in the same codex by *2* below).

2 Ad sororem suam omeliam 1   *Ut ego peccator . . . legentem inveniant*   15.74.61. 65

Pelagius, *De vita christiana*; *CPL* 730. *PL* 40. 1031. Location numbers may be repeated from *1* above. **61** Peterborough = BP21. 28c with *1* above, in the same codex cited below for Eusebius *162.5*, and BP21. 258c (preceded in the same codex by *1* above).

3 Ad populum omeliam 1   *Ait quosdam . . . durarent*

Ps. Eusebius Emesenus 'Gallicanus'; *CPL* 966 *serm.* 44 (*serm.* 45 in *CCSL*). *CCSL* 101A. 535–42, hom. 10 *Ad monachos* (cf. *1* above).

Constantinus *136*.

136 CONSTANTINUS monachus Cassinensis floruit A. Ch. <*blank*> et scripsit

> (Constantinus Africanus)
> This entry was probably based on Bury manuscripts.

1 De pantegni

> pantegnis *Add. 3470, queried by Tanner*
>
> See Thorndike/Kibre 1014. Printed with the works of Isaac Judaeus, Lyon 1515, pt 2, fol. 1r. [**82** Bury = B13. 110 = Cambridge, Trinity College, MS R. 14. 34 (Bury M. 37).]

2 De gradibus

> Source unidentified. Concerning the various forms of this work see note at B29. 3.

3 Librum qui dicitur Viaticum continentem lib. 7   *Quoniam quidam . . . multum*

> Printed, Lyon 1515 pt 2, fol. 144r. [**82** Bury = CUL MS Ii. 6. 5, fol. 3r (Bury U —), explicit 'multum valentur' (fol. 86r).]

137 CENSORINUS

> Source unidentified; the author and title appear in Cassiodorus II. 5. l, but it is not evident that Kirkestede used Book II of Cassiodorus as a source (Book II does not appear in the Bury bibliographic collection, Bodl. MS e Musaeo 31). For two other possible uses see Tullianus *589* and Victorinus *620.4*.

1 De die natali lib. 1

138 COLUMBANUS abbas floruit <*blank*> et scripsit

> Bale, *Index*, 56.
> Gale extracts, verso of penultimate back flyleaf.

1 De moribus metrice   *Haec tibi praecepta . . . corripit illum*   65

> tibi] sunt *Gale extracts*
>
> *CPL* 1112. *PL* 80. 287–91, incipit 'Haec praecepta'.

p. 57]

139 Sanctus DIONISIUS Areopagita episcopus Atheniensis floruit circa A.D.
<blank> et scripsit multa in lingua Graeca juxta Vincentium lib. 9°

> *Registrum* 5, Vincent IX 149 (references are followed by numbers in brackets [1, 2, etc.] that indicate the sequence of titles in the chapter), *Manipulus florum* I.
> The first fifteen titles and most of the incipits were supplied from the *Manipulus florum*. The *Manipulus florum* also provided explicits for the first four titles; other explicits were supplied from Bury manuscripts.
> See P. Chevallier, *Dionysiaca: Recueil donnant l'ensemble des traductions latins des ouvrages attribués à Denys de l'Aréopage*, 2 vols. (Bruges 1937).

1 De jerarchia coelesti lib. 1   *Omne datum ... honorificantes*   82.94.95.105.9.15

> R5. 1 (location numbers), Vincent IX 149 [1], *MF* I 2 (title, incipit, explicit). Ed. Chevallier, 2. 727. **82** Bury = B13. 63.

2 De jerarchia ecclesiastica lib. 1   *Quia quidam ... vapores*   82.94.95.105.9.15

> R5. 1 (location numbers), Vincent IX 149 [2], *MF* I 1 (title, incipit, explicit). Ed. Chevallier, 2. 1071. **82** Bury = B13. 63.

3 De divinis nominibus lib. 1   *Hunc o beati . . . duce Deo*   82

> Hunc] Nunc *MF*

> Vincent IX 149 [3], *MF* I 3. Ed. Chevallier, 1. 5. **82** Bury = BL MS Royal 7 B. IX, fol. 5r (Bury D. 6).

4 De mistica theologia lib. 1   *Trinitas . . .* Finis: *omni. Superessentialiter . . . perfectionem*   82.94.105

> *Incipit* Trinitas super essentialis, *explicit* perfectione et summitas omnium *MF*; a copying error has split the incipit and the explicit in two

> R5. 2, Vincent IX 149 [4], *MF* I 4. Ed. Chevallier, 1. 565.

5 Gayo monacho ep. 1   *Tenebras ... cognita*   105

> R5. 4, *MF* I 5. Ed. Chevallier, 1. 605.

6 Eidem ep. 1   *Quomodo ... participantes*

> *MF* I 5. Ed. Chevallier, 1. 608.

Dionisius   *139. 7*

7 Eidem ep. 1   *Subito* . . .

   MF I 5 (whole entry).

8 Eidem ep. 1   *Quomodo dicis* . . .

   MF I 5 (whole entry).

9 Dorotheo ep. 1   *Divina . . . causalem*

   MF I 5. Ed. Chevallier, 1. 620.

10 Sosipatro ep. 1   *Ne opineris . . . dicta sunt*

   MF I 5. Ed. Chevallier, 2. 1479.

11 Polycarpo episcopo ep. 1   *Ego quidem . . . veritatem*

   MF I 5. Ed. Chevallier, 2. 1482.

12 Dymophilo monacho ep. 1   *Hebraeorum . . . credo vera esse*

   MF I 5. Ed. Chevallier, 2. 1501.

13 Tito ep. 1   *Sanctus quidam . . . varietatibus*

   MF I 5. Ed. Chevallier, 1. 624.

14 Johanni evangelistae ep. 1   *Johanni . . . trade*

   MF I 5. Ed. Chevallier, 2. 1572.

15 Apoliphano ep. 1

   Apoliphano] de eclipsi solis in passione Christi *add. MF*

   MF I 5 (whole entry).

16 Passionarium

   R5. 3. [**82** Bury = B13. 242b 'Passio sancti Dionisii'.]

17 Theologia Ypotyposes

   Source unidentified. Perhaps a misinterpretation of two words at the beginning of the dedicatory letter prefixed to the translation of the *De diuinis nominibus* (*3* above): 'Nunc autem o beate post theologicas ypotyposes . . .'.

140 DIONISIUS episcopus Alexandriae et auditor Origenis floruit A. Ch. 258 et scripsit multa juxta Vincentium libro 12 et juxta Jeronimum

> Vincent XII 37 (except work *3*) and Jerome c. 69 (except works *3–4*) provide, in identical sequence, all the titles here. Kirkestede added work *3* and the incipit of *4* probably from the same Bury manuscript; the two works appear together, for example, in Bodl. MS Auct. F. 3. 14, fols. 116v–120v and Glasgow UL MS Hunterian 85, fols. 73v–92r.

1 De haereticis baptizandis lib. 1

2 De poenitentia ep. 1

3 De contradictione hominis ad Egipium lib. 1   *Venerationis* . . .

> Egipium *queried by Tanner*

> Dionysius Exiguus, preface (addressed to Eugippius) to Gregory of Nyssa's *De conditione hominis*. *CPL* 652a. *CCSL* 85. 33, incipit 'Sancto uenerationis', followed presumably by his translation of the work itself.

4 De Pascha ep. 1   *Beatissimo* . . .

> Dionysius Exiguus. Probably *CPL* 2286 (*PL* 67. 513), but see also *CPL* 2284 (*PL* 67. 483).

5 De immortalitate ep. 1

> De mortalitate *Jerome (edition, and Bodl. MS e Musaeo 31 p. 204)*

6 De sabbato ep. 1

7 De persecutione Decii ep. 1

8 De natura ad Thimotheum ep. 1

9 De temptationibus lib. 1

10 De poenitentia ad Laodicenses lib. 1

11 Item Catoni de poenitentia, secundum Jeronimum lib. 1

> Catoni] Cononi *Jerome edition*

12 De martirio ad Origenem lib. 1

Dionisius *140. 13*

  13 Adversus Paulum Samosatenum lib. 1

  14 Ad Basiliden epistolas multas

  15 Ad Dionisium Romanae ecclesiae episcopum lib. 4

  16 De exilio ad Alexandrinam ecclesiam lib. 1

  17 Ad B. Sixtum ep. 2

p. 58]

  18 Ad Romanum ep. 1

  19 Ad Philomenem et Dionisium Romanae ecclesiae presbyteros ep. 2

  20 Ad eundem Dionisium postea Romanum episcopum ep. 1

141 DIONISIUS monachus et abbas Romae floruit A. Ch. 528 et scripsit juxta Cassiodorum

    Cassiodorus I. 26. 2 (works *2–3*), Paulus Diaconus I 25 (work *1*).

  1 De pascali calculo lib. 8

  2 De canonibus ecclesiasticis lib. 1

  3 Item multa alia de Graeco transtulit in Latinum

142 DIONISIUS Corinthiorum episcopus floruit circa A. Ch. 158 et scripsit juxta Jeronimum et Vincentium lib. xi cap. 112°

    Vincent XI 112, Jerome c. 27 (probably through Vincent).

  1 Ad diversos ep. 8

    Vincent and Jerome list, and enumerate, letters to eight people.

143 DAMASUS papa ingenium habuit elegans in versibus componendis et floruit A. Ch. <*blank*> scripsitque juxta Jeronimum multa et brevia opuscula heroico metro, inter quae scripsit

Jerome c. 103 (no works are named).
Works *2–4* are letters of Damasus that appear in the collection of one hundred and twenty-three epistles of Jerome used in compiling the Jerome entry, *281.128–231*.

1 De mundi contemptu lib. 1

> Bernard of Clairvaux. The source of this entry was probably a manuscript with this attribution (as, for example, Edinburgh UL MS 181, and BNF lat. 8207, fol. 18r); cf. B. Hauréau, *Les poèmes latins attribués à St. Bernard* (Paris 1870) 3, 6; and R. W. Hunt in *Medium Aevum* 16 (1947) 8.

2 De 5 quaestionibus ad Jeronimum ep. 1   *Dormientem . . . benedixit*   82

> CPL 1633 *ep.* 9. CSEL 54. 265 (*ep.* 35).

3 De osanna ad Jeronimum ep. 1   *Commentaria . . . referant*

> CPL 1633 *ep.* 8. CSEL 54. 103 (*ep.* 19).

4 De egressione filiorum Israel de Egipto quaestionem   *Cur Deus . . .*

> Presumably *quaestio* 3 of *2* above, despite its brevity.

144 DIDIMUS Alexandrinus ab anno aetatis suae quarto caecus floruit A. Ch. 360 et plura edidit volumina juxta Jeronimum

> Kirkestede assembled this entry of twelve works from five secondary sources and a Bury manuscript: Jerome c. 109 (works *1–8*), *Registrum* 16. 2 (work *9*), *Historia tripartita* VIII 8 (*CSEL* 71. 478) and Palladius, *Historia Lausiaca* c. 3 (*PL* 74. 263) jointly (work *10*), Cassiodorus I. 5. 2 (work *11*), and Cassiodorus I. 8. 6 (work *12*). Both *Registrum* 16. 1 and a Bury manuscript supplemented Jerome at work *4*.
> *Speculum coenobitarum* 13.

1 In psalterium commentarios lib. 3

2 In evangelium Matthei et Johannis comment.

3 De dogmatibus contra Arrianos lib. 2

4 De Spiritu Sancto contra Ennomium lib. 1   *Omnibus quidem . . . sermonis* 82

> R16. 1 (location number). PL 23. 103. Same as Jeronimus *281.94*.

Didimus   *144. 5*

   5 In Ysaiam lib. 18

   6 In Osee lib. 3

   7 In Zachariam lib. 5

   8 In Job commentarios

   9 De Trinitate lib. 3

  10 Super Parierthon Origenis lib. 1

> Parierthon *queried by Tanner*
>
> Hic ab infantia sua, ut supradictum est, privatus oculis grammaticam, rhetoricam, arithmeticam, musicam, geometriam, astronomiam et silogismos Aristotilis et eloquentiam Platonis auditu didicit, et utrumque scilicet Vetus et Novum Testamentum perfecte cognovit, et de verbo ad verbum interpretatus est. Haec in Historia tripartita et Heraclidi libro De vitis patrum.

  11 Item super Proverbia Salomonis Graeco eloquio commentarium, quem transtulit Epiphanius in Latinum ad rogatum Cassiodori.

  12 Item super epistolas canonicas

p. 59]

145 DIDIMUS grammaticus floruit circa A. Ch. <*blank*> et scripsit juxta Senecam et Vincentium in Speculo historiali lib. 9 cap. 136 quatuor milia librorum

> Vincent IX 136. This information also appears in Vincent III 87. The information in Vincent comes from Seneca *ep.* 88, and thus Kirkestede probably does not quote Seneca directly here; however, he may demonstrate a first-hand knowledge of *ep.* 88 in the entry for Seneca *543*. See also Homerus *275* for another possible use of this letter.

146 DURANDUS Frater Praedicator floruit circa A. Ch. <*blank*> et scripsit secundum fratres

> *Script. Ord. Praed.* (whole entry), cf. Stams, 54.

   1 Super libros sententiarum lecturam 1

2 Sermones de tempore et sanctis

   om. Stams

147 DIACONTIUS floruit A. Ch. <*blank*> et scripsit juxta Ysidorum libro De viris illustribus

   Diacontius] Dracontius *Isidore*

   Isidore c. 24 (whole entry).

1 De creatione mundi Exameron

148 DIODORUS episcopus Tarsensis et Antiochenae ecclesiae presbiter floruit circa A. Ch. <*blank*> et scripsit juxta Jeronimum

   Jerome c. 119 (whole entry).

1 Super epistolas Pauli commentarium

2 Item multa alia ad Eusebii Emisseni carrecterem pertinentia, cujus cum sensum secutus sit, eloquentiam non potuit mutari propter ignorantiam secularium literarum

   mutari] imitari *Jerome*

149 DIOMEDES floruit circa A. Ch. <*blank*> et scripsit juxta Cassiodorum

   Cassiodorus I. 30. 2 (whole entry).

1 De ortographia lib. 1

150 DONATUS poeta et artis grammaticae scriptor et praeceptor B. Jeronimi floruit circa A. Ch. 344 et scripsit

   The source for both the author's name and the works was probably one or more Bury manuscripts.

1 De arte grammatica et de octo partibus orationis lib. 1   *Partes orationis* . . .

   Ed. L. Holtz, *Donat et la tradition de l'enseignement grammatical* (Paris 1981) 614. [**82** Bury = B13. 159a 'Donatus magnus.']

Donatus *150. 2*

2 De voce et litera, syllaba et pede   *Vox est . . . senas habent*

   ibid. 603–609.

3 De tonis sive accentibus   *Dicamus . . . commata*

   ibid. 609–610, incipit unidentified.

151 DOROTHEUS monachus sanctus floruit <*blank*> et scripsit subtiliter ut habetur in libro florum

   subtiliter] subtilitur *Add. 3470*

   Liber florum fol. 33v (whole entry). The name 'Jerotheus' appears in the chapter *De angelis* of the *Liber florum*; the Bury manuscript of the *Liber florum* may well have read 'Dorotheus'.

1 De angelis lib. 1

152 DARES Frigius floruit anno a creatione mundi <*blank*> et scripsit

   Same as Frigius Dares *192*. See also Dites *153*, Guido *236*.
   Bale, *Index*, 468.

1 De bello Trojano lib. 1   *Peleus rex . . . Daretis scripta est*   68.61

   Ed. F. Meister (Leipzig 1873). **61** Peterborough = BP21. 42a, 44b, 45b, 143k, 168b, and see BP21. 92m (excerpts); see also Fulgentius *185.1* which follows Dares in two of these codices.

   Hanc historiam quidam Cornelius Nepos magni Salustii in linguam Latinam transtulit, sed particularia illius historiae quae magis possunt allicere animos auditorum per nimiam brevitatem indecenter omisit. Haec Guido de Columpna Messana, qui scripsit plenissime quicquid de tota historia universaliter et particulariter gestum fuit. Vide in litera G.

   Guido de Columnis, *Historia destructionis Troiae* (ed. N. E. Griffin (Cambridge, MA, 1936)), prologue p. 4. The cross-reference is to Guido *236.1*.

153 DITES Graecus floruit <*blank*> et scripsit plenissime

   See also Dares *152*, Guido *236*.
   Guido de Columnis (ed. Griffin), 276.
   Bale, *Index*, 468.

1 De bello Trojano historiam lib.

Effrem *155. 4*

Sed Guido de Columpna hanc historiam ornavit dictamine pulcriori per ampliores metaphoras et colores et per transgressiones occurrentes, quae ipsius dictaminis sunt, picturis implens magnum defectum magnorum auctorum Virgilii, Ovidii et Homeri, qui in exprimenda veritate Trojani casus nimium defecerunt, quamvis opera eorum conscripserunt sive tractaverunt secundum fabulas antiquorum sive secundum apologias in stilo nimium glorioso, et specialiter ille summus poetarum, quem nihil latuit ne ejus veritas incognita remaneret ad ipsius operis perfectionem efficaciter laboravit.

    defecerunt] defecarunt *Add. 3470*   summus] simius *Add. 3470, queried by Tanner*   nihil] vel *Add. 3470, queried by Tanner*

    Guido, 276.

154 DIASCORIDES floruit circa annum <*blank*> et scripsit, disseruit et depinxit librum de herbis agrorum mirabili proprietate, qui quidem liber vocatur Herbarium Diascoridis.

    Cassiodorus I. 31. 2 (whole entry).
    [**82** Bury = Bodl. MS Bodley 130 (Bury M. 44) with Kirkestede's title 'Herbarium Dioscoridis' = B13. 95, 'Dioscorides'.]

p. 60]

155 EFFREM monachus et Edissenae ecclesiae diaconus floruit A.D. 360 et scripsit juxta Jeronimum et Vincentium libro 15° quae sequuntur

    Vincent XV 87 (works *3–8*), Jerome c. 115 (work *1*); *Registrum* 76 not used. Work *2*, and the incipits and explicits added to the other titles, came from manuscripts.
    Speculum coenobitarum 14.

1 De Sancto spiritu lib. 1

2 De transfiguratione Domini serm. 1   *De regionibus . . . sine errore*   82.65

    Printed, *Florilegium Casinense* 3 (1877) 28–31. **82** Bury perhaps = B13. 259.

3 De poenitentia omel. 1   *Dominus Jesus . . . laus et gloria*   82.65

    CPL 1143, iii, *De patientia* or *De paenitentia*. Works *3–8* form a corpus of homilies that circulated together. 'Ephraem Latinus'; CPL 1143. The titles come in sequence from Vincent with the incipits and explicits taken from manuscripts at **82** Bury = B13. 259b, 'Sermones Ephrem diaconi', and at **65** Ramsey.

4 De luctaminibus hujus saeculi omel. 1   *In luctaminibus . . . immortali*   82.65

Effrem *155. 5*

5 De compunctione cordis omel. 1   *Dolor me . . . praesumat*   82.65

6 De beatitudine animae omel. 1   *Beatus qui . . . pervenire*   82.65

7 De resurrectione et judicio Dei et regno coelorum omel. 1   *Gloria . . . infirmabuntur*   82.65

8 De die judicii omel. 1   *Venite . . . eternam*   82.65

156 EUAGRIUS monachus et presbiter Machariique discipulus et Antiochiae episcopus secundum Jeronimum floruit circa A. Ch. 360 et scripsit juxta Genadium, quae sequuntur

> Jerome c. 125 (Euagrius of Antioch, work *8*), Gennadius c. 11 (Euagrius Ponticus, works *1–4, 6–7*).
> *Speculum coenobitarum* 5.

1 De vitis patrum lib. 1

2 Contra 7 principalium vitiorum suggestiones lib. 7

3 Composuit et anachoritis sempliciter viventibus librum centum sententiarum per capita digestum

4 Composuit et coenobitis ac synodo doctrinam vitae communis lib. 1

5 De actuali vita lib. 1   *Obsecro vos . . . daemoni*

> Unidentified.

6 Ad virginem Deo sacratam libellum competentem religioni et sexui edidit

7 Item paucas sententiolas valde obscuras solis monachis congruentes

8 Item vitam S. Antonii de Graeco Athanasii in Latinum transtulit secundum Jeronimum libro De catholicis scriptoribus

> This work of Euagrius of Antioch, taken from Jerome is added to those of Euagrius Ponticus taken from Gennadius.

157 EUAGRIUS alter floruit A. Ch. <blank> et scripsit juxta Genadium

> Gennadius c. 51 (whole entry).

1 Altercationem Symonis et Judae et Theophili Christiani, et multa alia

158 EPIPHANIUS Ciprius Salaminae episcopus floruit circa A. Ch. 390 et scripsit multa juxta Jeronimum libro De viris illustribus

> Jerome c. 114 (work *1*), Cassiodorus I. 5. 4 (works *3–4*).

1 Adversus omnes haereses lib. 1

2 Johanni Chrysostomo ep. 1   *Oportebat . . . erroris*   82

> *Epistola ad Ioannem episcopum Ierosolymorum. CSEL* 54. 395 *ep.* 51.

3 Super Cantica Canticorum, secundum Cassiodorum

4 Super alios libros Salomonis secundum eundem Graeco sermone commentarios, quos postea alius Epiphanius ad praeceptum Cassiodori transtulit in Latinum

159 EUSEBIUS Caesariensis Palestinae episcopus floruit circa A.D. 339 et scripsit juxta Jeronimum libro De catholicis scriptoribus multa volumina

> Jerome c. 81 (works *1–4, 6–13*), Cassiodorus I. 7. 2 (work *14*); *Registrum* 13 not used.
> Titles in Greek from Jerome c. 81 are translated in the Bury text, Bodl. MS e Musaeo 31, p. 207 (Bury A. 31).

p. 61]

1 Ecclesiasticae historiae in lingua Graeca et postea per Rufinum in Latinum translatae lib. 9   *Successiones . . . meritorum*   82

> *GCS* 9/1–3. **82** Bury = B13. 239.

2 De evangeliorum dissonantia et in Ysaiam lib. 10

3 Quaestionum lib. 15

4 Theophaniarum lib. 5

5 De canonum diaconia lib. 1

> diaconia *queried by Tanner*

> Source unidentified.

Eusebius   *159. 6*

   6 De vita S. Pamphilii lib. 3

   7 Pro Origene lib. 6

   8 De martiribus opuscula multa

   9 Evangelicae expositionis lib. 20

  10 Cronicorum canonum historiam 1

  11 Contra Porphyrium lib. 25

  12 Moralium lib. 1

  13 Super psalterium commentarios eruditissimos

  14 Canones evangelicos collegit

160 EUSEBIUS presbyter floruit <*blank*> et scripsit juxta Genadium lib.

> *Registrum* 13, Gennadius c. 35. This chapter of Gennadius in Bodl. MS e Musaeo 31, p. 229 (Bury A. 31) comprises a single sentence, 'Eusebius scripsit de crucis domini misterio et apostolorum precipueque Petri constantia fidei uirtute indepta', from which Kirkestede crafted titles *1–3* and *5*.

   1 De cruce Domini lib. 1

   2 De apostolis lib. 1

   3 De misteriis lib. 1

   4 Tractatus qui dicitur Glosarium Eusebii

> Source unidentified. This is probably the *Onomasticon* of Eusebius of Caesarea which was emended and translated by Jerome (ed. F. Larsow and G. Parthey (Berlin 1862)).

   5 De constantia et fide Petri lib. 1

   6 De corpore et sanguine Domini   *Quia humane . . .*   10.45

> R13. 5. Incipit unidentified. The title is the same as Ysidorus *666.31* below.

161 EUSEBIUS natione Sardus ex lectore urbis Romae Bercellensis episcopus floruit circa A. Ch. 349 et scripsit secundum Jeronimum

> Jerome c. 96 (whole entry save the date).

1 Super psalmos commentarios

162 EUSEBIUS episcopus Emissenus floruit A. Ch. 312 et scripsit juxta Jeronimum libros innumerabiles e quibus

> Jerome c. 91 (works *1–3*).

1 Adversus Judaeos et gentes lib. 5

2 Ad Novicianos et Galathas lib. 5

3 Super evangelia omelias breves

4 De Pascha   *Exulta* . . .   45

> Ps. Eusebius Emesenus ('Gallicanus'). *CCSL* 101. 141 or 145 (*sermo de Pascha* 1 or 1A).

5 Omelias ad monachos omel. viii   *Exortatur . . . in futura*   11.15.61.74.65

> Ps. Eusebius Emesenus ('Gallicanus'). *CPL* 966 *serm.* 35–43. *CCSL* 101A. 419–529 (numbered *serm.* 36–44). There are ten *Homiliae ad monachos*; the incipit here is that of the first, the explicit that of the ninth ('. . . et in futuro praesidium' (and benediction)). **61** Peterborough = BP21. 28b (in the same codex cited above for Cesarius *135.1–2*).

163 EGESIPPUS historiographus floruit circa A. Ch. 158 et scripsit juxta Vincentium lib. xi cap. 112 [1] a passione Domini usque ad suam aetatem historias, multaque ad utilitatem credentium pertinentia composuit in libris quinque. Principium: *Bello*. Finis: *ignis*

> (Hegesippus)
> Vincent XI 112 (headnote and work 1), Diceto, 1. 20 (work *2*), Higden, 1. 20 (work *3*).

> [1] Josephus, *Historia de excidio urbis Hierosolymitanae*. *PL* 15. 963 among the works of St Ambrose. Incipit is that of c. 1. Same as Ambrosius *2.27*. See also Josephus *296.1*. [**82** Bury = B13. 11, 'Egesippus'.]

Egesippus   *163. 2*

  2 Item adversus ydola historiam 1

   Diceto, 1. 20 (whole entry).

  3 De excidio urbis lib. 1

   Higden, 1. 20 (whole entry). Same as Josephus *296.6*.

p. 62]

164 EUCHERIUS monachus et episcopus Lugdunensis floruit A. Ch. 451 et scripsit juxta Genadium et Ysidorum

   Whole entry save the date from Gennadius c. 64 (works *1, 3*) and Isidore c. 15 (work *2*).
   Speculum coenobitarum 26.

  1 De contemptu mundi lib. 1

  2 De laude vitae anachoriticae lib. 1

  3 Item opuscula Cassiani in uno coegit volumine tam clericis quam monachis necessaria

165 EUSEBIUS Arelatensis floruit <*blank*> et scripsit

   The source of this entry was presumably a manuscript at **65** Ramsey.

  1 De nativitate Domini serm. 1   65

   Probably *ps.* Eusebius Emesenus ('Gallicanus'), *CPPM* 1B. 4617. *CCSL* 101. 15.

166 EUTROPIUS monachus et presbiter floruit A. Ch. <*blank*> et scripsit juxta Genadium et Vincentium lib. 21 cap. 32

   See also Eutropius *176*.
   Registrum 40, Vincent XXI 26, Gennadius c. 50, Isidore c. 32.

  1 De ornatu honestae vitae   165

   R40. 1 (whole entry).

Eugipius   *167. 5*

2 Ad monachos omelias 10

   This work and its source are unidentified; perhaps a confusion with the ten homilies of Eusebius 'Gallicanus' (cf. Eusebius *162.5*).

3 Historiae Romanorum lib. 16   *Primus in . . . provenda sunt*   15.19.82

   in] mihi *Add. 3470*, queried by Tanner

   R40. 2. Paulus Diaconus; *CPL* 1181. Ed. A. Crivellucci (Rome 1914) 5–238. Same as *6* below.

4 De crismate et baptismate lib. 1

   Isidore 32 (whole entry), which refers to Eutropius Valentinensis. Same as Eutropius *176.1*.

5 Ad duas sorores ancillas Christi epistolas in modum libellorum consolatorias

   Whole entry from Vincent XXI 26 and Gennadius 50.

6 Item historiam Romanorum a tempore Justiniani

   Source unidentified. Same as *3* above.

167 EUGIPIUS abbas floruit A. Ch. 496 et scripsit juxta Ysidorum et Cassiodorum libro De viris illustribus

   Isidore c. 13 (the whole of entries *1–2*), Cassiodorus I. 23. 1 (the whole of entries *3–4*).
   Speculum coenobitarum 27.

1 Vitam S. Severini

2 De vita monachorum regulam 1

   A note by Kirkestede adds this work to the list of those who wrote monastic rules, in BL MS Campbell Roll XXI.1 (Bury —).

3 Ad Probam virginem

4 Ex operibus Augustini lib. 1

5 De floribus Paradisi lib. 1

   This work and its source are unidentified.

Ernaldus *168.*

168 ERNALDUS abbas Bonevallensis floruit A. Ch. <*blank*> et scripsit

> See also Arnulphus *31.*
> *Registrum* 36 (location number **94** for *1* below) and *Registrum* 69 (this version of the author's name), together with manuscripts presumably from Bury.

1 De 5 verbis Domini in cruce lib. 1   *Ultima . . . lucretur*   94

> 5] vi *R*

> R36. 2 and R69. 1. Explicit unidentified. Same as Arnulphus *31.3.*

2 Item librum 2^{dum} de vita S. Bernardi   *Virorum . . . serenitas*

> Vide supra verb. Arnulphus *add.* Add. 3470; *according to Tanner this was added in a recent hand*

> BHL 1212. *PL* 185. 267.

169 EGIDIUS frater de ordine Fratrum Heremitarum B. Augustini et doctor theologiae floruit A. Ch. <*blank*> et scripsit

> The report here came from an unidentified source, a list of the works of Giles of Rome, supplemented by manuscripts at **82** Bury, **65** Ramsey, and **173** Babwell.
> See G. Bruni, 'Catalogo critico delle opere di Egidio Romano', *Bibliofilia* 35 (1933) 7–69, 36 (1934) 78–110, and 37 (1935) 247–306.

1 De corpore Christi lib. 1

> Source unidentified.

2 De regimine principum lib. 3   *Ex regia . . . fidelibus*   82.65

> Printed, Rome 1607. **82** Bury = Cambridge, Gonville and Caius College, MS 113/182, fols. 1r–148r (Bury —), s. xv^1, perhaps copied from an earlier Bury exemplar.

3 De originali peccato tract. 1   *Ego sim . . . videre*

> Printed, *Opera* (Cordova 1712).

4 Super libros sententiarum lib. 4   *Candor . . .*

> Stegmüller *Sent.* 43. Printed, *Opera* (Cordova 1699–1706).

Edmundus *171.*

5 Quaestionum de angelis lib. 1

    Source unidentified.

6 Super librum de generatione

    Source unidentified.

7 Super librum phisicorum

    Source unidentified.

8 Super libros de anima

    Source unidentified.

9 De praedestinatione et praescientia

    Source unidentified.

10 De paradiso et inferno tract. 1   *Nobili militi . . . tantam gloriam*   173

    Same as *9* above. Printed, *Opera* (Cordova 1712).

170 ESICIUS Jerosolimorum episcopus floruit A. Ch. <*blank*> et scripsit

    See also Ysichius *672*.
    Mariale fol. 2r, *Registrum* 67.

1 Super Leviticum lib. 1

    R67 (whole entry).

p. 63]

171 EDMUNDUS archiepiscopus Cantuariensis floruit A. Ch. <*blank*> et scripsit

    Edmundus] Ed^{ius} *Add. 3470, queried by Tanner*

    (Edmund of Abingdon)
    Mariale fol. 2r.
    Bale, *Index*, 65.

Edmundus   *171. 1*

1 Librum qui vocatur Speculum Ed[mund]i   *Videte* . . .

> Edmundi] Ed¹ *Add. 3470, queried by Tanner*   Speculum Edmundi] Contemplande deitatis speculum *Bale*
>
> *Speculum ecclesiae siue Speculum sancti Edmundi*; ed. H. P. Forshaw, *Auctores britannici medii aevi* 3 (London 1973) 33.

172 EGIDIUS de Listiniis Frater Praedicator floruit A. Ch. <*blank*> et scripsit

> *Script. Ord. Praed.* (whole entry), cf. Stams, 11.

1 De unitate formarum lib. 2

2 De astrologia libros plures

173 EGIDIUS Aurelianus Frater Praedicator floruit A. Ch. <*blank*> et scripsit

> *Script. Ord. Praed.* (whole entry), cf. Stams, 43.

1 De eclipsibus solis et lunae

174 ELIZABETH

> *Mariale* fol. 2r.

175 EUGENIUS Cartaginensis Affricae civitatis episcopus floruit circa A. Ch. 495 et scripsit secundum Genadium

> Gennadius c. 98 (whole entry save the date).

1 De fide catholica lib. 1

2 Item epistolas et commonitoria fidei

3 Altercationum contra Arrianorum praesules lib. 1

4 Item preces pro quiete Christianorum velut apologias

176 EUTROPIUS abbas Sirbitanus et episcopus ecclesiae Valentinae floruit circa A. Ch. 587 et scripsit secundum Ysidorum

> Isidore c. 32 (whole entry save the date).
> *Speculum coenobitarum* 21.

1 De crismate et unctione post baptismum lib. 1

> Same as Eutropius *166.4*.

2 De distinctione monachorum ep. 1

177 EUSTASIUS genere Pamphilius primum Biriae Siriae episcopus, deinde Antiochenus episcopus floruit A. Ch. 321 et scripsit secundum Jeronimum

> Whole entry save the date from Jerome c. 85 (works *1–3*) and Cassiodorus I. 1. 1 (work *4*).

1 Contra Arrianum dogma

2 De anima contra Originem

3 Epistolas infinitas

4 Exameron B. Basilii transtulit in Latinum secundum Cassiodorum ubi supra

178 EMILIANUS facundissimus explanator floruit circa annum <*blank*> et scripsit secundum Cassiodorum ubi supra

> (Palladius)
> See also Palladius *423*.
> Cassiodorus I. 28. 6 (whole entry).

1 De ortis et pecoribus, apibus et columbis et piscibus alendis, aliisque rebus hujusmodi lib. xii

179 EUTICES quidam floruit circa annum <*blank*> et scripsit juxta Cassiodorum et Cathalogum Angliae

> Cassiodorus I. 30. 2 (whole entry). This author is not in the extant text of the *Registrum* (the 'Cathalogum Angliae').
> James extracts, p. 197.

1 De aspiratione lib. 4

Excolio *180.*

180 EXCOLIO doctor floruit circa A. Ch. <*blank*> et scripsit

> *Liber florum* fols. 3r, 33v.
> This 'author' is a misinterpretation of repeated marginal glosses in the *Liber florum* that begin, 'Ex scolio super Dionisium'.

1 Super libros Dionisii

181 EUCLIDES

> Source unidentified.

1 Triangulum aequaliter

> Probably *Elementa* version III, incipit 'Triangulum equilaterum'; see H. L. L. Busard and M. Folkerts, *Robert of Chester's (?) Redaction of Euclid's Elements* (Basel 1992), 1. 36.

182 ERODOTUS Quintilianus Angelius Suetonius floruit circa A. Ch. <*blank*> et scripsit

> Higden, 1. 22 (whole entry). While the edition of Higden reads 'Suetonius de gestis Romanorum', some manuscripts of Higden (for example Oxford, Magdalen College, MS 181, and Cambridge, St John's College, MS A. 12) read 'Herodotus, Quintillianus, Agellius, Suetonius de gestis Romanorum'.

1 De gestis Romanorum

183 ETHICUS philosophus floruit <*blank*> et scripsit

> Diceto, 1. 21.

1 Cosmographiam a Jeronimo translatam   *Philosophorum scedulae . . . distinxit*

> Philosophorum *queried by Tanner*

> 'Aethicus Ister'; *CPL* 2348. Ed. O. Prinz, MGH *Quellen zur Geistesgeschichte des Mittelalters* 14 (1993). Same as Jeronimus *281.III*. [**82** Bury = B13. 49a.]

p. 64]

184 FULGENTIUS monachus et episcopus Ruspensis floruit circa A.D. 492 et scripsit juxta Ysidorum et Vincentium in Speculo historiali lib. 21 cap. 108

Fulgentius *184. 8*

Registrum 25, Vincent XXI 108 (works *2–12* in sequence), Isidore c. 14 (works *1, 4–6, 13*). The entry was constructed initially from Vincent and Isidore followed by the remaining titles from the *Registrum* (works *14–16*); a manuscript or manuscripts at Bury provided the incipits and explicits, and the whole entries for works *17–20*.
Speculum coenobitarum 28.

1 De Trinitate lib. 1   65

    Isidore c. 14 refers to *De Trinitate ad Felicem* (*CPL* 819), but without an incipit one cannot be sure what Kirkestede saw at **65** Ramsey; cf. *CPL* 843, and the notes to R25. 2 and R25. 3.

2 De remissione peccatorum lib. 1

3 De fide ad Donatum lib. 1   *Multum* . . .   15

    R25. 2. *CPL* 817 *ep.* 8. *CCSL* 91. 257. Same as Augustinus *1.171*.

4 De ministerio mediatoris sive de incarnatione lib. 3   *Triumfalibus* . . .   15

    Triumfalibus *queried by Tanner*

    R25. 11. *CPL* 816. *CCSL* 91. 97. The title probably refers to Book I of *Ad Trasamundum*. See also *14* and *16* below.

5 De veritate et praedestinatione lib. 3   *Litterae tuae* . . . *veritatem*   15

    The title refers to *CPL* 823 (*CCSL* 91A. 458). However, the incipit and explicit belong to *Ad Monimum* Book III, the first book of which deals with predestination; location number **15** is taken from the *Registrum*'s entry for that book (R25. 1, 'De predestinacione ad Monimum lib. 1').

6 Responsionum ad objectiones Trasimundi lib. 3   *Objectio* . . . *dictum est*   15

    R25. 10. *CPL* 815. *CCSL* 91. 71; 'Dictum est' are the opening words of Trasamundus's objections (ib. 67) which normally accompany Fulgentius's responses.

7 De continentia conjugatorum servanda post votum lib. 1   *Ante menses* . . .   15

    R25. 15. *CPL* 817 *ep.* 2. *CCSL* 91. 197.

8 De virginitate et humilitate ad Probam lib. 1   *Spirituali* . . .

    R25. 16. *CPL* 817 *epp.* 3–4. *CCSL* 91. 212.

Fulgentius   *184. 9*

9   De oratione et compunctione ad eandem lib. 1

10   De caritate ad abbatem Eugipium lib. 1   *Utinam* . . .<u>15</u>

  R25. 17. *CPL* 817 *ep.* 5. *CCSL* 91. 235.

11   De contemptu mundi ad Theodorum lib. 1   *Ut ignotus* . . .   <u>15</u>

  R25. 18. *CPL* 817 *ep.* 6. *CCSL* 91. 240.

12   De poenitentia et indulgentia lib. 1   *Sicut verum* . . .   <u>15</u>

  R25. 19. *CPL* 817 *ep.* 7. *CCSL* 91. 244.

13   De libero arbitrio et gratia lib. 7

14   De immensitate Filii Dei lib. 1   *Quotiens* . . .   <u>15</u>

  R25. 12 (location number only). *Ad Trasamundum* Book II; *CCSL* 91. 120. See *4* above and *16* below.

15   De bono conjugali lib. 1   *Epistolam* . . .   <u>15</u>

  R25. 14. *CPL* 817 *ep.* 1. *CCSL* 91. 189.

16   De sacr\<ament\>o d\<omin\>i\<c\>e passionis lib. 1   *Quanquam* . . .   <u>15</u>

  sacro die *Add. 3470*

  R25. 13. *Ad Trasamundum* Book III; *CCSL* 91. 147. See *4* and *14* above.

17   De natali Domini serm.   *Cupientes* . . . *Deus Dei filius*   82

  CPL 829. *CCSL* 91A. 899. Explicit unidentified, though the text contains much similar language.

18   De S. Stephano serm.   *Heri celebr*[*av*]*i*[*mus*] . . . *salvatoris*   82

  CPL 830. *CCSL* 91A. 905.

19   De Epiphania serm.   *Nostis fratres* . . . *desiderium*   82

  CPL 831. *CCSL* 91A. 911.

20 Item de S. Stephano sermo *Jesus filius . . . conversus ad*   82

> Ps. Augustine. CPL 285 *serm.* 382; CPPM 1. 748. PL 39. 1684–6, explicit unidentified.

185 FABIUS PLANCIADES FULGENTIUS vir clarissimus floruit <blank> et scripsit ad Catum presbyterum Cartaginis

> Catum] Catim *Add. 3470, queried by Tanner*

1 Mithologiarum, id est fabularum lib. 3   *Diophantus . . . inportat*   61.10

> CPL 849. Ed. R. Helm (Leipzig 1898). **61** Peterborough = BP21. 45a and 143l, Fulgentius accompanied in both codices by Dares Frigius (as BP21. 45b and 143k, respectively), *152.1*.

186 FULBERTUS episcopus Carnotensis floruit circa A. Ch. 1001 et scripsit juxta Vincentium lib. 26 cap. 15

> Vincent XXVI 15 (names only a collection of letters). Despite Kirkestede's reference, the entry seems instead to have been based on manuscripts, at Bury and elsewhere.
> Works *1–3* appear together in BL MS Royal 6 A. XII, fols. 132v–146v (Rochester, s. xii).

1 Quae tria sunt necessaria ad perfectionem lib. 1   *Venerabili . . . refugiant*   82

> PL 141. 196 *ep.* 5. Authorship is questionable; see F. Behrends, *The Letters and Poems of Fulbert of Chartres* (Oxford 1976), lxii–lxiii. Same as *5* below. **82** Bury = B13. 83b.

2 Dialogum de quodam miraculo S. Martini   *Speciosa . . . aeternaliter*   82. 63.65

> *Dialogus Hugonis et Fulberti Carnotensis de S. Martino.* Ed. J. Mabillon, *Vetera Analecta* (Paris 1723) 213. **82** Bury = B13. 83a. / **63** Crowland = Lambeth Palace Library, MS 145, fol. 237v, with *5* and *6* below.

3 De quadam consuetudine, quam accepit sacerdos quando ordinatur ab episcopo lib. 1   *Domino suo . . . corrigere*

> consuetudine *queried by Tanner*

> PL 141. 192 *ep.* 3. Authorship is questionable; see Behrends, lxii–lxiii. Same as *6* below.

Fulbertus   *186. 4*

4   Responsoria, stirps Jesse et solem justitiae et ympnum, chorus novae Jerusalem

   Source unidentified.

5   Ad Deodatum ep. 1   63.65

   The source for this letter was `probably a manuscript. Same as *1* above. **63** Crowland = Lambeth Palace Library, MS 145, fol. 243r, with *2* above and *6* below.

6   Ad Finardum ep. 1   63.65

   The source for this letter was probably a manuscript. Same as *3* above. **63** Crowland = Lambeth Palace Library, MS 145, fol. 249r, with *2* and *5* above.

7   De muliere mala tract. 1   *Approbate* . . .   65

   This title probably refers to the *De poenitentia mulierum*, which is pt 2 of the *De peccatis capitalilbus*. Incipit is that of *8* below.

8   De nativitate B. Mariae serm. 1   *Beata Domini* . . .

   PL 141. 320 *serm.* 4. Incipit is that of the sixth sentence. [**82** Bury = Cambridge, Pembroke College, MS 24, fol. 140r (Bury O. 54); incipit given here occurs in the text on fol. 140va.]

p. 65]

187   FAUSTUS ex abbate Lirinensis ecclesiae episcopus Galliae floruit A. Ch. <*blank*> et scripsit juxta Genadium

   Gennadius c. 86 (whole entry).
   Speculum coenobitarum 29.

1   De gratia Dei lib. 1

2   De timore Domini lib. 1

3   Contra Arrianos et Macedonios lib. 1

4   Ad diaconum Graecum ep. 1

5   Ad Felicem praefectum ep. 1

6   De Sancto Spiritu lib. 1

188 FAUSTINUS presbiter floruit A. Ch. <*blank*> et scripsit juxta Genadium Gennadius c. 16 (whole entry).

1 Ad personam Facillae reginae adversus Arrianos et Macedonianos lib. 7

2 Item de Valentino, Theodosio et Archadio imperatoribus lib. 1

189 FIRMIANUS qui et LACTANTIUS, Arnobii discipulus, sub Dioclitiano principe accitus cum Flavio gramatico, cujus De rebus medicinalibus versu compositi extant libri. Floruit enim circa A. Ch. <*blank*> et docuit rethoricam Nicomediae, scripsitque juxta Jeronimum et Vincentium in Speculo lib. 14 cap. 89 quae sequuntur

> Same as Lactantius *345*.
> The first ten titles in sequence from Vincent XIV 89 (only *1–3, 5, 7–10*) and Jerome c. 80 (*1–10*). The Greek titles reported by Jerome have interlinear translations in Bodl. MS e Musaeo 31, pp. 206–207 (Bury A. 31) and therefore appear here.

1 Versus heroycos lib. 1

2 Librum qui inscribitur Grammaticus

3 De ira Dei et institutionum divinarum adversus gentes lib. 7

4 Breviarium ejusdem operis lib. 1

5 De persecutione lib. 1

6 Ad Asclepiadium lib. 2

7 Ad Probum epistolarum lib. 4

8 Ad Severum epistolarum lib. 2

> Severum *Add. 3470; Tanner, uncertain of this reading, has added* Servium *as a variant reading*

9 Ad Demetrianum epistolarum lib. 2

10 De formatione hominis ad eundem lib. 1

Firmianus *189. 11*

11 De falsa sapientia lib. 1

> The source for this entry was probably a manuscript. Book III of the *Institutiones*. Same as Lactantius *345.1*.

190 FASTIDIUS Britannorum episcopus floruit A. Ch. <*blank*> et scripsit secundum Genadium

> Gennadius c. 57 (whole entry).

1 De vita Christianorum ad Fatalem quendam lib. 1

2 De viduitate servanda et Deo digna doctrina lib. 1

191 FORTUNATUS poeta genere Ytalicus et episcopus Turonensis floruit circa A. Ch. 570 et scripsit secundum Paulum in Historia Longobardorum

> Vincent XXII 126, Paulus Diaconus II 13.

1 De laude virginum lib. 1

> Source unidentified. *CPL* 1044a.

2 Item actus B. Martini sub quatuor libris heroico contexuit metro

> Paulus Diaconus II 13 (whole entry).

3 Item ympnos singularum festivitatum anni

> Paulus Diaconus II 13 (whole entry).

4 Item vitam Manrilii Andegavensis episcopi

> Manrilii] Maurilii *Vincent*
>
> Vincent XXII 126 (whole entry).

5 Item vitam S. Hillarii Pictavensis episcopi

> Vincent XXII 126 (whole entry).

192 FRIGIUS Dares floruit anno a creatione mundi <*blank*> et scripsit

> Same as Dares Frigius *152*.

1 De bello Trojano   *Peleus rex* . . . *Daretis*   68

    Same as Dares *152.1*.

193 FLAVIANUS floruit <blank> et scripsit juxta Vincentium in Speculo lib. 3 cap. 87

    Flavianus] Flamianus *Vincent*

    Vincent III 87 (whole entry).

1 De vestigiis philosophorum lib. 1

p. 66]

194 FLACCIANUS floruit <blank> et scripsit

    Source and author unidentified. This entry may be a corrupt reference to the Flaccianus who appears in *exempla* collections of the later middle ages as the author of a *Gesta graecorum*. See B. Smalley in *Mélanges offerts à Etienne Gilson* (Toronto 1959), 547–62; and P. Lehmann, *Pseudo Antike Literatur des Mittelalter*, Studien der Bibliothek Warburg (Leipzig 1927), 25–6.

1 De gestis Romanorum

195 FLORENTIUS Wigorniensis monachus historiographus floruit A. Ch. <blank> et scripsit

    Perhaps this entry was to have contained the *Mariani Scoti Chronicon* found in Bodl. MS Bodley 297 (Bury C. 53). See Marianus *367.1*.
    Sharpe, *Latin Writers*, 116.

196 FLAVIUS primus episcopus Cambilonensis floruit A. Ch. <blank> et scripsit, ut habetur in libro Consuetudinum Cluniacensium

    Consuetudines cluniacenses I 12 (*PL* 149. 660; whole entry).

1 Ympnum qui cantatur in coena Domini ad mandatum   *Tellus ac* . . .

197 FERRANDUS Carthaginensis diaconus floruit circa A. Ch. <blank> et scripsit

    These three titles are just one work, *CPL* 848 *ep.* 7, *Qualis esse debeat dux religiosus in actibus militaribus seu de septem regulis innocentiae*. Work *1* is the introduction, *2* the seven rules, and *3* an abridgment of the title.

Ferrandus   *197. 1*

1 Qualis debet esse dux religiosus lib. 1   *Socialem . . . transmutatio*   15

   PL 67. 928.

2 Item de eodem lib. 1   *Prima proinde . . . ducibus Christianis*   15

   PL 67. 931.

3 De arte militari   20

   Source unidentified.

198 FRETHULFUS episcopus Luxoniensis floruit circa A. Ch. <*blank*> et scripsit

   (Frechulfus Lexoviensis)

1 Historiam vel librum temporum a principio mundi usque ad Christum lib. 7   *Cum aliquem . . . in me sunt*   83

   Historiae Part I Book I c. 1; ed. M. I. Allen, *CCCM* 169. 28, incipit 'Dum aliquam'. Explicit is that of Part I in the later version, ibid. 432. [**82** Bury = B13. 73; seen by Leland at Bury, B16. 20–21.]

2 Item a Christo usque ad obitum S. doctoris Gregorii papae secundum Trivet in commentario Boetii de consolatione philosophiae

   commentario] commento *queried by Tanner*

   Book II of the *Historiae*. The reference to Trivet's *Commentary*, which is unpublished, can be found, for example, in Bodl. MS Rawlinson G. 187, fol. 1r.

199 FULGERIUS Carnotensis

   Presumably an incomplete entry for Fulcherius Carnotensis.

200 FACUNDUS Ermanensis ecclesiae episcopus floruit circa A. Ch. 536 et scripsit juxta Ysidorum

   Isidore c. 19 (whole entry save the date).

1 Pro defensione trium capitulorum lib. 12

Gregorius   *203. 2*

201 FORTUNATIANUS natione Afer Aquilegiensis episcopus floruit circa A. Ch. 348 et scripsit juxta Jeronimum

>   Jerome c. 97 (whole entry save the date).

1   Super evangelia commentarios

202 FOCAS floruit circa annum <blank> et scripsit juxta Cassiodorum

>   Cassiodorus I. 30. 2 (whole entry). [Cf. **82** Bury = B13. 159c, 'Focas'.]

1   De differentia generis lib. 7

p. 67]

203 GREGORIUS sanctus monachus cardinalis et papa floruit circa A. Ch. 593 et scripsit multa

>   *Registrum* 2, *Manipulus florum* V.
>   This entry is based first on manuscripts, probably at Bury, and completed with titles from Kirkestede's bibliographic sources and a belated manuscript find. There is no obvious source of this entry's many unlikely location numbers, representing especially, though not exclusively, western monasteries.
>   *Speculum coenobitarum* 40.

1   Super librum Job lib. 35   *Inter multos ... lacrymas reddit*   89.79.94.92.93.95

>   R2. 5, *MF* V 1. *CPL* 1708. *CCSL* 143. 8–143B. 811. See also *8* below. [**82** Bury = B13. 168, 'Gregorius super Iob in iii^{bus} uoluminibus', part of which is Cambridge, Pembroke College, MS 15 (Bury —), containing Books XXVIII–XXXV; and B13. 203, 'Gregorii Moralium in Iob pars media', which B13. 203 tentatively identifies with Cambridge, Pembroke College, MS 14, containing Books XI–XXII, an individual volume from a multi-volume set. Cambridge, Pembroke College, MS 88 (Bury G. 18), containing Eclogues from the *Moralia*, has the same incipit (the end is mutilated).]

2   Pastorale lib. 4   *Pastorale ... manus levet*   89.94.79.95.92.93

>   R2. 3 (title), *MF* V 2 (title, incipit 'Pastoralis', explicit 'manus leuet'). *CPL* 1712. Ed. F. Rommel, SChr 381–2 (Paris 1992) 124–540, incipit 'Pastoralis', explicit 'manus me leuet'. The location numbers are repeated from *1* above. [**82** Bury = B13. 169.]

Gregorius   203. 3

3   Dialogorum lib. 4   *Quadam die . . . fuerimus*   89.117.92.93.94.95

>   R2. 4, *MF* V 3. *CPL* 1713. Ed. A. de Vogüé, SChr 260 and 265. The location numbers, save the suspect **117**, are repeated from *1* above. [**82** Bury = B13. 172; BL MS Royal 7 E. I, fol. 24v (Bury P. '1000'); BL MS Royal 8 F. XIV, fol. 7r (Bury G. 15), a book procured by Kirkestede.]

4   Super quodam evangelio omel. 40   43.79.94.92.93.81.82

>   R2. 2. *Homiliae XL in Euangelia*; *CPL* 1711. *PL* 76. 1075. **82** Bury = B13. 171 = Cambridge, Pembroke College, MS 16 (Bury G. 8), with title by Kirkestede in the upper margin of fol. 1r.

5   Registrum epistolarum 690 continens lib. 14   *Valde necessarium* . . .   83.84.95.81.43.42.15

>   R2. 7. *CPL* 1714. *CCSL* 140–140A. **42** Reading = B71. 63 = Bodl. MS Digby 214. / [**82** Bury = B13. 170 = BL MS Royal 6 C. II (Bury G. 16); the number of letters is not recorded there.]

6   Super Cantica Canticorum commentarios   *Os sponsi . . . antecessoribus*   163.118.102.95.83.8.5

>   95] 99 *R*   8.5 *should perhaps read* 85.

>   R2. 10. Perhaps the commentary by Robertus de Tumbalena which was often attributed to Gregory (Stegmüller *Bibl.* 7488). Partially printed in *PL* 150. 1364–70 and completed under Gregory's name in *PL* 79. 492–548. Explicit unidentified. See also Robertus Molendinensis *506.9*.

7   Super primam et ultimam partem Ezechielis omel. 22   *Deus prophetiae . . .*   161.118.79.94.92.99

>   161] 162 *R*   92.99] 99.93 *R*

>   R2. 6, *MF* V 4. *CPL* 1710. *CCSL* 142. [**82** Bury = B13. 149a; 201 = Cambridge, St John's College, MS B. 13, fol. 3r (Bury G. 6), in two books marked 'In primam partem Ezechielis' (fol. 3) and 'Super extremam partem eiusdem prophetie' (fol. 97); according to a note by Kirkestede (fol. 1r) this book was reserved for reading in the refectory.]

8   De sacramento altaris tract. 1   *Iccirco . . . fuerimus*   25

>   25] xxv *R*

>   R2. 18. The unidentified title and the location number come from the *Registrum*; the incipit is that of the *Moralia in Job* (*1* above) I 1, *CCSL* 143. 25; the explicit is unidentified.

Gregorius *203. 16*

9 Ad Augustinum Cantuariensem de polutione nocturna ep. 1   22.161.
8

> R2. 8 (whole entry). Location number **8** is presumably taken by mistake from R2. 9.

10 Dialogus inter Gregorium et Augustinum lib. 1   83

> The source for this entry was probably a manuscript. *CPL* 1327, 1714.

11 Epistolas breves ad diversos   50

> The source for this entry may have been a manuscript.

12 De conflictione vitiorum et virtutum lib. 1   *Apostolica vox . . . tradere*   83.65.63.74

> R2. 9. Ambrose Autpert. *CCCM* 27B. 909. Same as Augustinus *1.497* and Leo *343.3*.

> Quem tamen librum plures ascribunt Augustino, quidam Ambrosio; videtur tamen potius ascribendum Gregorio quia libellus ille continetur in libro Moralium ejusdem super Job de verbo ad verbum.

13 Decreta ejusdem   22.153

> R2. 1 (whole entry).

14 De fide ejusdem   1

> R2. 17 (whole entry).

15 Super Genesin, secundum quosdam   108

> R2. 15 supplied the title and the location number, but not the reservation.

16 Compilatio alternis   126.127.105.42.115

> compilatio] complinatio *Add. 3470, queried by Tanner*   alternis *queried by Tanner*

> R2. 13 ('Defloraciones eius') supplied the location numbers, but not the title (source unknown).

Gregorius   204.

204 GREGORIUS Nazanzenus monachus episcopus et praeceptor Jeronimi floruit A. Ch. 390 et scripsit multa secundum Jeronimum

> Jerome c. 117 (works *1–7, 15*); *Registrum* 18 not used.
> Works *6, 8–14* represent a collection of eight of the nine homilies of Gregory translated by Rufinus which travelled together; see BAV MS Vat. lat. 307, representative of a family of manuscripts that omit the homily *De Arrianis* and arrange the homilies in this sequence: 8, 9, 11, 12, 14, 6, 10, 13.
> [**82** Bury = B13. 254, 'Gregorius Nazanzenus'.]
> *Speculum coenobitarum* 16.

1 De morte fratris Caesarii lib. 1

> Jerome (whole entry).

2 Laudes Machabeorum lib. 1

> Jerome (whole entry).

3 Laudes Maximi philosophi lib. 1

> Jerome (whole entry).

4 Laudes Cipriani lib. 1

> Jerome (whole entry).

5 De nuptiis et virginitate lib. 2

> Jerome (whole entry).

6 De Sancto Spiritu contra Ennomium lib. 4   *De solempnitate . . . exultatio* 89.65

> Jerome, and cf. R18. 5. *CSEL* 46. 142.

7 Contra Julianum imperatorem lib. 1

> Jerome (whole entry).

8 Apologiticum lib. 3   *Victus sum . . . in Jesu Christo*   89.65

> Cf. R18. 2. *CSEL* 46. 7.

9 De nativitate Domini et de epiphania serm. 1   *Christus nascitur . . . possibile est*   89.65

> Cf. R18. 3. *CSEL* 46. 87.

Gregorius 205. 1

10 De reconciliatione monachorum serm. 1 *Linguam nostram . . . corda nostra* 89.65

    Cf. R18. 8. *CSEL* 46. 209.

11 De luminibus sive de secundis epiphaniis *Misterium . . . fulgebat* 89.65

    luminibus *queried by Tanner*

    Cf. R18. 4. *CSEL* 46. 111.

p. 68]

12 De agno regresso sive de semetipso *Desiderabam . . . probabili* 89.65

    Cf. R18. 6. *De semetipso de agro regresso*; *CSEL* 46. 167.

13 De grandinis vastatione lib. 1 *Quid laudabile<m> . . . in Christo Jesu* 89.65

    laudabile *Add. 3470, queried by Tanner*

    Cf. R18. 9. *CSEL* 46. 238.

14 De dictis Jeremiae lib. 1 *Ventrem meum . . . speramus* 99.65

    99 *should presumably read* 89.

    Cf. R18. 7. *CSEL* 46. 194.

15 Laudes Athanasii lib. 1

    Jerome (whole entry).

205 GREGORIUS alius floruit post Guidonem circa A. Ch. *<blank>* et scripsit

    The source and the author are unidentified.
    Bale, *Index*, 98, combining this entry with Gregorius de Bridelington *208*.

1 De musica lib. 3 *Debitum . . .*

    Unidentified; a longer incipit 'Debitum existimaui meum esse' is supplied by Bale's *Scriptores*, 346.

Gregorius *206.*

206 GREGORIUS Emisenus episcopus frater S. Basilii floruit tempore Jeronimi circa A. Ch. 390 et scripsit juxta Jeronimum et Vincentium lib. 15 cap. 86

> (Gregorius Nyssenus)
> Vincent XV 85 (works *1–2*), Jerome c. 128 (work *2*); *Registrum* 19 not used.

1 De ymagine, id est de hominis conditione lib. 1   *Si pecuniarum . . . cognoscere*   83

> The Latin translation by Dionysius Exiguus. *PL* 67. 347.

2 Contra Ennomium lib. 8

207 GREGORIUS Boeticus Heliberri episcopus floruit anno 390 et scripsit juxta Jeronimum De viris illustribus

> Jerome c. 105 (whole entry save the date).

1 De fide elegantem librum 1

2 Item ad diversos alios tractatus

208 GREGORIUS prior de Bridelington floruit <*blank*> et scripsit

> Bale, *Index*, 98, combining this author with Gregorius *205*.
> Sharpe, *Latin Writers*, 154.

1 Super Cantica Canticorum lib. 1   *Quisquis . . . Deus meus*   82

> Unidentified.

209 GREGORIUS archiepiscopus Turonensis floruit circa A. Ch. 586 et scripsit juxta Vincentium in Speculo lib. 22° cap. 125

> Vincent XXII 125 (whole entry save date).

1 Historiam regum Francorum lib. 1

2 Miracula B. Martini lib. 4

210 GENADIUS Massiliae presbiter floruit A. Ch. 495 et scripsit juxta Vincentium lib. 21 cap. ultimo et juxta ipsum Genadium

> *Registrum* 12, Vincent XXI 111, Gennadius c. 101, Diceto, 1. 22 and 80.
> To compile this entry Kirkestede used his bibliographic sources, supplemented with manuscripts of the two best-known works (*2* and *4* below). He perpetuates here the *Registrum*'s errors of attribution (*1*, *3*, *10* below).

1 De anima lib. 1

> R12. 1 (whole entry).

2 De viris illustribus lib. 1   *Jacobus... Romae episcopum*   83.<u>15</u>.<u>105</u>.<u>80</u>.<u>43</u>.<u>19</u>.<u>1</u>

> R12. 2, Vincent XXI 111. *CPL* 957. Ed. E. Richardson, *Texte und Untersuchungen* 14/1 (Leipzig 1896) 57. [**82** Bury = B13. 62g = Bodl. MS e Musaeo 31, p. 218 (Bury A. 31).]

3 Super libros Regum omelias   20

> R12. 5 (whole entry).

4 De ecclesiasticis dogmatibus lib. 1   *Credimus ... inveniri*   <u>105</u>.80.<u>43</u>.<u>19</u>.<u>15</u>.<u>1</u>.<u>9</u>

> 19] 139 *R*

> R12. 3. *CPL* 958. Ed. C. H. Turner in *JTS* 7 (1906–1907) 89–99; its history discussed by him, ibid. 77–99 and *JTS* 8 (1907) 103–114. Same as Augustinus *1.107*.

5 Adversus omnes hereses lib. 8

> Gennadius (whole entry).

6 Adversus Nestorium lib. 6

> Gennadius (whole entry).

7 Adversus Pelagium lib. 4

> Gennadius (whole entry).

8 Adversus Euticen lib. xi

> Gennadius (whole entry).

Genadius   *210. 9*

9 De mille annis in Apocalipsi lib. 1   65

> Gennadius c. 101 supplied the title, but the location number **65** Ramsey probably represents Kirkestede's first-hand knowledge.

10 Quid Christus de virgine natus est lib. 1

> R12. 4 (whole entry).

11 Cronicorum ubi Jeronimus dimisit lib. 1.

> Diceto, 1. 22 and 80 (whole entry).

p. 69]

211 GELASIUS papa floruit A.C. 494 et scripsit juxta Genadium et juxta Librum pontificalem

> Whole entry from Vincent XXI 101 (works *1–2, 4–6*) and Gennadius c. 95 (works *1–4*); *Liber pontificalis* c. 51 (ed. Duchesne, 1. 255) may be cited indirectly through Vincent (for works *1–2, 4–6*).

1 Adversus Euticen abbatem

> Vincent XXI 101, Gennadius 95.

2 Contra Nestorium grande volumen lib. 5

> Vincent XXI 101, Gennadius 95.

3 Adversus Petrum et Achaicum epistolas plures

> Gennadius 95.

4 Ympnos in similitudinem Ambrosii metrice

> Vincent XXI 101, Gennadius 95.

5 Adversus Arrium lib. 2

> Vincent XXI 101.

6 Sacramentorum praefationes et orationes et epistolas fidei

> Vincent XXI 101.

212 GILBERTUS Albus monachus et abbas de Swyneshed floruit A. Ch. <blank> et scripsit juxta Vincentium in Speculo historiali <blank> et juxta Cathalogum librorum Angliae

(Gilbert of Hoyland)
Registrum 56 ('Opera Gilberti') provided titles and locations, with added information from a manuscript for work 5. The allusion to Vincent (lacking here the customary book and chapter reference) is unidentified, and perhaps mistaken.
Bale, *Index*, 90.
Sharpe, *Latin Writers*, 145–6.

1 Super epistolas Pauli lib.   163.19

   R56. 2 (whole entry).

2 De sententiis lib. 1   12

   Sententias theologicas li. i *Bale (not in Registrum)*   12] xii *R*

   R56. 1 (whole entry).

3 Super psalterium   163.160.127.124

   R56. 3 (whole entry).

4 Super Mattheum   163

   163] 153 *R*

   R56. 4 (whole entry).

5 Super Cantica Canticorum omel. 47   *Varii sunt . . . qui approximant* 82.14.43.20.39.139

   Varii sunt] amantium affectus *add. Bale*   14] 114 *R*

   R56. 9. Stegmüller *Bibl.* 2493. *PL* 184. 11.

6 Super Apocalipsim   163

   R56. 5 (whole entry).

7 De anima lib. 1   165

   De anima] statu *add. Bale (not in Registrum)*

   R56. 7 (whole entry).

Gilbertus   *212. 8*

  8   De casu diaboli lib. 1   <u>163</u>

      163] 165 *R*

      R56. 6 (whole entry).

213   GILBERTUS episcopus Londoninensis floruit circa A. Ch. <*blank*> et scripsit devotissime

    (Gilbert Foliot)
    Gilbertus] Universalis *add. Add. 3470; according to Tanner this was added in a recent hand*

    Bale, *Index*, 90, 'ex Nicolai Brigan et Bostoni collectionibus'. The words 'et Bostoni' are inserted.

  1   Super Cantica   *Osculetur . . . pars mea*   11

      Stegmüller *Bibl.* 2490. *PL* 202. 1147.

214   GILBERTUS abbas Westmonasteriensis floruit circa A. Ch. <*blank*> et scripsit

    (Gilbert Crispin)

    Registrum 56 (a generic 'Opera Gilberti') evidently was used only for the location numbers This entry was presumably compiled from one or two manuscripts at **82** Bury or **168** Oxford Greyfriars. These three works are found together, for example, in BL MS Add. 8166, a collection of the works of Gilbert Crispin.
    Bale, *Index*, 91.
    Sharpe, *Latin Writers*, 142–3.
    A. S. Abulafia & G. R. Evans, *The Works of Gilbert Crispin, Abbot of Westminster*, Auctores Britannici medii aevi 8 (London 1986).

  1   De disputatione Judaei cum Christiano, id est cum seipso tunc abbate, ad Anselmum archiepiscopum lib. 1   *Reverendo . . . pronunciabatur*   82.<u>165</u>.11

      Reverendo] Venerabili patri *Bale*

      R56. 8. Sharpe, *Latin Writers*, 142. Abulafia & Evans, 8–53.

  2   De anima lib. 1   *Unde infanti . . . sub judice*   <u>168</u>

      168] 165 *R*

      R56. 7 (see Gilbert of Hoyland, *212.7*). Sharpe, *Latin Writers*, 142. Abulafia & Evans, 157–164.

3 De casu diaboli lib. 1   *De angelo* . . . *honoret*   168

    168] 165 *R*

    R56. 6 (see Gilbert of Hoyland, *212.8*). *Interrogationes et responsiones de angelo perdito*; Sharpe, *Latin Writers*, 142. Abulafia & Evans, 103, explicit 'honor et gloria per omnia s. s.'

215 GILBERTUS Porree floruit circa A. Ch. 1148 et scripsit

1 Super psalterium   Prologus: *Christus* . . . Principium: *Hinc* . . . *conclusit*   82.83

    Stegmüller *Bibl.* 2511. **82** Bury = B13. 133.

2 Super Trenos Jeremiae   *Quomodo* . . . *leguntur*   83

    Gilbert the Universal. Stegmüller *Bibl.* 2544. 2. Sharpe, *Latin Writers*, 149. Explicit unidentified.

3 Super Leviticum

    Gilbert the Universal. Stegmüller *Bibl.* 2538. Source unidentified.

4 Super Numeros

    Gilbert the Universal. Stegmüller *Bibl.* 2539. Source unidentified.

216 GALFRIDUS Cistertiensis monachus et abbas Claraevallensis floruit circa A. Ch. 1150 et scripsit

    (Geoffrey of Auxerre)
    Galfridus] Antisiodorensis *add*. Add. 3470; *according to Tanner this was added in a recent hand*
    See Gaufridus *238*.

    Registrum 55 ('Opera Galfridi').
    See J. Leclercq, 'Les écrits de Geoffroy d'Auxerre', *RB* 62 (1952) 274–91.

1 Super 5 libros Moysy   *Volentibus* . . .

    Unidentified.

2 Super Cantica Canticorum   105

    R55. 3 (whole entry).

Galfridus *216. 3*

   3 Super Mathaeum   *Dominus ac . . . personam Christi*   <u>105</u>.<u>153</u>.<u>115</u>.65

       105] 165 *R*

       R55. 1. (*Ps.?*) Geoffrey Babio. Stegmüller *Bibl.* 2604. *PL* 162. 1228. Explicit unidentified.

p. 70]

   4 Super Apocalypsin   <u>105</u>

       R55. 2 (whole entry).

   5 De vita et miraculis Bernardi lib. 3   *Clarissimi . . . sicut et tu*

       PL 185. 301–366.

217 GRACIANUS de Tuscia monachus S. Pauli de Bononia floruit circa A. Ch. 1151 et compilavit Decreta   83.82.44.63.53.14.15

       Tuscia] Tristia *Add. 3470;* Tusca *Higden;* Tuscia *James extracts*   Pauli] Proculi *Higden*   Decreta] Decretum *James extracts*

       Higden, 8. 10.
       Speculum coenobitarum 59.
       James extracts, p. 198.
       Ed. Friedberg, *Corpus iuris canonici* 1 (1879). **82** Bury = B13. 166.

218 GALIENUS

       Perhaps this entry was to have contained information found in Vincent XI 92.
       [**82** Bury = BL MS Royal 12 C. VI, fol. 49r (Bury M. 83), a manuscript procured by Kirkestede, which contains a late 14th-cent. list of twelve works of Galen and *ps.* Galen, each with incipit and explicit.]

219 GALFRIDUS Monumutensis floruit A. Ch. <*blank*> et scripsit

       Higden, 1. 24 (whole entry).
       Sharpe, *Latin Writers*, 127.

   1 Historiam Britonum

220 GUYMUNDUS episcopus Aversani floruit circa A. Ch. 1074 et scripsit

(Guitmund of Aversa)

Aversani] Averlani *Add. 3470, queried by Tanner*

1 De corpore et sanguine Christi lib. 3   Ad rem . . . referamus   82.65

PL 149. 1427. **82** Bury = B13. 13b = Bodl. MS e Musaeo 33, p. 213 (Bury A. —).

221 GERVASIUS floruit A. Ch. 1210 et scripsit ad imperatorem Ottonem IV De solaciis imperialibus

Gervasius] Tilberiensis *add*. *Add. 3470; according to Tanner this was added in a recent hand*

Étienne de Bourbon, prologue p. 7 (whole entry).
Bale, *Index*, 87.
Sharpe, *Latin Writers*, 141.

De rebus Anglicis lib. 1 *add. Bale as an entry; this work does not apppear in Étienne de Bourbon*

222 GORGIAS rethor floruit circa A. Ch. <*blank*> et scripsit juxta Vincentium lib. 4to cap. 54°

Vincent IV 54 (whole entry).

1. De concordia Graecismi lib. 1

223 GERARDUS Teutonicus Frater Praedicator floruit A. Ch. <*blank*> et scripsit

Script. Ord. Praed., cf. Stams, 25 (*om*. works 3–5).

1 Super methafisicam

2 Super Ecclesiasten

3 De naturis rerum

4 Super Porphyrium

5 Super quosdam libros Aristotelis

Guydo *224.*

224 GUYDO Argominensis Frater Praedicator floruit A. Ch. <blank> et scripsit

> (Guido Ariminensis)
> Argominensis *queried by Tanner;* Argommensis *Stams*
>
> *Script. Ord. Praed.* (whole entry), cf. Stams, 93.

1 Super libros phisicorum

2 Super librum de anima

3 Super ethicam

4 Super poleticam et rethoricam

225 GREGORIUS Viennensis Frater Praedicator floruit A. Ch. <blank> et scripsit

> *Script. Ord. Praed.* (whole entry), cf. Stams, 96.

1 De ecclipsibus solis et lunae

226 GODIUS Frater Praedicator floruit A. Ch. <blank> et scripsit

> Godinus *Stams, Pign. 41*
>
> *Script. Ord. Praed.* (whole entry), cf. Stams, 41.

1 Super libros sententiarum

2 Contra unitatem intellectus

3 Contra aeternitatem mundi

227 GALFRIDUS Vinesauf floruit A. Ch. <blank> et scripsit juxta *Mariale majus*

> *Mariale* fol. 2r.
> Bale, *Index*, 81, 'ex Bostono et Triueto'.
>
> De eloquentia lib. 1   Neustria sub clypeo regis . . .   *add. Add. 3470 as an entry; according to Tanner this was added in a recent hand; Mariale lists no title*

228 GAIUS sub Zepherino papa et Antonino Severi filio imperatore claruit <blank> et scripsit juxta Jeronimum ubi supra

> Jerome c. 59 (whole entry).

1 Contra Proculum Montani sectatorum librum insignem 1

p. 71]

> Et in eodem libro epistolas Pauli xiii tantum enumerans, quartam decimam quae fertur ad Hebraeos dicit non ejus esse, sed et apud Romanos usque hodie quasi Pauli apostoli non habetur.

229 GILDAS historiographus floruit <blank> et scripsit

> Ware extracts, fol. 132r.
> Sharpe, *Latin Writers*, 149–50.

1 De gestis Britonum historiam   *Britannia . . . fecerunt*

> Sharpe, *Latin Writers*, p. 150. MGH *Auct. Ant.* 13. III. [**82** Bury = London, College of Arms, MS Arundel 30, fols. 11r–21r (Bury —), an imperfect 'Gildas' (= Nennius) with this incipit, followed on fols. 21r–25r by an excerpt from the chronicle of Henry of Huntingdon (without rubric) with this explicit.]

230 GARGILIUS Martialis floruit circa annum <blank> et scripsit juxta Cassiodorum ubi supra

> Cassiodorus I. 28. 6 (whole entry).

1 De ortis et de virtutibus et nutrimentis olerum lib. 1

231 GODARDUS monachus Malmesbiriae floruit A. Ch. <blank> et scripsit

> This author and the source for his name are unidentified.
> Sharpe, *Latin Writers*, 150.

1 . . . . . lib. 1   *A Phoebo Phoebe . . .*

> The incipit is that of the Alan of Lille's *Doctrinale paruum* (PL 210. 581).

Giraldus   *232*.

232 GIRALDUS Cambrensis archidiaconus Landavensis historiographus floruit A.C. <*blank*> et scripsit

Higden, 1. 24.
Bale, *Index*, 421.
Sharpe, *Latin Writers*, 134–7.

1 Topographiam Hiberniae distinctione 3^{ci} lib. 1   *Placuit . . . injunctum*

   Placuit] excellentie vestre invictissime *add. Bale*

   Higden, 1. 24. Sharpe, *Latin Writers*, 137 (fourth state). Ed. J. F. Dimock, RS 21 (1867), 5. 20–202. [**82** Bury = CUL MS Ff. 1. 27 pt 2, p. 253 (Bury —).]

2 Itinerarium Walliae distinctione 4^{ci}

   Higden, 1. 24. [**82** Bury = CUL MS Ff. 1. 27 pt 2, p. 499 (Bury —).]

3 Vitam Regis Henrici II distinctione 3^{ci}

   Higden, 1. 24.

4 De ecclesiasticis ordinibus lib. 1

   Source unidentified; presumably this is *Gemma ecclesiastica*, Sharpe, *Latin Writers*, 135.

5 De principis instructione lib. 1

   Source unidentified; Sharpe, *Latin Writers*, 134.

233 GUIDO monachus Aretinus in Ytalia floruit circa A. Ch. 1022 et scripsit

   Works *1–3* represent four treatises of Guido d'Arezzo that circulated together, and are printed together in *PL* 141. 379–423. See the bibiographic discussion in B79. 171.

1 De musica mic[r]ologum lib. 1   *Gymnasio . . . viget saecula*

   micologum *Add. 3470, queried by Tanner*

   PL 141. 379.

2 Rithmum in musica   *Gliscunt . . . nosces*

   PL 141. 405. Explicit unidentified.

3 Super antiphonarium corectorium   *Temporibus . . . philosophis*

   corectorium *queried by Tanner*

   PL 141. 413, two works together. The incipit is that of the *Aliae regulae de ignoto cantu*; the explicit is that of *Ad Michaelem monachum de ignoto cantu*, *PL* 141. 423.

4 De figuris et numeris abaci   *Alligas . . .*

   Unidentified.

5 De divisionibus

   Source unidentified. This may represent a series of tracts beginning 'Diuisio monachorum'; cf. Sainte-Dié, Bibliothèque municipale, MS 42, fols. 59r, 117v, 130r. See *Theory of Music* 1 *International Inventory of Musical Sources*, ed. J. Smits van Waesberghe (Munich 1961), 131–3.

6 De mensura fistularum   *De hiis . . .*

   This work appears in several codices; cf. Bodl. MS Bodley 300 in which the *De mensura* appears on fol. 118v, followed by a 'Gilbertus de proporcionibus fistularum ordinandis', beginning 'De hiis instrumentis'. For further manuscripts and bibliography see Smits van Waesberghe 92–3.

234 GODEFRIDUS Parisiensis capellanus imperatoris floruit A. Ch. <*blank*> et scripsit

   Parisiensis] Parmensis *Étienne de Bourbon*

   (Godefridus de Viterbo)
   Étienne de Bourbon, prologue p. 8 (whole entry).

1 Papae Gregorii VIII librum qui vocatur Pantheon

235 GUNDISALVUS archidiaconus Tholetanus floruit   <*blank*> et scripsit

1 De anima   *Cum omnes . . . eructat verbum*   83.74

   Ed. J. T. Muckle in *Med. Stud.* 2 (1940) 23–103; explicit on p. 103 line 9.

2 De mentione scientiarum et de differentia inter scientias speculativas et practicas   *Felix prior . . . et inesse*

   De diuisione philosophiae. Ed. L. Baur in *BGPM* 4/2–3 (1903).

Guido   *236.*

236 GUIDO de Columpnis floruit circa A. Ch. 1287 et scripsit

See also Dares *152*, Dites *153*.

Guido de Columna, Messanensis in Sicilia, ornavit ac restauravit tam Ditem Cretensem quam Daretem Phrygium in historiis de bello Troiano. Et scripsit plenissime quicquid in tota historia universaliter ac particulariter fuerit gestum] *add. Bale, from Kirkestede's entries for Dares Frigius 152 and Dites 153*

Bale, *Index*, 111.

1 Historiam de bello Trojano lib. 36   *Licet cotidie . . . factum est*

Guido de Columnis, *Historia destructionis Troiae*. Ed. N. E. Griffin (Cambridge, MA, 1936).

237 GUIDO abbas S. Dionisii in Francia floruit A. Ch. <*blank*> et scripsit

(Guido de Castris)

1 Speculum legendarum sive sanctilogium vel martilogium lib. 14   *Legendas . . . pro gloria*   15

Sanctilogium; unprinted (see, for example, BL MS Royal 13 D. ix). Kirkestede cited this work as a source for Odo *405.15* and Usuardus *663*.

238 GAUFRIDUS Altisiodorensis B. Bernardi notarius floruit <*blank*> et scripsit

(Geoffrey of Auxerre)
See Galfridus *216*.
Source unidentified.

1 Contra Petrum Abelardum

This is probably the *Disputatio aduersus Abelardum* of William of Saint-Thierry. An anonymous manuscript of the *Disputatio* is attributed to Galfridus by C. Oudin, *De scriptoribus* (Leipzig 1722), 2. 1494–9.

239 GUIDO prior Cartusiae floruit A. Ch. <*blank*> et scripsit

(Guigo II of Chartreuse)
See also Wido *652*.

1 Meditationum lib. 1   *Bonum mihi . . . dimittet inanes*   61

Ed. E. Colledge and J. Walsh, SChr 163 (1970) 126–76, *Meditationes* 1–9.

Haimo 240. 6

p. 72]

240 HAIMO monachus S. Dionisii in Gallia et doctor theologiae floruit A. Ch. 1054 et scripsit multa

> (Haimo of Auxerre)
> *Registrum* 27 was probably not used.
> *Speculum coenobitarum* 54.
> Bale, *Index*, 155–6.
> On Haimo's exegetical writings see R. Riggenbach in 'Historische Studien zum Hebräerbrief', *Forschungen zur Geschichte des Neutestamentlichen Kanons*, ed. T. Zahn, vol. 8/1 (Leipzig 1907), esp. 56–110.

1 Super 5 libros Moysy

> Source unidentified. Fragments of a commentary on Genesis by Haimo have been discovered in Berlin, Deutsche Staatsbibliothek, MS theol. 2° 59, fols. 5v, 6r, etc.; V. Rose, *Verzeichniss der lateinischen Handschriften der Königlichen Bibliothek zu Berlin* (Berlin 1901), 2. 3–4 no. 223.

2 Super Ysaiam lib. 2   *Ysaias . . . liberatione*   83.13.65

> Cf. R27. 3. Stegmüller *Bibl.* 3083. *PL* 116. 715. [**82** Bury = B13. 85 = BL MS Egerton 2782 (Bury H. 1), with this title written by Kirkestede at the top of fol. 1r.]

3 Super epistolam Pauli expositionem   *A Corintho . . . perfectissima*   83.$\underline{9}$.65

> Cf. R27. 2. Stegmüller *Bibl.* 3101–112 (Rom–Tit). *PL* 117. 361–814. [**82** Bury = B13. 161.]

4 Super Apocalipsin lib. 8   *Planior . . . poneret*   83.5

> Planior] Legitur Genesis 28 *Bale*   5 should probably read 65, or possibly 15

> Cf. R27. 5. Stegmüller *Bibl.* 3122 and 3072. *PL* 117. 937.

5 Super epistolas et evangelia totius anni omel.   *Ad Romanos . . .*   83.2.65

> Cf. R27. 6. See the bibliographic discussion of this work in the *Registrum*.

6 In Christ[i]anarum rerum memoriam lib. 10   15

> The source for this entry may have been a manuscript. *Epitome sacrae historiae*; *PL* 188. 817.

Haimo *240. 7*

7 De detectione corporis S. Dionisii serm. 1   *Liquet nobis . . . clementia*   82

> **82** Bury = Cambridge, Pembroke College, MS 24, fols. 362v–374v (Bury O. 54).

8 Super libros Macabeorum   174

> The source for this entry may have been a manuscript; the work is unidentified.

9 De diversis rebus monachorum et monachatu   *Ut enim . . . facere debuisti*   65.63.62

> Unidentified. **65** Ramsey = B68. 19.

241 HAMONIUS Floriacensis floruit <*blank*> et scripsit

> Diceto, 1. 23 (whole entry).

1 Cronica a tempore Nini regis usque ad A. Ch. 843

> Same as Yvo *667.19*.
>
> Vitam Abbonis lib. 1 add. Add. *3470 as an entry; according to Tanner this was added in a recent hand*

242 HILLARIUS Pictavensis floruit circa A. Ch. 390 et scripsit multa juxta Jeronimum et Vincentium lib. 15

> *Registrum* 4, Vincent XV 24, *Manipulus florum* VII, Jerome c. 100. The *Registrum*'s entry for Hilary as transmitted is corrupt, including the heading, which is erased in one witness (Tanner 165) and lacking in the other (Peterhouse 169), and the location numbers, which are missing from several of the titles.

1 De synodis lib. 2   *Constitutum . . . intelligi*   94.105.128.9.19.15

> Probably the whole entry from R4. 1 (title and location numbers), Vincent XV 24, *MF* VII 2 (incipit and explicit), and Jerome 100. The text of the *Registrum* is corrupt at this point.

2 De Trinitate contra Arrianos lib. 12   *Circumspecte . . . in te et ex te*   94.105.82.83.42.32

> R4. 2 (title, location numbers), Vincent XV 24, *MF* VII 1 (incipit 'Circumspicienti' and explicit), Jerome 100; the text of the *Registrum* is corrupt at this point. *CPL* 433. *CCSL* 62–62A. See also *11* below.

Hillarius *242. 11*

3 Ad Constantium imperatorem lib. 1   *Beneficia* . . .   <u>94</u>

    R4. 3, Vincent XV 24, Jerome 100. *CPL* 459. *CSEL* 65. 181.

4 De Constantio imperatore lib. 1   *Tempus est . . . disponas*   <u>94</u>

    Whole entry from R4. 4 (title, location number), Vincent XV 24, *MF* VII 3 (incipit, explicit 'dissonans'), and Jerome 100.

5 Ympnorum et misteriorum lib. 1

    Whole entry from Vincent XV 24 and Jerome 100.

6 Super Cantica canticorum lib. 1

    Whole entry from Vincent XV 24 and Jerome 100.

7 Contra Auxentium lib. 1   *Dilectissimus . . . praedicabunt*   <u>94</u>.<u>161</u>.<u>158</u>

    Probably the whole entry from R4. 6 (title, location numbers), Vincent XV 24, *MF* VII 5 (incipit 'Dilectissimis', explicit), and Jerome 100. The text of the *Registrum* is corrupt at this point. See also *12* below.

8 Super epistolas canonicas lib. 7   <u>35</u>

    R4. 10 (whole entry save the number of books).

9 De fide lib. 1   <u>1</u>.<u>20</u>

    The whole entry, including the location numbers, comes from R3. 66, Ambrose *De fide*. The *Registrum*'s distinction between the works of Ambrose and the immediately following works of Hilary is blurred in both surviving manuscripts (see headnote above). Presumably the state of Kirkestede's *Registrum* was the source of this error.

10 Ad Augustinum ep. 1   <u>161</u>.<u>158</u>.<u>156</u>.<u>153</u>.<u>9</u>.<u>15</u>

    R4. 7 (probably the whole entry). The *Registrum* text is corrupt here.

11 De essentia Patris, Filii et Spiritus Sancti lib. 1   *Hos nunc* . . .   <u>23</u>

    23] 23.xxiii *R*

    R4. 12. The title is that of a pastiche from the *De Trinitate* (*2* above), *CPL* 469. The incipit is that of a different extract *De corpore et sanguine Domini* from Book VIII of *De Trinitate*, which also had a separate existence (see, for example, BL MS Royal 7 C. VIII, fol. 24r, and see BM *Cat. Royal*, 1. 119). *PL* 10. 246 and see *CCSL* 62A. 325; incipit 'Eos nunc. . .'.

Hillarius   *242. 12*

12 Exemplum blasphemiae Auxentii lib. 1   *Beatissimis . . . non oportet*   94

   Beatissimis *queried by Tanner*

   Whole entry from R4. 5 (title, location number) and *MF* VII 4 (incipit, explicit).

13 In Mattheum commentarios lib. 1   9.35.128.20

   20] xx *R*

   Whole entry from R4. 9, Vincent XV 24, and Jerome 100.

14 In Job tract. 1

   Whole entry from Vincent XV 24 and Jerome 100.

15 Adversus Valentem et Ursacium historiam

   Whole entry from Vincent XV 24 and Jerome 100.

16 Item historiam a principio mundi usque ad Christum

   MF VII 6 (whole entry).

17 In psalmum 1^{mum} et 2^{dum} commentarios   1

   Whole entry from R4. 11 ('Super Psalmos'), Vincent XV 24 and Jerome 100.

18 Item a 51° psalmo usque ad 62^m commentarios   1

   Jerome 100 (whole entry). Location number **1** is repeated from R4. 11 (=*17* above).

19 Item a 118° usque ad extremum psalmum   1

   Jerome 100 (whole entry). Location number **1** is repeated from R4. 11 (=*17* above).

20 Epistolarum ad diversos lib. 1

   Whole entry from Vincent XV 24 and Jerome 100.

p. 73]

243 HILLARIUS monachus et episcopus Arelatensis floruit circa A. Ch. 451 et scripsit juxta Genadium et Ysidorum

> Gennadius c. 70, Isidore c. 16 (whole entry save the date).
> *Speculum coenobitarum* 31.

1 Vitam S. Honorati monachi et abbatis et episcopi

244 HUGO S. Victoris Parisiensis canonicus literarum scientia clarus et in 7 liberalium artium peritia nulli sui temporis secundus obiit A. Ch. 1148 et scripsit multa et devota

> *Registrum* 97, Vincent XXVII 47 (references are followed by numbers in brackets [1, 2, etc.] that indicate the sequence of titles in the chapter), *Manipulus florum* XIV, Willelmus Durandus, *Rationale* IV 1 (ed. A. Davril and T. M. Thibodeau, *CCCM* 140 (1995) 240).
> The core of this entry was constructed from manuscripts of Hugh's works, at Bury and perhaps elsewhere. To this Kirkestede added information from his principal bibliographic sources, sometimes in a visible sequence: for example, Vincent of Beauvais determined the sequence of *15–22* below, while *34–39* and *45–48* represent two sequences from the *Manipulus florum* and *53–68* come in sequence from the *Registrum*, with two exceptions. At the end (*69–88*) the source of the titles is a mixture, presumably the result of repeated additions as Kirkestede found new items or noticed titles previously overlooked. Kirkestede's copying of *Registrum* location numbers, always eccentric, often follows a precisely reverse sequence for Hugh's works.
> See R. Goy, *Die Überlieferung der Werke Hugos von St Viktor*, Monographien zur Geschichte des Mittelalters 14 (Stuttgart 1976); we cite Goy's page numbers for those titles that have incipits here.

1 De sacramentis Veteris et Novi Testamenti lib. 2   *Librum de sacramentis ... erit in fine*   82.118.94.42.8.9.19

> R97. 17, Vincent XXVII 47 [13], *MF* XIV 1. Goy, 133. *PL* 176. 173–618. See also *58* below. **82** Bury = B13. 126, and cf. B13. 156; a versified version of *De sacramentis* survives in Cambridge, Gonville and Caius College, MS 145/195 (Bury H. 31), and Cambridge, Pembroke College, MS 109 (Bury H. 32); neither of these agrees with the incipit and explicit that Kirkestede gives here.

2 Didascalicon lib. 6   *Omni*[*um*] *expetendum ... animalibus*   82.118.94.116.8.19.9

> Omnium] Omni *Add. 3470*, queried by Tanner

Hugo 244. 2

> R97. 19 Vincent XXVII 47 [1], *MF* XIV 15. Goy, 14. Ed. C. Buttimer (Washington 1939) 4–130, incipit 'Omnium expetendorum'; explicit 'animalibus cenam', Book VI c. 13 of the edition. **82** Bury = Cambridge, Pembroke College, MS 111, fols. 161r–204v (Bury J. 20) with this explicit; and BL MS Royal 8 F. xiv, fol. 90r (Bury G. 15), explicit does not correspond (fol. 112v).

3 Super jerarchiam Dionisii angelicam expositionem lib. 1   *Judei . . . condescendit*   82.163.114.9.19.15.1

> R97. 14, Vincent XXVII 47 [4], *MF* XIV 33. Goy, 18. *PL* 175. 923.

4 Super Ecclesiasten lib. 6   *Verba . . . ignorant*   82.89.9.19.15.1.139

> R97. 12. Goy, 329. *PL* 175. 115. **82** Bury = Cambridge, Pembroke College, MS 90, fol. 1r (Bury H. 19) with this incipit and explicit.

5 Super Ecclesiasticum lib. 5

> Vincent XXVII 47 [2] (whole entry).

6 Super Lamentationes Jeremiae lib. 1   *Quomodo . . . quae sequuntur*   82.93.105.9.19.13.15

> R97. 16, Vincent XXVII 47 [3]. Goy, 67. *PL* 175. 255, explicit 'consequatur'. **82** Bury = London, Wellcome Historical Medical Library, MS 801A, fol. 126v (Bury B. 357).

7 De arra animae lib. 1   *Loquar . . . concupisco*   116.15.1.20.39.46.97

> R97. 10, Vincent XXVII 47 [5], *MF* XIV 19 (explicit does not correspond). Goy, 277. *PL* 176. 951.

8 Soliloquiorum lib. 1   *Solus . . . occupatione*   116.166.82.137.39.20

> 166] 165 *R*   137] 127 *R*

> R97. 9. The title is that of 7 above (R97. 10, *Soliloquium de arra anime*), and the location numbers also are taken from R97. 10. The incipit and explicit are those of *De interiori domo sive de conscientia aedificanda* cc. 29–41 often attributed to Hugh or to Bernard of Clairvaux. *PL* 184. 538–52. See also *10* below.

9 De amore sponsi ad sponsam lib. 1   *Ibo mihi . . . congregamus*   82

> *MF* XIV 25 (explicit 'congregamur'). Goy, 268. *PL* 176.987.

Hugo 244. 17

10 De conscientia lib. 1 *Domus haec . . .ubi nescitur* 82

> *MF* XIV 31 (title, incipit, explicit). Spurious, often attributed to Hugh or to Bernard of Clairvaux. *De interiori domo siue de conscientia edificanda* cc. 1–28. *PL* 184. 507–538. See also *8* above.

11 De rota praelationis et simulationis lib. 2 *Vita viri . . . contradicat*

> R97. 70. Hugo de Folieto; cf. B. Hauréau, *Oeuvres de Hugues de St-Victor: Essai critique* (Paris 1886, repr. 1963) 166.

12 De diligendo Deo lib. 1 *Omnia . . . affectus* 82.<u>43</u>

> R97. 52. Bernard; the misattribution to Hugh comes from the *Registrum*. *SBO* 3. 119, incipit 'Orationes a me'. Same as Bernard *85.2*.

13 De contemptu mundi et vanitate rerum mundanarum lib. 4 *O invide munde . . . mihi videtur* 82.<u>157</u>.<u>158</u>.<u>156</u>.<u>42</u>.15

> R97. 24 (incipit 'O munde immunde'), *MF* XIV 20 (incipit 'O munde immunde', explicit 'non mutetur'). Goy, 245. *PL* 176. 703.

14 Meditationum lib. 1 *Meditatio . . . apprehendit* 82.<u>39</u>.<u>115</u>.<u>15</u>.<u>9</u>.<u>111</u>.<u>128</u>

> R97. 8 (title, location numbers save **82** Bury), *MF* XIV. 3 (title, incipit, explicit). Goy, 196. Ed. R. Baron, *Hugues de Saint-Victor: Six opuscules spirituels* (Paris 1969) 44–58.

15 De virtute et modo orandi lib. 1 *Quo studio . . . sacrificium* 82.<u>43</u>.<u>9</u>.<u>13</u>.<u>20</u>.<u>116</u>.<u>15</u>

> R97. 29, 49, Vincent XXVII 47 [6], *MF* XIV 16 (incipit, explicit). Goy, 404. *PL* 176. 977. Location numbers **116** and **15** are taken from R97. 49, numbers **43** to **20** from R97. 29.

16 De institutione noviciorum lib. 1 *Quia fratres . . . det Deus Amen* 82.<u>20</u>.<u>1</u>.<u>15</u>.<u>19</u>.<u>89</u>

> R97. 6, Vincent XXVII 47 [7], *MF* XIV 17–18. Goy, 340. *PL* 176. 925. **82** Bury = BL MS Royal 8 F. XIV, fol. 149v (Bury G. 15), a manuscript procured, and this segment copied, by Kirkestede; Cambridge, St John's College, MS G. 2, fol. 1r (Bury H. 56).

17 De archa Noae lib. 5 *Cum sederem . . . provocet* 82.<u>49</u>.<u>46</u>.<u>39</u>.<u>20</u>.<u>1</u>.<u>15</u>

> R97. 4, Vincent XXVII 47 [8], *MF* XIV 14. Goy, 212 and 237, the four books of *De arca Noe morali* and, as fifth book, *De arca Noe mystica*. *PL* 176.

Hugo   244. 17

617–704. **82** Bury = Cambridge, Pembroke College, MS 90, fol. 139r (Bury H. 19) with this incipit and explicit, and Pembroke College, MS 9, fol. 159r (Bury B. 305), with Kirkestede's notes on fol. 177v ('Liber quintus de arca deficit' and 'Liber quintus principium *In planicie etc.* deficit') and the formal explicit in red on fol. 178v 'Explicit inperfecte de archis'.

18   De anima Christi lib. 1   *Queritis . . . praesumere*   82.<u>9</u>.15.1.<u>39</u>.<u>53</u>.<u>46</u>

R97. 27, Vincent XXVII 47 [9]. Goy, 124. *PL* 176. 847. Same as *37* below.

19   De perpetua virginitate B. Mariae lib. 1   *De incomperta . . . permansit*   <u>46</u>. <u>39</u>.<u>20</u>.<u>1</u>.<u>12</u>.<u>157</u>

12] xii *R*   157] 127 *R*

R97. 5, Vincent XXVII 47 [10]. Goy, 116. *PL* 176. 857; explicit is that of c. 3 (*PL* 176. 873). See also *57* below.

20   Super Magnificat expositionem 1   *Maximam . . . et semen ejus*   82

Vincent XXVII 47 [11], *MF* XIV. 22. Goy, 383. *PL* 175. 413. **82** Bury = Cambridge, Pembroke College, MS 90, fol. 66r (Bury H. 19).

21   Super Totum pulchrum es expositionem 1   *Verba ipsa . . . coronaberis*   <u>46</u>. <u>39</u>.<u>9</u>.<u>124</u>.<u>123</u>.<u>12</u>

12] xii *R*

R97. 3, Vincent XXVII 47 [12]. Goy, 438. *PL* 177. 1209.

22   Super quosdam versus psalmorum notulas   *Quosdam tibi . . . ego sum Deus*   82

Vincent XXVII 47 [14]. Goy, 58. *Miscellanea* II 1–78. *PL* 177. 589; explicit is that of c. 57.

23   Speculum   ecclesiae   lib.   1   *Ecclesiam   . . .   quoniam   disputant*   82.<u>39</u>.<u>114</u>.<u>153</u>.<u>160</u>.<u>165</u>

R97. 21 (title, location numbers save **82** Bury), *MF* XIV 29 (incipit 'De sacramentis ecclesiasticis', explicit 'quam disputans'). *Ps.* Hugh of Saint-Victor. *PL* 177. 335. Same as *88* below. **82** Bury = Cambridge, Pembroke College, MS 111, fol. 135v (Bury J. 20); BL MS Royal 8 F. XIV, fol. 113r (Bury G. 15), explicit 'quia disputans'.

Hugo 244. 30

24 Super regulam S. Augustini expositionem 1 *Haec praecepta . . . glorietur*
82.<u>9</u>.<u>127</u>.<u>166</u>.165

> R97. 23. Goy, 457. *PL* 176. 881.

25 De voluntate Dei lib. 1 *Prima rerum . . .*

> R97. 28 (whole entry).

26 Super Cantica Canticorum lib. 1 *In principio . . . gratias agamus* 82.<u>163</u>.<u>165</u>.<u>92</u>

> principio] primo Add. *3470*; principio *has been added by Tanner as a variant reading*
>
> R97. 35 (title, location numbers), *MF* XIV 37 (incipit, explicit). Honorius Augustodunensis; Stegmüller *Bibl.* 3573. *PL* 172. 347.

27 Super Dum medium silentium tenerent serm. <u>94</u>

> medium silentium *queried by Tanner*
>
> R97. 42 (whole entry). Same as Ambrose *2.81* and cf. Anselm *3.44*.

28 De claustro animae lib. 4 *Rogasti . . . immortalitatis* 82.<u>94</u>.<u>43</u>.<u>15</u>.<u>1</u>.<u>20</u>.<u>46</u>

> R97. 43, *MF* XIV 11 (title, incipit, explicit). Hugo de Folieto. Location numbers **94** and **43** come from R97. 43, but **15** to **46** are taken by mistake from R97. 44; a similar but not identical mistake occurs here in Peterhouse 169, suggesting an anomaly at this spot in the *Registrum* text. Same as Hugo de Folieto *245.1*.

29 De quinque septenis lib. 1 *Quinque . . . memento* 82.<u>9</u>.<u>1</u>.<u>15</u>

> R97. 1. Goy, 368. Ed. R. Baron, *Six opuscules spirituels*, SChr 155 (1969) 100–118, explicit 'memento mei'. **82** Bury = Cambridge, Pembroke College, MS 90, fol. 75v (Bury H. 19); Cambridge, Pembroke College, MS 9, fol. 178v (Bury B. 305), explicit does not correspond (fol. 180r); BL MS Royal 8 F. XIV, fol. 71v (Bury G. 15), the last two sentences of the text (expl. 'memento mei') are added in the margin in Kirkestede's hand.

30 De tribus maximis circumstantiis gestorum, id est personis, locis et temporibus lib. 1 *Fili sapientia . . . annis* 82.<u>63</u>.<u>139</u>.<u>1</u>.<u>15</u>.<u>9</u>.<u>153</u>

> R97. 34. Goy, 36. Prologue ed. W. M. Green in *Speculum* 18 (1943) 484; the list of historians' names from this text has been printed by G. H. Pertz in *Archiv* 11 (1858) 306; the chronological table of popes and emperors is edited by G. Waitz in MGH *Scriptores* 25. 90. See also *69* and *74* below.

Hugo *244. 31*

31 De laude caritatis lib. 1   *Jam multos . . . per omnia*   20.1.166

   Whole entry from R97. 66 (title, location numbers save the suspect **166**) and *MF* XIV 21 (title, incipit, explicit). See also *84* below.

32 De laude crucis lib. 1

   This work and its source are unidentified; probably it is a confused duplicate of *31* above.

33 De bestiis lib. 1   *Leo fortissimus . . . perveniat*

   MF XIV 38 (whole entry).

p. 74]

34 De medicina animae lib. 1   *Microcosmus . . . superponant*

   MF XIV 2 (whole entry).

35 De incarnatione Verbi lib. 1   *Quidam . . . glorificationes*

   MF XIV 4 (whole entry).

36 De potestate et voluntate Dei lib. 1   *Queritur . . . sed praescivit*   82.15

   praescivit] poscunt Add. *3470*, queried by Tanner

   R97. 63, *MF* XIV 6 (title, incipit, explicit). *PL* 176. 839.

37 De sapientia Christi lib. 1   *Quaeritis . . .*

   MF XIV 7 (whole entry). Same as *18* above.

38 De substantia dilectionis lib. 1   *Cotidianum . . . cupiditas*

   MF XIV 8 (whole entry).

39 De operibus trium dierum lib. 1   *Verbum bonum . . . ad resurrectionem*
   39.20.15.1.43.163.126

   Whole entry from R97. 18 (title, location numbers) and *MF* XIV 9 (title, incipit, explicit). Same as *42* and *67* below.

246

Hugo 244. 48

40 Super Decalogum lib. 1   *Audi Israel . . . pertinet ad*

> *Institutiones in decalogum legis Dominicae*. PL 176. 9–17. Same as *50* below. [**82** Bury = Cambridge, Pembroke College, MS 90, fol. 73v (Bury H. 19).]

41 De judicio veri et boni lib. 1   *Spiritualiter . . . naturam*   15.82

> R97. 61 (differently titled). Cf. Goy, 453 no. 2. *Miscellanea* I 1. PL 177. 469–77.

42 De contemplando sive de tribus diebus lib. 1   *Verbum bonum . . . ad resurrectionem*   168

> diebus] dietis Add. *3470*

> Printed as Book 7 of *Didascalicon*, *2* above. Goy, 98. PL 176. 811. Same as *39* above and *67* below. [**82** Bury = Cambridge, Pembroke College, MS 90, fol. 167r (Bury H. 19) with the rubric 'De tribus diebus'.]

43 De cibo Emanuelis lib. 1   *De cibo . . . non est appetendum*   168

> *Miscellanea* I 2. PL 177. 477.

44 Exameron lib. 2   *Librum istum . . . mihi videtur*   67

> The number of books pertains to Hugh's *De sacramentis christianae fidei*, Goy, 133, PL 176. 175, and the incipit is probably a variant of the first words of that work's preface ('Librum de sacramentis'); the explicit, however, is that of the *De sacramentis legis naturalis et scriptae dialogus*, Goy, 75, PL 176. 17–42. The title *Exameron* was used for both works.

45 Ad socium nubere volentem   *Dum te . . . eterna saecula*

> *MF* XIV 12 (whole entry).

46 De 7 donis Spiritus Sancti   *Scriptum est . . . operantur*

> *MF* XIV 24 (whole entry).

47 De sacra Scriptura   *Lectione . . . interfecit*

> *MF* XIV 26 (whole entry).

48 De 5 libris Moysy notulas   *Sciendum quod . . . capiet te*

> *MF* XIV 28 (whole entry).

Hugo   244. 49

49 De 3^bus voluntatibus in Christo lib. 1   *Quaeritis . . . vivit Deo*   82.<u>15</u>

> R97. 62 (title, location number), *MF* XIV 5 (title, incipit, explicit). Goy, 172. *PL* 176. 841.

50 De x praeceptis serm. 1   *Audi Israel . . . pertinent ad Dominum*   82

> Same as *40* above.

51 Super Ezechielem ad literam lib. 1   *Multis . . . complendum*   82

> *MF* XIV 36. Richard of Saint-Victor; Stegmüller *Bibl.* 7337. *PL* 196. 527.

52 De poenitentia lib. 1

> Source unidentified. This may refer to *Miscellanea* I 90, 104, 105, 106, IV 9, VII 29, etc.

53 De conflictu inter corpus et animam lib. 1   <u>127</u>

> R97. 7 (whole entry).

54 Super Novum Testamentum breviloquium   <u>167</u>.<u>126</u>

> Whole entry from R97. 11 (part of title and **126**) and R97. 60 (rest of the title and **167**).

55 Sententiarum lib. 1   <u>49</u>.<u>9</u>.<u>81</u>.<u>43</u>.<u>105</u>.<u>126</u>

> 81] 82 *R*

> R97. 13. Goy, 486. *PL* 176. 41. See also *56* below. [**82** Bury = cf. B13. 156.]

56 De fide, spe et caritate lib. 1   *De fide . . .*   <u>13</u>.<u>127</u>.<u>114</u>.<u>153</u>.<u>126</u>.<u>24</u>

> 24] xxiiii R

> R97. 22. *Tract.* 1 of *55* above. *PL* 176. 41, and see Goy, 486. Incipit is that of the preface.

57 Cur non fit conjugium inter eundem sexum   *Quoniam quidam . . .*   166. 19.143

> R97. 25 (title, incipit; location numbers lost). *De B. Mariae virginitate* c. 4. Goy, 116. *PL* 176. 873. The whole entry probably comes from the *Registrum*, but the *Registrum* text is corrupt at this point. See also *19* above.

Hugo   *244. 68*

58 Quod sacerdotes habeant potestatem etc.   *Potestatem* . . .   160

   R97. 26 (incipit, location number; title differs). *De sacramentis* II 14. 8. *PL* 176. 564. See also *1* above.

59 De quibusdam verbis Bibliae   *Hoc est aliis . . . a templo*

   Unidentified.

60 Epithalamium ejusdem   163.126

   R97. 36 (whole entry).

61 De profectione Jacob in Mesopotamiam   165

   R97. 39 (whole entry).

62 De resurrectione et anima lib. 1   126

   R97. 40 (whole entry, titled there *De ratione et anima*).

63 De anima lib. 4   126

   R97. 2 (whole entry save the number of books). Same as *76* below.

64 De viris illustribus   43

   R97. 51 (whole entry).

65 Super Vetus Testamentum   153.105.46

   R97. 56 (whole entry).

66 Super prologum Jeronimi ante Genesim   105.1

   R97. 58 (whole entry).

67 De tribus invisibilibus Dei   127

   R97. 59 (whole entry). Same as *39* and *42* above.

68 De creatione mundi lib. 1   1.166

   R97. 68 (whole entry save the suspect **166**).

Hugo   *244. 69*

69 Cronicorum a principio mundi lib. 1   *Divinarum* . . .   166.170.<u>63</u>.<u>1</u>.<u>15</u>.<u>9</u>

>   The same as *30* above, but beginning in the prologue where *74* below breaks off; Green, 491 line 3. The chronicle appears with this incipit in Erfurt, Collegium Amplonianum, MS Fol. 393, fols. 43r–51r. Location numbers **63** to **9** are probably taken from R97. 34 (=*30* above).

70 Ephitomiam in philosophiam lib. 1   *Saepe nobis . . . evadet*   165.158

>   *MF* XIV 27 (whole entry save the suspect location numbers)

71 De oratione Dominica expositionem

>   *MF* XIV 13 (whole entry).

72 Item de oratione Dominica expos.   *Haec autem obsecratio . . . adversitas*

>   A similar exposition of the Lord's Prayer appears in Lambeth Palace Library, MS 351, fol. 126v.

73 Item de oratione Dominica sermonem   *Septem sunt . . . inpotentes*

>   *MF* XIV 23 (whole entry).

74 De arte memorandi lib. 1   *Fili sapientia . . . solidum esse*   170.15

>   Part of the introduction to the chronicle (*30* above); Green, 488–91 line 2; see *69* above.

75 Collationum quaestionum super Genesin lib. 8   <u>160</u>.49

>   R97. 55 (whole entry, title 'Collecte questionum . . .').

76 De anima et homine lib. 1   <u>126</u>.166

>   R97. 2 (whole entry save the suspect **166**). Same as *63* above.

77 De consuetudinibus lib. 1   157

>   R97. 45 (whole entry). Location number **157** was presumably a mistake of Kirkestede's *Registrum*, which is shared with Peterhouse 169.

p. 75]

76 De misteriis ecclesiae lib. 1   *Oportet . . . saecula*

>   *MF* XIV 35 (whole entry).

Hugo 244. 85

79 Beniamin lib. 1 *Spiritualiter . . . ibi philosophus* 15

> Beniamin] Bemanin *Add. 3470, queried by Tanner* philosophus] plenis *Add. 3470, queried by Tanner*

> *MF* XIV 34 (title and incipit 'Spiritalis'; explicit does not correspond). This is error compounded. The title, provided by the *Manipulus florum*, mistakenly names a work by Richard, not Hugh, of Saint-Victor. However, the incipit (borrowed by Kirkestede) and the explicit in this *Manipulus florum* entry refer instead to Hugh's *Miscellanea* I 1 (*PL* 177. 469). The source of the explicit that Kirkestede gives here is unknown. **15** St Albans may = Bodl. MS Laud Misc. 409, fol. 64r, *Beniamin minor* without attribution of authorship, in a collection of works by Hugh; if so, that would imply that Kirkestede merely looked at the rubric in the St Albans book, or perhaps just the table of contents, and that his explicit came from elsewhere.

80 Ysogagasarum lib. 1 163

> R97. 33 (whole entry).

81 De duobus discipulis currentibus ad monumentum serm. 1 *Quaeris . . . resurgat* 82

> *Miscellanea* I 96, *PL* 177. 525. **82** Bury = Cambridge, Pembroke College, MS 90, fol. 77v (Bury H. 19).

82 De Balac et Balaam serm. 1 *Balac . . . reformaris* 82

> *Miscellanea* I 99, *PL* 177. 529. **82** Bury = Cambridge, Pembroke College, MS 90, fol. 78r (Bury H. 19).

83 De eo quod scriptum est: Vivus est sermo Dei *Semel locutus . . .*

> Vivus] Unius *Add. 3470, with* Vivus *inserted above the line, whether in Tanner's hand or not is unknown*

> Goy, 91. *PL* 177. 289. [**82** Bury = Cambridge, Pembroke College, MS 90, fol. 79v (Bury H. 19); also Cambridge, Pembroke College, MS 9, fol. 182v (Bury B. 305), without rubric, incipit does not correspond.]

84 Item de laude caritatis lib. 1 *Servo Christi . . .   Cogitanti . . .* 168

> The incipits are those of the prologue to *31* above. *PL* 176. 969.

85 De 3^{bus} ascensionibus Christi serm. *Beatus vir . . . videbimus*

> [**82** Bury = Cambridge, Pembroke College, MS 9, fols. 183r–188v (Bury B. 305), without rubric.]

Hugo   *244. 86*

86 Item super illud: Videte, vigilate et orate serm.   *Attende* . . .

> Unidentified.

87 Item super psalterium postillas   *Ego divinum . . . per unam etc.*   11

> Ego divinum *queried by Tanner*
>
> Unidentified.

88 Speculum ecclesiae intitulatur Innocentio III secundum W. Durandum in suo Rationali parte 4ta fol. 51 et in 2da columna ad finem et alibi frequenter.

> Same as *23* above.

245 HUGO de Folieto S. Petri Corbiensis dicitur fuisse monachus et scripsisse De claustro animae lib. 4 circa A. Ch. 1120 juxta Vincentium lib. 27 cap. 18. Sed dicti libri potius ascribendi sunt Hugoni de S. Victore et hoc patet in libro 2do capitulo de habitu, et infra, de habitu pretioso.

> Vincent XXVIII 18. The attribution is correct, but the work was often misattributed to Hugh of Saint-Victor. *PL* 176. 1017. Chapter 8 *De habitu, PL* 176. 1056; c. 18, *De habitu pretioso, PL* 176. 1070. Same as Hugo de S. Victoris *244.28*.

246 HILDEFONSUS monachus et archiepiscopus Toletanus floruit circa A. Ch. 616 et scripsit multa

> Titles *5–12* were taken in sequence from Julian's Life of Ildefonsus (BL MS Royal 6 B. x, fol. 21v (Bury A. 88)), a manuscript that also contains the text of *1* below. (Julian's Life is printed, *PL* 96. 43).
> See A. Braegelmann, *The Life and Writings of St. Ildefonsus of Toledo* (Washington, DC, 1942).

1 De virginitate B. Mariae sive de laudibus ejus contra 3 infideles lib. 1 *Deus lumen* . . .   82.65

> Julian, Life. *CPL* 1247. *PL* 96. 53. **82** Bury = B13. 5b, 189d; BL MS Royal 6 B. x, fol. 21v (Bury A. 88).

2 Contra eos qui disputant de virginitate ejus et parturitione lib. 1

> Source unidentified. Attributed to Radbertus; see Braegelmann, 165–6.

3 De assumptione B. Mariae serm. 4   65

> The source for this entry may have been a manuscript at **65** Ramsey comprising part of a collection of fourteen spurious sermons concerning the Virgin Mary; see Braegelmann, 158–63.

4 De puritate ejusdem opusculum 1

> Source unidentified. This may be a variant title for *1* above.

5 Prosopiae imbecillitatis propriae lib. 1

> Julian, Life (whole entry).

6 De proprietate personarum Patris et Filii et Spiritus Sancti lib. 1

> Julian, Life (whole entry).

7 Adnotationum in sacramentis lib. 1

> Julian, Life (whole entry).

8 Adnotationum in sacris lib. 1

> Julian, Life (whole entry).

9 De cognitione baptismi lib. 1

> Julian, Life (whole entry).

10 De progressione spiritualis deserti lib. 1

> Julian, Life (whole entry).

11 Epistolarum ad diversos lib. 1

> Julian, Life (whole entry).

12 Item librum partim metricum partimque prosaicum, in quo epithaphia et quaedam epigrammata sunt adnotata

> Julian, Life (whole entry).

Hildefonsus   *246. 13*

13 Item de sanctuario, secundum quosdam lib. 2   *In principio . . . mundi Domina*   86.65

> Unidentified. In the list of the works of Ralph of Flaix that Kirkestede recorded on fol. i^v of Cambridge, Pembroke College, MS 29 (Bury R. 14), he noted for this title 'Hunc tamen librum . . . quidam ascribunt sancto Hildefonso monacho et archiepiscopo Tholetano'. Kirkestede's ultimate source for the attribution may have been the *Mariale*, in which the work is cited repeatedly. Same as Radulphus *494.15*, where Kirkestede reiterates the possible attribution to Ildefonsus and gives a fuller description of the work.

247 HILDEBERTUS Cenomanensis episcopus floruit circa A. Ch. 1094, scilicet tempore Anselmi, et scripsit juxta Vincentium lib. 26 cap. 108

> Vincent XXVI 108 (works *1–2, 4, 6*).
> Bury manuscripts were even more instrumental than Vincent of Beauvais in shaping this entry.

1 De taedio hujus vitae, partim metrice, partim prosaice lib. 1   *Incendio . . . spiritus uxor*   82

> spiritus] Spc *Add. 3470, queried by Tanner*
>
> Vincent XXVI 108. *PL* 171. 989. **82** Bury = BL MS Add. 24199, fol. 45v (Bury P. 123).

2 De exilio suo versus elegantes   *Nuper eram . . .*

> Vincent XXVI 108 (whole entry).

[p. 76]

3 De misteriis missae versus   *Scribere proposui . . . redisse*   82

> *PL* 171. 1177–96 (treated as two works in *PL*). **82** Bury = BL MS Add. 24199, fol. 39r (Bury P. 123); BL MS Royal 8 B. iv, fol. 10r (Bury S. 184), in table of contents but without rubric; explicit does not correspond.

4 De eucaristia versus.

> Vincent XXVI 108 (whole entry).

5 De S. Maria Egiptiaca versus   *Sicut hiemps . . . historiam quievit*   82

> *PL* 171. 1321. **82** Bury = BL MS Add. 24199, fol. 49v (Bury P. 123).

6 De Trinitate pulcherrimam orationem   *Alpha et Omega . . . Alleluja*   82

> Vincent XXVI 108. *PL* 171. 1411.

7 Epistolarum ad diversos lib. 1   *Commissione . . .*   82

> Epistles of Hildebert are printed, *PL* 171. 141–312, incipit 'Conuersatione et conuersione'; 'commissione' is a plausible mistranscription of 'conuersione'.
> **82** Bury = B13. 116a.

8 De 3^{bus} vitiis, scilicet muliebri amore, avaritia et ambitione   *Plurima cum . . .*   82

> *PL* 171. 1428.

9 Sermones quamplures   *Facite elemosinam . . .*   11

> Incipit unidentified.

248 HELYNANDUS monachus Frigidi Montis de territorio Belvacensi floruit circa A. Ch. 1200 et scripsit juxta Vincentium in Speculo historiali lib. 30 cap. 108

> Vincent XXX 108 (whole entry).
> James extracts, p. 198.

1 De morte versus elegantes

2 De reparatione lapsi ad Galterum clericum qui fuerat novitius in ordine Cistertiensi ep. 1

3 Sermones peroptimos lib. 1

4 Item cronica ab initio mundi usque ad tempus suum in maximo volumine digessit, sed hoc quidem opus dispersum est ut nunquam totam simul reperiatur.

> totam] totum *James extracts*

249 HILDEGARDIS monacha tempore quo erat quinquennis spiritum habuit prophetiae et incepit prophetare anno aetatis suae 43° et A. Ch. 1242 et scripsit multa, quae fuerunt approbata a papa Eugenio in concilio Trevirensi praesentibus episcopis tam Francorum quam Teutonicorum et B. Bernardo magistro ejusdem. Ista patent plenius in Speculo temporum futurorum

Hildegardis   *249.*

Titles *1–9* were taken from the list of Hildegard's works in the *Speculum temporum futurorum* (partially printed, J. B. Pitra, *Analecta sacra* 8 (Montecassino 1882) 484–8), which appears in Cambridge, Corpus Christi College, MS 404, fol. 9r (Bury P. 163), a text copied by Kirkestede. The other titles, and the incipit and explicit for *6*, came from their respective texts in Cambridge, Corpus Christi College, MS 404, also copied by Kirkestede.

1 Librum Scyvias 1

   Scyvias] Scymas *Add. 3470, queried by Tanner*

   Hildegard list (whole entry).

2 Librum vitae meritorium 1

   Hildegard list (whole entry).

3 Librum divinorum operum 1

   Hildegard list (whole entry).

4 De coelesti armonia lib. 1

   Hildegard list (whole entry).

5 Simplicis medicinae secundum rerum creationem lib. 8

   Hildegard list (whole entry).

6 Speculum temporum futurorum sive pentachronon et continet lib. 3
   Et ecce . . . rapuisti   82

   pentachronon] pentatonon *Add. 3470, queried by Tanner*

   Hildegard list. Gebeno of Eberbach. Incipit is that of the *Sciuias, 1* above (*CCCM* 43–43A). **82** Bury = Cambridge, Corpus Christi College, MS 404, fol. 11v (Bury P. 163); although the explicit is on fol. 34r, the colophon that closely matches the wording of this title appears on fol. 38v, i.e. it treats works *10–13* below as if part of this work.

7 Super epistolas Pauli expositionem

   Hildegard list (whole entry).

8 Librum compositae medicinae de aegritudinum curis, causis et signis et continet lib. 3

   Hildegard list (whole entry).

9 Item omeliam ad ignotam linguam cum suis literis et scriptis aliis non paucis

> Hildegard list (whole entry).

10 Ad Cistertiensem ep. 1 *Ego fons . . . in aestimatione* 82

> Pitra, 8. 334–6, *Ad monachos Cistellenses*. **82** Bury = Cambridge, Corpus Christi College, MS 404, fols. 34r–35v (Bury P. 163).

11 Ad S. Bernardum ep. 1. *In spiritu . . . in certamine* 82

> PL 197. 189 *ep*. 29. **82** = Cambridge, Corpus Christi College, MS 404, fols. 35v–36r, 37v (Bury P. 163).

12 De discretione spiritum ep. 1 *Annuam . . . misceri* 82

> PL 197. 355 *ep*. 128. **82** Bury = Cambridge, Corpus Christi College, MS 404, fols. 37v–38r (Bury P. 163).

13 De regula S. Benedicti opusculum *Et ego . . . monet* 82

> PL 197. 1055 (explicit at end of first paragraph). **82** Bury = Cambridge, Corpus Christi College, MS 404, fol. 38r–v (Bury P. 163), with this explicit.

250 HELIODORUS presbiter floruit circa A. Ch. <*blank*> et scripsit juxta Genadium

> Gennadius c. 6 (whole entry).

1 De naturis rerum extraordinalium lib. 1

251 HELIODORUS alius Antiochiae presbiter floruit circa A. Ch. <*blank*> et scripsit juxta Genadium libro

> Gennadius c. 29 (whole entry).

1 De virginitate egregium volumen

Haly   *252. 1*

p. 77]

252 HALY filius Ambenragel et philosophus optimus floruit <blank> et scripsit multa

> This entry was compiled entirely from manuscripts, and contains the works of three different authors.
> See F. J. Carmody, *Arabic Astronomical and Astrological Sciences in Latin Translation* (Berkeley, CA, 1956).

1 Super centilogia Ptholomaei   *Quoniam res . . .*

> centilogia] sentilogia *Add. 3470, queried by Tanner*
>
> The title belongs to a work of Haly Abenrudian (Carmody, 16), incipit 'Dixit Ptolomaeus'. 'Quoniam res' is the incipit of an untitled item in a Bury astronomical compendium, CUL MS Add. 6860, fol. 43v (Bury A. 229) which has the name 'Haly' as a marginal heading beside the first line.

2 De judiciis stellarum et planetarum lib. 10   *Dixit Tholomaeus . . . Deus novit*

> Haly Abenragel. Carmody, 150–52. The incipit is that of *1* above. Printed, Venice: E. Radolt, 1485.

3 De electionibus horarum   *Rogasti me . . .*

> Haly Embrani. Carmody, 137–9. Ed. M. Vallicrosa, *Las traducciones de la Biblioteca Catedral de Toledo* (Madrid 1942) 328.

253 HERMANNUS

> (Hermannus Contractus)

1 De compoto   *Qui compoti . . .*

> Thorndike/Kibre 1204.

254 HUGO Pisanus floruit A. Ch. <blank> et scripsit

> (Hugutio)
> Higden, 1. 24 (whole entry).

1 De derivationibus lib. 1

255 HERENEUS Fotini episcopi Lugdunensis presbyter floruit A. Ch. 167 et scripsit juxta Jeronimum

    Whole entry from Jerome c. 35 save the date and save work *8*.

1 Adversus haereses lib. 5

2 Contra gentes lib. 1

3 De disciplina lib. 1

4 De apostolica praedicatione lib. 1

5 De scismate lib. 1

6 De monarchia lib. 1

7 De Pascha ep. 1

8 Adversus falsam scientiam lib. 3

    Source unidentified.

256 HERACLIDIS monachus vir religiosus et sanctus floruit A. Ch. 370 et scripsit juxta Vincentium lib. 18 cap. 64

    Vincent XVIII 64.
    Speculum coenobitarum 24.

1 Librum de vitis fratrum quos ipse viderat, qui quidem liber Paradisus vocatur   *Multi . . . adorare*   82

    Palladius of Hellenopolis, *Historia Lausiaca*, Latin tr. *PL* 74. 245. Same as Palladius *422.1*. **82** Bury = B13. 253.

257 HERMES, de quo Paulus apostolus meminit in epistola ad Romanos, floruit anno <blank> et scripsit juxta Jeronimum librum qui appellatur Pastor. Iste liber apud Graecos in ecclesiis publice legitur; revera utilis est, sed apud Latinos pene ignotus.

    Jerome c. 10 (whole entry).

Hesopus *258*.

258 HESOPUS philosophus claruit anno <blank> et scripsit tempore Tiri regis juxta Vincentium lib. 4to

> Vincent IV 2.

1 Fabulas elegantes et famosas lib. 1   *Agnus et lupus . . . alienos*   82

> A number of the fable collections printed by Hervieux begin with this tale; the explicit is unidentified. L. Hervieux, *Les Fabulistes latins*, 2 (Paris 1894²), 5, 157, 234, 302, 417, 455, 758.

259 HERMES qui et Trismegistus sive Mercurius floruit tempore Phillippi regis Macedonum A° M^{di} 3500° et scripsit De verbo perfecto et De Mathesi. Vide in litera T verbo Trimegistus.

> Vincent V 10 (whole entry).
> See also Apuleius *47*, Tremegistus *592*.

260 HENRICUS Huntedoniensis archidiaconus floruit A. Ch. 1135 et scripsit

> Works 2–6 probably formed a codex that began with Books I–VII of the *Historia Anglorum*, followed by *De summitatibus* (works *3–5*, otherwise Book VIII) and *De sanctis Anglorum* (work 6, otherwise Book IX); the eighth historical book (otherwise Book X) is not reported here.
> For a discussion of the author's various manuscript 'editions' of his work, see D. E. Greenway, *Henry, Archdeacon of Huntingdon*, Historia Anglorum*: The History of the English People*, OMT (1996), lxvi–lxxvii (versions), and cxvii–clx (manuscripts); and her 'Henry of Huntingdon and the manuscripts of his *Historia Anglorum*', in *Anglo-Norman Studies* 9 (1987) 103–126, with lists of manuscripts, 122–4; and see Sharpe, *Latin Writers*, 172. To judge from the *floruit* date that Kirkestede provides, the Bury version of the *Historia Anglorum* was one that included the date 1135, Greenway's 'third version' (edition, p. lxx).
> Bale, *Index*, 164, 'ex utroque Anglorum catalogo'.
> Sharpe, *Latin Writers*, 171–2.

1 Super Beati immaculati tract. 1   *Sanctissimo . . . fanum*   82

> Sharpe, *Latin Writers*, 171; Stegmüller *Bibl.* 3181. Not extant; unfortunately, discussing this work in her edition, Greenway (p. cxvi and nn. 214–15) has divided 'Boston of Bury' and Henry of Kirkestede into two cataloguers living in two different centuries.

2 De gestis regum Angliae historiam   *Cum in omni . . . nichil habens*   82.81.18.19

> *Historia Anglorum*; Sharpe, *Latin Writers*, 172. Ed. Greenway, 2–500.

3 De serie regum totius orbis ep. 1   *Cum maxime . . . perquirendum*
  82.19.63.64.65

  De summitatibus pt 1, letter to King Henry; Sharpe, *Latin Writers*, 171. Ed. Greenway, 502–556.

4 De serie regum Britanniae ep. 1   *Quaeris . . . videbis*   63.42.82

  De summitatibus pt 2, letter to Warinus; Sharpe, *Latin Writers*, 171. Ed. Greenway, 558–82.

5 De contemptu mundi tract. 6   *Waltere . . . scribendum est*   61.41.82.43

  De summitatibus pt 3, letter to Walterus; Sharpe, *Latin Writers*, 171. Ed. Greenway, 584–618.

6 De sanctis Angliae tract. 1   *De viris . . . liber novus*   34.42.82

  De miraculis Anglorum; Sharpe, *Latin Writers*, 171. Ed. Greenway, 622–96, explicit 'liber nonus explicit'.

p. 78]

261 HUMBERTUS Frater Praedicator floruit A. Ch. <*blank*> et scripsit

  Script. Ord. Praed. (whole entry), cf. Stams, 4.

1 Super regulam Augustini expositionem 1

2 De 7 gradibus contemplationis tract. 1

3 De officiis lib. 1

262 HUGO natione Burgundus vel de Vienna Frater Praedicator et cardinalis floruit A. Ch. <*blank*> et scripsit postillas

  Script. Ord. Praed. (whole entry), cf. Stams, 5.

1 Super omnes libros Bibliae

  The individual books of the bible are listed in Stams.

2 Super libros sententiarum

Hugo *262. 3*

   3 Item librum qui dicitur Speculum ecclesiae

   4 Concordantias Bibliae compilavit

     om. Stams

263 HAMBALDUS Frater Praedicator et magister theologiae floruit A. Ch. <blank> et scripsit

    Script. Ord. Praed. (whole entry), cf. Stams, 12.

   1 Super libros sententiarum

264 HUGO natione Gallicus Frater Praedicator et cardinalis floruit A.C. <blank> et scripsit

    Script. Ord. Praed. (whole entry), cf. Stams, 14.

   1 Super libros sententiarum

   2 De unitate formarum lib. 1

   3 De visione immediata lib. 1

   4 Contra coruptores Thomae lib. 1

265 HERVEUS Brito Frater Praedicator et magister theologiae floruit A.C. <blank> et scripsit

    Script. Ord. Praed. (whole entry), cf. Stams, 45.

   1 Super libros sententiarum lecturam 1

   2 Duo quodlibet

    Duo *Add. 3470, queried by Tanner*

   3 De peccato originali quaestiones

   4 De verbo lib. 1

Henricus *270. 1*

5 Contra Henricum de Gandavo ubi repugnat Thomam de Aquino

266 HUGO Argentinensis Frater Praedicator floruit A. Ch. <*blank*> et scripsit

> *Script. Ord. Praed.* (whole entry), cf. Stams, 51.

1 Compendium theologiae

267 HISPANUS Frater Praedicator floruit A. Ch. <*blank*> et scripsit

> *Script. Ord. Praed.* (whole entry), cf. Stams, 56.

1 Compotum manuale

268 HERMANNUS Teutonicus de Terwistis Frater Praedicator floruit A. Ch. <*blank*> et scripsit

> *Script. Ord. Praed.* (whole entry), cf. Stams, 69.

1 Postillas super Cantica

269 HEILWICUS Teutonicus Frater Praedicator floruit A. Ch. <*blank*> et scripsit

> *Script. Ord. Praed.* (whole entry), cf. Stams, 71.

1 De eo quod est mare magnum lib. 1

> quod est *queried by Tanner*   mare magnum] maximum mandatum *Stams, Pign.* 75

2 Librum exemplorum

270 HENRICUS Teutonicus Frater Praedicator floruit A. Ch. <*blank*> et scripsit

> *Script. Ord. Praed.* (whole entry), cf. Stams, 75, 78.
> A conflated entry for Hermannus de Minda Theutonicus and Hermannus Theutonicus, with the added confusion that the Christian name Henricus has been substituted.

1 De interdicto lib. 1

Henricus   *270. 2*

2 De assensu cordis lib. 1

3 Super Cantica lib. 1

4 De arte praedicandi tract. 1

271 HENRICUS de Costeseye Frater Minor et doctor theologiae floruit A. Ch. <*blank*> et scripsit

> (Henry Cossey)
> Bale, *Index*, 160, 'ex utroque Anglorum catalogo'.
> Sharpe, *Latin Writers*, 165–6.

1 Super Apocalypsin   *Quod vides . . . gloriae sanctorum*

> Sharpe, *Latin Writers*, 166. Stegmüller *Bibl.* 3158. Not printed; explicit unidentified. [**82** Bury = Bodl. MS Laud Misc. 85, fols. 67bis^v–172v (Bury J. 12, altered to J. 13), beginning cropped, end lacking.]

p. 79]

272 HELPRICUS floruit A.C. <*blank*> et scripsit

1 De arte calculatoria lib. 1   *Cum fratribus . . . facilius assequatur*   74

> *PL* 137. 17.

273 HERACLITUS floruit circa A. Ch. 189 et scripsit juxta Jeronimum libro De catholicis scriptoribus

> Jerome c. 46 (whole entry save date).

1 Super epistolam Pauli commentarios multos

274 HONORATUS Constantinae Affricae civitatis episcopus floruit circa A. Ch. <*blank*> et scripsit secundum Genadium ad quendam exulem, quod labores pro Christo ferendi sunt et quod confessionis fidei praeseverantia non solum praeterita purget peccata sed et meritum procuret martirii ep. 1

> Gennadius c. 96 (whole entry).

275 HOMERUS poeta in Graecia floruit tempore Salamonis circa A.D. <blank> et scripsit juxta Vincentium lib. 3 cap. 87

> Vincent III 87 (whole entry). The information in Vincent comes from Seneca, *ep.* 88; the letter is probably not quoted here directly, although first-hand knowledge of it is indicated in the entry for Seneca *543*. See also Didimus *145* for another possible use of this letter.

1 De bello Trojano Yliadem 1   *Trojani belli* . . .

> The 'incipit' is probably a corruption of the title.

2 Edisseam

> Unde Seneca in ep. 86 (*sic*) aiebat Homerum utraque m[ateri]a consummata Edissea et Yliade principium adjecisse operi suo, quo bellum Trojanum complexus est. Hujus rei argumentum asserebat quod duas literas in primo versu posuisset ex industria librorum suorum numerum continentes

>> materia] m^a *Add. 3470*, queried by Tanner

276 HENRICUS de Gandavo floruit <blank> et scripsit

1 Summam theologiae et continet articulos 75   *Quia theologiae . . . a voluntate*

> Stegmüller *Sent.* 318. Printed, Paris: Ascenius, 1520/repr. Franciscan Institute Publications, Text Ser. 5, ed. E. M. Buytaert, 2 vols. (St Bonaventure, NY, 1953), fol. 1r. Explicit unidentified.

2 Disputationes de quolibet xv   *Quaerebantur . . . ut miseratur nostri*

> Glorieux *Quodl.* 1. 177–99, fifteen quodlibets with this incipit and explicit. Ed. H. Macken & others, *Henrici de Gandavo Opera omnia* 5–19 (Leiden 1979–).

3 Prima pars summae sic incipit: *Quia theologia . . .*   Prima pars 2dae partis: *Pertractato hucusque* . . .   2da pars 2dae: *Expedito usque huc* . . .

> This entry analyzes *1* above: pt 1 = art. 1; first part of pt 2 = art. 53 (prologue, incipit 'Post tractata'); second part of pt 2 = art. 62.

277 HOLCOTE de ordine

> Same as Robertus de Holcote *515*.
> Sharpe, *Latin Writers*, 553–8.

Holcote   277. 1

1   De fautoribus, defensoribus et receptoribus haereticorum lib. 14   Principium 1^{mae} partis: *In omnibus curiosus existis* . . .   Principium 2^{dae} partis:

> William of Ockham, *Dialogus inter magistrum et discipulum*, also called *Dialogus de fautoribus, defensoribus et receptoribus hereticorum*; Sharpe, *Latin Writers*, 797. Ed. Lyon 1494/repr. London 1962.

2   Super librum Sapientiae librum bonum

> Sharpe, *Latin Writers*, 553. The source for this work was perhaps *Script. Ord. Praed.* (cf. Pign. 114). Same as Robertus de Holcote *515.3*.

278 HESIODUS floruit <blank> et scripsit

> Source unidentified. Cf. Higden, 2. 374 and Papias.

1   De natura deorum lib. 2

279 HILDEWINUS floruit circa A. Ch. <blank> et scripsit

> This author is probably Hilduin, chancellor of Notre Dame *c.* 1160–1189, who wrote sermons and a gloss on the gospels. Hilduin's name, but not this work, appears in Cambridge, Pembroke College, MS 7, fol. 1r (Bury B. 231); cf. B. Smalley in *Cambridge Historical Journal* 6 (1938) 103–113.

1   Super omelias Johannis   *In principio . . . velatum suum*   65

> Stegmüller *Bibl.* 6237,3. No longer extant. **65** Ramsey = B67. 120 = B68. 149.

280 HOUDEN <blank> scripsit

> Houden] *Tanner, uncertain of this reading, adds* Honden *as a variant reading*

(John of Howden)
Same as Johannes de Hovden *342*.

1   De processu Christi et redemptionis nostrae   *Ave verbum . . . verbum ens in principio*   Est inter Fratres Min. Norwic.

> Est inter Fratres Min. Norwic.] Vid. postea Ioh. Hovden *add Add. 3470; according to Tanner this was added in a recent hand*

> Same as Johannes de Hovden *342.1*. R. Bressie in *Modern Language Notes* 60 (1945), 253–4, suggested that the reference to the Norwich Franciscans represents an annotation by John Bale that was subsequently incorporated by Tanner in his transcription of the *Catalogus*, Add. 3470 (cf. Bale's record of

Howden at Norwich, *Index*, 220). Given Tanner's routine noting of additions by recent hands, Bressie's suggestion seems unlikely.

p. 80]

281 JERONIMUS monachus et presbyter cardinalis trium linguarum peritus Novum Testamentum Graecae fidei reddidit, et Vetus juxta veritatem Hebraicam transtulit in Latinum illudque commentatus est.[a] Solus ex antiquis doctoribus omnes 16 prophetias exposuit, et lxiv libris editis commentatus est. Danielem quoque Caldaico stilo locutum, et Job Arabico, in Romanam linguam mutavit. Evangelium etiam Mathaei ex Hebraeo fecit esse Romanum.[b] Psalterium a Soffrino postulatus ex Hebraeo Latina modulatione exposuit et Encheridion appellavit. Duos libros Salomonis explanavit. Cantica Canticorum ex Origenis interpretatione transtulit in Latinum. Epistolas Pauli et Johannis Revelationem disseruit. Quorundam etiam doctorum Graecorum opuscula in linguam nostram transtulit.[c] Floruit circa A. Ch. 390 et scripsit haec et alia ut patet infra. Nota quod B. Jeronimus correxit psalterium LXX interpretum, quod in omnibus ecclesiis primo cantabatur, quo iterum vitiato iterum novum composuit, quod papa Damasus rogatu Jeronimi cantari instituit in ecclesiis Gallicanis, et propter hoc Gallicanum vocatur, Romanis psalterio secundum LXX remanente. Tertium transtulit de Hebraica veritate in Latinum de verbo ad verbum.[d] Et sic patet quod triplex habetur psalterium, scilicet Gallicanum, quo utuntur Gallici communiter et Anglici, Romanum secundum LXX quo utuntur Romani, Hebraicum quo utuntur Judei.

[a] Vincent XVII 19. [b] Gennadius prologue. [c] Vincent XVII 19. [d] Vincent XVII 92.

Registrum 6, Vincent XVII 19 (references are followed by numbers in brackets [1, 2, etc.] that indicate the sequence of titles in the chapter), *Manipulus florum* IV, Jerome c. 135, Cassiodorus.

Two collections stand out, among the manuscripts used in compiling this entry. Works *61, 64, 92, 100, 102–103, 105–107, 109,* and *114* appear in a collection of items attributed to Jerome; we use Durham Cathedral, MS B. II. 11 here as a representative example of the collection. Works *128–231* (with interruptions at *208–212* and *214–215*) are taken from a codex of Jerome's letters similar to that found in Durham Cathedral, MS B. II. 10, Bodl. MS Bodley 365 pt 2, Oxford, New College, MS 129, and Cambridge, Pembroke College, MS 231. The Bury manuscript, no longer extant, is recorded as B13. 193, 'Ieronimi epistole'.

Exceptionally, Kirkestede arranged this entry primarily by subject, with occasional lapses: saints' lives (*1–6*); Marian works (*7–12*); scriptural studies (*13–55*); questions and interpretations (*56–65*); antiheretical tracts (*66–84*); a host of very brief Hieronymiana, mostly pseudonymous, mostly unprinted, from the collection similar to Durham B. II. 11 (*102–114*); titles not yet cited from other

Jeronimus *281.*

sources, taken in sequence from the *Registrum (115–123)*; and Jerome's epistles by recipient *(128–231)*, with the first four *(128–131)* gathered by subject, the monastic or clerical life. The end of the entry *(232–239)* is the usual assortment of afterthoughts and oversights.
Speculum coenobitarum 22.
See B. Lambert, *Bibliotheca hieronymiana manuscripta*, 4 vols. in 7 (Steenbrugge 1969–1972); references here are to item number.

1 Vitam S. Pauli pii heremitae   Inter multos . . . purpuras   82

    Jerome 135. *CPL* 617. *PL* 23. 17.

2 Vitam Malchi monachi   Qui navali . . . superari   82

    CPL 619. Ed. C. C. Mierow in *Classical Essays presented to James A. Kleist* (St Louis, MO, 1946) 33–60.

3 Vitam S. Hillarionis abbatis   Hillarion . . . dilexerat   82

    Jerome 28. *CPL* 618. Ed. A. A. R. Bastiaensen, in *Vite dei Santi*, ed. C. Mohrmann, 4 (Rome 1975) 74–142.

4 Vitam S. Frontoni monachi et episcopi

    BHL 2189 or 3192. The latter life of St Frontonius follows *5* below in, for example, Bodl. MS Bodley 386, fol. 51v, and Bodl. MS Hatton 84, fol. 22v. See *5* below.

5 Vitas patrum de Egipto   Primum sibi . . .   82.<u>127</u>.<u>117</u>.<u>79</u>.<u>8</u>.<u>1</u>

    R6. 67. Rufinus. *Historia monachorum*, commonly attributed to Jerome and often followed by other saints' lives. Ed. E. Schulz-Flügel, *Historia monachorum*, Patristische Texte und Studien 34 (Berlin 1990) 247, incipit 'Primum igitur'. Attributed to Jerome in Bodl. MS Bodley 386, fol. 1r, 'Narratio Sancti Hieronomi pres[b]iteri', followed by the lives of SS. Malchus and Frontinus, *2* and *4* above. **82** Bury = B13. 255b.

6 Adortationes et decreta patrum   Interrogavit . . . suffocabat   82

    Ps. Jerome. *PL* 73. 855. **82** Bury = B13. 165a.

7 De nativitate et infantia B. Mariae lib. 1   Petitis . . . docuerunt   82

    Cf. R6. 21. *Ps.* Jerome; *CPL* 633 *ep.* 50. *PL* 30. 297. **82** Bury = BL MS Royal 6 B. x, fols. 7r–9v (Bury A. 88), attributed to Jerome in Kirkestede's marginal title and in his table of contents; Cambridge, Pembroke College, MS 111, fol. 1r (Bury J. 20), attributed to Jerome in Kirkestede's table of contents.

Jeronimus *281. 12*

8 De Chromatio et Heliodoro episcopis   *Dominis sanctis ac . . . pervenire*
 82

> Chromatio] Coneaco *Add. 3470, queried by Tanner*
>
> Ps. Jerome. Supposedly Jerome's reply, to the request by Chromatius and Heliodorus to translate Matthew's recounting of the birth and childhood of the Virgin and the childhood of Christ; ed. J. Gijsel, *Corpus christianorum series apocryphorum* 9 (1997) 283–5. This usually appears as a preface to *9* below, but not in the two surviving Bury manuscripts: **82** Bury = BL MS Royal 6 B. x, fol. 7v, without rubric (Bury A. 88); Cambridge, Pembroke College, MS III, fol. 6r (Bury J. 20).

9 De Joachim et Anna et de ortu et infantia B. Mariae et de infantia Christi   *In diebus . . . Egiptiaca*   123.82.163.154

> Vincent XVII 19 [22] and cf. R6. 46 (neither title is a close match). *Ps.* Jerome, *De ortu beatae Mariae et infantia*, the *ps.*-Matthaean infancy gospel; ed. Gijsel (as *8*), 287. Explicit unidentified; see Gijsel's discussion of the work's conclusions, ibid. 478–80. Same as *239* below. See also *8* above.

10 De nativitate B. Mariae contra Elindium   *Benedictus . . .*   126.154.114. 82.111.128

> Elindium] Eluidium *R*
>
> R6. 66 (title and location numbers); incipit unidentified.

11 De perpetua virginitate B. Mariae contra Elindium   *Nuper rogatus . . . mater*   82.65

> Elindium] Eluidium *R*
>
> R6. 18, Vincent XVII 19 [7], *MF* IV 2, Jerome 135. *CPL* 609. *PL* 23. 183. **82** Bury = B13. 189c; BL MS Royal 6 B. x, fol. 9v (Bury A. 88), with Kirkestede's marginal rubric; Cambridge, Pembroke College, MS III, fol. 12r (Bury J. 20).

12 De assumptione B. Mariae ad Paulum et Eustachium   *Cogitis me . . . appareatis*   82.158.114.115.98

> R6. 43, and cf. Jerome 135. Paschasius Radbertus; *CPL* 633 *ep.* 9. *CCCM* 56C. 109–162. **82** Bury = B13. 189b; BL MS Royal 6 B. x, fol. 14v (Bury A. 88), with Kirkestede's marginal rubric; Cambridge, Pembroke College, MS III, fol. 27v (Bury J. 20).

Jeronimus *281. 13*

13 De libris historiae divinae ad Paulinum   *Frater Ambrosius . . . moriturum*
82

    Vincent XVII 19 [28]. *CPL* 620 *ep.* 53. *CSEL* 54. 442.

14 Breviarium majus super psalterium   *Quidam dicunt . . . adjungi*   164.<u>94</u>.
82.<u>8</u>.<u>95</u>.<u>42</u>

    R6. 2 (title) and R6. 68 (location numbers), Vincent XVII 19 [36]. *Ps.* Jerome; *CPL* 629, Stegmüller *Bibl.* 3333. *PL* 26. 823. See also *15* below.

15 Breviarium minus super psalterium   *Psalterium . . . benedicamus*   43.<u>108</u>.
<u>15</u>.82.139.94.65

    R6. 1, Vincent XVII 19 [36]. *CPL* 592. *CCSL* 78. 3–352. See also *14* above. **82** Bury = B13. 4 (and B13. 190) 'Ieronimus super psalterium' = Cambridge, Pembroke College, MS 91 (Bury J. 3), which has Kirkestede's contents note 'Breuiarium Jeronimi super quosdam psalmos'.

16 Super Ecclesiasten commentarium 1   *Tribus nominibus . . . vae hiis*   94.<u>9</u>.
<u>43</u>.<u>82</u>.<u>19</u>.<u>1</u>.<u>12</u>

    12] xii *R*

    R6. 63, Vincent XVII 19 [37], Jerome 135. *CPL* 583. *CCSL* 72. 250. **82** Bury = B13. 5a, 189a.

17 Super Ecclesiasticum commentarium 1   161.<u>128</u>.<u>102</u>

    R6. 65 (whole entry).

18 Super Ysaiam lib. 18   *Expletis . . . judicis*   93.<u>94</u>.<u>95</u>.83.<u>82</u>.<u>43</u>.<u>32</u>

    R6. 72, Vincent XVII 19 [38]. *CPL* 584. *CCSL* 73–73A. **82** Bury = B13. 3 (and 196) = Cambridge, Pembroke College, MS 17 (Bury J. 6), beginning with Book VIII and ending imperfectly.

19 Super Jeremiam lib. 20   *Prius explanationem . . .*   98.<u>13</u>.<u>10</u>.<u>12</u>.<u>1</u>.<u>15</u>.<u>35</u>

    13] xiii *R*   10] x *R*   12] xii *R*

    R6. 71, Vincent XVII 19 [39]. *CPL* 586. *CCSL* 74, incipit 'Post explanationes'. [**82** Bury = B13. 34a = BL MS Egerton 3776, fol. 3r (Bury J.7); incipit does not correspond.]

[p. 81]

20 Super Ezechielem lib. 14   *Finitis . . . ad consummationem*   39.10.102.1.15. 35.19.13

   10] x *R*

   R6. 70, Vincent XVII 19 [40]. *CPL* 587. *CCSL* 75. [**82** Bury = B13. 34b = BL MS Egerton 3776, fol. 90r (Bury J. 7), ends incomplete; Kirkestede's note on fol. 159r ('Deficit hic libri viii b. Jeronomi super Ezechielem') indicates that he has seen a fuller copy.]

21 Super Danielem lib.   *Contra prophetam . . .*   94.83.82.8.9.19.15

   R6. 73, Vincent XVII 19 [41]. *CPL* 588. *CCSL* 75A. 771.

22 Super Osee lib. 3   *Si in explanationibus . . . in Israel*   118.97.93.95.83.43

   97] 94 *R; location numbers for all twelve entries 22–33 are repeated from R74*

   R6. 74, 'Super xii prophetas', Vincent XVII 19 [42]. *CPL* 589. *CCSL* 76.1. [**82** Bury = B13. 191 = Bodl. MS e Musaeo 26, p. 1 (Bury J. 10).]

23 Super Johelem lib. 1   *Non idem . . . Jacob*   118.97.93.95.83.43

   97] 94 *R*

   R6. 74, Vincent XVII 19 [43]. *CPL* 589. *CCSL* 76. 159. See *22* above. [**82** Bury = B13. 191 = Bodl. MS e Musaeo 26, p. 124 (Bury J. 10).]

24 Super Amos lib. 3   *Amos . . . naturae est*   118.97.95.93.83.43

   97] 94 *R*

   R6. 74, Vincent XVII 19 [44]. *CPL* 589. *CCSL* 76. 211. See *22* above. [**82** Bury = B13. 191 = Bodl. MS e Musaeo 26, p. 163 (Bury J. 10).]

25 Super Abdiam lib. 1   *Cum essem . . . transgredere*   118.97.93.95.83.43

   97] 94 *R*

   R6. 74, Vincent XVII 19 [45]. *CPL* 589. *CCSL* 76. 349, incipit 'Dum essem'. See *22* above. [**82** Bury = B13. 191 = Bodl. MS e Musaeo 26, p. 261 (Bury J. 10), incipit 'Dum essem'.]

Jeronimus *281. 26*

26 Super Jonam lib. 1   *Triennium . . . assimulatur*   118.<u>97</u>.<u>93</u>.<u>95</u>.<u>83</u>.<u>43</u>

   97] 94 *R*

   R6. 74, Vincent XVII 19 [46]. *CPL* 589. *CCSL* 76. 377. See *22* above. [**82** Bury = B13. 191 = Bodl. MS e Musaeo 26, p. 278 (Bury J. 10).]

27 Super Micheam lib. 2   *Micheas . . . civitates*   118.<u>97</u>.<u>93</u>.<u>95</u>.<u>83</u>.<u>43</u>

   97] 94 *R*

   R6. 74, Vincent XVII 19 [47], Jerome 135. *CPL* 589. *CCSL* 76. 421. See *22* above. [**82** Bury = B13. 191 = Bodl. MS e Musaeo 26, p. 307 (Bury J. 10).]

28 Super Naum lib. 1   *Juxta LXX . . . non potest*   118.<u>97</u>.<u>93</u>.<u>95</u>.<u>83</u>.<u>43</u>

   97] 94 *R*

   R6. 74, Vincent XVII 19 [48], Jerome 135. *CPL* 589. *CCSL* 76A. 525. See *22* above. [**82** Bury = B13. 191.]

29 Super Abacuch lib. 2   *Usquequo . . . superabo*   118.<u>97</u>.<u>93</u>.<u>95</u>.<u>83</u>.<u>43</u>.<u>42</u>

   97] 94 *R*

   R6. 74, Vincent XVII 19 [49], Jerome 135. *CPL* 589. *CCSL* 76A. 581. See *22* above. [**82** Bury = B13. 191.]

30 Super Sophoniam lib. 1   *Antequam . . . non arbitror*   118.<u>97</u>.<u>93</u>.<u>95</u>.<u>83</u>.<u>43</u>.<u>42</u>

   97] 94 *R*

   R6. 74. Vincent XVII 19 [50], Jerome 135. *CPL* 589. *CCSL* 76A. 655. See *22* above. [**82** Bury = B13. 191.]

31 Super Aggeum lib. 1   *Anno secundo . . . multam*   118.<u>97</u>.<u>93</u>.<u>95</u>.<u>83</u>.<u>43</u>.<u>42</u>

   97] 94 *R*

   R6. 74, Vincent XVII 19 [51], Jerome 135. *CPL* 589. *CCSL* 76A. 713. See *22* above. [**82** Bury = B13. 191.]

32 Super Zachariam lib. 3   *Ultimo . . . auferendum*   118.<u>97</u>.<u>93</u>.<u>95</u>.<u>83</u>.<u>43</u>.<u>42</u>

   97] 94 *R*

   R6. 74, Vincent XVII 19 [52]. *CPL* 589. *CCSL* 76A. 747. See *22* above. [**82** Bury = B13. 191.]

Jeronimus *281. 39*

33 Super Malachiam lib. 1   *Ultimum . . . intelligens*   118.97.93.95.83.43.42

   97] 94 R

   R6. 74, Vincent XVII 19 [53]. *CPL* 589. *CCSL* 76A. 901. See *22* above. [**82** Bury = B13. 191.]

34 De Genesi et libris Veteris Testamenti   15

   R6. 56 (probably whole entry, title varies).

35 Super Mathaeum lib. 4   *In Ysaia . . . cum apostolis*   94.95.82.42. 43.8

   R6. 76, Vincent XVII 19 [54]. *CPL* 590. *CCSL* 77. 7. **82** Bury = B13. 192 = Bodl. MS e Musaeo 112, p. 5 (Bury J. 13).

36 Super Marcum et Lucam omel. 39   *Omnis scriba . . . enarrat*   94.95.19. 82.22.39

   R6. 77, Vincent XVII 19 [55], Jerome 135 (the added phrase 'et Lucam omel. 39'). The incipit and explicit are those of *ps.* Jerome on Mark, *CPL* 632. *PL* 30. 589. **82** Bury = B13. 194; Oxford, Balliol College, MS 175, fol. 105r (Bury B. 283), title added by Kirkestede.

37 Super Epistolam ad Ephesios lib. 3   *Si propositio . . . in corruptione*   95.82. 111.35.15.63

   R6. 33, Vincent XVII 19 [56], Jerome 135. *CPL* 591. *PL* 26. 443.

38 Super Epistolam ad Galathas lib. 3   *Non superbe . . . quid docetur*   95.82. 111.35.15.1

   R6. 33, Vincent XVII 19 [57], Jerome 135. *PL* 26. 311; incipit is that of Book I. All the location numbers save **1** are repeated from *37* above.

39 Super Epistolam ad Titum lib. 1   *Licet non . . . voluisset*   95.82.111. 35.15.1.63

   R6. 33, 6.91, Vincent XVII 19 [58], Jerome 135. *PL* 26. 555. The location numbers are repeated from *37* and *38* above. **82** Bury = B13. 101a = Bodl. MS Lat. th. c. 26, fol. 1r (Bury J. 16). / **15** St Albans = Bodl. MS Laud Misc. 363, fol. 47r.

Jeronimus *281. 40*

40 Super Epistolam ad Philemonem lib. 1   *Qui volunt . . . auditur*   95.82.111.
35.15.1.63

    R6. 33, 92, Vincent XVII 19 [59], Jerome 135. *PL* 26. 599. The location numbers are repeated from *37* and *38* above. **82** Bury = B13. 101b = Bodl. MS Lat. th. c. 26, fol. 23r (Bury J. 16), incipit 'Qui nolunt'; explicit (fol. 31) does not correspond. / **15** St Albans = Bodl. MS Laud Misc. 363, fol. 46v.

41 Super Actus apostolorum   95.18

    18] xviii *R*

    R6. 32 (whole entry).

42 Super Epistolas Johannis   95.53

    R6. 34 (whole entry).

43 Super Epistolas Petri   95.53

    R6. 35 (whole entry).

44 Super Epistolam Judae   95.53

    R6. 36 (whole entry).

45 Super Epistolam Jacobi   95.53

    R6. 61 (whole entry); location number **95** has been repeated from *42–44* above.

46 Super Apocalipsin lib. 1   *Principium . . . sentiunt*   15.161.94.8.9.35.20

    R6. 101. Jerome's recension of the commentary by Victorinus of Pettau; *CPL* 80, Stegmüller *Bibl.* 3457 and 8300. *CSEL* 49. 17–153.

47 Super Joshu Nave omel. 26   *Donavit . . . verus Israel*   95.82.114.1.20.
63.26.

    26] xxvi *R*

    R6. 75. Origen, Rufinus's translation. *GCS* 30 (*Origenes Werke* 7) 287–463; incipit is that of *hom.* 1. Same as Origines *404.6*.

48 De cantico Delborae lib. 1   *Baruch . . . in Jeremia*   161.94.95.82.15.1.139

    R6. 85. *Ps.* Jerome; Lambert 411, Stegmüller *Bibl.* 3413. *PL* 23. 1321.

Jeronimus *281. 56*

49 Super Parabolas Salomonis   19.10.12.109

> 10.12] xii.x *R*
>
> R6. 113 (whole entry).

50 Super Cantica Canticorum ad Damasum lib. 2   *Quomodo ... Christi Jesu*
   12.82.63.109

> 12] xii *R*
>
> R6. 114, Jerome 135. Origen; same as Origines *404.14*.

51 De psalmo 89mo ad Ciprianum ep.   *Frater karissime ... deseretur*

> *CPL* 620 *ep.* 140. *CSEL* 56/1. 269; incipit, absent from the edition, is that of the letter's introduction, 'Frater karissime Cipriane scito pronoscens quia'. Same as *159* below.

52 Ad Algasiam quaestiones 11   *De hac ... susceptura*

> Whole entry from Vincent XVII 19 [18] and *MF* IV 4 (incipit and explicit, 'suscepturi sunt').

53 Super Epistolas ad Timotheum lib. 1   95.82.111.35.15.1

> ?R6. 33. Source of this specific title is unidentified. The location numbers are repeated from *37* and *38* above.

54 Super psalmos a 10mo usque ad 16^{mum} tract. 7

> Jerome 135 (whole entry). Same as *169* below.

55 Breviarium super epistolas Pauli   *Paulus ... non remittunt*

> Doubtless a version of the commentary of Pelagius, which was frequently attributed in manuscript to Jerome and to which authentic interpolations by Jerome survive (*CPL* 759). See the discussion of the manuscript tradition by A. Souter, *Texts and Studies: Contributions to Biblical and Patristic Literature* 9/1 (Cambridge 1922); the explicit of Souter's edition (ib. pt 2) does not correspond, and unfortunately the incipit would fit any commentary on the Pauline epistles.

56 De quaestionibus Hebraicis in Genesin   *Plerique ... thema dicitur*
   94.93.95.82.43.9.8

> R6. 79, Vincent XVII 19 [29], Jerome 135. *CPL* 580. *CCSL* 72. 3; explicit unidentified. **82** Bury = B13. 24.

Jeronimus *281. 57*

57 De Hebraicis quaestionibus librorum Regum   *Fuit vir . . . emisse*
   19.1.82.94.95.156

   R6. 82, Vincent XVII 19 [34]. *Ps.* Jerome; Lambert 412, explicit is that of the *Quaestiones in II Reg.* See Stegmüller *Bibl.* 3414–15. *PL* 23. 1329.

58 De quaestionibus in Paralipomenon   *In diebus ejus . . . restauraret*   15.1.43.
   82.95.94

   R6. 83, Vincent XVII 19 [35]. *Ps.* Jerome; Lambert 412, inc. 'Quia in diebus ejus', expl. 'instauret'. *PL* 23. 1366.

59 Ad Hebaidam quaest. 12   *Ignota . . . extinguuntur*

   R6. 45, Vincent XVII 19 [17]. *CPL* 620 *ep.* 120. *CSEL* 55. 472, *Ad Hedybiam*.

60 De diversis quaestionibus ad Amandum epistolam   *Brevis . . . misereatur*

   CPL 620 *ep.* 55. *CSEL* 54. 486.

61 De interpretationibus Hebraicorum locorum et nominum   *Ethiopiam
   . . . tau signum*   95.43.82.42.8.90

   R6. 99, Vincent XVII 19 [26], Jerome 135. *CPL* 581. *CCSL* 72. 60. The explicit is that of a short note on the Hebrew and Greek alphabets which follows this work in Durham Cathedral, MS B. II. 11, fol. 61r. **82** Bury = BL MS Royal 8 F. xiv, fol. 172r (Bury G. 15), an abridgement.

62 De interpretatione literarum Hebraicarum in psalmo cxviii ad Marcellam ep.   *Nudius tertius . . . velociter*

   Ep. 30 *Ad Paulam*. Incipit and explicit are taken from *MF* IV 15, but the title there is just *De litterarum hebraicarum interpretatione*. This entry is the same as *194* below, for which the title, incipit, and explicit were taken from the Bury codex of Jerome's epistles; presumably Kirkestede added the fuller title to this entry as he was recording the title for *194*, since both *Catalogus* entries name the same mistaken recipient.

63 De optimo genere interpretandi lib. 1   *Paulus . . . scribere*

   Vincent XVII 19 [27]. *CPL* 620 *ep.* 57. *CSEL* 54. 503.

64 Super alphabetum Graecum et Hebraeum commentum   105.82.104

   R6. 24 (whole entry). A work beginning 'Aleph: mille vel doctrina. Beth: domus.' etc. occurs in Bury's collection of brief works of Jerome that mainly explain words in the bible. See also *65* below.

Jeronimus *281. 72*

p. 82]

65 Super alphabetum Hebraeum in Lamentatione Jeremiae *Et factum est . . . carnis* 166.161.94.95.105

> R6. 86 (title 'Super lamentationes Ieremie', location numbers). *Ps.* Jerome; *CPL* 630. *PL* 25. 787. In most surviving manuscripts of the minor collection of Hieronymiana (see Jerome headnote), the short work on the Hebrew and Greek alphabets (*64* above) is mislabelled *De lamentationibus Ieremie*; there was evidently a confusion of rubrics in the Bury collection as well, resulting in the conflated title here.

66 Contra Pelagianos ad Thesifontem lib. *Non audacter . . . comprobentur* 161.94

> R6. 96. *CPL* 620 *ep.* 133. *CSEL* 56/1. 241.

67 Contra Jovinianum lib. 2 *Pauci . . . susceperint* 93.94.95.89.43.83

> 43] 93 *Tanner 165*, 43 *Peterhouse 169*

> R6. 93, Vincent XVII 19 [5], *MF* IV 13 (explicit 'susceperunt'). *CPL* 610. *PL* 23. 211. See *118* below. [**82** Bury = B13. 195.]

68 Contra Luciferianum

> Vincent XVII 19 [6] (whole entry). See also *91* below.

69 Contra Vigilantium ep. 1 *Nec nos . . .*

> Vincent XVII 19 [8]. *CPL* 611, but only the last three paragraphs. *PL* 23. 350 para. 14, 'Nec nos negamus cunctis pauperibus'. See *77* below.

70 Contra Origenem de resurrectione carnis lib. 1

> Vincent XVII 19 [9] (whole entry).

71 Ad Minervium et Alexandrum de resurrectione carnis lib. 1 *In ipso . . . immutabimur*

> Minervium] Minermum *Add. 3470, queried by Tanner*

> Vincent XVII 19 [79]. *CPL* 620 *ep.* 119. *CSEL* 55. 446.

72 Ad Avitum de erroribus Origenis in primo libro Periarton lib. 1 *Ante annos . . . noverit*

> Vincent XVII 19 [10]. *CPL* 620 *ep.* 124. *CSEL* 56/1. 96.

Jeronimus *281. 73*

73 Ad Tranquillinum quomodo Origenem legere debeat ep. 1   *Majorum . . . salutat*   32.33.<u>9</u>.<u>19</u>.35.<u>15</u>.<u>1</u>

> *CPL* 620 *ep.* 62. *CSEL* 54. 583. Location numbers **9, 19, 15, 1** (and probably the others via copying error) are taken from R6. 78, 'Epistole Ieronomi'.

74 Item contra Pelagium ad Thesifontem lib. 3   *Dic michi . . . sequimini*

> Vincent XVII 19 [4]. *Dialogus adversus Pelagianos*; 'Ad Thesifontem lib. 3' is the title of a separate work taken from Vincent (XVII 19 [82]) and joined to this entry by mistake. *CPL* 615. *CCSL* 80. 6; incipit is that of Book I, expl. (ib. 124) 'sequamini'.

75 Contra Rufinum   105.<u>9</u>.<u>43</u>.<u>15</u>.<u>20</u>.<u>22</u>

> R6. 17 (whole entry).

76 Ad Pammachium et Marcellum contra Rufinum lib. 2   *Ex vestris . . . sustinere*   105.<u>154</u>.<u>104</u>.<u>163</u>.<u>164</u>

> Whole entry from R6. 16 (title and location numbers) and *MF* IV 11 (title, incipit 'Et uestris', explicit). Location numbers **163** and **164** are taken from R6. 78, 'Epistole eius'.

77 Item contra Vigilantium ep.   *Multa in . . . indignos*   94.<u>95</u>.<u>82</u>.<u>42</u>.<u>43</u>.<u>9</u>

> *CPL* 611. *PL* 23. 339. The location numbers are taken from R6. 78, 'Epistole Ieronimi'. See also *69* above.

78 Ad Riparium contra Vigilantium ep. 1   *Acceptis . . . mutetur*

> *CPL* 620 *ep.* 109. *CSEL* 55. 351.

79 Super Epistolas ad Corinthios

> Titles *79–81* are the same as *209–211* below.

> Cassiodorus I. 8. 14 (whole entry).

80 Super Epistolas ad Thessalonicenses

> Cassiodorus I. 8. 14 (whole entry)

81 Super Epistolam ad Colossenses

> Cassiodorus I. 8. 14 (whole entry)

Jeronimus *281. 89*

82 Contra Rufinum presbyterum Aquileiae lib. 2   *Lectis literis . . . videatur*   65

> Vincent XVII 19 [12], *MF* IV 9. *CPL* 614. *CCSL* 79. 73, explicit does not correspond; incipit and explicit may come from the *Manipulus florum*.

83 Contra blasphemias Vigilantii ep.   *Justum . . . loquaris*

> *CPL* 620 *ep.* 61. *CSEL* 54. 575.

84 Apologiticum ad Pammachium   *Quod a te . . . divitem*   161.43.104.166.126

> 104] 114 *R*   126] 26 *R*

> Vincent XVII 19 [80]. *CPL* 620 *ep.* 49 (48). *CSEL* 54. 350, incipit 'Quod ad te'. Location numbers are taken from R6. 78, 'Epistole Ieronomi'.

85 De ratione animae disputationum lib. 1   *Cum apud . . . anathema sit*   166.82.42

> R6. 110. Ps. Jerome; *CPL* 633 *ep.* 37. *PL* 30. 261 paragraphs 1–9. See also *86* below.

86 Sequitur dialogus Augustini et Jeronimi de eadem   *Sancte frater . . . fluenta sanctorum*

> R6. 112. Ps. Jerome; *CPL* 633 *ep.* 37. *PL* 30. 265, the dialogue which follows para. 9 of *85* above. Same as Augustinus *1.116*.

87 De regulis diffinitionum contra haereticos tract. 1   *Omne quod est . . . conferebantur*   94.95.166

> R6. 10, Vincent XVII 19 [3]. Syagrius; *CPL* 560. Ed. K. Künstle, *Antipriscilliana* (Freiburg 1905) 142. Attributed to Jerome in Lambeth Palace Library, MS 127, fol. 82v.

88 Ad Pammachium et Occeanum contra Origenem   *Scedulae . . . venustatem*   105.82.9.43.15.20.22

> Vincent XVII 19 [11], and cf. R6. 42. *CPL* 620 *ep.* 84. *CSEL* 55. 121. Location numbers **82** to **22** (and presumably **105** through error) are taken from R6. 78, 'Epistole Ieronomi'.

89 De distantia locorum lib. 1   *Ararath . . . fonte Rochel*   15.1.19.9.90.43.82.105

> R6. 81, Vincent XVII 19 [25]. Eusebius of Caesarea, tr. Jerome; Lambert 202. *PL* 23. 859–928. Same as *108* below.

90 De catholicis scriptoribus et viris illustribus lib. 1   *Symon . . . expleta*
94.42.82.95.8.80

R6. 23, 102 (location number **82** is taken from R6. 23, **94** and **8** from R6. 102, the title from both), Vincent XVII 19 [24]. *CPL* 616. Ed. E. Richardson, Texte und Untersuchungen 14 (Leipzig 1896). **82** Bury = B13. 62e = Bodl. MS e Musaeo 31, pp. 182–215 (Bury A. 31), explicit 'expleta sunt'.

91 De altercatione Luciferiani et Orthodoxi lib. 1   *Proxime . . . persuaderi*
94.43.105

R6. 9, Jerome 135. *CPL* 608. *PL* 23. 155. See also *68* above.

92 Super aedificium prudentiae tract. 1   *Gratia Dei . . . pertinet*   15.166.139

R6. 5. *Ps.* Jerome; Lambert 531. A commentary on Prudentius's *Psychomachia* vv. 821–44. Printed, J. B. Pitra, *Spicilegium Solesmense* 3 (Paris 1855) 421.

93 De essentia et immensitate Dei lib. 1   *Omnipotens . . . demonstrare*
50.63.39.1.15.9.82

R6. 90 (title, location numbers), R6. 94 (incipit), *MF* IV 14 (incipit, explicit). *Ps.* Jerome; *CPL* 633 *ep.* 14. *PL* 42. 1199; explicit is that of pt 1. Same as *101* below and Augustinus *1.162*.

94 Librum Didimi de Spiritu Sancto transtulit   *Omnibus quidem . . . sermonis*   161.82.39.164

R6. 98 (title, location numbers **161, 39**), R6.107 (title, location numbers **164, 161**), Jerome 135. Didimus Alexandrinus, tr. Jerome; Lambert 258. *PL* 23. 103–154. Same as Didimus *144.4*.

95 Temporale omnimodae historiae, secundum eundem Jeronimum in libro De viris illustribus et catholicis scriptoribus in fine

Jerome 135 (whole entry). Same as *119* below.

96 Omelias Origenis 28 transtulit de Graeco in Latinum et correxit

Jerome 135 (whole entry).

97 De xlii mansionibus filiorum Israel lib. 1   *Moverunt . . . corruerunt*   39.1.
15.43.82.161

R6. 80 (title, location numbers), Vincent XVII 19 [32], *MF* IV 1 (title, incipit, explicit). *CPL* 620 *ep.* 78. *CSEL* 55. 49.

Jeronimus *281. 104*

98 De x temptationibus et de x plagis in libro Numeri lib. 1   *Haec sunt*
   . . . 15.1.139.82.105.156

   R6. 84. *Ps.* Jerome; Lambert 409. *PL* 23. 1319.

p. 83]

99 De musicis instrumentis ep. 1   *Cogor a te* . . .   94.95.105.82.1.15

   R6. 88. *Ps.* Jerome; *CPL* 633 *ep.* 23. *PL* 30. 213.

100 De partibus minus notis Veteris Testamenti   *Sintagma* . . .   1.50.82

   R6. 89. *Ps.* Jerome; Lambert 468. A series of glossarial notes on the OT, beginning 'Syntagma: doctrina. Oeconicon : dispensatorem'.

101 De membris et motibus Jesu Christi et de essentia Dei lib. 1   *Omnipotens*
   . . . *demonstrare*   42.8.19.24.50.63

   24] xxiiii *R*

   R6. 51. Same as *93* above. **63** Crowland = B24. 31, 'epistole sue [Jeronimi]'.

102 De sphaera coeli et diversis scripturis   *Affirmatur* . . . *per eam*
   15.163.167.139

   R6. 57 (title, location numbers **15, 139**), R6. 104 (location number **163**). *Ps.* Jerome. The incipit is that of the *De sphaera coeli*; Lambert 625. In Durham Cathedral, MS B. II. 11, fol. 92r (see headnote above), this is followed by extracts beginning 'Paulus apostolus' and ending 'per eam', and the Bury manuscript must have been similar.

103 De mensura spaerae coeli   *Forma* . . . *ympnisonam*   15.1

   R6. 58. *Ps.* Jerome. The incipit is that of six hexameters entitled *Mensura spere* in Durham Cathedral, MS B. II. 11, fol. 105v; they are followed by a computistical note and another set of twenty-six hexameters, ending 'ymnisonam'; see headnote above.

104 De xii mensuris et ponderibus   *Ponderum* . . . *efficiunt*   15.1

   R6. 60. Location number **15** is repeated from *103* above. [**82** Bury = Cambridge, Pembroke College, MS 87, fol. 208r (Bury E. 11); explicit does not correspond; on the flyleaf Kirkestede added the attribution to Jerome to an older table of contents.]

Jeronimus   *281. 105*

105   De xii lapidibus pretiosis   *Jaspis . . . constantes*   15.1

   R6. 58. *Ps.* Jerome. Lambert 624a cites five manuscripts, none with this incipit and explicit. This work also appears in Durham Cathedral, MS B. II. 11, fol. 106v; see headnote above.

106   Item de mensuris et corporum altitudine   *Mensurarum . . . teneto*   15.1

   corporum *queried by Tanner*

   R6. 60. *Ps.* Jerome. This entry consists of two paragraphs which appear in Durham Cathedral, MS B. II. 11, fol. 105v; see headnote above. The first, incipit 'Mensurarum appellationes', explicit 'v stadia', is printed in *Die Schriften der römischen Feldmesser*, ed. F. Blume & others (Berlin 1848), 94. 13–95. 9; the second, beginning 'Ad estimandum cuiuscumque' and ending 'rei teneto', is ed. N. Bubnov, *Gerberti Opera mathematica* (Berlin 1899) 323. Location number **15** is repeated from *105* above.

107   De Romanis pontificibus   *Beatus . . . Romanus*   15.166

   R6. 69. *Ps.* Jerome. This work, an abridgement of the *Liber pontificalis* down to Constantine II (d. 767), is attributed to Jerome in Durham Cathedral, MS B. II. 11, fol. 103r; see headnote above. See L. Duchesne, *Études sur le Liber pontificalis* (Paris 1877) 108.

108   De situ locorum lib. 1

   Whole entry from R6. 44 and Jerome 135. Same as *89* above.

109   De vi civitatibus fugitivorum   *Prima . . .*   161.15

   R6. 95. *Ps.* Jerome; Lambert 408. A brief allegorical commentary on the Cities of Refuge (Deut 19), which appears in Durham Cathedral, MS B. II. 11, fol. 82v.

110   De gradibus Romanorum   *Decanus est . . . satrapa vocatur*   163.166

   R6. 105. *Ps.* Jerome spur. *ep.* 73; Lambert 373, inc. 'Decanus qui sit'.

111   Cosmographiam ethici philosophi transtulit   *Philosophorum . . .*   82.167

   'Aethicus Ister'. Same as Ethicus *183.1*. **82** Bury = B13. 49a.

112   De quibusdam capitulis 4 evangeliorum   95.166

   capitulis] causis *Add. 3470; Tanner, uncertain of this reading, has added 'capitulis' as a variant reading, probably from the Registrum*

   R6. 26 (whole entry save the suspect **166**).

Jeronimus *281. 121*

113 De naturis animalium et avium allegorice   95.42

   R6. 27. (whole entry).

114 Glosa septimae ebdomadae   *Non ad hoc . . . solares*   15.166.12

   12] xii *R*

   R6. 6. *Ps.* Jerome; Lambert 463. An extract from a commentary on Daniel 9 that appears in Durham Cathedral, MS B. II. 11, fol. 100v; see headnote above.

115 De usu psallendi tract. 1   166

   R6. 7 (whole entry).

116 De persecutione Christianorum tract. 1   94

   R6. 3 (whole entry). Same as Augustinus *1.505*.

117 De 7 mirabilibus tract. 1   166

   R6. 8 (whole entry).

118 De 5 sensibus tract. 1   122.12.163.161

   12] xii *R*

   R6. 47 (whole entry save the last two location numbers, derived perhaps from R6. 93 *Aduersus Jouinianum*). Book II of *Aduersus Jouinianum*, 67 above.

119 Cronicarum lib. 1   *Primus . . .*   15.42.19.29

   R6. 50. Eusebius, tr. Jerome; Lambert 203. *GCS* 47 (Berlin 1984³). Same as *95* above.

120 Sermones x   55.23

   23] xxiii *R*

   Whole entry from R6. 62 and Vincent XVII 19 [88].

121 Omelia super evangelia   94.114

   R6. 54 (whole entry, title varies).

Jeronimus *281. 122*

122 De accentibus tract. 1   <u>90</u>.<u>95</u>

R6. 30 (whole entry).

123 De literis tract. 1   <u>90</u>.<u>95</u>

R6. 31 (whole entry).

124 De verbo vitae tract. 1

This work and its source are unidentified.

125 De frugi et luxurioso ad Damasum

Whole entry from Vincent XVII 19 [15] and Jerome 135. Same as *135* below.

126 De homine perfecto tract. 1

Vincent XVII 19 [21] (whole entry).

127 De xv signis ante diem judicii tract. 1   *Primum signum . . . judicii*

Vincent XVII 19 [23]. Ps. Jerome *De xv signis diem iudicii praecedentibus*; Lambert 652, incipit of the introduction 'Quindecim signa', of the text 'Prima die'. *PL* 94. 555. [**82** Bury = Cambridge, Gonville and Caius College, MS 225/240, pp. 165–166, attributed to Jerome (Bury V. 12), explicit 'judicii Dei'.]

128 De institutione clericorum vel monachorum et de divinae historiae diversis expositionem ad Paulinum ep. 1   *Bonus homo . . . salutari*   63.<u>20</u>.<u>26</u>.98.85.<u>1</u>39.24

Vincent XVII 19 [62]. *CPL* 620 *ep*. 58. *CSEL* 54. 527. **63** Crowland = B24. 31, 'epistole sue [Ieronimi]'. Location numbers **20** and **26** (and probably others via miscopying) are taken from R6. 78, 'Epistole Jeronimi'.

129 De vita clericorum vel monachorum ad Nepotianum epistolam quasi librum 1   *Petis a me . . . confitebitur*   <u>8</u>.<u>42</u>.<u>82</u>.<u>32</u>.<u>9</u>.<u>19</u>.<u>35</u>.<u>1</u>

32] 22 *R*   35] 39 *R*

R6. 108, 60. *CPL* 620 *ep*. 52. *CSEL* 54. 413. Location numbers are taken from R6. 78, 'Epistole Jeronimi'. **82** Bury = B13. 193, 'Ieronimi epistole'.

Jeronimus *281. 133*

130 De vita monachi ad Rusticum ep. 1   *Nichil . . . praemia*   8.42.63.98.85. 82.139

R6. 49, Vincent XVII 19 [63]. *CPL* 620 *ep.* 125. *CSEL* 56/1. 118. Location numbers **8**, **42**, and **82** (and probably others via miscopying) are taken from R6. 78, 'Epistole Jeronimi'. **63** Crowland = B24. 31, 'epistole sue'. / **82** Bury = B13. 193, 'Ieronimi epistole'.

131 De vita clericorum ad Occeanum ep. 1   *Sofronius . . . affectu*   8.42.63. 82.32.9.19.35

35] 39 *R*

Vincent XVII 19 [64]. *Ps.* Jerome; *CPL* 633 *ep.* 42. *PL* 30. 288. All the location numbers save **63** are taken from R6. 78, 'Epistole Jeronimi'. **63** Crowland = B24. 31, 'epistole sue'. / **82** Bury = B13. 193, 'Ieronimi epistole'.

132 De contemptu mundi ad Heliodorum   *Quanto . . . labor durus est*   8.42. 63.82.32.9.19.35

Works *132–141, 148–149, 153–157, 159–207, 214–220, 222–231,* and *238*: The location numbers in these entries are repeated from *131* above, with the incidental addition of location number **115** (work *158*) and location number **15** (works *159, 168*). Some of these (those that are underlined) are obvious borrowings from R6. 78, 'Epistole Jeronimi', with the errors here of **32** for 22, **35** for 39, and **115** for 114, fairly consistently throughout; other location numbers no doubt also come from that source via miscopying.

Vincent XVII 19 [81], Jerome 135, and cf. R6. 106. *CPL* 620 *ep.* 14. *CSEL* 54. 44. Location numbers save **63** are taken from R6. 78, 'Epistole Jeronimi'. **63** Crowland = B24. 31, 'epistole sue'. / **82** Bury = B13. 193, 'Ieronimi epistole'.

133 De poenitentia ad Rusticum ep. 1   *Quid ignotus . . . non sum oblitus*   8.42. 63.82.32.9.19.35

Vincent XVII 19 [14]. *CPL* 620 *ep.* 122. *CSEL* 56/1. 56. **82** Bury = Cambridge, Pembroke College, MS 47, fol. 95r (Bury B. 40), with Kirkestede's marginal rubric at the beginning (fol. 95r top) and his marginal note fol. 97va (beside the words 'non sum oblitus') 'Explicit epistola Jeronomi'; he also inserted the title into the 12th-cent. table of contents on the front pastedown. / **63** Crowland = B24. 31, 'epistole sue'. For the other location numbers see the note to *132* above.

Jeronimus   281. 134

134 De morte Nepotiani epitaphium ad Heliodorum episcopum   *Grandes
      . . . desinamus*   8.42.63.82.32.9.19

   Vincent XVII 19 [61], and cf. R6. 106. *CPL* 620 *ep.* 60. *CSEL* 54. 548. **63**
   Crowland = B24. 31, 'epistole sue'. / **82** Bury = B13. 193, 'Ieronimi epistole'. For the other location numbers see the note to *132* above.

p. 84]

135 De filio prodigo ad Damasum ep. 1   *Beatudinis . . . non siliquis*
      8.42.63.82.32.9.19

   CPL 620 *ep.* 21. *CSEL* 54. 111. Same as *125* above. **63** Crowland = B24. 31, 'epistole sue'. / **82** Bury = B13. 193, 'Ieronimi epistole'. For the other location numbers see the note to *132* above.

136 De unius uxoris viro ad Occeanum   *Nunquam . . . concessum est*   8.42.63.
      82.32.9.19

   Vincent XVII 19 [16]. *CPL* 620 *ep.* 69. *CSEL* 54. 678. **63** Crowland = B24. 31, 'epistole sue'. / **82** Bury = B13. 193, 'Ieronimi epistole'. For the other location numbers see the note to *132* above.

137 De tribus virtutibus ep. 1   *Tres quondam . . .*   8.42.63.82.32.9.19

   Vincent XVII 19 [84], *MF* IV 7 (incipit 'Tres quodammodo'). *Ps.* Jerome; *CPL* 633 *ep.* 8. *PL* 30. 116. **63** Crowland = B24. 31, 'epistole sue'. / **82** Bury = B13. 193, 'Ieronimi epistole'. For the other location numbers see the note to *132* above.

138 De terra promissionis ad Dardanum   *Quaeris . . . caritatis est*   8.42.63.
      82.32.9.19

   CPL 620 *ep.* 129. *CSEL* 56/1. 162. **63** Crowland = B24. 31, 'epistole sue.' / **82** Bury = B13. 193, 'Ieronimi epistole'. For the other location numbers see the note to *132* above.

139 De veste sacerdotali ad Fabiolam ep. 1   *Usque hodie . . . aestimandus*
      8.42.63.82.32.9.19

   Vincent XVII 19 [31]. *CPL* 620 *ep.* 64. *CSEL* 54. 586. **63** Crowland = B24. 31, 'epistole sue.' / **82** Bury = B13. 193, 'Ieronimi epistole'. For the other location numbers see the note to *132* above.

Jeronimus *281. 145*

140 Ad Salianum diaconem lapsum ep. 1   *Samuel . . . combustio est*   8.42.63.
82.32.9.19

> Vincent XVII 19 [70], *Ad Sabinianum. CPL* 620 *ep.* 147. *CSEL* 56/1. 312, explicit 'combustionem'. **63** Crowland = B24. 31, 'epistole sue'. / **82** Bury = B13. 193, 'Ieronimi epistole'. For the other location numbers see the note to *132* above.

141 Ad Julianum diaconem ep. 1   *Antiquus . . . lectiorem*   8.42.63.82.32.9.19

> *CPL* 620 *ep.* 6. *CSEL* 54. 24, explicit 'laetiorem'. **63** Crowland = B24. 31, 'epistole sue'. / **82** Bury = B13. 193, 'Ieronimi epistole'. For the other location numbers see the note to *132* above.

142 Ad Niceam ypodiaconum ep. 1   *Turpilius . . . accipiam*   163.164.166.
118.127

> *142–144 and 146* : The location numbers have been taken in consecutive blocks from R6. 78, 'Epistole Ieronimi' (for 146, only the last four numbers were consecutive in Registrum*)*

> *CPL* 620 *ep.* 8. *CSEL* 54. 31.

143 Ad senatorem urbis Romanae ep. 1   *Sebesium nostrum . . . finienda est*
117.93.94.15.155.8

> Sebesium *queried by Tanner*   15] 95 *R*

> *CPL* 620 *ep.* 70. *CSEL* 54. 700. For location numbers see the note to *142* above.

144 De 7 vindictis Caym ad Damasum   *Postquam . . . dictasse*   116.42.43.
106.160.153

> 106] 156 *R*

> *CPL* 620 *ep.* 36 pt 1. *CSEL* 54. 268–75. For location numbers see the note to *142* above.

145 De egressione filiorum Israel de Egypto   *Hoc vero . . . simplicitatem*
115.32.9.108.19.35

> 115] 114 *R*   32] 22 *R*   108] 128 *R*   35] 39 *R*

> *CPL* 620 *ep.* 36 pt 2. *CSEL* 54. 276–81. Location numbers are taken, with many errors, from R6. 78, 'Epistole Jeronimi'.

Jeronimus   *281. 146*

146 De ignorantia Ysaac in benedicendis filiis   *Differo . . . salvus erit*   82.115.26.23.25.20

   115] 114 *R*

   CPL 620 *ep.* 36 pt 3. *CSEL* 54. 281–5. **82** Bury = B13. 193, 'Ieronimi epistole'. The location numbers are taken from R6. 78, 'Epistole Jeronimi', and see the note to *142* above.

147 De Osanna ad Damasum ep. 1   *Multi super . . . sententiam*   139.53.39.49.63.98.50

   MF IV 16, Jerome 8. *CPL* 620 *ep.* 20. *CSEL* 54. 104. **63** Crowland = B24. 31, 'epistole sue'. Location numbers **39** and **49** (and probably others via miscopying) are taken from R6. 78, 'Epistole Jeronimi'.

148 De seraphim et calculo ep. 1   *Septuaginta . . . non legimus*   8.42.63.82.32.9.19.35

   MF IV 5 (explicit 'et lingua'), Jerome 135. *CPL* 620 *ep.* 18b. *CSEL* 54. 97. **63** Crowland = B24. 31, 'epistole sue'. / **82** Bury = B13. 193, 'Ieronimi epistole'. For the other location numbers see the note to *132* above.

149 De morte Oseae regis et de seraphim et calculo in Ysaiam prophetam ep. 1   *Antequam . . . et lingua*   8.42.63.82.32.9.19.35

   Vincent XVII 19 [85]. *CPL* 620 *ep.* 18a. *CSEL* 54. 74. **63** Crowland = B24. 31, 'epistole sue'. / **82** Bury = B13. 193, 'Ieronimi epistole'. For the other location numbers see the note to *132* above.

150 Ad Damasum de fide cui in Antiochia communicare debeat ep. 1   *Quoniam vetus . . . mortuus est*   82.115.26.23.25.20.22

   115] 114 *R*

   Vincent XVII 19 [1]. *CPL* 620 *epp.* 15 and 16. *CSEL* 54. 62–9, inc. 'Quoniam uetusto'. **82** Bury = B13. 193, 'Ieronimi epistole'. Location numbers are taken from R6. 78, 'Epistole Ieronimi'.

151 De Melchisedech ep. 1   *Misisti . . . valitudini*   163.161.82.154.128.8

   R6. 100. *CPL* 620 *ep.* 73. *CSEL* 55. 13. **82** Bury = B13. 193, 'Ieronimi epistole'. Location numbers are taken from R6. 78, 'Epistole Ieronimi'.

152 De 7 gradibus ecclesiae ad Damasum   15.163.164.166

   Whole entry from R6. 78, 'Epistole Ieronimi' (location numbers) and Vincent XVII 19 [33] (title).

Jeronimus *281. 159*

153 De differentia presbyteri et diaconi   *Legimus . . . vendicent*   8.42.63.82. 32.9.19

    CPL 620 *ep.* 146. *CSEL* 56/1. 308. **63** Crowland = B24. 31, 'epistole sue'. / **82** Bury = B13. 193, 'Ieronimi epistole'. For the location numbers see the note to *132* above.

154 De judicio Salamonis ep. 1   *Multum . . . sustinuerimus*   8.42.63.82.32.9. 19

    R6. 39. *CPL* 620 *ep.* 74. *CSEL* 55.23. **63** Crowland = B24. 31, 'epistole sue'. / **82** Bury = B13. 193, 'Ieronimi epistole'. For the location numbers see the note to *132* above.

155 Quod Salamon et Achaz xi annorum genuisse dicantur filios ep. 1   *Zenon . . . suscipito*   8.42.63.82.32.9.19

    R6. 40. *CPL* 620 *ep.* 72. *CSEL* 55.8. **63** Crowland = B24. 31, 'epistole sue'. / **82** Bury = B13. 193, 'Ieronimi epistole'. For the location numbers see the note to *132* above.

156 De ortu amicitiae ad Florentinum ep. 1   *Quantus . . . invector*   8.42.63. 82.32.9.19

    CPL 620 *ep.* 4. *CSEL* 54. 19. **63** Crowland = B24. 31, 'epistole sue'. / **82** Bury = B13. 193, 'Ieronimi epistole'. For the location numbers see the note to *132* above.

157 Item ad eundem epistolam aliam   *In ea mihi . . . prosequatur*   8.42.63. 82.32.9.19

    CPL 620 *ep.* 5. *CSEL* 54. 21. **63** Crowland = B24. 31, 'epistole sue'. / **82** Bury = B13. 193, 'Ieronimi epistole'. For the location numbers see the note to *132* above.

158 Ad Castricianum ut de caecitate quae si contigit non debeat contristari ep. 1   *Sanctus filius . . . dupplicati*   115.8.82.63.32.9.19

    CPL 620 *ep.* 68. *CSEL* 54. 675. **82** Bury = B13. 193, 'Ieronimi epistole'. / **63** Crowland = B24. 31, 'epistole sue'. Other location numbers are taken from R6.78, 'Epistole Jeronimi'.

159 De psalmo 89° ad Ciprianum ep. 1   *Frater karissime . . . deseretur*   15.8.82. 63.32.9.19

    Same as *51* above. **82** Bury = B13. 193, 'Ieronimi epistole'. / **63** Crowland = B24. 31, 'epistole sue'. For the location numbers see the note to *132* above.

160 De septies percussa ad Innocentium Saepe a me . . .libertati 8.42.63.
82.32.9.19

> CPL 620 ep. 1. CSEL 54. 1. **63** Crowland = B24. 31, 'epistole sue'. / **82** Bury = B13. 193, 'Ieronimi epistole'. For the location numbers see the note to *132* above.

161 Ad Julianum exortatorium et de pignoribus consultum *Filius meus . . . faemina facti* 8.42.63.82.32.9.19

> Vincent XVII 19 [13]. CPL 620 ep. 118. CSEL 55. 434. **63** Crowland = B24. 31, 'epistole sue'. / **82** Bury = B13. 193, 'Ieronimi epistole'. For the location numbers see the note to *132* above.

162 Ad Pammachium ep. 1 *Christiani . . . generi* 8.42.63.82.32.9.19

> CPL 620 ep. 48 (49). CSEL 54. 347. **63** Crowland = B24. 31, 'epistole sue'. / **82** Bury = B13. 193, 'Ieronimi epistole'. For the location numbers see the note to *132* above.

163 Ad Theodorum Spanum de morte Lucini *Lugubri . . . brevis est* 8.42.63.82.32.9.19

> CPL 620 ep. 75. CSEL 55. 29, explicit unidentified. **63** Crowland = B24. 31, 'epistole sue'. / **82** Bury = B13. 193, 'Ieronimi epistole'. For the location numbers see the note to *132* above.

164 Ad Amagum Spanum ep. *Quamquam . . . salutamus* 8.42.63.82.32.9.19

> CPL 620 ep. 76. CSEL 55. 34. **63** Crowland = B24. 31, 'epistole sue'. / **82** Bury = B13. 193, 'Ieronimi epistole'. For the location numbers see the note to *132* above.

165 Ad Marcum presbyterum Calcidae ep. *Decreveram . . . brevis* 8.42.63.82.32.9.19

> CPL 620 ep. 17. CSEL 54. 70, explicit unidentified. **63** Crowland = B24. 31, 'epistole sue'. / **82** Bury = B13. 193, 'Ieronimi epistole'. For the location numbers see the note to *132* above.

166 Ad Exsuperantium ep. 1 *Inter omnia . . .* 8.42.63.82.32.9.19

> CPL 620 ep. 145. CSEL 56/1. 306. **63** Crowland = B24. 31, 'epistole sue'. / **82** Bury = B13. 193, 'Ieronimi epistole'. For the location numbers see the note to *132* above.

Jeronimus *281. 173*

167 Ad Lucinum haereticum ep. 1   *Nec opinanti . . . sentiamus*   8.42.63.82. 32.9.19

> *CPL* 620 *ep.* 71. *CSEL* 55. 1. **63** Crowland = B24. 31, 'epistole sue'. / **82** Bury = B13. 193, 'Ieronimi epistole'. For the location numbers see the note to *132* above.

168 De psalmo 44° ad Principiam virginem   *Scio me . . . totum canticum* 15.8.42.63.82.9.19

> Vincent XVII 19 [86]. *CPL* 620 *ep.* 65. *CSEL* 54. 616. **63** Crowland = B24. 31, 'epistole sue'. / **82** Bury = B13. 193, 'Ieronimi epistole'. For the location numbers see the note to *132* above.

169 Item super psalmos a 10mo usque ad 16^{mum} tractatus 7, secundum Jeronimum libro De catholicis scriptoribus in fine

> Jerome 135. Same as *54* above.

p. 85]

170 De virginitate servanda ad Eustochium virginem ep. 1   *Audi filia . . . cooperient*   8.42.32.82.9.19.35

> R6. 11, Vincent XVII 19 [65], Jerome 135. *CPL* 620 *ep.* 22. *CSEL* 54. 143. **82** Bury = B13. 193, 'Ieronimi epistole'. For the location numbers see the note to *132* above.

171 De viduitate servanda ad Furiam ep. 1   *Obsecras . . . cogitabis*   8.42.82. 32.9.19.35

> Vincent XVII 19 [72]. *CPL* 620 *ep.* 54. *CSEL* 54. 466. **82** Bury = B13. 193, 'Ieronimi epistole'. For the location numbers see the note to *132* above.

172 De morte Nebridii et de viduitate servanda ad Silvinam ep. 1   *Vereor . . . pertimesco*   8.42.82.32.9.19.35

> Vincent XVII 19 [73]. *CPL* 620 *ep.* 79. *CSEL* 55. 87. **82** Bury = B13. 193, 'Ieronimi epistole'. For the location numbers see the note to *132* above.

173 De monogamia ad Ageruciam   *In veteri . . . possidebit*   8.42.82.32.9. 19.35

> R6. 22, Vincent XVII 19 [71]. *CPL* 620 *ep.* 123. *CSEL* 56/1. 72. **82** Bury = B13. 193, 'Ieronimi epistole'. For the location numbers see the note to *132* above.

174 Ad Aletam de institutione filiae ep. 1   *Apostolus . . . offerendam*   8.42.82. 32.9.19

> Vincent XVII 19 [67], *Ad Laetam. CPL* 620 *ep.* 107. *CSEL* 55. 290. **82** Bury = B13. 193, 'Ieronimi epistole'. For the location numbers see the note to *132* above.

175 Ad matrem et filiam in Gallia commorantes ep. 1   *Retulit mihi . . . tempori*   8.42.82.32.9.19

> Vincent XVII 19 [68]. *CPL* 620 *ep.* 117. *CSEL* 55. 422. **82** Bury = B13. 193, 'Ieronimi epistole'. For the location numbers see the note to *132* above.

176 Ad Paulam de dormitione Blesillae   *Quis dabit . . . cum matre*   8.42.82. 32.9.19

> Vincent XVII 19 [74], Jerome 15. *CPL* 620 *ep.* 39. *CSEL* 54. 293. **82** Bury = B13. 193, 'Ieronimi epistole'. For the location numbers see the note to *132* above.

177 Ad Pammachium de morte Paulinae   *Sanato . . . patriarcham*   8.42.32. 82.9.19

> Vincent XVII 19 [75]. *CPL* 620 *ep.* 66 pt 1. *CSEL* 54. 647–60. **82** Bury = B13. 193, 'Ieronimi epistole'. For the location numbers see the note to *132* above.

178 Ad Oceanum de morte Fabiolae   *Plures . . . plus amat*   8.42.82.32.9.19

> Vincent XVII 19 [76]. *CPL* 620 *ep.* 77. *CSEL* 55. 37. **82** Bury = B13. 193, 'Ieronimi epistole'. For the location numbers see the note to *132* above.

179 De dormitione Sanctae Paulae epitaphium   *Si cuncta . . . viginti*   8.42. 82.32.9.19

> Paulae] Pauli *Add. 3470*

> Vincent XVII 19 [77]. *CPL* 620 *ep.* 108. *CSEL* 55. 306. **82** Bury = B13. 193, 'Ieronimi epistole'. For the location numbers see the note to *132* above.

180 Ad Tyrasium de morte filiae suae   *Benedicto . . . cum ille*   8.42.82.32.9.19

> Benedicto] Benedico *Add. 3470; Tanner, uncertain of this reading, has added* Benedictio *as a variant reading*

> R6. 4, Vincent XVII 19 [78]. *Ps.* Jerome; *CPL* 633 *ep.* 40, and cf. *CPL* 64 and 769. *PL* 30. 278. **82** Bury = B13. 193, 'Ieronimi epistole'. For the location numbers see the note to *132* above.

Jeronimus *281. 187*

181 Ad Marcellam ne contristaretur de aegrotatione et morte Blesillae
   Abraham . . . Belzebub   8.42.82.32.9.19

   Jerome 135. *CPL* 620 *ep.* 38. *CSEL* 54. 289. **82** Bury = B13. 193, 'Ieronimi
   epistole'. For the location numbers see the note to *132* above.

182 Ad Marcellam de quinque quaestionibus Novi Testamenti et de hiis qui
   Domino occasuri sunt ep.   *Magnis . . . dignatur*   8.42.82.32.9.19

   Domino] *Add. 3470*, queried by *Tanner*

   R6. 109, Jerome 135. *CPL* 620 *ep.* 59. *CSEL* 54. 541. **82** Bury = B13. 193,
   'Ieronimi epistole'. For the location numbers see the note to *132* above.

183 Ad Marcellam de Onaso ep. 1   *Medici . . . poteris*   8.42.82.32.9.19

   Jerome 135. *CPL* 620 *ep.* 40. *CSEL* 54. 309. **82** Bury = B13. 193, 'Ieronimi
   epistole'. For the location numbers see the note to *132* above.

184 Ad Marcellam de Hebraicis nominibus et verbis   *Nuper cum . . . tacita
   sunt*   8.42.82.32.9.19

   Jerome 135 *CPL* 620 *ep.* 26. *CSEL* 54. 220. **82** Bury = B13. 193, 'Ieronimi
   epistole'. For the location numbers see the note to *132* above.

185 Ad Marcellam de 10 nominibus quibus apud Hebraeos Deus vocatur
   ep. 1 *Nonagesimum . . . possumus*   8.42.82.32.9.19

   Jerome 135. *CPL* 620 *ep.* 25. *CSEL* 54. 218. **82** Bury = B13. 193, 'Ieronimi
   epistole'. For the location numbers see the note to *132* above.

186 Ad Marcellam de fide nostra et de dogmate haereticorum ep. 1
   Testimonia . . . sciscitari   8.82.42.32.9.19.35

   Jerome 135. *CPL* 620 *ep.* 41. *CSEL* 54. 311. **82** Bury = B13. 193, 'Ieronimi
   epistole'. For the location numbers see the note to *132* above.

187 De blasphemia in Spiritum Sanctum irremissibili ad Marcellam ep. 1
   Brevis . . . dictaremus   8.42.82.32.9.19.35

   irremissibili] irremissibilem *Add. 3470*

   Jerome 135. *CPL* 620 *ep.* 42. *CSEL* 54. 315. **82** Bury = B13. 193, 'Ieronimi
   epistole'. For the location numbers see the note to *132* above.

Jeronimus   *281. 188*

188 De detractoribus suis ad Marcellam   *Post priorem . . . calcant*   8.42.82. 32.9.19.35

>   Jerome 135. *CPL* 620 *ep.* 27. *CSEL* 54. 223. **82** Bury = B13. 193, 'Ieronimi epistole'. For the location numbers see the note to *132* above.

189 De fictis amicis qui sibi detractores habebunt ad Asellam   *Si tibi putem . . . precibus mitiga*   8.42.82.32.9.19.35

>   detractores] detractatores *Add. 3470, queried by Tanner*

>   *CPL* 620 *ep.* 45. *CSEL* 54. 323. **82** Bury = B13. 193, 'Ieronimi epistole'. For the location numbers see the note to *132* above.

190 De muneribus ad Marcellam   *Ut absentiam . . . gratum*   8.42.82.32.9. 19.35

>   *CPL* 620 *ep.* 44. *CSEL* 54. 322. **82** Bury = B13. 193, 'Ieronimi epistole'. For the location numbers see the note to *132* above.

191 De urbe secedenda ad Marcellam   *Ambrosius . . . cantationes*   8.42.82. 32.9.19.35

>   *CPL* 620 *ep.* 43. *CSEL* 54. 318; in one family of manuscripts parts of *ep.* 46, paragraphs 10–12 through the word 'cantiones', are added to the end of *ep.* 43; see *CSEL* 54. 321n. **82** Bury = B13. 193, 'Ieronimi epistole'. For the location numbers see the note to *132* above.

192 De Ephod ad Marcellam ep. 1   *Epistolare . . . perdentes*   8.42.82.32.9. 19.35

>   *CPL* 620 *ep.* 29. *CSEL* 54. 232. **82** Bury = B13. 193, 'Ieronimi epistole'. For the location numbers see the note to *132* above.

193 De psalmo 126° ad Marcellam   *Beatus . . . infirmitas*   8.42.82.32.9.19.35

>   *CPL* 620 *ep.* 34. *CSEL* 54. 259. **82** Bury = B13. 193, 'Ieronimi epistole'. For the location numbers see the note to *132* above.

194 De interpretatione Hebraicarum literarum in psalmo 118 ad Marcellam *Nudius tertius . . . velociter*   8.42.82.32.9.19.35

>   *CPL* 620 *ep.* 30. *CSEL* 54. 243, *Ad Paulam*. Same as *62* above. **82** Bury = B13. 193, 'Ieronimi epistole', which must have had the wrong addressee in its rubric, an error dating back at least to the 9th cent.; see *CSEL* 54. 243n. For the location numbers see the note to *132* above.

Jeronimus *281. 202*

195 De diaplasma ad Marcellam *Quae acceptis . . . nescientium* <u>8</u>.<u>42</u>.<u>82</u>.<u>32</u>. <u>9</u>.<u>19</u>.<u>35</u>

> *De diapsalmate. CPL* 620 *ep.* 28. *CSEL* 54. 227. **82** Bury = B13. 193, 'Ieronimi epistole'. For the location numbers see the note to *132* above.

196 De vita Asellae ad Marcellam *Nemo . . .* <u>8</u>.<u>42</u>.<u>82</u>.<u>32</u>.<u>9</u>.<u>19</u>.<u>35</u>

> *CPL* 620 *ep.* 24. *CSEL* 54. 214. Same as *198* below. **82** Bury = B13. 193, 'Ieronimi epistole'. For the location numbers see the note to *132* above.

197 Ad Marcellam de exitu Leae ep. 1 *Cum horum . . . perpetui* <u>8</u>.<u>42</u>.<u>82</u>. <u>32</u>.<u>9</u>.<u>19</u>.<u>35</u>

> *CPL* 620 *ep.* 23. *CSEL* 54. 211. **82** Bury = B13. 193, 'Ieronimi epistole'. For the location numbers see the note to *132* above.

198 Ad Marcellam ep. 1 *Nemo quod . . . sacerdotes* <u>8</u>.<u>42</u>.<u>82</u>.<u>32</u>.<u>9</u>.<u>19</u>.<u>35</u>

> Same as *196* above. **82** Bury = B13. 193, 'Ieronimi epistole'. For the location numbers see the note to *132* above.

199 Ad Marcellam ep. 1 *Nuper cum . . . invehatur* <u>8</u>.<u>42</u>.<u>82</u>.<u>32</u>.<u>9</u>.<u>19</u>.<u>35</u>

> *CPL* 620 *ep.* 37. *CSEL* 54. 286. **82** Bury = B13. 193, 'Ieronimi epistole'. For the location numbers see the note to *132* above.

200 Ad Marcellam et Pammachiam *Rursum . . . moriantur* <u>8</u>.<u>42</u>.<u>82</u>.<u>32</u>. <u>9</u>.<u>19</u>.<u>35</u>

> *CPL* 620 *ep.* 97. *CSEL* 55. 182. **82** Bury = B13. 193, 'Ieronimi epistole'. For the location numbers see the note to *132* above.

201 Ad Marcellam ep. 1 *Ut tam . . . mater* <u>8</u>.<u>42</u>.<u>82</u>.<u>32</u>.<u>9</u>.<u>19</u>.<u>35</u>

> *CPL* 620 *ep.* 32. *CSEL* 54. 252. **82** Bury = B13. 193, 'Ieronimi epistole'. For the location numbers see the note to *132* above.

202 De vita Marcellae ad Principiam *Saepe et . . . desiderans* <u>8</u>.<u>42</u>.<u>82</u>.<u>32</u>. <u>9</u>.<u>19</u>.<u>35</u>

> *CPL* 620 *ep.* 127. *CSEL* 56/1. 145. **82** Bury = B13. 193, 'Ieronimi epistole'. For the location numbers see the note to *132* above.

Jeronimus *281. 203*

203 Ad Demetriadium *Si summo ... adquiritur* 8.42.82.32.9.19.35

> Vincent XVII 19 [66]. Pelagius; *CPL* 633 *ep.* 1 and 737. *PL* 30. 15. See the medieval discussion of this work at *213* below. **82** Bury = B13. 193, 'Ieronimi epistole'. For the location numbers see the note to *132* above.

204 Ad Demetriadium *Inter omnes ...* 8.42.82.32.9.19.35

> Vincent XVII 19 [66]. *CPL* 620 *ep.* 130. *CSEL* 56. 175. **82** Bury = B13. 193, 'Ieronimi epistole'. For the location numbers see the note to *132* above.

p. 86]

205 De corruptione LXX in psalterio ad Summam et Fratelam lib. 1 8.42.82.32.9.19.35

> Vincent XVII 19 [19]. *Ad Sunniam et Fretelam. CPL* 620 *ep.* 106. *CSEL* 55. 247. **82** Bury = B13. 193, 'Ieronimi epistole'. For the location numbers see the note to *132* above.

206 Objurgationis Susannae virginis Deo consecratae super lapsu suo ep. 1 *Quid agis ...* 8.42.82.32.9.19.35

> Vincent XVII 19 [69]. *Ps.* Jerome; *CPL* 633 *ep.* 20 and 651. Ed. E. Cazzaniga, *Incerti auctoris 'De lapsu Suzannae'* (Turin 1948). Same as Ambrosius *2.91*. **82** Bury = B13. 193, 'Ieronimi epistole'. For the location numbers see the note to *132* above.

207 Ad Silvinam *Nec diviti ... futurorum* 8.42.82.32.9.19.35

> This work consists of excerpts from Jerome *ep.* 79 *Ad Saluinam* (*CSEL* 55. 87; cf. p. 87 line 13). These excerpts appear in Rome, Biblioteca Vallicelliana, T XVIII, fols. 74r–81r; see P. Fournier, *Mémoires de l'Institut de France, Académie des Inscriptions et Belles Lettres* 40 (1916) 103–104. **82** Bury = B13. 193, 'Ieronimi epistole'. For the location numbers see the note to *132* above.

208 Item scripsit juxta Cassiodorum annotationes brevissimas super epistolas Pauli, et vocatur Breviarium, ut patet infra

> Cassiodorus I. 8. 8 (whole entry). Same as *55* above.

209 Item diffusius super Epistolas ad Corinthios

> Epistolas] Epistolam *Add. 3470*

> All of entries *209–211*: Cassiodorus I. 8. 14. Same as *79–81* above.

Jeronimus *281. 215*

210 Super Epistolas ad Thessalonicenses

211 Super Epistolam ad Colocenses

212 Item historiam ecclesiasticam transtulit de Graeco in Latinum

> Cassiodorus I. 17. 2 (whole entry).

213 De epistola ad Demetriadem attitulata, quae sic incipit: *Si summo ingenio* . . ., dicit Augustinus ad Julianam matrem Demetriadis quod Pelagianam haeresin sapit; quam multum notat his verbis: Quod enim ait, Non possum ista bona esse nisi in te, optime et verissime dixit; quod vero ait, Non nisi ex te, hoc omnino virus est. Unde nullo modo Jeronimus hanc epistolam fecit, quia nec stilus nec fides congruit, quamvis in omnibus exemplaribus nomine ejus pertituletur, sed potius Julianus quidam Pelagianus, sicut dicit Beda in primo libro super C[anti]ca hiis fere verbis de illo scribens: In libro quem ad Demetriadium de institutione virginis scripsit, praedictus Julianus de potentia liberi arbitrii quomodo sentiat pandit. Quem videlicet librum nonnulli nostrum studiose legentes sancti et catholici doctoris Jeronimi esse temere arbitrantur, minime providentes quod suavitas eloquentiae demulcentis et haereseos perversitas seducentis manefestissime probat illius opusculum hoc non esse; quin potius ipse fidem ejus vel magis perfidiam in dialogo Accici et Cricoboli, quem vivente Pelagio edidit, cum adhuc Julianus ab eo puerulus quasi in caverna colubri nutriebatur, regulus divinis expugnaverit ac perculerit eloquiis.

> primo libro super cc[a] *Add. 3470, queried by Tanner*   Accici *queried by Tanner*
> caverna] caneria *Add. 3470, queried by Tanner*

> This note probably appeared in Bury's collection of Jerome letters, perhaps as a marginal gloss to work *203* above (cf. Oxford, New College, MS 129, fol. 158v) or at the end of the collection (cf. Bodl. MS Bodley 365, fol. 340r).

214 De cohabitatione clericorum et mulierum   *Promiseram . . . erit vobiscum*
     8.42.82.32.9.19.35

> *MF* IV 8 (title, incipit, explicit). Same as Augustinus *1.60* and Origines *404.23*. **82** Bury = B13. 193, 'Ieronimi epistole'. For the location numbers see the note to *132* above.

215 De disciplina et habitu virginali   8.42.82.32.9.19.35

> R6. 64. Same as Ciprianus *112.14*. **82** Bury = B13. 193, 'Ieronimi epistole'. For the location numbers see the note to *132* above.

Jeronimus *281. 216*

216 Ad virgines Enonenses ep. 1   *Carte exiguitas . . . nequam est*   8.42.82.
32.9.19.35

> *Hemonenses. CPL* 620 *ep.* 11. *CSEL* 54. 39. **82** Bury = B13. 193, 'Ieronimi epistole'. For the location numbers see the note to *132* above.

217 Ad Desiderium ep. 1   *Lectus sermo . . . volueris*   8.42.82.32.9.19.35

> *CPL* 620 *ep.* 47. *CSEL* 54. 345. **82** Bury = B13. 193, 'Ieronimi epistole'. For the location numbers see the note to *132* above.

218 Ad Paulum senem monachum   *Humanae . . . navigabunt*   8.42.82.35.
32.9.19

> *CPL* 620 *ep.* 10. *CSEL* 54. 35. **82** Bury = B13. 193, 'Ieronimi epistole'. For the location numbers see the note to *132* above.

219 Ad Crisotomum monachum   *Quocirca . . . scriberes*   8.42.82.32.9.19

> *CPL* 620 *ep.* 9. *CSEL* 54. 33, incipit 'Qui erga.' **82** Bury = B13. 193, 'Ieronimi epistole'. For the location numbers see the note to *132* above.

220 Ad Antonium monachum   *Dominus noster . . . impertias*   8.42.82.32.9.19

> *CPL* 620 *ep.* 12. *CSEL* 54. 41. **82** Bury = B13. 193, 'Ieronimi epistole'. For the location numbers see the note to *132* above.

221 Ad Theodosium et caeteros anachoritas intrinsecus commorantes ep. 1
Quam vellem . . . optati litoris   63.98.85.14.139.164

> *CPL* 620 *ep.* 2. *CSEL* 54. 10. **63** Crowland = B24. 31, 'epistole sue'. Location number **164** (and perhaps others via miscopying) is taken from R6. 78, 'Epistole eius'.

222 Ad Cromacium, Jovinianum et Eusebium   *Non debet . . . nescit*   8.42.82.
32.9.19.35

> Cromacium *queried by Tanner*

> *. . . Jouinum . . . CPL* 620 *ep.* 7. *CSEL* 54. 26. **82** Bury = B13. 193, 'Ieronimi epistole'. For the location numbers see the note to *132* above.

223 Ad Castorinam mat[e]rteram   *Johannes idem . . . absolvet*   8.42.82.32.
9.19.35

> materteram] matriteram *Add. 3470; Tanner, uncertain of this reading, has added the correction as a variant reading*

CPL 620 *ep.* 13. *CSEL* 54. 42. **82** Bury = B13. 193, 'Ieronimi epistole'. For the location numbers see the note to *132* above.

224 Ad Dommonem ep. 1   *Litterae tuae . . . ducere*   8.42.82.32.9.19.35

Vincent XVII 19 [83]. *CPL* 620 *ep.* 50. *CSEL* 54. 388. **82** Bury = B13. 193, 'Ieronimi epistole'. For the location numbers see the note to *132* above.

225 Ad B. Augustinum ep. 1   *In ipso . . . disceremus*   8.42.82.32.9.19

CPL 620 *ep.* 102. *CSEL* 55. 234. Explicit is that of paragraph 2; the final paragraph (3) is omitted in certain manuscripts; see *CSEL* 55. 236, note to line 13. **82** Bury = B13. 193, 'Ieronimi epistole'. For the location numbers see the note to *132* above.

p. 87]

226 Ad B. Augustinum ep. 1   *Anno . . . suscipiende*   8.42.82.32.9.19

CPL 620 *ep.* 103. *CSEL* 55. 237. **82** Bury = B13. 193, 'Ieronimi epistole'. For the location numbers see the note to *132* above.

227 Ad B. Augustinum ep. 1   *Crebras . . . pervenire*   8.42.82.32.9.19

CPL 620 *ep.* 105. *CSEL* 55. 242. **82** Bury = B13. 193, 'Ieronimi epistole'. For the location numbers see the note to *132* above.

228 Ad B. Augustinum ep. 1   *Tres simul . . . in angulo*   8.42.82.32.9.19

CPL 620 *ep.* 112. *CSEL* 55. 367. **82** Bury = B13. 193, 'Ieronimi epistole'. For the location numbers see the note to *132* above.

229 Ad B. Augustinum ep. 1   *Virum . . . amisimus*   8.42.82.32.9.19

CPL 620 *ep.* 134. *CSEL* 56/1. 261. **82** Bury = B13. 193, 'Ieronimi epistole'. For the location numbers see the note to *132* above.

230 Ad B. Augustinum ep. 1   *Omni quidem . . . beatissime papa*   8.42.82.32.9.19

CPL 620 *ep.* 141. *CSEL* 56/1. 290. **82** Bury = B13. 193, 'Ieronimi epistole'. For the location numbers see the note to *132* above.

231 Ad B. Augustinum et Alipium episcopos   *Sanctus . . . patres*   8.42.82.32.9.19

CPL 620 *ep.* 143. *CSEL* 56/1. 292. **82** Bury = B13. 193, 'Ieronimi epistole'. For the location numbers see the note to *132* above.

Jeronimus   *281. 232*

232 Expositionem fidei ad Augustinum et Alipium   *Credimus . . . comprobabit*

> *MF* IV 12 (whole entry); the words 'Ad Augustinum et Alipium' have been copied into this entry by mistake from *231* above. Pelagius; *CPL* 731. *PL* 45. 1716. [**82** Bury = Cambridge, Pembroke College, MS 108, fol. 50r (Bury F. 12).]

233 Symbolum fidei in Concilio Niceno editum   *Credimus in . . . sortiti sunt*   9.8.82.<u>166</u>

> R6. 111, Vincent XVII 19 [2], *MF* IV 6. *Ps.* Jerome; *CPL* 633 *ep.* 17 and 1746. *PL* 30. 176.

234 De fide S. Jeronimi   *Credo in unum . . . vitam aeternam*   94.<u>105</u>.15.<u>1</u>.82

> R6. 14. *Ps.* Jerome; *CPL* 553. *CCSL* 69. 273. This and *235* below often appear together in manuscripts: cf. Bodl. MS Bodley 147, fol. 78r-v.

235 De fide S. Jeronimi apud Betleem   *Credimus . . . praemia*   94.<u>105</u>.<u>1</u>.82

> 1.82] 182 *Add. 3470*

> R6. 15. *Ps.* Jerome; *CPL* 554. *CCSL* 69. 269. See *234* above.

236 De tribus quaestionibus ad Damasum omel. 3   82.<u>15</u>

> R6. 38, Vincent XVII 19 [30]. Same as *144–146* above.

237 De tribus naturis animae   *Anima tres . . . pacem cum Deo*

> *MF* IV 17 (whole entry).

238 Ad Marcellinum et Anapsichiam   *Tandiu . . . vera sancti*   <u>8</u>.<u>42</u>.<u>82</u>.<u>32</u>.<u>9</u>.<u>19</u>

> *CPL* 620 *ep.* 126. *CSEL* 56. 143, inc. 'Tandem'. **82** Bury = B13. 193, 'Ieronimi epistole'. For the location numbers see the note to *132* above.

239 Librum de ortu B. Mariae Virginis et de infantia Salvatoris a B. Matthaeo evangelista Hebraice scriptum transtulit in Latinum

> Source unidentified. Same as *9* above.

282 JOHANNES cognomento CRISOSTOMUS Antiochenae ecclesiae presbyter et monachus et postea Constantinopolitanus patriarcha et archiepiscopus floruit circa A. Ch. 394 temporibus Theodosii I et

Johannes Crisostomus *282.*

Archadii imperatorum, et scripsit in Graeca lingua ea quae sequuntur juxta Vincentium in Speculo.

Principium prologi Expositionis S. Johannis Crisostomi monachi et episcopi super evangelia Mathei a Burgundione, judice, natione et cive Pisano, de Graeco in Latinum perfecte et complete translatae A. Ch. 1147: Cum B. Johannis Crisostomi super evangelia S. Mathei duae expositiones impositae ab eo editae proferuntur et nulla earum debito fine integre translata esse perhibetur, d[ominu]s papa Eugenius III praedictas commentationes congrue consummationi tradere satagens ad Antiochenum patriarcham scripsit admonendo ut quod praedictis commentationibus deerat, ejus interventu ab aliquo interprete suppleretur. Ipse vero patriarcha sive desidia sive inscitia hoc minime complens expositionem tamen ejusdem S. Johannis Crisostomi perfectam super eundem evangelistam Graecis literis eidem summo pontifici mandare curavit. Quam cum praesul ille Romanus accepisset, mihi Burgundioni, judice suo natione Pisano mea enucleatione perficiendam commisit. Mea igitur relatione eam a praedictis duabus translationibus omnifariam discrepare cognoscens, et hanc tertiam translationem mihi praecepit promulgare, cujus omnino meritis confidens et mandatis ejus obtemperans, praedictum opus integre de Graeco in Latinum fideliter transtuli sermonem. Haec tertia reliquis duabus [p. 88] translationibus solertis lectoris judicio non immerito praeponatur. In 90 autem omeliis librum hunc divisit S. Johannes Crisostomus, nullamque fere totius evangelii secundum Mathaeum dictionem misterio vacuam dereliquit, et in morale semper unamquamque concludit omeliam. Prima omelia sic incipit: Oportebit quidem nos non indigere eo quod etc. 2da omelia: Liber generationis Jesu Christi etc. Tercia: Nunquid meministi mandati etc. Omelia nonagesima et ultima : Altera autem die quae est post Parasceven etc. Ubique error seipsum etc. Explicit perfectum Johannis Crisostomi super Mathaeum.[a]

Principium prologi Expositionis S. Johannis Crisostomi monachi et episcopi super evangelium Mathaei imperfecte et incomplete de Graeco in Latinum translatae: Sicut referunt Mathaeum scribere etc. Capitulum primum et omelia prima: Liber generationis etc. Liber quasi apotheca gratiarum etc. Capitulum 25 et homelia ultima: Simile est regnum coelorum decem virginibus etc. Notandum quod priorem quidem parabolam etc.[b]

Principium prologi Burgundionis judicis et civis Pisani in commentatione Johannis Crisostomi monachi et episcopi super evangelio S. Johannis evangelistae de Graeco in Latinum ab eo translata tempore papae Eugenii tertii: Omnibus in Christo fidelibus fratribus Burgundio judex et civis Pisanus in Domino salutem. Cum Cons[tan]tinopoli pro negotiis publicis patriae meae a concivibus meis ad imperatorem Manuelem etc. Et infra: Explanationem evangelii S. Johannis evangelistae a B. Johanne Crisostomo Constantinopoleως patriarcha et archiepiscopo mirabiliter editam de Graeco in Latinum vertere statui sermonem, tum quia ejus-

Johannes 282. 1

dem sancti patris commentationem super evangelia S. Mathaei, jam pridem papae Eugenio III integre translatam tradideram, tum quia hujus S. Johannis evangelistae expositionis penuria apud Latinos maxima erat. Nullum enim alium nisi S. Augustinum eum continue exponentem inveni. Et infra: Deinde per duos annos continuos Deo autore totum librum commentationis de Graeco in Latinum de verbo ad verbum transferens integre consummavi. Et infra: Partitur autem hic S. Johannes Crisostomus hunc librum in octaginta et octo omelias, quas in unaquaque septimana duabus diebus Sabbato scilicet Dominica populo in ecclesia coadunato confecit. In unaquaque fere omelia in initio prologum et in fide ex textu uniuscujusque omeliae materia sumpta morale componens etc. Omelia prima sic incipit: Quoniam agonum quae foris sunt inspectatores existunt. Omelia 2da: In primo erat Verbum. Siquidem Johannes nobis loqui etc. Omelia 88ma et ultima super capitulum evangeli 21^{mum} et ultimum: Simon Johannis amas me etc. Multa quidem alia sunt quae possunt dari nobis etc. Explicit perfectum Johannis Crisostomi super Johannem. Aliae sunt translationes expositionis Johannis Crisostomi super Johannem prius editae, quae communiter jam leguntur in ecclesiis et conventibus religiosorum.[c]

omeliae materia sumpta *queried by Tanner*

[a] Burgundio Pisanus, prologue, *Chrysostomus super Matthaeum*; part. ed. Martène & Durand, 1. 817. [b] Ps. Chrysostomus, *Opus imperfectum in Matthaeum*, prologue. [c] Burgundio Pisanus, *Chrysostomus*, ed. Martène & Durand, 1. 818.

Registrum 9, Vincent XVIII 42 (references are followed by numbers in brackets [1, 2, etc.] that indicate the sequence of titles in the chapter), *Manipulus florum* IX, Cassiodorus.
The sequence of the first six titles below may have been provided by Vincent but all of the first twenty-nine works (save *12*) either come from or are supplemented by manuscripts of Chrysostom's works, most or all at Bury; several of the sermons reported here appear together attributed to Chrysostom in an English manuscript, Hereford Cathedral, MS O. III. 13 (Hereford Cathedral, s. xii). The remainder of the entry, fourteen titles, is the usual mixture from Kirkestede's sources, including four more from manuscripts (*39–41, 49*).
Part of the entry for *4* below appears on the front paste-down of Cambridge, Pembroke College, MS 18 (Bury J. 28); see p. lxii above.
See A. Wilmart, 'La collection des 38 homélies latines de S. Jean Chrysostome', *JTS* 19 (1917–1918) 305–327.

1 De hoc quod nemo laeditur nisi a seipso lib. 1   *Scio quod . . . non laeditur*
8.90.42.82.13.15

Johannes Crisostomus   *282. 4*

R9. 10, Vincent XVIII 42 [1], *MF* IX 4. Wilmart 39. Ed. A. M. Malingrey in *Sacris erudiri* 16 (1965) 327–54. **82** Bury = B13. 82c.

2 De reparatione lapsi ad Theodorum monachum ejusdem monasterii cujus et ipse erat monachus lib. 1   *Quis dabit . . . alias non quaeras*   89.42.82.43. 8.90

quaeras *queried by Tanner*

R9. 7, Vincent XVIII 42 [2]. Wilmart 42. Ed. J. Dumortier, SChr 117 (1966) 257–322. Same as Augustinus *1.260*. Location numbers **82** to **90** were taken in error from R9. 8 (*3 below*), but Bury did possess this work. **42** Reading = B71. 101h. / **82** Bury = B13. 82a.

3 De compunctione lib. 2   *Dum te . . . opera negligenti*   8.90.9.42.82.13.15

R9. 8, Vincent XVIII 42 [3]. Wilmart 40. Ed. W. Schmitz, *Monumenta tachygraphica codicis Parisiensis latini 2718* 2 (Hanover 1883); explicit is that of Book I. **42** Reading = B71. 101g. / **82** Bury = B13. 82b.

p. 89]

4 Super Mathaeum imperfecte translatas omelias 90   *Liber quasi . . .*   43.35. 15.20.63.50.20

The second 20] xx R

R9. 31, Vincent XVIII 42 [4], *MF* IX 1. Ps. Chrysostom, *Opus imperfectum in Matthaeum. CPL* 707; Stegmüller *Bibl.* 4350. Erasmus edition, *Opera* 3 (Basel 1530) 474. [**82** Bury = B13. 38a = Cambridge, Pembroke College, MS 18, fol. 1r (Bury J. 28), incomplete and incipit does not match; Pembroke College, MS 19 (Bury J. 32), a 15th-cent. manuscript, was perhaps copied from an earlier Bury exemplar.]

Et nota quod istae omeliae raro inveniuntur omnes simul, nec servatur idem numerus illarum omeliarum in diversis libris, quia in quibusdam libris quotantur tres vel quatuor omeliae, ubi in aliis non quotatur nisi una omelia. Nec omeliae ponuntur in ordine juxta textum Mathaei, quia in quibusdam exemplaribus ab 8vo capite transit ad 19^{mum} caput et continuat usque ad 22^{m} caput evangelii. Deinde redit ad 10^{m} caput continuans usque ad 21^{m}, 23^{m}, 24^{m}, et sic procedit diversimode.

The words 'Et nota — simul' are taken from Vincent. The note ('nec seruatur—diuersimode') discussing the order of the homelies was written by Kirkestede in slightly longer form on the front pastedown of Cambridge, Pembroke College, MS 18 (Bury J. 28); printed above, p. lxii n. 138.

Johannes *282. 5*

5 Super Johannem omelias Burgundione translatas 88   *Qui agonum . . . nunc et semper*   9.104.108.94.173

> R9. 33 (location numbers **104, 108**) and R9. 29 (a sermon beginning 'Quis agnouir' that provided location number **9**), Vincent XVIII 42 [5], and *MF* IX 2 (incipit, explicit). Translation of Burgundio of Pisa; Stegmüller *Bibl.* 4355. Location number **94** arrived via the convoluted route described at *51* below. A manuscript at **173** Babwell may have been the source for the version of the title given here.

6 Super Epistolam ad Hebraeos omelias 35   *Multifarie . . . offerentes*   8.9.43. 15.82.20.63

> R9. 11, Vincent XVIII 42 [6]. *PG* 63. 237. **82** Bury = B13. 38b = Cambridge, Pembroke College, MS 18, fols. 57r–164r (Bury J. 28).

7 Super psalmum 50^m scilicet Miserere lib. 2   *Pictores . . . cum sanctis*   43.8. 15.1.63.46.82

> R9. 9. *Ps.* Chrysostom; Wilmart 1 and 2. Stegmüller *Bibl.* 4337,5. *Opera* (Basel 1547), 1. 723–51. **82** Bury = B13. 48b.

8 Super psalmum Qui habitat expositionem   *Psalmum 90^m Deo . . . tradam vobis*   15

> Psalmum 90^m Deo *queried by Tanner*   15] xv *R*

> R9. 40, 'Omelie super Psalterium'. *Ps.* Chrysostom. *PLS* 4. 786 *serm.* 19, expl. 'tradatur uobis'. Cf. Hereford Cathedral, MS O. III. 13, fol. 29v.

9 Super psalmum Dominus regit expos.   *Circulo . . . in gaudium*   15.82

> 15] xv *R*

> R9. 40, 'Omelie super Psalterium'. *Ps.* Chrysostom; cf. *CPL* 915 *serm.* 3. *PLS* 4. 825 *serm.* 30. Cf. Hereford Cathedrtal, MS O. III. 13, fol. 55r.

10 Super quosdam versus psalmorum omel. 16   *Deus generis . . .*   15.82

> 15] xv *R*

> R9. 40, 'Omelie super Psalterium'. *Ps.* Chrysostom; cf. *CPL* 915 *serm.* 2. *PLS* 4. 741 *serm.* 1. Cf. Hereford Cathedral, MS O. III. 13, fol. 1v.

11 De laudibus Pauli omel. 7   *Nichil . . . Jesu Christi*   42.13.15.1.20.39.63

> R9. 25, Vincent XVIII 42 [7], *MF* IX 5 (explicit does not correspond). *PG* 50. 473–514.

Johannes Crisostomus   *282. 19*

12   De decollatione S. Johannis   50.<u>63</u>.39.15

> R9. 3. Perhaps *ps.* Chrysostom (Petrus Chrysologus), *CPL* 930 = *PL* 52. 549; or perhaps the same as *13* below.

13   Contra mulierem bonam et malam serm. 1   *Heu me . . . commorem*   15.<u>63</u>.<u>39</u>.<u>82</u>.<u>104</u>

> 63] 53 *R*
>
> R9. 20 (title). *Ps.* Chrysostom, *In decollatione B. Iohannis Baptistae; CPL* 931. *PL* 96. 1508. Explicit unidentified. See also *12* above.

14   De exilio et expulsione sui ipsius   *Multi quidem . . . gratias ago*   8.<u>13</u>.<u>1</u>.<u>39</u>.<u>82</u>.<u>104</u>

> R9. 14. Wilmart 29. *PG* 52. 431. Location number **8** is taken from R9. 15–19, where it appears in company with these same *Registrum* location numbers. **82** Bury = B13. 82d.

15   De egressu suo ab Asia serm. 1   *Moyses . . . ad salutem*   8.<u>1</u>.<u>82</u>.<u>104</u>

> R9. 15. Wilmart 36. *PG* 52. 421. **82** Bury = B13. 82e.

16   Post exilii prioris redditum serm. 1   *Quid dicam . . . per immortalia*   63.<u>39</u>.<u>20</u>.<u>15</u>.<u>114</u>.<u>43</u>

> R9. 13, 'Sermones eiusdam' (location numbers only). *CPG* 4398. *PG* 52. 441–2. See also *18* below.

17   De praedictione Judae et passione Domini serm. 1   *Paucis hodie . . .*   8.<u>1</u>.<u>39</u>.<u>82</u>.<u>104</u>.<u>15</u>.<u>63</u>

> R9. 16, and R9. 13, 'Sermones eiusdem' (location numbers **15, 63**). Wilmart 10. *De proditione Iudae*. Printed Basel 1547, 3. 816. **82** Bury = B13. 82f.

18   De cruce et passione Domini serm.   *Quid dicam . . .*   8.<u>1</u>.<u>63</u>.<u>82</u>.<u>104</u>.<u>15</u>

> R9. 18, and R9. 13, 'Sermones eiusdem' (location number **15**). A second spurious sermon with this incipit (see *16* above); Wilmart 13. Printed Basel 1547, 3. 836.

19   De cruce et latrone serm. 1   *Hodierna . . . mereamur*   8.<u>1</u>.<u>39</u>.<u>82</u>.<u>63</u>.<u>15</u>

> R9. 17, and R9. 13, 'Sermones eiusdem' (location numbers **63, 15**). Wilmart 11. Printed Basel 1547, 3. 826. **82** Bury = B13. 82g.

Johannes   *282. 20*

20 De ascensione Domini serm. 1   *Quum de cruce . . .*   8.1.39.82.63.104.50

> R9. 19. Wilmart 14. Printed Basel 1547, 3. 865. Incipit 'Quando de cruce'.
> **82** Bury = B13. 82h.

21 Quomodo primus homo praelatus est omni creaturae serm. 1   *Dignitas . . . percipiat*   97.63.39.20.15

> R9. 39 (title, location number **97**), and R9. 13, 'Sermones eiusdem' (location numbers **63** to **15**). Ps. Chrysostom; CPL 921. PL 95. 1205.

22 De lapsu primi hominis serm. 1   *Deus sine . . . superhabundent*   70.97.63.39.20 15

> R9. 13, 'Sermones eiusdem' (location numbers **63** to **15**). Ps. Chrysostom; PLS 4. 793. Cf. Hereford Cathedral, MS O. III. 13, fol. 34r. Location number **97** is repeated from *21* above.

23 De Adam et Eva serm. 1   *Deus institutor . . . contrarium*   156.166.63.39.20

> R9. 2, and R9. 13, 'Sermones eiusdem' (location numbers **63** to **20**). Ps. Chrysostom; CPL 915 serm. 30. PLS 4. 797. Cf. Hereford Cathedral, MS O. III. 13, fol. 35v.

24 De Jacob et Esau serm. 1   *Portabat . . . alienum*   82.63.99.20.15

> 99] 39 *R*

> R9. 13, 'Sermones eiusdem' (location numbers **63** to **15**). Ps. Chrysostom; CPL 924. Ed. F. Liverani, *Spicilegium Liberianum* 1 (Florence 1863) 185.

25 De Joseph serm. 1   *Mittitur . . . defuerit*   82.63.99.39.20.15

> R9. 13, 'Sermones eiusdem' (location numbers **63, 39** to **15**). Ps. Chrysostom; CPL 925. Ed. Liverani, 1. 187. Location number **99** is perhaps an error compounded, a ghost from the mistake in *24* above.

26 De Moyse serm. 1   *Stabat . . . quod admisit*   82.63.39.20.15

> R9. 13, 'Sermones eiusdem' (location numbers **63** to **15**). Ps. Chrysostom; CPL 927. Ed. Liverani, 1. 190.

27 De Jeremia serm. 1   *Magnum . . . imperator*   82.63.39.20.15

> R9. 13, 'Sermones eiusdem' (location numbers **63** to **15**). Ps. Chrysostom; CPL 928. Printed Venice 1549, vol. 1, fol. 288v.

Johannes Crisostomus 282. 36

28 De nocturnis vigiliis et officiis diurnis   *Dominus filios . . . collocaverat*
82.20.19

19] xix *R*

R9. 37. Pseudonymous; unprinted. **82** Bury = Cambridge, Pembroke College, MS 18, fol. 164r (Bury J. 28), title added by Kirkestede.

29 Unde vivit anima et unde vivit caro meditationem   *Dum anima . . . creavit*
63.104.105.82

Ps. Anselm. *PL* 158. 733.

30 Quod nemo desperet de misericordia Dei tract. 1

R9. 38 (title varies).

31 De confessione et poenitentia tract. 1   8.15.63.97.104.21

21] xxi *R*

R9. 26 (whole entry).

32 De conversatione vitae et institutione morum lib. 1

Work and source unidentified.

33 De militia Christiana   82.166

R9. 23. *Ps.* Chrysostom; *CPL* 1148. Printed Basel 1547, 5. 739.

34 De militia spirituali   82.166

R9. 24. *Ps.* Chrysostom; *CPL* 1147. Printed Basel 1547, 5. 736.

35 Dialogorum ejus et Basilii de dignitate sacerdotali lib. 6   *Michi quidem
. . . tabernaculum*   15.39.21

21] xxi *R*

Whole entry from R9. 35 (part of the title, location numbers) and *MF* IX 3 (rest of the title, incipit, explicit).

p. 90]

36 De sacramento baptismatis tract. 1   136.144

Source unidentified.

Johannes   *282. 37*

37 Instituta fratrum   43

    fratrum] patrum *R*

    R9. 22 (whole entry).

38 De jejunio et eleemosina tract. 1   8.97.104.105

    R9. 12 (whole entry).

39 De fide Abrahae et immolatione Ysaac serm. 1   *Fides est . . . revocaverit*

    Ps. Chrysostom; *CPL* 923. *PL* 95. 1210.

40 De oratione Dominica expos. 1   *Annua nobis . . . bonae voluntatis*

    Annua] Anna *Add. 3470, queried by Tanner*

    Ps. Chrysostom; *CPL* 915. Cf. Hereford Cathedral, MS O. III. 13, fol. 50r.

41 De symbolo expos. 1   *Super fabricam . . . scribentur*

    Ps. Chrysostom; *CPL* 915 serm. 23. *PLS* 4. 481. Cf. Hereford Cathedral, MS O. III. 13, fol. 52v.

42 Super illud M[a]t[thaei]: Egrediente omel. 1

    Matthaei] Mt *Add. 3470, queried by Tanner*

    Perhaps whole entry from R9. 30, 'Super illud: Egressus Iesus etc.'.

43 Super illud Lucae: Erat Jesus ejiciens omel. 1

    Source unidentified.

44 Super illud Lucae: Erunt signa omel. 1

    Source unidentified.

45 Super omnes epistolas Pauli secundum Cassiodorum

    Cassiodorus I. 8. 15 (whole entry).

46 Super Actus Apostolorum omel. 55

    Cassiodorus I. 9. 1 (whole entry).

47 Vetus et Novum Testamentum a principio usque ad finem declaravit secundum Cassiodorum

> Cassiodorus I. *praef.* 4 (whole entry).

48 De Machabeis serm. 1

> Source unidentified.

49 De poenitentia epistolam vel sermonem 1   *Pura mente . . . promerebis*

> Bloomfield 4301 (inc. 'Prouida mente'). This sermon appears in, for example, BL MS Royal 5 C. VI, fol. 142r (Worcester, s. xiv).

50 Contra Judaeos lib. 1

> Source unidentified.

51 Super Cantica Canticorum   <u>94</u>

> Entries *51–53* derive wholly from R44. 1–3, 'Opera Iohannis' (which actually are works of John, abbot of Ford, recorded from a manuscript at <u>**94**</u> Ford); Kirkestede's remark after *53* below ('These are attributed to a certain Bishop John . . .') presumably refers not just to *53* but to all three of these, although the extent of the reference is not indicated by any mark in Add. 3470.
>
> R44. 1.

52 Super Jeremiam   <u>94</u>

> R44. 2. See note to *51* above.

53 Omelias   <u>94</u>

> R44. 3. See note to *51* above.

Ista attitulantur cuidam Johanni episcopo; utrum Crisostomo vel alteri dubitatur.

283 INNOCENTIUS III papa floruit circa A. Ch. 1198 et scripsit

> *Registrum* 30.
> *Registrum* was the initial basis for this entry, complemented and extended by manuscripts at Bury and neighbouring houses.

Innocentius III *283. 1*

1 De miseria hominis sive de contemptu mundi lib. 3   *Quare de vulva . . . ignis ardens*   12.20.25.82.19.9

> 12] xii *R*

> R30. 1 (half the title, and location number **12**), R30. 3 (rest of the title, and location numbers **20, 19**). *PL* 217. 701. Location number **25** (xxv *R*) probably comes by a copying error from R30. 2. **82** Bury = BL MS Royal 5 A. VIII, fols. 87rb–108r (Bury A. 52); BL MS Royal 8 F. XIV, fol. 180v (Bury G. 15).

2 De missa et ejus expositione lib. 3   *Cum apostolice . . . subscribendum*   114. 128.124.19.15.115

> R30. 2. *PL* 217. 773. [**82** Bury = Cambridge, Pembroke College, MS 94, fol. 135r (Bury O. 2).]

3 De sacramentis ecclesiae tract. 1   24

> 24] xxiiii *R*

> R30. 5 (whole entry).

4 De symonia tract. 1   24

> 24] xxiiii *R*

> R30. 7 (whole entry).

5 Super 7 psalmos poenitentiales tractatum elegantem   *Ne inter . . . nominis Jesu*   20.82

> R30. 6. *PL* 217. 967.

6 De festis sermones   *Cum venit . . .*   128

> R30. 4. *PL* 217. 313.

7 De conversione S. Pauli serm. 1   *Nolo mortem . . . Maximum ex[emplu]m . . .*

> exemplum] ex^m *Add. 3470, queried by Tanner*

> *Sermones de sanctis* 10. *PL* 217. 493. Incipit 'Nolo mortem . . . (Ez 33:11). Huius sententiae manifestum exemplum'.

Innocentius III *283. 14*

8 In dedicatione ecclesiae serm. 1 *Introibo . . . in secula*

   Sermones de tempore 27. PL 217. 433; incipit is that of the biblical verse, explicit that of the benediction. Same as *14* below.

9 In dedicatione ecclesiae serm. 1 *Egressus . . . Duo sunt . . .*

   Sermones de tempore 29. PL 217. 441. Incipit 'Egressus . . . (Lc 19:1). Duo sunt'.

10 Epistolae decretales lib. 5 *Devotioni vestrae . . .*

   The *Compilatio tertia decretalium*, drawn from the decretals of Innocent III; ed. A. Agustín, *Antiquae collectiones decretalium* (Lérida 1576) 424–600.

11 Epithalamium de nuptiis sponsi et sponsae lib. 3 *Gaude frater . . . in domo tua*

   Epithalamium] Phiam *Add. 3470, queried by Tanner*

   PL 217. 949.

12 Constitutiones in concilio generali Laterani anno pontificatus sui 17° *Firmiter credimus . . .*

   [**82** Bury = Cambridge, Pembroke College, MS 101, fol. 69r (Bury S. 65), without rubric.]

13 De scaccario moralem tractatum *Mundus ille . . . nulla est*

   scaccario] sanctuario *Add. 3470, queried by Tanner*

   [**82** Bury = Bodl. MS Bodley 240, p. 762 (Bury H. 55), attributed to Innocent; this manuscript is almost certainly too late to have been used for this entry, but its contents were copied from earlier Bury books. Explicit unidentified.]

14 De latria et dulia lib. 1 *Universorum . . . propter salvationem* 63

   Iste liber continet cap. 19

   The incipit and explicit are those of the text. Same as *8* above.

Ignatius *284.*

p. 91]

284 IGNATIUS episcopus Antiochenae ecclesiae et discipulus B. Johannis evangelistae floruit anno <*blank*> et scripsit juxta Jeronimum

> Vincent XI 57, Jerome, c. 16.
>
> Works *6–8* represent a collection of spurious Ignatius letters allegedly translated by Robert Grosseteste; see S. H. Thomson, *The Writings of Robert Grosseteste* (Cambridge 1940), 58–62.

1 Ad Ephesios ep. 1

> Jerome 16 (whole entry).

2 Ad Magnensiones ep. 1

> Jerome 16 (whole entry).

3 Ad Trojenses ep. 1

> Jerome 16 (whole entry).

4 Ad Romanos ep. 1

> Jerome 16 (whole entry).

5 Ad Philadelphios et Smirneos et Policarpum ep. 1

> Jerome 16 (whole entry).

6 Ad B. Mariam matrem Christi ep. 1   *Christofera . . . confortentur*   82

> Spurious; ed. J. B. Lightfoot, *The Apostolic Fathers*, 2/3 (London 1889²) 70, *ep.* 3.

7 Ad S. Johannem evangelistam ep. 1   *Johanni sancto . . . nostro*   82

> Spurious; Lightfoot, 69 *ep.* 1.

8 Ad S. Johannem evangelistam ep. aliam   *Johanni sancto . . . jubeas et*   82

> Spurious; Lightfoot, 70 *ep.* 2.

9 Epistolas alias ad diversos xii

> Vincent XI 57 (whole entry).

285 JOHANNES CASSIANUS vir illustris, prudens et facundus monachus, in Massilia Galliae presbiter ordinatus, multa scripsit utilia, inter quae Patrum antiquorum instituta et 24 seniorum collationes eorundem conscripsit. Quae certe opuscula multam aedificationem continent animarum et luculento sermone nitescunt. Nec inter multa antiquorum opuscula quicquam ad spirituales profectus atque perfectionis apicem tendenti utilius quidam doctores arbitrantur se legisse, licet apocrifa reputari videantur ejus opuscula in decreto papae Gelasii et etiam juxta Genadium libro De viris illustribus. Prosper scribat adversus ejusdem opuscula et infamet ea velut nociva, quae tamen ecclesia Dei salutaria probat.[a] Nam Beatus Dominicus, ut in ejus vita legitur, librum illum qui Collationes patrum dicitur studiose legens ac vigilanter intelligens salutis in eo rimatus semitas magnum perfectionis apicem apprehendit. Agit siquidem liber ille de cordis puritate, de vitiis, et de perfectione omnium virtutum, cujus frequens lectio Christi discipulum ad multam cordis puritatem, ad contemplationis arcem et totius spiritualis disciplinae perfectionem gratia opitulante perducit. Haec Vincentius in Speculo historiali lib. xx cap. 14.[b] Item B. pater Benedictus opuscula Johannis Cassiani, videlicet Instituta patrum et Collationes eorum monachis suis recommendat ad collationem in capitulo legenda, ut habetur in regula sua cap. xlii et cap. lxxiii. Quae quidem regula a B. Gregorio papa et ab universali ecclesia est approbata, ut habetur in 2do libro Dialogorum B. Gregorii et 18 q. 11 ca. *Perniciosam.* Et sciendum quod B. Benedictus nihil in regula monachorum praecepit sacris canonibus obvians vel repugnans. Probatur enim in canone monachis esse licita quae in regula conceduntur vel etiam inducuntur, sicut patet 16 q. i *Superiori autoritate* et Extra. *Ne clerici vel monachi* c. 1. Item monachi sunt ad observantiam regulae compellendi Extra. comm. *Relatum.* Item monachis non solum legenda est regula sed quam vulgariter exponenda Extra. *De regula*, et *Ne magistro* lib. vii. Decretum etiam Gelasii non obviat supra dictis. Licet enim opuscula Cassiani de quibus loquitur publice in ecclesia legi non debeant, in capitulo tamen monachorum sicut praecipit regula S. Benedicti sine periculo legi possunt. Floruit autem Johannes Cassianus circa A. Ch. 460.

Cassiodorus libro De institutione divinarum literarum sic ait ad monachos suos: Cassianus de libero arbitrio a B. Prospero jure culpatus est; ejus [p. 92] tamen opuscula sedulo legite et libenter audite. Sed in rebus talibus excedentem monemus ut sub cautela legere debeatis.[c]

Bernardus Cassinensis, expositor super regulam S. Benedicti, super illud: Collationes patrum et Instituta et Vita eorum, etc. Tres tibi libros B. Bened[ictus] specialiter nominavit, ut scias eas non negligendos sed a monachis perfecti volentibus et ad perfectionem tendentibus frequenter esse legendos. Primus est Collatio patrum habens 24 libros. Secundus Instituta patrum, qui liber in 12 libros partitur. Tertius liber est, quem Vitas patrum appellamus, in quo nonnulla aedificatio nobis patrum

Johannes Cassianus *285*.

ostenditur per exempla. Item capitulo regulae xlii: Mox ut surrexerunt a coena etc., et infra: Legat unus Collationes vel Vitas patrum, super quo idem expositor: Has duas nominatim non sine causa expressit scripturas quam multum habent fidei devotionem sanctosque mores aedificare et nutrire et ad contemplationis altitudinem promovere.[d]

> Prosper] Prospero *Add. 3470, queried by Tanner*   Beatus Dominicus] Beatus Vincentius *Add. 3470, queried by Tanner*   sedulo] sedule *Cassiodorus*   Bernardus Cassinensis] Bern. Cassiodorus *Add. 3470, queried by Tanner*   exempla] extra *Add. 3470, queried by Tanner*

[a] Vincent XX 14–15; *Decretum Gelasianum* V; Gennadius c. 85. [b] Vincent XX 14. [c] This lengthy passage with its several citations (beginning 'Item B. pater Benedictus'), which also appears in the *Catalogus*' introduction (p. 17), is supplied from an anonymous notice on Cassian found in Cambridge, Pembroke College, MS 92, fol. ii[r–v], a manuscript provided for the abbey by Kirkestede; the last part of the notice was written by Kirkestede. [d] Bernard of Cassino, *In regulam S. Benedicti expositio*, ed. A. M. Caplet (Monte Cassino 1894) 433 ('Tres tibi — per exempla') and 295 ('Mox ut—promouere').

Registrum 32, Vincent XX 14, 15 (works *1–5, 7–8*); Gennadius c. 85 (work *11*).
For this entry Kirkestede listed the contents of Cambridge, Pembroke College, MS 92 (Bury J. 35), a manuscript commissioned by him; the contents of the manuscript mirror the sequence in Vincent. Kirkestede added to these an **82** for Bury, supplemented by location numbers from the *Registrum*; and he added to the end six titles from his bibliographic sources. Portions of this entry appear in his hand on fol. 2r–v of Pembroke 92 (see preceding paragraph).
Speculum coenobitarum 25.

1 De institutis et regulis coenobiorum et de habitu monachi et canonica oratione et de psalmorum modo lib. 4   *Veteris . . . possidetur*   93.156.82.114.43

> R32. 4, Vincent XX 14–15. CPL 513. CSEL 17. 3–78, Books I–IV. **82** Bury = B13. 257; Cambridge, Pembroke College, MS 92, fol. 1r (Bury J. 35).

2 De origine et qualitate et remediis octo principalium vitiorum lib. 8 *Quintus . . . credamus*   93.156.82.114.43

> R32. 7, Vincent XX 14–15. Books V–XII of the *De institutis* (*1* above). CSEL 17. 81–231. The location numbers are repeated from *1* above. **82** Bury = Cambridge, Pembroke College, MS 92, fol. 25v (Bury J.35); manuscripts often treated Books I–IV as *De institutis* proper, and Books V–XII had the title 'De origine [etc.]' and though Pembroke 92 has no separate rubric for this section of the *De institutis*, it lists the title separately in the table of contents: 'Libri [Johannis Cassiani] de origine et remediis .viii. principalium uiciorum'.

Johannes Cassianus 285. 9

3 Ad Leontium et Elladium x collationes patrum in S[c]ithi[otica] commorantium quas ab eis audierat   *Debitum . . . servaverint*   93.82.89.114. 105.43

> Sithi *Add. 3470, queried by Tanner*

> R32. 3, Vincent XX 14–15. *CPL* 512. *Collationes* Books I–X. *CSEL* 13. 3–308. **82** Bury = B13. 258; Cambridge, Pembroke College, MS 92, fol. 73r (Bury J. 35); the *Collationes* in Pembroke 92 are referred to in a note by Kirkestede on a flyleaf of Lambeth Palace Library, MS 218 pt 2, see p. xlvi and n. 66 above.

4 Ad Honoratum et Eucherium collationes 7   *Dum virtutem . . . displicet*   82.83

> Vincent XX 14–15. *CPL* 512. *Collationes* Books XI–XVII. *CSEL* 13. 312–500. **82** Bury = B13. 259, 'Collationes patrum'; Cambridge, Pembroke College, MS 92, fol. 163r (Bury J. 35); Lambeth Palace Library, MS 218, fol. 91r (Bury J. 23).

5 Ad Invenianum, Minervium, Leontium et Theodorum alias collationes 7   *Emissis . . . domitetur*   82.83

> Vincent XX 14–15. *CPL* 512. *Collationes* Books XVIII–XXIV. *CSEL* 13. 503–711, explicit 'comitetur'. **82** Bury = B13. 259, 'Collationes patrum'; Cambridge, Pembroke College, MS 92, fol. 219r (Bury J. 35), explicit 'domitetur' (fol. 281r).

6 De vita monachorum regulam 1   127.126.114.108.1.20

> R32. 6 (whole entry).

7 Item quatuor res omnia monachorum professioni necessaria continentes

> Vincent XX 14–15 (whole entry).

8 De incarnatione Domini contra Nestorium lib. 7   15.20.98.23

> 23] xxiiii *R*

> Whole entry from R32. 8 and Vincent XX 14–15.

9 Librum poenitentialem   24

> 24] xxiiii *R*

> R32. 1 (whole entry; title *Penitenciarius eius*).

Johannes Cassianus   *285. 10*

  10 De Aegiptiacis monachis <u>166</u>

      R32. 2 (whole entry).

  11 De libero arbitrio lib. 1

      Gennadius 85 (whole entry).

286 JOHANNES DAMASCENES monachus et presbiter, cui beata virgo Maria manum abscissam miraculose restituit, floruit circa A.D. 387 et scripsit

    Manipulus florum XI, 'Libri Prosperi et Damasceni'.
    Works *1–5* represent a Latin corpus of five works of Damascenus that travelled together; see, for example, Oxford, Magdalen College, MS 192. Source of the rest of the entry is unidentified.
    Speculum coenobitarum 23.

  1 Libros sententiarum 4   *Deum nemo . . . fructificantes*   82

      MF XI 3 (incipit, explicit; title does not correspond). *De fide orthodoxa.* Ed. E. M. Buytaert (St Bonaventure, NY, 1955). **82** Bury = BL MS Royal 7 B. ix, fol. 83r (Bury D. 6), in which Kirkestede has labelled this title 'rarus liber' on the table of contents (fol. ii^v); Cambridge, Pembroke College, MS 20, fol. 1r (Bury J. 57); Cambridge, Pembroke College, MS 34, fol. 211v (Bury T. 7); Cambridge, Pembroke College, MS 94, fol. 185r, modern foliation (Bury O. 2).

    Quos quidem libros quidam Burgundio nomine transtulit de Graeco in Latinum A. Ch. 1146 in quibus libris continetur orthodoxae fidei traditio

      A version of this notice concerning Burgundio of Pisa appears in the rubric of Cambridge, Pembroke College, MS 94, fol. 185r (Bury O. 2), and in many of the manuscripts of his translation.

  2 Ad Cosmam episcopum logicarum lib. 1   *Ens commune . . . invertibile*   82

      invertibile] imitibile *Add. 3470, queried by Tanner*

  3 De 100 haeresibus   *Omnium haeresium . . . alterum*

  4 De introductione dogmatum lib. 1   *In nomine Patris . . . vestigia*

  5 De trisagio ep. 1   *Ejus quod ad . . . orantes*

      [**82** Bury = Bodl. MS Bodley 240, pp. 753–759 (Bury H. 55); see the note to Innocentius *283.13*.]

6 De assumptione B. Mariae sermonem

    Source unidentified.

7 Item scripsit de medicina

    Source unidentified.

8 Item scripsit de grammatica

    Source unidentified.

9 Item historiam sanctorum Barlaam et Josaphat transtulit de Graeco in Latinum

    Source unidentified.

10 Item scripsit vitam S. Johannis Eleemosynarii

    Source unidentified.

p. 93]

287 JOHANNES SCOTUS philosophus et monachus et B. Bedae discipulus, unus de fundatoribus studii Parisiensis, floruit circa A. Ch. <*blank*> et scripsit juxta Vincentium lib. 28 cap. 83

    Vincent XXV 42.
    Bale, *Index*, 247, 'ex utroque Anglorum catalogo'.
    Ware extracts, fol. 133v.
    Sharpe, *Latin Writers*, 311–12.
    See especially M. Lapidge and R. Sharpe, *A Bibliography of Celtic-Latin Literature 400–1200* (Dublin 1985) 695–713.

1 Librum quem Perisicion merimorum De divisione naturae intitulavit

    Vincent XXV 42 (whole entry).

2 Jerarchiam Dionisii de Graeco transtulit in Latinum et commentavit

    Vincent XXV 42 (whole entry).

3 De Eucharistia lib. 1

    Vincent XXV 42 (whole entry).

Johannes Scotus *287. 4*

    4 Ad regem Carolum ep. 1   *Valde quidam* . . .

        PL 122. 1031. The incipit is that of the prefatory letter of this author's translation of the Dionysius corpus, Lapidge/Sharpe 696.

    5 Ad regem Carolum versus 24   *Hanc libavi* . . .

        libavi] libam *edition;* libavi Add. *3470, Ware extracts*

        PL 122. 1029. Lapidge/Sharpe 696.

    6 Item versus   *Lumine sidereo* . . .

        PL 122. 1037. This is a prefatory verse to *2* above.

288 JOHANNES SARISBURIENSIS egregius philosophus et episcopus Carnotensis floruit tempore S. Thomae martiris et post circa A. Ch. 1177 et scripsit

    These six works probably formed a single Bury volume; a similar collection can be seen in BL MS Royal 13 D. IV, which contains *1–3* and *5*.
    Cf. James extracts, p. 200.
    Sharpe, *Latin Writers*, 309–310.

    1 Policraticon de nugis curialium etc. et continet lib. 8   *Inter omnia . . . in eo gressus*   173.82.65

        Sharpe, *Latin Writers*, 309. Ed. C. C. J. Webb (Oxford 1909).

    2 Metalogicon continens lib. 4   *In humanis . . . cultorem*   82

        Sharpe, *Latin Writers*, 309. CCCM 98. 9–184.

    3 De dogmate philosophorum Enteticum   *Dogmata . . . curam semper*   82

        Sharpe, *Latin Writers*, 309. Ed. R. E. Pepin in *Traditio* 31 (1975) 137–93, explicit 'cura semper uiuere lege Dei'.

    4 Item vitam et passionem S. Thomae archiepiscopi Cantuar[iensis]   82

        Sharpe, *Latin Writers*, 309.

    5 Item librum qui dicitur Euticus, id est Fortunatus   *Si mihi credideris* . . .   82

        Sharpe, *Latin Writers*, 309, *Entheticus*. Ed. J. van Laarhoven, *Entheticus Maior and Minor*, 3 vols. (Leiden 1987), 1. 231.

6 Item librum qui dicitur Architrenius   *Velificatur . . . dilectus et ultra*   82.65

> Iohannes de Hauvilla. Ed. P. G. Schmidt (Munich 1974) 127–284. **65** Ramsey = B68. 198.

289 JOHANNES GERUNDIENSIS episcopus floruit circa A. Ch. 594 et scripsit juxta Ysidorum libro De viris illustribus

> Isidore c. 31 (whole entry).
> *Speculum coenobitarum* 20.

1 De vita monachorum regulam 1

> A note by Kirkestede adds this work to the list of those who wrote monastic rules, in BL MS Campbell Roll XXI.1 (Bury —).

2 Item cronicas ab anno Justiniani usque ad annum 8^{vum} Mauricii imperatoris

> imperatoris] imperatorem *Add. 3470*

290 JOHANNES BELETH floruit circa A. Ch. <*blank*> et scripsit

> *Registrum* 73.
> Sharpe, *Latin Writers*, 215.

1 De officiis ecclesiae librum   *In primitiva* . . .   160.114.128.82.111.166

> R73. 1. *CCCM* 41A. **82** Bury = Lambeth Palace Library, MS 105, fol. 113r (Bury R. 36); Hereford Cathedral, MS P. III. 1, fol. 1r (Bury J. 47).

2 Librum pontificalem

> Unidentified.

291 JOHANNES Antiochenae ecclesiae presbyter, Eusebii Emisseni Theodorique sectator, floruit A. Ch. 390 et juxta Jeronimum multa composuisse dicitur, de quibus unum legit B. Jeronimus. Item Genadius libro De viris illustribus sic dicit: Johannes Antiochenae parochiae ex grammatico presbyter scripsit contra eos qui in una tantum substantia adorandum asserunt Christum, nec duas in Christo asserunt naturas. Item aliquas Cirilli Alexandrini episcopi sententias impugnat contra Nestorem prolatas. Vivere adhuc ducitur, et ex tempore declamare. Haec Jeronimus et Genadius.

> Whole entry save the date from Jerome c. 129 and Gennadius c. 94.

Jacobus *292*.

292 JACOBUS monachus cognomento Sapiens Nizibene Persarum <*blank*> civitatis episcopus fuit, unus ex numero sub Maximiano persecutore confessorum et eorum qui in Nicena synodo Arrianam perversitatem dampnarunt, et floruit circa A. Ch. 336 et scripsit multa juxta Genadium libro De viris illustribus

> Gennadius c. 1 (whole entry save the date).
> *Speculum coenobitarum* 33.

p. 94]

1 De fide contra omnes haereses

2 De caritate generali

3 De jejunio

4 De oratione

5 De dilectione erga proximum

6 De resurrectione

7 De vita post mortem

8 De humilitate

9 De poenitentia

10 De satisfactione

> *This title is written twice in Add. 3470*

11 De virginitate

12 De sensu animae

13 De circumcisione

14 De acino benedicto pro quo in Ysaia legitur: Non est exterminatus botrus

15 De Christo quod Filius Dei sit et consubstantialis Patri

16 De castitate adversus gentes

17 De constructione tabernaculi

18 De gentium conversatione

19 De regno Persarum

20 De persecutione Christianorum

21 Composuit et Ypoandi minoris quidam Graecorum curiositatis sed majoris fiduciae, quia divinarum Scripturarum tantum auctoritate constructurus ora eorum comprimit, qui praesumptuosa suspitione de adventu Christi inaniter philosophantur.

> Ypoandi *is an attempt to imitate the Greek title in Bodl. MS e Musaeo 31 p. 220, reading queried by Tanner*   Christi] antichristi *Gennadius (edition and e Musaeo 31)*

293 JOACHIM abbas de Flor in Calabria floruit circa A. Ch. <*blank*> et scripsit multa, videlicet

> Flor *queried by Tanner*
>
> This entry seems entirely based on manuscripts, at **168** Greyfriars Oxford, and at Bury itself.
> See P. F. Russo, *Bibliografia Gioachimita*, Biblioteca di Bibliografia Italiana 28 (Florence 1954).
> *Speculum coenobitarum* 55.

1 Super Apocalypsin lib.   *Quia profundius . . . sicut illorum*   168

> Stegmüller *Bibl.* 4016. Printed, Venice 1527 (repr. Frankfurt 1964), fols. 1r–224r. Incipit is that of pt 1 (fol. 26v).

2 Super libros Prophetarum commenta

> Source unidentified. Cf. Stegmüller *Bibl.* 4038–4048.

3 De seminibus lib. 1   *Semen cecidit . . .*

> *Ps.* Ioachim; Russo, 30. Stegmüller *Bibl.* 4033. Unprinted. [**82** Bury = Cambridge, Corpus Christi College, MS 404, fol. 44r (Bury P. 163), copied by Kirkestede, and cf. fol. 43v.]

Joachim *293. 4*

4 De moribus paparum qui post eum venturi essent usque ad ultimum lib.
  1 *Genus nequam* . . .

   paparum *queried by Tanner*

   Ps. Ioachim; Russo, 41–8. Printed before 1485 (Hain 9376). [**82** Bury = Cambridge, Corpus Christi College, MS 404, fols. 88r–95r (Bury P. 163), a book that Kirkestede assembled; see p. lxxvii above.]

5 De oneribus prophetarum   *Henrico 6to . . . interibunt*

   Ps. Ioachim; Russo pp. 37–38; cf. Stegmüller *Bibl.* 4036. Ed. O. Holder–Egger, *Neues Archiv der Gesellschaft für ältere deutsche Geschichtskunde* 33 (1907–1908) 139–187.

6 De duobus ordinibus prophetantium   *Offendent . . . angelus*

   This title appears in a catalogue of John Erghome's books, 361d in the 1372 catalogue of the Austin Friars in York (*Friars*, 86): 'Joachim de duobus ordinibus'; incipit and explicit unidentified. The work may be related to portions of *ps.* Ioachim, *Super Hieremiam et super Esaiam* (Venice 1516–1517); cf. M. Reeves, *Recherches de théologie ancienne et médiévale* 25 (1958) 112, 124.

7 De concordia   *Universa . . . civitatem*   168

   Ed. E. R. Daniel, *Transactions of the American Philosophical Society* 73/8 (Philadelphia, PA, 1983) 4, incipit 'Uniuersis'; the explicit occurs on p. 422 line 315.

8 Super oraculum Cirilli commenta   *Stellae . . . a terga*

   Ps. Ioachim; Russo, 50–51. Ed. P. Plur in *Vom Mittelalter zur Reformation*, ed. K. Burdach, 2/4 (1912) 246–51 and 254–327. [**82** Bury = this entry contains two commentaries on Cyril that appear in the same sequence, copied by Kirkestede in Cambridge, Corpus Christi College, MS 404, fols. 68v and 70r (Bury P. 163), explicit fol. 87v.]

294 JOHANNES Jerosolymitarum episcopus floruit A. Ch. <*blank*> et scripsit secundum Genadium

   Gennadius c. 31 (whole entry).

1 Adversus obtrectatores studii sui lib. 1   In quo ostendit se Origenis ingenium, non fidem, secutum

Josephus 296. 5

295 JOHANNES Constantinopolitanus episcopus natione Capadox floruit circa A. Ch. 591 et scripsit secundum Ysidorum Graeca eloquia ad Leandrum episcopum

> Isidore c. 26–27 (whole entry save the date).

1. De sacramento baptismatis lib. 1

   > Huic B. Gregorius papa scribit librum Regulae pastoralis et Leandro episcopo praedecessori Ysidori Moralia super Job in libris 35

p. 95]

296 JOSEPHUS dux belli Judaeorum floruit A. Ch. 73 tempore Vespasiani et scripsit juxta Jeronimum

> See also Egesippus *163*.
> *Registrum* 31, Jerome c. 13 (works *1–5*).
> See *The Latin Josephus*, ed. F. Blatt, Acta Jutlandica 30/1, Humanistisk Serie 44 (Copenhagen 1958).

1 De captivitate Judaica et de subversione urbis Jerusalem lib. 7   *Cum potentes . . . conjecturam*   94.155.82.157.156

   > R31. 1, Jerome 13. Printed, Cologne 1534, fol. 217r; incipit is that of c. 1. See also Ambrosius *2.27* and Egesippus *163.1*. **82** Bury = B13. 10, 236–7.

2 Libros antiquitatum ab initio saeculi usque ad Domitianum lib. 22 *Historiam . . .*   94.155.82.156.50

   > R31. 2, Jerome 13. Ed. Blatt (Books I–IV only); printed, Cologne 1534, fol. 1r. **82** Bury = B13. 10, 236–7.

3 Contra Apinionem grammaticum Alexand[rinum] lib. 2

   > Jerome 13 (whole entry).

4 De vituperatione Judaeorum lib.

   > Jerome 13 (whole entry).

5 De gestis Machabeorum lib.

   > Jerome 13 (whole entry).

Josephus   *296. 6*

   6 De excidio urbis Jerusalem lib.   <u>82</u>

> R31. 4. Same as Egesippus *163.3*. **82** Bury = B13. 11, 'Egesippus'.

297 JUSTINUS philosophus et martir, Trogi Pompeii abbreviator, floruit circa A. Ch. <blank> et scripsit juxta Jeronimum De viris illustribus

> Same as Trogus Pompeius *588*.
> Diceto, 1. 20 provided information for the headnote; the rest of this entry comes entirely from Jerome c. 23.
> [Kirkestede seems not to have had recourse to the manuscript recorded at **82** Bury = B13. 23b, 'Iustinus'.]

   1 De Christiana religione lib. 1

   2 Contra gentiles, cui praenotavit titulum Castigatio lib. 1

> Castigatio *is the interlinear Latin translation found in the text of Jerome in Bodl. MS e Musaeo 31 p. 193*

   3 De monarchia Dei lib. 1

   4 Librum quem praenotavit Salten

> Salten *is the transliteration from the Greek available in Bodl. MS e Musaeo 31 p. 193*

   5 De anima lib. 1

   6 Contra Judaeos dialogorum lib. 1

   7 Contra Marcionem volumina insignia

   8 Contra haereses lib. 1

298 JUSTINIANUS imperator et legis lator floruit A. Ch. <blank> et scripsit juxta Ysidorum

> Isidore c. 18 (whole entry save concluding statement).

   1 De incarnatione Domini lib.

   2 Contra Illiricianam synodum lib. 1

3 Contra Affricanos episcopos lib. 1

> Hic ex duobus pene millibus librorum et tricesies centenis milibus versum jura Digestorum redintegravit

>> This statement perhaps comes from the *Historia Romana* of Paul the Deacon, I 25.

299 JUSTUS Orgillitanae ecclesiae episcopus floruit circa A. Ch. <*blank*> et scripsit secundum Ysidorum

> Isidore c. 21 (whole entry).

1 Super Cantica Canticorum expos. 1

> Hujus quoque fratres uterini Justinianus, Imbridius et Hilpidius episcopi quaedam scripsisse feruntur

300 JUSTINIANUS praedicti Justi germanus et ecclesiae Valentinae episcopus floruit A. Ch. <*blank*> et scripsit juxta Jeronimum et Ysidorum

> Isidore c. 20 (whole entry); this author does not appear in Jerome.

1 De Spiritu Sancto lib. 1

2 De baptismo Christi lib. 1

3 Contra Bonosiacos lib. 1

4 De distinctione baptismi Johannis et Christi lib. 1

5 Quod Filius sicut Pater invisibilis sit lib. 1

301 JULIUS FIRMICUS floruit circa A. Ch. <*blank*> et scripsit

> (Firmicus Maternus)

1 Matheseos lib. 4   *Olim tibi . . . exempla*

> *CPL* 101. Ed. W. Kroll & others (Leipzig 1897–1913).

Julius *302.*

p. 96]

302 JULIUS Affricanus floruit circa A. Ch. 240 et scripsit juxta Jeronimum et Vincentium in Speculo lib. 12 cap. 23

> See also Affricanus *32.*
> Vincent XI 32, Jerome c. 63, Cassiodorus I. 25. 1.

1 De temporibus vol. 5

> Whole entry from Vincent XI 32 and Jerome 63.

2 De re militari lib. 4   *Cum ad instruendum . . . milites habent*   82

> Iulius Frontinus. Same as Julius Frontinus *303.2.*

3 Ad Aristidem ep. 1

> Whole entry from Vincent XI 32 and Jerome 63.

In hac epistola agit super diaphoniam quae videtur esse in genealogia Salvatoris apud Mathaeum et Lucam plenissime disputata. Hujus est epistola ad Origenem super quaestionem Susannae, eo quod dicat in Hebraico hanc fabulam non haberi nec conveniri cum Hebraica proprietate, id est: Sub hoc prino secet et sub hoc scino scindat, contra quam doctam epistolam scripsit Origenes.[a] Item scripsit juxta Cassiodorum libro De institutione divinarum literarum libellum, qui maria, insulas, montes famosos, provincias, civitates, flumina, gentes ita quadrifaria distinctione complexus est, ut pene nichil libro ipsi desit quod ad cosmographiae notitiam cognoscitur pertinere.[b]

> [a] Jerome 63; 'proprietate—scindat' appears as an interlinear translation of the Greek in Bodl. MS e Musaeo 31, p. 203 (Bury A. 31).   [b] Cassiodorus I. 25. 1 (p. 66 lines 12–15), referring to the *De cosmographia* of Iulius Orator.

303 JULIUS Frontinus floruit circa A. Ch. <blank> et scripsit

1 Stratagematicon

> Same as 2 below.

2 De scientia rei militaris lib. 4   *Cum ad instruendum . . . victi sunt*

> Ed. G. Gundermann (Leipzig 1888). Same as *1* above and as Julius Affricanus *302.2.*

Julianus *306. 2*

304 JULIUS CELSUS floruit tempore Julii Caesaris et scripsit juxta Vincentium in Speculo historiali lib. 7 cap. 5

>(Julius Caesar)
>Vincent VII 5.

1 De bello Gallico Caesaris lib. 8   *Gallia est . . . belli gerandi*

>Vincent VII 5. Ed. O. Seel (Leipzig 1961). [**82** Bury = B13. 52, 'Gesta Cesaris'.]

2 De bello civili lib. 3   *Litteris . . . fuerunt*

>Ed. A. Klotz (Leipzig 1957).

3 De bello Alexandrino, Hispaniae et Affricano lib. 3   *Bello Alexandrino . . .*

>Ed. A. Klotz (Leipzig 1927).

305 JULIUS papa floruit A. Ch. 341 et scripsit juxta Genadium libro De viris illustribus

>Gennadius c. 2 (whole entry save the date).

1 De incarnatione Domini ep. 1

306 JULIANUS quidam cognomento Pomerius episcopus Toletanus floruit A. Ch. <*blank*> et scripsit juxta Ysidorum

>This conflation of the works of Iulianus Pomerius and Julian of Toledo comes from *Registrum* 65; but the conflation of their names probably derives from the manuscript of the *Prognosticon* from which Kirkestede copied the note into entry *4* below.
>See also Promeritus *468*.
>*Registrum* 65 (Iulianus Pomerius), 70 (Julian of Toledo); Isidore c. 12 (Iulianus Pomerius).

1 De virginibus instituendis lib. 1

>Isidore 12 (whole entry).

2 De futurae vitae contemplatione vel actuali conversatione nec non de vitiis et virtutibus lib. 3   <u>105</u>

>Whole entry from R65. 1 and Isidore 12.

Julianus *306. 3*

3 De animae natura more dialogi lib. 8

Quorum primus continet quid sit anima et qualiter credatur ad Dei ymaginem facta; in 2do loquitur utrum anima corporea an incorporea sit; in 3^{io} disserit primo homini unde sit anima facta; in 4to utrum nova sine peccato fiat et peccatum primi hominis ex illo propagata originaliter trahat; in 5to describat quae sit facultas animae; in 6to eloquitur unde sit ea discordia, quae carni spiritus vel caro spiritui adversatur; in septimo scribit de differentia vitarum ac mortium vel resurrectione carnis et animae sive de morte carnis et ejus resurrectione; in 8vo loquitur de hiis quae in fine mundi futura sunt vel de quaestionibus quae solent de resurrectione proponi sive de finibus bonorum et malorum. Hic tamen Julianus in 2do ejusdem operis libro Tertulliani erroribus consentiens animam corpoream esse dixit, quibusdam hoc fallacibus argumentis astruere contendens. Haec Ysidorus ubi supra.

Isidore 12 (whole entry).

4 Item de origine mortis humanae lib. 1   *Peccato primi* . . .   105.**80**.82.**90**. 65.74

R65. 2 (location number **105**), R70. 1 (location numbers **80, 90**). Julian of Toledo, *Prognosticon*; CPL 1258. CCSL 115. 19.

Iste liber intitulatur Pronosticon futuri saeculi, videtur autem extractus esse de duobus ultimis libris ejusdem Juliani De animae natura

p. 97]

307 JUNILIUS Constantinopolitanus floruit circa A. Ch. <*blank*> et scripsit juxta Cassiodorum ubi supra

(Iunilllus Africanus)
Cassiodorus I. 10. 1.

1 Super Vetus Testamentum et Novum

This work and its source are unidentified.

2 De regularibus institutis divinarum Scripturarum   *In quot primas* . . . *confitemur*   15

Cassiodorus I. 10. 1. CPL 872. Ed. H. Kihn, *Theodor von Mopsuestia und Junilius Africanus als Exegeten* (Freiburg 1880) 471–528.

308 JORDANUS magister ordinis Fratrum Praedicatorum secundus post S. Dominicum floruit A. Ch. <blank> et scripsit

> Script. Ord. Praed. (whole entry), cf. Stams, 2.

1 Super Apocalipsin postillas

2 Super Priscianum juniorem

> Priscianum] Precianum *Add. 3470, queried by Tanner*

309 JOHANNES de Deo canonicus Blistonensis floruit A. Ch. 1243 et scripsit

> Blistonensis *read* Lisbonensis
>
> Titles *1–10* were taken from a list of this author's works similar to the one that appears in the epilogue of Bonn, Universitätsbibliothek, MS 269c, printed in Schulte, 2. 95 n. 4; it was expanded with incipits and explicits from Bury manuscripts wherever possible. Works *11–16* presumably come from one or more Bury manuscripts.
> See M. C. Díaz y Díaz, *Index scriptorum latinorum medii aevi hispanorum* (Salamanca 1958), cited by number, and J. F. von Schulte, *Die Geschichte der Quellen und Literatur des canonischen Rechts*, 3 vols. (Stuttgart 1875–1880), 2. 94–107, cited by page and reference-letter.

1 Breviarium super toto corpore decretorum

> Díaz 1267, Schulte, 2. 96B.

2 Casus decretalium   *Quoniam quidam . . . ex diligenti*   82

> Díaz 1270, Schulte, 2. 97E. Explicit unidentified. Same as *3* below.

3 Concordantias decretorum et decretalium   *De constitutionibus . . . est notatum*   81.83.45.82.33

> Schulte, 2. 97E, an alternative title for *2* above. The prologue begins 'Quoniam quidem' and the text 'De const.'. Explicit unidentified.

4 Distinctiones super toto jure canonico

> Díaz 1274.

Johannes de Deo *309. 5*

5 Libellum judicum lib. 4   *Ad honorem* . . .   82

>   To judge from the title this is Díaz 1271, Schulte, 2. 97F. The inadequate incipit is the invocation 'Ad honorem summe Trinitatis et indiuidue unitatis in nomine Patris et Filii et Spiritus sancti' that invariably opens the works of Iohannes de Deo. Usually Kirkestede ignored it, but see *16* below.

6 Summam super titulum decretalium

>   Díaz 1272.

7 Super epistolas 7 canonicas

>   Works *7–8*: The list in Bonn, Universitätsbibliothek, MS 269c (Schulte, 2. 95 n. 4) reads, '. . . cum epistolis canonicis de decretis persoluendis'.

8 De decimis solvendis tract. 1

9 Cronica a tempore Petri usque ad tempus papae Innocentii IV

>   Díaz 1287.

10 Apparatum super toto corpore decretorum cum historiis et casibus uniuersis

>   Díaz 1266.

11 De poenitentia et confessione lib. 7   *Ea est regula* . . . *regnum Dei*

>   The title is Díaz 1275 and Schulte, 2. 102M, but the incipit is Díaz 1286, *Summa moralis*; explicit unidentified.

12 De dispensationibus lib. 1   *Primo de* . . . *brevitatis*

>   Works *12–14*: Schulte, 2. 96–7 and n. 11 describes the *Liber dispensationum* from its contents in manuscripts that were then in the Prague Museum (MS I. B. 4, fols. 294r–301r) and the Bonn Universitätsbibliothek (MS 269c), where the text is divided into three parts that comprised these three works in the *Catalogus*. We have not seen these manuscripts, nor do we know English manuscripts that conform to this description.
>
>   Díaz 1269, Schulte, 2. 96D pt I. Explicit unidentified.

13 De formandis sententiis lib. 1   *Dictum est* . . . *alleluja*

>   Schulte, 2. 96D pt II, 'Formatio sententiarum et opinionum dispensationum et interlocutoriarum et definitiuarum' (p. 97 n. 11); incipit and explicit unidentified.

14 De relationibus tract. 1   *Incipit . . . praenotatur*

> Schulte, 2. 96D pt III, 'Formatio relationum et consultationum' (p. 97 n. 11); incipit unidentified, explicit 'pernotatur'.

15 Pastorale lib. 7   *Noverit tua . . . concordiam*

> The title is Díaz 1268, Schulte, 2. 96C. Incipit and explicit unidentified.

16 Cavillationum lib. 7   *Ad honorem . . . ex ratione*

> Díaz 1280 and Schulte, 2. 104Q cite several 16th-cent. printings (not seen). See also the note to *5* above.

310 JUVENCUS Hispanus presbiter poeta, rethor et orator optimus floruit circa A. Ch. 318 et scripsit tempore Constantini secundum Jeronimum

> Jerome c. 84 (works *1–2*).

1 Super quatuor evangelia metrice lib. 4   *Rex fuit . . . in saecula regant*

> Jerome 84. *CPL* 1385. *CSEL* 24. 3, explicit '. . . regnat'.

2 De sacramentis metrice lib. 2

> Jerome 84 (whole entry).

311 JUVENALIS vel JUNIUS Aquinias id est de Aquino oppido oriundus poeta floruit circa A. Ch. 58 et scripsit

1 De satiris lib. 5   *Semper ego . . . torquibus omnis*

> Ed. W. V. Clausen (Oxford 1992) 37–175. [**82** Bury = B13. 15.]

312 JORDANUS archiepiscopus Ranensis floruit <*blank*> et scripsit

> Ranensis] Ravennensis *Diceto*

> *Registrum* 82, Diceto, 1. 22.

1 De origine Gothorum historiam 1

> Whole entry from R82. 1 and Diceto, 1. 22.

Jordanus   *312. 2*

2 De numeris lib. 21

> The works of two authors are conflated by the addition here of the *Tractatus de numeris libri iv* of Jordanus de Nemore, the late 12th- or early 13th-cent. mathematician. See G. Sarton, *Introduction to the History of Science*, 3 vols. (Baltimore 1927–48), 2/2. 613–16.

313 JOHANNES Parisiensis magister theologiae et Frater Praedicator floruit A. Ch. <*blank*> et scripsit

> *Script. Ord. Praed.* (whole entry), cf. Stams, 32.

1 Super primum librum sententiarum

2 Item super omnes libros sententiarum lecturam

p. 98]

3 De iride lib. 1

4 Contra corruptores Thomae

5 Super librum metheororum

6 De sacramento altaris tract. 1

7 De unitate esse et essentiae in creatis

8 De adventu Christi lib. 1

314 INNOCENTIUS V papa et Frater Praedicator. Hic priusquam fuit papa vocabatur Petrus de Tharentasia doctor egregius et scripsit

> Same as Petrus de Tharenta *446*.
> *Script. Ord. Praed.* (whole entry). This entry does not correspond to Stams, 9, 'Petrus de Tarenhentasia'.

1 Super libros sententiarum

> Same as Petrus de Tharenta *446.8*, Petrus Carnotensis *483.1*.

2 Item multa alia

315 JOHANNES DE ERDENBERS Frater Praedicator et magister theologiae floruit A. Ch. <*blank*> et scripsit

> *Script. Ord. Praed.* (whole entry), cf. Stams, 31, 106.

1 Super libros sententiarum lecturam

2 Super omnes libros Bibliae postillam

316 JOHANNES FAVENTINUS Frater Praedicator floruit A. Ch. <*blank*> et scripsit

> *Script. Ord. Praed.* (whole entry), cf. Stams, 36

1 De unitate formarum

317 JOHANNES Pingens Asinum Frater Praedicator et magister theologiae floruit A. Ch. <*blank*> et scripsit

> Pingens] Pungens *Stams, Pign. 40*; Pingens *Add. 3470, queried by Tanner*
>
> *Script. Ord. Praed.* (whole entry), cf. Stams, 38.

1 Super omnes libros sententiarum

318 JACOBUS DE BENEVENTO Frater Praedicator floruit A. Ch. <*blank*> et scripsit

> *Script. Ord. Praed.* (whole entry), cf. Stams, 60.

1 Super Lucam et Johannem postellam

319 JACOBUS DE FRUMANNO Frater Praedicator floruit anno <*blank*> et scripsit

> *Script. Ord. Praed.* (whole entry), cf. Stams, 61.

1 De arte praedicandi tract. 1

2 Sermones de tempore et sanctis

Jacobus   *320.*

320 JACOBUS Frater Praedicator et episcopus Januensis floruit A. Ch. <*blank*> et scripsit

>Iacobus de Voragine.
>*Script. Ord. Praed.*, cf. Stams, 65.
>Works *1, 3* and *4* represent the Dominican list supplemented by manuscripts.

1 Legendam Lumbardicam   *Universum* . . .

>*Legenda aurea* (also called *Historia Lombardica*); Kaeppeli 2154. Ed. G. P. Maggioni (Florence 1998).

2 De beata Virgine lib. 1

>om. *Stams*

3 Sermones de tempore et sanctis   *Humane* . . .

>Kaeppeli 2156. Pr. Cologne *c.* 1478 (Goff J193), &c.

4 Opus quadragesimale   *Filia populi* . . .

>om. *Stams*

>Kaeppeli 2157. Pr. Brescia [1493] (Goff J186), &c.

321 JOHANNES Teutonicus Frater Praedicator floruit A. Ch. <*blank*> et scripsit

>*Script. Ord. Praed.* (whole entry), cf. Stams, 67.

1 Tres summas juris

2 Summam confessorum

>om. *Stams*

3 Librum qui dicitur Confessionale

322 JOHANNES de Fano Frater Praedicator floruit A. Ch. <*blank*> et scripsit

>*Script. Ord. Praed.* (whole entry), cf. Stams, 77.

1 Summam juris

2 Tabulam super decretales

    Tabulam] Summam *Stams*

323 JOHANNES Januensis Frater Praedicator floruit A. Ch. \<blank\> et scripsit

    Iacobus Ianuensis] *Stams*

    Script. Ord. Praed. (whole entry), cf. Stams, 82, Pign. 68.

1 De modis significandi lib. 1 et vocatur Catholicon

    De modis significandi *om. Pign.*   et vocatur Catholicon *om. Stams*

p. 99]

324 JACOBUS DE VITRIACO Frater Praedicator et episcopus Achonensis et Tusculanensis et tandem cardinalis floruit A. Ch. \<blank\> et scripsit

    Script. Ord. Praed. (cf. Pign. 117), Vincent XXXI 10–11, Étienne de Bourbon, prologue p. 6.
    Kirkestede has conflated the names and careers of the early 14th-cent. Dominican Iacobus de Teriace (Iacobus de Cessolis, author of *1* below) with the cardinal Iacobus de Vitriaco (Jacques de Vitry, author of *2–3* below).

1 De ludo scaccarii moraliter tract. 4   *Inter omnia . . . maxime ludentium*

    Iacobus de Cessolis, *Liber de moribus hominum et officiis nobilium ac popularium super ludo scaccorum.* Kaeppeli 2066. Ed. F. Vetter, *Das Schachzabelbuch Kunrats von Ammenhausen nebst den Schachbüchern des Jakob von Cessole und des Jakob Mennel* (Frauenfeld 1892) [not seen]. ·

2 Vitam S. Mariae de Oegnies

    Oegnies] Oigines *Add. 3470, queried by Tanner*

    Vincent XXXI 10–11 (whole entry).

3 Item historiam transmarinam

    Étienne de Bourbon, prol. (whole entry).

Johannes de Saxonia *325.*

325 JOHANNES DE SAXONIA Frater Minor et doctor Juris utriusque floruit A. Ch. <*blank*> et scripsit

1 Summam confessionum et continet lib. 2   *De confessoribus . . . commemorasse*   173

> John of Erfurt, *Summa confessorum*, ed. N. Brieskorn, 3 vols. (Frankfurt 1980); incipit is at vol. 2, p. 2, explicit, 'commemorasse sufficiant', at vol. 3, p. 1548.

326 IZACHIUS vel IDACIUS Fenicae civitatis Hispaniarum episcopus cognomento Clarus et eloquio decorus floruit A. Ch. 377 et scripsit secundum Isidorum

> Isidore c. 2 and another *pseudo*-Isidorian source.
> The works of two authors, Idacius of Spain and Itacius of Gaul, are conflated in this entry .

1 Contra Priscillianum apologeticum lib. 1

> Isidore 2.

2 Cronica a tempore Theodosii usque ad A. Ch. 500

> This entry pertains to Itacius, bishop of Galicia, as described in the 'long version' of Isidore's *De uiris illustribus* with additions; ed. G. von Dzialowski, *Isidor und Ildefons als Literarhistoriker*, Kirchengeschichtliche Studien 4/2 (Münster 1898) 15 c. 9. This (as with all the added matter) is absent from the Bury Isidore (Bodl. MS e Musaeo 31). Kirkestede ignored the discrepancy between the chronicle's date and the *floruit* date of his composite author.

327 JUDAS unus ex LXX[a] floruit circa A. Ch. <*blank*> et scripsit juxta Jeronimum plenissime

> Jerome c. 52 (whole entry).

1 Super Danielem de ebdomadibus

328 JOHANNES Cornubiensis floruit circa A. Ch. 1169 et scripsit

> Bale, *Index*, 196.
> Sharpe, *Latin Writers*, 229–30.

1 Eulogium ad papam Alexandrum III   *In concilio . . . salvus esse non concilio*] Turonensi quod dudum *add.* Bale

> Sharpe, *Latin Writers*, 230. Ed. N. M. Häring in *Med. Stud.* 13 (1951) 257–300.

2 Super canonem missae

    Source unidentified. Spurious; Sharpe, *Latin Writers*, 230.

    Commentarios scripturarum   li. pl. *add. Bale as an entry*

329 JACOBUS DE VITERBIO frater ordinis Heremitarum B. Augustini floruit circa A. Ch. \<blank\> et scripsit

1 Duo quodlibet   *In disputatione . . . non excaecatur*   82

    Ed. E. Ypma, *Cassiciacum* suppl. 1–4 (Würzburg 1968–72), only vols. 1 and 2; explicit 'non excedatur'

330 JOHANNES DE RUPELL[A]

    (Jean de La Rochelle)

1 De quatuor virtutibus cardinalibus lib. 1   *Sicut dicit Aristo[ti]les in . . . superpositorum*

    The title presumably refers to the *Summa de uitiis et uirtutibus*, Stegmüller *Sent.* 493,2 (unprinted), but the incipit and explicit are unidentified.

331 JOHANNES DE GARLANDIA floruit circa A. Ch. 1040 et scripsit

    Bale, *Index*, 207.
    Sharpe, *Latin Writers*, 253–7.

1 Libellum de dictionibus obscuris   *Dictionarius . . .*

    Sharpe, *Latin Writers*, 255. Ed. Hunt, *Teaching Latin*, 1. 196.

2 Librum de accentu   *Ecclesiae sacrae . . .*

    sacrae] sacra *Add. 3470*

    Ars lectoria ecclesiae siue Accentarius; Sharpe, *Latin Writers*, 253.

3 Librum misteriorum ecclesiae   *Anglia quo . . .*

    Sharpe, *Latin Writers*, 254. Ed. F. W. Otto in *Commentarii critici in codice a Bibliothecae Academicae Gissensis* (Giessen 1842) 131–51. Same as Alexander de Hales *54.3*.

Johannes de Garlandia   *331. 4*

  4 Librum qui dicitur Unus omnium   *Commoda . . .*

    Sharpe, *Latin Writers*, 256.

  5 Librum satiricum   *Scribo novam . . .*

    Morale scholarium; Sharpe, *Latin Writers*, 255. Ed. L. F. Paetow (Berkeley, CA, 1927).

  6 Librum de miraculis B. Mariae   *Fecit Deus . . .*

    Stella maris; Sharpe, *Latin Writers*, 256. Ed. E. F. Wilson (Cambridge, MA, 1946). [**82** Bury = BL MS Royal 8 C. IV, fols. 16r–23v (Bury R. 42), with a marginal title by Kirkestede but with no attribution of authorship.]

  7 Item compotum et tabulam

    Source unidentified. Spurious; Sharpe, *Latin Writers*, 256.

332 JOHANNES SCOLASTICUS abbas montis Synay dictus Climacus floruit A. Ch. <*blank*> et scripsit

    Kirkestede probably took the biographical information from the prologue and colophon of a Bury manuscript that contained the works below; see the similar information provided in, for example, Bodl. MS Canon. Misc. 333, fols. 4r, 110v. The two works follow one another in a late 15th-cent. manuscript, Prague UL MS XIII. C. 8, dated 1462.
    See O. Bardenhewer, *Geschichte der altkirchlichen Literatur* (Freiburg im Breisgau 1912), 5. 79–82, for a discussion of the Latin translations.

  1 Abbati Johanni monachorum de Raythu librum qui Scala vocatur. Principium: *A bono*. Finis: *causalitas in est erat et erit*.

    The Latin translation of the *Scala* by Angelus Clarenus (Angelus de Cingulo); see *DS* 8. 369–89, at 385. Printed Paris *c.* 1505 (Goff J311) [not seen]. A Latin translation with this incipit and explicit is reported in Prague UL MS XIII. C. 8, fols. 2v–121r [not seen]. For a list of manuscripts (without incipits and explicits) see R. G. Musto in *Archivum Franciscanum Historicum* 76 (1983) 215–38 and 589–645.

  2 Item ad Pastorem serm. 1   *Beata ferens . . .*

    The entry cites only the explicit; the incipit has been lost, by Kirkestede or in transmission to Tanner. See Prague UL MS XIII. C. 8, fols. 121r–128r, incipit 'In inferiori quidem libro', explicit 'beata ferens'.

Titulus Scalae paradisiacae talis est: Primus gradus coelestis hujus intellectualis Scalae Johannis Scolastici abbatis montis Synay a libro cognominati Climaci. Climax enim Graece Latine dicitur Scala, et continet iste liber de Scala 30 gradus in 30 capitulis distinctos.

paradisiacae] praedcae *Add. 3470*

333 JOHANNES MANDUYT doctor theologiae floruit circa A. Ch. 1342 et scripsit

(John Maudith)
Bale, *Index*, 231.
Sharpe, *Latin Writers*, 282.

1 De doctrina theologica lib. 1   *Legimus* . . .

A copy of this work survives in Salisbury Cathedral, MS 167, fol. 18r (s. xiv).

334 JOHANNES de Alba Villa

(Iohannes Halgrinus de Abbatisvilla)
Johannes de Albavilla] Abbatisvilla add. *Add. 3470, superscript; according to Tanner this was added in a recent hand*

1 Super epistolas et evangelia in Dominicis diebus totius anni omelias   *Cum sacro sancta . . . Dominum laudans*

Schneyer *Rep*. 3. 510 (incipit), and 523 (explicit). [**82** Bury = Cambridge, Pembroke College, MS 85 pt 3, fol. 27r (Bury B. 340), ends imperfect; BL MS Royal 2 E. IX, fol. 2r (Bury T. 40), with Kirkestede's marginal rubric at the beginning of the text.]

2 Super epistolas et evangelia in festis sanctorum totius anni   *Licet cum . . . gaudiis*

Schneyer *Rep*. 3. 523 or 527 (incipit), explicit unidentified.

p. 100]

335 JOHANNES Carpinus floruit <*blank*> et scripsit

(Iohannes de Plano Carpini)
Vincent XXXII 3 and 25 (whole entry).

1 Itinerarium

336 JOHANNES Ocreatus floruit <blank> et scripsit

Sharpe, *Latin Writers*, 287–8.

1 De numeris   *Virtus amicitiae* . . .

Helcep sarracenicum; Sharpe, *Latin Writers*, 287. Ed. C. S. F. Burnett in *Mathematische Probleme im Mittelalter: Die lateinische und arabische Sprachbereich*, ed. M. Folkerts (Wiesbaden 1996) 262.

337 JOHANNES Walensis Frater Minor

(John Waleys)
This entry was compiled entirely from manuscripts at Bury and neighbouring houses, especially **173** Babwell.
Bale, *Index*, 212–13.
Sharpe, *Latin Writers*, 337–40; L. Wadding, *Scriptores ordinis minorum*, new edn (Rome 1906) 141–2. See also J. Swanson, *John of Wales: a Study of the Works and Ideas of a Thirteenth-Century Friar* (Cambridge 1989), who lists the works and surviving manuscripts on pp. 229–89; Swanson's report (p. 238, no. 91) that CUL MS Add. 3470 contains two works of John Waleys is mistaken.

1 Breviloquium antiquorum   *Quoniam misericordia . . . permanere est vita*

Sharpe, *Latin Writers*, 337. Printed, Venice 1496, fols. 240r–259v. Explicit 'permanere ego uita'. Same as 9 below.

2 Floriloquium   *Cum enim . . . in vita et*

Sharpe, *Latin Writers*, 338. Printed, Venice 1496, fols. 167r–232r. Explicit unidentified. Same as 7 below.

3 Communeloquium   *Cum doctor . . . advenire*   173

Sharpe, *Latin Writers*, 338. Printed, Venice 1496, fols. 1r–166v.

4 Miniloquium sive collectiloquium   *Cum almus . . . regnum aeternum*   173

Moniloquium; Sharpe, *Latin Writers*, 338.

5 Dietarium religiosorum lib. 3

Prima pars vocatur Ordinarium sive decretarium vitae religiosae, et sic incipit: *Nunquid nosti*. Secunda pars vocatur Locarium et incipit: *Volo viros*. Tertia pars Itinerarium, et incipit: *Quum vir*.

Johannes *338.*

Ordinarium; Sharpe, *Latin Writers*, 338. Printed, Venice 1496, respectively fols. 260r–289r, 289r–293r, 293r–305v. [**82** Bury = Cambridge, St John's College, MS G. 2, fols. 13r–45r (Bury R. 56).]

6 De oculo morali lib. 1   *Si diligenter . . . eriguntur*   173

> Peter of Limoges; see Sharpe, *Latin Writers*, 296. Printed, Venice 1496, under John Pecham's name.

7 Compendiloquium

> Source unidentified. Same as *2* above.

8 De disciplina tract. l   *Disciplina . . . sapientia*   173.65

> Unidentified.

9 De quatuor virtutibus tract. 1   *Quoniam misericordia . . .*

> Same as *1* above.

10 De correptione sive correctione   *Probata virtus . . . commorabitur*   15

> Unidentified. Wadding, 142, gives a longer incipit, 'Probata uirtus quasi per ignem'; explicit unidentified.

11 De exortatione tractatum 1   *Qui exortatur . . . moderantis*

> Unidentified. Wadding, 142, gives a longer incipit, 'Qui exortatur in doctrina'; explicit unidentified.

12 De cura pastorali tract. 1   *Licet beatus . . . et haec ad David*

> beatus] bos *Add. 3470*

> *Pastoralia*; Sharpe, *Latin Writers*, 338, who says it is not known to survive.

338 JOHANNES de Bromyerd frater floruit A.D. <*blank*> et scripsit

(John Bromyard)
See Wilhelmus Brumyard *650*.
Bale, *Index*, 185.
Sharpe, *Latin Writers*, 220–21.

Johannes *338. 1*

1 Tabulam de jure canonico et civili moraliter   *Ab infantia . . . praecollector*

> *Opus triuium siue Tractatus iuris civilis et canonici ad moralem materiam applicati*; Sharpe, *Latin Writers*, 221. A version of this work was printed under the name of Philippus de Bronnerde, Cologne, not after 1473 (Goff J258); reprinted under Bromyard's name, Lyons 1500 (Goff J259). The incipit is that of the *tabula*.

339 JOHANNES Peccham Frater Minor doctor theologiae et archiepiscopus Cantuar[iensis] floruit A.C. 1278 et scripsit multa sancta et devota

> Bale, *Index*, 236.
> Sharpe, *Latin Writers*, 290–97.

1 De Domini passione tract. 1   *Pullus aquilae . . . cum custodibus*

> Glorieux *Rép.* 316bt gives a longer incipit, 'Pullus aquile sanguinem'; the work and its explicit are unidentified.

2 Sermones de Dominicis per annum 25   *Honeste . . . congregabit*

> Honeste] ambuletis *add. Bale*

> *Collationes dominicales*; Sharpe, *Latin Writers*, 294. [**82** Bury = Bodl. MS Laud Misc. 85, fols. 1r–31r (Bury J. 12, altered to J. 13); incipit lacking, explicit 'congregabit electos'.]

340 IGNIUS floruit <*blank*> et scripsit

> Source unidentified. This is presumably a garbled reference to 'Iginus', i.e. Hyginus or, more likely, *ps.* Hyginus, *De astrologia*, ed. A. Boutemy in *Latomus* 3 (1939) 128–37.

1 De signis et sideribus

341 JOHANNES dictus ANGLICUS vicarius de Tynmuithe floruit A. Ch. 1366 et scripsit

> Even though the incipits and explicits to these works are not supplied, the entry was apparently compiled from a first-hand knowledge of the manuscripts at **82** Bury and **15** St Albans. Only works *1* and *3* (BL MS Cotton Tiberius E. 1) have survived, while excerpts from the *Martyrologia*, work *4*, appear in the Bury manuscript of the *Historia aurea*, work *1* below (Bodl. MS Bodley 240, pp. 583–623).
> Bale, *Index*, 176–7; the same works appear, slightly rearranged.
> Sharpe, *Latin Writers*, 333–4.

1 Historiam auream collectam de diversis historiis et eventibus orbis terrarum a creatione mundi usque ad tempora regis Edw[ardi] III inclusive in tribus voluminibus   15.162.147.82

> Sharpe, *Latin Writers*, 334. Cambridge, Corpus Christi College, MSS 5–7, which probably date from the 15th cent., are too late to be the volumes reported here from **15** St Albans. / **82** Bury = Bodl. MS Bodley 240, pp. 1–582 (Bury H. 55); this manuscript is too late to have been the source of the entry, but the contents of Bodley 240 were compiled from earlier Bury manuscripts.

2 Librum servorum Dei majorem qui vocatur Martirilogium in maximo volumine   15

3 Librum servorum Dei minorem qui vocatur Sanctilogium ex vitis et miraculis sanctorum Angliae, Walliae, Scotiae et Hiberniae collectum in magno volumine   15

> Sharpe, *Latin Writers*, 334.

4 Martirologio quoque venerabilis Bedae sanctorum nomina nonnulla martirum et confessorum et virginum virtutes et miracula breviter et succincte adjecit

5 Scripsit etiam super Genesim, Exodum, et Leviticum, Numerum, Deuteronomium, Josue, Judicum, Regum, et Apocalipsin morales expositiones et allegoricas, et plerique in locis literales, ex opusculis sanctorum doctorum et patrum antiquorum diligenter extractas maximo volumine

6 De omnibus vero sanctis usus ecclesiae Sarisburiensis lectiones vitas eorum breviter continentes compilavit in uno volumine, quem quidem librum Lectionarium nominare decrevit.

p. 101]

342 JOHANNES DE HOVDEN clericus dominae Alienorae reginae matris regis Edwardi primi post conquestum scripsit meditationem devotissimam de nativitate Christi, passione et resurrectione ejusdem, ut mens legentis affectione in Christi amore perficiat et coelitus accendatur. Liber autem istius meditationis vocatur.

> (John of Howden)
> Same as Houden *280*.
> Bale, *Index*, 221.

Johannes de Hovden *342.*

> This entry was compiled from manuscripts of Howden's works at **173** Babwell and **82** Bury similar to Bodl. MS Laud. Lat. 368, BNF MS lat. 3757 (s. xiv, London Franciscans), or especially BL MS Cotton Nero C. ix, which also contains (fol. 218v) most of the biographical note above.
> Sharpe, *Latin Writers*, 266–7.

1 Philomela   *Ave verbum . . . ens in principio*   173

> ens] enu *Add. 3470,* queried by Tanner

> Sharpe, *Latin Writers*, 266. Ed. C. Blume, *John Hoveden's Nachtigallenlied,* Hymnologische Beiträge 4 (Leipzig 1930). Same as Houden *280.1.*

2 Quindecim gaudia B. Virginis   *Virgo vincens . . . portum patriae*   173

> Virgo vincens] balsamum, odore *add. Bale*

> Sharpe, *Latin Writers*, 267. Ed. F. J. E. Raby, *Poems of John of Hoveden,* Surtees Society 154 (1939) 1.

3 Quinquaginta cantica edita ab eodem   *Summe . . . omnis exultet*   173

> Sharpe, *Latin Writers*, 267. Ed. Raby, 8; incipit is that of verse 12, which is the first verse of *Cantica* II.

4 Meditationem de nativitate et passione Christi et vocatur Canticum amoris   *Princeps . . . coeli regia*   82

> Sharpe, *Latin Writers*, 266. Ed. Raby, 206–240; explicit is that of a portion of the poem that no longer survives.

343 LEO papa II natione Tuscus floruit circa A.D. 446 et scripsit multa et in omeliis declamandis multum valuit et sermones plures composuit unde sermonologus dictus est

> (Leo I)
> *Registrum* 28, Gennadius c. 71, *Decretum Gelasianum* IV 3, *Decretum* Di. 37 cc. 5, 6.

1 De incarnatione Verbi ad Flavianum lib.   *Lectis . . .*   151.15.1.58

> R 28.1. *CPL* 1656 *ep.* 28. Ed. C. Silva-Tarouca, Pontificia Universitas gregoriana: Textus et documenta, ser. theol. 9 (Rome 1932) 20. Location number **151** is perhaps a doublet of the numbers 15 1 in the (edited) *Registrum,* but in fact both manuscript transcripts of the *Registrum* at this point incorrectly read 151 (a number not used in the *Registrum*), indicating a corruption of some sort here.

Leo *343.* 8

2 Super missam tract. 1 128

   R28. 5 (whole entry).

3 De conflictu vitiorum et virtutum, secundum quosdam 128.39.104.25

   25] xxv *R*

   R28. 4 (whole entry). Same as Augustinus *1.497* and Gregorius *203.12*.

4 Adversus Euticen abbatem Constantinop[olitanum] lib.1

   Gennadius 71.

5 De constitutione et symbolo Calcedonensis synodi adversus haereses Nestorii et Euticii 15

   R28. 6 (whole entry).

6 Epistolas decretales 70

   Source unidentified.

7 Epistolas alias quamplures 42.94.53.10.20

   42] 43 *R*   10.20] x.xx *R*

   R28. 3 (whole entry).

8 Sermones ad populum 79 *Salvator* . . . 126.153.105.9.19.115

   R28. 2. *CPL* 1657. *CCSL* 138–138A; incipit is that of *serm.* 21 (*CCSL* 138. 85). None of the English collections in the edition contains seventy-nine sermons nor begins with *serm.* 21.

Si quis textum istius Leonis De incarnatione Verbi et alia scripta ejus ad Flavianum vel Fabianum episcopum Constantinop[olitanum] usque ad unum iota disputaverit et non ea in omnibus venerabiliter receperit, anathema sit. In Decret[o] Gelasii, Di. 15 *Sancta Romana* et Di. 37 *Legimus.* Hujus S. Leonis festum celebratur in vigilia apostolorum Petri et Pauli.

Decretum Gelasianum IV 3, *Decretum* Di. 37 cc. 5, 6.

Lanfrancus *344.*

344 LANFRANCUS monachus et prior de Becco et postea abbas Cadomensis et tandem archiepiscopus Cantuariae floruit circa A. Ch. 1079 et scripsit

> *Registrum* 51 and Higden, 7. 208, supplemented by an unidentified source.
> *Speculum coenobitarum* 48.
> Bale, *Index*, 218.
> James extracts, p. 90.
> Sharpe, *Latin Writers*, 357–8.

1 Contra Berengarium in modum dialogi De corpore et sanguine Domini lib. 1   *Lanfrancus . . . ergo vera etc.*   8.1.105.9.20.53.24

> 24] xxiiii *R*

> R51. 2, 5. Sharpe, *Latin Writers*, 357. *PL* 150. 407. Location number **8** comes inadvertently from R51. 3.

2 De casibus in missa et de corpore et sanguine Domini summas   8.1.82

> Source unidentified; cf. R51. 5. Concerning two pseudonymous works with these titles see M. T. Gibson, *Lanfranc of Bec* (Oxford 1978) 239–48, and her handlist of manuscripts of Lanfranc's works at 240. Concerning the authentic *De corpore et sanguine domini* (*PL* 150. 407–442) see the list and discussion of manuscripts by R. B. C. Huygens in *Sacris Erudiri* 16 (1965) 358–69 and partial edition 370–77. Location numbers **8 1** are copied by mistake from *1* above.

p. 102]

3 Omnes libros Veteris et Novi Testamenti qui vitio scriptorum corrupti erant, nec non scripta sanctorum patrum, secundum ortodoxam fidem correxit et commentavit

> commentavit] commutavit *James extracts*

> Source unidentified.

4 Epistolas plures ad diversos   1

> R51. 1 (whole entry).

5 Item contra Berengarium lib. 1 id est Scintillarium

> Scintillarium quoddam *is entered as a separate title in Bale*

> Whole entry from R51. 2 and Higden (in MSS C and D).

6 Item regulam, secundum quosdam

> R51. 3 (whole entry).
>
> Consuetudines monachorum lib. 1 *add. Bale as an entry, habet Speculum coenobitarum; Bury's library had a copy of this work (B13. 246, 'Consuetudinarium Lanfranci'); it is possible that this title was originally part of the Lanfranc entry in the* Catalogus.

345 LACTANTIUS qui et FIRMIANUS floruit circa A. Ch. <blank> et scripsit juxta Jeronimum et Vincentium lib. 14 cap. 89

> Same as Firmianus *189*.
> Neither title appears in Jerome or in Vincent XIV 89.

1 De falsa sapientia lib. 1

> Source unidentified. Same as Firmianus *189.11*.

2 De ave quae vocatur Phoenix lib. 1   *Est locus . . . habere nocendi*   65

> *CPL* 90. Ed. M. C. Fitzpatrick (Philadelphia, PA, 1933) 40; the explicit is that of Claudian's *Phoenix auis* (in his *carmina minora*: ed T. Birt, MGH *Auct. Antiq.* 10. 311–15), which often was coupled in manuscripts with the similar work of Lactantius.

346 LEANDER natus in Cartaginensi provincia Spaniae et monachus Spalensis ecclesiae et postea Bethicae provinciae episcopus floruit A. Ch. 593 et scripsit secundum Ysidorum

> Whole entry save the date from Isidore c. 28 and (the final comment) c. 27. *Speculum coenobitarum* 19.

1 Adversus haereticorum dogmata lib. 2

2 Adversus Arrianorum instituta lib. 1

3 De institutione virginum et contemptu mundi

4 De baptismo ad Gregorium papam ep.

5 De morte non timenda ep. 1

6 In toto psalterio duplici versione conscripsit orationes

7 In sacrificiis quoque laudibus atque psalmis multa duplici sono composuit

Leander   *346. 8*

    8 Ad caeteros quoque coepiscopos plurimas promulgavit epistolas.

    Huic B. papa Gregorius scripsit Moralia super Job et quasdam epistolas, secundum Ysidorum

347 LUCIANUS presbyter floruit A. Ch. <blank> scripsit Graeco eloquio juxta Genadium

    Gennadius cc. 47–8 (whole entry).

  1 Revelationem de inventione sanctorum Stephani et Nicodemi etc. ad omnes ecclesias, quam transtulit Avitus presbiter, ut patet supra in litera A.

    See Avitus *11.7*.

348 LUCANUS poeta claruit A. Ch. 54 et scripsit juxta Vincentium in Speculo historiali lib. 9 cap. 137

    Vincent IX 137.

  1 De incommodo civilis discidii lib. x   *Bella per . . . moenia magnum*

    De bello ciuili; ed. A. E. Housman (Oxford 1927).

349 LUDOLDUS Frater Praedicator floruit A. Ch. <blank> et scripsit

    Script. Ord. Praed. (whole entry), cf. Stams, 90.

  1 Flores grammaticae

350 LENTIUS floruit <blank> et scripsit secundum Miletum episcopum Laodociae

    (Leutius)
    Ps. Mileto, prologue to the *Transitus B. Mariae* (*BHL* 5352), *PG* 5. 1239 (whole entry).

  1 Actus Apostolorum, Johannis scilicet et Andreae et Thomae, qui de virtutibus quae per eos fecit Dominus vere dixit, sed de doctrina eorum multa mentitus est. Dixit enim eos docuisse duo principia, quae execratur ecclesia Christi

351 LUCIANUS alius vir disertissimus Antiochenae ecclesiae episcopus et martir floruit A. Ch. 236 et scripsit secundum Jeronimum

> ecclesiae episcopus] ecclesiae presbyter *Jerome edition;* ecclesie episcopus *Jerome, Bodl. MS e Musaeo 31 p. 206*
>
> Jerome c. 77 (whole entry save the date).

1 De fide libellum

2 Epistolas ad diversos

352 LUCIFER Caralitanus episcopus floruit circa A. Ch. 344 et scripsit secundum Jeronimum

> Jerome c. 95 (whole entry save the date).

1 De fide contra Constantium imperatorem

p. 103]

353 LUCIUS Alexandrinus episcopus floruit circa A. Ch. 387 et scripsit juxta Jeronimum

> Jerome c. 118 (whole entry save the date).

1 De Pascha solennes epistolas

354 LEPORIUS monachus et presbyter praesumens de puritate vitae Pelagianum dogma coeperat sequi, sed per B. Augustinum admonitus et emendatus scripsit

> Gennadius c. 60 (whole entry).
> Bale, *Index*, 283.

1 De emendatione sua libellum 1

2 Item de incarnatione Christi lib. 1

355 LICINIANUS Cartaginis Spartariae episcopus floruit tempore Mauritii circa A. Ch. 589 et scripsit juxta Ysidorum

> Spartariae *queried by Tanner*
>
> Isidore c. 29 (whole entry save the date).

Licinianus   *355. 1*

   1 De sacramento baptismi lib. 1

   2 Ad Eutropium ep. 1

   3 Item epistolas plurimas et multa alia

356 LONGUS floruit circa A. Ch. <blank> et scripsit juxta Cassiodorum libro De institutione divinarum literarum

> Same as Velius *611*.
> Cassiodorus I. 30. 2 (whole entry).

   1 De ortographia lib.

357 LUITPRANDUS diaconus Titinensis ecclesiae floruit A. Ch. <blank> et scripsit

> Diceto, 1. 23 (whole entry).

   1 Historiam Longobardorum

358 LAURENTIUS prior Dunelmiae et postea abbas Westmon[asteriensis] floruit circa A. Ch. 1160 et scripsit

> Kirkestede has conflated Lawrence of Durham with Lawrence of Westminster.
> Bale, *Index*, 279–80.
> Ware extracts, fol. 132r, work *4* only.
> Sharpe, *Latin Writers*, 359–61 and 365.

   1 Sermones   *Ut tota cum . . .*   11

> Ut tota cum] devotione Domini celebremus *add. Bale*

> Collected, not composed, by Lawrence of Westminster; Sharpe, *Latin Writers*, 365. **11** Westminster = Oxford, Balliol College, MS 223; the rubricator of the manuscript neglected to fill in the opening words 'Dignum est, fratres', and Kirkestede reproduced the faulty incipit, confirming that this manuscript was his source.

   2 De consolatione mortis amici   *Saepe et supra . . . nostrae disputationi*

> Saepe et supra] modum multis anxietatibus *add. Bale*

> Lawrence of Durham; Sharpe, *Latin Writers*, 359.

3 Dialogorum in metro lib. 4   *Carmina . . . omnis ei*

    Lawrence of Durham; Sharpe, *Latin Writers*, 359.

4 Vitam S. Brigidae prosaice

    Like the other works, this entry was probably based on a manuscript. Lawrence of Durham; Sharpe, *Latin Writers*, 361.

5 Yponosticon lib. 9   *Principium rerum . . .*   Finis: de S. Cuthberto et de confessoribus et de virginibus; ultimum verbum est: *hic et homo*   83

    Principium rerum] sine tempore tempora formans *add. Bale*

    Lawrence of Durham; Sharpe, *Latin Writers*, 360.

Iste Laurentius sic scribit in suo Yponosticon de S. Edmundo martire: Utque cruore suo Gallos Dionisius ornat/ Graecos Demetrius gloria quisque suos/ Sic nos Edmundus nulli virtute secundus/ Lux patris et patriae gloria magna suae/ Sceptra manu, diadem caput, sacra purpura corpus/ Ornat ei, sed plus vincula, mucro, cruor.

    The poem is edited by J. Raine, Surtees Society 70 (1880) 69.

p. 104]

359 MAXIMUS Tauriensis vel Taurinensis ecclesiae episcopus floruit A. Ch. 412 et scripsit juxta Genadium et Vincentium lib. 20mo

    Registrum 48, Vincent XX 5 (works *1–7, 9–10*); Gennadius (c. 41) is cited indirectly through Vincent.

1 De gratia baptismi lib. 1

    Vincent XX 5 (whole entry).

2 De avaritia et hospitalitate lib. 1

    Vincent XX 5 (whole entry).

3 De defectu lunae lib. 1

    Vincent XX 5 (whole entry).

4 De jejunio lib. 1

    Vincent XX 5 (whole entry).

Maximus 359. 5

   5 De elemosyna generali et speciali lib. 1

       Vincent XX 5 (whole entry).

   6 De passione Domini tract. 1

       Vincent XX 5 (whole entry).

   7 De Juda traditore lib. 1

       Vincent XX 5 (whole entry).

   8 De symbolo expos. 1

       Source unidentified.

   9 In laudem apostolorum et Johannis baptismate et S. Eusebio tract. 1

       Vincent XX 5 (whole entry).

  10 De baptismo S. Cipriani tract. 1

       Vincent XX 5 (whole entry).

  11 Epistolas plures ad diversos

       Source unidentified.

  12 Omelias quamplures et sermones   15.50.63.105

       R48. 1. *CPL* 220–23; it is impossible without a surviving manuscript to know the contents of the manuscript at **50** Pipewell.

360 MAXIMUS philosophus et post episcopus Constantinopolitanus floruit circa A. Ch. <*blank*> et scripsit juxta Jeronimum

       Jerome c. 127 (whole entry).

   1 De fide contra Arrianos lib. 1

361 METHODIUS Tiri episcopus et martir floruit A. Ch. 254 tempore Decii et Valeriani in Calcide Graeciae et scripsit juxta Jeronimum

       Jerome c. 83, Higden, 1. 22; *Registrum* 77 was not used.

1 Contra Porphirium libros plures

   Jerome 83 (whole entry).

2 De resurrectione contra Origenem lib. 1

   Jerome 83 (whole entry).

3 De Phitonissa et de exitu animae contra eundem lib. 1

   Jerome 83 (whole entry).

4 Super Genesin et Cantica Canticorum

   Jerome 83 (whole entry).

5 Item multa alia quae vulgo lectitantur

   Jerome 83 (whole entry).

6 De principio et fine mundi juxta magistrum in historiis et alios doctores lib. 1   *Sciendum . . . eripere dignetur*

   Higden, 1. 22 . [**82** Bury = Cambridge, Corpus Christi College, MS 404, fols. 4r–6v (Bury P. 163), copied by Kirkestede; another copy of this work was formerly in Cambridge, Gonville and Caius College, MS 225/240 (Bury V. 12), according to Kirkestede's table of contents there (p. 2).]

7 De similitudine 10 virginum lib. 1

   Jerome 83 (whole entry).

362 MACHARIUS monachus et abbas Egiptius floruit anno Christi <*blank*> et scripsit juxta Genadium

   Gennadius c. 10.
   Speculum coenobitarum 3.

1 Ad juniores monachos ep. 1

   In illa epistola docet illum perfecte posse servire Deo qui conditionem creationis suae cognoscens ad omnes semetipsum inclinaverit labores, et luctando atque Dei auxilium adversum omne quod in hac vita suave est implorando, ad natalem quoque proveniens puritatem continentiam velut naturae debitum munus optinuit.

   Gennadius 10 (whole entry).

Macharius 362. 2

2 Item scripsit multa alia juxta Genadium in libro De viris illustribus

> Gennadius 10 (whole entry)

3 De ea quae est secundum Spiritum perfectione lib. 1   *Gratia . . . et vivificante*

> The *De perfectione in spiritu* is part of an extract from the spiritual homilies of Macharius made in the 10th cent. by Simeon Logotheta; cf. O. Bardenhewer, *Geschichte der altkirchlichen Literatur* (1912), 3. 89.

363 MACHARIUS alius monachus et abbas Alexandriae floruit A. Ch. 303 et scripsit juxta Genadium

> Gennadius c. 28.
> *Speculum coenobitarum* 4.

1 Adversus mathematicos lib. 1

> Gennadius 28 (whole entry).

In quo labore orientalium quaesivit solacia scripturarum et obiit in Thebaida 4 Non. Januarii A. Ch. 363°.

> Source of this statement is unknown.

364 MARTINUS Dumiensis monasterii episcopus floruit A. Ch. 527 et scripsit secundum Ysidorum libro De viris illustribus cap. 22°

> Dumiensis] Diumensis *Add. 3470*, queried by *Tanner*

> (Martin of Braga)
> *Registrum* 41, Isidore c. 22 (works *1, 5*).

1 De quatuor virtutibus tract. 1   *Quatuor . . . ignaviam*. Et intitulatur Formula vitae honestae   82.15.126.156.105.8

> R41. 1 (second title, location number **15**), R41. 3 (first title, location numbers **126** to **8**), Isidore 22. *CPL* 1080. Ed. C. W. Barlow, *Martini episcopi Bracarensis opera omnia* (New Haven, CT, 1950) 236; incipit is that of c. 1a. Same as Augustinus *1.488* and Seneca *543.18*. **82** Bury = BL MS Royal 8 F. xiv, fol. 140r (Bury G. 15), a manuscript procured, and this segment copied, by Kirkestede; BL MS Royal 8 C. iv, fol. 13v (Bury R. 42), fragment.

2 De 10 virtutibus tract. 1   126

> R41. 4 (whole entry).

p. 105]

   3 De sententiis lib. 1 <u>161</u>

       R41. 5 (whole entry).

   4 Ad Neronem lib. 1 <u>166</u>.163

       166] 161 *R*

       R41. 6 (whole entry save the suspect **163**).

   5 Sermones plures et epistolas in quibus ortatur vitae emendationem et conversationem fidei, orationis instantiam, eleemosinarum largitionem, pietatem, cultum virtutum <u>126</u>

       Whole entry from R41. 2 and Isidore 22.

MARCUS TULLIUS. Quaere literam T vocabulo **TULLIUS**

365 **MARCUS VARRO** floruit tempore Octaviani Augusti A. Ch. <*blank*> et scripsit juxta Vincentium in Speculo lib. 7 cap. 58

       Same as Varro *609*.
       Vincent VII 58 (whole entry).

   1 Libros antiquitatis xli

       Quorum xxv humanis rebus divinisque xvi tribuit

366 **MARCELLINUS ILLIRICANUS** floruit A. Ch. 529 et scripsit juxta Cassiodorum tempore Justiniani

       Cassiodorus I. 17. 1–2 (whole entry save the date).

   1 De temporum qualitatibus et locorum positionibus lib. 4

   2 Cronica usque ad tempora Justiniani

367 **MARIANUS SCOTUS** et monachus floruit A. Ch. <*blank*> et scripsit

       Diceto, 1. 23.
       Ware extracts, fol. 132r.

Marianus Scotus   *367. 1*

1 Cronicorum

> Diceto, 1. 23 (whole entry).

2 Super Lucam abbreviationes   *Fuit in diebus . . .   Per moysen . . . formam Domini*

> [**82** Bury = Bodl. MS Bodley 297, p. 147 (Bury C. 53), with Kirkestede's marginal rubric 'Abbreuiationes Mariani super Lucam'; explicit on p. 194.]

368 MARCION disertissimus Antiochenae ecclesiae presbiter floruit circa A. Ch. 272 et scripsit secundum Jeronimum

> Marcion] Malchion *Jerome edition;* Marcion *Bodl. MS e Musaeo 31 p. 205*
>
> Jerome c. 71 (whole entry).

1 Contra Paulum Samosatenum dialogorum lib. 1

2 Item ex persona synodi epistolam grandem

369 MACROBIUS presbiter floruit anno <*blank*> et scripsit secundum Genadium ante lapsum

> Gennadius c. 5, *MF* XVI, 'Libri diuersorum auctorum'.

1 Ad virgines et confessores tantum

> tantum *Add. 3470, queried by Tanner; perhaps* librum
>
> Gennadius 5 (whole entry).

2 De sompno Cipionis   *Cum in Africa . . . continetur*

> *MF* XVI 5 (whole entry, incipit 'Cum in Affricam', explicit 'continetur integritas'); this title correctly belongs to Macrobius Ambrosius Theodosii (370).

3 Ad confessores et virgines lib. 1

> Gennadius 5 (whole entry).

370 MACROBIUS AMBROSIUS THEODOSII vir consularis floruit <*blank*> et scripsit

> *Registrum* 90 (the name 'Macrobius' with location numbers but without a list of works) was not used.

1 Librum Saturnaliorum

   Source unidentified. Same as *2* below. [**82** Bury = B13. 53.]

2 De tribus diebus conviviorum Saturnalium lib. 1   *Multas . . . humori*

   Ed. J. Willis, Teubner (1970²). [**82** Bury = CUL MS Ff. 3. 5, fol. 7r (Bury A. 130).]

3 De viribus herbarum

   Source unidentified. Spurious; same as Macer *388*.

371 MILETO vel MILETUS Asianus Sardensis vel Sardinensis episcopus floruit A. Ch. 88 et scripsit juxta Jeronimum libro De catholicis scriptoribus cap. 26

   Jerome c. 24 (whole entry save work *18*), *Mariale* fol. 2r (work *18*).

1 De Christiano dogmate lib. 1

2 De vita prophetarum lib. 1

3 De Pascha lib. 2

4 De ecclesia lib. 1

5 De die Dominica lib. 1

6 De fidelibus lib. 1

7 De psalmis lib. 1

8 De sensibus lib. 1

9 De anima et corpore lib. 1

10 De baptismo lib. 1

11 De veritate lib. 1

12 De generatione Christi lib. 1

Mileto   *371. 13*

   13 De prophetia Christi lib. 1

   14 Librum qui dicitur Clavis

p. 106]

   15 De diabolo lib. 1

   16 De Apocalipsi lib. 1

   17 Eglogarum lib. 7

   18 De assumptione B. Mariae lib. 1   *Cum nobis* . . .   77

       Mariale fol. 2r. Spurious. *CPG* 1096. The incipit 'Nunc uobis petentibus' or 'Nos uobis petentibus' occurs in continental manuscripts (for example, Troyes, BM MS 1876 and Brno UL MS Mk 99).

   19 De philoximia lib. 1

       philoximia *Add. 3470; Tanner, uncertain of this reading, added* philoxumia *as a variant*

372 MUSSEUS Massiliensis ecclesiae presbyter floruit tempore Leonis et Marchiani et scripsit juxta Genadium et excerpsit de Sanctis Scripturis

      Gennadius c. 80 (whole entry).

   1 Lectiones totius anni festivis diebus aptas et responsoria et psalmorum capitula tempori et lectionibus congruentia

   2 De sacramentis et officiis divinis ad Eustasium episcopum egregium volumen 1

   3 Omelias quamplures

373 MILITIADES floruit A. Ch. <*blank*> et scripsit secundum Jeronimum libro De viris illustribus

      Militiades] Miltiades *Jerome edition;* Militiades *Bodl. MS e Musaeo 31 p. 197*

      Jerome c. 39 (whole entry).

Martinus   376. 1

1 Contra gentes et Judaeos libros plures

2 Adversus alios lib. 1

3 Apolegiticum lib. 1

374 MINUCIUS Felix Romae causidicus floruit A. Ch. <*blank*> et scripsit juxta Jeronimum ubi supra

> Jerome c. 58 (whole entry).

1 De fato vel contra mathematicos lib. 1

2 Dialogum Christiani et haeretici qui Octavus inscribitur

> De isto Minutio meminit Lactantius in libris suis.

375 MONAGALDUS floruit A. Ch. <*blank*> et scripsit

> (Manegoldus de Lautenbach)
> Source of *1* and *3* unidentified.

1 Super psalterium

2 Super epistolas Pauli xiv   *Paulus . . . dignum quidem*

> Stegmüller *Bibl.* 5445. [**82** Bury = seen by Leland at Bury, B16. 6.]

3 Super Platonem   10

376 MARTINUS Frater Praedicator Polonus episcopus et poenitentiarius papae floruit A. Ch. 1276 et scripsit

> poenitentiarius] primarius *Add. 3470; Tanner, uncertain of this reading, added* poenitentiarius *as a variant*

> *Script. Ord. Praed.* (cf. Stams, 35), supplemented by Bury manuscripts.

1 Cronica de papis et imperatoribus   *Quoniam scire . . . Johannes papa*

> MGH *Scriptores* 22. 377–475. This is the later recension of this text ending with John XXI in 1277.

Martinus   *376. 2*

2 Tabulam super decretales   *Inter alia . . . nobilitas*

   om. Stams

   Margarita Decreti; Kaeppeli 2973. Printed, Nuremberg 1481, &c. [**82** Bury = Cambridge, Pembroke College, MS 40 (Bury T. 47), annotated by Kirkestede.]

3 De conditione urbis Romae lib. 1

   om. Stams

377 MONETA Frater Praedicator in Lumbardia floruit A. Ch. <*blank*> et scripsit

   Script. Ord. Praed. (whole entry), cf. Stams, 76.

1 De sectis haereticorum lib. 1

378 MATHEUS Ripensis Frater Praedicator Daciae floruit A. Ch. <*blank*> et scripsit

   Script. Ord. Praed. (whole entry), cf. Stams, 103.

1 Sermones de tempore et sanctis

379 MATHEUS PARISIENSIS floruit circa A. Ch. <*blank*> et scripsit

   Source unidentified.
   Bale, *Index*, 289.
   Sharpe, *Latin Writers*, 373.

1 Historiam sive librum cronicorum

   Historia Anglorum; Sharpe, *Latin Writers*, 373. Ed. F. Madden, RS 44 (1866–1869).

MERCURIUS TRISMEGISTUS infra in T.

380 MUSANUS non ignobilis doctor floruit A. Ch. <*blank*> sub imperator Marco Antonino secundum Jeronimum et scripsit

   Jerome c. 31 (whole entry).

1 Ad quosdam fratres errantes lib. 1

381 MODESTUS floruit A. Ch. <*blank*> sub imperatore Marco Antonino et Lucio Aurelio Commodo secundum Jeronimum et scripsit

>   Jerome c. 32 (whole entry).

1 Adversus Marcionem lib. 1

382 MARCELLUS ANCHERANUS episcopus floruit circa A. Ch. 340 et scripsit secundum Jeronimum De catholicis scriptoribus

>   Ancheranus] Aucheranus *Add. 3470; Tanner added the correction as a variant reading*
>
>   Jerome c. 86 (whole entry save the date).

1 Contra Arrianos disputationum multa volumina

p. 107]

383 MOTHUNUS Mesopotamiae presbiter apud Antiochiam floruit circa A. Ch. <*blank*> et scripsit juxta Genadium tempore Genadii

>   Mothunus] Mothimus *Bodl. MS e Musaeo 31 p. 236*
>
>   Gennadius c. 72 (whole entry).

1 Adversus Eutichen egregium libellum

384 MENNADIUS Constantinopolitanae ecclesiae episcopus floruit circa A. Ch. 458 et scripsit secundum Genadium

>   Mennadius] Gennadius *Gennadius edition, Bodl. MS e Musaeo 31 p. 240*
>
>   Gennadius c. 91 (whole entry save the date).

1 Super Danielem prophetam commentarios

2 Item omelias multas

385 MAXIMUS Augustanae civitatis episcopus floruit circa A. Ch. 495 et scripsit secundum Ysidorum brevi stilo Historiam de hiis quae temporibus Gothorum in Spaniis acta sunt storico et composito sermone. Sed et multa alia versu prosaque scripsisse dicitur.

>   Isidore c. 33 (whole entry save the date).

Maximus   *386.*

386 MAXIMUS alius floruit circa A. Ch. 190 et scripsit secundum Jeronimum ubi supra Quaestionem insigni volumine: Unde malum et quod materia a Deo facta sit.

> Jerome c. 47 (whole entry save the date).

387 MARTIRIUS floruit circa A. Ch. <*blank*> et scripsit secundum Cassiodorum

> Cassiodorus I. 30. 2 (whole entry).

1 De ortographia lib. 1

388 MACER

1 De viribus herbarum   *Herbarum quasdam . . . nasci perhibebunt*   74

> perhibebunt] *Add. 3470; Tanner has added* prohibebunt *as a variant reading*
>
> Ed. L. Choulant, *Macer Floridus de uiribus herbarum* (Leipzig 1832). Explicit 'prohibebit' is that of c. 63. Same as Macrobius Ambrosius Theodosii *370.3.*

389 MARCIUS VALERIUS MARTIALIS Cocus floruit <*blank*> et scripsit

1 Epigrammatωn lib. xii   *Spero me . . . ferre potest*

> Ed. W. Heraeus and I. Borovskij, *Epigrammaton libri*, Teubner (1976²) 11–307.

2 Xenia lib. 1   *De toga . . . rosa est*

> Book XIII of the Epigrams; Heraeus and Borovskij, 307–320, incipit 'Ne toga'.

3 Apophoreta lib. 1   *Cinthesibus . . . lucis aves*

> Book XIV of the Epigrams; Heraeus and Borovskij, 321–43.

4 De seriis lib.

> Source unidentified.

390 MARCIANUS FELIX CAPELLA floruit <*blank*> et scripsit

> Vincent V 37.

1 De nuptiis Philologiae et Mercurii metrice et prosaice lib. 1   *Tu quem
   . . . faveantque Musae*

   Ed. J. Willis, Teubner (1983) 1–58 line 6. [**82** Bury = B13. 56.]

2 De geometria lib. 7

   Hoc probat Vincentius in Speculo libro 5° cap. 37°

   Vincent V 37 (whole entry).

391 MARBODIUS floruit <blank> et scripsit

1 De natura lapidum lib. 1

   PL 171. 1737. [**82** Bury = BL MS Add. 24199, fol. 46r (Bury P. 123).]

392 MARCUS PAULUS DE VENETIIS floruit <blank> et scripsit

1 Itinerarium de consuetudinibus et conditionibus Orientalium regionum et de mirabilibus ibidem lib. 3   *Librum prudentis* . . .   Ultimum capitulum: De regione tenebrarum et provincia Ruthenorum

   prudentis] pdentis *Add. 3470*

   The translation of Francesco Pipino; Kaeppeli 1114. See C. W. Dutschke, 'Francesco Pipino and the Manuscripts of Marco Polo's *Travels*', PhD diss. (UCLA 1993).

393 MARIUS SALERNITANUS floruit <blank> et scripsit

1 De proficuo humano lib. 1

   The work is not known to have survivied. In his *De elementis*, which survives in a single manuscript from Bury (BL MS Cotton Galba E. IV = Bury M. 21), Marius mentions having written this book ('[librum] De humano proficuo feci'; ed. R. C. Dales (Berkeley, CA, 1976), 179).

394 MAURICIUS

   Sharpe, *Latin Writers*, 374.

Mauricius   *394. 1*

1 Distinctiones   *Circa abjectionem . . . multiplex est*   11

> Sharpe, *Latin Writers*, 374, Stegmüller *Bibl.* 5566. Partially printed, *Dictionarium S. Scripturae Mauritii Hybernici* (Venice 1603). **11** Westminster = B105. 33, probably the same as Bodl. MS Bodley 46, fols. 1r–297v; 'multiplex est' are the opening words of the last *distinctio*.

395 MAXIMIANUS

> Source unidentified.

1 De bello Gildonico

> Claudius Claudianus; *Texts and Transmission*, 143–5. See also Claudius *120*.

p. 108]

396 NOVATIANUS urbis Romae presbyter floruit A. Ch. <*blank*> et scripsit juxta Jeronimum ea quae sequuntur

> Jerome c. 70 (whole entry).

1 De Pascha lib. 1

2 De Sabbato lib. 1

3 De circumcisione lib. 1

4 De sacerdote lib. 1

5 De oratione lib. 1

6 De cibis Judaicis lib. l

7 De instantia lib. 1

8 De Attalo

9 De Trinitate grande volumen, quod plurimi nescientes Cipriani aestimant

397 NICHOLAUS Ambianensis floruit circa A. Ch. <*blank*> et scripsit papae Clementi III

1 De arte fidei catholicae lib. 5

> *PL* 210. 595. [**82** Bury = BL MS Royal 8 C. IV, fol. 8r (Bury R. 42), with marginal rubric and attribution of authorship by Kirkestede.]

398 NICHOLAUS TRIVET Frater Praedicator floruit A. Ch. <*blank*> et scripsit

> *Script. Ord. Praed.*, which presumably supplied the titles below that have no incipits and explicits (*2, 4–5, 7*). This author is omitted by Stams, and Pign. 43 gives a version different from this entry.
> Bale, *Index*, 308–309.
> Sharpe, *Latin Writers*, 394–8.

1 Super Boetium de Consolatione philosophiae explanationem   *Carmina . . . cernentis omnia*

> Sharpe, *Latin Writers*, 395. Only parts are printed; cf. Sharpe, *Latin Writers*. [**82** Bury = seen by Leland at Bury, B16. 9.]

2 Super regulam B. Augustini

> Inter multas et varias religiosam *add. Bale as an incipit*
>
> Sharpe, *Latin Writers*, 395.

3 De missa tract. 1   *Fons sapientiae . . . usque ad salutem*   63

> Sharpe, *Latin Writers*, 396. Kaeppeli 3142; incipit is that of the prologue; explicit 'usque in finem ad laudem' etc. Presumably the same as *9* below.

4 Cronicorum lib. 1

5 De astronomia multa

> multa *om. Bale*

6 Super tragedias Senecae lib. 9   *Tria genera . . . fulmine etc.*   173.158.165

> Sharpe, *Latin Writers*, 395. Parts have been printed; cf. Sharpe, *Latin Writers*.

7 Super declamationes Senecae

Nicholaus Trivet *398. 8*

8 Super Exodum cum doctoribus super eodem   *Deus visitabit . . . laudabunt*

   Sharpe, *Latin Writers*, 394. The work does not survive.

9 De missa tractatum alium   *Rogatus a . . . participationem*   147.61

   Presumably the same as *3* above; incipit and explicit unidentified.

399 NICHOLAUS DE GORHAM Frater Praedicator floruit A. Ch. <*blank*> et scripsit

   Script. Ord. Praed., cf. Stams, 30, 105. Kirkestede's additions from **82** Bury have been supplied with incipits and explicits, but the references to **65** Ramsey were probably added from memory, without his verifying the incipits and explicits. Bale, *Index*, 301 (works 7–9).

1 Super Ecclesiasticum postillas   65

2 Super Lucam et Matheum   65

3 Super epistolas Pauli   65

4 Super epistolas canonicas

5 Super Apocalipsin

6 Distinctiones   *Abeuntium . . . cum Domino*   65.82

   Stegmüller *Bibl.* 5740; Kaeppeli 3090. **82** Bury = Cambridge, Pembroke College, MS 99, fols. 1r–193ra (Bury S. 38).

7 Themata vel sermones de Dominicis   *Hora est jam . . . prodigia ejus*   82

   Hora] Hominum *Add. 3470*   Hora est jam] nos de somno *add. Bale*

   82 Bury = Cambridge, Pembroke College, MS 99, fols. 195r–257r (Bury S. 38).

8 Tabulam super decreta et decretales

9 Themata vel sermones de festis   *In baculo . . . unum sunt*

   baculo *Add. 3470, queried by Tanner*   In baculo] meo transivi Iordanem *add. Bale*

   [**82** Bury = Cambridge, Pembroke College, MS 99, fol. 257r (Bury S. 38).]

400 NICEAS Romacianae civitatis episcopus floruit circa A. Ch. <*blank*> et scripsit secundum Genadium

> Gennadius c. 22 (whole entry).

1 De instructione baptismi lib. 1

2 De errore gentilitatis lib. 1

3 De fide unicae majestatis lib. 1

4 Adversus genealogiam lib. 1

5 De symbolo lib. 1

6 De agni Paschalis victima lib. 1

7 Ad virginem lapsam lib. 1

p. 109]

401 NICETUS episcopus floruit circa A. Ch. <*blank*> et scripsit juxta Cassiodorum libro De institutione divinarum literarum

> Cassiodorus I. 16. 3 (whole entry).

1 De fide sancti Trinitatis lib. 1

> Si quis de Patre et Filio et Spiritu Sancto aliquid summatim peroptat attingere nec se mavult longa lectione fatigare, hunc librum Niceti De fide, quem doctrinae coelestis claritate completum in contemplationem divinam compendiosa brevitate conscripsit. Qui quidem liber voluminibus S. Ambrosii sociatus est quae ad Gratianum imp[eratorem] destinavit.

402 NENNIUS Brito discipulus Eldugi presbyteri floruit A. Ch. <*blank*> et scripsit

> scripsit] historiam aedidit *Bale*

> Source unidentified. No doubt this was meant to record the *Historia Britonum* (MGH *Auct. Antiq.* 13. 111).
> Bale, *Index*, 297.

Nicholaus de Lyra   *403*.

403 NICHOLAUS DE LYRA Frater Minor floruit circa A. Ch. <blank> et scripsit

1 Super totam Bibliam

> The source was probably a Bury manuscript. Stegmüller *Bibl.* 5829–5923. Printed, Rome 1471–2, &c. [**82** Bury = Cambridge, Pembroke College, MS 11, fol. 1r (Bury —), Genesis–Kings, beg. imperfect; this is too late to be reported in the *Catalogus* but may descend from the manuscript Kirkestede used.]

2 Super psalterium   *Propheta magnus . . . perducat*   65

> Stegmüller *Bibl.* 5853. Printed, *Nicholaus de Lyra postilla super Psalterium* (Paris: Ulrich Gering, 1483)

3 Super evangelia   *Quatuor facies . . . ad faciem*

> Stegmüller *Bibl.* 5896–5900. Printed, *Nicholaus de Lyra postilla super Evangelia* (Basel: Berthold Ruppel, n.d.), &c.

404 ORIGINES doctor super omnes post apostolos in ecclesia Dei floruit circa A. Ch. 222 et scripsit 6000 et amplius tractatus. Licet enim Origines iste in multis erraverit, tamen quia multa scripta reliquit utilia, quaedam eorum ecclesia recipit. Nam et papa Gelasius in Decretis suis illa opuscula Origenis approbat, quae B. Jeronimus non reprobat.

> *Registrum* 10, Vincent XII 11 and 13, Cassiodorus I. 1. 9 and I. 2. 11.
> Vincent provides the initial sequence of titles, fleshed out from manuscripts and from the *Registrum*. The end of the entry (works *23–30*), as usual, comprises an unsystematic record of afterthoughts and oversights from all sources. See also Adamantius *33*.
> *Speculum coenobitarum* 1.

1 Super Genesin omel. 17   *Quod est principium . . . posuimus*   98.128.114. 154.105

> R10. 18, Vincent XII 11. Stegmüller *Bibl.* 6170. *GCS* 29. 1. The so-called 17th homily is composed of parts of Rufinus's *De benedictionibus patriarcharum*; see *CCSL* 20. 186–7. [**82** Bury = B13. 39a which perhaps = Cambridge, Pembroke College, MS 94, fol. 1r (Bury O. 2), incipit 'Quid . . .'.]

2 Super Exodum omel. 13   *Videtur . . . Deo Jacob*   105.154.114.35.23.104

> R10. 19, Vincent XII 11. Stegmüller *Bibl.* 6174. *GCS* 29. 145. [**82** Bury = B13. 39b which perhaps = Cambridge, Pembroke College, MS 94, fol. 41r (Bury O. 2).]

Origines   *404. 11*

3 Super Leviticum omel. 16   *Sicut in novissimis . . . imposuit*   105.154.114.
   8.35.23

   R10. 20, Vincent XII 11. Stegmüller *Bibl.* 6176. *GCS* 29. 280. [**82** Bury = B13.
   39c, which perhaps = Cambridge, Pembroke College, MS 94, fol. 77r (Bury
   O. 2).]

4 Super Numeros omel. 28   *Divinis . . . numerati sunt*   105.43.42.114.
   124.9

   R10. 24, Vincent XII 11. Stegmüller *Bibl.* 6178. *GCS* 30. 3.

5 Super Deuteronomium serm. 4   65

   Vincent XII 11 (whole entry save **65** Ramsey, perhaps added by Kirkestede
   from memory without record of incipit and explicit).

6 Super Josue vel Jehu Nave omel. 26   *In divinis . . . Israel*   80.42.82.9.
   19.35.39

   R10. 11, Vincent XII 11. Stegmüller *Bibl.* 6181. *GCS* 30 (*Origenes Werke* 7)
   286–463; incipit is that of the prologue. Same as Jeronimus *281.47*. [**82** Bury
   = B13. 212.]

7 Super Judicum omel. 8   *Lector . . . mereamur*   105.42.154.35.104

   R10. 21, Vincent XII 11. Stegmüller *Bibl.* 6283. *GCS* 30. 464. [**82** Bury = B13.
   97 = Cambridge, Pembroke College, MS 95, fol. 1r (Bury O. 4).]

8 De Elcana tract. 1   *Non tunc . . . in Christo*

   Vincent XII 11. *GCS* 33. 1. [**82** Bury = Cambridge, Pembroke College, MS
   95, fol. 19v (Bury O. 4).]

9 Super libros Regum lib. 11   105.154.104

   R10. 22 (whole entry).

10 Super principium libri Job lib. 3

   Vincent XII 11 (whole entry).

11 Super psalmum 36^m omel. 5

   Vincent XII 11 (whole entry).

Origines *404. 12*

12 Super psalmum 37ᵐ omel. 2

> Vincent XII 11 (whole entry).

13 Super psalmum 38ᵐ omel.2

> Vincent XII 11 (whole entry).

14 Super Cantica Canticorum   *Quomodo dicimus . . . Christi Jesu*   42.83.9.15.
39.23.63

> 83] *a repeated* 82 *R*

> R10. 5, Vincent XII 11. *GCS* 33. 27. Same as Jeronimus *281.50*. [**82** Bury = Cambridge, Pembroke College, MS 95, fol. 29v (Bury O. 4).]

15 Epitalamium super Cantica   *Epitalamium . . . in fide*   84.82.42.19.20.39

> 84] 89 *R, but Tanner 165 and Peterhouse 169 both have* 84 *(a number not otherwise used in Registrum)*

> R10. 6, Vincent XII 11. *GCS* 33. 61. Same as Petrus Commestor *440.8*. **82** Bury = B13. 213.

16 Super Ysaiam omel. 9   *Quidam . . . efficieris*   105.154.82.43.39.104

> R10. 10, Vincent XII 11. Stegmüller *Bibl.* 6202. **82** Bury = Cambridge, Pembroke College, MS 95, fol. 42r (Bury O. 4), incipit 'Quamdiu'.

17 Super Jeremiam omel. 14   *Deus ad . . . Christo Jesu*   105.154.43.39.82.104

> R10. 7, Vincent XII 11. Stegmüller *Bibl.* 6205. *PL* 25. 585. **82** Bury = Cambridge, Pembroke College, MS 95, fol. 64r (Bury O. 4).

18 Super Ezechiel omel. 4   *Magnum . . .*   105.43.63.104.107

> R10. 23, Vincent XII 11. Stegmüller *Bibl.* 6208. *GCS* 33. 318; incipit is that of the prologue. [**82** Bury = Cambridge, Pembroke College, MS 95, fol. 119v (Bury O. 4), which contains only two homilies according to the rubrics (fols. 119v, 128r).]

19 Super Mattheum lib. 26   20

> Quorum 12 primi raro inveniuntur

> 20] xx *R*

> Whole entry from R10. 33 (title and location number) and Vincent XII 11 (title and comment on rarity).

Origines 404. 27

p. 110]

20 Super Lucam omel. 38   20.63.35.105.9

>   R10. 26, Vincent XII 11. The location numbers are a compilation: **20** and **63** are taken from R10. 29, 'Omelie eius'; **105** and **9** from R10. 12–17, a list of individual homilies on gospel texts; and **35** from R10. 26 itself.

21 Super principium Johannis tract. 1

>   Vincent XII 11 (whole entry).

22 Super Epistolam ad Romanos lib. 10   *Volentem . . . offerent*   163.94.9.15. 53.39.63

>   R10. 4, Vincent XII 11. Stegmüller *Bibl.* 6221. *PG* 14. 831; explicit unidentified. [**82** Bury = B13. 215.]

23 De singularitate clericorum   *Emiseram . . . erit vobiscum*   63.15.82.35. 43.10

>   10] x *R*

>   R10. 8. *Ps.* Cyprian; *CPL* 62. *CSEL* 3/3. 173. Same as Augustinus *1.60* and Jeronimus *281.214*. **82** Bury = B13. 33d.

24 De natali Domini serm. 1   *Quia mortuus . . .*   108

>   R10. 1 (whole entry, incipit 'Quod mortuus').

25 De circumsisione Domini serm. 1   8.108

>   R10. 25 (whole entry).

26 Libros Periarthon, in quibus maximae ejus haereses inveniuntur

>   Vincent XII 11 (whole entry). Same as Rufinus *508.10*.

27 Extat etiam libellus qui planctus Origenis dicitur et a B. Jeronimo translatus inscribitu   12

>   12] xii *R*

>   Whole entry from R10. 28 and Vincent XII 13.

Origines   404. 28

28 Epistolas scripsit plures ad diversos

   R10. 27 (whole entry).

29 Super Paralipomenon libro 2do prolixam omeliam secundum Cassiodorum

   Cassiodorus I. 1. 9 (whole entry).

30 Super Ruth secundum Cassiodorum expositionem

   Cassiodorus I. 2. 11 (whole entry).

405 ODO primus abbas Cluniacensis floruit circa A. Ch. <*blank*> et scripsit

   Registrum 50, Guido de Castris's *Sanctilogium* (unedited; cited from BL MS Royal 13 D. ix), fol. 1r.
   The conflation here of several authors with similar names originated with the *Registrum*.
   Speculum coenobitarum 47.

1 De Trinitate lib.

   This work and its source are unidentified.

2 Super 5 libros Moysy lib.   *Primus nobis* . . .   19.15.45

   R50. 1. *Ps*. Odo of Morimond; Stegmüller *Bibl*. 6124–8. **45** Warden = Z26. 3, Odo of Canterbury on the Pentateuch (incipit 'Operis subditi materia lex') seen by Leland there in the 16th cent.

3 De libro vitae   8

   R50. 4 (whole entry).

4 De onere Philistiim   8

   R50. 5 (whole entry).

5 Librum partium compositarum   159.82

   R50. 6. Unidentified; cf. Stegmüller *Sent*. 793.

6 De vitiis et virtutibus animae lib. 3   *Auctor* . . . *parebit*   82.115.50.74

   R50. 8. *Collationes* of Odo of Cluny. *PL* 133. 519. **82** Bury = B13. 167b; a note by Kirkestede (BL MS Harley 1005, fol. 35v = B14. 13) names this as a work read in the refectory at Bury.

Odo   405. 15

7 Cronicarum lib. 1   *Breves . . . moritur*   15

   R50. 7. Ado of Vienne. *PL* 123. 23.

8 De ternario lib. 1   105

   R50. 2 (whole entry).

9 Medullam Moralium Gregorii compilavit in unum volumen

   Source unidentified.

10 De translatione S. Benedicti serm. 1   *Festina . . . per ipsum*   82

   PL 133. 721–9, incipit 'Festiua'.

11 Epistolarum lib. 1

   Source unidentified.

12 Item sermones alias quamplures   43.50.73.74.147

   R50. 3. **147** Spalding = B95. 11, 'Sermones Odonis'.

13 De arte musica dialogum   *Quid est musica . . . benedictus*

   Ps. Odo of Cluny; *PL* 133. 759–73.

14 De confessione capitula 42   Primum: *Poenitentiam.* Ultimum: *Qui peregrinos.*   65

   Odo of Cheriton. *Summa de poenitentia*, unprinted; Bloomfield 3871. Explicit unidentified.

15 Martilogium, ut scribit Guido in Sanctilogio suo multis locis

   Guido de Castris (see headnote) ascribes this to Ado of Vienne.

Odo de Tyrentona   *406.*

406 ODO DE TYRENTONA doctor theologiae floruit post tempus S. Bernardi 1180 et scripsit omelias vel sermones de tempore et sanctis. Prologus: *Ante quatuor . . .* Principium sermonum: *Cum appropinquasset . . .* et *Praesens evangelium bis legitur in anno . . .*   79.65

> Ante *queried by Tanner*
>
> (Odo of Cheriton)
> Bale, *Index*, 313–14.
> Schneyer *Rep.* 4. 483–99. The 'principium sermonum' includes the biblical text (Mt 21:1) and the opening words of the sermon.

407 OROSIUS historiographus et presbiter Hispanus discipulusque B. Augustini floruit circa A. Ch. 442 et scripsit secundum Genadium

> *Registrum* 79, Gennadius c. 40, Higden, 1. 22.

1 De Ormesta, id est miseria, mundi a prima creatione usque ad tempora sua ad B. Augustinum Ypponensem lib. 7   *Majores . . . si deleas*   8.82

> R79. 1, Higden, 1. 22. *Historiae aduersus paganos*; *CPL* 571. Ed. M. P. Arnaud-Lindet, 3 vols. (Paris 1990–91), 1. 13–3. 132. Same as *4* below. **82** Bury = B13. 23a.

2 Quaestiones ad B. Augustinum lib. 1   *Licet . . . prodesse*   8

> R79. 2. *Ps.* Augustine; *CPL* 373a. *PL* 40. 733. Same as Augustinus *1.325*, *1.405*.

3 Apolegiticum lib. 1

> Source unidentified. *CPL* 572; *CSEL* 5.

4 Adversus gentes lib. 7

> Gennadius 40. Same as *1* above.

408 ODO archiepiscopus Vienensis floruit A. Ch. <*blank*> et scripsit

> (Ado of Vienne)
> Whole entry from *Liber florum* fols. 91r, 95r–96r, or Étienne de Bourbon, prologue p. 7.

1 Cronica

p. 111]

409 OSSIUS Cordubensis episcopus floruit circa A. Ch. 284 et scripsit juxta Ysidorum

> Isidore c. 1 (whole entry save the date).

1 De laude virginum ep. 1

2 Item sententias multas in concilio Sardinensi

410 ODILO abbas Cluniacensis floruit circa A. Ch. <blank> et scripsit

1 De purificatione serm. 1   *Omnipotentis . . .*

> PL 142. 999.

411 ORATIUS FLACCUS Satirus poeta floruit tempore Octoviani et scripsit juxta Vincentium lib. 7mo cap. 67

> Vincent VII 67.

1 Epistolarum lib. 2   *Prima . . . licentius aetas*   82.63.27

> Vincent VII 67. Ed. S. Borzsák, Teubner (1984) 230–91, explicit 'decentius aetas'. **82** Bury = B13. 173, 'Oratius totus in uno uolumine'.

2 Sermonum lib. 2   *Qui fuit . . . serpentibus Afris*   82.92.27

> Vincent VII 67. Ed. Borzsák, 151. **82** Bury = B13. 173, 'Oratius totus in uno uolumine'.

3 Carminum secularium lib. 1   *Phoebe . . .*   82.92.37

> Vincent VII 67. Ed. Borzsák, 125. **82** Bury = B13. 173, 'Oratius totus in uno uolumine'.

4 Odarum vel carminum lib. 4   *Mecaenas . . . cavemus*   82.63.37

> Vincent VII 67. Ed. Borzsák 1. **82** Bury = B13.173, 'Oratius totus in uno uolumine'.

Oratius Flaccus *411. 5*

5 Poesiam vel poetriam vel de arte poetica lib. 1   *Humano . . . hirudo*
   82.75.22

   Vincent VII 67. Ed. Borzsák, 292. **82** Bury = B13. 173, 'Oratius totus in uno uolumine'.

6 Inopodon ad Mecaenatem lib. 1   *Ibis lib[ur]nis . . . exitum*   82.42.53

   liburnis] lib. . .nis *Add. 3470, queried by Tanner*

   Ed. Borzsák, 128–50, explicit 'exitus'. **82** Bury = B13. 173, 'Oratius totus in uno uolumine'. / **42** Reading = B71. 203, 'Ode et poetria et sermones et epistole Oratii'.

412 OVIDUS PUBLIUS NASO poeta floruit circa A.D. 22 et scripsit juxta Vincentium lib. 7

Vincent VII 106 (works *1–6, 8–10, 14*).
This entry appears to be primarily based on Vincent and on manuscripts, at **82** Bury and at **10** Holy Trinity, Aldgate. However, lists of Ovid's works circulated in manuscript, and Kirkestede may have made use of one of these as well; a list similar to Kirkestede's appears in Krakow UL MS 2115 fol. 2r. Work *11*, which the Krakow list omits, appears in a shorter list in Madrid, Escorial, Real Biblioteca, MS V.III.10. See P. Lehmann, *Pseudo–Antike Literatur des Mittelalters*, Studien der Bibliothek Warburg 13 (Leipzig 1927), 89.
In this entry, Kirkestede frequently lists as 'explicit' the initial words of the last line of verse.

1 De nuce lib. 1   *Nux ego . . . ipsa meis*   10.82

   Vincent VII 106. Attribution is questionable. Ed. M. Pulbrook (Maynooth, Ireland, 1985) 46–62, explicit at line 164, 'ipsa meos'.

2 Epistolarum lib. 1   *Hanc tua . . .*

   Vincent VII 106. Ed. H. Dörrie (Berlin 1971) 47.

3 De arte amandi lib. 4   *Si quis . . .*

   Vincent VII 106. *Ars amatoria*; ed. E. J. Kenney (Oxford 1961) 113.

4 Metamorphoseos lib. 15   *In nova . . . si quid habent veri*

   Vincent VII 106. Ed. R. Ehwald, 2 vols. in 1 (Berlin 1915–16).

5 De fastis lib. 6   *Tempora . . .*   82

   Vincent VII 106. Ed. D. E. W. Wormell & E. Courtney, Teubner (1978).

Ovidus Publius Naso *412. 16*

6 De tristibus lib. 5   *Parve nec . . . laudis habet*   10

   Vincent VII 106. Ed. J. André (Paris 1968) 2; explicit (p. 162) 'laudet et hortatu' etc.

7 De remedio amoris lib. 2   *Legerat . . .*

   Ed. Kenney 205.

8 De Ponto lib. 4   *Naso . . . plaga locum*   10.82

   Vincent VII 106. Ed. J. A. Richmond (Leipzig 1990).

9 Librum sine titulo continens lib. 3

   Vincent VII 106.

10 Invectionis in Ibin lib. 1   *Tempus . . . et pede quo*   10.82.65

   Vincent VII 106. Ed. F. W. Lenz (Turin 1956) 3–83.

11 De mirabilibus mundi lib. 1   *Hic serpens . . . rapinam*   10

   Thierry of Saint-Trond, according to J. G. Préaux in *Latomus* 6 (1947) 353–65. Ed. M. R. James in *Essays and Studies presented to William Ridgeway* (Cambridge 1914) 290–96.

12 De cuculo lib. 1   *Conveniunt . . . salvae*   10

   Ps. Ovid. *PL* 121. 983.

13 De pulice lib. 1   *Parve pulex . . . si me socium*   10.82

   Ps. Ovid. Ed. N. E. Lemaire, *Poetae latini minores* (Paris 1826) 275.

14 De vetula lib. 3   *O quam . . . nescia vita*   82.83

   Vincent VII 106. Ps. Ovid. Ed. D. M. Robathan (Amsterdam 1968) 50.

15 De anulo lib. 1   *Anule . . . esse fidem*   10.82

   Amores lib. 2 c. 15. Ed. Kenney, 58.

16 De sompno lib. 1   *Nox erat . . . alta meos*   10.82

   Amores lib. 3 c. 5. Ed. Kenney, 76.

Ovidus Publius Naso *412. 17*

17 De medicamine faciei lib. 1   *Sistite . . . illineretque genis*   10.82

   illineretque] aluminatque *Add. 3470, queried by Tanner*

   Ed. Kenney 103; incipit 'Discite'.

18 De medicamine aurium lib. 1   *Nec tibi . . . assumat in auras*   10.82

   Ps. Ovid. Ed. C. Pascal, *Studi Medievali* 2 (1906) 249–54.

19 De philomena lib. 1

   Ps. Ovid.

413 OLIVERUS Brito Frater Praedicator floruit circa A. Ch. 1292 et scripsit

   Brito *Add. 3470; according to Tanner this was added in a recent hand; however, Brito appears also in Stams, and in Pign., the stand-ins for Kirkestede's source, and in Bale, his early witness*

   Script. Ord. Praed. (whole entry), cf. Stams, 26.
   Bale, *Index*, 314.

1 Super libros sententiarum

2 Super libros elencorum

3 Super Lucam lecturam 1

   om. Stams

4 Sermones de tempore

   om. Stams

414 ORESIESIS monachus amborum Pachomii et Theodori collega, vir in Scripturis ad perfectum instructus, secundum Genadium composuit librum divino sale conditum totiusque monasticae disciplinae instrumentis constructum, et in totum pene Vetus et Novum Testamentum compendiosis dissertationibus juxta monachorum duntaxat necessitatem invenitur expositum, quem vice testamenti prope diem obitus fratribus optulit. Floruit circa A. Ch. <*blank*>

   ambo2] *Add. 3470.*

   Gennadius c. 9 (whole entry).
   Speculum coenobitarum 10.

p. 112]

415 OLIMPIUS natione Hispanus, episcopus, floruit circa A. Ch. <*blank*> et scripsit secundum Genadium librum fidei contra eos qui naturam et non arbitrium in culpam vocant, ostendens non creatione sed inobedientia insertum naturae malum.

>Gennadius c. 23 (whole entry save the date).

416 ORIANUS floruit circa A. Ch. <*blank*> et scripsit juxta Ysidorum

>Isidore c. 4 (whole entry).

1 Vitam et obitum Paulini lib. 1

417 OSBERTUS DE CLARA monachus et prior Westmon[asteriensis] floruit circa A. Ch. 1136 et scripsit

>Bale, *Index*, 315. Bale's editors note that the incipits which appear in the *Index* 'have been extended from some other authority in a different ink'.
>Sharpe, *Latin Writers*, 409–410.

1 Epistolas ad diversos in 2 voluminibus. Principium primi voluminis: *Innocentii summi pontificis etc. Frater Osbertus etc.* Principium epistolarum in 2do volumine: *Praeclaros etc.* Ultima epistola 2dae partis sic incipit: *Opinionis etc.*

>Sharpe, *Latin Writers*, 409. Ed. E. W. Williamson (Oxford 1929). Book II of the letters no longer survives.

2 Item miracula S. Edmundi regis et martiris ad rogatum A[nselmi] abbatis. Principium: *A[nselmus] abbas etc.* Item principium epistolae Osberti: *Sanctitate etc.* Item principium prologi: *Cum laureatus etc.* Principium miraculorum quae scripsit Osbertus: *In provincia et.*

>Sharpe, *Latin Writers*, 409. See Williamson, 26–32, for a discussion of the manuscripts and authorship of this work. The incipits given here indicate a manuscript of the *Miracula* that began with Abbot Anselm's letter asking Osbert to write the work, followed by Osbert's reply, the prologue, and the text of what was probably Book II of the *Miracula*. [**82** Bury = several manuscripts of the *Miracula* survive, though none is identical with this description: BL MS Cotton Titus A. VIII, fol. 109r (Bury S. 153), after fol. 78r; Pierpont Morgan Library, MS 136, fols. 43r–149r (Bury —); and an abbreviated version in the late manuscript Bodl. MS Bodley 240, p. 655 (Bury R. 55; see the note to Johannes Anglicus *341.1*). The *Miracula* in Cotton Titus A. VIII were printed by T. Arnold, RS 96, 3 vols. (1890–96), 1. 107–208.]

Osbertus de Clara   417. 3

3   Item vitam et miracula S. Edburgae. Prologus: *Fidelibus*. Principium vitae: *Imperante*. Finis: *omnium populorum*   65.170

> Sharpe, *Latin Writers*, 410. Ed. S. J. Ridyard, *The Royal Saints of Anglo-Saxon England* (Cambridge 1988); the prologue, an introductory letter, is ed. Williamson, 119, *ep.* 43.

4   Item vitam et miracula S. Adelberti vel Ethelbricti regis. Principium: *Gloriosus*

> Sharpe, *Latin Writers*, 410.

418   OSBERNUS monachus Christi Cantuariae floruit A.C. 1074 et scripsit

> Source unidentified.
> Bale, *Index*, 315.
> Sharpe, *Latin Writers*, 407.

1   Vitam et miracula S. Dunstani

> Sharpe, *Latin Writers*, 407. Ed. W. Stubbs, RS 63 (1874) 69.

2   Vitam et miracula S. Alphegi

> Sharpe, *Latin Writers*, 407. Ed. H. Wharton, *Anglia Sacra* (London 1691), 2. 122.

> De musica quoque lib. 1 *add. Bale as an entry*

419   PAPIAS sanctus et sancti Johannis apostoli auditor et postea episcopus Jeropolitanus floruit circa A. Ch. 160 et scripsit juxta Jeronimum libro De catholicis scriptoribus quinque volumina quibus praenotavit explanatio sermonum Domini. Item scripsit secundum alios librum grammaticalem qui entitulatur Glosarium. Scripsit etiam mille annos futuros post resurrectionem, quibus corporaliter regnum Christi in hac terra futurum sit; hanc opinionem mille annorum secuti sunt Hireneus et Apollinaris et caeteri, qui post resurrectionem aiunt in carne Dominum cum sanctis regnaturum. Tertullianus quoque in libro de spe fideli et Victorinus Pictabionensis et Lactantius in hanc opinionem ducuntur. Igitur Papias autor fuit haereticorum qui dicuntur Ciliastae, id est Millenarii; non tamen inter haereticos sed inter sanctos in Martilogio computatur, sicut nec Hireneus Lugdunensis nec Victorinus haeretici appellantur, qui gloriosi martires fuerunt et tamen in hac opinione Papiam secuti sunt. Multi enim sancti in aliquibus simpliciter errasse leguntur, sicut B. Ciprianus de rebaptizandis, qui tamen error eis non imputatur propter caeteras virtutes, quae in eis praecellebant

et quare non ex obstinatione animi sed ignorantiae simplicitate errabant. Haec in Martilogio Johannis Anglici et Jeronimus in libro De catholicis scriptoribus.

> Whole entry from Jerome c. 18 and Iohannes Anglicus (i.e. John of Tynemouth). The Martyrology of John of Tynemouth survives only as a few extracts in Bodl. MS Bodley 240, fol. 582r (Bury H. 55); the life of Papias is not among them.

p. 113]

420 PAPIAS alius floruit circa A. Ch. <*blank*> et scripsit librum de grammatica per alphabetum qui vocatur Eleucidarium et doctrinae erudimentum. Principium: *Fili uterque* . . . *A. ideo prior est literarum* . . . Finis: *Zoria signa*

> (*Registrum* 92, the single word 'Papias' and location numbers, was not used.) Printed, Venice 1496/repr. Turin 1966. The first incipit is that of the prologue 'Alii utique'; the second is that of the text.

421 PACHOMIUS monachus et abbas floruit circa A. Ch. <*blank*> et scripsit juxta Genadium

> Gennadius c. 7 (whole entry).
> *Speculum coenobitarum* 8.

1 Regulam utrique monachorum generi aptam, quam angelo dictante susceperat

2 Ad abbatem Sirum ep. 1

3 Ad abbatem Cornelium ep. 1

4 De Pascha ep. 1

5 De die remissionis ep. 1

6 De fratribus extra monasterium laborantibus ep. 1

422 PALLADIUS monachus et discipulus Euagrii floruit circa A. Ch. <*blank*> et scripsit secundum Historiam tripartitam

> *Historia tripartita* VIII 1 (*CSEL* 71. 462).
> *Speculum coenobitarum* 34.

Palladius   *422. 1*

1 De vitis fratrum lib. 1

>   Source unidentified; this title is not in *Historia Tripartita*. Same as Heraclidis *256.1*.

423 PALLADIUS alius floruit circa A. Ch. <*blank*> et scripsit

>   Same as Emilianus *178*.
>   (*Registrum* 93 not used.)
>   *Speculum coenobitarum* 34.

1 De agricultura lib. 13   *Pars est prudentiae . . . pedes*   29

>   Cf. R1. Ed. R. H. Rodgers, Teubner (1975) 2–240.

424 PAULINUS monachus et Nolanus episcopus floruit A. Ch. 425 et scripsit juxta Genadium et Vincentium in Speculo lib. 21 cap. 26 et lib. 19 cap. 37

>   Vincent XXI 26, XIX 36, XIX 39, and Gennadius c. 49.

1 De morte Christi et baptizati infantis lib. 1

>   Whole entry from Vincent XXI 26 and Gennadius 49.

2 De virginitate ad sororem suam epistolas multas

>   Whole entry from Vincent XXI 26 and Gennadius 49.

3 De contemptu mundi et diversis causis lib. 2

>   Whole entry from Vincent XXI 26 and Gennadius 49.

4 De poenitentia lib. 1

>   Whole entry from Vincent XXI 26 and Gennadius 49.

5 Ad Severum epistolas plures

>   Whole entry from Vincent XXI 26 and Gennadius 49.

6 De laude generali omnium martyrum lib. 1

>   Whole entry from Vincent XXI 26 and Gennadius 49.

7 Sacramentorium et ympnarium

    Whole entry from Vincent XXI 26 and Gennadius 49.

8 Ad Theodosium super victoria tirannorum Panigericum

    Whole entry from Vincent XXI 26 and Gennadius 49.

9 Ad S. Augustinum vitam S. Ambrosii

    Vincent XIX 36 (whole entry).

10 Vitam S. Felicis martiris

    Vincent XIX 39 (whole entry).

425 PAULINUS presbiter floruit circa A. Ch. 413 et scripsit secundum Genadium

    Gennadius c. 69 (works *1–5*), Isidore c. 4 (works *6–7*), and a manuscript.

1 De initio quadragesimae tractatus 100

    Gennadius 69 (whole entry).

2 De Dominico die Paschae

    Gennadius 69 (whole entry).

3 De obedientia

    Gennadius 69 (whole entry).

4 De poenitentia

    Gennadius 69 (whole entry).

5 De neophitis

    Gennadius 69 (whole entry).

6 De benedictionibus patriarcharum secundum 3^{cem} sensum lib. 1

    Isidore 4 (whole entry).

Paulinus *425. 7*

7 Vitam S. Ambrosii ad petitionem S. Augustini

> Isidore 4 (whole entry).

8 Vitam S. Felicis in Pi<n>cis lib. 6   *Annam . . . sume coronam*   82

> pīcis *Add. 3470, queried by Tanner*

> Paulinus Nolanus. *Carmina natalicia. CSEL* 30. 51–118, 194–206, 246–261. The incipit is that of *carm.* 15 (p. 51), 'Annua'; the explicit is that of *carm.* 17 (p. 96). Cf. editor's preface, pp xii–xiv. Same as Paulinus Nolanus *424.10*.

426 PAULUS Romanus diaconus et monachus Cassinensis floruit circa A. Ch. 809 et scripsit

> James extracts, p. 198.

1 Historiam Longobardorum lib. 6   *Septentrionalem . . . pacem custodiens*   82

> *CPL* 1179. Ed. L. Capo (Milan 1992) 12–364. **82** Bury = B13. 61b.

2 Historiam Romanorum lib.   *Res Romanas . . .*   61.10

> *CPL* 1181. Ed. A. Crivellucci (Rome 1914); for the incipit see p. 10 note k. **61** Peterborough = BP21. 42c. [**82** Bury = B13. 61a.]

3 Iste Paulus fecit ympnos de S. Johanne baptista, scilicet Ut queant laxis, cum aliis. Et est unum notabile in primo versu ympni Ut queant etc. Habetur enim ibi [p. 114] illud musicae: ut, re, mi, fa, sol, la; Ut, Ut queant laxis; Re, Resonare fibris; Mi, Mira gestorum; Fa, Famuli tuorum; Sol, Solve polluti; La, Labii reatum etc. Iste enim Paulus cum deberet quodam anno cereum Paschalem consecrare, fauces ejus raucae factae sunt; ut igitur vox ejus restitueretur, ympnos praedictos ad honorem S. Johannis baptistae, quem devote diligebat composuit, ubi in primo petit vocem sibi restitui.

> ubi in primo *Add. 3470; Tanner has added* principio *as a variant reading*; pº *James extracts*

> *PL* 95. 1597.

427 PAULUS quidam episcopus floruit circa A. Ch. <*blank*> et scripsit secundum Genadium

> Gennadius c. 32 (whole entry).

Paulus   *432. 3*

1 De poenitentia et modo poenitendi lib. 1

In quo libro dat legem poenitentibus ita dolere debere pro peccatis ne supra mensuram tristitiae immensitate desperationis mergantur

428 PETRUS Edissenae ecclesiae presbyter floruit circa A. Ch. <*blank*> et scripsit secundum Genadium varios tractatus, et in morem S. Effreni diaconi psalmos metro composuit

> Gennadius c. 75 (whole entry).

429 POSSIDONIUS Affricanae provinciae episcopus floruit A. Ch. <*blank*> et scripsit juxta Ysidorum libro De viris illustribus

> Isidore c. 8 (whole entry).

1 Vitam S. Augustini

2 Item Indiculum librorum B. Augustini, in quo plus quam 400 librorum volumina supputantur

430 PASCASINUS Ciciliensis episcopus floruit circa A. Ch. 444 et scripsit juxta Ysidorum

> Isidore c. 11 (whole entry save the date).

1 Ad Leonem papam Pascalem epistolam

431 PASTOR episcopus floruit circa A. Ch. <*blank*> et scripsit juxta Genadium libellum in modum symboli totam pene ecclesiasticam credulitatem continentem

> Gennadius c. 77 (whole entry).

432 PAULUS alius presbyter natione Pannonius floruit circa A. Ch. 495 et scripsit juxta Genadium

> Gennadius c. 76 (whole entry save the date).

1 De virginitate servanda lib. 1

2 De contemptu mundi lib. 1

3 De vitae instructione lib. 1

433 PETRUS ABELARDI episcopus Parisiensis floruit A. Ch. 1150 et scripsit

    John of Tynemouth's *Historia Aurea* XIX 44 (Bodl. MS Bodley 240).
    Kirkestede has made Peter Abelard bishop of Paris, probably through confusion with Peter Lombard, and has attributed to him Peter of Capua's distinction collection.
    Cf. James extracts, p. 200.

1 Librum qui dicitur Sic et non   *Dominus Jesu . . . non recipimus*

    Ed. B. B. Boyer & R. McKeon (Chicago 1977); incipit and explicit unidentified. Same as Adelardus *51.2*.

2 Librum qui vocatur Alphabetum magistri Petri   *Petierunt . . . alpha altissimus*
  83

    Peter of Capua. Not edited; see Rouse & Rouse, *Authentic Witnesses*, 211-14, and the list of manuscripts in W. Maleczek, *Petrus Capuanus* (Vienna 1988), 239-43. The incipit indicates that Kirkestede saw a manuscript that began with the *Responsio*, for which the common rubric was 'Responsio magistri Petri facta scolaribus in ipsis scolis insistentibus pro presenti opere inchoando'; rather than an explicit attribution to Abelard, the rubric was probably the source of Kirkestede's mistaken identification of 'Magister Petrus'.

Hujus scripta incendio et scriptorem silentio condempnavit papa Innocentius secundum Historiam Auream

    John of Tynemouth XIX 44.

434 PATRICIUS archiepiscopus Hiberniae floruit A. Ch. 429 et scripsit

    Bale, *Index*, 317.
    Ware extracts, fol. 132r.
    Sharpe, *Latin Writers*, 414.
    See A. Gwynn, *The Writings of Bishop Patrick, 1074-1084*, Scriptores Latini Hiberniae 1 (Dublin 1955).

1 De tribus habitaculis coeli, mundi et inferni   *Tria sunt . . . misericordem*
  83

    Sharpe, *Latin Writers*, 414. Ed. Gwynn, 106. Same as Augustinus *1.185 and 1.206*. [**82** Bury = Bodl. MS Bodley 240, p. 811 (Bury H. 55); concerning this manuscript see note to Johannes Anglicus *341.1*.]

435 PAPIRIANUS floruit circa A. Ch. <blank> et scripsit juxta Cassiodorum

Cassiodorus I. 30. 2 (whole entry).

1 De ortographia lib.

436 PASCHASIUS RADBERTUS monachus et ecclesiae Romanae diaconus floruit circa A. Ch. <blank> et scripsit

Registrum 22.

1 De sacramentis lib. 1   <u>19</u>

R22. 1 (whole entry).

2 De corpore et sanguine Domini lib. 1   *Dilectissimo* . . .   95.<u>156</u>. <u>32</u>.<u>20</u>.<u>98</u>

20] xx *R*

R22. 3. *CCCM* 16. 3.

3 Super Lamentationes Jeremiae lib. 5   *Multo . . . flagella cessant*   <u>163</u>.<u>43</u>. <u>82</u>.<u>105</u>.<u>80</u>.<u>15</u>

R22. 2. Stegmüller *Bibl.* 6262. *CCCM* 85. 3. **82** Bury = B13. 14.

4 Super Genesin

This work and its source are unidentified.

5 Vitas patrum Graecorum   *Vitas patrum . . . pauca non etc.*   168

Liber septimus siue Verba seniorum, translated from the Greek Lives of the Fathers by Paschasius of Dumium. See C. W. Barlow, *Martini episcopi Bracarensis opera omnia* (New Haven 1950), 11–28. *PL* 73. 1025.

6 Scolia de generatione Jesu Christi   *Libet inquit . . . apparere*   82

The incipit is that of the *Expositio in Matheo evangelista*, *CCSL* 56. 20 ('Liber inquit'), explicit does not correspond. The work appears with a similar title (*Scholia ex libro Paschasii Diaconi romane ecclesie de Christi et Salvatoris nostri genealogia*) and with this incipit and explicit in Cambridge, Corpus Christi College, MS 332, p. 153 (Rochester, s. xii[in]).

Paterius   *437.*

p. 115]

437 PATERIUS discipulus Gregorii papae floruit circa A. Ch. <blank> et scripsit

1 Super Vetus et Novum Testamentum   *Virtutes . . . ostendit*   82.16.105. 13.166.139

   CPL 1718. *PL* 79. 683. Explicit unidentified. **82** Bury = B13. 45.

438 PAMPHILIUS presbiter Eusebii Caesariensis episcopi et martir floruit circa A. Ch. <blank> et scripsit juxta Jeronimum

   Whole entry from Jerome c. 75 (works *1–2*) and Hugh of St Victor, *Didascalicon* IV 13 (final comment).
   Cited in the 1660s by A. Wood, *Survey of the Antiquities of the City of Oxford*, ed. A. Clark, OHS 17 (Oxford 1890), 2. 379.

1 Super 12 prophetas lib. 25

2 Apolegiticum pro Origene

   Hic tanto bibliotecae divino amore flagravit, ut maximam partem Origenis voluminum sua manu descripserit. Hic etiam in biblioteca sua prope 30,000 voluminum habuit, juxta Hugonem in Didascalicon.

439 PETRUS LUMBARDUS sive LONGOBARDUS Parisiensis episcopus floruit A. Ch. 1154 et scripsit

   Vincent XXX 1.

1 Sententiarum libros 4^r qui leguntur in scolis   *Cupientes . . . Christo duce pervenit*

   Vincent XXX 1. Ed. I. Brady (Grottaferrata 1971–81), explicit (vol. 2, p. 560) 'Via duce peruenit'. [**82** Bury = B13. 234 = Cambridge, Pembroke College, MS 28 (Bury P. 64), with Kirkestede's (and other Bury monks') school notes; Book IV only is also found in Cambridge, Pembroke College, MS 97, fol. 1r (Bury P. 81), in Pembroke College, MS 118, fol. 63r (Bury Y. 12), and in Hereford Cathedral, MS P. III. 1, fol. 103r (Bury J. 47).]

2 Majores glosas psalterii collegit   *Cum omnes . . . laudet Dominum*

   Vincent XXX 1. Stegmüller *Bibl.* 6637. *PL* 191. 55. [**82** Bury = B13. 227.]

3 Majores glosas epistolarum Pauli   *Principia rerum . . . munera cum sint*

> Vincent XXX 1. Stegmüller *Bibl.* 6654–68. *PL* 191. 1301–1696, *PL* 192. 9–520. [**82** Bury = Oxford, St John's College, MS 43, fol. 1r (Bury P. 58), explicit 'munera sit cum omnibus vobis. Amen' (fol. 234r).]

4 Sermones quosdam utiles composuit

> Vincent XXX 1 (whole entry).

440 PETRUS COMMESTOR frater uterinus Petri Lumbardus floruit circa A. Ch. 1154 tempore S. Thomae martiris et scripsit

> *Registrum* 60, Vincent XXX 1 (works *1, 4*).

1 Historiam scolasticam super Bibliam   *Imperatoriae . . . in catacumbis*   73.74. 15.35.93.13

> Vincent XXX 1. Stegmüller *Bibl.* 6543–65. *PL* 198. 1055. **15** St Albans = BL MS Royal 4 D. VII, fol. 9r; the work also appears in early 15th-cent. St Albans borrowing lists (B87. 40 and 56). / [**82** Bury = Cambridge, Pembroke College, MS 26 (Bury P. 11).]

2 Sermones allegoricos super Bibliam 14   *In praecedentibus . . . bonus Deus*   105.13.82.35.94.80

> R60. 3. Richard of Saint-Victor, *Allegoriae* (= *Liber exceptionum* pt 2). This often circulated with the *Historia scholastica*, at times under the Comestor's name. Ed. Jean Châtillon, Textes philosophiques du Moyen Âge 5 (Paris 1958), incipit is that of the second prologue. See Châtillon's introduction, 28–30. [**82** Bury = Cambridge, Pembroke College, MS 27, fols. 57r–116v (Bury P. 25) = Châtillon MS 57, both incipit and explicit correspond; BL MS Royal 7 C. II, fol. 58r (Bury R. 40) = Châtillon MS 86, with rubric in Kirkestede's hand in the margin; explicit (fol. 88v) does not correspond.]

3 Sermones quamplures alios 42   *Erudimur . . . immortalia*   13.105.82

> R60. 2. See Schneyer *Rep.* 4. 636–51. **82** Bury = Cambridge, Pembroke College, MS 27, fol. 1r (Bury P. 25), a collection of forty-one sermons, incipit 'Erudimini'.

4 Item nonnulla alia opuscula

> Vincent XXX 1 (whole entry).

5 Super visiones Danielis ad literam   105

> R60. 1 (whole entry).

Petrus Commestor   *440. 6*

6 De oratione Dominica serm. 1   *Inter omnia . . . devotionis*

> Peter Abelard. *PL* 178. 611.

> Iste liber continetur inter sermones allegoricos lib. xi in fine

>> [**82** Bury = occurs in Cambridge, Pembroke College, MS 27 (Bury P. 25), on fols. 99r–101v, at the end of Book XI of the *Allegoriae*.]

7 De conceptione B. Mariae serm. 1   *Conceptionem . . .*

> Reportedly in an edition of Comestor's works (Antwerp 1536; not seen), incipit 'Conceptionem beate virginis Marie corde et voce'.

8 Super Cantica epitalamium   *Epitalamium . . . florebit*   11

> Origen. Same as Origines *404.15*.

441 PETRUS PICTAVENSIS Parisiensis cancellarius floruit circa A. Ch. 1154 et scripsit

> *Registrum* 59.
> See P. S. Moore, *The Works of Peter of Poitiers* (Washington 1936).

1 Sententiarum lib. 5   *Invisibilia . . . homo est omnis homo*   82.163.94. 73.74

> Stegmüller *Sent.* 679, explicit 'hoc enim est omnis homo'. Books I and II are edited by P. S. Moore & M. Dulong (Notre Dame, IN, 1943, 1950).

2 Super tabernaculum Moysi lib.   *Secretum . . .*   82.15.39.35

> Ed. P. S. Moore & J. A. Corbett (Notre Dame, IN, 1938). **82** Bury = Cambridge, Pembroke College, MS 96 (Bury P. 35).

3 Super Boetium de Trinitate   124

> R59. 1 (whole entry).

4 De ebdomadibus   124

> R59. 2 (whole entry).

5 De officiis divinis lib. 1   *Nota quod officium* . . .   74

> See Moore, 166 and n. 12, who cites a 17th-cent. reference to this title (otherwise unknown to him) at the abbey Ter Duinen in Belgium. Incipit unidentified.
>
> De istis tribus qui vocantur nomine Petri sunt isti versus subsequentes compositi:
>   Tres fuerant Petri magni nobis paedagogi
>   Commestor, Pictavus, Lumbardus theologi
>   Historiat primus (id est Commestor), bene disputat ille secundus (id est Pictavus),
>   Tertius (id est Lumbardus) hic quaerens solvens praecellit utrosque.
>
> *The words in parentheses appear as interlinear glosses in Add. 3470*
>
> Source unidentified.

442 PETRUS Cantor Parisiensis floruit circa A. Ch. 1170 et obiit anno 1197 et scripsit

> *Registrum* 53. The principal manuscript (?at Bury) with which Kirkestede supplemented the *Registrum*'s information resembled the collection of Peter the Chanter's works in BL MS Royal 10 C. v (England, s. xiii).

1 Super Vetus Testamentum   *Quam durum* . . .   161.105.160.115.12

> 12] xii *R*
>
> R53. 1. The incipit is that of Petrus Cantor's *Glossae super Genesim*, ed. in part by A. Sylwan (Göteborg 1992); incipit ('Quod durum') is on p. 18; without its explicit one cannot tell how much or which parts of the Chanter's OT exegesis this manuscript contained.

2 Super Novum Testamentum   105

> R53. 10 (whole entry).

3 Super psalterium   *Beatus vir* . . . *firmavi tamen*   160.8.108.20.74

> firmavi tamen *queried by Tanner*
>
> R53. 8. Stegmüller *Bibl.* 6475. Explicit unidentified.

4 Super Ecclesiasticum   9

> R53. 11 (whole entry).

Petrus   *442. 5*

p. 116]

5 Super Ysaiam   <u>161</u>.<u>160</u>

    R53. 5 (whole entry).

6 Super Jeremiam   <u>160</u>.<u>161</u>

    R53. 6 (whole entry).

7 Super Ezechielem   <u>160</u>

    R53. 7 (whole entry).

8 Super epistolas canonicas   *Os meum . . .*   <u>161</u>

    R53. 3. Stegmüller *Bibl.* 6524–30.

9 Super Actus Apostolorum   *Liquefacta est . . . coronatus*   <u>161</u>

    R53. 4. Stegmüller *Bibl.* 6508.

10 Super Apocalipsin   *Apocalipsis haec . . . attollimus*   <u>161</u>

    R53. 2. Stegmüller *Bibl.* 6531.

11 Tractatum de poenitentia   *Primum est . . .*   74

    Discussed and described by A. Teetaert, *Aus der Geisteswelt des Mittelalters: Studien und Texte Martin Grabmann . . . gewidmet* (Münster 1935), 310–31, with a list of manuscripts (313).

12 Super 4 evangelia id est Unum ex quatuor   *Quatuor . . . vanae sunt*   83

    Cf. R53. 10. Stegmüller *Bibl.* 6504–6507.

13 Consiliarium   *Quaeritur . . .*   65

    Summa de sacramentis et animae consiliis. Ed. J. A. Dugauquier in *Analecta Mediaevalia Namurcensia* 4 (1954), 7 (1957), 11 (1961), 16 (1963), and 21 (1967). See also *11* above.

14 Summam quae vocatur Verbum abbreviatum cap. 40   *Verbum abbreviatum . . . jocunditas*   65

> R53. 9. Stegmüller *Bibl.* 6447. *PL* 205. 23. [**82** Bury = BL MS Royal 7 C. xi, fol. 1r (Bury V. 21), with chapters numbered to 102; explicit does not correspond. The final column of text from this work, in a quire formerly bound at the end of Cambridge, Pembroke College, MS 25 (Bury O. 55), was identified by Kirkestede with the marginal note 'hic est finis illius notabilis summe que vocatur verbum abbreuiatum, quem quidem continet cii capitula'; the quire is now in a box of fragments and binding scraps, Pembroke College, MS 313. Concerning this fragment see also Alanus *16.1.*]

443 PETRUS DAMIANUS episcopus et monachus Hostiensis floruit A. Ch. 1075 et scripsit

> Vincent XXVI 52; *Registrum* 74 probably not used.

1 De officiis ecclesiae lib.   *Ea quae . . .*   82

> Rupert of Deutz, *De diuinis officiis*, ed. R. Haacke, *CCCM* 7. 5. Attributions to Peter Damian seem to have been common, for reasons not apparent.

2 Librum qui vocatur Dominus vobiscum   *Non ignorat . . . sacramentum*   74.82.65

> *PL* 145. 231; 'sacramentum' is the explicit of cc. 11, 17, and 18.

3 Item sermones

> Source unidentified. *CCCM* 57.

4 Item narrationes notabiles secundum Vincentium in Speculo historiali lib. 26 cap. 52°

> Vincent XXVI 52 (whole entry).

5 Epistolarum lib. 1

> Source unidentified.

6 Item vitam et miracula Odilonis abbatis Cluniacensis

> Source unidentified. *PL* 144. 925.

444 PETRUS BLESENSIS archidiaconus Bathoniensis floruit circa A. Ch. <blank> et scripsit

> *Registrum* 46, Peter of Blois, *Inuectiua in deprauatore* = *PL* 207. 1115 (works *1, 5, 7–8, 12–17*).
> Bale, *Index*, 319 (*3–5, 7, 9–10, 12, 15–17*); Bale consistently offers much longer incipits for this author's works.
> Sharpe, *Latin Writers*, 418–23.

1 Super Job ad Henr[icum] regem Angliae lib. 1   *Vir erat . . . triumphat*
   1̲2̲4̲.1̲2̲.3̲9̲.4̲9̲.82.163

   > 12] xii *R*

   > R46. 2, *Inuectiua*. Sharpe, *Latin Writers*, 418. *PL* 207. 797.

2 De vera amicitia Christianorum lib. 2   *Subsannabit . . . plenitudo*   82.86

   > Sharpe, *Latin Writers*, 418. Ed. M. M. Davy, *Un traité de l'amour du XIIe siècle: Pierre de Blois* (Paris 1932) 106–584. **82** Bury = BL MS Harley 4025, fols. 98v and 92r (Bury S. 97), imperfect; this manuscript was procured and its parts put together by Kirkestede, later misbound.

3 De transfiguratione Christi lib. 1   *Magistri . . . sine fine*   3̲9̲.1̲2̲

   > Magistri celestis Iesu Christi   *Bale*   12] xii *R*

   > R46. 3. Sharpe, *Latin Writers*, 420. *PL* 207. 777.

4 De conversione S. Pauli serm. 1   *Recolenda . . . gloriae Domini*   1̲2̲.14.82

   > Recolenda divi Pauli memoria   *Bale*   12] xii *R*

   > R46. 5. Sharpe, *Latin Writers*, 419. *PL* 207. 791.

5 Dialogorum inter Henricum r[egem] Angl[iae] et abbatem Bonevallensem lib. 1   *Filios . . . assumam*   82.166

   > Filios enutriui ipsi autem spre   *Bale*

   > *Inuectiua* Sharpe, *Latin Writers*, 420. Ed. R. B. C. Huygens, *RB* 68 (1958) 87. **82** Bury = Lambeth Palace Library, MS 105, fol. 130v (Bury R. 36).

6 De periculis praelatorum ep. 1   *Reverendo . . . in librum*   73.82

   > *PL* 207. 314 *ep.* 102. **73** Norwich Holy Trinity = cellarer's rolls (B57. 19), payment to have seven quires of Peter of Blois's letters copied in the late 13th or early 14th cent.

7 Contra perfidiam Judaeorum   *Quaerebam* . . . *inconstans*

    Querebam a visione noctes *Bale*

    Inuectiua Sharpe, *Latin Writers*, 421. PL 207. 825

8 Epistolarum 145 lib. 1   *Rogatus* . . . *suppellex*   <u>12</u>.<u>120</u>.<u>24</u>.1.2.83

    12.120.24] xii.xxiiii.xx *R*   *location numbers 1.2 probably* = 12 *R, copied by error from 9 below*

    R46. 1, *Inuectiua* Sharpe, *Latin Writers*, 420. PL 207. 1. The incipit is that of *ep*. 1; the explicit is that of *ep*. 107.

9 Item sermones quamplures   *Dum medium etc.* . . .

    Dum medium silentium tenerent omnia *Bale*

    R46. 4. Sharpe, *Latin Writers*, 422. PL 207. 559.

10 De testimoniis fidei catholicae lib. 1   *Cum infundamur* . . . *in aeternum*

    Cum infundamento ecclesie catholice *Bale*

    Sharpe, *Latin Writers*, 420.

11 Vitam S. Cuthlaci monachi et anachoritae

    Source unidentified. Sharpe, *Latin Writers*, 422.

12 De peregrinatione Jerosolimitana

    Inuectiua.

13 De praestigiis Fortunae lib. 1

    Inuectiua.

14 De confessione et poenitentia

    Inuectiua.

15 Librum qui Canon episcopalis dicitur

    Inuectiua.

Petrus Blesensis *444. 16*

16 Opus novellum de assertione fidei

Inuectiua.

17 Librum exortationum

Librum exortationum] Piarum exhortationum lib. *Bale*; *Inuectiua confirmis Add. 347⁰*

Inuectiua.

445 PETRUS Afulfi quondam Judaeus et ad fidem Christi conversus floruit circa A. Ch. 1106 et scripsit

(Petrus Alphonsus)
Registrum 52.

1 Contra Judaeos et Saracenos librum elegantem in modum dialogi   *Dixit operis* . . .   126.82.43.105.8.19

R52. 1. Ed. K. P. Mieth (1982), in Pedro Alfonso de Huesca, *Diálogo contra los judíos*, ed. J. Tolan & others (Huesca 1996) 5; incipit 'Dixit sequentis operis'.

2 Librum dialogorum qui dicitur Clericalis disciplina lib. 1   *Dixit Petrus . . . coelesti*   126.82.105

R52. 2–3. Ed. A. Hilka & W. Söderhjelm (Heidelberg 1911). Location number **126** is taken from R2, **105** from R3. / **82** Bury = BL MS Royal 10 B. XII, fol. 1r (Bury D. —), already imperfect at the end in Kirkestede's day; his note fol. 19v, 'Deficiunt viii capitula parua de isto opusculo, videlicet .i. folium et dimidium'.

3 Dialogorum libros 3   Quorum primus de 7 artibus, 2^{dus} de sectis, legibus et credulitatibus, 3^{ius} liber sive 3^{ia} distinctio de humano proficuo *Cum haberem discipulum* . . . *obfirmavit*   43.15

R52. 4, source of the location numbers. The title, incipit, and explicit are unidentified.

p. 117]

446 PETRUS DE THARENTA Frater Praedicator archiepiscopus Lugdunensis et cardinalis et papa dictus Innocentius V floruit A. Ch. 1276 et scripsit

Same as Innocentius V *(314)*.
Script. Ord. Praed., cf. Stams, 9. The titles are taken in sequence from the Dominican list, with added information from a Bury manuscript for work *8*.

1 Super Genesim

2 Super Exodum

3 Super Leviticum

4 Super Numerum

5 Super Deuteronomium

6 Super Lucam

7 Super epistolas Pauli

8 Super libros sententiarum quaestiones   *Nunquid nosti . . . vitam in praemio* 82

> Kaeppeli 3340. Printed, Toulouse 1649–52. Same as Innocentius V *314.1* and Petrus Carnotensis *483.1*.

9 De unitate formae

10 De magnitudine coeli

11 De aeternitate mundi

12 De intellectu et voluntate

447 PETRONIUS monachus et episcopus Bononiensis floruit circa A. Ch. 388 tempore Theodosii et Valentiniani et scripsit secundum Genadium

> Whole entry (save the date) doubly from Vincent XXI 25 and Gennadius c. 42; they name the title of *2* below only to state that it is not in fact Petronius's.
> *Speculum coenobitarum* 17.

Petronius   *447. 1*

1 Vitas patrum monachorum Egypti

2 De ordinatione episopi lib. 1

3 Item quendam tractatum partim metricum et partim prosaicum

448 PETRUS HELI

Source unidentified. This was probably meant to refer to the *Summa in Priscianum*, ed. L. Reilly (Toronto 1993).

449 PERSIUS floruit A. Ch. 58 et scripsit

Vincent IX 137.

1 De quatuor satiris metrice lib. 4   *O curas . . . acervi*

Ed. W. V. Clausen (Oxford 1959). [**82** Bury = B13. 159b.]

450 PETRUS abbas S. Remigii floruit A. Ch. <*blank*> et scripsit

(Probably Peter II, abbot 1162–81)

1 De claustrali disciplina lib.

(Work and source unidentified.)

451 PETRUS Ravennatis episcopus floruit A. Ch. <*blank*> et scripsit

(Petrus Chrysologus)

1 Sermones 150   *Hodie nobis . . .*   Omel. ult.: *Omnibus quidem . . .*

CPL 227. *CCSL* 24, 24A, 24B. The incipits are those, respectively, of *serm.* 1 (*CCSL* 24. 15) and *serm.* 165 (*CCSL* 24B. 1017).

2 De oratione Dominica   *Accepistis . . . subjectum*

CPL 227 *serm.* 67. *CCSL* 24A. 402.

3 Item de eadem   *Fratres karissimi . . . non videbunt*

CPL 227 *serm.* 71. *CCSL* 24A. 424.

452 PHILO Judaeus natione Alexandrinus scriptor insignissimus floruit circa A. Ch. 39 et scripsit juxta Jeronimum

    Whole entry save *4* and *10* (and save the date) from Jerome c. 11.

1 In 5to libro Moysy in confusione linguarum lib. 7

2 De natura et inventione lib. 1

3 De hiis quae sensu precamur et testamur lib. 1

    sensu precamur *queried by Tanner*

4 De benedictionibus lib. 1

    Source unidentified.

5 De eruditione lib. 1

6 De haerede divinarum rerum lib. 1

7 De divisione aequalium et contrariorum lib. 1

8 De tribus virtutibus lib. 1

9 Cur quorundam in Scripturis mutata sunt nomina lib. 1

10 De vita theor[et]ica vel supplicum lib. 1

    Source unidentified; this work is cited in the *Speculum coenobitarum* as a history of monasticism (ed. Hall, 162 and 163).

11 De pactis lib. 2

12 De gigantibus lib. 1

13 Quod sompnia mittantur a Deo lib. 5

14 Quaestionum et solutionum in Exodo lib. 5

Philo   *452. 15*

15   De tabernaculo decalogo lib. 4

16   De victimis et repromissionibus lib. 1

17   De maledictis lib. 1

18   De Judeis et vita urbana lib. 2

19   De providentia Dei lib. 1

20   De Alexandro lib. 1

21   De apostolicis viris et contemplativa vita lib. 1

   apostolicis *queried by Tanner*

22   De agricultura lib. 2

23   De ebrietate lib. 2

24   Quod omnis peccans servus sit et quod liber sit qui bonis studiis operam dat lib. 1

25   De vita sapientum lib. 1

453   PHILEAS episcopus et martir floruit circa A. Ch. 237 et scripsit secundum Jeronimum libro De catholicis scriptoribus

   Jerome c. 78 (whole entry save the date).

1   De laude martirum lib. 1

454   PHILIPPUS Cretensis episcopus floruit A. Ch. 158 et scripsit juxta Jeronimum et Vincentium in Speculo historiali lib. 11 cap. 112

   The whole entry save the date comes from Vincent XI 112 and Jerome c. 30.

1 Ad Marcionem lib. 1

455 PONTIUS diaconus S. Cipriani floruit circa A. Ch. 258 et scripsit juxta Jeronimum ubi supra

> Jerome c. 68 (whole entry save the date).

1 De vita et passione S. Cipriani lib. 1

456 PHILIPPUS presbiter optimus et auditor Jeronimi floruit circa A. Ch. 390 et scripsit juxta Genadium

> Gennadius c. 63 (whole entry save the date).

1 Super librum Job commentarios

2 Epistolas ad diversos

457 PIERIUS presbiter Alexandriae floruit circa A. Ch. 289 qui juxta Jeronimum in tantum sermonis diversorumque tractatum floruit elegantia ut Origines minor vocaretur. Hujus est longissimus tractatus in Osee.

> Jerome c. 76 (whole entry save the date).

458 POLICARPUS presbyter et B. Johannis apostoli discipulus floruit A. Ch. 140, et scripsit juxta Jeronimum ubi supra

> Jerome c. 17 (whole entry save the date).

1 Ad Philippenses epistolam utilem, quae usque hodie in Asiae legitur conventu

459 PORPHIRIUS philosophus floruit A. Ch. 239 et scripsit

1 Ysagogas (Introductiones) in categorias (id est praedicamenta) Aristotelis
Cum sit . . . traditionem

> *The words in parentheses appear as interlinear glosses in Add. 3470*
>
> Ed. L. Minio-Paluello, *AL* 1/6–7 (1966) 5–31.

460 POLICRATES Ephesiorum episcopus floruit A. Ch. 213 et scripsit juxta Jeronimum et Vincentium in Speculo historiali lib. 12 cap. 16

> Whole entry save the date from Vincent XII 16 and Jerome c. 45.

1 Adversus Victorem papam epistolam synodicam

461 PORCHETUS floruit circa A. Ch. <blank> et scripsit

> Source unidentified.

1 De victoria Judaeorum

> This anti–Semitic tract of Porchetus, a Genoese Carthusian, survives in Eton College, MS 130, fols. 3r–91r.

p. 119]

462 PLINIUS Secundus floruit circa A. Ch. 110 et scripsit juxta Vincentium in Speculo lib. 11mo

> *Registrum* 91, Vincent XI 67 (works *1–3*), *Manipulus florum* XVI ('Libri diuersorum auctorum').
> The works of the younger and elder Pliny are combined in this entry.

1 De historia naturali lib. 37   *Plinius . . . constant*

> R91. 1, Vincent XI 67, *MF* XVI 1 (explicit 'constant primum pondere'). Pliny the Elder. Ed. K. Mayhoff, 5 vols. (Leipzig 1892–1909). [**82** Bury = B13. 96.]

2 Epistolas ad diversos circiter 100

> Whole entry from R91. 2 and Vincent XI 67.

3 De omnibus bellis Romanorum lib. 38

> Vincent XI 67 (whole entry).

463 PLUTARCHIUS floruit circa A. Ch. 100 et scripsit juxta Vincentium in Speculo lib. 11

> Vincent XI 48 (whole entry).

1 Ad Trajanum imperatorem librum pulcherrimum

2 De constitutione politica   *Plutarchius . . .*

464 PLATO philosophus discipulus Socratis floruit anno <blank> et scripsit multa. Hujus consuetudo erat libros suos intitulare nominibus magistrorum suorum vel eorum qui magistros suos docuerant, ut majorem auctoritatem verbis suis adquireret, et rationibus hiis sunt libri ejus appellati

> Vincent IV 77 (works *1–3*), Higden, 3. 350.

1 Thimeus de universali justitia lib. 2   *Ysocrates* . . . *perspicuo*

> Vincent IV 77. Ed. J. H. Waszink, *Plato Latinus* 4 (London 1962).

2 Phelton vel Faedron de immortalitate animae lib. 1

> Vincent IV 77 (whole entry).

3 Gorgias

> Vincent IV 77 (whole entry).

4 De vacca

> Source unidentified. This is an alchemical treatise attributed to Plato; Thorndike/Kibre 246, 383, 576. Presumably the same as Virgilius *630.13* below.

5 Phaedron, ut supra

> Source unidentified.

465 PLACENTINUS BARRE floruit anno <blank> et scripsit

> This entry and its source are unidentified.

466 PROSPER natione Aquitannicus monachus et B. Leonis papae notarius et postea episcopus in Italia factus floruit A. Ch. 460 et scripsit

> *Registrum* 23, Vincent XXI 58 (quoting Gennadius), *Manipulus florum* XI, Gennadius c. 85, Cassiodorus I. 1. 7.
> This entry includes two works that Kirkestede saw in manuscript (*3* and *4*), and the remainder is taken with little perceptible order (probably representing insertions over time) from his secondary sources.
> Portions of this entry appear on fol. ii^v of Wisbech, Wisbech and Fenland Museum, Town Library, MS 1 (Bury P. 119).
> *Speculum coenobitarum* 38.

Prosper   *466. 1*

1 Cronica a primi hominis conditione usque ad obitum Valentiniani Augusti et captivitatem urbis Romae a Genserico rege Wandalorum factam   167

> Whole entry from R23. 1, Vincent XXI 58, and Gennadius 85.

2 Adversus opuscula Cassiani lib. 1

> Quae quidem opuscula ecclesia Dei salutaria probat, sed ille infamat velut nociva

> Whole entry from Vincent XXI 58 and Gennadius 85.

3 Sententiarum sive epigrammatum lib. 1   *Haec Augustini . . . spiritus unus alat*   22.82

> Qui liber partim est metricus, partim prosaicus, et ex dictis B. Augustini collectus; alio nomine dicitur liber B. Augustini De vera innocentia, ut patet in litera A.

>> 22] xxi *R*

>> R23. 10, *MF* XI 2. *CPL* 525. *CCSL* 68. 219. In certain manuscripts this work is preceded by two epigrams, the first of which begins 'Haec Augustini'; see *CPL* 518. Explicit unidentified. Same as Augustinus *1.223*. **82** Bury = Cambridge, Pembroke College, MS 87, fol. 145r (Bury E. 11).

4 De vita contemplativa lib. 3   *Contemplativa . . . instituta*   42.43.19.15. 1.20.22

>> 20.22] 23.22 *Peterhouse 169*

>> R23. 6 (location numbers), *MF* XI 1 (title, incipit, explicit). Julianus Pomerius; *CPL* 998. *PL* 59. 415. [**82** Bury = B13. 101e = Bodl. MS Lat. th. c. 26, fol. 76v (Bury J. 16); Wisbech, Wisbech and Fenland Museum, Town Library, MS 1 (Bury P. 119).]

5 Super Vetus et Novum Testamentum lib. 3

> Qui libri secundum Cassiodorum continent 153 titulos

>> Cassiodorus I. 1. 7 (whole entry).

6 Ad Augustinum et alios epistolas   161.158.156.153.15

>> R23. 2 (whole entry).

Primasius *467. 3*

7 Contra blasphemias Pelagianorum lib. 1   166.108

    R23. 4 (whole entry).

8 De institutione canonicorum lib. 1   166

    R23. 5 (whole entry).

9 Ad Rufinum in quaestionibus solvendis   166.152

    R23. 7 (whole entry).

10 Soliloquia   43

    R23. 8 (whole entry).

11 Epistolae S. Leonis papae adversus Euticen de vera Christi incarnatione ad diversos datae ab isto Prospero dictatae creduntur

    Whole entry from Vincent XXI 58 and Gennadius 85.

12 De vitiis et virtutibus, secundum quosdam   127.42.9.15.25

    25] xxv *R*

    R23. 3 (whole entry).

467 PRIMASIUS Affricanus episcopus floruit circa A. Ch. 554 et scripsit juxta Ysidorum

    Whole entry save date from Isidore c. 9 (works *1, 3*) and Cassiodorus I. 9. 4 (works *2–3*).

1 Contra haereses lib. 3

    Isidore 9 (whole entry).

2 Super Apocalipsin secundum Cassiodorum lib. 5

    Cassiodorus I. 9. 4 (whole entry).

3 Item Quid faciat haereticum lib. 1

    Whole entry from Isidore 9 and Cassiodorus I. 9. 4.

Promeritus   *468.*

p. 120]

468 PROMERITUS episcopus Galliae floruit circa A. Ch. 495 et scripsit juxta Genadium

> Pomerius *Gennadius edition*; Promeritus *Gennadius in Bodl. MS e Musaeo 31 p. 241*
>
> Same as Julianus Pomerius *306*.
> Gennadius c. 99 (whole entry).

1 De natura et qualitate animae et de resurrectione lib. 8

2 De contemptu mundi lib. 1

3 De vitiis et virtutibus lib. 1

469 PRUDENTIUS poeta floruit circa A. Ch. <blank> et scripsit juxta Genadium et Vincentium lib. 18

> *Registrum* 29, Vincent XVIII 62 (works *1–3, 6–9*), Gennadius c. 13 (works *2–3, 5–9*).

1 De conflictu vitiorum et virtutum lib. 1   Senex . . . regnet   82.65

> R29. 5, Vincent XVIII 62. *Psychomachia. CPL* 1441. *CCSL* 126. 149. **82** Bury = BL MS Add. 24199, fol. 1r (Bury P. 123); Bodl. MS Rawlinson C. 697, fol. 64r (Bury A. 119), incipit and explicit do not correspond.

2 De Novo et toto Veteri Testamento personis excerptis Tirocheum commentatus est   Eva columba . . . pandere solus   7.94.65

> 7] 1 R
>
> R29. 2, Vincent XVIII 62, Gennadius 13. *Tituli historiarum*; *CPL* 1444. *CCSL* 126. 390.

3 Exameron de mundi fabrica commentatus est in morem Graecorum usque ad conditionem primi hominis et praevaricationem ejus

> Whole entry from Vincent XVIII 62 and Gennadius 13.

4 Contra haereticos lib. 1   Plurima . . . cucurrit   82

> *CPL* 1439. *Liber Apotheosis* lines 1–177, *CCSL* 126. 77–83.

Prudentius 469. 11

5 Invitatorium ad martirium lib. 1

 Gennadius 13 (whole entry).

6 De laude martirum lib. 1 1.10

 10] x R

 Whole entry from R29. 6, Vincent XVIII 62, and Gennadius 13.

7 Ympnorum lib. 1 *Per quinquennia . . .* Post hymnus: *Ales d<i>ei nuncius . . .* 1.82

 Per quinquennia *queried by Tanner*

 R29. 1, Vincent XVIII 62, and Gennadius 13. *CPL* 1438. *CCSL* 126. 1; incipits are those of the prologue and of hymn 1, respectively. **82** Bury = B13. 79a.

8 Adversus Symmachum ydolatriam defendentem lib. 2 *Paulus . . . sequatur* 1

 R29. 7, R29. 9, Vincent XVIII 62, and Gennadius 13. *CPL* 1442. *CCSL* 126. 182.

9 Item libellos quos Graece intitulavit Apotheos, Sichomachia, Amarchigenia, id est de divinitate et compugnantia animi et de origine peccatorum 1.10.94.65

 10] x R

 R29. 3–5, R29. 8. A blanket reference to titles *1* and *4* above and *15* below; taken verbatim from Gennadius 13 (also available in Vincent XVIII 62, but the wording fits Gennadius). **65** Ramsey = B68. 319–20, and B67. 188. The other location numbers come from the four *Registrum* entries.

10 Idem contra Sabellianos *Cede profanator . . . utraque*

 profantator *Add. 3470, queried by Tanner*

 Liber Apotheosis lines 178–320, *CCSL* 126. 83–8.

11 Idem contra Judeos *Haec si Judaicos . . . fideles*

 Liber Apotheosis lines 321–551, *CCSL* 126. 89–96.

407

Prudentius *469. 12*

12 Idem contra Homuncionitas   *Sunt qui . . . abisse*

    Homuncionitas] *a space left in Add. 3470, queried by Tanner*

    Liber Apotheosis lines 552–781, *CCSL* 126. 96–104.

13 Idem de natura animae   *Occurrit . . . in se*

    Liber Apotheosis lines 782–952, *CCSL* 126. 104–110.

14 Idem contra Fantasmaticos   *Est opere . . . provocat*

    Liber Apotheosis lines 953–1085, *CCSL* 126. 110–15, explicit 'prouocat ite'.

15 Idem contra Marcionitas   *Quo te . . . adurat*

    Amartigenia; *CPL* 1440. *CCSL* 126. 118.

470 PRISCIANUS floruit circa A. Ch. 528 et scripsit duo volumina 1^{mum} majus, 2^{dum} minus.

    Vincent XXII 50, Higden, 1. 22. The secondary sources have been supplemented with manuscripts, doubtless from Bury.

1 In primo agit de ortographia, cosmographia et de ethimologia et de veritate orationum vel viii partium orationis et continet lib. 16   *Cum omnis . . . siderea polus*

    Vincent XXII 50. *Institutiones grammaticae* Books I–XVI; *CPL* 1546. Ed. M. Herz in *GL* 2 and 3. 1–105. [**82** Bury = B13. 44, 'Prisciani magni tres'.]

2 In 2do de constructione et continet lib. 2   *Quoniam mihi . . . omnium rerum*

    Vincent XXII 50. *Institutiones grammaticae* Books XVII–XVIII; *CPL* 1546. Ed. Herz, 3. 105–377.

3 Quidam dicunt quod composuit 3^{ium} librum, scilicet librum de accentu qui sic incipit: *Litera est. . .* Finis: *pape evax*

    Vincent XXII 50. *De accentibus*; *CPL* 1552. Ed. Herz, 3. 519–28.

4 Item scripsit cosmographiam   *Lectionum . . . divisiones*

    Kirkestede took this title from Higden, 1. 22. The incipit and explicit refer to the work edited by A. Riese, *Geographi latini minores* (Heilbronn 1878) 71.

5 Item de xii versibus Virgilii   *Arma virum . . . facientes*

   CPL 1551. Ed. Herz, 3. 459–515.

6 Item ad Cosdram de naturalibus lib. 1

   Cosdram *queried by Tanner*   naturalibus] natura libri *Add. 3470, queried by Tanner*

   Vincent XXII 50 (whole entry).

471 PREPOSITINUS floruit A. Ch. <blank> et scripsit

1 Summam theologiae   *Qui producit . . . claritatem*   74.173

   Summa de quaestionibus theologicis; Glorieux *Rép.* 109g; the work appears with this incipit and explicit in, for example, Oxford, Balliol College, MS 210, fols. 3r–72r.

472 PROBA uxor Adelphi floruit A.D. <blank> et scripsit juxta Mariale et juxta Ysidorum De viris illustribus

   Isidore c. 5; *Mariale* fol. 2r has the name only, 'Proba uxor Adelphi'.

1 Centonam de Christo Virgilianis coaptatum versiculis et intitulatur Virgilio Centona   *Jam dudum . . . in religione*   82.65

   Isidore 5. CPL 1480. CSEL 16. 569, explicit (609) 'in religione nepotes'.

2 Item Homero-Centonam lib. 1

   Hujus Homero-Centonam non habet Latinitas, sicut Virgilio-Centonam ejus non habet Graecia; studuit enim haec mulier utramque gentem ad fidem catholicam invitare priorum documentis auctorum. Proba uxor Adelphi proconsulis inter ecclesiasticos scriptores computata foemina sola, eo quod ex operibus Virgilii sparsim dicta compingens Veteris ac Novi Testamenti quoddam quasi vaticinium collegit; cujus non solum miramur ingenium sed laudamus diligentiam.

   Source unidentified. 'Proba — diligentiam' is partially quoted, partially paraphrased from Isidore.

Pebadius *473.*

p. 121]

473 PEBADIUS episcopus Galliae floruit circa A. Ch. 390 et scripsit juxta Jeronimum libro De catholicis scriptoribus

    Jerome c. 108 (whole entry save the date).

1 Contra Arrianos lib. 1

2 Item opuscula alia

474 PACACIANUS episcopus floruit circa A. Ch. 387 et scripsit juxta Jeronimum ubi supra varia opuscula de quibus est [1.] Cervus

    Jerome c. 106 (whole entry save the date).

2 Item contra Novatianos lib. 1

475 PINITUS Cretensis Gnosiae urbis episcopus floruit circa A. Ch. 164 et scripsit juxta Jeronimum ad Dionisium Corinthiorum episcopum epistolam valde elegantem, in qua docet non semper lacte populos nutriendos, ne quasi parvuli ab ultimo occupentur die, sed solido vesci debere cibo ut in spiritalem proficiant senectutem.

    urbis episcopus] urbis Romae episcopus, *Add. 3470*

    Jerome c. 28 (whole entry save the date).

476 PANTHENUS philosophus tantae prudentiae et eruditionis tam in Scripturis quam in seculari literatura fuit, ut in Indiam a Demetrio Alexandriae episcopo mitteretur, ubi Bartholomaeum apostolum repperit adventum Domini nostri Jesu Christi juxta Mathei evangelium praedicasse, quod Hebraeis literis scriptum revertens Alexandriam secum detulit. Hujus multi sunt in Sacra Scriptura comentarii, sed magis viva vox ejus profuit ecclesiis. Floruit circa annum 208 juxta Jeronimum ubi supra.

    Jerome c. 36 (whole entry save the date).

477 PRISCILLIANUS Pamphiliae episcopus floruit circa A. Ch. <*blank*> et scripsit juxta Jeronimum opuscula multa de quibus aliqua pervenerunt ad Jeronimum

Pamphiliae] Abilae *Jerome*

Jerome c. 121 (whole entry).

478 PELAGIUS abbas ante lapsum suum in haeresin scripsit juxta Genadium studiosis juris necessarios tres de Trinitate libros et pro actuali conversatione Eglogarum ex divinis Scripturis librum unum, capitulorum indiciis in modum S. Cipriani martiris praesignatum.

Gennadius c. 43 (whole entry).

479 POTERIUS Alexandrinae ecclesiae antistes et martir floruit circa A. Ch. 458 et scripsit juxta Ysidorum

Isidore c. 10 (whole entry save the date).

1 De festivitate Paschali ad Leonem papam lib. 3

480 PETRUS abbas Tripolitanae provinciae S. Pauli epistolas exempli opusculorum Beati Augustini subnotasse narratur, ut per os alienum sui cordis declararet archanum, quae ita locis singulis competenter aptavit, ut haec magis studio B. Augustini credas esse perfectum. Mirum est sic alterum ex altero dilucidasse, ut nulla verborum suorum adjectione permixta desiderium cordis proprii complesse videatur. Haec Cassiodorus in libro De institutione divinarum literarum.

Cassiodorus I. 8. 9. Kirkestede has copied this passage into Bodl. MS e Musaeo 9, fol. i^r (Bury B. 290), with the comment 'Iste liber Petri rarissimus est'.

481 PETRUS DE AUREOLA Frater Minor floruit A. Ch. <*blank*> et scripsit

Source unidentified.
Works *3* and *4* appear together in Erfurt, Collegium Amplonianum, MS Quarto 131, fols. 91–104, 104–114, and in Rome Bibl. Naz. Fondo Sessoriano 1405, fols. 1–23, 25–44.

1 De principio naturae

2 Quodlibet

3 De conceptione B. Mariae   *Non dum . . . constituta est*

Ed. Bibliotheca Franciscana scholastica medii aevi 3 (Quaracchi 1904) 23–94.

Petrus de Aureola   *481. 4*

   4 Repercussorium contra adversarium innocentiae martiris Dei   *Justificationem . . . reprehendit me*

      ibid. 95–153.

   5 Super quatuor libros sententiarum

   6 Compendium super Bibliam

482 PARISIENSIS episcopus dictus Will[elmu]s de Avernys secundum alios floruit A. Ch. <blank> et scripsit

> (William of Auvergne)
> The basis for this entry was a manuscript, or more than one, at **82** Bury, and another at **173** Babwell.
> See P. Glorieux, *Répertoire des maîtres en théologie de Paris au XIIIe siècle*, 2 vols (Paris 1933–4) no. 141; id. *La Faculté des Arts et ses maîtres au XIIIe siècle*, Études de philosophie médiévale 59 (Paris 1971) no. 148; O. Weijers, *Le Travail intellectuel à la Faculté des arts de Paris: textes et maîtres* 3, Studia artistarum 6 (Turnhout 1994) 96–9.

   1 De fide et legibus lib. 5   *In ordine . . . imputantes*   82

> Printed, *Guilielmi Alverni . . . Opera omnia*, 2 vols. (Paris 1674), 1. 1.

p. 122]

   2 De immortalitate animae   *Nosse . . . consistit*   82

> Ed G. Bülow in *Beiträge zur Geschichte der Philosophie des Mittelalters* 2/3 (1897) 39; printed, Paris 1674, 1. 329.

   3 De gratia   *Post haec . . . gratiam*   82

> Ed. G. Corti, *Corona Lateranensis* 7 (Rome 1966) 47–66; Glorieux *Rép.* 141p.

   4 Cur Deus homo   *Ponam . . . famulatum*   82

> Printed, Paris 1674, 1. 555. **82** Bury = Bodl. MS Laud Misc. 85, fols. 57r–67*bis* (Bury J. 12, altered to J. 13), without attribution of authorship.

   5 De claustro animae   *Ortus . . . officium janitoris*   82

> Printed, with the *De claustro anime* of Hugh of Saint-Victor (Paris 1507), fols. 1v–23v; explicit unidentified.

6 De praebendis lib. 1   *Behemoth . . . relinquentes*   82

> Printed as *Tractatus de collatione beneficiorum*, Paris 1674, 2/2. 248, incipit 'Umbram Behemoth'.

7 De virtutibus lib. 1   *Postquam . . . de medio eorum*

> Printed, Paris 1674, 1. 102.

8 De universo spirituali lib. 3   *Honoret . . . gratiarum actionem*   173

> *De uniuerso*, second principal part. Printed, Paris 1674, 1. 807.

9 De universo corporali lib. 3   *Scientia . . . in sequentibus*   173

> *De uniuerso*, part 1 of the first principal part. Printed, Paris 1674, 1. 593–682.

10 De bono et malo tract. 1

> Source unidentified.

11 De profunditatibus coelorum lib. 1

> This work and its source are unidentified.

12 De sacramentis et sacramentalibus lib. 1   82

> The source for this work was presumably a manuscript. See Glorieux *Rép.* 1410. Printed, Paris 1674, 1. 407–555.

13 Contra exemptiones lib. 1

> Giles of Rome; Glorieux *Rép.* 400bd.

483 PETRUS Carnotensis floruit circa A. Ch. <blank> et scripsit

(Petrus de Tharentasia = Pope Innocent V).

1 Super libros sententiarum   *Numquid . . . via duce*

> Same as Innocentius V *314.1* and Petrus de Tharenta *446.8*.

484 PETRUS de Vineis floruit circa A. Ch. <blank> et scripsit

1 Epistolarum lib. 1   *Collegerunt . . . minutum*

> Ed. J. R. Iselius (Basel 1740).

485 PLAUTUS

[**82** Bury = B13. 94, 'Plautus et Terentius', evidently a codex containing these eight plays of Plautus and the six plays of Terence; see Terentius 577. Cambridge, Gonville and Caius College, MS 225/240, pp. 5–13 (Bury V. 12), contains *sententiae* excerpted from these same eight plays in sequence.]

1 In Amphitrione   *Amore captus . . . plaudite*

   Ed. W. M. Lindsay (Oxford 1904), unpaginated.

2 In Asinaria   *Amanti . . . satis*

   ibid. (explicit 'datis').

3 In Aulularia   *Aulam . . . ferens a me*

   ibid.

4 Captivorum   *Hos quos . . . plausum date*

   ibid.

5 In Curculione   *Quo ted hanc . . . plaudite*

   ibid.

6 In Casina   *Non mihi . . . nausea*

   ibid. (explicit 'nautea').

7 In Cistellaria   *Dum autem . . . in comoedia*

   ibid. (incipit 'Cum ego ante').

8 In Epidico   *Meus adolescens . . . extollite*

   ibid. (incipit 'Heus').

486 PROCULUS

1 De causis lib. 1   *Omnis causa . . . generatio simul*

   S. Thomas exponit hunc librum et etiam Alfarabius commentator. Est enim liber bene autenticus et frequenter in quaestionibus allegatur, sed non sub nomine proprio, sed tantum sic: Auctor de Causis. [2.] Expositio S. Thomae sic incipit: *Sicut dicit philosophus 4to ethicorum etc.* Finis: *probatio inducitur quae praemissa est.* [3.] Expositio Alfarabii sive commentum sic incipit: *Cum ergo removet etc.*, et finit sic: *adquisitum sicut ostendimus etc.*

1. and [3.] together are *ps.* Proclus, *Liber de causis*, ed. A. Pattin in *Tijdschrift voor Filosofie* 28 (1966). The incipit and explicit of *1* are those of the propositions only, beginning with proposition 1 para. 1 and ending with proposition 31 para. 214 (Pattin, 134–200 line 76); probably the same as Aristotle *46.38*. The incipit and explicit of *3* are those of the demonstrations of the propositions, beginning with proposition 1 para. 2 and ending with proposition 31 para. 219 (Pattin, 134 line 3–203 line 16), which were thought to be a commentary on the *De causis* by Alpharabius; cf. BL MS Royal 12 D. xiv, fol. 142r and BNF MS lat. 16082, fol. 311r. Same as Alpharabius *75.1*.

[2.] Ed. H. D. Saffrey, *Textus philosophici Friburgenses* 4–5 (Fribourg 1954). Same as Thomas de Aquino *567.15*.

487 PORTUMANUS floruit et scripsit juxta J[ohannem] Sarisb[uriensem] in Policratico lib. 8°

John of Salisbury, *Policraticus* VIII 6, 7; ed. C. C. J. Webb (Oxford 1909). Book VIII contains, without the mention of any specific works, a discussion of this author's philosophy taken from Macrobius's *Saturnalia*. The name appears as 'Postumianus' in Macrobius and as 'Portunianus' in the *Policraticus*.

488 POMPONIUS Porphirionis floruit <*blank*> et scripsit

Source unidentified.

1 Commentaria super omnes libros Oracii

489 QUADRATUS episcopus et apostolorum discipulus floruit circa A. Ch. 61 et scripsit juxta Jeronimum

Jerome c. 19 (whole entry save the date).

1 De Christiana religione lib. 1

490 QUINTILIANUS floruit circa A. Ch. 71 et scripsit juxta Vincentium lib. 9no

Vincent X 121; *Registrum* 85 not used.

Quintilianus *490. 1*

1 De oratoria institutione lib. 8   *Subtilius . . . angustiae faciunt*

> Vincent X 121. Ed. M. Winterbottom, 2 vols. (Oxford 1970); the incipit and explicit are unidentified. [**82** Bury = B13. 162a, 261.]

2 De 17 causis lib.   *Ex incendio . . . ne dicas*

> *Ps.* Quintillian, *Declamationes.* Ed. L. Håkanson (Stuttgart 1982) 20–389. [**82** Bury = B13. 90; Cambridge, Gonville and Caius College, MS 154/204, p. 157 (Bury P. 162), with colophon by Kirkestede, but the explicit does not correspond (p. 202).]

491 QUINTUS CURTIUS Rufus floruit <*blank*> et scripsit

1 De Alexandro Magno historice lib. 9   . . . *honos habetur*

> Ed. K. Müller (Munich 1954). [**82** Bury = B13. 61c.]

p. 123]

492 RABANUS monachus et S. Bedae discipulus sophistaque sui temporis poetarum nulli secundus et theologus optimus, abbas Fuldensis et postea Magontiae archiepiscopus est ordinatus A.D. <*blank*> Hic unus erat de primis fundatoribus Parisiensis studii, ut patet in verbo Alcuinus, et scripsit multa.

> *Registrum* 11, Vincent XXIV 173 (works *1–6, 9–16, 20*) and XXV 28, *Manipulus florum* X, Martinus Polonus (MGH *Scriptores* 22. 462).
> The sequence of the titles is governed by Vincent of Beauvais, fleshed out with Bury manuscripts, with incipits and explicits from the *Manipulus florum,* and with location numbers from the *Registrum.* As usual there are brief interruptions in the sequence, and additions from other sources at the end.
> *Speculum coenobitarum* 45.
> Bale, *Index,* 326 (biographical notice and works *24–25* only).

1 De laude crucis lib. 2   *De ymagine . . .*   42.32.19.35.13.20

> R11. 14, Vincent XXIV 173. *PL* 107. 133.

2 De institutione clericorum lib. 1   *Ecclesia . . . admittitur*   15.19.10.82.43.42

> 10] x *R*

> R11. 11, Vincent XXIV 173. *PL* 107. 297; explicit is perhaps that of the penultimate chapter of Book II, 'credulitas amittitur' (*PL* 107. 371).

Rabanus *492. 10*

3 Super Genesim lib. 4   *In principio . . . usque in finem*   15.<u>19</u>.<u>10</u>.<u>82</u>.<u>43</u>.<u>124</u>

   10] x R

   R11. 10 (title, location numbers), Vincent XXIV 173, *MF* X 1 (title, incipit, explicit). Although some of them are borrowed from the *Manipulus florum*, the incipits and explicits of the five entries here (works *3–5, 7–8*) generally represent a Bury codex containing Walafrid Strabo's *Abbreuiatio Rabani Mauri in Pentatheucum* (?B13. 71); cf. Stegmüller *Bibl.* 8316, 8318–21. The *Abbreuiatio* often circulated with the genuine commentaries of Hrabanus or were attributed to Hrabanus. See, for example, Cambridge, Trinity College, MS B. 2. 4, which begins with Hrabanus' *Super Genesim* followed by the *Abbreuiatio*; and BNF MS lat. 12307, in which Strabo's *Abbreuiationes* on Genesis and Leviticus are attributed to Hrabanus. **82** Bury = B13. 71, 'Rabbanus super v libros Moysi'.

4 Super Exodum lib. 4   *Hujus libri . . . obsecraris*   124.<u>156</u>

   R11. 1, Vincent XXIV 173, *MF* X 2 (explicit 'obsecratis', incipit does not correspond). See note to *3* above. Location number **124** was included here because it was supplied for the other four books of the Pentateuch in the *Registrum* (*3* above and *5, 7, 8* below).

5 Super Numerum lib. 1   *Locutus . . .*   <u>124</u>

   R11. 18, Vincent XXIV 173. See note to *3* above.

6 Super libros Regum lib. 4   <u>163</u>

   Whole entry from R11. 4 and Vincent XXIV 173.

7 Super Leviticum lib. 1   *Sequentis . . . intelliguntur*   <u>124</u>

   R11. 17, *MF* X 3 . See note to *3* above. *PL* 114. 795; explicit unidentified.

8 Super Deuteronomium lib. 1   *Haec sunt . . . idem per omnia*   <u>124</u>

   Whole entry from R11. 19 (title, location number) and *MF* X 4 (title, incipit, explicit). See note to *3* above.

9 Super Paralipomenon lib. 4

   Vincent XXIV 173 (whole entry).

10 Super Judith lib. 1

   Vincent XXIV 173 (whole entry).

Rabanus   *492. 11*

11   Super Hester lib. 1

   Vincent XXIV 173 (whole entry).

12   Super librum Sapientiae lib. 3

   Vincent XXIV 173 (whole entry).

13   Super Ecclesiasticum lib. 10

   Vincent XXIV 173 (whole entry).

14   Super Jeremiam lib. 1

   Whole entry from R11. 16 and Vincent XXIV 173.

15   Super libros Machabeorum lib. 1   *Reverentissimo* . . .   19.42.43.82.127

   R11. 12, Vincent XXIV 173. Stegmüller *Bibl.* 7058–7059. *PL* 109. 1127.

16   Super Mathaeum lib. 8   *Expositionem . . . curavimus*   93.9.19.82.42.13.15

   R11. 5, Vincent XXIV 173, *MF* X 5. Stegmüller *Bibl.* 7060. *PL* 107. 729. **82**
   Bury = B13. 68.

17   Super Parabolas Salomonis lib. 1   125

   R11. 8 (whole entry).

18   Super epistolas Pauli ad Corinthios, Galatas et Ephesios   19.9.166

   R11. 20 (whole entry save two suspect location numbers).

19   Super Apocalipsin   139

   R11. 23 (whole entry).

20   De naturis rerum et ethimologiis verborum et de mistica earundem rerum significatione lib. 22   *Primum . . . cooperatio*   13.15.80.42.82.123

   R11. 3, Vincent XXIV 173. Stegmüller *Bibl.* 7020. *PL* 111. 13. Concerning the title see E. Heyse, *Hrabanus Maurus' Enzyklopädie 'De rerum naturis'* (Munich 1969), chapter 1. Same as *21* below.

21   De significationibus verborum   82

   R11. 13 (whole entry). Same as *20* above.

22 De compoto   35.95

   Rɪɪ. 9 (whole entry).

23 De ecclesiasticis officiis   *Officium* . . .   35.23.46

   Rɪɪ. 21. Book II of *2* above, *PL* 107. 325.

24 De praedestinatione   35

   Rɪɪ. 22 (whole entry).

25 De opere Christi   26

   26] xxxvi *R*

   Rɪɪ. 24 (whole entry).

26 De corpore et sanguine Domini   20.53.46.1.42.161

   Rɪɪ. 6 (whole entry).

493 RABY MOYSES Judaeus floruit <*blank*> et scripsit

   (Maimonides)
   Cf. *Manipulus florum* XVI ('Libri diuersorum auctorum').

1 De duce dubiorum lib. 6   *In nomine . . . lux orietur*

   Et procedit per dubia totius Bibliae

   The incipit and explicit ('lux oriatur eis') come from *MF* XVI 2. But the *Manipulus florum* offers a title phrased differently, describes the work as containing three parts, and offers no basis for the concluding comment. Kirkestede knew a manuscript of this at Babwell (see his note in BL MS Royal 8 F. xɪv, fol. 132r [Bury G. 15], and see p. lvi above), which may have been the source of this information.

494 RADULFUS Flaviacensis monachus et abbas floruit circa A. Ch. 1094 et scripsit multa

   Registrum 37.
   This entry combines information from manuscripts with information from the *Registrum*.
   Portions of this entry appear on Cambridge, Pembroke College, MS 29, fol. i^r (Bury R. 14), including locations copied from the *Registrum* and the biographical statement from an unknown source; see p. lxiii above.
   Speculum coenobitarum 46.

Radulfus   *494. 1*

1 Super Leviticum lib. 20   *Cum inter . . . in monte Sinay*   **8**.63.20.15.82.31

   31] 13 *R*

   R37. 1. Stegmüller *Bibl.* 7093. *Maxima Bibliotheca Patrum* 17 (Lyon 1677) 48. **82** Bury = Kirkestede noted on the flyleaf of Pembroke College 29 (*4* below) that Bury owned a handsome two-volume copy of this work, no longer extant: 'In librario Sancti Edmundi in .ii. pulcris et magnis voluminibus'; and he took note as well, in two copies of a glossed Leviticus (Cambridge, Pembroke College, MSS 49, fol. 77v (Bury B. 48), and 50, fol. 54r (Bury —)), of Ralph's commentary on this book ('Hunc librum exponit etiam Radulfus Flauiacensis monachus et abbas' or (in the second instance) '. . . exponit plenius Radulfus abbas Flauiacensis').

2 Super epistolas Pauli   61

   61] 161 *R;* 61 *Peterhouse 169*

   R37. 2 (whole entry).

3 Super Apocalipsin   161

   R37. 3 (whole entry).

4 Super Parabolas Salomonis lib. 15   *Post negotia . . . sine manu*   82.83

   R37. 4. Richard de Préaux; Stegmüller *Bibl.* 7095, 7293. **82** Bury = Cambridge, Pembroke College, MS 29 (Bury R. 14), explicit 'siue malum'.

p. 124]

5 Super libros Regum

   R37. 5 (whole entry).

6 Super psalmos

   Source unidentified.

7 Super Ecclesiasten lib.

   Source unidentified.

8 Super Mathaeum   20

   20] xx *R*

   R37. 11 (whole entry).

Radulfus   *494. 15*

9 De vi aetatibus et de hiis quae post futura sunt   <u>8</u>

   R37. 9 (whole entry).

10 De diversis miraculis et meditationibus   <u>8</u>

   meditationibus] mirabilibus *R*

   R37. 10 (whole entry).

11 De orationibus et meditationibus lib. 1   *Si quis . . . gaudere*   175.109.122

   Unidentified.

12 De episcopo et clerico lib. 3   *Multi . . . concedat*   175.109.168

   Unidentified.

13 De expositione missae tract. 1   *Quando . . . primum*   175

   Unidentified.

14 De abbate et monacho lib. 1   *Qui bonus . . . redempti sumus*   <u>8</u>.82.175. 165.167

   R37. 8 (title, of a work unidentified in the *Registrum*). Kirkestede has added the incipit and explicit, which also are unidentified.

15 De sanctuario Dei quod est S. Maria lib. 2   *In principio . . . in aeterna*   <u>8</u>.86

   De sanctuario Dei quod est S. Maria queried by *Tanner*; the wording of the title is confirmed by Kirkestede's note on Pembroke College 29 fol. i^v

   R37. 7. Unidentified. See the discussion of this and the preceding work at *Registrum* 37. 7. Same as Hildefonsus *246.13*.

Hunc tamen librum De sanctuario quidam ascribunt Hildefonso archiepiscopo Toletano; intitulatur autem a quibusdam sic: Liber de sacro templo Dei quod est tabernaculum coeleste, et hoc patet in prologo illius libri. Primus enim liber De sanctuario agit de electione et conceptione B. Mariae et de nativitate et annunciatione ejusdem, et de nativitate Domini. Secundus de virginitate et de assumptione B. Mariae. Secundum quosdam dividitur in quatuor libros.

495 RADULPHUS Niger floruit tempore S. Thomae archiepiscopi et martiris circa A. Ch. 1164 et scripsit, sicut ipsemet testatur in libro Cronicorum suorum

> Ralph Niger, *Chronicum*, ed. H. Krause (Frankfurt 1985) 287, source of all the titles, to which has been added information from a manuscript or manuscripts at **82** Bury.
> Bale, *Index*, 331–2.
> Sharpe, *Latin Writers*, 450–51.

1 Super libros Regum lib. 24   *In canonica . . . ascendere merear*   **82**

> Stegmüller *Bibl.* 7148,7.

2 Super Eptaticum lib. 7   *Microcosmus* . . .   **82**

> Eptaticum] Pentatheucum Bale; Niger p. 287 confirms Add. 3470

> Incipit unidentified.

3 Epitome in Paralipomenon

4 Remediarium in Esdram

5 De re militari et de tribus viis peregrinationis Jerosolumitanae lib. 4   *Militia . . . convalescam*   **82**

> Divided into two works in Bale; but Niger p. 287 and the surviving Bury manuscript confirm Add. 3470.

> Sharpe, *Latin Writers*, 451. Ed. L. Schmugge (Berlin 1977) 98. *Speculum coenobitarum* 46. 6 (attrib. to Ralph of Flaix). **82** Bury = Cambridge, Pembroke College, MS 27, fols. 120r–156v (Bury P. 25); cf. fol. 149ra. Kirkestede corrected the misattribution of this work to Ralph of Flaix, in a list of works he copied from the *Registrum* on fol. i[r] of Cambridge, Pembroke College, MS 29 (Bury R. 14).

6 De quatuor festivitatibus B. Mariae lib. 1

7 De interpretationibus Hebraeorum nominum lib. 1

8 Cronica a principio mundi usque ad tempus suum lib. 1   *In principio . . .*   **82**

> Sharpe, *Latin Writers*, 450. Ed. H. Krause (Frankfurt 1985).

RADBERTUS monachus supra in litera P nomine Paschasius.

496 RADULFUS monachus Westmon[asteriensis] floruit circa A. Ch. 1180 et scripsit abbati suo Laurentio

> Bale, *Index*, 335.
> Not in Sharpe, *Latin Writers*.

1 Omelias nobiles, et continet partes 2   *Ecce dies . . . terrestria* Secunda pars illarum omeliarum incipit: *In illo tempore . . . veniam autori*

> Bale labels the two parts Homelias epistolarum *and* Homelias evangeliorum *respectively*

> These homilies have not been identified and do not appear to have survived.

497 REMIGIUS ALTISIODORENSIS <blank> in exponendis Scripturis divinis et humanis floruit A. Ch. <blank> et scripsit

1 Super quatuor evangelia

> Source unidentified.

2 De missa tract. 1   *Celebratio . . . consecratur*   74

> Chapter 40 of his *De diuinis officiis*, which had a separate existence. *PL* 101. 1246; explicit unidentified.

3 Super prologum Bibliae   *Epistola . . . in Dei templo*   168

> Unidentified.

4 Super alium prologum Bibliae   *Desiderii . . . exempla*   168

> *PL* 131. 51–4, explicit comes from the last lemma: 'exemplaria Latina quam Graeca, Graeca quam Hebraea.'

5 Super epistolas Pauli

> Source unidentified.

6 Super Donatum commentum

> Source unidentified.

Richardus 498.

498 RICHARDUS de S. Victore Parisiensis canonicus floruit A. Ch. <*blank*> et scripsit

> *Registrum* 98, Vincent XXVIII 58 (works *1, 4, 6–9, 11–16*), *Manipulus florum* XIII, *Mariale* fol. 75r.
> Bale, *Index*, 361–2 (works *1–9, 17–18, 23, 29–38* only).
> Sharpe, *Latin Writers*, 506–508.

1 De Sancta Trinitate lib. 8   *Si ad sublimia . . . doctrinam*   94

> Whole entry from R98. 5 (title, location number), Vincent XXVIII 58, *MF* XIII 1 (title, incipit 'Si ad sublimium', explicit 'doctrinam discens').

2 De patriarchis seu de contemplatione lib. 1   *Benjamin . . . ratio*   63.12.115.124.82.159

> 12] xii *R*

> R98. 17 (location numbers), R98. 15 (title), *MF* XIII 11 (title, incipit, explicit 'ratio applaudit'). *Beniamin minor*; Sharpe, *Latin Writers*, 506. Stegmüller *Bibl.* 7325. *PL* 196. 1.

3 Item de contemplatione lib. 5   *Misticam . . . locuti sumus*   74.155

> R98. 20. *Beniamin maior*; Sharpe, *Latin Writers*, 506. Stegmüller *Bibl.* 7324. *PL* 196. 63–192; explicit is that of V 19. Same as *34* below. A note by Kirkestede in BL MS Royal 8 F. xiv, fol. 132r mentions the copy at **74**, Holme St Benets (see p. lvi above). / [**82** Bury = BL MS Royal 8 F. xiv, fol. 132r (Bury G. 15)]

[p. 125]

4 De exterminio mali et promotione boni lib. 1   *Quid est . . . meretur*   94.43.114.123.12.53

> 12] xii *R*

> Whole entry from R98. 7 (location numbers), Vincent XXVIII 58, *MF* XIII 12 (title, incipit, explicit).

5 De statu interioris hominis lib. 1   *Omne caput . . . oleo*   94.43.127.9.12.26

> 12] xii *R*   26] xxv *R*

> Whole entry from R98. 23 (title), R98. 10 (location numbers), and *MF* XIII 13 (title, incipit, explicit).

Richardus   *498. 14*

6 Ad novitios tract. 1   *Afferte . . . pax vestra*   82

   Vincent XXVIII 58. *Adnotatio in Psalmum 28*. Cf. Sharpe, *Latin Writers*, 508. *PL* 196. 285.

7 De 4 ventis lib. 1   *Videbam . . . destruitur*   82

   Vincent XXVIII 58. Book III of *De eruditione hominis interioris*; cf. Sharpe, *Latin Writers*, 506. *PL* 196. 1347.

8 Super Danielem et de mistico sompno Nebuchadonosor lib. 1   *Quid est illud*
   . . .   163.43.127.94.95

   illud] idem *Add. 3470*; illud *Bale, MF*   95] 92 *R*

   Whole entry from R98. 14 (title, location numbers **163** to **127**), R98. 9 (location numbers **94**, **95**), Vincent XXVIII 58, and *MF* XIII 9 (title, incipit 'Quid illud').

9 De arbore Nabugodonosor lib. 1   166.163.127.12.95

   12] xii *R*   95] 92 *R*

   Whole entry from R98. 14 and R98. 9 (location numbers) and Vincent XXVIII 58 (title), save the suspect **166**.

10 Super Ezechielem ad literam   9.93.94.12

   93] 43 *R*   12] xii *R*

   R98. 4 (whole entry).

11 De officiis ecclesiae lib.

   Vincent XXVIII 58 (whole entry).

12 De sacrificio Abrahae lib. 1

   Vincent XXVIII 58 (whole entry).

13 Super illud: In die illa nutriet homo vaccam

   Vincent XXVIII 58 (whole entry).

14 Super illud: Ecce virgo concipiet

   Whole entry from R98. 6 and Vincent XXVIII 58.

Richardus *498. 15*

15 Contra Andream Judaizantem   *In quendam . . . delectat*   9.15.94.86

   Vincent XXVIII 58. Book I of *De Emmanuele*; Sharpe, *Latin Writers*, 506. *PL* 196. 601; the incipit is that of the prologue. Same as *36* below. Location numbers **9** to **94** were mistakenly copied here instead of with *14* above (R98. 6).

16 Librum qui dicitur Excerptiones, in quo breviter continetur divisio et materia omnium scientiarum ac series historiae praecedentium temporum et quaedam morales expositiones sacrarum scripturarum

   Vincent XXVIII 58 (whole entry).

17 Super Joelem expos. 1   *Joel . . . dignetur*   154.43.15.82

   Joel propheta *Bale*

   R98. 21. Works *17* and *18* (a single entry in *Registrum*) usually circulated together. They are perhaps attributable to Richard or to Hugh of Saint-Victor; Sharpe, *Latin Writers*, 508. *PL* 175. 321.

18 Super Naum prophetam expos. 1   *Naum . . .*   154.43.15.82

   R98. 21. See the note to *17* above. *PL* 96. 705.

19 De potestate ligandi et solvendi   *Quodcunque . . . peccatum*

   MF XIII 2 (whole entry).

20 De spiritu blasphemiae   *Qui in evang*[*elio*] *. . . coegisti*

   MF XIII 3 (whole entry, incipit 'Que in euangelio').

21 De tribus appropriatis   *Quaeris a . . . munda*

   MF XIII 4 (whole entry, explicit 'munda et bona').

22 De verbis apostoli   *Quaeris quomodo . . . intellectum*

   MF XIII 5 (whole entry, explicit 'intellectum nostrum').

23 Super illud Ysaiae: Ad me clamat   *Ad me . . . tu me*

   Ad me clamat *add. Bale*

   MF XIII 6 (whole entry, explicit 'tu me coegisti').

Richardus 498. 34

24 Item de verbis apostoli *Si ea quae . . . retribuitur*

    MF XIII 8 (whole entry).

25 De potestate judiciaria *In regeneratione . . . poterit credi*

    MF XIII 10 (whole entry).

26 De differentia peccati mortalis et venialis *Quum quaestioni . . .*

    MF XIII 7 (whole entry, incipit 'Quoniam questioni').

27 De studio sapientiae et ejus commendatione 163

    R98. 16 (whole entry).

28 De tribus processionibus 115.12

    12] xix *R*

    R98. 24 (whole entry).

29 Super Ecclesiasten 15

    R98. 22 (whole entry).

30 Super Exiit edictum 94

    R98. 8 (whole entry).

31 Sermones plures et devotos 166.94

    R98. 11 (whole entry save the suspect **166**).

32 Librum qui dicitur Poenitentiale ejusdem *Humanum . . . sufficiant* 94.93

    R98. 19. The *Registrum*'s entry (title, and location number **93**) refers to the penitential of Robert of Flamborough; but the incipit and explicit that Kirkestede gives here are unidentified.

33 De oratione Dominica expos. 1

    This work and its source are unidentified.

34 De 6 generibus contemplationis tract. 1 163.82.94

    R98. 13. Same as *3* above. **82** Bury = BL MS Royal 8 F. xiv, fol. 132r (Bury G. 15).

Richardus   *498. 35*

  35 De conceptione B. Mariae tract. 1

     Mariale fol. 75r (whole entry).

  36 Dialogorum ejus de Emanuele lib. 1   *Post illum . . . sermone*   86

     R98. 18. Book II of *De Emmanuele*. PL 196. 633. Same as *15* above.

  37 Super psalterium expos. 1   *Beatus . . . laudare possit*

     R98. 12. The work represented by this incipit and explicit is unidentified.

  38 Super quosdam psalmos et de sententiis quarundam scripturarum
     Quare fremuerunt . . . Quid per gentes desiderio . . .   82

     Cf. Stegmüller *Bibl.* 7377. PL 196. 265; the two incipits are those of Psalm 2 and of the text, respectively. For the complex manuscript tradition of Richard of Saint-Victor's commentaries on the psalms see *Dictionnaire de spiritualité* 13. 618–20. **82** Bury = Ipswich, Central Library, MS 8 pt 1, fol. 6r (Bury B. 240), attributed to Richard of Saint-Victor.

499 RICARDUS DE MEDIA VILLA Frater Minor floruit circa A. Ch. <*blank*> et scripsit

     (Richard Middleton)
     Sharpe, *Latin Writers*, 493–4.

  1 Super libros sententiarum lib. 4   *Abscondita . . . humiliter*

     Sharpe, *Latin Writers*, 493. Stegmüller *Sent.* 722. The four are printed, *Ricardus de Mediavilla: questiones super quarto libro sententiarum* (Venice: Dionysius Bertochus, 1489).

  2 Super primum sententiarum lib. 1   *Abscondita . . . mihi tribuat*

  3 Super 2^{dum} sententiarum lib. 1   *Omnia per . . . me Dominus*

  4 Super 3^{ium} sententiarum lib. 1

  5 Super 4^{tum} sententiarum lib. 1   *In nova . . . essem humiliter*

     In nova] Innona *Add. 3470, queried by Tanner*

p. 126]

[R]   *501. 2*

500 RADULPHUS DE DICETO decanus ecclesiae S. Pauli Londoninensis floruit A. Ch. 1147 et scripsit

> 1197 *corrected to* 1147 *in Add. 3470, in what looks like Tanner's hand*
>
> Diceto, 1. 23–4.
> Bale, *Index*, 329.
> Twysden, *Scriptores*, xxix.
> Sharpe, *Latin Writers*, 446.

1 Librum cronicorum qui dicitur Ymagines historiarum   *Cronica sunt ymagines historiarum . . . et finit A. Ch. 1195*

> Diceto, 1. 23–4. The incipit is that of the *Abbreuiationes chronicorum*, ed. W. Stubbs, RS 68 (1876), 1. 34, which extends to the year 1147; the explicit, unidentified, must come from Ralph's continuation, which begins with the year 1148 (printed as *Ymagines historiarum*, beginning ib. 1. 291), but the exact year of the chronicle's conclusion differs from one manuscript to another.

501 [R] . . . de Frisingfeld floruit circa A. Ch. <*blank*> et scripsit

> Frisyngfelde magister quidam Anglus numeratus a Bostono Buriensi in R. littera   *Bale fol. 45r*
>
> Frysyngfelde Sudovolcas grammaticus peritus   *Bale fol. 48r*
>
> Bale, *Index*, 73. The first entry ('ex Bostoni Buriensis catalogo') appears on fol. 45r of Bale's notebook. A second entry ('ex Bostono Buriensi monacho') for this author appears on fol. 48r. The variants noted below occur only in this second entry. Each of Bale's notebook entries appears among authors whose names begin with F, which indicates that the christian name was already absent from Bale's manuscript, just as it is from Add. 3470.
>
> Sharpe, *Latin Writers*, 828. This author and his two works are unidentified.

1 Librum metricum qui dicitur Practica grammaticae   *Commoda . . . per saecula cuncta*

> Commoda provenire pueris   *Bale*

2 Librum prosaicum qui vocatur Verbarius   *Cum sit necessarium . . . per aeterna saecula*

> Cum sit necessarium ante omnia   *Bale*

429

502 RICARDUS DE CYRENCESTRIA

Bale, *Index*, 343.
Sharpe, *Latin Writers*, 464.

1 De officio ecclesiastico lib. 7   *Officium ut* . . .

Sharpe, *Latin Writers*, 464. This work is not known to survive. It was cited extensively by Kirkestede's younger contemporary William Woodford; see J. I. Catto, 'William Woodford, OFM (*c.* 1330–*c.* 1397)', DPhil. diss. (Oxford 1969) 119–20, 244, 324–5.

503 RATHAMIUS floruit circa A. Ch. <blank> et scripsit

(Ratramnus Corbiensis)
These two works are found in the same order with the same titles in Cambridge, Sidney Sussex College, MS 71, fols. 66r–91r (Warden, s. xii–xiii).

1 De anima lib. 1   *Suo quantum* . . . *arguatis*   15.65.82

Ed. A. Wilmart, *RB* 43 (1931) 210, incipit 'Duo quantum', explicit (p. 223) 'arguatis et corrigatis'.

2 De eo quod Christus de virgine natus est per naturalem corporis partem lib. 1   *Fama est* . . . *complacebit*   15.65.82

De natiuitate Christi. PL 121. 81. **82** Bury = Cambridge, Pembroke College, MS 22, fol. 230r.

504 RICARDUS DE WITHRINGSETE cancellarius Cantebriggiae floruit <blank> et scripsit

Bale, *Index*, 364.
Sharpe, *Latin Writers*, 519.

1 De vitiis et virtutibus et de sacramentis lib.   *Qui bene praesunt* . . . *erit consummatus*

This appears as two titles in Bale

Sharpe, *Latin Writers*, 519. [**82** Bury = Cambridge, Pembroke College, MS 118, fols. 24r–52v (Bury Y. 12), untitled; Kirkestede's table of contents calls it 'Summa Ricardi *Qui bene present*'.]

505 ROBERTUS Lincoln[iensis] episcopus qui et GROSTESTE dicitur, floruit A. Ch. 1250 et obiit anno 1253 et scripsit multa. Hic fuit doctor in theologia, in triplici lingua eruditus, Latina, Hebraica, et Graeca. Multa de glosis Hebraeorum extraxit, de Graeco multa transferri fecit, utpote libros Dionisii, quorum novam translationem perlucide commentavit.[a] Item in logica et astrologia et in cunctis liberalibus artibus excellenter erat eruditus. Ad papam Innocentium misit epistolam invectivam satis tonantem pro eo quod ecclesias Angliae exactionibus indebitis vexare videretur. Hac de causa vocatus est ad Curiam, et cum ibi molestaretur appellavit constanter a Curia papae Innocentii ad tribunal Christi; unde contigit quod eodem Roberto in Anglia obeunte audita est vox in Curia papae: Veni miser ad judicium, et papa in crastino inventus est exanimis: quasi cuspide baculi in latere percussus. Hiis de causis licet perspicuus effulserit Robertus miracula transferri, tamen nec in sanctorum cathalogo poni non est a Curia permissus.

[a] Nicholas Trevet, *Annales*, ed. T. Hog (London 1845) 243.

Mariale fol. 141v.
Consistent with the rest of the entry, works *1, 3, 6–7, 10, 12, 18–19, 21–23*, and *40*, even though they lack incipits and explicits, were probably supplied from manuscripts.
Ely extracts, fol. 149v.
Bale, *Index*, 375. A slightly condensed form of the biographical note reappears at the end of the *Index* entry.
Sharpe, *Latin Writers*, 539–51.
See also S. H. Thomson, *The Writings of Robert Grosseteste* (Cambridge 1940), cited here by page number; and the edition of L. Baur, *Die philosophische Werke des Robert Grosseteste, Bischof von London*, BGPM 9 (Münster 1912).

1 Super Dionisium de coelesti et ecclesiastica jerarchia lib. 2

Sharpe, *Latin Writers*, 546–7. Thomson, *Grosseteste*, 78–9.

2 De originali peccato lib. 1   *Quocirca . . .*

Untraced; Thomson, *Grosseteste*, 272.

3 Super Dionisium de divinis nominibus

Thomson, *Grosseteste*, 79.

4 De libero arbitrio quaestiones lib. 1   *Cum per . . . contrarium*

Sharpe, *Latin Writers*, 541. Thomson, *Grosseteste*, 91. Recension II; ed. Baur, 150–225.

Robertus   505. 5

5   De spaera lib. 1   *Intentio* . . .

   Sharpe, *Latin Writers*, 542. Thomson, *Grosseteste*, 115–16. Ed. Baur, 10–32.

6   De astrolabio lib. 1

   Spurious; Thomson *Grosseteste*, 243.

7   De compoto lib. 1

   Sharpe, *Latin Writers*, 540. Thomson, *Grosseteste*, 95–6.

8   Super librum posteriorum   *Intentio . . . posteriorum*

   Sharpe, *Latin Writers*, 542. Thomson *Grosseteste*, 84–5. Ed. P. Rossi (Florence 1981) 93; the explicit is presumably part of the colophon (cf. ib. 408 note).

9   Super libros physicorum notulas   *Cum scire* . . .

   Sharpe, *Latin Writers*, 543. Thomson, *Grosseteste*, 82. Ed. R. C. Dales (Boulder, CO, 1963).

10   Super Dionisium de mistica theologia

   theologia *Add. 3470, queried by Tanner*

   Sharpe, *Latin Writers*, 546–7. Thomson, *Grosseteste*, 79–80.

11   Super prologum Bibliae expos. 1   *Hanc epistolam . . . pleni sunt sensibus*   168

   The proemium to *12* below; explicit unidentified.

12   Exameron

   Sharpe, *Latin Writers*, 542. Thomson, *Grosseteste*, 100–101. Ed. R. C. Dales & S. Gieben, Auctores Britannici medii aeui 6 (1982). See *11* above.

13   Super psalterium   *Beatus vir* . . .

   Sharpe, *Latin Writers*, 543. Thomson, *Grosseteste*, 75–6.

14   Super Epistolam ad Galathas   *Ut apostolus . . . quid docetur*

   Sharpe, *Latin Writers*, 543. Thomson, *Grosseteste*, 73. *CCCM* 130. 41; explicit unidentified.

15 De 10 praeceptis   *Sicut dicit . . . sex mandatis*

> Sharpe, *Latin Writers*, 543. Thomson, *Grosseteste*, 131–2. *De decem mandatis*. Ed. R. C. Dales & E. B. King, Auctores Britannici medii aeui 10 (1987). [**82** Bury = Bodl. MS Laud Misc. 85, fols. 32r–56v (Bury J. 12, altered to J. 13), without rubric but with title and attribution in the explicit; BL MS Royal 11 B. III, fols. 319v–328v (Bury V. 18), with rubric by Kirkestede in the margin but without attribution of authorship.]

16 De cessatione legalium   *Fuerunt . . .*

> Sharpe, *Latin Writers*, 543. Thomson, *Grosseteste*, 121–2. Ed. R. C. Dales & E. B. King, Auctores Britannici medii aeui 7 (1986).

17 De confessione tract.1   *Quum cogitabo . . . potentiam*

> Sharpe, *Latin Writers*, 543. Thomson, *Grosseteste*, 172 *serm.* 15.

18 De cura pastorali

> Sharpe, *Latin Writers*, 543. Thomson, *Grosseteste*, 129. Ed. H. R. Luard, RS 25 (London 1861) 357, as *ep.* 127.

19 De eo quod oportuit Deum fieri hominem

> Unidentified.

p. 127]

20 De veritate serm. 1   *Ego sum . . . in singulis*

> Sharpe, *Latin Writers*, 542. Thomson, *Grosseteste*, 119–20, explicit 'in angulis'. Ed. Baur, 130.

21 De resurrectione serm.1

> Sharpe, *Latin Writers*, 545. Thomson, *Grosseteste*, 218 *dict.* 20.

22 De civitate Dei compendium

> Unidentified.

23 Super Job

> Untraced; Thomson, *Grosseteste*, 271.

24 De prima forma et forma omnium   *Rogavit . . . corripias*   168

   Sharpe, *Latin Writers*, 541. Thomson, *Grosseteste*, 98–9. Ed Luard, 1–17 as *ep.* 1, explicit 'corrigas'.

25 De luce   *Formam . . . temporibus*

   Sharpe, *Latin Writers*, 541. Thomson, *Grosseteste*, 108–109. Ed. Baur, 51.

26 De colore vel coloribus   *Color est . . . ostenduntur*

   Sharpe, *Latin Writers*, 540. Thomson, *Grosseteste*, 93–4. Ed. Baur, 78; explicit 'ostendere possunt'.

27 De potentia   *Omne quidem . . . ad effectum*

   Sharpe, *Latin Writers*, 542. Thomson, *Grosseteste*, 112, incipit 'Omne quod est'. Ed. Baur, 126.

28 De yride   *Et perspectim . . . variationis*

   Sharpe, *Latin Writers*, 541. Thomson, *Grosseteste*, 105–106, incipit 'Et perspetiui'. Ed. Baur, 72.

29 Secundum opus ejusdem de libero arbitrio   *Quia circa . . . dicenda*

   Thomson 90–91. Recension I; ed. Baur, 150–241. This work appears with the following three works (30–32) in Oxford, Exeter College, MS 28; see D. A. Callus in *Studies in Medieval History presented to F. M. Powicke* (Oxford 1948), 180–208.

30 De scientia Dei   *Quaeritur . . . recte*

   Sharpe, *Latin Writers*, 542. Thomson, *Grosseteste*, 113 (nos. i and ii). *Questiones theologicae* I, ed. Callus, 194. See *29* above.

31 De misericordia et justitia Dei   *Consequitur . . . per Dei gratiam*

   Consequenter *Bale*

   Sharpe, *Latin Writers*, 542. Thomson, *Grosseteste*, 113 (no. iv). *Questiones theologicae* III (or perhaps II and III), ed. Callus, 199–204, 204–205. See *29* above.

32 De locali praesentia Dei   *Hic quaeritur . . . filius*

   Sharpe, *Latin Writers*, 542. Thomson, *Grosseteste*, 113 (no. v). *Questiones theologicae* IV, ed. Callus, 205. See *29* above.

33 Summam de articulis fidei et de omnibus quae pertinent ad officium sacerdotale   *Templum . . . a servitute*

> Sharpe, *Latin Writers*, 544. Thomson, *Grosseteste*, 138–40. *Templum Domini*, ed. J. W. Goering & F. A. C. Mantello, Toronto Medieval Latin Texts 14 (Toronto 1984) 29–68, explicit 'ab eius seruitute est esse in temperancia' etc. [**82** Bury = BL MS Royal 8 C. IV, fols. 2r–7v (Bury R. 42); BL MS Royal 8 B. IV, fol. 92r (Bury S. 184), explicit does not correspond (fol. 100r); BL MS Royal 12 F. xv, fol. 165r (Bury S. 55); and in the table of contents in Cambridge, Pembroke College, MS 101 (Bury S. 65), but now missing from that volume.]

34 Dicta quaedam   *Amor . . . et misericordiae*

> Sharpe, *Latin Writers*, 545. Thomson, *Grosseteste*, 214–32.

35 Item testamenta 12 patriarcharum de Graeco transtulit in Latinum quae per multa tempora incognita et abscondita fuerunt per invidiam Judeorum nec ad notitiam Jeronimi vel alterius interpretis pervenerunt. Manifeste enim in eis de Salvatore propheciae reperiuntur. Principium autem sic est: *Transcriptum . . . exi de terra*   74.168.164.154

> Sharpe, *Latin Writers*, 548. Thomson, *Grosseteste*, 42–4. *PG* 2. 1025; explicit 'exitus eorum ex terra Egiipti'.

36 Item summam de septem vitiis capitalibus, secundum quosdam   *Primo videndum . . . plangit*   82.1

> Primo videndum] Providendi *Add. 3470*; Primo videndum *Bale*

> Spurious. Sharpe, *Latin Writers*, 551. Thomson, *Grosseteste*, 268, incipit 'Primo uidendum'.

37 Item transtulit de Graeco in Latinum librum qui dicitur Suda, quem composuerunt viri sapientes, scilicet Eudemius Rhetor, Elladius qui fuit tempore Theodosii juvenis, Eugenius Frigius, Zosimus Gazeus, Caecilius Siculus, Longinus Casineus, Lupertus Beritius, Justinus, Julius Sophista, Pacatus, Pamphilius, Zophirion et Polion.

> *Mariale* fol. 141v. Sharpe, *Latin Writers*, 548. Thomson, *Grosseteste*, 63–4. This paragraph ('dicitur Suda — Polion') is the opening sentence of the text. [**82** Bury = BL MS Royal 8 B. IV, fol. 72r (Bury S. 184), an eight-leaf quire acquired for Bury by Kirkestede and bound with other things at Bury in his day. His note on fol. 80r refers to other copies (see p. lvii above), at King's Lynn and at the Oxford Greyfriars, not reported here.]

Robertus   *505. 38*

   38 Sermones   *Erunt signa . . . attemptatum*

   Sermones per adventum *Bale*   Erunt signa in sole et luna *Bale*

   Sharpe, *Latin Writers*, 544–5. Thomson, 160–182. The incipit is that of *serm.* 2, the explicit of *serm.* 14. While this does not correspond to any of the collections of sermons described by Thomson (see table 164–165), three are quite similar. *Serm.* 2 appears first only in BL MS Royal 7 D. xv (Revesby, s. xiii).

   39 De natura luminis et diafoni   *Considerandum . . .*

   Spurious; Thomson, *Grosseteste*, 256. Extract from Book II *lect.* 19 of Thomas Aquinas's treatise on Aristotle's *De anima*.

   40 Encheridion

   Spurious; Thomson, *Grosseteste*, 249–50. [**82** Bury = Cambridge, Pembroke College, MS 87, fol. 2r (Bury E.11).]

506 ROBERTUS MOLENDINENSIS vel MELUDINENSIS et episcopus Herefordensis floruit A. Ch. <*blank*> et scripsit

   Registrum 54, 'Opera Roberti', Higden, 1. 38 (work *16*).
   Kirkestede took the ambiguous *Registrum* entry to be the works of Robert of Melun, and he based his own list of sixteen titles almost entirely on the *Registrum* list—with its sequence rearranged to conform to biblical order, and with added information from manuscripts.
   Bale, *Index*, 369 (Robertus Crickladensis, works *1–4, 6–15*, not in sequence), 'ex utroque catalogo Anglorum', and 384 (Robertus Lorayn, works *13, 15–16*), 'ex Bostono Buriensis'.
   Sharpe, *Latin Writers*, 567.

   1 Super Genesin   46

   R54. 14 (whole entry).

   2 Super Exodum   160.108

   R54. 8 (whole entry).

   3 Super Leviticum   166.15.30

   R54. 2 (title; source of location numbers unknown).

   4 Super Numerum   160.46

   R54. 9 (whole entry save the suspect **46**).

Robertus Molendinensis 506. 13

5 De connubio Jacob   <u>126</u>.<u>114</u>.115.<u>120</u>

    120] 124 *R*

    R54. 3 (whole entry save the suspect **115**).

6 Super libros Regum   <u>57</u>

    R54. 12 (whole entry).

7 Super psalterium   <u>161</u>

    R54. 5 (whole entry).

8 Super 12 prophetas   <u>160</u>.<u>57</u>

    R54. 7 (whole entry).

9 Super Cantica   *Vox sponsi . . . cor[p]us debemus*   <u>124</u>.63

    corus *Add. 3470, queried by Tanner*

    R54. 11. Robertus de Tumbalena; Stegmüller *Bibl.* 7488. *PL* 150. 1361–70, completed *PL* 79. 492–548. **63** Crowland = B25. 3.

10 Super Mathaeum   <u>156</u>.<u>161</u>.<u>126</u>

    R54. 4 (whole entry).

11 Super epistolas Pauli   <u>63</u>

    R54. 13 (whole entry). **63** Crowland = B24. 65.

12 Super Apocalipsin lib. 1   166.163

    Revelatio quae Graeca dicitur Apocalips. *add. Add. 3470; according to Tanner this was added in a recent hand*

    R54. 1 (title; source of location numbers unknown).

13 De sacramentis Veteris et Novi Testamenti

    Same as *14* below.

Robertus Molendinensis   506. 14

14 Sententiarum lib. 2   *Quemadmodum . . . rubrica de inferno*   82

rubrica   *queried by Tanner*

R54. 6. Stegmüller *Sent.* 745. Ed. R. M. Martin in *Spicilegium sacrum Lovaniense* 21 (1947) and 25 (1952); explicit unidentified. Works *13* and *14* are the same. Kirkestede probably took the title of *13* above from the two-volume Bury manuscript (no longer extant) that Leland called, presumably on the basis of its rubric, 'Super Sententias sive de sacramentis veteris testamenti' (B16. 8); but Kirkestede gave *13* no incipit and explicit and no location number **82** for Bury. The title of *14* may have come from the *Registrum*, but it too may instead have come from the Bury manuscript; and here Kirkestede does supply incipit and explicit and the number **82**. In a surviving Bury manuscript that contains only three chapters of this *summa*, BL MS Royal 7 C. II, fol. 2r (Bury R. 40), Kirkestede's note on fol. 57v refers to the two-volume Bury copy: 'Deficiunt de ista summa partes siue libri tres de fine et XI partes siue libri de principio. Vide summam istam plenarie completam in armario claustri in duobus pulcris et magnis voluminibus'. Leland also emphasized that the volumes were handsome, 'duo pulcherrima . . . ac doctissima volumina'.

Primus liber istarum sententiarum continet partes 16 et capitula <blank> 2^{dus} liber non per partes dividitur sed tantum per capitula 201.

15 Item scripsit sermones quamplures

R54. 10 (whole entry).

16 Cronica Mariani splendide defloravit

Higden, 1. 38 (whole entry).

Super Ezechielem *entry inserted by Bale at a later time, Index, 369*

507 ROBERTUS PULLUS floruit circa A. Ch. <blank> et scripsit

Source unidentified.
Bale, *Index*, 386.
Sharpe, *Latin Writers*, 570–71.

1 Super psalmos

Doubtful; Sharpe, *Latin Writers*, 570. Stegmüller *Bibl.* 7747. Information concerning this work originates with the *Catalogus*.

2 Sententiarum lib.

The source for this entry was probably a manuscript. Sharpe, *Latin Writers*, 570; Stegmüller *Sent.* 748. *PL* 186. 639.

[p. 128]

508 RUFINUS monachus et presbyter Aquilinensis et interpres eloquentissimus floruit circa A. Ch. 350 et scripsit multa juxta Genadium et Vincentium in Speculo lib. 18 cap. 99

> Vincent XVIII 99 (works *1–4, 5–6*), Gennadius c. 17 (works *1–7*), *Liber florum* fol. 33v; *Registrum* 24 not used.

1 De simbolo lib. 1

> Whole entry from Vincent XVIII 99 and Gennadius 17.

2 Historiam ecclesiasticam Eusebii Caesariensis transtulit de Graeco in Latinum et addidit praedictae historiae lib. 2   *Successiones . . . meritorum*

> Vincent XVIII 99, Gennadius 17. *PL* 21. 467. [**82** Bury = B13. 239.]

3 Item transtulit libros Basilii, Gregorii Nazianzeni, Clementis, Euagrii, et Pamphilii martiris

> Whole entry from Vincent XVIII 99 and Gennadius 17.

4 Item maximam partem Bibliae de Graeco transtulit in Latinum.

Horum omnium quaecunque praemissis prologis a Latinis leguntur, a Rufino interpretata sunt; quae autem sine prologo, ab alio translatae sunt.

> Whole entry from Vincent XVIII 99 and Gennadius 17.

5 Item benedictionem Jacob super patriarchas 3^{ci}, id est historico, morali et mystico sensu disseruit, quae sic incipit:

> Whole entry from Vincent XVIII 99 and Gennadius 17.

6 Epistolas ad timorem Dei exor[ta]torias

> Whole entry from Vincent XVIII 99 and Gennadius 17.

7 Ad Probam virginem ep. 1

> Gennadius 17 (whole entry).

8 Ad Jeronimum apolegiae lib. 2   *Relegi . . . datam*

> *CPL* 197. *CCSL* 20. 37.

Rufinus *508. 9*

  9 Ad papam Anastasium apolegiam   *Audivi . . . livorem*

       CPL 198. *CCSL* 20. 25.

  10 Libros Pariarchon Origenis de Graeco transtulit in Latinum   *Scio quam . . .*

       CPG 1482. Ed. H. Crouzel & M. Simonetti, SChr 252 (incipit on p. 68) and 268 (1978–80). Same as Origines *404.26*.

  11 De angelis

       Liber florum fol. 33v (whole entry).

509 RAYMUNDUS Frater Praedicator et poenitentiarius papae floruit A. Ch. 1227 et scripsit

       Script. Ord. Praed. (whole entry), cf. Stams, 3.

  1 Summam juris quae suo nomine intitulatur

       [**82** Bury = BL MS Royal 6 B. x, fol. 93r (Bury A. 88), but not with this title which comes from *Script. Ord. Praed.*; excerpts are found in Cambridge, Pembroke College MS 87, fol. 1r (Bury E. 11).]

  2 Item quinque libros decretarium compilavit

510 ROBERTUS KYLWARDEBY natione Anglicus, Frater Praedicator, doctor theologiae et archiepiscopus Cant[uariensis] cardinalisque Portuensis floruit circa A. Ch. 1272 et scripsit

       Script. Ord. Praed. (whole entry save work *13*), cf. Stams, 6.
       Bale, *Index*, 383 (works *3, 4, 13* only).
       Sharpe, *Latin Writers*, 560–64.

  1 Super Porphirium commentarium

  2 Super libros Aristotelis commentarium

       In place of this title, Stams and Pign. list the seventeen commentaries on Aristotle.

  3 Super librum Divisionum Boetii

  4 Super librum Topicorum Boetii

5 Super Priscianum minorem expositionem

6 Super librum de natura relationis lib. 1

7 Sophistriam grammaticalem

8 Sophistriam logicalem

9 De ortu scientiarum lib. 1

10 De rebus praedicabilibus lib. l

11 De unitate formarum

12 Super libros sententiaru[m]

13 Tabulam super originalia Augustini, Ambrosii, Boetii, Ysidori et Anselmi
   Abymelech . . . zizania   168.1.2.119.8

>Sharpe, *Latin Writers*, 364. See esp. D. A. Callus in *Studia mediaevalia in honorem R J. Martin* (Bruges 1948), 243–70, and in *Dominican Studies* 2 (1949) 38–45. The location numbers, save **168** (Oxford Greyfriars, a sensible place for Kilwardby's *tabulae*), are all suspect, referring to libraries that Kirkestede did not know. [**82** Bury = Cambridge, Pembroke College, MS 39, fol. 1r (Bury T. 29); the 'explicit' is the last entry, fol. 77va.]

511 ROBERTUS Tracensis episcopus floruit circa A. Ch. <*blank*> et scripsit

>(Rupert von Deutz)
>Source unidentified.

1 De divinis officiis

>Same as Petrus Damianus *443.1*.

512 RICARDUS de Capwell Frater Praedicator floruit A. Ch. <*blank*> et scripsit

>(Richard Knapwell)
>*Script. Ord. Praed.* (whole entry), cf. Stams, 19.
>Bale, *Index*, 354.
>Sharpe, *Latin Writers*, 487.

1 Super libros sententiarum lecturam

Ricardus *512. 2*

2 Contra coruptores Thomae de Aquino

3 De unitate formarum

4 De immediata visione Dei

513 RICARDUS FICHACRE vel FISAKEL Frater Anglicus de ordine Praedicatorum floruit A. Ch. <blank> et scripsit

> *Script. Ord. Praed.*, supplemented by information from manuscripts (Stams, 97, has title *2* only).
> Bale, *Index*, 347.
> Sharpe, *Latin Writers*, 476–8.

1 Super psalterium

> Not known to survive; Sharpe, *Latin Writers*, 476. Stegmüller *Bibl.* 7267.

2 Super libros sententiarum *O altitudo . . .* 74.83.65

> O altitudo diviciarum sapientie *Bale*
>
> Sharpe, *Latin Writers*, 477. Stegmüller *Sent.* 718.

3 De poenitentia lib. 1 *Quia ut . . .* 74

> Not known to survive. Attributions of this work to Richard Fishacre stem from this entry in the *Catalogus*.

[p. 129]

514 ROBERTUS DE OXFORD Frater Praedicator floruit circa A. Ch. 1340 et scripsit

> Rubertus, natione Anglicus, de Erfort *Stams*
>
> *Script. Ord. Praed.* (whole entry), cf. Stams, 17.
> Bale, *Index*, 385.
> Sharpe, *Latin Writers*, 567–8, identifies this author with the Franciscan Robert of Orford (d. after 1293). Since the author in question here appears in a list of Dominican writers and was the author of polemics in defence of Aquinas, it is possible that there are still problems with this identification.

1 Contra dicta Henr[ici] de Gandavo, quibus impugnat S. Thomam de Aquino

2 Contra primum Egidii super libros sententiarum ubi impugnat S. Thomam de Aquino

515 ROBERTUS DE HOLCOTE Anglicus de ordine Praedicatorum et magister theologiae floruit A. Ch. *<blank>* et scripsit

> Same as Holcote 277.
> *Script. Ord. Praed.* (whole entry save for location numbers), cf. Pign. 114; this author (d. 1349) is not in Stams (datable before 1350). The two references to **65** Ramsey must represent Kirkestede's knowledge that these works were to be found there.
> Bale, *Index*, 381; Bale combines the two Holcote entries.
> Sharpe, *Latin Writers*, 553–8.

1 Lecturam et quaestiones super librum sententiarum

2 Sermones de tempore et sanctis per totum annum

3 Super Sapientiam lecturam nobilem et famosam   65

4 Super Ecclesiasticum lecturam aliam

5 Super evangelia Mathaei   65

516 ROBERTUS CURSON doctor theologiae et Sedis apostolicae legatus in Anglia floruit circa A. Ch. *<blank>* et scripsit

> Bale, *Index*, 370.
> Sharpe, *Latin Writers*, 534.

1 Summam theologiae   *Videndum* . . .

> Sharpe, *Latin Writers*, 534. Stegmüller *Sent.* 731.

2 De salvatione Origenis

> This work and its source are unidentified. Attributions of it to Robert Curson stem from this entry in the *Catalogus*.

517 RHODON genere Asianus a Tatiano Romae eruditus floruit circa A. Ch. *<blank>* et scripsit juxta Jeronimum temporibus Commodi et Severi

> Jerome c. 37 (whole entry).

1 Adversus Marcionem lib. 1

Rhodon   517. 2

2 Ad Castallionem lib. 1

3 In Exameron elegantes tractatus

4 Adversus Cathafrigas lib. 1

518 RETHICIUS Eduorum, id est Augustudunensis episcopus sub Constantino celeberrimae famae habitus est in Gallia, et scripsit secundum Jeronimum

> Jerome c. 82 (whole entry).

1 Super Cantica Canticorum commentarium

2 Adversus Novatianum grande volumen

519 ROBERTUS DE S. VICTORE floruit circa A. Ch. <*blank*> et scripsit juxta *Mariale*

> *Mariale* fol. 2r (whole entry).

520 <RIDEVALES>

> (John Ridewall)
> The author's name and the biographical note have been lost or were not written. The source for this entry was probably a manuscript which contained the works listed below. Bale copied this *Catalogus* entry in his notebook, along with information from five other sources, under the letter I for Ioannes; but Kirkestede's entry appears among the Rs in the *Catalogus*, suggesting that he knew this author simply as Ridevales (see *1* below) or something similar. (For a variety of forms in common use see Sharpe, *Latin Writers*, 901, *s.n.* Ridewall.) Bale, *Index*, 242.
> Sharpe, *Latin Writers*, 301–302.

1 Commentum Ridevales super Mithologias Fulgentii continens picturam poeticam virtutum et vitiorum sub ymaginibus deorum et dearum quos antiquitus coluit varia superstitio paganorum, et continet

> Sharpe, *Latin Writers*, 301–302.

2 Item super Augustinum de civitate Dei

> Sharpe, *Latin Writers*, 301.

> *Entry* Questiones ordinarias viii lib. 1   Primus articulus questionis qua querebatur . . .   *add. Bale*

521 REGIO abbas Prumiensis floruit <*blank*> et scripsit

> Prumiensis] Prinicensis *Add. 3470, queried by Tanner*

> (Regino of Prum)
> Diceto, 1. 23 (whole entry).

1 Cronica a nativitate Domini usque ad annum ejus 910

522 ROBERTUS abbas de Monte S. Michaelis in Normannia floruit <*blank*> et scripsit

> (Robert of Torigny)
> Diceto, 1. 23 (whole entry).
> Bale, *Index*, 384.
> Sharpe, *Latin Writers*, 574–5.

1 Cronicorum lib. 1

523 RICARDUS BARRE archidiaconus Luxoviensis floruit circa A. Ch. 1188 et scripsit

> Perhaps this entry was to have contained Richardus Barre, *Super Bibliam*, which appears in Lambeth Palace Library, MS 105, fol. 1r (Bury R. 36), with heading and classmark in Kirkestede's hand.

Memorandum quod D<ominu>s RICARDUS DE BURY quondam episcopus Dunelmensis edidit nuper tractatum quem intitulavit Philobiblon, id est amore librorum.

> See Ricardus de Bury 527.

> vide pag. seq. *post* id est amore librorum *add. Add. 3470; according to Tanner this was added in a recent hand*

524 ROBERTUS rex Franciae fecit sequentia<m> *Sancti Spiritus* et r<esponsoriu>m *O Juda et Jerusalem*, cum notis suis, et r<esponsoriu>m *Cornelius centurio* cum notis. Hic Robertus in ecclesiasticis cantibus non mediocriter eruditus in magnis sanctorum festis in aliquo regni sui monasterio cum monachis aut cantavit aut capam tenendo chorum rexit. Unde cum semel in festo S. Aniani Aurelianis dimisso exercitu suo circa quoddam castrum quod obsidebat, Agnus Dei capam gerens ter personaret, muri obsessi castri subito corruerunt.

> sequentia *Add. 3470, queried by Tanner*   responsorium] R^m *(twice) Add. 3470, both times queried by Tanner*   ter *Add. 3470, queried by Tanner*

> Part of this information has been supplied by Vincent XXV 107, the rest by an unidentified source.

Ricardus   *525.*

525 RICARDUS Radulfi archiepiscopus Armachanus Hiberniae floruit A. Ch. 1349 et scripsit

> (Richard Fitzralph)
> Ware extracts, fol. 132r.
> Sharpe, *Latin Writers*, 478–81.

1 De quaestionibus Armeniorum lib. 19   *Reverendis . . . amplissimam*   82

> *Summa de quaestionibus Armenorum*; Sharpe, *Latin Writers*, 481. Printed, Paris 1512. **82** Bury = Cambridge, Pembroke College, MS 5 (Bury A. 143), a late acquisition 'ex dono Johannis Gosford', but the gift dates from before Gosford became prior (1382).

p. 130]

526 RICARDUS prior Eliensis floruit circa A. Ch. <*blank*> et scripsit

> Bale, *Index*, 344.
> Sharpe, *Latin Writers*, 467–8.

1 Sermones   *Ascendet . . .*   Sermo ult.: *Praevaluit . . .*   169

> See Sharpe, *Latin Writers*, 467; unidentified. A longer incipit, 'Ascendet sicut virgultum coram', is offered by Bale's *Scriptores*, 269.

527 RICARDUS DE BURY episcopus Dunelm[ensis] floruit A. Ch. 1342 et scripsit

> Sharpe, *Latin Writers*, 462.

1 Librum qui dicitur Philobiblon, id est amor librorum

> Sharpe, *Latin Writers*, 462. Ed. E. C. Thomas & M. Maclagan (Oxford 1960). [**82** Bury = BL MS Royal 8 F. xiv, fol. 76r (Bury G. 15), procured for the abbey by Kirkestede.]

528 RICARDUS heremita de Ampole floruit circa A. Ch. <*blank*> et scripsit

> (Richard Rolle)
> This list is probably compiled from a manuscript or manuscripts of Richard Rolle's works at Bury.
> Bale, *Index*, 351.
> Sharpe, *Latin Writers*, 501–503.

Ricardus 528. 9

For lists of works see H. E. Allen, *The Writings Ascribed to Richard Rolle Hermit of Hampole* (New York, NY, 1927), esp. pp. 22–50 and consideration of the *Catalogus* list, 418–19; and N. Marzac, *Richard Rolle de Hampole (1300–1349)* (Paris 1968) 35–66.

1 Incendium amoris lib. 1   82

    Sharpe, *Latin Writers*, 502. Ed. M. Deanesly (Manchester 1915). See also *3* below.

2 Melos amoris lib. 1   82

    Sharpe, *Latin Writers*, 502. Ed. E. J. F. Arnould (Oxford 1957). Same as *11* below.

3 De amore divino   82

    In initio et fine bonorum operum   add. Bale; cf. Allen, *357*

    Probably *Contra amatores mundi* which is commonly known as *De amore dei* (Allen, 204–205); however, Bale cites the *Incendium amoris* (*1* above) by this title twice in the *Index* (pp. 348, 352).

4 De timore Domini et contemptu mundi   82

    Perhaps another variant of the title of *Contra amatores mundi*; see *3* above.

5 Vehiculum vitae sive xii capitula   82

    Probably the *Emendatio uitae*; cf. Allen, 230–45.

6 Super lectiones de officio mortuorum   82

    Commentary on Job; Allen, 130–44.

7 Super psalmum: Domine in virtute

8 Super psalterium duntaxat Latin[e] et Angl[ice]

    duntaxat   *queried by Tanner (probably* dupliciter)   Latine et Anglice] in Latin. et Angl.   *Add. 3470;* In psalterium Latine et Anglice   *Bale*

    See Allen, 165–92.

9 Super Lamentationes Jeremiae

    Jeremiae   *queried by Tanner*

    Sharpe, *Latin Writers*, 502. Stegmüller *Bibl.* 7310. Printed Cologne 1536.

Ricardus   528. 10

    10 Super 4^{tum} librum sententiarum, secundum quosdam

        Doubtful; the *Catalogus* is the only authority for attributing such a work to Rolle.

    11 De glorificatione sanctorum

        Same as *2* above; cf. E. J. F. Arnould, *The* Melos amoris *of Richard Rolle of Hampole* (Oxford 1957), xvi and 15 line 6.

529 SALUSTIUS floruit tempore Gaii Julii Caesaris et scripsit juxta Vincentium in Speculo lib. 7 cap. 32

    Vincent VII 32.

    1 In Catilinam Accilanario sive de bello Accilanarum lib. 1   *Omnes homines . . . agitabantur*

        Vincent VII 32. Ed. A. Kurfess (Leipzig 1957) 2–52. Works *1* and *2* customarily circulated together. [**82** Bury = Cambridge, Pembroke College, MS 114, fol. 1r (Bury S. 1), evidently misbound in part, explicit on a folio numbered 38 (after *De bello Jugurthino*); seen by Leland at Bury, B16, note between 15 and 16. The foliation of this manuscript is erratic.]

    2 De bello Jugurthino sive in Jugurtham lib. 1   *Falso . . . triumphavit*

        Vincent VII 32. Ed. Kurfess, 53–147. See *1* above. [**82** Bury = Cambridge, Pembroke College, MS 114, fol. 14r (*recte* fol. 15r) (Bury S. 1), end mutilated.]

    3 Invectivas contra Thitonem

        Vincent VII 32 (whole entry).

530 SALMANUS Massiliensis ecclesiae presbiter floruit tempore Genadii A. Ch. <*blank*> et scripsit juxta Genadium

    (Salvianus)
    Gennadius c. 68 (whole entry); Kirkestede added the interlinear note 'qui et Sidonius' to the text of Gennadius in Bodl. MS e Musaeo 31, p. 235 (Bury A. 31). See the discussion at Sidonius *544*.

    1 De bono virginitatis lib. 3

    2 Contra avaritiam lib. 4

    3 De peccati judicio lib. 5

4 In Exameron lib. 1

5 Super ultimam partem Ecclesiastici expositionem

6 Epistolarum lib. 1

7 Omeliarum super evangelia lib. 1

531 SEDULIUS poeta et presbiter Achaiae floruit A. Ch. 434 tempore Theodosii minoris et scripsit juxta Ysidorum libro De viris illustribus

> Isidore c. 7 (works *1–3*), *Decretum Gelasianum* IV 5 (work *3*).
> Ely extracts, fol. 149v.
> Bale, *Index*, 406.

1 De signis et virtutibus Veteris <Testamenti>   Prologus: *Domino meo* ...

> Isidore 7. *Epistola ad Macedonium*, dedication to *2* below. CPL 1448. CSEL 10. 1 (see *variae lectiones*).

2 <Dactylico> eroico metro lib. 1   *Pascales ... manipulos*   83.74.65

> Dactylico *lacking in Add. 3470, queried by Tanner*; Dactylico heroico metro *Isidore*

> Isidore 7. *Carmen Pascale* preface and Book I; CPL 1447. CSEL 10. 14–42.

Iste Sedulius primo fuit laicus saeculari sapientiae deditus et in Ytalia philosophiam didicit, postea vero in servicium Dei totum se transtulit et cum aliis metrorum generibus heroicum metrum docuit, et hunc librum inter alios libros suos in Achaia scripsit de Veteri et Novo Testamento, quem protitulavit Paschale carmen

> Isidore 7.

3 Item de gestis Christi sacramentis et miraculis lib. 4   *Expulerat ... volumina libros*   83.65.74

> Isidore 7. *Carmen Pascale* libri II–V. CSEL 10. 44–146.

Et vocantur isti libri in Decretis Gelasii papae Opus Paschale et alibi Carmen Paschale, prout in prologo libri

> *Decretum Gelasianum* IV 5 (line 251); the other source ('et alibi') was probably the *Mariale* fol. 28r.

Sedulius *531. 4*

    4 Item scripsit ad exitum ympnum continentem versus 110   *Cantemus Domino socii . . . gloria magna Patri*   78.74.83

        CPL 1449. Ed. G. Dreves, *AH* 50 (1907) 53–6.

p. 131]

    5 Item composuit ympnum *A solis ortus cardine*, et continet 7 versus incipientes per 7 primas literas alphabeti videlicet A. B. C. D. E. F. G. Item composuit ympnum *Hostis Herodes <impie>* etc., et continet 15 versus per reliquas literas alphabeti videlicet ab H usque etc. Vide apud 83, et vocantur isti ympni Carmen alphabeti

        impie *Bale, Ely extracts*

        Ed. Dreves, *AH* 50 (1907) 58–9.

532 SABBATIUS Galliae episcopus floruit A. Ch. <*blank*> et scripsit juxta Genadium

        Gennadius c. 25 (whole entry).

    1 De fide adversus Marcionem lib. 1

    2 De Christo et de Deitate adversus Eunomium lib. 1

533 SEVERIANUS Gavelensis episcopus floruit A. Ch. <*blank*> et scripsit juxta Genadium

        Gennadius c. 21 (whole entry).

    1 Super Epistolam ad Galathas lib. 1

    2 De baptismo et de epiphania lib. 1

    3 Omelias quamplures

534 SEVERUS Malactanae sedis antistes floruit A. Ch. <*blank*> et scripsit juxta Ysidorum

        Isidore c. 30 (whole entry).

    1 Adversus Vincentium episcopum haereticum

2 Librum de virginitate

3 Ad sororem suam qui dicitur Anulus

535 SEVERUS presbiter Aquitannicus cognomento Sulpitius floruit apud urbem Tholosam A. Ch. 398 et scripsit juxta Genadium

> Vincent XIX 8 (whole entry save the date), Gennadius c. 19 (whole entry save the date and work *2*).
> Ely extracts, fol. 149v.

1 Vitam S. Martini monachi et episcopi Turonensis

2 Ad Basulam socrum suam de transitu ejusdem

3 Collationem Postumiani et Galli se mediante et judice de conversatione monachorum orientalium et ipsius S. Martini habitam et in dialogi speciem duobus incisionibus comprehendit

4 De amore Dei et contemptu mundi ad sororem suam epistolas multas

5 Ad Paulinum episcopum ep. 2

6 Epistolas alias ad diversos

7 Cronicorum lib. 1

536 SEVERINUS episcopus

1 De innocentibus serm. 1

> The source for this work may have been a manuscript. A homily of Petrus Chrysologus (*hom.* 152), with this title and attributed to Severianus, is found in Manchester, John Rylands Library, MS 12, fol. 6r. See Schenkl 4817,2.

537 SERGIUS monachus floruit A. Ch. <*blank*> et scripsit juxta Vincentium lib. 24 cap. 51 et juxta cronicas

> Vincent XXIV 51.

Sergius   537. 1

1 Alchoran, scilicet librum Legis Machometi   *Domino suo . . . et liberet*

> The translation of Robert of Ketton; Sharpe, *Latin Writers*, 559–60. Printed, Basel 1543. [**82** Bury = Bodl. MS Selden supra 31, fol. 32r (Bury M. 10).]

Iste Sergius propter scelera sua multa, quae in monasterio perpetraverat, de ecclesia expulsus, iratus cogitans se vindicare ad partes ulteriores Arabiae accessit, et Machometum jam se prophetam dicentem et ydolatriam invenit, cui se conjungens

538 SEXTUS sub imperatore Severo floruit, anno scilicet Ch. <*blank*> et scripsit secundum Jeronimum De catholicis scriptoribus

> Jerome c. 50 (whole entry).

1 De resurrectione lib. 1

539 SERVUS DEI episcopus floruit circa A. Ch. <*blank*> et scripsit juxta Genadium

> Servus *queried by Tanner*
>
> Gennadius c. 88 (whole entry save the date).

l. De fide catholica lib. 1

540 SAMUEL Edissenae ecclesiae presbiter floruit circa A. Ch. 495 et scripsit juxta Genadium sermone Syro contra Nestorianos et Euticianos et Thimothianos libros plures. Item ad diversos alios haereticos.

> Gennadius c. 83 (whole entry save the date).

541 SIMPLICIANUS episcopus Mediolanensis multis epistolis ortatus est Augustinum Yponensem adhuc presbiterum agitare ingenium, et expositionibus Scripturarum vacare, ita ut jam novus quidam Ambrosius Origenis <*blank*> videretur, et multas ad ejus personam absolvit Scripturarum quaestiones. Est hujus epistola propositionum in qua interrogando quasi disciturus docet doctrinam. Haec Genadius.

> Gennadius c. 37 (whole entry). The blank corresponds to Greek in Gennadius.

542 SIRICIUS papa floruit Anno Ch. 389 et scripsit juxta Ysidorum libro De viris illustribus

> Isidore c. 3 (whole entry save the date).

Seneca   543. 4

1 Opusculum decretale

2 Contra Jovinianum et Ausentium lib. 1

p. 132]

543 SENECA patruus Lucani poetae floruit A. Ch. 58° tempore Neronis et scripsit multa juxta Jeronimum et alios

> *Registrum* 83 , Vincent IX 102 (references are followed by numbers in brackets [1, 2, etc.] that indicate the sequence of titles in the chapter), *Manipulus florum* XIX, Jerome c. 12.
> The sequence of works *1–13* is governed by Vincent of Beauvais, frequently combined with incipits and explicits from the *Manipulus florum* and with location numbers from the *Registrum*, and probably supplemented from Bury manuscripts. Among the titles that represent Bury manuscripts are the rare Tragedies (*11* below).

1 De morte Claudii imperatoris qui dicitur Ludus Senecae lib. 1   *Quid actum . . .*

> Vincent IX 102[1], *MF* XIX 7 (incipit; title varies). [**82** Bury = perhaps the problematic catalogue entry B13. 116b, 'plures libri Senece'.]

2 De beneficiis lib. 7   *Inter multos . . . et dare*   163.49.82.43.42.15

> 49] 94 *R*   15] 105 *R*

> R83. 1 (title, location numbers), Vincent IX 102[2], *MF* XIX 3 (title, incipit, explicit 'dare et perdere'). **82** Bury = perhaps the problematic catalogue entry B13. 116b, 'plures libri Senece'.

3 De clementia ad Neronem lib. 2   *Scribere . . . flectantur*   163.94.82.114.105.1

> R83. 5 (location numbers), Vincent IX 102[3], *MF* XIX 4 (title, incipit, explicit). **82** Bury = perhaps the problematic catalogue entry B13. 116b, 'plures libri Senece'.

4 De 4ʳ virtutibus ad Paulum lib. 1   *Credo tibi . . . properantem*   126

> Whole entry from R83. 6 (part of title, location number), Vincent IX 102[4], *MF* XIX 1 (rest of the title, incipit, explicit). The title *De quattuor uirtutibus*, from Vincent and *Registrum*, presumably referred to Martin of Braga's work of this name, CPL 1080 (*18* below). It is not apparent why Kirkestede confused or conflated this with the entry in the *Manipulus florum* for the letters to Paul (*12* below), for which (as for work *4*) Kirkestede's report seems to be completely second-hand.

453

Seneca   *543. 5*

5   De moribus lib. 1   *Omne peccatum . . . licuit*   153.82.105.163.15

> R83. 4 (title, location numbers), Vincent IX 102[5], *MF* XIX 14 (title, incipit, explicit). **82** Bury = perhaps the problematic catalogue entry B13. 116b, 'plures libri Senece'.

6   De remediis fortuitorum bonorum   *Licet cunctorum . . . felicitas*   163.82. 105.43

> 43] 46 *R*

> R83. 2 (title, location numbers), Vincent IX 102[6], *MF* XIX 15 (title, incipit, explicit). **82** Bury = perhaps the problematic catalogue entry B13. 116b, 'plures libri Senece'.

7   De immatura morte

> Vincent IX 102[7] (whole entry).

8   De naturalibus quaestionibus lib. 10   *Grandinem . . . dulcior*   161.94.92. 105.9.20

> Whole entry from R83. 8 (title, location numbers), Vincent IX 102[8], and *MF* XIX 20 (title, incipit, explicit 'dulcior gustus').

9   Declamationum vel causarum lib. 10   *Exigitis . . . inventus*   94.82.9

> R83. 15 (title, location numbers), Vincent IX 102[9], *MF* XIX 6 (incipit, explicit). **82** Bury = perhaps the problematic catalogue entry B13. 116b, 'plures libri Senece'.

10   De sententiis diversorum oratorum   *Deliberat . . . nolite a me*

> Whole entry from Vincent IX 102[10] and *MF* XIX 8 (explicit 'nolite a me omnia exigere que scio').

11   Tragediarum lib. 9   *Soror . . . fulmina montes*   166.82

> montes *queried by Tanner*

> R83. 10, Vincent IX 102[11]. Ed. O. Zwierlein (Oxford 1986). **82** Bury = extracts from the Tragedies survive in Cambridge, Gonville and Caius College, MS 225/240 (Bury V. 12), pp. 1–8.

12   Epistolas ad Paulum apostolum et e contra 14   *Credo . . . ad Deum istinc*   94.95.153.8.9.43.1

> istinc *queried by Tanner*

Seneca 543. 20

Whole entry from R83. 9, Vincent IX 102[13], Jerome 12, and *MF* XIX 1 (title, incipit, explicit 'ad Deum istinc properantem'). See *4* above

13 Epistolarum moralium ad Lucillium lib. 22   *Ita fac . . . felices*   124.43.82. 1.15.166

  R83. 11, Vincent IX 102[12], *MF* XIX 2. Ed. L. D. Reynolds (Oxford 1965); explicit is the end of Book XX. **82** Bury = B13. 27, 'Epistole Senece'; BL MS Royal 8 C. IV, fol. 24r (Bury R. 42), beginning and end imperfect.

14 Ad Lucillium quare mala bonis viris accidunt

  MF XIX 17 (whole entry). Same as *30* below.

15 Proverbiorum lib. 1   *Alienum . . . vitiosum est*   153.135.1.108

  R83. 12. *Ps.* Seneca. Any of several collections of sentences in alphabetical order that circulated under the title *Prouerbia Senecae* in the Middle Ages. [**82** Bury = perhaps the problematic catalogue entry B13. 116b, 'plures libri Senece'.]

16 De paupertate lib.   *Honesta . . . insolentiam*   163.94.92.46

  R83. 3 (title, location numbers), *MF* XIX 16 (title, incipit, explicit). [**82** Bury = Cambridge, Gonville and Caius College, MS 225/240, p. 232 (Bury V. 12), explicit does not correspond; BL MS Royal 11 B. III, fol. 337r (Bury V. 18).]

17 De copia verborum ad Paulum lib. 1

  MF XIX 5 (probably whole entry; *MF* title does not include the words 'ad Paulum').

18 De quatuor virtutibus lib. 1   *Quatuor . . . obtemperare*   126

  R83. 6, *MF* XIX 5. Martin of Braga, *Formula honestae uitae. CPL* 1080. Explicit unidentified. Same as Augustinus *1.488*, and Martinus *364.1*, and see *4* above.

19 Rethoricam

  MF XIX 6 (whole entry).

20 Apotheosin   105

  R83. 14 (whole entry).

Seneca   *543. 21*

21 De vita beata ad Gallionem   *Vivere . . . navigatorem*

    MF XIX 10 (whole entry, title '. . . ad Gallicionem').

22 De ira ad Novatum lib. 3

    MF XIX 19 (whole entry).

23 De tranquillitate animi ad Serenum lib.   *Inquirent . . . labentem*

    MF XIX 11 (whole entry, incipit 'Inquirenti').

24 De brevitate vitae ad Paulinum   *Major . . . circumsonant*

    MF XIX 12 (whole entry, explicit 'circumsonat').

25 Ad Martiam de consolatione filii sui   *Nisi de . . . non novit*

    MF XIX 9 (whole entry, incipit 'Nisi te').

26 Ad Helbiam de consolatione filii sui   *Cum . . . insurgat*

    MF XIX 13 (title; incipit and explicit do not correspond). *Dial.* 12. *Dialogi*, ed. L. D. Reynolds (Oxford 1977) 291 line 3–316 line 29. [**82** Bury = perhaps the problematic catalogue entry B13. 116b, 'plures libri Senece'.]

27 Item ad Martiam   *Fiduciam . . . lucet*

    Dial. 6; ed. Reynolds, 129 line 7–166 line 7. [**82** Bury = perhaps the problematic catalogue entry B13. 116b, 'plures libri Senece'.]

28 Ad Serenum quomodo in sapientem non cadit injuria   *Tantum inter . . . generis haec*

    MF XIX. 18 (whole entry, explicit 'generis humani est').

29 De 7 artibus liberalibus lib. 1   *De liberalibus . . . nihil scire*

    Ad Lucilium (*ep.* 88); ed. L. D. Reynolds (Oxford 1965) 312–23.

30 De providentia ad Lucillium lib. 1

    MF XIX 17 (whole entry). Same as *14* above.

Sidonius 544. 9

544 SIDONIUS qui et SALMANUS juxta Vincentium in Speculo, Gayus Sollius Apollinaris episcopus Arvernensis floruit tempore Perpetui episcopi Turonensis circa A. Ch. 456 juxta Genadium et Vincentium lib. 22° cap. 46 et scripsit

> See also Salmanus *530*.
> Vincent XXII 46, Gennadius c. 68. Works 1–8 are taken in this order from Vincent and Gennadius
> Vincent is responsible for the identification of Sidonius with Salvianus. Under Sidonius's name Vincent lists the works of Salvianus which, through Vincent's source Helinandus, ultimately come from Gennadius. Although there is a separate entry above in the *Catalogus* for Salvianus (*530*; see further there), the conflation is reproduced here from Vincent and two authentic works of Sidonius are added, *9–10* below.

1 De praesenti judicio lib. 5

2 De virginitate ad Marcellum lib. 3

3 Adversus avaritiam lib. 4

4 Super <extremam> partem <Ecclesiastici> lib. 1

> Super ... partem ...   *Add. 3470, queried by Tanner*
>
> Same as *6* below.

5 De principio Geneseωs quasi Exameron lib. 1

6 Ad Claudium episcopum Menevensem epistolarum lib. 1

> Menevensem] Viennensem *Vincent, Gennadius*

7 Ad Salomium episcopum lib. 1

8 Omelias plures

9 Item 150 epistolas ad diversos lib. 9   *Dum percipis ... videatur*

> Apollinaris Sidonius. *CPL* 987. Ed. A. Loyen, Collection Budé, 2–3 (Paris 1970). [**82** Bury = B13. 27b.]

Seneca *544. 10*

10 Panegirica, id est laudes metrice lib. 1   *Cum juvenem . . .*

Apollinaris Sidonius. *CPL* 986. Ed. A. Loyen, Collection Budé, 1 (Paris 1960) 2.

11 Sacramentorum lib. 1

Gennadius 68 (whole entry).

545 SIAGRIUS floruit circa A. Ch. <blank> et scripsit juxta Genadium

Gennadius c. 66 (whole entry).

1 De fide lib. 1

2 Item de regulis fidei lib. 7

p. 133]

546 SIMACHUS Patricius floruit circa A. Ch. 493 et scripsit

Vincent XXI 14 (whole entry).

1 Epistolarum lib. 1

Hic autem fere omnes artes liberales de Graeco transtulit in Latinum

547 SERAPION Tmieus episcopus cognomento Scolasticus et carus Antonii monachi floruit A. Ch. <blank> et scripsit secundum Jeronimum

Tmieus] tymeus *text of Jerome in Bodl. MS e Musaeo 31 p. 210*

Jerome c. 99 (whole entry).
Speculum coenobitarum 7.

1 Adversus Manicheos lib. 1

2 De psalmorum titulis lib. 1

3 Epistolas utiles ad diversos

548 SERAPION alius Antiochiae episcopus floruit tempore Commodi A. Ch. <blank> et scripsit juxta Jeronimum

Jerome c. 41 (whole entry).

1 De haeresibus Montani lib. 1

2 Epistolarum lib. 1

3 De evangelio S. Petri ad Rofensem Ceciliae ecclesiam lib. 1

549 SOCRATES philosophus Ethicae inventor fuisse dicitur, qui de ea 24 libros secundum positivam justitiam conscripsit

> Vincent IV 56 (whole entry).

550 SIBILLA floruit anno a creatione mundi <*blank*> et scripsit

1 Prophetias de Christo et aliis lib. 1   *Novem . . . cum illo*   83.82.74.63.43.44

> *PL* 90. 1181, among the works of Bede. This series of location numbers is the longest in the *Catalogus* referring entirely to libraries that Kirkestede knew, or probably knew, first-hand. **82** Bury = Cambridge, Corpus Christi College, MS 404, fol. 1v–3v (Bury P. 163), copied by Kirkestede.

551 SOFRONIUS vir apprime eruditus floruit A. Ch. <*blank*> et scripsit juxta Jeronimum libro De viris illustribus

> Jerome c. 134 (whole entry).
> *Speculum coenobitarum* 32.

1 De laude Betleem librum insigne

2 De subversione Sirapis lib. 1

3 De virginitate ad Eustochium lib. 1

4 Vitam S. Hilarionis monachi

5 Quaedam opuscula Jeronomi in Graecum sermonem transtulit

6 Psalterium et prophetas transtulit de Hebraeo in Graecum

552 STRABUS discipulus Rabani floruit A. Ch. 813, qui dictante Rabano plurima excepit et scripsit

> Source unidentified.

Strabus   *552. 1*

1 Item super quosdam libros Pentateuci commenta edidit

> Presumably Walafrid Strabo's *Abbreuiatio Rabani Mauri in Pentatheucum*; cf. Stegmüller *Bibl.* 8316, 8318–21. See Rabanus *492.3*.

553 SMARAGDUS abbas floruit A. Ch. <blank> et scripsit

> (*Registrum* 81 not used.)
> *Speculum coenobitarum* 58.

1 Diadema monachorum   *Hoc est remedium . . . mereamur*   83.82.63.61.65

> *PL* 102. 593. **82** Bury = B13. 255a. / **61** Peterborough = BP2. 38 , BP21. 330d.

2 Super regulam S. Benedicti cum concordantia aliarum regularum sanctorum patrum praedecessorem S. Benedicti expos. 1 *Obsculta . . . felix qui etc.*   82.65

> Ed. A. Spannagel and P. Engelbert, *Corpus consuetudinum monasticarum* 8 (1974) 7–337 (cf. lines 9, 10, and 12).

3 Super quaedam evangelia expos.

> Source unidentified. Cf. Stegmüller *Bibl.* 7695.

554 STEPHANUS DE LANGETON archiepiscopus Cantuariae floruit A. Ch. 1225 et scripsit

> *Registrum* 57, Higden, 8. 204.
> Kirkestede's borrowings from the *Registrum* were supplemented by information from manuscripts, at Bury and at other houses whose books he knew. The titles' sequence is sometimes governed by the sequence of the books of the bible and sometimes by the sequence of the *Registrum*, before any semblance of method disappears at the end.
> Bale, *Index*, 416–17.
> Sharpe, *Latin Writers*, 624–32.
> See esp. G. Lacombe and B. Smalley, 'Studies on the Commentaries of Cardinal Stephen Langton', *Archives d'histoire doctrinale et littéraire du Moyen-Age* 5 (1930) 5–220; and R. Quinto, *Doctor Nominatissimus: Stefano Langton (†1228) e la tradizione delle sue opere*, BGPTM, new ser. 39 (1994).

1 Super Genesin   *Tabernaculum . . . coelestem*   106.<u>160</u>.<u>43</u>.<u>115</u>.<u>49</u>.65

> R57. 7. Sharpe, *Latin Writers*, 625. [**82** Bury = Cambridge, Pembroke College, MS 101, fol. 86r (Bury S. 65).]

Stephanus de Langeton   554. 10

2 Super Exodum   *In ingressu . . . fragile est*   106.160.43.115.49.65

    R57. 8. Sharpe, *Latin Writers*, 625. Incipit is that of the prologue; explicit unidentified. Location numbers are repeated from *1* above.

3 Super Numerum   106.43.115.49.65

    106] 160 *R*

    R57. 9 (whole entry); location numbers are repeated from *1* above.

4 Super Deuteronomium   106.43.115.49.65

    106] 160 *R*

    R57. 11 (whole entry); location numbers are repeated from *1* above.

5 Super Leviticum   99

    99] 49 *R*

    R57. 18 (whole entry).

6 Super Josue   *Ego visiones . . . et modicum*   65

    Sharpe, *Latin Writers*, 625. Explicit unidentified.

7 Super libros Regum expos.   *Rectoribus . . . novissimo*   163.49.122.42.12

    49] 94 *R*   42.12] 43.xii *R*

    R57. 3. Sharpe, *Latin Writers*, 626.

8 Super Paralipomenon   43

    R57. 13 (whole entry).

9 Super libros Machabeorum   160.43

    R57. 10 (whole entry).

10 Super Ysaiam   *Audite . . . quo novi*   127.94.92.12.20.10

    quo novi] quomodo *Add. 3470; Tanner, uncertain of this reading, has added* quo novi *as a variant*   12] xii *R*   10] x *R*

Stephanus de Langeton   554. 10

> R57. 4. *Isaias moralisatus*; Stegmüller *Bibl.* 7818. Cf. Sharpe, *Latin Writers*, 628.

p. 134]

11 Super xii prophetas   *Ossa 12 . . . secura*   <u>163</u>.<u>160</u>.<u>114</u>.<u>122</u>.<u>127</u>

> R57. 2. Sharpe, *Latin Writers*, 627. Explicit unidentified.

12 Super Thobiam   49.<u>43</u>

> R57. 14 (whole entry save the suspect **49**).

13 Super Judith   <u>43</u>

> R57. 15 (whole entry).

14 Super Hester   <u>43</u>

> R57. 16 (whole entry).

15 Super Esdram   <u>43</u>

> R57. 17 (whole entry).

16 Super Ecclesiasticum   <u>94</u>.<u>92</u>.<u>127</u>

> Hoc nomen ecclesiastes interpretatur *add. Bale as the incipit; Registrum, Kirkestede's source, has no incipit*
>
> R57. 5 (whole entry).

17 Super Cantica   <u>92</u>.166.163

> R57. 6 (whole entry, save the two suspect location numbers).

18 De Magdalena et poenitentia tract.1   *Miserator . . . de nomine*   <u>8</u>

> R57. 12. Sharpe, *Latin Writers*, 630. The explicit may be that of the first sentence of the second tract, as it appears in Oxford, Balliol College, MS 152, fol. 25r (St Osyth, s. xiii).

19 De similitudinibus lib. 1   *Nec miles* . . .

> Sharpe, *Latin Writers*, 631, considers that Bale's record, drawn from Kirkestede, of a *De similitudinibus* with the incipit 'Nec miles' remains untraced. Sharpe also reports a text with the title *Similitudinarium* (inc. 'Infernus. Ita sunt anime') ascribed to Langton in Lincoln, Lincolnshire Records Office, MS Ancaster 16/1, fols. 76r–92r (not seen by us).

20 Summam quae vocatur Adam ubi es, de vitiis et virtutibus   *Adam ubi* . . .   **163**.61

> R57. 1. Sharpe, *Latin Writers*, 631. **61** Peterborough = BP21. 83e, in the same codex with *23* below, and perhaps BP21. 228c.

21 Vitam Ricardi regis Anglorum

> Higden, 8. 204 (whole entry).

22 Super librum Judicum   *Restituam* . . . *de oculo tuo*

> Sharpe, *Latin Writers*, 625.

23 Sermones lx   *Filia* . . . *studeamus*   61.86

> Sharpe, *Latin Writers*, 631. Concerning the incipit see P. B. Roberts, *Studies in the Sermons of Stephen Langton* (Toronto 1968), 35; explicit unidentified. **61** Peterborough = BP21. 83d, in the same codex with *20* above, and cf. BP21. 92d.

24 Super Job   65

> lib. xxxiiii Licet cum malis valde laudabile . . . *add.* Bale

> The source of this entry was presumably the Ramsey manuscript. Spurious; see Sharpe, *Latin Writers*, 626. An abbreviation of Gregory the Great's *Moralia on Job*. **65** Ramsey = BL MS Royal 8 F. x, fol. 116r, attributed to Langton.

25 Super Ecclesiasten   *Hoc nomen* . . .   11

> The incipit is that of the commentary on Ecclesiasticus, *16* above; Sharpe, *Latin Writers*, 626.

26 De vera poenitentia tract. 1

> Source unidentified. This is perhaps a variant title for *18* above.

Stephanus Burgundus 555.

555 STEPHANUS Burgundus et Frater Praedicator floruit A. Ch. <*blank*> et scripsit

> Script. Ord. Praed. (whole entry), cf. Stams, 21.

1 Postilla super Ecclesiasten

2 Super Apocalipsin

3 De auctoritatibus sanctorum et philosophorum lib. 1

556 STEPHANUS Gallicus et Frater Praedicator floruit A. Ch. <*blank*> et scripsit

> Script. Ord. Praed. (whole entry), cf. Stams, 39.

1 Librum de oculo

557 SYMON de Borastona Anglicus et Provincialis Fratrum Praedicatorum floruit A. Ch. <*blank*> et scripsit

> Script. Ord. Praed. (this author is omitted by Stams and Pign.), supplemented by manuscripts.
> Bale, *Index*, 409–410.
> Sharpe, *Latin Writers*, 609–610.

1 Distinctiones, quae suo nomine appellantur   *Abjicere 2^{dum} autorem* . . .

> Sharpe, *Latin Writers*, 609. [**82** Bury = Bodl. MS Bodley 216 (Bury B. 46), probably too late in date to have served for this entry, but the majority of its folios were written at Bury by the monk William Barrow (sacrist 1407–1426), presumably copied from an earlier Bury manuscript (cf. fol. 1r top).]

2 Sermones bonos et subtiles

3 De ordine judiciario

4 Contra crimina corrigenda   *Corripiet . . . compilantis*

> *De ordine iudiciario circa crimina corrigenda*; Sharpe, *Latin Writers*, 609. See *3* above.

558 SOLINUS FLACCUS GAIUS JULIUS grammaticus floruit <*blank*> et scripsit

Probably the whole entry is from Higden, 1. 22, but Bury possessed a manuscript of Solinus [**82** Bury = B13. 49].

1 De mirabilibus mundi

559 SERVIUS grammaticus floruit circa annum <*blank*> et scripsit commenta

This entry comes from a manuscript or manuscripts at Bury.

1 Super Virgilii Bucolicorum lib. 9   *Bucolica . . . bucolicis*

Ed. G. Thilo & H. Hagen, *Servii Grammatici qui feruntur in Vergilii carmina commentarii*, Teubner (1881–1902) 3/1. 1–127. [**82** Bury = B13. 74, 'Seruius super Virgilium'.]

2 Georgicorum lib. 2   *Virgilius . . . titulum*

Ed. Thilo & Hagen, 3/1. 128–360. [**82** Bury = B13. 74, 'Seruius super Virgilium'.]

3 Super libros ejusdem Eneydos lib. 12   *In exponendo . . .*

Ed. Thilo & Hagen, vols. 1–2. [**82** Bury = B13. 74, 'Seruius super Virgilium'.]

4 De metris elementis et sillabis   *Igitur primas . . . longa sunt*

sunt] fiunt *Add. 3470, queried by Tanner*

Ed. H. Keil, *Probi Donati Servii qui feruntur De arte grammatica libri*, GL 4 (1864) 449.

5 Tractatus qui dicitur Centimetrum   *Licet audacter . . . exsolvat*

Ed. Keil, 456.

560 STATIUS Tholosensis poeta floruit A. Ch. 75 tempore Vespasiani et scripsit

Vincent VI 61.

1 Thebaidos lib. 12   *Fraterna . . . honores*

Statius   *560. 1*

> Vincent VI 61. Ed. H. W. Garrod (Oxford 1906), incipit 'Fraternas'. [**82** Bury = B13. 108, 'Statius', probably a manuscript that contained both works *1* and *2*.]

2 Achilleydos lib.   *Magnanimum* . . .

> Vincent VI 61. Ed. O. A. W. Dilke (Cambridge 1954) 31. [**82** Bury = B13. 108, 'Statius', probably a manuscript that contained both works *1* and *2*.]

561 SECUNDUS philosophus floruit tempore <*blank*> et scripsit

> Higden, 5. 16, 18.

562 SERLO

> (Serlo of Wilton)
> Bale, *Index*, 407.
> Twysden, *Scriptores*, xxvii.
> Sharpe, *Latin Writers*, 605–606.

1 De oratione Dominica   *Protector noster* . . .

> Sharpe, *Latin Writers*, 605. Ed. L. C. Braceland, *Serlo of Savigny and Serlo of Wilton: Seven Unpublished Works* (Kalamazoo 1988) 76.

2 De dictionibus dissilabis lib. 1   *Dactile* . . .

> Sharpe, *Latin Writers*, 605. Ed. J. Öberg, *Serlon de Wilton* (Stockholm 1965) 79.

p. 135]

563 SUETONIUS GAIUS TRANQUILLUS floruit <*blank*> et scripsit

> See also Erodotus *182*.

1 De vita Caesarum xii, scilicet a Julio usque ad Domitianum lib. 1   *Annum agens . . . insequentium*

> Ed. M. Ihm, Teubner (1908). [**82** Bury = San Marino, Huntington Library, MS HM 45717 (Bury S. 18), explicit (fol. 117v) 'insequentium principum'.]

564 SCIPIO

The source for this unfinished entry was probably Vincent VI 47, 48, 57.

565 SIGEBERTUS floruit <blank> et scripsit

Diceto, 1. 21 (whole entry).

1 Cronographiam

566 SYMPHOSIUS poeta floruit circa A.D. <blank> et scripsit

1 Enigmata in quibus continentur versus obscurissimi   *Haec quoque . . . ad auras*

  CPL 1518. CCSL 133A. 621.

567 THOMAS DE AQUINO natione Siculus, Albus monachus et postea Frater Praedicator floruit A. Ch. 1264 et scripsit multa

et scripsit multa excellencia   *Ely extracts fol. 119v; no works are listed there*

All ninety-two titles were taken from *Script. Ord. Praed.*, complemented by information from manuscripts from Bury and neighbouring libraries, especially **170** Thetford and **65** Ramsey. Stams, 8, contains all the ninety-two titles listed below (with eight exceptions: *16–17, 48–49, 69, 85–86, 92*), but in the following order: *1–3, 18–38, 43–46, 78–81, 42, 47, 82–84, 87–90, 4–15, 91, 51–53, 55, 39, 56, 41, 40, 54, 76–77, 57–68, 70–75, 50*.
Ely extracts, fol. 119v.
See M. Grabmann, *Die Werke des Hl. Thomas von Aquin*, BGPTM, new ser. 22 (1949).
S. Thomae Aquinatis opera omnia jussu impensaque Leonis XIII P.M. edita, 1– (1882–), cited here as *STO*; *Doctoris angelici divi Thomae Aquinatis . . . opera omnia*, ed. S. E. Frette, P. Maré & others, 34 vols. (L. Vives: Paris, 1871–80), cited here as Vives.

1 Scripsit autem fallacias minores

2 Super Periarmenias   *Dilecto sibi . . .*

  STO 1/1. 3.

3 Super librum posteriorum

4 Super libros physicorum   *Quum quid . . .*

  STO 2. 3, incipit 'Quoniam quidem'.

Thomas de Aquino *567. 5*

5 Super libros de coelo et mundo *Sicut philosophus . . . Opinamur . . .*

    STO 3. 1, incipit 'Sicut philosophus dicit in I Physicorum, Tunc opinamur . . .'.

6 Super libros metheororum

7 De generatione et corruptione *De generatione . . .*

    STO 3. 261.

8 Super librum de anima *Bonorum . . .*

    STO 45/1. 3.

9 Super librum de somno et vigilia

10 Super librum de memoria et reminiscentia lib. 1 *Sicut dicit philosophus . . . quam causam*

    STO 45/2. 103–133.

11 Super librum de sensu et sensato lib. 1 *Sicut dicit . . . futurorum*

    STO 45/2. 3–101.

12 Super methafisicam

13 Super libros ethicorum lib. 10 *Sicut dicit . . . ethicorum*

    STO 47. 3–607.

14 Super librum de morte et vita

15 Super librum de causis *Sicut dicit . . . praemissa est*

    Ed. H. D. Saffrey, *Textus philosophici Friburgenses* 4–5 (Fribourg 1954). Same as Proculus *486.2*.

16 Super poleticam

17 Super yconomicam

18 De ente et essentia *Quia primis . . . sufficiant* 170

    STO 43. 369, incipit 'Quia paruus'. Explicit unidentified.

19 De elementis in mixto *Dubium* . . .

    STO 43. 155.

20 De materia prima

21 De dimensionibus interminatis

    divisionibus *Stams*

22 De principio individuationis *Quum duae* . . . 170

    Vives 27. 465, incipit 'Quoniam . . .'.

23 De principiis naturae *Quoddam* . . . 170

    STO 43. 39, incipit 'Nota quod quoddam'.

24 De operibus occultis naturae *Quum mihi* . . . 170

    STO 43. 183, incipit 'Quoniam in'.

25 De eo quod est et quo est

26 De motu progressivo animalis

27 De motu cordis *Quum omne* . . . 170

    STO 43. 127, incipit 'Quia omne'.

28 De aeternitate mundi *Supposito* . . . 170

    STO 43. 85.

29 De sortibus *Postulavit* . . . 170

    sortibus *queried by Tanner*

    STO 43. 229.

30 De judiciis astrorum

31 Contra unitatem intellectus

Thomas de Aquino   567. 32

32 De unitate formae   *Quaeritur autem* . . .   170

  Vives 28. 50. Spurious; see Grabmann, 236.

33 De genere   *Quum omnis* . . .   170

  Vives 28. 5.

34 De accidente   *Quum omnis cognitio* . . .   170

  Vives 28. 1.

35 De instantibus   *Quum omnem* . . .   170

  Vives 27. 512.

p. 136]

36 De relatione lib. 1   *Quae de natura* . . .

  Spurious; see Grabmann, 230, 237.

37 De fato   170

38 Super Boetium de Ebdomadibus   *Praecurrere* . . .

  Vives 28. 467.

39 Super Boetium de Trinitate quaestiones

40 Super Dionisium de Coelesti jerarchia

41 Super Dionisium de Divinis nominibus

42 De duabus naturis in una essentia

43 De fide, spe et caritate ad Urbanum papam

44 De virtutibus

45 De decem praeceptis tract. 1   *Tria sunt . . . mandata*   10.61

  Vives 27. 144. **61** Peterborough = BP21. 176g, in the same codex with *47, 49, 86,* and *87* below.

Thomas de Aquino 567. 57

46 De verbo   *Quum circa* . . .   170

>   Vives 27. 268.

47 De articulis fidei tract. 1   *Postulat . . . nativitatem*   10.61

>   *STO* 42. 245–52. **61** Peterborough = BP21. 176h, in the same codex with *45* above, and *49*, *86*, and *87* below.

48 De quatuor oppositis   *Quoniam 4ʳ* . . .   170

>   Vives 27. 520.

49 De 7 sacramentis tract. 1   *Nunc restat . . . offensam*   61

>   *STO* 42. 252; explicit unidentified. **61** Peterborough = BP21. 176i, in the same codex with *45* and *47* above, and *86* and *87* below.

50 Super primum nocturnum psalterii, 2^{dum} et 3^{ium} 158

>   Location number **158** should probably read **15**.

51 Super Job   15

52 Super Ysaiam   65

53 Super Jeremiam   15

54 Super Cantica Canticorum

55 Super 4^r evangelia dupliciter per modum postillae et glosae

>   dupliciter] duntaxat *Add. 3470, queried by Tanner*

56 Super 15 capitula Mathei per se

57 Super 1um librum sententiarum scripturam 1   *Ego sapientia . . . initiavit*   65

>   *57–60* Vives vols. 7–11.
>
>   [**82** Bury = Cambridge, Pembroke College, MS 33, fol. 1r (Bury T. 1).]

Thomas de Aquino 567. 58

58 Super 2^{dum} sententiarum script. 1   *Species ejus . . . corumpetur*   65

> *58–60*: The medieval library catalogue from **65** Ramsey abbey, lists a set comprising the last three of the four books of Thomas on the Sentences, but no four-volume set and no copy of volume 1 (*57* above); B68. 552–4 (and see also odd volumes, B68. 65, 121, 487). [**82** Bury = Cambridge, Pembroke College, MS 33, fol. 136r (Bury T. 1).]

59 Super 3^{ium} sententiarum script. 1   *Ad locum . . . vincibile*   65

> Explicit unidentified. See *58* above.

60 Super 4^{tum} sententiarum script. 1   *Misit . . . ordinantur*   65

> See *58* above. [**82** Bury = Cambridge, Pembroke College, MS 34 (Bury T. 7).]

61 Summam theologiae 4^r volumina continentem, videlicet:
Primam partem in primo volumine, *Quia catholice . . . decebat*   65
Primam partem 2^{dae} partis in 2do volumine, *Quia sicut . . . mali*   65
Secundam partem 2^{dae} partis in 3^{io} volumine, *Post communem . . . animarum*   65
Tertiam et ultimam partem in 4to volumine   65

> *STO* vols. 4–12, presumably; the last explicit quoted ('. . . animarum') appears at *STO* 10. 553, the end of the *secunda secundae* as the entry says, but Kirkestede evidently did not see the fourth volume. Sets of the multi-volume *Summa theologica* from **65** Ramsey are recorded (B68. 118–20a and B68. 547–9) but none seems to fit the four-volume presentation described here. / [**82** Bury = Cambridge, Pembroke College, MS 35 (Bury (T. 9)), vol. 1; Cambridge, Pembroke College, MS 36 (Bury T. 10), vol. 2, with Kirkestede's title on fol. 1r.]

62 Summam contra gentiles de fide catholica quae continet libr. 4   *Veritatem . . . in sempiternum*

> *STO* vols. 13–15, explicit 15. 299. [**82** Bury = Cambridge, Pembroke College, MS 37, fol. 1r (Bury T. 12).]

63 Quaestiones: De veritate 27   *Quaestio est de veritate . . . sufficienter*   65

> Quaestiones *written once at the left, with bracket connecting it to works 63–70 in Add. 3470*

> *STO* 22. 3. **65** Ramsey = B68. 567. / [**82** Bury = Cambridge, Pembroke College, MS 37, fol. 113r (Bury T. 12).]

64 <Quaestiones> de potentia Dei 10   *Qu<aestio> est de potentia . . . peccatum*   65

 Vives 13. 1. **65** Ramsey = B68. 120b and 556a.

65 <Quaestiones> de spiritualibus creaturis 11   *Qu<aestio> est de spiritualibus . . . potentiae*

 Vives 14. 1.

66 <Quaestiones> de anima 21   *Qu<aestio> est de anima . . . corporaliter*

 STO 24/1. [**82** Bury = Cambridge, Pembroke College, MS 37, fol. 267r (Bury T. 12).]

67 <Quaestiones> de virtutibus 6   *Qu<aestio> est de virtutibus . . . actiones*

 STO 41A. 51. [**82** Bury = Cambridge, Pembroke College, MS 37, fol. 278v (Bury T. 12).]

68 <Quaestiones> de malo 16   *Qu<aestio> est de malo . . . in arepticiis*

 STO 23. 3–334. [**82** Bury = Cambridge, Pembroke College, MS 37, fol. 237v (Bury T. 12).]

69 <Quaestiones> de simplicitate divinae essentiae 12   *Qu<aestio> est de simplicitate . . . Damasceni*

 Vives 13. 214. *De potentia Dei quaes. VII–X.*

70 <Quaestiones> item xi quodlibet   *Quaesitum est de Deo . . . sequentem*

 Vives 15. 583. *Questiones quodlibetales.*

71 Determinationes 52 quaestionum

72 Determinationes 36 quaestionum

73 Determinationes 6 quaestionum

74 Declarationes quarundam quaestionum ad Ducissam Brabantiae

75 Contra errores Graecorum

76 Sermones de angelis

Thomas de Aquino 567. 77

77 Sermones de quadragesima

78 Contra impugnantes religionem   67

79 De correctione fraterna

80 De forma absolutionis

81 De perfectione vitae spiritualis

82 De sacramentis et de missa lib. 1

83 De angelis

84 Super orationem Dominicam expositionem

85 Super Mathaeum expositionem   *Qui fecit . . . petimus*   10.61

> Vives 19. 226.

86 De salutatione angelica expositionem   *In salutatione . . . benedictus*   10.61

> Vives 27. 199. **61** Peterborough = BP21. 176f, in the same codex with *45*, *47*, and *49* above, and *87* below.

87 Super simbolum expositionem   *Primum . . . imprimatur*   10.61

> Vives 27. 203. **61** Peterborough = BP21. 176e, in the same codex with *45*, *47*, *49*, and *86* above.

88 Super Magnificat   10

89 De genealogia B. Mariae

90 Super primum decretalium

91 De regno et regi Cipri

92 Coruptorium contra opera S. Thomae et primo contra primam partem Summae suae   *Quaestione 12 . . . articulo*

> The *Correctorium fratris Thomae* of William de Mara; Sharpe, *Latin Writers*, 787. Ed. P. Glorieux, *Les premières polémiques thomistes* (Le Saulchoir 1927), 1. 1–208; the unremarkable explicit does not correspond.

p. 137]

568 TATIANUS floruit circa A. Ch. <*blank*> et scripsit juxta Jeronimum infinita volumina in quibus extat unus contra gentiles liber florentissimus

> Whole entry from Jerome c. 29 and Zacharias (*PL* 186. 37).

1 Item unum ex quatuor compaginavit evangelium juxta Zachariam

569 THOMAS subdiaconus Sarisberiensis floruit A. Ch. <*blank*> et scripsit

> (Thomas of Chobham)
> Bale, *Index*, 434.
> Sharpe, *Latin Writers*, 649–50.

1 Librum poenitentialem   *Cum miserationes . . . sufficiant*

> Cum miserationes] domini   *add. Bale in a different ink*

> Sharpe, *Latin Writers*, 649. Ed. F. Broomfield, *Analecta medievalia Namurcensia* 25 (1968).

570 THOMAS archiepiscopus Cantuariae et martir floruit A. Ch. <*blank*> et scripsit

> (Thomas Becket)
> Source unidentified. The source may have been a manuscript of the letters.
> James extracts, p. 198.
> Sharpe, *Latin Writers*, 641.

1 Epistolarum lib. 1

> lib. 1] lib. 2 *James extracts*

> Sharpe, *Latin Writers*, 641. Ed. A. Duggan, 2 vols. (Oxford 2000).

571 THEODORUS Siriae provinciae Ciprae civitatis episcopus floruit A. Ch. 450 et scripsit juxta Genadium

> Theodoretus *Gennadius edition;* Theodorus *Bodl. MS e Mus. 31*

> Gennadius c. 90 (whole entry).

Theodorus   571. 1

1 De incarnatione Domini contra Euticen lib.

2 Libros ecclesiasticae historiae imitatus Eusebium Caesar[iensem] conscripsit, a fine scilicet Eusebii usque ad imperium Leonis, sub quo et mortuus est

572 THEODORUS Heracliae et Trachiarum episcopus floruit tempore Constantini, anno scilicet Christi <blank> et scripsit juxta Jeronimum commentarios

> Jerome c. 90 (whole entry).

1 Super Mathaeum

2 Super Johannem

3 Super apostolum

4 Super psalterium

573 THEODORUS monachus et successor abbatis Pachomii floruit A. Ch. <blank> et scripsit juxta Genadium

> Gennadius c. 8 (whole entry).
> *Speculum coenobitarum* 9.

1 Plures epistolas ad monasteria Sanctarum Scripturarum sermone digestas

2 Exortationum ep. 3

574 THEOPHILUS episcopus Antiochenae ecclesiae sextus floruit A. Ch. 158 et scripsit secundum Jeronimum

> Whole entry from Jerome c. 25 and, for work 6, Zacharias (*PL* 186. 39).

1 Contra Marcionem lib. 1

2 Ad Antholicum vol. 3

3 Contra haeresim Hermogenis lib. 1

4 Super Proverbia Salomonis commentarium

5 Super evangelia commentarium

6 Item 4ʳ evangelia in unum opus compinxit juxta Zachariam

7 Alios autem breves et quamplures tractatus ad aedificationem ecclesiae conscripsit

575 THIMOTHEUS episcopus floruit circa A. Ch. <*blank*> et scripsit juxta Genadium

> Gennadius c. 59 (whole entry).

1 De nativitate Domini 2ᵈᵘᵐ carnem

576 THEOPHILUS Alexandriae episcopus floruit A. Ch. 387 et scripsit juxta Genadium

> Gennadius c. 34 (whole entry save the date).

1 Contra Originem lib. 1

2 Contra Antropoformitas haereticos lib. 1

3 De fide catholica lib. 3

4 De ratione Paschali lib. 1

5 Compotum cursus 100 annorum

577 TERENTIUS comoediarum scriptor floruit tempore Octoviniani anno 41° A. Ch. 1 et scripsit

> Vincent VI 73 (works *1–6*).
> [**82** Bury = B13. 94b 'Plautus et Terentius'; see Plautus *485*.]

1 In Andria   *Vos istaec . . . finito*

> Vincent VI 73. Ed. R. Kauer & W. M. Lindsay (Oxford *c.* 1936), unpaginated. Incipit of act 1; explicit unidentified. [**82** Bury = Cambridge, Gonville and Caius College, MS 225/240 (Bury V. 12), which formerly contained excerpts from works *1*, *2* and *6*, according to Kirkestede's table of contents (p. 3).]

Terentius 577. 2

2 In Eunucho *Quid faciam . . . ite haec*

> Vincent VI 73. Kauer & Lindsay, incipit of act 1. [**82** Bury = Cambridge, Gonville and Caius College, MS 225/240 (Bury V. 12), which formerly contained excerpts from works *1*, *2* and *6*, according to Kirkestede's table of contents (p. 3).]

3 In Eautontimorumenos *In militiam . . . fiat*

> Vincent VI 73. Kauer & Lindsay, incipit is that of C. Sulpici Apollinaris Periocha.

4 In Adelphios *Storax . . . recte*

> Vincent VI 73. Kauer & Lindsay, incipit is that of act 1.

5 In Echira *Orator . . . diem nunquam*

> Vincent VI 73. Kauer & Lindsay, incipit is that of the second prologue.

6 In Phormio *Amicus . . . aderit*

> Vincent VI 73. Kauer & Lindsay, incipit is that of act 1. [**82** Bury = Cambridge, Gonville and Caius College, MS 225/240 (Bury V. 12), which formerly contained excerpts from works *1*, *2* and *6*, according to Kirkestede's table of contents (p. 3).]

578 TERTULLIANUS presbiter Affricanus floruit circa A. Ch. 212 et scripsit juxta Jeronimum

> Jerome cc. 18, 53 (whole entry save work *8*).

1 De spe fidelitatis lib. 1

> Jerome 18 (whole entry).

2 De pudicitia lib. 1

> Jerome 53 (whole entry).

3 De persecutione lib. 1

> Jerome 53 (whole entry).

4 De jejuniis lib. 1

> Jerome 53 (whole entry).

5 De monogamia lib. 1

    Jerome 53 (whole entry).

p. 138]

6 De extasi lib. 1

    Jerome 53 (whole entry).

7 Adversus Appollonium lib. 1

    Jerome 53 (whole entry).

8 Apolegiticum lib. 1

    CPL 3. *CCSL* 1. 77. The source for this entry was probably a manuscript; this is one of the few works of Tertullian that circulated during the Middle Ages.

9 Item post lapsum suum scripsit adversus ecclesiam libros plures secundum Jeronimum

    Jerome 53 (whole entry).

579 THOLOMAEUS Philadelphius rex Aegipti floruit A.M. <*blank*> et scripsit juxta Cassiodorum libro De institutione divinarum literarum <1.> librum in quo sic omnia loca evidenter expressit, ut eum cunctarum regionum pene incolam fuisse credatur, eoque fiat ut monachi in uno loco positi sicut decet animo percurrant in legendo, quod aliorum peregrinatio plurimo labore collegit

    cunctarum] [ ]tarum *Add. 3470, queried by Tanner*

    Cassiodorus I. 25. 2, Vincent VI 15, Higden, 5. 26 and 4. 36.
    Ely extracts, fol. 149v.
    James extracts, p. 198.

    <1> Cassiodorus I. 25. 2 (whole entry).

2 Bibliotecam per LXX interpretes transferri fecit

    Vincent VI 15 (whole entry).

Tholomaeus 579. 3

3 Centilogium   *Non obliviscaris* . . .

> Higden, 5. 26. The title refers to *ps.* Ptolemy, *Liber fructus*, but the incipit does not correspond. Perhaps what Kirkestede saw instead was John Ashendon, *De significatione conjunctionis Saturni et Martis in Cancro* . . . (ed. K. V. Snedegar, *John Ashendon and the Scientia astrorum Mertonensis*, DPhil. diss. (Oxford 1988)), which begins 'Sicut dicit Ptolemeus in centilogio proposicio 50ª, Non obliuiscaris . . .'. For manuscripts of Ashendon's work, composed before 1357, see Sharpe, *Latin Writers*, 205. [**82** Bury = 'Centilogium Tholomei cum commento' in Kirkestede's contents note in Cambridge, Pembroke College, MS 46, flyleaf (Bury A. 222), but the work is no longer there.]

4 Almagistum

> Higden, 4. 36 (whole entry).

5 Quadrupertitum

> Higden, 4. 36 (whole entry).

6 De 100 verbis id est centilogium

> Iste Tholomaeus 70 milia librorum in sua bibliotheca fertur habuisse, secundum Ysid[orum libro] Eth[imologiarum] 6.
>
> Higden, 4. 36 (whole entry). Isidore is cited through Higden.

580 TRIPHON Origenis auditor floruit A. Ch. <*blank*> et scripsit secundum Jeronimum

> Jerome c. 57 (whole entry).

1 De vacca rufa in Deuteronomio lib. 1

2 De dichomatibus quae cum columba et turture ab Abraham ponuntur in Genesi

581 TRIPHILIUS Cipri episcopus floruit A. Ch. <*blank*> tempore Constantii et scripsit secundum Jeronimum

> Jerome c. 92 (whole entry).

1 Super Cantica Canticorum commentarium

582 TULLIUS MARCUS qui et CITHERO dicitur floruit tempore Gaii Julii Caesaris primi imperatoris et scripsit

(Cicero)
Vincent VII 6, *Manipulus florum* XVII. *Registrum* 84 was probably not used (but see work *29*).

1 De officiis lib. 3   *Quamquam . . . praeceptis*   83

Vincent VII 6, *MF* XVII 5 (incipit, explicit 'preceptisque letabere'). Ed. C. Atzert (Leipzig 1963), explicit 'Praeceptisque laetabere'.

2 De amicitia lib. 1   *Quintus . . . praestabilius esse*   83

Vincent VII 6, *MF* XVII 4 (incipit, explicit 'prestabilius esse putetis'). Ed. J. G. F. Powell (Warminster 1990) 28–72, explicit 'Praestabilius putetis'.

3 De senectute lib. 1   *Scire si . . . possitis*   83

Vincent VII 6, *MF* XVII 6 (incipit 'O Tite si'). Ed. P. Wuilleumier (Paris 1981) 82–135, incipit 'O Tite si'.

4 Philippicarum lib. 2   *Quousque . . . possit*

Whole entry from Vincent VII 6 (title), with the incipit and explicit by mistake from *MF* XVII 12, the *Catilinarians* (*5* below). See also *19* below.

5 Cautelinarium, quod dicitur Philosophia ejusdem

MF XVII 12 (whole entry); see also *4* above.

6 Rethoricorum lib. 2   *Saepe et . . . restat*

Vincent VII 6, *MF* XVII 1 (explicit does not correspond). *De inuentione.* Ed. E. Stroebel, Teubner (1915); explicit (p. 156) 'restant in reliquis dicemus'. [**82** Bury = B13. 160, 260.]

7 Tusculanorum lib. 5   *Malum . . .*

Vincent VII 6. Ed. M. Pohlenz (Leipzig 1918), incipit at the beginning of I 5 (p. 221).

8 Orationum lib. 12

Vincent VII 6 (whole entry).

Tullius Marcus *582. 9*

9 Invectivarum lib. 6

    Vincent VII 6 (whole entry).

10 De legibus lib. 3

    Vincent VII 6 (whole entry).

11 De divinatione lib. 2   *Vetus . . . naturaliter*

    Whole entry from Vincent VII 6 and *MF* XVII 11.

12 De fine boni et mali lib. 5

    Vincent VII 6 (whole entry).

13 Rethoricam novam quae continet lib. 6   *Et si in . . . exercitationis*

    MF XVII 2 (whole entry, incipit 'Etsi negociis').

14 Epistolarum lib. 7   *Oticio salutem . . .*

    MF XVII 13 (whole entry, incipit 'M. Cicero salutem').

15 De paradoxis lib. 7   *Animadverti . . . existimandi sunt*   83.82

    Vincent VII 6, *MF* XVII 10 (incipit 'Animaduerte', explicit 'estimandi sunt'). Ed. R. Nickel (Munich 1994) 200–244.

16 De republica et de sompno Scipionis lib. 6

    Source unidentified. *Macrobius de sompnio Sipionis* (*Manipulus florum* XVI 5) immediately precedes the list of Cicero's works in the *Manipulus florum*, which may have contributed to the confusion here.

17 De universitate   *Multa . . .*

    universitate *Add. 3470, queried by Tanner*

    MF XVII 9 (whole entry, title *De universalitate*).

18 Dispositionum lib. 7   *Non eram . . .*

    MF XVII 7 (whole entry).

19 De actione   *Antequam* . . .

   MF XVII 3 (whole entry, title *De accusatione*). The Philippics; see *4* above.

20 De deo Socratis vel de natura deorum lib. 3   *Quam multae . . . propensior*   61

   Vincent VII 6, MF XVII 8 (incipit as here 'Quam multe', explicit). Ed. W. Ax (Stuttgart 1961), incipit 'Cum multae'. **61** Peterborough = BP21. 130, note.

21 De fato lib. 1   *Inter* . . .   61

   Vincent VII 6. Ed. R. Giomini, Teubner (1975) 149; incipit unidentified. **61** Peterborough = BP21. 130c.

22 De creatione mundi lib. 1

   Vincent VII 6 (whole entry).

23 Dialogorum ad Ortensium lib. 1

   Vincent VII 6 (whole entry).

24 Topicorum lib.   *Omnis ratio* . . .

   Ed. K. Bayer (Munich 1993) 8, incipit 'Cum omnis ratio'.

25 De partitione orationis lib. 1

   partitione] perditione *Add. 3410, queried by Tanner*

   Vincent VII 6 (whole entry).

26 De academiis lib. 1

   Vincent VII 6 (whole entry).

27 De oratore lib. 1

   Vincent VII 6 (whole entry).

28 De adornatione verborum   *Omne genus . . . ab auditore*   83

   Unidentified.

Tullius Marcus *582. 29*

  29 Contra Salustium

    Cf. R84. 1.

p. 139]

583 TYCONIUS Affer et Donatista in divinis literis eruditus floruit A. Ch. 398 et scripsit secundum Genadium et Augustinum lib. 3^{io} De doctrina Christiana

    Gennadius c. 18 (works *1–3, 5*), Augustinus, *De doctrina Christiana*, III 30 (works *4, 6*); *Registrum* 80 not used.

1 De intestino bello lib. 4

    Gennadius 18 (whole entry).

2 Expositiones diversarum causarum

    Gennadius 18 (whole entry).

3 Expositionem super Apocalipsin

    Gennadius 18 (whole entry).

4 Contra Donatistas, secundum Augustinum libros plures

    Augustine III 30 (whole entry).

5 Regulas ad investigandum et inveniendam intelligentiam Scripturarum quae continent libros 8

    Gennadius 18 (whole entry).

6 Item librum quem Regularem vocavit, quia in eo 7 regulas executus est, quarum primam ponit de Domino et ejus corpore, 2^{dam} de Domini corpore bipertito, 3^{iam} de promissis et lege, 4^{tam} de specie et genere, 5^{tam} de temporibus, 6^{tam} de recapitulatione, 7^{mam} de diabolo et ejus corpore

    Augustine III 30 (whole entry).

584 THOMAS DE SUTTON Anglicus et Frater Praedicator floruit A. Ch. <*blank*> et scripsit

> *Script. Ord. Praed.* (whole entry), cf. Stams, 16.
> Bale, *Index*, 455–6.
> Sharpe, *Latin Writers*, 682–4.

1 Super praedicamenta

2 Super 6 principia

3 Super libros priorum et posteriorum

> et posteriorum *om. Stams*

4 Item complevit scripturam Thomae de Aquino super Periarmenias

5 De unitate formarum

6 Duo quodlibet

7 De relatione

8 Summam theologiae

9 Super psalterium

10 De concordia librorum theologiae

> *om. Stams*

585 THOMAS DE LINDUNO Frater Praedicator et patriarcha floruit A. Ch. <*blank*> et scripsit

> *Script. Ord. Praed.* (whole entry), cf. Stams, 79.

1 Postillas super epistolas Pauli

> *Stams and Pign. 82 list the individual Pauline epistles.*

586 THOMAS WALEYS Anglicus Frater Praedicator floruit A. Ch. <blank> et scripsit

> Script. Ord. Praed. This author is omitted by Stams; Pign. 110 gives a version different from the Catalogus.
> Bale, Index, 457.
> Sharpe, Latin Writers, 685–7.

1 Lecturam super psalterium

> Sharpe, Latin Writers, 686. [**82** Bury = B16. 10.]

2 De visione faciali contra papam Johannem 22   Mementote . . .   170

> Sharpe, Latin Writers, 686, De uisione beatifica.

3 De temporibus et instantibus quae Pater posuit in sua potestate   Non est vestrum . . . approbatur   170

> vestrum] nosse tempora vel modus add. Bale

> Sharpe, Latin Writers, 686. Ed. T. Kaeppeli, Le procès contre Thomas Waleys, O.P., étude et documents (Rome 1936) 157.

4 Sermones multos

> Sharpe, Latin Writers, 687 notes spurious sermons.

5 Super omnem Methaium comment. 1 continens lib. 15   A veritate . . . tota die

> In Methamorfosin Bale

> Pierre Bersuire; Sharpe, Latin Writers, 687. Printed, Paris 1509.

587 THEODORICUS THEUTONICUS Frater Praedicator floruit A. Ch. <blank> et scripsit

> Script. Ord. Praed. (whole entry), cf. Stams, 28.

1 De tempore

2 De yride

3 De mensuris rerum

4 De origine rerum praedicabilium

5 De corpore Christi in sacramento

6 De corpore Christi mortuo

7 De habitibus

8 De entium universitate

9 De tribus difficilibus

10 De quiditatibus entium

11 De generatione lucis

12 De coloribus

13 De majus et minus

14 De ente et essentia

15 De elementis in mixto

> *This is two works in Stams,* De miscibilibus in mixto, De elementis in quantum sunt partes mundi

16 De efficacia Dei

17 De intelligentiis

18 De cognitione entium separatorum

19 De substantia orbis

20 De substantiis spiritualibus

21 De dotibus corporum gloriosorum

22 De theologia et ejus subjecto

23 De intellectu et intelligibili

Theodoricus Theutonicus   *587. 24*

24   De immaterialitate angelorum

25   De cirurgia lib. 4   Isti libri intitulantur Filia principis

   om. Stams

26   De defensione privilegiorum Ordinis Praedicatorum lib. 1

   Stams adds six other titles: De natura contrariorum, de causis, de voluntate, de viribus inferioribus intellectu in angelis scilicet de animatione coeli, de visione beatifica et de accidentibus.

p. 140]

588   TROGUS POMPEYUS floruit tempore Nini regis Assiriorum et scripsit

   (Justin Martyr)
   Same as Justinus *297.*
   Vincent XI 94.

1   Chronicorum lib. 1

   Source unidentified. Same as *2* below.

2   Item composuit historiam totius pene orbis continentem libros 44 quam abbreviavit discipulus suus Justinus

   Vincent XI 94 (whole entry).

589   TULLIANUS presbiter Cartaginensis floruit <*blank*> et scripsit

   Source unidentified; the author appears in Cassiodorus II. 3. 13, but it is questionable whether Kirkestede used Book II. For other possible uses of this source see Censorinus *137* and Victorinus *620.4.* (Book II of the Institutes does not appear in the Bury bibliographic codex, Bodl. MS e Musaeo 31.)

590   THEODORUS papa et sanctus floruit A. Ch. 643 et scripsit juxta Radulphum Nigrum in libro De moralibus super Regum et juxta Cronica Martini

   Radulphus Niger (Lincoln Cathedral, MS 25, fols. 5r–88r), Martinus Polonus (MGH *Scriptores* 22. 423). The author and work are the same as Theodorus *591* below; the duplication was Kirkestede's (aided by Ralph Niger and the *Decretum*), not Martinus's.

488

1 Librum poenitentialem

591 THEODORUS archiepiscopus Cantuariae monachus et natione Graecus floruit A. Ch. 659 et scripsit juxta cronica Martini Librum poenitentialem cauta et mirabili discretione distinguens modum singularum culparum, de quo libro in jure canonico frequenter fit mentio et specialiter 36 q. 6 c. ultimo.

> Martinus Polonus (MGH *Scriptores* 22. 423), *Decretum* (ed. Friedberg, *Corpus iuris canonici* 1 (1879)) c. 32 q. 1 c. 6; same as Theodorus *590* above.
> James extracts, pp. 198–199.

592 TREMEGISTUS vel TRISMEGISTUS qui et MERCURIUS vel HERMES floruit A.M. tempore <*blank*> et scripsit juxta Vincentium in Speculo historiali lib. 5to

> See also Apuleius *47* and Hermes *259*.
> Vincent V 10 (works *1–3*).

1 Ad Asclepium lib. 1   *Asclepius iste . . . coenam*   83

> Vincent V 10. Ed. A. D. Nock, *Corpus Hermeticum* 2 *Asclepius* (Paris 1973) 296.

2 De verbo perfecto lib. 1

> Vincent V 10 (whole entry).

3 De mathesi et constellatione lib. 2

In hiis duobus libris de mathesi fatalem constellationem conatur asserere, ipsamque negantibus et improbantibus respondere.

> Vincent V 10 (whole entry).

4 De Hellera, id est de Deo deorum lib. 1

> Hellera *queried by Tanner*

> This work and its source are unidentified.

5 Logoscolios magnum librum

> The *Logos teleios*; Kirkestede may have seen this work mentioned by Robert Holcot in his Commentary on Wisdom (printed as *M. Roberti Hokoth in librum Sapientiae regis Salomonis praelectiones 213* [Basel 1586] 540 lecture 164). Same as *1* and *2* above.

Theodorus   593.

593 THEODORUS qui postea Gregorius appellatus est Gneocesareae episcopus floruit circa A. Ch. 223 et scripsit juxta Jeronimum

> Jerome c. 65 (whole entry save the date).

1 Panegiricum, id est gratiarum lib. 1 ad Originem

2 Super Ecclesiasten interpretationem valde utilem

3 Epistolas plures ad diversos

594 THEOPHILUS Palestinae Cesareae episcopus sub Severo principe floruit, anno scilicet Ch. <blank> et scripsit juxta Jeronimum adversus eos qui xiv^a luna cum Judeis Pascha faciebant sinodicam et utilem epistolam

> Jerome c. 43 (whole entry).

595 TITUS BOSTRENUS episcopus floruit circa A. Ch. 363 et scripsit juxta Jeronimum

> Jerome c. 102 (whole entry save the date).

1 Adversus Manichaeos libros plures

2 Item scripsit alia volumina

596 THEOTIMUS Scythiae Thomorum episcopus floruit circa A. Ch. 390 et scripsit in morem dialogorum et veteris eloquentiae breves commaticosque tractatus.

> commaticosque *queried by Tanner*
>
> Jerome c. 131 (whole entry save the date).

597 TITUS Livius scriptor historicus floruit tempore Julii Caesaris et scripsit

> Vincent VI 58 (whole entry).

598 THEODORUS alius Antiochenae ecclesiae presbyter floruit circa A. Ch. <blank> et scripsit juxta Genadium

> Gennadius c. 12 (whole entry).

1 Contra Apolinaristas et Anomeos de incarnatione Domini lib. xv

599 THEODORUS Anchiranus Galatiae episcopus floruit circa A. Ch. <blank> et scripsit juxta Genadium

> Gennadius c. 56 (whole entry).

1 Contra Nestorem lib. 1

600 THEODORUS presbyter in Coeleusiria floruit circa A. Ch. 476 et scripsit juxta Genadium

> Theodolus *Gennadius edition*; Theodorus *text of Gennadius in Bodl. MS e Musaeo 31 p. 240*

> Gennadius c. 92 (whole entry save the date).

1 De consonantia Veteris et Novi Testamenti contra haereticos lib. 1

601 THEOCTISCUS floruit circa annum <blank> et scripsit juxta Cassiodorum

> Cassiodorus I. 30. 2 (whole entry).

1 De ortographia lib. 3

602 THEOFRASTUS philosophus et discipulus Aristotelis floruit A.M. <blank> et scripsit juxta Vincentium lib. 6

> Whole entry from Vincent VI 2 and John of Salisbury, *Policraticus*, Book VIII = ed. C. C. J. Webb (Oxford 1909), 2. 296, 234.

1 De amicitia lib. 1

> Vincent VI 2 (whole entry).

2 De nuptiis aureolum librum

> John of Salisbury VIII 11 (ed. Webb, 2. 296) (whole entry).

3 De divitiis, secundum J<ohannem> Sarisburiensem in Polycratico lib. 8vo, lib. 1

> John of Salisbury VIII 2 (ed. Webb, 2. 234) (whole entry).

Thinredus   *603.*

p. 141]

603 THINREDUS monachus Doveriae floruit circa A. Ch. <*blank*> et scripsit

> (Theinred of Dover)
> Bale, *Index*, 429.
> Sharpe, *Latin Writers*, 636.

1   De musica et de legitimis ordinibus pentacordorum et tetracordorum lib. 3   *Quoniam musicorum* . . .

> *Divided into two titles,* De legitimis ordinibus musice *and* Pentacordorum et tetracordorum libri *by Bale, wrongly it seems*
>
> Sharpe, *Latin Writers*, 636.

604 TROTA et TROTULA filia ejus floruerunt anno <*blank*> et scripsit Trotula

1   De passionibus mulierum lib. 1   *Cum auctor . . . aqua tepida*

> The incipit and explicit indicate that the manuscript recorded here contained both the *Trotula maior* and the *Trotula minor.* Two versions of this text are printed, Strasbourg 1544 and Basel 1556. The explicit is that of the *Trotula minor* c. 61 (pr. Basel, p. 304). [**82** Bury = a codex that contains this text, belonging to Mr P. L. Robinson, London (Bury M. 36).]

605 TURPINUS Remensis archiepiscopus floruit A. Ch. <*blank*> et scripsit

> Whole entry from Higden, 1. 272 and 6. 40, 252, 264, or Étienne de Bourbon, prologue, p. 7.

1   Historiam de bello Karoli Magni contra Saracenos apud Runcevallem

606 VALERIUS MAXIMUS GAYUS VALERIUS FLACCUS BALBUS SENNUS floruit A. Ch. 19 tempore Augusti imperatoris et scripsit

> Vincent VII 123, *Manipulus florum* XVI ('Libri diuersorum auctorum').
> Kirkestede conflated in the heading the names of Valerius Maximus the historian and Valerius Flaccus the epic poet.

1 De dictis et factis memorabilibus antiquorum lib. 9   *Urbis Romae . . . coegit*

> Vincent VII 123, *MF* XVI 3 (title and explicit do not correspond). Ed. C. Kempf (Leipzig 1888). [**82** Bury = Cambridge, Pembroke College, MS 105 (Bury V. 1), with Kirkestede's note on the flyleaf that it was useful for composing popular sermons ('pro sermonibus ad populum').]

2 De dissuasione nuptiarum ad Rufinum lib. 1   *Loqui . . . vale*

> *MF* XVI 4 (title does not correspond). Walter Map; Sharpe, *Latin Writers*, 737. Ed. M. R. James, C. N. L. Brooke & R. A. B. Mynors (Oxford 1983) 288–312. [**82** Bury = formerly in Cambridge, Gonville and Caius College, MS 225/240 (Bury V. 12), according to Kirkestede's contents note on the flyleaf (p. 3) describing a part of the volume now missing.]

3 Commentum super Valerium ad Rufinum   *Mulier . . . et gratia*

> An anonymous commentary that survives in Cambridge, Clare College, MS 14, fol. 143r (St Albans, s. xiv; not seen), incipit 'Mulier si primatum teneat contraria est viro suo [Eccl 25:30]. Sicut dicit glosa,' explicit 'Si quid satis, dei munus et gratia'; described by M. R. James, *Walter Map, De nugis curialium* (Oxford 1914), xxxi–xxxii.

607 WALTERUS DE MAURITANIA episcopus Parisiensis floruit A. Ch. <*blank*> et scripsit

> The works in this entry (save work *9*) and the source for them are unidentified. For a discussion of this author and his letters see L. Ott, *BGPTM* 34 (1937) 126–347.

1 De fide et legibus

2 De gratia

3 De immortalitate animae

4 Librum qui dicitur Cur Deus homo

5 De virtutibus

6 De claustro animae

7 De universo

8 De praebendis

Walterus de Mauritania   607. 9

   9 De sententiis lib. 1

      See Stegmüller *Sent.* 837, and cf. 271, 632.

608 WARNERIUS monachus Westmonast[eriensis] floruit A. Ch. 1092 et scripsit

      Westmonasteriensis] vir eruditus, multa scripsit opuscula, praecipue homelias ad vulgum, et claruit *add. Bale*

      Source unidentified.
      Bale, *Index*, 465.
      Sharpe, *Latin Writers*, 744.
      No works of Warner's are known to survive.

609 VARRO philosophus Romanus et historiographus floruit anno Caesaris Augusti <*blank*> et scripsit

      Same as Marcus Varro *365*.
      Vincent VII 57–58 (whole entry).

   1 De rebus humanis sententias 25

      Vincent VII 58 (whole entry).

   2 De rebus divinis sententias 16

      Vincent VII 58 (whole entry).

   3 Ad Atheniensem auditorem sententias morales

      Vincent VII 58 (whole entry).

   4 Item de cultu deorum lib. 1

      Vincent VII 57 (whole entry).

610 VEGETIUS Renatus floruit <*blank*> et scripsit

      Registrum 95.

   1 De re militari lib. 5   *Antiquis . . . monstraverunt*

      R95. 1. Ed. C. Lang (Leipzig 1885).

611 VELIUS floruit circa annum <*blank*> et scripsit juxta Cassiodorum

> Same as Longus *356*.
> Cassiodorus I. 30. 2 (whole entry).

1 De ortographia lib.

612 VICTOR Mauritaniae civitatis episcopus floruit A. Ch. <*blank*> et scripsit secundum Genadium

> Gennadius c. 78 (whole entry).

1 Adversus Arrianos lib. 1

2 De poenitentia lib. 1

3 Ad Basiliam consolatoriam epistolam

4 De resurrectione lib. 1

5 Omelias multas

613 VICTOR papa floruit circa A. Ch. 199 et scripsit juxta Jeronimum tempore Severi imperatoris

> Jerome c. 34 (whole entry save the date).

1 Super quaestione Paschae lib. 1

2 Item alia opuscula

614 VICTOR alius Affricanus episcopus floruit anno 528 et scripsit juxta Ysidorum

> Isidore c. 25 (whole entry save the date).

1 Historias a principio mundi usque ad tempora Justini imperatoris

p. 142]

615 VINCENTIUS natione Gallus presbiter monasterii Lirinensis insulae floruit circa A. Ch. 387 et scripsit secundum Genadium

> Gennadius cc. 65 (Vincentius Lerinensis) and 81 (Vincentius Gallus); Kirkestede combined here the works of two writers.

Vincentius   *615. 1*

    1 Ad evitanda haereticorum collegia lib. 1

        Gennadius 65 (whole entry).

    2 Super quosdam psalmos commentarium

        Gennadius 81 (whole entry).

616 VICTORIUS Massiliensis rethor floruit A. Ch. 440 et scripsit secundum Genadium

    Victorinus *Gennadius edition*; Victorius *Bodl. MS e Musaeo 31 p. 233*

    Gennadius c. 61 (whole entry).

    1 A principio Geneseωs usque ad obitum Abrahae metrice lib. 4

617 VICTORIUS alius natione Aquitannicus calculator Scripturarum invitatus ab Hillario papa composuit juxta Genadium Paschalem cursum indagatione cautissima post quatuor priores qui composuerunt, id est Ypolitum, Eusebium, Theophilum et Prosperum

    Gennadius c. 89 (whole entry).

618 VICTORIUS Pictavensis episcopus floruit A. Ch. <*blank*> et scripsit

    Source unidentified. This entry appears to be a confusion of Victorius of Aquitaine (*617*) and Victorinus, bishop of Pettau.

    1 De pascha lib. 1

    2 Librum ympnorum

619 VICTORINUS ex oratore Pictabionensis episcopus et martir floruit A. Ch. <*blank*> et scripsit secundum Jeronimum

    Petabionensis *Jerome edition*; Pictabionensis *text of Jerome in Bodl. MS e Musaeo 31 p. 205*

    Jerome c. 74 (whole entry save work *11*).

    1 Super Genesin

    2 Super Exodum

3 Super Leviticum

4 Super Ysaiam

5 Super Ezechielem

6 Super Abacuch

7 Super Ecclesiasten

8 Super Cantica Canticorum

9 Super Apocalipsin

10 Adversus omnes haereses

11 Super Mathaeum, secundum Cassiodorum

> Cassiodorus I. 7. 1 (whole entry).

620 VICTORINUS natione Afer rethor et doctor grammaticus floruit A. Ch. 343 et scripsit juxta Jeronimum

> Jerome c. 101.

1 Adversus Arrium more dialetico libros valde obscuros

> Jerome 101 (whole entry).

2 Item super apostolum Paulum commentarios

> Jerome 101 (whole entry).

3 Super Rethoricam Tullii lib. *Omnis quicunque . . . proveniunt*

> *CPL* 1544. The explicit is that of an anonymous commentary on Cicero's *De inuentione* frequently found with Victorinus's commentary on *De inuentione*. Both are ed. C. Halm, *Rhetores latini minores* (Leipzig 1863) 155–304, 305–310.

4 Super Topica Tullii lib. 4

> Source unidentified. *CPL* 94a. The work survives only in *testimonia* of Martianus Capella (who does not mention Victorinus by name), Cassiodorus

Victorinus   *620. 4*

  and Boethius; see P. Hadot, *Marius Victorinus: Recherches sur sa vie et ses oeuvres* (Paris 1971) 313–21. Cassiodorus names Victorinus in Book II of the Institutes (II. 3. 19): 'Topica Aristotelis Cicero transtulit in Latinum; cuius commenta prospector atque amator Latinorum Victorinus quattuor libris exposuit'. It is questionable whether Kirkestede knew Book II (Book II of the Institutes does not appear in the Bury bibliographic codex, Bodl. MS e Musaeo 31); for two other possible uses of this source see Censorinus *137* and Tullianus *589*. Boethius mentions Victorinus in his own commentary on the Topics (*CPL* 888; at *PL* 64. 1041): 'Quattuor enim voluminibus Victorinus in Topica conscriptis . . .'. This is not a work that Kirkestede included in the *Catalogus*; see Boetius *94*.

621 VICTRUVIUS floruit A. Ch. <*blank*> et scripsit

 1 De architectura lib. 10 *Architecti . . . explicata*

  Ed. V. Rose & H. Müller-Strübing (Leipzig 1867) 2–284. [**82** Bury = B13. 152; seen by Leland at Bury, B16. 19.]

622 VIGILIUS papa floruit A. Ch. <*blank*> et scripsit

 Registrum 71 (whole entry).

 1 Contra Nestorium et Euticen lib. 4 105

623 VIGILIUS diaconus floruit A. Ch. 432 et scripsit secundum Genadium ex traditione patrum monachorum regulam totius professionis monasticae continentem disciplinam.

  patrum] fratrum *Add. 3470;* patrum *Ely extracts fol. 119v, Gennadius, Speculum coenobitarum*
  Gennadius c. 52 (whole entry save the date).
  Ely extracts, fol. 119v.
  Speculum coenobitarum 18.

624 VIGILIUS episcopus floruit A. Ch. 433 et scripsit secundum Genadium

 Gennadius c. 38 (whole entry save the date).

 1 De laude martirum lib. 1

 2 De gestis sui temporis apud barbaros epistolam unam

625 WILHELMUS DE MONTE vel **MONTIBUS** floruit A.C. <*blank*>
et scripsit

> *Mariale*, as cited. This entry is based largely on manuscripts.
> Ely extracts, fol. 119v.
> Bale, *Index*, 131–2.
> Sharpe, *Latin Writers*, 793–4.
> See J. W. Goering, *William de Montibus (c. 1140–1213): The Schools and the Literature of Pastoral Care* (Toronto 1992).

1 Speculum poenitentiae   *De peccatorum . . . non curat*   65

> De peccatorum agnitione tractatum *Bale*

> Sharpe, *Latin Writers*, 793. Ed. Goering, 187–210; explicit unidentified. See also *8* below.

2 Distinctionum lib. 1   65

> Distinctionum theologicarum. lib. 1   Arcus dicitur Christus et propiciatio . . . *Bale*

> *Mariale* fol. 19r. Sharpe, *Latin Writers*, 793. Goering, 268–303 prints extracts, including the incipit that Bale offers. [**82** Bury = BL MS Royal 6 B. x, fol. 43v (Bury A. 88).]

3 De adventu Domini serm. 1   *Benedictus . . .*

> Benedictus qui venit in nomine *Bale*

> William de Montibus's sermons are unprinted; Sharpe, *Latin Writers*, 793, and see discussion in Goering, 515–66.

4 De bonitate mulierum ad moniales ep. 1   65

> *Mariale* fol. 63r. Sharpe, *Latin Writers*, 793. Ed. Goering, 225–6.

5 Concordantias literales super Bibliam

> *Mariale* fol. 13r.

6 Expositiones evangeliorum   *Cum appropinquasset . . .*

> Cum appropinquasset Iesus *Bale*

> Not found in Sharpe, *Latin Writers*, or Goering.

Wilhelmus de Monte *625. 7*

7 Numerale ejusdem   *Unus est Deus . . . virtutibus*   65.63

>Unus est Deus] et hoc natura docet *add. Bale; this longer incipit unidentified*

>Sharpe, *Latin Writers*, 793. Goering, 236–60, prints excerpts, including the opening words. This is probably the 'quedam summa magistri Willelmi de Montibus' in the medieval catalogues of **65** Ramsey = B68. 152c and 546. / [**82** Bury = London, Wellcome Historical Medical Library, MS 801A, fol. 88r (Bury M. 27), a fragment of the *Numerale* with the rubric *Unus Deus* (inc. 'Deus unus est').]

8 Speculum poenitentis   *Dicit Ysaias . . . culpae*   61

>Dicit Ysaias] parate viam domini *add. Bale*

>The title is that of *1* above; incipit and explicit unidentified. **61** Peterborough = BP21. 232b.

9 Versus ejusdem glosae   *Quis veniat . . . terrent*   61

>Quis veniat] videas quo quando *add. Bale*

>The *Versarius*, Sharpe, *Latin Writers*, 794. Ed. Goering, 389–471. **61** Peterborough = BP21. 90d, and see also an early 13th-cent. donation to Peterborough (BP7. 7).

p. 143]

626 WILHELMUS DE BURGO monachus de Ramesia doctor theologiae floruit A. Ch. 1188 et scripsit subtiliter et devote

>(William of Peterborough)
>This entry is based on manuscripts at **65** Ramsey abbey.
>*Speculum coenobitarum* 56.
>Bale, *Index*, 118.
>Sharpe, *Latin Writers*, 800–801.

1 Super Cantica ab eo loco: Dilectus meus candidus usque ad finem omelias   *Qui in . . . Wilhelmum*   65

>usque — qui in *om. Bale*   Dilectus meus candidus *Bale treats this as the incipit*

>This work appears in Prague UL MS Lobkowitz 431, fols. 187r–191r. See P. Lehmann, *Mitteilungen aus Handschriften* III, Sitzungsberichte der Bayerische Akademie der Wissenschaften. phil.-hist. Abteilung 6 (Munich 1931–2) 11–18.

2 Distinctiones *Alpha . . . nunc materia* 65

   Distinctiones varias *Bale*

   Unidentified. A longer incipit, 'Alpha prima graecorum litera', can be supplied from Bale, *Scriptores*, 225.

3 Omelias notabiles et sermones *Aspiciens . . .*

   Aspiciens vel Reverenter *Bale*

   Unidentified. A longer incipit, 'Aspiciens a 'longe' vidi turbi', can be supplied from Bale, *Scriptores*, 225.

4 Eufrastica, id est bene exposita et continet capitula 100 *Quid est . . . deficere* 65

   Sharpe, *Latin Writers*, 801. **65** Ramsey = Bodl. MS Bodley 833, fol. 5r, the only known manuscript; quite unexpectedly, this codex has a Ramsey *ex libris* written by Kirkestede on fol. 1r ('Liber monasterii de Rameseya').

5 Librum partium

   Secunda pars vel potius prima pars sermonum ejus sic incipit: *Reverenter.* Ultima capitula: *Quum superius.* 65

   partium *queried by Tanner*

   Unidentified. A longer incipit, 'Reverenter docet experiri ea', can be supplied from Bale, *Scriptores*, 225. **65** Ramsey = B68. 63, B68. 517.

627 WILHELMUS PARVUS floruit A. Ch. 1197 et scripsit

   Same as Wilhelmus Neubrigensis *658*.
   Bale, *Index*, 144.
   Sharpe, *Latin Writers*, 794.

1 Super Cantica *Crebra . . . commendare*

   Sharpe, *Latin Writers*, 794. Ed. J. C. Gorman, *Explanatio sacri epithalamii in matrem sponsi*, Spicilegium Friburgense 6 (Fribourg 1960) 71.

628 VALERANUS floruit A. Ch. <*blank*> et scripsit juxta Cassiodorum

   Same as Curtius *117*.

   Cassiodorus I. 30. 2 (whole entry).

1 De ortographia lib.

629 WILHELMUS DE PAGULA vicarius de Wingfeld prope forestam de Windesor floruit A. Ch. <*blank*> et scripsit

> (William of Paull)
> The whole entry, including titles without incipits, was probably based on a manuscript or manuscripts at Bury.
> Ely extracts, fol. 119v.
> Bale, *Index*, 143.
> Ware extracts, fol. 132.
> Sharpe, *Latin Writers*, 799–800.

1 Summam summarum de jure canonico pariter et divino et continet lib. 5   *Ad honorem . . . respondendum*

> Sharpe, *Latin Writers*, 800. Excerpts ed. L. E. Boyle, *Proceedings of the Second Congress of Medieval Canon Law* (Vatican City 1965) 415–56.

2 Speculum praelatorum

> Sharpe, *Latin Writers*, 799.

3 Speculum religiosorum   *Accipite . . . passionem Christi*

> Accipite] vos religiosi *add. Ely extracts fol. 119v*
>
> Sharpe, *Latin Writers*, 799.

4 Summam quae vocatur Oculus sacerdotis   *Ignorantia . . . coronam vitae*

> Sharpe, *Latin Writers*, 799. The incipit and explicit indicate that this work included only the *Sinistra pars* and the *Dextra pars*.

5 Ad regem Angliae Edw[ardum] III ep. 1

> Sharpe, *Latin Writers*, 799. Ed. J. Moisant (Paris 1891) 83.

630 VIRGILIUS MARO floruit tempore Caesaris Augusti et scripsit

> Vincent I 61–2 (works *1–3, 6–7, 12*).
> The major Virgilian corpus (works *1–3*) was presumably recorded from a manuscript at **82** Bury [= B13. 107, 'Virgilius ij°']. The collection of *carmina minora* reported from **61** Peterborough was similar to that in Bodl. MS Auct. F. 1. 17, fols. 39r–42r.

1 Bucolicarum lib. 1   *Tityre tu . . . capellae*

> Vincent I 61–2. Ed. M. Geymonat (Turin 1973) 3–54.

Virgilius Maro   *630. 9*

2 Georgicarum lib. 4   *Quid faciat . . . fagi*

   Vincent I 61–2. Ed. R. A. B. Mynors (Oxford 1969).

3 Æneydos lib. 12   *Arma . . . sub umbras*

   Vincent I 61–2. Ed. Geymonat, 173–667. [**82** Bury is presumably not Cambridge, Trinity College, MS R. 3. 50 (Bury —), a 12th-cent. manuscript procured for Bury by Abbot Curteys (1429–46) after Kirkestede's death.]

4 Librum qui dicitur Copa vel Cona secundum quosdam   *Copa . . . aratrum*   61

   Ps. Virgil. Ed. R. Giomini, *Appendix Vergiliana*, Biblioteca di studi superiori 26 (Florence 1953) 83. Explicit is that of the *Moretum*, *15* below. **61** Peterborough = BP21. 132e (in the same codex with *7*, *9*, *11*, *14*, *15*, and *16* below).

5 Item librum qui vocatur Sirina

   Source unidentified. *Ciris*.

6 Item librum Ætnan

   Vincent I 61–2 (whole entry).

7 Item Culicen   *Lusimus . . . reddit*   61

   Vincent I 61–2. *Ps.* Virgil. Ed. Giomini, 3. **61** Peterborough = BP21. 132c (in the same codex with *4* above, and *9*, *14*, *15*, and *16* below).

8 Item Priapea

   Priapea] napeya *Add. 3470, queried by Tanner*

   Source unidentified.

9 Item Catelepton est et non   *Vir bonus . . . rectis*   61

   Catalepton est et non   *queried by Tanner*

   Ps. Virgil. In the title, *De est et non* has been joined to the *Catalepton*, which is an alternate name for works *8* and *10*. The incipits and explicits of the *De est et non* (ed. Giomini, 143), and of *14* below, *De uiro bono* (ed. Giomini, 146), have been exchanged. Perhaps the muddle reflects the state of the Peterborough manuscript. **61** Peterborough = BP21. 132f (in the same codex with *4* and *7* above, and *14*, *15*, and *16* below).

Virgilius Maro   *630. 10*

10 Epigrammata

> Source unidentified.

11 Item Dyras vel Driades

> Source unidentified. *Dirae*. This work appears in BP21. 132d, the same Peterborough codex that supplied works *4, 7, 9, 14, 15,* and *16*; but (unlike his treatment of the other six) for this work Kirkestede does not give incipit or explicit or the location number for Peterborough (**61**).

12 De musca lib. 1

> Vincent I 61–2 (whole entry).

13 De vacca Platonis

> Source unidentified. Presumably the same as Plato *464.4* above.

14 De viro justo   *Est et non . . . versant*   61

> *Ps.* Virgil, *De uiro bono*. For the incipit and explicit see *9* above. **61** Peterborough = BP21. 132g (in the same codex with *4, 7,* and *9* above, and *15* and *16* below).

15 De moreto vel simbolo lib. 1   *Jam nox . . . aratrum*   61

> *Ps.* Virgil. *Moretum*. Ed. Giomini, 93. **61** Peterborough = BP21. 132i (in the same codex with *4, 7, 9,* and *14* above, and *16* below). See also *4* above.

16 Egloga Virgilii de rosis   *Ver erat . . . properare tuum*   61

> *Ps.* Virgil. Ed. Giomini, 149. **61** Peterborough = BP21. 132h (in the same codex with *4, 7, 9, 14,* and *15* above).

631 VITELLIUS Affer floruit A. Ch. <*blank*> et scripsit secundum Genadium

> Gennadius c. 4 (whole entry).

1 De eo quod odio sint mundo servi Dei

2 Adversus gentes et alios traditores in persecutione divinarum Scripturarum

3 Ad regulam ecclesiasticam pertinentia multa disseruit

632 WILHELMUS monachus et abbas S. Theodorici floruit A. Ch. <blank> et scripsit secundum Bernardum

> (William of Saint-Thierry)
> The reference to Bernard is unidentified.
> See J. M. Déchanet, *Guillaume de S. Thierry, l'homme et l'oeuvre* (Bruges 1942).

1 De corpore et sanguine Domini   *Cum Christianae . . . reficit*

> PL 180. 345.

2 Ad fratres de mon[t]e lib. 1

> mone *Add. 3470, queried by Tanner*

> Same as Bernardus *85.17.*

3 Idem Wilhelmus scripsit vitam s. Bernardi abbatis   *Scripturus . . .*

> PL 185. 225.

p. 144]

633 WILHELMUS Durandi episcopus Munacensis in Aquitannia floruit A. Ch. 1265 et scripsit

> Five, and perhaps all six, of these titles derive from manuscripts presumably at Bury.
> Ely extracts, fol. 119v; for the works in this entry the extracts consistently offer more, or different, information.

1 Rationale de officiis divinis partes 8   *Quaecunque . . .*   Finis: *de compoto et Xalendario*

> Quaecunque] in ecclesiastic' add. *Ely extracts fol. 119v*

> Printed, Mainz 1459 &c.

2 Pontificale et continet partes 3   *Pontificale . . .*   Finis: *de benedictionibus solempniter dandis post etc.*

> Pontificale cum solemnis benediccionibus et statuta synodalia   *a substitute title in Ely extracts fol. 119v; cf. title of 6 below*

> Ed. M. Andrieu, *Le pontifical romain au Moyen–Age* 3, Studi e Testi 88 (Rome 1940); explicit unidentified. See also 6 below.

Wilhelmus   633. 3

3 Reportorium lib. 5   *Quid sit . . . episcopus*

   Quid sit] Fides *add. Ely extracts fol. 119v*   episcopus] nullus episcopus *add. Ely extracts fol. 119v (in error from 4 below)*

   Printed, Frankfurt 1592 &c.

4 Aureum confessorum et memoriale sacerdotum   *Cum sit ars . . . nullus episcopus*

   Cum sit ars] arcium   *add. Ely extracts fol. 119v*

   Ed. J. Berthelé, *Mémoires de l'Académie des sciences et lettres de Montpellier*, Section des lettres sér. 2 (Montpellier 1900), vol. 3 no. 1.

5 Speculum judiciale lib. 4   *De trono . . . sempiternum*

   trono *queried by Tanner*   De trono] dei procedunt *add. Ely extracts fol. 119v*

   Printed, Frankfurt 1592 &c.

6 Statuta synodalia

   Source unidentified. This may be a reference to part 3 of *2* above.

634 URSINUS monachus floruit circa A. Ch. <blank> et scripsit secundum Genadium

   Gennadius c. 27 (whole entry).

1 De baptismo lib. 1

635 VIGILLIUS episcopus Affricae floruit circa A. Ch. <blank> et scripsit

   (Vigillius Thapsensis)
   This entry is based on a manuscript or manuscripts, presumably at Bury.

1 De incarnatione Verbi lib. 5   *Magnum . . .*

   CPL 806. PL 65. 95.

2 De altercatione Athanasii, Sabellii, Fortini et Arrii lib. 1   *Cum apud . . . pervenire*

   PL 62. 155–80. Same as Athanasius *6.10*.

3 De 1000 annorum intelligentia in Apocalipsi lib. 1

   This work and its source are unidentified.

636 VINCENTIUS Burgundus alias Belvacensis Frater Praedicator floruit A. Ch. 1244 et scripsit

   Script. Ord. Praed. fleshed out from manuscripts; cf. Stams, 29.

   1 Speculum naturale quod continet lib. 22   *Mundi factura . . . illuminabit eam*   73.173

   Printed, Strasbourg: Adolf Rusch, *c.* 1473–6.

   2 Speculum doctrinale quod continet lib. 1

   3 Speculum morale quod continet lib.

   4 Speculum historiale quod continet lib. 32   *Quum multitudo . . .*

   Printed, Strasbourg: Johann Mentelin, 1473, incipit 'Quoniam . . .'.

   5 De laudibus B. Virginis lib. 1

   6 De gratia lib. 1

   7 De morte amici consolatoriam epistolam

   8 De detractione lib. 1

   9 De morali principis institutione lib. 1   *Clarissimus . . . utilitatis fides*   168

   Ed. R. J. Schneider, *CCCM* 137. 3–143.

   10 De puerorum eruditione nobilium lib. 1   *Devotissime . . . honorari*   168

   Ed. A. Steiner, Medieval Academy of America Publications 32 (Cambridge, MA, 1938).

   11 De Trinitate lib. 1

   12 De Filio Dei lib. 1

637 WILHELMUS DE HOTHUN Anglicus Frater Praedicator et archiepiscopus Dublinensis floruit A. Ch. <blank> et scripsit

> de Hothun *om. Stams, habet Ware*

> Script. Ord. Praed. (whole entry), cf. Stams, 13.
> Bale, *Index*, 129.
> Ware extracts, fol. 132r.
> Sharpe, *Latin Writers*, 778.

1 Super primum librum sententiarum

2 Item super omnes libros sententiarum lecturam

3 De unitate formarum lib. 1

4 De immediata visione divinae essentiae

638 WILHELMUS DE ALTONA natione Anglicus Frater Praedicator floruit A. Ch. <blank> et scripsit

> Script. Ord. Praed. (whole entry), cf. Stams, 15.
> Bale, *Index*, 113.
> Sharpe, *Latin Writers*, 747–50.

1 Super Mathaeum postillam 1

2 De x virginibus

3 Super Ecclesiasten

> Quaestiones varias lib. 1 *add. Bale; not in Stams*

639 WILHELMUS DE MAUNFELD Anglicus Frater Praedicator floruit A. Ch. <blank> et scripsit

> Maunfeld] Masfelt *Stams*

> Script. Ord. Praed. (whole entry), cf. Stams, 18.
> Bale, *Index*, 137.
> James extracts, p. 199.
> Sharpe, *Latin Writers*, 784.

1 Contra Henricum de Gandavo quibus impugnat Thomam de Aquino

2 Contra coruptores Thomae de Aquino

3 De angelis quaestiones

640 WLRICUS Frater Praedicator floruit A. Ch. <*blank*> et scripsit

>Script. Ord. Praed. (whole entry), cf. Stams, 24.

1 Super libros metheororum

2 Super 4 libros sententiarum

3 Summam theologiae

641 WILHELMUS LUMBARDUS Frater Praedicator floruit A. Ch. <*blank*> et scripsit

>Script. Ord. Praed. (whole entry), cf. Stams, 42.
>The title *Postillam super Dionisium totum* appears in Stams and Pign. 42 in place of works *1–3*.

1 Super Dionisium de Divinis nominibus

2 Super Dionisium de Coelesti jerarchia

3 Super Dionisium de Ecclesiastica jerarchia

4 Super Boetium de Consolatione philosophiae

p. 145]

642 WILHELMUS DE PARALDO Frater Praedicator et archiepiscopus Lugdunensis floruit A. Ch. <*blank*> et scripsit

>Script. Ord. Praed., cf. Stams, 47. Although the whole entry seems to have come from the list, Bury had two manuscripts with works of William's.

1 Summam virtutum

>[**82** Bury = BL MS Royal 11 B. III, fol. 29r (Bury V. 18), without rubric or attribution of authorship; this title came from *Script. Ord. Praed.*]

Wilhelmus de Paraldo   *642. 2*

    2 Summam vitiorum

        [**82** Bury = Cambridge, St John's College, MS F. 1 (Bury S. 26), without rubric or attribution of authorship; a similar title appears on the table of contents but again the author's name is absent. This title came from *Script. Ord. Praed.*]

    3 Sermones de tempore et sanctis

643 WILHELMUS Aurelianensis Frater Praedicator floruit A. Ch. <*blank*> et scripsit

        Script. Ord. Praed. (whole entry), cf. Stams, 74.

    1 Super Apparatum Raymundi

644 WILHELMUS GALLICUS Frater Praedicator floruit A. Ch. <*blank*> et scripsit

        Script. Ord. Praed. (whole entry), cf. Stams, 80.

    1 Librum qui dicitur Praeparate

        Properate *Add. 3470, queried by Tanner*

645 WILHELMUS BRIXENSIS Frater Praedicator floruit A. Ch. <*blank*> et scripsit

        Wilhelmus] Albertus *Stams*

        Script. Ord. Praed. (whole entry), cf. Stams, 81.

    1 De officio sacerdotis lib. 1

646 WILHELMUS PARISIENSIS Frater Praedicator floruit A. Ch. <*blank*> et scripsit

        Script. Ord. Praed. (whole entry), cf. Stams, 84.

    1 Tabulam juris

647 WILHELMUS GALLICUS Frater Praedicator floruit A. Ch. <*blank*> et scripsit

        Script. Ord. Praed. (whole entry), cf. Stams, 87.

1 Super Apocalypsin postillam 1

648 WILHELMUS DE ENKOURT Anglicus Frater Praedicator floruit A. Ch. <*blank*> et scripsit

> (William Deyncourt)
> *Script. Ord. Praed.* (whole entry). This author is omitted by Stams and Pign.
> Bale, *Index*, 124.
> Sharpe, *Latin Writers*, 764.

1 Super Ecclesiasten lecturam optimam

2 Sermones plures et bonos

649 WILHELMUS DE KINGESHAM Anglicus Frater Praedicator floruit A. Ch. <*blank*> et scripsit

> *Script. Ord. Praed.* (whole entry). This author is omitted by Stams and Pign.
> Bale, *Index*, 130.
> Sharpe, *Latin Writers*, 780.

1 Super Ecclesiasticum lecturam 1

650 WILHELMUS BRUMYARD Anglicus Frater Praedicator floruit A. Ch. 1349 et scripsit

> A confused reference to John Bromyard. See Johannes de Bromyerd *338*.
> *Script. Ord. Praed* (whole entry). This author is omitted by Stams and Pign.
> Bale, *Index*, 118.
> Sharpe, *Latin Writers*, 756, 220–21.

1 Summam bonam quae vocatur Brumyard

2 Item distinctiones

651 WILHELMUS BRABANTINUS Corinthiensis Frater Praedicator floruit A. Ch. <*blank*> et transtulit omnes libros naturalis et moralis philosophiae de Graeco in Latinum. Item transtulit librum Procli.

> *Script. Ord. Praed.* (whole entry), cf. Stams, 33.

Wido *652.*

652 WIDO monachus Cartusiensis floruit \<blank\> et scripsit

>   (Guigo II of Chartreuse)
>   See also Guido *239.*
>   *Mariale* fol. 44r (whole entry).

1 De annunciatione sermonem 1   *Ciba nos* . . .

653 WALTERUS DE BOKEDENE Frater Praedicator floruit A. Ch. \<blank\>

>   *Script. Ord. Praed.* (whole entry). This author is omitted by Stams and Pign.
>   Bale, *Index,* 100.
>   Sharpe, *Latin Writers,* 709.

>   Quaestiones theologiae lib. 1 *entry add. Bale*

654 WILHELMUS monachus Gemeticensis floruit A. Ch. \<blank\> et scripsit

>   (William of Jumièges)
>   Source unidentified.
>   Bale, *Index,* 125.

1 De regibus Anglorum historiam 1

>   Officiarium ecclesiae lib. 1 *entry add. Bale; Bale's editors note that this entry has been inserted between the lines*

655 WILHELMUS DE CONCHES philosophus floruit circa A. Ch. \<blank\>

>   Bale, *Index,* 122.
>   The works appear together in this sequence in BL MS Arundel 377 (Ely, s. xii/xiii).

1 Philosophiam primam de naturis inferiorum et superiorum lib. 2   *Cum dudum* . . . *regnare est*

>   *Incorrectly divided into two works in Bale*

>   Daniel of Morley, *Philosophia.* Ed. G. Maurach in *Mittellateinisches Jahrbuch* 14 (1979) 212–45.

2 Philosophiam secundam   *Quaeris . . . vivere*

> *Dragmaticon.* Ed. I. Ronca, *CCCM* 152. 3–270. [**82** Bury = Cambridge, Gonville and Caius College, MS 225/240, p. 19 (Bury V. 12), with Kirkestede's title ('Secunda philosophia') and attribution in the upper margin.]

656 VERECUNDUS floruit A. Ch. <*blank*> et scripsit

1 Super quaedam cantica prophetarum   *Cantica . . . fulgebimus*

> cantica] circa *Add. 3470*   prophetarum *queried by Tanner*

> *CPL* 870. *CCSL* 93. 1–203. [**82** Bury = B13. 79b.]

657 WILHELMUS DE MALMESBIRIA monachus floruit circa A. Ch. <*blank*> et scripsit

> Bale, *Index*, 135.
> Sharpe, *Latin Writers*, 784–6.

1 De gestis regum Angliae lib. 5   *Domino venerabili . . . ornamento ubique*

> Ed. R. A. B. Mynors, R. M. Thomson & M. Winterbottom, OMT (1998), 1. 10–798; explicit is that of paragraph 446. [**82** Bury = BL MS Harley 447, fol. 1r (Bury C. 49).]

2 De gestis pontificum

> Prima sedes episcoporum *add. Bale as incipit*

> The source of this entry was probably a manuscript. Sharpe, *Latin Writers*, 785. Ed. N. E. S. A. Hamilton, RS 52 (1870).

658 WILHELMUS NEUBRIGENSIS ecclesiae canonicus floruit A. Ch. 1160 et scripsit abbati Rievalliae

> Same as Wilhelmus Parvus 627.
> Bale, *Index*, 144. Bale has correctly combined the two entries for this author under the name 'Guilhelmus Parvus, Neubrigensis ecclesiae canonicus'.
> Sharpe, *Latin Writers*, 794.

1 Historiam de gestis Anglorum lib. 5   *Historiam . . . illi essent*   170

> Sharpe, *Latin Writers*, 794. Ed. R. Howlett, RS 82/1–2 (1884–5); explicit (ib. 2. 500) 'illi esset'.

659 WALTERUS Exon[iensis] archidiaconus floruit A.D. <blank> et scripsit

> Exoniensis] sive Excestriensis *add. Bale*   scripsit Britannorum chronica *Bale*
>
> Higden, 1. 24 (whole entry).
> Bale, *Index*, 104.
> While the printed edition of the *Polichronicon* reads 'Walterus Oxon.' (i.e. Walter Map), some manuscripts read 'Walterus Exon.' (for example, Oxford, Magdalen College, MS 181, and Cambridge, St John's College, MS A. 12).
> Sharpe, *Latin Writers*, 734, a ghost.

660 WILHELMUS Rivallensis floruit A. Ch. <blank> et scripsit

> Higden, 1. 24 (whole entry)
> Sharpe, *Latin Writers*, 803; a ghost.

[p. 146]

661 WINDICHINDUS floruit A. Ch. <blank> et scripsit

> (Widukind)
> Diceto, 1. 23 (whole entry).

1 Historiam Saxonum

662 WINDOCINENSIS floruit <blank> et scripsit

> (Matthew of Vendôme)
> Bale, *Index*, 291.

1 Summam quae vocatur <blank>   Ne videar magnificare . . . biberunt   61

> *Ars versificatoria* (the name is of modern coinage). Ed. F. Munari, *Mathei Vindocinensis Opera* 3, Storia e letteratura 171 (Rome 1988) 39–221; incipit 'Ne meas uiderer magnificare'. **61** Peterborough = BP21. 160k.

663 USUARDUS monachus floruit A. Ch. <blank> et scripsit ad Carolum regem Franciae et imperatorem secundum librum de donis et secundum sanctilogium Guidonis

> Whole entry from the secondary sources cited. The passage in Guido de Castris' *Sanctilogium* (unpublished) may be found in BL MS Royal 13 D. IX, fol. 1r, prologue; Étienne de Bourbon (the 'liber de donis'), prologue p. 8. Ely extracts, fol. 119v.

Ysidorus 666.

1 Martilogium 1 quo communiter utitur ecclesia Gallicana

> Gallicana] Anglicana *Ely extracts fol. 119v*

664 XPOFORUS Nolhamsensis Frater Praedicator floruit A. Ch. <*blank*> et scripsit

> Nolhamsensis] Molhusensis *Pign.*
> Script. Ord. Praed. (whole entry), cf. Pign. 108. This author is omitted by Stams.
> Bale, *Index*, 53.
> See Sharpe, *Latin Writers*, 85.

1 Super quatuor evangelia postillas

2 Super omnes epistolas Pauli

3 Super epistolas canonicas

4 Sermones de tempore et sanctis

665 XPOFORUS Lumbardus Frater Praedicator floruit A. Ch. <*blank*> et scripsit

> Script. Ord. Praed. (whole entry), cf. Stams, 44.

1. Super Mathaeum, Marcum et Lucam postillas

666 YSIDORUS sanctus Hispalensis episcopus quondam B. Gregorii magni discipulus et B. Leandri successoris floruit A. Ch. 616 et scripsit multa

> *Registrum* 8, Vincent XXIV 31 (references are followed by numbers in brackets [1, 2, etc.] that indicate the sequence of titles in the chapter), *Manipulus florum* VIII.
> Works *1–10* come from a manuscript once at **82** Bury (= B13. 9, 'Ysidorus super uetus testamentum'); it is not recorded among the location numbers, however, which are all evidently taken from the corresponding *Registrum* entries, though often with groundless extrapolation from one entry to another. Of the thirty-nine remaining titles, nearly half (eighteen) are taken entirely from the *Registrum*, and slightly more than half (twenty-one) represent manuscripts. It is hard, however, to imagine the principle that might have determined their sequence, and instead we suppose repeated insertions over the years. This entry presents an above-average quantity of unlikely location numbers, representing widely-scattered ecclesiastical institutions that Kirkestede surely did not know first-hand; the explanation is not obvious.
> Ely extracts, fol. 119v.
> James extracts, p. 199.

Ysidorus   *666. 1*

1   Super Genesin allegorias lib. 1   *Creatura . . . carnem*   20.53.10.27.102.94

    10.27] x.xxvii *R*

    R8. 59, Vincent XXIV 31 [1]. *CPL* 1195. *PL* 83. 209; incipit is that of c. 1. Location number **94** comes from R8. 17, 'Super Vetus Testamentum'. / [**82** Bury = B13. 9.]

2   In Exodum lib. 1   *Primo . . . credentibus*   94.93.89.9.19.35.39

    2–5 below: Location numbers are taken from R8. 17, 'Super Vetus Testamentum'; consistently, 89] 97 *R*

    R8. 17, Vincent XXIV 31 [8]. *CPL* 1195. *PL* 83. 281; incipit is that of c. 1. [**82** Bury = B13. 9.]

3   In Leviticum lib. 1   *In exordio . . . approbatur*   94.93.95.89.9.19.35

    R8. 17, Vincent XXIV 31 [9]. *CPL* 1195. *PL* 83. 321; incipit is that of c. 1, explicit unidentified. For the location numbers see the note to *2* above. / [**82** Bury = B13. 9.]

4   In Deuteronomium lib. 1   *Liber Deuteronomii . . . inveniemur*   94.93.95.89.9.19.35

    R8. 17, Vincent XXIV 31 [11]. *CPL* 1195. *PL* 83. 359. For the location numbers see the note to *2* above. / [**82** Bury = B13. 9.]

5   In Numerum lib. 1   *Cathalogus . . . extinguamus*   94.93.95.89.9.19.35

    R8. 17, Vincent XXIV 31 [10]. *CPL* 1195. *PL* 83. 339; incipit is that of paragraph 3 of the preface. For the location numbers see the note to *2* above. [**82** Bury = B13. 9.]

6   In Josue et Jehu Nave lib. 1   *Post mortem . . . subiciat*   154.8.35.15.115.12

    12] xii *R*

    R8. 44, Vincent XXIV 31 [12]. *CPL* 1195. *PL* 83. 371. [**82** Bury = B13. 9.]

7   In librum Judicum lib. 1   *Historiam . . . triumphant*   154.8.35.15.115.12

    12] xii *R*

    R8. 45, Vincent XXIV 31 [13]. *CPL* 1195. *PL* 83. 379. Incipit is that of c. 8. [**82** Bury = B13. 9.]

Ysidorus   666. *14*

8 In librum Regum lib. 1   *Post librum . . . requiescit*   154.13.35.15.115.12

   13] 8 *R*   12] xii *R*

   R8. 46, Vincent XXIV 31 [14]. *CPL* 1195. *PL* 83. 391. [**82** Bury = B13. 9.]

9 Super Ruth   *Videamus . . . Salvatorem*   8.82.35.15

   82 *may be* 80 *R*

   R8. 48. *CPL* 1195. *PL* 83. 390 (printed as c. 9 of 7 above). **82** Bury = B13. 9.

10 Super Esdram   *Namque*. . .   15.95.64.166

    R8. 56. *CPL* 1195. *PL* 83. 421; incipit 'Iam quod'. [**82** Bury = B13. 9.]

11 Super Cantica Canticorum lib. 3   166.42.163

    R8. 22 (whole entry save the suspect **163**).

12 De quatuor evangelistis   *Quibus modis . . . in coelo*

    Unidentified.

13 De nominibus sanctorum patrum Veteris et Novi Testamenti allegoriam et quid tipice significent   *Quaedam . . . saturabuntur*   163.94.95.43.19.12

    12] xii *R*

    R8. 18. *Allegoriae*; *CPL* 1190. *PL* 83. 97.

14 De ortu et obitu sanctorum patrum Veteris et Novi Testamenti et ubi sepulti sunt   *Adam prothoplastes . . .*   163.74.82.94.95.80

    In quibusdam vero locis, sicut apud Holm S. Benedicti, liber iste sic incipit: *Adam homo primus 6ta feria factus sine patre etc.* et sic finit: *de S. Stephano adoratur.*

    6ta feria] 6 fratrum *Add. 3470, queried by Tanner*

    R8. 13. *CPL* 1191. Ed. C. Chaparro Gómez (Paris 1985) 109. **74** Holme St Benets had a manuscript of this work similar to Cambridge, Corpus Christi College, MS 439, fol. 51v, incipit 'Adam homo primus sexta feria factus', explicit 'de S. Stephano'. / **82** Bury = B13. 62d and B13. 199b = Bodl. MS e Musaeo 31, p. 142 (Bury A. 31).

Ysidorus   666. 15

15 Cathalogum de viris illustribus   *Ossius . . . dum legi*   166.163.82.94.95.80

> R8. 16. *CPL* 1206. Ed. C. Codoñer Merino (Salamanca 1964) 133–53. **82** Bury = B13. 62h and B13. 199c = Bodl. MS e Musaeo 31, p. 243 (Bury A. 31).

16 Prohemiorum de libris Veteris et Novi Testamenti lib. 1   *De librorum . . . praenotabo* 1.3.19

> R8. 57 ('Prohemiorum libri Noui et Veteris Testamenti'). Despite the title (cf. *CPL* 1192 and see *19* below), the incipit and explicit are those of an extract consisting of Book I cc. 11–12 of Isidore's *De ecclesiasticis officiis*, *PL* 83. 745. See also *19* below. [**82** Bury = Bodl. MS e Musaeo 31, pp. 127–140 (Bury A. 31); Kirkestede's table of contents entitles this work, 'De libris Veteris et Noui Testamenti'.]

17 De mistico intellectu veteris legis   *Paradisus . . . ministerium*

> An excerpt from the *Etymologiae* XIV 3. 2–4, found in (for example) Cambridge, Corpus Christi College, MS 316, fol. 191r; explicit does not correspond.

18 De nominibus significatis in lege et in evangelio   166.95

> Whole entry from R8. 25 and Vincent XXIV 31 [6].

p. 147]

19 De libris Veteris et Novi Testamenti   *Plenitudo . . . lignum vitae*   166.94. 155.19.49

> 155] 105 *R*
>
> R8. 23. *In libris Veteris ac Noui Testamenti prooemia*; *CPL* 1192. *PL* 83. 155; incipit is that of the prologue, explicit is that of the text. [**82** Bury = B13. 62c and B13. 199a = Bodl. MS e Musaeo 31 (Bury A. 31); but this is the title that Kirkestede's table of contents there gives to *16* above; incipit and explicit do not correspond.]

20 Soliloquiorum vel sinonimorum   *Anima <mea> . . . places*   94.81.82.43. 9.19

> Anima *queried by Tanner;* Anima mea *Ely extracts fol. 119v*
>
> R8. 20, Vincent XXIV 31 [1]. *CPL* 1203. *PL* 83. 827; incipit is that of c. 1. **82** Bury = B13. 48c and B13. 200; Bodl. MS Laud Misc. 233, fol. 1r (Bury Y. 7), with Kirkestede's table of contents.

Ysidorus   666. 28

21 Sententiarum quae intitulantur De summo bono lib. 3   *Summum bonum
   ... includit*   94.79.92.89.19.15

   94 *may be* 9.43 *R*

   R8. 10, Vincent XXIV 31 [2], *MF* VIII 1. *CPL* 1199. *PL* 83. 537. [**82** Bury
   = B13. 197, 198a; BL MS Royal 5 A. VIII, fol. 19r (Bury A. 52); the guard
   leaves at the head of Cambridge, St John's College, MS G. 2 (Bury H. 56),
   are the beginning of an abandoned text of the *De summo bono*, present in St
   John's G. 2 in Kirkestede's time.]

22 De origine officiorum lib. 2   *Primum ... firmaretur*   65

   Vincent XXIV 31 [4], *MF* VIII 3. *De ecclesiasticis officiis. CPL* 1207. *CCSL* 113.
   4–108. Same as Augustinus *1.332*, and see *23* below.

23 De officiis ecclesiasticis   *Tonsura ... mereantur*   156.114.111.105.35

   R8. 3. The title is that of *22* above, and the incipit and explicit are those of
   39 below, the anonymous *Regula canonicorum*; cf. G. Morin in *DTC* 1. 934. *PL*
   105. 821–934, incipit 'Tonsurae'.

24 Contra Judaeos ad sororem lib. 2   *Judei ... in aeternum*   95.43.82.35.63.42

   R8. 7, 36, Vincent XXIV 31 [5]. *CPL* 1198. *PL* 83. 449. **82** Bury = B13. 101c
   = Bodl. MS Lat. th. c. 26, fol. 32v (Bury J. 16); B13. 198b; Cambridge,
   Pembroke College, MS 118, fol. 1r (Bury Y. 12). / **42** Reading = B71. 48c
   = Chicago, Newberry Library, MS 12. 2, fol. 57r.

25 Explanationum lib. 1   *Mirum ...*   166.94

   R8. 8 (whole entry).

26 De sapientia Dei lib. 1   *Omnis ...*   139.104.97

   R8. 11 (whole entry).

27 De flagellis lib. 1   *Omne ...*   139.104

   R8. 12 (whole entry, incipit 'Diuine').

28 Differentiarum lib. 1   *Inter Deum et Dominum ... diliguntur*   82.94.95.8.9.
   35

   Nonnulli norunt quod iste liber sub tempore Sigisberti regis Gothorum
   scriptus sit. Locus est a peritis et Ytalia prima civitas Gothorum vocatur,
   quae de Gallis et Francis occidentalis est. Persona vero istius codicis

Ysidorus   *666. 28*

　　Ysidorus Minor fertur fuisse. Requirunt etiam periti quare iste Minor appellatur, vel quia alter sub uno vocabulo in eodem loco ante ipsum fuit, vel quod caeteris tractatoribus minor erat. Ergo ille auctor sponte hunc scripsisse librum noscitur contra haereticos male putantes de Trinitate, de anima, et de homine. Explicit prologus.

　　R8. 27. *CPL* 1202. *PL* 83. 69, explicit perhaps that of the penultimate paragraph, 'diligere fratrem'. The note 'Nonnulli norunt' appears as the prologue. **82** Bury = B13. 198c.

29 De Creatore et ordine creaturarum lib. 1   *Universitatis . . . timemus*   161. 94.82.95.8.139

　　R8. 30. *CPL* 1189. Ed. M. C. Díaz y Díaz (Santiago de Compostela 1972) 84–204.

30 Super libros Virgilii   82.166.163

　　R8. 38. Unidentified.

31 De corpore et sanguine Domini serm. 1   *Magnitudo . . . assumant*   165. 153.15.1

　　R8. 21. *Ps.* Eusebius Emesenus ('Gallicanus'); *CPL* 966 *serm.* 16. *CCSL* 101. 195. The title is the same as Eusebius *160.6* above.

32 De sacramento baptismi   105.143

　　R8. 60 (whole entry except the suspect location numbers).

33 Regulam ad monachos   *Plura . . . gratiam*   86.83.82.15.35

　　Plura] sunt precepta *add. Ely extracts fol. 119v*

　　R8. 39. *CPL* 1868. Ed. J. C. Ruiz, *San Leandro, San Isidoro, San Fructuoso* (Madrid 1971) 90.

34 Scintillarum lib. 1   117.161.163

　　R8. 40 (whole entry save the suspect **117**).

35 A semetipso ad semetipsum   114.119.35

　　R8. 53 (whole entry save two suspect location numbers).

36 De anima   94.139

　　R8. 51 (whole entry).

37 Dialogorum lib. 1   42.117.119

> R8. 43 (whole entry save two suspect location numbers).

38 Enigmata metrica   95.128.113

> R8. 15 (whole entry save two suspect location numbers).

39 Regulam ad canonicos   *Cum in nomine . . . signatur*   82

> Anonymous. *PL* 105. 815; the incipit is that of the preface, explicit unidentified. See also *23* above.

40 Ethimologiarum lib. 37   *Disciplina . . . siccetur*   8.94.42.9.82.13

> R8. 9, Vincent XXIV 31 [3], *MF* VIII 2. *CPL* 1186. Ed. W. M. Lindsay (Oxford 1911). **42** Reading = Bodl. MS Bodley 396, fol. 29r, and B71. 115. / **82** Bury = B13. 8.

41 De numero et ejus mistico misterio lib. 1   *Unum . . .*   154.9

> R8. 1. Stegmüller *Bibl.* 5175.

42 De virtutibus et viciis lib. 1   95

> R8. 6 (whole entry).

43 De naturis rerum lib. 1   *Dies est . . . formula*   95.13.15.1.63.10.46

> 10] x *R*

> R8. 33. *CPL* 1188. Ed. J. Fontaine (Bordeaux 1960) 173; explicit unidentified.

Iste liber rarus est sed bonus, et continet capitula xlix.

44 De naturis bestiarum et lapidum lib.   *De naturis . . .*   65

> This is probably an anonymous text similar to BL MS Royal 2 C. xii, fol. 133r (St Peter's abbey, Gloucester, s. xiii[in]), 'Liber de natura quorundam animalium et lapidum', inc. 'De natura leonis', described as a version of the Latin *Physiologus* with additions from the corresponding passages in Isidore's *Etymologiae*; BM *Cat. Royal*, 1. 53–4. See G. R. Mermier in *Beasts and Birds of the Middle Ages: the Bestiary and its Legacy*, ed. W. B. Clark & M. T. McMunn (Philadelphia, PA, 1989), 69–85, at 75.

45 De operibus sex dierum   89

> R8. 34 (whole entry).

Ysidorus   *666. 46*

46   De situ terrae Jerosolymitanae   80.89

> R8. 50 (whole entry; location number **89** is repeated from *45* above).

47   Sermones quamplures   91.43.115.116.105

> R8. 47. No collection of Isidore's sermons circulated in the middle ages. Presumably Kirkestede took the title from the *Registrum*, but the source for this group of location numbers is unknown.

48   Extat etiam Liber decretorum apostolicorum, quem prius compilavit iste Ysidorus, in unum grande volumen compingens scilicet epistolas decretales pontificum Romanorum canonesque conciliorum, ex quo volumine manifestum est Yvonis et Gratiani decreta fuisse excerpta, qui quidem liber Ysidori nullum alium habet ordinem nisi secundum tempora Romanorum pontificum per successiones temporum. De hoc fit mentio xix Di. c. i.[a] Hoc vero volumen Ysidori Yvo Carnotensis abbreviavit, quia non sine magno sumptu scribi poterat, et quia hoc etiam non parvae practicatis erat opus. Hic cathalogum ex eodem volumine abbreviato libellum portatilem legitur composuisse, qui Summa decretorum Yvonis appellatur. Post hunc Gratianus fecit et compilavit decreta paparum sicut scribit Vincentius in Speculo historiarum. Scias tamen quod ante compilationem Gratiani fuit alia compilatio, quae vocatur Breviatio canonum Fulgentii; de hac habetur lxiii Di. *Cum ergo*. Item fuit alia compilatio canonum composita a Burgardo episcopo, de quo habetur lxxiii Di. *In nomine Domini*, et illam compilationem in xx libros divisit, de qua Gratianus multa extraxit.[b] Haec omnia Archid[iaconus] i Di. c. i.

> practicatis] practitatis *Add. 3470 queried by Tanner*, practicatis *James extracts*   cathalogum] chatalogum *James extracts*   historiarum] historiali *James extracts*

> [a] Vincent XXIV 31.   [b] Guido de Baysio, *Rosarium*, Di. 1 c. 1, pr. Venice 1601, fol. 3r.

49   Cronica cronicorum lib. 1

> R8. 4 (whole entry).

667   YVO monasterii Belvacensis canonicus et praepositus et postea Carnotensis episcopus floruit A. Ch. 1094 et scripsit multa

> *Registrum* 35, Vincent XXVI 84.
> Works *1–2, 4* come from a Bury manuscript, and works *6–12* from another manuscript, perhaps at **50** Pipewell. The remaining dozen titles come almost entirely from the *Registrum*, with information from manuscripts complementing about half of those.

Yvo   667. 6

1 De sacramentis neophitorum serm. 1   *Quum populus . . . reddant*   15.104. 13.14

13.14] xiii.xxiiii R *(Peterhouse 169)*

R35. 1. *PL* 162. 505 *serm.* 1. [**82** Bury = Cambridge, St John's College, MS D. 19, fol. 1r (Bury Y. 24).]

2 De sacramentis dedicationis ecclesiae serm. 1   *Quum ad dedicationem . . . studeatis*   15.9.1.115.22.128

22] 12 R

R35. 4. *PL* 162. 527 *serm.* 4. [**82** Bury = Cambridge, St John's College, MS D. 19, fol. 70v (Bury Y. 24).]

3 De officio et vestibus sacerdotum et ecclesiae vasorum lib. 1   15.1.9.128.153

R35. 8 (whole entry).

4 De excellentia sacrorum ordinum et de vita ordinandorum   *Quia Christiana . . . perficiat*   15.166.156.19.1

R35. 15. *PL* 162. 513 *serm.* 2. [**82** Bury = Cambridge, St John's College, MS D. 19, fol. 23r (Bury Y. 24).]

p. 148]

5 De modo et ordine et veritate sacramentorum Christi et ecclesiae 1.161.139

R35. 19 (whole entry save two suspect location numbers).

6 De significatione sacerdotalium et indumentorum serm.   *Quia sanctitas . . . sufficiunt*   14.128.9.50

6–12: Location numbers **128** and **9** are taken from R35. 12, 'Sermones eius'. This unit of seven entries is perhaps based on a manuscript at **50** Pipewell abbey; however, several of the works (*6, 8–10*) are found in Cambridge, St John's College, MS D. 19 (Bury Y. 24), and in Kirkestede's table of contents there, and their rubrics, incipits, and explicits correspond with these entries, suggesting that Kirkestede may have followed his frequent practice of relying instead or in addition on a Bury book. (Cambridge, Corpus Christi College, MS 269, a surviving Pipewell manuscript of Ivo's works, contains no sermons.)

PL 162. 519 *serm.* 3. [**82** Bury = Cambridge, St John's College, MS D. 19, fol. 46v (Bury Y. 24).]

Yvo   667. 7

7 De mistica interpretatione dedicationis ecclesiae serm. 1   *Morem . . . erit eis*   15.128.9.50

>   R35. 17. This is the title of a genuine sermon (*PL* 162. 535 *serm.* 4), but the incipit and explicit refer to a different work of uncertain authorship, *PL* 131. 845. Concerning the location numbers see the note to *6* above. Same as Ambrose *2.28*. [A catalogue entry from Bury, B13. 84e, describes the copy of this work attributed to Ambrose that Kirkestede cited at *2.28*.].

8 De cruce Domini serm. 1   *Coruptum . . . comprehendere*   1.128.9.50

>   R35. 21. *PL* 162. 562 *serm.* 6. [**82** Bury = Cambridge, St John's College, MS D. 19, fol. 132v (Bury Y. 24), with its rubric 'Quare dominus natus et passus sit' changed by Kirkestede in the margin to 'Sermo de cruce domini'.] / Concerning the location numbers see the note to *6* above.

9 De adventu Domini serm. 1   *Quum praesentes . . . interpellat*   128.9.50

>   *PL* 162. 562 *serm.* 7. [**82** Bury = Cambridge, St John's College, MS D. 19, fol. 149r (Bury Y. 24).] / Concerning the location numbers see the note to *6* above.

10 De nativitate Domini serm.   *In divinae . . . pacificavit*   128.9.50

>   divinae] dīne Add. *3470*, queried by Tanner

>   *PL* 162. 568 *serm.* 8. [**82** Bury = Cambridge, St John's College, MS D. 19, fol. 155r (Bury Y. 24).] / Concerning the location numbers see the note to *6* above.

11 De S. Jacobo serm. 1   1.24.128.9.50

>   R35. 22. Concerning the location numbers see the note to *6* above.

12 Ad Paschalem serm.   128.9.50.166

>   R35. 13. Concerning the location numbers see the note to *6* above.

13 De corpore et sanguine Domini   8

>   R35. 10 (whole entry).

14 De non tenenda praelatione sine fructu   8

>   R35. 11 (whole entry).

15 Librum qui vocatur Poculum mellitum   153

    R35. 9 (whole entry).

16 De convenientia veteris et novi sacerdotii   *Beneficia . . . voluit*   15.1

    R35. 16. *PL* 162. 535. [**82** Bury = Cambridge, St John's College, MS D. 19, fols. 98v–132v (Bury Y. 24), with this title. Concerning this manuscript see the note to *24* below.]

17 Super psalterium postillas   161

    R35. 5 (whole entry).

18 De multimoda distinctione scripturarum   108.23.6

    23.6] xxiii.vi *R*

    R35. 14 (whole entry).

19 Cronicorum et gestorum a Nino rege Assiriorum usque ad Karolum filium Ludovici lib. 1 *Assiriorum* . . .   126.157.156.43.153

    R35. 2. Hugh of Fleury. Printed, Westphalia 1638. Same as Haimo *241.1*.

20 Epistolarum cclx lib. 1   *Urbanus . . . quidem*   9.13.1.39.63.57.20

    R35. 3. *PL* 162. 11. Explicit unidentified. [**82** Bury = B13. 17; a few of Ivo's letters appear in Cambridge, Pembroke College, MS 69, fols. 63r–65v, 74r–76v (Bury B. 95), but they have no rubric nor any entry in the table of contents.]

21 Pannomiorum vel decretorum lib. 8   *Exceptiones* . . .   93.80.82.13.115.39.71

    R35. 7. *Panormia. PL* 161. 1041; incipit is that of the prologue. **82** Bury = B13. 16, 'Canones Yvonis'. The remaining location numbers probably were taken from the *Registrum*, but its text is corrupt here.

22 Decreta etiam apostolica abbreviando compilavit, quae quidem prius Ysidorus in unum magnum volumen redegerat, quae compilatio intitulatur Summa decretorum Yvonis exceptiones

    Vincent XXVI 84 (whole entry).

23 De regulis ecclesiasticis   *Exceptiones* . . .   15.1

    R35. 18. The *Exceptiones ecclesiasticarum regularum*, printed by *PL* as the prologue for both *21* and *22* (*PL* 161. 47) above, also circulated alone.

24 De missa tract. 1

> This work and its source are unidentified. The words 'et de misteriis misse' appear at the end of the title of *16* above, in Kirkestede's table of contents in Cambridge, St John's College, MS D. 19 (Bury Y. 24), but there is no mention of the mass in the work's rubric (fol. 98v).

25 De Minerva dea sapientiae

> This work and its source are unidentified.

668 YPOLITUS episcopus floruit circa A. Ch. 235 et scripsit juxta Jeronimum ubi supra et juxta Vincentium in Speculo lib. 12 cap. 30

> The whole entry save the date comes jointly from Vincent XII 30 and Jerome c. 61.

1 Exameron super Genesin

2 Super Exodum

3 Super Cantica Canticorum

4 Super Zachariam

5 Super psalterium

6 Super Ysaiam

7 Super Danielem

8 Super Apocalipsin

9 De Proverbiis

10 De Ecclesiaste

11 De Saul [et] Phitonissa

12 De Antichristo

13 De resurrectione contra Marcionem

14 De Pascha contra omnes haereses

15 De laude Domini Salvatoris

16 De ratione Paschae et canone temporum

669 YSAAC floruit circa A. Ch. <*blank*> et scripsit juxta Genadium libro De viris illustribus

    Gennadius c. 26 (whole entry).

1 De Trinitate

2 De incarnatione

670 YSAAC alius Antiochenae ecclesiae presbyter floruit circa A. Ch. 458 et scripsit juxta Genadium

    Gennadius c. 67 (whole entry save the date).

1 Contra Nestorianos et Euticianos

2 De ruina Antiochiae

671 YPOCRAS

1 De judiciis infirmitatis   *Sapientissimus* . . .

    Ps. Hippocrates. This is probably the translation made by William of Moerbeke; see L. Thorndike in *Janus* 49 (1960) 103–129. A manuscript of this translation (Leipzig UL MS 1143) is edited by K. Sudhoff in *Archiv für Geschichte der Medizin* 16 (1925) 95–102.

p. 149]

672 YSICHIUS monachus et discipulus Hilarionis floruit anno <*blank*> et scripsit multa secundum Cassiodorum

    See also Esicius *170*.
    The reference to Cassiodorus has not been identified.

YSUARDUS supra in U verbo **USUARDUS**

    See Usuardus *663*.

Zacharias *673.*

673 ZACHARIAS Crisopolitanus floruit A. Ch. <*blank*> et scripsit

Registrum 62.

1 Unum ex quatuor seu concordiam evangelistarum et desuper expositionem continuam   *De excellentia . . . ascensionis*   43.108

R62. 1. *PL* 186. 11.

674 ZOROASTES qui et CHAM dicebatur magicae artis inventor floruit tempore Abrahae

Higden, 2. 276 (whole entry).

1 Hic vii ar

Add. 3470, the whole queried by Tanner   qui septem liberales artes in quatuordecim columnis . . . conscripsit *Higden*

NOMINA DOCTORUM qui scribunt super Bibliam

Numbers in brackets refer to the author and work in the text of the *Catalogus*. Names without a number were added to this table by Kirkestede from other sources.

SUPER GENESIN

Augustinus super Genesin ad literam [*1.184*]

Augustinus de Genesi contra Manichaeos [*1.186*]

Augustinus de 7 diebus in Genesi [*1.198*]

Augustinus de Adam et temptatione Abrahae [*1.2, 26*]

   Adam *queried by Tanner*

Augustinus de benedictionibus Jacob et Esau [*1.37*]

Augustinus quod homo factus est ad imaginem Dei [*1.207*]

Augustinus de S. Joseph et de connubio Jacob [*1.221, 240*]

Augustinus de locutionibus in Genesi [*1.258*]

Augustinus de cataclismo [*1.90*]

Augustinus de luctatione Jacob [*1.259*]

Augustinus de lapsu et reparatione hominis et de paradiso [*1.260*]

Ambrosius de operibus sex dierum [*2.23*]

Ambrosius de arca Noe [*2.1*]

Ambrosius de Abraham et de Abel et Caym [*2.2–3*]

Ambrosius de Assenech [*2.4*]

   Asseneth *Add. 3470, queried by Tanner*

Ambrosius de benedictionibus patriarcharum [*2.12*]

Ambrosius de Jacob et Joseph [*2.39–40*]

Ambrosius de paradiso [*2.57*]

Ambrosius de Ysaac [*2.95*]

Alcuynus super Genesin ad literam [*7.5*]

Andreas Auctus episcopus [*13.1*]

   Entry queried by Tanner

Apion Exameron [*23.1*]

Abbas de Pratellis super Genesim in libris 31

Basilius Exameron [*78.1*]

Beda [*84.1*]

Bruno [*91.1*]

Gregorius papa [*203.15*]

Gregorius Emissenus [cf. *206*]

Galfridus abbas Clarevallensis [*216.1*]

Haymo [*240.1*]

Hugo de S. Victore [*244.48*]

Jeronimus de Genesi [*281.34*]

Jeronimus de ignorantia Ysaac in benedicendo filios [*281.146*]

Johannes Crisostomus de Adam et Eva, Jacob et Esau et Joseph [*282.23–25*]

   Jacob et Esau et Jacob *Add. 3470*

Johannes Crisostomus de fide Abrahae et immolatione Ysaac [*282.39*]

Methodius de Genesi [*361.4*]

Origenes [*404.1*]

Rabanus [*492.3*]

Odo [*405.2*]

Prudentius [*469.3*]

NOMINA DOCTORUM

Radulfus Niger [495.2]
Petrus de Tharnetesia [446.1]
Philo Judaeus [452.1]
Robertus Herfordensis [506.1]
Robertus Lincolniensis Exameron, item testamenta xii patriarcharum [505.12, 35]
Paschasius monachus [436.4]
Stephanus Cantuariensis [554.1]
Strabus [552.1]
Victorinus [619.1]
Ysidorus [666.1]
Ypolitus [668.1]
Sidonius [544.5]

SUPER EXODUM
Augustinus de Cantico Exodi [1.48]
Andreas [13.2]
Beda [84.1]
Haymo [240.1]
Hugo [244.48]
Origenes [404.2]
Odo [405.2]
Petrus de Tharnetersia [446.2]
Philo Judaeus [452.1]
Rabanus [492.4]
Radulfus Niger [495.2]
Robertus Herfordensis [506.2]
Stephanus Cantuariensis [554.2]
Victorinus [619.2]
Ysidorus [666.2]
Ypolitus [668.2]
Strabus [552.1]
Galfridus Clarevallensis [216.1]
Bruno [91.1]

Johannes Crisostomus de Moyse [282.26]
Petrus Pictavensis de tabernaculo Moysy [441.2]
Ammonius de constantia Moysi [30.1]
Gregorius [cf. 203]

SUPER LEVITICUM
Andreas [13.3]
Beda [84.1]
Bruno [91.1]
Esicius [170.1]
Gilbertus [215.3]
Galfredus [216.1]
Haymo [240.1]
Hugo [244.48]
Origenes [404.3]
Odo Cluniacensis [405.2]
Philo Judaeus [452.1]
Petrus de Tharneteysia [446.3]
Rabanus [492.7]
Radulphus Flaviacensis [494.1]
Radulphus Niger [495.2]
Robertus Herefordensis [506.3]
Stephanus Cantuariensis [554.5]
Victorinus [619.3]
Ysidorus [666.3]
Augustinus [1.258]
Gregorius [cf. 203]
Jeronimus [281.34]
Strabus [552.1]

p. 150]

SUPER NUMERUM
Andreas [*13.4*]
Beda [*84.1*]
Bruno [*91.1*]
Galfridus [*216.1*]
Haymo [*240.1*]
Hugo [*244.48*]
Origenes [*404.4*]
Odo [*405.2*]
Petrus de Tharnetersia [*446.4*]
Philo Judaeus [*452.1*]
Rabanus [*492.5*]
Radulphus Niger [*495.2*]
Robertus Herfordensis [*506.4*]
Stephanus Cantuariensis [*554.3*]
Ysidorus [*666.5*]
Augustinus [*1.258*]
Gregorius [cf. *203*]

SUPER DEUTERONOMIUM
Andreas [*13.5*]
Beda [*84.1*]
Bruno [*91.1*]
Gilbertus [cf. *215*]
Galfridus [*216.1*]
Haymo [*240.1*]
Hugo [*244.48*]
Odo [*405.2*]
Origenes [*404.5*]
Petrus de Tharnet. [*446.5*]
Philo Judaeus [*452.1*]
Rabanus [*492.8*]
Radulphus Niger [*495.2*]
Stephanus Cantuariensis [*554.4*]
Ysidorus [*666.4*]
Adamantius [cf. *33*]

Jeronimus [*281.109*]
Augustinus [*1.258*]
Gregorius [cf. *203*]

SUPER JOSUE VEL JEHU NAVE
Andreas [*13.6*]
Adamantius [*33.3*]
Augustinus [*1.258*]
Beda [*84.16*]
Origenes [*404.6*]
Jeronimus [*281.47*]
Stephanus Cantuariensis [*554.6*]
Ysidorus [*666.6*]
Gregorius [cf. *203*]

SUPER JUDICES
Andreas [*13.7*]
Adamantius [*33.3*]
Augustinus [*1.237*]
Beda [*84.17*]
Origenes [*404.7*]
Jeronimus [*281.34?*]
Stephanus Cantuariensis [*554.22*]
Ysidorus [*666.7*]
Claudius [cf. *119*]
Augustinus [*1.258*]
Gregorius [cf. *203*]

SUPER RUTH
Bellator presbyter [*105.1*]
Origenes [*404.30*]
Isidorus [*666.9*]
Quidam monachus

SUPER LIBROS REGUM
Angelonius [*10.1*]
Andreas [*13.8*]
Beda [*84.5*]
Jeronimus [*281.57*]
Origenes [*404.9*]
Rabanus [*492.6*]
Radulphus Flaviacensis [*494.5*]
Radulphus Niger [*495.1*]
Robertus Herefordensis [*506.6*]
Stephanus Cantuariensis [*554.7*]
Ysidorus [*666.8*]
Ypolitus de Saul et Phitonissa [*668.11*]
Augustinus de S. Helia [*1.210*]
Augustinus de pugna David et Goliae [*1.376*]
Augustinus de praevaricatione Salomonis [*1.433*]
Ambrosius de judicio Salomonis inter duas mulieres [*2.78*]
Ambrosius de Davide [*2.22*]
Ambrosius de Helia [*2.36*]
Ambrosius de poenitentia Salamonis [*2.79*]
Methodius de Phitonissa [*361.3*]
Genadius [*210.3*]
Alcuynus [cf. 7]

SUPER YSAIAM
Augustinus [*1.511*]
Ambrosius [*2.96*]
Andreas [*13.12*]
Albertus [*56.33*]
Beda [*84.8*]
Bernardus [*85.31*]
    Bernardus queried by Tanner

Eusebius [*159.2*]
Haymo [*240.2*]
Jeronimus [*281.18*]
Origenes [*404.16*]
Petrus Cantor Parisiensis [*442.5*]
Richardus de S. Victore [*498.23*]
Stephanus [*554.10*]
Victorinus [*619.4*]
Ypolitus [*668.6*]
Didimus [*144.5*]
Thomas de Aquino [*567.52*]

SUPER JEREMIAM
Andreas [*13.13*]
Albertus [*56.34*]
Beda [*84.10*]
Cassiodorus [*111.9*]
Gilbertus [*215.2*]
Gregorius Nazianzenus [*204.14*]
Hugo [*244.6*]
Jeronimus [*281.19*]
Johannes Crisostomus de Jeremia [*282.27*]
Origenes [*404.17*]
Paschasius [*436.3*]
Petrus Cantor Parisiensis [*442.6*]
Rabanus [*492.14*]
Thomas de Aquino [*567.53*]
Pascasius tantum super Lamentationes [*436.3*]

SUPER EZECHIELEM
Albertus [*56.35*]
Gregorius papa [*203.7*]
Origenes [*404.18*]
Jeronimus [*281.20*]

Petrus Cantor Parisiensis [*442.7*]
Robertus Crikeladensis [cf. *506*]
Hugo de S. Victore [*244.51*]
Victorinus [*619.5*]

SUPER DANIELEM
Andreas [*13.14*]
Albertus [*56.36*]
Beda [*84.9*]
Jeronimus [*281.21*]
Origenes [cf. *404*]
Richardus de S. Victore [*498.8*]
Ypolitus [*668.7*]
Petrus Commestor [*440.5*]
Mennadius [*384.1*]
Porfirius [cf. *459*]
Judas unus de LXX [*327.1*]

SUPER XII PROPHETAS
Ambrosius [*2.56*]
Albertus [*56.37*]
Beda [*84.11*]
Jeronimus [*281.22–33*]
Stephanus [*554.11*]
Robertus de Herfordensis [*506.8*]
Didimus [*144.6–7*]
Andreas [*13.15*]
Pamphilius [*438.1*]
Joachim abbas [*293.2*]
Pierius presbiter super Osee [*457*]
Verecundus super quaedam cantica prophetarum [*656.1*]
Ypolitus super Zachariam [*668.4*]
Ricardus super Johelem et Naum [*498.17–18*]
Victorinus super Abacuch [*619.6*]

SUPER JOB
Augustinus [*1.17, 255*]
Ambrosius [*2.43*]
Ambrosius alius [*20.2*]
Albertus [*56.31*]
Beda [*84.19*]
Didimus [*144.8*]
Gregorius [*203.1*]
Origenes [*404.10*]
Petrus Blesensis [*444.1*]
Philippus [*456.1*]
Robertus Lincolniensis [*505.23*]
Hillarius [*242.14*]
Jeronimus [*281 headnote*]

SUPER PSALTERIUM
Augustinus [*1.347*]
Ambrosius super Beati immaculati et notulas super totum psalterium [*2.13, 65*]
Alexander Nequam [*4.3*]
Anselmus [*3.37*]
Cassiodorus [*III.2*]
Didimus [*144.1*]
Gilbertus [*212.3*]
Hugo super quosdam versus psalmorum [*244.22*]
Jeronimus [*281.14–15*]
Henricus Huntedoniensis super Beati immaculati [*260.1*]
Petrus Cantor Parisiensis [*442.3*]
Radulphus Flaviacensis [*494.6*]
Ricardus de S. Victore [*498.37*]
Menegaldus [*375.1*]
Robertus Lincolniensis [*505.13*]
Robertus Herfordensis [*506.7*]

Robertus Pullus [507.1]
Ricardus Fisacre [513.1]
Nicolaus de Lyra [403.2]
Thomas de Aquino [567.50]
Theodorus [572.4]
Thomas de Sutton [584.9]
Yvo [667.17]
Serlo [cf. 562]
Gilbertus [212.3]
Eusebius [159.13]
Eusebius alius [161.1]
Petrus Lumbardus [439.2]
Johannes Crisostomus super quosdam psalmos [282.7–10]
Ypolitus [668.5]
Remigius [cf. 497]
Hillarius [242.17–19]

Achacius [19.1]
Beda [84.20]
Bernardus de Trilia [97.3]
Epiphanius [158.4]
Gerardus [223.2]
Hugo [244.4]
Jeronimus [281.16]
Radulphus Flaviacensis [494.7]
Richardus de S. Victore [498.29]
Theodorus [593.2]
Victorinus [619.7]
Ypolitus [668.10]
Wilhelmus de Altona [638.3]
Sidonius [544.4]
Origenes [cf. 404]
Gregorius [cf. 203]
Rabanus [cf. 492]

SUPER PARABOLA SALOMONIS
Andreas [13.11]
Beda [84.6]
Didimus [144.11]
Epiphanius [158.4]
Jeronimus [281.49]
Bernardus de Trilia [97.1]
Rabanus [492.17]
Radulphus Flaviacensis [494.4]
Theophilus [574.4]
Ypolitus [668.9]
Gregorius [cf. 203]

SUPER ECCLESIASTEN
Alexander Nequam [4.7]
Alcuynus [7.8]
Andreas [13.10]

SUPER CANTICA CANTICORUM
Augustinus [1.68]
Anselmus [3.31]
Alexander Nequam [4.2]
Adelredus [5.8]
Alcuynus [7.6]
Albertus [56.32]
Epiphanius [158.3]
Berengaudus [82.2]
Beda [84.7]
Bernardus [85.12]
Bernardus de Trilia [97.2]
Cassiodorus [111.8]
Gregorius [203.6]
Gregorius de Bridelington [208.1]
Gilbertus [212.5]
Galfridus [216.2]

Hillarius [242.6]
Hugo [244.26]
Jeronimus [281.50]
Justus episcopus [299.1]
Origenes [404.14]
Robertus Herfordensis [506.9]
Rethicius [518.1]
Stephanus [554.17]
Thomas de Aquino [567.54]
Triphilius [581.1]
Wilhelmus Parvus [627.1]
Wilhelmus de Ramesia [626.1]
Victorinus [619.8]
Ysidorus [666.11]
Ypolitus [668.3]
Methodius [361.4]
Henricus Teutonicus [270.3]

SUPER ECCLESIASTICUM
Hugo [244.5]
Jeronimus [281.17]
Nicholaus Gorham [399.1]
Petrus Cantor [442.4]
Rabanus [492.13]
Robertus Holcote [515.4]
Stephanus [554.16]
Wilhelmus de Kingesham [649.1]

SUPER LIBRUM SAPIENTIAE
Bellator presbyter [105.2]
Bernard de Trilia [97.4]
Rabanus [492.12]
Robertus de Holcote [515.3]

SUPER PARALIPOMENON
Andreas [13.9]

Origenes [404.29]
Rabanus [492.9]
Stephanus [554.8]
Radulphus Niger [495.3]

SUPER ESDRAM
Beda [84.12]
Stephanus [554.15]
Ysidorus [666.10]
Bellator [105.3]
Radulphus Niger [495.4]

SUPER HESTER
Cassiodorus [111.12]
Rabanus [492.11]
Stephanus [554.14]
Bellator [105.5]

SUPER JUDITH
Cassiodorus [111.13]
Rabanus [492.10]
Stephanus [554.13]
Bellator [105.6]

SUPER TOBIAM
Andreas [cf. 13]
Beda [84.14]
Cassiodorus [111.11]
Stephanus [554.12]
Bellator [105.4]

SUPER MACHABAEOS
Bellator [105.7]
Cassiodorus [111.14]
Gregorius Nazianzanus [204.2]
Rabanus [492.15]
Stephanus [554.9]

Johannes Crisostomus [*282.48*]
Beda [cf. *84*]

p. 151]

SUPER 4ʳ EVANGELIA

Augustinus super Johannem omelias et super Mathaeum et Lucam quaestiones [*1.215, 160, 407, 410*]

Augustinus de concordia evangeliorum [*1.83*]

Ambrosius super Lucam, omelias in ejusdem super evangelia [*2.47*]

Adelredus super evangelium Cum factus esset Jesus annorum, et super Nemo accendit [*5.1, 17*]

Alcuynus super Johannem [*7.9*]

Albertus super quatuor evangelia [*56.38–39*]

Beda super Mathaeum, Marcum et Lucam, et super quaedam evangelia omelias 50 [*84.55, 22–24*]

Bernardus super Missus e[s]t, Magnificat, Intravit, Cum esset desponsata, et Ecce nos reliquimus [*85.13–14, 28, 30*]

    Magnificat] Magister Add. 3470, queried by Tanner

Bernardus de Trilia super Johannem [*97.5*]

Claudius super Mathaeum et Johannem [*119.1*]

Eusebius Caesariensis super omnia evangelia [*159.9*]

Eusebius Emissenus super omnia evangelia [*162.3*]

Gregorius papa omelia super evangelia [*203.4*]

Galfridus super Matthaeum [*216.3*]

Haymo super evangelia totius anni [*240.5*]

Babio super Mathaeum [*107.1*]

Hilarius super Mathaeum [*242.13*]

Jeronimus super 4ʳ evangelia [*281.35–36*]

Johannes Crisostomus super Mathaeum et Johannem [*282.4–5*]

Juvencus super 4ʳ evangelia [*310.1*]

Maximus super evangelia [cf. *359.9*]

Nicolaus de Gorham super Lucam et Mathaeum [*399.2*]

Origenes super Mathaeum et Lucam et principium Johannis [*404.19–21*]

Petrus de Tharnet. super Lucam [*446.6*]

Rabanus super Mathaeum [*492.16*]

Radulphus Flaviacensis super Mathaeum [*494.8*]

Remigius super 4 evangelia [*497.1*]

Robertus Herfordensis super Mathaeum [*506.10*]

Salmanus super evangelia [*530.7*]

Johannes de Alba Villa super evangelia [*334.1–2*]

Theodorus super Mathaeum et Johannem [*572.1–2*]

Theophilus super quatuor evangelia [*574.5*]

Victorinus super Mathaeum [*619.11*]

Wilhelmus de Montibus super evangelia [*625.6*]

Christoforus Nolhamsensis super 4 evangelia [*664.1*]

    Nonhamsensis Add. 3470, queried by Tanner

Christoforus super Mathaeum, Marcum et Lucam [665.1]
Ysidorus super 4 evangelia [666.12]
Zacharias de concordantia evangeliorum [673.1]
Anselmus super Mathaeum et Johannem [3.51]
Clemens Lantoniensis de concordia evangeliorum [115.1]
Tatianus de concordia evangeliorum [568.1]
Marianus super Lucam [367.2]
Augustinus super evangelia omelias 50 [1.337]
Ammonius canones evangeliorum excogitavit, quos postea Eusebius plenius collegit [30.2]
Gilbertus super Mathaeum [212.4]
Petrus Cantor super evangelia [442.12]

SUPER EPISTOLAS PAULI

Augustinus super epistolas ad Romanos et Galathas [1.143, 145, 159]
Augustinus de verbis apostoli sermo [1.480–481]
Ambrosius super epistolas omnes [2.61]
Anselmus super omnes epistolas [3.38]
Alcuynus super epistolam ad Hebraeos [7.7]
Albertus super omnes epistolas [56.40]
Beda super omnes epistolas [84.61]
Cassiodorus super epistolam ad Romanos [111.15]
Gilbertus super omnes epistolas [212.1]
Haymo super omnes epistolas [240.3]
Hildegardus super omnes epistolas [249.7]
Heraclitus super omnes epistolas [273.1]
Jeronimus super omnes epistolas [281.37–40]
Johannes Crisostomus super omnes epistolas [282.45]
Bruno super omnes epistolas [91.2]
Menegaldus super omnes epistolas [375.2]
Nicholaus de Gorham super omnes epistolas [399.3]
Origenes super epistolam ad Romanos [404.22]
Petrus Lumbardus super omnes epistolas [439.3]
Petrus de Tharnet. super omnes epistolas [446.7]
Petrus Tripolitanae super omnes epistolas [480]
Rabanus super epistolas Colicenses et Galatas et Ephesios [492.18]
Radulphus Flaviacensis super omnes epistolas [494.2]
Remigius super omnes epistolas [497.5]
Robertus Lincolniensis super epistolam ad Galatas [505.14]
Thomas de Linduno super omnes epistolas Pauli [585.1]
Victorinus rethor super omnes epistolas Pauli [620.2]
Christoforus Norhamsensis super omnes epistolas Pauli [664.2]

SUPER EPISTOLAS CANONICAS

Augustinus super epistolas Jacobi et Johannis [*1.139–140*]

Beda super omnes epistolas canonicas [*84.27*]

Bernardus super epistolam Jacobi [*85.32*]

Cassiodorus super omnes epistolas canonicas [*111.16*]

Didimus super omnes epistolas canonicas [*144.12*]

Jeronimus super omnes epistolas canonicas [*281.42–45*]

Nicholaus de Gorham super omnes epistolas canonicas [*399.4*]

Christoforus Nolhamsensis super omnes epistolas canonicas [*664.3*]

Haymo super epistolas totius anni [*240.5*]

Johannes de Alba Villa super epistolas totius anni [*334.1–2*]

Johannes Crisostomus super omnes epistolas canonicas [cf. *282*]

SUPER ACTUS APOSTOLORUM

Arator poeta [*22*]
Jeronimus [*281.41*]
Lentius [*350.1*]
Petrus Parisiensis Cantor [*442.9*]
Johannes Crisostomus [*282.46*]
Rabanus [cf. *492*]
Beda [*84.26*]

SUPER APOCALIPSIN

Augustinus [*1.23*]
Ambrosius [*2.7*]
Anselmus [*3.52*]
Apringius [*18.1*]
Albertus [*56.74*]
Berengaudus [*82.3*]
Berengarius [*96.1*]
Beda [*84.28*]
Gilbertus [*212.6*]
Galfridus [*216.4*]
Haymo [*240.4*]
Henricus Costesay [*271.1*]
Jeronimus [*281.46*]
Nicholaus de Gorham [*399.5*]
Petrus Cantor Parisiensis [*442.10*]
Primasius [*467.2*]
Rabanus [*492.19*]
Radulphus Flaviacensis [*494.3*]
Robertus Herfordensis [*506.12*]
Victori[n]us [*619.9*]
Wilhelmus Gallicus [*647.1*]
Ypolitus [*668.8*]
Joachim abbas [*293.1*]

SUPER TOTUM VETUS ET NOVUM TESTAMENTUM

Augustinus [*1.403, 454*]
Ambrosius [*2.67*]
Alexander Nequam [*4.9*]
Alcuinus [*7.14*]
Adrianus [*45.1*]
    Adamantius Add. 3470, queried by Tanner
Albertus [*58.1*]
Basilius [*78.9*]
Clemens [*114.9*]
Didimus [*144.10*]
Hugo [*244.54, 65*]

NOMINA DOCTORUM

Jeronimus [*281 headnote*]
Johannes Crisostomus [*282.47*]
Junilius [*307.1*]
Lanfrancus [*344.3*]
Optatus [*44.2*]
Paterius [*437.1*]
    Paterius *queried by Tanner*
Petrus Commestor [*440.1–2*]

Petrus Cantor Parisiensis [*442.1–2*]
Nicolaus de Lyra [*403.1*]
Sedulius [*531.2*]
Ysidorus [*666.19*]
Robertus Herefordensis [*506.13*]
Hugo de S. Victore [*244.54, 65*]
Petrus Lumbardus [cf. *439*]

p. 152]
    Qui legis hunc librum scriptoris Rex miserere.
    Dum scripsit vere non fecit ut aestimo pigrum.
    Si tibi displiciat veniat tua gratia grandis
    Quam cunctis pandis haec sibi sufficiat.
    Scriptoris nomen Botulphi villa vocatur,
    Qui condempnatur, nisi gratum det Deus omen.

APPENDIX

KIRKESTEDE'S LOCATION NUMBERS

A large proportion of the information that the *Catalogus* appears to provide about the location of its authors' works is second-hand, borrowed directly from the information that the Oxford Franciscans had recorded from first-hand reports early in the 14th cent., in the *Registrum Anglie de libris doctorum et auctorum veterum*. Nevertheless, Kirkestede included in his catalogue a significant body of additional information on the location of books, representing his own knowledge pertinent to the mid 14th cent. In this appendix we attempt to single out the information that is new and specific to the *Catalogus*, setting forth the evidence on which our judgment is based. In the process we also take into account the fact that numbers easily fall victim to copyists' errors.

Each ecclesiastical library is listed here in the numerical order of the *Nomina locorum* in the *Catalogus*; we record its name as spelt in that list, followed by its modern identification. The heading also includes references to Ker, *MLGB* (for surviving manuscripts from the library), and to the relevant volume of the Corpus of British Medieval Library Catalogues (for surviving medieval catalogues or booklists). In the notice for each library we list the works reported from it, divided among four categories depending on the faithfulness of the reference, in detailed list or in summary. We first list in detail the occasions where the library's number appears with works that Kirkestede added to the information in his sources. Second, we state the number of times that the location number was added to a title copied from the *Registrum* (i.e. the title, but not the number, is a copy); and if it seems possible that these additions may be genuine rather than mistakes of some sort, we list those instances in detail too. An asterisk (*) beside a title indicates the existence of external evidence that corroborates the presence of this work – or something that Kirkestede assumed to be this work – in the library concerned (such as a surviving manuscript or a medieval catalogue reference). Third, we give in summary the total instances when the number was simply copied, along with the title, from the *Registrum*. Fourth, we point out any appearances of a library's number that are clearly erroneous (details are provided in the relevant entry in the *Catalogus*). In a concluding statement, we evaluate the likelihood that Kirkestede's report reflects his personal knowledge of the books at this location.[1]

1. By 'personal knowledge' we mean that Kirkestede had current information about an institution's books beyond what was available in the *Registrum*. Normally, that would mean that he visited the library in question, but we realize it is also possible that he occasionally took his information from a booklist, from the report of a visiting monk, from a borrowed codex that came temporarily to Bury, or from some similar source.

APPENDIX

In summary, these are the book collections about which Kirkestede had, or probably had, direct and current knowledge: **10** Holy Trinity Aldgate, **11** Westminster, **15** St Albans, **45** Warden, **50** Pipewell, **61** Peterborough, **63** Crowland, **65** Ramsey, **68** Saffron Walden, **73** Norwich cathedral priory, **74** Holme St Benets, **77** Sibton, **79** Butley, **81** Ipswich St Peter's, **82** Bury St Edmunds, **83** Colchester St John's, **84** Colchester St Botulph's, **85** St Osyth's, **86** Coggeshall, **147** Spalding, **168** Oxford Greyfriars, **169** Ixworth, **170** Thetford Blackfriars, **173** Babwell, **175** Barking. He possibly also had first-hand knowledge of the following: **14** Stratford Langthorne, **19** London St Paul's, **42** Reading, **43** Woburn, **44** Dunstable, **62** Thorney, **64** Barnwell, **67** Ely, **78** Leiston, **80** Ipswich Holy Trinity, **166** Hexham, and **174** Earls Colne. The names of these thirty-six libraries are printed in capitals in the list below.

1   *Cantuariae Trinitatis*: Canterbury (Kent), Benedictine cathedral priory of Holy Trinity or Christ Church. Ker, *MLGB*, 29.

With works added by Kirkestede this number appears once: Robert Grosseteste *505.36*. In thirteen instances this number is added to works taken from the *Registrum*: Augustine *1.53, 338, 418, 450, 456*, Bernard *85.8, 21*, Jerome *281.38*, Ivo *667.4, 16*. In 190 instances this number is copied with works taken from the *Registrum*. In eight instances its presence is an obvious error: Augustine *1.70, 459*, Ambrose *2.94*, Jerome *281.39, 40, 53*, Lanfranc *344.2*, Peter of Blois *444.8*, and Peter Kilwardby *510.13*. Kirkestede had no personal knowledge of this library.

2   *Cantuariae Augustini*: Canterbury (Kent), Benedictine abbey of St Augustine. Ker, *MLGB*, 40.

This number appears once with a work added by Kirkestede, Kilwardby *510.13*, in a dubious number-series. In two instances this number is added to works taken from the *Registrum*: Augustine *1.6* and Haimo *240.5*. In two cases it is an obvious mistake, Bernard *85.12* and Peter of Blois *444.8*. This number was not used by the compilers of the *Registrum*. Kirkestede had no personal knowledge of this library.

3   *Cantuariae Gregorii*: Canterbury (Kent), Augustinian priory of St Gregory. Ker, *MLGB*, 47; Webber & Watson, *Augustinians*, A7.

With a work added by Kirkestede this number appears once, Aristotle *46.29*. In one instance, Isidore *666.16*, the number is added to a work taken from the *Registrum*. In another instance this number is copied with a work taken from the *Registrum*. This number was not used by the *Registrum*'s compilers. Kirkestede had no personal knowledge of this library.

5   *Ledes*: Leeds (Kent), Augustinian priory of B.V.M. and St Nicholas. Ker, *MLGB*, 112.

APPENDIX

This number appears twice only, Gregory *203.6* and Haimo *240.4*, in both cases as an obvious mistake. The *Registrum* makes no use of this number. Kirkestede had no personal knowledge of this library.

7 *Rofa*: Rochester (Kent), Benedictine cathedral priory of St Andrew. Ker, *MLGB*, 160; Sharpe & others, *Benedictines*, B77–83.

This number appears once, Prudentius *469.2*, as a mistake for **1**. The *Registrum* makes no use of this number. Kirkestede had no personal knowledge of this library.

8 *Batalie*: Battle (Sussex), Benedictine abbey of St Martin. Ker, *MLGB*, 7; Sharpe & others, *Benedictines*, B9.

This number appears once with a work added by Kirkestede, Kilwardby *510.13*, in a series of numbers of doubtful authenticity. In four instances this number is added to works taken from the *Registrum*: Augustine *1.67*, Anselm *3.15*, Bede *84.6*, and Isidore *666.40*; in each case a plausible emendation would be **83**. In eighty-eight instances **8** has been copied with works taken from the *Registrum*. This number also appears with eighty-nine epistles of Jerome *281*, an extrapolation from *Registrum*'s single entry 'Epistole Ieronimi'. Eight other appearances are obvious errors: Augustine *1.390*, Bernard *85.5*, Gregory *203.6, 9*, Chrysostom *282.2, 14*, Lanfranc *344.1, 2*. Kirkestede had no personal knowledge of this library.

9 *Merthone*: Merton (Surrey), Augustinian priory of B.V.M. Ker, *MLGB*, 130.

With works added by Kirkestede this number appears twice: Augustine *1.183* and Hilary *242.1*. In seven instances this number is added to works taken from the *Registrum*: Augustine *1.34, 74, 225, 330*, Ambrose *2.38*, Bede *84.6*, Innocent *283.1*. In 133 instances this number is copied with works taken from the *Registrum*. This number appears also with eighty-nine epistles of Jerome *281*, extrapolated from *Registrum*'s single entry 'Epistole Ieronimi'. In eleven other instances the appearance of this number is an obvious error: Augustine *1.311*, Bernard *85.5*, Origen *404.20*, Richard of St Victor *498.15*, Ivo *667.6–12*. Although Kirkestede knew various libraries in the London area (see **10**, **11**, **19** below), it is doubtful that he travelled as far south as Merton. Kirkestede probably had no personal knowledge of this library.

10 LONDON. TRINITATIS: London, Augustinian priory of Holy Trinity, Aldgate. Ker, *MLGB*, 123.

With works added by Kirkestede this number appears twenty-two times: Augustine *1.182 Extrema verba Augustine de fide*, Bonaventure *89.5 Meditationes et contemplationes*, Eusebius presbyter *160.6 De corpore et sanguine Domini*, Fabius Planciades Fulgentius *185.1 Mithologiarum*, Ovid *412.1 De nuce, 6 De tristibus, 8 De Ponto, 10 Invectionis in Ibin, 11 De mirabilibus, 12 De cuculo, 13 De pulice, 15 De

APPENDIX

anulo, *16 De sompno*, *17 De medicamine faciei*, *18 De medicamine aurium*, Paul the Deacon *426.2 Historiam Romanorum*, Thomas Aquinas *567.45 De 10 praeceptis*, *47 De articulis fidei*, *75 Super Mathaeum*, *76 De salutatione angelica*, *77 Super simbolum*, *78 Super Magnificat*. In three instances this number is added to works taken from the *Registrum*: Augustine *1.167 Contra Felicem Manichaeum*, Bede *84.4 De templo Salomonis*, *6 Super Proverbia Salomonis*. The *Registrum*'s compilers made no use of this (arabic) number. In seventeen instances this number is copied (for **x**, an unidentified *Registrum* location) with works taken from the *Registrum*. Kirkestede had personal knowledge of this library.

11   WESTMONASTERIVM: Westminster, Benedictine abbey of St Peter. Ker, *MLGB*, 195; Sharpe & others, *Benedictines*, B104–108.

With works added by Kirkestede this number appears eight times: Eusebius Emesenus *162.5 Omelias ad monachos*, Gilbert Foliot *213.1 Super Cantica*, Hugh *244.87 Super Psalterium*, Hildebert *247.9 Sermones quamplures*, Lawrence **358.1 Sermones*, Mauricius **394.1 Distinctiones*, Petrus Comestor *440.8 Super Cantica epitalamium*, Stephen Langton *554.25 Super Ecclesiasten*. Of these eight, every work is given its incipit and, in every case but Eusebius, **11** is the only location number given; the Westminster manuscript of Lawrence's sermons can be positively identified by its anomalous incipit (see p. cxx above). In two instances this number is added to works taken from the *Registrum*, Aelred *5.14 Vitam S. Edwardi confessoris*, and Gilbert Crispin *214.1 De disputatione Iudaei cum Christiano*. **11** was not used by the *Registrum*'s compilers. Kirkestede had personal knowledge of this library.

12   *S. Maria ultra pontem*: Southwark (Surrey), Augustinian priory of St Mary Overy. Ker, *MLGB*, 180.

In thirty-seven instances this number is copied (for **xii** in thirty-five of these; for **xix**, at Richard of St Victor *498.28*) with works taken from the *Registrum*. Kirkestede had no personal knowledge of this library.

13   *Waltham*: Waltham (Essex), Augustinian abbey of Holy Cross. Ker, *MLGB*, 192; Webber & Watson, *Augustinians*, A38–39.

With works added by Kirkestede this number appears twice: Paterius *437.1 Super Vetus et Novum Testamentum*, amid a suspicious series of numbers, and Petrus Comestor *440.1 Historiam scolasticam super Bibliam*. In four instances **13** is added to works taken from the *Registrum*: Augustine *1.4*, Anselm *3.22*, Haimo *240.2*, and Rabanus *492.16*; and in fifty-three instances (for **xiii** on one occasion) this number is copied with works taken from the *Registrum*. At Bernard *85.5* the appearance of this number is an obvious error. Kirkestede had no personal knowledge of this library.

14   STRATFORDIA: Stratford Langthorne (Essex), Cistercian abbey of B.V.M. Ker, *MLGB*, 183; Bell, *Cistercians*, Z24.

APPENDIX

With works added by Kirkestede this number appears twice: Gratian *217.1 Decretum* and Jerome *281.221 Ad Theodosium*. In two instances this number is added to works taken from the *Registrum*, Peter of Blois *444.4 De conversione S. Pauli*, and Ivo of Chartres *667.6 De significatione sacerdotalium et indumentorum*. In one instance, Ivo *667.1*, it is copied, for **xxiiii**, from the *Registrum*. Kirkestede possibly had personal knowledge of this library.

15 S. Albanvs: St Albans (Hertfordshire), Benedictine abbey of St Alban. Ker, *MLGB*, 164; Sharpe & others, *Benedictines*, B85–91.

With works added by Kirkestede this number appears twenty-four times: Augustine *1.434 De spiritu et anima*, Aristotle *46.29 De coloribus*, Cassiodorus *111.7 De anima*, Caesarius *135.1 Omelias ad monachos*, *2 Ad sororem suam*, Eusebius Emesenus *162.5 Omelias ad monachos*, Ferrandus *197.1 Qualis debet esse dux religiosus*, *2 De eodem*, Gratian *217.1 Decretum*, Guido de Castris *237.1 Sanctilogium*, Haimo *240.6 In Christianarum rerum memoriam*, *74 De arte memorandi*, and **79 Beniamin*, Junilius *307.2 De regularibus institutis divinarum Scripturarum*, John of Wales *337.10 De correptione sive correctione*, John of Tynemouth *341.1 Historiam auream*, *2 Librum servorum Dei maiorem*, *3 Librum servorum Dei minorem*, Petrus Comestor **440.1 Historiam scolasticam super Bibliam*, Peter of Poitiers *441.2 Super tabernaculum Moysi*, Ratramnus *503.1 De anima*, *2 De eo quod Christus de Virgine natus est*, Thomas Aquinas *567.51 Super Job* and *53 Super Jeremiam*. For most of these works, **15** appears either alone or in company with the numbers of other libraries that Kirkestede knew at first hand. In twelve, or perhaps eighteen, instances this number is added to titles taken from the *Registrum*: Augustine *1.170 De fide ad Petrum*, *269 De mendacio*, *293 Meditationes*, *347 Super Psalterium*, Ambrose *2.26 De observantia episcoporum*, Anselm **3.21 Monologion*, Jerome *281.21 Super Danielem*, *37 Super Epistolam ad Ephesios*, *114 Glosa septimae ebdomadae*, *234 De fide S. Jeronimi*, Chrysostom *282.12 De decollatione S. Johannis*, Robert of Melun *506.3 Super Leviticum*, and perhaps six Jerome epistles, *281.73*, *78*, *143*, *152*, *159*, *168*, which may instead be extrapolations of the *Registrum* entry for epistles of Jerome. In 196 instances (four times in place of **xv**) this number is copied with works taken from the *Registrum*. In twenty instances the appearance of this number is an obvious error: Anselm *3.30*, Hugh *244.28*, Jerome *281.38–40*, *53*, *104*, *106*, Chrysostom *282.16–19*, *21–22*, *24–27*, Richard of St. Victor *498.15*, and Seneca *543.2*. Kirkestede had personal knowledge of this library.

16 *Prioratus Roberti*: Robertsbridge (Sussex), Cistercian abbey of B.V.M. Ker, *MLGB*, 160.

With works added by Kirkestede this number appears once, Paterius *437.1*. In two instances this number is copied with works taken from the *Registrum*; the *Registrum* makes no use of this (arabic) number. In two other instances the appearance of this number is an obvious error: Augustine *1.15*, *70*. Kirkestede had no personal knowledge of this library.

544

APPENDIX

18 *Novus Locus*: Newark (Surrey), Augustinian priory of B.V.M. and St Thomas the Martyr. Ker, *MLGB*, 133.

This number appears once with a work added by Kirkestede, Henry of Huntingdon *260.2*. In one instance, Jerome *281.41*, this number is copied (for **xviii**) with a work taken from the *Registrum*. This (arabic) number was not used by the compilers of the *Registrum*. Kirkestede had no personal knowledge of this library.

19 LONDON. S. PAVLI and *Waverleye*: London, cathedral church of St Paul, and Waverley (Surrey), Cistercian abbey of B.V.M. Following his copy of the *Registrum*, Kirkestede has used this number in his initial list to represent two different places. Ker, *MLGB*, 120 and 194; Bell, *Cistercians*, Z27 (Waverley).

With works added by Kirkestede this number appears twice: Henry of Huntingdon *260.2–3*. In nine instances, **19** is added to works taken from the *Registrum*: Augustine *1.4 De adulterinis coniugiis*, *269 De mendacio*, *276 De musica*, *497 De conflictu vitiorum et virtutum*, Ambrose *2.50 De misteriis*, Hugh *244.57 Cur non fit coniugium inter eundem sexum*, Rabanus *492.18 Super Epistolas Pauli ad Corinthios, Galatas, Ephesios*, Isidore *666.16 Prohemiorum de libris V. et N.T.*, Ivo *667.4 De excellentis sacrorum ordinum et de vita ordinandorum*. In eighty-three instances (three times for **xix**) this number is copied with works taken from the *Registrum*. Number **19** also appears with eighty-one epistles of Jerome *281*, extrapolated from a single *Registrum* entry 'Epistole Ieronimi'. In two other instances the appearance of this number is an obvious error: Augustine *1.311* and Bernard *85.5*. If Kirkestede understood **19** to represent St Paul's, it is possible that his additions of this number represent personal knowledge of this library.

20 *Lewes*: Lewes (Sussex), Cluniac priory of St Pancras. Ker, *MLGB*, 114; Sharpe & others, *Benedictines*, p. 260.

With works added by Kirkestede this number appears twice: Bernard of Cassino *86.1*, and Ferrandus *197.3*; for the latter no incipit and explicit are given. This number is added to a work taken from the *Registrum*: Augustine *1.4*. In seventy instances (twelve times for **xx**) this number is copied with works taken from the *Registrum*. In twelve instances the appearance of this number is an obvious error: Bernard *85.22*, Hilary *242.9*, Hugh *244.28*, Chrysostom *282.16, 21–27*, and Origen *404.20*. Kirkestede had no personal knowledge of this library.

21 Left blank in Add. 3470.

Kirkestede's use of **21** is restricted to three instances (twice for **xxi**) in which it is copied with works from the *Registrum*. Kirkestede's use of this number does not represent personal knowledge.

APPENDIX

22 *Cicestria*: Chichester (Sussex), cathedral church of Holy Trinity. Ker, *MLGB*, 50.

This number appears once with a work added by Kirkestede: Horace *411.5*. Once it is added to a work taken from the *Registrum*, Augustine *1.388*. In ten instances it is copied with works taken from the *Registrum*. In one other instance the appearance of this number is an obvious error: Ivo *667.2*. Kirkestede had no personal knowledge of this library.

23 *Suthwych*: Southwick (Hampshire), Augustinian priory of B.V.M. Ker, *MLGB*, 181; Webber & Watson, *Augustinians*, A31.

In fourteen instances (four times for **xxiii**) this number is copied with works taken from the *Registrum*. Kirkestede had no personal knowledge of this library.

24 *Tichefeld*: Titchfield (Hampshire), Premonstratensian abbey of the Assumption. Ker, *MLGB*, 190; Bell, *Cistercians*, P6.

This number appears once with a work added by Kirkestede, Jerome *281.128*. In one instance, Ivo *667.11*, it is added to a work taken from the *Registrum*. In eleven instances this number is copied, for **xxiv**, with works taken from the *Registrum*. Kirkestede had no personal knowledge of this library.

25 *Quareria*: Quarr (Isle of Wight), Cistercian abbey of B.V.M. Ker, *MLGB*, 153.

This number is added once to a work taken from the *Registrum*, Ambrose *2.38*. In nine instances (six times for **xxv**) **25** is copied with works taken from the *Registrum*. Its appearance at Innocent III *283.1* is an obvious error. Kirkestede had no personal knowledge of this library.

26 *Bellus Locus*: Beaulieu (Hampshire), Cistercian abbey of B.V.M. Ker, *MLGB*, 9; Bell, *Cistercians*, Z1.

This number is added once to a work taken from the *Registrum*, Augustine *1.4*. In six instances (twice for **xxvi**) **26** is copied with works taken from the *Registrum*. Kirkestede had no personal knowledge of this library.

27 *Rumesia*: Romsey (Hampshire), abbey of Benedictine nuns of B.V.M. and St Elfleda. Ker, *MLGB*, 164.

With works added by Kirkestede this number appears twice: Horace *411.1–2*. In one instance, Augustine *1.73*, the number is added to a work taken from the *Registrum*. In three instances **27** is copied, for **xxvii**, with works taken from the *Registrum*. Kirkestede had no personal knowledge of this library.

28 *Modesfonte*: Mottisfont (Hampshire), Augustinian priory of Holy Trinity. Ker, *MLGB*, 132.

This number appears once added to a work taken from the *Registrum*: Alexander Nequam *4.5*; *Registrum* made no use of this number. Kirkestede had no personal knowledge of this library.

APPENDIX

29 *Christi Ecclesia*: Christchurch, Twinham (Hampshire), Augustinian priory of Holy Trinity or Christ Church. Ker, *MLGB*, 51; Webber & Watson, *Augustinians*, A8.

This number appears twice, Jerome *281.119* and Palladius *423.1*, added to works taken from the *Registrum*; the *Registrum* made no use of this number. Kirkestede had no personal knowledge of this library.

30 *S. Swithini*: Winchester (Hampshire), Benedictine cathedral priory of SS. Peter, Paul, and Swithun. Ker, *MLGB*, 199; Sharpe & others, *Benedictines*, B113.

This number appears only twice, once with a work added by Kirkestede, Bernard of Cassino *86.2*, and once added to a work taken from the *Registrum*, Robert of Melun *506.3*; the *Registrum* made no use of this number. Kirkestede had no personal knowledge of this library.

31 *S. Barnabae*: Hyde (Hampshire), formerly New Minster, Winchester, Benedictine abbey of Holy Trinity, B.V.M., and St Peter. Ker, *MLGB*, 103; Sharpe & others, *Benedictines*, B51–52.

This number appears only once, Ralph of Flaix *494.1*, as an error for **13**. Kirkestede had no knowledge of this library.

32 *S. Mariae Winton.*: Winchester, abbey of B.V.M. of Benedictine nuns, commonly called Nunnaminster. Ker, *MLGB*, 201; Sharpe & others, *Benedictines*, p. 651.

In one instance (Augustine *1.63*) this number is added to a work taken from the *Registrum*. In twenty instances this number is copied with works taken from the *Registrum*. In addition, **32** appears with eighty-seven epistles (Jerome *281*), as a misreading for **22** in the *Registrum* entry 'Epistole Ieronimi'. Kirkestede had no personal knowledge of this library.

33 *S. Dionisii*: Southampton (Hampshire), Augustinian priory of St Denis. Ker, *MLGB*, 180.

This number appears twice with works added by Kirkestede: Jerome *281.73*, an epistle, and Johannes de Deo *309.3*. The *Registrum*'s compilers did not use this number. Kirkestede had no personal knowledge of this library.

34 *Werewell*: Wherwell (Hampshire), abbey of Holy Cross, of Benedictine nuns. Ker, *MLGB*, 197.

This number appears only once, with a work added by Kirkestede: Henry of Huntingdon *260.6*. The *Registrum*'s compilers made no use of this number. Kirkestede had no personal knowledge of this library.

APPENDIX

35 *Saresbiria*: Salisbury, cathedral church of B.V.M. Ker, *MLGB*, 171.

With works added by Kirkestede this number appears twice: Petrus Comestor *440.1 Historiam scolasticam*, and Peter of Poitiers *441.2 Super tabernaculum Moysi*. In nine instances this number is added to works taken from the *Registrum*: Augustine *1.4, 34, 293, 338, 347, 497*, Jerome *281.37*, Comestor *440.2*. In seventy-three instances this number is copied with works taken from the *Registrum*. This number also appears with forty-seven Jerome epistles, in company with numbers taken from the single *Registrum* entry 'Epistole Ieronimi'; **35** is presumably a misreading for *Registrum*'s **39**, perhaps a mistake in Kirkestede's copy of the *Registrum*. In five other instances in which this number is found, its presence is an obvious error: Augustine *1.126*, Jerome *281.38–40, 53*. Kirkestede had no personal knowledge of this library.

36 *Herles*: ?Ivychurch (Wiltshire), Augustinian priory of B.V.M. Not in Ker, *MLGB*.

This number appears only once, added to a work taken from the *Registrum*, Anselm *3.22*. The *Registrum*'s compilers made no use of this number. Kirkestede had no personal knowledge of this library.

37 *Oseneya*: Osney (Oxfordshire), Augustinian abbey of B.V.M. Ker, *MLGB*, 140; Webber & Watson, *Augustinians*, A26.

This number appears only twice, with works added by Kirkestede, Horace *411.3–4*. Kirkestede had no personal knowledge of this library.

39 *Eynesham*: Eynsham (Oxfordshire), Benedictine abbey of B.V.M., St Benedict, and All Saints. Ker, *MLGB*, 86; Sharpe & others, *Benedictines*, B33–34.

This number appears once with a work added by Kirkestede, Peter of Poitiers *441.2*. It is added once to a work taken from the *Registrum*, Chrysostom *282.12*, and in forty-two instances it is copied with works from the *Registrum*. In seven cases the appearance of this number is an obvious error: Chrysostom *282.16, 21–23, 25–27*. Kirkestede had no personal knowledge of this library.

41 *Thame*: Thame (Oxfordshire), Cistercian abbey of B.V.M. Ker, *MLGB*, 188.

This number appears with one work added by Kirkestede, Henry of Huntingdon *260.5*. It is added to one work taken from the *Registrum*, Augustine *1.142*. At Bernard *85.5* it appears as a mistake for **43**. The *Registrum*'s compilers made no use of this number. Kirkestede had no personal knowledge of this library.

42 RADINGIA: Reading (Berkshire), Benedictine abbey of B.V.M. Ker, *MLGB*, 154; Sharpe & others, *Benedictines*, B71–74.

With works added by Kirkestede this number appears three times: Henry of Huntingdon **260.4 De serie regum Britanniae* and *6 De sanctis Angliae*, and Horace

APPENDIX

411.6 Inopodon ad Mecaenatem. In twenty instances **42** is added to works taken from the *Registrum*: Augustine *1.59 De conjugio bono*, *105 De doctrina christiana*, *137 Epistolae*, *142 Encheridion*, *199 Contra quinque haereses*, *342 De poenitentia*, Ambrose 2.31 *De fuga saeculi*, *58 De poenitentia unica*, *86 De laude virginum*, *91 De lapsu virginis consecratae*, Anselm *3.1 De conceptu virginali*, *4 De libero arbitrio*, Bede *84.2 De tabernaculo Moysi*, *22 Super evangelium Marci*, *23 Super evangelium Lucae*, Gregory *203.5 Registrum epistolarum*, Chrysostom *282.2 De reparatione lapsi*, *3 De compunctione*, Isidore *666.24 Contra Judaeos ad sororem*, *40 Ethimologiarum*. In eighty-four instances this number is copied with works taken from the *Registrum*. Number **42** appears with eighty-eight epistles of Jerome *281* extrapolated from the single *Registrum* entry 'Epistole Ieronimi'. In seven other instances the appearance of this number is an obvious error: Augustine *1.416*, Anselm *3.29–30*, Bede *84.27*, Bernard *85.22–23*, and Boethius *94.4*. Kirkestede possibly had personal knowledge of this library.

43 WOBVRNE: Woburn (Bedfordshire), Cistercian abbey of B.V.M. Ker, *MLGB*, 205.

With works added by Kirkestede this number appears four times: Babio *107.1 Super Mattheum*, *2 Sermones*, Henry of Huntingdon *260.5 De contemptu mundi*, and Sibyl *550.1 Prophetias de Christo*. In eighteen instances **43** is added to works taken from the *Registrum*: Augustine *1.34 De baptismo*, *137 Epistolae*, *170 De fide ad Petrum*, *282 De moribus ecclesiae et moribus Manichaeorum*, *347 Super psalterium*, *402 De 8 quaestionibus Dulsinii*, *497 De conflictu vitiorum et virtutum*, Ambrose *2.22 De S. David apologia*, *50 De misteriis*, *58 De poenitentia unica*, *77 Ad Susannam virginem*, *86 De laude virginum*, *91 De lapsu virginis consecratae*, Anselm *3.5 Cur Deus homo*, Bede *84.2 De tabernaculo Moysi*, Gregory *203.4 Super quodam evangelio*, *5 Registrum epistolarum*, Isidore *666.47 Sermones*. In 162 instances this number is copied with works taken from the *Registrum*. In seven instances the appearance of this number is an obvious error: Augustine *1.126*, *311*, *381*, *407*, *416*, Bernard *85.6*, *14*, and Chrysostom *282.2*. Although the number of cases in the first category is small, the facts that in the Babio and Sibyl entries **43** appears with the numbers of libraries that Kirkestede knew, and that Woburn is conceivably within Kirkestede's travelling range, support the validity of this number. Kirkestede possibly had personal knowledge of this library.

44 DVNSTABLE: Dunstable (Bedfordshire), Augustinian priory of St Peter. Ker, *MLGB*, 60.

This number appears twice with works added by Kirkestede, Gratian *217.1 Decretum*, and Sibyl *550.1 Prophetias de Christo*, both times in company with the numbers of libraries that Kirkestede knew. The rarity of the number's occurrence suggests it to be a mistake in both instances; but the location of Dunstable along the Bury–Cambridge–St Albans route to London, to the contrary, makes its validity plausible. The *Registrum*'s compilers made no use of this number. Kirkestede possibly had personal knowledge of this library.

APPENDIX

45   WARDONA: Warden (Bedfordshire), Cistercian abbey of B.V.M. Ker, *MLGB*, 193; Bell, *Cistercians*, Z26.

With works added by Kirkestede this number appears seven times: Augustine *1.257 Sermo de latrone et cruce*, Bernardus Morlanensis *88.1 De contemptu mundi*, Berengar *96.1 Super Apocalipsim*, Claudius Viennensis *121.1 De statu et substantia animae*, Eusebius presbyter *160.6 De Corpore et sanguine Domini*, Eusebius Emesenus *162.4 De Pascha*, and Johannes de Deo *309.3 Concordantias Decretorum et Decretalium*. For four of these, **45** is the sole location given, for a title with an incipit; for the other three times, **45** appears principally with the numbers of libraries that Kirkestede knew. This number appears once added to a work, Odo **405.2 Super 5 libros Moysi*, taken from the *Registrum*; **45** was not used by the compilers of the *Registrum*. Kirkestede had personal knowledge of this library.

46   *S. Neotus*: St Neots (Huntingdonshire), Benedictine alien priory of St Neot (cell of Bec). Ker, *MLGB*, 170; Sharpe & others, *Benedictines*, p. 589.

In one instance, Robert of Melun *506.4*, this number is added to a work taken from the *Registrum*. In nineteen instances this number is copied with works taken from the *Registrum*. In one other instance, Hugh *244.28*, the appearance of **46** is an obvious error. Kirkestede had no personal knowledge of this library.

49   *Northampton S. Jacobi*: Northampton, Augustinian abbey of St James. Ker, *MLGB*, 135.

This number does not appear with works added by Kirkestede. In two instances **49** is added to works taken from the *Registrum*: Augustine *1.342* and Stephen Langton *554.12*. In fourteen instances this number is copied with works taken from the *Registrum*. In two instances, Bede *84.14* and Langton *554.7*, the appearance of **49** is an obvious error. Kirkestede had no personal knowledge of this library.

50   PIPEWELLE: Pipewell (Northamptonshire), Cistercian abbey of B.V.M. Ker, *MLGB*, 152.

With works added by Kirkestede this number appears three times: Augustine *1.241 De non jurando*, Gregory *203.11 Epistolas breves*, and Jerome *281.147 De Osanna ad Damasum*. This number is added twenty-eight times to works taken from the *Registrum*: Augustine *1.39 De boni natura, 227 De justitiae perfectione, 276 De musica, 302 De mensura numero et pondere, 342 De poenitentia, 406 Quaestiones de Eptatico, 488 De 4 virtutibus cardinalibus*, Ambrose *2.68 De tribus quaestionibus Salomonis*, Alcuin *7.31 De virtutibus et vitiis*, Bede *84.1 Super Genesin Exodum Leviticum Numerum et Deuteronomium*, Bernard *85.13 Super Missus est*, Jerome *281.93 De essentia et immensitate Dei, 100 De partibus minus notis Veteris Testamenti, 101 De membris et motibus Jesu Christi*, Chrysostom *282.4 Super Mathaeum imperfecte, 12 De decollatione S. Johannis, 20 De ascensione Domini*, Josephus *296.2 Libros antiquitatum*,

APPENDIX

Maximus *359.12 Omelias*, Odo *405.6 De vitiis et virtutibus animae, 12 Sermones*, Ivo *667.6 De significatione sacerdotalium, 7 De mistica interpretatione dedicationis ecclesiae, 8 De cruce Domini, 9 De adventu Domini, 10 De nativitate Domini, 11 De S. Jacobo, 12 Ad Paschalem*. In fifteen of the twenty-eight instances, **50** is the only non-*Registrum* number added to a series of library numbers taken from the *Registrum*. The number **50** was not used by the compilers of the *Registrum*. Pipewell is within plausible travelling distance of places like Peterborough and Crowland which Kirkestede almost certainly visited. Kirkestede had personal knowledge of this library.

53 *Lentona*: Lenton (Nottinghamshire), Cluniac priory of Holy Trinity. Ker, *MLGB*, 113.

With works added by Kirkestede this number appears three times: Gratian *217.1*, Jerome *281.147*, and Horace *411.6*; none of these appearances is especially persuasive. In two instances it is added to works taken from the *Registrum*: Augustine *1.347* and Bede *84.24*. In eleven instances this number is copied with works taken from the *Registrum*. Kirkestede probably had no personal knowledge of this library.

55 *Thurgertone*: Thurgarton (Nottinghamshire), Augustinian priory of St Peter. Ker, *MLGB*, 190; Webber & Watson, *Augustinians*, A36.

This number is copied from the *Registrum* twice. Kirkestede had no personal knowledge of this library.

57 *Rucheforde*: Rufford (Nottinghamshire), Cistercian abbey of B.V.M. Ker, *MLGB*, 164.

In one instance this number is added to a work taken from the *Registrum*, Augustine *1.402*. In four instances this number is copied with works taken from the *Registrum*. In one other instance, Bernard *85.14*, its appearance is an obvious error. Kirkestede had no personal knowledge of this library.

58 *Crokestone*: Croxton (Leicestershire), Premonstratensian abbey of St John. Not in Ker, *MLGB*.

This number appears twice added to works taken from the *Registrum*, Ambrose *2.26* and Leo *343.1*. The *Registrum*'s compilers made no use of this number. Kirkestede had no personal knowledge of this library.

60 *Blanchewell*: This house (*Banchewelle* and *Bankewale* in the *Registrum* manuscripts) remains unidentified.

This number appears once with a work added by Kirkestede, Augustine *1.182*. It appears once added to a work taken from the *Registrum*, Augustine *1.88*. In both cases **50** would be a credible emendation. The *Registrum*'s compilers made no use of this number. Kirkestede had no personal knowledge of this library.

APPENDIX

61 BVRCH: Peterborough (Northamptonshire), Benedictine abbey of SS. Peter, Paul, and Andrew. Ker, *MLGB*, 150; Friis-Jensen & Willoughby, *Peterborough*.

With works added by Kirkestede this number appears twenty-nine times: Augustine *1.19 *De libero arbitrio*, Bernardus Morlanensis 88.1 *De contemptu mundi*, Bonaventure *89.5 *Meditationes et contemplationes*, Caesarius *135.1 *Omelias ad monachos*, *2 *Ad sororem suam*, Dares Frigius *152.1 *De bello Trojano*, Eusebius Emesenus *162.5 *Omelias ad monachos*, Fulgentius *185.1 *Mithologiarum*, Henry of Huntingdon 260.5 *De contemptu mundi*, Nicholas Trevet 398.9 *De missa*, Paul the Deacon *426.2 *Historiam Romanorum*, Smaragdus *553.1 *Diadem monachorum*, Stephen Langton *554.23 *Sermones*, Aquinas *567.45 *De 10 praeceptis*, *47 *De articulis fidei*, *49 *De 7 sacramentis*, 85 *Super Mathaeum*, *86 *De salutatione angelica*, *87 *Super simbolum*, Cicero *582.20 *De deo Socratis*, William de Montibus *625.8 *Speculum poenitentia*, *9 *Versus eiusdem glosae*, Virgil *630.4 *Copa vel Cona*, *7 *Culicen*, *9 *Catelepton*, *14 *De viro justo*, *15 *De moreto vel simbolo*, *16 *Egloga*, and Matthew of Vendôme *662.1 *Summam*. In three instances it is added to titles taken from the *Registrum*: Bernard *85.21 *Meditationes*, Stephen Langton *554.20 *Summam quae vocatur Adam ubi es*, and Cicero *582.21 *De fato*. In all thirty-two of its appearances, **61** stands either alone or in company with other libraries that Kirkestede knew; in each instance the work is given its incipit and, with two exceptions, its explicit as well. This number is not used in the *Registrum*. Kirkestede had personal knowledge of this library.

62 THORNEYE: Thorney (Cambridgeshire), Benedictine abbey of B.V.M. and St Botolph. Ker, *MLGB*, 189; Sharpe & others, *Benedictines*, B100–101.

This number appears once, Haimo 240.9 *De diversis rebus monachorum et monachatu*, an unidentified work added by Kirkestede; **62** appears there in a series with two other libraries from roughly the same neighbourhood, **65** Ramsey and **63** Crowland, which Kirkestede knew. Kirkestede possibly had personal knowledge that this work was in this library; it is more likely that the single appearance of **62** is an error.

63 CROYLANDE: Crowland (Lincolnshire), Benedictine abbey of B.V.M., St Bartholomew, and St Guthlac. Ker, *MLGB*, 55; Sharpe & others, *Benedictines*, B24–25.

With works added by Kirkestede this number appears seventeen times: Augustine *1.294 *Ad Maximum*, 434 *De spiritu et anima*, Bernard 85.14 *Super Magnificat*, Babio 107.1 *Super Mattheum*, Fulbert *186.2 *Dialogum de quodam miraculo S. Martini*, *5 *Ad Deodatum*, *6 *Ad Finardum*, Gratian 217.1 *Decretum*, Henry of Huntingdon 260.3 *De serie regum totius orbis*, 4 *De serie regum Britanniae*, Innocent III 283.14 *De latria et dulia*, Nicholas Trevet 398.3 *De missa*, Horace 411.1 *Epistolae*, 4 *Odarum vel carminum lib.*, Sibyl 550.1 *Prophetias de Christo*, Smaragdus 553.1 *Diadema*, and William de Montibus 625.7 *Numerale*. In addition it appears thirty-three times with Jerome epistles (*281*), principally in company with numbers taken from the *Registrum* entry 'Epistole Ieronimi'; since no emendation suggests itself, since there is independent evidence of Kirkestede's use of this number, and since Crowland did indeed possess a codex of Jerome's letters (B24. 31), it is possible that the Jerome references in this case are genuine, or—more plausibly—that they reflect Kirkestede's first-hand knowledge that a codex of Jerome letters existed at Crowland. In ten instances aside from Jerome's letters this number is added to works taken from the *Registrum*: Augustine *1.142 Encheridion*, *215 *Super evangelium Johannis*, 227 *De justitiae perfectione*, 370 *De perfectione justitiae*, Bernard *85.17 Ad fratres de monte*, 21 *Meditationes*, Gregory *203.12 De conflictu vitiorum et virtutum*, Jerome *281.37 Super Epistolam ad Ephesios*, 101 *De membris et motibus Jesu Christi*, Robert of Melun *506.9 *Super Cantica*. In thirty-nine instances this number is copied with works taken from the *Registrum*. In fifteen instances the appearance of this number is an obvious error: Bernard *85.29*, Jerome *281.39–40*, Chrysostom *282.16–17, 19, 21–27, 29*, and Origen *404.20*. Finally, it seems probable that much of the information that Kirkestede ostensibly contributes concerning **163** Newminster in fact refers to **63**; see below. Kirkestede had personal knowledge of this library.

64 BERNEWELL: Barnwell (Cambridgeshire), Augustinian priory of St Giles. Ker, *MLGB*, 7; Webber & Watson, *Augustinians*, A2.

This number appears twice with works added by Kirkestede: Augustine *1.294 Ad Maximum* and Henry of Huntingdon *260.3 De serie regum totius orbis*. In one instance, Isidore *666.10 Super Esdram*, this number is added to a title taken from the *Registrum*. **64** is not used in the *Registrum*. Because of the proximity of Barnwell to Bury and because of the appearance of **64** with two works that Kirkestede added, each time in the company of other numbers representing libraries that Kirkestede knew, Kirkestede possibly had personal knowledge of this library.

65 RAMESIA: Ramsey (Huntingdonshire), Benedictine abbey of B.V.M. and St Benedict. Ker, *MLGB*, 153; Sharpe & others, *Benedictines*, B67–70.

With works added by Kirkestede this number appears ninety-two times: Augustine **1.434* De spiritu et anima*, Anselm *3.33 De assumptione B. Mariae*, Aldhelm *8.1 Enigmata*, 2 *De virginitate et laude sanctorum et sanctarum*, Abbo **9.5 Cathegoriarum*, 15 *Sermo in coena Domini*, Anticlaudianus **64*, Bede *84.43 De temporibus et luna*, Bernard *85.14 Super Magnificat*, 18 *De 6 alis seraphim*, Bonaventure *89.3 Breviloquium*, Caesarius *135.1 Omelias ad monachos*, *2 *Ad sororem suam*, Columbanus *138.1 De moribus*, Ephraem *155.2 De transfiguratione Domini*, 3 *De poenitentia*, 4 *De luctaminibus huius saeculi*, 5 *De compunctione cordis*, 6 *De beatitudine animae*, 7 *De resurrectione et judicio Dei*, 8 *De die judicii*, Eusebius Emesenus *162.5 Omelias ad monachos*, Eusebius Arelatensis *165.1 De nativitate Domini*, Giles of Rome *169.2 De regimine principum*, Fulgentius *184.1 De trinitate*, Fulbert *186.2 Dialogum de quodam miraculo S. Martini*, 5 *Ad Deodatum*, 6 *Ad Finardum*, 7 *De muliere mala*, Gregory of Nazianzus *204.6 De S. Spiritu*, 8 *Apologeticum*, 9 *De nativitate Domini*, 10 *De reconciliatione monachorum*, 11 *De luminibus*, 12 *De agno regresso*, 13 *De*

APPENDIX

grandinis vastatione, *14 De dictis Jeremiae*, Gennadius *210.9 De mille annis in Apocalipsi*, Guymundus *220.1 De corpore et sanguine Christi*, Haimo *240.9 De diversis rebus monachorum, Ildefonsus *246.1 De virginitate B. Mariae*, *3 De assumptione B. Mariae*, *13 De sanctuario*, Henry of Huntingdon *260.3 De serie regum totius orbis*, Hilduin **279.1 Super omelias Johannis*, Jerome *281.82 Contra Rufinum*, John of Salisbury *288.1 Policraticon*, **6 Architrenius*, John Waleys *337.8 De disciplina*, Lactantius *345.2 De ave quae vocatur Phoenix*, Nicolas de Gorham *399.1 Super Ecclesiasticum*, *2 Super Lucam et Matheum*, *3 Super epistolas Pauli*, *6 Distinctiones*, Nicolas de Lyre *403.2 Super Psalterium*, Origen *404.5 Super Deuteronomium*, Odo of Cluny *405.14 De confessione*, Odo of Cheriton *406.1 Sermones de tempore et sanctis*, Ovid *412.10 Invectionis in Ibin*, Osbert of Clare *417.3 Vitam et miracula S. Edburgae*, Petrus Cantor *442.13 Consiliarium*, Peter Damian *443.2 Librum qui vocatur Dominus vobiscum*, Proba *472.1 Centonam de Christo*, Ratramnus *503.1 De anima*, *2 De eo quod Christus de virgine natus est*, Richard Fishacre *513.2 Super libros Sententiarum*, Robert Holcot *515.3 Super Sapientiam*, *5 Super evangelium Mathaei*, Sedulius *531.2 De signis et virtutibus*, *3 De gestis Christi sacramentis et miraculis*, Smaragdus *553.1 Diadema monachorum*, *2 Super regulam S. Benedicti*, Stephen Langton *554.6 Super Josue*, *24 Super Job*, Aquinas *567.52 Super Isaiam*, *57 Super primum librum Sententiarum*, **58 Super secundum lib. Sent.*, **59 Super tertium lib. Sent.*, **60 Super quartum lib. Sent.*, **61 Summam theologiae*, **63 Quaestiones de veritate*, **64 Quaestiones de potentia Dei*, William de Montibus *625.1 Speculum poenitentiae*, *2 Distinctiones*, *4 De bonitate mulierum*, **7 Numerale*, William of Peterborough *626.1 Super Cantica*, *2 Distinctiones*, **4 Eufrastica* (Bodl. MS Bodley 833, with an *ex libris* note in Kirkestede's hand), *5 Liber partium*, and Isidore *666.22 De origine officiorum*, *44 De naturis bestiarum et lapidum*. In thirty-four other instances, this number was added to works taken from the *Registrum*: Augustine *1.1 De Academicis*, *383 Super praedicamenta*, *506 De doctrina christiana*, Anselm *3.41 Sermones*, Alexander Nequam *4.10 Super symbolum Athanasii*, *12 Quaestiones*, *13 Sermones ab adventu*, *14 Regulas super theologiam*, Basil *78.1 In exameron*, Baldwin *80.1 De sacramentis*, *3 Sermones*, Bachiarius *81.1 De reparatione lapsi*, Bede *84.53 Lamentationes in diem Judicii*, *63 Super Psalmos*, Bernard *85.17 Ad fratres de monte*, *21 Meditationes*, *35 Quaestiones quatuor*, Cassiodorus *111.2 Super Psalterium*, Gregory *203.12 De conflictu vitiorum et virtutum*, Geoffrey of Auxerre *216.3 Super Mathaeum*, Haimo *240.2 Super Isaiam*, *3 Super epistolas Pauli*, *5 Super epistolas et evangelia totius anni*, Jerome *281.11 De perpetua virginitate B. Mariae*, *15 Breviarium minus*, Julianus Pomerius *306.4 De origine mortis humanae*, Petrus Cantor *442.14 Verbum abbreviatum*, Prudentius *469.1 De conflictu vitiorum et virtutum*, *2 De Novo et toto Veteri Testamento*, **9 Apotheos, Sichomachia, Amarchigenia*, and Stephen Langton *554.1 Super Genesin*, *2 Super Exodum*, *3 Super Numerum*, *4 Super Deuteronomium*; in many of these thirty-four instances, either **65** is the only number added, with incipit, to a work with a series of numbers copied from the *Registrum*, or it appears in company with other numbers representing libraries that Kirkestede knew. **65** was not used by the compilers of the *Registrum*. At least some of the report ostensibly for **165** Brinkburne is probably an error for **65**; see below. Kirkestede had personal knowledge of this library.

APPENDIX

67 ELY: Ely (Cambridgeshire), Benedictine cathedral priory of St Peter and St Etheldreda. Ker, *MLGB*, 77; Sharpe & others, *Benedictines*, B27–28.

With works added by Kirkestede this number appears twice: Hugh *244.44 Exameron*, with incipit and explicit, and Aquinas *567.78 Contra impugnantes religionem*, without incipit. In each case **67** is the only location number given. In one instance, Augustine *1.424*, this number is copied with a work from the *Registrum* (R1. 137, where the appearance of **67** is presumably an error). The *Registrum*'s compilers made no use of this number. Despite the rarity of the number's appearance, Ely's proximity to Bury suggests that Kirkestede possibly had personal knowledge of this library.

68 WALDEN: Saffron Walden (Essex), Benedictine abbey of B.V.M. and St James. Ker, *MLGB*, 192; Sharpe & others, *Benedictines*, B84.

This number appears three times in all, with works added by Kirkestede: Alexander the Great *55.3–4* and Dares *152.1*. In the first two instances **68** is the only number given, and in the third it appears with **61** Peterborough, a library which Kirkestede did know. In all three cases the titles are supplied with incipits and explicits. This number is not used by the *Registrum*. In addition, there is external evidence of Kirkestede's knowledge of Walden's library, in the form of a location note in his hand in Cambridge, Gonville and Caius College, MS 113/182, fol. 138r (see p. lvii above). All four works (*55.3*, *55.4*, *152.1*, and the 'Alexander' epistles mentioned in Caius 113) circulate together in, for example, London, College of Arms, MS 1 (Canterbury Franciscans, s. xiv). Therefore, despite the rarity of this number's appearances, Kirkestede probably had personal knowledge of this library, or at least of one of its codices.

69 *Huntyngdon*: Huntingdon, Augustinian priory of B.V.M. Ker, *MLGB*, 103.

This number appears once, added to a work taken from the *Registrum*, Bernard *85.21*. This number is not used in the *Registrum*. Kirkestede had no personal knowledge of this library.

70 *Westacre*: Westacre (Norfolk), Augustinian priory of B.V.M. and All Saints. Ker, *MLGB*, 195.

This number appears once with a work added by Kirkestede, Chrysostom *282.22*. Despite the fact that Westacre is as close to Bury as are some libraries that Kirkestede surely did see, this single appearance is likely to be an error. Kirkestede probably did not have personal knowledge of this library.

71 *Castelacre*: Castle Acre (Norfolk), Cluniac priory of B.V.M. Ker, *MLGB*, 48; Sharpe & others, *Benedictines*, B18–19.

This number appears twice, in obvious error: Augustine *1.10*, and Ivo *667.21*. Kirkestede had no personal knowledge of this library.

APPENDIX

73 NORWIC. S. TRINITATIS: Norwich, Benedictine cathedral priory of Holy Trinity. Ker, *MLGB*, 135; Sharpe & others, *Benedictines*, B57–61.

With works added by Kirkestede this number appears eleven times: Anselm *3.18 De beatitudine et miseria*, *30 Sigillum S. Mariae*, *33 De assumptione B. Mariae*, Albertus Magnus *56.67 Super librum de animalibus*, Astulphus *72.1 Cantelarium*, Bernard of Cassino *86.1 Speculum monachorum*, *2 Super regulam S. Benedicti*, Petrus Comestor *440.1 Historiam scolasticam*, Peter of Poitiers *441.1 Sententiae*, Peter of Blois *444.6 De periculis praelatorum*, Vincent of Beauvais *636.1 Speculum naturale*. In one instance, Odo *405.12 Sermones*, **73** has been added, with a series of libraries that Kirkestede knew, to a title taken from the *Registrum*. This number was not used by the compilers of the *Registrum*. There is evidence that Kirkestede had knowledge of the Norwich library in the form of a location note at Astulphus *72.1* (and see also p. cxxi above). Kirkestede had personal knowledge of this library.

74 S. BENEDICTVS DE HOLM: Holme St Benets (Norfolk), Benedictine abbey of St Benedict. Ker, *MLGB*, 102; Sharpe & others, *Benedictines*, B49.

With works added by Kirkestede this number appears twenty-six times: Alcuin *7.10 De ratione animae*, Alanus *15.3 De planctu*, Alanus *16.1 De modo et arte praedicandi*, Bernard *85.43 De gemitu animae*, Babio *107.1 Super Mattheum*, *2 Sermones*, Caesarius *135.1 Omelias*, *2 Ad sororem suam*, Eusebius *162.5 Omelias ad monachos*, Gundisalvus *235.1 De anima*, Helpricius *272.1 De arte calculatoria*, Macer *388.1 De viribus herbarum*, Petrus Comestor *440.1 Historiam scolasticam*, Peter of Poitiers *441.1 Sententiae*, *5 De officiis divinis*, Petrus Cantor *442.11 Tractatum de poenitentia*, Peter Damien *443.2 Librum qui vocatur Dominius vobiscum*, Prepositinus *471.1 Summam theologiae*, Remigius *497.2 De missa*, Robert Grosseteste *505.35 Testamenta 12 patriarcharum*, Richard Fishacre *513.2 Super libros Sententiarum*, *3 De poenitentia*, Sedulius *531.2 Dactylico*, *3 De gestis Christi*, *4 Ympnum*, Sibyl *550.1 Prophetias de Christo*. In eleven instances it is added to works taken from the *Registrum*: Basil *78.8 Sermones*, Baldwin *80.3 Sermones*, Bernard *85.8 Apologeticum*, *10 De laude novae militiae*, Gregory *203.12 De conflictu vitiorum et virtutum*, Julianus Pomerius *306.4 De origine mortis humanae*, Odo *405.6 De vitiis et virtutibus animae*, *12 Sermones*, Petrus Cantor *442.3 Super Psalterium*, Richard of St Victor *498.3 De contemplatione*, Isidore *666.14 De ortu et obitu sanctorum patrum*. **74** is not used in the *Registrum*, and there is no reason to doubt the validity of these eleven additions; one of them underscores Kirkestede's first-hand knowledge of the Holme St Benets library, in the form of a comment on Isidore *666.14*, 'sicut apud Holm S. Benedicti, liber iste sic incipit . . .'. There is external evidence, in a location note by Kirkestede in BL MS Royal 8 F. xiv on fol. 132r (see *498.3*). Kirkestede had personal knowledge of this library.

75 *Langeley*: Langley (Norfolk), Premonstratensian abbey of B.V.M. Ker, *MLGB*, 108.

This number appears once, with a work added by Kirkestede, Horace *411.5*. Despite the propinquity of Langley to Norwich and Holme St Benets—places that Kirkestede visited—the number **75**'s sole appearance in the Horace entry, which has many unexplained numbers, is not persuasive. The *Registrum*'s compilers made no use of this number. Kirkestede probably had no personal knowledge of this library.

77 SIBBETONE: Sibton (Suffolk), Cistercian abbey of B.V.M. Ker, *MLGB*, 180.

This number appears once with a work added by Kirkestede, Miletus *371.18 De assumptione B. Mariae*. In two instances, Bernard *85.8 Apologeticum* and *38 Epistolae*, this number is added to titles taken from the *Registrum*. The *Registrum*'s compilers made no use of this number. There is external evidence of Kirkestede's knowledge of the Sibton library, in a location note in his hand in Cambridge, Corpus Christi College, MS 404, fol. 66r (see p. lviii above). Kirkestede's report, though small, probably represents personal knowledge of this library.

78 LEYSTONE: Leiston (Suffolk), Premonstratensian abbey of B.V.M. Ker, *MLGB*, 113.

This number appears with one work added by Kirkestede, Sedulius *531.4 Ympnum continentem versus 110*. The *Registrum*'s compilers made no use of this number. Despite its single appearance, other facts—that **78** appears in company with two other East Anglian libraries (Holme St Benets and Colchester St John's), and that Leiston is certainly within reasonable travelling distance from other libraries that Kirkestede visited—suggest that Kirkestede's single reference possibly represents personal knowledge of this library.

79 BVTLEYE: Butley (Suffolk), Augustinian priory of B.V.M. Ker, *MLGB*, 22.

This number appears twice with works added by Kirkestede, Augustine *1.413 De resurrectione*, and Odo of Cheriton *406.1 Omelias de tempore et sanctis*. In seven instances—Bernard *85.8 Apologeticum, 39 Sermones*, Gregory *203.1 Super librum Job, 2 Pastorale, 4 Super quodam evangelio, 7 Super Ezechielem*, Isidore *666.21 De summo bono*—this number is added to titles taken from the *Registrum*. In two instances this number is copied with titles taken from the *Registrum*. **79** appears very rarely (three or four times) in the *Registrum*. Kirkestede probably had personal knowledge of this library.

80 GYPEWIC TRINITATIS: Ipswich (Suffolk), Augustinian priory of Holy Trinity. Not in Ker, *MLGB*.

In eight instances **80** is added to works taken from the *Registrum*: Augustine *1.199 Contra quinque haereses, 215 Super evangelium Johannis, 304 Contra Manicheos*, Anselm *3.5 Cur Deus homo*, Gennadius *210.4 De ecclesiasticis dogmatibus*, Jerome *281.90 De catholicis scriptoribus et viris illustribus*, Petrus Comestor *440.2 Sermones allegoricos*, Isidore *666.14 De ortu et obitu sanctorum patrum*. In twenty-three other instances this number is copied with works taken from the *Registrum*. The

APPENDIX

appearance of this number at Ivo *667.21* is an obvious error. Ipswich is in the East Anglian area where Kirkestede appears to have had considerable knowledge of the libraries, including another Ipswich Augustinian house (**81** below); and **80** appears frequently, though by no means always, in company with the numbers of libraries that Kirkestede knew. Although the evidence is not compelling, Kirkestede possibly had personal knowledge of this library.

81 GYPEWIC PETRI: Ipswich (Suffolk), Augustinian priory of SS. Peter and Paul. Not in Ker, *MLGB*.

This number appears twice with works added by Kirkestede: Henry of Huntingdon *260.2 De gestis regum Angliae* and Johannes de Deo *309.3 Concordantias Decretorum et Decretalium*. In seven instances this number is added to works taken from the *Registrum*: Augustine *1.12 De animae quantitate, 29 De 12 abusivis saeculi, 142 Encheridion, 497 De conflictu vitiorum et virtutum*, Ambrose *2.23 Exameron*, and Gregory *203.4 Super quodam evangelio, 5 Registrum epistolarum*. In eight other instances this number is copied with titles taken from the *Registrum*. Kirkestede probably had personal knowledge of this library.

82 S. EDMUNDVS DE BVRY: Bury St Edmunds (Suffolk), Benedictine abbey of St Edmund, King and Martyr. Ker, *MLGB*, 16; Sharpe & others, *Benedictines*, B12–16.

Kirkestede's use of this number, that of his own abbey, is ubiquitous; he supplied it (to works that he added, and as addition to titles taken from the *Registrum*) more than 400 times, and beyond that he employed information from the Bury library on a great many occasions without recording the number **82**.

83 COLCESTRIAE S. JOHANNIS: Colchester (Essex), Benedictine abbey of St John the Baptist. Ker, *MLGB*, 53; Sharpe & others, *Benedictines*, B22.

With works added by Kirkestede this number appears seventy-three times: Augustine *1.44 Ad Bonefacium, 45 Item ad Bonefacium, 93 Ad Consentium, 98 Ad quendam comitem, 121 Ad Donatum et Donatistam, 155 Ad Enodium, 156 Ad Emeritum, 157 Ad Eleusium, 178 Ad Fortunatianum, 179 Ad Festum, 182 Extrema verba Augustini, 183 De concordia fratrum, 190 Ad Glorium et Eleusinum, 209 Ad Honoratum, 218 Ad Julianum, 306 Ad Marcellinum, 307 Item ad eundem, 308 Item ad eundem, 366 De praedestinatione, 369 Ad Pascentium, 391 Ad Paulinam, 434 De spiritu et anima*, Anselm *3.18 De beatitudine*, Alcuin *7.3 Dialogorum inter ipsum et Karolum librum*, Alanus *15.6 Anticlaudianus*, Aristotle *46.1 Periarmeniarum, 3 Elencorum, 4 Priorum analeticorum, 6 De physica et naturali scientia, 9 De anima, 10 De sensu et sensato, 12 De memoria et reminiscentia, 13 De sompno et vigilia, 14 De morte et vita, 15 De vegetabilibus et plantis, 16 De animalibus, 17 De differentia spiritus et animae, 18 Metheororum, 20 De regimine principum, 36 De intelligentia, 37 De progressu animalium, 38 De causis, 39 De motu animalium*, Apuleius *47.1 De deo Socratis*, Basil *78.3 De institutione monachorum, 4 De vita communi monachorum, 5 De vita solitaria,*

APPENDIX

Cassiodorus *111.7 De anima*, Cyril *126.5 Sermones*, Freculph *198.1 Historiam*, Gregory *203.10 Dialogus*, Gregorius Emesenus *206.1 De ymagine*, Gilbert de la Poree *215.1 Super Psalterium, 2 Super Trenos Jeremiae*, Gratian *217 Decretum*, Gundisalvus *235.1 De anima*, John Cassian *285.4 Ad Honoratum et Eucherium, 5 Ad Invenianum, Minervium Leontium et Theodorum*, Johannes de Deo *309.3 Concordantias Decretorum et Decretalium*, Lawrence of Durham *358.5 Yponosticon*, Ovid *412.14 De vetula*, Peter Abelard *433.2 Alphabetum magistri Petri*, Patrick *434.1 De tribus habitaculis*, Petrus Cantor *442.12 Super 4 evangelia*, Richard Fishacre *513.2 Super libros Sententiarum*, Sedulius *531.2 Dactylico eroico metro, 3 De gestis Christi, 4 Ympnum continentem versus 110, 5 Carmen alphabeti*, Sibyl *550.1 Prophetias de Christo*, Smaragdus *553.1 Diadema*, Cicero *582.28 De adoratione verborum*, Tremegistus *592.1 Ad Asclepium*; In more than a dozen of these entries Kirkestede gives both **82** (Bury) and **83** as locations, excluding the possibility that **83** is merely an error for **82** throughout. Moreover, for Sedulius *531.5* the *Catalogus* entry describes the contents and then specifies 'Vide apud **83**'. In fifty-one instances this number is added to works taken from the *Registrum*: Augustine *1.49 De cantico novo, 51 De civitate Dei, 52 De laude caritatis, 56 De confessionibus, 65 De correctione Donatistarum, 90 De cataclysmo, 102 Ad Deogratias, 107 De definitionibus fidei rectae, 137 Epistolae, 139 Super epistolam Johannis, 142 Encheridion, 158 Ad Edicciam, 159 Epistolae ad Romanos expos., 165 Contra Felicianum de unitate, 166 De feria quarta, 168 De fide vel symbolo, 180 De eo: Fundamentum, 184 Super Genesin ad literam, 199 Contra quinque haereses, 215 Super evangelium Johannis, 279 Super Mulierem fortem, 303 Ad Memorum episcopum, 304 Contra Manicheos, 305 De modis locutionum, 310 De nuptiis et concupiscentia, 311 De natura et gratia, 330 De obedientia et humilitate, 347 Super Psalterium, 374 De bono perseverantiae*, Ambrose *2.94 De virginitate*, Anselm *3.35 Epistolas*, Bernard *85.21 Meditationes, 24 De colloquio Simonis et Jesus, 39 Sermones*, Gregory *203.5 Registrum epistolarum, 6 Super Cantica, 12 De conflictu vitiorum et virtutum*, Gennadius *210.2 De viris illustribus*, Haimo *240.2 Super Isaiam, 3 Super epistolam Pauli, 4 Super Apocalipsin, 5 Super epistolas et evangelia totius anni*, Jerome *281.18 Super Isaiam, 67 Contra Jovinianum*, Peter of Blois *444.8 Epistolae*, Ralph of Flaix *494.4 Super Parabolas*, Cicero *582.1 De officiis, 2 De amicitia, 3 De senectute, 15 De paradoxis*, Isidore *666.33 Regulam ad monachos*; in several of these **83** may be an error for **82** Bury. In thirty instances this number is copied with titles taken from the *Registrum*. In four instances, the appearance of this number is an obvious error: Augustine *1.154, 305, 358, 416*. Kirkestede had personal knowledge of this library.

84 COLCESTRIAE BOTVLPHI: Colchester (Essex), Augustinian priory of St Botulph. Ker, *MLGB*, 53.

With works added by Kirkestede **84** appears twenty times: Augustine *1.31 Ad Asellicum, 32 Ad Apringium, 33 De adventu Domini secundo, 129 Ad Dioscorum, 131 Ad Donatistas, 132 Ad eosdem, 392 Ad Paulinam et Therasiam, 393 Ad Paulinam, 394 Ad Pammachium, 395 Ad Possidium*, and Aristotle *46.2 Topicorum lib., 5 Posteriorum analeticorum lib., 8 De generatione et corruptione, 25 De mundo ad Alexandrum, 28 De*

559

APPENDIX

mineris, 29 De coloribus, 33 De inundatione Nili, 35 De juventute et senectute, 40 De proprietatibus elementorum, 41 De phisonogmia. In twenty-five instances this number is added to titles taken from the *Registrum*: Augustine *1.3 Contra adversarium legis et prophetarum, 4 De adulterinis conjugiis, 6 De agone christiano, 10 De natura animae ad Renatum, 11 De natura animae ad Petrum, 12 De animae quantitate, 13 De immortalitate animae, 14 De 2 animabus contra Manicheos, 15 De natura et origine animae ad Vincentium, 29 De 12 abusivis saeculi, 30 Ad Armentarium et Paulinam de voto, 34 De baptismo contra Donatistas, 36 De unico baptismo, 41 De tempore barbarico, 66 De credendi utilitate, 67 De cura pro mortuis gerenda, 268 Contra mendacium, 269 De mendacio, 270 Unde malum contra Fortunatum, 273 Ad Macedonium, 276 De musica, 278 De mirabilibus, 279 Super Mulierem fortem,* and Gregory *203.5 Registrum epistolarum*; some of these may be errors for **82** Bury. Location number **84** was not used by the compilers of the *Registrum*. In two instances, Augustine *1.74* and Origen *404.15*, the appearance of **84** is an error. Kirkestede had personal knowledge of this library.

85 S. Ositha: Chich (Essex), Augustinian abbey of St Peter, St Paul, and St Osyth. Ker, *MLGB*, 170.

With works added by Kirkestede this number appears twice: Jerome *281.128 De institutione clericorum, 221 Ad Theodosium*. In nine instances this number is added to works taken from the *Registrum*: Augustine *1.1 De Academicis, 4 De adulterinis conjugiis, 36 De unico baptismo, 43 Super Beati immaculati, 91 Contra cartulam Valerio commissam, 215 Super evangelium Johannis*, Ambrose *2.23 Exameron*, Bede *84.55 Super Mattheum*, and Jerome *281.130 De vita monachi ad Rusticum*; all but three of the nine (*1.43, 1.91, 84.55*) are supplied with incipits and explicits. The *Registrum*'s compilers made no use of this number. Kirkestede probably had personal knowledge of this library.

86 Coggeshale: Coggeshall (Essex), Cistercian abbey of B.V.M. Ker, *MLGB*, 52; Bell, *Cistercians*, Z5.

With works added by Kirkestede this number appears seven times: Basil *78.3 De institutione monachorum*, Bernard *85.40 De viis vitae, 41 De 7 gradibus obedientiae*, Ildefonsus *246.13 De sanctuario*, Peter of Blois *444.2 De vera amicitia christianorum*, Richard of St Victor *498.15 Contra Andream judaizantem*, and Stephen Langton *554.23 Sermones*. In five instances this number is added to titles taken from the *Registrum*: Bernard *85.38 Epistolae, 39 Sermones*, Ralph of Flaix *494.15 De sanctuario Dei quod est S. Maria*, Richard of St Victor *498.36 Dialogorum de Emanuale lib.*, and Isidore *666.33 Regulam ad monachos*; all but the Bernard works (*85.38–39*) have been supplied with incipits and explicits. **86** was not used by the compilers of the *Registrum*. There is external evidence, in the form of a location note by Kirkestede in Cambridge, Corpus Christi College, MS 404, fol. 66r (see p. lviii above), that he was acquainted with Coggeshall's books. Kirkestede had personal knowledge of this library.

APPENDIX

89 *Bomeneye*: Bodmin (Cornwall), Augustinian priory of St Petroc. Ker, *MLGB*, 10.

This number appears with a work added by Kirkestede, Gregory of Nazianzus *204.6*. In four instances this number has been added to titles taken from the *Registrum*: Gregory *203.1*, Jerome *281.67*, Isidore *666.21*, *46*. In thirty-nine instances this number is copied with titles taken from the *Registrum*. In nine instances the presence of this number is an obvious error: Augustine *1.142*, *323*, Ambrose *2.23*, Gregory *203.2*, *3*, Gregory of Nazianzus *204.8–14*, and Isidore *666.3*, *4*, *5*. Kirkestede had no personal knowledge of this library.

90 *Lancenetone*: Launceston (Cornwall), Augustinian priory of St Stephen. Ker, *MLGB*, 112.

In five instances this number is added to titles taken from the *Registrum*: Augustine *1.13*, *63*, *115*, *199*, *386*. In twenty-seven instances this number is copied with titles taken from the *Registrum*. In one other instance the presence of this number is an obvious error, Augustine *1.416*. Kirkestede had no personal knowledge of this library.

91 *Plomtone*: Plympton (Devon), Augustinian priory of St Peter. Ker, *MLGB*, 152; Webber & Watson, *Augustinians*, A27–28.

This number appears once, added to a work taken from the *Registrum*, Isidore *666.47*. The *Registrum*'s compilers made no use of this number. Kirkestede had no personal knowledge of this library.

92 *Duncawile*: Dunkeswell (Devon), Cistercian abbey of B.V.M. Ker, *MLGB*, 59; Bell, *Cistercians*, Z6.

With works added by Kirkestede this number appears twice, Horace *411.2–3*, both times among the problematic numbers in the Horace entry. In eight instances this number is added to works taken from the *Registrum*: Augustine *1.115*, *139*, Anselm *3.23*, Aelred *5.14*, Gregory *203.1*, *4*, Isidore *666.21*. In twelve instances this number is copied with works taken from the *Registrum*. In seven other instances the appearance of this number is an obvious error: Anselm *3.24–26*, Bernard *85.5*, *12*, and Gregory *203.2–3*. Dunkeswell is a great distance from Bury. Kirkestede probably had no personal knowledge of this library.

93 *Buckfestar*: Buckfast (Devon), Cistercian abbey of B.V.M. Ker, *MLGB*, 14; Bell, *Cistercians*, Z3.

With works added by Kirkestede this number appears three times: Augustine *1.121*, Aelred *5.17*, and Petrus Comestor *440.1*. In three instances **93** is added to works taken from the *Registrum*: Augustine *1.274*, Gregory *203.1*, *4*. In thirty-five instances this number is copied with works taken from the *Registrum*. In four other instances the appearance of this number is an obvious error: Albertus Magnus *56.73*, Gregory *203.2–3*, and Ivo *667.21*. Kirkestede probably had no personal knowledge of this library.

APPENDIX

94   *Forda*: Forde (Dorset), Cistercian abbey of B.V.M. Ker, *MLGB*, 88; Bell, *Cistercians*, Z8.

With works added by Kirkestede this number appears once: Peter of Poitiers *441.1*. In ten instances this number is added to works taken from the *Registrum*: Ambrose *2.23*, Anselm *3.5*, *15*, Bernard *85.38*, Gregory *203.1*, *4*, *7*, Petrus Comestor *440.2*, Richard of St Victor *498.32*, Isidore *666.40*. In 156 instances this number is copied with works taken from the *Registrum*. In six other instances the appearance is an obvious error: Bernard *85.5*, *12*, Gregory *203.2–3*, Richard of St Victor *498.15*, and Isidore *666.21*. This number was heavily used by the compilers of the *Registrum* (including about ninety other titles that Kirkestede did not borrow), providing wide scope for addition by misinterpretation. Kirkestede probably had no personal knowledge of this library.

95   *Exonia*: Exeter (Devon), cathedral church of St Peter. Ker, *MLGB*, 81.

In eleven instances this number is added to works taken from the *Registrum*: Augustine *1.63*, Ambrose *2.23*, *87*, Alcuin *7.31*, Gregory *203.1*, *5*, Jerome *281.87*, *90*, Isidore *666.10*, *28*. In 140 instances this number is copied with works taken from the *Registrum*. In five other instances the appearance of this number is an obvious error: Augustine *1.126*, *416*, Gregory *203.2–3*, and Jerome *281.45*. Kirkestede had no personal knowledge of this library.

96   *Tantonia*: Taunton (Somerset), Augustinian priory of SS. Peter and Paul. Ker, *MLGB*, 188; Webber & Watson, *Augustinians*, A34.

This number appears twice added to works taken from the *Registrum*, Augustine *1.76*, and Bede *84.6*, and once copied with a work taken from the *Registrum* (Augustine *1.232*). Kirkestede had no personal knowledge of this library.

97   *Alingeleya*: Athelney (Somerset), Benedictine abbey of St Saviour, St Peter, and St Paul. Ker, *MLGB*, 5.

This number appears once with a work added by Kirkestede, Augustine *1.121*. In two instances, Augustine *1.73* and *147*, this number is added to works taken from the *Registrum*. In ten instances **97** is copied with works taken from the *Registrum*. In fifteen other instances the appearance of this number is an obvious error: Augustine *1.340*, Anselm *3.21*, Jerome *281.22–33* and Chrysostom *282.22*. Kirkestede had no personal knowledge of this library.

98   *Glastonia*: Glastonbury (Somerset), Benedictine abbey of B.V.M. Ker, *MLGB*, 90; Sharpe & others, *Benedictines*, B36–45.

This number is added to one work taken from the *Registrum*: Augustine *1.227*; and it appears with four Jerome epistles listed by Kirkestede: *281.128*, *130*, *147*, and *221*, doubtless the result of a single error in copying the *Registrum*'s numbers for 'Epistole Ieronomi' (R6. 78). In ten instances **98** is copied with works taken from the *Registrum*. Kirkestede had no personal knowledge of this library.

APPENDIX

99 *Totonia*: Totnes (Devon), Benedictine alien priory of B.V.M. (cell of St Serge, Angers). Ker, *MLGB*,190; Sharpe & others, *Benedictines*, B103.

In nine instances this number is copied with works taken from the *Registrum*. In one other instance the appearance of this number is an obvious error, Chrysostom *282.25*. Kirkestede had no personal knowledge of this library.

101 *Tore*: Torre (Devon), Premonstratensian abbey of St Saviour or Holy Trinity. Not in Ker, *MLGB*.

This number appears once with a work added by Kirkestede, Albertus Magnus *56.73*; the title is not furnished with its incipit or explicit. Kirkestede had no personal knowledge of this library.

102 *Bristollia S. Augustini*: Bristol (Gloucestershire), Augustinian abbey of St Augustine. Ker, *MLGB*, 13; Webber & Watson, *Augustinians*, A6.

This number appears once added to a work taken from the *Registrum*, Augustine *1.72*. In four instances **102** is copied with works taken from the *Registrum*. Kirkestede had no personal knowledge of this library.

103 *Malmesbira*: Malmesbury (Wiltshire), Benedictine abbey of B.V.M. and St Aldhelm. Ker, *MLGB*, 128; Sharpe & others, *Benedictines*, B53–54.

In thirty-three instances **103** is copied with works taken from the *Registrum*. Kirkestede had no personal knowledge of this library.

104 *Cirencestria*: Cirencester (Gloucestershire), Augustinian abbey of B.V.M. Ker, *MLGB*, 51; Webber & Watson, *Augustinians*, A9.

This number appears with one work added by Kirkestede, Chrysostom *282.29*. In one instance this number is added to a work taken from the *Registrum*: Ambrose *2.38*. In thirty-four instances this number is copied with works taken from the *Registrum*. One appearance is an obvious error, Jerome *281.84*. Kirkestede had no personal knowledge of this library.

105 *Clammorgan*: Margam (Glamorganshire), Cistercian abbey of B.V.M. Ker, *MLGB*, 129.

With works added by Kirkestede this number appears twice: Chrysostom *282.29* and Paterius *437.1*. Once this number is added to a title taken from the *Registrum*: Isidore *666.32*. In 101 instances it is copied with works taken from the *Registrum*. In four other instances the appearance of this number is an obvious error: Augustine *1.40*, Bernard *85.7*, Jerome *281.88*, and Origen *404.20*. Kirkestede had no personal knowledge of this library.

106 *Dore*: Dore or Abbey Dore (Herefordshire), Cistercian abbey of B.V.M. Ker, *MLGB*, 58.

APPENDIX

This number appears once added to a title taken from the *Registrum*, Stephen Langton *554.1*. The *Registrum*'s compilers made no use of this number. In four instances the appearance of this number is an obvious error: Jerome *281.144*, and Langton *554.2–4*. Kirkestede had no personal knowledge of this library.

107 *Wigemore*: Wigmore (Herefordshire), Augustinian abbey of St James. Ker, *MLGB*, 198.

This number appears once, Origen *404.18*, copied from the *Registrum*. Kirkestede had no personal knowledge of this library.

108 *Glovernia S. Petri*: Gloucester, Benedictine abbey of St Peter. Ker, *MLGB*, 91; Sharpe & others, *Benedictines*, B46–49.

In one instance this number is added to a work taken from the *Registrum*, Augustine *1.137*. In thirty instances it is copied with works taken from the *Registrum*. Its appearance at Jerome *281.145* is an obvious error. Kirkestede had no personal knowledge of this library.

109 *Lantonia*: Lanthony II (Gloucestershire), Augustinian priory of B.V.M. and St John the Baptist. Ker, *MLGB*, 293; Webber & Watson, *Augustinians*, A16–18.

With works added by Kirkestede this number appears twice: Ralph of Flaix *494.11–12*. In four instances this number is copied with works taken from the *Registrum*. Kirkestede had no personal knowledge of this library.

111 *Evesham*: Evesham (Worcestershire), Benedictine abbey of B.V.M. and St Egwin. Ker, *MLGB*, 80; Sharpe & others, *Benedictines*, B29–31.

This number is added to two works taken from the *Registrum*, Ambrose *2.58* and Bede *84.22*, perhaps a misreading of **xii** in both cases. In thirteen instances **111** is copied with works taken from the *Registrum*. Kirkestede had no personal knowledge of this library.

113 *Persover*: Pershore (Worcestershire), Benedictine abbey of St Edburga. Ker, *MLGB*, 294; Sharpe & others, *Benedictines*, B65.

This number is added to a work copied from the *Registrum*, Isidore *666.38*. The *Registrum*'s compilers made no use of this number. Kirkestede had no personal knowledge of this library.

114 *Bordesle*: Bordesley (Worcestershire), Cistercian abbey of B.V.M. Ker, *MLGB*, 11; Bell, *Cistercians*, Z2.

In thirty-two instances this number is copied with works taken from the *Registrum*. In four other instances its appearance is an obvious error: Anselm *3.4*, Aelred *5.6*, Bernard *85.25*, and Cassian *285.2*. Kirkestede had no personal knowledge of this library.

APPENDIX

115 *Wenelach*: Wenlock or Much Wenlock (Shropshire), Cluniac priory of St Milburga. Ker, *MLGB*, 195.

In four instances this number is added to works taken from the *Registrum*: Bede *84.51*, Bernard *85.6*, Robert of Melun *506.5*, and Isidore *666.47*. The number **115** also appears with four Jerome epistles, *281.145, 146, 150, 158*; in each instance as a misreading for **114**, found in the *Registrum* entry 'Epistole Ieronimi'. In twenty-seven instances this number is copied with works taken from the *Registrum*. Kirkestede had no personal knowledge of this library.

116 *Salopia*: Shrewsbury (Shropshire), Benedictine abbey of SS. Peter and Paul. Ker, *MLGB*, 179; Sharpe & others, *Benedictines*, p. 592.

This number is added to one work taken from the *Registrum*, Isidore *666.47*. In seventeen instances it is copied with works taken from the *Registrum*. Kirkestede had no personal knowledge of this library.

117 *Lilleshulle*: Lilleshall (Shropshire), Augustinian abbey of B.V.M. Ker, *MLGB*, 115.

This number is added to four works taken from the *Registrum*: Augustine *1.76*, Gregory *203.3*, and Isidore *666.34, 37*. In four instances this number is copied with works taken from the *Registrum*. Kirkestede had no personal knowledge of this library.

118 *Cestriae abbatia*: Chester (Cheshire), Benedictine abbey of St Werburg. Ker, *MLGB*, 49; Sharpe & others, *Benedictines*, B21.

This number is added to two works taken from the *Registrum*: Ambrose *2.54*, and Gregory *203.7*. In twenty instances **118** is copied with works taken from the *Registrum*. Kirkestede had no personal knowledge of this library.

119 *Basingwerch*: Basingwerk (Flintshire), Cistercian abbey of B.V.M. Ker, *MLGB*, 7.

This number appears, in a suspect number series, with one work added by Kirkestede, Kilwardby *510.13*. In two instances, Isidore *666.35* and *37*, this number is added to works taken from the *Registrum*. The appearance of **119** at Ambrose *2.47* is a mistake for **114**. The number **119** is not used in the *Registrum*. Kirkestede had no personal knowledge of this library.

120 *Planagustel*: Llanegwast or Llanegwist, otherwise Valle Crucis (Denbighshire), Cistercian abbey of B.V.M. Ker, *MLGB*, 191.

This number is added to a work taken from the *Registrum*, Augustine *1.72*. This number appears twice in obvious error, at Peter of Blois *444.8* as an error for **xx**, and at Robert of Melun *506.5* as an error for **124**. This number is not used in the *Registrum*. Kirkestede had no personal knowledge of this library.

APPENDIX

122 *Deulacresse*: Dieulacres (Staffordshire), Cistercian abbey of B.V.M. and St Benedict. Ker, *MLGB*, 57.

This number appears once with a work added by Kirkestede, Ralph of Flaix *494.11*. In three instances this number is copied with works taken from the *Registrum*. Kirkestede had no personal knowledge of this library.

123 *Crokesden*: Croxden (Staffordshire), Cistercian abbey of B.V.M. Ker, *MLGB*, 56.

This number is copied seven times with works taken from the *Registrum*. Kirkestede had no personal knowledge of this library.

124 *Mirevallis*: Merevale (Warwickshire), Cistercian abbey of B.V.M. Ker, *MLGB*, 130.

This number is added to one work taken from the *Registrum*, Augustine *1.63*. In nineteen instances this number is copied with works taken from the *Registrum*. The appearance of **124** at Rabanus *492.4* is an obvious error. Kirkestede had no personal knowledge of this library.

125 *Coventria*: Coventry (Warwickshire), Benedictine cathedral priory of B.V.M. Ker, *MLGB*, 54; Sharpe & others, *Benedictines*, B23.

This number is copied with one work taken from the *Registrum*, Rabanus *492.17*. Kirkestede had no personal knowledge of this library.

126 *Cumbe*: Combe (Warwickshire), Cistercian abbey of B.V.M. Ker, *MLGB*, 54.

In thirty-two instances this number is copied with works taken from the *Registrum*. In four other instances the appearance of **126** is an obvious error: Augustine *1.51*, Anselm *3.30*, Aelred *5.6*, and Jerome *281.84*. Kirkestede had no personal knowledge of this library.

127 *Stanle*: Stoneleigh (Warwickshire), Cistercian abbey of B.V.M. Ker, *MLGB*, 183; Bell, *Cistercians*, Z23.

In twenty instances this number is copied with works taken from the *Registrum*. Two appearances of **127** are obvious errors: Augustine *1.40*, and Aelred *5.6*. Kirkestede had no personal knowledge of this library.

128 *Kelineworthe*: Kenilworth (Warwickshire), Augustinian priory of B.V.M. Ker, *MLGB*, 105.

This number is added to one work taken from the *Registrum*, Isidore *666.38*. In twenty-five instances it is copied with works taken from the *Registrum*. In seven other instances the appearance of **128** is an obvious error: Ivo *667.6–12*. Kirkestede had no personal knowledge of this library.

APPENDIX

129 *Burtonia*: Burton-on-Trent (Staffordshire), Benedictine abbey of B.V.M. and St Modwenna. Ker, *MLGB*, 15; Sharpe & others, *Benedictines*, B11.

This number is added to one work taken from the *Registrum*, Augustine *1.91*. In two other instances this number is copied with works taken from the *Registrum*. Its appearance at Anselm *3.8* is an obvious error. Kirkestede had no personal knowledge of this library.

133 *Revesby*: Revesby (Lincolnshire), Cistercian abbey of B.V.M. and St Lawrence. Ker, *MLGB*, 158; Bell, *Cistercians*, Z17–18.

This number is added to a work taken from the *Registrum*, Augustine *1.24*. The number **133** is not used in the *Registrum*. Kirkestede had no personal knowledge of this library.

135 *Torkeseye*: Torksey (Lincolnshire), Augustinian priory of St Leonard. Not in Ker, *MLGB*.

This number is added to one work taken from the *Registrum*, Augustine *1.119*; it is copied once with a work from the *Registrum*. The appearance of **135** at Augustine *1.15* is an error for **139**. Kirkestede had no personal knowledge of this library.

136 *Luya*: Louth Park (Lincolnshire), Cistercian abbey of B.V.M. Ker, *MLGB*, 127; Bell, *Cistercians*, Z13.

This number appears with one work added by Kirkestede, Chrysostom *282.36*, without incipit or explicit. The *Registrum*'s compilers made no use of this number. Kirkestede had no personal knowledge of this library.

137 *Grymesby*: Grimsby (Lincolnshire), probably the convent of Austin friars. Ker, *MLGB*, 93.

This number appears as a mistake for **127** at Hugh *244.8*. The *Registrum*'s compilers made no use of this number. Kirkestede had no knowledge of this library.

139 *Eborac. S. Mariae*: York, Benedictine abbey of B.V.M. Ker, *MLGB*, 217; Sharpe & others, *Benedictines*, B120–124.

With works added by Kirkestede this number appears twice: Augustine *1.120* and Paterius *437.1*. It also appears with four Jerome epistles, *281.128*, *130*, *147*, and *221*, doubtless as a copying error. In two instances this number is added to works taken from the *Registrum*: Ambrose *2.74* and Ivo *667.5*; and in thirty-three instances this number is copied with works taken from the *Registrum*. In three other instances the presence of **139** is an obvious error: Augustine *1.147*, Anselm *3.30*, and Bernard *85.22*. Kirkestede had no personal knowledge of this library.

APPENDIX

143 *Bridelington*: Bridlington (Yorkshire), Augustinian priory of B.V.M. Ker, *MLGB*, 12; Webber & Watson, *Augustinians*, A4–5.

This number was added to a work taken from the *Registrum*, Isidore *666.32* (without incipit and explicit). The *Registrum*'s compilers made no use of this number. The appearance of **143** at Hugh *244.57* is an obvious error. Kirkestede had no personal knowledge of this library.

144 *Whiteby*: Whitby (Yorkshire), Benedictine abbey of St Peter and St Hilda. Ker, *MLGB*, 197; Sharpe & others, *Benedictines*, B109–110.

This number appears once, with a work added by Kirkestede, Chrysostom *282.36* (without incipit or explicit). The *Registrum*'s compilers made no use of this number. Kirkestede had no personal knowledge of this library.

145 *Meltone*: Malton (Yorkshire), Gilbertine priory of B.V.M. Not in Ker, *MLGB*.

This number is added to a work taken from the *Registrum*, Augustine *1.117*. The *Registrum*'s compilers made no use of this number. Kirkestede had no personal knowledge of this library.

147 Spaldinges: Spalding (Lincolnshire), Benedictine priory of B.V.M. and St Nicholas. Ker, *MLGB*, 181; Sharpe & others, *Benedictines*, B95–96.

With works added by Kirkestede this number appears five times: Adalbert **53.1 De moralibus Gregorii*, Albertus Magnus *56.67 Super librum de animalibus*, Bonaventure *89.5 Meditationes*, John of Tynemouth *341.1 Historiam auream*, and Nicolas Trevet *398.9 De missa*. It is added to one work taken from the *Registrum*, Odo **405.12 Sermones*. This number was not used by the compilers of the *Registrum*. Kirkestede probably had personal knowledge of this library.

148 *Thornhom*: Thornholm (Lincolnshire), Augustinian priory of B.V.M. Ker, *MLGB*, 189; Webber & Watson, *Augustinians*, A33.

This number is added to one work taken from the *Registrum*, Augustine *1.71*. The number **148** was not used by the *Registrum*'s compilers. Kirkestede had no personal knowledge of this library.

149 *Karleolum*: Carlisle (Cumberland), Augustinian cathedral priory of B.V.M. Ker, *MLGB*, 48.

This number is added to one work taken from the *Registrum*, Augustine *1.26*. The appearance of **149** at Augustine *1.89* is an obvious error. This number was not used by the *Registrum*'s compilers. Kirkestede had no personal knowledge of this library.

APPENDIX

150 *Holmcoltram*: Holme Cultram (Cumberland), Cistercian abbey of B.V.M. Ker, *MLGB*, 102.

This number is not used in the *Registrum*. The appearance of **150** at Augustine *1.89* is an obvious error. Kirkestede had no knowledge of this library.

151 *Fornayse*: Furness (Lancashire), Cistercian abbey of B.V.M. Ker, *MLGB*, 89.

This number is added to one work taken from the *Registrum*, Anselm *3.22*. Once it is copied with a work taken from the *Registrum*. At Augustine *1.15* and *40*, the number **151** appears in error for the *Registrum*'s *15.1*. Kirkestede had no personal knowledge of this library.

152 *Gedesworth*: Jedburgh (Roxburghshire), Augustinian abbey. Not in Ker, *MLGB*.

This number is added to one work taken from the *Registrum*: Augustine *1.137*. In forty-four instances this number is copied with works taken from the *Registrum*. This number's appearances at Augustine *1.89* and *358* are obvious errors. Kirkestede had no personal knowledge of this library.

153 *Kelcom*: Kelso (Roxburghshire), Benedictine abbey of B.V.M. Ker, *MLGB*, 105.

In four instances this number is added to works taken from the *Registrum*: Augustine *1.67*, *1.71*, Ambrose *2.77*, Bernard *85.8*. In thirty-six instances this number is copied with works taken from the *Registrum*. In four other instances, Anselm *3.2*, and Bernard *85.7* and *22-23*, the appearance of this number is an obvious error. Kirkestede had no personal knowledge of this library.

154 *Melros*: Melrose (Roxburghshire), Cistercian abbey of B.V.M. Ker, *MLGB*, 130.

With works added by Kirkestede this number appears once, Grosseteste *505.35*. In two instances this number is added to works taken from the *Registrum*: Augustine *1.67* and Jerome *281.9*. In forty-seven instances **154** is copied with works taken from the *Registrum*. The appearance of **154** at Bernard *85.23* is an obvious error. Kirkestede had no personal knowledge of this library.

155 *Neubotle*: Newbattle (Midlothian), Cistercian abbey of B.V.M. Ker, *MLGB*, 133.

This number is added to one work taken from the *Registrum*, Anselm *3.23*. In seven instances this number is copied with works taken from the *Registrum*. In four other instances this number's appearance is an obvious error, Augustine *1.27*, and Anselm *3.24–26*. Kirkestede had no personal knowledge of this library.

APPENDIX

156 *De S. Andreæ*: St Andrews (Fife), Augustinian cathedral priory of St Andrew. Ker, *MLGB*, 169.

This number appears with one work added by Kirkestede, Augustine *1.120*. In three instances it is added to works taken from the *Registrum*: Augustine *1.26*, Bernard *85.13*, and Ivo *667.4*. In thirty-three instances this number is copied with works taken from the *Registrum*. In three other instances the presence of **156** is an obvious error: Augustine *1.147, 207*, and Cassian *285.2*. Kirkestede had no personal knowledge of this library.

157 *De S. Cruce*: Holyrood (Midlothian), Augustinian abbey of Holy Cross, B.V.M., and All Saints. Ker, *MLGB*, 102.

This number appears with one work added by Kirkestede, Aelred *5.10*. In two instances this number is added to works taken from the *Registrum*, Augustine *1.338* and Anselm *3.23*. In five instances it is copied with works taken from the *Registrum*. In four other instances the appearance of this number is an obvious error: Anselm *3.24–26*, and Hugh *244.19*. Kirkestede had no personal knowledge of this library.

158 *Dumfermyn*: Dunfermline (Fife), Benedictine abbey of Holy Trinity. Ker, *MLGB*, 59.

With works added by Kirkestede this number appears twice, Hugh *244.70* and Nicolas Trevet *398.6*. In one instance, this number is added to a work taken from the *Registrum*, Augustine *1.26*. In fourteen instances it is copied with works taken from the *Registrum*. The occurrences of **158** at Augustine *1.89* and Aquinas *567.50* are obvious errors. Kirkestede had no personal knowledge of this library.

159 *S. Agathae*: Easby (Yorkshire), Premonstratensian abbey of St Agatha. Ker, *MLGB*, 76.

This number is added to two works taken from the *Registrum*, Augustine *1.71*, and Odo *405.5*. In three instances it is copied with works taken from the *Registrum*. Kirkestede had no personal knowledge of this library.

160 *Jorevallis*: Jervaulx (Yorkshire), Cistercian abbey of B.V.M. Ker, *MLGB*, 105; Bell, *Cistercians*, Z10.

In twenty-eight instances this number is copied with works taken from the *Registrum*. Appearance of this number at Augustine *1.23* is an obvious error. Kirkestede had no personal knowledge of this library.

161 *Giseborne*: Guisborough (Yorkshire), Augustinian priory of B.V.M. Ker, *MLGB*, 94; Webber & Watson, *Augustinians*, A11.

This number is added to four works taken from the *Registrum*: Augustine *1.295*, Ambrose *2.51*, Jerome *281.118*, and Ivo *667.5*; none of them is provided with

APPENDIX

an incipit. In ninety-one instances this number is copied with works taken from the *Registrum*. In two other instances the appearance of **161** is an obvious error: Ambrose *2.94*, and Bernard *85.14*. Kirkestede had no personal knowledge of this library.

162 *Tynemutha*: Tynemouth (Northumberland), Benedictine priory of B.V.M. and St Oswin, cell of St Albans. Ker, *MLGB*, 191; Sharpe & others, *Benedictines*, B93.

This number appears once with a work added by Kirkestede, John of Tynemouth *341.1*; the location must have been an assumption on Kirkestede's part. In five instances this number is copied with works taken from the *Registrum*. Kirkestede had no personal knowledge of this library.

163 *Novum Monasterium*: Newminster (Northumberland), Cistercian abbey of B.V.M. Ker, *MLGB*, 134.

With works added by Kirkestede this number appears three times: Ambrose *2.11* (probably for **63**), Alcuin *7.32* and Peter of Poitiers *441.1*. Twelve times this number is added to works taken from the *Registrum*, all probably in error for **63**: Augustine *1.235*, *418*, Ambrose *2.51*, *69*, Andrew of St Victor *13.2*, Jerome *281.9*, *118*, Peter of Blois *444.1*, Robert of Melun *506.12*, Stephen Langton *554.17*, Isidore *666.11*, *30*. In four other cases in which no emendation is obvious, this number is added to works taken from the *Registrum*: Augustine *1.237*, Bernard *85.31*, Martin of Braga *364.4*, Isidore *666.30*. In seventy-two instances this number is copied with works taken from the *Registrum*. In three entries for Jerome epistles (*281.76*, *142*, *152*) **163** is taken from the *Registrum* entry *6.78* 'Epistole eius [Ieronimi]'. In four other instances this number's appearance is an obvious error: Ambrose *2.11*, Andrew of St Victor *13.3–4*, and Boethius *94.4*. Kirkestede had no personal knowledge of this library.

164 *Dunelmia*: Durham, Benedictine cathedral priory of St Cuthbert. Ker, *MLGB*, 60.

With works added by Kirkestede this number appears twice: Alcuin *7.32*, and Grosseteste *505.35*. In twelve instances this number is copied with works taken from the *Registrum*. In three entries for epistles of Jerome (*281.76*, *152*, and *221*) this number is taken from *Registrum 6.78* 'Epistole eius'. Kirkestede had no personal knowledge of this library.

165 *Bringeborne*: Brinkburn (Northumberland), Augustinian priory of SS. Peter and Paul. Not in Ker, *MLGB*.

With works added by Kirkestede this number appears twice as a probable error for **65**: Ambrose *2.11*, and Nicolas Trevet *398.6*. This number also appears with another work added by Kirkestede, Hugh *244.70*, where the emendation is not obvious. In two instances this number is added to works taken from the *Registrum*, Augustine *1.117*, and (probably for **65**) Ralph of Flaix

APPENDIX

494.14. In fifteen instances this number is copied with works taken from the *Registrum*. Once this number's presence is an obvious error, Augustine *1.70*. Kirkestede had no personal knowledge of this library.

166 HEMLDESHAM VEL HECLESHAM: Hexham (Northumberland), Augustinian priory of St Andrew. Ker, *MLGB*, 101.

With works added by Kirkestede this number appears five times: Aelred *5.10 De diversis virtutibus*, Arnulph *31.2 De corpore et sanguine Domini*, Hugh *244.69 Cronica*, Paterius *437.1 Super V et NT*, and Peter of Blois *444.5 Dialogorum inter Henricum regem Angl. et abbatem Bonevallensem lib*. In twenty-four instances it is added to works taken from the *Registrum*: Augustine *1.43 Super Beati immaculate*, *237 De libro Judicum*, *338 De die ordinationis suae*, *380 Contra paganos et Judaeos*, Ambrose *2.89 De morte Valentiniani*, Alexander Nequam *4.10 Super symbolum Athanasii*, Bernard *85.32 Super epistolam Jacobi*, Hugh *244.31 De laude caritatis*, *68 De creatione mundi*, *76 De anima et homine*, Jerome *281.87 De regulis diffinitionum contra haereticos*, Chrysostom *282.33 De militia Christiana* and *34 De militia spirituali*, John Beleth *290.1 De officiis ecclesiae*, Richard of St. Victor *498.9 De arbore Nabugodonosor*, *31 Sermones plures et devotos*, Robert of Melun *506.3 Super Leviticum*, *12 Super Apocalipsin*, Seneca *543.11 Tragediarum lib*., Stephen Langton *554.17 Super Cantica*, Isidore *666.10 Super Esdram*, *30 Super libros Virgilii*, Ivo *667.4 De excellentia sacrorum ordinum et de vita ordinandorum*, *12 Ad Paschalem*; of these titles, an incipit has been supplied to only six. In fifty-five instances this number is copied with works taken from the *Registrum*. In eight cases the appearance of the number is an obvious error: Augustine *1.184*, Anselm *3.21*, Bernard *85.31*, Boethius *94.7–8*, Jerome *281.112* and *152*, and Martin of Braga *364.4*. The distance of Hexham from Bury makes it unlikely that Kirkestede visited this library; but no plausible emendation presents itself for the twenty-nine instances of apparent addition. The number of times Kirkestede adds this number to the *Catalogus* makes one suspect that he had some sort of report, hearsay or perhaps a list, of the books at Hexham; transmission of information by such a route would explain the absence of incipits. Kirkestede possibly had direct knowledge of this library.

167 *Cern. S. Mariae*: Cerne (Dorset), Benedictine abbey of B.V.M., St Peter, and St Ethelwold. Ker, *MLGB*, 49.

This number appears with one work added by Kirkestede, Jerome *281.111*. In five instances this number is added to works taken from the *Registrum*: Augustine *1.28*, Ambrose *2.4*, *89*, Jerome *281.102*, Ralph of Flaix *494.14*. In five other cases it is copied with works taken from the *Registrum*. Kirkestede had no personal knowledge of this library.

168 FRATRVM MINORVM OXON: Oxford, Franciscan convent. Ker, *MLGB*, 141.

The name and number of this library are added to the basic *Registrum* list of libraries by Kirkestede. With works added by Kirkestede **168** appears

APPENDIX

seventeen times: Ambrose 2.81 *De silentio triplici*, Ansbertus 21.1 *De assumptione Beatae Mariae*, Hugh 244.42 *De contemplando*, 43 *De cibo Emanuelis*, 84 *De laude caritatis*, Joachim 293.1 *Super Apocalypsin*, 7 *De concordia*, Paschasius 436.5 *Vitas patrum Graecorum*, Ralph of Flaix 494.12 *De episcopo et clerico*, Remigius 497.3 *Super prologum bibliae*, 4 *Super alium prologum bibliae*, Grosseteste 505.11 *Super prologum bibliae*, 24 *De prima forma et forma omnium*, 35 *Testamenta duodecim patriarcharum de graeco trans.*, Kilwardby 510.13 *Tabulam super originalia*, Vincent of Beauvais 636.9 *De morali principis institutione*, 10 *De puerorum eruditione nobilium*. The two other appearances of **168**, Gilbert Crispin 214.2–3, are obvious errors. A location note by Kirkestede in BL MS Royal 8 B. IV, fol. 81r, along with other evidence, suggests that Kirkestede and other Bury monks spent time at Oxford (see pp. xxxiii and lvii above). Kirkestede had personal knowledge of this library.

169 YXWORTH: Ixworth (Suffolk), Augustinian priory of B.V.M. Not in Ker, *MLGB*.

Kirkestede added the name and number of this library to the list of locations. It appears only once, with a work added by Kirkestede, Richard of Ely 526.1 *Sermones*. **169** is the only location given, and the incipits of the first and last sermons are given. No probable alternative reading suggests itself, and Kirkestede probably added Ixworth to the list for the express purpose of including these sermons. Kirkestede's use of this number probably represents personal knowledge.

170 FRATRVM PRAEDIC. THEFFORDIAE: Thetford (Norfolk), Dominican priory. Not in Ker, *MLGB*.

The name and number of this library were added to the list by Kirkestede. The only Dominican priory on the list, Thetford must have been added especially for its holdings of the works of Aquinas. **170** appears twenty times in all, each time with a work added by Kirkestede: Hugh of Saint-Victor 244.69 *Cronica*, 74 *De arte memorandi*, Osbert of Clare 417.3 *Vitam et miracula S. Edburgae*, Thomas Aquinas 567.18 *De ente et essentia*, 22 *De principio individuationis*, 23 *De principiis naturae*, 24 *De operibus occultis naturae*, 27 *De motu cordis*, 28 *De aeternitate mundi*, 29 *De sortibus*, 32 *De unitate formae*, 33 *De genere*, 34 *De accidente*, 35 *De instantibus*, 37 *De fato*, 46 *De verbo*, 48 *De quatuor oppositis*, Thomas Waleys 586.2 *De visione faciali contra papam Johannem*, 3 *De temporibus et instantibus quae Pater posuit in sua potestate*, and William of Newburgh 658.1 *Historiam de gestis Anglorum*. For the fourteen works of Aquinas **170** is the only number cited, and incipits are provided for all but one. Kirkestede had personal knowledge of this library.

173 BABEWELLE MINORVM: Babwell (Suffolk), Franciscan convent. Ker, *MLGB*, 5.

The name and number of this library were added to the list by Kirkestede. With works added by Kirkestede **173** appears eighteen times: Alanus 15.1 *De maximis theologicis*, 4 *Principium commenti*, and 16.1 *De modo et arte praedicandi*, Giles

573

APPENDIX

of Rome *169.10 De paradise et inferno*, John of Salisbury *288.1 Policraticon*, John of Erfurt *325.1 Summam confessionum*, John Waleys *337.3 Communeloquium, 4 Miniloquium, 6 De oculo morali, 8 De disciplina*, John of Howden *342.1 Philomela, 2 Quindecim gaudia Beatae Virginis, 3 Quinquaginta cantica*, Nicolas Trevet *398.6 Super tragedias Senecae*, Praepositinus *471.1 Summam theologiae*, William of Auvergne *482.8 De universo spirituali, 9 De universo corporali*, Vincent of Beauvais *636.1 Speculum naturale*. This number is added to one work taken from the *Registrum*, Chrysostom *282.5 Super Johannem*. There is repeated external evidence of knowledge of the Babwell library in the form of location notes by Kirkestede in Cambridge, Pembroke College, MS 87, fol. 188r, BL MS Royal 8 F. xiv, fol. 132r, and Cambridge, Corpus Christi College, MS 404, fol. 6v. Kirkestede had personal knowledge of this library.

174 COLNE: Earls Colne (Essex), Benedictine priory of B.V.M., St John the Evangelist, and St Andrew. Not in Ker, *MLGB*.

The name and number of this library were added to the list by Kirkestede. This number appears with one work added by Kirkestede, Haimo *240.8 Super libros Macabeorum*; this is the only location reported for the work, but no incipit is given to substantiate that Kirkestede had seen a manuscript. The number **174** is added to one work taken from the *Registrum*, Augustine *1.206 De tribus habitaculis*. The evidence is not compelling, but given proximity, and given that Earls Colne was added to the list by Kirkestede, his report possibly represents personal knowledge of this library.

175 BERKYNGE: Barking (Essex), Benedictine abbey of nuns of B.V.M. and St Ethelburga. Ker, *MLGB*, 6; Sharpe & others, *Benedictines*, B7.

The name and number of this library were added to the list by Kirkestede. With works added by Kirkestede **175** appears three times: Ralph of Flaix *494.11 De orationibus et meditationibus, 12 De episcopo et clerico, 13 De expositione missae*. It appears added to one work taken from the *Registrum*, Ralph of Flaix *494.14 De abate et monacho*. Presumably Kirkestede added Barking to the list specifically to report these works. Kirkestede had personal knowledge of a manuscript at Barking that contained four works attributed to Ralph of Flaix, none of them known today.

The following location numbers were not used in the *Catalogus*: **4, 6, 17, 38, 40, 41–8, 51–2, 54, 56, 59, 66** (a number left blank in the list in Add. 3470 and in one copy of the *Registrum*, Tanner 165), **72, 76, 87–8, 100** (another number left blank in the list in Add. 3470 and in both copies of the *Registrum*), **110, 112, 121, 130–32, 134, 138, 140–42, 146, 171–2, 176–95**.

ALPHABETICAL LIST OF HOUSES

Athelney 97
Babwell 173
Barking 175
Barnwell 64
Basingwerk 119
Battle 8
Beaulieu 26
Blanchewell 60
Bodmin 89
Bordesley 114
Bridlington 143
Brinkburn 165
Bristol 102
Buckfast 93
Burton-on-Trent 129
Bury St Edmunds 82
Butley 79
Canterbury Christ Church 1
Canterbury St Augustine 2
Canterbury St Gregory 3
Carlisle 149
Castle Acre 71
Cerne 167
Chester 118
Chichester 22
Cirencester 104
Coggeshall 86
Colchester St Botulph 84
Colchester St John 83
Combe 126
Coventry 125
Crowland 63
Croxden 123
Croxton 58
Dieulacres 122
Dore 106
Dunfermline 158
Dunkeswell 92
Dunstable 44
Durham 164
Earls Colne 174
Easby 159
Ely 67
Evesham 111
Exeter 95

Eynsham 39
Forde 94
Furness 151
Glastonbury 98
Gloucester 108
Grimsby 137
Guisborough 161
Hexham 166
Holme Cultram 150
Holme St Benets 74
Holyrood 157
Huntingdon 69
Ipswich Holy Trinity 80
Ipswich St Peter 81
?Ivychurch 36
Ixworth 169
Jedburgh 152
Jervaulx 160
Kelso 153
Kenilworth 128
Langley 75
Lanthony 109
Launceston 90
Leeds 5
Leiston 78
Lenton 53
Lewes 20
Lilleshall 117
London Holy Trinity 10
London St Paul †19
Louth Park 136
Malmesbury 103
Malton 145
Margam 105
Melrose 154
Merevale 124
Merton 9
Mottisfont 28
Newark 18
Newbattle 155
Newminster 163
Northampton 49
Norwich 73
Osney 37
Oxford 168
Pershore 113

Peterborough 61
Pipewell 50
Plympton 91
Quarr 25
Ramsey 65
Reading 42
Revesby 133
Robertsbridge 16
Rochester 7
Romsey 27
Rufford 57
St Albans 15
St Andrews 156
St Neots 46
St Osyth 85
Salisbury 35
Shrewsbury 116
Sibton 77
Southampton 33
Southwark 12
Southwick 23
Spalding 146
Stoneleigh 127
Stratford Langthorne 14
Taunton 96
Thame 41
Thetford 170
Thorney 62
Thornholm 148
Thurgarton 55
Titchfield 24
Torksey 135
Torre 101
Totnes 99
Twinham 29
Tynemouth 162
Valle Crucis 120
Walden 68
Waltham 13
Warden 45
Waverley †19
Wenlock 115
Westacre 70
Westminster 11
Wherwell 34
Whitby 144

575

Wigmore 107
Winchester cathedral 30
Winchester Hyde 31
Winchester Nunnaminster 32
Woburn 43
York St Mary 139

ALPHABETICAL LIST OF AUTHORS

Abbo Floriacensis K9
Absolon K62
Acacius Caesariensis K19
Achardus de S. Victore
 K71
Acilius Severus K43
Adalbertus Metensis
 K7.18; K53
Adelardus Bathoniensis
 K51
Ado Viennensis K405.7;
 K408
Adrianus K45
Aegidius Aurelianus K173
Aegidius de Lessines
 K172
Aegidius Romanus K169;
 K482.13
Aelredus Rievallensis K5
Aesop K258
'Aethicus Ister' K183;
 K281.111
Africanus K32
Agrippa Castor K41
Aimoinus Floriacensis
 K241
Alanus ab Insula K4.14;
 K15–16; K85.18
Albericus de London
 K4.21; K73
Albertanus Brixiensis K67
Albertus Brixiensis K645
Albertus Erfordensis K57
Albertus Laudensis K58
Albertus Magnus K46.28;
 K56
Albumasar K63
Alcuinus K7; K84.45
Aldhelmus K8
Aldobrandinus de
 Tuscanella K60
Alexander Altissiodorensis
 → Willelmus
 Altissiodorensis
Alexander Cantuariensis
 K3.14, 59

Alexander Cappadociae
 ep. K39
Alexander de Hales K54
Alexander Magnus K55
Alexander Nequam K4
Alfarabius K68.8; K75;
 K486
Alfredus Beverlacensis
 K74
Alfredus Magnus K65.2;
 K76
Alfredus Presbyter K65;
 K68.1
Algazel K69
Alkindus K70
Alvarus Pelagius K77
Amalarius Metensis K14
'Ambrosiaster' K1.384,
 454; K2.67
Ambrosius Alexandrinus
 K20
Ambrosius Autpertus
 K1.497; K2.7; K3.33;
 K21.1–2; K203.12;
 K343.3
Ambrosius Diaconus K37
Ambrosius Mediolanensis
 K1.433; K2; K242.9
Ammonius K30
Amphilocius K25
Anatholius Alexandrinus
 K24
Andreas de S. Victore
 K13
Angelomus Luxoviensis
 K10
Angelus Clarenus K332.1
Ansegisus K50
Anselmus Cantuariensis
 K1.19, 80, 111, 424, 468;
 K3; K282.29
Anselmus Laudunensis
 K3.31, 37–8, 51–2
†Anspertus Rotomagensis
 K21
Anthiochus K28

†Anticlaudianus K64
Antonius monachus K12
Apion K23
Apollinaris Hieropolitanus
 K17
Apollinaris Laodicensis
 K35
Apollonius K36
Apollonius senator K38
Apringius K18
L. Apuleius K47
Aquila Ponticus K66
Arabianus K40
Arator K22
Archelaus K42
Aristides K49
Aristoteles K46; K486
Arnaldus → Ernaldus
Arnobius K26
Arnulfus → Ernulfus
Asclepius K34
Astulphus K72
Athanasius Alexandrinus
 K6
Atticus Constantino-
 politanus K27
Audentius K29
Augustinus de Dacia
 K61
Augustinus Hibernicus
 K1.278
Augustinus Hipponensis
 K1
Aulus Gellius K48
Avicenna K68
Avitus Bracarensis K11

Bachiarius K81
Bachillus K104
Baldwinus Cantuariensis
 K80
Bardesanes K95
Bartholomaeus Anglicus
 K93
Bartholomaeus Brixiensis
 K109

Bartholomaeus Pisanus K100
Basilius Anchiranus ep. K79
Basilius Magnus K1.421, †507; K7.30; K78
Beda Venerabilis K84; K111.5; K281.49
Bellator K105
Berengarus Turonensis K82.4
Berengaudus K2.7; K82; K96
Bernardus Aiglerius K86
Bernardus Claraevallensis K85; K144.1; K244.10, 12
Bernardus de Claromonte K98
Bernardus Morlanensis K88
Bernardus Papiensis K108
Bernardus Silvestris K87
Bernardus de Trilia K97
Beryllus K83
Birgitta Sueciae K110
Boethius K94
Boethius Dacus K101
Bombolonius de Bononia K102
Bonaventura K89
Bruno Carthusiensis K91.2
Bruno de Segni K91
Buconius → Voconius
Burchardus Anerbe K99
Burcardus Wurmaciensis K106
Byrhtferthus K90

Caecilius K133
Caelestinus I papa K131
Caelestius K128
Caelius Aurelius K125
Caesar, C. Iulius K304
Caesarius Arelatensis K1.5, 23, 106, 147, 180, 221, 228, 240, 281, 286, 359–60, 415, 432, 486, 502; K235

Candidus K123
Cassiodorus Senator K111
Cato, M. Porcius K122
Censorinus K137
Cerealis K134
Christopherus Lombardus K665
'Christopherus Nolhamsensis' K664
Cicero, M. Tullius K582
Claudianus Claudius K120; K395
Claudianus Mamertus K121
Claudius Taurinensis K119
Clemens Alexandrinus K114
Clemens Lanthoniensis K115
Clemens papa ps. K112.25; K113
Columbanus K138
Columella, L. Iunius K116
Commodianus K129
Constantinus Africanus K136
Constantius Lugdunensis K124
Cornelius K118
Costa ben Luca K46.17
Crispinus K127
Curtius → Valeranus
Q. Curtius Rufus K491
Cyprianus Carthaginensis K1.60, 150, 211, 329; K112; K281.215
Cyprianus Gallus ps. K112.25
Cyrillus Alexandrinus K126
Cyrillus Hierosolomitanus K130
Cyrus Alexandrinus K132

Damasus I papa K143
Daniel de Morley K655.1
Dares Frigius K152; K192

Defensor Locogiacensis K666.34
Diacontius → Dracontius
'Dictys Cretensis' K153
Didymus Caecus Alexandrinus K144; K281.94
Didymus Grammaticus K145
Diodorus K148
Diomedes K149
Dionysius Alexandrinus K140
Dionysius Areopagita ps. K139
Dionysius Corinthiorum ep. K142
Dionysius Exiguus K140.3–4; K141
Dioscorides K154
Dominicus Gundisalvi K235
Donatus Grammaticus K150
Dorotheus K151
Dracontius K147
Durandus de S. Porciano K146

Eadmerus Cantuariensis K3.19, 28, 32
Edmundus Rich K171
Egidius → Aegidius
Elizabeth K174
Ephraem Syrus ps. K1.72; K155
Epiphanius Cyprius K158
Ernaldus Bonaevallis K31.1, 3; K85.37; K168; K666.45
Ernaldus Leodiensis K59
Ernulfus Roffensis K31
Eucherius Lugdunensis K1.162; K164; K281.93
Euclides K181
Eugenius Carthaginensis K175
Eugippius K167
Eusebius Arelatensis K165

Eusebius Caesariensis
  K159; K160.4;
  K281.89, 95, 108, 119;
  K508.2
Eusebius Emesenus K162
'Eusebius Gallicanus'
  K1.256, 389, 415;
  K135.1, 3; K160.6;
  K161.5; K162.4–5;
  K165.1; K166.2;
  K666.31
Eusebius Presbyter K160
Eusebius Vercellensis
  K161
Eustathius K177
Eutropius Presbyter
  K166; K281.126
Eutropius Valentinensis
  K166.4; K176
Eutyches K179
Evagrius Antiochenus
  K156.8
Evagrius Monachus K157
Evagrius Ponticus K156
Evodius Uzaliensis K1.411

Facundus Ermanensis
  K200
Fastidius Britannorum
  K190
Faustinus Presbyter K188
Faustus Rhegiensis K187
Ferrandus Carthaginensis
  K197
Firmicus, Iulius Maternus
  K301
'Flaccianus' K194
Flavianus K193
Flavius K196
'Florentius Wigornensis'
  K195
Florus Lugdunensis
  K84.25, 61, 65
Fortunatianus K201
Freculphus Lexoviensis
  K198
Frontinus, Sextus Iulius
  K302.2; K303
Fulbertus Carnotensis
  K186

Fulcherius Carnotensis
  K199
Fulgentius Mythographus
  K185
Fulgentius Ruspensis
  K1.170–71; K184

Gaius K228
Galandus Regniacensis
  K3.34
Galenus K218
Galfridus Altissiodorensis
  K85.24; K216; K238
Galfridus de Babion
  K1.90, 344; K107;
  K216.3
Galfridus Monemutensis
  K219
Galfridus de Vino Salvo
  K227
Galfridus Viterbiensis
  K234
Q. Gargilius Martialis
  K230
Gaunilo K3.11
Gelasius K211
Gennadius K1.107; K210
Gerardus Teutonicus
  K223
Gervasius de Tilbury
  K221
Gilbertus Crispinus
  K3.12–13; K212.7–8;
  K214
Gilbertus Foliot K213
Gilbertus de Hoylandia
  K212
Gilbertus Porretanus
  K46.32; K212.1–3, 6;
  K215
Gilbertus Universalis
  K215.2–4
'Gildas' → 'Nennius'
Giraldus Cambrensis
  K232
Godardus K231
Gorgias K222
Gratian K217
Gregorius K205
Gregorius I papa K203

Gregorius IX papa
  K509.2
Gregorius de Bridlington
  K208
Gregorius Illibertanus
  K2.68, 80; K207;
  K281.234–5; K666.25
Gregorius Nazianzenus
  K204
Gregorius Nyssenus
  K206
Gregorius Turonensis
  K209
Gregorius Viennensis
  K225
Guibertus Tornacensis
  K89.4
Guido Aretinus K233
Guido Ariminensis K224
Guido de Castris K237
Guido de Columpnis
  K152.1; K236
Guigo II Carthusianus
  K239; K652
Guitmundus Aversanus
  K220

Haimo K240.9
Haimo Altissiodorensis
  K82.2; K111.8; K240;
  K492.19
Haimo de Bazochiis
  K240.6
Haimo monachus
  K240.7
Haly ibn Regel K252
Haly ibn Ridwan K252.1
Haly Imbrani K252.3
Hamonius → Aimoinus
Hannibaldus de Hannibaldis K263
Hegesippus K2.27; K163;
  K296.6
Helinandus de Frigidomonte K248
Heliodorus K250
Heliodorus Antiochenus
  K250
Helpericus Altissiodorensis
  K272

Helwicus Teutonicus
K269
Henricus Cossey K271
Henricus de Gandavo
K276
Henricus Huntingdonensis
K260
Henricus Teutonicus →
Hermannus Teutonicus
Heraclidis → Palladius
Heraclitus K273
Hermannus Contractus
K253
Hermannus Teutonicus
K270
Hermannus de Zerbst
K268
Hermas K257
Hermes Trismegistus ps.
K259; K592
Hervaeus Natalis K265
Hesiodus K278
Hesychius Hierosolo-
mitanus K170;
K672
Hieronymus K1.116, 330,
505; K281
Hilarius K242.10; K243
Hilarius Arelatensis
K242.8
Hilarius Pictaviensis
K242
Hildebert Cenomanensis
K247
Hildegardis Bingensis
K249
Hilduinus K279
Hippocrates K671.1
Hippolytus K668
Hispanus K267
Homerus K275
Honoratus K274
Honorius Augustodunensis
K1.86, 148, 487; K3.30;
K244.26
Q. Horatius Flaccus
K411
Hrabanus Maurus
K1.208; K492
Hugo K264

Hugo Ambianensis
K666.37
Hugo de Folieto K244.11,
28, 34, 45; K245;
K667.19
Hugo Ripelinus K266
Hugo de S. Caro K262
Hugo de S. Victore
K1.134; K2.81; K85.14;
K244
Hugutio Pisanus K254
Humbertus de Romanis
K261
Hyginus K340

Iacobus K667.11
Iacobus ep. K292
Iacobus Beneventanus
K318
Iacobus de Cessolis
K324.1
Iacobus de Fusignano
K319
Iacobus Viterbiensis
K329
Iacobus de Vitriaco
K324
Iacobus de Voragine
K320
Idacius Hispanus K326
Ignatius Antiochenus
K284
†Ignius K340
Ildefonsus Toletanus
K246
Innocentius III papa
K283
Innocentius IV papa
K283.13
Innocentius V papa →
Petrus Tarentasiensis
Ioachim de Flore K293
Iohannes Halgrinus de
Abbatisvilla K334
Iohannes de Alta Villa
K288.6
Iohannes Antiochenus
presbyter K291
Iohannes de Ardenburgo
K315

Iohannes Ashendon
K579.3
Iohannes Beleth K290
Iohannes de Bromyard
K338; K650
Iohannes Cassianus K285
Iohannes de Caulibus
K89.6
Iohannes Chrysostomus
K1.2, 260, †507; K282
Iohannes Climacus K332
Iohannes Constantino-
politanus K295
Iohannes Cornubiensis
K328
Iohannes Damascenus
K286
Iohannes de Deo K309
Iohannes de Erfordia
K325
'Iohannes de Fano' →
Martinus Fanensis
Iohannes Faventinus
K316
Iohannes Fiscannensis
K1.429; K7.15
Iohannes Fordensis
K282.52
Iohannes Friburgensis
K321
Iohannes de Garlandia
K54.3; K331
Iohannes Gerundiensis
K289
Iohannes Hierosolomitanus
K294
Iohannes de Howden
K280; K342
Iohannes Ianuensis K323
Iohannes Maudith K333
Iohannes Mediocris
K282.9–10
Iohannes Ocreatus K336
Iohannes Parisiensis
Quidort K313
Iohannes Pecham K339
Iohannes de Plano Carpini
K335
Iohannes Pungensasinum
K317

Iohannes Ridewall K520
Iohannes de Rupella K330
Iohannes de S. Geminiano K269.2
Iohannes Sarisburiensis K288
Iohannes Scottus Eriugena K287
Iohannes Tynemutensis K341
Iohannes Walensis K337; K339.2
Iohannes Wigornensis → 'Florentius Wigornensis'
Iordanes K312
Iordanus de Nemore K312.2
Iordanus de Saxonia K308
Iosephus Flauius K296
Irenaeus Lugdunensis K255
Isaac K669
Isaac presbyter K670
Isidorus Hispalensis K1.332; K666
Itacius Galliensis K326
Iudas K327
Iulianus Pomerius K306; K466.4; K468
Iulianus Toletanus K1.388; K306.4
Iulius I papa K305
Iulius Africanus Sextus K303
Iulius Valerius K55.3
Iunillus Africanus K307
Iustinianus K298
Iustinianus Valentinensis ep. K300
Iustinus, M. Iunianus K297; K588.1
Iustus K299
Iuuenalis, D. Iunius K311
Iuuencus, C. Vettius Aquilinus K310
Ivo Carnotensis K666.5–6, 16; K667

Ivo Carnotensis, magister K667.17

Lactantius Firmianus K189; K345
Lanfrancus K344
Laurentius Dunelmensis K358
Laurentius Westmonasteriensis K358
Leander K346
Lentius K350
Leo I papa K343
Leporius K354
Licinianus K355
Liudprandus K357
T. Livius K597
Longus, Velius K356; K611
Lucanus, M. Annaeus K348
Lucianus Antiochenus K351
Lucianus presbyter K347
Lucifer Calaritanus ep. K352
Lucius Alexandrinus K353
Ludolfus de Hildesheim K349

Macarius K363
Macarius ps. K362
'Macer Floridus' K388
Macrobius K370
Macrobius ep. K369
Malchion K368
Manegoldus Lautenbachensis K375; K376.2
Marbodus Redonensis K391
Marcellinus Comes K366
Marcellus K382
Marcus Paulus K392
Marianus Scottus K367
Marius K393
Martialis, M. Valerius K389
Martianus Capella K390

Martinus Bracarensis K1.488; K364; K543.4, 18
Martinus Fanensis K322
Martinus Polonus K376
Martyrius K387
Matthaeus Paris K379
Matthaeus Vindocinensis K662
Matthias Ripensis K378
Mauricius Hibernicus K394
Maximianus → Claudianus Claudius
Maximus K386
Maximus ep. K385
Maximus Constantinopolitanus K360
Maximus Taurinensis K1.257; K359
Melito K371
Mennadius K384
Methodius K361
Miltiades K373
Minucius Felix K374
Mochimus K383
Modestus K381
Moneta Cremonensis K377
Moses Maimonides K493
Musaeus K372
Musanus K380

'Nennius' K229; K402
Nicetas Remesianensis K1.493; K400
Nicetus ep. K401
Nicholaus Ambianensis K15.2, 5; K397
Nicholaus de Byard K103
Nicholaus Damascenus K46.15
Nicholaus de Gorran K399
Nicholaus de Lyra K403
Nicholaus Trevet K198.2; K398
Novatianus K396

Odilo Cluniacensis K410
Odo Cantuariensis K405.2–5, 12
Odo de Cheriton K405.12, 14; K406
Odo Cluniacensis K405
Odo Morimundensis K405.8
Oliverius Trecorensis Brito K413
Olympius K415
Optatus K44
Oresiesis K414
Orianus K416
Origen K1.68; K33; K281.47, 50, 137; K404; K440.8; K508.10
Orosius K407
Osbernus Cantuariensis K418
Osbertus de Clara K417
Ossius K409
P. Ovidius Naso K412

Pachomius K421
Pacianus K474
Palladius, Rutilius Taurus Aemilianus K178; K423
Palladius Helenopolitanus K256.1; K422
Pamphilius K438
Pantaenus K476
Papias K420
Papias ep. K419
Papirianus K435
Paschasinus K430
Paschasius Dumiensis K436.5
Paschasius Radbertus K281.12; K436; K492.26
Pastor K431
Paterius K437
Patricius Dublinensis K1.185, 206; K434
Paulinus Aquileiensis K1.98, 136, 152, 498; K94.15
Paulinus Mediolanensis K425

Paulinus Nolanus K424; K425.8
Paulus ep. K427
Paulus presbyter K432
Paulus Diaconus K166.3, 6; K426
Pelagius K1.467, 504; K135.2; K281.55, 203, 213, 232; K478
Aulus Persius Flaccus K449
Petronius K447
Petrus presbyter K428
Petrus Abaelardus K51.2; K433
Petrus Alfonsi K445
Petrus Aureoli K481
Petrus Berchorius K586.5
Petrus Blesensis, Bathoniensis archidiac. K444
Petrus Cantor K442
Petrus Capuanus K433.2
Petrus Cellensis K450
Petrus Chrysologus K2.41; K282.12; K451; K536.1
Petrus Comestor K440
Petrus Damiani K443
Petrus Elias K448
Petrus Lemovicensis K337.6
Petrus Lombardus K439
Petrus Pictaviensis K441
Petrus Tarentasiensis K314; K446; K483
Petrus Tripolitanus K480
Petrus de Vinea K484
Phileas K453
Philippus Cretensis ep. K454
Philippus Presbyter K456
Philo Iudaeus K452
Phocas K202
Phoebadius K473
Pierius K457
Pinytus K475
'Placentinus Barre' K465
Plato K464
Plautus, T. Maccius K485

C. Plinius Secundus K462
Plutarchus K463
Polycarpus K458
Polycrates K460
†Pompeius Trogus K588
Pomponius Porfyrio K488
Pontius K455
Porchetus de Salvaticis K461
Porphyrius K459
Possidius K429
'Postumianus' K487
Poterius K479
Praepositinus Cremonensis K471
Primasius K467
Priscianus Caesariensis K470
Priscillianus K477
Proba K472
Proclus K486
Prosper Aquitanus K1.61, 223; K2.46; K466
Prudentius K469
Ptolemaeus, Claudius K579

Quadratus K489
Quintilianus, M. Fabius K490
Quodvultdeus K1.33, 41, 49–50, 90, 166, 199, 443–4, 447, 457, 511

R. de Frisingfeld K501
Rabanus → Hrabanus
Radbertus K246.2
Radulphus de Arundel K496
Radulphus de Diceto K500
Radulphus Flaviacensis K494
Radulphus Niger K494.2–3, 5; K495
Radulphus de Turbine K3.29

Ratramnus Corbeiensis K492.24; K503
Raymundus de Penaforti K509
Regio Prumiensis K521
Remigius Altissiodorensis K84.54; K497
Reticius K518
Rhodo K517
Richardus Barre K523
Richardus de Bury K527
Richardus de Cirencester K502
Richardus Eliensis K526
Richardus Fishacre K513
Richardus Fitzralph K525
Richardus de Furnival K412.14
Richardus Knapwell K512
Richardus de Mediavilla K499
Richardus Pratellensis K494.4
Richardus Rolle K528
Richardus de S. Victore K244.51, †79; K440.2, 6; K498
Richardus de Wetheringsett K504
Robertus II rex Franciae K524
Robertus de Bridlington K506.1–5, 8, 10–11
Robertus de Courson K516
Robertus de Flamborough K498.32
Robertus Grossesteste K505
Robertus Herefordensis ep. K506.16
Robertus Holcot K277; K515
Robertus Kilwardby K510
Robertus Melodunensis K506
Robertus de Oxford K514

Robertus Pullus K507
†Robertus de S. Victore K519
Robertus Toriniacensis K522
Robertus de Tumbalena K203.6; K506.9
Rogerus Shepshed K505.36
Rufinus K508
Rupertus Tuitiensis K443.1; K511

Sabbatius K532
C. Sallustius Crispus K529
Salvianus K530; K544
Samuel Edissenae K540
Scipio K564
Secundus Philosophus K561
Sedatus Nemausensis K1.313
Sedulius K531
Seneca, L. Annaeus K364.4; K543
Serapion, Antiochiensis ep. K548
Serapion Scholasticus K547
Sergius K535
Serlo Wiltoniensis K562
Servius K559
Servus Dei K539
Severianus K533; K536
Severus ep. K534
Sextus K538
'Sibylla' K550
Sidonius, C. Sollius Apollinaris K544
Sigebertus Gemblacensis K565
Simon Boraston K557
Simplicianus K541
Siricius K542
Smaragdus S. Michaelis K553
Socrates K549
Solinus K558
Sophronius K551

Statius, P. Papinius K560
Stephanus Burgundus K555
Stephanus Gallicus K556
Stephanus Langton K554
C. Suetonius Tranquillus K182; K563
Sulpicius Severus K535
Syagrius K281.87; K545
Symmachus, Q. Aurelius K546
Symphosius K566

Tatian K568
P. Terentius Afer K577
Tertullian K578
Theinredus Doverensis K603
Theoctiscus K601
Theodolus K600
Theodoretus K571
Theodoricus Carnotensis K441.3–4
Theodoricus Fribergensis K587
Theodoricus de S. Trudonis K412.11
Theodorus qui postea Gregorius K593
Theodorus monachus K573
Theodorus presbyter K598
Theodorus Ancyranus K599
Theodorus Cantuariensis K590.1; K591
Theodorus Heracliae ep. K572
Theodulphus Aurelianensis K666.32
Theophilus Alexandriae ep. K576
Theophilus Antiochenae ep. K574
Theophilus Caesareae ep. K594
Theophrastus K602
Theotimus K596

Thomas Aquinas K68.1;
    K567
Thomas Becket K570
Thomas de Chobham
    K569
Thomas de Linduno
    K585
Thomas Sutton K584
Thomas Walensis K586
Ticonius K1.†462; K583
Timotheus K575
Titus K595
Triphylius K581
Trogus Pompeius K55.4
'Trotula' K604
Trypho K580
Tullianus K589
Turpinus ps. K605
Tyconius K1.462

Ulricus Engelberti K640
Ursinus K634
Usuardus K663

Valeranus K117; K628
Valerianus K1.135
Valerius Maximus K606
Varro, M. Terentius
    K365; K609
F. Vegetius Renatus
    K610
Venantius Fortunatus
    K191
Verecundus K656
P. Vergilius Maro K630
Victor I papa K613
Victor Cartennensis
    K2.58; K612
Victor de Vita K614
Victorinus, Marius
    K94.6; K281.46; K620
Victorinus Massiliensis
    K616
Victorinus Poetovionensis
    K619

Victorius Aquitanus K617
Vigilius ep. K624
Vigilius Diaconus K623
Vigilius Thapsensis
    K1.†110, 165; K6.10;
    K622; K635
Vincentius Bellovacensis
    K636
Vincentius Gallus K615
Vincentius Lerinensis
    K615.1
Vitellius Afer K631
M. Vitruvius Pollio K621
Voconius K92

Walahfridus Strabo
    K492.3–5,7–8; K552
Walterus Buckden K653
Walterus de Castellione
    K55.2
'Walterus Exoniensis'
    K659
Walterus de Mauritannia
    K3.53; K607
Warnerius Westmonast-
    eriensis K608
Widukindus K661
Willelmus Altissiodorensis
    K52
Willelmus de Alton K638
Willelmus de Alvernia
    K482
Willelmus Aurelianensis
    K643
Willelmus Brixiensis →
    Albertus Brixiensis
Willelmus de Bromyard
    → Iohannes de
    Bromyard
Willelmus de Conchis
    K655
Willelmus de Cortemlia
    Lombardus K641
Willelmus Deyncourt
    K648

Willelmus Durandus
    Senior K633
Willelmus de la
    Furmenterie K89.4
Willelmus Gallicus K644
Willelmus Gallicus K647
Willelmus Gemeticensis
    K654
Willelmus Godinus K226
Willelmus de Hotham
    K637
Willelmus de Kingsham
    K649
Willelmus de Macclesfield
    K639
Willelmus Malmesburi-
    ensis K657
Willelmus de Mara
    K567.92
Willelmus de Moerbeke
    K651; K671.1
Willelmus de Montibus
    K625
Willelmus de Novo Burgo
    K627; K658
Willelmus de Ockham
    K277.1
Willelmus de Pagula
    K629
Willelmus Parisiensis
    K646
Willelmus Peraldus K642
Willelmus Petroburgensis
    K626
'Willelmus Rievallensis'
    K660
Willelmus de S.
    Theodorico K2.21;
    K85.3, 17, 20, 27;
    K168.2; K216.5; K238.1;
    K632

Zacharias Chrysopolitanus
    K673
Zoroastes K674

INDEX OF MANUSCRIPTS

BONN, Universitätsbibliothek
269c   K309

CAMBRIDGE, Clare College
14   K606.3

CAMBRIDGE, Corpus Christi College
19   K1.164
135   xliv n; K3.16–17, 19, 35–6
269   K667.6
316   K3.43, 57; K666.17
332   K436.6
404   xxx n, lvii–lviii, lxxv, lxxvii–lxxxii, lxxxiii, lxxxix n; K110; K249.6, 10–13; K293.3–4, 8; K361.6; K550.1
439   K666.14

CAMBRIDGE, Gonville and Caius College
113/182   K169.2
145/195   liv; K244.1
154/204   lvi–lvii; K55; K490.2
225/240   K46.30; K281.127; K361.6; K485; K543.11, 16; K577.1–2, 6; K606.2; K655.2
230/116   cxxvii n, cxxxiv n
480/476   K68.2

CAMBRIDGE, King's College
3   K1.12, 15, 450; K94.1
7   K84.27–8

CAMBRIDGE, Pembroke College
1   lxviii, cvi; K1.24, 105, 142; K2.52; K3.1–11, 14–17, 21–2, 45–6; K84.47
2   K52.1–2
3   K52.3
4   K52.4
5   K525.1
7   K279
9   K85.12; K244.17, 29, 83, 85
10   K89.2
11   K403.1
12   K119.1
14   K203.1
15   K203.1
16   xlvii n; K203.4
17   xliv n; K281.18
18   xliv n, li n, lxii–lxiii; K282.4, 6, 28
19   K282.4
20   K1.107, 278; K3.14; K286.1
22   xcix; K503.2
23   xlv
24   xliv n, xlv; K186.8; K240.7
25   xliv n, lii–liii; K16.1; K442.14
26   xliv n; K440.1
27   xliv n, lxiii–lxiv; K440.2–3, 6; K495.5
28   xxxiii; K439.1
29   xliv n, xlviii n, lxiii, clxvi; K246.13; K494.1, 4
33   K567.57–8

34	K1.107, 278, 404; K286.1; K567.60		K286.1–2; K404.1–3
35	K567.61	95	K404.7–8, 14, 16–18
36	K567.61		
37	K567.62–3, 66–8	96	K441.2
39	K510.13	97	K439.1
40	lxviii; K376.2	99	K399.6–7, 9
41	liv; K1.142	101	K283.12
42	xliv n; K2.14, 20, 22, 26, 29, 35, 52–3, 72, 75, 84	105	xlvii n; K606.1
		107	xliv n; K89.3
		108	K1.182; K6.10; K281.232
43	li; K54.1–2		
44	xlvii n; K14.1	109	K244.1
45	K13.12–14	111	K244.2, 23; K281.7–8, 11–12
46	K579.3		
47	xliii, xliv n; K281.133	114	K529.1–2
		118	xliv n; K85.4–5, 13; K439.1; K504.1; K666.24
49	xliv n, lxiv n; K494.1		
50	lxiv n; K494.1	231	K281
59	xliv n	313	K16.1; K442.14
63	liv		
69	K667.20	CAMBRIDGE, Peterhouse	
72	xlvii n	164	xcvii
80	K89.3	169	xciii n, cxii; K244.28, 77
81	K84.4–5, 13		
83	K84.23	245	K3.30
84	xliv n, lxi n; K94.1, 3–4, 16	CAMBRIDGE, St John's College	
		A. 12	xcviii; K659
85	liv–lv; K82.3; K334.1	B. 13	xlix n; K203.7
		D. 19	xliv n; K667.1–4, 6, 8–10, 16, 24
87	lv, lvi; K1.278, 487, 496–7; K15.1; K281.104; K466.3; K505.40; K509.1	F. 1	K642.2
		F. 3	K5.6
		G. 2	xxxviii, lxxv; K244.16; K337.5; K666.21
88	xliv n; K203.1		
90	K244.4, 17, 20, 29, 40, 42, 81–3	CAMBRIDGE, Sidney Sussex College	
91	K281.15	71	K503
92	xxx n, xxxvii, xlvi n, lxi, lxiii, xci, cxxxviii; 17 n; K285	CAMBRIDGE, Trinity College	
		B. 2. 3	K492.3
		R. 3. 50	K630.3
94	K283.2;	R. 14. 9	K4.21

R. 14. 34   K136.1
CAMBRIDGE, University Library
   Add. 850   xxxvi, xlii–xliii
   Add. 3470   lxi n, cxv,
                      clxxiv–clxxvii,
                      clxxx,
                      clxxxiv–clxxxviii,
                      cxci, cxcv,
                      cxcviii–cci,
                      cciv–ccvii,
                      ccxi–ccxii
   Add. 4220   xlvii
   Add. 4406/1   K111.2
   Add. 6006   xxxix, lxxv
   Add. 6860   K252.1
   Ee. 3. 60   xliii
   Ff. 1. 14   K1.507
   Ff. 1. 27   K232.1–2
   Ff. 3. 5   K47.1; K370.2
   Gg. 1. 25   K1.479
   Gg. 4. 4   lxix n, lxx n
   Ii. 1. 28   K1.480
   Ii. 1. 29   K1.141
   Ii. 1. 35   K1.389
   Ii. 3. 23   K1.480
   Ii. 4. 23   K1.241, 329
   Ii. 6. 5   K136.3
   Kk. 2. 21   K86.2
   Kk. 4. 11   K1.2
   Peterborough
      Cathedral 3   K85.21

CAMBRIDGE, MA, Harvard University, Houghton Library
     Richardson 26   K1.35–6, 323,
                          340, 442

CHICAGO, Newberry Library
   12   K1.105, 199;
           K666.24

COLUMBIA, MO, University of Missouri Library
     Rare-L/PA/3381.A1/F7 no. 14
                  K111.2

DOUAI, Bibliothèque municipale
   553   lxviii n

DUBLIN, Trinity College
   492   K84.38

DURHAM, Dean and Chapter Library
   B. II. 10   K281
   B. II. 11   K281.102–103,
                105–107, 109, 114
   B. III. 30   cxxvii n,
                cxxxiv n
   B. IV. 30   K4.17
   B. IV. 41   cxxvii, cxxxiv n,
                cxxxv

EDINBURGH, University Library
   104   K3.1, 4
   181   K144.1

GLASGOW, University Library
   Hunterian 85   K140
   Hunterian 110   K68.9
   Hunterian 209   lxviii; K93.1

HEREFORD, Cathedral Library
   O. III. 13   K282. 8–10,
                22–3, 40–41
   P. III. 1   K290.1; K439.1

IPSWICH, Central Library
   2   clxxx
   4   lxviii, xcix n
   6   clxxx
   8   clxxx; K498.38

LONDON, British Library
   Add. 4787   cxciii
   Add. 8166   K214
   Add. 24199   K247.1, 3, 5;
                K391.1; K469.1
   Arundel 34   cxlii n
   Arundel 507   cxxvii, cxxxiv
   Campbell Roll
      XXI.1   lxv, cxxxix, cl;
                K167.2; K289.1

Cotton Claudius		Royal 5 A. VIII	K1.434; K85.21;
A. XII	xxxiv, xlii, cxxvii n,		K283.1; K666.21
	cxxxiv n	Royal 5 B. I	K1.413
Cotton Claudius		Royal 5 C. V	K1.415
E. IV	cxxvii, cxxxii,	Royal 5 C. VI	K282.49
	cxxxiii n	Royal 5 D. VI	K1.137
Cotton Galba		Royal 5 E. XIV	K3.44
E. IV	K393.1	Royal 5 F. X	K135.1
Cotton Nero		Royal 5 F. XV	K1.434
C. IX	K342	Royal 6 A. XII	K186
Cotton Otho		Royal 6 B. X	lii; K3.32; K246;
B. IV	cxlii		K281.7–8, 11–12;
Cotton Tiberius			K625.2
B. II	xl, xli, xlix, lii,	Royal 6 B. XI	K85.17
	liv, lxxv	Royal 6 C. II	xlvii n; K203.5
Cotton Titus		Royal 7 B. IX	cvi; K1.18, 39,
A. VIII	xl, xli n, lii, liv;		142, 282, 404,
	K9.3; K417.2		425, 434; K3.1–4,
Cotton Vitellius			8–11, 15, 17,
E. XII	cxxvii, cxxxii,		21–2; K139.3;
	cxxxiv		K286.1
Egerton 2204	K84.23	Royal 7 C. II	li–lii; K85.12;
Egerton 2782	xlix n; K240.2		K440.2; K506.14
Egerton 3776	xlvii n;	Royal 7 C. VIII	K242.11
	K281.19–20	Royal 7 C. XI	liii; K16.1;
Harley 447	xli n; K657.1		K442.14
Harley 1005	xxxv, xxxix, xlvii,	Royal 7 D. XV	K505.38
	xlix, lxix n,	Royal 7 E. I	K203.3
	lxxii–lxxiv;	Royal 8 B. IV	xxx n, lvii;
	K405.6		K94.4; K247.3
Harley 1206	K86.1–2	Royal 8 C. IV	K94.2; K331.6;
Harley 3027	K1.13, 20, 29,		K364.1; K397.1;
	98, 143, 154,		K505.33, 37;
	325, 358, 364,		K543.13
	402, 425, 427,	Royal 8 D. VIII	K3.44
	495	Royal 8 E. X	lxviii; K554.24
Harley 3775	cxxvii, cxxxiv n	Royal 8 F. XIV	xxxiii, xxxviii,
Harley 3977	xxxix n		liii–liv, lvi, lvii n;
Harley 4025	li n; K444.2		K78.5; K85.7;
Harley 4843	cxxvii n, cxxxiv n		K112.1; K203.3;
Royal 2 C. XII	K666.44		K244.2, 16, 23,
Royal 2 E. IX	K334.1		29; K281.61;
Royal 3 B. XI	lix n		K283.1; K364.1;
Royal 3 D. I	xciii n, cxcii n		K493.1; K498.3,
Royal 4 D. VII	K440.1		34; K527.1

Royal 10 B. XII	liv–lv; K85.21; K445.2	175	K84.6, 14; K281.36
Royal 10 C. v	K442	210	K471.1
Royal 11 B. III	K505.15; K543.16; K642.1	223	K358.1
		232	cxxi
Royal 12 C. VI	lvii; K46.41		
Royal 12 D. XIV	K486		

OXFORD, Bodleian Library

Royal 13 A. I	K55.5
Royal 13 D. IV	K288
Royal 13 D. IX	c; K237.1; K663
Royal 15 C. VI	K55.1
Sloane 1128	K68.9

Add. C. 181	K1.225, 310
Auct. F. 1. 17	K630
Auct. F. 3. 14	K140
Auct. F. inf. 1. 2	K1.342
Ballard 4	cxcviii n
Ballard 5	cci
Ballard 33	cxcviii
Bodley 46	K394.1
Bodley 77	K65
Bodley 130	xlvii n; K154
Bodley 136	K1.171
Bodley 147	K281.234
Bodley 159	K1.479
Bodley 204	K1.176, 349
Bodley 216	lxviii; K557.1
Bodley 240	xxx n, xxxvi n, lxxi, c, cxxvii, cxxix–cxxxi, cxxxvi; K5; K283.13; K286.5; K341.1; K417.2; K419; K434.1
Bodley 297	xl–xli; K195; K367.2
Bodley 300	K233.6
Bodley 356	cx; K4.2
Bodley 365	K281.213
Bodley 386	K281.4–5
Bodley 396	K666.40
Bodley 833	lix; K626.4
Canon Misc. 333	K332
Digby 11	lvii n
e Musaeo 6	K1.215
e Musaeo 7	xlvii n; K1.347
e Musaeo 8	xlvii n; K1.347
e Musaeo 9	lx; K84.25; K480
e Musaeo 26	cxxii; K281.22–7

LONDON, College of Arms

1	lvii n; K55.4
Arundel 30	xl n, xlviii n, lxxxiii n; K229.1

LONDON, Lambeth Palace Library

52	xcix n
61	cxc n
67	xliv n, lxi; K94.7–8
105	K108.1; K290.1; K444.5
127	K281.87
145	K186.2, 5–6
218	xlvi, lxi; K7.32; K285.3–4
448	lxi n, clxxviii–clxxx, clxxxvi
594	cxcvi n

LONDON, Mr P. L. Robinson
K604.1

LONDON, Wellcome Historical Medical Library

801A	K1.445; K4.20; K85.18; K244.6; K625.7

NEW YORK, Pierpont Morgan Library

136	K417.2

OXFORD, Balliol College

152	K554.18

e Musaeo 27	K2.47	Rawlinson C.	
e Musaeo 31	xliv n, lx, xc,	531	K1.493
	xciv–xcv, ciii–cvi;	Rawlinson C.	
	5 n; K1.416;	697	cvi, clxiii;
	K111.4; K130;		K8.1–3; K469.1
	K159–60;	Rawlinson G.	
	K210.2; K281.90;	187	c; K198.2
	K326.2; K530;	8° Rawlinson	
	K589; K620.4;	470	clxxxix
	K666.14–16, 19	Selden supra 31	K537.1
e Musaeo 32	K1.163	Selden supra 64	clxxxvii
e Musaeo 33	cx; K1.83, 228;	Tanner 24	cxcv
	K220.1	Tanner 25	cxcvii–cxcviii
e Musaeo 36	K84.1	Tanner 165	xciii n, cxii,
e Musaeo 86	cxc n		cxcvi, cc, ccvii
e Musaeo 112	cvi; K3.1, 3;	Tanner 469	cxcix n
	K281.35	Twyne 22	cxci–cxcii
Gough Essex 1	cxxvii n,	Wood E. 4	cxciii–cxciv
	cxxxiv n	OXFORD, Exeter College	
Hatton 84	K281.4	28	K505.29
James 11	cxci		
Lat. hist. d. 4	xxxiv, lxvi–lxvii,	OXFORD, Magdalen College	
	lxx	7	K67
Lat. th. c. 26	K1.278;	181	xcviii; K659
	K281.39–40;	192	K286
	K666.24		
Lat. th. d. 29	K3.54	OXFORD, Merton College	
Lat. th. d. 30	c	118	K2.28
Laud Lat. 4	cxxxi n		
Laud Lat. 368	K342	OXFORD, New College	
Laud Misc. 85	K271.1; K339.2;	129	K281.213
	K482.4;	OXFORD, Oriel College	
	K505.15		
Laud Misc. 136	K1.481	75	cxxxi n
Laud Misc. 233	xlv; K666.20	OXFORD, The Queen's College	
Laud Misc. 264	K3.21	304	cxxvi–cxxvii,
Laud Misc. 277	K3.53		cxxxi–cxxxiii,
Laud Misc. 363	K281.39–40		cxxxvi,
Laud Misc. 409	K244.79		cxliv–clxxiii
Laud Misc. 578	?K1.59		
Malone 3	cxcv	OXFORD, St John's College	
Rawlinson A.		43	K439.3
376	K2.86, 91	OXFORD, Trinity College	
Rawlinson C.		B 89	K1.293
259	lxx n		

PARIS, Bibliothèque de l'Arsenal
   903   K126.6

PARIS, Bibliothèque nationale de France
   lat. 2152   K1.94
   lat. 2601   K80.3
   lat. 3757   K342
   lat. 3833   K1.90
   lat. 6443   K68.1
   lat. 8207   K144.1
   lat. 12307   K492.3
   lat. 16082   K486

PRAGUE, National and University Library
   XIII. C. 8   K332
   Lobkowitz 431   K626.1

ROME, Biblioteca Apostolica Vaticana
   Reg. lat. 125   K1.164
   Reg. lat. 127   cxxvii–cxxix, cxxx–cxxxi, cxxxii, cxxxiii n, cxxxvii, cxliii
   Reg. lat. 424   K16

SALISBURY, Cathedral Library
   62   xcix n
   167   K333.1

SAN MARINO, Huntingdon Library
   HM 26560   xcix n
   HM 31151   K1.3, 22, 165, 186, 225–6, 366, 373
   HM 45717   K563.1

TROYES, Bibliothèque municipale
   1961   K2.19

WISBECH, Wisbech and Fenland Museum
   Town Library 1   xxxviii, xlix, l, lxiii; K466

YORK, Minster Library
   XVI.K.5   cxxvii, cxxxiv n

GENERAL INDEX

References are to page numbers in the Introduction

Abbo of Fleury liv
Adam of Hempnall xxxv
Ælfheah, archbishop of Canterbury xli
Ailwin xl, xli
Aimoin de Fleury xcix
Alain de Lille lv
Alanus Porretanus lii–liii
Alexander of Hales li
Allen, Thomas cxci
Andrew Ashton xxxiv, cxxxiv n
Anstis, John, the elder cciii
Antichrist and prophecies lvii–lviii, lxxvii–lxxxii
Augustine xxxiii, l, liv, lvi, lx, ci, cii
autobibliographies ci

Babwell (Suffolk), Franciscan convent lv n, lvi, lviii, lxxxvi, cxiv, cxxi, cxxx
Baldwin, abbot xlv
Bale, John lxxxix, cxxxv–cxxxvi, cxlii, clxxiv–clxxviii, clxxxii–cxc, cci, cciv, ccv, ccix
Barking (Essex), abbey cxiv, cxxi
Barlow, Thomas cxciv n
Battle abbey (Sussex) xlviii n
beaver stencil lxxxi, lxxxii
Bede lx–lxi, ci
Benedict, saint xxxvii
Benedict XII, pope xxxiii, xxxiv
Bernard of Clairvaux xxxviii
Bodley, Thomas cxcii
Boethius lxi
'Boston of Bury' xxix n, cxxvi, cxxxv–cxxxvi, cxlii, clxxiv–clxxv, clxxvi, clxxxi–clxxxiv, ccv; → Henry of Kirkestede
Bressie, Ramona ccix
Bridges, John cciii
Buckenham, Richard clxxx
Bury St Edmunds (Suffolk), Benedictine abbey
  archives xliii, xlvi–xlvii
  disputed election of 1379 lxix n, lxxv, lxxvi
  exemption from episcopal control xxxii, xxxv–xxxvi
  homicide lxxi–lxxii
  library
    catalogue xliii–xliv, xlvi
    classification system xlv–xlviii, xlix–li
    contents lists xlv
    ex libris notes xliv, xlvi
    refectory books xlix, l
    site of xlviii–xlix
    size of l–li
  ordination of monks xxxi, xxxii, lxiv–lxv
  plague lxiv–lxvii, lxxvii
  riots of 1327–29 xxxi–xxxii, xlviii
  tempest and collapse of bell-tower lxx–lxxi
  university training of monks xxxiii–xxxiv
  → Edmund, saint; Peasants' Revolt

Caius, John clxxxix
Caius, Thomas clxxxix
Cambridge, Carmelite convent cxxxiv n
Camden, William cxc, cciv
Cassian → John Cassian
Cassiodorus xxxvii, xciv–xcv, lx–lxi, xciv–xcv, xcix
Catalogus de libris autenticis et apocrifis
  'Catalogus minor' cxc, cxcii–cxciii
  date of compilation lxxxvii–lxxxix
  editorial principles ccxi–ccxiv
  Ely cathedral extracts clxxviii–clxxx, clxxxvi
  incipits and explicits cix–cxi

introduction xc–xci
location numbers (list of libraries)
   cxi–cxxiv
interpretation cxviii–cxx
medieval copies clxxiv–clxxviii
method of compilation cii–cxxiv
*Nomina doctorum qui scribunt super
   Bibliam* cxxiv–cxxv
Norwich copy clxxv–clxxviii
preface xci–xcii
projected publication cxcv–cciv,
   ccviii–ccx
purpose lxxxiv–lxxxvii
record of vanished works cvii
sources xcii–cii
title lxxxix, clxxv–clxxvi,
   clxxxii–clxxxiv
transcript cxcvii–cci, cciv–ccvii
transmission clxxiv–ccx
Cavendish, Sir John lxxvi
Charlett, Dr Arthur cxcviii, ccii
Chichester (Sussex), cathedral church
   cxxiii
Chichester, Sr Josephine ccviii–ccix
Churchill, Awnsham, the elder cxcv,
   cxcvii–cxcix, cciii, cciv, ccv
Churchill, Awnsham, the younger cciv
Churchill, John cxcvii
Churchill, Joshua cciv
Churchill, William cciii
Cnut, king of Denmark, England, and
   Norway xl n
Coggeshall (Essex), abbey lviii, cxxi
Colchester (Essex), abbey of St John
   cxxxiv n
Colchester (Essex), priory of St
   Botulph lvii n
Cotton, Sir Robert cxc, cxci, cxcii,
   cciv
Cromwell, Thomas clxxx n, clxxxii
Crowland (Lincs), abbey cxxiii

David ab Augusta xxxix
De viris illustribus lxxxiv–lxxxv,
   xciv–xcv, cii, ciii, civ–cvi

Decretum Gelasianum xcix
Dugdale, Sir William cxcv n
Dunkeswell (Devon), abbey cxxiii
Durham, cathedral priory
   cxxxi–cxxxii, cxxxiv, cxxxv

Earls Colne (Essex), priory cxiv
Edmund, saint, life and miracles
   xxxvi, xl–xli, xlix, l, lii, liv, lxiv,
   lxx–lxxi, lxxiii, cxxix–cxxx
Edmund Bromfeld lxxv, lxxvi
Edmund Brundish, prior xxx n, xxxv,
   lxvi–lxvii, lxix
Edmund Wirlington lxix, lxx n
Edward II, king of England xxix,
   xxxi–xxxii
Edward III, king of England xxix,
   xxxii, xxxvi, lxxvii
Elmswell (Suffolk) lvii
Ely, cathedral priory lxv, lxxiv; →
   Catalogus de libris autenticis et apocrifis,
   Ely cathedral extracts
Etienne de Bourbon xcix
†Excolio c

Fairfax, Robert, seventh Baron Fairfax
   of Cameron ccvi
'Florence of Worcester' ci
Fulgentius c
Fuller, Thomas cxciii, cxcvi, cciv

Gale, Thomas cxciv–cxcv, cci,
   ccv
Gennadius xciv–xcv; → *De viris
   illustribus*
Geoffrey of Hemblington xxx n
Ghellinck, Fr Joseph de ccviii
Gibson, Edmund cxcvii, cci, cciv
Gilbert le Barbour lxvii n
Glastonbury (Somerset), abbey
   cxxxi–cxxxiii; → John Moorlinch
Gransden, Antonia ccix
Gratian xc, c
Greek words cv
Gregory I, pope xxxviii, l, liv

Greyfriars, Oxford → Oxford,
    Franciscan convent
Guido of St-Denis c
Guillelmus Durandus → Willelmus
    Durandus

H. de Brigham lviii
Hall, Anthony cxxvi, cxxxvi, cci, cciii
Hatton, Capt. Charles cxcviii
Hearne, Thomas cxci, cxcii n, cxcix n,
    cci–cciii
Henry of Hunstanton, abbot
    lxvi–lxviii, cxxvii
Henry of Kirkestede xxix–clxxiii, ccv
    as abbot's chaplain xxxii, xxxv
    as author of revised *Speculum
        coenobitarum* cxxxv–cxliii
    bibliographic notes li–lv
    birthplace xxx–xxxi
    death-date lxxiv–lxxxii
    hand of xxx, lxxv, lxxxiii
    knowledge of other libraries lv–lix,
        cxx–cxxiv
    as librarian xlii–lxiv
    name → birthplace
    as novice master xxxvii–xlii
    ordination xxxi
    as prior lxix–lxxiv; resignation
        refused lxxii
Hereford, cathedral church xlvii n
Herman xli, xlix
Hildegard of Bingen ci
Hinton (Somerset), charterhouse
    cxiv–cxv
Holinshed, Raphael clxxxix
Holme St Benets (Norfolk), abbey lvi,
    cxxx
Holt, Ailot clxxx n, clxxxi–clxxxii,
    ccv
Hugh de Chiverey, abbot cxxvii
Hugh of Fleury c
Hugh of Saint-Victor xxxiii, xxxviii,
    liii, liv, xc, c, cix
Hugh of Saxham xxx n
Hunt, R. W. ccix

Innocent III, pope xxxviii
Innocent VI, pope lxviii
Iohannes → John
Isidore of Seville xc, xciv–xcv, cxxxix;
    → *De viris illustribus*
'Ivo' → Hugh of Fleury
Ixworth (Suffolk), priory cxiv, cxxi

James, M. R. lxxxiv, ccvi–ccvii, ccviii
James, Richard cxci–cxcii, ccii
James, Thomas cxcii–cxciii, cciv
Jerome lxxxiv, xc, xciv–xcv, cxvii; →
    De viris illustribus
Joachim of Fiore xlii, lviii,
    lxxvii–lxxxii, cxxxviii, clxxvi
'John Boston' clxxxix; → 'Boston of
    Bury'
John Brinkley, abbot xxxiii, xl, lxvii,
    lxviii–lxx, lxxi, lxxv, xcix n
John of Cambridge, prior xxx n, xlii
    n, lii, lxix n, lxx, lxxiv, lxxvi
John Cassian xxxvii–xxxviii, xlvi, lxi,
    cxxxvii
John Chrysostom li n, lxii
Iohannes de Deo ci
John Erly xxxvii n
John Ernstede xxxv
John of Gosford xxx n, lxix n
John of Grafton lxxi, lxxii n
John of Lakenheath xliii, xlvi, lxxvi
John Langwood cxxx
John of Lavenham xxx n, lxvii n,
    lxix–lxx, lxxi
John Moorlinch cxxxi
John of Norton lxxi
John of Salisbury c
John of Snailwell xxxv, lxix, lxx n
John Tebaud lvii
John Timworth, abbot lxix n, lxxv,
    lxxvi
John Totyngton xxxiv–xxxv
John of Tynemouth xxxvii n, lxxxviii,
    cxxix, c, cxxix
John of Wales xxxviii–xxxix
John Whethamstede, abbot cxlii–cxliii

John of Worcester xl n, xli
John Wrawe lxxiv, lxxvi
John Wyclif xxix
Josephus cxxxviii
Julian of Toledo c
Julianus Pomerius lxiii; → Prosper of Aquitaine

Ker, N. R. lxxxiii
King's Lynn (Norfolk) lvii
Kirstead Green (Norfolk) xxx

Langley (Norfolk), abbey cxxiii
Laurent Pignon xcvi–xcvii, civ
Leland, John lxxi n, clxxx, clxxxii
Lenton (Notts), priory cxxiii
Liber albus lxxii–lxxiii
Liber florum c
Liber pontificalis c
Little, A. G. ccviii
London, charterhouse cxxx

Maimonides lvi
Malone, Edward cxcv n
Manipulus florum → Thomas of Ireland
Mariale maius xcviii–xcix, cxi, cxli
'Marianus' xl–xli
Martin of Braga xxxviii
Martinus Polonus c, ci
Ps. Miletus c
Mount Grace (Yorks), charterhouse cxxxiv n
Mynors, Sir Roger ccix

Nicholas Trevet c, cvii
Nicholas of Wortham xxx n
Nicolson, William cxcvi–cxcvii, ccii
Norwich, cathedral priory lxx n, cxx–cxxi, cxxiv, cxcix; → *Catalogus de libris autenticis et apocrifis*, Norwich copy; William Bateman

Oldys, William cxcv
Osbert of Clare lii

Osney (Oxon), abbey cxxiii
Oxford, Franciscan convent xxxiii, lvii, lxxxv–lxxxvi, xciv, cxiv, cxix; → *Registrum Anglie*
Oxford, Gloucester College xxxiii–xxxiv, lxviii, cxiv
Oxford, Magdalen College cxxxv

Palladius c
Pantin, W. A. cxxvi, ccix
Parker, Matthew, archbishop of Canterbury cxciv n
Paul the Deacon c, ci
Peasants' Revolt xxix, lxxiv, lxxvi
Peter of Blois ci
Peter of Clopton xxx n
Peter Lombard xxxiii
Phillipps, Sir Thomas ccvi–ccvii
Pignon, Laurent → Laurent Pignon
Pits, John cxcii
prophecies of the popes lxxviii–lxxxii; → Antichrist; Joachim of Fiore
Prosper of Aquitaine xxxviii, l, lxiii; → Julianus Pomerius

Ralph of Caston xxx n
Ralph of Coggeshall, abbot lviii
Ralph de Diceto xcviii, ci
Ralph of Flaix xlviii n, lxiii–lxiv
Ralph Niger lxiii, ci
Ramsey (Hunts), abbey liii n, lix, cxiv, cxx, cxxiii–cxxiv, cxxx
Ranulf Higden lxxxviii, xcviii, ci
Reginald of Denham xxx n
Registrum Anglie de libris doctorum et auctorum veterum lxi, lxiii, lxxxv–lxxxvi, xciii–xciv, xcv, cxi–cxxiii, cxl, cxli–cxlii, clxxxvii, cxc, cxcvi, cc–cci, ccv–ccvi, ccvii, ccviii, ccx; → Oxford, Franciscan convent
Richard II, king of England lxxvi, lxxix–lxxx
Richard de Bury, bishop of Durham lxxxviii, lxxxix

Richard of Denham xxx n
Richard le Palmer lxvii n
Richard of Saint-Victor lvi,
 lix n
Robert, abbot xlviii n
Robert Grosseteste cvii
Robert of Icklingham xxx n
Robert Lyrlyngges xxxv
Robert of Melun li
Roger of Huntingdon cxxix
Romsey (Hants), abbey cxxiii

Saffron Walden (Essex), abbey lvii,
 cxxi, cxxx
St Albans (Herts), abbey cxxxi–cxxxii,
 cxxxiii–cxxxiv; → John
 Whethamstede; Thomas de la Mare,
 Thomas Walsingham
Samson, abbot xli, liv, lxvi
Sancroft, William, archbishop of
 Canterbury cxcvi, cc, ccvii
Savage, E. A. ccix
Scriptores ordinis Praedicatorum xcvi–xcvii,
 ciii–civ
Sibton (Suffolk), abbey xxxi n, lviii,
 cxxi
Simon of Langham xxx n, lxvii
Smart, William clxxx–clxxxi
Smith, Thomas ccii
Speculum coenobitarum xlii, lxxvii,
 lxxxvii–lxxxviii, cxxvi–clxxiii; revised
 version cxxxi–cxxxiv; → Henry of
 Kirkestede
Stams catalogue xcvi–xcvii, civ
Stanbrook (Worcs), abbey ccviii
Stigand, bishop of Elmham and
 Winchester and archbishop of
 Canterbury xl n
Sweyn, king of Denmark and England
 xxxvii n, xl, xli

T. de Saxham xlvii, lxxiii
Tanner, Joseph ccv
Tanner, Thomas cxlii, cxcv n,
 cxcvii–ccvii

Thetford (Norfolk), Cluniac priory
 cxiv, cxxx
Thetford (Norfolk), Austin convent cxiv
Thetford (Norfolk), Dominican convent
 cxiv
Thomas of Ireland lxxxvi, xci–xcii,
 xcv, xcvii, cix, cxi, cxvi
Thomas de la Mare, abbot lxxii
Thomas of Sutton lxvii n
Thomas Thakstede cxxx
Thomas Walsingham, abbot lxx, lxxii n,
 cxxxiii–cxxxiv
Thomson, Rodney M. ccix
Thorpe, Thomas ccvi
Tournus (Burgundy), abbey
 cxxvii–cxxix
Twyne, Brian cxci–cxcii, cxciii, cci,
 ccvii
Twysden, Sir Roger cxciii–cxciv,
 cxcvii, cciii, cciv, ccv
Twysden, Sir William ccv
Tyrrell, James cxci, ccii

Ulric of Regensburg c
Urban V, pope lxxxii
Urban VI, pope lxxv, lxxxii
Ussher, James, archbishop of Armagh
 cxc–cxciv, ccii, cciv, ccv

Vincent of Beauvais xxxviii, lxi, xc,
 xcv, cvii–cx, cxl
Vossius, Isaac ccii

Walter Pinchbeck xliii
Ware, James cxciii
Westminster, Benedictine abbey xxx n,
 cxx–cxxi
Wharton, Henry cxcv, cxcvi, cc
Wilkins, David ccv–ccvi
Willelmus → William
William Andrew xxxvii n
William Bateman, bishop of Norwich
 xxxv–xxxvi, lxv
William of Bernham, abbot xxxii,
 xxxv–xxxvi, lxiv–lxv, lxvi–lxvii

William of Blundeston lxxi, lxxii n
William of Colchester xxxiv n
William Curteys, abbot xlvii
Willelmus Durandus c
William Hengham xxxvi
William Langland lxx
William of Malmesbury ci
William of Peterborough lix, cxiv
William of Rockland xxx n

William of Stow xxx n
Master William Wyvelyngham xxxv
Witham (Somerset), charterhouse
   xlviii n
Wood, Anthony cxciii–cxciv, ccii, cciv
Woolpit (Suffolk) xxxiv–xxxv
Wyclif, John → John Wyclif

Zacharias Chrysopolitanus c